GALATIANS

GALATIANS

A Commentary for Students

Mark J. Keown

Morphe Publishers

Auckland

Galatians: A Commentary

paperback isbn: 978-0-473-51269-9
ebook isbn: 978-0-473-51270-5

Cover Photo: Javier Art Photography

Manufactured in USA.

CONTENTS

Preface   1

Abbreviations   iii

Other Books by Mark J. Keown   vii

PART I. PART ONE: AN INTRODUCTION TO GALATIANS

1. Chapter One: An Introduction to Galatians   11

PART II. PART TWO: PRESCRIPT AND SITUATION (GAL 1:1–10)

2. Chapter Two: Prescript (Gal 1:1–5)   69
3. Chapter Three: No Other Gospel (Gal 1:6–10)   97

PART III. PART THREE: PAUL'S NARRATIVE IN WHICH HE DEFENDS HIS GOSPEL AND APOSTLESHIP(1:11–2:14)

4. Chapter Four: The Revelation of the Gospel (Gal 1:11–12)   123
5. Chapter Five: Paul's Former Life in Judaism (1:13–14)   131
6. Chapter Six: Paul's Conversion and Call (1:15–16b)   139
7. Chapter Seven: Paul's Gospel Remains the Same (1:16c–21)   149

8. Chapter Eight: Paul Otherwise Unknown in   165
    Judea (1:22–24)

9. Chapter Nine: Paul, His Gospel, and His   175
    Mission Endorsed in Jerusalem (2:1–10)

10. Chapter Ten: Paul and Peter Clash in Antioch   219
    (2:11–14)

PART IV. PART FOUR: THE BODY OF THE
LETTER—DO NOT YIELD TO THE
JUDAIZING 'GOSPEL!'

11. Chapter Eleven: Thesis Statement—Justified   243
    by faith and Not Law (2:15–16)

12. Chapter Twelve: The Judaizers Rather than   267
    Christ Serve Sin (2:17–18)

13. Chapter Thirteen: Dead to the Law, Alive in   279
    Christ, By Grace, Not Law (2:19–21)

14. Chapter Fourteen: Remember the Spirit Was   293
    Received by Faith, Not Law (3:1–5)

15. Chapter Fifteen: Children of Abraham by   313
    Faith (3:6–9)

16. Chapter Sixteen: Redeemed by Christ from the   327
    Curse of the Law (3:10–14)

17. Chapter Seventeen: The Abrahamic Promise   343
    Fulfilled Through Christ Not Law (3:15–18)

18. Chapter Eighteen: The Law's Function to   359
    Prepare for Justification by Faith in Christ
    (3:19–24)

19. Chapter Nineteen: The Inclusion, Unity, and   379
    Equality of All Believers in Christ (3:25–29)

20. Chapter Twenty: No Longer Slaves but   401
    Redeemed Children and Heirs (4:1–7)

21. Chapter Twenty-One: Do Not Return to   427
    Slavery (4:8–11)

22. Chapter Twenty-Two: Remember Your   447
    Conversion (4:12–20)

23. Chapter Twenty-Three: Be Children of Sarah, Not Hagar (4:21–4:31) — 481

24. Chapter Twenty-Four: A Final Appeal: Do Not Accept Circumcision (5:1–6) — 517

25. Chapter Twenty-Five: Get Back in the Race (5:7–12) — 539

PART V. PART FIVE: HOW THEN TO LIVE? FREEDOM, LOVE, BY THE SPIRIT (5:13–6:10)

26. Chapter Twenty-Six: The Freedom to Love! (5:13–15) — 567

27. Chapter Twenty-Seven: Walk in the Spirit (5:16–18) — 595

28. Chapter Twenty-Eight: Walk Away from the Works of the Flesh (5:19–21) — 613

29. Chapter Twenty-Nine: Cultivate the Fruit of the Spirit (5:22–26) — 653

30. Chapter Thirty: Bear One Another's Burdens (6:1–6) — 687

31. Chapter Thirty-One: Sow to the Spirit for Eternal Life (6:7–10) — 719

PART VI. PART SIX: POSTSCRIPT (6:11–18)

32. Chapter Thirty-Two: Postscript (6:11–18) — 747

Works Referenced — 792

This commentary on Galatians grows out of my teaching at Laidlaw College, Auckland, NZ. It is designed as a tool for students giving them a basic but comprehensive and readable understanding of the text of Galatians. I also throw in thoughts from my own reflections and experiences, which are more devotional, and church orientated. An analysis of the Greek used in Galatians with some engagement with primary and secondary sources is mainly dealt with in footnotes which cover the uses of the Greek terms in comparative literature. Similarly, textual variants are discussed in the notes. The Greek is also transliterated throughout the commentary and in the notes to aid understanding. There is not a huge amount of engagement with secondary literature, and students and readers are encouraged to read a wider range of commentaries, monographs, essays, and articles to supplement this work. It is critical to read a range of scholars when studying Scripture as each brings fresh insights and ideas. May the Lord bless you and keep you.

ABBREVIATIONS

AYB	Anchor Yale Bible
AYBD	*The Anchor Yale Bible Dictionary*
BADG	Arndt et al. *A Greek-English Lexicon of the New Testament and Other Early Christian Literature,* 1979.
BDAG	Arndt et al. *A Greek-English Lexicon of the New Testament and Other Early Christian Literature,* 2000.
BDF	Blass et al. *A Greek Grammar of the New Testament and Other Early Christian Literature,* 1961.
BECNT	Baker Exegetical Commentary on the New Testament.
BJRL	*Bulletin of the John Ryland's Library*
BNTC	Black's New Testament Commentary
CCGNT	Classic Commentaries on the Greek New Testament.
CCS	Continental Commentary Series
Charlesworth	*The Old Testament Pseudepigrapha,* 1983.
COQG	Christian Origins and the Question of God.
CS	Cornerstone Series
DNTB	Porter et al. *Dictionary of New Testament Background,* 2000.
DBL Hebrew	Swanson. *Dictionary of Biblical Languages with Semantic Domains: Hebrew (Old Testament),* 1997.
DPL	Hawthorne et al. *Dictionary of Paul and His Letters,* 1993.
DJG	Green et al. *Dictionary of Jesus and the*

	Gospels, 1992.
ECHC	Early Christianity in its Hellenistic Context
EDEJ	Collins et al. *The Eerdmans Dictionary of Early Judaism*, 2010.
EEC	Evangelical Exegetical Commentary.
EDNT	Balz, et al. *Exegetical Dictionary of the New Testament*, 1990.
Eng.	English
ERT	*Evangelical Review of Theology*
ESV	English Standard Version
FCCGRW	First Century Christianity in the Graeco-Roman World
Gk	Greek
HibJ	*Hibbert Journal*
HTR	*Harvard Theological Review*
ICC	International Critical Commentary
JSNT	*Journal for the Study of the New Testament*
JSNTSup	Journal for the Study of the New Testament Supplement Series
KNT	Kommentar zum Neuen Testament
LBD	Barry et al. *The Lexham Bible Dictionary*, 2016.
Louw & Nida	*Greek-English Lexicon of the New Testament: Based on Semantic Domains*, 1996.
LSJ	Liddell et al. *A Greek-English Lexicon*, 1996.
NAC	New American Commentary
NASB95	New American Standard Bible (1995)
NET	New English Translation
NIGTC	New International Greek Testament Commentary
NIV	New International Version
NIVAC	The NIV Application Commentary
NovTSup	Supplements to Novum Testamentum
NTC	New Testament Commentary.
parr.	parallels

PBM	Paternoster Biblical Monographs
PDBS	*Pocket Dictionary of Biblical Studies,* 2002.
PDSNTG	*Pocket Dictionary for the Study of New Testament Greek,* 2001.
PDTT	*Pocket Dictionary of Theological Terms,* 1999.
PNTC	Pillar New Testament Commentaries
NICNT	New International Commentary on the New Testament
NTS	*New Testament Studies*
SP	Sacra Pagina
ST	*Studia Theologica*
s.a.	See also
TDNT	*Theological Dictionary of the New Testament,* 1964.
TENTS	Texts and Editions for New Testament Study
TMSJ	*The Masters Theological Journal*
THK	Theologischer Handkommentar zum Neuen Testament
WBC	Word Biblical Commentary
WUNT	*Wissenschaftliche Untersuchungen zum Neuen Testament*

OTHER BOOKS BY MARK J. KEOWN

Congregational Evangelism in Philippians (Wipf & Stock, 2008)
What's God Up to on Planet Earth (Wipf & Stock, 2011)
Philippians, 2 vols, Evangelical Exegetical Commentary
  (Lexham, 2017)
Jesus in a World of Colliding Empires, 2 vols (Wipf & Stock, 2018)
Discovering the New Testament, Vol 1: The Gospels and Acts
  (Lexham, 2018)
Discovering the New Testament, Vol 2. The Pauline Letters
  (Lexham, 2021)
*Discovering the New Testament, Vol 3. Hebrews and the General
Epistles*
  (Lexham, 2022)
The New Testament: A Taster (Morphe, 2020)
Romans and the Mission of God (Wipf & Stock, 2022)
Understanding Mark's Gospel (Wipf & Stock, 2022)

PART ONE: AN INTRODUCTION TO GALATIANS

CHAPTER ONE: AN INTRODUCTION TO GALATIANS

INTRODUCTORY COMMENTS

Galatians is one of Paul's most vehement and passionate letters. He writes as God and Christ's apostle urging the Galatians to remember the gospel that he preached among them. Unlike his other letters, there is no thanksgiving or blessing, an indicator of his trenchant concern for his converts. Rather, he gets straight down to work, stating his horror that the Galatians are deserting the gospel—not that there is another gospel for Paul (or anyone who believes in Jesus). He reminds them of his conversion and call—Galatians giving valuable information concerning Paul's life. This is all to serve his greater purpose of calling them back to the gospel of grace—his gospel having been given the thumbs up by the respected Jerusalem apostolic core. He reminds them of his clash with Peter (Cephas) in Antioch where he daringly challenged the respected pillar of the church that his retreat from table fellowship with the gentiles would inadvertently play into the hands of the Judaizers;[1] those who want new gentile converts to come under the law for salvation and inclusion in God's

---

1. The term Judaizer is based on a Greek verb *ioudaizō* used in Gal 2:14. The Greek means 'live as one bound by Mosaic ordinances or traditions, live in Judean or Jewish fashion' (BDAG 478). *PDBS* 68 defines Judaizers as '[a] group of Jewish Christians who believed that all gentile Christians should "live like Jews" (Gal 2:14) by embracing Jewish customs. Although the word *Judaizer* does not appear in the NT, such attempts at "judaizing" conflicted with Paul's insistence that salvation is "not by the works of the law but through faith in Jesus Christ" (Gal 2:16). It is important to understand that Paul never encouraged Jewish Christians to abandon their Jewish way of life and national identity, though he was falsely accused of doing so (Acts 21:21).'

people. He then vigorously and emotionally calls the gentiles back to justification by faith and not by the law. Indeed, for Paul now that he is in Christ, justification has always been based on faith since Abraham (and even earlier, e.g., Noah, Enoch). The law cannot achieve justification; only Christ can, and through faith in him, the Galatians received the Spirit. The law is valuable and valid, but not as a means of justification—rather, it functions to lead people to the need of Christ.

Once in Christ by faith, there are no social boundaries—all are one in Christ. There is no basis for rank or status, sexism, or racism within the body of Christ. No ethnicity, Jew or otherwise, has any priority in God's people. Those who believe are set free from enslavement to law and sin and are children of God through faith. So, the Galatians must not go back into enslavement to the law. To do so puts them in a place parallel with their former experience as pagans when they worshiped false gods and were subjugated to demonic forces and the religious and philosophical powers of their world. Paul outlines a fresh ethic, one not governed by law, but one led by the Spirit who bears virtuous fruit in the believer—especially love. Those governed by the inside-out ethic of the Spirit put to death the deeds of the flesh; things excited but not extinguished by the law. Only believers by the Spirit have that internal power to do so, even if they are never fully perfected this side of eternity. Hence, the Galatians must persevere in the Spirit, supporting and bearing with each other, sowing to please the Spirit, and yielding eternal life. All that matters is Christ crucified.

Galatians is a veritable treasure trove of Pauline theology and speaks powerfully today of the essence of Paul's Gospel—Christ and Christ crucified. It reminds readers that one is justified and included in God's people by grace through faith, and that alone. It challenges us to work hard to understand Paul's view of the law—a field of vibrant critical debate in the last forty years—the New Perspective on Paul. It calls believers to refute syncretism, whereby the gospel is violated. It calls for radical unity among believers, regardless of social standing, race, gender, talent, or other typical worldly way of ranking people. Galatians has some of the clearest ethical teachings in Scripture. It gives important biographical and chronological data concerning Paul's Jewish life, his conversion, and his movements early in his Christian career. In what follows, the authorship, dating, and setting, along with other critical issues, will be discussed.

AUTHORSHIP

Galatians begins with the words, 'Paul, an apostle,' indicating that Paul is the author. While Paul's authorship has been challenged on occasion,[2] even F. C. Baur of the skeptical Tübingen *Religionsgeschichte* School, famous for questioning the authorship of Paul's letters, does not question Paul's authorship writing,[3]

In the Homologoumena, there can only be reckoned the four great Epistles of the Apostle, which take precedence of the rest in every respect, namely, the Epistle to the *Galatians*, the two Epistles to the Corinthians, and the Epistle to the Romans. There has never been the slightest suspicion of unauthenticity cast on these four Epistles, and they bear so uncontestably the character of Pauline originality, that there is no conceivable ground for the assertion of critical doubts in their case.

In verse 2, Paul adds, 'and with all the brothers with me.' Whereas in other epistles, individuals are named alongside Paul and may indicate that they are co-authors, co-senders, or

---

2. See Richard N. Longenecker, *Galatians*. WBC 41 (Dallas: Word, Incorporated, 1998), lviii who notes that Bruno Bauer in the nineteenth century denied Paul's authorship dating the letter in the second century AD (*Kritik der paulinischen Briefe* [Berlin: Hempel, 1852]). Others followed (A. D. Loman, A. Pierson, S. A. Naber, Rudolf Steck, Daniel Volter, W. C. van Manen, C. H. Weisse, and Jacob Cramer). In the twentieth century, L. G. Rylands, *A Critical Analysis of the Four Chief Pauline Epistles* (London: Watts, 1929); F. R. McGuire, "Did Paul Write Galatians?" *HibJ* 66 (1967–68): 52–57; and J. C. O'Neill, *The Recovery of Paul's Letter to the Galatians* (London: SPCK, 1972) also followed. O'Neill finds thirty passages in Galatians that are supposedly inserted by someone other than Paul. These ideas are not to be taken seriously.
3. See F. C. Baur, *Paul the Apostle of Jesus Christ, His Life and Work, His Epistles and his Doctrine*. Vol. 1, trans. E. Zeller (London: Williams and Norgate, 1876), 246, 250–57 (italics mine). The Homologoumena is those books of the New Testament acknowledged as authoritative and canonical from the earliest time, compared with what Baur calls the Antilogoumena, which is made up of the disputed letters.

secretaries,[4] the mention of a group does not necessarily indicate any actual involvement in the production of the letter, but an agreement with its appeal. As Paul is in Syrian Antioch, and as 'brothers' is inclusive, it likely includes every Christian present with Paul in the city[5] and so adds immense authority to the letter[6]—all of us in Antioch agree with it! The Judaizers are in error!

He may have used a secretary (amanuensis)[7] for this letter, as in the case of Tertius who penned Romans on Paul's behalf (Rom 16:22). In 2 Thess 3:17 Paul states that he has added a greeting with his own hand, and 'this is the sign of genuineness in every letter of mine.' Galatians 6:11 is an example, Paul showing that he dictated his letter to an amanuensis (cf. 1 Cor 16:21; Col 4:18; Phlm 19).[8] Who the amanuensis involved with Galatians was, is unclear. Timothy is a possibility if we date Galatians in the 50s. If earlier, any of a number of brothers in Antioch are possible (e.g., Barnabas, Lucius, Manaen, or Simeon Niger). The similarity of style with the other undisputed letters suggests that the letters were closely dictated, rather than an amanuensis using a greater degree of freedom as in Ephesians, Colossians, and the Pastorals.

SETTING AND DATE

If authorship is a well-settled matter, the same cannot be said of the setting and date of Galatians. There has been ongoing and engaged debate about when Galatians was written and the situation at the time. This is based on some uncertainties. First,

---

4. Sosthenes, 1 Cor 1:1; Timothy, 2 Cor 1:1; Phil 1:1; Col 1:1; 1 Thess 1:1; 2 Thess 1:1; Phlm 1; Silvanus (Silas), 1 Thess 1:1; 2 Thess 1:1.

5. So, we can think of the likes of Barnabas, Lucius, Manaen, Niger, perhaps John Mark and Agabus, and others.

6. See further on authorship, Longenecker, *Galatians*, lvii–lix.

7. An amanuensis is 'A person who takes dictation, a secretary (Lat. "by hand").' The difference in style between New Testament letters that are signed by the same person (e.g., 1 and 2 Pet) is sometimes accounted for by the use of an amanuensis, who would have been given a degree of freedom in the writing process. See Romans 16:22; 1 Peter 5:12.' (See *PDSNTG* 17).

8. Longenecker, *Galatians*, lx.

who are the 'Galatians' Paul writes to? Second, how do the visits to Jerusalem in Acts line up with Galatians? And so, when should it be dated? Finally, how does the theological situation in Galatians relate to Acts and Romans in particular? Each issue will be discussed in turn.

THE NORTH AND SOUTH GALATIAN THEORIES

The English 'Galatians' comes from the Latin *Galatae* and refers to the Celts and Gauls. Around 500 BC, the Celts came from the area of the Danube, which runs from western Germany to the Black Sea. They spread out, some settling in France (Gaul), some in Britain (Wales, Ireland, and Scotland),[9] and some in the Balkans (the region north of Greece), moving from there into Asia Minor (Turkey). In the third century BC, some took control of central Asia Minor and eventually were contained in the region of the Anatolian plain around Ancyra, the modern capital toward the north-east of modern Turkey. When Rome took over, they allowed the Galatians to remain a client-kingdom under their own king (Amyntas)[10] until 25 BC when Augustus Caesar reorganized Galatia into a Roman province, including the original Galatian territory around Ancyra ('North Galatia') and the southern regions of Phrygia and Lycaonia ('South Galatia').

At the time of Paul, Galatia was a Roman province stretching all the way across the center of Asia Minor from Pontus in the north on the Black Sea, to Pamphylia on the Mediterranean (where Paul started his missionary journey in Acts 13). However, it is debated to what region of Galatia the letter was written. It could be that the letter is addressed to the Christian churches throughout this whole region (the Pan-Galatian Theory, popular

---

9. My dad's family are from Ireland originally. On the basis of this, I (the writer) must be part Celtic myself (and Saxon, Viking, and Norman).

10. King Amyntas was Tetrarch of the Trocmi and ruled from 36 BC to 25 BC (Strabo, *Geogr.* xii). He originally ruled Lycaonia and then added Derbe and other areas. In the Roman Triumvirate wars, he backed Brutus and Cassius but deserted to Mark Antony before the battle of Philippi 42 BC. Mark Antony gave him rule over Cappadocia in 37 BC. He then deserted to Octavian before the battle of Actium in 31 BC. He was eventually killed by an ambush set up by his wife in 25 BC.

in the nineteenth century). However, this is unlikely in that Galatians addresses the specific issues of a group of people that Paul had previously ministered to.[11]

Until the late nineteenth century, it was believed by most, including Luther and Calvin, that Galatians was written to the ancient Celts in north Galatia (the 'North Galatia Theory'). They reached this conclusion because of political changes after the time of the NT when *Provincio Galatia* (the Roman Province of Galatia) was confined mainly to the north. These changes included Vespasian expelling almost all of Pisidia from Galatia in AD 74, while in AD 137 Lycaonia was taken out of Galatia and joined to the province of Cilicia. In AD 297, southern Galatia was joined to a new province of Pisidia.[12] In addition, Christianity thrived in northern Galatia in the fourth and fifth centuries and so scholars such as Lightfoot (1865), Moffatt (1911), and modern commentators such as Betz, Lührmann, and others believe the letter was addressed to the north. They argue that the people in the letter of 'Galatians' resembled the Celts in their fickleness, superstition, and licentiousness. They felt that Galatians contained the same thinking as the letter to the Romans and so it must be a work from late in Paul's apostolic mission (mid–50s AD). Luke's mention of Galatia in Acts 16:6 and 18:23 at the beginning of Paul's second and third Antiochian journeys suggests that Paul visited these areas on these journeys. He may have planted churches there. If so, Galatians was written to the churches in the central-northern cities of Ancyra, Pessinus, and Tavium.

Ramsay and Bruce have argued persuasively against this view.[13] They contend that Galatians was written to the churches of South Galatia, which Paul evangelized on his first missionary journey, i.e., Perga, Pisidian Antioch, Iconium, Lystra, and Derbe (Acts 13–14) (the 'South Galatia Theory'). Ramsay believes Paul

11. George, *Galatians*, 40.
12. Longenecker, *Galatians*, lxiii.
13. W. M. Ramsay, *St. Paul the Traveller and the Roman Citizen* (London: Hodder & Stoughton, 1907), 130–51; F. F. Bruce, *The Epistle to the Galatians: A Commentary on the Greek Text*, NIGTC (Grand Rapids, MI: Eerdmans, 1982), 3–18.

intended to go to Ephesus but was forced to head inland to Pisidian Antioch to find relief for malaria. Whether it was malaria or not, it could be that illness did cause Paul to get medical help in Pisidian Antioch (Gal 4:13). In addition, the cities of Paul's first journey were undoubtedly considered part of the Roman Galatian province at the time. These cities lay on the major trade route west from Syria and Cilicia to Ephesus, the Sebastian Way. Pisidian Antioch was the base for the Roman governor of the province.

George has noticed a number of parallels between the themes of Galatians and Paul's initial evangelization in Acts 13–14 including 1) justification (cf. Acts 13:38–39); 2) the gentile nature of the churches (cf. Acts 13:46, 48 where Jews reject the message and gentiles accept it); 3) signs and wonders (Gal 3:5, cf. Acts 14:3, 8–10); 4) an angel of God (Gal 4:14, cf. Acts 14:12: Paul as Hermes?); and 5) the persecution of Paul (Gal 6:17, cf. Acts 13:45, 50–52; 14:5–6, 19–20). The references in Acts 16:6 and 18:23 then do not refer to the evangelization of the north, but to trips to strengthen these first Christians (cf. 1 Cor 16:1 [the same churches]; 2 Tim 4:10; 1 Pet 1:1 [the province in general]).

All things considered, 'the weight of evidence falls strongly in support of the view that Paul addressed his letter to the congregations in South Galatia that he and Barnabas established on their first missionary journey.'[14]

PAUL'S VISITS TO JERUSALEM

There is some difficulty in lining up the visits of Paul to Jerusalem from Acts and Galatians and Romans.

The visits in Acts are:

1) Visit 1 (Acts 9:26–29): After Paul's conversion and escape from Damascus.

2) Visit 2 (Acts 11:27–30): The Antiochian Collection Visit.

3) Visit 3 (Acts 15:1–19): The Jerusalem Council Visit.

4) Visit 4 (Acts 18:23): The Second Antiochian Missionary Journey Visit.

---

14. George, *Galatians*, 38.

5) Visit 5 (Acts 21:17–23:30): The Jerusalem Collection and Third Antiochian Missionary Journey Visit (imprisonment).

The visits in Galatians and Romans are:

1) Visit 1 (Gal 1:18–19): Three years after his conversion and trips to Arabia and Damascus.

2) Visit 2 (Gal 2:1–10): Fourteen years later, a trip to discuss the gospel he proclaimed and where the poor are specifically mentioned (cf. Gal 2:10).

3) Visit 3 (Rom 15:25–33): The Jerusalem Collection and Third Missionary Journey Visit (imprisonment).

Most likely, the first visit in Acts 9 is the first visit mentioned in Gal 1:18–19. The fourth visit in Acts 18:23 after his second Antiochian mission is mentioned only in passing by Luke and is probably not noted by Paul at all because it was of little significance—he simply passed through Jerusalem en route to Syrian Antioch. The fifth visit in Acts 21:17 in which Paul is imprisoned is clearly the third visit anticipated in Romans 15. So, the key question is: is the second visit in the Epistles the second or third visit in Acts, i.e., *is it the Antiochian Collection visit (Acts 11:27–30)*—date, ca. AD 46? Or is it the *Jerusalem Council visit* (Acts 15:1–19), ca. AD 48–49?

In favor of correlating the Galatians 2 visit with the Jerusalem Council visit in Acts 15 is that Galatians 2 refers to key themes common to Luke's account including the shape of Paul's gospel (v. 2), circumcision (v. 3), Judaizers (esp. v. 4), and reference to Jacob (James)[15] and Peter (Cephas) (vv. 8–9)—both of whom

---

15. Throughout this commentary, I will be calling James, Jacob. This is because the Greek *Iakōbos* translates as 'Jacob' and not 'James.' As William Varner, *James,* EEC (Bellingham, WA: Lexham, 2012), 84 tells us, 'The name is the Graecized form of the Hebrew name for the OT "Jacob" (Gen 27:36; Isa 41:8; 43:22; Jer 26:28 [lxx 30:10]; Ezek 28:25). Jacob (יַעֲקֹב), was a common name among Jewish men, appearing as the name of three prominent leaders in the early church: James the brother of John; James the Apostle, and James the brother of Jesus.' Arnold G. Fruchtenbaum, *The Messianic Jewish Epistles: Hebrews, James, First Peter, Second Peter, Jude.* 1st ed. (Tustin, CA: Ariel Ministries, 2005), 207 explains that when *Iakōbos* was translated into Latin, it was initially similar to *Iakobus* but evolved into *Jacobus* and then the "B" changed to an "M," and his name became *Jacomus.* Then, the English translation of *Jacomus* became *James.* As such, I will retain the name 'Jacob' in this commentary. Retaining 'Jacob,' enables

played significant roles in the Jerusalem Council (Peter, Acts 15:7–11; Jacob, Acts 15:13–21). Another factor is the dating of the material in Gal 1:15–2:10. If we take the crucifixion as AD 33,[16] then Paul's conversion was in AD 33–35, add the three years in Damascus/Arabia (taking us to AD 36–38), then another fourteen years to AD 50–52, and this fits nicely with the Jerusalem Council visit at the end of the first Antiochian missionary journey around AD 51–52 after which Paul launched the second missionary journey delivering the Jerusalem letter through the Pauline churches. Galatians would be written after this, perhaps around the same time as Romans and the Corinthian correspondence (c. 55–56).[17]

In favor of the Antiochian collection visit in Acts 11:26–30 is the appeal to Paul to 'always remember *the poor*' in Gal 2:10, which would concur with the Acts 11:30 collection delivery. In addition, with the gospel exploding among Greeks in Antioch, it makes sense that Paul would make a visit to Jerusalem with the Jerusalem local Barnabas to gain support for his law-free gospel from the Jerusalem Apostles. Furthermore, the acceptance of his ministry and the splitting up of the mission between Peter and Paul in Gal 2:7–10 fits a setting before the first Antiochian missionary journey (Acts 13). The chronological question, which appears at first hand insurmountable, can be resolved if the fourteen years are taken as inclusive of the three years and not

---

NT readers to recognize that the many men named James in the NT are in fact named after Israel's founder, Jacob who became Israel.

16. See H. W. Hoehner, 'Chronology,' in *DJG* 121–22 who argues for a crucifixion date of AD 33 based on a range of arguments: 1) Caiaphas' high priesthood (AD 18–37), Pilate's procuratorship (AD 26–36), and Herod Antipas' tetrarchship (4 BC–AD 39) suggest that he died between AD 26 and 36; 2) Jesus died Nisan 14, between 26–36. Astronomical events fit with AD 27, 30, 33, and 36 and the most likely, AD 30; 3) AD 27 and 36 can be eliminated as they are outside his ministry period. Hoehner argues AD 30 is unlikely as John the Baptist's ministry began in the fifteenth year of Tiberius, AD 29; 4). The relationship between Pilate and Herod Antipas fits best with AD 33. Hence, he believes Jesus died April 3 or 4 AD 33.

17. See, for example, Joseph Baber Lightfoot (ed.), *St. Paul's Epistle to the Galatians. A Revised Text with Introduction, Notes, and Dissertations* (4th ed), CCGNT (London: Macmillan and Co., 1874), 1–56. For further references see Douglas J. Moo, *Galatians*, BECNT (Grand Rapids, MI: Baker Academic, 2013), 4 n. 5.

as consecutive to it, i.e., eleven years after the first visit. This would mean that the visit to Jerusalem was AD 47–49, which fits with the Antiochian Collection visit and the date of the Jerusalem Council. Moreover, if Jesus actually died in AD 30, as is argued by a good number of scholars,[18] Paul's conversion would be in the immediate period after this (AD 31–32). If we then add the three years in Arabia with the fourteen years later when he again went to Jerusalem, we come up with a date of around AD 48.

Another problem for later dates is the Jerusalem Collection taken up during Paul's third Antiochian mission. If Galatians precedes the third Antiochian visit, then one would expect mention of it as it was one of the primary motivations for the mission. Such mentions are made in 1 Cor 16:1–4; 2 Cor 8–9; and Rom 15:28–31 but are completely absent from Galatians. Of special interest is 1 Cor 16:1 where Paul writes, 'now concerning the collection for the saints: *as I directed the churches of Galatia, so you also are to do.*' If Galatians is written near Romans and the Corinthian letters, then the lack of mention of the Jerusalem Collection seems problematic.

Finally, if we link Gal 2 to Acts 15, one asks why Paul would write Galatians at all or in the form it is if he had just attended the Jerusalem Council at which the key Christian leaders, including Peter and Jacob, had agreed on a circumcision-free gospel. They had written the Jerusalem letter to be delivered to the churches by Judas and Silas (Acts 15:22–35). Surely, Paul would simply ensure the letter was received and understood. Or, if he still chose to write the letter, his narrative would mention the Jerusalem letter. Or, he would have gone to Galatia himself with the Jerusalem letter to deal with the Judaizers.

---

18. See K. P. Donfried, 'Chronology (New Testament),' in *AYBD* 1015–16 who argues notes that caution needs to be taken concerning the fifteenth year of Tiberius as it could be AD 28, the date he ruled as co-emperor with Augustus (AD 25–26). More importantly, he rightly states that the popular idea of Jesus' three-year ministry is vague with the evidence indicating a ministry of anything from one to three years. He argues that Jesus was either crucified in AD 30 on the day before Passover (in John, Nisan 14) or the day of Passover (Synoptics, Nisan 15). If this is correct, then seventeen years from Paul's conversion if in AD 31–32 would fit snugly with a date in the late 40s.

THE VERACITY OF ACTS

The previous discussion concerning the most intriguing dilemma of reconciling the visits of Paul to Jerusalem often depends on the differing attitudes of scholars to Acts and the way they view Galatia. Those who are skeptical of the historicity of Acts usually align Galatians 2 with Acts 15 and pay little attention to trying to reconcile Galatians and Acts—they see no need to, as Acts is more theological than historical. They rely purely on the letters for a Pauline chronology. They usually argue Paul evangelized the Galatians envisaged in the letter on the second Antiochian missionary journey (Acts 16–18), rather than the first (Acts 13–14). They tend to date Galatians after the Jerusalem Council and the clash with Peter in Antioch, and so date it to Paul's third Antiochian missionary journey, anytime in the period AD 52–57.[19] Those who have a more positive view of the historicity of Acts tend to harmonize the accounts and come up with the solution that Gal 2 is the visit of Acts 11 dating Galatians around AD 48. This resolves the dilemma and allows for the Acts chronology to stand.

RESOLUTION

All in all, while we cannot be completely sure, and although it goes against a large portion of NT scholarship, the weight of the above analysis suggests that is better to align the Galatians 2 visit to Jerusalem with the Antiochian collection visit in Act 11:26–30 (c. 46). I see no reason to discredit Luke's account and consider there are good reasons to align Gal 2 with Acts 11 rather than Acts 15.

During this visit, Paul's gospel is endorsed. After his return to Antioch, Judaizers, who differed on their view of the gospel, visited the Antiochian church and taught the believers 'unless you are circumcised according to the custom of Moses, you cannot be saved' (Acts 15:1). It is likely that they also visited

---

19. For example, D. Lührmann, *Galatians*, CCS (Minneapolis: Fortress, 1992).

Paul's recently planted churches in the south Galatian area (Acts 13–14).

The visit to Antioch led to a debate between Paul and Barnabas sparking the trip to Jerusalem to resolve the issue once and for all. This likely occurred in AD 49. Galatians then was written from Antioch after the famine visit and *before* the Jerusalem Council around AD 47–48 at which the issue was resolved for the wider church (although the issue remained into the 60s to some extent, as is evident in Phil 3).[20] It was written to urge the Galatians not to listen to the Judaizers and to adhere to the gospel of grace.

After the Jerusalem Council visit, Judas and Silas traveled back to Antioch with Barnabas and Paul to deliver the letter to reinforce that his teaching in Galatians was 'kosher' (Acts 15:22–35). Sometime after this, Paul and Barnabas agreed to return to the churches 'in every city where we proclaimed the word of the Lord and see how they are' (Acts 15:36)—this clearly refers to those towns evangelized on the first Antiochian mission journey in Acts 13–14. After the rift between Paul and Barnabas (and Mark), Paul set out with Silas carrying the letter to reinforce the law-free gospel articulated in Galatians. They visited and strengthened these churches, including Derbe and Lystra, where Paul took Timothy under his wing and set out west (Acts 15:40–16:5).

A SUGGESTED CHRONOLOGY OF PAUL'S LIFE AND MINISTRY

As an aside, it is good to see how Galatians fits into a full chronology of Paul's life. Scholars form their chronologies in two main ways depending on how they view Acts. Those with a negative view of the historicity of Acts and the disputed Paulines create a chronology from his seven undisputed letters. With little chronological information in the letters, this has creativity and flexibility. The key markers from the letters include reference to his escape from Damascus during the reign

---

20. See also Colossians 2:13 and 1 Tim 1:8–9, which may indicate Judaizing activity in the 60s.

of King Aretas, which dates it between AD 37–40 (2 Cor 11:32), the movements mentioned in Galatians 1:11–2:14, the hardship catalogs in 2 Corinthians (6:4–10; 11:21–33; 12:1–10), travel plans in the letters,[21] and his undisputed prison letters Philippians and Philemon.

As the imprisonment in question is disputed, some set the prison letters during a supposed Ephesus imprisonment during his stay 52–55, which is not explicitly mentioned but deduced from references to extreme suffering (e.g., 1 Cor 15:32; 2 Cor 1:2–2:4). Others prefer imprisonment in Caesarea (AD 57–59), and some in Rome (AD 60–61). As a result, some schemes date Philippians early in the 50s (Ephesus), and Galatians in the mid-50s (at the same time as Romans and Corinthians). Jewett has come up with a chronology like this (outlined below). Note that Galatians is placed in the period 52–54 from Ephesus before Philippians, the Corinthians letters, and Romans. You will also note that the Jerusalem Council for Jewett aligns with Acts 18:22 rather than Acts 11 or 15, which is creative but unlikely:[22]

34	Paul's conversion (Gal 1:15, 16; 2 Cor 12:2)
35–37	Activities in Arabia, return to Damascus (Gal 1:17)
37	Escape Damascus; Jerusalem 1 (2 Cor 11:32–33; Acts 9:23–26)
37–46	Activities in Syria and Cilicia
43–45	First missionary journey: Cyprus, South Galatia
46–51	Second missionary journey: North Galatia, Macedonia, Achaia

21. See Rom 1:13–15; 15:19–32; 1 Cor 16:1–9; 2 Cor 7:5–16; 1 Thess 1:9; 2:17; 3:1–8.
22. See R. Jewett, *A Chronology of Paul's Life* (Philadelphia: Fortress Press), 1979), foldout. He aligns the Jerusalem Conference visit with Acts 18:22. Other chronologies of Paul from his letters can be found in J. Knox, *Chapters in the Life of Paul* (Nashville: Abingdon Press, 1950), 83–88 and G. Lüdemann, *Paulus, der Heidenapostel, vol 1, Studien zur Chronologie* (Göttingen: Vandenhoeck & Ruprecht, 1980), 272–73. These two scholars think Paul engaged in his mission in Syria, Cilicia, and Galatia in AD 36–39, and in Macedonia and Achaia in AD 38–51. They place Paul in Corinth in AD 41, the date they ascribe to the Claudian Edict; and the conference in Acts 15 = Gal 2:1, and so place it in AD 50/51. They believe Paul was in Ephesus AD 51–53. 1 Thessalonians is written in 41, 1 Corinthians in AD 52, 2 Corinthians and Galatians in AD 53, Romans in AD 54, and they see the AD 54/55 as the end of any Pauline chronology due to lack of information.

49	Claudius Edict (expulsion of Jews from Rome)
51	Hearing before Gallio at Corinth (Gallio Inscription)
51	**1 Thessalonians**
51	Second Jerusalem visit: apostolic conference (Acts 18:22/Gal 2:10)
52	Conflict with Peter (Gal 2:14–17)
52–57	Third missionary journey North Galatia
52–54	Ephesus; **Galatians**
54/55	Ephesian imprisonment; **Philemon, Philippians**
55	Visit to Corinth; return to Macedonia and Asia; **1 and 2 Corinthians**
56/57	Back to Corinth; **Romans**
57	Philippi to Jerusalem, Arrest
57–59	Imprisonment in Caesarea
61	Imprisonment in Rome
61	Execution in Rome

Scholars who regard Acts highly, me included, tend to use Acts as the main basis for Paul's life and argue that you can reconcile his letters with Acts. With this in mind, below is a proposed chronology of Paul's life. It assumes the general accuracy of Acts and that the scant chronological material in the letters can be harmonized with Luke's account. In this more traditional chronology, Galatians falls in AD 48 after Paul's first mission in AD 47–48 with the visit in Gal 2 aligning with Acts 11:30 (see the earlier discussion). This chronology is adapted from F. F. Bruce.[23]

1–10	Paul's Birth
Aut 27–Aut 28	Ministry of John the Baptist
Spring 28	Baptism of Jesus (Mark 1:9–11 par)
Summer 28	Early Judean ministry of Jesus (John 2:13–4:3)
Autumn 28–Aut 29	Galilean ministry of Jesus (Mark 1:14–9:50 and parr.)
Aut 28–Spring 30	Jesus in Judea and Perea

---

23. F. F. Bruce, *The Acts of the Apostles: The Greek Text with Introduction and Commentary* (Grand Rapids: Eerdmans, 1951), 55–56. I have made one or two minor adjustments and additions.

	(Mark 10:1 and parr.)
April–May 30	Crucifixion, Resurrection, Ascension, and Pentecost (Luke 23–24; Acts 1–2)
c. 33	Conversion of Saul of Tarsus (Acts 9:1–22; Gal 1:15–17)
c. 35	Paul's first visit to Jerusalem (Acts 9:26–30; Gal 1:18–20)
c. 43	Death of Jacob, brother of John, and Peter's escape from prison (Acts 12:1–17)
March 44	Death of Herod Agrippa I (Acts 12:20–23)
45–48	Famine in Judea and the first Jerusalem Collection (Acts 11:28)
c. 46	Paul and Barnabas visit Jerusalem (Acts 11:30; Gal 2:1)
c. 47–48	Paul and Barnabas' mission journey to Cyprus and SE Galatia (Acts 13:4–14:26)
c. 48	Peter and Paul clash in Antioch (Gal 2:11–14)
c. 48	**Galatians** (from Antioch on return)
49	Claudian Edict expelling Jews from Rome due to conflict over Christ (Suet, *Claud.* 25.4; Acts 18:2)
c. 49	Apostolic Council in Jerusalem (Acts 15:6–29)
c. 49–50	Paul's missionary journey to Macedonia including Philippi, Thessalonica, Berea, Illyricum? (Acts 16:9–17:14; 1 Thess 1:2–2:2)
Aut 50–Spring 52	Paul in Corinth (Acts 18:1–18; 1 Cor 2:1–5)
Late 50	**1 & 2 Thessalonians**
c. May 51	Gallio proconsul of Achaia (Acts 18:12)
Spring–Summer 52	Paul's return to Judea and Syria

	(Acts 18:22)
Aut 52–Sum 55	Paul in Ephesus on his third major missionary journey (Acts 19:1–20:1)
Early 55	Paul sends Timothy and Erastus to Macedonia (Acts 19:22)
Spring 55	**1 Corinthians** (1 Cor 16:8)
Summer 55	Paul's sorrowful visit to Corinth (2 Cor 2:1; 13:2)
Sum/Aut 55	Titus' reconciling mission in Corinth (2 Cor 2:13; 7:5–16)
Aut 55	Paul in Troas (2 Cor 2:12)
Wint 55–Aut 56	Paul in Macedonia, Illyricum? (second Jerusalem Collection) (Acts 20:1f; Rom 15:19)
56	**2 Corinthians**
Winter 56–57	Paul in Achaia (Corinth) (Jerusalem Collection) (Acts 20:2f; Rom 15:25–28; 16:23)
Early 57	**Romans**
May 57	Paul's arrival to deliver the collection. His arrest in Jerusalem (Acts 21:15–33)
57–59	Paul imprisoned at Caesarea (Acts 23:23–26:32)
Sept 59	Paul sails to Italy after an appeal to Caesar (Acts 27:1f)
Wint 59–60	Paul in Malta (Acts 28:1–10)
Feb/March 60	Paul arrives in Rome (Acts 28:14–16)
c. 60	**Colossians, Philemon, Ephesians**
c. 62–63	**Philippians**
Late 62–63	End of Paul's Roman detention (Acts 28:30)
62	Death of Jacob the Just in Jerusalem (Josephus, *Ant.* 20.9)
62–64	Fourth Missionary Journey to Spain? East to Greece and Asia
July 64	Great fire in Rome
64–65	Imprisonment in Rome, **1 Timothy, Titus,**

Neronian persecution
65–67 **2 Timothy,** Peter and Paul killed
70 Destruction of Jerusalem

This chronology suggests that Paul was converted around AD 33 in his twenties, some three years after the resurrection. He began his Antiochian missionary journeys in about AD 47–48 in his mid–40s. His letters were written between AD 48–64. He died in his early 60s in Rome under Nero. It places Galatians in AD 48 after his first Antiochian mission and before the Jerusalem Council.

PURPOSE AND SEQUENCE

Assuming the correctness of the setting and date above, we can construct the situation and see the purpose of Galatians clearly. Paul had been on his first Antiochian missionary journey, taking the Gospel to the area of South Galatia (Acts 13–14). After this journey, Judaizers from Jerusalem had gone to Syrian Antioch and into the Pauline churches of Galatia and had challenged Paul's gospel, telling the new gentile converts that belief in Jesus was not enough. Male converts also needed to be circumcised and all gentile converts were expected to adhere to the law of Moses (and particularly its boundary markers, like circumcision) to be Christian and to be included in God's people.[24] These Judaizers ('false brothers') had also visited Antioch, where Paul has resisted them (Gal 2:4–5). Paul had also had a clash over table fellowship in Antioch with Peter and Jacob who, in order not to offend the Judaizers, withdrew from table fellowship with the new gentile converts (Gal 2:11–14).

We can also possibly discern in the letter things that they have said that have maligned Paul at a personal letter—things that have buttressed their false gospel. They have accused him of corrupting the gospel to gain converts, rather than being concerned with God's will (Gal 1:10–11). They may have put him down as a second-rate Jew (Gal 1:13–14) and accused him of

24. Female converts would not need to be circumcised but would be expected to adhere to other laws. Any male children would be circumcised on the eighth day.

creating a false gospel without the confirmation of the Jerusalem apostles (Gal 2:1–10). They are challenging his gospel of grace, arguing that it makes Christ a servant of sin (Gal 2:17). They have perhaps argued that Paul places no value in the law at all (Gal 3:21). He is being accused of preaching circumcision elsewhere, but softening the gospel to win converts in Galatia, something he is clearly not guilty of as he preaches the same gospel everywhere (Gal 5:11).

As one might expect from the one who pioneered these churches with love and passion, Paul is deeply offended—seeing this as a violation of the gospel of grace through faith in Jesus Christ, which sets Jew and gentile on an equal footing. Paul wrote Galatians to urge his converts to resist these Judaizers. He thus wrote the letter *in AD 48 a year before the Jerusalem Council.*

In the letter, he refers to an earlier discussion he had with the apostles in Jerusalem on his famine visit, at which time he was set apart to take the gospel to the gentiles. He states that this gospel does not require circumcision and adherence to the law. Later on, some of these same Judaizing preachers traveled again to Antioch, and this time clashed even more dramatically with Paul and Barnabas (Acts 15:1–2). Due to this event, and with the blessing of the multicultural Antiochian church, Paul and Barnabas met again with the leaders of the church in Jerusalem. At the meeting, it was formally agreed that new gentile converts did not need to be circumcised or adhere to the law of Moses to be part of God's saved people.

After that meeting, Paul traveled back to Antioch accompanied by two Jerusalem prophets, Judas, and Silas, to reinforce that the decree was the decision of the leaders of the whole church. He then set out with Silas through these same Galatian churches on his second Antiochian mission carrying with them the Jerusalem decree (Acts 15:23–29). It is also possible that the letter was delivered to Rome on this trip, perhaps by Luke, during the time that the Jews had been expelled from the city by Claudius. If so, it may have accelerated the gentilization of the Roman church and added to tensions when the Jews returned. This may give background to the letter to Rome some eight or so years later and perhaps the conflict referred to in Phil 1:14–18.[25]

It is clear then that the letter was written to reinforce that the gospel is a gospel of grace and that new gentile converts do not need to be circumcised and come under the law of Moses to be saved and included in God's people. Contrasting the demand for law adherence, for Paul, all that gentile converts require is genuine faith in God and his Son. The letter is an appeal to resist and reject the teaching of the Judaizers who were demanding this. It asserts that the only human response required to be declared righteous in God's sight (justified) is faith (*pistis*)—justification by faith. The letter also reasserts Paul's apostolic authority, although, as always, Paul subordinates his own maltreatment to the concerns of the gospel (cf. Phil 1:12–18a). Paul does not mess around in this letter. He is deeply concerned that forcing gentile believers to adhere to the law of Moses will dramatically curtail the spread of the gospel among the gentiles, while simultaneously spreading the wrong gospel to those who do accept it.

GALATIANS AND THE 'NEW PERSPECTIVE' ON PAUL

In recent years, the study of Paul in Galatians and Romans, in particular, has been affected by the so-called 'New Perspective on Paul.' As it is important to be familiar with this when reading both these letters (and Phil 3), here, I will first outline the Old Perspective (OP), then the New Perspective (NP), and assess its value and importance for the study of Paul's letters and Galatians.[26]

---

25. See Mark J. Keown, *Philippians*, EEC (Bellingham, WA: Lexham, 2017), 1:5–9.
26. See also Mark M. Mattison, 'A Summary of the New Perspective on Paul,' http://www.thepaulpage.com/a-summary-of-the-new-perspective-on-paul/; Dennis M. Swanson, 'Bibliography of Works on the New Perspective on Paul,' *TMSJ* 16/2 (Spring 2005): 317–24 (this whole edition of TMSJ is worth a read as it is devoted to the issue).

THE 'OLD PERSPECTIVE'

The 'old perspective' on Paul dominated Protestant scholarship from the Reformation until the late twentieth century. It sees Paul as responding to a Jewish legalism concerning the law, i.e., that the Jewish view was one of legalistic works-righteousness for salvation, seeking to be saved through merit achieved through flawless living out of the law (cf. Gal 3:10–11; Deut 27:26; Lev 18:5; Rom 2:5–29). It was believed that Judaism had degenerated into graceless legalism, hypocrisy, and a lack of compassion. The 'Jew' represented religion off the rails, a religion based on human works and merit instead of reliance on God's grace and human action as a response to grace, i.e., a 'works theology.'

Protestant scholars used the lens of Luther's critique of Roman Catholicism to read Rabbinic Judaism. It was held that Rabbis believed salvation was earned through merit, keeping the law so that God the judge would grant salvation and reward. Many commentaries of Romans, Galatians, and other books are based on this viewpoint.[27] Romans 7:7–25, for Sanday and Headlam, is read as Paul's pre-conversion tortured experience as he sought to satisfy the demands of God for salvation. While a few scholars in this period challenged this prevailing view (see below), this view was completely dominant over NT scholarship including Paul. Some works were important for supporting this view, such as Ferdinand Weber, who worked through rabbinic literature to find examples to demonstrate this view of Judaism as legalism.[28] His work was followed by the works of the likes of Emil Schürer and Wilhelm Bousset.[29]

27. For example, see W. Sanday and A. C. Headlam, *A Critical and Exegetical Commentary on the Epistle to the Romans*, ICC (Edinburgh: T & T. Clark, 1895); R. K. Bultmann, *Primitive Christianity in Its Contemporary Setting*, trans. R. Fuller (London: Collins, 1960).

28. F. Weber, *System der altsynagogalen palästinischen Theologie aus Targum, Midrasch und Talmud* (Leipzig: Dörffling & Franke, 1880), revised as *Jüdische Theologie auf Grund des Talmud und verwandter Schriften* (Leipzig: Dörffling & Franke, 1897).

29. D. Emil Schürer, Geschichte des Jüdischen Volkes im Zeitalter Jesu Christi (Leipzig: J. C. Hinrichs'sche Buchhandlung, 1886); Wilhelm Bousset, *Kyrios Christos: A History of*

THE NEW PERSPECTIVE

The Jewish scholar Montefiore critiqued this dominant view of Christian theologians for painting a Rabbinic Judaism negatively so that Paul's theology would shine more brightly (grace and faith over law and works).[30] Montefiore argued Weber had misread rabbinic literature and that the God of Israel was a compassionate, merciful, and forgiving God who would grant forgiveness to the repentant. He believed that the Rabbis, rather than seeing the law as a horrendous burden, saw it as a gift and delight (cf. Ps 19; 119). He argued the Rabbis valued faith as highly as Paul, but his appeal had little effect.

In 1927, G. F. Moore's two-volume study on rabbinic theology argued that Weber had little first-hand knowledge of rabbinic literature and took most of his quotes from Christian works against Judaism.[31] He emphasized the role of grace, forgiveness, and repentance in rabbinic literature. In 1948, W. D. Davies' work, *Paul and Rabbinic Judaism* argued Paul's doctrine of justification by faith apart from works was one metaphor among others. He contended that Paul was a Pharisee who had realized that the messianic age had dawned.[32]

A critical turning point in questioning the consensus is Krister Stendahl's 'The Apostle Paul and Introspective Conscience of the West' written in 1963/76,[33] a year before Sander's epoch-creating work (below). Stendahl argued that Paul had been misread by Luther through his own experience, and others subsequently had incorrectly read Paul through Luther's eyes. Stendahl argues that Paul of the NT does not speak of his tremendous struggle with guilt (like Luther) due to seeking to

the *Belief in Christ from the Beginning of Christianity to Irenaeus*, trans. J. E. Steely (Nashville: Abingdon, 1970).

30. C. G. Montefiore, *Judaism and St. Paul* (London: Max Goscen, 1914).
31. G. F. Moore, Judaism in the First Centuries of the Christian Era: The Age of the Tannaim (2 vols.; Cambridge, MA: Harvard University, 1927).
32. W. D. Davies, *Paul and Rabbinic Judaism*: Some Rabbinic Elements in Paul's Theology (London: Society for Promoting Christian Knowledge Publishing, 1955), 71-73.
33. Krister Stendahl, 'The Apostle Paul and the Introspective Conscience of the West' in *The Harvard Theological Review* 56. 3 (July 1963): 199-215. Republished in *Paul Among Jews and gentiles*, (Augsburg: Fortress), 1976.

satisfy God through perfect obedience to the law. Rather, Paul demonstrates the opposite. For example, in Acts 23:1, Luke records Paul stating, 'Brothers, I have lived before God *in all good conscience* up to this day.' Stendahl argues that Paul was not wracked with guilt as a Jew as he sought to please God through the law. Stendahl contends that Rom 7 does not represent Paul's despairing cry at his failure to live the law but represents Paul's larger argument against the law. Paul then does not deny the law but acknowledges it as holy and good. His guilt relates to human sin and fleshly weakness, proneness to sin, rather than the law itself. To read Rom 7 as Paul's guilt over law is to read into it a western individualistic introspective consciousness. Where guilt is expressed in Paul, it is over his persecution of the Christian movement and not a failure to live up to the law (1 Cor 15:9; 1 Tim 1:13–16). Stendahl also argued that as a Christian, Paul does not demonstrate excessive over-confidence in his righteousness. He testifies to a clear conscience (2 Cor 1:12a) and confidence (1 Cor 9:27). Yet he also recognizes his need to continue on (Phil 3:12–14) and awaited judgment (2 Cor 5:10) with the hope of a positive verdict (2 Cor 5:11–12; 1 Cor 4:4).

The watershed moment in the discussion came with E.P. Sanders' 1977 book *Paul and Palestinian Judaism*.[34] He worked through the major works of NT scholarship to demonstrate how scholars had denigrated ancient Judaism as a religion based on salvation by merit and obedience to the law. He worked through the Tannaitic literature,[35] the literature of Qumran (DSS), the Apocrypha, and the Pseudepigrapha to answer the question, 'what must one do to be saved?' He concluded that almost all of the literature of Judaism answered the question 'what must one do to be saved' *not* with legalistic, perfect righteousness, but through *belonging* to the covenant people of God. While obedience was appropriate, atonement was available through repentance, prayer, and sacrifice, through the mercy of God, for

---

34. E. P. Sanders, *Paul and Palestinian Judaism: A Comparison of Patterns of Religion* (Philadelphia: Fortress Press, 1977).
35. Rabbinic works from AD 10–220 including the Mishnah, Baraita, Tosefta, and Tannaitic Midrash.

those who do not flawlessly obey the law. Sanders called this 'covenantal nomism.'[36] He defines this as 'the view that one's place in God's plan is established on the basis of the covenant and that the covenant requires as the proper response of man his obedience to its commandments while providing means of atonement for transgression.'[37] As such, obedience is *not the means of entering into the covenant*, which cannot be earned through merit. In his words: 'the intention and effort to be obedient constitute the *condition for remaining in the covenant*, but they do not *earn* it.'[38] Rather, inclusion comes through the grace of God. Obedience then is about *maintaining one's position* in the covenant. The only dissenting voice in Second Temple Judaism is *4 Ezra*, who Sanders considered atypical. Thus, Judaism was redefined as a religion not of works and merit, but of grace. At its heart are the free election of Israel and its religious system centered on repentance, atonement through sacrifice, and God's forgiveness. To this grace, Israel's right response was gratitude and faithfulness.

This work led to a swing in NT scholarship whereby it has become a point of agreement that the 'old perspective' distorted the Jewish perspective on law and misread the notes of grace and mercy in Judaism. Since then, prominent scholars like James Dunn[39] and Tom Wright[40] among others have argued for the New Perspective on Paul. They particularly emphasize the cultural implications of the Judaizing debate referred to in the Pauline writings. In recent years, the debate has died down, but it is fair to say that the New Perspective on Paul has changed the way that Paul is understood—liberating him from the

---

36. Sanders, *Paul and Palestinian Judaism*, 75.
37. Sanders, Paul and Palestinian Judaism, 75.
38. Sanders, *Paul and Palestinian Judaism*, 180 (emphasis his).
39. See James D. G. Dunn, 'The New Perspective on Paul,' *BJRL* 65 (1983): 95-122; idem, 'Yet Once More— "The Works of the Law,"' *JSNT* 46 (1992): 99-107.
40. See N. T. Wright, *Paul and the Faithfulness of God*, COQG 4 (Minneapolis: Fortress Press, 2013), idem, *What Saint Paul Really Said: Was Paul of Tarsus the Real Founder of Christianity?* (Grand Rapids: Eerdmans, 1997); idem, The Climax of the Covenant. Minneapolis: Fortress, 1992.

Reformation and understanding his perspective within first-century Second Temple Judaism.

THE POSITION OF THIS COMMENTARY

While siding with the Old Perspective, this commentary accepts validity in both views. The NP proponents rightfully recognize that Judaism at the time of Paul was not concerned with doing works to gain salvation; rather, second Temple Jews believed that they were elect as a people by God's grace. Hence, one was born into the covenant community. They kept the law to maintain their relationship with God (not to enter it). They also rightfully recognize that the debate Paul was engaged in was a cultural Jewish question—does a gentile have to become a Jew to be justified and included in God's people. Judaizers said yes. Paul says no. They also correctly recognize the huge ecclesiological questions this raises in terms of culture—is there a superior or primary culture? Or are all human beings on the same level before God, both Jew and gentile?

Yet, the NP fails to deal with Paul's overall argument. They limit the works of the law to boundary markers, especially circumcision. These are the presenting issues, but Paul's overall argument is that a believer, Jew or gentile, is not under the law in any sense. They are free from it. For gentile converts to accept the demand for boundary markers was to enter what is now a false religion. For Jewish evangelists to demand submission to the boundary markers of Judaism was to preach a corrupted gospel with a deficient Jesus. New gentile converts could come to Christ from their cultural perspective and did not need to also convert to Judaism.

NP advocates also fail to recognize that whether Jews were concerned about keeping the law to enter the covenant people or remain in it, it led to legalism. Judaism at the time was legalistic as Jews, especially Pharisees, demanded people keep the law slavishly to please God. We see this powerfully in Jesus' constant clashes with the Pharisees and Scribes. Paul recognizes that to acknowledge the demands of the boundary markers is to bring people into legalism. Further, it leads to seeking to please God by behavior and can lead to pride in oneself and judgmentalism of self and others. It brings them into a religious system that has no power to save them. Indeed, the Jewish religious system for Paul continues in Christianity and as we will see in our discussion of Gal 4:8–1, Judaism that rejects Jesus is no better than a pagan religion advocating self-mutilation (as with some in Galatia at the time).

Paul's perspective on the law in Galatians demonstrates that there is truth in the NP where culture is concerned. However, this commentary sides with the OP overall. Put another way, the event of the cross ended the demand of the law for salvation and inclusion in God's people. It ended any notion of a privileged race, gender, or social status. It inaugurated a new era where people are free from bondage to demands that are impossible to keep. All these demands do is illuminate the law. People are set free to live in a loving relationship with God, their father. They are emancipated to live in love with one another, forever putting aside petty human divisions. They are one with God and each other in Christ. Paul ends up by recognizing that while believers are not under the law, by the Spirit of God they live out the central impulses of God; supremely, love.

GALATIANS AND THE LAW

Galatians has been at the heart of the debate on the law in Paul. Older scholars read Galatians as Paul's critique of legalistic Judaism. It was held that whereas Judaism held that one had to fulfill the law to be justified before God the judge, Paul argues that one is justified by faith and saved on the basis of grace. New Perspective advocates have critiqued this view of Judaism, Paul, and Galatians. They argue Judaism was always a religious system of grace. law-observance was not to earn God's salvation but to remain a part of God's covenant people. They argue that the issue at hand is not the whole law, but those things Jews upheld to distinguish themselves from the gentiles; the so-called boundary markers: circumcision, Sabbath, and eating protocols. They see the real issue as inclusion. They are concerned about the cultural questions raised by Jewish believers: does a new gentile convert need to become a Jew to be included in God's people? Because of their passion for Jewish law, which enshrined circumcision (esp. Gen 17; Lev 12:3), Sabbath (e.g., Exod 20:8–11), and food laws (e.g., Lev 11), they wanted gentile Christians to uphold these laws. New Perspective thinkers believe Paul's problem is not with the whole law, but with these boundary markers. Otherwise, new converts should uphold the law. Old perspective thinkers have critiqued this, arguing that while there is clearly a cultural dimension to the debate, Paul's concern goes further than boundary markers. He argues that Christians are no longer under the law in any sense. They are justified by faith. They enter God's people by faith. They remain in God's people by faith.

The position of this commentary is that of the Old Perspective but accepting aspects of the New Perspective position. The New Perspective thinkers have rightly located the argument in the first-century context with the focus on what a gentile must do to be justified by God. They recognize that what is at issue is cultural; one does not have to be a Jew to be saved. No culture has supremacy. This extends to gender and social status in 3:28: a Jew, a man, and a citizen are not superior beings within the body of Christ who are elite over gentiles, women, and slaves. Believers are one and all on the same level. The theology of Galatians challenges all attitudes of cultural supremacy (e.g., Nazism, white supremacy, apartheid, Israel over Palestine, etc.), patriarchy, and slavery.

However, the Old Perspective argument that Galatians is about salvation is correct. Paul's argument is that all that is required to be justified before God the King and Judge is faith. At the moment of faith, a person is saved and included in God's people and remains so where there is genuine faith. A believer is not *under* the law in any sense. They are free from it. The law has served its purpose of being a tutor for Israel and is now fulfilled by Christ and in Christ. The Christian does not live by the outward governance of a set of rituals, but by the internal impulsion of the Spirit. In this way, a Christian will live out the essence of the law, especially the 'laws' of faith and love. However, they are not under the law.

We will now have a closer look at Paul's argument concerning the law through Galatians, demonstrating that both the OP emphasis on salvation by grace and faith but not works and the NP stress on culture are merited to some degree. In Galatians, Paul is dealing with Judaizers, who advocated that gentile converts needed not only to place their trust in Jesus but be circumcised and submit to the Torah, especially the boundary markers of Sabbath, ritual purity, and eating laws. They are to yield to the requirements of the law.

The first reference to 'law' (*nomos*) is found in Gal 2:15–16. After discussing the clash with Peter over fellowship with gentiles, Paul writes, 'We are by nature Jews and not sinners from the gentiles, having known that a man is not justified by *works of the law* except through faith in Jesus Christ. And we also believed in Christ Jesus, so that we will be justified by faith in Christ and not by works of the law, because from works of the law no flesh shall be justified.'

This is a controversial text with many questions to be answered. First, there is the relationship of what is said to the previous clash in Antioch. Second, there is the meaning of the participle *eidotes* ('having known'), which launches Gal 2:16. Is it consecutive or contrasting in some way? Third, what is the meaning of 'works of the law' here? Are they boundary markers or badges of inclusion in the people of God, i.e., circumcision, Sabbath and Jewish calendar, and food laws? Or is it the whole law that Paul has in mind? Finally, there is the question of the meaning of *pisteōs Iēsou Christou* or *pisteōs Christou*. Traditionally, these are taken objectively as 'faith in Jesus Christ' or 'faith in Christ.' Many scholars are now arguing that it should be read as 'faithfulness of Jesus Christ/Christ,' emphasizing that Christ's faithfulness saves people who place their trust in him.

The final question, while extremely interesting and important theologically, is incidental to this discussion, so I will not deal with it here (see 2:16).[41] The first three questions are important. Dunn and others read Rom 2:15–16 in light of the problem of eating rituals in Antioch. For them, 'works of the law' are not the whole law but *boundary markers* because that is the immediate contextual issue (eating 2:11f). 'We know' are the Jews who have always known that works of the law do not justify. God, through the grace of the covenant and election, justifies. Now, it is faith in Jesus Christ as his Messiah who justifies.

However, this reading has a number of problems. First, the 'we' who know that a person is not justified by works of the law except through faith in Jesus Christ is clearly Christian-speak, not Jewish language, i.e., it is not historic Israel and faith *in God*. If it were, it would read, 'we know that a man is not justified by works of the law but through faith in God.' That is, 'we' *must* refer to *Christians* for almost all Jews *do not know this*, having rejected Jesus as Christ and Lord. However, it is likely in this text Paul has *particularly* in mind the Jewish Christians like the ones mentioned through chs. 1–2 of Galatians (himself, Peter, John, Jacob, and others).

'Having known' then relates to Christian or Jewish Christian knowledge. There are three possibilities, then, for the participle *eidotes*, 'knowing.' Either Paul is speaking *ironically* of all believers as 'Jews,' i.e., 'We are by nature Jews' includes all believers grafted into Israel whether Jews or gentiles—the new Israel. The participle *eidotes* then can be read as 'having known.' Second, it

---

41. The construct *pistou Christou* (faith/faithfulness in/of Christ) in different forms is found six times in Paul (Rom 3:22; Gal 2:16, 20; 3:22; Eph 3:12; Phil 3:9). Hays and other modern scholars take it objectively arguing that believers are saved in the faithfulness of Christ. That is, he is the faithful one in whom we are saved. Examination of the texts shows that if 'faith in Christ' is intended there is a double-up of the idea of faith and it is redundant. However, outside of these *pistis Christou* verses, Paul never speaks of the faithful life of Christ and always speaks of him as the object of faith. As such some take it as a general emphatic statement making clear that it is faith in Christ. The first view mentioned does not change the traditional view that we are saved through faith in Christ. What it does is shift the emphasis to Christ, our faith is in *his faith* and *his faith* saves us (if we believe). It is fair to say that it could go either way. This will be discussed in the commentary on 2:16 where I side with the 'faith in Christ' school but admit it is a close call and that arguably, both-and could be in view (see the commentary on the text). See for a summary Matthew C. Easter, 'The Pistis Christou Debate: Main Arguments and Responses in Summary,' *CBR* 9.1 (2010): 33–47.

can be read as 'nevertheless knowing' (NASB95) or 'yet we know' (ESV). A third possibility is that Paul does not mean all Jews (which is impossible with their rejection of Christ) but means 'we *Christians* who are Jews by nature and not gentile sinners.' Thus the 'we' refers to Peter, Jacob, Paul, and other Jewish Christians who know it to be true that salvation is in Christ alone. This would appear to be the best reading. Here, Paul is saying that 'no man [person]' and even 'no flesh' is justified by works of the law. The only justification is found through faith in Christ. The real question is, 'what are the works of the law?' Boundary markers? The whole law? Both?

Second, while in the immediate context it might seem justified to take 'works of the law' (*ergōn nomou*) as food laws, this idea crumbles as we read further into Paul's use of *nomos* in Galatians where it becomes clear that Paul is speaking generally of law and not just certain works. Now, this is a huge issue and, in my view, one of the blind spots for New Perspective thinkers. At *no point* does Paul define 'works of the law' as merely boundary markers. He certainly does not at the first use in Gal 2:16. Rather, as we will see as we discuss law further in Galatians, *he moves freely between 'the law' and 'works of the law.'* To read all references to 'the law' as 'works of the law' as boundary markers *requires assuming this definition was known to the Galatians.*

It is argued by many NP thinkers that the term 'works of the law' is a technical term in Judaism, which is possible. As I will discuss in more detail in the commentary on Gal 2:16, the only evidence for this is Qumran, and this is hardly justification for assuming that Paul held this view. Even more problematic is that the Galatians and the Romans are thousands of miles from Qumran, whose writings are those of a Jewish sect. Further, Rome was not a Pauline church and cannot be assumed to hold this perspective. This is a very weak argument.

In addition, we will see through this commentary that Paul's polemic in Galatians as it develops cannot be limited to merely boundary markers. Rather circumcision, in particular, *is representative of coming under all the law for salvation, ecclesiology, mission, and ethical behavior*—entry into a system of salvation that requires flawless obedience to the law! It is better to read the relationship between 'the law' and 'works of the law' the other way around, i.e., living out all the precepts of law whether boundary markers or not. Circumcision is like *a wedge* for Paul: to be circumcised is to enter law as the basis for salvation and inclusion in God's people and to add to Christ. It is to render Christ's death insufficient in and of itself. Paul is opposed to adding *anything* to Christ whether circumcision, Sabbath, eating laws, or any other OT precept. Christianity is not Jesus-plus! It is Jesus! Today we could add baptism, having a quiet time, turning up to church every Sunday, tithing, and so on—none of these contribute to our justification before God, our salvation. We are justified by faith.

The next reference to the law in Galatians is not to 'works of the law' but to 'the law' in 2:19. Paul states that 'for through *the law* I died to *the law,* so that I might live to God. I have been crucified with Christ.' Here Paul is stating that he is dead to *the law* not merely 'the works of the law' and not boundary markers—it is 'the law!' Paul is now *dead* in Christ and as such, he is *free* of law (cf. Rom 7:1–3). Paul now lives in and through Christ by faith (Gal 2:20). In Gal 2:21, Paul says that he does not render grace null, pointing out that if justification comes through *the law* (note it is not 'works of the law'), then Christ's death is pointless and avails nothing. In other words, to claim that law has validity *in any sense* (boundary markers or otherwise) removes the need for Christ and makes salvation based on doing the law and not grace. Salvation then would be in Judaism and law, not Christ which it must be for Paul. Thus, for Paul, there is *no going back* to the law system. For the Galatians, of course, it is not going back; it is leaving grace to enter a system that cannot save!

In Galatians 3, Paul goes on. He asks who has bewitched the Galatians to disobey the truth, i.e., the gospel of grace. Christ has died and so the era of law is ended. He then asks them two important questions in Gal 3:2, 5 returning to the phrase 'works of the law.' He asks did the Galatians receive the Spirit (or God do miracles among them) by becoming Jews and coming under the law and doing its precepts (note there is no reference to certain precepts) or by believing? Clearly, the answer is by believing when they heard the gospel. So, for them to return to law is to return to 'flesh.' It is to seek to please God, be saved, and be included in God's people through self-effort rather than through grace, faith, and Spirit (Gal 3:3). In Gal 3:6–9, Paul illustrates this from the law itself with Abraham who 'believed God, and it was credited to him as righteousness,' i.e., he was justified by faith and not any work (remember this is before the law was given; cf. Gen 15:6; Rom 4). Salvation and becoming a child of Abraham and God, which are coterminous events, occur through faith (Gal 3:7). All nations are blessed through Abraham's faith by faith.

In Gal 3:10–29, Paul defines 'works of the law' and his understanding in regard to the whole law. In fact, even if 'works of the law' does not refer to covenantal entry points, his argument here is about the whole law and shows that it is the law which one enters that is the issue more than the entry itself—the law cannot save. Through this passage he draws on the law itself to prove his point; the law is good (cf. Rom 7:12), but it is useless to save, and it always has been—this is the fault of people and not of God for no flesh can fulfill the law because of sin (aside from Jesus who did). The law's value lies in that it leads people to recognize sin and realize their need for the grace of Christ.

In Gal 3:10, Paul states that *every person* (including the Galatians and Jews) who seeks to rely on the works of the law for salvation and inclusion in God's people is *under a curse*. The curse is drawn from the law itself; Deut 27:26: 'Cursed is *everyone* who does not observe and obey *all the things* written in the book of the law.' Note it is 'everyone' and 'all the things written in the book of the law.' This issue cannot be narrowed to merely boundary markers or entry points. Paul is writing off *the whole system* based on law and obedience as a means of salvation. It did not save the Jews before Jesus; faith did. It won't save Christians now, faith does. 'Works of the law' then are 'everything written in the book of the law' and not merely boundary markers or badges of Judaism. Even if they are 'boundary markers,' this text clarifies that the problem is the *whole law!* Boundary markers, particularly circumcision, are included and of great importance as markers of inclusion and entry points, but they are starting points and symbolic of the *whole law*. We can note here too that as Paul cites the OT, he draws on the whole corpus and not merely the Torah; for him, the law is the whole OT (cf. 1 Cor 14:21).

Paul, in Gal 3:11, then quotes another of his favorite texts on faith, Hab 2:4 (cf. Rom 1:17): 'the righteous one will live by faith.'[42] Again this emphasizes that faith, and not the law, brings life. In Gal 3:12, he states that law is not based on faith but on obedience to the law. He quotes Lev 18:5 in support: 'whoever does the works of the law, will live by them.' Note it is 'whoever,' i.e., all, Jew or gentile (including the Galatians, the Romans, or the Philippians, etc.—we can add Māori, Pakeha, Asian, Polynesian, African, British, American, and so on). 'Works of the law,' previously defined as all the law, here means doing *everything written in the book of the law* (the OT cf. Gal 3:22, 'the Scripture').

In Gal 3:13, Paul tells his readers that Christ has redeemed them from the curse of the law, i.e., *the need to do the law*. Christ became the curse of the cross for humanity, dying on a tree after completing the law. Paul quotes Deut 21:23 in support. For the Jew, being hanged on a tree was considered a curse, yet Christ took the curse of the law in his death on a cross. In so doing, he redeemed humanity, fulfilled the promise of gentile blessing given to Abraham (Gen 12:3), brought salvation by faith, and inaugurated the age of the Spirit (Gal 3:14). The Spirit is key, for it is by the Spirit that one now lives, not the law. The promise to Abraham is fulfilled in the seed of Abraham, an individual, namely Christ (Gal 3:15–16). The law which antedated Abraham by 430 years has not nullified this promise (Gal 3:17), and therefore, inheritance comes through the promise and not the law (Gal 3:18).

Using diatribe, in Gal 3:19, Paul asks an interlocutor's question: 'why/what then the law?' That is, what is its function?

42. Note that this can equally be 'the righteous through faith, will live.' This does not really affect the meaning, retaining the centrality of faith but shifting 'will live' to eternal life rather than a life of faith. In that ongoing life and not just eternal life is in view here, it is better to translate it as 'the righteous one will live by faith.'

Why bother bringing it to Israel if it cannot save? Paul explains that it was introduced by God (angels) because of sin until the promised one (Messiah, the seed of Abraham) would come (Gal 3:20). As Paul sees Jesus as the promised one, the Messiah, seeing Jesus as the exclusive seed of Abraham is an innovative view of the law in Judaism—no one outside of the Christian faith held this view (although the idea might have been held that the Spirit would come and place the law on the heart, and the external code would then not be required).

Paul's interlocutor responds, 'is the law then opposed to the promises of God?' Paul emphatically denies this, 'absolutely not' (*mē genoito*). Paul states that if there was a law that could give humanity eternal life, then righteousness would come through obedience to the law (Gal 3:21). But that hasn't happened in Israel or anywhere else (aside from Jesus)—it can't, because of sin, whether the people in view are Jews or gentiles. However, the Scripture (a cipher for the law and including the whole OT), rather than bringing life, has effectively functioned as a jailor, imprisoning all humanity ('the whole world,' i.e., Jew and gentile alike) under sin. This prepared the way for the promise to be fulfilled in Messiah Jesus. As all are in sin and helpless before God, *faith in God and Christ alone saves* (Gal 3:22; see Rom 4 on faith in God and justification). We can observe here that Paul uses 'the Scripture' or 'writing' (*graphē*), i.e., the written code here of the law, the OT. Furthermore, it is the 'whole world;' Jew and gentile that is imprisoned. The law has no redemptive power; its power is to prepare the way for redemption by revealing sin and need. Note there is nothing on 'works of the law' or certain parts of the law here, it is 'the law.'

Paul then develops the notion of imprisonment in Gal 3:23–24. Before faith came (i.e., the promised Abrahamic seed that is Christ, his death, resurrection, and salvation by faith), humanity, and most particularly Jews ('we'), were held captive without hope of freedom under law. The law functioned as a *paidogōgos* ('tutor, guide') to superintend or guide the Jews until the Messiah. The purpose of the law is 'so that we might be justified by faith' (Gal 3:24). Paul states emphatically in Gal 3:25

that the supervisory role of the law has ended now that faith
has come. Humanity is justified by faith, saved by faith, and the
law has no role in salvation, whether boundary markers or the
whole Torah or Scriptures. By faith in Christ, all of humankind
can become children of God (Gal 3:26).

This idea has huge social implications. All who are in Christ
are one. Social factors separating people in the ancient world
are blown apart. There is now no longer Jew nor gentile, slave
nor free, male and female (3:28). While people remain in these
states, they are bound together on one basis—faith. They are one
people. There is no status differentiation before God. This sets
the agenda for a new humanity.

When we look back at 2:11–14, the problem Paul had with
Peter is clear. In withdrawing from gentiles to dine with Jews,
Peter was reinforcing a Torah view of the world. Those who
withdrew were bad enough, but the leading apostle of the early
church! Paul calls him out for his non-gospel conduct. At this
point, NP thinkers are correct to make a big deal of this verse, for
it brings to the fore the social and ecclesiological implications of
the issue. A church should be genuinely intercultural without any
cultural superiority (beyond a *lingua franca*, cf. 1 Cor 14:1–25),
without gender bias, and without class differentiation.

In Gal 3:27–29, these people who believe and are baptized in
the Spirit[43] are Abraham's seed and heirs of the world. As Paul
clearly teaches in Rom 9–11, this is not a completely new people
without reference to historic Israel, but a people from every
nation included in the people of God *by faith* from history—a
remnant of grace. Salvation, visually symbolized by baptism, sees
all humanity from all nations ('Jew nor Greek'), from every class
('slave nor free'), and both genders ('male and female'), included
in God's people on the same basis—faith and not law, boundary
markers, or otherwise!

In Gal 4:1–3, Paul likens imprisonment under the law (which
is the experience of all who live by law) to a son in an ancient

---

43. As I will argue in the commentary, while this can be water baptism it may be that
Spirit-baptism fits the context and Paul's wider theology better (similarly Dunn,
Witherington). Again, meaning is not overly shifted by the decision either way.

home before the coming of age; he is effectively a slave, even if he is the heir. In Gal 4:4–6, Christ came as God's Son, born under the law, to redeem those under the law, and set them free into sonship, inheritance, and life by the Spirit. Implied is that Jesus fulfilled the law, and by doing so, became our savior. Hence, his obedience becomes ours as we are 'in Christ' by faith.

In Gal 4:8–10, Paul appeals to the Galatians not to allow themselves to be enslaved to the elemental principles of the world (*stoicheia*), which here means the law. This is an incredible statement that shows how he views the law and Judaism. Paul elsewhere uses *stoicheia* of empty pagan philosophies and traditions which enslave (Col 2:8, 20). By calling Jewish law *stoicheia* and warning the Galatians not to go 'back' to them, he is effectively likening the law (now that Christ has come) to a pagan and demonic religious system.

In Gal 4:10, we get insight into what the Galatians are beginning to do aside from circumcision. They are effectively taking on the Jewish calendar ('special days and months and seasons and years'). New Perspective thinkers make this determinative of 'works of the law;' rather, this calendar symbolizes coming under the whole law, and so rendering believers' initial acceptance of Christ void. In a broad theological sense, they are returning to works, not faith. The contrast between Hagar and Sarah (Gal 4:21–31) illustrates Paul's concern. Hagar represents slavery *to law*, the *Sinai covenant*, and the earthly Jerusalem where the now-defunct Temple stands (to the west from Galatia). Note it is the *whole law*, the whole Sinai covenant. In contrast, Sarah, represents freedom, promise, the Jerusalem above, and the spiritual motherhood of the children of the promise. In mind are all the Galatian believers and all believers, Jew and gentile alike. Paul tells the Galatians to rid themselves of the 'slave women and her son,' i.e., the Judaizers, the Mosaic covenant which is now unnecessary as it is fulfilled in Christ, the system of Israel, righteousness by the law, and the earthly Jerusalem with its temple system, the law as a religious system, etc.

In Gal 5:1, Paul states his view emphatically: 'it is for freedom that Christ has set us free. Stand firm, then, and *do not let yourselves be burdened again by a yoke of slavery.'* Slavery to what? Not merely to a part of the law, but to the law as a religious system, as indicated in Gal 3:15–4:6. Paul reintroduces the notion of circumcision here. This is the first direct reference to circumcision since the reference to Titus (Gal 2:3), 'the circumcision party' (2:1). To be circumcised will mean that the Galatians who have been justified by faith have turned to reliance on the law and this will render Christ's death of no value to them (Gal 5:2). It will see them exit Christ and enter the system Christ came to relieve the Jewish people from—the Mosaic covenant and law (although they can be regrafted in, cf. Rom 11:23). This system has had its day.

Galatians 5:3 is the most important verse in Galatians for defining the presenting issue. Here, Paul states that if a man is circumcised at the demand of the Judaizers, 'he is obliged to obey the entire law.' This verse more than any other is fatal to any thinker who claims the issue is merely about boundary markers. Circumcision is indeed a boundary marker, the key indicator of a man's inclusion in the Jewish people. However, circumcision for Paul is just the thin end of the wedge. To be circumcised at their insistence is to leave Christianity and become a Jew and so, to leave the Christian faith that is antithetical to justification by law (of any kind) and to place one's reliance on law and one's ability to fulfill it.

Now the Jew Jesus has come and fulfilled the law. He has been preached to Israel (Rom 10:14–21). He is the only way to be saved or justified, for Jews and gentiles alike. When a gentile enters Judaism through its boundary markers, they join all Jews who fail to live the law but who have rejected Jesus and are (like all sinful humanity) lost. To do so means that one is no longer relying on grace but *must obey the whole law for salvation.* As such, the cross on which Jesus died to complete the work of obedience to the law, is no longer the means of salvation for such a person, the law is. Paul is saying you can't have it both ways. While the law was important for Israel during its period (Moses–Christ), now that

Christ has come, it is Christ or the law. This is not a both-and situation!

In Gal 5:4, Paul rams this home—'you who want to be justified by the law have *cut yourselves off from Christ*; you have *fallen from grace*.' As in Romans, this means being broken off from the olive tree of God's people. Here we see that it is possible to believe and fall away. The good news is that one can also be grafted back in (Rom 11:17–24).

Paul's argument against the law raises the matter of ethics and the Christian life. What code does a Christian live by? If not law, then what? Surely, we are to live by the law. God has spoken in the law! Is there any other way? In Gal 5:5, Paul begins to shift his attention to these types of questions introducing two things that govern Christian ethics: *The Spirit and love.* Indeed, for Paul, love is poured into a believer's heart by the Spirit, and the Spirit and love govern every aspect of our lives (Rom 5:5). He states: 'By faith, we eagerly await through the Spirit the righteousness for which we hope.' 'We' refers to all believers. For believers, righteousness is generated by the internal work of the Spirit, not imposed by an external code. The ethics of God are written on the human heart by the Spirit.

In Gal 5:6, Paul rules out the physical operation of circumcision being of any significance. It means nothing, avails nothing, and does nothing. It is needless mutilation (Phil 3:3). In Gal 5:6b, he makes clear the second critical dynamic in Christian ethics, 'what counts is faith working through *love*.' The guiding principle is internal, the Spirit; the 'law' if there is one, is love springing forth from faith. Yet 'love' is not for Paul a law as much as an internal code on the heart, out of which one lives by non-coerced compulsion, e.g., 'the love of Christ compels us' (2 Cor 5:14).

After a strong final appeal to reject the Judaizers who are bringing the Galatians back under law (Gal 5:7–13), Paul turns to what life in Christ looks like under grace and not law. In Gal 5:13, he reaffirms their freedom, most notably, freedom from the law. Paul warns them not to use their freedom for licentiousness, which could be seen as a logical outcome of his seeming antinomianism (cf. Rom 6:1–23). This is perhaps what some Corinthians were doing, seeing his theology as a lead-in to licentiousness. It is not a freedom *to* sin; it is a freedom *from* sin. It is a freedom from bondage to live lives of love by the Spirit. Believers are to serve one another (and the world) in love. This verse sums up Christian ethics and mission. It is service through love, something impelled by the Spirit. At other points, Paul emphasizes that this is indeed Christ's example in his ministry and culminating on the cross (Phil 2:6–11).

In Gal 5:14, the *whole law*, including boundary markers and the full injunctions of the Decalogue and Scriptures, along with all casuistic law that can be created out of these (e.g., oral law), is fulfilled in *one message (heni logō)*. The single message is the second commandment: '*Love your neighbor as yourself.*' This one statement is the guiding principle for Christian ethics.[44] Critically, this statement is drawn from the law itself, indicating that, while believers are not under the law, there is continuity between the OT law and life in Christ. The continuity is found in the Spirit. This Spirit has inscribed the law on our hearts (Jer 31:33; 2 Cor 3:3, s.a. Rom 2:15). Hence, we live inside-out lives, faithful to God's divine law, especially love, by the Spirit. The original law was Spirit–generated as well, from the heart of God on Mt Sinai—as such, there is no disjunction between the heart of the OT law and Christian ethics. It is the law on the heart generated through lives in submission to Christ. This one 'law of love' sums up all laws.

In Gal 5:16–6:10, the emphasis falls on the internal power of the Spirit by which believers are to live and be led in every moment of every day. They are to reject seeking self-gratification, lust, and the excessive passions that characterize fallen humanity and they are to live by the internal unction of the Spirit according to love. The Spirit bears fruit in the believer. If they live by the Spirit, they will reject sin and support each other out of love. As they live in this wonderful *koinōnia* of *agapē*, they will 'fulfill the law of Christ' (Gal 6:3). The law of Christ is

---

44. See Lev 19:18; Mark 12:32, and parr.; John 13:34; Rom 13:8–10; 1 Cor 13; Jas 2:8.

the supreme law of neighborly love as led by the Spirit. Believers must live their lives to please the Spirit and will receive eternal life and reward (Gal 6:7–9). They are to do good to all people (Gal 6:10). It is an internally generated life—'from the inside out' not 'the outside in.'

As such, believers are to reject circumcision not merely as a boundary marker, but as a symbol that represents subjugation to the law as a means of salvation and living. Such subjugation is a rejection of grace, of Christ, of the cross, and the essence of Christianity is violated. What matters is not circumcision or uncircumcision, law or no law, but 'a new creation' by the Spirit, characterized by love (Gal 6:12–16).

In conclusion, then, Paul's view of the law rejects it as a religious system. No one can be justified by the law because we all sin. One person has fulfilled the law, Jesus. He has died and risen and now if we believe in him, we are justified before God in him. We are pardoned of all legal transgressions. Those that return to law fall from this status of justification by faith. Grace is no longer theirs. They join all humankind who have rejected Jesus and God's salvation. Adding any legal requirements to faith destroys salvation. It introduces status differentiation into the church whereby those who do what is required are seen as superior to others, whatever it may be. It devastates mission, as now we must preach a gospel not merely of faith in God and his Son for salvation, but we must require converts to do these other things (circumcision, baptism, or whatever we introduce). Ethics shifts from an inside-out love by the Spirit to seeking to please God through legal observance—an impossibility! Even the great Paul, who lists his credentials in Phil 3:4–6, could not achieve justification even though his fleshly claims were so great. Paul is adamant in Galatians: we are justified by faith on the basis of God's grace extended to us in Jesus Christ, who died for our sins to set us free from this evil age for lives of service and ultimately, eternal life.

WHO WERE THE GALATIAN JUDAIZERS?

Before starting the exegetical analysis, it is worth pausing to consider just who Paul is dealing with in this letter. As noted earlier on setting and date, Galatians was likely written around 48, a year prior to the Jerusalem Council (Acts 15). As such, through consideration of the data in Galatians and Acts, we can get a general feel for who these Judaizers are and what they argued.

We can note first of all that the people involved are seeking to turn the Galatians to a different gospel and, as such, to the desertion of God (1:6–7). The description of God as the one who called the Galatians in grace also suggests that their teaching violates the gospel of grace, whereby salvation is granted as a gift. In Paul's response, grace is mentioned here and there, regarding his call (1:15; 2:9) and justification (2:21) indicating that their teaching in some way rendered the idea of a gospel of grace obsolete. In 5:4, to accede to these people means to have 'fallen away from grace.' As such, the grace of the gospel is at stake. Hence, this speaks of something incredibly serious, rather than some discussion of whether one should celebrate the Sabbath or simply church interpersonal relationships. The Judaizers' teaching cuts to the core of the gospel. They are described in 1:7 as troubling the Galatians (s.a. 5:10). The term *tarassō* is strong, used of agitated rioting crowds in Acts 17:8, 13, and so speaks of a real disturbance (see further 1:7).

Paul's long narrative of his apostleship and gospel in 1:10–2:14 indicates a strong need for Paul to defend his gospel and authority. In this section, we get strong hints of the Judaizers' perspective. There are 'false brothers' who infiltrated gatherings in Jerusalem (2:4). The use of *adelphos* language (brothers) indicates that these are either people who are seemingly Christians but who are not (e.g., members of the church who are actually false whether they know it or not) or are people pretending to be Christians (e.g., Jews feigning Christian belief). As we move through the letter, it becomes clear that they fall into the former category; they are people who believe themselves to be Christians, but for Paul, they are not. We know that they are Jewish (or gentiles convinced by Judaism) because circumcision is at stake; Paul was pleased that Titus was not forced to be circumcised (2:3). Forced circumcision comes up again in 6:12, and circumcision features frequently in the letter.[45]

The clash of Paul with Peter referenced in 2:11–14 tells us more about the Judaizers. These people are part of a group from Jacob, the brother of Jesus, and a respected leader in the Jerusalem Church (2:12). This indicates that they are not merely Jews, but Jewish members of the Jerusalem Church. They must then hold a belief in Jesus, but also consider that aspects of the law must be maintained by all Christians, including Jewish converts. They did not eat with the Galatian Christians, indicating that they practiced Jewish eating protocols, including separation from uncircumcised gentiles. Although it is not explicit, they likely also kept kosher food practices. So, thus far, they are Jewish Christ believers who wish to compel new converts to be circumcised and who likely eat kosher food.

We get a further hint as to their concerns in 4:10 where Paul refers to the Galatians observing days, months, seasons, and years. As will be discussed in detail on this verse, these refer to Jewish calendric observances including Sabbath, new moons, and festivals (s.a. Col 2:16). So, we have a picture of their demands: circumcision of male converts, forbidding eating with the uncircumcised, kosher food, and the observance of the Jewish calendar of Sabbaths, new moons, and festivals. That they are prepared to infiltrate meetings suggests dubious ethics, prepared to engage in political intrigue to achieve their ends (further below).

It is not unreasonable to suggest that as they were clearly enforcing these aspects of the Torah, other laws were also being enforced. This might include such things as women being marginalized after birth and during menstruation (Lev 12:1–8; 15:19–24), people avoiding touching dead bodies and corpses

---

45. See 2:7, 8, 9, 12; 5:2, 3, 6, 11; 6:12, 13, 15.

(Lev 11:29–36, 39; 21:1–4), and the marginalization of people with diseases (Lev 13–14) and bodily discharges (Lev 15).

The statement 'neither male and female' may be in part a response to expectations that women are excluded from the community after childbirth and during menstruation (3:28). Similarly, the backdrop to Paul's mention of the Galatians' welcoming him may be in part because of Judaizing expectations of separation from diseased people (4:13–15). The problem with enforcing certain Torah regulations on new converts is deciding which laws must be enforced.

Paul's argument throughout the letter enables us to discern what the Judaizers are arguing. They likely believe that a gentile who believes in Jesus and is baptized is partway there. They also need to adhere at least to these core markers of Jewish identity to be full participants in God's people. The emphasis on justification suggests, further, that they are arguing that right standing before God requires faith along with observance of core markers of the Torah. So, faith is a good start, but it must be followed by the Jewish rituals of incorporation. As such, both conversion (salvation) and perseverance are at stake. Paul will counter that all that is needed to be justified is faith and ongoing faith for perseverance (esp. 2:16).

Galatians 2:17 suggests Paul is being charged by the Judaizers with encouraging sinfulness among converts by his repudiation of law and reliance on faith (cf. Rom 3:8; 6:1, 14). They are concerned that the law is required to ensure gentile converts please God. How else will they live the right way before him? After all, Israel has the Torah to show them how to live. Paul's solution is that believers have died to the law (2:19), and in Gal 5–6, it is the Spirit who generates in us the required life. He recognizes that if the law is required for justification, then Christ's coming and cross are meaningless, for a person is then justified by law.

The Judaizers also seem also to have no real pneumatology. If so, they may be arguing that receipt of the Spirit requires yielding to the Jewish national identity markers. Alternatively, they play down the role of the Spirit. Paul counters with a strong pneumatology, reminding the Galatians that they have received the Spirit by faith (3:2, 5, 14). Further, by Christ, they are redeemed from the law and by the Spirit are adopted as God's children (4:5). Finally, the ethical life of the believer is not a law-enforced life, but a Spirit-impelled one. Implied is the internal law of Christ, the law inscribed on the heart, a life lived inside out by the Spirit's power.

It is likely that the Judaizers made a big deal of the Abrahamic covenant. Paul's response indicates that they drew on Genesis 15–17. The new gentiles have come into the people of Abraham and of his grandson Israel (Jacob). Having believed in God through Christ, as with the men of Abraham's family, they must then be circumcised to seal the salvation process. They almost certainly felt that the Mosaic Covenant was still operative for Christians, and so the law was as important for Christians as for Jews. Effectively, they believed that new gentile converts must *become Jews*. New converts must be circumcised and adhere to the culture prescribed by the law to be true children of Abraham; Paul is then repudiating God's word through Moses.

Paul responds by arguing that all that is required is a faith like that of Abraham (Gen 15:6). He explains the Mosaic Covenant as an interim period in God's salvation plan, which served its purpose but has now had its day. The law's purpose was akin to a Roman pedagogue or tutor. The role of the law was to constrain Israel (3:23) until faith came, i.e., until Christ came. The law it prescribed is fulfilled in the one born under the law who redeems Israel from the law (4:5). Its period is complete now that faith in Christ has come (3:19, 21). Now in Christ, all who have been baptized in the Spirit are clothed in Christ. The social boundaries which prevail in the world are now subsumed in unity and impartiality (3:28). All people, Jew and gentile alike, are children of Abraham through faith in Christ (3:29).

In Romans 4, Paul will extend his argument by showing that Abraham was a gentile at the time of faith, uncircumcised. Only subsequent to his point of faith was he circumcised. As such, again using Gen 15:6 as the basis for his argument (Rom 4:3, cf. Gal 3:6), Paul contends that justification has always been by faith and not works of the law. The law never saved and never can. To yield to the Judaizers is for the Galatians to place themselves in a now-defunct version of Judaism, akin to a pagan religion (4:8–11). Using brilliant sarcasm, Paul writes of circumcision as false mutilation of the flesh akin to pagan mutilation and something that achieves nothing before God (5:2–3, 7, 12). It is nothing to boast about. If one wants to boast of mutilation, one should boast in the mutilated Jesus on the cross (6:13–14) and one's own suffering for him—the marks of Jesus we carry on his behalf (6:17). Indeed, if one does yield to the demand for circumcision *as a basis for justification*, one is lost to Christ, as one must then keep the whole law, which is an impossibility (5:3–4).

The Hagar and Sarah narrative in 4:21–31 also calls on the Abrahamic story from the perspective of his wife and slave. The Judaizers may be arguing that the uncircumcised gentiles are effectively Ishmaelites. They may even advocate that those who refuse circumcision should be expelled. Paul argues the converse, stating that it is the children of the free woman Sarah who must expel the Judaizers. This passage also highlights the importance of the Mosaic Covenant and Jerusalem to the Judaizers. They likely had a proto-Zionistic hope of Jerusalem's restoration, the Temple as the center of a world religion, and the nations flowing to Jerusalem with tribute. Paul counters again, stating that the Jerusalem that counts is the heavenly new Jerusalem, and the Mosaic Law received at Mount Sinai is no longer the constitution of God's people. Rather, it is freedom in the Spirit.

One of their core strategies appears to be their repudiation of Paul. This has been hinted at in his narrative of his early years. It is again touched on in his reference to sin in 2:17 where they appear to argue that Paul's law-free gospel makes Christ a servant of sin. Again, in 4:12–20, Paul gives another narrative, one of his coming to Galatia as he remembers fondly the way he and his gospel were received. He effectively appeals to the Galatians to rediscover their love and acceptance of him and repudiate his critics who are troubling him (6:17). Another aspect of their repudiation of Paul is the false idea that Paul elsewhere preaches circumcision and only preached against circumcision in

Galatia to win them over (5:11). Hence, Paul must defend himself from this charge. Since his conversion to Christ, he has never preached circumcision, and if he was doing so, why are Jews continuing to persecute him?

Another aspect that is likely driving the Judaizers is persecution (5:11). While it is argued by some that the Judaizers are urging the Christians to get circumcised to avoid Roman persecution, more likely, this speaks of Jewish persecution. This was a time of rising nationalism in Israel that would culminate in the war with Rome and the destruction of the nation (see further in the exegetical notes). It may be that the Jewish Christians who do not see a need for law-observance are being persecuted not just for their belief in Jesus, but for breaking Mosaic tradition. They are thus bringing impurity into the nation. For Paul, the Judaizers are seeking to stop this problem by having the Christians circumcised. They are likely motivated here by a concern for the Jewish mission. By having them circumcised, other Jews may also be prepared to convert. The problem is that if this is so, the mission to the gentile world will be stymied.

As already mentioned, the ethical passage through 5:13–6:10 likely counters the deficient pneumatology of the Judaizers. The Judaizers want to retain the law as a basis for the Christian life. Only by doing so will they be able to repudiate idolatry, immorality, and relational breakdown. For Paul, this is out of the question because the law does not constrain sin; it excites it (esp. Rom 7) and reveals it. Rather, the Spirit is the way to live. We also get further insight into the ethical fruit of their teaching. As they have imposed law, the Galatians have fallen prey to violent arguments, envy, conceit, and provocation (5:15, 21, 26). With the help of the Judaizers, obsessed with legalistic law observance, they are becoming participants in a loveless, joyless, divided form of the faith (which is so often the case when Christians get bogged down in litigious concerns). There may be other things from the works of the flesh manifesting amongst them as they turn from Spirit to law. Paul counters by telling them to live by the Spirit and sow to produce its fruit.

So, who are these people? They are likely Jewish converts who are passionate about maintaining the Jewishness of the faith. We know that some are from Jerusalem (2:11–14). This is confirmed in Acts 15:1, where it is men *from Judea* who come to Antioch to teach that new converts must be 'circumcised according to the custom of Moses' to be saved. Others may be Jewish converts from within Galatia where persecution of Christians was experienced from the first (Acts 13:44–45, 50; 14:4–5, 19). Other possibilities include Jews from Damascus (Acts 9:19–22) or from Antioch who had heard Paul in the past in synagogues or otherwise and who may have gone to Jerusalem to stir up such trouble. At this stage of the church, Jerusalem is likely the main breeding ground for Judaizers. Later, Thessalonica will be another center for their activity (Acts 16–17, Phil 3?).

From Acts, we get further possibilities. Some may have been from the 3000 converted at Pentecost and had not worked through the extent of the freedom of the gospel (Acts 2:5–13, 41). They may have come from the Hellenistic Jews in the church (Acts 6:1), although they could equally come from the Hebraic Jews repudiating Hellenistic Christianity as a corruption of Palestinian Christianity. Luke mentions a number of Jerusalem priests that converted, and people with such a strong Jewish heritage could be involved (Acts 6:7). In Acts 15:5, those who stand to debate Paul and Barnabas on the question of circumcision include some 'who belonged to the party of the Pharisees.' This suggests they are former Pharisaic colleagues of Paul. Paul had formerly led the charge in the destruction of the emerging Christian church (Acts 7–9). Now, he was not only preaching the Christian gospel but also repudiating Mosaic protocols considered essential. This likely provoked his former peers greatly. This suggests that the dispute was very personal indeed.

CONCLUSION

In sum, they are Jewish believers, mainly from Jerusalem. This group likely included some of the priests and Pharisees, some of whom may have had a personal agenda against Paul.

They believed in Jesus but also argued passionately that the protocols of Mosaic law should be upheld by new converts. The theological basis of their view was a high view of the importance of Genesis 17, and particularly, the Mosaic tradition. Their core demands were the circumcision of male converts, Jewish food protocols, and Jewish calendric expectations. However, by arguing for the importance of the law, the whole Torah is up for grabs. Women during periods would need to be marginalized, and so on. If a male was not circumcised, he was not right with God. Circumcision was a condition of justification, salvation, and inclusion into God's people. Perseverance required not only faith but law-observance. Their problem was not promoting circumcision per se, but as a condition for salvation, and as an entry point into Mosaic law observance as essential. As Paul stresses, circumcision and uncircumcision mean nothing (5:6; 6:15, s.a. 1 Cor 7:18–19). It is much the same as a haircut or cutting one's nails. However, where it is a condition of salvation alongside other Mosaic requirements, being circumcised is to effectively leave Christianity. It is to become a Jew, a religion (like all religions) that saves no one. Only faith can justify. Now that Christ is preached, only faith in Christ can bring the status of justification.

The Judaizers also repudiated and maligned Paul's version of the faith as a promotion of morality and sin. They rejected Paul himself and were prepared to spread false ideas about him to turn people from him. They likely rejected his apostolic status. They turned the Galatians against him. They were falsely motivated. They exhibited false ethics—being arrogant, envious, self-promoting, divisive, and deceitful.

While, for Paul, their motivations were dubious, they were probably motivated to some extent missionally, wanting to win their own Jewish people to Christ. They recognized that a law-free non-circumcision gospel would be too big a hurdle for most Jews. Wanting to win their people, they fatally syncretized the gospel to their culture. This is a warning to us concerning the syncretization of the gospel to our own cultures. We can inadvertently destroy the gospel in our zeal. This is unacceptable.

What they failed to see is that such a gospel would stop Christianity in its tracks in the remainder of the world. They failed to see that their version of the gospel was ethnocentric and violated the core idea that the gospel is for all peoples. They had a deficient understanding of the grace of God, the effectiveness of Christ's sacrifice on the cross, the role of the Spirit in Christian life, the oneness of people in Christ, the repudiation of sexism, racism, and elitism in the gospel, and the sole requirement of faith for justification. They thus had a deficient soteriology, Christology, pneumatology, missiology, ecclesiology, and ethical theology. So, while they were full of noble intentions, they were wrong in their reading of the gospel, and were for Paul, paving the road to hell. Paul's passion makes sense when we realize what would have happened if the Judaizers had won the day. At best, the church would have ended up as a small Jewish sect. Like Qumran, all that might be left of such a faith would be ruins and a fragmented underground library in Israel/Palestine.

The problem of the Judaizers persisted after the letter to the Galatians and the Jerusalem Council. The Letter of Romans speaks of ongoing issues between Jews and gentiles. There may be a Judaizing dimension in the problems in Corinth (2 Cor 10–12). Colossians 2, Ephesians 2, Philippians 3, and 1 Timothy 1:8–11, to varying degrees, also indicate that Judaizers were threatening the Philippians as late as AD 63. John's Gospel suggests ongoing issues, perhaps as late as the 80s.

While we are not beset often with Christians demanding Christians Judaize, Judaizing lives on in some extreme forms of Zionism, which can suggest two paths of salvation, one for the Jew and another for the gentile. It can be seen in the favoring of the land of Israel over other lands, rampant expectations of a theocratic millennial state in Israel, and a favoring of the Jewish people at the expense of others (e.g., the Palestinians). Paul's theology speaks of all peoples on an equal footing before God. Salvation came to the Jew first and then to the gentiles, but on the same basis—grace and faith. The world and all its lands are God's property, a *cosmos* he is restoring (Rom 8:19–23; 1 Cor 15:20–28). Salvation is certainly from the Jews, or better, from *the* Jew. In that we are in Christ, we are clothed in Jewishness. Yet, we remain the people we are by descent, gender, and status. And we are equal! No race or place has precedence. The law still has validity, in Christ, who is the law, who has fulfilled the law, and who generates the life of God from within us by his Spirit. However, we are free to be who we are without partiality as we live by the Spirit.

The Judaizers anticipate works theologies that have beset the church through its history, as in the case of Pelagius and pre-Reformation Roman Catholicism. Galatians does warn us that we can and must add nothing to Jesus. As Paul himself says best, 'we are saved by grace, through faith' (Eph 2:8). However, understood rightly, Judaizing also challenges us at a cultural level to repudiate all forms of racism or ethnocentricism, calling for a truly multicultural and intercultural church—a church that is free of gender domination and elitism of any sort. A church must then be wary of false theologies, however noble, that subtly bring division.

When the gospel comes into a new culture, it will always need to be adapted to the language and culture of the people to whom the gospel is preached. This process is contextualization. However, if we allow the essence of the gospel to be corrupted, we end up with syncretism, whereby the gospel becomes so perverted that it is not the gospel any longer. The Judaizers are syncretizing the gospel to Judaism. Every culture has aspects of its life that are challenged by the gospel. The Jewish dependence on law observance needs to be set aside and they are failing to do this. As such, this controversy warns us against syncretism as we seek to contextualize the gospel. All of us must examine our practices as the people of God in light of Galatians. Are we corrupting the gospel in the direction of certain works that are prioritized over faith? Are we violating the social unity of the people of God the gospel must produce?

Galatians tells us that while the unity of the Spirit is one of our governing gospel ideals, there is a time to cast out those who sow such syncretized gospels. However, we seek to do all we can to correct this before resorting to such extreme measures. It tells us that we must not quench the Spirit with law, and if we live by the Spirit, we will see God's law, supremely love, lived among us in communities through which God changes suburbs, cities, and nations.

GENRE AND STRUCTURE

GENRE

Scholars have recently argued for a variety of genres and structures for Paul's letters, including Galatians. The very influential Betz understands Galatians as a 'magical letter' and an 'apologetic letter,' which reflects *forensic rhetorical patterns*.[46] The Galatians are the jury, Paul, the defendant, and the Judaizers are the accusers. Betz argues it includes these elements:

1. Epistolary prescript (1:1–5).
2. *Exordium* (introduction) (1:6–11).[47]
3. *Narratio* (narration) (1:12–2:14).[48]
4. *Propositio* (proposition) (2:15–21).[49]
5. *Probatio* (confirmation) (3:1–4:31).[50]
6. *Exhortatio* (exhortation) (5:1–6:10).[51]
7. Epistolary Postscript, including *Peroratio* (conclusion, vv. 12–17) (6:11–18).[52]

---

46. H. D. Betz, 'The Literary Composition and Function of Paul's Letter to the Galatians,' *NTS* 21 (1975): 353–79. Ancient writers were concerned with rhetorical forms, the structure, and the intent of speeches. Three key forms are commonly identified: "'forensic" (rhetoric that seeks to persuade people about a past event), "deliberative" (rhetoric that seeks to persuade people to take action), and "epideictic" (rhetoric that seeks to persuade people to reaffirm a particular view in the present).' See Moo, *Galatians*, 64.
47. The *exordium* is an introduction establishing the speaker's character and the key issues.
48. A statement of the related issue-related facts.
49. The central issue with points of agreement/disagreement.
50. The development of the central argument.
51. Rebuttal of the arguments of the opponents.
52. Summary of the case seeking sympathy.

Witherington also reads Galatians through the rhetorical lens and follows others such as Kennedy and Hall who classify Galatians as deliberative rhetoric that seeks *to persuade* readers/hearers of a particular course of action. He thus does not see Galatians as forensic apologetic, but as deliberative rhetoric framed by epistolary prescript and closing. He structures the letter like this:[53]

Epistolary Prescript: 1:1–5

Exordium: 1:6–10—Two Gospels?

Narratio: The Origin and Character of the Gospel of Grace (1:11–2:14)

The Gospel of Christ—1:11–12

A Narrative of Surprising Developments: Jerusalem, Antioch, and beyond—1:13–2:14

    Propositio: 2:15–21—By the Faithfulness of Christ, Not by Works of the law

Probatio: 3:1–6:10

Argument 1: The Faith of Abraham and the Foolishness of the Galatians—3:1–18

    Division 1: The Appeal to Spiritual Experience—3:1–5

    Division 2: The Appeal to Scripture—3:6–15

    Division 3: The Appeal to Legal Covenants—3:15–18

Argument 2: The Goal of the Guardian, the Function of the Faithful One—3:19–4:7

    Division 1: Why the law was added—3:19–22

    Division 2: The Guardian's Goal—3:23–29

    Division 3: The Heirs Apparent—4:1–7

Argument 3: Shared Experience—4:8–20

    Division 1: Déjà Vu—4:8–11

    Division 2: Paul's Labor Pains—4:12–20

Argument 4: The Allegory of Antipathy—4:21–5:1

Argument 5: The Unkindest Cut of All—5:2–15

    Division 1: Testimony from the Top—5:2–6

    Division 2: What Cuts and What Counts—5:7–12

---

53. Ben Witherington III, Grace in Galatia: A Commentary on St. Paul's Letter to the Galatians (Grand Rapids, MI: Eerdmans, 1998), 34–35.

Division 3: Freedom's Service, Love's law—5:13–15
Argument 6: Antisocial Behavior and Eschatological
Fruit—5:16–26
Division 1: Foiling the Fulfilment of the Flesh—5:16–21
Division 2: The Spirit's Fruit—5:22–26
Argument 7: Bearable Burdens and the Yoke of Christ—6:1–10
Division 1: The law of Christ—6:1–5
Division 2: Doing Good to Teachers and Others—6:6–10
Paul's Autograph: 6:11
Peroratio: 6:12–17
Epistolary Closing: 6:18
Witherington's analysis is actually very similar to Betz, with
the only change the *probatio* running right through from 3:1 to
6:10. However, others have found mixed rhetorical approaches.
For example, Hansen[54] and Longenecker[55] consider Paul begins
forensically but utilizes deliberative rhetoric in the second part
of the letter. These various schemes call into question tightly
classifying the letter with any one form. So, while there is an
apologetic feel to the letter and rhetoric is used, it is not clear that
Galatians should be classified in such a way.[56]
Another alternative is John Bligh, who has argued that
Galatians as a whole should be read as a macro-chiasmus with an
A-B-B'-A' symmetrical structure:[57]

A1   Prologue, 1:1–1:12
    B1   Autobiographical Section, 1:13–2:10
        C1   Justification by Faith, 2:11–3:4
            D1   Arguments from Scripture,
            3:5–3:29
                E   *Central Chiasm, 4:1–4:10*
            D1   Argument from Scripture,
            4:11–4:31
        C2   Justification by Faith, 5:1–5:10
    B2   Moral Section, 5:11–6:11

54. G. W. Hansen, *Galatians*, IVPNTCS 9 (Downers Grove, IL: InterVarsity, 1994), 57–67.
55. Longenecker, *Galatians*, c–cxix.
56. Moo, *Galatians*, 64.
57. J. Bligh, *Galatians: A Discussion of St. Paul's Epistle* (London: St. Paul, 1969), 37–42.

A2   Epilogue, 6:12–6:18

One familiar with Galatians can instantly see an issue with this; namely, in what sense does an autobiographical section mirror a moral section? Other problems become evident quickly. First, does 4:1–10 bear the weight of the central statement of the letter? Second, while there are Scriptures mentioned in D and D', 4:11–20 does not mention the Scriptures but includes direct first-person appeal. While justification and faith are mentioned in 5:1–5:10, it hardly mirrors 2:11–3:4! As with most attempts to see Paul's letters as chiasms, Galatians is not to be classified as a macro-chiasm.

As such, I concur with Moo when he says, 'Galatians does not appear to fit neatly into any of the major rhetorical categories.'[58] As he goes on to say, '[o]f course, this is not to deny that Paul may use certain rhetorical conventions in his argument. But we judge that the attempt to analyze and interpret Galatians in terms of ancient rhetoric has only limited value.'[59] As such, the structure I have set out below seeks to discern the flow of the letter without concern to squeeze its every part into rhetorical patterns, but rather, to break the letter down into its component sections and pick out the main point being made in each unit.

A STRUCTURE OF GALATIANS

1) PRESCRIPT (1:1–5)

1. Author and senders (1:1–2a)
2. Recipients (1:2b)
3. Greeting (1:3)
4. The self-giving delivering death of Christ (1:4)
5. Doxology (1:5)

2) NO OTHER GOSPEL (1:6–10)

1. Desertion of the gospel (1:6)

---

58. Moo, *Galatians*, 64.
59. Moo, *Galatians*, 64.

---

2. No different gospel (1:7)
3. A curse on false preachers (1:8–9)I seek God's approval (1:10)

3) A NARRATIVE OF PAUL'S CONVERSION AND EVANGELISTIC COMMISSION (1:11–2:14)

1. The gospel revealed to Paul by Christ (1:11–17)
2. Paul's post-conversion movements—Arabia, Damascus, Jerusalem, Syria, and Cilicia (1:17–22)
3. Paul's second visit to Jerusalem (2:1–10)
4. Paul and Peter clash in Antioch (2:11–14)

4) THE CENTRAL APPEAL: DO NOT YIELD TO THE JUDAIZING GOSPEL (2:15–5:12)

1. Thesis statement: Justified by faith and not law (2:15–16)
2. The Judaizers rather than Christ serve sin (2:17–18)
3. Dead to the law, alive in Christ, by grace, not law (2:19–21)
4. Remember that the Spirit was received by faith, not law (3:1–5)
5. Children of Abraham by faith (3:6–9)
6. Redeemed by Christ from the curse of the law (3:10–14)
7. The Abrahamic promise is not through the law but through Christ (3:15–18)
8. The Function of the law—to prepare for justification by faith in Christ (3:19–24)
9. Inclusion, oneness, and equality of all believers in Christ (3:25–29)
10. No longer slaves but redeemed children and heirs (4:1–7)
11. Do not return to slavery (4:8–11)
12. Remember your conversion (4:12–20)
13. Be children of Sarah, not Hagar (4:21–4:31)
14. A Final Appeal: Do not accept circumcision (5:1–12)

5) HOW THEN TO LIVE? FREEDOM, LOVE, IN THE SPIRIT (5:13–6:10)

1. Freedom to love (5:13–15)
2. Walk in the Spirit (5:16–25)
3. Bearing burdens (6:1–5)
4. Sow to the Spirit for eternal life (6:6–10)

6) POSTSCRIPT (6:11–18)

1. Signature (6:11)
2. Final appeal—do not be circumcised but boast in Christ (6:12–17)
3. Farewell (6:18)

PART TWO: PRESCRIPT AND SITUATION (GAL 1:1–10)

Chapter Two: Prescript (Gal 1:1–5)

AUTHOR AND SENDERS (GAL 1:1–2A)

Paul begins the letter in *Galatians 1:1* identifying himself as sender with a description of his apostleship and the brothers and sisters in his locale, a qualification concerning God who raised Jesus, and the recipients:

Paul (*Paulos*),[1] **an apostle** (*apostolos*),[2] **not** (*ou*)[3] **from** (*apo*)[4]

1. The common name Παῦλος (*Paulos*) is used twice in Galatians, both times of Paul (1:1; 5:2).
2. The noun ἀπόστολος (*apostolos*) is found three times in the letter: 1:1 of Paul; 1:17, of those apostles before him in Jerusalem; see also 1:19. It is not a widely common Greek word but has an ambassadorial and marine background. In Judaism it is linked to the OT notion of God sending
3. The common negation οὐ (*ou*) is found thirty-seven times in Galatians. With other negations like *mē* and *ouki*, *ou* is important to the argument of the letter, used often of what is not. These include: Paul's gospel *not* from people (1:1), *not* another gospel (1:7), *not* a slave of Christ (1:10), *not* a human gospel (1:11), *not* immediately going to Jerusalem (1:16), seeing *none* of the other apostles (1:19), Paul *not* lying (1:20), God shows *no* partiality (2:6), conduct *not* in step with the gospel (2:14), *not* being gentile sinners (2:15), *not* by works of the law (2:16), *no* one justified by works of the law (2:16), *not* nullifying the grace of God (2:21), *not* abiding in every command of the law (3:10), the law is *not* of faith (3:12), what a verse does *not* say (3:16), a covenant *not* annulling an earlier one (3:17), a mediator is *not* only one (but between parties) (3:20), no social barriers in the gospel (3:28), did *not* know God (4:8), the Galatians did *not* scorn or despise Paul (4:14), *no* good purpose (4:17), *not* listening to the law (4:21), does *not* bear children ... *not* in labor (4:27), shall *not* inherit (4:30; 5:21), *not* children of the slave (4:31), persuasion *not* from God (5:8), *not* gratifying the flesh (5:16), *not* under law (5:18), *no* law against love (5:23), boast *not* in the neighbor (6:4), and God is *not* mocked (6:7). See also *oude*.
4. The preposition ἀπό (*apo*) is found eight times in Galatians. Each use has the meaning 'from'—'not *from* people' (1:1), grace ... peace *from* God ... (1:3), 'turning *from* the one

people (genitive plural *anthrōpos*)[5] **nor** (*oude*)[6] **through** (*dia*)[7] a **person** (genitive *anthrōpos*), **but** (*alla*)[8] **through** (*dia*) **Jesus** (genitive *Iēsous*)[9] **Christ** (genitive *Christos*)[10] **and** (*kai*)[11] **God** (*Theos*)[12] **the Father** (*patēr*)[13] **who** (*ho*)[14] **raised** (aorist participle[15] *egeirō*)[16] **him** (*autos*)[17] **from** (*ek*)[18] **the dead** (*nekros*).[19]

who called you' (1:6), 'from those who seemed to be influential' (2:6), 'from Jacob' (2:12), 'this I want to learn *from* you' (3:2), 'one is *from* Mount Sinai' (4:24), 'severed *from* Christ' (5:4).

5. The noun ἄνθρωπος (*anthrōpos*) is used fourteen times in Galatians. Often it is used of a person or people as opposed to God, as the source of Paul's apostleship, gospel, and desire to please (1:1, 10, 11, 12), God showing no partiality (2:6), of people before God and in human behavior (2:16; 5:3; 6:1, 7), and a human example of a will formed by people (3:15).

6. The conjunction οὐδέ (*oude*) compounds *ou*, 'not' and *de*, 'but, and' yielding 'and not, nor, also not, not either, neither, not even' (BDAG 734). It is found nine times in the letter in the sense 'nor' (1:1, 17; 3:28; 4:14), 'not' (1:12; 2:5), 'not even' (2:3), or 'even not' (6:13).

7. The preposition διά (*dia*), 'through, because of,' is found nineteen times in Galatians usually meaning 'through' (1:1, 12, 15, 16, 19, 21; 3:13, 18, 19, 26; 4:7, 23; 5:6, 13; 6:14), and sometimes 'after' (2:1) or 'because of' (2:4, 13).

8. The contrastive conjunction ἀλλά (*alla*) is found twenty-three times in Galatians. Mostly it has the strong adversative sense, 'but' (1:1, 8, 12, 17; 2:3, 7, 14; 3:12, 16, 22; 4:2, 7, 8, 13, 17, 23, 29, 30, 31; 5:6, 13; 6:13, 15). It is an important term in his argument, where Paul sets up a scenario and then strikes a strong contrast.

9. The name Ἰησοῦς (*Iēsous*), the Greek for the Hebrew Joshua meaning 'save,' is found seventeen times in Galatians: Jesus Christ (1:1, 12; 2:16; 3:1, 22; 6:14), Lord Jesus Christ (1:3; 6:18), Christ Jesus (2:4, 16; 3:14, 26, 28; 4:14; 5:6, 24), and Jesus (6:17). Clearly, it is Jesus' earthly name.

10. The title Χριστός translates the Hebrew Messiah, 'anointed one.' It is assigned to Jesus (see previous note). It is found thirty-four times in Galatians in a range of forms including Jesus Christ, Lord Jesus Christ, Christ Jesus (see previous note). Otherwise, it is found absolutely, 'Christ' (1:6, 7, 10, 22; 2:16, 17, 19, 20, 21; 3:13, 16, 24, 27, 29; 4:19; 5:1, 2, 4; 6:2, 12).

11. The conjunction καί (*kai*) is used seventy–two times in Galatians mostly with the meaning 'and' (1:1, 2, 3, 4, 7, 9, 13, 14, 15, 16, 17, 18, 21, 24; 2:1, 2, 9, 12, 13, 14, 15, 16, 20; 3:5, 6, 16, 17, 28; 4:2, 7, 9, 10, 14, 18, 20, 22, 27, 30; 5:1, 12, 15, 16, 21, 24; 6:2, 4, 16). Otherwise, it connotes 'also' (2:8, 10, 16, 17; 4:3, 29; 5:25; 6:1, 17), 'even' (1:8; 2:13) or 'indeed' (3:4).

12. The name θεός (*Theos*) is used thirty-one times in Galatians. Aside from the second reference in 4:8, all refer to the Jewish God Yahweh with the Greek standard term for God (1:1, 3, 4, 10, 13, 14, 20, 24; 2:6, 19, 20, 21; 3:6, 8, 11, 17, 18, 20, 21, 26; 4:4, 6, 7, 9, 3; 21; 6:7, 16). He is 'God the Father' on three occasions (1:1, 3, 4, cf. 4:6), and paired with Jesus twice (1:1, 3).

13. The common Greek term for 'father,' *patēr*, is found five times. Three times it is

As he always does, Paul begins by simply stating his name, *Paulos*. Raised as Saul (*Saulos*), he likely assumed the name Paul in Greek settings like his hometown Tarsus due to its similarity of sound.[20] At this stage of life in the late 40s, Saul is probably in his early to mid-forties, as it is likely that he was born in the first decade of the first century. He was a Roman citizen from birth, indicating that his parents were freed-people (Acts 22:25–29; 23:37). This gave him certain legal exemptions and traveling privileges. He was raised in Tarsus, and a citizen of that town (Acts 21:39). He was born an Israelite, from the tribe of Benjamin, circumcised on the eighth day, and thoroughly versed in Hebrew culture, religion, and language (2 Cor 11:22; Phil 3:6). When young, he was sent to Jerusalem to train to become a member of the most religious sect in Judaism, the Pharisees (Acts

applied to God as supreme Father of all (1:1, 3, 4) and once of God absolutely (4:6). Once it is used of a human father in an analogy of a household (4:2).

14. The masculine article *ho* is found 277 times in Galatians. They are not always translated and noted in the translations due to their frequency.

15. Wallace, *Greek Grammar*, 307 notes that this is an example of a noun-article-adjective construct, with τοῦ ἐγείραντος (*tou egeirantos*) functioning as an adjective. The article is added to the adjectival participle to bring out the force of God as resurrecting agent: '*the one who raised him* from the dead.'

16. The verb *egeirō*, 'raise,' is only used once in Galatians, of Jesus resurrection by God who *raised* him from the dead (1:1).

17. The common pronoun αὐτός (*autos*) recurs twenty-six times in Galatians: 1) Masculine (he, them) (1:1, 15, 16, 18; 2:2, 9, 11, 13, 17; 3:6, 16; 4:4, 6, 17; 6:13, 16); 2) Neuter (it, them) (1:12, 13; 2:10; 3:10, 12); 3) Feminine (her) (4:25, 30).

18. The preposition ἐκ (*ek*) is used thirty-five times in Galatians. It is an important preposition, as it is used in the contrast between 'from faith' and 'from works of the law/from the law.' 1) 'Raised *from* the dead' (1:1); 2) 'Deliver us *from* this present evil age' (1:4); 3) 'Angel *from* heaven' (1:8); 4) 'Set me apart *from* my mother's womb' (1:15), '*from* a woman' (4:4), '*from* a slave woman' and '*from* a free woman' (4:22, 23); 5) '*From* the circumcision' (2:12); 6) 'Not *from* gentile sinners' (2:15); 7) 'Not *from* works of the law' (2:16, 3x; 3:2, 5, 10), '*from* the curse of the law' (3:13), '*from* the law' (3:18, 21), '*from* the flesh' (6:8); 8) '*From* faith' (2:16; 3:7, 8, 9, 11, 12, 22, 24; 5:5), '*from* hearing with faith' (3:2, 5), '*from* promise' (3:18), '*from* the Spirit' (6:8); 9) 'From him who calls you' (5:8).

19. The Greek noun for 'dead,' νεκρός (*nekros*) occurs once in Galatians, in 1:1, in the masculine, speaking of the 'dead people' from whom God raised Jesus.

20. I have noticed the South Korean immigrants to English speaking NZ often assume English names; sound is sometimes the basis for this.

22:3; 23:6; 26:5). As he will intimate in Gal 1:14, he was a brilliant young Pharisee, dedicated to the Jewish traditions. This is seen in his determination to destroy the Christian movement in Jerusalem and Syria.[21]

He was dramatically converted through experiencing a vision of Jesus while en route to Damascus to plunder the church and commissioned to be an emissary of God and his Son Jesus, carrying the gospel to the gentile world.[22] He writes around seventeen or so years after that event (Gal 1:17–2:1). In that time, he had engaged in mission engagement in Jerusalem, Arabia, Syria (especially Antioch), Cilicia, and the south Galatian cities of Pisidia, Derbe, Lystra, Iconium, and Pisidian Antioch. By the time of writing, he had gained extensive mission experience and seen the Christian movement established from Jerusalem to southwestern Turkey (Acts 9–14; Gal 1:17–2:10). His great zeal and brilliance as a Pharisee will be seen through this letter as he writes with real theological depth, expressing passionate concern for his new converts who are falling prey to Jewish false teachers—the nascent Christian movement is at stake.

Paul describes himself as an 'apostle' (apostolos—'a sent one').[23] The term was not widely used in Greek sources, sometimes associated politically with naval military expeditions or people sent for a particular ambassadorial purpose.[24] It likely draws its religious sending significance from Israel's prophetic tradition. Initially, apostles were those who witnessed the ministry, death, and resurrection of Jesus (Acts 1:22). The NT literature gives evidence of a broader range of apostles, including Barnabas (Acts 14:4, 14), Silas and Timothy (1 Thess 2:6), and others (e.g., 1 Cor 15:7). Paul commonly labels himself an apostle (Rom 11:13; 1 Cor 9:1) in the prescripts of letters as here.[25] Paul also mentions

---

21. See Gal 1:13; Phil 3:6; Acts 7:58–8:3; 9:1–2, 21, 26; 22:4–5; 26:9–11.
22. See Gal 1:15, 2:7–10; Acts 9:4–18; 22:6–21; 26:12–18; Rom 11:13; Eph 3:7–12; 1 Tim 2:7.
23. Used three times in Galatians. The others are in Gal 1:17, 19 of Jerusalem apostles—'those who were apostles before me,' including Peter and Jacob, the brother of Jesus.
24. K. H. Rengstorf, 'ἀπόστολος,' in *TDNT* 1:408.
25. See Rom 1:1; 1 Cor 1:1; 2 Cor 1:1; Eph 1:1; Col 1:1; 1 Tim 1:1; 2 Tim 1:1; Tit 1:1.

apostles who serve within the ministry of the local church, perhaps establishing new congregations.[26] The basis for his claim is that he has seen the risen Lord (1 Cor 9:1), although he concedes he is the 'least of the apostles unworthy to be called an apostle' (1 Cor 15:9) and that his apostleship is questioned (1 Cor 9:2). It is likely that those threatening the Galatians question his apostleship, and his use of the term here is an immediate assertion of his status and authority.

Not only is he an apostle, but he is an apostle 'not from people' but 'through Jesus Christ and God the Father.' 'Not from people' indicates that he was not appointed an apostle by the Jerusalem leaders, or any other ordaining group as could be argued of Justus/Matthias (Acts 1:23). Rather, his apostleship is direct from Jesus Christ on the Damascus Road. He will give more detail on this in 1:11–2:10, where he describes his conversion and commission by Jesus, which was endorsed by the Jerusalem apostles (though he was not called by them). They had appointed other apostles to replace Judas. Jacob was verified as an apostle as was Barnabas (Acts 14:4, 14; Gal 1:9, cf. 1 Cor 15:7)—perhaps in a similar way. Paul was not.

'Not from a man' has two levels of significance. First, he does not trace his apostleship to an individual person who appointed him, whether Peter, Jacob, John, or another agency. Second, it has a certain irony as he will state in the next clause, 'but through Jesus Christ and God the Father …' Of course, at one level for Paul, the first Christians, and orthodox theology, Jesus was and is a man. So, in saying 'not from a man,' he is in effect saying Jesus is more than a man; he is God's Son, God being designated 'the Father.' It is through what appears to be just a man, Jesus, that he is set apart an apostle. However, Jesus is the means of God's appointing him. Further, this hints at Paul's recognition of the deity of Christ while recognizing God's unique status as 'the Father.'

With 'but through Jesus Christ and God the Father,' Paul invokes the names of God and Jesus, giving a theological and

---

26. See 1 Cor 12:28, 29; Eph 4:11, cf. 2 Cor 8:23; Phil 2:25.

Christological basis to his apostleship. 'Through' (*dia*) connotes agency,[27] and Christ and his Father have commissioned Paul for his apostolic work. He will explain more of this in the latter parts of Ch. 1. The significance of his beginning with his apostleship sourced in God and Christ and not human agency is critical as the letter unfolds as Paul gives considerable attention to the defense of his gospel and apostleship to the Galatians. His opponents are clearly undermining him as they seek to convince the Galatian gentile Christians to be circumcised. By beginning this way, Paul begins to undermine their claims.

The name 'Jesus Christ' speaks first of the human Jesus who was born, lived, died, and rose again some two decades earlier. However, as noted in discussing the previous clause, for Paul, Jesus is more than a mere *anthrōpos*. The name Jesus is the Greek for Joshua (and Hebrew variants), meaning 'savior,' and as such, is a fitting name for the one who is the savior of the world (Phil 3:20). From a biblical theology perspective, the name invokes memories of the first Joshua who cleansed the land (Joshua) and the High Priest Joshua at the time of Zechariah (e.g., Zech 3:1)—Jesus is bringing God's salvation to the world beginning in Israel. He is a high priest of the order of Melchizedek, as the writer of Hebrews uniquely articulates.[28] Paul will use the term Jesus seventeen times in the letter.

'Christ' speaks of Jesus *the Messiah, Christos* translating the Hebrew/Aramaic term. While in Greek circles, the term had no religious significance, in Israel's story, it is a term replete with theological importance. It speaks of a long-awaited eschatological figure, a descendant of King David who would restore the Davidic monarchy, who would bring redemption for Israel from gentiles and evil doers, who would gather God's people, and bring God's reign. The use of the term indicates

---

27. The preposition *dia* is used nineteen times; here twice with genitive speaking of agency ('*through* a person'); similarly, '*through* a revelation' (1:12), '*through* grace' (1:15), '*through* faith' (2:16; 3:14, 26), '*through* the law' (2:19, 21), '*through* a promise' (3:18; 4:23), '*through* angels' (3:19), *through* God (1:1; 4:7), '*through* love' (5:6, 13), and '*through* Christ' (1:1; 6:14). Of time, 'after' (2:1). It can be causal as in 2:4; 4:13.

28. See Heb 5:6, 10; 6:20; 7:1–17, cf. Gen 14:18; Ps 110:4.

that Paul believes Jesus to be this Christ. He has come, not as expected with armies and power, but as a humble servant, giving himself to the most humiliating form of death in the Roman world—crucifixion. Whereas prior to his experience of the risen Christ, he repudiated the notion of a crucified Messiah—for cursed is anyone hung on a tree (3:13; Deut 21:23)—now Paul believes that this is central to God's self-revelation in the Christ. As a crucified Messiah, Jesus is both savior and life-example. Paul will use the term Christ of Jesus thirty-seven times in Galatians.

'God the Father' speaks of the Jewish God, whom Jesus addressed as *Abba* (the Aramaic intimate term for Father), and now Paul does the same (4:6; Mark 14:36; Rom 8:15). Invoking God's name is indicative of the cataclysmic religious transformation that is spreading through the non-Jewish world. Uncircumcised gentile converts across Turkey are now believers in this Jewish God, who sent his Son as Messiah, and who died for them, as Paul will mention in this prescript (v., 4). They have renounced the idolatry of the worshiping the many Greek and Roman gods and goddesses, the Roman Emperor, and the many eastern gods (e.g., Isis) who have been welcomed into the polytheistic Roman world (Gal 4:8). Now there is one God, and one Lord, this God's Son, and *all* others are renounced (e.g., 1 Cor 8:6). He is 'the Father,' the paterfamilias and patron of this new and ever-growing family of believers, Jew and gentile. Jesus is his Son (Gal 1:16; 2:20; 4:4). The Galatians are part of this family, adopted as his children by faith and signed and sealed by the Spirit (Gal 3:26; 4:5–7). God will be mentioned specifically twenty-nine times in the letter.[29] Just in the use of this name, the Galatians are subtly urged to reject the 'gospel' of the Judaizers.

God is further described as the one 'who raised (aorist passive *egeirō*) him from death.' 'Him' is clearly Jesus, and so this speaks of the moment when Jesus was resurrected from the dead. This, of course, was an event no human, Paul included, witnessed. Nor did Paul see the empty tomb. According to the Gospels, only

29. Absolutely (1:10; 2:21; 3:6, 8, 11, 17, 18, 20, 21, 26; 4:4; 4:6, 7, 8, 9 [twice], 14; 5:21; 6:7, 16). Otherwise, God the father (1:1), God our Father (1:3), our God and Father (1:4, 13, 22, 24; 2:6, 19), 'Son of God' (2:20).

some of the first disciples, women, and men, were so privileged. However, he has met the risen Christ (1:15) and is now a believer.

The agency of God in Jesus' resurrection recurs throughout the NT.[30] Other texts indicate that God did this by the agency of his Spirit (Rom 8:11). For Paul, who once ridiculed Christian claims, his vision of Jesus has made him a believer that God indeed raised Jesus from the dead. Elsewhere he lists six people or groups who give witness to meeting the risen Lord—Peter, Jacob, the Twelve, the 500, the apostles, and himself as one abnormally born. For him, the resurrection of Jesus is central to the gospel he preaches, the gospel which saves those who hold firm to it until the end (1 Cor 15:1–11). There is no room for a Greco-Roman merely spiritual resurrection; the Jesus who died and was buried was raised (1 Cor 15:12). Without Christ's resurrection, Christianity falls, sin holds sway, destruction awaits, and all hope is gone (1 Cor 15:12–19). But, because Christ has been raised as the firstfruits of the resurrection, believers too can have immense confidence in their own future resurrection at the coming of Christ (1 Cor 15:24–28).

The reference to the resurrection of Christ by God here is pivotal to the argument that follows through the letter. It speaks of vindication of Jesus Messiah being raised; thus, nothing else is required for justification, not law or any works thereof. They raise no-one; rather, because of sin, the law imprisons as it condemns. As 1:5 will add, Jesus is the one who gave himself for humanity so that people would be delivered from this present evil age characterized by sin, law, death, and the spiritual forces of evil.

This preceding reference to the resurrection shows that God endorses Jesus as the sinless one who gave himself according to God's will and lived a sinless life, fulfilling the law and so, was raised from the dead. Hence, the gospel is a gospel of Christ, not Christ plus anything else other than the faith that a person has to connect them to the Christ and so be 'in Christ' and

---

30. See the use of the divine passive—God the agent of his resurrection (Matt 17:9; John 2:22; 21:14; Rom 6:9; 7:4; 1 Cor 15:12, 20; 2 Tim 2:8). God is explicitly agent in Acts 3:15; 4:10; 13:30, 34; 17:31; Rom 8:9; 10:9; Eph 1:20; Col 2:12; Heb 13:20; 1 Pet 1:21).

so justified. We see here the function of the resurrection as the central miracle on which Christianity is founded. It is the lens through which we look back to the cross and see its spiritual significance. Those who place their faith in the one who gave himself for him/her will experience that same resurrection. First, there is spiritual rebirth as eternal life is implanted in believers by the Spirit. Finally, and ultimately, believers will experience full bodily resurrection as in the twinkling of an eye when the perishable mortal believer becomes imperishable and immortal. Death is swallowed up in victory (1 Cor 15:50–56). The antidote for death's sting is available to be taken. Eternal life, the gift of God, has been given (Rom 6:23). Praise God! Little wonder Paul cannot hold back from breaking into doxology in v. 5.

In *Galatians 1:2a*, Paul also adds to himself as sender:
and (*kai*, 1:1) **all** (*pas*)[31] **the brothers** (plural *adelphos*)[32] **who** (*ho*, 1:1) **[are]**[33] **with** (*syn*)[34] **me** (dative *egō*).[35]

31. The common adjective πᾶς (*pas*), 'all, everyone, everything,' is found fifteen times in Galatians: '*all* the brothers' (Gal 1:2), all those present in Antioch when Paul challenged Peter (2:14), all people (2:16; 6:10), all the nations (3:8), all people who rely on the law, accepts circumcision (3:10; 5:3), all hung on a tree (3:13), all things (3:22), all Christians (3:26, 28), everything a master owns (4:1), the whole law (5:14), and all good things (6:6).
32. The noun ἀδελφός (*adelphos*), 'brother,' is found eleven times in Galatians: the brothers with Paul (1:2)—which could be the whole church or his team. One literal use, Jacob the blood brother of Jesus (1:19). As with all of Paul's letters, the dominant use (nine times) of *adelphos* is in the plural (*adelphoi*) as a term of epistolary address to the Galatian church, including women (1:11; 3:15; 4:12, 28, 31; 5:11, 13; 6:1, 18).
33. Where bracketed words are used these are added either to give clearer meaning or to supply an implied verb missing in the Greek. Such verbs (most often the verb 'to be') are common.
34. The preposition σύν (*syn*), 'with' is used four times in Galatians: 1) of people; '*with* me' (1:2; 2:3), '*with* Abraham' (3:9), 'the flesh *with* its passions and desires' (5:24). He also uses nine terms with *syn-* as prefix (as he commonly does): 1) *synēlikiōtēs*: 'a contemporary' (someone *with* the same age) (1:14), 2) *symparalambanō*: 'take along *with*' (2:1), 3) *synēstheō*, 'eat together *with*' (2:12); 4) *synypokrinomai*: 'join *with* someone in hypocrisy' (2:13); 5) *synapagō*, 'lead away *with*' (2:13); 6) *synistēmi*, 'recommend, commend' (*stand* with) (2:18); 7) *systauroō*, 'crucify *with*' (2:19); 8) *synkleiō*, 'imprison *with*' (2:22, 23); 9) *systoicheō*, 'stand together *with*' (4:25).
35. Variant forms of the personal pronoun ἐγώ (*egō*) (cf. the English 'ego'), 'I,' are found fifty–nine times in Galatians: me, 'I' (1:2, 11, 12, 14 [2x],15 [2x], 16, 17, 24; 2:3, 6 [2x], 8, 9 [2x], 19, 20, 12 [2x], 14 [2x], 15, 18, 19, 20 [4x], 21; 5:2, 10, 11; 6:14 [2x], 17 [3x]);

If Paul is writing from Antioch, this could indicate his group of co-workers—Paul sometimes using *adelphos* in the technical sense of co-workers (e.g., 1 Cor 16:12; 2 Cor 1:1; Phil 2:25). Alternatively, as with Paul's main uses of the term of other Christians, it here is inclusive, speaking of all the believers in Antioch. Either way, it adds authority to his letter. He writes, and all those in his team and the Antiochian church concur, i.e., all participants together in the one true gospel. They stand apart from the Judaizers who are most definitely *not* true 'brothers', but are 'false brothers' (*pseudadelphous*, 2:4)—who are really not brothers at all. They are not family, but enemies of the gospel. The family must come together against them. In a sense, the Galatians are being challenged to decide 'whose side are you on?' Are you in the family? Or are you opting for Judaizers? From our knowledge of the Antiochian church, this group of brothers likely includes Barnabas and John Mark (who have not yet split with Paul), and the likes of Simeon Niger, Lucius of Cyrene, and Manaen (Acts 13:1). As Paul uses 'brothers' inclusively of women, this should not be limited to the men of the Antiochian church. It would include women, the elite, slaves, and anyone who stands with Paul in the theology of the letter. The mention of the brothers also speaks of unity in what we know to be a multicultural church (cf. Gal 3:28). The Galatians need to come together as brothers and sisters in Christ, Jew and gentile, slave and free, and male and female, without partiality.

RECIPIENTS (1:2B)

Galatians 1:2b states the recipients:

---

plural 'our', 'us', 'we' (1:3, 4 [3x], 8, 23; 2:4 [2x], 9, 15, 16; 3:13 [2x], 24; 4:3, 6, 26; 5:1, 3; 6:14, 18). 64% singular dominant, esp. in Chs. 1–2, 6. Chapters 3–4 have more plurals, 'we, us,' speaking corporately of Christian experience.

'To the churches (plural *ekklēsia*)[36] of Galatia[37] (genitive *Galatia*).[38]'

The 'churches' uses the plural of *ekklēsia*, a term used in the Greek world of the gathering of the citizens of a city for political decision making (e.g., Acts 19:32, 39) and in the LXX of the gathering of God's people (e.g., Deut 4:10; Josh 9:8; Judg 20:2; 1 Kings 8:14). Now, the *ekklēsia* (plural) are gatherings of the reconstituted people of God in Christ who gather in particular locations for worship, hearing the word, participating in the sacraments of baptism and Eucharist, fellowship, edification, and from that central point, radiate out to engage in mission as they go about their lives.

The first churches met in homes, often the villas of the wealthy. While initially they likely met on the Sabbath, by the mid–50s there is evidence that their primary meeting point was the first day (Acts 20:7; 1 Cor 16:2) otherwise known as 'the Lord's Day' (Rev 1:10). With that said, the early church probably met more often as the church became the primary gathering point for the people as they abandoned their idols, temple worship, and even the *collegia* (voluntary associations), which were dedicated to patron gods. For example, those in the Jerusalem church met daily in the temple courts (Acts 2:46). While there were likely multiple gathering points in each locale, the people of God formed a church within that city.[39] There were no denominations, although there may be flavors, some of which clashed, e.g., Jewish, gentile.

36. There are three uses of the noun ἐκκλησία (*ekklēsia*) in Galatians. The term has a rich history in Greek thought concerning the gathered citizens of the city, the *demos*, and in Jewish thought of Israel gathered. Its root meaning is the 'called out ones.' The uses are in 1:2 of the churches of Galatian; in 1:22 of those in Judea; and in 1:13 of the whole Christian church. Paul now builds what he sought to destroy (cf. 2:17).

37. The dative ταῖς ἐκκλησίαις (*tais ekklēsiais*, 'to the churches') is a dative of recipient. Wallace explains, 'This is a dative that would ordinarily be an indirect object, except that it appears in *verbless constructions* (such as in titles and salutations). It is used to indicate the person(s) who receives the object stated or implied. This usage is not common.' (Wallace, *Greek Grammar*, 148).

38. This is the only use of noun Γαλατία (*Galatia*) in Galatians (cf. 1 Cor 16:1)—also 2 Tim 4:10; 1 Pet 1:1.

39. See Rom 16:1, 23; 1 Cor 1:2; 11:8; 14:23; 2 Cor 1:1; Col 4:16; 1 Thess 1:1; 2 Thess 1:1.

The church was not identified with a building. The church met in the home, but the church was the people. While the church remained in existence, whether gathered or not, essential to its existence was gathering. There was no notion of a 'churchless faith,' such an idea is an oxymoron and an expression of today's almost narcissistic, western hyper-individualism.

In Paul's letters overall, there is the church of God, as in the case of the whole movement persecuted by Paul,[40] the churches of God (1 Cor 11:16, 22; 2 Thess 1:4), all the churches of Christ (Rom 16:16), every church (1 Cor 4:17; 7:17), all the churches of the saints (1 Cor 14:33), the churches (1 Cor 14:34; 2 Cor 8:19, 23, 24), all the churches (2 Cor 8:18; 11:28), and the rest of the churches (2 Cor 12:13).

We have here reference to the churches of Galatia, made up of the churches in the main centers (below) and any others now established by the Galatians and other believers after Paul left. These new churches would also be made up of multiple house churches (e.g., Rom 16:5; Col 4:15; Phlm 2). The churches in Galatia are again singled out in 1 Cor 16:1, speaking of Paul's request for them to contribute to the Jerusalem Collection (however, not in this letter indicating it precedes or postdates it). Similarly, he speaks of regional groupings including the churches of Asia (1 Cor 16:19), the churches of the gentiles (Rom 16:4), the churches of Macedonia (2 Cor 9:1), the churches of Judea (Gal 1:22; 1 Thess 2:14).

As discussed in the Introduction, while some scholars claim this refers to the northern region of the Roman province of Galatia, this most likely refers to the southern churches evangelized in Paul's first Antiochian missionary journey described in Acts 13–14. Tracking Paul's journey indicates the churches in Perga (Acts 13:13; 14:25), Pisidian Antioch (Acts 13:14–49, 21), Iconium (Acts 13:51–14:6, 21), Derbe (Acts 14:6, 20–21), Lystra (Acts 14:6–21), Pamphylia (Acts 14:24), Perga (Acts 14:25), perhaps Attalia (Acts 14:24), along with any other

---

40. See Gal 1:13, cf. 1 Cor 10:32; 11:22; 15:9; Eph 1:22; 3:10, 21; 5:23, 24, 25, 27, 29, 32; Phil 4:15; Col 1:18, 24; 1 Tim 3:5, 15.

churches established in the region through those who took the gospel from these churches (esp. Acts 13:49). In those cities, Paul had appointed elders (Acts 14:23), no doubt to whom this letter was especially focused, as they were charged with the leadership of the churches.

Some of the members were Jews, especially in Pisidian Antioch, where Paul's mission included proclamation in the Synagogue, and Luke records Jews and God-worshipers (*sebōmenōn*, Acts 13:43, 50) were among those converted (Acts 13:14–43)—similarly, in Iconium (Acts 14:1). There is also substantial evidence of Jewish resistance to Paul's mission on this trip, and this could have added Judaizer pressure that new converts not only believe but pay homage to Israel's traditions—especially including circumcision and the law (Acts 13:45, 50; 14:2, 4, 5, 19). Later emotional warnings to the Ephesian elders in Miletus to pay careful attention to the protection of their flocks from 'fierce wolves' who will attack them mercilessly and 'speaking twisted things' likely has such situations as these Judaizers in mind (Acts 20:28–30).

Notably, whereas later Paul describes the church as 'the church of God' (1:13) and 'the churches of Judea *that are in Christ Jesus*' (1:22), here they are simply 'the churches of Galatia.' The genitives in 1:13 and 22 indicate Paul recognizes them as authentic gatherings of people faithful to the gospel. The lack of such a genitive here is telling—the Galatians are churches, but are they churches of God? Are they churches in Christ Jesus? That depends on their response to the letter.

GREETING (1:3)

Galatians 1:3, Paul pronounces his favored blessing,[41] found in

---

41. **Variant**: There is a textual variant on 1:3. The chosen text, *apo theou patros ēmōn kai kyriou Iēsou Christou*, is found in a wide range of witnesses, including ℵ A P Ψ 33 and a number of Greek fathers. Other texts including P46, P51vid, B D F G H move *ēmōn* to after *Kyriou* ('our Lord'). Yet others simply have *patros kai kyriou* ('father and Lord'). While a good external case can be made for the moving of *ēmōn*, the consistency of this blessing with the seven other similar greetings of Paul suggests this should read as the others.

eight of his letters (Rom 1:7; 1 Cor 1:3; 2 Cor 1:2; Eph 1:2; Phil 1:2; 2 Thess 1:2; Phlm 3):[42]

Grace (*charis*)[43] **and** (*kai*, 1:1) **peace**[44] (*eirēnē*)[45] **to you** (plural *sy*)[46] **from** (*apo*)[47] **God** (*Theos*, 1:1) **our** (plural *egō*, 1:2) **Father** (*patēr*, 1:1) **and** (*kai*) **the Lord** (*kyrios*)[48] **Jesus** (*Iēsous*, 1:1) **Christ** (*Christos*, 1:1), …

The pronouncement of the blessing accords with the Greek pattern of greeting, *chairein*, 'rejoice, greetings,' and the Jewish *Shalom*, 'peace.' Paul utilizes the Greek *eirēnē*, which stands for Shalom, and blends it with *charis*, 'grace.' He brings the two great cultural traditions, Jewish and Greek, and Christianizes them in the greeting, 'from God our Father and the Lord Jesus Christ.' As with 1:1, we have the Father and Jesus combined.

42. *Charis* is also used in other greetings (Col 1:2; 1 Tim 1:2; 2 Tim 1:2; Tit 1:4).
43. The noun χάρις (*charis*) is used seven times in Galatians: in the greeting and farewell (1:3; 6:18); the grace of Christ (1:6); similarly, the grace of God (2:21), or just grace where stands in contrast to the law (5:4); and Paul called by grace (1:15; 2:9).
44. Wallace, *Greek Grammar*, 51 notes that in these greetings the nominative nouns χάρις (*charis*, grace) and εἰρήνη (*eirēnē*, peace) are nominative absolutes without the verb. He notes, 'The verb never appears in the *corpus Paulinum*, however. This may be significant, especially if the suggestion that Paul invented (or at least popularized) the "grace and peace" salutation is taken seriously, for what would be a "signature" item for him (and hence so understood by his churches) may have needed expansion via an explicit verb in other writers.'
45. The noun εἰρήνη (*eirēnē*), 'peace,' is found only three times in Galatians: in the greeting prayer wish (1:3), as the third fruit of the Spirit (5:22), and as a blessing upon Israel (6:16).
46. The pronoun σύ (*sy*), 'you,' is found fifty–two times in Galatians; all plural, as a term of address: 1:3, 6, 7, 8, 9, 11, 20; 2:5, 14; 3:1, 2, 5, 8, 16, 28, 29; 4:11, 12, 13, 14, 15, 16, 17, 18, 19, 20, 28; 5:2, 7, 8, 10, 12, 13, 14, 14, 21; 6:1, 11, 12, 13, 14, 18. Its common use indicates the directness of Paul's appeal. It includes the whole church.
47. The preposition ἀπό (*apo*) is used eight times in the letter. It always has the sense 'from'; see 1:1, 'Paul's apostleship not *from* people;' 1:3, 'grace and peace *from* God;' 1:6, 'turning *from* him;' 2:6, '*from* those who seemed to be influential …;' 2:12, '*from* Jacob;' 3:2, 'learn *from* you;' 4:24, '*from* Mt Sinai;' and 5:4, '*from* Christ.'
48. The noun κύριος (*kyrios*) is only used six times in Galatians, much less than other Christological terms (Jesus, 17x; Christ, 38x) aside from Son (which is used of Christ four times). The full name, '*Lord* Jesus Christ,' is found thrice, in the greeting, farewell (1:3; 6:18) and once elsewhere (see below, 6:14). 'Christ' is the dominant Christological term in Galatians as in all Paul's letters aside from the Thessalonian correspondence. Other uses are 'the *Lord's* brother' (1:19), 'confidence in the *Lord*' (5:10), 'cross of our *Lord* Jesus Christ' (6:14), the 'grace of our *Lord* Jesus Christ' (6:18).

The greeting is a prayer-wish, first for grace, a term central to his theology found 100 times in his letters. *Charis* has the sense of God's generous beneficence toward humankind despite our hapless state. The term recurs eight times in Galatians. Aside from the greeting and final farewell (Gal 6:18), it lies at the center of his appeal—the Galatians deserting the 'grace of Christ' in favor of a different gospel based on works of the law (Gal 1:6). Grace sums up God's work in Christ—it is salvation given freely by the lavish generosity of God received by faith alone.[49] Paul does not turn to the works of the law for righteous standing before God; otherwise, it would nullify grace for human effort and merit (Gal 2:21). To receive circumcision is to annul grace as one comes under the law and must keep it in toto, something that is implausible and thus, the circumcised one has 'fallen away from grace' (Gal 5:4). The term *charis* links nicely to the next verse where Jesus '*gives himself* for our sins,' a gift of God, an act of amazing grace. This is done in conformity with God's will; hence, at the heart of both Father and Son is self-giving on behalf of others, including even the undeserving—this is grace!

Paul develops his theology of grace most fully in Romans and Ephesians, where the term is used twenty-four times and eleven times respectively. Paul also employs grace in Galatians and elsewhere when speaking of his conversion and call to mission.[50] It then is a lavish term, Paul asking God to bless the Galatians with the fullness of salvation and life in Christ (cf. Eph 1:6, 7).[51] With the bite of the letter concerning their turning from grace to

---

49. *Charis* is commonly related to salvation, cf. Rom 3:24; 4:16; 5:2, 15, 17, 20, 21; 6:1, 14, 15, 17; 11:5, 6; 1 Cor 1:4; 2 Cor 1:12, 15; 4:15; 6:1; 2 Cor 8:9; 9:8, 14; Col 1:6; 2 Thess 1:12; 2:16; 2 Tim 1:9; 2:1; Tit 2:11; 3:7.

50. See Gal 1:15; 2:9, cf. Rom 1:5; 12:3; 15:15; 1 Cor 3:10; 15:10; Eph 3:2, 7, 8; Phil 1:7.

51. *Charis* can also mean 'thanks' toward God (Rom 7:25; 1 Cor 10:30; 1 Cor 15:57; 2 Cor 2:14; 8:16; 9:15; Col 3:16; 1 Tim 1:12; 2 Tim 1:3). It is associated with the giving of spiritual gifts (*charismata*) (Rom 12:6; Eph 4:7). It is used in farewells (Rom 16:20; 1 Cor 16:23; 2 Cor 13:14; Eph 6:24; Phil 4:23; Col 4:18; 1 Thess 5:28; 2 Thess 3:18; 6:21; 2 Tim 4:22; Tit 3:15; Phlm 25); of graciously contributing to the Jerusalem Collection gift (1 Cor 16:3; 2 Cor 8:1, 4, 6, 7, 19); God's grace revealed in Paul's weakness (2 Cor 12:9); favor through speech (Eph 4:29); and grace-filled speech (Col 4:6).

law, it has a special edge—you have been saved by grace through faith (Eph 2:5, 7, 8), so do not desert the grace of Christ! Live in and from it!

'Peace' (*eirēnē*) is used less often than grace in Paul (forty-three times), but it is still an important term. As noted above, it is used eight times in greetings. He also uses it sparingly in his farewells (Eph 6:23). In a world of people who do not know the way of peace (Rom 3:17) and who yearn for peace (1 Thess 5:3), it is used for the character and action of God as a God of peace who generates Shalom through his work in people.[52] Jesus 'is our peace' uniting people with historic enmities in Christ (Eph 2:14, 15, 17). He is 'the Lord of peace' who gives the fullness of peace to believers (2 Thess 3:16); peace with God (reconciliation) (Rom 5:1; 1 Cor 7:15), internal peace in the midst of struggle through prayer (Phil 4:7), peace between believers (concord, community, unity, *koinōnia*) (Rom 14:17, 19; 1 Cor 16:11; Eph 4:3; Col 3:15), the sharing of the gospel that brings peace (Eph 6:15), peace with others beyond the Christian community, and eschatological peace in the fullest sense of eternal Shalom in God's restored world (Rom 2:10). Peace as a virtue is generated in believers through the Spirit (Rom 8:6; 14:17; 15:13). It is a fruit of the Spirit in 5:22 (cf. 2 Tim 2:22). Paul also prays a blessing of peace and mercy upon the Israel of God (see Gal 6:16). It has a special import to the situation Paul is addressing in which the Galatians' peace with God is being threatened by their abandonment of the gospel of grace, not to mention the conflict going on in Galatia (esp. Gal 5:15).

'From God our Father and the Lord Jesus Christ,' speaks of the source of grace and peace. While grace and peace can come from others, they can only truly come from God and his Son. Peace in our world tends to be achieved through war. We know this from recent history as when Nazi Germany was quelled in WW2 or more recent ongoing clashes in the Middle East. This phrase also recalls 1:1, where Paul's apostolic call comes from Christ and God—now grace and peace come from the same source.

---

52. See Rom 15:33; 16:20; 1 Cor 14:33; 2 Cor 13:11; Phil 4:9; 1 Thess 5:23.

Here, the order is reversed; 'Jesus Christ and God the Father.' The varying order speaks of how much authority Paul ascribes Jesus, which is astonishing considering that he used to put people into prison for such 'heresy.'

The addition of 'our' is inclusive of all Christians, Galatians included—so don't desert him and his Son! 'Our' can go with either 'God the Father' or with 'Lord Jesus Christ,' and its placement may indicate both are in mind. It speaks of intimate union believers have with God and Jesus Christ, a deeply comforting thought to ruminate upon. He adds 'Lord' (*kyrios*) to 'Jesus Christ.'

In formal terms, Roman citizens had three names, the praenomen (given name), nomen (name of the *gens* or clan), and the cognomen (family name), e.g., Marcus Tullius Cicero. An agnomen was sometimes added, especially in honor of military achievements, e.g., Gaius Cornelius Scipio Africanus.[53] While 'Lord Jesus Christ' does not necessarily line up perfectly with this, it speaks of the three-fold Roman name.

'Lord' has rich meaning for Paul and his readers. First, *kyrios* is used some 6156 times in the LXX of Yahweh.[54] Its use implies Jesus' divinity, especially in quotes and allusions to OT texts which are applied to Christ.[55] Second, *kyrios* was used in the Greek and Roman world of gods and the Emperor.[56] By calling Jesus Lord, Paul has elevated him above the pantheon, and the Emperor. Hence, in both Jewish and Greco-Roman worlds, and especially the provinces, this is religiously and politically subversive. The political threat to the Imperium is especially acute in the provinces where the Imperial Cult was important as in Asia Minor, and no less so in the Synagogue.

53. C. E. Bennett, *New Latin Grammar* (Boston; New York; Chicago: Allyn and Bacon, 1908), 390.
54. B. Witherington, III. 'Lord,' in *DJG* 485.
55. See Rom 4:8/Ps 32:2; 9:28/Isa 10:23; 9:29/Isa 1:9; 10:13/Joel 2:32; Rom 14:11/Phil 2:10/Isa 45:23; Rom 15:11/Ps 117:1; 1 Cor 1:31/2 Cor 10:17/Jer 9:23–24; 1 Cor 10:26/Ps 24:1.
56. Witherington, III. 'Lord,' 485 who notes its use (and *kyria*, feminine) of Isis, Serapis, and Osiris. He also notes it was used of Nero and Augustus. There also are many other uses.

Paul's prayer for grace and peace has real meaning—may you re-establish yourselves in the gospel of grace so that you are at peace with God, with each other, and take the gospel of peace to the world as you should.

THE SELF-GIVING DELIVERING DEATH OF CHRIST (1:4A–B)

In *Galatians 1:4a–b*, very unusually, Paul adds a tag to his prayer for blessing:

who (*hos*)[57] **gave** (aorist *didōmi*)[58] **himself** (*heauton*)[59] **for** (*hyper*)[60] **our sins** (plural *hamartia*),[61] **so that** (*hopōs*)[62] **he might deliver** (aorist middle subjunctive *exaireō*)[63] **us** (accusative plural *egō*, 1:2) **from** (*ek*, 1:1) **this present** (genitive *enestōtos*)[64] **evil** (genitive *ponēros*)[65] **age** (*aiōnos*),[66] ...

57. The relative pronoun ὅς (*hos*), which can also be feminine (ἥ, *hē*), or neuter (ὅ, *ho*) recurs twenty-four times in Galatians (who, which, what, that): dative 'to whom' (1:5); 'that' (1:7; 2:2, 4); 'the one' (1:8, 9), 'in what' (1:20), 'who' (1:23; 3:10, 16), 'them' (2:5), 'the thing(s)' (2:10; 5:17), 'what' (2:18), 'which' (2:20), 'to whom' (3:1), 'which time' (3:19; 4:19), 'whose' (4:9), 'for whom' (4:19), 'such things' (5:21), 'whatever thing' (6:7), and by which' (6:14).
58. Galatians' six uses of the verb δίδωμι (*didōmi*), 'give,' are of Christ *giving* himself (1:4), the three pillar-apostles *giving* Paul the right hand of fellowship (2:9), the *giving* of the law (3:21), the *giving* of faith in Christ Jesus (3:22), and the Galatians' *giving* their eyes to Paul (4:15).
59. Seven times the reflexive pronoun ἑαυτοῦ (*heautou*), 'himself, itself, herself, themselves,' is used in Galatians—of Christ giving *himself* (1:4; 2:20), Peter separating *himself* (2:12), of the arrogant deceiving *himself* (6:3), *one's own* work (6:4), boasting in *oneself* (6:4), and *one's own* flesh (6:8).
60. Four times the preposition ὑπέρ (*hyper*) is employed in Galatians. With the genitive, 'on behalf of, for the sake of, for'—'our sins' (1:4)—similarly, 2:20 ('died for me'), and 3:13 ('becoming a curse for us'). Otherwise, with accusative, 'beyond' (1:14).
61. Three uses in Galatians of the noun ἁμαρτία (*hamartia*), sin; 'our sins' (1:4), Christ is certainly not a 'servant of sin' (2:17), but everything, people and world included, is imprisoned under sin (3:22).
62. This use in 1:4 is the only use of ὅπως (*hopōs*) in Galatians. It is not particularly common in Paul, used nine times (Rom 3:4; 9:17; 1 Cor 1:29; 2 Cor 8:11, 14; 2 Thess 1:12; Phlm 6). For purpose, he usually uses *hina*, which is interchangeable with *hopōs* (A. Kretzer, 'ὁ´πως,' in *EDNT* 2:525).
63. This use in 1:4 is the only use of the verb ἐξαιρέω (*exaireō*) in Galatians. It is synonymous with *rhyomai*.
64. The verb ἐνίστημι (*enistēmi*) is found only once in Galatians, of 'the *present* age' (1:4).
65. Galatians 1:4 is the only use in the letter of the common noun for evil, πονηρός

Usually, at this point, Paul moves into thanksgiving and prayer. However, in Galatians, Paul uniquely develops the blessing with addition clauses that highlight the redemptive work of Christ that accords with God's will, and then he pronounces a blessing upon God. This unique feature throws the spotlight on these words, which are utterly central to the argument he will mount in the letter—the death of Christ is sufficient. Circumcision and submission to the law are not required. Place your faith in the crucified one, and you will experience that resurrection. Do not go back!

'Who gave himself for our sins.' 'Who' is the genitive singular masculine *tou*, and so refers to the one just mentioned—'the Lord Jesus Christ' (all genitive singular masculine). He is the 'one who *gave* himself.' 'Gave' translates *didōmi*, a common Greek word for 'give.' It is commonly used by Paul (seventy-two times) especially of God's giving to humanity a diversity of things such as the Spirit,[67] and more.[68]

(*ponēros*). We have here a nice example of the reflexive pronoun ἑαυτοῦ (*heautou*) being used to 'highlight the participation of the subject,' here Christ. See Wallace, *Greek Grammar*, 351.

66. There are three uses of the noun αἰών (*aiōn*) in Galatians; here, in the sense of 'age' (the present one); whereas in 1:5 Paul uses *eis tous aiōnas tōn aiōnōn*, 'into the ages of ages,' i.e., 'forever, for all eternity.'

67. For *didōmi*, see Rom 5:5; 2 Cor 1:22; 5:5; Eph 1:17; 1 Thess 4:8; 2 Tim 1:7.

68. Other uses of *didōmi* include: 1) the giving of God and/or Christ: This includes a range of things God gives including the Spirit (Rom 5:5; 2 Cor 1:22; 5:5; Eph 1:17; 1 Thess 4:8; 2 Tim 1:7); grace generally including salvation (1 Cor 1:4; 2 Tim 1:9); to be generous in monetary gifts (2 Cor 8:1, 5); in speech (Eph 5:29); in spiritual gifts or mission roles (Rom 12:3, 6; 15:15; 1 Cor 3:5, 10; 12:7, 8, 24; 2 Cor 5:18; Eph 3:2, 7, 8; 4:7, 8, 11; Col 1:25; 1 Tim 4:14); victory in Christ (1 Cor 15:57); a spirit of stupor to Israel (Rom 11:8); the ability to live in unity (Rom 15:5); long hair as a gift of God to women (1 Cor 11:15); differing plant bodies (1 Cor 15:38); care into a heart (2 Cor 8:16); good gifts to the poor (2 Cor 9:9); authority (2 Cor 10:8; 13:10); suffering (2 Cor 12:7); Jesus as head of the church (Eph 1:22); inner strength (Eph 3:16); evangelistic words to preach (Eph 6:19); judgment (2 Thess 1:8); comfort (2 Thess 3:9); peace (2 Thess 3:16); mercy (2 Tim 1:16, 18); understanding (2 Tim 2:7); and repentance (2 Tim 2:25). 2) People giving to God: Abraham gave glory to God (Rom 4:20); give room for God's wrath (Rom 12:19); give an account of oneself before God at judgment (Rom 14:12). 3) People giving to others: Paul giving a judgment (1 Cor 7:25; 2 Cor 8:10), of avoiding giving an obstacle that someone may stumble on (1 Cor 9:12; 2 Cor 6:3), reason to boast (2 Cor 5:12), instructions in a letter (1 Thess 4:2). 4) People not

As noted on v. 3, *didōmi* speaks of grace, the heart of which is self-giving for the good of the other, even if undeserving. Later in 2:9, the verb will be used of the right hand of fellowship being *given* to Paul by Jacob, Cephas, and John. The law was also *given* by God through angels (3:21)—an act of grace, now transcended in Christ's self-giving. Whereas here, Jesus gave himself, in 3:22, the promise of Abraham is *given* to believers in Christ Jesus. It is used of the Galatians who, with cruciform selflessness, were prepared to gouge out their eyes to *give* them to Paul in 4:15—an astonishing statement of their welcome to him. Here we have Jesus giving himself to deliver people from sin and this evil age.

Similarly, in 1 Tim 2:6, Jesus 'gave himself as a ransom for all.' Again, Jesus '*gave himself* for us to redeem us from all lawlessness' (Tit 2:14). Other texts speak of Christ's self-sacrifice in differing ways. In Romans 15:3, Christ did not please *himself* but took upon himself reproach. Later in 2:20, Paul can say, 'I have been crucified with Christ. It is no longer I who live, but Christ who lives in me. And the life I now live in the flesh I live by faith in the Son of God, who loved me and *gave himself* for me.' The self-giving of Jesus here calls to mind the Christ-hymn of Phil 2:7–8, 'but he *emptied himself*, by taking the form of a servant, being born in the likeness of men ... And being found in human form, he *humbled himself* by becoming obedient to the point of death, even death on a cross' (cf. Heb 5:5; 7:27; 9:14, 25).

This self-giving cruciformity is the pattern for the Christian life. In 2 Cor 5:18–19, Christ reconciled believers 'to *himself*,' gifting them the ministry of reconciliation as 'in Christ God was reconciling the world *to himself*.' This he did by dying 'for all, that those who live might no longer live *for themselves* but for him who for their sake died and was raised' (2 Cor 5:15). Similarly, in Ephesians 5:2, Paul urges his readers to 'walk in love, as Christ loved us and *gave himself up for us*, a fragrant offering and sacrifice to God.' This self-giving is the pattern of love a husband must show his wife (Eph 5:25)—they must love their

---

giving opportunity for Satan (Eph 4:27; 1 Tim 5:14). 5) Abstract usages: a musical instrument giving sound (1 Cor 14:7, 8), and a tongue giving speech (1 Cor 14:9).

wives, 'as Christ loved the church and *gave himself* up for her.' Generally, Christians are not to seek their 'own good, but the good of his/her neighbor' (1 Cor 10:24). They are 'do nothing from selfish ambition or conceit, but in humility, count others more significant than yourselves.' Each is to 'look not only to *his/ her own* interests but also to the interests of others' (Phil 2:3–4, f. Phil 2:21). Christ is our life pattern of self-giving.

'For our sins' uses the plural of *hamartia*, the most common NT word for sin, found in Paul sixty-four times. For Paul, humanity, Jew and gentile alike, are under sin's sway (Rom 3:9), enslaved to sin (Rom 6:17), due to Adam's sin and all humanity's willing participation in it, including us (Rom 5:12, 21). Sin precedes the law (Rom 5:13), but the law brings knowledge of sin (Rom 3:20; 7:6–11). It functions as death's sting empowered by the law, which makes sin apparent (1 Cor 15:56). Unless sin is dealt with in a person's life, that person will die and experience destruction (Rom 6:23, cf. Eph 2:1). Thus, Paul can say in 3:22; the Scripture imprisoned everything under sin—all the cosmos and all its people.

As this text says, Christ, who is not a servant of sin (2:17), gave himself 'for our (*hyper ēmōn*) sins.' He 'died for our (*hyper ... ēmōn*) sins' (1 Cor 15:3). Despite his knowing no sin, God made him to be sin for us (*hyper ēmōn*) so that believers may become the righteousness of God (2 Cor 5:21). His death then becomes the believers' death (Rom 6:2); believers are crucified with him and released from sin's bondage in his death (Rom 6:6–7, 11). In him then, 'we have redemption, the forgiveness of sins' (Col 1:14). Jesus has set believers free from sin and law (Rom 8:2–3). Believers are thus under grace and not sin; hence, we are set free from sin, and so sin must no longer be allowed to reign in our bodies (Rom 6:12–22).

What stands out here is Jesus' voluntary self-giving on behalf of our sins. That this was fully effective is seen in v. 1, God raised him from the dead! Wow! Let us never lose our awe at such a thing! Christ's work then is fully complete—*tetelestai*! (It is finished! John 19:30), and believers need to do nothing more than to believe in him. Already, Paul is going to work disarming the

Judaizers and challenging the Galatians to remember the essence of the gospel. Jesus is sufficient to deal with the problem of sin; don't compromise him! We need to hear this today too.

The use of *hopōs* in 1:4b signals a purpose clause—'with the purpose of delivering us ....' So then, the self-giving of Christ for the sins of fallen humanity is with the express intent of 'delivering us from the present evil age'—the death of Christ was an act of deliverance, a rescue mission so to speak. 'Us' is the first use of the plural of *egō* in Galatians (see v. 2), speaking of all believers, including Paul and the Galatians. 'Deliver' is *exaireō*, which compounds *ek* ('from') and *aireō* (pick, choose, e.g., 2 Thess 2:13; Phil 1:22) yielding 'pick out of.' While it can have the vivid negative sense of 'tear out' as in an offending eye (Matt 5:29; 18:29), it has the positive meaning 'rescue' or 'deliver' in Luke's writings; as in Joseph's deliverance in Egypt (Acts 7:10), the Exodus (Acts 7:34), Peter rescued from prison (Acts 12:11), and Paul delivered from Jew and gentile (Acts 23:37; 26:17). Its reference to the Exodus in Acts 7:34 reminds the Galatians (and us) that the Jesus-event is a new Exodus where God saves his people from bondage to false powers to be his people. They must live in the reality of the new Exodus and not stop at Mt Sinai.

'From the age of present evil' uses an attributed genitive and indicates 'the present evil age.'[69] 'Present' is *enistēmi* which can mean a time that has arrived or will come (2 Thess 2:2; 2 Tim 3:1), but here speaks of things present or contemporary (Rom 8:38; 1 Cor 3:22; 7:26). The idea of the present age is also found in Heb 9:9.[70] *Ponēros* is one of the standard terms used across Paul (eleven times) and the NT (seventy-eight times) for something corrupted by evil.

'The present evil age' conforms to Paul's historical understanding where time is broken into three eras (also thought of a two-age perspective). First, there is 'before the ages' in which God (the King of Ages, 1 Tim 1:17) decreed his work (1 Cor

---

69. On this genitive see Wallace, *Grammar*, 89.
70. The text of Heb 9:9 reads: 'By this the Holy Spirit indicates that the way into the holy places is not yet opened as long as the first section is still standing (which is symbolic for the present age).'

2:7), his eternal purpose (3:11), and hid the mystery of salvation through the death of Messiah which is now revealed in Christ (Eph 3:9; Col 1:26; Tit 1:2; 2 Tim 1:9).

Second, as in the following verse, there is 'the age *to come*.' This is the eternal age described as into the ages, 'forever,'[71] 'the coming ages' (Eph 2:7), and as in the next verse (1:5), 'the age of ages' (Eph 3:21; Phil 4:20; 1 Tim 1:17; 2 Tim 4:18). The mystery of the gospel was hidden from before the ages into the present age, in which, totally unexpectedly, it is now revealed in the crucified Messiah (Eph 3:9).

Between these two eras, 'before the ages,' and 'the eternal age to come,' as in this text, there is 'this age' characterized by fallenness, sin, evil, and death. A similar sentiment is found in Eph 5:16, 'the days are evil (*ponēros*).' This age is dominated by people who walk in the age of this world, as Christians once did (Eph 2:2). These include people who do 'evil (*ponēros*) deeds' (Col 1:21), arrogant debaters (1 Cor 1:20), false wisdom (1 Cor 2:6; 3:18), the rich living at the expense of the poor (1 Tim 6:17), and evil, ignorant, and violent rulers—some of whom killed Jesus, and who will be brought to nothing (1 Cor 2:6, 8). In its fallenness, the world is governed (not ruled, that is done by God and his Son) by the ruler of this age, Satan, who blinds human minds to the gospel (2 Cor 4:4). Indeed, in Eph 6:16 and 1 Thess 3:2, Paul calls Satan 'the *ponēros* (evil) one'—a spiritual being completely consumed and characterized by corruption. However, while Satan has power due to human sin, Christ rules even over this fallen age as he will without any opposition (1 Cor 15:25–27) in the one to come (Eph 1:21).

Unlike Demas who 'loved the present age' (2 Tim 4:10) and the false teachers of Ephesus who were evil (*ponēros*, 2 Tim 3:13), Christians, on whom the end of the ages has come (1 Cor 10:11), are not to be 'conformed to this age' (Rom 12:2). Rather, they are to abandon earthly wisdom for the wisdom of the cross (1 Cor 3:18) and live godly lives renouncing worldly passion (Tit 2:12). They are to abhor what is *ponēros* (evil) and cling to what is

---

71. See Rom 1:25; 9:5; 11:36; 16:27; 1 Cor 8:13; 2 Cor 9:9; 11:31.

good (Rom 12:9). They are to abstain from 'every form of *ponēros*' (1 Thess 5:22). At times they are even to expel the *ponēros*, 'evil person or thing,' from the church (1 Cor 5:13). Christians, then, live in this fallen evil age but are delivered from it, 'left behind' to do the work of resisting evil and sowing goodness into it; supremely, sowing the gospel of grace. They are to live out of goodness and not *ponēros*.

In 2 Thessalonians 3:2, similarly, Paul speaks of 'evil men' from whom he hopes to be delivered (*rhyomai*) by the prayers of the Thessalonians. In 2 Timothy 4:18, on the eve of his death, Paul confidently states that God will deliver (*rhyomai*) him from 'every evil deed' and bring him safely into eternity.

In the other seven uses of the grace and peace blessing, Paul does not develop it with a subordinate sentence as he does here. As such, the way he extends it here is significant. He does this for a number of reasons. It reminds the Galatians of Christ's death for sins that delivered them from this evil age. What law completely fails to do; Jesus has done. Consequently, it sets up what will follow as he appeals for them not to turn from grace and faith. To do so is to put themselves back in the hideous position of being under sins that are not dealt with; they are 'lost in sin,' and they are captive again to this 'present evil age.' They are thus under Satan's thralldom. They must live in their freedom from sin and this age. This has two temporal edges: 1) Life in the present, by faith, free of sin's dominion, free of law's bondage, and life in the Spirit—freedom, despite living in this present evil age; 2) The future full freedom whereby evil is quenched, and they live eternally, free of sin and death in a restored world, with millions of other fully restored people, experiencing 'the freedom of the glory of the children of God' (Rom 8:21).

DOXOLOGY (GAL 1:4C–5)

In *Galatians 1:4c–5*, Paul concludes his greeting with reference to God's will and a doxology:

according to (*kata*)[72] **the will** (*thelēma*)[73] **of our** (genitive plural *egō*, 1:2) **God** (*Theos*, 1:1) **and** (*kai*, 1:1) **Father**[74] (*patēr*, 1:1)—**to**

whom (dative *ho*) **[be] the glory** (*doxa*)[75] **into** (*eis*, 1:2) **the ages** (*aiōn*, 1:4b) **of ages** (*aiōn*) **[forever and ever], amen** (*amēn*).

The final clause of 1:4 turns the spotlight back on God, Yahweh: 'according to (*kata*) the will (*thelēma*) of our God and Father'—Paul continuing the pairing of Christ and God (1:1, 3). This constant pairing is no accident. The Judaizers are strong on God but diminish Christ by demanding circumcision. They have a deficient Christology and a false soteriology. God is again 'our God and Father' (cf. 1:1, 3).

'The will of our God and Father' emphasizes that the self-sacrificial death of Christ to deal with human sins and deliver people from this present evil age is God's will. The God who created the world; who called Abraham; who led Israel into Egypt for salvation; who, through Moses, led them out and gave them the law at Sinai; who led them into the Land; who walked in relationship with them in Israel's story despite their sin; and

72. The preposition κατά (*kata*) is found seventeen times in Galatians. Most uses have the meaning 'in accordance with ...' including: 'the will of God' (1:4) which contrasts with 'humankind' (1:11; 3:15); 'a revelation'—(causal, 'because') (2:2); 'a promise' (3:29); and 'the flesh' (4:23, 39), which contrasts with 'the Spirit' (4:29). Other uses include, '*beyond* measure,' (*kath hyperbolēn*) of Paul's powerful persecution of the church (1:13). Other uses also include: '*Toward/to* his face' (2:11) and '*before* your eyes' (3:1). *Contrary* to or *against* is found five times (2:11; 3:21; 5:17 [twice], 23). In 4:28, it has the sense 'like.' These show that *kata* is a preposition with diverse meanings.

73. This is the only use of θέλημα (*thelēma*) in Galatians, otherwise, twenty-four times in Paul (1:4).

74. There is no article attached to πατρὸς in τοῦ θεοῦ καὶ **πατρὸς** ἡμῶν (*tou Theou kai patros ēmōn*). This is a nice example of Granville Sharp's rule which Wallace, *Greek Grammar*, 271–74 defines in this way: *When the copulative* καὶ *connects two nouns of the same case, [viz. nouns (either substantive or adjective, or participles) of personal description, respecting office, dignity, affinity, or connexion, and attributes, properties, or qualities, good or ill], if the article* ὁ*, or any of its cases, precedes the first of the said nouns or participles, and is not repeated before the second noun or participle, the latter always relates to the same person that is expressed or described by the first noun or participle*: i.e., it denotes a farther description of the first-named person. (Emphasis his). Wallace adds: 'In other words, in the TSKS construction, the second noun refers to the *same* person mentioned with the first noun when: (1) neither is *impersonal*; (2) neither is *plural*; (3) neither is a *proper* name.' Wallace calls this the TSKS construction ([the] article-substantive-καί-substantive) where the second noun is a substantive. This is one of eighty constructions in the NT which fit the requirements of Sharp's rule.

75. The noun δόξα (*doxa*) is found only once in Galatians (1:5).

who sent the Prophets who spoke of God's coming deliverance, has acted decisively in history in Jesus. This was always his plan, conceived before creation (1 Cor 2:7). Christ's work is sufficient. As such, they must not yield to the false teachers calling them to law adherence.

Here *thelēma* speaks of God's will, which was that Christ would die to save humankind. The associated verb *thelō* is used through Galatians. Sometimes, it is the desires of the Judaizers in view. As in 1:7 where they want to pervert the gospel of Christ. They want to shut out the Galatians (4:17), to make a good showing of them in their flesh (6:12), by wanting to have them circumcised (6:13). At other times it is Paul's desires. So, in 3:2, he wants to know the answer to his rhetorical question concerning on what basis they received the Spirit. He wants to change his tone but cannot in 4:20. Yet other times, it is the Galatians' will. Hence, in 4:9, he asks them whether they want to be enslaved again to the *stoicheia*. Some want to be under the law (4:21). Paul wants them to live by the Spirit and not what the flesh wills (5:17). This all adds up to a battle of wills in Galatians. Will God's will prevail? Will Paul's will, which represents that of God, convince them? Or will the Judaizers desires override the Galatians' will to yield to the gospel of grace?

Galatians 1:5 is a classic Pauline doxology:

to whom (dative *hos*) **be the glory** (*doxa*) **into** (*eis*)[76] **forever and ever** (*aiōnas tōn aiōnōn*, see the previous verse)**, amen.**[77]

---

76. The common preposition εἰς (*eis*) is found thirty times across Galatians with six nuances: 1) 'To:' 'to another gospel' (1:5, 6); 'to Jerusalem ... to Arabia ... to Damascus ... to Jerusalem ... to Syria ... to Jerusalem' (1:17, 18, 21; 2:1); 'to the gentiles' (2:8, 9; 3:14); 'to the circumcised' (2:9); 'to Antioch' (2:11); 'to his own flesh ... to the Spirit' (6:8); 2) '**Into:**' 'into the ages of ages' (1:5); '[run] *into* emptiness' (2:2); 'baptized *into* Christ' (3:27); '[Spirit] *into* our hearts' (Gal 4:6); '*into* slavery' (4:24); 3) '**In:**' 'believed *in* Christ Jesus' (2:16); '[confidence in the Lord] *in* you' (5:10); '*for* opportunity' (5:13); '*for* himself only ... not *for* the other' (6:4); 4) To, **until:** 'until the coming faith' (3:23); '*until* Christ came' (3:24); 5) '**For:**' '*for* his [Peter] apostleship' (2:8); '*for* righteousness' (3:6); '*for* you' (4:11); 6) **Purposive:** '*in order to* make the promise void' (3:17).

77. *PDBS* 38 defines doxology as: 'In the NT, a form of praise, blessing or glory to God (Gk *doxa*, "praise, glory," *legō*, "to speak") used in the context of worship and often ending with an "Amen." Examples include Rom 1:25; 16:27; Eph 3:21; Phil 4:20; 1 Tim 1:17; Rev 1:6; 7:12.

Paul delights in breaking forth into spontaneous praise using *doxa* in the midst of a letter. Such doxologies are found in the Hebrew Scriptures (e.g., Ps 72:19; 104:31) and other Jewish writings. For example, the Apocalypse of Sedrach (second–fifth-century AD) and 4 Macc 18:24 (first-century AD) both end with the same words found in Gal 1:4.

Other Pauline examples include: 'To him be glory forever (*eis tous aiōnas*), amen' (Rom 11:36); 'to the only wise God be glory forevermore through Jesus Christ! Amen' (Rom 16:27); 'to the praise of his glorious grace, with which he has blessed us in the Beloved' (Eph 1:6); 'to the praise of his glory' (Eph 1:14); 'to him be glory in the church and in Christ Jesus throughout all generations, forever and ever. Amen' (Eph 3:21); 'to the glory and praise of God' (Phil 1:11); 'to the glory of God the Father' (2:11); 'to our God and Father be glory forever and ever. Amen' (Phil 4:20); 'To the King of the ages, immortal, invisible, the only God, be honor and glory forever and ever. Amen' (1 Tim 1:17). The praise utterance here in Gal 1:5 is also found verbatim in 1 Tim 4:18 (cf. 2 Cor 1:20; 4:15; 1 Tim 1:11).

Paul, along with other biblical writers, knows that God is completely and utterly glorious. His glory is unimaginable and complete; and to him, nothing can be added. This is a prayer that humanity will offer him the glory he deserves in his total gloriousness. Here it is '*the* glory'—creation and redemption are his work, and he deserves all the glory—not Paul, not any other Christian, and certainly not the Judaizers. 'Forever and ever' uses the emphatic *eis tous aiōnas tōn aiōnōn*, literally, 'into the ages of ages.'[78]

'Forever and ever,' or literally, 'into the ages of ages' (*eis tous aiōnas tōn aiōnōn*) is found regularly in the NT, and especially in Revelation.[79] It is found in doxologies that bear a close resemblance to Gal 1:5 (Rev 1:6; 5:13); similarly, the doxology of 1 Tim 1:17 (above). 1 Peter 4:11 is very similar to Gal 1:5: 'to him is the glory and the power forever and ever, amen.' Philippians

78. See Ps 83:5 [Eng. 84:4]; *Apoc. Sed.* 16.7; *Pr. Jac.* 1.8; *Gk. Apoc. Ezra* 7.16.
79. See Rev 1:18; 4:9, 10; 10:6; 11:15; 15:7; 19:3; 20:10.

ends with a very similar construction: 'To our God and Father be glory forever and ever. Amen' (Phil 4:20). 2 Timothy and Hebrews end with these same words (2 Tim 4:18; Hebrews 13:21). Thus, we can conclude that this is a familiar doxology, used in Jewish and Christian thought. Its placement here rather than near the conclusion of the letter draws attention. By placing it here, the Galatians are reminded of the greatness of God's redemptive work in Christ and challenged to yield to him fully and turn from their flirtation with Judaizing heresy.

CHAPTER THREE: NO OTHER GOSPEL (GAL 1:6–10)

One of the outstanding features of Galatians (and Titus) is the complete absence of the characteristic thanksgiving and intercession[1] found in most of Paul's letters,[2] or a blessing like those found in 2 Corinthians and Ephesians (2 Cor 1:3–7; Eph 1:3–14). Considering Paul's emphasis on gratitude, prayer, and blessing, this is remarkable and gives insight into the depth of Paul's concern. He does not have a lot to be thankful for with the Galatians, and while he cries out a blessing to God in the previous verse, he does not yet pronounce a direct blessing on his readers. Rather, he wants nothing to hinder the Galatians from hearing him loud and clear. His plea is urgent because the gospel and their salvation are at stake.

In this section, Paul expresses his amazement and concern that some of the Galatians are turning away from the gospel of grace to 'another gospel.' He reasserts that there is only one gospel and that false teachers are disturbing the Galatians and distorting it to the point that it is not the gospel. Paul's concern is seen in the pronouncement of an imprecation (curse) on anyone who preaches a different gospel (for there is no other one), whether angel or human being. The reference to 'angel' calls to mind the giving of the law to Moses so important to the Judaizers and thus is a subtle challenge to their claims (cf. Gal 3:19). 'Let him be accursed' is a proclamation that they experience eternal torment.[3] Very unusually for Paul in his letters, he repeats this

---

1. However, 1:3 is a prayer-wish for the Galatians and 1:4–5 a doxology.
2. See Rom 1:8–14; 1 Cor 1:4–9; Phil 1:3–11; Col 1:3–14; 1 Thess 1:2–10; 2 Thess 1:3–4; 1 Tim 1:12–17; 2 Tim 1:3–7; Phlm 4–7.
3. George, *Galatians*, 98–99 rightly says. 'To be anathematized then means far more than

statement. Clearly, this is emphatic to drive home his warning (v. 9).

DESERTION OF THE GOSPEL (1:6)

In *Galatians 1:6* Paul launches his challenge to the Galatians with a statement of his astonishment that they are deserting the grace of Christ for a false gospel:

I am amazed (*thaumazo*)[4] **that** (*hoti*, 1:6)[5] **so** (*outos*)[6] **quickly** (*tacheōs*)[7] **you are turning away** (present middle *metatithēmi*)[8] **from** (*apo*, 1:1) **the One Who Called** (aorist participle[9] *kaleō*)[10] **you** (plural *sy*, 1:3) **by** (*en*)[11] **the grace** (*charis*, see 1:3) **of Christ**

to be excommunicated. It means nothing less than *to suffer the eternal retribution and judgment of God.'* (Italics mine).

4. This use in 1:6 is the only use of the verb θαυμάζω (*thaumazo*), 'I am amazed' in Galatians. It is common in the Gospels of people's amazement at Jesus.

5. There are twenty-nine uses of ὅτι (*hoti*) in Galatians: 1) As a 'marker of narrative or discourse content, direct or indirect, *that'* (BDAG 731): 1:6, 11, 13, 20, 21; 2:7, 14, 16; 3:7; 3:11; 4:13, 15; 5:3, 10, 21; 2) Causal, 'because, for:' 2:11, 16 [2nd use]; 4:6, 12, 20; 4:27; 6:8; 3) Marker of speech (effectively a speech mark): 3:8 [2nd use], 10, 11 [2nd use]; 3:13; 4:22; 5:2.

6. Five times the adverb οὕτως (*houtōs*) is used in Galatians: with *tacheos*, 'so quickly' (1:6); with *anoētos*, 'so foolish' (3:3); with *anaplyroō*, 'so fulfil;' 'so also, similarly, in the same way' (4:3, 39).

7. Galatians 1:6 is the only use of the adverb ταχέως (*tacheōs*) in Galatians—here meaning 'quickly,' or 'so soon.' Either way, Paul is stunned at the speed of their desertion of the gospel.

8. The only use of the compound verb μετατίθημι (*metatithēmi*) in Galatians is in 1:6. Here it connotes 'desert' or 'turn away from.'

9. The participle τοῦ καλέσαντος is a neat example of a substantival (independent) participle where the participle is not related to a noun, but is independent, and functions as a substantive. So, God is described as 'the caller of you, the one calling you.' See Wallace, *Greek Grammar*, 619.

10. The verb καλέω (*kaleō*) is used four times, all of God's call to people: 1) To the Galatians, to salvation, and to freedom (1:6; 5:6, 13); 2) To Paul, 'by his grace' (1:15).

11. The common preposition ἐν (*en*) is found forty-one times in Galatians. It is slippery in meaning with each of these listed here subject to discussion: 1) Signaling the **means** by which something is done, '*by grace*' (1:6); '*by faith*' (2:20); '*by the law*' or '*by them*' (3:11, 12; 5:4); '*by an intermediary*' (3:19); 2) **Within a sphere**: '*within* Judaism' (1:13, 14); '*in Christ*' or '*in Christ Jesus*' (1:22; 2:4, 17; 3:14, 26, 28; 5:6), '*in the flesh*' (2:20; 6:12, 13), '*in you* [Abraham]' (3:8); '*in the Lord*' (5:10); '*in the cross*' (6:14); 3) **Socially**, 'among,' '*among* my contemporaries' (1:14); '*among* the gentiles' (1:16; 2:2),

(Christos, 1:1) **to** (*eis*, 1:5) **another** (*heteros*)[12] **gospel** (*euangelion*)[13]— ...

Paul continues with the verb *thaumazō*, 'I am amazed,' which is placed first for prominence, emphasizing the level of his amazement (already shown in his lack of thanksgiving or blessing). The verb is common in the wider NT[14] but is used by Paul only here and in 2 Thess 1:10 of the return of Christ when he is 'marveled at' by the saints. Paul is clearly utterly stunned. The verb is present tense, here a progressive present (or descriptive present) whereby the present 'describes a scene in progress, especially in narrative literature.'[15] It is also a continuous experience.

'*among* you' (3:5); 4) '**To**:' 'reveal his Son *to* me' (1:16); 5) **Causal**, 'because,' '*because* of me' (1:24); 6) '**In, within**,' '*in* me' (2:20); 'in/within the book of the law' (3:10); '*in* my flesh' (4:14); '*in* you' (4:19); 7) **Temporal**, 'when:' '*when* I am present'—'*in* my presence' (4:18); 8) '**About**:' 'perplexed *about* (in) you;' 9) **Locative**, '*in* Arabia' (4:25); 10) '**with**:' '*with* a good purpose' (4:18); '*with* (in) one word;' '*with* a spirit of gentleness' (6:1); '*with* the one who teaches' (6:6); 10) Active, 'doing:' 'caught *doing* (in the action of) any transgression; 11) '**On/in**:' 'bear *in/on* my body.'

12. The adjective ἕτερος (*heteros*), 'another, other,' is used three times. '*Another* gospel' (1:5), 'the *other* apostles' (1:19), 'in the *other* (person)' (6:4). It is used interchangeably with *allos* (1:7; 5:10), there being no significant difference in meaning in the NT. In Classical Greek, *heteros* speaks of 'another, other' where there are two options, whereas *allos* to 'another, other' when there are many. By NT times this distinction had broken down. This is seen here where, although 'another' could be argued to be the Judaizing gospel, in principle, there could be any number of possibilities here.

13. There are seven uses of εὐαγγέλιον (*euangelion*) in Galatians of: 'a different *gospel*' (there is no one) (1:6); 'the *gospel* of Christ' (the only *gospel*, 'about Christ') (1:7); 'the *gospel* that was preached by me,' 'the *gospel* that I proclaim among the gentiles,' 'the *gospel* of the uncircumcised' (which is the *gospel* of Christ, 1:7) (1:11; 2:2; 2:7); and 'the truth of the *gospel*' (2:5, 14). The emphasis is on its content in Galatians. He also uses the verb *euangelizomai* seven times (see further 1:8) and *proeuangelizomai*, 'preach beforehand' once (3:8).

14. The verb *thaumazō* is used regularly in the Gospels of Jesus' amazement at times such as the Roman centurion (Matt 8:10; Luke 7:9, also Mark 6:6;), or more commonly of the amazement at Jesus found in the crowds, the disciples, the Jewish leaders, or Pilate (Matt 8:27; 9:33; 15:31; 21:20; 22:22; 27:14; Mark 15:5, 44; Luke 4:22; 8:25; 9:43; 11:14, 38; 20:26; 24:12, 41; John 3:7; 4:27; 5:20, 28; 7:15, 21). Other uses of amazement at other things are found in Luke 1:21, 63; 2:18, 33. In Acts it is found of the amazement of the Jewish leaders and people at events and the disciples (Acts 2:7; 3:12; 4:13; 13:21, cf. Acts 7:31). See also 1 John 3:13; Jude 16; Rev 13:3; 17:6, 7, 8.

15. Wallace, *Greek Grammar*, 518.

The content of his ongoing state of amazement is signaled by *hoti*, 'that.' What gives him such shock is that the Galatians are turning away from God who called them by the gospel. 'So quickly' (or 'so soon') can be translated 'so easily' but all of Paul's uses of *tacheōs* are temporal.[16] Hence, it is suggestive of a short period since their conversion by Paul on his first Antiochian mission journey. This fits a traditional chronology in which Paul and Barnabas evangelized Turkey in AD 47–48, and Paul writes Galatians later in AD 48. A date in the mid-50s seems less likely.

Metatithēmi carries the idea of change (Heb 7:12),[17] and sometimes, as here, of 'desert' or 'turn away from. The associated verb *metastrephō* is found in v. 7, 'wanting to *distort* the gospel of Christ.' While the issue is the gospel of grace (below), by turning from the gospel, they are deserting God, here described as 'the one (he) who called you.' Through the preaching of the gospel by whomever (e.g., Paul, Billy Graham), God speaks, sending his clarion call to people to yield to him as Sovereign. The verb for 'call' is *kaleō* which can simply mean 'invite' (e.g., Matt 22:3). However, in Paul's thought, it carries the sense of effective call—God summons, and we come (see further 1:16). The Judaizers are claiming that faith in Christ without subjection to circumcision and law is a rejection of God. Paul is countering; the converse is the case—to reject the gospel of grace by adding to faith in Christ circumcision, law, or any law (works), one actually turns away from the God who willed to save humanity through the grace demonstrated in his son, who died voluntarily for humanity's sins, and was raised again (1:4–5).

'The grace of Christ' (*chariti Christou*)[18] sums up the gospel message. While the exact nature of the genitive 'of Christ' is slippery,[19] this construct defines the gospel as grace and Christ.

---

16. See 1 Cor 4:19; Phil 2:19, 2:24; 2 Thess 2:2; 1 Tim 5:22; 2 Tim 4:9.
17. *Metatithēmi* can also connote 'transfer' as to another place as in the case of Joseph's bones from Egypt to Shechem (Acts 7:16), or Enoch to God (Heb 11:5).
18. **Variant:** Some witnesses do not include 'of Christ,' so it simply reads 'by grace.' Yet others have 'of Jesus Christ' and some 'of God.' While P46vid G and F* omit 'of Christ,' the external support for the inclusion of 'of Christ' is very strong and widespread including P51 א A B and many early Fathers. As such, it should be included.

The two are intertwined. 'Grace' here connotes 'gift,' God's lavish offer of salvation in and through Christ, which is received by faith alone (which will become evident) (see further on grace 1:3). Faith is merely assent to the proclaimed gospel of grace bound up in Christ. The references to grace before any mention of faith are important to note. While on the human side of the salvation 'event,' faith is the only and right response that justifies, grace precedes faith. As Paul expresses cleverly in Eph 2:8, salvation is 'by grace through faith.' God is the initiator, the one who calls, as this verse says. His grace is the motivator of his action for a world that has rebelled.

'Christ' speaks of Jesus Christ Lord, who gave himself to deal with humanity's sin and is raised (1:4), who Paul serves as an apostle (1:1), and who bestows grace and peace (1:3). There is no mention of the law or any particular law because justification is a gift of grace through Christ. This the Galatians are deserting. They must remember it is justification by grace through faith, or as Paul more often speaks 'from grace' (*ek pistou*).

The phrase 'to a different gospel,' or more literally, 'to another gospel,' uses *euangelion*, the primary term used by Paul to sum up the Christian message (seventy-six times, verb *euangelizomai* twenty-one times, *euangelistēs*, 'evangelist,' twice)—overall ninety-nine uses of this language.[20] It has powerful antecedents in Judaism, in particular, its use of the good news of God's redemption of Israel from Babylon through his anointed (Cyrus) proclaimed by the prophet to Israel (Isa 40:9; 52:7; 60:6; 61:1).[21]

---

19. The genitive is slippery with a wide range of possibilities: 1) 'The grace described by Christ' (descriptive/aporetic genitive); 2) 'The grace belonging to Christ' or 'Christ's grace' (possessive genitive, so Longenecker, *Galatians*, 15); 3) 'The grace which is Christ' (genitive of apposition [epexegetical genitive or genitive of definition]);' 4) 'The grace produced by Christ' (genitive of production); 5) 'The grace dependent on/ derived from Christ' (genitive of source, origin); or 6) 'The grace Christ has for us' (subjective genitive).

20. Outside of Paul: *Euangelion*: 4x Matt; 8x Mark; 2x Luke-Acts; 1x 1 Peter; 1x Rev. *Euangelizomai*: 1x Matt; 25x Luke-Acts; 2x Heb; 3x 1 Peter; 2x Rev; *Euangelistēs*, 1x Acts. John prefers witness language.

21. See also 1 Sam 31:9; 2 Sam 1:20; 4:10; 18:19, 20, 26, 31; 1 Kings 1:42; 1 Chron 10:9; Ps 39:10 [Eng. 40:9]; 67:12 [68:11]; 95:2 [96:2]; Joel 2:32; Nah 1:15; Jer 20:15.

Equally significant is the *euang–* terms being used across the
Roman world of the good news of the Emperor proclaimed by
heralds throughout the Empire. The best example is the Priene
Inscription (9 BC).[22] Its use in the NT is powerful, speaking of
political (in a kingdom sense), spiritual, and ultimately complete
redemption by Christ the King.

Here, 'another gospel,' speaks of the alternative form of the
Christian message being presented by the Judaizers. This gospel
does not deny the story of Christ but wants to place it within the
framework of Jewish law and particularly its boundary markers,
especially circumcision. So, their 'good news' involves the
proclamation of God, Christ, and Torah, with Christ aside from
the Torah being insufficient. As Paul will go on to state directly
in the next verse and throughout the letter, this one is not the
gospel, and there is no other. In fact, their 'good news' is in fact
'bad news,' as in it, humankind remains lost under sin and its
consequences. Only Jesus is sufficient to deal with sins once and
for all, and the Galatians must not abandon him!

NO DIFFERENT GOSPEL (1:7)

Paul continues from v. 6 into *Galatians 1:7*:

22. The Priene inscription, 9 BC, was commonly found in throughout Asia Minor
(Priene, Apameia, Eumeneia, Dorlyaion, and Maioneia) in Greek and/or Latin. It
includes the official letter of Paulus Fabius Maximus (lines 30–41 below), which
begins with an honorific official motion by the high Priest, followed by political
motions (lines 41–77). It is entitled 'The Letter of Paulus Fabius Maximus and
Decrees by Asians Concerning the Provincial Calendar.' It reads (see Major
Contributors and Editors, 'Ephesians,' in *LBD*):It seemed good to the Greeks in Asia,
by the opinion of the high priest Apollonius, the son of the Asiatic Menophilos: Since
Providence, divinely ordering our life, having displayed earnestness and love of
honor, arranged for the most perfect good, by bringing in Augustus, whom for the
benefit of humanity she has filled with moral excellence, even as she gave
(*charisamenē*) to us and those who will come after us a Savior (*sōtēra*) who not only
stopped war, but who shall arrange peace (*kosmēsonta de eirēnēn*); and Caesar, when he
was manifest, surpassed the hopes of all who had anticipated the good news
(*euangelia*), not only by surpassing the benefactors which occurred before him, but
neither leaving hope of surpassing him in future ones. And the birthday of the god
(*tou theou*)] began the good tidings (*euangelion*) for the world (*tōi kosmōi*) because of
him.

—which (neuter *hos*, 1:5) **is** (*eimi*)[23] **not** (*ou*, 1:1) **another** (*allos*) **[gospel]**,[24] **but** (*ei*[25] *mē*[26])[27] **[there are] some men** (plural masculine *tis*)[28] **who are** (*eimi*, 1:7) **troubling** (present participle *tarassō*)[29] **you** (plural *sy*, 1:3) **and** (*kai*, 1:1) **wanting** (present

23. The common verb εἰμί (*eimi*), indicating 'I am/to be' is frequent in Galatians, fifty–three times (and implied a number of other times). The singular present third person *estin*, 'is' (1:7, 11; 3:12, 16, 20 [2x]; 4:1, 2; 4:24 [2x], 25, 26 [2x]; 5:3, 19 [2x], 22, 23; 6:15), the present plural third person *eisin*, 'they are' (1:7; 3:7, 10 [2x]; 4:24), present singular third person imperative, *estō*, 'let him/her/it be' (1:8, 9), imperfect middle singular first person *ēmēn*, 'I would not be' (1:10, 22), imperfect active third person plural *ēsan*, 'they were' (1:23; 2:6), present participle *ōn*, 'being' (2:3, concessive, 'though;' 4:1; 6:3, temporal, 'when he is'), present infinitive *einai*, 'to be' (2:6, 9; 4:21; 6:3), imperfect third person singular *ēn*, 'was' (2:11; 3:21), present second person plural *este*, 'you are' (3:3, 26, 28, 29; 4:6; 4:28; 5:18), plural first person present *esmen*, 'we are' (3:25; 4:31), imperfect first person plural *ēmen*, 'we were' (4:3), imperfect middle first person plural *ēmetha*, 'we were' (4:3), present second person singular *ei*, 'you are' (4:7), present plural participle *ousin*, 'being' (4:8), and subjunctive third person singular *ē*, 'he is' (5:10).
24. The adjective ἄλλος (*allos*) is used twice; 1:7: 'another [gospel];' 5:9: 'another perspective.' See also *heteros* in 1:6 where I discussed how the terms are interchangeable (although their use differed in classical Greek—*heteros*, 'another' in relation to two options—'one or other'; *allos*, 'another' in regard to many).
25. The conditional adverbial conjunction εἰ (*ei*), 'if,' is used twenty times in Galatians: 1) In the form *ei mē* (lit. 'if not'), in 1:7 connoting 'but' and 'except' in 1:19 and 6:14; 2) In 'if ... then' conditional sentences (1:9, 10; 2:14, 17, 18; 2:21; 3:18, 21, 29; 4:7; 5:11, 15, 18, 24; 6:3); 3) *ei ge*, 'if indeed' (3:4); 4) Simple 'if' (4:15). On the forms of the conditional sentences, see each passage in this commentary.
26. The negation μή (*mē*) is found twenty-four times in Galatians: 1) *Ei mē*, 'but, except' (see previous note) (1:7, 19; 6:14); 2) Like *ou*, 'not,' (2:2; 4:8, 8, 30; 5:1, 7, 13, 15, 17, 26; 6:1, 7, 9 [2x], 12); 3) *ean mē*, 'but' (2:16); 4) *mē genoito*, 'absolutely not' (2:17, 21; 6:14); 5) *mē pōs*, 'lest;' 6) *ou mē*, emphatic 'not' (5:16).
27. The construct εἰ μή (*ei mē*) is used three times in Galatians. Literally, it means 'if not.' It is translated 'but,' as in 1:7: 'which [gospel] there is no other, *but* (*ei mē*) some are troubling you.' The other two uses carry the sense 'except.' In 1:9: 'I saw none of the other apostles *except* Jacob.' In 6:14: 'but may it never be for me to boast *except* in the cross.' The construct is found eighty–six times in the NT of which twenty-six are in Paul. See on *ei mē*, BDAG 278.
28. There are nine uses of the indefinite pronoun τις (*tis*) in Galatians: 1) Plural masculine *tines, tinas* 'some men, some people' (1:7); 2) Singular masculine *tis*, 'anyone, any man, any person, any angel' (1:9; 6:3); 3) Singular neuter *ti, tini*, 'something' (2:6; 6:3), 'anything' (5:6; 6:15).
29. The verb ταράσσω (*tarassō*), 'trouble, shake, unsettle, confuse' is found twice in Galatians, 1:7; 5:10, both of Judaizers who are troubling the Galatians.

participle *thelō*)[30] **to distort** (aorist infinitive *metastrephō*)[31] **the gospel** (*euangelion*, see 1:6) **of Christ** (genitive *Christos*, 1:1).

'Which is (*estin*) not another (*allos*),' in **Galatians 1:7**, clarifies Paul's opinion of this so-called Judaizing gospel—it is *not* another gospel as there is no other one. These agitators have so distorted the gospel of grace, that it is no longer the gospel.

Those troubling the Galatians (you) refers to the Judaizers who are not named; they are merely described as 'some men.' Throughout Galatians, Paul refuses to name these people indicating his disdain for them. They are not 'brothers' as in 1:1; rather, they are false brothers (*pseudadelphous*, 2:4). They have clearly come to the Galatian churches preaching their false gospel. Just who these people are is not clear. We can rule out Barnabas (2:1, 9, 13), Cephas/Peter (1:18; 2:11), Jesus' brother Jacob (1:19),[32] and John, with the three pillar-apostles distinguished from the false brothers in 2:7–10; similarly, Titus (2:1, 3).

When Paul was in Jerusalem discussing the gospel, these false brothers spied on Paul and Barnabas (2:4). In the Antiochian dispute, they are described as 'the circumcision party,' indicating their desire for new gentile converts to be circumcised (2:12; 6:12). They have bewitched the Galatians (3:1). They are likely expecting the Galatians to observe Jewish Sabbaths, feasts, and perhaps the Jubilee (4:10). They are making much of the Galatians (4:17). Like pushy athletes, they are cutting in on the Galatians (5:7) and seeking to persuade them (5:8). They are those 'troubling you' (5:10) and 'unsettling you' (5:12). They may be telling the Galatians that Paul preaches circumcision

---

30. The verb θέλω (*thelō*), 'I want, will, wish,' related to *thelēma* (will) in 1:4, is used nine times: 1) The will of the Judaizers (3:2; 4:17; 6:12, 13); 2) Paul wanting to know something from the Galatians (3:2), to be with them (4:20); 3) The will of the Galatians (4:9, 21; 5:17). He does not use the verb of God but does so with *thelēma*.

31. There is one use of the verb μεταστρέφω (*metastrephō*, *meta*, 'with, after' plus *strephō*, 'turn') in 1:7, here meaning 'distort, corrupt, pervert' the gospel.

32. Paul is careful in 2:11–14 to distinguish between certain people who came from Jacob with the 'circumcision party,' there being no need to consider that Jacob is responsible.

elsewhere, which he does not (5:11). This is causing infighting (5:15).

These are likely the same group or kind of people as those who infiltrate Antioch in Acts 15:1 saying to gentile converts, 'unless you are circumcised according to the custom of Moses, you cannot be saved.' Luke also records there that some believers 'who belonged to the party of the Pharisees' and who at the Jerusalem Council argued against the gospel of grace stating, 'it is necessary to circumcise them and to order them to keep the law of Moses' (Acts 15:5).

The verb *tarassō* suggests real agitation. It is used for the stirring of the pool in John 5:7. Otherwise, it indicates being disturbed as Herod was when he heard the news of the birth of a rival king (Matt 2:3). Oft-times, the term has greater strength, used of being terrified, as were the disciples when they saw Jesus walking on water and thought he was a ghost (Matt 14:26; Mark 6:50), of Zechariah's terror at the appearance of the angel (Luke 1:12), of the grief of the disciples when Jesus was killed (Luke 24:38) or when Jesus saw Mary weeping over Lazarus (John 11:33), Jesus' travails at his forthcoming betrayal and the cross (John 12:27; 13:21), and city disturbances over the arrival of the gospel (Acts 17:8, 13, cf. John 14:1, 27; 1 Pet 3:14). The term is used again in 5:10 of the Judaizers who are troubling them and who must bear the consequences for their behavior. It is used by Luke in his account of the Judaizers in Acts 15:24—they are throwing the Galatians into disarray, as they did in Antioch (Acts 15:1–4).

They want to turn the Galatians from the gospel of Christ. In these opening seven verses, Paul has already spoken of the death of Christ for sin, his resurrection, and 'the grace of Christ.'

A CURSE ON FALSE PREACHERS (1:8–9)

In *Galatians 1:8*, having written off the gospel and described the opponents, Paul now boldly calls a curse on them. He repeats it for good measure:

'But (*alla*, 1:1) **even** (*kai*, 1:1) **if** (*ean*)[33] **we** (*egō*, 1:2) **or** (*ē*)[34] **an**

angel (*angelos*)[35] **from** (*ek*, 1:1) **heaven** (*ouranos*)[36] **preach a gospel** (*euangelizomai*)[37] **to you** (dative *sy*, 1:3)[38] **contrary** (*para*)[39] **to the gospel which we preached** (*euangelizomai*) **to you** (dative *sy*), **let that person be** (present imperative *eimi*) **accursed** (*anathema*).[40]

'But' is *alla*, introducing a strong contrasting thought to the Judaizing false gospel that has come to Galatia. *Kai* here connotes 'even' rather than the usual 'and' (see 1:1). *Ean* introduces a third-class conditional sentence, indicating something hypothetical and unlikely for the sake of argument.[41] 'We' is emphatic and

---

33. The conditional particle ἐάν (*ean*) is used seven times in Galatians. Sometimes it signals 'if' in conditional sentences (1:8; 5:2; 6:1, 7). Otherwise, it is found in the form *ean mē* ('but') (2:16), *hostis ean ē*, 'whoever he may be' (5:10), or *ha ean thelēte tauta poiēte*, 'the things if he wishes these things to do' (5:17).

34. The logical disjunctive conjunction ἤ (*ē*) is found eight times in Galatians, seven times introducing an alternative perspective, 'or' (1:8, 10 [2x]; 2:2; 3:2, 5, 15). Once it introduces comparison, 'more *than*' (4:27).

35. The noun ἄγγελος (*angelos*), 'angel' is found thrice in Galatians: 1) An angel bringing another gospel (anathema) (1:8); 2) The law put into effect by angels (3:19); 3) The Galatians received Paul as an angel (4:14).

36. The noun οὐρανός (*ouranos*), 'heaven, sky,' receives only one mention, in 1:8 where it means 'heaven,' the abode of God and angels who delivered the law to Moses and from which no new gospel will come.

37. The verb εὐαγγελίζομαι, *euangelizomai*, is the middle of εὐαγγελίζω (*euangelizō*) but with the same meaning, 'preach the gospel.' It is also related to *euangelion*, 'gospel.' Euangelizomai is used seven times in Galatians; each time concerning the preaching of the gospel whether a false message (1:8, 9), the true gospel (1:8), or the gospel preached by Paul (1:11, 16, 23; 4:13). See also on *euangelion* on 1:6; *proeuangelizomai*, 'preach beforehand' in 3:8; and the synonym *kērussō* in 2:2 and 5:11.

38. **Variant:** There are a whole host of variants to the phrase *euangelizētai hymin* (proclaim [mid subjunctive] the gospel to you). These include: 1) *hymin euangelizētai* (reverse order); 2) *euangelizetai hymin* (proclaim the gospel [present tense] to you); 3) *euangelisetai hymin* (proclaimed [aorist] the gospel to you); 4) *euangelisētai hymin* (proclaim the gospel to you); 5) *euangelizētai* (without *hymin*); 6) *euangelizetai*, (without *hymin*) (proclaim [present tense]). It is clear that the text is uncertain. Those with good textual support include the chosen reading and 1) above. Metzger, *Commentary*, 521 is right to favor the chosen reading. The meaning is unaffected.

39. The preposition παρά (*para*) is only used four times in Galatians. It is used of a gospel 'contrary' to the true gospel Paul preached (1:8, 10); otherwise, it indicates 'from' (1:12; 3:11).

40. The imprecation ἀνάθεμα (*anathema*) is not common in the NT, six times overall—twice in Galatians, in 1:8, 9, in parallel.

41. On this category see Wallace, *Grammar*, 696.

likely refers to Paul's team or himself, and the brothers and sisters of Antioch.[42] Its use here is powerful. Even if those who founded the church there, Paul and Barnabas, were to come with a different gospel, they should reject it, and may that person be cursed. This reminds me of Rom 9:1–3 where Paul, with great sorrow and anguish, wishes that he could be accursed and cut off from Christ if it would mean that his people, Israel, would yield to the gospel of Christ and grace with faith. However, he will not compromise the gospel to Judaism or any other worldview to achieve that end. Christian history is littered with people who corrupt the gospel. Parallel to the Judaizing heretics are those who have preached a 'works' gospel through history (e.g., Pelagius, Medieval Catholicism). Today we face massive challenges from false gospels such as the prosperity gospel that violates Christian economics, as well as liberal gospels that corrupt sexual ethics. We have to be ever vigilant.

'Or an angel from heaven' speaks of one of God's messengers appearing in a vision with a gospel that differs from the gospel first preached by Paul which is consistent with the gospel preached by all Christians across the church. This has a special sharpness as it was believed in Judaism that the law was mediated to Israel through angels (see 3:19). The gospel of Christ supersedes any appearance from a so-called angel. Of course, this also calls to mind Satan, who delights in masquerading as an angel of light corrupting humanity and God's church with false gospels.[43] This has special relevance for us because a faith like Mormonism is in good part based on the so-called 1823 vision of the angel Moroni to Joseph Smith, the cult's founder.[44] Similarly,

---

42. Wallace, *Greek Grammar*, 395 sees this as a text which may indicate the editorial 'we,' so indicating 'I.' Yet he also notes that '[t]he brothers in v 2, then, seem to function in a supporting role, as witnesses to the truth of Paul's gospel.' If so, and I agree with him, it is not the editorial 'we' per se. Rather, Paul and others are known to be authentic believers. So, Peter, Barnabas, John, Jacob—if any such luminaries were to preach another gospel, it is spurious.

43. See 2 Cor 11:12–14, cf. Eph 6:11; 1 Tim 3:7; 5:15; 2 Tim 2:26; 1 Pet 5:8.

44. See e.g., J. P. Eckman, The Truth about Worldviews: A Biblical Understanding of Worldview Alternatives (Wheaton, IL: Crossway Books, 2004), 99.

one of the core traditions of Islam is the appearance of the angel Gabriel in AD 610 when,

> [o]n the seventeenth night of the month of Ramadan, Muhammad was in solitary meditation in a cave at the foot of Mount Hira, near the city of Mecca, when he suddenly saw a vision. The angel Gabriel commanded him to 'recite.' Not understanding what he was to recite, Muhammad heard Gabriel exclaim that he was the prophet of God (Allah). Muhammad's newfound monotheism was controversial among the polytheistic tribes of Mecca. Resistance from Mecca intensified, and his life was in danger. According to Muslim tradition, Allah confirmed Muhammad's prophethood in 620, miraculously bringing him at night to Jerusalem. There he conversed with Jesus, Moses, and Abraham, and there he and Gabriel were taken by a ladder to the seventh heaven. (Muslims believe that the Dome of the Rock is built on the site of this ascension). Still, his monotheistic message was rejected by his people.[45]

Galatians 1:8–9 takes on great significance as we consider the claims of these religions. Of course, in context, the issue is someone who preaches a gospel of Jesus plus circumcision and Mosaic law, as do the Judaizers. Paul is here repudiating this. Even if angels appear in dazzling white and full of supernatural power, if their message is not consistent with Paul's gospel, it is spurious and must be rejected.

The final clause, which forms the apodosis to the conditional sentence signaled by *ean*, is powerful: *anathema estō*, 'let that person be cursed.' The verb *estō* (present active imperative *eimi*), is the first imperative in the letter.[46] Paul tends to use the

---

45. Eckman, *Worldviews*, 76.

46. The first use of the imperative in direct appeal is 4:12 in his appeal for the Galatians to imitate him, 'be (imperative *ginomai*) as I.' Other imperatives include: 'tell me' (4:21); 'stand firm' (5:1), 'do not submit again' (5:1), 'become slaves of one another' (5:13), 'watch that you care for one another' (5:15), 'live by the Spirit,' 5:16), 'restore on another gently' (6:1), 'bear one another's burdens' (6:2), 'test their own work' (6:4), 'share with their teachers in all good things' (6:6), 'do not be deceived' (6:7), 'see what large letters …' (6:11), and 'let no one make trouble for me' (6:17). He also uses imperatives in some citations: Isa 54;1 in 4:27: 'rejoice,' 'break forth,' and 'shout;' Gen 21:10: 'Cast out …' What stands out in these uses is that almost all are in the ethical

indicative and is sparing with the imperative. He urges response to God on the basis of indicative status rather than a direct appeal. As such, when he uses the imperative, it has some heightened force.

This is the first of twenty-three imperatives in the letter in twenty verses. *Estō* here and in v. 9 are directed to the person in mind, rather than the Galatians. There are only two other imperatives in the first three chapters, both targeting the Galatians: 'behold' (1:20), and 'know' (3:7). In Ch. 4–6 where Paul is more direct in commanding response, there are nineteen, with sixteen directed at the Galatians.[47] Not unusually, the imperatives are clustered in the second half of his letter as Paul uses the indicative to lay down his case and summon readers to the right response, and then is more direct in his paraenesis.

Anathema is a word replete with meaning. In the LXX *anathema* can be positive—used of something devoted to the Lord for offering at the temple (2 Macc 2:13) and firstborn animals who are devoted to the Lord (Lev 27:28; Deut 13:17).[48] However, the notion of destruction is implied—devoted to destruction as an offering to God.

It also translates the Hebrew *ḥē·rĕm*, employed of destruction in the context of a military invasion whether destroying a town (Deut 13:15) or annihilating the inhabitants of Canaan (Deut 20:17). In the attack on Jericho, it is employed of the devotion of the city and everything in it to destruction. If Israel failed to do this, Israel's camp would itself be an object of destruction

---

sections. This is characteristic of Paul—he uses the indicative before moving to imperative.

47. Three of these are in the citation Isa 54:1 in 4:27 and one from Gen 21:10 in 4:30 (although this has a double meaning, implicitly directed the Galatians to expel the Judaizers). Those directed at the Galatians include: 'become as I am' (4:12); 'tell me' (4:21); 'stand firm' and 'do not submit to a yoke of slavery' (5:1), 'look, see' (5:2; 6:11); 'serve one another' (5:13); 'watch out' (5:15); 'walk by the Spirit' (6:1); 'bear one another's burdens' (6:2); 'let each test his/her own work' (6:4); 'let … share all good things' (6:6); 'do not be deceived' (6:7); and 'let no one cause me trouble' (6:17).

48. Josephus uses it of things devoted as gifts to the building of the temple in Jerusalem (*Ant.* 17.162; *Ag. Ap.* 1.113) and of publicly devoted monuments (*Ag. Ap.* 1.11). Philo's one use is of the whole of Israel as an offering to God (*Mos.* 1.253).

(Josh 6:17, 18; 7:1).[49] While Israel was faithful to this in Jericho, in the invasion of Ai, Achan took devoted things (*anathema*), and as a result, he and his family were killed.[50] Destroyed places were named *ḥār·mā(h)*, translated *anathema*, implying 'devoted, destroyed, given to the ban, accursed' (Num 21:3; Judg 1:17). In Zech 14:11, Jerusalem will be free of ever again being destroyed, *anathema*.

Luke uses the term once in Acts 23:14 of a sacred vow to God to see Paul destroyed. Otherwise, all NT uses are found in Paul. As noted above, in Rom 9:3, he employs it in his wish to be 'accursed (*anathema*) and cut off from Christ' if this would see his people saved. This is reflected in his preparedness to offer himself up to destruction if that could save his people. Ironically, in his ministry, this is what Paul does, but only at a physical level as he spends himself in ministry—'I die every day' (1 Cor 15:31), to yield eternal life. In 1 Cor 12:3, he employs *anathema* in his criteria for Spirit-reception, no one with the Spirit of God would ever consider saying 'Jesus be cursed!'—meaning to offer up Jesus to destruction by God. Rather, one who has the Spirit will confess, 'Jesus is Lord.'

There is also an irony here in Galatians, for Jesus *is* the sacred offering of God for sin, set apart for destruction (3:10–14). He has taken the curse of sin upon himself; those who reject the gospel of Christ, remain accursed before God. By calling down this imprecation on the Judaizers, Paul is merely stating their certain fate, unless they return to the gospel of grace. Consequently, the Galatians must reject it, or they will be similarly anathematized.

In 1 Cor 16:22, Paul uses a similar construction to Gal 1:8 and 9: 'if anyone has no love for the Lord, *let him be accursed* (*anathema*). Our Lord come!' This speaks of eternal destruction for that person. Behm rightly says, '[t]he Pauline use of ἀνάθεμα is along the lines of the LXX. For Paul, the word denotes the object of a curse.'[51] Behm goes on, '[t]he controlling thought here

---

49. It is also used of a destroyed place named 'Anathema' (Num 21:3).
50. Josh 7:1, 11, 12, 13; 22:20; 1 Chron 2:7.
51. J. Behm, 'ἀνάθεμα,' in *TDNT* 1:354.

is that of the delivering up to the judicial wrath of God of one who ought to be ἀνάθεμα because of his sin.'[52]

This then speaks of the preacher of the false gospel being utterly repudiated, rejected from the Christian community, and left for God's judgment—set apart for destruction. While Paul has a strong theology of inclusion within the church (3:28), he also sets limits whereby those who violate the gospel are to be excluded. Where the gospel is violated in its core tenets, through the extremes of ethical compromise, or divisive behavior, relationships with those people are to be severed.[53] Ultimately, if there is no repentance, 'let that person be cursed' speaks of their condemnation to eternal destruction. If the people who are seeking to Judaize the Galatians are in the hearing of the reading of the letter, this is powerful stuff—they are being cursed in the severest possible way through Paul. Those who preach the false gospel are being handed over to God to be judged (cf. 1 Cor 5:5; 1 Tim 1:19–20). It also looks forward to the destruction of demonic beings who corrupt the Christian faith (see above on Mormonism and Islam). All demonic beings will be brought to nothing (Rom 16:20; 2 Thess 2:8–9; 1 Cor 15:24, cf. Matt 25:41; Rev 20:6–10). Similarly, those who reject the gospel will be destroyed at the judgment. Paul shows here that someone can appear to be a dedicated believer who is very passionate and active in mission yet in actual fact, is not one of God's people and will face God's wrath. This is consistent with Jesus' warning in Matt 7:21–23.

Galatians 1:9 includes an introductory statement recalling 1:8, and then restates with slightly different language v. 8:

as (*hōs*)[54] **we have said before** (perfect *proeipon*)[55] **and** (*kai*,

---

52. Behm, 'ἀνάθεμα,' 354.

53. See Rom 16:17; 2 Cor 10–12; 1 Cor 5; Phil 3; 1 Tim 1:20; 2 Tim 2:17–19; Tit 3:10–11.

54. The common comparative conjunction ὡς (*hōs*) is used nine times in Galatians. Seven times it connotes 'as' (1:9; 4:12 [2x], 14 [2x]; 5:14; 6:10). In 3:16 with *epi*, *hōs* twice connotes 'referring to.'

55. The verb προεῖπον (*proeipon*) compounds *pro*, 'before' and *eipon*, 'say, tell' and so means 'say before.' Paul uses it in 1:9 as he repeats what he said in 1:8, and in 5:21, he uses it of previous warnings against the misdeeds of the flesh.

1:1) **now** (*arti*)[56] **say** (*legō*)[57] **again** (*palin*),[58] **if** (*ei*, 1:7) **anyone** (*tis*, 1:7) **preaches a gospel** (*euangelizomai*, 1:8) **to you** (dative *sy*, 1:3) **contrary** (*para*, 1:8) **to the one which** (neuter *hos*, 1:5) **you received** (*paralambanō*),[59] **let that person be** (present imperative *eimi*) **accursed** (*anathema*, 1:8).

The introductory clause is non-complicated, merely introducing his repetition of the previous warning; however, two things stand out. First, Paul uses *proeipon* ('say before) in the perfect tense, indicating something just said (past) but which stands with the present effect (stative). Second, this double stating is unique in Paul and is emphatic—he wants to stress his warning.[60]

The second statement is in the form of a first-class conditional statement (*ei* plus indicative mood), where something is assumed true for the sake of argument. [61] The protasis reads, 'if anyone proclaims a gospel to you contrary than what you received, let that person be accursed.' This speaks again of the Judaizers preaching a gospel other than what the Galatians received through Paul during his initial evangelization of the region described in Acts 13–14 (s.a. Gal 3:1–5; 4:13).

The Greek term 'chosen,' *paralambanō*, can simply mean 'take' or take along' someone somewhere.[62] Here, however, it carries

---

56. The adverb ἄρτι (*arti*) is used three times in Galatians, all indicating the temporal present, 'now' (1:9, 10; 4:20).
57. The common Greek verb for speaking, λέγω (*legō*) is found nine times in Galatians: 1) Of Paul's speech through the letter (1:9; 3:15, 17; 4:1, 21; 5:2, 16); 2) Of [God's] speech through Scripture (3:16; 4:30).
58. The adverb πάλιν (*palin*), is found nine times in Galatians, each time meaning 'again:' 'say *again*' (1:9), 'returned *again*' (1:17; 4:9), 'went up *again*' (2:1), 'build *again*' (2:18), 'be *again*' (4:9), 'I am *again*' (4:19), 'be subjected *again*' (5:1), and 'testify *again*' (5:3).
59. The verb παραλαμβάνω (*paralambanō*) means to accept or to receive; and is used twice in this letter, first, in 1:9, of the gospel received/accepted by the Galatians, and in 1:12, of Paul's reception of the gospel.
60. The verb *legō* is extremely common in the NT, 1,329 times. 100 of these are in Paul. As discussed in the notes, it is found nine times in Galatians either of Paul's speech in the letter (1:9; 3:15, 17; 4:1, 21; 5:2, 16); or of [God's] speech through Scripture (3:16; 4:30).
61. See Wallace, *Grammar*, 690 who notes '[t]his class uses the particle εἰ with the indicative (in any tense) in the protasis.'
62. *Paralambanō* can have the meaning 'take someone' or 'take someone along' including

its technical sense of the passing on of a tradition as in the case of 1 Cor 11:23 (the tradition of the Last Supper), 1 Cor 15:1 (the tradition of the resurrection), 1 Cor 15:3 (the traditions of the appearances of Christ), the Christian tradition (Phil 4:9; 1 Thess 4:1; 2 Thess 36), and Paul's gospel received through revelation from and of Christ in v. 9.[63]

On those trips, he and Barnabas passed on the gospel, and the Galatians willingly received it (cf. John 1:11; Col 2:6; 1 Thess 2:13). As such, why would they consider abandoning it for something new?—a Judaizing Gospel. For Paul, this is anathema—for the Judaizing message is like the 'gospel' he himself advocated as a Jewish Pharisee. That is, one must become a Jew by circumcision and ritual cleansing, and then one must come under Jewish cultural and legal expectations of the observance of the Jewish calendar including Sabbath observance, the Day of Atonement and other feasts, Jewish kosher eating and table fellowship, Jewish concern for purity, and other legal expectations. If anyone preaches a gospel of Jesus plus such things, they are devoted to God for destruction. By analogy, if anyone subsequent to the writing of Galatians does the same, violating the gospel at its core, they face eternal destruction. This warning from Paul is not to be sniveled at.

AS CHRIST'S SERVANT, I SEEK GOD'S APPROVAL (1:10)

The relationship of *Galatians 1:10* to the context is difficult. Some see it as part of the previous paragraph. Others see it as an introduction to what follows. Yet others consider it a literary transition from the *exordium* (introduction) to the *narratio,* which begins at 1:12. Another possibility is that it is a parenthetical

---

taking a wife (Matt 1:20, 24) or taking people (take with) somewhere (Matt 2:13, 14, 20, 21; 4:5, 8; 12:45; 17:1; 18:16; 20:17; 24:40, 41; 26:37; 27:27; Mark 4:36; 5:40; 9:2; 10:32; 14:33; Luke 9:10, 28; 11:26; 17:34, 35; 18:31; John 14:3; 19:16; Mark 15:39; 16:33; Acts 21:24, 26, 32; 23:18).

63. See also Mark 7:4. It is used in 'did not *receive* [Jesus]' in John 1:11. Similarly in Col 2:6 where the Colossians *received* Christ, and 1 Thess 2:13 where the Thessalonians *received* the word of God. It is also used of *receiving* from the Lord a ministry (Col 4:17). See also Heb 12:28—*receive* a kingdom.

emotional outburst. Most likely, it is the conclusion to the introduction to the letter and states emphatically that his whole purpose in life is to gain God's approval, to please him, as he should as a slave of Christ. However, it also functions parenthetically to transition to what follows where he will defend his apostleship.

The verse includes two questions with a conditional response:

For (*gar*)[64] **am I now** (*arti*)[65] **[pursuing] the approval** (*peithō*)[66] **of people** (plural *anthrōpos*, 1:1) **or God** (*Theos*, 1:1)? **Or** (*gar*) **am I seeking** (present *zēteō*)[67] **to please** (present infinitive *areskō*)[68] **people** (dative plural *anthrōpos*)? **If** (*ei*, 1:7) **I am still** (*eti*)[69] **pleasing** (imperfect *areskō*) **people** (dative plural *anthrōpos*), **then I am** (imperfect *eimi*, 1:7) **not** (*ou*, 1:1) **a slave** (*doulos*)[70] **of Christ** (genitive *Christos*).

The first part of the verse is difficult because of the slippery nature of the verb *peithō*. While in the passive and middle it can

64. The conjunction γάρ (*gar*), which always sits second or third in a clause, is 'used to express cause, clarification, or inference' (BDAG 189). It is found thirty-six times in Galatians, mostly with the sense of 'for' with varying shades of relationship to the former: 1:10, 11, 12, 13; 2:6, 8, 12, 18, 19, 21; 3:10, 18, 21, 26, 27, 28; 4:15, 22, 24, 25, 27, 39; 5:5, 6, 13, 14, 17; 6:3, 5, 7, 9, 13, 15, 17. Runge, *Discourse Grammar*, 52 notes that '[t]he books of Romans and Hebrews have the greatest concentration of usage, followed closely by 1–2 Corinthians and Galatians.'

65. Three uses of ἄρτι (*arti*) are found in Galatians. It means 'now,' the present, in all three (1:9, 10; 4:10).

66. The verb (*peithō*) recurs thrice in Galatians. In 1:10 it is difficult to interpret, possibly meaning 'mislead, persuade, or seek the approval of.' In 5:7 it perhaps has the sense of obeying or being persuaded. The other use is 5:10 where it is used in a common Pauline manner, in the perfect tense, of his *confidence* in the Lord.

67. The common verb ζητέω (*zēteō*), 'to seek,' is found twice in Galatians: 'seeking to please people?' (1:10); 'seeking to be justified in Christ' (2:17).

68. The verb ἀρέσκω (*areskō*) is found only in 1:10, of pleasing God rather than people.

69. The adverb ἔτι (*eti*), which stresses continuation, is used thrice in Galatians, each time meaning 'still'—1:10, 'if I am *still* trying to please people ...;' 5:11 [2x]: 'if I, brothers and sisters, *still* preach circumcision, why am I *still* being persecuted?'

70. The noun δοῦλος (*doulos*), 'slave,' is found four times in Galatians. First, it is used of Paul as a slave of Christ (Gal 1:10). Second, he employs it of the breakdown of the social boundary of slave and freeperson in Christ in 3:28. Thirdly, it is used of the distinction between a slave and a son (child)—the Galatians who were slaves to sin, law, death, and the elemental powers, are now free children of God (4:1, 7). The verb *douloō* is found once in 4:3.

mean 'obey' as in Gal 5:10 (cf. Rom 2:8), which would fit nicely
here—am I now seeking to obey people or God?' implied answer,
God—in the present tense it would usually have the sense of
'persuade, convince.'

If so, what does it mean to persuade people here?[71] It can
mean to persuade people to believe in God as in 2 Cor 5:11:
'therefore, knowing the fear of the Lord we persuade (peithō)
people.' However, what then does it mean to persuade God?
Witherington suggests Paul seeks to persuade people to believe
and God to judge the Judaizers. However, taking peithō in its
normal persuasion sense here seems strained. Or, one could say,
the answer is people, rather than God—his purpose is to
persuade people to believe as befits a servant of Christ.[72] Another
possibility is that he seeks to persuade neither people nor God.

However, it is more likely that the two questions asked in this
verse are parallel, and so 'persuade' parallels 'to please' (areskein)
(see below). So peithō here implies Paul's desire is not to persuade
people to approve of him (say the Judaizers) but to persuade
God to approve of his ministry, i.e., another way of saying he
seeks to please God. Hence, the implied answer is that he is not
seeking the approval of people in his ministry, but God, who
is his master—he is truly a slave of Christ.[73] This could then
respond to criticism of Paul as one who seeks the approval of
people rather than God through preaching a different gospel
in different circumstances (see further 5:11). For Paul, this is
nonsense.

The second question is simpler as Paul then answers it with
a conditional statement indicating the answer is 'no.' It
also explicates the first question: 'or am I seeking (present zēteō)
to please (present infinitive areskō) people (dative plural
anthrōpos)?'

---

71. We can rule out the common use of the perfect tense of peithō in Paul where it means
    to be 'persuaded, convinced, or confident' (Rom 2:19; 8:38; 14:14; 15:14; 2 Cor 2:3;
    10:7; Gal 5:10; Phil 1:6, 14, 25; 2:24; 3:3, 4; 2 Thess 3:4; 2 Tim 1:5; 2 Tim 1:12; Phlm
    21). It can also mean 'rely, place confidence' in (2 Cor 1:9).
72. See Bruce, Galatians, 84.
73. Moo, Galatians, 83–84.

The common verb *zēteō* (117 times NT) here speaks of what Paul seeks to do in his ministry. Paul uses it for his own ministry in 1 Cor 10:33, where he does not seek his own advantage but the good of the many so that they may be saved—his focus is the purposes of God, not his own good or advancement (cf. Phil 2:21). Similarly, in 1 Thess 2:5–6, he reminds the Thessalonians that he and his co-workers did not use flattery as a pretext for greed or seek the glory of people.[74]

Areskō is used in Paul's statement that 'those who are in the flesh cannot *please* God' (Rom 8:8). For him, the Christian obligation is to bear with the weak, and not to please oneself but to please one's neighbor for his good, as did Christ (Rom 15:1–3). So, Paul can say he is a people-pleaser, but only in the sense of the purposes of God in their lives—their good before God, their salvation (1 Cor 10:33). Overall, what matters is pleasing the Lord, even if at times this comes at the expense of pleasing one's spouse (1 Cor 7:32–34). Christians, as good soldiers of Christ, should aim to please Christ as soldiers please their enlisting officer (2 Tim 2:4). So, he urges the Thessalonians to live up to his urgings to 'please God' (1 Thess 4:1). The imperative to please God is clear in 1 Thess 2:4 preceding the reference cited above on *zēteō*, where Paul tells the Thessalonians that he and his team, having been approved by God to be entrusted with the gospel, speak 'not to please people, but to please God who tests our hearts' (1 Thess 2:4). This is unlike the Jewish people who killed prophets, Christ, and rejected Christians—they 'displease God and oppose all humankind' (1 Thess 2:15). The Judaizers, in

---

74. The verb *zēteō* is also used in Paul (22x in all) of people who seek eternal life (Rom 2:7), seeking to establish one's own righteous status before God (Rom 10:3), of people seeking God (Rom 10:20), people seeking Paul's life (Rom 11:3), of Greeks seeking wisdom (1 Cor 1:22), of what is sought in a steward—faithfulness (1 Cor 4:2), seeking freedom or a wife (1 Cor 7:27), seeking the good of the neighbor, not oneself (1 Cor 10:24), love not seeking its own way (1 Cor 13:5), seeking to excel in gifts that build the church (1 Cor 14:12), Paul seeking the Corinthians, not their wealth (2 Cor 12:14), the Corinthians seeking proof Christ is speaking in him (2 Cor 13:3), seeking to be justified in Christ (2:17), seeking one's own interests, not Christ's (Phil 2:21), seeking things above (Col 3:1), and Onesiphorus seeking Paul in Rome (2 Tim 1:17).

their quest for righteousness through law, are also opposing the gospel and will face God's wrath to the end.

Paul then is not seeking his own gain, glory, or the approval of others; he seeks only to please God as is befitting of anyone who names Christ as Lord. Simply put, Paul is asking the Galatians who they think he seeks to please, God and his Son, or people (to win them to faith). As a true apostle, a servant of Christ and God, the answer is clearly, no, for his whole modus operandi is to please God. They should know this, for he has been serving among them.

Paul answers his own question with a second-class 'if … then' conditional statement (ei plus indicative past tense, here imperfect)—this assumes something untrue for the sake of argument as it is untrue[75] because Paul would not for one minute consider seeking to be a people pleaser rather than a God-pleaser: 'if (ei, 1:7) I am still (eti) pleasing (imperfect areskō) people, then I am (imperfect eimi) not a slave (doulos) of Christ.' The imperfect tense here is chosen because Paul is speaking of his so-called pleasing of people from an internal aspect rather than a summative angle (aorist).[76] It is the past reaching into the present, 'still.' This does not point back to a time when Paul was a people-pleaser, as in his pre-conversion Jewish ministry, but to his earlier ministry in Galatia. His opponents charge him with this as he is supposedly fickle, circumcising some (e.g., Timothy, Acts 16:3) and not others (e.g., Titus, 2:3) He supposedly preaches circumcision at other times (5:13) and not others (e.g., when among the Galatians). Thus, he merely seeks to please people to win them to Christ. They are then distorting Paul's understanding of gospel and culture and his desire to please people only in the sense of pleasing the God who desires to save

---

75. See on this Wallace, *Grammar*, 694.

76. On the imperfect see Wallace, *Grammar*, 541 who notes 'Like the present tense, the imperfect displays an *internal aspect*. That is, it portrays the action from within the event, without regard for beginning or end. This contrasts with the aorist, which portrays the action in a summary fashion. For the most part, the aorist takes a *snapshot* of the action while the imperfect (like the present) takes a *motion picture*, portraying the action as it unfolds. As such, the imperfect is often incomplete and focuses on the *process* of the action.'

them. They may find evidence in this in 1 Cor 9:19–22 where Paul adapts his behavior to different cultural settings. What they are not acknowledging is that Paul does do this, but never at the expense of the essence of the gospel. The point of this type of conditional sentence is that it is contrary to fact—Paul has never sought to please people at the expense of the gospel and certainly does not do so in the present.[77]

He brings home his argument in 1:10–11 in the apodosis: 'then I am not (*ouk*) be a slave (*doulos*) of Christ.' The Roman world in which Paul and the Galatians dwell is premised on slavery (s.a. on slavery, 3:28). Slaves were drawn from

warfare, piracy, brigandage, the international slave trade, kidnapping, infant exposure, natural reproduction of the existing slave population, and the punishment of criminals to the mines or gladiatorial combat. Above all else, warfare remained throughout classical antiquity, an important supplier of slaves.[78]

In urban areas, slaves were somewhere between fifteen and thirty-three percent of the population.[79] They were involved throughout society, working among the freeborn and some, when manumitted, held positions of considerable power including those in Caesar's household (e.g., Phil 4:22) and the 'most excellent Felix,' who was an imperial freedman of Claudius (Acts 24:22–27).[80] Most struggled as laborers and domestics. For Romans, to be a slave violated the glorious ideal of freedom. It was thus abhorred and despised to be in a state of slavery.

For Paul, however, in the light of Christ's coming, slavery carries a different status. One can be a slave in the Roman world,

---

77. Paul does acknowledge the need to please people for the good of the gospel as indeed Christ did. However, we do not do this at the expense of the gospel's theological and ethical core (Rom 15:1–3; 1 Cor 10:33). What is most important, is pleasing God (2 Cor 5:9).

78. J. A. Harrill, 'Slavery,' in *DNTB* 1125.

79. Harrill, 'Slavery,' 1125.

80. Harrill, 'Slavery,' 1125 notes, 'In cities throughout the ancient Mediterranean world, slaves were trained and served as physicians, architects, craftspeople, shopkeepers, cooks, barbers, artists, thespians, magicians, prophets (e.g., Acts 16:16–24), teachers, professional poets and philosophers. Some slaves could accumulate considerable wealth from their occupations.'

as many Christians were (1 Cor 12:13; Eph 6:5) but be Christ's freedman or woman—a child of God who is no longer a slave (3:28; 4:7; 1 Cor 7:21–23). Being a peasant or slave or from the senatorial or equestrian classes makes no difference in Christ. All God's adopted daughters and sons are royal, with full rights as children of the world's supreme Emperor, brothers and sisters of Jesus the Christ and Lord of the world. As such, all God's people of whatever status, gender, and race are equal as sisters and brothers before God (Gal 3:28; 1 Cor 12:13; Col 3:11; Phlm 16).

Those who are in slavery should not make their priority gaining freedom but pleasing their masters 'as slaves of Christ, doing the will of God from the heart' knowing he will reward them.[81] Conversely, masters are to treat their slaves with justice and fairness (Col 4:1; Eph 6:9). Further, God made himself known in the Roman world as one in the form of God who became human in the form of a slave (Phil 2:6–7). He gave up heaven's riches and became poor so that his people could be liberated from poverty to wealth (spiritual in the present, total in the consummation) (2 Cor 8:9). As such, slavery takes on a fresh nuance.

Christ is so glorious, that to be a slave of Christ, as Paul describes himself here, is the greatest of all honors! (cf. Rom 1:1; 2 Cor 4:5; Phil 1:1; Col 4:12; Tit 1:1). It is an honor to be in his service because we are slaves of the Creator and King of the Cosmos who has called us his children. Later he will tell the Galatians that they are no longer slaves (of law and sin) but are free children and heirs (4:1–7; 5:1, cf. 2:4; 4:9, 22–31). Yet, while this is true, in his ministry, Paul can willingly take the language of slavery on himself, doing as Jesus did, and emptying himself and taking the form of a slave for the purpose of the gospel (Phil 2:7–8, cf. Phil 3:4–11). And, as a slave of Christ, his sole purpose is to please his master through obedience (Rom 6:16–22). Hence, he is not a people pleaser; he pleases Christ and Christ alone. This teaches us too that our sole goal is to please God and to

81. See Eph 6:6, 8, cf. 1 Cor 7:21–23; Col 3:22; 1 Tim 6:1; Tit 2:9.

voluntarily enslave ourselves to God and his mission—this is where joy is found in Christ.

Later, Paul will mention *eritheia*, 'selfish ambition,' in his vice list (5:20). This is likely a characteristic of the Judaizers. They are probably telling the Galatians that it is Paul who is not a God-worthy slave. By implication, in light of 5:20, 1:10 is effectively stating that it is the Judaizers who are not true slaves of Christ.

PART THREE: PAUL'S NARRATIVE IN WHICH HE DEFENDS HIS GOSPEL AND APOSTLESHIP(1:11–2:14)

CHAPTER FOUR: THE REVELATION OF THE GOSPEL (GAL 1:11–12)

Paul now moves into a defense of his apostleship and gospel. He does so with a *narratio*, a narration of his prior Jewish life, his conversion, his receipt of the gospel direct from Christ, his apostolic commission, his subsequent movements, his encounters with the apostles in which his gospel and mission were vindicated, and his clash with Peter in Antioch. This deals in one fell swoop with the question of his authority and whether his gospel is indeed the gospel. This prepares the way for the rhetorical and theological assault he makes on the Judaizing gospel in 2:15–4:7, and his appeal to the Galatians not to put themselves into slavery to law, sin, and death. Rather, they are to live freely, by faith, expressed in love and the fruit of the Spirit, whom they are to please (4:8–6:10).

THE GOSPEL IS NOT A HUMAN MESSAGE (1:11)

The body of the letter proper is launched in *Galatians 1:11*:

For (*gar*, 1:10),[1] **I make known** (*gnōrizō*)[2] **to you** (dative plural *sy*) **[that] the gospel** (*euangelion*, 1:6) **which was preached** (*euangelizomai*, 1:8) **by** (*hypo*)[3] **me** (genitive *egō*, 1:2) **is** (present

---

1. **Variant**: It is disputed whether Paul begins *gar*, 'for,' or *de*, 'but, and.' The textual evidence is split evenly, perhaps with *de* having a better case. I have gone with the adopted reading *gar*, but this one could go either way.
2. Galatians 1:11 is the only use of γνωρίζω (*gnōrizō*), here, as with all of Paul's uses, signaling, 'I want you to know.'
3. The preposition ὑπό (*hypo*) is used eleven times in Galatians, in two main ways: 1) With the genitive, agency, 'by:' 'preached *by* me' (1:11); 'ratified *by* God' (3:17); 'to be known *by* God' (4:9); 'consumed *by* one another' (5:15); 2) With accusative, 'under:'

eimi, 1:7) **not according to** (*kata*, 1:4) **humankind** (accusative *anthrōpos*, 1:1).

Burton rightly notes that the assertion of this verse is in effect the proposition that the narratio of 1:13–2:21 will seek to prove: Paul's gospel is from God.[4] The verse begins with a disclosure formula, which is 'a common epistolary formula used at the beginning of the body,' which 'signals a new thematic unit.'[5] The formula uses 'a verb of knowing (here, *gnōrizō*, 'make known') and derives its name from the fact that the writer wishes to make known to the recipient some information.'[6] As here, it 'frequently introduces the letter body.'[7] Here what is disclosed in the formula is, 'for, I make known (*gnōrizō*) to you …' While in wider literature *gnōrizō* can mean 'know,' here, as in all NT uses, it means 'made known.'[8] As here, Paul uses the verb in other disclosure formulas (1 Cor 12:3; 15:1; 2 Cor 8:1).

As he commonly does across his letters, with his customary form of epistolary address (sixty-nine times),[9] he calls the Galatians *adelphoi*, the plural of *adelphos* (see on 1:2), an inclusive term indicating 'brothers and sisters.'[10] The use of the terms speaks of the family bond that he and the Galatians have in

---

'under a curse' (3:10); 'under sin' (3:22); 'under the law' (3:23; 4:4, 5, 21; 5:18); 'under a guardian' (3:25), 'under guardians' (4:2), 'under the elementary principles' (4:3).

4. Ernest De Witt Burton, *A Critical and Exegetical Commentary on the Epistle to the Galatians*, ICC (New York: Charles Scribner's Sons, 1920), 35.

5. Jeffrey T. Reed, *A Discourse Analysis of Philippians: Method and Rhetoric in the Debate over Literary Integrity*, JSNTSup 136 Sheffield: Sheffield Academic Press, 1997), 388. See also Longenecker, *Galatians*, cvii who finds them in 1:11, 13: 3:7; 4:13, 15. However, S. E. Runge, *Discourse Grammar of the Greek New Testament: A Practical Introduction for Teaching and Exegesis* (Bellingham, WA: Lexham Press, 2010), 104 notes that they function as a metacomment with pragmatic effect relative to context, i.e., not necessarily to launch a new section.

6. J. A. D. Weima, 'Letters, Greco-Roman,' in *DNTB* 643.

7. Weima, 'Letters,' 643. He notes Rom 1:13; 2 Cor 1:8; Gal 1:11; Phil 1:12; 1 Thess 2:1.

8. Other uses of *gnōrizō* include God or Christ disclosing something (Luke 2:15; John 15:15; 17:26 [2x]; Acts 2:28; Rom 9:22, 23; 16:26; Eph 1:9; 3:3, 5, 10; Col 1:27); people making known something (Luke 2:17; Col 4:7, 9; 2 Pet 1:16) including in prayer (Phil 4:6) and Paul in his proclamation ministry (Eph 6:19, 21), or in a letter—not making known (see Phil 1:22).

9. Other terms used less frequently include 'beloved,' and 'children' (e.g., 4:19).

10. See 3:15; 4:12, 28, 31; 5:11, 13; 6:1, 18.

and with Christ the Son and big brother (1:16; 2:20; 4:4, 6), and as sons and daughters of Abraham (3:7) and Sarah (4:31). Equally significantly in this letter, the Galatians' inclusion in God's family came as a result of the ministry of their older brother (and father, 1 Cor 4:15), Paul (4:19). Now, with Paul and in Christ, they are adopted as children of God (3:26; 4:5, 6, 7, 28) who is *the* Father and *their Patros* (1:1, 3, 4). They are also bonded by the Spirit with the 'brothers' in Antioch who co-send the letter (1:2).

They stand in stark contrast to the *pseudadelophous*, the 'false brothers,' the Judaizers, who, for Paul, are no longer a part of this family of God but believe themselves to be the core of God's household (2:4). Their choice is to join Judaizers in their false gospel and leave the family of God forming across the nations of the world. Or they will reject their 'gospel' and live by faith and not law. This analysis shows that although Paul does not stress the church as the family of God in direct terms, he only uses 'household of God' twice (Eph 2:19; 1 Tim 3:15, cf. 1 Pet 4:17), the church as God's family is his dominant ecclesial motif (cf. 'body of Christ,' 'temple of the Spirit,' 'bride of Christ,' etc.). The use of the term *adelphos* calls them as a family to take notice. It draws them in, assuring them that their status remains in place, at least for now if they do not yield completely to the Judaizers. It is thus a term with hortatory power, calling the Galatians to be what they have become, true brothers and sisters of Paul and Christ.

The content of what he wants them to know is now given: '[that] the gospel (*euangelion*, 1:6) which was preached (*euangelizomai*, 1:8) by (*hypo*) me is not according to humankind (*kata anthrōpon*).' In 1:1 Paul tells the readers that his apostleship is not from people or through a person. Here, Paul tells the Galatians that the message of God he brought to the cities of Galatia on his mission journey did not originate from other people. In the verses that follow, he will narrate where his gospel did come from. As with his apostleship, it came from Christ directly by revelation. Subsequently, he has journeyed with that gospel across the regions along the eastern shores of the Great Sea (Mediterranean) and talked with people concerning the gospel, and learned of other elements of the gospel tradition like the resurrection appearances and the Last Supper (1 Cor 11:23–26; 1 Cor 15:5–8). However, the gospel itself came from Christ on the Damascus Road. The Judaizers on the converse, have gained their gospel from hearing the preaching of others and have amended it in accordance with their Jewish tradition.

THE GOSPEL RECEIVED BY REVELATION (1:12)

In *Galatians 1:12* Paul continues:

For (*gar*, see 1:10) I (*egō*, see 1:1) [did] not (*oude*, see 1:1) receive (aorist *paralambanō*, see 1:9) it (neuter *autos*, 1:1) from a person (*anthrōpos*, 1:1), nor (*oute*)[11] by being taught it (aorist passive *didaskō*),[12] but (*alla*, 1:1) through (*dia*, 1:1) the revelation (*apokalypseōs*)[13] of Jesus (genitive *Iēsous*, 1:1) Christ (genitive *Christos*, 1:1).

The *gar*, 'for,' here is explanatory indicating that Paul is explicating his statement that the gospel is not from people. While the first-person verb *paralabon* would suffice, Paul adds an emphatic 'I' (*egō*). As noted in discussing 1:9, the verb *paralambanō* can have the sense of the handing on of a tradition (as the Galatians received the gospel from Paul). Here, Paul is stating he did not receive the gospel in this way. He did not sit at the feet of the Twelve or any other Christian teacher and hear the gospel proclaimed so that faith was born in his heart. As he will explain, he saw Jesus directly. He is like those people we meet in the churches of God who had a revelation of Christ that brought about their conversion.

11. Five times the correlative conjunction οὔτε (*oute*) is used, it connotes 'nor' (1:12; 5:6 [2nd use]; 6:15 [2nd use]) or 'neither' (5:6; 6:15). In strings invoking 'neither ... nor' it is used twice.
12. The verb διδάσκω (*didaskō*) is used only here in Gal 1:12—it speaks of receiving instruction, teach.
13. The noun ἀποκάλυψις (*apokalypsis*), 'unveil, uncover,' is only used twice in Galatians: 1) Of Paul's experience of the revelation of Jesus Christ (1:12); 2) Paul's trip to Jerusalem based on a 'revelation' (2:2). It is related to *apokalyptō*, see 1:15.

Didaskō is a common verb for 'teach' (ninety-seven times NT, sixteen times Paul). It carries the simple sense of someone (Rom 2:21; Eph 4:21) or something (1 Cor 11:14) transmitting knowledge and wisdom to another person or, as here, of a person receiving learning (Col 2:7). 'Teaching' is also one of the spiritual gifts that the so-gifted should be liberated and encouraged to exercise (Rom 12:7); Christians are to teach one another with wisdom (Col 3:16; 1 Tim 4:11; 2 Tim 2:2), and Timothy is instructed concerning how to teach in Ephesus (1 Tim 4:11; 6:2). In 1 Tim 2:12, Paul either absolutely prohibits women from teaching men, or, as I consider more likely, gives instructions to this effect specific to the Ephesian church due to women being embroiled in the false teaching besetting the church. Those who teach for shameful gain must be silenced (Tit 1:11). Paul himself teaches as he travels the churches (1 Cor 4:17; Col 1:28; 2 Thess 2:15), and through letters (2 Thess 2:15), as in Galatians.

Part two of Gal 1:12 focuses on how Paul did learn the gospel. Rather than from other Christians passing on the tradition (as is the case with the Galatians), he received it through 'a revelation (*apokalypsis*) of Christ Jesus.' 'Revelation' is *apokalypsis*, which is the title of the final book in the NT, which contains a revelation from Christ to the Apostle John on Patmos. The term is drawn from *kalyptō*, 'cover, hide, conceal,' and has the sense of unveiling or uncovering. In the NT, it is always associated with God's revealing of himself including Christ being 'a light for revelation to the gentiles' (Luke 2:32), the revelation of the mystery of the gospel which is Christ in the present (Rom 16:25), a personal revelation from God passed on from one to another (1 Cor 14:6, 26), revelation through the Spirit to a Christian (Eph 1:17), a profound revelatory experience (2 Cor 12:1, 7; Gal 2:2), John's Patmos revelation experience (Rev 1:1), the future revelation of Christ at his coming,[14] the future ultimate revelation of God's judgment (Rom 2:5), and the future revelation of the children of God (Rom 8:19). Here, it is the revelation of Christ that Paul experienced on the Damascus Road, described three times by

---

14. See 1 Cor 1:7; 2 Thess 1:7; 1 Pet 1:7, 13; 4:13.

Luke in Acts (Acts 9:1–19; 22:2–21; 26:4–18), and referred to elsewhere in Paul's letters (Eph 3:3). He refers to it in 1:15–16, writing of God 'who called me by his grace, was pleased to reveal his Son to me, in order that I might preach him among the gentiles.' At that time, Paul did not consult with anyone concerning this.

The construct 'revelation *of Jesus Christ*' can be an objective genitive—'the revelation of Jesus Christ' so Christ is the actual content of the gospel. Or, it can also be a subjective genitive—'[What/the fact that] Jesus Christ reveals'—the content of the gospel revealed by Jesus Christ.[15] Most likely, this is a false distinction, and this is what Wallace calls a plenary genitive, Paul utilizing intentional ambiguity with a construct that is both subjective and objective.[16] While in most cases, the subjective produces the objective, in this case, the objective revelation of Christ Jesus to Paul generates the content of the gospel. This is supported by 1:16, where God was 'pleased to reveal his Son' to Paul, with the purpose that he would preach him to the gentiles. Further, the same construct is found in Rev 1:1 (the revelation of Jesus Christ), and Wallace also considers this a plenary genitive.[17]

The content of the gospel here then is 'him'—Jesus Christ. As a brilliant Pharisee with an extraordinary grasp of the Jewish Scriptures and traditions, the revelation of Jesus Christ to Paul led him to completely rethink his understanding of the gospel. The gospel still retains much of the shape of the Jewish story—Creation, Fall, sin, Abraham, law, Messiah, people of the nations believing, the Spirit poured out, the church formed, the mission enacted, future judgment, a restored cosmos, and eternal

---

15. Wallace, *Grammar*, 113; Longenecker, *Galatians*, 24.

16. On this genitive, Wallace, *Grammar*, 119–20. He writes (italics his), 'If *both* ideas seem to fit in a given passage, *and do not contradict but rather complement one another*, then there is a good possibility that the genitive in question is a plenary (or full) genitive.' This would seem to be the case here. Other examples may be 2 Cor 5:14; Rom 5:5 (both 'the love of God'—him for us [subjective], and us for him [objective]); John 5:42; 2 Thess 3:5; and 'gospel of God'—'Gospel about God' or 'God's gospel given' (Mark 1:1, 14; Rom 1:1; 15:16; 1 Thess 2:2, 8, 9).

17. Wallace, *Grammar*, 120. I find it extremely surprising he does not consider Gal 1:12 in the same way.

destiny. But now Christ has come into that story, it is now reframed around Jesus (as it was always intended to be but was hidden from humanity, cf. Rom 16:25; 1 Cor 2:7).

He came as a servant (Luke 22:24–30), died on a cross, rose from death, appeared to his disciples, and commissioned and empowered them to take the message of his coming to the world (Luke 23:26–24:48). He ascended, poured out the Spirit, rules as Lord, and will return (Acts 1:1–11; Rom 8:24). He will judge all people (Rom 2:6–11). The world will be set free from bondage to sin and death (Rom 8:20–21). In the revelation of Jesus Christ, Paul the persecutor became Paul the Christian and theologian, and he rethought the whole gospel. He needed no other agency. Now he is consumed with a passion to preach the gospel to the nations so that the gentiles will know this Jesus and become children of God. He yearns for the same for his people, but most reject this Jesus, as he himself once did. These Judaizers have recognized Jesus as Messiah but have not grasped the full implications of Jesus.

In the context of the argument of Galatians, the key is that Paul received the gospel directly from Jesus. It is then *the* gospel; there is no other. The Judaizers cannot make this claim and are preaching a different gospel, and so it is to be rejected utterly and they with it. They want more than Jesus as the gospel; they want the law. They want more than faith; they want circumcision. This diminishes Christ as if he is not sufficient.

CHAPTER FIVE: PAUL'S FORMER LIFE IN JUDAISM (1:13–14)

Having laid down the premise that he did not receive the gospel from people but direct from Jesus Christ himself, Paul begins the full narration of his former Jewish life, his conversion, and the events subsequent that saw that gospel endorsed by those that are considered the leading Christians of the day—the Jerusalem apostles.

In Galatians 1:13, he begins with a summary of his past life as a Jew. These verses sit alongside Phil 3:4–6, 2 Cor 11:22, and in a different way Rom 7, along with Luke's material on Paul's pre-Christian life, as important for us to understand Paul. As with Phil 3 and 2 Cor 11, a brief mention of his past life is found in the context of others challenging his apostolicity and authority. This indicates that at the time of Paul, there circulated Jewish Christians who considered Paul a false Christian apostle and leader, preaching a corrupted gospel and who repudiated his credentials. While Paul generally abhors any claims to self-righteousness and boasting other than Christ as he intimates in 6:13–14,[1] especially from his life before Christ (Phil 3:3–8), at times he has to assert his authority, reminding readers of just who he was. This is never done for his own glory but to add force to his letters intended to correct the false teachers' claims and call his converts back to the gospel. This is one of those situations, with the Judaizers claiming superior authority to Paul. He takes them on at their own game.

This material is gold for knowing who Paul was. In 2 Cor 11:22, we learn that Paul is a Hebrew, an Israelite, and a son

---

1. See cf. 1 Cor 1:29–30; 3:21; 13:4; 2 Cor 10:17.

of Abraham (in a literal Jewish sense)—just like his opponents who malign him. In Phil 3:4–6, he reminds the Philippians that he has superior credentials to any Judaizer. Like them, he was 'circumcised on the eighth day' and is a covenant member 'of the people of Israel.' Moreover, he is from the highly favored 'tribe of Benjamin' that produced Israel's first king (after whom he is named) and which supported the Davidic monarchy. Despite being from Tarsus in Cilicia, he is no proselyte or merely a Diaspora Greek-speaking Jew. He is 'a Hebrew of Hebrews'—raised in a Hebrew family (not Greek-speaking), immersed in Israel's language and traditions. He can claim even to be a Pharisee—a member of the elite strict Jewish legalists. He can claim that he lived a life fulfilling the law and even more righteous and blameless (in Jewish terms) than any Judaizer. More than any of the Judaizers, he, with great zeal, was a persecutor of the Christian movement in its early days. Luke adds detail to this account, by telling us Paul was trained under the great Gamaliel in Jerusalem and narrating his persecution as he sought to destroy the Christian movement in Israel and Syria—even becoming an accessory to the killing of Christians (Acts 7:58; 26:10).

A PERSECUTOR (1:13)

Here in *Galatians 1:13–14,* Paul reminds them of what they have heard of him. In *Galatians 1:13,* the focus is his persecution of the church:

For (*gar,* 1:10) **you have heard** (aorist *akouō*)[2] **of my** (accusative *emos*)[3] **former** (*pote*)[4] **life** (*anastrophē*)[5] **in** (*en,* 1:6) **Judaism**

---

2. The common Greek word for 'hear,' ἀκούω (*akouō*) is found three times in Galatians: 1) The Galatians previously having heard of Paul's persecution of the church (1:13); 2) The Judean churches hearing of the conversion of their former persecutor (1:23); 3) Listening to the law (4:21). The final use carries the Hebrew sense of עָמַע (šā·maʻ) which often carries the meaning 'hearing with understanding and obedience' (e.g., Deut 4:1).

3. Twice the adjective ἐμός (*emos*) is used in Galatians; both indicating 'my'—'former way of life' (1:13); 'own hand' (6:11).

4. The indefinite adverb ποτέ (*pote*) refers to past time and is found in Galatians four

(*Ioudaismos*);[6] **that** (*hoti*, 1:6) **I, with** (*kata*, 1:4) **violence** (*hyperbolē*),[7] **persecuted** (imperfect *diōkō*)[8] **the church** (*ekklesia*, 1:2) **of God** (genitive *Theos*, 1:1) **and** (*kai*, 1:1) **plundered** (imperfect *portheō*)[9] **it** (feminine *autos*, 1:1).

Again, the conjunction *gar* is here explanatory, further developing what he has just said. 'You have heard' uses the very common *akouō* (428 times NT, thirty-four Paul)—the Galatians have clearly had Paul's story narrated to them, no doubt in his evangelization of the cities and teaching in the newly formed churches. The verb is placed first, giving it prominence; he is reminding them of what he knows they know. 'My former way of life in Judaism' uses *anastrophe*, a term used only thirteen times in the NT and referring to one's manner of life or conduct.[10] He thus here refers to his manner of life as a Jew, from the cradle in his Hebrew family and synagogue in Tarsus in Cilicia,[11] through his training as a Pharisee under the Hillel Rabbi Gamaliel I in Jerusalem,[12] and his time as a Pharisee.

The second half of the verse focuses on one portion of his former way of life, his final period of time as a Pharisee in which he persecuted the church. *Hoti* (that) here signals what he is

---

times: Paul's past life (1:13); Paul's former persecution (1:23 [2x]); 'ever'—'what they (the apostles) *ever* were' (2:6).

5. The verb ἀναστροφή (*anastrophe*) is used once of Paul's former 'way of life.' Paul usually uses *peripateō* rather than *anastrophē*. They are synonyms.

6. *Ioudaismos* is used twice in 1:13–14 of Judaism as Judea's religious system—can be 'Judeanism,' the religion of the Jews or Judeans.

7. The noun ὑπερβολή (*hyperbolē*) invokes something to an extraordinary degree (BDAG 1032) (cf. Eng. 'hyperbole'). It is used once in Galatians (1:13), with *kata* (*kath*) and speaks of 'persecuting the church of God to an extreme degree,' i.e., violently.

8. There are five uses of διώκω (*diōkō*) in Galatians. The term is from hunting and means to pursue, either with positive intent (e.g., pursue love) or maliciously (persecute). As befitting the tone of the letter, all five uses concern persecution, whether Paul's persecution of the church (1:13, 23), the persecution of Isaac (4:29), Paul being persecuted (5:11), and people persecuted for the cross of Christ (6:12).

9. The verb πορθέω (*portheō*) features twice in the letter, both speaking of Paul's desire to plunder the church (1:13, 23).

10. See Eph 4:22; 1 Tim 4:12; Heb 13:7; Jas 3:13; 1 Pet 1:15, 18; 1 Pet 2:12; 3:1, 2, 16; 2 Pet 2:7; 3:11.

11. See Acts 21:39; 22:3 cf. 9:11, 30; 11:25.

12. See Acts 22:3; 23:6; 26:5; Phil 3:5, cf. Acts 5:34.

reminding them of; hence, it almost carries the sense, 'namely.' Persecuted is *diōkō*, a hunting term, which Paul also uses athletically (Phil 3:12–14). It is sometimes used of pursuing a positive attribute or thing, such as righteousness and law (falsely) (Rom 9:30, 31), hospitality (Rom 12:13), peace (Rom 12:14; 14:19), love (1 Cor 14:1), the heavenly prize (Phil 3:12, 14), good (1 Thess 5:15), and other attributes (1 Tim 6:11; 2 Tim 2:22).[13]

However, it is used often in the NT in its negative sense—'pursue,' 'hunt to hurt,' or 'persecute,'[14] including Paul's persecution of the church (1 Cor 15:9; Phil 3:6, further below). All five uses in *diōkō* indicates persecution (1:13, 23; 4:29; 5:11; 6:12). Paul elsewhere speaks of his persecution of the church of God (1 Cor 15:9).

Here, *diōkō* is imperfect—a customary (habitual or general) imperfect—referring to 'an event that occurred regularly.'[15] He persecuted it *kath hyperbolēn*. *Hyperbolē* speaks of 'an extraordinary degree.'[16] It is found only in Paul who uses it of being 'sinful *beyond measure*' (Rom 7:13), of love as '*the most excellent* way' (1 Cor 12:31), of being '*utterly* burdened' (2 Cor 1:8), of '*the surpassing* power' (2 Cor 4:7), 'an eternal weight of *superlative to superlative* glory (2 Cor 4:17), '*the surpassing greatness* of the revelations' (2 Cor 12:7). In the context of persecution, it speaks of extremely violent persecution.

Paul describes the object of his persecution here as the 'church of God,' speaking of the church *in toto* as it was at that time. The genitive 'of God' here is astonishing when we consider that Paul formerly thought of the church as anything but the church of God. Rather, to Paul, the church was a false cult worshiping the Satanic deceiver Jesus and so Satan himself—how his thoughts have changed! The use of 'of God' here cuts a vivid contrast with 1:2 where the readers' communities are simply 'the churches of

13. See also Luke 17:23; Heb 12:14; 1 Pet 3:11.
14. See Rom 12:14; 1 Cor 4:12; 2 Cor 4:9; 2 Tim 3:12, s.a., Matt 5:10, 11, 12, 44; 10:23; 23:34; Luke 11:49; 21:12; John 5:16; 15:20; Acts 7:52; 9:4, 5; 22:4, 7, 8; 26:11, 14, 15; Rev 12:13.
15. Wallace, *Greek Grammar*, 548.
16. BDAG 1032.

Galatia.' Whether they remain churches 'of God' will be seen in their response to the letter.

The verb for the destruction of the church is *portheō*. This is a strong word used for the plundering of cities,[17] and violent persecution (e.g., 4 Macc 11:4). Its three NT uses are all of Paul, two in Galatians of his violent destruction of the church (1:13, 23), and the other in Acts 9:21 in the same sense. It thus speaks of Paul's violent attack on the Christian church. The imperfect is conative, which portrays an action desired or attempted and not completed.[18]

Paul's desire to destroy the church aligns with Luke's accounts of his testimony, which Luke records three times. In Acts 7:58 the young man Saul is present at the stoning of Stephen, with witnesses who would then stone him, laying their garments at his feet, while in Acts 8:1 Saul approved of this act. He then set about a 'great persecution against the church in Jerusalem,' scattering all bar the apostles into Judea, Samaria, and Syrian Antioch (Acts 8:1; 11:19–21). Ironically, this spread the church further (Acts 8:4; 11:19–21). Indeed, it is one of the great ironies of Paul's life that even as a Pharisee opposing Christianity, his actions served to enhance its mission! We see the sovereignty of God over the world, the church, and the lives of his people at play.

Paul destroyed the church by breaking into homes and dragging men and women off to prison (Acts 8:3). In Acts 22:4, Luke records Paul's speaking of his persecution at the Temple, describing how he 'persecuted the Way to the death, binding and delivering to prison both men and women.' This is again confirmed in Acts 26:10–11, where in Jerusalem, 'he locked up many of the saints in prison ... and when *they were put to death, I cast my vote against them. I punished them often in all the synagogues and tried to make them blaspheme*' (Acts 26:10–11). He then gained letters of endorsement from the High Priest Caiaphas and set about the destruction of the Christians of the synagogues of Damascus to bring them bound to Jerusalem (Acts

---

17. See, e.g., 4 Macc 4:23; Josephus, *Ant.* 5.31; *J.W.* 7.44, 425; Philo, *Conf.* 47; Sib. Or. 3.510; 3 Bar. 1.1.

18. Wallace, *Greek Grammar*, 549–51.

8:1–2). Acts 26:11 suggests he may have done similarly in other foreign cities. Thankfully, for the church, en route to Damascus, this plan was disrupted by Jesus' appearance to him.

In all three Lukan accounts of his persecution, Jesus addresses Paul with 'Saul, Saul, why are you persecuting me?' To this, Paul responds, 'Who are you, Lord?' Each time Jesus replies, 'I am Jesus of Nazareth, whom you are persecuting' (Acts 9:4–5; 22:7–8; 26:14–15).

The overall effect of Paul's argument is that he was a Jew par excellence before his conversion; so much so, that he plundered the church. His opponents cannot claim this. The Galatians who know his story should stop being hoodwinked by the Judaizers' malicious and slanderous gossip concerning him.

A ZEALOT FOR JUDAISM (1:14)

In *Galatians 1:14,* he explains more about his way of life under Judaism:

And (*kai*, 1:1) **I was advancing** (imperfect *prokoptō*)[19] **in** (*en*, 1:6) **Judaism** (dative *Ioudaismos*, 1:13) **beyond** (*hyper*, 1:4) **many** (plural *polys*)[20] **my own age** (*synlikiōtēs*)[21] **among** (*en*) **my** (genitive *egō*, 1:2) **people** (*genos*),[22] **being** (*hypachō*)[23] **far more**

---

19. Galatians 1:14 is the only use of προκόπτω (*prokoptō*) in Galatians, it is used militarily and ethically of advancing—here, Paul, in the traditions of Judaism.
20. The adjective πολύς (*polus*) is used three times: '*many* of my own age' (1:14); many descendants of Abraham (3:16); and many children of the desolate one (4:27).
21. The noun συνηλικιώτης (*synēlikiōtēs*) indicates a person one's own age or a contemporary (BDAG 971). Galatians 1:14 is the only use in the NT—*a hapax legomenon.*
22. The noun γένος (*genos*) (cf. Eng. 'genus') is used only once in Galatians in 1:14 in the sense of 'my people.'
23. The verb ὑπάρχω (*hyparchō*) is used twice in Galatians, both synonymous with the verb 'to be,' so '*being* extremely zealous …' and '*being* a Jew' (2:14). It can speak of a state as in Phil 2:6, while in Galatians it is a synonym for *eimi*, although something of the stative idea may flow over into both uses.

(*perissoterōs*)[24] **zealous** (*zēlōtēs*)[25] **[than them] for my ancestors'** (genitive *patrikos*)[26] **traditions** (*paradosis*).[27]

Paul continues speaking of what the Galatians already have heard—his former way of life in Judaism. He was 'advancing in Judaism.' 'Advancing' is *prokoptō*, used of Jesus advancing in wisdom and stature (Luke 2:52), of the night being far advanced (Rom 13:12), negatively of people advancing into ungodliness (2 Tim 2:16), of people failing to advance far (2 Tim 3:9), and of evil people advancing from bad to worse (2 Tim 3:13). The imperfect here is a customary imperfect which is continuous, so Paul was 'continually advancing in Judaism.'[28] Here, Paul was advancing in learning. He was doing so, 'beyond many of his age group.' The noun *synlikiōtēs* compounds *syn*, 'with' and *hēlikia*, 'age, period of life, era,' and yields people of the same age, contemporaries. 'Among my people' use *genos*, a term that can mean 'his people,' 'his nation,' or 'his kind.'[29]

In part two of the verse, he assumes the term zealous (*zēlōtēs*). It is found in the NT of Simon the Zealot (Luke 6:15; Acts 1:13), of Jews who are 'zealous for the law' (Acts 21:20), and of Christians being 'zealous for what is good.' Paul elsewhere uses it of the Corinthians being '*zealous* for manifestations of the Spirit' (1 Cor 14:12) and of Christians '*zealous* for good works' (Tit 2:14). In Acts, Luke recalls Paul stating he was '*zealous* for God' before Agrippa (Acts 22:3). Before his conversion, Paul was not a Zealot in the technical sense of wanting to overthrow Rome. However,

24. The adverb περισσοτέρως (*perissoteros*) expresses abundance. Galatians 1:14 is its only use in this letter, 'extremely zealous.'

25. The noun ζηλωτής (*zēlōtēs*), 'zealot' or 'one zealous for' is used once in Galatians in 1:14, verbally meaning 'zealous.' It doesn't carry the technical sense of being a Zealot opposing Rome. Rather, he is like Phinehas, zealous for Israel's traditions (cf. Num 25).

26. The adjective πατρικός (*patrikos*), comes from one's *patēr*, father, and so what is handed down from one's fathers (ancestors); used only once in Gal 1:14—another *hapax legomenon*.

27. The only use of the noun παράδοσις (*paradosis*) is in 1:14 where it speaks of the traditions of Paul's ancestors to which he was zealously devoted.

28. Wallace, *Greek Grammar*, 548.

29. BDAG 194 offers a range of options in the NT: 'descendant, family, relatives, nation, people, class, kind.'

he is an enthusiast for his nation and its traditions, prepared to use violence if need be. One wonders whether Paul would have supported the rebellion against Rome in the late 60s if he had not been converted.

'My ancestors/fathers' translates the Greek *patrikos*, a term found only here in the NT, but in the Greek OT of one's fathers.[30] It is a patriarchal way of describing one's forebears. 'Traditions' is *paradosis*, used of the 'traditions of the elders' in relation to ritual washing before meals in Matt 15:2 and Mark 7:3.[31] Paul also uses it of traditions in general (Col 2:8), and Christian traditions he passed onto the Corinthians (1 Cor 11:2) and Thessalonians (2 Thess 2:15; 3:6). Here, in particular, it refers to the core distinctives of Judaism enshrined in the Scriptures and oral law—Sabbath, circumcision, ritual purity, sacrifice, feasts, eating protocols, food laws, Temple, synagogue, and the preservation of the Jewish faith. His passion is seen in his vehement reaction to the claim that Jesus is the Messiah and Son of God, the contention that his work saves people from sin, and that faith justifies without concern for the law. By establishing his past credentials, he declares himself formerly the Judaizer of Judaizers to whom the gospel has been revealed. Hence, he undermines the critique of the Judaizers. He is every bit a Jew as they are, a brilliant one in fact, as zealous for the Jewish faith as they are and even more so because he alone set out on a pogrom to destroy the Christian movement.

---

30. See e.g., Gen 50:8; Lev 22:13; Num 36:8; Josh 6:25; 1 Chron 7:4.
31. Cf. Matt 15:3, 6; Mark 7:3, 5, 8, 9, 13.

CHAPTER SIX: PAUL'S CONVERSION AND CALL (1:15–16B)

Galatians 1:15–17 is one long Greek sentence launched with 'when' followed by a description of his conversion, and then resolved with the emphatic 'I did not immediately consult with anyone' at the end of v. 16. He then explicates this further, explaining that he did not go to Jerusalem to discuss things with the apostles but went first to Arabia and Damascus. Again, he is emphasizing to the Galatians that his gospel is sourced in God's direct revelation to him on the Damascus Road and perhaps developed further as he went away into the desert of Arabia. There, he may have meditated at length on his experiences in light of the Scriptures and preached his newly discovered gospel in Arabia's key centers.

SET APART, CALLED, AND COMMISSIONED

Galatians 1:15–16b reads:
  15 **But** (*de*)[1] **when** (*hote*)[2] **God** (*Theos*, 1:1)[3] **who** (masculine *ho*,

---

1. The conjunction δέ (*de*) is extremely common, found fifty–eight times alone in Galatians. It is often difficult to translate depending on how you discern Paul's intent, so these are disputable. With this in mind, it can be consecutive, 'and' (1:20, 22, 23; 2:4, 6, 9; 2:20 [1st, 3rd]; 3:8, 17, 20 [1st], 29; 4:1, 6, 7, 18, 20, 25 [2x]; 5:3, 10, 24; 6:6, 9, 10). Alternatively, it is a mild adversative 'but' (1:15, 19; 2:2, 11, 12, 16, 17; 2:20 [2nd]; 3:11, 12, 18, 20 [2nd], 23, 25; 4:4, 9 [2x], 26, 28; 5:11, 15, 16, 17, 18, 19, 22; 6:4, 8, 14). At times it is better translated as 'now' (3:16; 4:13), or 'while' (4:23).
2. The temporal adverb ὅτε (*hote*) is found six times, 'when' (1:15; 2:11, 12, 14; 4:4).
3. **Variant**: Most texts read *eudokēsen ho Theos* while P46 B F G and others delete *ho Theos*. In support of non-inclusion is that: 1) It clarifies what is implied (God is the agent), so maybe additional; 2) The shorter reading is often to be preferred. I have included it in my translation; however, the words *ho Theos* may well be additional.

1:1) **set me** (accusative *egō*, 1:1) **apart** (aorist participle *aphorizō*)[4] **from** (*ek*, 1:1) **my** (genitive *egō*) **mother's** (genitive *mētēr*)[5] **womb** (*koila*)[6] **and** (*kai*, 1:1) **called** (aorist participle[7] *kaleō*, 1:6) **[me] by** (*dia*, 1:1) **his** (*autos*, 1:1) **grace** (*charis*, 1:3), 16 **was pleased** (aorist *eudokeō*)[8] **to reveal** (aorist infinitive *apokalyptō*)[9] **his** (*autos*) **Son**

4. The verb ἀφορίζω (*aphorizō*), 'set apart,' has the sense of separation and is used twice in Galatians; of Paul 'set apart' for the gospel—a person selected (1:15), and of Peter 'separating' or 'setting himself apart' in 2:12.
5. The standard Koine word for 'mother,' μήτηρ (*mētēr*) (Eng. 'matron') is used twice of Paul's mother (1:15), and of Jerusalem above which is the mother of the children of promise (4:26).
6. The noun κοιλία (*koilia*), can mean things like belly, heart, innards, stomach, womb, and genitals. It is used once in the letter, clearly of a mother's womb (1:15).
7. We have an example of Sharp's rule in this verse (see the discussion in the Greek notes on 1:4). This time it is with a participle which forms the substantive in the TSKS Personal Construction: Ὅτε δὲ εὐδόκησεν [ὁ θεὸς] **ὁ ἀφορίσας** με ἐκ κοιλίας μητρός μου **καὶ καλέσας** διὰ τῆς χάριτος αὐτοῦ. Hote de eudokēsen [ho Theos] **ho aphorisas me** ek koilias metros mou **kai kalesas** dia tēs charitos autou. 'But when God **who set me** apart from my mother's womb and **called** [me] by his grace.' The rule tells us that the one who set him apart (God) is the same as the one who called.
8. The one use of the verb εὐδοκέω (*eudokeō*) in Galatians has the meaning 'pleased,' God *pleased* to reveal his Son to Paul (1:16).
9. The verb ἀποκαλύπτω (*apokalyptō*), 'reveal, uncover, unveil,' is found twice, of God revealing Jesus to Paul (1:15), and of faith being revealed (3:23). The noun *apokalypsis* used in 1:12 and 2:2 (see discussion on 1:12).

(*huios*)[10] **to** (*en*, 1:6) **me** (dative *egō*), **so that** (*hina*)[11] **I might preach him** (*euangelizomai*) **in** (*en*) **the nations** (*ethnos*)[12] …

Paul describes his conversion theologically. As noted above, *hote*, 'when,' sets up a sentence that will be resolved in the final clause of v. 16. 'But when' (*hote de*) has the same sense as *nyni de* (but when), a strong forceful adversative phrase Paul uses on occasion to mark a sharp transition.[13] *De* can mean 'and' or 'but' here is used with strong adversative force as with *alla*, which is not common. It is thus prominent and draws attention as it does in 4:4 where we have a shift from a state of enslavement to God sending Jesus in the fulness of time (cf. 2:11, 12).

Here *hote de* refers to the moment on the road to Damascus where Paul saw the risen Christ, an encounter that reshaped his life and theology forever. For Paul, this is an act of God. He defines God as 'the one who set me apart' using *aphorizō* (cf. Eng.

---

10. The noun υἱός (*huios*), 'Son,' is found thirteen times across the letter. Four times of Jesus as 'his [God's] *Son*' (1:16; 4:4, 6), 'the *Son* of God' (2:20); otherwise, of believers as sons (children) of Abraham (3:7) or sons (children) of God (3:26, cf. 4:6, 7); and Abraham's two sons, Ishmael and Isaac (4:22) who are Hagar's son (the slave woman) (4:30) and that of Sarah (the free woman) (4:30).

11. The conjunction ἵνα (*hina*) is used seventeen times in Galatians. Along with the majority of Paul's uses (83% according to P. Lampe, "ἵνα, hina," in *EDNT* 2:190): 1) Of purpose (final): 'so that I might preach him' (1:16); 'so that they might bring us into slavery' (2:4); 'so that the truth of the gospel might be preserved for you' (2:4); 'so that we should go to the gentiles' (2:9); 'we have also believed in Christ Jesus, *so that* we might be justified by faith' (2:16); 'so that I might live to God' (2:19); 'so that we might be justified by faith' (3:24); 'so that we might receive adoption as sons' (4:5); 'so that you may make much of them' (4:17); 2) Consecutive use, 'only the poor that we remember' (2:10); 'that you do not want to do these things' (5:17); 'so that they may not be persecuted for the cross of Christ' (6:12); 'so that they may boast in your flesh' (6:12); 3) Result: 'with the result that in Christ Jesus the blessing of Abraham might come to the gentiles (3:14); 'with the result that we might receive the promised Spirit through faith' (3:14); and 'with the result that the promise of faith in Jesus Christ might be given to those who believe' (3:22). Note: some of these are open to interpretation and some potentially carry both purpose and result.

12. There are ten uses of the noun ἔθνος (*ethnos*) in Galatians. It can mean 'pagans, gentiles, or nations' and all mentions in Galatians refer to the gentiles except perhaps the citation of Gen 12:3 in 3:8, where it invokes 'nations,' although gentiles is implied as it is the nations beyond Abraham's family—as recipients of Paul's mission (1:16; 2:2, 8, 9), in the Antioch church (2:12, 14), and generally (2:15; 3:8).

13. E.g., Rom 3:21; 6:22; 7:6; 1 Cor 15:20; Eph 2:13; Col 3:8.

'horizon'). *Aphorizō* can mean separate in the sense of exclusion (Luke 6:22). It also has the meaning 'separate,' as in 2 Cor 6:17 where believers are to separate themselves from unholiness. There may be some irony as it calls to mind the Pharisees. [14] The name 'Pharisee' is drawn from the Aramaic *prsh*, which means 'to separate,' 'divide,' or 'distinguish.' This formerly 'separated one' is now truly set apart by God for service to Christ.' This sense of separation is found in its only other use in the letter in 2:12 where Peter withdrew and separated himself from the gentiles while eating in Antioch (cf. Matt 13:49; 25:32; Acts 19:9). It can have the sense of people being set apart for a specific task as when Paul and Barnabas were appointed to take the gospel to Galatia (Acts 13:2). Paul uses it in this sense in Rom 1:1, where he is 'set apart for the gospel of God.' Here, Paul is set apart by God and called by his grace so that he would preach him to the world.

'From my mother's womb' invokes the Hebrew idea of God's sovereignty over one's life from conception (Job 31:15; Ps 58:3; Hos 12:3). So, Samson is 'a Nazirite *from my mother's womb*' (Judg 16:17, cf. Judg 13:7). God says to Jeremiah, 'before I formed you *in the womb*, I knew you, and *before you were born* I consecrated you; I appointed you a prophet to the nations' (Jer 1:5). David sings '*from my mother's womb*, you have been my God' (Ps 22:10, cf. Ps 71:6; 139:13). God formed Israel '*from the womb*' (Isa 44:3, cf. 44:23; 46:3). The Servant says in Isa 49:1: 'The Lord called me *from the womb*, from the body of my mother he named my name' (Isa 49:5). The angel states to Elizabeth that John will be filled with the Spirit 'even *from his mother's womb*' (Luke 1:15). Paul here is likening himself to Jeremiah and the Servant, set apart from God from conception. This presupposes that his pre-Christian life as a Pharisee also fits into God's purposes of setting him apart. Now God's ultimate purposes have come to pass, and he is fulfilling his destiny to be the apostle to the nations.

As an aside, the notion also calls into question the practice of abortion, the child's life under God's sovereignty from

---

14. See Dunn, James D. G. *The Epistle to the Galatians*, BNTC (London: Continuum, 1993), *Galatians*, 63. See also Bradley T. Johnson, 'Pharisees,' in *LBD*.

conception in Jewish and early Christian thought. Indeed, while it was practiced widely in the Roman world along with the exposure of unwanted infants,[15] it was viewed negatively in Judaism.[16] Although it is not explicitly repudiated in the NT, Christians opposed it vehemently.[17]

Paul describes this as being 'called (*kaleō*) through his grace.' *Kaleō* has a range of meanings, including calling a person or thing by name, inviting, or summoning.[18] While Paul uses it with

15. So, for example, Plato accepted a fetus was a living being (Plutarch, *[Plac. philos.]* 5.15) but recommended abortions for women after forty (Plato, *Resp.* 5.9). Aristotle accepted abortions up to forty days for male babies, ninety for females (*Pol.* 7.15.25[1335b]; *Hist. an.* 7.3; *Gen. an.* 4. 1). Stoics held that the baby was part of the mother until birth and Musonius Rufus forbade induced abortions. The exposure of unwanted children was widely tolerated especially if deformed. While the Hippocratic Oath forbids abortifacients except to expel a dead fetus, there are other recommended medical methods for Greek physicians to abort the fetus. Induced abortion was common in the early Empire. However, Ovid and Seneca were positive toward those who did not abort children (Ovid, *Am.* 2.14. 5–6; Seneca, *Helv.* 16.3). See S. B. Ricks, 'Abortion in Antiquity,' in *AYBD* 1:32.
16. Outside of Israel, ancient legal codes were negative towards abortion on the grounds that it robbed society of the contribution of the child. The meaning of Exod 21:22–25 is disputed with some seeing this as referring to death for someone who causes an abortion and others believing it refers to harm to the mother. The LXX of the text argues for the death penalty if one causes a fully developed fetus to abort (as with Aristotle). Philo interprets Exod 21:22–23 as stipulating a fine for an abortion of an unformed fetus and death if it is formed as an outrage against nature (*Spec. Leg.* 3.108–109). Josephus interprets Exod 21:22–25 as harm to the woman (*Ant.* 4.278). However, in *Ag. Ap.* 2.202 he repudiates abortion. Rabbinic writings are concerned for both fetus and mother. Exodus 22 leads to the view of a fine for violence that induces an abortion (*Mek. Nez.* 8). In *m. Nid.* 5:3 it is a capital offense to kill a newborn and a fetus is a person after birth (*m. Ohol.* 7:6; *Nid.* 3:5). Abortion is permitted if a mother's life is endangered (*m. Ohol.* 7:6). See Ricks, 'Abortion,' 1.32–33.
17. Early Christians opposed both abortion and infanticide. *Pharmakoi* may refer to using abortifacients (Rev 21:8; 22:15, cf. Rev 9:21; 18:23; Gal 5:20). The *Didache* and *Epistle of Barnabas* condemn both abortion and infanticide (*Did.* 2:2; *Ep. Barn.* 19:5, cf. *Apos. Con.* 7.3.2; *Did.* 5:2; *Ep. Barn.* 20:2. See further Ricks, 'Abortion,' 1.33–35.
18. Outside of Paul: to call a person or group a name—Jesus, Immanuel, a Nazarene, children of God, the least in the kingdom, Lord, rabbi, father, teachers, John, Son of the Most High, holy, barren, Zechariah, prophet of the Most High, Zealot, Magdalene, Mary, your son, Zacchaeus, Iscariot, benefactors, Cephas, Barsabbas, Solomon's Porch, Saul, Great, Italian Cohort, Niger, Zeus, Mark, brothers, friend of God, and the Devil (Matt 1:21, 23, 25; 2:23; 5:9, 19; 22:43, 45; 23:7, 8, 9, 10; Luke 1:13, 31, 32, 35, 36, 59, 60, 61, 62, 76; 2:21 23; 6:15, 46; 8:2; 10:39; 15:19, 21; 19:2; 20:44; 22:3, 25;

some range,[19] in cases like this, it, and related language, have the sense of God's effective call which encompasses the human response. God is the one who calls things that don't exist into existence (Rom 4:17); he predestines, calls, justifies, and glorifies believers (Rom 8:30). His call is effective. The call is not irrespective of faith and human volition—it speaks of the whole shebang—he calls, we yield. Nor does this mean God is not summoning others to him by his Spirit through the gospel. It is just that Paul does not use the language of *kaleō* in this sense. They refuse him, so they are not called. There is still room for human volition in Paul's theology. Here, as in 1:15, it encompasses his call to faith and his vocation as the apostle to the gentiles (cf. 1 Cor 15:9).[20]

'Through (*dia*) his grace,' emphasizes the gift dimension of his experience, with 'his' here being *God's* grace. Paul has just prayed that the Galatians experience this grace (1:3). He earlier spoke

---

John 1:42; Acts 1:23; 3:11; 7:58; 8:10; 10:1; 13:1; 14:12; 15:22; 15:37; Heb 2:11; Jas 2:23; 1 Pet 3:6; 1 John 3:1; Rev 12:9); to name a place or geographical feature—house of prayer, field of blood, Bethlehem, Nain, Bethsaida, Olivet, the Skull, Straight Street, Fair Havens, the Northeaster, Cauda, Malta, Patmos, Sodom, Armageddon, Faithful and True, the Word of God (Matt 21:13; 27:8; Mark 11:17; Luke 2:4; 7:11; 9:10; 19:29; 21:37; 23:33; Acts 1:12, 19; 9:11; 27:9, 14; 27:16; 28:1; Rev 1:9; Rev 11:9; 16:16; 19:11, 13); to name a time—today (Heb 3:13). Used of a person summoning someone—the wise men, laborers, a servant, Jesus, the Sanhedrin, or Paul (Matt 2:7, 8; 25:14; Mark 3:31; Luke 19:13; Acts 4:18; 24:2). With the sense, 'invite' someone—wedding feast, a Pharisee's home, a Banquet, and a wedding (Matt 22:3, 4, 8, 9; Luke 7:39; 14:7, 8, 9, 10, 12, 13, 16, 17, 24; John 2:2; Rev 19:9). For God to 'summon'—Jesus out of Egypt (Matt 2:15). Of Jesus calling disciples—the first (Matt 4:21; Mark 1:20), sinners (Matt 9:13; Mark 2:17; Luke 5:32).

19. Paul: Called, as in named—'children of the living God' (Rom 9:26). Israel called—through Isaac's line (Rom 9:7, cf. Heb 11:8)—this is arguably also a theological use of the term. Also theological, it is used for being called *to or into something*—freedom (Gal 5:13), peace (1 Cor 7:15), role in life (1 Cor 7:17), one hope (Eph 4:4), to one body (Col 3:15), kingdom (1 Thess 2:12), holiness (1 Thess 4:7), eternal life (1 Tim 6:12), and a holy calling (2 Tim 1:9) (cf. 1 Pet 3:9; 5:10; 2 Pet 1:3). Invited—to an unbeliever's home (1 Cor 10:27).

20. See also Rom 9:12, 24, 25; 1 Cor 1:9, 18, 20, 21, 22, 24; Eph 4:1; 1 Thess 5:24. The call is through the gospel (2 Thess 2:14). See also the noun *klēsis*, 'calling,' (Rom 11:29; 1 Cor 1:26; 7:20; Eph 1:18; 4:1, 4; Phil 3:14; 2 Thess 1:11; 2 Tim 1:9). This Pauline sense of God's effective call is found in two other NT writers, Hebrews and Peter (*kaleō*: Heb 5:4; 9:15; 11:8; 1 Pet 1:15; 2:9, 21; *klēsis*: Heb 3:1; 2 Pet 1:10).

of the 'the grace of Christ' which the Galatians are deserting (1:6). Here, he was called through the agency (*dia*, 1:1) of God's undeserved beneficence. So, the Galatians were called 'by the grace of Christ' through the gospel, whereas the gospel was revealed when Paul was 'called through the grace of Christ.' All is grace, whether our creation, our conversion, the gifting of the Spirit, our call, our gifts, our very lives, and eternal futures.

Our salvation is a call by grace, God summoning us through the grace of Christ to him. We should yield and stay ever yielded, as did Paul. If our call is God's, we will, for his call is effective. Our vocation will also be called. We remain in the vocation and situation from which we were previously called before our conversion (1 Cor 7:17–24), but we are always ready to accept a fresh call. In my case, I was a schoolteacher at the time of my call and remained so until some two years later when I was called to leave teaching to serve in ministry. I remain in this now. I will continue to do so until I am called out of it or to the upward call of God in Christ Jesus—the heavenly prize (Phil 3:14). The Galatians are threatening to desert grace. 'God forbid,' thinks Paul.

In 1:16, we find out the purpose of God's calls for Paul is 'to reveal his Son to me.' The verb *apokalytō* means to 'unveil, reveal,' and here speaks of the same event as the *apokalypsis* (revelation) of Jesus Christ in 1:12. Here, the content of the revelation is again Jesus Christ, described as 'his Son.' While Paul uses Christ and Lord commonly of Jesus, and never uses Son of Man, he uses Son as a descriptor of Jesus on occasion as here in 1:16 whether it be 'his Son,'[21] or 'the Son' (1 Cor 15:28).[22] The idea of 'son of God' is used in Jewish thought of Israel (Deut 32:8), angels,[23] and the king in texts which also invoke it of the Messiah.[24] The idea of

---

21. See also 4:4, 6, cf. Rom 1:3, 9; 5:10; 8:29; 1 Cor 1:9; 1 Thess 1:10), 'Son of God' as in 2:20 (cf. Rom 1:4; 2 Cor 1:19; Eph 4:13).
22. He also uses *huios* of 'sons (children) of Abraham' (3:7), Christians as 'sons (children) of God' (3:26; 4:6, 7), the literal sons of Abraham (4:22), Ishmael 'the son of the slave,' and Isaac, 'the son of the free woman' (4:23, 30).
23. See Gen 6:2, 4; Ps 29:1; 89:6; Job 1:6; 2:1; 38:7; Hos 11:1.
24. See Ps 2:7; 89:26–27; 2 Sam 7:14; 1 Chron 22:10; 4Q174; 4Q246.

the Messiah as Son is seen in the High Priest's interrogation of Jesus (Mark 14:61).

In Greco-Roman thought, it was applied to the emperor and gods. Homer employs it to describe the sons of Zeus (e.g., Homer, *Il.* 5.683) and other gods (Homer, *Il.* 13.345), consistent with the Olympian gods as a family dynasty. Eastern rulers were known as sons of God as were specific deities like Helios or Zeus, especially in Egypt. Alexander the Great was labeled 'son of Zeus,' similarly, the Ptolemies. Augustus was described as *Divi filius* (Son of God).[25] As such, like the terms, Lord and Savior, 'Son of God' is an idea that is rich in meaning.

By ascribing to Jesus divine sonship, Paul speaks of Jesus as divine from a Greco-Roman perspective, and in Jewish thought, as Messiah. Paul's full theology indicates that he uses it in a sense beyond mere Messiah, seeing Jesus as divine as hinted in 1:1 (above),[26] while distinct from God the Father (esp. 1 Cor 8:6). 'To reveal his Son' summarizes what he has said earlier in v. 12—'a revelation of Jesus Christ.'

'In me' can refer to a subjective experience and may include this,[27] but likely it should be translated 'to me,' with *en* (in) rather than *eis* chosen by Paul to explain that this experience worked through his senses into his inner being, transforming him fully. So, it has the sense of 'to and into me.' It was both an objective experience (as Luke describes thrice), and a subjective transformation.

The purpose of Christ's revelation is 'so that (*hina*) I might proclaim (*euangelizomai*) him among the nations (plural *ethnos*).' As noted earlier on *hina* (see note in translation), this is a purpose clause, as are most of Paul's *hina* uses; so, it gives the purpose for which God set Paul apart—to proclaim Christ.

'I might proclaim' uses *euangelizomai*, the verb attached to *euangelion* (gospel, 1:6–9). Here, the verb has an object—'him,' i.e., Christ (not God in this instance). Elsewhere, Paul also speaks preaching 'Christ.'[28] Such constructions speak of Christ as the

---

25. See Peter Wülfing von Martitz, 'υἱός,' in *TDNT* 8:335–40.
26. See Rom 9:6; Phil 2:6–11; Col 1:15–20; 2:9; Tit 2:10.
27. See Dunn, *Galatians*, 64.

essence of his message, most particularly his crucifixion and resurrection (1 Cor 2:2; 15:3–5). However, his full message spans pre-creation in which God formed his plan, creation, fall, Israel's story read through the lens of Christ, Christ, the Spirit, the church, mission, faith, hope, love, cruciformity, Christ's return, judgment, eternal destruction for unbelievers, eternal life for believers, and the transformation of the cosmos. Christ is the center of this salvation-historical view of the cosmos.

'In the nations' uses *ethnos*, speaking of the gentiles, Paul's particular mission focus (2:2, 8, 9). In Paul's time, this speaks of wide swathes of land to the east, south, west, and north, of which much was known at his time. The Galatians are some of the recipients of his God-sent mission. He has visited them and preached Christ among them, and many believed in the gospel of grace. There is an implicit claim to authority here—he has done this among them, and so they should listen, and reject the Judaizers.

28. See 1 Cor 1:23; Phil 1:15, 17, 18, cf. Eph 3:8; Col 1:28.

CHAPTER 7

CHAPTER SEVEN: PAUL'S GOSPEL REMAINS THE SAME (1:16C–21)

NO HUMAN CONSULTATION (1:16C)

Paul signals his intent in 1:16c as he explains that he did not immediately go to Jerusalem or elsewhere to consult others. As in v. 12, this is to confirm to the Galatians that the gospel revealed to him was not fiction, created by people, but came from God through the revelation of Jesus Christ. He narrates his movements—Arabia, Damascus, then three years later, Jerusalem for fourteen days meeting Peter and Jacob, Syria, and Cilicia. He did not engage with the Judean churches. His gospel remains based on the revelation of Christ, and this is *the* gospel, despite the Judaizers maligning Paul and his message.

Galatians 1:16c is effectively a heading for what follows through to 2:14:

I **did not** (*ou*, 1:1) **immediately** (*eutheōs*)[1] **consult** (aorist

---

1. The adverb εὐθέως (*eutheōs*), which connotes 'immediately,' is found only once in Galatians, of Paul's immediate move after his conversion (1:16).

passive *prosanatithēmi*)[2] **with flesh** (dative *sarx*)[3] **and** (*kai*, 1:1) **blood** (dative *haima*)[4] ...

'Immediately' prepares the way for his later visits to Jerusalem; the first, three years after his conversion, and the other some fourteen years later. It is prominently placed first. The verb *anatithēmi* is found elsewhere in the NT in Acts 25:14–of the Roman Governor Festus setting forth Paul's case to Agrippa II for his 'counsel, approval or decision.'[5] Paul uses *anatithēmi* in 2:2 speaking of presenting his gospel before the Jerusalem leaders. *Prosanatithēmi*, adding the prefix *pros*, used here in this verse, originally had the sense of 'present one's cause ... to another.' As such, here it carries the meaning 'I did not expound it to' flesh and blood 'for their approval or submit it to their judgment.'[6] Paul uses it again in 2:6, where it means that the Jerusalem leaders imposed no additional requirement concerning the gospel, e.g., circumcision; they merely asked that he continue to remember the poor.[7]

---

2. The verb προσανατίθημι (*prosanatithēmi*) is only used in Galatians in the NT meaning: 1) Consult with someone—Paul did not do so after his conversion (1:16); 2) Add or contribute to—the apostles did not do this for Paul's gospel (2:6).

3. The noun σάρξ (*sarx*), 'flesh,' is found eighteen times in Galatians: 1) In the construct 'flesh and blood,' it refers to people—'I did not consult anyone' (1:16). Similarly, in Gal 2:16 where 'no one (*ou pasa*) of *flesh* will be justified from works of the law'—this is due to flesh's fallenness. Paul speaks of his life as 'the life I now live in the *flesh*' (2:20). He refers to a 'sickness of *flesh*' which led to him preaching in Galatia (4:13, cf. 4:14). Again in 4:23, someone born according to the flesh—their human state, born of another (4:23, 29); 2) Contrasted with Spirit, flesh in its fallen sense, which is flawed and unable to save (3:3), which seeks to enslave with sin (5:13), is full of false desires (5:16), which stand in enmity to the Spirit (5:17), and is full of false works Paul's lists (5:19–21). In contrast, believers in Christ have crucified the flesh with its corrupted passions and desires and must live by the Spirit (5:24). If one sows to please the flesh (lives out these desires and passions), one is destroyed (6:8); whereas, if one sows to please the Spirit, one reaps eternal life (6:8). 3) In 6:12–13, there may be a double sense where 'a good showing in the *flesh*' and 'they may boast in your *flesh*' may refer to fleshly non-Spirit life by law, and/or circumcision of the flesh.

4. The only reference to αἷμα (*haima*), 'blood' (English, hematology), is in 1:16, paired with flesh, referring to people who are made of flesh and blood, i.e., no one.

5. J. Behm, 'ἀνατίθημι (προσανατίθημι),' in *TDNT* 1:253.

6. Behm, 'ἀνατίθημι (προσανατίθημι),' 1:253.

7. 'προσανατίθεμαι,' in *EDNT* 3:162.

'Flesh and blood' here mean mortal people, who are formed physically of 'flesh and blood' (Matt 16:17) and are subject to death and require bodily transformation to eradicate corruption from their beings to enter eternity (1 Cor 15:50, cf. Eph 6:12). The use of the clause here may be intentional to contrast with the divine origin of the gospel—Paul did not get it from mortal humanity characterized by flesh and blood, but from the one who has died and risen, and is no longer flesh and blood—Jesus Christ. The use of 'flesh' in Paul's thought, always, to some degree or another, carries that notion of fallenness, weakness, mortality, prone to passion and desire, sinfulness, and so subject to death. He didn't talk to any mortal—he received it by a revelation from God who revealed himself in and through his Son. One can hear him muttering, 'Can the Judaizers claim this? No. Stop listening to them!'

This verse creates a slight problem when compared with Luke's account, as Luke refers to Ananias being instrumental in conveying to Paul his mission commission (Acts 9:10–19). Some see here a basis to question Luke's historical reliability. However, in Luke's account, Paul did not consult Ananias, rather, Ananias was *sent by Christ* through a vision and so it is likely that Paul saw his involvement as part of his revelatory experience. Ananias was sent by God and his role was to lay his hands upon Paul, through whom Jesus healed Paul and filled him with the Spirit, and to relay to him his apostolic commission from Christ (also Acts 22:12–16). After this encounter, Paul was for some days with the Damascus disciples. However, Luke gives no account of Paul seeking out other disciples for guidance concerning the gospel. Most likely, Paul sees the encounter with Ananias as part of the same visionary experience.

TO ARABIA AND BACK TO DAMASCUS (1:17)

In *Galatians 1:17*, Paul adds:
nor (*oude*, 1:1) **did I go up** (aorist *anerchomai*)[8] **to** (*eis*, 1:5)

---

8. The verb ἀνέρχομαι (*anerchomai*) compounds *ana*, 'up' and *erchomai*, 'go, come' so here speaks of 'go up' to Jerusalem. The use of 'up' of approaching the holy city is standard.

Jerusalem (*Hierosolyma*)[9] **to** (*pros*)[10] those (plural *ho*) **who were apostles** (plural *apostolos*, 1:1) **before** (*pro*)[11] **me** (genitive *egō*, 1:2), **but** (*alla*, 1:1) **I went** (*aperchomai*)[12] **to** (*eis*, 1:5) **Arabia** (*Arabia*)[13] **and** (*kai*, 1:1) again (*palin*, 1:9) **returned** (*hypostrephō*)[14] to (*eis*) **Damascus** (*Damaskos*).[15]

This is a critical statement as it indicates that Paul's gospel was set in place in his mind and heart by Christ before consulting with any who were already apostles—those called by Christ to leadership, and with him his ministry.

This is used twice for going up to Jerusalem in 1:17, 18. It is synonymous with *anabainō*, 'go up,' used in 2:1, 2 of also going up to Jerusalem.

9. The city name (noun) Ἱεροσόλυμα (*Hierosolyma*) is used thrice in Galatians, each referring to the historical city in relation to Paul's visits (1:17, 18; 2:1). This is the Hebraized Greek name. In Gal 4:25, 26, Ἱερουσαλήμ (*Ierousalēm*), the general Greek term is used.

10. The preposition πρός (*pros*) which speaks of movement to the side of, usually with the genitive meaning 'from,' with dative meaning 'at,' or with accusative as is most often in the NT, 'to.' It can also connote, 'with' or 'for.' There are nine uses in Galatians: 1) 'To:' '*to* those who were apostles before me' (1:17); '*to* everyone' and '*to* those who are of the household of faith' (6:10); 2) 'With:' 'remained *with* him fifteen days' (1:18); 'not walking in accordance *with/to* the truth of the gospel' (2:14); and '*with* you' (4:18, 20); 3) 'For'—'*for* a moment' (2:5), and '*for* you' (2:5).

11. The preposition πρό (*pro*), 'before,' is found three times of 'before' (1:17; 2:12, 23). *Pro* is also common as a prefix (eleven words): *proeipon*, 'say beforehand' (1:9; 5:21); *prokoptō*, 'progress, advance' (1:14); *proanatithēmi*, 'consult with' (1:16); *prographō*, 'portray publicly' (3:1); *prooraō*, 'foresee' (3:8); *proeuangelizomai*, 'preach beforehand' (3:8); *prokyraō*, 'ratify beforehand' (3:17); *prothesmia*, 'previously appointed day' (4:1); *prolegō*, 'tell beforehand' (5:21); *prokaleō*, 'provoke, challenge' (5:25); *prolambanō*, 'overtake' (6:1).

12. This reference in 1:18 is the only use of *aperchomai* in Galatians. It compounds *apo* (from) and *erchomai* (come, go) and so literally ('come from,' 'go from') and refers to his going to Arabia after his conversion. Paul's only other use is in Rom 15:28 of his hoped-for departure to Spain.

13. Arabia is mentioned twice in Galatians; in 1:17 and 4:25, which mentions Mt Sinai being in the area. The term derives from the Semitic terms for 'desert' and stretched south of Damascus into the Arabian Peninsula.

14. Galatians 1:17 is the only use of *hypostrephō* in Galatians. It compounds *hypo* (by, under) and *strephō* (turn) and the compounds indicates 'turn back, return' (BDAG 1041). This is Paul's only use of the verb.

15. *Damaskos* is used here and in 2 Cor 11:32 of Paul's escape from the city. Here, he speaks of his return to the city after his time in Arabia. It correlates with the modern city in Syria.

The second part of the verse explains Paul's movements. Rather than head to Jerusalem, he went into Arabia and returned again to Damascus. The name Arabia likely derives from *arabat* or *araba*, Semitic terms for 'desert.' The region is likely part or all of the Sinai Peninsula. As with the whole region, it was affected by the ebb and flow of kingdoms, including Assyria, Babylon, Persia, and Greece. After Alexander died, the Nabataeans controlled large northern parts of the region. Their capital was Petra, the region described by Josephus as 'Arabia Petrea' (Josephus, *J.W.* 1.267). The remainder was politically chaotic. Damascus came under Rome in 64 BC and was no longer part of Arabia. In 55 BC, it was pillaged by the governor of Syria. At the time of Christ, for the Romans, Arabia was the region south of the province of Syria. Aside from Petra, there were other key centers. It was not until AD 106 that Nabataea was annexed and came under Rome. So, at the time of Paul, Arabia was not joined politically to Damascus. Galatians is the only NT document that refers to Arabia.[16]

There are differing views of what Paul did in Arabia. Some, like Hengel and Schnabel, argue that Paul preached in the main centers. Schnabel argues that it is most likely Paul preached, beginning in the synagogues, in the Nabataean cities of Petra, Selaima, Shabba, Kanatha, Soada, Bostra, and possibly Pella and Scythopolis, both of which belonged to Judea. He may also have gone to the cities of the Decapolis—Philadelphia, Gerasa, Dium, and Adraa.[17] In support of this, Luke tells us in Acts that Paul immediately began preaching Christ in the Damascus synagogues; it is then likely that he extended this into the other areas he visited in Arabia (Acts 9:20–22). His need to escape from Damascus also indicates that he was active; otherwise, why expel him? (Acts 9:23–25; 2 Cor 11:32–33).

Another possibility arises from 4:25 and Paul's theology. He mentions 'Mt Sinai *in Arabia*,' which could mean that the site

16. Further on Arabia, see R. L. Drouhard, 'Arabia,' in *LBD*; E. J. Schnabel, *Early Christian Mission, Volume Two: Paul and the Early Church* (Leicester/Downers Grove, Ill.: Apollos/IVP, 2004), 1033–34.
17. Schnabel, *Paul*, 1037–35.

of the giving of the law is located in the Hedjaz Mountains. Some think that Paul, during these three years, spent substantial time contemplating his experience of seeing Christ and worked through his understanding of the gospel. He may have spent time on Mt Sinai working through his understanding of the Mosaic law in relation to the Messiah's coming.

While some scholars seem determined to decide between the two as if they need to be mutually exclusive, the two ideas do not actually need to be in tension. A three-year period is a substantial enough time for Paul to move about preaching in the main centers and also to spend much time in prayer and meditation. A visit to Mt Sinai would make sense if it was in the region. His worldview was so shaken that it seems implausible that he did not spend substantial time on his knees and pouring over the Scriptures. Similarly, it seems unlikely Paul would not preach if there were synagogues in the area. Hence, the two concepts fit together nicely, so, we need not decide between the two.

After he left Arabia, he returned to Damascus. As such, his time in Damascus and Arabia is as much a mission journey as his later forays from Syrian Antioch to Asia Minor and Greece. Damascus appears to have functioned as his base in much the same way as Antioch did later. He likely traveled at least 300 km by land in this period—some twelve days of walking. Of course, this was spaced over three years and could be substantially more.[18]

Aside from his time in Arabia, this fits with the Lukan chronology in Acts. Luke states, 'for *some days* he was with the disciples at Damascus' (Acts 9:19). After a period of preaching, in which he engaged in a mission to the south in Nabataea, 'when *many days* passed, the Jews plotted to kill him' (Acts 9:23). While Luke's chronology is vague, there is no reason one cannot see here Paul's three-year period.

---

18. See Schnabel, *Paul*, 1031–72 who devotes a whole chapter to this seeing it as his first mission journey including his time in Syria and Cilicia. On the travel figures see Schnabel, *Paul*, 1288: overall, he estimates Paul traveled some 25,000 km (15,500 mi) as a missionary, some 14,000 km (8,700 mi) by land. He notes Alexander the Great traveled around 32,000 km (19,900 mi) meaning that Paul's travels were not much less than the great Macedonian military leader.

JERUSALEM WITH CEPHAS (1:18)

In *Galatians 1:18*, Paul tells the Galatians that only then did he go
to Jerusalem:

Then (*epeita*)[19] **after** (*meta*)[20] **three** (*tria*)[21] **years** (*etos*),[22] **I went
up** (aorist *anerchomai*, 1:17) **to** (*eis*, 1:5) **Jerusalem** (1:17) **to
become acquainted with** (*historeō*)[23] **Cephas**[24] (*Cephas*),[25] **and**
(*kai*, 1:1) **he remained** (aorist *epimenō*)[26] **with** (*pros*, 1:17) **him
[for] fifteen** (*dekapente*)[27] **days** (*hēmera*).[28]

Only three years after Paul's conversion he traveled up to

---

19. The adverb of time or position ἔπειτα (*epeita*), in Galatians is always used of time
    signifying 'then,' three times in quick succession in Paul's narratio of his conversion
    and post-conversion encounters (1:18, 21; 2:1).
20. The preposition μετά (*meta*), is found seven times in Galatians signifying: 1) 'After,
    afterward, later' (*meta* plus accusative): '*after* three years' (1:18); '430 years *later*;' 2)
    'With' (*meta* plus genitive): '*with* Barnabas (2:1); '*with* the gentiles' (2:12), 'slavery *with*
    her children' (4:25), 'shall not inherit *with* the son' (4:30); and 'the grace ... be *with* your
    spirit' (6:18).
21. The number τρεῖς (*treis*) is found once, '*three* years later' (1:18).
22. The noun ἔτος (*etos*) means 'year.' It is used thrice in Galatians, in 1:18 (three *years*); 2:1
    (fourteen *years*); and 3:17 (430 *years*). In classical Greek, *enautios* speaks of a fixed
    cyclic period of time in distinction from the more fixed meaning of *etos*, year (see R.
    Kratz, 'ἐνιαυτός,' in *EDNT* 1:454). See also on *eniautos*, 4:10.
23. The verb ἱστορέω (*historeō*) (cf. English, history), is used once in 1:18 with the sense of
    'visit to get to know.'
24. **Variant**: *Petros* (Peter) is preferred in a small group of texts. However, the wide
    support for *Cēphan* and the logic that *Petros* would be supplied for Greek readers
    makes *Cēphan* almost certainly original.
25. Paul four times refers to Peter by his Aramaic name Κηφᾶς (*Cēphas*) in Galatians
    (1:18; 2:9, 11, 14). Yet, in 2:7, 8, he uses *Petros*, Peter, his Greek name. This is
    fascinating and leads to speculation concerning his attitude toward Peter. However,
    the interchangeability in 2:7–10 suggests that we should not read anything malicious
    into it. Both terms mean 'rock.' Most likely, Paul chose to use the Aramaic name to
    show his intimate familiarity with Peter as one Jew to another. Like the Judaizers, he
    knows Peter in this way.
26. Paul uses the compound verb ἐπιμένω (*epimenō*) combining *epi* (upon) and *menō*
    (remain), in the sense of '*stay* with' in 1:18. Here, the verb ἐπέμεινα (*epemeneina*) is
    stative and the preposition πρὸς (*pros*) is transitive. Hence, the verb does not indicate
    motion whereas the preposition does. See Wallace, *Greek Grammar*, 359.
27. The number, δεκαπέντε (*dekapente*), compound *deka* (ten) and *pente* (five), producing
    fifteen. It is used once in Gal 1:18—'*fifteen* days.'
28. There are two uses of ἡμέρα (*hēmera*), 'day'—fifteen days stay with Peter (1:18), and
    'you observe *days* and months' (4:10), i.e., holy days.

Jerusalem. This implies to readers that his gospel was already set in place. On one of his two departures from Damascus (either to Arabia or to Jerusalem), Paul had to escape in a basket lowered from the wall of the city. He describes this himself in 2 Cor 11:32 when the governor under King Aretas[29] was guarding the city ready to seize him. Luke also records this event, placing it at the end of his three years in Damascus and Arabia, from whence Paul went to Jerusalem after staying in Damascus 'some days' (Acts 9:25). Depending on when we date Paul's conversion, this either happened within a short period after Jesus' death, either AD 30 or AD 33. As such, the three years (which is an approximation and could be anything from two and a half to three and a half years, or 'the third year' as in 'the third day') would take us to somewhere between 33 and 36 (see earlier on Paul's Visits to Jerusalem).

The Greek used to describe his time is a *hapax legomenon* (unique in the NT), *historeō*, from which we get the English 'history.' The verb connotes 'visit (for the purpose of coming to know someone or something …).'[30] So, the purpose of Paul's visit is to get to know Cephas. Paul remained there with him for fifteen days, a period in which there were no doubt amazing discussions concerning Peter's time with Jesus, and Paul's recent conversion, one of those moments in Scripture where we wish we had a video recorder handy!—kind of like the Emmaus Road encounters between Jesus and the two travelers.

This fortnight with Peter is important in discussions concerning what Paul knew of the historical Jesus. On the basis of 2 Cor 5:16 and the paucity of references to the earthly life of Jesus in Paul's letters, Bultmann and others have argued that Paul knew little of the Jesus of history. However, a two-week

---

29. This is King Aretas IV (ca. 9 BC-AD 40). His daughter married Herod Antipas, the son of Herod the Great, the one who killed John and interrogated Jesus. When Antipas married his brother Philip's wife, Aretas attacked and defeated Antipas. Antipas then appealed to Tiberius the emperor, and the governor of Syria Vitellas instigated an attack on Aretas. See, Major Contributors and Editors, 'Aretas IV,' in *LBD*.

30. BDAG 483. In the LXX it is used of 'the histories concerning the kings' (1 Esdr. 1:31, 40).

intensive with Peter no doubt filled Paul in on what he didn't know already concerning Jesus' life. He was also in Jerusalem in the early days of the church and in contact with Christians whom he persecuted. No doubt, he learned a lot in this time prior to becoming a Jesus follower. He also traveled with two Gospel writers, Luke (the 'we passages' in Acts) and Mark (Acts 12:25, cf. Col 4:10; 2 Tim 4:11; Phlm 24), so the idea that Paul knew little about the earthly Jesus does not hold much merit. The few references to Jesus' earthly life show Paul's emphasis on the cross and resurrection rather than ignorance.[31]

MEETING JACOB (JAMES) (1:19)

In *Galatians 1:19*, Paul continues:

But (*de*, 1:15) **other** (accusative *heteros*, 1:6) **apostles** (plural *apostolos*, 1:1) **I did not** (*ou*, 1:1) **see** (aorist *eidon*)[32] **except** (*ei mē*, both 1:7) **Jacob** (*Iakōbos*)[33] **the brother** (accusative *adelphos*, 1:2) **of the Lord** (genitive *Kyrios*, 1:3).

Paul stayed with Peter and saw none of the other apostles. The only other apostle he saw was Jacob, not the brother of John (James and John) who died at the hands of Herod Agrippa I in AD 44 (Acts 12:1–2), but Jesus' blood brother Jacob. This testifies to a real change of heart on the part of Jacob who, like his other brothers Joseph (Joses), Judas (Jude), and Simon, according to

---

31. See the excellent essay, S. Kim, 'Jesus, Sayings of,' in *DPL* 474–91 who gives a comprehensive analysis of the sayings and allusions to Jesus' teaching in Paul—they are more substantial than earlier scholars believed. See also the similarly superb essay by John M. G. Barclay, 'Jesus and Paul,' in *DPL* 492–503 who summarizes the history of the debate, Bultmann, and more recent developments. He notes a range of ways Paul reflects the Jesus tradition.

32. The verb εἶδον (*eidon*), 'see,' is found four times in Galatians—'I saw none of the other apostles' (1:19); 'when they saw that I had been entrusted with the gospel' (2:7); 'when I saw that their conduct was not in step with the truth of the gospel' (2:14); 'See with what large letters I am writing' (6:11).

33. There are three mentions of Ἰάκωβος (*Iakōbos*), James, or, as I have translated it, 'Jacob,' in Galatians. In 1:19 he is described as 'the Lord's brother' and an apostle. In 2:9 he is named alongside John and Peter as those considered 'pillars'—he seems to have replaced John's brother Jacob who was killed by Herod Agrippa I in AD 44, some three to four years before Galatians. In 2:14 there were 'certain men sent from Jacob.'

the Gospel writers, did not believe in Jesus during his earthly ministry.[34] Paul elsewhere reports that Jesus appeared to Jacob (1 Cor 15:7). In Acts, he is indirectly mentioned among the first Christians in Acts 1:14 ('and his brothers'). He is not referenced again until after the death of Jacob, John's brother. However, after Herod Agrippa I sought Peter's life, Jacob emerged as the Jerusalem church leader (Acts 12:17; 15:13; 21:18). Here it is implied that he is an apostle, perhaps appointed to the role after the death of Jacob the brother of John. He also wrote the letter of Jacob. Josephus records his death in AD 62 after the death of Governor Felix and before the arrival of the new governor Albinus, the High Priest the Sadducee Ananua, a bold and insolent man, assembled the Sanhedrin who tried Jacob for breaking Jewish law, and he was stoned to death (Josephus, *Ant.* 20.200).

As with his time with Peter, during the same time, Paul undoubtedly learned a lot talking to Jacob, of his experience of his brother Jesus and the Christian life now that Jacob had met the risen Christ and had come to believe in him. What matters for the Galatians letter is that, while Paul no doubt had a lot of blanks filled in, they added nothing to his gospel.

The visit of Paul to Jerusalem is narrated in Acts, although some of the details are at variance with Galatians. Luke tells us Paul tried to join the disciples, but there was a great fear of him as their former persecutor. Barnabas took him under his wing and brought him to the apostles (plural). Paul then went out preaching in Christ's name and fled to Caesarea and onto Tarsus in Cilicia (below). The only real issue here is the plural 'apostles.' Paul does state he met with two apostles, Peter and Jacob. However, there is some inconsistency between the accounts (Acts 9:26–30). While for some this leads them to write off Luke's historicity; rather, this account is scant and a few minor detail inconsistencies are hardly enough to lead us to reject Acts completely. This is a historical summing up of events

34. See Matt 12:46–50; 13:55–58; Mark 3:20–21, 31–35; 6:3–6; Luke 8:19–21; John 7:5.

in a manner that fits Luke's agenda as a historian (remembering that all history is biased).

PAUL'S CLAIM TO VERACITY (1:20)

In *Galatians 1:20*, Paul pauses to tell his readers that what he is saying is utterly truthful:

And (*de*, 1:15) **these things** (neuter plural *hos*) **I write** (*graphō*)[35] **to you** (dative *sy*), **take note** (middle imperative *eidon, idou*),[36] **that** (*hoti*, 1:6) **before** (*enōpion*)[37] **God** (genitive *Theos*. 1:1), **I do not** (*ou*, 1:1) **lie** (*pseudomai*).[38]

This verse is parenthetical and so is rightly placed in parentheses in the English Bible. It is as if Paul pauses to swear on the Bible, as one might in court. 'These things I write to you' refers to the narration of events from his conversion to his trip to Jerusalem, and what will follow. 'I write' still leaves space for an amanuensis, but if so, Paul is dictating—it is his letter, as the first person indicates.

'Take note' (*idou*), the middle imperative of *eidon* (see), is the first imperative directed at the Galatians in the letter. It literally means 'look, see, behold' and calls attention to what Paul is saying. It is used widely in the NT (200 times), but sparingly by Paul including in an OT quote (Rom 9:33). The other use is in climactic statements which are highlighted by the term. For example, 'Behold! I tell you a mystery. We shall not all sleep, but we shall all be changed.'[39]

'Before God' (*enōpion Theou*) features across Paul's letters

---

35. There are seven uses of the verb γράφω (*graphō*) in Galatians, the common Greek term for writing, which he uses in two ways: 1) Of Paul's writing in the letter (1:20; 6:11); 2) Of things written in the OT, usually in the form *gegraptai*, the perfect, mostly introducing a quotation but sometimes in other settings—it stands written, i.e., it still speaks (3:10 [2x], 21; 4:22, 27).
36. The interjection ἰδού (*idou*) connotes 'behold, see, take note, hearken,' etc. It is the middle imperative of the verb εἶδον (*eidon*), 'see.' It is used once in Galatians in 1:19 in his statement of his integrity in the writing of the letter.
37. The preposition ἐνώπιον (*enōpion*) occurs once in Gal 1:20, meaning 'before.'
38. The verb ψεύδομαι (*pseudomai*) meaning 'to lie' is used once in Gal 1:20 where Paul states that he is not lying in the narration of his trips to Jerusalem.
39. See 1 Cor 15:51, cf. 2 Cor 5:17; 2 Cor 6:2, 9; 7:11; 12:14.

speaking of 'in God's sight' or 'in the presence of God.'[40] Here, God is witness and judge, and if Paul is lying, he is calling judgment on himself. As such, he invokes God as his witness, something he does elsewhere; for a Jew or a Christian, the most solemn statement of one's veracity.[41]

'I do not lie' uses *pseudomai* (Eng. 'pseudo'), a term that brings to mind similar parenthetical outbursts: Romans 9:1: 'I am speaking the truth in Christ, I am not lying …' Similarly, in 2 Cor 11:31: 'The God and Father of the Lord Jesus, he who is blessed forever, knows that I am not lying.' And again, 'For this I was appointed a preacher and an apostle (I am telling the truth, I am not lying), a teacher of the gentiles in faith and truth' (1 Tim 2:7).[42]

The manner of this outburst suggests that the Judaizers are maligning his story. They are likely arguing that he knows that circumcision is essential and expects it of his converts elsewhere while compromising it in Galatia to win converts. Paul is emasculating the idea with all that he has—what he is narrating here is the truth before God—God be his judge!

SYRIA AND CILICIA (1:21)

In *Galatians 1:21*, he continues:
  Then (*epeita*, 1:18) **I went** (aorist *erchomai*)[43] **into** (*eis*, 1:1) **the**

---

40. See Rom 3:20; 14:22; 1 Cor 1:29; 2 Cor 4:2; 7:12; 2 Cor 8:21; 1 Tim 2:3; 5:4, 21; 6:13; 2 Tim 2:14; 4:1.
41. Compare Rom 1:9; Phil 1:8; 1 Thess 2:5, cf. 2 Cor 1:23.
42. In Col 3:9 he uses *pseudomai* as he urges the Colossians not to lie to one another using the term (cf. Jas 3:14; 1 John 1:6). Essential to this is the idea of Heb 6:18—'it is impossible for God to lie.' So, we should not lie either. See also *pseudomai* in Matt 5:11; Acts 5:3, 4; Rev 3:9.
43. The verb ἔρχομαι (*erchomai*) is used for movement, 'come, go.' It is found eight times in Galatians: 'I *went* into the regions' (1:21); 'when Cephas *came* to Antioch' (2:11), 'certain men *came* from Jacob … when they *came* …' (2:12); 'until the offspring should *come*' (3:19); 'before faith *came*' (3:23); 'now that faith has *come*' (3:25), 'when the fullness of time had *come*' (4:4).

regions (plural *klima*)[44] **of Syria** (genitive *Syria*)[45] **and** (*kai*, 1:1) **Cilicia** (genitive *Kilikia*).[46]

After his first visit to Jerusalem, Paul then left for Syria and Cilicia. From the Hellenistic period, the region of Syria was well-defined, similar to the modern state. It was bounded to the west by the Mediterranean, to the south by Palestine, to the north by the Taurus Mountains, and to the east by the Euphrates region.[47] In the OT, Syria is referred to as Aram.

The leading centers were Damascus and Antioch, which became the first real center for gentile Christianity. After being under Greek rule (Seleucids, Ptolemy's), it was annexed to Rome in 64 BC. It became a province that at the time included Palestine, with Antioch its capital—a major city in the Roman world.[48] Syria is mentioned eight times in the NT.[49] Syria is again referenced in relation to Paul's returns to Antioch from mission journeys (Acts 18:18; 20:3; 21:3). It is paired with Cilicia in Acts 15:23 in the letter from the Jerusalem Council to the gentiles of these churches and in Acts 15:41 of Paul's travel through there with the letter. Schnabel notes the main urban centers of the region Paul may have evangelized—in accordance with his approach of planting churches in the main centers.[50] Some of this

---

44. Galatians 1:21 is the only use of the noun κλίμα (*klima*), signifying *regions* (uncommon in the NT, only used elsewhere by Paul in Rom 15:23; 2 Cor 11:10).

45. The place-name Συρία (*Syria*) is used once in Galatians, in 1:21. BDAG 978 notes that Syria was 'the part of Western Asia bounded on the north by the Taurus Mts., on the east by the lands of the Euphrates, on the south by Palestine, on the west by the Mediterranean Sea.' This is roughly coterminous with modern Syria.

46. The place-name Κιλικία (*Kilikia*) (Cilicia) is found once, in 1:21. BDAG 544 describes it as 'a province in the southeast corner of Asia Minor, whose capital is Tarsus; home of Paul.' This is the southeastern corner of modern Turkey.

47. BDAG 978.

48. D. D. Lowery, 'Syria,' in *LBD*.

49. Syria features twice in the Gospels, of Jesus whose fame spread from Palestine through to Syria (Matt 4:24)—perhaps indicating Antioch is the point of origin for the Gospel; Quirinius who was governor (Luke 2:2).

50. Schnabel, *Paul*, 1048–54 notes Abla, Helioplis, Laodikeia, Emesa, Arethusa, Epiphaneia, Larissa, Apameia, Mariamme, Raphaneai, Marysia, Seleucia and Belum, Platanoi, Alesandreai, Imma, Gindaros, Kyrrhos, Nikoplis, Germanikeia, Litarba, and Beroia.

may have been achieved with co-workers, as he does elsewhere (e.g., Epaphras in Col 1:6).

Cilicia is a region to the south-east of Asia Minor (modern Turkey) with the Mediterranean Sea to the south (Cyprus), Pamphylia to the west, Lycaonia and Cappadocia to the north, and Syria to the east. Tarsus was the main center. It lay on the major roads with the Cilician Gates opening the way to the Taurus Mountains to the north and the Syrian Gates (Belen Pass) marking the eastern route to Syria connecting Asia Minor to Palestine and Egypt. It came under the Greeks' control in 334 BC at the Battle of Issus, and after this, the Seleucids and Ptolemies vied for control. Rome took Cilicia in 102 BC. The well-known philosopher and Roman politician Cicero governed Cilicia for a year, 51–50 BC. Cleopatra ruled it from 37 BC. Then, with the victory of Octavian at Actium in 31 BC, Augustus ruled Cilicia personally.[51]

Cilicia features in the NT early in the story of the church. Some Cilicians were members of the Synagogue of the Freedmen in Jerusalem. They were critical in disputes with Stephen and his martyrdom (Acts 6:9). It is likely Paul was a member of this group. Tarsus was Paul's hometown, he was described by Luke as 'a man of Tarsus' (Acts 9:11), is quoted by Luke as being 'a Jew, from Tarsus in Cilicia, a citizen of no obscure city' (Acts 21:39), and as 'a Jew, born in Tarsus in Cilicia' (Acts 22:3, cf. Acts 23:34). As noted above, Cilicia is paired with Syria in the Jerusalem Council letter (Acts 15:23, 41). En route to Rome to trial, Paul passed by his home province (Acts 27:5). Apart from Tarsus, there were a number of other urban centers where Paul and his co-workers may have evangelized.[52]

In Acts, Luke confirms Paul's departure from Jerusalem via Caesarea Maritima to Tarsus in Acts 9:30. He also tells us that

---

51. See R. L. McMillan, 'Cilicia,' in *LBD*.
52. Schnabel, *Paul*, 1058–1069 notes Tarsus, Anazarbos, Mallos, Soloi-Pompeiopolis, Sebaste, Korykos, Seleucia, Olba, Baiae, Issos, Katabolos, Aigai, Epiphaneia, Hierapolis, Mopsuestia, Adana, Augusta, Zephyrion, Palaiai, Aphrodisias, Anemurion, Kalanthia, Saha, Bozburun, Koramsali, Lamos, and Kanytela.

Paul was in Tarsus when Barnabas went looking for him to bring him to Antioch to work in the burgeoning church (Acts 11:25).

Schnabel rightly considers this a mission journey of Paul after Arabia (see above). In fact, this mission period is the longest of his career—Schnabel suggests it extended from AD 33/34 to 44/45.[53] As such, this is an understated period of Paul's mission engagement. Some would say that it is a good example of the premise, 'mission begins at home.' In his hometown, Paul developed the skills he would take to the world. Christians today who want to be cross-cultural missionaries should take note and begin among their own people.

---

53. Schnabel, *Paul*, 1047 considers Jesus died in AD 30 and Paul was converted in AD 31/32 and was in Arabia (Nabataea) during AD 32/33. Others, like Hengel and Schwemer, suggest he was in Syria-Cilicia from AD 36/37 to 46/47, thirteen years (AD 36/37–39/40 in Tarsus; 38/39 in Antioch; 41–46/47 in Syria and Phoenicia).

CHAPTER EIGHT: PAUL OTHERWISE UNKNOWN IN JUDEA (1:22–24)

PAUL UNKNOWN AMONG JUDEAN CHURCHES (1:22)

Paul continues his narrative, emphasizing that his gospel is from a divine source rather than any human agency. He refers to his relative obscurity among the churches in Judea after he left Jerusalem to go to Tarsus and later Antioch, from where he worked in mission.

In *Galatians 1:22*, he states:

And (*de*, 1:15) **I was** (imperfect[1] *eimi*, 1:7) **unknown** (present passive *agnoeō*)[2] **in person** (dative *prosōpon*)[3] **to the churches** (plural dative *ekklēsia*, 1:2) **of Judea** (genitive *Ioudaia*)[4] **that** (dative plural feminine *ho*, 1:1) **[are] in** (*en*, 1:6) **Christ** (dative *Christos*, 1:1).

---

1. The combination of ἤμην (*ēmēn*, was) and the anarthrous participle ἀγνοούμενος (*agnooumenos*, 'unknown') is periphrastic. A periphrastic construction 'refers to a construction in which a participle occurs with a form of εἰμί.' (*PDSNTG* 96). It is a round-about way of saying something. Here, 'I was unknown to the face of the churches.' See on this Wallace, *Greek Grammar*, 648.
2. The only use of the verb ἀγνοέω (*agnoeō*) in Galatians is 1:22: 'I was *unknown*,' i.e., the Judean churches did not know Paul in person (to the face).
3. The noun πρόσωπον (*prosōpon*) is used three times in Galatians. It speaks of *the face* in a literal sense but can indicate the entire bodily presence, a person, the surface of something, or appearance. In 1:22 it connotes 'unknown by face, personally, or in person;' while in 2:6, 'God does not receive the face of a person,' speaks of God not welcoming people by appearance or view (status)—'does not show favoritism.' In 2:11 Paul opposes Peter 'to his face,' i.e., not in secret or behind his back.
4. The only reference to the place name Ἰουδαία (*Ioudaia*) (Judea) is in 1:22. BDAG 477 describes the meaning as 'the southern part of Palestine in contrast to Samaria, Galilee, Perea and Idumea, *Judea*.'

Paul now qualifies his relationship with the churches in the region of Jerusalem in the period after he left the city. The imperfect 'was' speaks of that period between his two Jerusalem visits, the other being Gal 2. He was 'unknown,' uses the present passive of *agnoeō* (cf. Eng. 'agnostic'). The term *agnoeō* is used twenty-two times in the NT, most of which are in Paul (sixteen).[5] As in 2 Cor 6:9 where he speaks of his being '*unknown* yet well known (*epignōskō*),' here it refers to personal, relational knowledge—they had not met him, although they had heard something of him. The use of the imperfect of the verb suggests that at the time of writing, he is now known to them. This may indicate that on his Jerusalem trip referred to in 2:1–10, he became familiar with them as they traveled among them after delivering the Asian, Macedonian, and Achaian collection.

'In person' literally means 'to the face'—the Christians of Judea have not met him in person. 'The churches of Judea' refer to those churches in Jerusalem and the region of Judea, which here likely constitutes the whole Jewish nation spread through Palestine.[6] It recalls the 'churches of Galatia' in 1:2; Paul often

---

5. Paul uses *agnoeō* five times in disclosure formulas: of his not wanting people to be *unaware* including his travel plans (Rom 1:13), a mystery concerning Israel (Rom 11:25), the things that Israel experienced in the wilderness (1 Cor 10:1), spiritual gifts (1 Cor 12:1), his afflictions in Asia (2 Cor 1:8), and that Christians should not grieve over the dead as if there is no hope. He uses it twice in questions: asking the Romans if they do not know that those baptized in Christ are baptized into his death (Rom 6:3) and asking them if they do not know about the law binding a person while alive (Rom 7:1). Otherwise, he applies it to people being ignorant that God's kindness leads to repentance (Rom 2:4), being ignorant of the righteousness of God (Rom 10:3), not recognizing the authority of Paul, and then that person being unrecognized (1 Cor 14:38), being ignorant of Satan's plans (2 Cor 2:11), and the pre-Christian Paul acting ignorantly in unbelief (1 Tim 1:13). Outside of Paul it is used of understanding a saying (Mark 9:32; Luke 9:45). It is used relationally of people not recognizing Jesus (Acts 13:27), the unknown God (Acts 17:23), of people who are ignorant Christian (Heb 5:2), or those who blaspheme about things of which they are ignorant (2 Pet 2:12).

6. Paul, as here, uses it of the whole nation (Rom 15:31; 2 Cor 1:16; 1 Thess 2:14). Other NT writers use it in the same way (Matt 24:16; Mark 13:14; Luke 1:5; 3:1; 7:17; 21:21; Acts 2:9; 10:37; 11:1, 29; 15:1; 21:10; 26:20; 28:21). At times, it refers just to the southern region around Jerusalem rather than the whole nation (Matt 2:1, 5, 22; 3:1, 5; 4:25; 19:1; Mark 3:7; 10:1; Luke 1:65; 2:4; 4:44; 5:17; 6:17; 23:5; John 4:3, 47, 54;

thinking regionally in terms of his understanding of the church (cf. the churches of Auckland).

Of these churches, we know a little. If Judea, in this instance, includes the three parts of Israel—Galilee, Samaria, and Judea—we know that there were churches established in the Samaritan region through the ministry of Philip who traveled preaching the gospel 'to many villages of the Samaritans' (Acts 8:5–25). One of these was likely Sychar, a town with many followers of Jesus after his encounter with the Samaritan woman (John 4:1–45).

In Judea proper, there were many Christians (e.g., Acts 11:29). From Acts we know that from the earliest days of the church in Jerusalem there were at least Jacob and the Lord's other brothers (e.g., Acts 1:14; 12:17), Jacob the brother of John (until a few years prior), the prophet Agabus (Acts 11:28), John Mark, his mother, and their servant Rhoda (Acts 12:12–13).

There was likely a church formed by Philip in Azotus (Ashdod), just south of Tel Aviv (Joppa) on the coast (Acts 8:40). There was certainly a church in Caesarea Maritima, through the ministries of Philip and his family (Acts 8:40), Peter (Acts 10–11), and Paul (Acts 9:30). This included the Roman centurion Cornelius and his family (if he remained there), and perhaps other Romans he and his family had shared Christ with (Acts 10–11).

Other churches were probably found in Lydda, where Peter healed Aeneas (Lod, ten km/six mi inland from Tel Aviv), and Sharon (just north of Tel Aviv) (Acts 9:32–35). There is good evidence of a church in Joppa, where Peter raised Tabitha/Dorcas from the dead and from where he traveled to see Cornelius. This included at least Tabitha and Simon the Tanner (Acts 9:36–10:7). There is no reference to churches in Galilee, but we can be confident there were churches throughout the region from the earliest days. Paul is not known to them personally, only by reputation.

'Which are in Christ' speaks of authentically Christian

7:1, 3; 11:3; Acts 1:9; 8:1; 9:31; 12:19). BDAG 477 takes Paul here in the narrower sense, however, this could equally refer to the whole Jewish nation in Palestine (including Galilee).

churches. This is the first use of 'in Christ' in Galatians. Paul uses 'in Christ' commonly across his letters (seventy-six times)—also 'in him' (twenty-four times), and 'in the Lord' (forty-eight times)—a total of 148 times. The language is rich, speaking of believers who at conversion by grace and through faith are included in Christ signifying their new identity in him; the status of righteousness, sanctification, adoption into the family of God, redemption, reconciliation, cleansing, Spirit-reception, and inclusion in the covenantal people of God. Here, it is churches who are in Christ which means groups of genuine Christians who gather in particular locations forming bodies of Christ who together with all believers form the cosmic body of Christ. It is a collective belonging to Christ.

'In Christ' is a glorious concept. It is arguably the center of Paul's theology, although this is disputed. Of course, in the context of a debate with Judaizers, 'in Christ' has real significance, for these are churches too are shaped by the same gospel of grace, the gospel of faith, *not law*, the gospel that does not expect circumcision of gentile converts like Cornelius—collectives who are saved and included by grace through faith.

In contrast to 1:2 where the Galatians are 'churches of Galatia' (1:2), these Judean churches are 'in Christ.' The status of the Galatians is not clearly 'in Christ,' as they flirt with the Judaizers. If they yield to their demands, they will no longer be churches in Christ, but effectively synagogues of those who seek justification through the works of the law. This is implausible, for the law merely leads people to Christ now that he has come.

In Galatians 'in Christ' is used six times of 'the freedom we have in Christ Jesus'—a freedom from enslavement to sin and death empowered by the law which functions to imprison (Gal 2:4). Having been justified in Christ (2:16), for recipients of the Abrahamic blessings 'in Christ Jesus' (3:14), being unified as one in Christ Jesus (3:28), and in Christ Jesus, circumcision or uncircumcision has no value (5:6). Once, he uses the language of 'in the Lord' of his confidence 'in the Lord' (5:10).

FROM PERSECUTOR TO PREACHER (1:23)

Galatians 1:23–24 is one sentence in which Paul states what these churches of Judea in Christ knew of him:

But (*de*, 1:15) **they were** (third-person plural *eimi*) **only** (*monos*)[7] **hearing** (aorist participle *akouō*, 1:13) **that** (*hoti*, 1:6) **'the one who was** (imperfect *eimi*, 1:7) **formerly** (*pote*, 1:13) **persecuting** (present participle *diōkō*, 1:13) **us** (plural *egō*, 1:2) **[is] now** (*nyn*, 1:23) **preaching** (present *euangelizomai*, 1:8) **the faith** (*pistis*)[8] **which** (feminine singular *ho*, 1:5) **he was formerly** (*pote*) **destroying** (imperfect *portheō*, 1:13),' **and** (*kai*, 1:1) **they glorified** (*doxazō*)[9] **God** (*Theos*, 1:1) **because** (*en*, 1:6) **of me** (dative *egō*).

The churches of Judea did not know Paul by face, personally, but they had heard about him, likely through the ministries of Jerusalem Christians like Peter, Jacob, the prophet Agabus, and others as they shared the word and people traveled through the churches. What they had heard is signaled by *hoti*, which marks the discourse—that Paul, who was the one who had persecuted them,[10] is now preaching the faith which he formerly plundered.

Of note here is the use of 'the faith' (*tēs pistēs*) as a summative term for the Christian religion signaling the introduction of a central motif of the letter. 'The faith' is likely chosen because the response of faith is the dominant issue in the Judaizing controversy—is faith sufficient? Does one need to be

---

7. The adverb μόνος (*monos*), 'only, features seven times in Galatians, all in the form *monon* connoting 'only' (1:23; 2:10; 3:2; 4:18; 5:13; 6:4, 12).

8. The noun πίστις (*pistis*), 'faith, faithfulness,' is used twenty-two times in Galatians: 1) Of the 'Christian faith' as a whole (1:23); 2) In the much disputed *pisteōs Iēsou Christou* (or just *Christou*), 'faith of Jesus Christ/Christ' constructions, meaning either: a) Faith in Christ (objective genitive, my preference); b) Faith/faithfulness of Christ (subjective genitive) (2:16; 3:22); 3) 'Faith' as in the response that justifies a person (2:20; 3:2, 5, 7, 8, 9, 11, 23, 24, 26; 5:5), in contrast to law (3:12, 25), the means of receiving the Spirit (3:14), which brings people into God's family (3:26); 4) Which works out in love (5:6); 5) Faithfulness as a fruit of the Spirit (5:22); 6) The church is the household of faith (6:10).

9. The verb δοξάζω (*doxazō*), 'glorify' is used once in Galatians, in 1:24, in the imperfect, it speaks of the Judean churches glorifying God because of Paul's conversion—the language of praise and worship.

10. See Acts 8:1–3; 9:1, 13, 21; 22:4, 19; 26:10, 11; 1 Cor 15:9; Gal 1:13; Phil 3:6; 1 Tim 1:13.

circumcised? Does one need to yield to other Jewish religious protocols like Sabbath, feasts, etc.? Here, as sparingly elsewhere in Paul and especially in the Pastorals,[11] 'the faith' sums up the religion as a religious system of the response of faith to God and his Son; it is this faith that justifies. He likely chooses this way of describing Christian religion because faith is at stake in Galatians.

The term *pistis* will feature throughout the letter. This is the only use of 'the faith' in a summative religious sense. Otherwise, it features twenty-one other times (see the note above), most in relation to the question of whether faith is enough. For Paul, it clearly is. For the Judaizers, it is not enough; one must enter salvation and the covenantal people of God through circumcision and Jewish religious boundary markers. For Paul, this is an accursed idea. Rather, faith in Christ *is* enough.

Faith in Christ justifies Jew and gentile alike, not works of the law (2:16; 3:8), for the law is not from faith (3:12). One lives as a Christian by faith in the Son, and by faith alone (2:20). The Spirit is received, and miracles are worked when the gospel is received through faith and not through works of the law (3:2, 5, 14). Those with faith are children of Abraham (3:7) and blessed with him (3:9), receiving the Abrahamic promise (3:22). By faith, people are declared righteous and live (3:9, 11). Faith sets people free from captivity to sin under the law (3:23). The law guarded them until Christ came; now that he has come and died for sin, they are no longer under the law's guardianship, they are justified by faith (3:24)—they are 'out of sins' prison,' and the law's guidance is no longer required. They are children of God through faith (3:26). They await with eager expectation the hope that righteousness by faith yields and the Spirit who now resides—the consummation (5:5). In the meantime, they live by faith working itself out through love (5:6). They live by the Spirit, and the Spirit yields even more faith and faithfulness in the believer's life (5:22). They do good to all those in the household of faith (6:10).

11. See 1 Cor 16:13; 2 Cor 13:5; Eph 4:13; Phil 1:25, 27; Col 1:23, 27; 1 Tim 1:2; 3:9; 4:1, 6; 5:8; 6:10, 12, 21; 2 Tim 3:8; 4:7; Tit 1:13; 3:15. Elsewhere only Luke and Jude use the phrase 'the faith' in a similar way (Acts 6:7; 13:8; 14:22; 16:5; Jude 3).

Christianity must always remain 'the Faith' and not degenerate into a system of works, of 'ought' and 'ought not to,' or a system of rules for justification. The starting point is that if we believe, we are 'in.' We need no other thing to be 'in' to belong. We simply are in—summoned by God, called by him, and faith has been borne, and we are his. So, we receive the Spirit—woosh!

In an instant, at that first moment of faith—God downloads his glorious Essence. This is the same power that worked as God and Christ formed the Cosmos. Instantly, at that moment of faith, we are born (as John would say) children of the living God (John 1:12), adopted as God's sons and daughters (4:5). As such, to God we yield, and by the Spirit we live, out of faith and faith alone, expressing it with the fruit of the Spirit, supremely love! As we yield to Christ as Lord walking in faith, the Spirit cultivates in us Christlike attitudes. He generates the fruit of the Spirit. We do good works, not to be justified, but *because we are justified*! Out of gratitude—grace giving birth to grace.

We will do a lot of those many things the law demands, for of course, the law comes from the heart of God. Supremely, we will love God wholeheartedly and passionately, and we will love our neighbors (even our enemies) as we long to be loved and are loved in Christ—both laws found in the law.[12] *Many* other things we will also do. However, these are done not because they are in the law which we are under and because they must be kept for us to remain in God's people, but because we *are in*! It is the Spirit who etches the law into our broken beings (2 Cor 3:3), writes the law on our hearts (Jer 31:33; Rom 2:15), generating God's ideals within us that flow over, softening and healing our hard and broken hearts, so that, if we remain yielded, over time, he makes us more and more like Jesus.

The key is that *we do not add to faith*, wittingly or unwittingly (often we do not even know we are doing it), for when we do, we quench the Spirit. It can never be more than 'the faith!' If we add to faith, we become joyless legalists bound to the demands of the law. We become judgmental of ourselves and others, critical and

12. See Deut 6:5; Lev 19:18, cf. Gal 5:14; Mark 12:29–31.

cynical people who are hard and harsh, loading up burdens on our own backs and those of others. No! We belong to 'the Faith' and 'the Faith' it must remain.

GLORY TO GOD (1:24)

In *Galatians 1:24*, Paul concludes the response of the Judean churches to him: "and they glorified (*doxazō*) God because of me." 'Glorified' is *doxazō*, related to 'glory' (*doxa*), and signifies 'to influence one's opinion about another so as to enhance the latter's reputation, praise, honor, extol.'[13] When used of God, it speaks not of adding to God's glory, for his glory is complete, infinite, eternal, and unchangeable. Rather, it speaks of acknowledging it. It is thus the language of praising God who is fully glorious in his person and actions. It adds nothing to him but is the right response of a human to God in his glorious Godness.

In the LXX, *doxazō* is used of glorifying God[14] and even more so in the Pseudepigrapha, especially in the *Testament of Solomon*.[15] The hope of Isaiah that the Lord 'will be glorified in Israel' finds fruition here because of Paul's conversion (Isa 44:23). Throughout the NT, and especially in Luke's writings, God is similarly ascribed glory.[16] In Paul's writings, Christians are gifted from God 'so that together you may with one voice glorify the God and Father of our Lord Jesus Christ' (Rom 15:6).[17] Here, it

---

13. BDAG 258.
14. See Exod 15:2; Ps 21:24 [Eng. 22:23]; 85:9, 12 [Eng. 86:9, 12]; Sir 43:30; Mal 1:11; Isa 25:1; 42:10; 66:5; Dan 3:26, 51, 55, 56.
15. See 3 Bar. 17.4; T. Naph. 8.4; T. Jos. 8.5; T. Job 14.3; 16.7; T. Ab. (A) 14.9; 15.5; T. Sol. 1.8; 2.5, 9; 3.5, 7; 5.13; 8.1; 10.10; 13.7; 14.7; 15.13, 15; 18.41; 20.21; 25.9; Jos. Asen. 20.5; Apoc. Mos. 43; 4 Bar. 7.17; 9.14; Hist. Rech. 9.2; Pss. Sol. 10.7; 17.5, 30.
16. See Matt 5:16; 9:8; 15:31; Mark 2:2; Luke 2:20; 5:25, 26; 7:16; 13:13; 17:15; 18:43; 23:47; John 14:13; 15:8; 21:19; Acts 4:21; 11:18; 13:48; 21:20; 1 Pet 2:12; 4:11, 16; Rev 15:4. In John, the verb has special significance related to Jesus' glorification on the cross and in the subsequent resurrection and exaltation (John 7:39; 8:54; 11:4; 12:16, 23; 13:31; 16:14; 17:1, 4, 5, 10), and God through him (John 12:28; 13:31–32; 17:1).
17. Otherwise he uses *doxazō* of idolatry as a failure to glorify God (Rom 1:21), believers being glorified in the eschaton (Rom 8:30), his own ministry (Rom 11:13); believers glorifying God with their bodies (1 Cor 6:20), people being honored (1 Cor 12:26), the

is people in the Judean churches who are raising their hearts and voices to God and glorifying him.

'Because of me' uses *en*, which here is causal; 'because of me.'[18] This is again important—the Judean Churches, full as they are with Jewish converts, many of whom who witnessed the ministry of Jesus some fifteen to twenty years prior, were not maligning Paul for preaching a false gospel because they had heard of his heretical views; rather, they praised God because of Paul. Hence, the Galatians should do the same and send these Judaizing heretics packing.

glory of the law now superseded by the glory of Christ and the gospel (2 Cor 3:10), and the word of the Lord (2 Thess 3:1); believers glorifying God through obedience, confession of the gospel, and generosity (2 Cor 9:13), and the eschatological hope now being realized that the gentiles might 'glorify God for his mercy' (Rom 15:9).

18. See meaning 9 in BDAG 329. It can hardly mean 'with me,' or 'in me,' as these are churches in Christ. BDAG suggest this may mean 'for me,' which is also possible, but prefer 'in my case,' which is not as likely as the causal interpretation.

CHAPTER 9

CHAPTER NINE: PAUL, HIS GOSPEL, AND HIS MISSION ENDORSED IN JERUSALEM (2:1–10)

Signaled by 'then' (*epeita*), Paul continues his narrative. He narrates how after fourteen years (either from his conversion, or from his last visit), he again visited Jerusalem. This time he had Barnabas and Titus with him. This is either the famine visit described in Acts 11:26–30 or the Jerusalem Council trip in Acts 15. As already proposed in the introduction, the former is more likely. The trip was catalyzed by a revelation, this time not of Christ, and perhaps referring to Agabus' prophecy of a famine (2:2; Acts 11:28). He set before them the gospel that he preaches in the gentile world to be confident he had it right.

He notes that the Jerusalem church and its leaders made no demand that Titus had to be circumcised. However, some whom he considers 'false brothers' surreptitiously sought to force new gentile converts to be circumcised. Paul and his team did not yield to them so that the gospel would be preserved for the Galatians and other gentiles. Not only was his gospel accepted, but the leading Jerusalem Christians, including Jacob, Peter, and John, welcomed him warmly and did not add anything to his understanding. Rather, they endorsed his ministry, acknowledging that just as God endorsed Peter's role as the one leading the mission to Jews, Paul was the apostle to whom God had entrusted the gospel mission to the gentiles. The only caveat was that Paul continues to be concerned for the poor, which was his intention, and which he demonstrated on his third Antiochian missionary journey, which was devoted to raising funds from the Galatians, Macedonians, and Achaians for the again famine-beleaguered Jerusalem Christians.

JERUSALEM AGAIN (2:1)

In *Galatians 2:1*, Paul states:

Then (*epeita*, 1:18), **after** (*dia*, 1:1) **fourteen** (*dekatessares*)[1] **years** (*etos*, 1:18), **again** (*palin*, 1:9) **I went up**[2] (*anabainō*)[3] **to** (*eis*, 1:1) **Jerusalem** (*Hierosolyma*, 1:18) **with** (*meta*, 1:18) **Barnabas** (*Barnabas*),[4] **taking along with** (*symparalambanō*)[5] [us] **also** (*kai*, 1:1) **Titus** (*Titos*).[6]

The sequence of 'then' (*epeita*) continues from 1:18, 21. 'After fourteen years' seems most naturally to refer to fourteen years since his first visit to Jerusalem. If Jesus' death and resurrection were in AD 30 and Paul's conversion within a year or so of this, this would take us to around AD 47. If his death was in AD 33, then it could take us into the 50s. However, if fourteen years are inclusive of the three years, we are again in the second half of the 40s AD. If this is the 50s, this could be the Jerusalem Council trip after Paul's second Antiochian mission to Macedonia and Achaia and before his Jerusalem Collection trip in the mid–50s. Otherwise, it is the trip to Jerusalem recorded in Acts 11:26–30 stimulated by Agabus' prophecy of the famine. Deciding between these options is tricky.

In both Acts 11 and 15, Paul is with Barnabas (Acts 11:30; 15:2). Titus is not mentioned in either of these Acts texts and only features in the third of Paul's journeys from Antioch (2 Cor

---

1. This is the only use of *dekatessares* in Galatians (*deka*, 'ten,' plus *tessares*, 'four' produces fourteen). See 'fourteen generations' thrice in Matt 1:17 and 'fourteen years ago' in 2 Cor 12:2.

2. **Variant**: There are three readings for 'went up' including: 1) *palin anebēn*; 2) *anebēn palin* (reversing the order); 3) *palin anēlthon* (C). Reading 1) has much better support and is certainly correct.

3. There are two uses of ἀναβαίνω (*anabainō*), 'to go up,' in Galatians, both of going up to the Jerusalem in 2:1, 2. It is synonymous with *anerchomai*, used in the same way in 1:18.

4. The transliteration of the name Βαρναβᾶς (*Barnabas*) is identical to the English name—he is mentioned three times in Galatians (2:1, 9, 13).

5. The only use of the verb συμπαραλαμβάνω (*symparalambanō*) is in 2:1. It compounds three terms: *syn* (with), *para* (alongside), *lambanō* (take)—hence 'take along with.' It is used in Acts 12:25; 15:37, 38.

6. The name Τίτος (*Titos*) (Titus) is mentioned twice in Galatians, in the narration of Paul's visit to Jerusalem (2:1, 3).

2:13; 7:6, 13, 14; 8:6, 16, 23; 12:18) (further below). However, one can argue that there is no reference to his involvement with Paul in his first missionary endeavor to Galatia and he fits a later time in his ministry. Paul's concern for the poor is relevant to both (cf. 2:10); in Acts 11:26–30 his trip to Jerusalem was stimulated by Agabus and he brought gifts, while his mission journey after the Jerusalem Council was for the purpose of raising funds for Jerusalem (1 Cor 16:1–4; 2 Cor 8–9; Rom 15:25–31). Our uncertainty over the date of the death of Jesus and the intention of the years (fourteen or seventeen), means that either a date in the later 40s or very early 50s fits.

In favor of Acts 11 is the reference to a revelation, which could be Agabus' prediction (Acts 11:28). However, there is nothing referring to Agabus or the famine in 2:2, unless we see 2:10 as endorsing the collection and doing similar things in the future—so a second collection later. In favor of the Jerusalem Council, is that Paul states in 2:2 that his purpose in visiting is the gospel.

However, there are aspects of Gal 2 that call into question the correlation of Gal 2 and Acts 15. There is no actual reference to a gathering to discuss the gospel at which Peter, Jacob, Paul, Barnabas, and the Judaizers shared their views. All that is mentioned is a subversive attempt to influence Paul's team toward circumcision and a private presentation of his gospel before those who appeared to be of influence in the church—who could be 'those who seemed influential (2:2). However, there is no reference to much debate (Acts 15:7), the final decision, the contents or sending of the Jerusalem Council letter, Silas, Judas Barsabbas, or the Galatian churches. Moreover, if this is the Jerusalem Council trip, why send Galatians when he is about to embark on a mission journey through the Galatians churches? Wouldn't he simply take the Jerusalem Council letter as he and Silas went west? It makes the Galatians letter redundant. So, seeing this as Acts 11 makes sense. Galatians, then, is an earlier letter sent before the Jerusalem Council. The Council resolved the problem once for all. Paul then took the Council's letter (15:30) with him on his second Antiochian mission to reinforce

Galatians. There is no reference in Galatians to Paul coming to
Galatia himself, which he does after the Jerusalem Council.

All in all, the question of which Acts visit aligns with Gal 2 is
most difficult to resolve. However, I consider the better of the
two options is the visit was prior to the Jerusalem Council when
Paul traveled from Antioch to Jerusalem with the first collection
after the revelation of the famine to Agabus (Acts 11). After this,
Paul returned to Antioch from where he and Barnabas set off
to preach in Cyprus and among the Galatians (Acts 13–14). He
returned and reported on the conversion of the Galatians (Acts
14:26–28). Then, Judaizers came to both the Galatian churches
(as evidenced in the letter) and Antioch, preaching circumcision
for salvation and inclusion (Acts 15:1). This led to conflict. Paul
wrote Galatians. Then, he and Barnabas set off to Jerusalem to
the Jerusalem Council meeting (Acts 15). After this, he returned
to Antioch with Judas and Silas to deliver the letter. Then, after
his split with Barnabas and Mark, he traveled with Silas to the
Galatian churches reinforcing Galatians with the Jerusalem
Council letter. He then went further west in mission, led by the
Spirit to bypass western Asia Minor and established the churches
in Macedonia and Achaia. As such, 'I again went up to Jerusalem'
likely refers to Acts 11:26–30.

This is the first reference to Barnabas in Galatians. He will
be mentioned again in 2:9 of the same Jerusalem visit, and in
2:13 of the incident with Peter in Antioch. Our knowledge of
Barnabas comes from Luke. We learn from him that he also goes
by the name Joseph and that his name Barnabas is from the
Aramaic term ברנבו—*bar*, 'Son' and *Nabas*, meaning prophet or,
as Luke translates it, 'consolation.' Barnabas then means 'son of
consolation or encouragement' (*paraklēsis*). His name is a good fit
for the man Luke describes.

He was a Levite from Cyprus (Acts 4:36). As a Levite, he was
a descendant of Levi, Jacob and Leah's son. We don't know if he
was a Gershonite, Kohathite, or Merarite Levite (1 Chron 6:17).
The Levites represented the firstborn of the nation set apart
for God for the Passover (Num 3:40–51; Exod 13:1–2). They
were mainly custodians of worship, with duties based on clan.

Whereas priests are strictly from Aaron's line, Levites are from the wider tribal descent. Swann notes that there

is little indication of bitterness or tension between the Levites and the priests. A symbiotic relationship between the Levites and the priests continued in the postexilic era—the Levites' primary duties were to guard the places of worship and the priests (see Neh 12:44–47).[7]

Meyer notes that their duties are primarily liturgical, either leading worship and singing, reading Scripture, policing the temple, keeping the doors, assisting in sacrifices, and participation in community governance.[8] Interestingly, Levites could not possess land, yet Luke records that Barnabas generously sold some land to provide money for the poor in the Jerusalem Church. This could indicate that Barnabas was not living strictly, but more likely suggests that Levitical land ownership was now permitted.[9] Whatever the case, his preparedness to sell land to contribute to the needs of the poor in the Jerusalem church shows both his generosity and how Jesus had captured his heart (Acts 4:37).

His goodness is seen in the way he took Paul under his wing in Jerusalem after his time in Damascus and Arabia and brought him to Peter and Jacob (Acts 9:27, cf. Gal 1:18). He was later sent from Jerusalem to Antioch and sought out Saul from Tarsus, and together they worked in the Antiochian church (Acts 11:22–25). He and Saul are together on this trip, likely to deliver the Antiochian Jerusalem Collection.

They returned from Jerusalem to Antioch with John Mark (his cousin, below), and he and Saul/Paul worked in the church with other leaders (Acts 13:1). Due to the leading of the Spirit, Mark, Barnabas, and Saul/Paul, set out on the first Antiochian mission (Acts 13:2), first traveling to his home island Cyprus where they

7. J. T. Swann, 'Levites,' in *LBD*.
8. R. Meyer, 'Λευ(ε)ίτης,' in *TDNT* 4:239–41.
9. J. B. Polhill, *Acts*, NAC 26 (Nashville: Broadman & Holman Publishers, 1992), 154 who notes Jeremiah owned land (Jer 32:6–15). See also B. Witherington III, *The Acts of the Apostles: A Socio-Rhetorical Commentary* (Grand Rapids, MI: Eerdmans, 1998), 209 who notes also Josephus, *Life* 68–83.

ministered and then to the Galatian region to which Paul writes. Luke names Paul and Barnabas together, so it seems they shared ministry responsibilities (Acts 13:7, 43, 50; 14:14, 20) including some preaching (Acts 13:46), although Luke sees Paul as the chief speaker (Acts 14:12). In Lystra, after the healing of the man lame from birth, he is labeled Zeus, indicating his seniority, while Paul was identified as Hermes as he is the keynote speaker (Acts 14:12). Luke also uses the plural 'apostles' twice in Acts 14 of Barnabas along with Paul, perhaps indicating that Barnabas was accepted (at least by Luke) into the apostolic guild (Acts 14:4, 14).

On their return from the trip, Barnabas and Paul clashed with Judaizers who are likely the same group that came to Galatia. As a result, the pair traveled to Jerusalem for the Jerusalem Council (Acts 15:2) where he and Paul shared their mission experiences (Acts 15:12). They returned to Antioch with Judas Barsabbas and Silas (Acts 15:22, 25), and remained there for some time (Acts 15:35).

Deciding to return to the Galatian churches, Luke records that Barnabas and Paul clashed over John Mark's return to Jerusalem in Perga (Acts 15:36). Barnabas wanted to take John Mark which Paul resisted. Clearly, neither Paul nor Barnabas were perfect. Not finding agreement, they separated their mission efforts with Paul heading to Galatia and Barnabas and John Mark going to Cyprus (Acts 15:39). He is not mentioned in Acts after this event. It is possible that he traveled to Corinth at some point (1 Cor 9:6). The only other mention is Col 4:10 where we learn he is a cousin of Mark, who appears to be reunited with Paul in Rome some years later (Col 4:10).

Barnabas is mentioned by Clement of Alexandria, who believed Barnabas was one of the seventy-two in Luke 10 (*Strom.* 2.20). Tertullian considered that Barnabas is the author of Hebrews (*Pud.* 20), which makes good sense as the letter reflects much Pauline thought but is very interested in Levitical and OT ideas. Two later works are attributed to him. First, the *Acts of Barnabas* bears his name and was supposedly written by John Mark. However, it is likely written pseudonymously in the fifth century. The *Letter of Barnabas* is a pseudonymous second-century work, although Clement of Alexandria thought it was original to Barnabas.[10] Here, he is with Paul on this trip to Jerusalem. His presence does little to decide whether this is Acts 11 or Acts 15, as Luke states, he went on both trips.

ENSURING THE GOSPEL IS NOT IN VAIN (2:2)

In *Galatians 2:2*, Paul continues:

And (*de*, 1:15) **I went up** (aorist *anabainō*, 2:1) **in accordance with** (*kata*, 1:4) **a revelation** (*apokalypsis*, 1:12) **and** (*kai*, 1:1) **privately** (*kat idian* [*kata*, 1:4, plus the feminine of *idios*])[11] **set before** (aorist middle *anatithēmi*)[12] **them** (dative plural *autos*, 1:1) **the gospel** (*euangelion*, 1:6) **that I preach** (present *kērussō*)[13] **among** (*en*, 1:6) **the gentiles** (*ethnos*, 1:16) **to those seeming to be of repute** (present participle *dokeō*),[14] **lest** (*mē*, 1:7 plus *pōs*)[15] **I am running** (present *trechō*)[16] **or have run** (aorist *trechō*) **in** (*eis*, 1:1) **vain** (*kenos*).[17]

---

10. See further on Barnabas, A. K. Tresham, 'Barnabas,' in *LBD*.

11. The adjective ἴδιος (*idios*), indicates what belongs to oneself, 'own.' It is found thrice in Galatians: 'privately' or 'by myself' (*kat idian*) (2:2); one's own load (6:5); 'in one's own time' or 'at the time that is appropriate' (6:9).

12. The only reference to the verb ἀνατίθημι (*anatithēmi*) is found in Gal 2:2. Here, it has the sense of 'communicate, refer, declare' (BDAG 73).

13. The proclamatory verb κηρύσσω (*kēryssō*) is found twice in Galatians, 2:2; 5:11. It is a synonym with *euangelizomai*, used seven times in the letter (also *proeuangelizomai* in 3:8). It has the sense of 'herald' the gospel.

14. The cognitive verb δοκέω (*dokeō*) is used five times in Galatians. It is a thinking word, but with a particular nuance of subjective knowledge or opinion, 'seem, suppose.' It is used of 'the *seeming* ones' referring to 'those *seeming* to be something' (2:2) and again in 2:9, of those '*seeming* to be pillars.' In Gal 6:3, 'if anyone *supposes* he/she is something, when he/she is nothing, he/she deceives oneself.'

15. The particle πώς (*pōs*) is an indefinite particle signifying 'how, somehow,' and it is used twice in Galatians each time in the construct μὴ πως (*mē pōs*), 'not how,' which suggests 'a negative perspective expressing misgiving' and is best translated, 'lest' (2:2: 'lest I am running ...' 2:2; 4:1: 'lest I may have labored over you in vain').

16. The verb τρέχω (*trechō*) is an athletic term meaning 'run.' Paul uses it three times in relation to the Christian life (which he often calls a 'walk,' *parakaleō*). In 2:2 he uses it in the present and aorist subjunctive of his Christian ministry among the Galatians. In 5:7 he uses it of the Galatians life of faith as a race, in which they were running well, but have been hindered by 'the cheating Judaizers.' It has the sense we often hear today, of someone's 'journey.'

Paul says again that he went *up to* Jerusalem (see on 1:18), referring to the second visit mentioned in the previous verse. 'In accordance with a revelation' uses the same language (verb) as 1:12 (see further on *apokalypsis* 1:12), whereby he received the gospel 'by a revelation (noun) of Jesus Christ' (cf. 1:16, 'to reveal his Son'). Here, it refers to a different event. We know of a stunning revelation Paul received fourteen years before the writing of 2 Corinthians in AD 56, so around AD 42, in which he was caught up to the third heaven, to paradise, where he heard astonishing things (2 Cor 12:1–7). However, this revelation does not fit the chronology of Galatians nor Paul's trips to Jerusalem. As already argued, a far better alternative is Agabus' prophecy that there would be a widespread famine (Acts 11:28). However, this could equally be another revelatory experience Paul had of which we know no more than this.

As a result of this revelation, he set before[18] them his gospel that he preaches among the gentiles. 'Them' is vague but clarified by what follows—'the seeming ones' (cf. 2:6, 'those seeming to be something;' 2:9, 'those seeming to be pillars'). As such, it is set before those who had been apostles with Jesus and may include some other disciples (like Jesus' brothers) and the elders of the church (see Acts 11:30, cf. Acts 15:2). So then, this includes at least Peter, Jacob, and John, who are all named in v. 9.

Paul's description of them as 'those seeming (*dokeō*) to be of repute' is intriguing. *Dokeō* is a cognitive verb which highlights subjective opinion rather than more concrete terms like *oida* and *gnōskō*. Plato philosophically distinguished between the way things actually are and the way they seem (Plato, *Resp.* 2.361b/ 362a).[19]

Paul uses it eighteen times always with a subjective edge of a view of oneself as wise (1 Cor 3:18), one who claims knows

---

17. The noun κενός (*kenos*) is literally 'empty,' and is used once in 2:2 of Paul running in vain, i.e., to no avail, with no positive outcome, 'in vain.' The synonym *eike* is found in 3:4 and 4:11.

18. *Anatithēmi* is used once else in the NT, of Festus laying Paul's case before King Agrippa II (Acts 25:14). This is forensic, and it may have a forensic sense.

19. G. Kittel, 'δοκεʹω,' in *TDNT* 2:232.

something (1 Cor 8:2), one who is self-confident (1 Cor 10:12), one who considers being contentious with Paul (1 Cor 11:16), a person who considers him/herself a prophet (1 Cor 14:37), those who consider Paul foolish (2 Cor 11:16), and others who consider they have reasons for confidence in the flesh (Phil 3:4). He employs it of the parts of the body that *seem* weaker or less honorable (1 Cor 12:22, 23), and of not wanting to *seem* to be frightening the Corinthians (2 Cor 10:9). Paul employs it of his own opinion including such things as apostles being last of all, people sentenced to death as a world-spectacle (1 Cor 4:9), and his view that he has the Spirit (1 Cor 7:40).

Here it is used three times in quick succession of the Jerusalem apostolic leaders who are the '*seeming* ones' (2:2, 6, 9). In 2:2, it is 'those *seeming* to be something' and in the third, 'those *seeming* to be pillars' clarifying what he has in mind in 2:2. This carries the sense of 'seeming to be influential' (ESV), 'those who held in high regard.' Later, in 6:3, he will again use it of 'anyone who thinks he is something when he is nothing' being guilty of self-deception. Here in Ch. 2, the verb has the sense of those held 'to be of repute.'[20] We find this kind of idea in Mark 10:42: 'those *seeming* to be (*hoi dokountes*) rulers of the gentiles.'

While the language is not necessarily ironic or facetious,[21] Paul is using it here to speak of the way that these people are perceived by others rather than his own actual view. Paul is not necessarily trying to denigrate the Jerusalem Apostles but contrasts them with the way he is being viewed by his opponents who see him not as a 'seeming one,' while they esteem the Jerusalem Apostles. Rather, he is to be repudiated as inferior. However, as he is here narrating, there is no reason for him to be differently viewed as he has seen the risen Christ, been commissioned by him, and has had his gospel and apostolic status and ministry accepted by the so-called 'seeming ones.'[22] He is in fact, one of those who 'seems to be something' and a 'pillar'

---

20. Kittel, 'δοκε´ω,' in 232. He notes Josephus, *Ant.* 19.307; *J.W.* 4.141, 159.
21. Kittel, 'δοκε´ω,' 233.
22. Similarly, Moo, *Galatians*, 124.

and so should be listened to rather than the Judaizers who keep putting him down.

The gospel Paul refers to is also vague. If we take Acts as constitutive, we have messages of Paul at Lystra (Acts 14:15–17), Pisidian Antioch among the Galatians at the synagogue (13:16–41), to the Areopagus in Athens (Acts 17:22–31), and before various authorities (Acts 22:3–21; 24:10–21; 25:8–11; 26:2–29). These are extremely diverse including a classical salvation-historical message in Antioch, reference to Greco-Roman philosophy and religion in Lystra and Athens, and testimonies in his defenses.

Arguably, the closest to 'a Pauline gospel' is Romans, although this is shaped to the context he is addressing. Likely, Romans helps us, as many of the same key issues dominate Romans as in Galatians—grace, faith, not law, righteousness/justification, the Spirit, and so on. The particular question at hand appears to be the required response to the gospel—does a person need to enter the family of God through the Jewish covenantal boundary markers, particularly circumcision? Or is faith enough? However, as this encounter precedes both Galatians and Romans, it may have been a more general conversation of the gospel in relation to the Jewish understanding. Certainly, the gospel as per the law would have been central to this discussion, as would the required response.

'That I proclaim' uses a different verb of proclamation to *euangelizomai* used consistently to this point in the letter (1:8, 9, 11, 16, 23, cf. 4:13), *kēryssō*. *Kērussō* speaks of the proclamation of a herald. It is used in the LXX more extensively than *euangelizomai* (sixty-one times), including the proclamation of Aaron (Exod 32:5). It is also used of heralds of significant political figures, especially kings.[23]

---

23. Including Moses (Exod 36:6), Jehu (2 Kings 10:20), Jehoshaphat (2 Chron 20:3), Joash (2 Chron 24:9), Cyrus (2 Chron 36:22; 1 Esdr 2:2), Ahasuerus (Add Esth 6:9, cf. 6:11), the king of Nineveh (Jon 3:7), and Nebuchadnezzar (Dan 3:4). It is also used of prophets heralding God's word to Israel (Hos 5:8; Mic 3:5; Joel 2:1, 15; 3:9; Jon 1:2; 3:2, 4, 5) and the Messiah (Isa 61:1). See also Zech 9:9; 1 Macc 5:49; 10:63, 6, cf. Acts 15:21.

Outside of Paul in the NT, it connotes a messenger heralding the reign of God whether the prophet John, Jesus, an angel, or disciples, who will herald the gospel 'throughout the whole world' as Paul is now doing.[24] Luke uses it of Paul's heralding ministry (Acts 9:20; 19:13; 20:35; 28:31).[25]

Paul employs it nineteen times of Jewish preaching (Rom 2:21), false preaching (2 Cor 11:4), and of gospel preaching by apostles and others,[26] and of his own preaching (1 Cor 9:27). He makes use of it again in 5:11 of his own preaching, which decidedly does not include circumcision, despite claims to the contrary. Hence, it speaks of the gospel he is commissioned by Jesus Christ the Lord to herald.

'Among the gentiles' refers to the nations beyond Israel. At the time of Paul, this encompassed significant swathes of land. He was likely conscious of Europe north to Britain as Caesar had attacked it fifty years before Christ and Claudius had invaded it merely a few years before Galatians in AD 43. There is good evidence that Europe to Scandinavia was well known. To the northeast and east India was recognized (supposedly evangelized by Thomas), and China (*Sēres*). To the south, there is substantial awareness of large parts of Africa.[27] For Josephus for example, the 'ends of the earth' to the north included the Germans and Scythians; to the west, Gades in Spain (*J.W.* 2.363); to the south, Ethiopia (E.g., *J.W.* 2.382); and to the east, India (*J.W.* 2.385) and China (*Sēres, Ant.* 1.147).[28] Paul was then commissioned by God to lead the mission of the gospel to these areas. What a challenge!

24. See Matt 24:14; Mark 13:10; Luke 24:47, cf. Matt 26:13; Mark 14:9; 16:15, 20.
25. In detail: of John the Baptist (Matt 3:1; Mark 1:4, 7; Luke 4:3); Jesus (Matt 4:17; 9:35; 11:1; Mark 1:14, 38; Luke 4:18, 19, 44; 8:1; Acts 10:37; 1 Pet 3:19); an angel (Rev 5:2), or disciples (Matt 10:7, 27; Mark 1:45; 3:14; 5:20; 6:12; 7:36; Luke 8:39; 9:2; 12:3; Acts 8:5; 10:42; see also the texts of global mission above).
26. See Rom 10:8, 14, 15; 1 Cor 1:23; 15:11, 12; 2 Cor 1:19; 4:5; 11:4; Phil 1:15; Col 1:23; 1 Thess 2:9; 1 Tim 3:16; 2 Tim 4:2.
27. Schnabel, *Mission*, 1:444–99, e.g., the *Peutinger Table*, likely based on first-century sources, is a map from Britain to China. Pliny the Elder (a.d. 23/24–79) describes an area including large parts of Europe including Spain, Gaul, and Germany; the Russian Steppe area (e.g., Scythians with uncountable numbers of tribes); north Africa; and west including India, China (*Sēres*), and the Malay Peninsula.
28. Schnabel, *Mission*, 1:468–69.

Thus far, he had ventured into Syria, Cilicia, and the regions of his first Antiochian mission journey into Asia Minor (the recipients of this letter). Much remained to do including the rest of Asia Minor, Macedonia, Achaia, and Rome—these he evangelized on his second and third Antiochian missions (Acts 16–20). Beyond that lay the lands west to Spain (they did not know of the Americas), which he planned to reach after Rome (Rom 15:24, 28), although it is unclear whether he ever made it there.

It is often argued Paul expected an imminent Parousia and that by the time of Romans in the later 50s, he believed the job was done. This is ridiculous, as the Roman Empire spanned only a small part of the known world and huge areas north, south, and east remained untouched (and perhaps even Spain still). Paul knew he would never get the job done, but he was heaven-bent on getting as much done as he could with this strategy of planting churches in key urban contexts beginning among the Jews, and the gospel being extended by his converts.[29]

At this stage of his missionary career, with much left to do, it was essential he established that his gospel was on the button, 'lest I am running and have run in vain.' *Mē pos* is a strictly Pauline clause in the NT that conveys misgiving and often translated 'lest.'[30] Here it conveys 'lest,' 'in the hope that I did not ...,' or 'somehow I did not run ...' In 4:11, he expresses a similar misgiving over the Galatians, this time using a business metaphor, 'labored' (*kopiaō*): 'I am afraid lest (that I may have) I labored over you in vain (*eikē*).'

'Vain' is *kenos*, which comes from a set of terms which speak of 'empty.' It can have a literal sense of 'empty-handed' (Mark 12:3; Luke 20:10) or the rich being empty (Luke 1:53). Jacob uses it of an empty person (foolish, Jas 2:20), and Luke applies

---

29. See M. J. Keown, 'An Imminent Parousia and Christian Mission: Did the New Testament Writers Really Expect Jesus' Imminent Return?' in *Christian Origins and the Establishment of the Early Jesus Movement*, eds. Stanley E. Porter and A. W. Pitts, TENTS; ECHC 4 (Leiden: Brill, 2018), 242–64.

30. See 1 Cor 8:9; 9:27; 2 Cor 2:7; 9:4; 11:3; 12:20; 1 Thess 3:5, cf. Rom 11:21; 2 Cor 9:4.

it figuratively to the gentiles who plot against God's anointed in vain—to no avail (Acts 4:25).

Eleven of eighteen uses of *kenos* in the NT are in Paul.[31] In 1 Cor 15 he speaks of God's 'grace toward me was not *in vain*' (1 Cor 15:10, similarly 2 Cor 6:1), and of Christian labor in the Lord not being *in vain* (because of the resurrection)—it is worthwhile, it brings eternal reward (1 Cor 15:58). On three other occasions, he uses it in a manner similar to this. In 1 Cor 15:14, he states that if Christ has not been raised, then Christian preaching and faith is *kenos*—empty, worthless, valueless achieving nothing, 'to no avail,' 'in vain' (1 Cor 15:14). In 1 Thessalonians, while his coming to Thessalonica was 'not in *vain* (*kenos*)' (1 Thess 2:1), he expresses concern that Satan had drawn the Thessalonians into temptation and 'our labor (*kopos*, cf. Gal 4:11) would be in *vain* (*kenos*)' (1 Thess 3:5). In Philippians 2:16 Paul pairs running (used here) and laboring (in Gal 4:11) in a statement concerning the Philippians ongoing gospel engagement: 'so that in the day of Christ I may boast that I did not run in vain or labor in *vain* (*kenos*).'

Here in 2:2, his sentiment is similar. In terms of the metaphor, this does not mean that Paul will not finish the race himself, but that the Galatians will not press on to win the prize for which they have been called heavenward. They will fail to finish and will not receive the wreath. Paul himself is confident that he will finish, but if they turn away, he will no longer be able to boast about the Galatians before God. Worse still, they will fall short and be destroyed. Hence, he places the gospel he preaches before the Jerusalem leaders to make sure that what he preached was 'kosher,' so that those whom he considered had come to Christ (including the Galatians) were indeed God's people. Otherwise, he would be running and have run 'to no avail.'

Paul loves the athletic metaphor, not because Jews were into athletics, for indeed devoted Jews repudiated athletics as idolatrous, but because of its popularity across the Greco-Roman world. Among non-Jews, athletics was a prime source of

---

31. Other uses include uses include 'empty words' (Eph 5:6) and 'empty deceit' (Col 2:8).

entertainment, with the PanHellenic Games (Olympic, Pythian, Namean, and Isthmian) held regularly throughout the Empire.[32] As such, as it is in our culture, it was a ready-made metaphor for the Christian life. There are hints of this in the OT used of those who 'run the way of your commandments' (Ps 118:32 [Eng. 119:32]), of God's word running swiftly (Ps 147:4)—an idea Paul employs (2 Thess 3:1)—and of seven martyred brothers 'running the course toward immortality' (4 Macc 14:5).

The writer of Hebrews is the only other NT writer who also employs the running metaphor.[33] He urges Christians to run with perseverance the race set before them with eyes fixed on Jesus' (Heb 12:1–2). Paul uses it of human effort to please God (Rom 9:16). He likens the Christian life to a race, urging the Corinthians to run toward the prize of immortality so as to win, with self-control, and not aimlessly (1 Cor 9:24–26)—with discipline including bodily control. He speaks of his own ministry as a 'run' (Phil 2:16) and of the word 'running' (2 Thess 3:1). In Phil 3:12–14, he utilizes the hunting metaphor *diōkō* (persecute, pursue) of the Christian life as a pursuit of the prize of eternal life with Christ with all its wonderful blessings. Believers are to 'press on' to the finishing tape and to attain the receiving of the victory wreath from the Lord Jesus Christ on the rostrum.

In 5:7, he employs *diōkō* of the Galatians who, before the Judaizers *cut in on them,* 'were *running* well.' In light of its pagan associations, this is a somewhat daring example of contextualization among Jews. However, it is a ready-made

32. The Olympics (776 BC onwards) were held at Olympia to honor Zeus every four years; the prize, an olive wreath. The Pythian Games were held every four years (mid Olympic cycle) in Delphi to honor Apollo; the prize, a laurel wreath. The Namean Games were held every two years in Nemea, Corinthia, in honor of Zeus and Heracles; the prize, wild celery. The Isthmian Games were held in Isthmia Sicyon every two years in honor of Poseidon; the prize, pine. Participants came from the Greek (Roman) world at great expense with events like chariot racing, wrestling, boxing, pankration (similar to cage fighting), stadion, pentathlon (wrestling, stadion, long jump, javelin, discus), and aside from chariot racing, these sports were conducted naked. Winners were lauded with gifts and honor on return to their homes. See 'Panhellenic Games' in *Wikipedia*, https://en.wikipedia.org/wiki/Panhellenic_Games.

33. Other uses are all of people running in a literal sense (Matt 27:48; 28:8; Mark 5:6; 15:36; Luke 15:20; 24:12; John 20:2, 4; Rev 9:9).

metaphor in a gentile context conveying the effort that is implicit to the Christian life and ministry. Thankfully, God enables. He uses the term twice here in 2:2 (*trechō* [present subjunctive] and *edramon* [aorist])—these uses point to his ministry, past and present—he wanted to be sure that the gospel he had been preaching and was continuing to preach, and by implication, will preach, is the truth from God and not some corruption thereof.

TITUS NOT COMPELLED INTO CIRCUMCISION (2:3)

In *Galatians 2:3*, circumcision, the core issue, is somewhat suddenly and yet innocuously introduced:

But (*alla*, 1:1) **not even** (*oude*, 1:1) **Titus** (*Titos*, 2:1) **who** (*ho*, 1:1) [was] with (*syn*, 1:2) me (dative *egō*, 1:2), being (present participle *eimi*, 1:7) a Greek (*Hellēn*),[34] **was compelled** (aorist *anagkazō*)[35] **to be circumcised** (aorist passive *peritemnō*).[36]

This is no incidental comment as it not only introduces the core issue, circumcision, but it indicates that the Jerusalem leaders did not demand the circumcision of Titus. This is hardly surprising, as the Roman soldier Cornelius and his family had received the Spirit despite the men of the house not being circumcised (Acts 10:45–46).

---

34. The noun Ἕλλην (*Hellēn*), from which we get terms like Hellenism (Helen, etc.), is found twice in Galatians. First, here it is used of Titus who is a Greek, and second, of the body of Christ in which there is no distinction between Jew and Greek (3:28). In the latter use, it carries the same force as 'gentile.'

35. The verb ἀναγκάζω (*anagkazō*) carries the sense of force, compulsion, or to strongly urge or press upon someone (BDAG 60). It is used three times in Galatians. First, here it is used of Titus who was not compelled to be circumcised (2:3). Whereas, in 2:14, it is applied of Peter inadvertently compelling gentiles to live like Jews. In 6:12, it is used of the Judaizers who compel the Galatian gentiles to be circumcised.

36. The verb περιτέμνω (*peritemnō*), compounds *peri* (around) and *temnō* (cut—a term not found in the NT) and so it literally means to 'cut around.' It is used six times in Galatians, indicating its importance, of: Titus not compelled to be circumcised (2:3), in 5:2–3, twice in Paul's insistence that the Galatians do not be circumcised or else Christ is of no avail to them as they will be obligated to keep the whole law. In 6:12–13, it is used thrice of the Judaizers who compel the Galatians to be circumcised, even though they do not obey the law themselves, and want to boast over the Galatians' circumcision.

Titus (*Titos*) is mentioned here. Surprisingly, he is not referred to outside of the Pauline epistles including Acts despite playing a significant role in Paul's Jerusalem Collection trip. He is particularly prominent in 2 Corinthians, which is written during the third Antiochian mission from Macedonia (c. AD 56). This is used as support for matching Gal 2 with Acts 11, and this is not an insignificant argument as Titus is not mentioned in Paul's early ministry. Still, this is not conclusive evidence when other factors are considered.

In 2 Corinthians, Paul indicates that Titus was not in Troas as he expected, something that caused him great concern (2 Cor 2:13). Hence, he went on to Macedonia in search of him and found him after Titus had been to Corinth (2 Cor 7:6, 13, 14). It seems he was sent on ahead from Macedonia to Corinth with other significant gospel figures (2 Cor 8:7, 16, 23; 12:18). In Galatians, at the point Paul narrates, he is with Paul and Barnabas as they go to Jerusalem. In Titus 1:4, he is in Crete and the recipient of the letter (likely toward the end of Paul's life). Finally, he is mentioned in 2 Tim 4:10 where he had gone to Dalmatia on the eve of Paul's death.[37]

We know nothing of his origins, although it is speculated that he was from Syrian Antioch,[38] which is an educated guess as it is from Antioch that he and Barnabas traveled to Jerusalem. In reality, he could be from anywhere that Paul has ministered including Antioch in Syria, Cilicia (including Tarsus), or even Galatia. For example, he may have brought news to Paul of the Judaizing problem in Galatia. Wherever he is from, he is clearly much loved by Paul. He describes him as a 'brother' (2 Cor 2:13). Paul is prepared to abandon an opportunity to preach the gospel in Troas to find him when he is not there (2 Cor 2:13). He is described as having joy and earnestness (2 Cor 7:13; 8:6, 16). He is a partner (*koinōnos*) and co-worker (*synergos*), terms reserved

---

37. Dalmatia is a mountainous region on the eastern shore of the Adriatic Sea across from Italy and part of the province of Illyricum which Paul reached in his missions prior to Romans in AD 57 (Rom 15:19). The region is part of modern Croatia. See Major Contributors and Editors, 'Dalmatia,' in *LBD*.

38. R. Lokkesmoe, 'Titus,' in *LBD*.

for those who are in a close missional relationship with Paul. In the Jerusalem Collection visit, he played a key role, especially in Corinth, treating the Corinthians with integrity (2 Cor 12:18). In the letter to Titus, he is described as his true or legitimate (*gnēsios*) child in the common faith. This could indicate he is a convert of Paul[39] and certainly speaks of his genuineness and close relationship.

His mention in Paul's first letter (Galatians) in the late 40s (as this commentary argues), Corinthians in the middle of the 50s, and Titus in the early 60s indicate that he was with Paul through much of his ministry. In later tradition, supposedly, Titus was appointed bishop of the churches of Crete (Eusebius, *Eccl. hist.* 3.4). This is uncertain and likely a backreading of the role of individual bishops in the next century.

Titus is described as a Greek, which can mean that he is from Greece itself, or as the term is most commonly used in the NT and often in contrast to 'Jews' (see Gal 3:28),[40] he is a gentile. Here, the key point is that he is not a Jew, and therefore, uncircumcised, with circumcision normally repudiated by non-Jews.

He was not forced to be circumcised uses *anagkazō*, a term which indicates compulsion with varying degrees of force. Sometimes, it is used in a softer sense of legitimate compulsion, such as Jesus telling his disciples to get into a boat (Matt 14:22; Mark 6:45), a servant urging people to come into the banquet (Luke 14:23), or Paul feeling compelled to appeal to the Caesar (Acts 28:19). Paul uses it ironically, of the Corinthians forcing him to have to boast like a fool (2 Cor 12:11). At other times, it is stronger, used of illegitimate force such as forcing people to blaspheme Christ (Acts 26:11). In that circumcision is a painful operation that makes most men wince at the very thought, this is the sense in its three uses in Galatians—of gentiles being forced

---

39. Lokkesmoe, 'Titus.'
40. There is actually no certain example of the term *Hēllēn* being used of a Greek per se. On occasion it is ambiguous, e.g., Acts 16:1, 3; 17:4. Generally, it is clearly a synonym for gentile: John 7:35; 12:20; Acts 14:1; 18:4; 19:10; 20:21; 21:28. In Paul: Rom 1:14, 16; 2:9, 10; 3:9; 10:12; 1 Cor 1:2, 24; 10:32; 12:13; Col 3:11.

to live as Jews and to be circumcised (cf. 2:14; 6:12). Paul is thankful that Titus was not so forced. This indicates that his law-free gospel had gained acceptance in Jerusalem. The Jerusalem leaders were not Judaizers.

The term for circumcision here is *peritemnō*, meaning 'cut around,' which can also mean to cut around something like a person's neck.[41] However, here it clearly means to cut around the penis to remove the foreskin—circumcise. Although modern historians question this, according to ancient Greek historians who were much more proximate to the times, the Jewish practice of circumcision can be traced to Egypt.[42] They mention other nations who practiced it including the Colchi east of the Black Sea,[43] the Troglodytes of north Africa (Diodorus Siculus, *Hist*, 3.32.4), the Ethiopians, the Phoenicians, and the Syrians (Herodotus, *Hist*. 2.104.2–4).

The practice is central to the Jewish faith, with the Abrahamic covenant requiring every Jewish male to undergo circumcision on day eight.[44] Any male convert (proselyte) must be circumcised to be accepted into the covenant people. As such, the Jews are called 'the circumcised' or 'the circumcision,' i.e., the Jewish people including those in Palestine and the world (Gal 2:7–9; Eph 2:11; 4:11).

Both Jesus (Luke 2:21, cf. Luke 1:59) and Paul (Phil 3:5) were circumcised, and we can assume this of every other Jewish male Christian in the NT. The act was repudiated as barbaric by the Greeks and Romans. As such, it is not surprising that it was a massive issue in the NT church. Jesus never gave instructions on circumcision, so it was left to the church to work it through. As with other core Jewish rites such as Sabbath, festivals, food laws, and purity laws, which Jesus did not demand his followers adhere to, circumcision for Paul, Barnabas, and others working

---

41. See Diodorus Siculus, *Hist*. 3.39.9; Appian *Bell. civ.* 1.71; Herodotus, *Hist*. 4.64.2.

42. See Herodotus, *Hist*. 2.36.3 (fifth-century BC); Diodorus Siculus, *Hist*. 1.28.3 (60–30 BC); Strabo, *Geogr*. 17.2.5 (64/63 BC-AD 24).

43. See Diodorus Siculus, *Hist*. 1.55.5; Herodotus, *Hist*. 2.104.2.

44. See Gen 17:10–14, 23–27; 21:4; Exod 12:44, 48; Lev 12:3; Josh 5:2–7; John 7:22–23; Acts 7:8.

in gentile mission, was not a requirement. Paul reasoned that God's grace was sufficient. All that is required is faith for the circumcised and the uncircumcised alike (Rom 3:30; 4:9–12). As such, as he preached through the churches of Galatia, he did not expect his converts to be circumcised, nor did he want them to seek to remove the marks of circumcision if already circumcised (epispasm) (cf. 1 Cor 7:18–19). Now, they were being challenged by Judaizers who believed that faith was not enough—one *had* to be circumcised. As such, one had to become a Jew and yield to works for justification. For Paul, as with Deuteronomy and Jeremiah, to be circumcised is a matter of the heart.[45]

Paul believes that a Jew being circumcised was something cultural and legitimate in those terms. However, for a Christian to be circumcised at the beckoning of the circumcision party as necessary for salvation and inclusion in God's covenant people is to enter into the Jewish system that is now completed and continuing in Christ. That is, it is to enter a system that has no power to save or transform. It has had its day so to speak.

The circumcision party had come to Galatia demanding that these new converts be circumcised (2:12; 6:12–13, cf. Tit 1:10). But to be so as an entry marker to God's people means reliance on law and, therefore, Christ is of no benefit, for one becomes a Jew and enters the Jewish religious system and must obey the whole law to be justified before God (5:2–3).

For Paul, circumcision (being a Jew) and uncircumcision (being a gentile) count for nothing; what matters is faith working through love (5:6) and a new creation (6:15). As previously noted, one of the charges against Paul is that he preached circumcision on occasions but not on others (Acts 16:1–3), so as to win converts—i.e., he was fickle with the gospel. He turns this on his head, repudiating this for if so, the offense of the cross is removed (Gal 5:11). In Philippians, he goes even further, calling the church, male and female, Jew and gentile, 'the circumcision.' That is, in Christ, Christians are the true circumcised people of God—those in God by faith saved in the circumcised one (Phil

---

45. See Deut 10:16; 30:6; Jer 4:4; Rom 2:25–29.

3:3). In a sense, just as Christ's death is ours by faith, so is Christ's circumcision. Another nuance is that Christians are circumcised of the heart with a spiritual circumcision by faith, signified by baptism (Col 2:11–12).

Unlike Timothy, who is a Jew and is circumcised for missional reasons so that he can be a Jew among Jews and share Christ, Titus has no need to be circumcised. For Titus to be circumcised is to remove him from reliance on Christ and the cross and place him in the old system, which was good while it lasted, but not good enough to deal with sin forever. Now that Christ has come, it is superfluous. If one enters the Jewish system, one becomes a Jew and relies on the law and so on self-righteousness. This cannot justify. Only Christ can. By faith.

This does not mean every Jew living prior to Christ is lost. Abraham was 'justified by faith.' By analogy, every Jew or non-Jew who had that faith is also justified, his/her faith reckoned to him as righteousness. However, this is achieved in and through Christ, whose death justifies all humans who have saving faith in God before, during, and after his earthly life (Rom 4; Gal 3).

THE DECEITFUL JUDAIZERS (2:4)

In *Galatians 2:4–5*, using a range of rare biblical words, Paul describes the infiltration of false Christians, Judaizers, and Paul and his team's refusal to yield to them for the sake of the Galatians:

But (de, 1:15) **because** (dia, 1:1) **of false brothers** (plural *pseudadelphos*)[46] **who sneaked in** (*pereisaktos*)[47]—**those** (*hostis*)[48]

---

46. The ψευδάδελφος (*pseudadelphos*) compounds *pseudēs* (false, lying, cf. Acts 6:14, Rev 2:2; 21:8) and *adelphos* (brother, cf. 1:1) and so means, 'false brother.' It is found once in Galatians, in 2:4, and in 2 Cor 11:26 where Paul says he is ever in 'danger from *false brothers*.' The meaning is clear—those who claim to be Christians but are false (pseudo-Christians). In Galatians, these are the Judaizers.

47. The noun παρεισέρχομαι (*pereisaktos*) is found once in Galatians and once in the whole NT. In fact, it is super-rare. In a Bible Word Study in Logos, it is found once else in the Greek literature available to Logos in Strabo, *Geogr.* 17.1.8, as a nickname for Ptolemy IX Alexander I who became ruler against the wishes of the people and was nicknamed *Pereisactus*, 'usurper.' In Gal 2:4 it has the sense 'those secretly bought

who slipped in (*pareiserchomai*)'[49] **to spy on** (*kataskopeō*)[50] **the freedom** (*eleutheria*)[51] **we** (plural *egō*, 1:2) **have** (present *echō*)[52] **in Christ** (*en Christō*, 1:22), **in order** (*hina*, 1:16) **to enslave** (future *katadouloō*),[53] **us** (plural *egō*)—**to them** (dative *hos*)[54] **not even** (*oude*, 1:1)[55] **for** (*pros*, 1:17) **a moment** (*hōra*)[56] **did we yield** (aorist

in.' It is related to *pareisagō* which can mean 'I bring forward,' 'I present,' 'I introduce' neutrally, but more commonly of something unlawful and subversive, e.g., letting enemies into a city—something 'illegal, secret or unobserved.' The verb is found in 2 Pet 2:1 of false prophets (*pseudoprophētai*) who are like false teachers (*pseudodidaskaloi*) who secretly (*pareisagō*) bring in destructive heresies. In Gal 2:4, *pareisaktos*, a verbal adjective, has the same sense of their infiltrating the Christian community. See W. Michaelis, 'παρει´σακτος,' in *TDNT* 5.825–26.

48. The relative pronoun ὅστις (*hostis*) is found seven times in Galatians: 1) In the masculine plural form *hoitines* of *those men* who slipped in as false brothers (2:4), of you *who* want to be justified by the law (5:4), and *whoever* it is that is confusing the Galatians (5:10); 2) In the plural neuter *hatina*, of Hagar and Sarah forming an allegory (these) and the works of the flesh *which* are obvious (Gal 4:24, 26) and in 5:19; 3) In the feminine singular, *ētis*, conveying 'who' (4:26).

49. The verb παρεισέρχομαι (*pareiserchomai*) literally means 'come in,' as in 'the law came in' (Rom 5:2), or 'slipped in' or 'snuck in' as in 2:4. These are the only two uses in the NT.

50. The only use of κατασκοπέω (*kataskopeō*) in the NT is found in Galatians 2:4. It compounds *kata* (which as a wide range) and *skopeō*, 'watch, look for, notice,' used more commonly. It means to 'spy out.'

51. The noun ἐλευθερία (*eleutheria*) is a Greek word meaning 'freedom,' used four times in Galatians. It speaks of the freedom from law, sin, and death in Christ (2:4; 5:1). Those called to this freedom, are not to use it for the flesh, but for love. Paul also uses *eleutheros* of 'free' in contrast to slavery (3:28) and in the Sarah/Hagar allegory (4:22, 23, 26, 30, 31). See discussion on 3:28.

52. The common verb ἔχω (*echō*), 'have, hold,' is found five times in Galatians, all in the sense 'have' (has, had, have): 'the freedom we *have* in Christ' (2:4), 'Abraham *had* two sons' (4:22), 'the one who *has* a husband' (4:27), 'the boast he *has*' (6:4), and 'as we *have* time.'

53. The verb καταδουλόω (*katadouloō*), which compounds *kata* (which as a wide range) with *douloō*, 'enslave,' and has the sense of 'bring into slavery.' It is found only in 2:4 and elsewhere in 2 Cor 11:20.

54. This is an example of a parenthetic nominative whereby the subject of an explanatory clause **within** another clause.' (Emphasis his). In this case the subject is found in 2:4, the false brothers. See Wallace, *Greek Grammar*, 53.

55. **Variant**: There are five readings for 'to them not' (*ois oude*). However, the wide support makes it certain to be original with the other readings unlikely (*ois; oude*; omit; omit *ois oude ... hypotagē*).

56. The common Greek term ὥρα (*hōra*) indicating 'hour, time,' is used once of Paul and his team not yielding to the Judaizers for an 'hour,' or a moment (2:5).

eikō)[57] **in submission** (dative *hypatagē*),[58] **so that** (*hina*) **the truth** (*alētheia*)[59] **of the gospel** (genitive *euangelion*, 1:6) **might remain** (aorist subjunctive *diamenō*)[60] **with** (*pros*, 1:17) **you** (plural *egō*).

Here Paul narrates how false brothers, pseudo-Christians secretly slipped into their gatherings. The verb *pareisaktos* and associated verb *pareiskagō* are very rare. The verb is used in 2 Peter 2:1–2 of 'false prophets (*pseudoprophētes*) who arose among the people' of Israel. 'Likewise, there will be false teachers (*pseudodidaskalos*) among' Peter's recipients' context. They 'will secretly bring in (*pareisagō*) destructive heresies, even denying the Master who brought them ....' There are similarities with Peter's thought here, with *pseudo*-language alongside *pereisaktos*.

Pereisaktos can be neutral 'bring forward, present, introduce' but is often used for 'something unlawful and furtive' such as letting enemies into a city, introducing strange gods, the term using *eis* which suggests 'what is illegal, secret, or unobserved,'[61] i.e., secretive. As mentioned in the note on the translation, it was used of Ptolemy IX Alexander I, the unpopular usurper king (*pareisaktos*).[62] This is the stuff of thrillers, with spies sneaking into the Christian community to observe them. It also calls to mind Judas and the Jewish leaders conspiring to destroy Jesus (Mark 14:1–2, 10–11). It shows the character of Paul's

---

57. The verb εἴκω (*eikō*) is a hapax *legomenon*, found only in 2:5: Paul and his team 'did not *yield* in submission' to the Judaizers.
58. The noun ὑποταγή (*hypotagē*) (related to *hypotassō*, 'submit'), is found in 2:5 of Paul and his team not yielding in submission or subjugation to the Judaizers. Paul alone uses it of 'submission to the gospel' (2 Cor 9:13), and of wives and children (1 Tim 2:11; 3:4).
59. The noun ἀλήθεια (*alētheia*), 'truth' is found three times in Galatians either of 'the *truth* of the gospel' (2:5, 14) or 'the *truth*' (5:7). The associated verb, 'tell the *truth*' (*alētheuō*) is used in 4:16.
60. The compound of *dia* (through, because) and *menō* (stay, remain) is διαμένω (*diamenō*) which is found only in 2:5, where it speaks of the truth of the gospel 'remaining' for the Galatians. Another compound, *epimenō*, 'stay,' is used in 1:18. As in 1:18; 4:18, 20 we have a stative verb (διαμείνῃ, *diameinē*) with a transitive preposition (*pros*). See further 1:18.
61. W. Michaelis, 'παρεισάγω,' in *TDNT* 5:824–85.
62. Michaelis, 'παρεισάγω,' 824–85.

opponents; they are prepared to use subterfuge and deception. Paul repudiates such ideas elsewhere (2 Cor 4:1–2; 1 Thess 2:3).

'False brothers' uses *pseudadelphos*, a term used only once else in the NT, also by Paul in 2 Cor 11:26 in his list of sufferings, 'in danger from *false brothers*.' These false brothers in Jerusalem are the very sort of people he has in mind. He further describes them as 'those who slipped in to spy on the freedom we have in Christ Jesus.' The term warns us as Christians that it is possible to appear to be one of God's children, but in fact, we are not. Here, this is so of these people with a gospel so corrupted that it is no longer God's message. We must follow Paul's advice in 2 Cor 13:5: 'Test yourself to see if you are in the faith, examine yourself.' If we hold fast in our faith and rely on God's Spirit, we will pass the test.

'Slipped in' is *pareiserchomai*,[63] another term with *eis*, and so speaking of something secretive. It is another rare word in the NT, only found in Rom 5:20 of the 'law *coming in* to increase the trespass.'[64]

'To spy' uses *kataskopeō*, a term found only here in the NT (*hapax legomenon*) and used three times in the LXX of *spying* on a city (2 Sam 10:3), the land (1 Chron 19:3), or a camp (1 Macc 5:38). Here, it has the sense of their sneaking in to spy on the law-free Pauline Christian group.

'The freedom we have in Christ Jesus,' in Galatians speaks particularly of freedom from the law—the freedom to live by faith and not works of the law, especially circumcision, and likely focused on other boundary markers like Sabbath, kosher food, purity, and other specifically Jewish protocols. This freedom from the law is due to Christ's work. Where he is believed in, freedom from sin is generated, sin's consequences are resolved,

---

63. It compounds three Greek words: *para* (alongside), *eis* (to), and *erchomai* (come, go)—to go into get alongside, i.e., sneak into a setting to spy.

64. It is not used in the LXX. In the Pseudepigrapha, *pareiserchomai* is employed of drunkenness and shamefulness sneaking in through excessive drinking (T. Jud. 16.2) and a demon sneaking into the place where the ill lie sick and stop the recovery (T. Sol. 11.2). Philo uses it of weakness, sickness, and disease sneaking into the rational nature (*Opif.* 150), light or reason entering the soul (*Ebr.* 157), and cares entering a person's mind (*Abr.* 96).

and eternal freedom is experienced—'the freedom of the glory of the children of God' (Rom 8:21).[65] This is a freedom granted by the Spirit for 'where the Spirit of the Lord is, there is *freedom*.' The term for freedom, *eleutheria*, features in 5:1; again, in the sense of freedom from the law because in Christ, one has freedom from sin and death.

'We' here speaks of those present in the meeting but is here also inclusive of all believers who have this freedom.[66] As Paul will make clear later, believers are not to use their freedom from the law as a pretext for sin but are to live out their freedom in love (5:13, cf. 1 Pet 2:16, 19). Here, the focus is definitely on freedom from the law, to which the Judaizers seek to enslave the Galatians again (see on *katadouloō* below).

'In order to enslave us' (*katadouloō*)[67] speaks of the Judaizers' desire to compel the uncircumcised of the Pauline team and church including Titus to be circumcised. This would bring Titus under the system of law observance, which would mean he would be under the law and again enslaved to the sin, death, and destruction from which Jesus had set him free. Again, the term used is very rare in the NT, only used elsewhere by Paul of the false teachers in Corinth who 'make slaves of' the Corinthians (2 Cor 11:20). For gentiles converted to Christ to be circumcised as an act of covenantal obedience that enslaves them to the Sinai covenant and also the elemental spirits of the world from which they have been freed (4:3, 9). These are spiritual forces that are decidedly *not* from God (4:8). Those who are no longer slaves but children (4:7), born of the free woman Sarah and not Hagar

---

65. Paul also uses it in 1 Cor 10:29 of his freedom to eat as he likes. He will willingly condition his behavior where non-essential things are concerned for love's sake if his liberty causes others to stumble. He also uses *eleutheros*, 'free,' of those literally free in contrast to those in slavery (3:28; 4:22, 23, 26, 30, 31). Jacob uses *eleutheria* somewhat ironically of the 'law of freedom' (Jas 1:25; 2:12), which is likely 'the law of Moses as interpreted and supplemented by Christ' (Douglas J. Moo, *The Letter of James*, PTNC (Grand Rapids, MI; Leicester, England: Eerdmans; Apollos, 2000), 94).

66. Wallace, *Greek Grammar*, 398.

67. Wallace, *Greek Grammar*, 571 notes that this future stands in the place of an aorist subjunctive. This is the case here with καταδουλώσουσιν (*katadoulōsousin*) where one might expect an aorist subjunctive.

(4:22–31), who must not again be yoked in slavery to the law (5:1).

STANDING STRONG FOR THE GOSPEL AND GALATIANS (2:5)

'For an hour' is non-literal, and while it can carry the sense 'for a while' (John 5:35; 2 Cor 7:8; Phlm 15), here it connotes 'for a moment.'[68] The verb for yield is another *hapax legomenon*—*eikē*. It is used three times in the LXX, of the angel of death (the destroyer) yielding to Moses and Aaron (Wis 18:21, cf. Num 16:41–50), the nations yielding to Israel (Mic 7:12), and of human reason yielding to (supposedly) inferior emotions (4 Macc 1:6). It thus carries that sense of submission or surrender.

'In submission' is the indirect object of the verb. *Hypotagē* is only used by Paul in the NT, of '*submission* to the confession of the gospel of Christ' (2 Cor 9:13), a woman learning in quietness with full *submission* (1 Tim 2:11), and children submitting (1 Tim 3:14). The construction speaks of Paul's resistance to these Judaizers—not for an instant did they yield to their arguments that Titus and other gentiles must be circumcised.

Using a purposive *hina*, he gives the purpose for their refusal to yield, 'so that the truth of the gospel might remain for you.' 'The truth of the gospel' specifically focuses on its content and right response—a gospel of the grace of Christ (1:6, 7) which Paul received from Christ directly and proclaims in all places (1:11–12). Central to this is that the only response required is faith. There is no requirement of law-obedience as would be understood in Judaism. Peter violates the 'truth of the gospel' when he withdraws from table fellowship with gentiles. As such, the radical equality of all humanity before God is central to Paul's understanding. There is to be no racial superiority for God (and ideally us) has no prejudice. Jew and gentile alike stand before God as those under sin and the gospel deals with it the same way in all peoples—through the atoning work of Christ. To come

---

68. BDAG 1102.

under the law means to be prevented from 'obeying the truth' (5:7).

'Might remain for you,' uses *diameno*, compounding *dia* (through) and *meno* (remain, stay), and literally 'remain through,' i.e., is preserved or remains in place. Again, Paul employs a word rarely used in the NT, only found in Luke of Zechariah, who *remained* unable to speak' (Luke 1:22) and of those who *remained* by Jesus in his trials (Luke 22:28). Otherwise, it is employed of God's *constancy* (Heb 1:11), and all things on earth *continuing* (2 Pet 3:4). Thus, here it speaks of the gospel remaining a message of grace and not law-observance for the gentile converts of Galatia. They need not be circumcised for salvation and inclusion in God's covenant people. They must not preach a gospel to Asia calling for new converts to submit to circumcision for inclusion. There cannot be *any* ethnic privilege within their communities of faith. They cannot allow the gospel to become one of works, for one cannot be justified by works (Rom 3:20; 4:2).

THE APOSTOLIC LEADERS ADDED NOTHING TO THE GOSPEL (2:6)

Having dealt with the direct intervention of the Judaizers, or the 'circumcision party,' in *Galatians 2:6* Paul turns to the response of the prominent Christians in the Jerusalem community:

And (*de*, 1:15) **from** (*apo*, 1:1) **those seeming** (present participle *dokeo*, 2:2) **to be** (infinitive *eimi*, 1:7) **something** (neuter *tis*, 1:7)—**what sort of people** (plural nominative *hopoios*)[69] **they ever** (*pote*, 1:13) **were** (imperfect *eimi*) **[makes] not one [jot]** (*oudeis*)[70] **of difference** (*diaphero*) [71] **to me** (dative *ego*); **God**

---

69. The adjective ὁποῖος (*hopoios*) connotes 'what sort of' and is used once in 2:6, of *what sort* of Christians the Jerusalem leadership were.

70. The adjective οὐδείς (*oudeis*), 'no one' is found eight times in the letter: In 2:6 of it making 'not one' or 'no' difference to Paul; of *no one* being justified by the law (3:11), *no one* being able to nullify or add to a will once ratified (3:15). It can simply mean 'no' as in 4:1, 'no different' (4:1), 'no wrong' (4:12), 'no benefit' (5:2), or 'no other view' (5:10).

71. The compound verb διαφέρω (*diaphero*) joins *dia* (through) and *phero* (carry) and has the literal sense 'carry through' (e.g., Matt 11:16) or 'carry beyond' (Acts 27:27).

(*Theos*, 1:1)⁷² **does not** (*ou*, 1:1) **receive** (*lambanō*)⁷³ **the face** (*prosōpon*, 1:22) **of a person** (*anthrōpos*, 1:1) **(show favoritism)—for** (*gar*, 1:10) **to me** (dative *egō*) **those seeming [to be something]** (participle *dokeō*, 2:2) **contributed** (*prosanatithēmi*, 1:16) **nothing** (*oudeis*, see 2:6).

This may be a chiastic structure

A1   And from those seeming (*dokeō*) to be something.

   B1   What sort of people they ever were makes not one jot of difference to me.

   B2   God does not show favoritism.

A2   For to me those seeming to be something (participle *dokeō*) contributed nothing.

These things mark this as a possible chiasm. A and A' both use the present participle of the verb *dokeō* (seeming). B and B' both focus on impartiality and non-discrimination. B focuses on Paul's attitude that mirrors God's attitude in B'. B and B' may actually be the whole center in one statement. What calls the chiasm into question is the longer A' and B and B' having no verbal parallels.

Whether this is a chiasm or not, Paul's argument is clear. 'From those seeming to be something' recalls 2:2 (those seeming to be). Here, it is given more clarity: 'those seeming to be something.' As discussed on 2:2, this is taking the view of the Judaizers who accept the primacy of the Jerusalem Apostles and denigrate Paul. Paul's intent is not to put them down; indeed, he has met with Peter for fifteen days and is narrating a meeting with them in

---

However, the term has elided to the sense 'be unlike' or 'differ, be different.' It is found twice in Galatians. First, in 2:6, it is used where ie makes 'no *difference*' to Paul whether the Jerusalem leaders are influential or not. Second, in 4:1 of an infant being no different from a slave in terms of inheritance, although owner of everything.

72. θεὸς (*Theos*, 'God') here is another example of the parenthetic nominative where 'God shows no partiality' is 'within a larger parenthesis with its subject embedded in the verb "they were" (ἦσαν).' See further Wallace, *Greek Grammar*, 54 and 2:5.

73. The standard Koine term for 'take, receive,' λαμβάνω (*lambanō*), is found thrice in Galatians and used in two ways. First, in the interesting clause, 'God does not *receive* the face of a person.' This means God does not judge a person by external appearances; he does not show favoritism or partiality (2:6). Second, he uses it of the Galatians *receiving* the Spirit (3:2, 14).

Jerusalem where he was offered the right hand of fellowship. Rather, he is somewhat ironically stating that he should be considered one of them because the 'seeming to be ones' have vindicated him. Those in mind include at least the apostles (especially Peter), Jesus' brother Jacob, and John, and likely a broader group of those who knew Jesus directly, e.g., John Mark.

Paul drops in a caveat concerning these influential people—'what sort of people they ever were makes not one jot of difference to me.' This can sound very arrogant and negative as if Paul does not respect them. However, this is a comment on equality of status rather than a negative jibe. It also speaks to the whole problem that the Judaizers' viewpoint raises. By saying this, Paul is putting all Christians on a level playing field. No one is of superior status, certainly not because someone is a Jew or because someone knew Jesus directly. Paul is not going to base his gospel on people, no matter how great they are, for he received it directly from Christ by revelation. The gospel calls for radical equality of status among men or women, Jew and Greek, slave and free. In stating this, his intention is not to demean any person, least of all Peter, Jacob, John, and the other apostles; rather, he seeks to demonstrate the point of the letter in his attitude. As the next clause says, he is emulating God in this attitude. Further, if they are ones who seem to be of repute, so is he! They have vindicated this themselves as he is narrating.

Turning to the next sentence, Paul does not use a connective (asyndeton)[74] which causes the sentence to stand out (one might expect *gar*, 'for'). Read literally, the sentence is strange: 'a face (or an appearance) of a person God does not receive.' However, this is a Hebrew idiom whereby God does not judge a person by appearances. For example, in 1 Sam 16:7 in the LXX, God tells Samuel not to look at the physical appearance of the sons of Jesse when anointing the king 'because not as a person does God see for a person will look to the face (*prosōpon*), but God looks to the heart.'[75]

---

74. Asyndeton is 'a construction in which clauses are joined without the use of connecting particles or conjunctions.' See S. E. Porter, *Idioms of the Greek New Testament*. Sheffield: JSOT, 1999), 309. The expected particle is absent.

We get this sense in Matt 22:16 (Mark 12:14) where Herodians say to Jesus, 'you do not care about anyone's opinion, for you are *not swayed by appearances*' (lit. 'the face of a man,' *prosōpon anthrōpōn*). Similarly, in Luke 20:21, 'teacher, we know that you speak and teach rightly, and *show no partiality*' (lit. 'receive a face,' *lambaneis prosōpon*). Paul also speaks to the Corinthians of 'those who boast about outward appearance (*prosōpon*) and not what is in the heart' (2 Cor 5:12).

Romans 2:11 expresses the same idea with differing language: 'for there is no favoritism (*prosōpolēmpsia*) with God' (cf. Eph 6:9; Col 3:25; Jas 2:1; Jude 16).

God then does not judge people on appearances, but on the basis of their hearts, the quality of their faith, and character. Paul is taking the same approach to the Jerusalem rulers. What matters is the gospel, not a person's reputation.

The Judaizers in their zeal for a gospel including circumcision are inadvertently setting up a status-based community—the circumcised and the uncircumcised. The appearance of one's penis is neither here nor there; what matters is a heart circumcised by faith. There is no partiality with God nor Paul, and there should be none among Christian ministers of the gospel, or in communities of faith.

This is a sobering warning to those of us in Christian traditions that claim superiority over others or where people venerate their leaders in hierarchical churches. Similarly, we are warned of putting down immigrants or in other situations where people are judged on appearance, status, gender, disability, race, age, body, intelligence, a sinful past, a present struggle with sin, and so on. Christianity is radically egalitarian; it is about the heart of a person.

The final sentence is linked by *gar*, 'for,' here expressing continuity and the resolution of the whole construct. 'They added nothing' speaks of those in Jerusalem who seem to be highly esteemed in the church and nascent Christian movement.

---

75. See also Ps 81:2 (Eng. 82:2)—'How long will you judge unjustly and *show favoritism* (*lambanete prosōpa*) to sinners?' In Sirach 32:15 we read 'for the Lord is the judge, and with him there is *no partiality* (*prosōpon*).' See also Sir 32:16.

'Added nothing' uses *prosanatithēmi* which is used in 1:16 with the sense of presenting a case for approval. Here, having presented his gospel to them, they came back with no additional material to be added, e.g., circumcision. They simply endorse the mission leadership roles of Peter and Paul and ask Paul to continue to remember the poor.

ENTRUSTED WITH THE GOSPEL TO THE UNCIRCUMCISED (2:7-8)

In Galatians 2:7–10, Paul states what they did decide to do—they agreed that Paul was entrusted with the gospel mission to the uncircumcised. Galatians 2:7–9 is one long sentence spanning the acceptance of Paul and his gospel by Jacob, Cephas, and John, and them offering the right hand of fellowship to Paul and Barnabas and dividing the mission between the two core apostolic leaders; Paul to the gentiles and Cephas to the circumcised.

He begins in *Galatians 2:7*:

but (*alla*, 1:1) **in contrast** (*tounantion*)[76] **when they saw** (aorist participle *eidon*, 1:19) **that** (*hoti*, 1:6) **I have been entrusted** (perfect *pisteuō*, 2:7) **with the gospel** (*euangelion*, 1:6) **to the uncircumcised**[77] (genitive *akrobystia*),[78] **just as** (*kathōs*)[79] **Peter** (*Petros*)[80] **to the circumcised** (genitive *peritomē*).[81]

---

76. The adverb τοὐναντίον (*tounantion*) compounds the article (*ho*) with *enantion*, the neuter of *enantios*, 'in front of, in the sight of, before,' to form an adverbial crasis yielding 'on the other hand, on the contrary.' This is the only use in Galatians.

77. The genitives τῆς ἀκροβυστίας (of uncircumcision) and τῆς περιτομῆς (of circumcision) are good examples of genitives of destination whereby '[t]he genitive substantive indicates where the head noun is going (or the direction it is "moving" in) or the purpose of its existence. This is a somewhat rare category.' Wallace, *Greek Grammar*, 100.

78. The noun ἀκροβυστία (*akrobystia*), connotes 'the uncircumcised,' those who are not Jews. It is found three times in the letter (2:7; 5:6; 6:15).

79. The common (182 times NT, eighty-eight times Paul) comparative adverb καθώς (*kathōs*), 'just as, likewise, in the same way' is found thrice in Galatians: 1) Comparing the scope of Paul's ministry to that of Peter, 'to the uncircumcised, *just as* Peter had been ... circumcised;' 2) Comparing faith as the basis for Galatian receipt of the Spirit, '*just as* Abraham, "believed God ...";' 3) Likening a prior warning to a current one, 'I warn you, *just as* (or *as*) I warned you before.'

Paul starts with the stronger adversative, *alla*, here with the usual contrasting sense of 'but,' and pairs it with the very uncommon adverb *tounantion*,[82] which together express 'but on the other hand,' 'but on the contrary,' or 'but in contrast,' stating with a strong adversative feel what the Jerusalem leaders did do. 'When they saw' is the aorist participle of a common Greek word *eidon* and is temporal ('when they saw') or perhaps causal ('because they saw'). It refers here to the spiritual insight of the Jerusalem leaders who perceived that Paul's gospel was consistent with the gospel as they understood it after their experiences of Christ's earthly ministry, death, and resurrection.

'That I had been entrusted with the gospel' uses *pisteuō*, not its dominant sense of 'believe, trust' but of someone believing in another person and so placing something in their trust. The verb is perfect passive, speaking statively of something entrusted in the past and active in the present and by another agency—here God who set Paul apart from conception, called him, and revealed his Son to him so that he would preach him to the world (1:14–15). The verb is in the first person—Paul himself has been so entrusted (not Barnabas, Titus, or others). As such, they perceived that despite Paul's persecution of his Son and people, God in his grace 'believed' in him and entrusted him with the gospel of the uncircumcised.

'The gospel of the uncircumcised' is a clear example of the rare genitive of destination or purpose whereby the genitive (of the uncircumcised) indicates the direction or purpose toward which it is moving. So, here it implies 'the gospel for/to the uncircumcised/uncircumcision.'[83]

---

80. The name Πέτρος (*Petros*), meaning 'rock,' the personal name of Simon Peter or Cephas (Aramaic), is mentioned twice in Galatians 2:7, 8. Otherwise, it is found 156 times in the NT.

81. The noun περιτομή (*peritomē*) compounds *peri* (cut) and *tomē* (around) producing 'cut around.' It is found seven times in Galatians of 'the *circumcised*' (2:7, 8, 9), the '*circumcision* group'—the Judaizers (2:12), or 'the *circumcision*' (5:6, 11; 6:15).

82. The crasis *tounantion* (a single word is formed with two words) suggests 'on the contrary' and is only used twice else in the NT, 2 Cor 3:7; 1 Pet 3:9. It is extremely uncommon, not found in Philo, the LXX, and a few wider Greek sources. Josephus uses it ten times.

The uncircumcised here are the *akrobystia*, technically meaning the foreskin and which is used for being circumcised (Rom 4:10, 11, 12), the state of being uncircumcised (Rom 2:25, 26; 4:11; 1 Cor 7:18, 19; Col 2:13), the uncircumcised (Rom 2:27), or as here, as a term for gentiles—the uncircumcision (Acts 11:3; Rom 2:26; 3:30; 4:9; Eph 2:11; Col 3:11).[84] As there were other peoples who were circumcised (e.g., Egyptians, see 2:3), this refers exclusively to those (including Egyptians and others) who were not circumcised in the Jewish setting as an initiation into God's covenantal people. Paul uses it twice else in Galatians of the state of uncircumcision as compared with the state of circumcision—which both count for nothing when what counts is faith working through love and a new creation (5:6; 6:15). Paul then has been entrusted with the gospel mission to the non-Jewish world. In v. 8, he uses *ethnē*, 'gentiles, nations' in parallel.

When one considers the general knowledge of the world at the time, this is an astonishing ministry in scope. As argued concerning 2:2, Paul was well aware of the world from Spain to China, from Scandinavia, Britain, and the Russian Steppes, to sub-Saharan Africa.[85] Paul was then commissioned by God to lead the mission of the gospel to these areas. What a challenge!

Galatians 2:8 is a further parenthetical explanatory note:

For (*gar*, 1:10) **the one** (*ho*, 1:1) **who worked** (aorist participle *energeō*)[86] **in Peter** (dative[87] *Petros*, 2:7) **for** (*eis*, 1:5) **apostleship**

---

83. On this genitive, see Wallace, *Grammar*, 100–101. Another example is 'sheep *of slaughter*,' i.e., 'sheep *destined for slaughter*' (Rom 8:36).

84. In the LXX, *akrobystia* is used of foreskins (Gen 17:11, 14, 23, 24, 25; 34:24; Exod 4:25; Lev 12:3; Josh 5:3; 1 Sam 18:25, 27; 2 Sam 3:14; Judith 14:10), someone who has not had it removed (Gen 34:14), or the restoration of the foreskin—epispasm (1 Macc 1:15).

85. Schnabel, *Mission*, 1:468–69.

86. The term ἐνεργέω (*energeō*), compounds *en* (in, among) and *ergos* (work) and so means literally 'work in.' Paul uses *energeō*, 'work' four times in Galatians: here twice of God *working in* Peter's and Paul's apostolic commissions (2:8); his *working* (producing) miracles among the Galatians (3:5); and of faith *working* through love (5:6). Paul uses two other *erg-* (work) words in Galatians. This includes *ergon*, 'works,' used eight times (*works* of the law, 2:16; 3:2, 5, 10; *works* of the flesh, 5:10; test his own *work*, 6:4). He also uses the verb *ergazomai*, 'work, accomplish, carry out, do' in his injunction to the Galatians to 'do good (*work* good among) to all people' in 6:10. Hence, Paul

(*apostolē*)[88] **to the circumcised** (genitive *peritomē*, 2:7) **worked** (aorist *energeō*) **also** (*kai*, 1:1) **in me** (dative *egō*, 1:2) **for** (*eis*) **the gentiles** (plural *ethnos*, 1:16).

The *gar* is causal clarifying the reason for their recognition of Paul's commission from God—'for, because.' 'The one who worked in Peter' can be Christ or God, by the Spirit. As the language of call is used of God in Paul's letters, this refers to God who worked in and through Christ by the Spirit commissioning Peter to apostleship. This same God also called Paul (1:14–15). Paul here is drawing together his and Peter's callings. Peter's call occurred when Jesus called him and commissioned him as an apostle (further below), while Paul was called on the Damascus Road. They are both called of God, and so Paul should be held in the same esteem as those seeming to be something and considered pillars of the church. As such, the Judaizers should listen to Paul as much as the so-called Jerusalem pillars; he too, is a pillar of God's church.

The verb 'worked' here is *energeō*, literally 'work (*ergon*) in (*en*).' It is used only three times outside Paul of miraculous powers supposedly at work in a raised John the Baptist (Matt 14:2; Mark 6:14) and the power of prayer (Jas 5:16). The other eighteen uses are in Paul who employs it of sinful passions at work in the flesh (Rom 7:5), comfort working in suffering (2 Cor 1:6), death at work in gospel workers (2 Cor 4:12), Satan at work in the children of disobedience (Eph 2:2), lawlessness at work (2 Thess 2:7). As here, it is most often employed of God working spiritual

repudiates works of the law but expects the Galatians to repudiate works of the flesh and do good work to all. He acknowledges his and Peter's dependence on God for their missionary work.

87. The datives Πέτρῳ (*Petrō*, Peter) and ἐμοί (*emoi*, me) are datives of instrument in which, '[t]he dative substantive is used to indicate the means or instrument by which the verbal action is accomplished. This is a very common use of the dative, embracing as it does one of the root ideas of the dative case.' (Wallace, *Greek Grammar*, 162). Peter and Paul are the instruments through or by which God is reaching both the circumcised and uncircumcised (i.e., the whole world, Jew and gentile).

88. The noun ἀποστολή (*apostolē*) connotes 'office of a special emissary, apostleship, office of an apostle, assignment' (BDAG 121). It is used once in Galatians—in 2:8 of Peter's apostolic commission and implied of Paul. It is clearly related to *apostolos*, used of Paul and other apostles, see 1:1.

gifts (1 Cor 12:6) by his Spirit (1 Cor 12:11), working all things according to his will (Eph 1:11), working in resurrecting and exalting Christ (Eph 1:20), working his power in us (Eph 3:20), working in believers for his good pleasure (Phil 2:13), working in Paul's ministry (Col 1:29), and God's word working in believers (1 Thess 2:13). This divine sense is in Galatians—of God working miracles because of faith through the Spirit (3:5). The other use in Galatians is of faith outworked through love (5:6).

We can trace God and his Son's work in Peter to the Gospels and Acts with Peter called by Christ to follow him to fish for people (Mark 1:16–20; Matt 4:18–22; Luke 5:1–11) and his commissioning as an apostle (Mark 3:13–19; Matt 10:2–4; Luke 6:14–16). In the lists of the Twelve, he is always named first indicating his prominence. Further, we read of his re-commissioning after Christ's resurrection to feed Christ's sheep (John 21:1–23, cf. Luke 24:33), Pentecost, and his role as the prime spokesperson in Jerusalem (Acts 2:1–41; 3:1–4:22; 51–42).

This statement by Paul indicates that the Jerusalem church recognized Peter's missional leadership role. This is seen in Acts, where Peter ministers across Judea, including Lydda, Joppa, and Caesarea Maritima (Acts 9–10). We see further evidence of Peter moving through churches in other regions, including those of Paul in Antioch (see what follows 2:11–14), Corinth (1 Cor 1:12; 3:22; 9:5), and the churches of the whole of Asia Minor (1 Pet 1:1). Peter is without question the dominant figure in early Christianity in its first phase. While he was instrumental in the conversion of Cornelius and his family (Acts 10–11), we can surmise from this text that his emphasis was on the mission to the circumcised (*peritomē*), the Jews in Israel and the Diaspora (see on 2:7). Of course, even Cornelius was a God-worshiper and his ministry to Jews in synagogues would bring him into contact with many other similar God-fearing gentiles. As such, while his ministry focused on the circumcised, it would touch many gentiles as well (the converse being true of Paul). Peter may have focused much of his work beyond Judea after his arrest and escape from Agrippa I (Acts 12:1–19). However, in this passage, he is in Jerusalem again.

The God who worked in Peter to bring him to apostleship also worked (same term, *energeō*) in Paul, bringing him to apostleship. This refers to Paul's stunning transformational experience on the road to Damascus, already discussed above on 1:12–17 (cf. Acts 9:1–19; 22:1–21; 26:1–23), including his call to be the apostle to the gentiles (*ta ethnē*). Elsewhere Paul speaks of his apostleship, gifted by grace (further below), 'to bring about the obedience of faith for the sake of his name among all the gentiles.'[89] The point Paul is making to the Galatians is that he and Peter are called by the same God, and both are authorized as his apostles. They should refuse to take heed of the denigration of Paul by the Judaizers.

It is rather astonishing to read that these apostles who traveled the dusty streets of Palestine with Jesus to his death and who were first witnesses to the resurrection, would see in Paul the same light as that which they see Peter. Their former persecutor is indeed an apostle as they are. It is also astonishing to again consider the scope of Paul's mission. He is entrusted with the mission to the nations. As noted on 2:2 and 7, this was a huge region. The work, of course, is not yet complete. Many people groups remain unevangelized. Both Peter's and Paul's commission lives on in the church. It is up to us to continue it to Jews and gentiles wherever we encounter them. We are to go to all nations bearing the good news of God and in so doing we continue the ministries initiated by Christ and begun by Peter and Paul.

THE RIGHT HAND OF FELLOWSHIP (2:9)

In *Galatians 2:9*, Paul signaled by *kai*, 'and,' Paul continues:
    And (*kai*, 1:1) **acknowledging** (participle *gnōskō*)[90] **the grace**

---

89. See Rom 1:5, cf. 1:13; 11:13; 15:16–18; 3:1–8; Col 1:28; 1 Thess 2:16; 1 Tim 2:7; 2 Tim 4:17.

90. One of the most common Greek words for knowing, γινώσκω (*gnōskō*), is found four times in Galatians: 1) The Jerusalem leaders knowing or acknowledging Paul's commission (2:9); 2) The Galatians knowing that those of faith are children of Abraham 3:7); 3) Coming to know God (4:9, 1st use); 4) Being known by God (4:9, 2nd use).

(*charis*, 1:3) **given** (aorist passive *didōmi*, 1:4) **to me** (dative *egō*, 1:2), **Jacob** (*Iakōbos*, 1:16) **and** (*kai*) *Cephas* (1:18)[91] **and** (*kai*) **John** (*Iōannēs*)[92]—**those seeming** (present participle *dokeō*, 3:18) **to be** (infinitive *eimi*, 1:7) **pillars** (plural *stylos*)[93]—**gave** (aorist *didōmi*, 1:4) **to me** (dative *egō*) **and** *Barnabas* (2:1) **the right hand** (*dexios*)[94] **of fellowship** (genitive *koinōnia*),[95] **so that** (*hina*, 1:16) **we** (plural *egō*) [would go] **to** (*eis*, 1:5) **the gentiles** (plural *ethnos*, 1:16), **and they to** (*eis*) **the circumcision** (*peritomē*, 2:7) …

Paul continues his narrative of the gospel's acceptance in Jerusalem. Jacob, Cephas, and John acknowledge that his gospel mission is a gift of grace from God. As discussed concerning 1:3, grace refers to God's beneficence toward unworthy humanity. The construct 'grace given to me' is a common way for Paul to define his conversion and commission.[96] He also uses the phrase 'grace given' of salvation (1 Cor 1:4), the differing spiritual gifts conferred on all Christians (Rom 12:6; Eph 4:7), and the desire of the Macedonians to give lavishly to the Jerusalem Collection (2 Cor 8:1). With the verb *didōmi*, 'give,' the construct is emphatic.

For Paul, his call was definitively an act of grace on God's part. Paul had been heaven-bent (in his view) in his determination to snuff out the nascent Christian movement. He met Jesus on the Damascus Road who completely turned his world upside down (see 1:12–17). This Jesus had indeed risen and *is* Messiah, Son of God, and Lord. While he remained a committed Yahwist, Paul's

---

91. **Variant:** As with 1:18, some texts amend *Cēphas* to *Petros*, including P46 D F G. However, the word order is also rearranged in most of these texts and so it is clear *Cēphas* is original.

92. The name Ἰωάννης (*Iōannēs*), 'John,' is mentioned only once in Galatians, in 2:9. This is the only reference to John in the Pauline Epistles.

93. The noun στῦλος (*stylos*), 'pillar,' is found once in Galatians, in 2:9, of the three Jerusalem apostles, Peter, Jacob, and John. This is the only use of the term by Paul.

94. Galatians 2:9 is the only use of the noun δεξιός (*dexios*), 'right,' in Galatians. It refers to the 'right hand of fellowship'—full acceptance and welcome.

95. The noun κοινωνία (*koinōnia*) is only found once in Galatians, in 2:9, speaking of the 'fellowship' into which Paul and Barnabas were welcomed by the Jerusalem Christian leadership. Barnabas was already one of them, but this may speak of his admission to apostolic status. The associated verb *koinōneō* is used in 6:6 of the Galatian Christians sharing in good things with their teacher.

96. See Rom 12:3; 15:15; 1 Cor 3:10; Eph 3:2, 7, 8, cf. Phil 1:7.

theology now included God's Son, both human and divine, who called him by his grace to take his message to the world. Here, his call is endorsed. Now he is truly heaven-bent on propagating the message to the world.

The conversion and call experience of Paul is one of the great stories of Scripture. God's grace is seen powerfully, as he takes this religious zealot—prepared to imprison and kill for the faith—and turns his life around. God disrupted his life, radically calling him, and then sent him out to preach his gospel and to suffer for his name.

I know this grace myself. Raised in a non-Christian home, I had a brief encounter with God in my early teens in which the word was planted in my heart. However, I did not follow through on this and went about my life into my late teens and early twenties. Life was seeking glory in sport, yet experiencing brokenness played out in drinking, recreational drugs, living with my girlfriend, and partying. The truth was I was lost in despair. Thankfully God intervened and drastically disrupted my life. The word that had been sown in my heart as a boy came to life. I heard God's summons. I yielded, as did my girlfriend Emma on Feb 24, 1985. By the grace given to me, I have been able to serve him in ministry to this day. Similarly, my wife was called and commissioned by God and has now served for decades in Presbyterian ordained ministry. To the praise of his glory, Amen.

Cephas is again Peter, as in the other uses of Peter's Aramaic name in Galatians and the other Paulines.[97] Paul probably prefers the Aramaic to show his familiarity with Peter. Jacob is clearly the brother of Jesus (Mark 6:3; Matt 13:55) as Jacob, the brother of John, had died three to four years prior to Galatians at the hands of Herod Agrippa I (Acts 12:1).

While the John mentioned here could be John Mark as he is in Jerusalem and returns to Antioch with them after this trip (Acts 12:25), this is certainly the Apostle John. This is the only mention of him in Paul's letters. As with Peter, he was a fisherman, working in a business with Jacob, Andrew, Peter, Zebedee, and

---

97. See 1:18; 2:9, cf. 1 Cor 1:12; 3:22; 9:5; 15:5; John 1:42.

other hired hands (Mark 1:20). With Jacob, Peter, and Andrew, he is also one of the first disciples called by Christ (Matt 4:21; Mark 1:19; Luke 5:10), and likely the other disciple in John 1:29–40. He is also one of the Twelve (Matt 10:2; Mark 3:17; Luke 6:14).

He and his brother were labeled Boanerges, 'sons of thunder,' which could indicate that they were loud, hot-tempered, and/or had a zealot's zeal. With Peter and his brother Jacob, John was one of the Synoptics' apostolic inner circle, being present at the Transfiguration[98] and at Jesus' Gethsemane agony (Mark 14:33; Luke 22:8). Some of his involvement in the Synoptics includes his seeking to stop exorcists using Jesus' name (Mark 9:38; Luke 9:49), with Jacob seeking the prime seats beside Jesus in his glory and so suffering the indignation of the others (Mark 10:35, 41), and again with Jacob seeking to call fire down on a Samaritan town (Luke 9:54).

If he is the loved disciple of John, as I consider most likely, he reclines beside Jesus at the Last Supper (John 13:23), is at the cross (John 19:26), ran to the empty tomb with Peter (John 20:2), was one of the seven at the Sea appearance (John 21:7, 20), was reputed to not die until Jesus returned (John 21:23), and wrote the Gospel (John 21:24). He is part of the early Jerusalem church (Acts 1:13), where in the early chapters, he is consistently named alongside Peter, involved in healings, appearances before the Sanhedrin, floggings, and imprisonments (Acts 3:1–4:19). After Philip's evangelization of Samaria, he and Peter also traveled to Samaria to minister, imparting the Spirit to the new converts (Acts 8:14–17). He is not mentioned in Acts after the Samaria mission. However, he is also likely the writer of the three letters of John (1, 2, 3 John), and most likely Revelation while in exile on Patmos, after an extraordinary vision of Christ (Rev 1:1, 4, 9; 22:8). At this time, he is in Jerusalem, but tradition places him in Ephesus in the years to come where he died as an old man.

The three leaders are described as 'those seeming to be pillars.' Paul again uses *dokeō*, a term of subjective knowledge, used in 2:2, 6, and again in 6:3 (see further 2:2). Here, they are not just

---

98. See Matt 17:1; Mark 9:2; Luke 9:28, cf. Mark 1:29; 5:37; 13:3; Luke 8:51.

'seeming to be,' or 'seeming to be something,' but 'those seeming to be pillars' (*stylos*). This is an architectural term used for a pillar or column.

In the LXX, it is frequently used of God leading Israel as a pillar of fire and cloud.[99] More interestingly for this reference, it is used of pillars in the tabernacle[100] and temple[101] including the eschatological temple of Ezekiel (Ezek 40:49). The description of these three as pillars may connote them as pillars sustaining God's Temple, the people of God (cf. Eph 2:20). Whether this is correct or not, they are seen by many as critical people in God's church (cf. 'pillars of the community'). As noted concerning 2:2 and 2:6, this is not a denigration of their status but Paul's challenge to the Galatians to recognize that he too is a pillar and to repudiate the put-downs of Paul by the Judaizers.

'They gave to me and Barnabas the right hand of fellowship (*koinōnia*)' speaks of their warm inclusion of the two in the apostolic guild. In ancient cultures, the right side was held in high estimation as more dominant, active, and powerful. Conversely, 'the left' is often seen negatively (Prov 4:27a LXX; Eccl 10:2). This prejudice for the right side is reflected in Gen 48:13–18, where Joseph places his right hand on Joseph's younger son, Ephraim, and his left on the older Manasseh. Joseph then tried to reverse Jacob's hand, only for Jacob to refuse to do so.

It is God's right hand through which he exercises his power,[102] including creation (Isa 48:13) and judgment (Hab 2:16). Sacrificial blood to cleanse from sin is placed on the right hand and foot.[103] The right hand of someone of importance is the place of highest honor[104] and the Psalmist sings of God at his right hand (Ps 16:8). This is true of God where his right hand is the place of highest honor, where one finds the angelic hosts (1

---

99. E.g., Exod 13:21–22; Num 14:14; Deut 31:15.
100. E.g., Exod 26:15–37; 27:10–17; 35:10–12; 37:4–17; Num 4:31–32.
101. E.g., 2 Kings 11:14; 23:3; 25:13–17; 1 Chron 18:8; 2 Chron 3:15–17; 4:12–13; Jer 52:17, 20–22.
102. E.g., Exod 15:6, 12; Deut 33:2; Ps 21:8; 89:13; Ezek 21:22.
103. See Lev 8:23; 14:14, 17, 25, 28.
104. See 1 Chron 6:39; Neh 8:4 [2 Esd 18:4].

Kings 22:19; 2 Chron 18:18), pleasure (Ps 16:11), refuge (Ps 17:7), support (Ps 18:35; Isa 41:10), salvation (Ps 20:6), victory (Ps 44:3), and righteousness (Ps 48:10; 60:5).

Sisera is killed by Yael's right hand (Judg 5:26). The signet ring for sealing was also on the right hand (Jer 22:24). Satan stands at the right hand of the angel of the Lord to accuse (Zech 3:1). The taking of another by the right hand is honorific, as when Joab took Amasa by the right hand, but then betrayed him and killed him with the left (2 Sam 20:9)—a dishonorable act. God himself takes his anointed, Cyrus, by the right hand (Isa 45:1). In 2 Macc 12:11, defeated nomads ask Judas to grant them the right hand, a sign of friendship.

The right hand is the place of the Messianic Lord, fulfilled in Christ in the NT (Ps 110:1, NT texts below). So, in the NT, the 'right hand' gives to the poor (Matt 6:3) while the 'right eye' and 'right hand' must be removed if they cause sin (Matt 5:29). To sit at the right hand of someone is of the highest status,[105] and this is the seat of Christ in relation to God.[106] The sheep destined for salvation are at the right hand of God at the judgment (Matt 25:33, 34). An injured right hand was particularly problematic in most cases; hence, the healing of that hand is critical, enabling the person to work (Luke 6:6–10). The royal scepter is held in the right hand; hence, the reed is placed in Jesus' right hand by the Roman soldiers (Matt 27:29). Jesus holds seven stars in his right hand (Rev 1:16, 20; 2:1) and also lays his right hand on John (Rev 1:17). The scrolls in Revelation are held in the right hand of God (Rev 5:1, 7). The angel lifts his right hand to heaven (Rev 10:5) and the beast's mark is placed on the right hand (Rev 13:16).[107] Hence, the offering of the right hand of fellowship by Peter, Jacob, and John, to Paul and Barnabas is the highest of honors.

---

105. See Matt 20:21, 23; Mark 10:37, 40; Luke 20:42; 22:69; Acts 2:25, 33, 34; 5:31; 7:55, 56; Rom 8:34; Eph 1:20; Col 3:1; Heb 1:3, 13, 8:1; 10:12; 12:2; 1 Pet 3:22.
106. Matt 26:64, cf. Matt 22:44; Mark 12:36; 14:62.
107. There are also many examples of the right and left being neutral, e.g., Josh 23:6—'turning aside neither to the right hand or the left.' See further on the right in the NT, P. von der Osten-Sacken, 'δεξιός,' in *EDNT* 1:285.

'Fellowship' is *koinōnia*, which is a term with wide associations in the Greek world for a wide range of common endeavors including business, marriage, and friendship.[108] The term is used in the NT to describe Christian friendship or fellowship. It is used for fellowship with God (1 John 1:3), with Christ (1 Cor 1:9; 1 John 1:3, 6), participation in the Lord through the Lord's Supper (1 Cor 10:16), participation in the Spirit (2 Cor 13:14; Phil 2:1), Christian fellowship (Acts 2:42; 1 John 1:3, 17), specific material acts of fellowship like the Jerusalem Collection (Rom 15:26; 2 Cor 8:4; 9:13, cf. Heb 13:16), partnership in the life and mission of the gospel (Phil 1:5), partnership in Christ's sufferings (Phil 3:10), and fellowship in faith (Phlm 6).[109]

The right hand of fellowship here is more than Christian fellowship. It is an acceptance of Paul and Barnabas in missional terms, as 'fellow missionaries,' or 'fellow apostles,' on a par with those who ministered with Christ and others they commissioned (e.g., Stephen, Philip, Acts 6:1–7). Both Paul and Barnabas are offered this status, perhaps indicating the point at which Barnabas was accepted as an apostle. Hence, Luke can use the plural of Paul and Barnabas as apostles in Acts 14:4, 14. This absolute acceptance is critical and should put to bed any sense Paul is inferior or that his gospel is to be rejected in favor of the Judaizers' teaching.

The purpose of their acceptance is that 'we to the gentiles (nations), and they themselves to the circumcision.' 'Gentiles' is a better translation than 'nations' here, as the task of preaching the gospel to the circumcision is not exclusively limited to the Palestine region, it is inclusive of the Diaspora—the circumcised throughout the nations. No verb is found, but 'might go,' or 'might preach' is implied. We have here implicit evidence of the Great Commission to take the gospel to all nations in Paul's writings.[110] Paul and Barnabas are to lead the way in sharing the gospel among the swathes of gentiles across the known world

---

108. See Friedrich Hauck, 'κοινωνία,' in *TDNT* 3:797–809.
109. *Koinōnia* is also used in terms of ethical dualism, light having no fellowship with darkness (2 Cor 6:14, cf. 1 John 1:6).
110. See Matt 28:18–20; Luke 24:46–49; John 20:21; Acts 1:8.

(a huge task, see on v. 2). While Peter, John, and Jacob are to focus on the circumcised, i.e., the Jews in Palestine and the wider world, Paul is commissioned to take the gospel to the rest.

This is, then, like a mission society gathering where two missions come together and agree that they are all on the same team and allocate the world to the two groups (e.g., the North and South Islands of NZ; Asia and Europe, etc.). The key thing is that Paul and Barnabas and their gospel are endorsed, and it is agreed that they are commissioned by God for the work of the gospel. As such, the Galatians must recognize this and turn back from their flirtation with Judaizing heresy. They are a part of the gentile world and as such, are under Paul's authority as agreed by the Jerusalem church leadership. They should then yield to the instructions of the letter.[111]

REMEMBER THE POOR (2:10)

In *Galatians 2:10*, we get the only condition placed on Paul and Barnabas by the Jerusalem leadership:

—**[Asking] only** (*monos*, 1:23) **that** (*hina*, 1:16) **we remember** (present subjunctive *mnēmoneuō*)[112] **the poor** (genitive *ptōchos*);[113] **this** (neuter *houtos*)[114] **same** (neuter *autos*, 1:1) **thing which**[115] (neuter *hos*, 1:5) **I was also** (*kai*, 1:1) **eager** (aorist *spoudazō*)[116] **to do** (aorist infinitive *poieō*).[117]

---

111. On obedience to Paul and leaders, see such texts as 6:6; 2 Cor 10:6; 1 Thess 4:2; 5:12–13; 2 Thess 3:14; Phlm 21.
112. The verb μνημονεύω (*mnēmoneuō*), 'remember' (English, mnemonic, a device for remembering) is found once in Galatians 2:10—'remember the poor.'
113. The noun πτωχός (*ptōchos*), the Greek for 'poor,' features twice in the letter; in 2:10 literally of those in material need, and in 4:9, figuratively as an adjective of 'poor' or 'beggarly' *stoicheia*, elemental principles of the world.
114. The adjectival pronoun οὗτος (*houtos*), 'this,' features ten times in Galatians, neuter: *'this* thing' or 'this' (2:10; 3:2, 17; 6:7, 16), plural *'these* things' (2:18; 5:17 [2x]; 5:21); masculine: plural *'these* people' (3:7; 6:7, 12); and feminine: *'these* women' (4:24).
115. The article ὁ καὶ ἐσπούδασα is an example of the generic article: 'While the *individualizing* article distinguishes or identifies a particular object belonging to a larger class, the *generic* article distinguishes one class from another. This is somewhat less frequent than the individualizing article (though it still occurs hundreds of times in the NT). It categorizes rather than particularizes.' Wallace, *Greek Grammar*, 227.

Only (*monos*) specifies the one caveat on their acceptance of Paul. 'That' (*hina*) is likely imperatival.[118] If this encounter correlates with Acts 11:26–30, as I have argued, then Paul and Barnabas have come to Jerusalem in part to deliver the Antiochian collection gathered after Agabus' predicted famine. Indeed, this request from the Jerusalem leadership makes good sense and is suggestive that linking Acts 11 and Gal 2 is appropriate.

Scholarship generally argues that this request is specifically targeted at the poor saints in Jerusalem—please continue to remember the poor here in Jerusalem (as you have just done). However, there are good reasons to consider that this should be read generally. 'The poor' is *ptōchos* that is used sparingly in a spiritualized sense.[119] Here, as it is usually used in the NT, it is a general term for the material poor and wider sources.[120] This is how Paul uses it in Rom 15:26: 'the poor of the saints who are in Jerusalem' (Rom 15:26), and somewhat ironically in contrast to 'rich' in 2 Cor 6:10. His only other use is Gal 4:9 where it is adjectival and figurative; so 'poorly, beggarly' of the *stoicheia*, the elemental spirits or principles (see on 4:9). Here then, it should be read as a general command. Paul and Barnabas are urged to continue to do as they have done in their recent collection from Syrian Antioch (Acts 11:30) and continue to care for the poor. This is further evidence (as if any is needed in light of Jesus' teaching) that basic to the Christian mission is caring for the poor. As I note in *Congregational Evangelism*, doing so is a basic component of apostolic ministry.[121]

---

116. The verb σπουδάζω (*spoudazō*) is used once in Galatians in 2:10 of Paul's 'zeal, eagerness, or devotion' to remember the poor.
117. The common verb ποιέω (*poieō*), 'do, make,' is found six times in Galatians of *doing* something including doing what was asked, remembering the poor (2:10), '*doing*' the things of the law (3:10, 12; 5:3), '*doing* the things you want to do' (5:17), and '*doing* good' (6:9).
118. Wallace, *Greek Grammar*, 475.
119. Spiritualized: *poor* in spirit (Matt 5:3), spiritually *poor* (Rev 3:17).
120. See Matt 11:5; 19:21; 26:9, 11; Mark 10:21; 12:42–43; 14:5, 7; 4:18; 6:20; 7:22; 14:13, 21; 16:20, 22; 18:22; 19:8; 21:3; John 12:5, 6, 8; 13:29; Jas 2:2, 3, 5, 6; Rev 13:16.
121. Mark J. Keown, Congregational Evangelism in Philippians: The Centrality of an

Paul's response is positive. This is the very thing he is eager to do. 'Eager' is *spoudazō*. It is used once in Hebrews of believers being *eager* to enter God's Sabbath rest (Heb 4:11). Peter uses it three times of 'being eager:' to confirm one's calling and election (2 Pet 1:10), to recall Peter's teaching after his death (2 Pet 1:15), and to be 'found in him' spotless (2 Pet 3:14). Paul's other uses include being eager to maintain Spirit-unity (Eph 4:3), his eagerness to see the Thessalonians face to face (1 Thess 2:17), in injunctions to Timothy to be eager to present himself as an approved worker (2 Tim 2:15), and to come to Paul (2 Tim 4:9, 21)—similarly, to Titus (Tit 3:12). It speaks here of Paul's *eager zeal for the poor*. He will demonstrate this again in the second Jerusalem Collection, this time gathering funds from the Galatians themselves, the Macedonians, and the Achaians (Rom 15:26–31; 1 Cor 16:1–4; 2 Cor 8–9). There is no mention of this collection in Galatians, indicating that it is written earlier—in fact, before Paul's second Antiochian mission (Acts 16–18).

This injunction to Paul speaks to us as Christians passionate about the sharing of the gospel in our contexts. We need to allow the words of Peter, Jacob, and John to Paul to nestle in our spirits and move us to action—we must remember the poor. Our response should be the same as Paul's—eagerness and zeal. This emulates 'the grace of our Lord Jesus Christ, that though he was rich, yet for your sake, he became poor so that you by his poverty might become rich' (2 Cor 8:9). A constituent element of authentic mission is caring for the poor and marginalized. We must not fall into the error of some evangelicals in the past who have seen care for the poor as secondary to preaching the gospel—the gospel calls for caring for both spiritual and material needs. We should be zealous to do both. Indeed, preaching the gospel involves word and deed as evidenced by Luke's Gospel where 'to preach good news to the poor' involves feeding them material food, healing them, and nourishing them with God's word.[122]

Appeal for Gospel Proclamation to the Fabric of Philippians, PBM (Milton Keynes: Paternoster, 2008), 175–78.

122. E.g., Luke 9:10–17; 12:33; Acts 4:32–37; 9:36.

CHAPTER TEN: PAUL AND PETER CLASH IN ANTIOCH (2:11–14)

PAUL CONFRONTS PETER (2:11)

While Galatians 2:11–14 is a new section, it is still a component of Paul's narrative of his life in the gospel written to remind the Galatians of his apostolic credentials and the authenticity of the gospel they had believed. They must not yield to a Judaizing gospel, which is no gospel at all. Rather, they must continue to walk in the truth of the gospel of grace and justification by faith.

Here, Paul narrates an earlier time when subsequent to Paul's visit to Jerusalem, Peter came north to Antioch in Syria. On this occasion, Paul felt the need to challenge Peter publicly. In an honor-shame culture, this is an amazing and potentially humiliating moment. Furthermore, in that Peter is one of the three 'seeming to be something/pillar' ones, the gravity of the moment is even more pronounced.

Peter had come to Antioch and was initially quite comfortable eating with the gentile uncircumcised converts in the church. However, at some unspecified point, some Christians came from Jacob in Jerusalem to Antioch. When these people arrived, Peter withdrew from table fellowship with the gentiles, for fear of 'the circumcision party.' It seems that some from Jerusalem were Judaizers. This should not surprise us as the issue of Judaizing was not resolved in Jerusalem until the meeting of Acts 15 at the end of the 40s AD. Moreover, up to the point of the conversion of Cornelius' household, all converts were probably already Jews or expected to Judaize. It was only subsequent to the Jerusalem Council a year or two after Galatians that orthodox theology absolutely refuted Judaizing. It often takes the church a while to work through difficult issues. This is particularly the case where there is a dominant and assumed cultural perspective (e.g., concerning women in ministry).[1]

When they came, Peter was torn between dining with the gentiles and violating Jewish table protocols that forbade such fellowship or dining with the Jews. As they sat apart, Peter was challenged to keep to his Jewish culture or continue to uphold shared table fellowship in the new culture of the gospel. Peter chose the latter, not wanting to offend his Jewish brethren, and so withdrew from table fellowship with the gentiles. Others joined Peter, including Barnabas, much to Paul's consternation. As such, the church became racially segregated at its meals. Jews dine with Jews on the basis of concerns over ritual purity and gentiles with gentiles. It seems that Paul alone remained in table fellowship with the gentiles seeing that the gospel called for an end to such segregation.

Peter and Barnabas' act infuriated Paul who saw the old enmity of Jew and gentile in play; the gospel was then violated into a gospel of apartheid or racial supremacy. He dared to confront Peter publicly, a presumptuous and provocative action toward one of the church pillars, the one whom Jesus had set apart as the rock. For Paul, the gospel is racially inclusive; the old barriers are gone including that of Jew and gentile. Ritual purity concerns are things of the past for Christians whether Jews or gentiles, we are all sinners now purified in Christ through the Spirit. In an age where table fellowship was basic to *koinōnia* and demonstrated one's familial bond, eating together was an essential visible expression of their oneness in Christ in which there is neither Jew nor Greek (3:28). Separation is a violation of Christology—'in Christ' we are bound together in oneness. It is

---

1. Another such issue is the current worldwide debates on sexuality and gender. Over time the church will engage with Scripture, theological, and cultural perspectives and establish an orthodox perspective. In my opinion, it will be the so-called 'conservative' position but lavished with grace and warmth and love toward all of broken humanity. I stand to be corrected.

a violation of pneumatology, whereby the Spirit is forming Jew and gentile into one Temple of the Spirit (1 Cor 3:16).

The purpose of this encounter again is not to draw attention to Paul, to demean Peter or Barnabas, or to suggest an irrevocable division between Paul and Peter, Paul and Jacob, or Pauline and Petrine theology, but to add further support to Paul's claim that the gospel is a gospel of grace, faith, and inclusion. One does not have to Judaize to be a Christian. To Judaize is, in fact, to violate the gospel, as it (unwittingly perhaps) suggests racial supremacy (for the Jews) and demeans gentiles, forcing them to conform to the Jewish culture. It degrades Christ who came to break down such divisions.

As such, the Galatian Christians must not allow themselves to be so divided. They, Jew and gentile, circumcised or uncircumcised, are one people, and they are formed in Christ by faith in the one crucified to make them one. This must be demonstrated in their community meals. There is no place for a fragmented church at meals, at which the Lord's Supper is celebrated. This calls to mind 1 Cor 11:17–34 where the Corinthians are not one at communion. This has no place in Christianity.

In *Galatians 2:11*, Paul writes:

But (*de*, 1:15) when (*hote*, 1:15) Cephas (1:18)[2] came (aorist *erchomai*, 1:21) to (*eis*, 1:18) Antioch (*Antiocheia*),[3] I opposed (*anthistēmi*)[4] [him] to (*kata*, 1:4) his (dative *autos*, 1:1) face (*prosōpon*, 1:22), because (*hoti*, 1:6) he was (imperfect *eimi*) condemned (*kataginōskō*).'[5]

This is the only evidence we have of Peter traveling to Syrian

---

2. **Variant**: As in other earlier instances (1:18; 2:9), *Cēphas* is amended to *Petros* in some texts. As with the other texts, *Cēphas* is to be preferred.
3. There is one reference to the place name Ἀντιόχεια (*Antiocheia*), 'Antioch,' in Gal 2:11, this is most likely Syrian Antioch rather than Pisidian Antioch.
4. The verb ἀνθίστημι (*anthistēmi*) compounds *anti* (against) and *tithēmi* (stand) and has the sense 'stand against.' It is found once in Gal 2:11, of Paul *opposing* Peter to his face or setting his face to Peter.
5. The verb καταγινώσκω (*kataginōskō*) compounds *kata* (according to, against) and *ginōskō* (know, acknowledge) and yields 'know something against' and so Peter being 'condemned' or 'convicted.'

Antioch and it would seem likely that it is quite recent, sometime after the delivery of the Antiochian gift and the encounter with Peter, Jacob, and John just narrated, and the sending of the letter; i.e., sometime in 46–47.[6] A visit from Peter to Antioch is not surprising as Luke records that he had escaped Jerusalem about two to three years earlier after Agrippa I killed John's brother Jacob and also sought to kill Peter. He had also traveled to Caesarea (Acts 12:19).

The term for opposed is *anthistēmi*, used in Jesus' teaching, 'do not *resist* the one who is evil' (Mark 5:39). Luke uses it of withstanding adversaries (Luke 21:15) or Stephen's wisdom (Acts 6:10) and of Elymas, who opposed Paul and Barnabas (Acts 13:8). Both Jacob and Peter use it of *resisting* Satan (Jas 4:7; 1 Pet 5:9), as does Paul (Eph 6:13). Otherwise, Paul uses it of humanity's inability to resist God's will (Rom 9:19) and in his injunctions not to resist the state; otherwise, one is *resisting* God (Rom 13:2). His other three uses are of opposing false teachers (2 Tim 3:8; 4:15). One can see it is a strong word, speaking of real opposition to Peter. 'To his face' (*kata prosōpon*) uses *kata* in its less common meaning 'against;' 'against his face.' Of Paul's 194 uses of *kata*, he only uses it in this way eleven times. Of the seventeen in Galatians, he uses it this way four other times (3:21; 5:17, 23).[7]

This speaks of doing it directly (and not behind his back) and in public.[8] Paul's preparedness to do this speaks of how strongly he felt about the violation of the integrity of the gospel of grace and its violation of unity in Christ. This would be a shocking move in cultures that value honor above all else.

We might question Paul here and ask why he did not take Peter, Barnabas, and others aside, and challenge them. Perhaps

---

6. Or, if we go for the alternative chronology, AD 52.

7. See also Rom 8:33; 11:2; 1 Cor 4:6; 2 Cor 13:8; Col 2:4; 1 Tim 5:19. Outside of Paul, see Matt 5:11, 23; 10:35; 12:14, 25, 30, 32; 26:59; 27:1; Mark 3:6; 9:40; 11:25; 14:55, 56, 57; Luke 9:50; 11:23; 23:14; John 18:29; Acts 4:26; 6:13; 14:2; 16:22; 21:28; 24:1; 25:2, 3, 15, 27; Jas 5:9; 1 Pet 2:11; 2 Pet 2:11; Jude 15; Rev 2:4, 14, 20. Such use is absent from Hebrews and the Johannine epistles. In 3:21: 'against the promise;' in 5:17: flesh against the Spirit and Spirit against the flesh; and in 5:23: 'against such things there is no law.'

8. See Luke 2:31; Acts 3:13; 25:16; 2 Cor 10:1, 7.

this was a better way of doing it. But, sometimes, directly challenging someone in public may be the right thing to do to get the desired response. There is a time to 'carefront' someone and to do it in public, especially when the stakes are super high.

'Because he stood condemned' uses *kataginōskō*, found only elsewhere in the NT twice in 1 John 3:20–21 of the heart condemning believers. In the LXX, as in 1 John, it is used of the heart condemning a person (Sir 14:2) and of the condemnation of one who rejoices in wickedness (Sir 19:5). It can have the sense of 'see through' someone's apparent goodness, as with an intelligent needy person seeing through an arrogant rich man (Prov 28:11). In Deut 25:1 it has the sense of charging a married partner with an offense. So, here it can mean to be charged or as is more likely, Peter was condemned by the gospel. The use of the imperfect of *eimi* (*ēn*) (was) suggests something past, rather than something that has continued to the present. The implication is that he and Peter are fine now.

THE INFLUENCE OF THE JUDAIZERS (2:12)

In *Galatians 2:12*, Paul gives the context for his public rebuke of Peter:

For (*gar*, 1:17) **before** (*pro*, 1:17) **some people** (plural, accusative *tis*, 1:7)[9] **came** (aorist infinitive[10] *erchomai*, 1:21) **from** (*apo*, 1:1) **Jacob** (*Iakōbos*, 1:19), **he ate** (*synesthiō*)[11] **with** (*meta*, 1:18) **the gentiles** (plural *ethnos*, 1:16). **But** (*de*, 1:15) **when** (*hote*, 1:15) **they came** (plural *erchomai*),[12] **he drew back** (aorist *hyperstellō*)[13] **and** (*kai*, 1:1) **separated** (*aphorizō*, 1:15) **himself**

---

9. **Variant**: Some texts amend the plural *tinas* to the singular *tina*. However, this is clearly erroneous.

10. The infinitive is sometimes used of time after πρὸ τοῦ, πρὶν, or πρὶν ἤ. This is called the subsequent infinitive. With *pro*, it connotes 'before.' See Wallace, *Greek Grammar*, 596 (see also 3:23).

11. The compound verb συνεσθίω (*synesthiō*), which compounds *syn*, 'with,' plus *esthiō*, 'eat,' producing 'eat together with.' It is found once in Galatians of Peter who ate with the gentiles.

12. **Variant**: While a good number of texts include the singular *ēlthen* (P46vid ℵ B D*, etc.), the plural *ēlthon* is clearly a better reading as a group is in mind.

(*heautos*, 1:4), **fearing** (present passive participle *phobeō*)[14] **those** (plural *ho*,[15] 1:1) **from** (*ek*, 1:1) **the circumcision** (genitive *peritomē*, 2:7).

Before the arrival from Jerusalem of a group that clearly included Jews (the circumcision), Peter ate with the gentiles, who in the Second Temple period, were increasingly seen by devoted Jews as impure. What occurs is premised on understanding the importance of table fellowship in ancient cultures. Barchy writes,

It would be difficult to overestimate the importance of table fellowship for the cultures of the Mediterranean basin in the first century of our era. Mealtimes were far more than occasions for individuals to consume nourishment. Being welcomed at a table for the purpose of eating food with another person had become a ceremony richly symbolic of friendship, intimacy, and unity.[16]

As such, as we come to a text like this, we need to realize the social significance of what is going on. The choice of whether to dine with someone is laden with social significance. Peter's decision to eat with the gentiles was extremely radical considering his upbringing (below). However, his subsequent decision to pull back is insulting and repudiates the gentile Christians; similarly, the refusal of the Jews from Jerusalem is also insulting. Further, Paul rebuking him in the context of a meal is also daring and a potential violation of food protocols.

In Jewish culture, there were strict protocols for eating kosher food (Lev 11; Deut 14), and violating these causes impurity and 'symbolizes and reinforces her separation from other nations.'[17]

---

13. The compound verb ὑποστέλλω (*hypostellō*) blends *hypo*, 'by, under' and *stellō* forming 'avoid, keep away from,' and with the prefix, is intensive—'draw back, withdraw, shrink back.' In 2:12, it is emphatic.

14. The verb φοβέω (*phobeō*) is found twice in Galatians, the verb used in 2:12 of Peter's fear of the circumcision group causing him to withdraw from table fellowship, and in 4:11, of Paul's fear that his work among the Galatians is wasted due to their desertion of the gospel.

15. The final phrase τοὺς ἐκ περιτομῆς is a neat example of the article substantivizing a prepositional phrase, the preposition being *ek*; **the ones** from the circumcision.' See Wallace, *Greek Grammar*, 236.

16. S. S. Barchy, 'Table Fellowship,' in *DJG* 796.

17. H. K. Harrington, 'Purity and Impurity,' in *EDEJ* 1121.

As such, eating with gentiles was seen as defiling. This is seen in Jubilees 22:16: 'Separate yourself from the gentiles, and do not eat with them.' In Qumran

The Qumran sectarians were careful to maintain the purity of their communal food and drink, 'the purity.' Members bathed before eating (1QS 5:13; 4Q514 frg. 1 cols. i–ii lines 2–4; 4Q274 1, i 3–9). Food had to be harvested in a state of purity lest it transmits impurity to produce through the liquid of its juice (4Q284a frg. 1 lines 2–8). Outsiders, even Jews, were considered impure along with their belongings and forbidden to eat with the sect.[18]

This is seen in the NT where Peter is cited in Acts stating, 'you yourselves know how unlawful it is for a Jew to associate with or to visit anyone of another nation' (Acts 10:28).

Jesus, of course, challenged this. He directly repudiated Jewish food laws in Mark 7/Matt 15 where he declared that it is not what goes into the mouth that makes a person unclean, but what comes forth from the heart (Mark 7:18–23). In Luke 7/Matt 8, Jesus is willing to go to the Capernaum home of a Roman Centurion when he requests the healing of his servant. Only the intervention of the Centurion stopped him as the Roman was concerned that Jesus would violate Jewish protocols. Jesus' also healed gentiles and the second of his feeding miracles occurred in the Decapolis (Mark 7:31–9)—a gentile region likely with gentile participants. He also dined with sinners, for which he was criticized.[19] The freedom Christians have in table fellowship is derived from Christ's table fellowship with sinners.[20] Peter should have known this from this encounter recorded in both Mark and Matthew.

Luke does not take account of Mark 7's food material but does tell us of God directing Peter through a vision to lay aside

---

18. Harrington, 'Purity,' 1122.
19. See Matt 9:10–13; 11:19; Mark 2:15–17; Luke 5:30–32; 7:34; 15:1–2.
20. One can also argue that Jesus dining in the homes of the Pharisees is another example of his dining with sinners (e.g., Luke 7, 11, 14), as the Jewish leaders were sinners as much as any other humans and arguably, more so. He also healed gentiles, touching them and driving sickness and demons from them (e.g., Mark 7:24–30).

concerns to avoid gentiles in table fellowship. He records that
prior to Paul and Barnabas' visit to Jerusalem (2:1–10), Peter
had been at the center of the Cornelius' conversion episode.
While praying around midday, Peter had been granted a vision
three times of a sheet of unclean animals from heaven lowered
to him, and a voice commanding him to kill and eat. Peter's
response was initially negative due to purity concerns. However,
God spoke from heaven stating 'what God has made clear, do not
call common'—after this occurred three times, the sheet returned
to heaven (Acts 10:9–16; 11:5–10). This spurred Peter's trip to
Cornelius' home where the Spirit fell on the gentiles as they
heard him preach. He said to Cornelius, 'God has shown me that
I should not call any person common or unclean' (Acts 10:28).
In his sermon, he states, 'Truly I understand that *God shows no
partiality*, but in every nation, anyone who fears him and does
what is right is acceptable to him' (Acts 10:34–35). As such, Peter
clearly had a good understanding of the freedom of the gospel
where eating is concerned. The cross of Christ has dealt with
all impurity, and so people of every nation can eat freely. When
Peter pulled back from eating with gentiles for table fellowship
with the Jews, he violated his own theological understanding
gained through revelation from Christ. He stood condemned on
many fronts.

Paul also expresses his desire that Christians eat with all people
including gentiles, urging the Corinthians to accept invitations
to meals at the homes of gentiles without concern for purity
and eating what is set before them—unless someone raises issues
of conscience, then the believer may choose not to eat for the
sake of the other (1 Cor 10:24–11:1). Peter then was acting in
accordance with a gospel without partiality as he dined with the
gentiles.

Paul's words are emphatic in his description of Peter dining
with the gentiles—he uses *synesthiō*, 'dine together with,'[21] and the
preposition *meta*, which gives emphasis to his action. The verb is

---

21. The verb *synesthiō* is found five times in the NT. It is used in the Pharisees' critique of
Jesus for 'dining with' sinners (Luke 15:2) and of those who ate and drank with Jesus
in his ministry (Acts 10:41). It is used in Acts 11:3 of Peter eating with Cornelius'

imperfect, indicating a habitual past practice.[22] Scholars debate whether Peter was still eating only kosher food while eating with them,[23] or whether he ate as did the gentiles. We cannot know for sure; however, 'live like a gentile' in 2:14 likely suggests the latter, as does the vision of Acts 10.[24]

However, some people came from Jacob.[25] We have no idea who these people are, except that some are clearly Jewish Christians as indicated by the circumcision group.[26] The implication is that these are some from the Jerusalem church who hold to a Judaizing theology. This does not necessarily indicate that Jacob is a Judaizer,[27] or that he held a 'conservative position' on table fellowship—that Jews should eat separately.[28] Nor does it indicate that we can reduce this to a group that was purporting to be from Jacob falsely[29]—after all, Peter and Barnabas would hardly join them if that were so because they too were from Jerusalem and would know the people involved. Indeed, in my view, such ideas can be ruled out on the basis of the prior visit of Paul to Jerusalem where Jacob, with John and Peter, endorsed Paul's gospel (2:1–10). Further, while his letter can be argued to suggest that faith in some sense includes works (although this is debatable to me), Jacob does not endorse circumcision or law-observance in the letter. We can also note that Jacob would have been among those in Acts 11 who endorsed Peter's experience with Cornelius based on a vision that allowed for the eating of non-kosher food.[30]

---

family. Paul's other use is 1 Cor 5:11 where the Corinthians should not eat with those who are willfully and unrepentantly engaged in gross sinful activity.

22. Longenecker, *Galatians*, 73.

23. Dunn, *Galatians*, 121–22.

24. Moo, *Galatians*, 146.

25. There is a slight dispute among scholars as to whether the verb 'from Jacob' is to be attached to 'some men' (some men from Jacob came) or to 'came' (some men came from Jacob). As Moo, *Galatians*, 147 notes, the difference is minimal.

26. Some may be gentiles who had converted; however if so, they are now Jews (proselytes).

27. Some scholars believe that separate table fellowship is Jacob's view (e.g., Longenecker, *Galatians*, 73).

28. Moo, *Galatians*, 147.

29. Lightfoot, *Galatians*, 112.

Neither does this suggest that the whole group were Jewish and Judaizers, for there may have been others among them. However, it does show that there were Judaizers in the Jerusalem Church at this point. This could indicate that the Jerusalem Church allowed them to function, that they had not worked through the issue sufficiently (which they would later, see Acts 15), or that Jacob was the sort of leader who allowed a range of views (as we might see on the homosexual issue in some denominations). So, it is not likely that Jacob was conservative, but as a leader, he was inclusive and perhaps had not fully worked through the issue. They may then not represent Jacob's actual view, but he may not have sought to deal with Judaizers at this point allowing them to live together with those with a Pauline view. Considering that prior to the Jerusalem Council the majority (if not all) of the Jerusalem Christians were likely living faithfully to Jewish protocols and many would-be Judaizers, it is not surprising that Jacob took this inclusive leadership position.

The make-up of the circumcision group is a little vague. The Greek reads *tous ek peritomēs* which can simply mean 'those who are Jews,' 'those who are from the circumcision,' or 'those who are from those insisting on circumcision' ('the circumcision party' [ESV], 'the circumcision group' [NIV], 'those who were pro-circumcision' [NET], 'the circumcision faction' [NRSV]). Some claim that here the phrase is neutral, simply connoting 'Jews' as in Acts 10:45 (and possibly Acts 11:2;[31] Rom 4:12; and Col 4:11). However, these are clearly not just Jews;[32] they are Jewish Christians as they have come from Jacob.[33] Others claim that

---

30. Moo, *Galatians*, 147.

31. It is disputed whether 'those from the circumcision' should be read as Jews or Judaizers. Likely it should be the former as it would have the same meaning as in 10:45 and this predates the Judaizing resolution in Acts 15.

32. Lightfoot, *Galatians*, 112; Longenecker, *Galatians*, 74. However, why would they be eating among the Galatian Christians at all if they are just Jews? Some have attempted to argue that these are gentile Christians with a Jewish perspective. This is hardly the best way to read 'from the circumcision' because, if they were circumcised, they would be Jews either by birth or conversion.

33. Moo, *Galatians*, 148; Witherington, *Grace*, 154–55.

these are merely Jewish Christians in a bland and broad sense. However, they are distinguished in the text from Peter, Barnabas, Paul, and 'the rest of the Jews [Jewish Christians]' (next verse) and so this group would not merely be Jewish Christians, but those who insist that faith is not enough arguing for circumcision and law-observance for salvation and inclusion in God's people.

They are of a similar ilk to the group who afflict Antioch in Acts 15:1–2 and to whom Paul refers in Tit 1:10–11.[34] Perhaps some of them are from the priests who believed in Christ in Acts 6:7. They likely include those Pharisees who contended with Paul and Barnabas at the Jerusalem Council in Acts 15: who argued that 'it is necessary to circumcise them and order them to keep the law of Moses.'

Some connect this concern for purity to the socio-political situation. Under the gentile rule, many Jews at the time were concerned about preserving their religious identity. With Paul's libertine view of the boundary markers, it is then not surprising some were concerned about his theology. This was also the time of the rise of the Zealots who argued for strict separation from gentiles. These Jewish Christians may have been influenced by this Jewish nationalism and so were moved to push for Christian converts to be Jewish. It may be that this is connected with the persecution referred to in Gal 6:12 and so part of their motivation for wanting to have the gentiles circumcised was due to their being persecuted for not doing so (see further 6:12).

Witherington also notes that just after the writing of Galatians (if an earlier date is correct), in AD 49, thousands of Jews were killed during Passover at the instigation of Zealots instigated by xenophobia (Josephus, *J.W.* 2.224–27; *Ant.* 20.1–12). This shows the tension that existed at the time.[35] Further, they may have been motivated missionally, concerned that such free Jew-gentile relationships would drive a further wedge between the Jewish

---

34. ESV of Tit 4:11: 'For there are many who are insubordinate, empty talkers and deceivers, especially those of the circumcision party (*hoi ek tēs peritomēs*). They must be silenced since they are upsetting whole families by teaching for shameful gain what they ought not to teach.'

35. Witherington, *Grace*, 155.

Christians and other Jews. 'But Paul rightly sees that such an accommodation cannot be allowed because of what it would say about the gentiles' status within the community.'[36] At this point in the church's history, the question of circumcision and the law was not fully resolved. Hence, Judaizers and law-free Christians co-existed. Jacob appears to be very conciliatory, nicknamed Jacob the Just, and perhaps this gives evidence of his capacity to retain unity across diverse theology. Acts 21:20 may indicate that he continued to be inclusive concerning those zealous for the law.

One final point needs to be made. While Paul here repudiates Peter (and by implication, the Jews who came from Jacob) for their failure to eat with the Galatian gentiles, Paul's vision for unity at the table is not unlimited. Elsewhere he urges the Corinthians to disassociate themselves from table fellowship with those who claim to be Christians but are unrepentantly and blatantly involved in a range of sinful activities—sexual immorality, greed, idolatry, abusiveness, alcoholism, or theft.[37] Social barriers like race, culture, gender, social status, and rank must not divide believers; these are false divisions. The Corinthians mistakenly thought this meant disassociation from unbelievers, which Paul corrects in 1 Cor 5. However, where someone claims Christian faith but is engaged in such sinful activities, they are to be cut off from table fellowship. Hence, Christian unity is not without its limits. Disassociation comes where the core of the gospel is violated theologically or ethically.

So, when these Jewish Christians who demanded circumcision came to Antioch, Peter 'drew back' (aorist *hyperstellō*). The verb *stellō* means to 'keep away, stand aloof' (2 Thess 3:6), or 'avoid' (2 Cor 8:20). With the prefix *hypo*, it is intensive—he not only kept away but actively did so.

He 'separated' (*aphorizō*) himself. As noted regarding 1:15, the verb *aphorizō* is a rather strong term indicating separation as

36. Moo, *Galatians*, 149. On the socio-political argument see further R. Jewett, "The Agitators and the Galatian Congregation," *NTS* 17 (1970–71): 198–212.
37. See 1 Cor 5:11–13, cf. 2 Thess 3:10, 14; Tit 3:10–11, cf. Matt 7:21–23; 18:15–19; Rom 16:17; 2 Cor 6:14–18; Phil 3:2.

with God and Jesus separating humanity at the judgment (Matt 13:49; 25:32), of people excluding Christians (Luke 6:22), and God setting people apart for mission (Acts 13:2; Rom 1:1; Gal 1:15). It is used in 2 Cor 6:17 of believers separating themselves from extremely sinful people as in 1 Cor 5 (also 2 Cor 6:17). The use of 'he' and 'himself' indicates his own agency—Peter is culpable. He bowed to the pressure and violated the gospel's call for the oneness of all ethnicities in Christ.

The reason that is given is fear, with Paul using the common Greek term *phobeō*. The common verb (ninety-five times) has a range from reverent awe (Rom 11:22), fear (as in the fear of authorities if you do wrong) (Rom 13:3–4), respectful submission (Eph 5:33), and abject terror. Paul uses it in 4:11 again of his own fear that his work among the Galatians is coming to nothing because they are selling out to the Judaizers (cf. 2 Cor 11:3; 12:20). Here it likely indicates Peter's fear of offending his Jewish brothers.

The final phrase 'the circumcision' (cf. NKJV) can simply mean 'the Jews,' but as they came from Jacob, likely indicates those in the group who were Jewish believers in Jesus and/or those who were Judaizers. Further, Paul uses 'the circumcision' here but 'the Jews' in the next verse, indicating a distinction—the former is the Judaizing group, the latter, all the Jewish Christians. Hence, it is most often translated as 'the circumcision group' (NIV84, NIV, TNIV), 'party' (ESV, cf. NASB95), 'faction' (NRSV), or 'those who were pro-circumcision' (NET).

Peter was in a difficult situation. He was in a room with Jewish believers who were still concerned about ritual purity. They were not fully aware of the freedom in Christ. As a Jew himself, and as a highly respected Christian leader, he did not want to offend or cause humiliation for Peter or anyone else for that matter. On the other hand, the gospel of racial oneness in Christ called for him to stand firm and continue in table fellowship with the gentiles. Furthermore, Peter himself should have been challenging his Jewish brethren to stop separating themselves and mingle together as one. This is the call of the gospel. At this early stage in the expansion of the gospel, the separation was a reinforcement of old enmities. Peter erred, and so much so that the other Jews followed his lead including Paul's colleague Barnabas. As the key Jewish leader to those from Jerusalem, it was critical that he demonstrated the unity of the gospel and urged all to dine in a mixed way.

Elsewhere in 1 Cor 9:19–21, Paul speaks of his flexibility of approach where culture is concerned. He was comfortable when among Jews to 'be a Jew,' but, when he was among gentiles, he was equally relaxed 'becoming' one of them in cultural terms. Such decisions are easy when there is no ethnic diversity in one setting. However, here in Antioch, there were young gentile Christians mixing with Jewish Christians. The freedom of the gospel was imperative: people are to lay aside social divisions and come together as one.

This is something we need to bear in mind *every time* we enter a Christian gathering that is multicultural. In my setting in Auckland, NZ, this is the case in every setting. The natural tendency is to cluster together with those 'like us,' whether it be others of the same age, mindset (e.g., love of sport), intellectual level, gender, or race. This is why so many churches in NZ and other western countries are ethnically based—we all prefer to be with people like us. It is simpler and has even been argued to be a good strategy to further the gospel. Like the characters of the sitcom *Friends*, we naturally look for those we blend with and inadvertently become cliquey and violate the gospel. What we all need to do more and more is look around for those who are different and seek out fellowship with them. We need to go the extra mile to incorporate others so that they are not only included but feel that sense of belonging we yearn for. So, at church, I encourage you to sit among those who are of a different culture. At church morning teas and meals, dine with those who are different. Invite people who are different into your homes. After the services at the usual coffee and tea session, break down those barriers, seek out the immigrant, and talk to those of different cultures. The gospel calls for a radical new community—this is as basic to the gospel as telling people about

Jesus. One of the things we preach is the formation of a new humanity that breaks down the enmities of our world.

OTHERS INCLUDING BARNABAS ALSO SEPARATE (2:13)

Galatians 2:13 continues what happened:
And (*kai*, 1:1) **the rest** (*loipos*)[38] **of the Jews** (plural *Ioudaios*)[39] **also** (*kai*) **joined with him** (dative *autos*, 1:1) **in hypocrisy** (*synypokrinomai*),[40] **so that** (*hōste*)[41] **even** (*kai*) **Barnabas** (2:1) **was led away** (*synapagō*)[42] **by their** (genitive plural *autos*) **hypocrisy** (*hypokrisis*).[43]

'The rest of the Jews' likely indicates the Jewish Christians other than Paul among the Antiochians. This may include the likes of those scattered in the Sauline persecution who came to Antioch and initially evangelized the Antiochians (Acts 11:16) including the likes of Simeon (Niger), Lucius (of Cyrene), and Manaen (a friend of Herod) (Acts 13:1) (if they are all Jews), and John Mark, who had come to Antioch with Paul and Barnabas after the collection visit (Acts 12:25). Whoever they were, they

---

38. The adjective λοιπός (*loipos*) is used twice in the letter; first, in 2:10 of 'the *other* Jews' or 'the *rest* of the Jews;' second, in 6:17 it has the sense 'for the rest,' 'from now on, in the future,' or 'finally.'
39. The adjective Ἰουδαῖος (*Ioudaios*) means the Jews in Galatians in all four uses; Gal 2:13, 14, 15; 3:28. It can also mean Judean.
40. The verb συναπάγω (*synypokrinomai*) is another *syn* compound (with) this time with *hypokrinomai*, 'pretend, make believe, act the part, dissemble' (BDAG 1038) and yields 'join in playing a part or pretending, join in pretense/hypocrisy'—'join together in dissimulation (meaning, 'cunning, dissemblance, duplicity, guile') (BDAG 977–78). This is the only use in the NT, a hapax *legomenon*. It is very rare in wider sources.
41. The adverbial result conjunction ὥστε (*hōste*) is used five times in Galatians. With the result sense, 'so that,' in 2:13; 'consequently, therefore, so then' in 3:9, 24; 4:7, 16.
42. The verb συναπάγω (*synapagō*) compounds *syn*, 'with' and the more common verb *apagō*, 'lead off, take away,' yielding 'lead away with.' It is used once in Galatians of Barnabas being led by the examples of Peter and the other Jews to shrink back from table fellowship with the gentiles to dining with Jews only. It can also mean associate (Rom 12:16).
43. The noun ὑπόκρισις (*hypokrisis*) compounds *hypo* (under) and *krisis* (judgment). It carries the idea of 'playing a stage role' and has the sense, of 'play-acting, pretense, outward show' (BDAG 1038) (Eng. 'hypocrisy'). It is found once in Galatians, in 2:13 of those who withdrew table fellowship. This is the only use in Galatians.

were influenced by Peter to separate themselves from the gentile believers and eat only with Jews. Paul describes this as joining Peter in hypocrisy. The particular term compounds *syn*, 'with' and *hypokrinomai*, 'pretend, make believe, act the part, dissemble' and so yields 'join in playing a part or pretending,' or as *EDNT* suggests, 'be hypocritical together.'[44]

The *hypokrin–* word group has meaning drawn from the context of acting, whereby someone plays a part. Whereas in the wider Greek world it was not in the main negative, in the NT, the terms are used in the sense of someone acting a part, faking and deceiving through duplicity.[45] The only other use of *hypokrinomai* is in Luke 20:20 of spies who 'pretended' to be honest, sent to trap Jesus.[46] Here, they joined Peter in his duplicity—on the one hand, he (and they) knew the freedom of the gospel and that he and other Jews in Christ should eat and drink with gentiles, but acceded to cultural pressure and separated. They were thus not living by the gospel they cherish, but by a double standard.

'So that even Barnabas was led astray (*synapagō*) by their hypocrisy' shows that even the great Barnabas, the 'Son of Encouragement' (see further 2:1) who, together with Paul, established the churches of Galatia, was led astray. Paul here uses another *syn* compound verb, compounding *syn*, 'with' and *apagō*, 'lead off, take away.' The term *synapagō* is only used three times in the NT. It can have a positive connotation of being led away with someone for good intent, so 'associate,' as in Rom 12:16 where one should 'associate with the lowly.' Peter uses it in his warning to his readers not to be '*carried away* with the error of lawless people' (2 Pet 3:17). Barnabas allowed himself to be taken away by the hypocrisy (*hypokrisis*) of Peter and the other Jews.

Hypokrisis is used by Jesus of the Jewish leaders who are

---

44. See Horst Robert Balz and Gerhard Schneider, *EDNT* 'συνυποκρι´νομαι,' 3:311.

45. See U. Wilckens, 'ὑποκρίνομαι,' in *TDNT* 8:559–63.

46. The more common *hypokritēs* is found in Jesus' teaching especially in his challenge to the duplicity and double standards of the Jewish leadership (Matt 6:2, 5, 16; 15:7; 22:18; 23:13, 15, 23, 25, 27, 28, 29; Mark 7:6; 12:15; Luke 12:1, 56; 13:15). Christians are not to be so duplicitous (Matt 6:2; 1 Pet 2:1). They are not to judge others, standing in self-righteousness while themselves being sinners (Matt 7:5; Luke 6:42). The destiny of such hypocrites is eternal judgment (Matt 24:51).

duplicitous—outwardly appearing righteous, but inwardly 'full of hypocrisy and lawlessness' (Matt 23:28, cf. Mark 12:15; Luke 12:1). Peter employs it in his injunctions to believers to put away all forms of hypocrisy (1 Pet 2:1). It is a feature of false teachers of Ephesus (1 Tim 4:2). Barnabas (even Barnabas!), who had been involved from the early days of the Antiochian church and who had evangelized Galatia, should have known better. He allowed himself to be led astray from the gospel. This is a classic case of peer pressure leading a believer to yield to something they deep down do not uphold. To be Christ's disciples, we must be strong in such situations.

FORCING GENTILES TO JUDAIZE (2:13)

Galatians 2:14 gives the setting and content of Paul's public rebuke of Peter:

But (*all*, 1:1) **when** (*hote*, 1:5) **I saw** (*eidon*, 1:19) **that** (*hoti*, 1:6) **they were not** (*ou*, 1:1) **acting in accordance** (*orthopodeō*)[47] **with** (*pros*, 1:17) **the truth** (*alētheia*, 2:5) **of the gospel** (genitive *euangelion*, 1:6), **I said** (*eipon*)[48] **to Cephas** (dative *Cephas*, 1:18)[49] **before** (*emprosthen*)[50] **them all** (genitive plural *pas*, 1:2), '**if** (*ei*, 1:7) **you** (*sy*, 1:3), **being** (present participle *hypachō*) **a Jew** (*Ioudaios*, 1:14), **live** (present *zaō*)[51] **like a gentile** (*ethnikōs*)[52] **and** (*kai*, 1:1)

---

47. The verb ὀρθοποδέω (*orthopodeō*), is from *orthopous*, 'with upright feet,' so 'to stand erect on the feet,' 'not to waver,' 'not to tumble,' and is found only in the NT (*hapax legomenon*) in 2:14 of 'stand uprightly' according to the gospel, which Peter was not doing in breaking table fellowship with the gentiles in favor of the Judaizers. It is not found at the time in other Greek literature, hence, is a Pauline neologism.

48. The verb εἶπον (*eipon*) is a less common verb of speech, which suggests 'say, tell,' is found twice in Galatians—in 2:14, where Paul '*said* to Cephas ...' and of promises that were *told* to Abraham and to his offspring in 3:16.

49. **Variant:** As with other references to *Cēphas* some texts (including Textus Receptus) amend it to *Petros*. For the same reasons, *Cēphas* is to be preferred (see 1:18; 2:9, 11).

50. The term ἔμπροσθεν (*emprosthen*) is a common Greek preposition meaning 'before, in front of,' and is found once in Galatians of Paul who spoke to Peter before all in the Antiochian church (2:14).

51. The verb *zaō* is used nine times in Galatians and means 'live.' In 2:14 it is used of Peter's living as a Jew. Paul employs it five times in 2:19–20 of himself: '*live* to God,' 'it is no longer I who *live* but it is Christ who *lives* in me. And the life I *live* in the flesh, I

not (*ouki*)[53] **a Jew** (*Ioudaikōs*),[54] **how** (*pōs*)[55] **can you compel** (present *anagkazo*, 2:3) **the gentiles** (plural *ethnos*, 1:16) **to Judaize** (infinitive *Ioudaizō*)?'[56]

Paul observed what occurred as the Jews from Jerusalem sat separately—Peter broke table fellowship with the Antiochian gentiles, sat with the Jewish Christians of Jerusalem, and other local Jews then followed even including Barnabas. This left Paul alone among the gentiles, creating an otherwise completely segregated situation. One thinks of the USA during the era of racial segregation, especially in the South. Or, more recently, apartheid in South Africa. Not to mention NZ's own story, where, in many instances, Māori and Pakeha were segregated, if not always by law. More insidiously, there is the uncritical segregation that goes on all over the world as people prefer the company of their own 'kind' and do not welcome aliens and strangers. We see it in our city each Sunday as people gather in ethnic churches, where many are mainly European, and where even within multicultural churches, there is a lack of interculturality.

He saw that they (plural) were 'not acting in accordance

---

live by faith in the Son of God…' Otherwise, it is used in *'live* by faith' (3:11), *'live* by them [the works of the law]' (3:12); *'live* by the Spirit' (5:25). The noun *zoē* is used in 6:8 of *'life* eternal.' Aside from 2:14 and 2:19 where it speaks of Peter and Paul's current life, it invokes eternal living in the other instances. Life is an important theme in Galatians. Like Moses in Deut 30:19, he is summoning the readers to 'choose life and not death.'

52. The adverb ἐθνικῶς (*ethnikōs*) is found only once in the NT, in 2:14 (*hapax legomenon*), and with the verb 'live,' speaks of Peter, who, although a Jew, does 'live the manner of a *gentile*' (cf. *ethnos*, 1:16). It contrasts with *Ioudaikōs*, 'live like a Jew,' in the same verse (see below).

53. The adverb οὐχὶ (*ouki*), 'not,' is found once in Galatians, 2:14—'not like a Jew.'

54. The adverb Ἰουδαϊκῶς (*Ioudaikōs*) is another adverb that contrasts with *ethnikōs*, and speaks of living in accordance with Judaism, 'like a Jew.' As with *ethnikōs*, it is a hapax *legomenon* (only in 2:14 in the NT).

55. The common interrogative adverb πῶς (*pōs*), 'how, in what way,' is used twice in Galatians: 1) *'How* can you compel the gentiles to live like Jews?' 2) *'How* can you turn back to the weak and beggarly stoicheia?'

56. The verb ιουδαΐζω (*Ioudaizō*) is found in the NT only in 2:14 (*hapax legomenon*)—the only use in the NT and means to 'become a Jew,' Judaize, from which the term 'Judaizers' comes.

(*orthopodeō*) with the gospel. As noted in the translation, the *hapax legomenon* and Pauline neologism *orthopodeō* indicates not walking rightly with the gospel. Peter, Barnabas, and the others are not standing firm on the gospel of grace, faith, and inclusion. The truth of the gospel speaks of a range of ideas that their action violates. By their actions, they are contravening the unity of Jew and gentile in Christ by faith. Further, they are pressuring new gentile converts to Judaize—become Jews, be circumcised, and come under the law—only in this way do they get to eat together. It causes them to turn to a religious system requiring works that will leave them as sinners before God with the effect of the cross void. As such, it violates the gospel in its horizontal (inclusion by enculturation, communal, culture, egalitarian) dimensions, and its vertical (salvation by works and not grace through faith).

Seeing this, Paul could not help himself and dared to speak to Cephas 'before all.' Cephas is singled out as he is arguably the more influential early church leader and because he initiated the break from table fellowship with the gentiles. 'All' here is the whole church—Jews and gentiles.

Paul asks a first-class conditional (*ei* plus indicative in the protasis) question ('if … then …?'), where there is an assumption of truth for the sake of argument (see on 1:9)—here, it is clearly a true situation. The protasis reads, 'if you being a Jew live like a gentile (*ethnikōs*) and not like a Jew (*Ioudaikōs*)…' 'You being a Jew,' refers to Peter's ethnicity as a Jewish man, which is not in question as he was clearly a Jewish fisherman from Galilee, no doubt circumcised on the eighth day. 'Being' is *hyparchō* which can merely be a synonym for the verb 'to be' (*eimi*), but in Classical Greek, it carries the sense of a state of 'being,' a notion found at times in the NT.[57] While we should not push this distinction too hard, this is arguably one of those cases.[58]

---

57. See Acts 16:20, 37; 17:24, 27; 1 Cor 7:26; 11:7; Phil 2:6; 3:20.

58. See also on 1:14. *Hyparchō* can be used of one's possessions (material state): Matt 19:21; 24:47; 25:14; Luke 7:25; 8:3, 21; 12:15, 33, 44; 14:33; 16:1; 19:8; Acts 4:32, 37; 1 Cor 13:3; Heb 10:34. It is often merely the verb 'to be:' Luke 8:41; 9:48; 11:13; 16:14, 33; 23:50; Acts 2:30; 3:2, 6; 4:34; 5:4; 7:55; 8:16; 10:12; 16:3; 17:29; 19:36, 40; 21:20; 22:3; 27:12, 21, 34; 28:8, 18; Rom 4:19; 1 Cor 11:18; 12:22; 2 Cor 8:17; 12:16; Gal

'Live (*zaō*)[59] like a gentile (*ethnikōs*) and not like a Jew (*Ioudaikōs*)' at first blush is confusing because, on the face of it, Peter has just done the very opposite—choosing to live like a Jew in renouncing table fellowship with the gentile converts and sitting with the Jewish believers. However, this likely refers to the manner in which Peter, both during and since the Cornelius event and including his time in Antioch up to the point of his self-separation, has lived among the gentiles sharing table fellowship with them. The verb *zaō* is present tense, speaking of his present lifestyle (despite crossing the floor to the Jews)—he 'lives like a gentile' among them. He is not concerned to uphold Jewish purity concerns, which would rule out such living.

The two adverbs used here stand in contrast and in first-century Jewish terms are antonyms. The first, *ethnikōs*, is closely related to the noun *ethnikos* that signals 'national' (Josephus, *Ant.* 12.36) or the gentiles (Matt 5:47; 6:7; 18:17; 3 John 7). Here, the adverb speaks of Peter's participation in gentile custom. This does not mean participation in gentile sins (e.g., sexual

1:14; Jas 2:15; 2 Pet 1:8; 2:19; 3:11. However, in many of these, the verb may have been chosen rather than *eimi* because it is more stative, having a sense of permanence.

59. *Zaō*, 'live,' is very common in the NT (140 times) and in Paul (fifty–nine times). It can simply relate to a life lived, while alive (Rom 7:1, 2, 3; 14:7; 1 Cor 7:39; 2 Cor 6:9; 1 Thess 4:15, 17; 2 Tim 5:6), life in the flesh (Phil 1:22), the living (Rom 14:9; 2 Tim 4:1), a living being (1 Cor 15:45), as a vow, 'as I live' (Rom 14:11; 2 Cor 5:15), 'life itself' (2 Cor 1:8), making a living (1 Cor 9:14). Elsewhere it is used for living 'by faith,' the essence of being a Christian (Rom 1:17; Hab 2:4). Other positive ideas include to live to God (Rom 6:10, 12; 14:7), from death to life (Rom 6:13), 'you will *live*' (Rom 8:13, cf. 2 Cor 4:11), '*lives* by the power of God' (2 Cor 13:4), to 'live with him' (2 Cor 13:14; 1 Thess 5:10), living in the Spirit (Gal 5:25), 'to *live* is Christ' (Phil 1:21), we live (1 Thess 3:8), '*live* a godly life' (2 Tim 3:12), and 'to *live*' by gospel ethical values (Tit 2:12). Negative ideas include living 'in sin' (Rom 6:2), 'according to the flesh (Rom 8:12, 23; Gal 3:12), living by law (Rom 10:5), living to oneself (Rom 14:7; 2 Cor 5:15), '*living* in the world' (Col 2:20), and living in false ethics (Col 3:7). It can mean '*alive* apart from the law' (before the law is understood) (Rom 7:9). It can be a descriptor, 'living God' (Rom 9:26; 2 Cor 3:3; 6:16; 1 Thess 1:9; 1 Tim 3:15; 4:10), a '*living* sacrifice' (Rom 12:1). Of resurrection, '*lived* again' (Rom 14:9). Here it speaks of a mode of living in ethnic terms. In Galatians Paul uses it again in 2:20 of the life he lives being Christ living in him, a life in the flesh lived by faith (four uses of *zaō*). He speaks of the righteous living by faith (3:11, Hab 2:4), living by law (3:12), as opposed to living by the Spirit (5:25).

immorality), which he repudiates (see 1 Pet 1:14–17; 2:11–12; 4:2–6; 2 Pet 2:2, 14, 17–19). Rather, it means table fellowship including such things as not being concerned with kosher food or for contamination due to contact with gentiles. In contrast, *Ioudaikōs* speaks of living in a Jewish manner—kosher food, separate table fellowship, Sabbath and other calendric expectations, ritual purity, and so on.

The apodosis (the 'then' clause) is a question drawn from the previous statement that Peter has been living as a gentile—if so, how can you compel the gentiles to Judaize? 'Compel' is *anagkazō*, used in 2:3 of Titus not being 'forced' or 'compelled' to be circumcised in Jerusalem. In 6:12, it is used to describe the Judaizers who actively force the new converts to be circumcised (see further 2:3). Here, in his actions, Peter is inadvertently pressuring the new gentile converts to Judaize. That is, if they want to participate fully with the Jews in life in Christ, including table fellowship with the likes of Peter, they must be circumcised and come under Mosaic law. Paul is calling Peter on the implications of his behavior.

The verb *Ioudaizō* forms the basis of the name 'Judaizer'—someone becoming a Jew. In Esther 8:17 (Greek LXX), it is used for gentiles who were circumcised to become Jews. Similarly, it is found in Josephus of a man becoming a Jew (Josephus, *J.W.* 2.454) and in the form 'the Judaizers' (Josephus, *J.W.* 2.463)—gentiles who converted to Jews. Plutarch also uses it of a freedman Caecilius who was suspected of Judaizing (*Cic.* 7.5). Here, Peter is challenged at causing people to do this very thing—to Judaize, to become Jews.

PART FOUR: THE BODY OF THE LETTER—DO NOT YIELD TO THE JUDAIZING 'GOSPEL!'

CHAPTER ELEVEN: THESIS STATEMENT—JUSTIFIED BY FAITH AND NOT LAW (2:15–16)

Having completed his narrative in which he has defended the authenticity of his call and gospel, and in so doing, laid siege to the claims of the Judaizers, in 2:15 Paul begins the body of Galatians, in which he mounts a long, complex argument to convince the Galatians not to yield to the Judaizers. His argument is creative and complex, full of theological assertions like justification by faith and not law (2:15–21), direct appeals and rhetorical questions concerning spiritual experience (3:1–5), quotes, echoes, and allusions to the fulfillment of OT hopes in Abraham (3:7–29), statements of Christian status such as their not being slaves, but children who have received the Spirit (4:1–7), appeals not to go back into bondage (4:8–11), recollections of past encounters (4:12–20), the creative allegorization of the Genesis accounts of Hagar and Sarah (4:21–31), assertions of freedom and the futility of circumcision (5:1–6), and a final appeal and wish that the Judaizers would completely emasculate themselves (5:7–12).

JEWS AND NOT GENTILE SINNERS (2:15)

Without using a connective linking this to the previous section (asyndeton, see 2:6), Paul begins in 2:15–16 with a long statement emphasizing justification by faith, the proposition he will defend. He speaks as a Jew bought up under the law, yet he and other Christian Jews know that it is not by the law that a person is justified, it is by faith and faith alone.

Galatians 2:15 indicates Paul is speaking as a Jewish Christian on behalf of others:

We (plural *egō*, 1:3) **are by birth** (dative *physis*)[1] **Jews** (plural *Ioudaios*, 2:13) **and** (*kai*, 1:1) **not** (*ou*, 1:1) **sinners** (plural *hamartōlos*)[2] **from** (*ek*, 1:1) **the gentiles** (*ethnos*, 1:16).

Paul begins his theological argument with a statement as a Jewish Christian. 'We' is placed first indicating prominence, and so can be translated 'we ourselves.' Who the 'we' appears somewhat ambiguous but becomes understandable as we consider its context.

'Jews by birth' ('naturally,' *physis*),[3] clearly indicates he is speaking for the Jews, as does the contrast he makes with the gentiles. However, he is not speaking as a Jew who is not a Christian, for such a Jew would argue that while faith is important, works of the law are critical for justification. Nor is he speaking for Judaizers who are arguing the very converse of Paul—justification requires not only faith in Jesus Christ but circumcision and law-observance (cf. Acts 15:1, 5). Hence, he is speaking on behalf of Jewish Christians, most especially those mentioned through the preceding narrative—Jacob, Peter, John, Barnabas, the other Jerusalem leaders, other Christian Jews, and of course, himself. 'We' then is inclusive of Jewish Christians other than Judaizers.

'Not sinners (*hamartōlos*) from the gentiles' strikes the contrast.

---

1. The noun φύσις (*physis*) (cf. Eng. 'physical,' 'physics,' etc.) is found twice in Galatians—in 2:15 it speaks of being Jews by birth (naturally). Whereas in 4:8, it speaks of those who are enslaved to those things that are by nature not gods.
2. The noun ἁμαρτωλός (*hamartōlos*) is one of the *hamart-* nexus of terms indicating 'sinner,' and is used twice in Galatians, 2:15 (not gentile sinners) and 2:17 (found to be sinners).
3. *Physis* is a term found fourteen times in the NT, all but two in Paul. Outside of Paul, it is used in Jas 3:7 of the natural state of animals. Peter employs it of believers being partakers in the divine nature (2 Pet 1:4). Paul uses it for natural sexual relations (heterosexual) (Rom 1:26), gentiles who 'by nature' do the law's requirements (Rom 2:14), of being physically uncircumcised (Rom 2:27), natural branches of an olive tree as opposed to those grafted on (Rom 11:21, 24), nature (culture) teaching that long hair is a disgrace to a man (1 Cor 11:14), of those who are Jews by natural descent (2:15), supposed gods who are not so by nature (4:8), and sinful people who are 'by nature, children of wrath' (Eph 2:3).

It is an intriguing description. *Hamartia* was discussed in 1:4. Here he uses *hamartōlos*, which can designate 'sinful' or 'sinner,' the latter implied here. It speaks of those who are in a state of sinfulness and corruption.[4] In Paul, it is used of someone who is condemned for sin (Rom 3:7), sinful (Rom 7:13), as a general descriptor (1 Tim 1:9), and of those whom Jesus came to save (1 Tim 1:15) (like me). He uses it again in 2:17 of Christians seeking justification in Christ who are 'found to be sinners.'

Here, it can be read as if Jews are not sinners, whereas gentiles are. However, in Rom 5:8 *hamartōlos* is used as a descriptor of humanity before Christ—'while we were yet *sinners*'—the 'we' inclusive of Jew and gentile alike (cf. Rom 5:19). So, the point here is not that Jews are not sinners while gentiles are, but that Jewish Christians ('we') are not *by nature gentile sinners* (they are, in actual fact, Jewish sinners). Now, they are in Christ, and he will focus on what these Jewish Christians know and uphold—that justification is by faith and not works of the law. Indeed, it always has been and ever will be until Christ returns.

JUSTIFIED BY FAITH AND NOT OBSERVING THE LAW (2:16)

In *Galatians 2:16*, in a long and theologically complex verse, Paul states the premise of the letter. He declares what these Jewish Christians know, though they are Jews by birth who once claimed justification required works of the law:

Nevertheless ([*de*, 1:15]), **we know** (perfect participle *oida*)[5]

---

4. In the Synoptics, *harmatōlos* is used of Jesus' sinful eating companions (Matt 9:10, 11; 11:19; Mark 2:15, 16; Luke 5:30; 7:34; 15:2), those he came to save (Matt 9:13; Luke 5:32), those who killed him (Matt 26:45; Mark 14:41; Luke 24:7), 'sinners' in a generic sense (Luke 6:32, 33, 34; 15:1), individuals like the woman in Luke 7 (Luke 7:37, 39; Luke 15:7, 10; 19:7), and Galilean sinners (Luke 13:2). As an adjective, it is used of a *sinful* generation (Mark 8:38), and Peter's self-description—'I am a *sinful* man' (Luke 5:8, cf. Luke 18:13). In John, it is a denigrating descriptor of Jesus (John 9:16, 24, 25, 31). In Heb–Rev, it is used for humanity (Heb 7:26; 1 Pet 4:18), those who killed Jesus (Heb 12:3), people who need purification (Jas 4:8), a backslidden Christian (Jas 5:20), and humanity in enmity to God (Jude 15).

5. The common cognitive verb οἶδα (*oida*), a term of concrete knowledge, is found in Galatians on three occasions: 1) Knowledge that justification is by faith and not works of the law (2:16); 2) the Galatians who prior to Paul's evangelization 'did not *know*

that (*hoti*, 1:6) **a person** (*anthrōpos*, 1:1) **is not** (*ou*, 1:1) **justified** (present passive *dikaioō*)[6] **from** (*ek*, 1:1) **works** (genitive *ergon*)[7] **of the law** (genitive *nomos*),[8] **except** (*ean*, 1:8 plus *mē*, 1:7) **through** (*dia*, 1:1) **faith** (genitive *pistis*, 1:23) **in Jesus** (genitive *Iēsous*, 1:1) **Christ** (genitive *Christou*, 1:1); **and** (*kai*, 1:1) **we** (plural *egō*, 1:1) **believed** (aorist *pisteuō*, 1:23) **in** (*eis*, 1:5) **Jesus** (accusative *Iēsous*) **Christ** (accusative *Christos*), **so that** (*hina*, 1:16) **we have been justified** (aorist passive *dikaioō*) **by** (*ek*) **faith** (genitive *pistis*) **in Christ** (genitive *Christos*) **and** (*kai*) **not** (*ou*) **from** (*ek*) **works** (genitive *ergon*) **of the law** (genitive *nomos*), **because** (*hoti*) **from** (*ek*) **works** (genitive *ergon*) **of the law** (genitive *nomos*) **no** (*ou* plus *pas*) **flesh** (*pas*, 1:2) (*sarx*, 1:16) **will be justified** (future passive *dikaioō*).

The first part of the verse may be a chiasm:[9]

A1   And we know that a person (*anthrōpos*) is not (*ou*) justified (*dikaioō*) from (*ek*) works of the law (*ergōn nomou*)

God' (4:8), and 3) of the Galatian's knowledge that Paul preached first there due to an illness (4:13).

6. The verb δικαιόω (*dikaioō*), 'justified, declared righteous, innocent, not guilty, pardoned, acquitted,' is used eight times in Galatians, in one of two ways: 1) '*Justified* by faith' (2:16; 3:24), '*justified* in Christ' (2:17), 'God would *justify* the gentiles by faith' (3:8), which is the only means of justification; 2) Justification by faith is set in contrast to '*justified* by works of the law' (2:16) or '*justified* before God by the law' (3:11; 5:4), which is implausible to the Christian Jew Paul.

7. The noun ἔργον (*ergon*), the most common Greek word for 'work,' is used eight times in Galatians: 1) '*Works* of the law' (2:16, three times; 3:2, 5, 10); 2) '*Works* of the flesh' (5:19); 3) One's own work which each must test (6:4). Other *erg-* terms are found in Galatians adding to the picture of Paul's works theology (not for justification, but to work it out through love). These include *energeō*, 'be at work, work' used in 2:8 of God working in Peter and Paul's ministries, and of God working miracles among the Galatians in 3:5. The other work term is *ergazomai* meaning 'work, accomplish, carry out, do' and used in 6:10 of the Galatians doing good to all people.

8. The noun νόμος (*nomos*) is used thirty-two times in Galatians, emphasizing its importance to Paul's argument: 1) 'Works of the *law*' (2:16, three times; 3:2, 5, 10, 11, 12, 13, 17, 18, 19, 21 [twice]); 2) 'The *law*' (2:19, two times; 2:21; 3:23, 24; 4:4, 5, 21; 5:4, 18; 6:13); 'the whole *law*' (5:3, 14)—the Mosaic *law*; 3) 'The Book of the *law*' (3:10); 4) 'a *law*' (3:21); 'no *law*' (5:23); 4) 'The *law* of Christ' (6:2). All references to law aside from the last three mentioned are of the Mosaic law and/or the works required by it; the final 'law' is the one that brings justification.

9. The chiasm may begin in v. 15 and end in v. 17 as evidenced by the repetition of the language of sinners (*hamartōlos*).

B1   but through faith (*pistis*) in/of Jesus Christ (*Iēsou Christou*)

      C   and we have believed in Christ Jesus

B2   so that we have been justified (*dikaioō*) from the faith (*pistis*) of/in Christ (*Christou*)

A1   and not (*ou*) from works of the law (*ergōn nomou*) because from works of the law (*ergōn nomou*) no (*ou*) fleshly creature will be justified (*dikaioō*).

The chiastic contrast is seen in repeated themes and the reverse orders of B and B'. The center of the chiasm provides the emphasis—we have believed in Christ, and so we must go on believing and not turn to reliance on works of the law as the Judaizers are urging.

'Nevertheless,' translates *de* (usually, 'but,' 'and'), the particle introducing something contrasting with the usual views of Jews by birth. Sometimes 2:15 is translated concessively to draw this out—'*although* we are Jews from birth, nevertheless ...'

'We know' speaks of these Jewish Christians' understanding. 'Know' is *oida*, which in classical thought is a strong cognitive verb speaking of something concrete and proven through testing and observation, rather than something one is coming to know, relational, or in a sense, subjective knowledge (for which *ginōskō* would be used). Thus, it is something they have come to know and trust.[10] The participle is not causal,[11] but functions as an adverbial participle of attendant circumstance ("circumstantial participle") and so adds an associated fact or conception to what was stated in v 15. It is best translated as a coordinate verb with καί ("and we know").[12]

'A person is not justified by works of the law' requires some

---

10. On has to be careful as *oida* and *ginōskō* are often synonyms, but sometimes, as here, and usually in Paul, it is concrete (see the discussion in A. Horstmann, 'οἶδα,' in *EDNT* 2:494. I have discussed *oida* at some length in my article Mark J. Keown, 'Did Paul Plan to Escape from Prison? (Philippians 1:19–26),' *JSPL* 5.1 (Summer 2015): 89–108.

11. Wallace, *Greek Grammar*, 631 notes that adverbial perfect participles like this one almost always belong to this category. Yet here it makes little sense.

12. Longenecker, *Galatians*, 83.

unpacking. 'A person' is general, *anthrōpos* signaling all people—male and female, Jew nor gentile, slave nor free.

'Works of the law' is disputed. Traditionally, the phrase has been understood as all the works required of the law, i.e., 'doing the law,' in a comprehensive sense, particularly inclusive of the key works required in Second Temple Judaism, i.e., circumcision, Sabbaths, festivals, eating laws, purity rituals, sacrificial, and penitential requirements. The alternative view (held by Dunn and Wright in particular) argues that it is not the whole law that is in mind, but specifically *the boundary markers of Judaism*, most especially circumcision.

Support for this is drawn in particular from a Qumran document, the *Miqsat Maase Hatorah* or 4QMMT,[13] where the phrase 'works of the law' in Hebrew is used. So Dunn writes: 'the obligations laid upon Israelites by virtue of their membership of Israel.'[14] 'In principle that meant all that the law required.'[15] However, it would 'mean in principle all that the faithful Israelite had to do as a member of the chosen people, that is, as distinct from "gentile sinners."'[16] As such, Paul is not ruling out 'doing the law' in its entirety, but specifically the boundary markers.[17] This leaves room to say that Paul is not repudiating the whole law, but only these key markers.

An exploration of Paul's use of *nomos* (law) in Galatians affirms that boundary markers *are* of key importance, but Paul is saying more than this. 'Works of the law' features in Galatians six times (and twice in Romans, Rom 3:20, 28). He uses it twice in 2:16 stating that one cannot be justified by 'works of the law.' Not only is justification achieved through faith rather than works of the law, but the Spirit is also received, and miracles are worked by God through faith and not works of the law (3:2, 5). Reliance

---

13. On this document see Michael Morrison, 'Miqsat Maase Hatorah,' in *LBD*.

14. Dunn, *Galatians*, 135–36.

15. Dunn, *Galatians*, 136.

16. Dunn, *Galatians*, 136.

17. See N. T. Wright, '4QMMT and Paul: Justification, "Works" and Eschatology (2006),' in N. T. Wright, *Pauline Perspectives: Essays on Paul, 1978–2013*. Minneapolis, MN: Fortress Press, 2013), 332–55.

on works of the law means a person is 'under the law' and
fulfillment of every aspect of the law is required—as this is
impossible, the person is accursed (3:10)—subject to sin's
consequences including physical death and eternal destruction.

At other points, he uses 'the law' in an absolute sense. For
example, 'through the law I died to the law' (2:19). As with 'works
of the law,' righteousness is not achieved through 'the law'—if
so, then Christ died for nothing because Christ would not be
necessary (2:21). No one is justified before God by the law (3:11).
The law is counter to faith (3:12). The curse of the law is sorted
by Christ, who 'became a curse for us,' dealing with the problem;
ironically, by becoming accursed through being hung on a tree
(3:13). The law was given 430 years after the Abrahamic promise
and does not annul that covenant or make the promises void
(3:17), inheritance is not subject to the law (3:18). The law
functioned in a temporary manner, not to bring justification, but
as a guide to the people of faith concerning how to live (3:19), and
to imprison them to be released; justified by faith (3:21–24).

Jesus was born under the law (4:4) to redeem those trapped
in sin under the law (4:5), that they might be children of God.
Those in Galatia desiring to be under the law, do not listen to
the law and follow the free woman Sarah (4:21). To accede to
circumcision is to place oneself under the obligation to keep the
whole law, as circumcision achieves nothing (5:3). The severing
of the foreskin to Judaize in actual fact amputates a person from
Christ as the person has turned aside from grace to legal
observance for justification (5:4). If there is a law, it is the law of
love, that fulfills all law (5:14), the fruit of the Spirit, 'against such
things there is no law' (5:23), and the bearing of one another's
burdens, which also fulfills the law (6:2). This happens when
believers are led by the Spirit, and if so, they are not under the
law (5:18). Paul's last mention in Galatians is 6:13, repudiating
the Judaizers who do not keep the law (no one can) but desire to
bring the Galatians under the law so that they can boast in their
circumcised flesh. As such, while works of the law are without
doubt inclusive of the core boundary markers like circumcision,

'works of the law' take one into a whole system of doing 'works of the law' (the law in toto).

In sum, for Paul, the law per se is now a redundant religious system as understood in Judaism and by the Judaizers. The Galatians are 'in Christ' and to accede to the Judaizers and do the 'works of the law' is to leave Christ and place oneself under law, a system that has had its time and is now completed in Christ. No human can fulfill it, aside from Christ, who came under the law, lived it, died, and rose again, and now satisfies all legal requirements before God. Believers must remain in Christ and not allow themselves to be seduced into the legal requirements of Judaism, whatever is asked;[18] they must simply believe. They then receive the Spirit. They live a life from the law inscribed by God on their hearts, an inside-out life. This life is expressed in love and the fruit of the Spirit (Gal 5:22–23). This is the life he wants for the Galatians rather than returning to the fruitless legalism of Judaism.

The verb *dikaioō*, 'justified,' is part of the *dikaio–* nexus of terms (cf. *dikaios*, 'just, righteous,' *dikaiosynē*, 'righteousness, justice'). Specifically, in Paul, it is a legal term that speaks of a person being in 'right standing' before God who is King and Judge. For the Jew, God alone is righteous and just (Sir 18:2; Isa 42:21). His ordinances are true and righteous (Ps 18:10 [Eng. 19:9]). Conversely, humanity is utterly sinful, unrighteous, and unjust before him. So, in the LXX, we read, 'all in vain I have *justified* my heart, and washed my hands in innocence' (Ps 72:13 [Eng. 73:13]). Similarly, in Ps 142:2 [Eng. 143:2]: 'no one living is *righteous* before you' (cf. Sir 7:5; 9:12).

For Paul, no one is and can be righteous before God on one's own merits whether through law or any other religious system,

---

18. For example, one might expect a gentile to celebrate Passover or another religious festival. One might insist on kosher food. One might expect drawing back from touching a dead body, expect women to remain separate during menstruation, expect people to tithe, adhere to Sabbath, withdraw from fellowship with sinners, and so on. As Paul says in Col 2:23: 'These have indeed an appearance of wisdom in promoting self-made religion and asceticism and severity to the body, but they are of no value in stopping the indulgence of the flesh.'

including Christianity itself where it strays from a gospel of Christ, grace, and faith. This is due to the universal problem of sin, which brings death and eternal destruction unless resolved by the righteousness of God. As such, how can a person be justified before God? Or how can one be 'declared righteous,' 'acquitted,' 'pardoned,' or declared 'not guilty?'

The Jewish answer is through being a faithful Jew under God's covenant. In Judaism, this is possible either by birth or through conversion to Judaism by becoming a proselyte, which is, to Judaize. For the Judaizers who do accept Jesus as Messiah, they have not fully left this system behind. For them, belief in Jesus is not enough. New converts must also yield to the Jewish law and *especially* (but not exclusively) those Jewish legal protocols that distinguished them from the world—circumcision, Sabbath, feasts, eating laws, ritual purity, and so on. Conversely, for Paul, the only way to be declared righteous by God the King and Judge is through faith in his Son, sent as Messiah, crucified for the sins of the world, raised and justified, who conveys to believers the status of 'justified ones.'

The verb *dikaioō* is used twice in this verse. The first use of the verb *dikaioō* is present tense and speaks of the *present* status of being righteous based on their faith *at the point of conversion*. So, if one is joined to Jesus by faith, that person *is* justified! Not guilty! Pardoned! Acquitted! Righteous! Vindicated! This is the present God-declared status of a Christian on the basis *of faith*. The second use is the future tense, speaking of the final decision of God on the basis of the believers' perseverance in faith. This is what is at odds with the Judaizers. After beginning with faith (and receipt of the Spirit), they are seeking to complete their justification through works of the law (the flesh) (cf. 3:2).

The construct 'from faith' (*ek pisteōs*) is found twenty-three times in the NT, all but two in Paul (cf. Heb 10:38; Jas 2:24). In Paul, it is found in Romans and Galatians only; significantly, it is found in letters in which he is dealing with Jewish perspectives on justification and so emphasizing the centrality of faith for justification. The construct is commonly linked to justification/ righteousness language. So, in Romans, the 'righteousness of God is revealed from (*ek*) faith to faith' and 'the one who is righteous will live from (*ek*) faith' (Rom 1:17, cf. Hab 2:4). God justifies a person from (*ek*) faith in/of Jesus (Rom 3:26). He justifies the circumcised 'from (*ek*) faith and the uncircumcised through (*dia*) faith' (Rom 3:30). Since Christians are 'justified from (*ek*) faith,' they 'have peace with God' through Christ (Rom 5:1). Believers have gained righteousness 'from (*ek*) faith' (Rom 9:30, cf. 9:32; 10:6; 14:23) (s.a. Rom 4:16).

In Galatians 'those from (*ek*) faith are the children of Abraham' (3:7). God justifies the gentiles 'from (*ek*) faith' (3:8). Those 'from (*ek*) faith are blessed with the faith of Abraham' (3:9). As in Rom 1:17, he cites Hab 2:4 (cf. Heb 10:38): 'the righteous one from (*ek*) faith will live' (3:11). Conversely, the law is not 'from (*ek*) faith' but requires the doing of its works (3:12). In 3:22, all humanity is imprisoned to sin's power, 'so that the promise from (*ek*) faith in/of Jesus Christ might be given to those who believe.' In 3:24, the law has been a tutor to Israel 'so that we might be justified from (*ek*) faith.' Finally, in 5:5, 'through the Spirit from (*ek*) faith,' believers 'eagerly await the hope of righteousness (*dikaiosynē*).' In such contexts, *ek* speaks of cause[19] or instrument[20]—so, 'by faith,' or 'through faith.' Thus, while the Godward side of justification is grace, the humanward basis of one being declared righteous by God is 'faith' (*pistis*).

Pistis is discussed regarding 1:23 where it meant 'the faith' speaking effectively of 'the authentic Christian religion.' Here, *pistis* is the agency through which a person is justified by God. The term is used twice in this verse. Elsewhere in Galatians, Paul lives by faith (2:20), the Galatians received the Spirit through 'hearing with *faith*' (Gal 3:2, 5), and in 3:14, simply *faith*. Those who believe are children of the God-believer Abraham (3:7) and receive God's blessing and promise through him (3:8, 11, 22, cf. Gen 12:3).

The law, however, does not rest on faith but on its works, which avail nothing (3:12). Still, the law maintained Israel until

---

19. A. T. Robertson, A Grammar of the Greek New Testament in the Light of Historical Research (Logos Bible Software, 2006), 598; BDAG 659.

20. BDF §195(1e); Porter, *Idioms*, 155.

faith was revealed (3:23, 25). As in this passage, believers are 'justified from faith' (3:24). Believers then are 'children of God through faith' (Gal 3:26) and so are 'the family of faith' (Gal 6:10). They await the hope of righteousness by faith (5:5). This faith *works* out in love (5:6).

Hence, we get a hint of Paul's strong works theology. People are not saved or justified by works. Faith is what is required. However, Paul strongly advocates Christians do good works. These are an outworking of faith, believers working out their own salvation through love. Yet, for Paul, this outworking is still by God's power (cf. Phil 2:12–13). The Spirit in those of faith produces the fruit of faith/faithfulness (5:22, cf. 5:6; Eph 2:10).

When one places such an emphasis on faith as the basis of justification, it is crucial to define faith. Adapting the classic Reformer's three-fold perspective on faith, faith in Christian terms is first cognitive (*notitia*)—an intellectual belief in the elements of the gospel (in Galatia; that which Paul preached). For us, this is the gospel handed down to us in the Scriptures. Second, it is assent to God (*assensus*)—a yielding 'yes' to God, initially (as when Paul preached to the Galatians), and ongoing until their death or the return of Christ (they are threatening to turn this into a 'no!'). Thirdly, it is trust (*fiducia*)—trusting God and his Son who work in us by the Spirit, *no matter what!* The world may throw a universe load of *skybala* at us, but we continue to trust in God, his Son, his Spirit, his salvation, and his providence (cf. Rom 8:28). Additionally, it is relational (*affinitas*)—a deep inner knowing that we are one in God in Christ and he in us through the Spirit who testifies with our spirit that we are God's children (Rom 8:16).[21] It is knowing God or better, being known by him! (4:9, cf. 1 Cor 13:12). So, Calvin defined faith as 'a firm and sure knowledge of the divine favor towards us, founded on the truth of a free promise in Christ, and revealed to our minds and sealed on our hearts by the Holy Spirit.'[22]

It is important to note here that *pistis* can also mean

---

21. A variant on the classical reformed understanding of faith. See J. I. Packer, *Concise Theology: A Guide to Historic Christian Beliefs* (Wheaton, IL: Tyndale House, 1993). I have added *affinitas*, which speaks of relationality which lies at the essence of faith.

'faithfulness,' as it likely does in 5:22 in the list of the 'fruit of the Spirit.' It is used this way in Rom 3:3 of God, who of course, does not have 'faith' as we might have it, but is faithful—so 'will their faithlessness nullify the faithfulness of God?' (cf. Matt 23:23). Whether it means 'faithfulness' or 'faith' depends on whose faith is in mind—that of Christ or the believer.

As just noted, the great question (one of the great NT questions of recent times) this text brings up is 'whose faith?' As in the other instances of faith with a genitive referring to Christ (twice here; 3:12),[23] the genitive 'of Jesus Christ,' *Iēsou Christou* (*pistis Christou*) has traditionally been rendered as an objective genitive—'through/by faith *in* Christ'[24] (e.g., ESV, NIV, NRSV, NKJV, CEV). As such, Christ is the object of the faith of people who believe in him. *Pistis* then is translated as 'faith' not 'faithfulness'—'through *faith* in Jesus Christ.'

So then, on the basis of a person's faith, if authentic in God's eyes, a person is declared righteous by God because of the work of Christ who was sinless, fulfilled the law, died for our sins, rose from death, is exalted as Lord, and conveys to us the status of righteous, justified. We believe and at that moment of belief are joined with him 'in Christ' and are declared righteous on the basis of his righteousness. This righteousness is conferred to us as it was with Abraham. Jesus is the justified one, and we are so justified on the basis of his work.

The converse position has gained much popularity in recent times. This takes the genitive as a subjective genitive[25] and translates it as 'the faith of Christ' or 'the faithfulness of Christ' (see the NET Bible, 'by the faithfulness of Jesus Christ'). In this way of thinking, Jesus' life of faith/faithfulness saves people, and it is his faith/faithfulness that is in mind. However, people must

22. Jean Calvin, *Institutes of the Christian Religion: The Originals* (Raleigh, NC: Hayes Barton Press, 2005), 498.

23. See Rom 3:22, 26; Gal 2:16 [twice]; 3:22; Phil 3:9, cf. 'faith in him' (Eph 5:12).

24. In an objective genitive, Christ is the object of faith—we direct our faith toward Christ for justification. Similarly, an objective reading of *agapē theou* is our love for God (2 Cor 5:14).

25. A subjective genitive treats the genitive *Christou* (Christ) as the subject of faith—it is his faith or his faithfulness (or both) that justifies.

still believe in him as the next clause indicates, 'and we believed (*pisteuō*) in Christ Jesus.' As such, the life of Jesus, the faithful believing one, has completed the work required of all humans. Our faith joins us to him, the Faithful One, and we are justified by faith. While the former view also sees Jesus' work as the basis for justification, this viewpoint throws even more emphasis on his faithfulness and work. However, this view, while recognizing that we as humans must respond to Jesus by faith (for the 'faith of Christ' passages also include the response of faith),[26] there is a diminution of our role in salvation.

The debate between these two positions has been going on for a number of years. In favor of the traditional reading 'faith in Christ' are these arguments (among others):

1. This is the traditional position that was held by the early church and Reformation thinkers.
2. Other than these seven "of Christ" texts,[27] faith (*pistis*) is never used by Paul of Christ.
3. Aside from Eph 3:12, the constructs are only found in letters where Paul is dealing with the question of whether faith is sufficient—as such, the double reference to faith is intentional and emphatic, not a redundancy—he is emphasizing that it is faith and faith alone that justifies (Rom 3:22).[28] Furthermore, if the verse is a chiasm, the emphasis is seen in the central statement, 'and we have believed in Christ Jesus.
4. Although genitives with faith like this one in Paul and the NT are *always* subjective referring to the faith of the person (e.g., faith of Abraham, Rom 4:16, 'your faith,' e.g., Rom 1:8, etc.),[29] this is not a valid argument as

---

26. E.g., Rom 3:22: 'through the faithfulness of Christ, *for all who believe;*' Gal 2:16: 'by the faithfulness of Christ … And *we have come to believe in Christ Jesus,* so that we may be justified by the faithfulness of Christ;' Gal 3:22: 'because of the faithfulness of Christ—*to those who believe*' (NET).

27. Romans 3:22, 26; Gal 2:16 [2x]; 3:22; Phil 3:9; also, Eph 3:12 (of him).

28. '*Faith* in Jesus Christ for all who *believe*' (Rom 3:22).

29. See also Rom 1:12; 1 Cor 2:5; 15:14, 17; 16:13; 2 Cor 1:24; 10:15; Eph 1:15; Col 1:4; 2:5; 1 Thess 1:8; 3:2, 5, 6, 7, 10; 2 Cor 1:3, 4; Phlm 5, 6, cf. 2 Cor 8:7; Phil 1:25; 1 Thess

Christ is not a mere person who directs faith to God but is the Son of God in whom we believe.

5.   Where God is used genitivally with faith (*pistin Theou*), 'faith in God' is the best translation (Mark 11:22). Similarly, Rev 14:12, *pistin Iēsou* should be translated as 'faith in Jesus.' In Paul, in Col 2:12 he uses the genitive to define the object of faith: 'faith in the power of God' (*tēs pisteōs tēs energeias tou Theou*); 'faith in the truth' (*pistei alētheias*)—so it is argued, it should be with *pistis Iēsous*. Further, the genitive is used with the verb of the object of believing; for example, 'believed *in* God' (*episteusen Theou …*) (Rom 4:17). Similarly, in Rom 10:14, Christ is implied as the object of belief using a genitive (verb): 'how can they call upon *one* in whom they have not believed? And how can they believe *in* (*ou*) one [Christ] of whom they have not heard …?'

6.   The contrast with 'faith' is 'works of the law' or 'works,' and the actor is the person seeking righteousness (they seek to do the works of the law for justification). By analogy, the converse is more likely; the actor in terms of faith is the believer and Christ the object (e.g., Phil 3:9).

7.   All other references to faith that do not express an object become ambiguous and could possibly be 'Christ's faith/faithfulness' rather than the believer's faith. This means that texts aside from these texts in Galatians, Romans, Phil 3,[30] and in the other Paulines[31]—that refer to believing or faith without specification concerning the object or agency of

---

1:3; 2 Thess 1:11. See too Matt 9:2, 22, 29; 15:28; Mark 2:5; 5:34; 10:52; Luke 5:20; 7:9, 50; 8:25, 48; 17:5, 19; 18:42; 22:30; Heb 11:39; 12:2; 13:7; Jas 1:3; 2:18; 1 Pet 1:7, 9, 21, 5:9; 2 Pet 1:5; 1 John 5:4; Rev 2:13, 19, cf. 2 Pet 1:1; Rev 13:10.

30. Whose faith in Rom 3:25, 27, 28, 30, 31; 4:16; 5:1, 2; 9:30; 10:6, 8; 11:20; Gal 3:8, 9, 12, 14, 23, 24, 25, 26; 5:5, 6; 6:10; Phil 3:9?

31. So, for example, 1 Cor 13:13 ('faith, hope, and love'—whose faith?); 2 Cor 5:7 ('we walk by faith'— whose faith?); Eph 2:8 ('through faith'—whose faith?); Eph 3:17; 4:5 ('one faith.' Which? Whose?); Eph 6:17 & 1 Thess 5:8 (the shield or breastplate of faith? Whose faith?). The same questions can be asked of any faith text in Paul.

faith—in each case is unclear. Are they referring to
Christ's faith or that of the believer? As such, 'faith in
Christ' makes more sense in terms of Paul's wider
pistis-theology.

8. Paul uses faith language 196 times including the noun
pistis (142 times), and the verb *pisteuō* (fifty-four times).
Only once does he *explicitly* speak of God's faithfulness,
and never Christ's (Rom 3:3). In the vast majority of
Paul's uses of the noun *pistis*, he does not express the
object of faith. However, faith in God and his son Christ
is implied.[32] Christ as the object of faith for Paul is
explicitly stated;[33] similarly, God.[34]As such, in light of

---

32. See on *pistis*: Rom 1:5, 8, 12, 17; 3:28, 30, 31; 4:5, 9, 11, 12, 13, 14, 16, 19, 20; 5:1, [2];
9:30, 32; 10:6, 8, 17; 11:20; 12:3, 6; 14:1, 22, 23, 26; 1 Cor 2:5; 12:9; 13:2, 13, 14, 17;
16:13; 2 Cor 1:24; 4:13; 5:7; 8:7; 10:15; 13:5; Gal 1:23; 3:2, 5, 7, 8, 9, 11, 12, 14, 23, 24,
25, 26; 5:5, 6, 22; 6:10; Eph 2:8; 3:17; 4:5, 13; 6:16, 23; Phil 1:25, 27; 2:17; Col 1:4, 23;
2:7; 1 Thess 1:3; 3:2, 5, 6, 7, 10; 1 Thess 5:8; 2 Thess 1:3, 4; 2 Thess 1:11; 2 Thess 3:2; 2
Tim 1:2, 4, 5, 19; 2:7, 15; 3:9; 4:1, 6, 12; 5:8, 12; 6:10, 11, 12, 21; 2 Tim 1:5, 18, 22; 3:8,
10; 4:7; Tit 1:1, 4, 13; 2:2, 10; 3:15; Phlm 6. See on *pisteuō*: Rom 1:16; 3:22, second use;
6:8; 10:4; 13:11; 15:13; 1 Cor 1:21; 3:5; 13:7; 14:22; 15:2, 11; 2 Cor 4:13; Gal 3:22; Eph
1:19; 1 Thess 1:7; 2:10, 13; 2 Thess 1:10.

33. Using *Pistis*: Faith in Christ, he often uses *en* (in): *pisteōs en tō autou* (faith **in** him) (Rom
3:25); *en pistie zō tē tou huiou tou Theou* (faith **in** the Son of God) (Gal 2:20); *pistin en tō
kyriō Iēsou* (faith **in** the Lord Jesus) (Eph 1:15); *tēn pistin hymōn en Christō Iēsou* (your
faith **in** Christ Jesus) (Col 1:4); *pisteōs tēs en Christō Iēsou* (faith **in** Christ Jesus) (cf. 1
Tim 1:14; 3:9, 13; 2 Tim 1:13). Otherwise, he uses prepositions that speak of 'toward:'
eis (toward) or *pros* (toward): *eis Christon pisteōs hymōn* (faith **in** Christ Jesus) (Col 2:5);
tēn pistin, ēn exeis pros ton kyrion Iēsoun (the faith, which you have **in** the Lord Jesus)
(Phlm 5); *ē pistis hymōn ē pros ton Theon* (your faith **in** God) (1 Thess 1:8). Using
pisteuō: Christ implied using a genitive (Rom 10:14): 'how can they call upon *one* in
whom they have not believed? And how can they believe *in* (**ou**) one of whom they
have not heard …' Also uses eis: *eis auton pisteuein* (to believe **in** him) (Phil 1:29). Also
uses **epi**, 'believe **in** him for eternal life' (*pisteuein ep autō …*) (1 Tim 1:16). Also, the
simple dative, '**in** whom I have believed' (**ō** *pepisteuka*) (2 Tim 1:12); 'who believed in
God' (*hoi pepisteukotes **Theō***) (Tit 3:8).

34. God: (Rom 4:3, simple dative, 'believed **in** God' [*episteusen ... **tō Theō**]); 'believed **in**
God' (*episteusan tō Theō*) (Gal 3:6); 'and **in** him you believed' (*en hō kai pisteusantes*)
(Eph 1:13); Rom 4:5 uses epi, 'upon' 'believed **in** the one who justifies...' (*pisteuonti de
epi to dikaiounta ...*); again uses epi, *tois pisteuousin **epi** ton egeiranta Iēsoun ...* (Rom 4:24);
whoever believes **in** him (*ho pisteouōn ep autō*) (Rom 9:33); 'who believes **in** him'
(*pisteuōn ep autō*) (Rom 10:11). In other Romans 4 uses, God is implied (Rom 4:11,
18).Also, uses the genitive, (*episteusen Theou ...*) (Rom 4:17).

the overwhelming support that Paul uses explicit and implicit references to faith in Christ, and never elsewhere speaks of Christ's faith or faithfulness, it seems preferable to translate the *pistis Christou* constructs objectively: 'faith in Christ.'[35]

9. The example of Abraham as a prototype of Jesus, the faithful one, is flawed. In Rom 4, Abraham's faith is directed toward God whereas in Rom 3 faith is directed toward God and Christ. As such, the parallel is not Abraham to Christ, but Abraham to us!—we are to emulate Abraham's faith in God in the manner of trust and belief in God and his Son. Further, while Jesus is an example in Phil 2, he is also the object of faith, and faith language is not used of him in this passage.

However, good arguments can be garnered for the subjective reading 'faith/faithfulness of Christ.'

1. Although 'in Christ' is the traditional position, this does not rule out 'faith/faithfulness of Christ.' It is a legitimate interpretation of the genitive. Extremely competent scholars support it.[36]

2. While there are only seven texts that speak of Christ's faith/faithfulness in Paul, their difference from other texts stands out and draws attention, supporting that Paul is making a different point.

35. Other *pisteuō* constructs speak of faith in content: 'that God raised him from the dead' (cf. Rom 10:9, cf. Rom 10:10); 'that Jesus died and rose again' (*pisteuomen hoti Iēsous* ...) (1 Thess 4:14). 'Our message,' dative, lit. 'Our hearing,' i.e., what they heard; 'our testimony to you was believed' (*episteuthē to martyrion ēmōn* ...). (cf. 2 Thess 2:11, 12, both dative; see also Rom 14:2; 1 Tim 3:16). He also uses it of 'entrusted' (Rom 3:2; 1 Cor 3:5; 9:17; Gal 2:7; 1 Thess 2:4; 1 Tim 1:11; Tit 1:3) or to 'believe' something about a church (1 Cor 11:18).

36. For example, R. N. Longenecker, *Paul, Apostle of Liberty* (New York: Harper & Row, 1964), 149–52; Richard B. Hays, *The Faith of Jesus Christ: An Investigation of the Narrative Substructure of Galatians 3:1–4:11* (SBLDS 56; Chico: Scholars, 1983); M. D. Hooker, "Πίστις Χριστοῦ," *NTS* 35 (1989): 321–42'; Wright, N. T. *Paul and the Faithfulness of God*. Vol. 4 of *Christian Origins and the Question of God*. Minneapolis: Fortress Press, 2013.

3. While it is true that these constructs only fall in letters where faith is at issue, the point is that it is Jesus' faith that justifies people. It does emphasize faith but focuses faith on Jesus, the faithful one. This highlights Christology which is always a good thing.

4. As noted above, the genitive constructions 'faith of Abraham,' 'your faith,' in Paul, *always* point to the person's own faith—should not this be the case where Christ is the genitive?

5. Faith is used in terms of Christ in Hebrews 3:2 where Jesus 'was faithful to him [God] who appointed him, just as Moses also was faithful in God's house.' Revelation 14:12 can be translated as 'faith of Jesus.'

6. The contrast arguing that the agency with works is the person and so it should also be with faith is flawed, as this creates a 'works' theology whereby the work of faith is required. The subjective moves the emphasis on works to Christ as it should.

7. Where God is used in the genitive with faith in Paul (*pistin tou Theou*), God's faithfulness is in mind, and so it should be translated 'faithfulness of God' (Rom 3:3); similarly, Christ.

8. The ambiguity this interpretation creates should be welcomed each time faith is mentioned. On each occasion, the question of whose faith or faithfulness should be asked in each occurrence.

9. While God and Christ are objects of faith in Paul, as the data above (in the footnotes) indicates, Paul has other ways of stating this, he usually prefers other prepositions rather than the genitive, whether *en*, 'in,'[37] or the simple dative.[38] Otherwise, he uses prepositions that speak of 'toward' including *eis* (Col 2:5; Phil 1:29), or *pros* (Phlm 5; 1 Thess 1:8).

10. While Christ's faith is not mentioned, his obedience is

37. See Rom 3:25; Gal 2:20; Eph 1:15; Col 1:4, cf. 1 Tim 1:14; 3:9, 13; 2 Tim 1:13), *epi*, 'upon' (Rom 4:5, 24; 9:33; 10:11; 1 Tim 1:16.
38. See Rom 4:3; Gal 3:6; Eph 1:13; 2 Tim 1:12; Tit 3:8.

stressed as the example to be emulated, especially in Phil
2:5–8 (cf. 1 Cor 11:1), so it is implied. Further, Abraham
is the example of faithfulness in Rom 4, and so Jesus is
faithful and we are in him.

In conclusion, we have a fascinating debate with a somewhat
uncertain decision. People line up on both sides, some
passionately defending 'faith in Christ,' others 'faith/faithfulness
of Christ.' Yet others consider both are in mind, a kind of plenary
genitive,[39] with Paul being intentionally ambiguous (further
below).

Personally, in a split decision, I veer toward the traditional
view for the reasons above. In particular, the evidence that early
church thinkers took it objectively—that, for Paul, God and his
Son are the object of faith to an overwhelming extent; that these
texts are only found in contexts where Paul is passionately
defending the gospel of faith alone for justification against
Judaizers who want faith plus law; and that the contrasts with
works/works of the law and Abraham indicate that the issue
at hand is what we do as humans to be justified—we believe,
we do not do works. Finally, the subjective reading creates

---

39. On the plenary genitive see Wallace, *Grammar*, 119–21 who states that with the
plenary genitive, 'the noun in the genitive is *both* subjective and objective.' Wallace
goes on, 'Almost universally, when a particular gen. is in question, commentators
begin their investigation with the underlying assumption that *a decision needs to be
made. But such an approach presupposes that there can be no intentional ambiguity or
pregnant meaning on the part of the speaker*. Yet if this occurs elsewhere in human
language (universally, I believe, even if somewhat rare in every culture), why is it that
we tend to deny such an option to biblical writers?' (Emphasis mine). He argues that
the key to identification is that if both subjective and objective ideas fit, '*and do not
contradict but rather complement one another*, then there is a good possibility that the
genitive in question is a plenary (or full) genitive.' (Italics his). Some examples include
hē agapē tou Christou (2 Cor 5:14) which can be 'the love Christ has for us' (Christ
subject, subjective) which produces 'the love we have for Christ' (Christ object,
objective) (cf. Rom 5:5). Similarly, 'the revelation of Jesus Christ' (Rev 1:1) can be 'the
revelation that comes from Christ' (subjective) or 'the revelation about Christ'
(objective). Here the subjective interpretation produces the objective, where Jesus
makes the revelation and his concerns are that revelation (in the book of Revelation).
Other examples are John 5:42; 2 Thess 3:5 and 'gospel of God' (Mark 1:1, 14; Rom 1:1;
15:16; 1 Thess 2:2, 8, 9).

overwhelming ambiguity concerning the other texts in Paul which have no subject.

Still, it is an outstanding debate, one that will interest scholarship for ages to come. It may, in fact, be another case of the *plenary genitive* (see previous note). The plenary sees the genitive as both subjective and objective usually where the subjective produces the objective. This could be argued to apply here. The subjective reading, 'the faith of Jesus Christ' (Jesus Christ as the subject of the faith) produces the objective, 'our faith in Jesus Christ' (Jesus Christ as the object of our faith, the objective genitive). So, this may be one of those moments where Paul takes the grammatical form that is intentionally ambiguous and capable of being read in both ways. It is then akin to 'the love of God' which can be the 'love God has for us' and 'our love for God' with the love God has for us producing our love. Overall, while I am drawn to the subjective and plenary views, I remain convinced this is an objective genitive.

In whatever way we read the 'faith of Jesus Christ,' in the next clause, the response of faith is still found: 'and we have believed (*pisteuō*) in (*eis*) Christ Jesus.' 'We' here is inclusive of all Christians, Jews and gentiles. If we read it subjectively, we believe in Christ the faithful one, joined to his faithful life by our belief in him. For the traditional objective reader (faith in Christ), this is emphatic; no person can be justified through works of the law but only through faith, and we are those who have done so, and so we are justified. The Galatians and all Christians must not Judaize, for they are justified on the basis of faith.

The use of 'we' draws the Galatians into the whole body of believers including Paul, Barnabas, his team, the brothers and sisters with him in Antioch, Peter, Jacob, John, and others. For those of us who believe today some 2000 years later, we too are justified by our faith in Jesus Christ, and we have believed in Christ Jesus.

The response of believing is what sees the verdict, 'acquitted!' declared over a person. In humility, they can then claim the status as those justified by faith. Here, Paul is more explicit, using the preposition *eis* of faith, something he does uncommonly (Phil

1:29; Col 2:5)—something more frequent in other NT writings, especially John.[40] *Eis* carries the sense of 'to or into,' and so faith directed toward or to Christ.

Believed is *pisteuō*, discussed in 2:7, where it means 'entrusted.' Here, it has the sense 'believe' as in 3:6 where Abraham 'believed God' and 3:22, of 'those who believe' or 'the believing ones.' With *eis*, it carries the sense 'to entrust oneself to an entity in complete confidence.'[41]

For Paul, as discussed with reference to *pistis* and *pisteuō* language in the epistle, faith is the required response of a human to God in prior to Christ as in the case of Abraham (Gal 3:7–9, 14, cf. Rom 4). It is also the required response of Christian believers who believe in Jesus Christ and his Father for justification. Faith alone is sufficient. Here it is aorist tense, the perfective aspect incorporating the whole idea of initial faith to present ongoing faith.

'So that we might be justified (*dikaioō*, see above) by faith in Christ' restates what has previously been said with the same ambiguity concerning whose faith is involved. It is a *hina* clause representing the result of this belief (rather than purpose)—namely, that they are justified. Justified is *dikaioō*, used earlier in the verse, here in the subjunctive (which is required after *hina*). Whereas the previous reference to being *dikaioō* was aorist and so covers the period from conversion to the present, the future here speaks of final judgment, where one's status as justified is ratified. The only basis for this ratification is ongoing faith, not observing works. However, this is still justification by works in the sense that Jesus has fulfilled the required works, and we are in him.

This verse vividly shows how Paul views justification. Christ is the fully justified one, living a sinless life under the law (2 Cor 5:21; Gal 4:4). Of all flesh and blood, he alone is justified on his own merits. He is thus raised from the dead, vindicated by God,

---

40. See Matt 18:6; Mark 9:42; John 1:12; 2:11, 23; 3:16, 18, 36; 4:39; 6:29, 35, 40; 7:5, 31, 38, 39, 48; 8:40; 9:35, 36; 10:42; 11:25, 26, 45, 48; 12:11, 36, 37, 42, 44, 46; 14:1, 12; 16:9; 17:20; Acts 10:43; 14:23; 24:24; 26:18; Col 2:5; 1 John 5:10, 13.

41. BDAG 817.

and not only has eternal life as God the Son but has earned it (as if he needed to!).

We are *justified in him* at the moment of conversion—a status which is ratified (sealed) by God who imprints us with his Spirit on the basis of faith. At the final judgment, this is finalized as we are accepted into God's eternal kingdom and experience the fullness of transformation from perishability and mortality to imperishability and immortality. This final justification at the final judgment is due to our status as justified ones in the present *by faith*. As with the first use of *dikaioō* in the verse with the aorist passive, the passive refers to God's agency—he justifies believers at the moment of faith and at the final judgment, declaring them 'not guilty,' 'acquitted,' 'pardoned,' 'justified,' 'righteous,' and *gerechtfertigt!*[42]

'Faith in Christ' is literally the genitive *pisteōs Christou*, and so can be 'faithfulness/faith of Christ' (subjective) or 'faith in Christ' (objective). As discussed above, scholarship is divided. While I remain committed to the objective view, it could be that both are in mind (see above on *pisteōs Iēsou Christou*).

'And not from works of the law' restates the earlier part of the verse—no person is justified by works of the law. Faith is the only response through which a human can be justified before God. The final clause gives the reason (causal *hoti*)—'because from works of the law no *flesh* (**sarx**) will be justified (future passive *dikaioō*).

Whereas Paul used the standard term for human earlier (*anthrōpos*), here he says literally: 'not all flesh,' connoting 'no fleshly being.' Paul perhaps uses *sarx* here as for him, *sarx* often speaks of the fallen human state, riddled with sin and destined for death. Further, this is the problem of the whole living world, in which all vegetation and creatures of flesh are subject to decay and death. This is due not to animal sin, but the violation of God's injunctions by the supreme fleshly creature, humans, made in God's image, to rule over his world on his behalf. We have usurped God's prerogatives, and so the whole created order is

---

42. German for 'justified,' a favorite term of Luther.

corrupted, yearning to be set free from sin, decay, and death (Rom 5:12; 8:19–23).

This problem of decay and death must be dealt with for people to dwell eternally with God, who is pure goodness as is his realm. The world itself will be set free from its bondage to decay. We and our world must be purified. The means of this is Jesus' death, to which we are joined by faith, justified and sanctified, so that we experience by the Spirit internal transformation and freedom from sin, and await our final transformation eagerly into 'spiritual bodies' (1 Cor 15:44)—bodies freed from sin and fully animated by the Spirit. The world itself also awaits this, the revelation of the children of God, when the Spirit of God floods the world washing away all sin and corruption. Then, the creation itself will experience its full transformation into the world God created it to be—eternal, glorious, and free from death. The final state of justification requires this transformation, or should I say, the final transformed state requires this justification. For those who believe in Christ, and so are justified, this is a certainty—'their labor in the Lord is not in vain' (1 Cor 15:58).

In sum, this astonishing verse states the premise of Galatians. No human being who is mere fallen flesh corrupted by sin can be justified through obedience to the law—other than Jesus that is. He alone did it. Rather, the only path to being justified is by faith in this law-fulfilling Christ Jesus. In him, they are justified as he is, and if they remain in him, will hear God's voice in the final day cry out, 'innocent! Come into the kingdom prepared for you since the beginning of creation.' This is a renewed world without pain, tears, suffering, death, and torment (Matt 25:34; Rev 21:4). As such, the Galatians must not yield to the false gospel of the Judaizers who are telling them faith is *not enough*. In addition to believing in Christ, they must yield to Judaism's boundary markers and come under the Torah. For Paul, this is to return to a system that has had its day. Now and until the return of Christ, faith in Christ is required and faith alone. After that, faith will no longer be required for we will not only be fully known, but we

ourselves will have full relational and revealed knowledge of God
for all eternity (cf. 1 Cor 13:13).

CHAPTER TWELVE: THE JUDAIZERS RATHER THAN CHRIST SERVE SIN (2:17–18)

Galatians 2:17–18 is extremely challenging. How do these verses fit into Paul's argument against the Judaizers? Moo notes that there are two main interpretations. First, it could be that Paul is considering the Jewish Christian experience *as they came to Christ in conversion*. At this time, they found themselves to be sinners like the gentiles and in need of Christ for justification. This does not cause Christ to be sin's servant, as they were always sinners. Verse 18 then is the explanation—it is when they go back under the Torah (as do Judaizers) that they become transgressors either because they become guilty for their sins again (severed from Christ), or through breaking the 'law of the gospel.' This idea fails to convince because there is no sense in which Paul felt like a gentile sinner before his conversion. Rather, he was confident in his Jewishness, as expressed most clearly in Phil 3:4–6, especially 'concerning the law, blameless' (cf. 1:13–14). His conversion came about not through a deep awareness of sin (as in the case of Luther) and perceived need, but through Christ who surprisingly disrupted his self-confident Pharisaic life on the road to Damascus. It was subsequent to this experience that he realized that he and other Jews are no different from the gentiles (see Rom 7:13–25).

The alternative is that Paul is considering the Jewish Christians *in their post-conversion context*. They are presently seeking justification in Christ and have abandoned the law as a means of justification (v. 16). They, therefore, are themselves found (or acknowledge themselves) to be 'sinners' like the gentiles who live without the law (cf. 'gentile sinners,' v. 15).

Knowing this, however, does not make Jesus a servant of sin through the abandonment of the law, as some of his opponents are likely claiming. Absolutely not! But if Jewish Christians or any other Christians seek to rebuild the law as their ultimate authority subsequent to conversion by faith in Christ to God, they return to the legal system and become transgressors of the law. Otherwise, if they resist this, they are free of the law. This view is to be preferred as it makes much better sense of the reality of the experience of Paul and fits the context.[1]

These two verses are brilliantly ironical. Reference to being found as sinners is clearly true—for all have sinned (Rom 3:23). The idea that Christ is a servant of sin is clearly revolting to Paul (and any genuine Christian, cf. 1 Cor 12:3). The Judaizers are seemingly charging Paul for doing this in revoking law observance. Then Paul turns this on its head. If he rebuilds the law (as *they* are doing), this is what would prove him to be a transgressor. Of course, he is not rebuilding the law; they are! So, ironically, they are proving their own sinfulness in doing so, revoking Christ for the law (which avails nothing). Further, by using the first person, Paul reminds readers of his own destruction of the church. If he rebuilds the law, he does it again, this time not through persecution but through false teaching. This is indeed what the Judaizers are doing! They are continuing the persecution work of Paul, if unwittingly and inadvertently!

CHRIST IS NOT A SERVANT OF SIN? (2:17)

In *Galatians 2:17* Paul writes:

But (*de*, 1:15) **if** (*ei*, 1:7) **in seeking** (present participle *zēteō*, 1:10) **to be justified** (aorist passive infinitive *dikaioō*, 2:16) **in** (*en*, 1:6) **Christ** (*Christos*, 1:1) **we ourselves** (plural *autos*, 1:1) **have also** (*kai*, 1:1) **been found** (aorist passive *heuriskō*)[2] **[to be] sinners** (*hamartōlos*, 2:15), **[is] Christ** (*Christos*) **then** (*ara*)[3] **a servant**

---

1. Moo, *Galatians*, 164.

2. Galatians 2:17 is the only use of the common Greek verb εὑρίσκω (*heuriskō*) meaning 'find.' In 2:17, Jewish Christian believers are *'found* to be sinners' like the gentile sinners (v. 15).

(*diakonos*)[4] **of sin** (genitive *harmartia*, 1:4)? **May it never** (*mē*, 1:7) **be** (aorist middle optative *ginomai*)![5]

The sentence is conditional, linked to the previous by *de* (here connoting 'but'), and so building on the previous statement of justification by faith and not works of the law. The conditional conjunction *ei* denotes 'if,' and with the present indicative, it indicates a first-class condition, which speaks of something real (see on 1:9)—indeed, as with all humans, 'we' *are* found to be sinners.

The protasis picks up 'justified' from the previous verse where Paul stresses that justification is in Christ alone—so 'if in seeking (on *zēteō*, see 1:10) to be justified in Christ' is indeed correct (on 'in Christ,' see 1:22). Seeking justification is what he, Peter, Jacob, John, and other authentic Jewish Christians are seeking to do, for they know that this is the only way to receive justification, by faith in Christ (or of and in Christ) (2:15–16) (on justification see 2:16). Conversely, the Judaizers want more as they are concerned that faith is not enough; they must also come under the law as the basis for their salvation, ethics, ecclesiology, and mission.

'We ourselves have also been found to be sinners' completes the protasis. 'We' for consistency must be Jewish Christians like

---

3. The interrogative particle ἆρα (*ara*), is found once in 2:17. It is a 'marker of a tone of suspense or impatience in interrogation, *then* w. the onus for a correct answer put on the addressee' (BDAG 127)—it has the sense 'then.' It is not to be confused with ἄρα.

4. Paul only uses διάκονος (*diakonos*) once in Galatians, in 2:17, in asking whether Christ is a 'servant' or 'minister' of sin, now that gentile Jewish Christians have abandoned the law as a means of justification and gentile 'sinners' are included in God's people without circumcision and law submission.

5. The verb γίνομαι, *ginomai*, which has a range including 'become, be, be born, come to pass, etc.' is used twelve times in Galatians. The formula μὴ γένοιτο, used commonly by Paul, is found in 2:17 where *ginomai* is aorist optative, a verbal mood 'used in prayers, wishes and other instances to denote verbal action that is possible' (*PDSNTG* 91). *Mē genoito* is an exclamation meaning literally 'may it not be,' 'may it not happen,' or 'never!' *nein!* 'not at all!' 'absolutely not,' etc. (see also 3:21; 6:14). *Ginomai* carries the meaning 'become' in 3:13 (Christ *becoming* a curse for us). In 3:14 it connotes 'come' (the blessing of Abraham might *come* to the gentiles); similarly, 'came' in 3:17 (law *came* 430 years after). It means 'was' (or 'became') in Gal 3:24 (the law **became** our guardian). 'Become' is appropriate in 4:12 (*become* as I am); 4:16 (have I then *become* your enemy); 5:26 (let us not *become* arrogant). It means 'born' in Gal 4:4 (*born* of woman, *born* under the law).

Paul, Jacob, and John. 'Ourselves' (*autoi*) is not required; hence, its inclusion is for emphasis. As noted above, this speaks of the reality of the situation for all who seek justification by faith in Christ—all are sinners. Paul amplifies this type of thinking in Romans 1:18–3:20, showing that 'Jews and gentiles alike are all under the power of sin' (Rom 3:9).' Jews are in the same position as gentile sinners before God, even with all their advantages (2:15, cf. Rom 3:1–8; 9:1–5). As such, Jewish Christians cannot keep the law, which they are required to do if they are to be justified by the works of the law. He has also just ruled this out (v. 16). As he will discuss later, this does not mean Jews prior to Christ are lost. Those with faith like Abraham are justified as he is. Of course, Abraham was at the time of Gen 15:6 a gentile! So, justification has always been by faith for gentiles and Jews alike.

So then (*ara*),[6] does the fact that Jews seeking justification in Christ (and by inference gentiles, v. 15), make Jesus a servant (*diakonia*) of sin (*hamartia*, see 1:4)? *Diakonia* can have the sense of a minister or servant, the former more an anachronistic institutionalized interpretation of the term. Paul uses the term of a governing authority who, in actual fact, is a servant of God in his governance of the world, wittingly or unwittingly (Rom 13:4). He also uses it of the office of deacon of those who serve in the church alongside elders, perhaps in secondary roles (Rom 16:1; Phil 1:1; 1 Tim 3:8, 12). Satan's emissaries are described this way (2 Cor 11:15). Most commonly, it is used for one who serves in the gospel mission—a *diakonia*.[7] As here, in Rom 15:8, he uses it positively of Christ who 'became a servant to the uncircumcised' in his mission.

Here, he speaks of Christ as a servant of sin. This is likely a charge used against Paul by the Judaizers who are saying that in preaching freedom from the law, Paul is encouraging sinfulness

---

6. *Ara* is a relatively uncommon marker of suspense, impatience, or interrogation so signifying '*then*' (BDAG 127). It is not particularly common in the NT where it is used eighteen times. See only once else in Paul in 2 Cor 1:17. Here, it may carry that sense of impatience and frustration with the Galatians. It is not to be mistaken for ἄρα, also transliterated *ara*, see 2:21.

7. See Rom 4:3; Gal 3:6; Eph 1:13; 2 Tim 1:12; Tit 3:8.

among converts as they fail to uphold Jewish protocols and fall into uncleanness—things like ritual purity and eating requirements, Sabbath violation, and so forth. The Judaizers are misguidedly concerned for the ethical lives of converts. Certainly, they are in Christ, but how then must they live? Must they not uphold the law given by God through Moses years ago? Paul will deal with this question with his doctrine of the Spirit in Chs. 5–6 in particular—believers live out of the supreme law of love by the Spirit who generates in them Spirit-fruit. By advocating a law-free Christian life, Paul is not an antinomian or a repudiator of ethics; his opponents fail to understand him. They have a deficient Christology—Christ's death deals with the problem of ethical impurity. Equally, they have a flawed Pneumatology—the Spirit is the power that brings the ethical life God requires.

Paul deals with this type of stuff in Romans. For example, in Romans 3:8 he deals with the accusation 'why not do evil that good may come?—as some people slanderously charge us with saying?' He responds—'their condemnation is just.' In Romans 6:1, his opponents state, 'are we to continue in sin that grace may abound?' He answers as here, 'may it never be!' He tells the Romans that their baptism symbolizes their death to sin, and so they are under grace. In Romans 6:14, mimicking his opponents, he asks, 'Are we to sin because we are not under law but under grace?' Again, he replies, 'may it never be!' Believers are slaves of righteousness and not of sin. Such arguments distort Paul's works theology. By repudiating justification by works, Paul is not repudiating works! They simply cannot bring justification for no one can fulfill the requirements of the law before a perfect, holy God. However, once a person is gifted justification on the basis of faith, that individual's life's goal is to continue to please their Savior God by living the good works he has prepared for them to do.

Here he replies abruptly and emphatically, 'may it never be' (*mē genoito*). Aside from Luke 20:16, the other fourteen uses of this clause are found in Paul. For him, it is a favorite device drawn from diatribe.[8] He uses it twice else in Galatians (3:21;

6:14) and elsewhere especially in Romans.[9] Literally, the aorist optative *ginomai* and emphatic negation *mē* can be translated, 'may it never be!' In all his uses apart from 6:14 where it is used mid-sentence of his determination never to boast of anything other than the cross of Christ, he uses it to answer a question—whether one of his opponents literally or potentially (anticipated).

Concerning Paul's use of the emphatic clause, Wallace rightly states, 'Here it indicates, as it usually does, his repulsion at the thought that someone might infer an erroneous conclusion from the previous argument.'[10] So Paul, here, utterly repudiates the idea of Christ being a servant of sin. For Paul, Jesus 'knew no sin' (2 Cor 5:21), so the idea that he is a servant of sin is preposterous and repulsive. Jesus certainly came as the one who fulfills Isaiah's prophetic expectation of God's Servant to serve (e.g., Rom 15:8; Phil 2:7). However, he did not come to be a servant of sin in the sense of overlooking sin or leading people into sin.

Conversely, Jesus came to deal with sin! He 'died for our sins'

---

8. *PDNTG* 46 defines 'diatribe' as '[a]n ancient literary style that employs the device of an imaginary dialogue partner or opponent [interlocutor], and which is often drawn out or acrimonious.'

9. For *mē genoito* see Rom 3:4, 6, 31; 6:2, 15; 7:7, 13; 9:14; 11:1, 11; 1 Cor 6:15. The term *ginomai* is very common in the NT, 668 times, with Paul using it 140 times. Aside from *mē genoito*, Paul uses it in Galatians in four other ways: 1) 'Become, became' (3:13; 4:12, 16; 5:26, see also Rom 2:25; 4:18; 7:13; 9:29; 10:20; 11:9, 17; 15:8; 1 Cor 1:30; 3:13, 18; 4:9, 13; 7:21, 23; 8:9; 9:20, 22; 10:7; 11:19; 13:1, 11; 15:45; 2 Cor 5:17, 21; Eph 3:7; Phil 1:13; 2:8; 3:6; Col 1:23, 25; 1 Thess 1:6, 7; 2:8, 14; 1 Tim 2:14; 2 Tim 3:9; Tit 3:7; Phlm 6). 2) 'Born' (4:4, see also Rom 1:3; Phil 2:7). 3) 'Be, been' (3:24, see also Rom 3:4, 19; 6:5; 7:3, 4; 11:5, 6, 34; 12:16; 15:16, 31; 16:3, 7; 1 Cor 4:16; 7:36; 9:15, 23, 27; 10:20, 32; 11:1; 14:20, 25, 26, 40; 15:10, 37, 54, 58; 16:2, 14; 2 Cor 1:19; 6:14; 7:14; 8:14; 12:11; Eph 4:32; 5:1, 7, 17; 6:3; Phil 2:15; 3:17; Col 1:18; 3:15; 4:11; 1 Thess 1:5; 2:1, 7, 10; 1 Thess 3:5; 1 Tim 4:12). 4) 'Come, came' (3:14, 17, see also Rom 11:25; 1 Cor 2:3; 4:5; 2 Cor 3:7; Eph 2:13; 1 Thess 1:5; 2:5; 1 Tim 6:4; 2 Tim 1:17). Other meanings include 'happen' or 'happened' ('came to be,' 'to pass') (1 Cor 10:6; 2 Cor 1:8; 1 Thess 3:4; 2 Tim 2:18; 3:11); 'do,' 'done' (Eph 5:12); and 'removed' (been taken) (2 Thess 2:7); is (1 Tim 5:9).

10. Wallace, *Greek Grammar*, 482 who adds: 'The apostle could have expressed his sentiment with οὐ μὴ γένηται, except that the optative seems to appeal to the volition: *You should never conclude such a thing! God forbid that you should think this! No way!* and the like.'

(1 Cor 15:3) and 'gave himself for our sins to deliver us from the present evil age' (Gal 1:4). In him, believers have 'redemption, the forgiveness of sins' (Col 1:14). He releases people from the power of sin and death to live lives that please God (Rom 6:6–7, 17, 22, cf. Eph 2:1). He is the killer of sin in the believer (Rom 6:11). The body of sin is crucified to be spiritually raised into life in the Son of God (2:20). Faith releases people from the prison of sin (3:22). Going back under the law (despite its essential goodness) stings the person bringing alive the poison of sin and spiritually kills the person (Rom 7:9, 11; 1 Cor 15:56). Jesus, who is without sin, takes sin to himself and annihilates it so that believers 'might become the righteousness of God' (2 Cor 5:21). As such, they don't have to face destruction, for Jesus has taken this to himself as our representative and substitute.

If Scripture had emoticons, no doubt we would see Paul's revulsion at the charge that Christ is a servant of sin. The converse is the case. He alone deals with it; the law excites it. 'Galatians, do not go under law!' Because you will have to do it all flawlessly if you do. And you will fail! That is the case with every human who seeks justification through law or any works system (Pelagian, Medieval Roman Catholicism, or otherwise). If it could be done, Christ would then have died for nothing!

IF I REBUILD JUDAISM, I AM A TRANSGRESSOR (2:18)

In *Galatians 2:18*, Paul turns to the first person stating:
For (*gar*, 1:10) if (*ei*, 1:7) **the things** (plural neuter *hos*, 1:5) I destroyed (aorist *kataluō*),[11] **these things** (neuter plural *houtos*, 2:10) **I again** (*palin*, 1:9) **build** (*oikodomeō*),[12] **I demonstrate**

---

11. There is only one use of καταλύω (*kataluō*) in Galatians 2:18. It compounds *kata*, 'down' and *luō*, 'loose, untie, destroy' and speaks of destroying something (as in a building or destroyed city)—'destroy, demolish, dismantle, tear down.' In context, it is the Jewish legal system. It is only found twice else in the NT both in Paul of the destruction of the work of God for the sake of food laws (Rom 14:20), and the destruction of the human body (2 Cor 5:1).

12. The common verb οἰκοδομέω (*oikodomeō*) which means 'build' is used once in 2:18 with *palin* (again), of the rebuilding (build again) of that which was previously torn down. In this context, the Jewish legal system (as the Judaizers do). It is ironic, as Paul

(present *synistēmi*)[13] **myself** (*emautou*)[14] **[to be] a transgressor** (*parabatēs*).[15]

Paul begins with an explanatory *gar*, 'for,' explaining why Christ is not a servant of sin; instead, it is those who reinstate the law that serve corruption. Paul again uses a conditional sentence signaled by *ei*, with the protasis proposing that he rebuilds things torn down, and the apodosis speaking of the consequence—he is a transgressor. Whereas the previous verse included a first-class condition, this is a second-class condition indicating something *contrary to fact*, unreal[16]—the opposite, of course, is the case!

Difficult though this text is, in context, it must speak of the rebuilding of the legal system of the Jews—the law as they know it. Of course, this is the very thing the Judaizers are seeking to do—to syncretize Christianity with their understanding of Jewish law. By using the first person 'I,' Paul likely has in mind others who may do the same and adds vividness and force to his statement. He is putting on himself the perspective of the Judaizers.[17]

'The things he has torn down' uses *kataluō*, which is a building metaphor here, speaking of the destruction or tearing down of something. It is used by Jesus to describe the throwing down of the stones (destruction) of the Temple.[18] 'The things' here would

once destroyed the church in the name of Judaism. Now, if he rebuilds Judaism at the expense of the church, he does that same thing in a different way. The Judaizers are of course doing this. Paul uses two other oik- terms in Galatians: *oikonomos*, household manager, in 4:2, of those the child is under until reaching maturity; and *oikeios*, of the members of a household in 6:10, here, the household of faith. The English *econom-* terms come from it (economy, economic, etc.).

13. The verb *synestēmi* which compounds *syn*, 'with, together' and *histēmi*, 'stand, establish,' is used once in Galatians of 'establish' or 'demonstrate,'—Paul establishing himself as a transgressor if he rebuilds Judaism.
14. The personal reflexive pronoun ἐμαυτοῦ (*emautou*) indicates 'myself' and is used once, 'I *myself*,' in Gal 2:18.
15. Paul uses παραβάτης (*parabatēs*) once in Gal 2:18, one of only three uses in the NT, all in Paul (cf. Rom 2:25, 27). It speaks of a 'violator, transgressor.' In wider Greek sources, it has the idea of a warrior beside the charioteer, a foot-soldier (BDAG 759).
16. See Wallace, *Grammar*, 694.
17. Wallace, *Greek Grammar*, 391 suggests that here Paul is politely condemning the readers; perhaps. More likely, however, he is condemning the Judaizers and warning any Galatians who would submit to them.

most naturally speak of the Jewish legal system which is now completed in Christ (Rom 10:4). We could limit these to boundary markers, but in fact, as throughout the whole letter, the entire law is in play.

The use of the first person 'I' gives witness to Paul's primary role in the development of the law-free theology. One of our great debts of gratitude to Paul is the development of a theology that is completely based on grace on the side of God, and faith as the only human response. In the Lukan narrative in Acts, we see this development, particularly in Syrian Antioch. Preceded by Peter observing God pour his Spirit out on the uncircumcised in Cornelius' household, which was not fully appreciated until the Jerusalem Council (below); it was there in Antioch that the gospel was first preached with intent among uncircumcised Greeks (Acts 11:20–21).

As noted previously regarding 1:13, in one of the great historical ironies, Paul was instrumental in causing this to happen, by decimating the Jerusalem Church. As they fled his brutal persecution, they took the gospel with them. Paul was drawn to Antioch by Barnabas (Acts 11:25–26). It was there that the law-free gospel appears to have really taken hold. Overall, however, it is Paul who had met Christ who fully realized that Jewish boundary markers and legal obedience are secondary to salvation and inclusion in God's people. While his law-free gospel was accepted in Jerusalem, it seems it was not until the Jerusalem Council that it became the only acceptable understanding of Christian salvation and inclusion in God's people (Acts 15). The use of the first person is completely appropriate.

'I again build' uses *palin* (again) and *oikodomeō* (build again), a common term for construction. For example, it is used for Christ building the church (Matt 16:18) and the rebuilding of the torn down temple.[19] Paul uses it of building his churches (Rom

18. See its use on the destruction of the Temple: Matt 24:2, 61; 27:40; Mark 13:2; 14:58; 15:29; Luke 21:6. Otherwise, *kataluō* is used seventeen times in the NT: 1) Of the abolishment or destruction of the law or the prophets (Matt 5:17); 2) To find rest or lodging (Luke 9:12; 19:7).

15:20) and of people building them up through the prophetic gifts (1 Cor 14:4, cf. Acts 9:31; 20:32). Paul here is countenancing the idea that he would shift from a law-free gospel to one that requires law. There is then irony in its use, Paul building up Judaism and its law at the expense of the church. In a sense, it is rebuilding the Temple and repudiating the Temple that is Jesus Christ and his people (1 Cor 3:11–16; 6:19; Eph 2:19–22). The destruction of the church of God is, of course, what Paul himself did as a persecutor (1:14) and something he now reviles (1 Cor 3:17). Here, if he rebuilt the law into the system of Christian soteriology, ecclesiology, ethics, and mission, he would be doing the same thing, but in a different way; not with violent force, but with a false theology that effectively renders *Christ*-ianity merely Judaism with Christ syncretized into it. It is essentially ripping Jesus out of the cornerstone of the renewed Temple God is forming with people in him.[20] It is diminishing Christ the Son of God from his status as savior of believers, by grace, through faith.

Later in 6:10, he will use *oikeios*, 'members of a household,' in his injunction to the Galatians to do good to all, 'especially those who are of the *household* of faith.' The use in 6:10 speaks of the renewed people of God in Christ, the true Temple. This speaks of all people from history who believe in God as did Abraham, and now that Christ has come and the gospel heard, it speaks of those who believe in Jesus, Jew or gentile. In my view, this is parallel to the 'Israel of God' (see 6:16).

---

19. See Matt 26:61; 27:40; Mark 14:58; 15:29; John 2:29, cf. Acts 7:47, 49. *Oikodomeō* relates to the *oikos* (house, household). It speaks of construction. It is used forty times in the NT. Other uses include metaphorically building one's house (life) on Jesus' teaching (the rock) or conversely on the sand (not Jesus' teaching) (Matt 7:24–26; Luke 6:48–49); building in a general sense (Luke 17:28); building a tower (Matt 21:33; Mark 12:1; 14:28, 30); builders rejecting the cornerstone/capstone (Matt 21:42; Mark 12:10); building tombs (Matt 23:29; Luke 11:47, 48); a town (Luke 4:29); a synagogue (Luke 7:5); and barns (Luke 12:18). Paul also uses it of 'love' which 'builds up' (1 Cor 8:1, cf. 1 Cor 10:23; 1 Thess 5:11), and of negative upbuilding (1 Cor 8:10). Two other *oik-* terms are found in Galatians: *oikonomos* ('household manager,' 4:2), and *oikeios* (members of a household; specifically, 'the household of faith,' in 6:10).

20. Cf. Matt 21:42; Mark 12:10; Luke 20:17; 1 Pet 2:5, 7.

Again, there is an irony here. Paul sought to destroy this Temple. To reinstate law is to rebuild the Jerusalem temple and destroy the church. The household of faith is now being built, a renewed Israel of God, and he is focused on this. Not so the Judaizers, who are unwittingly destroying what is being built up. They are still living in the Jerusalem below, Mt Sinai where the law was received, and are not working to build the Temple of the Jerusalem above, the free city (4:24–26).

By demanding new Christians circumcise and yield to Jewish boundary markers and law, Judaizers are effectively rebuilding Judaism as it formerly was. Christ is insufficient and subordinated to the law. As noted, the use of a building metaphor is ironic—they are rebuilding 'the Temple,' which is now Christ and his people. What Christian servants should be doing is building on the foundation of the church (Christ) and the work of the 'pillars' (2:9; Eph 2:20), Paul included, and teaching the gospel consistent with Christ crucified and raised as presented in the NT (esp. 1 Cor 3:10–17). The Judaizers unwittingly are continuing the work of Paul in his pre-Christian state, destroying the church of God by Judaizing.

In the apodosis, the 'then' clause is then given: 'then I demonstrate myself to be a transgressor.' 'Demonstrate' is *synistēmi*, which here has a range of senses including 'demonstrate, show, or establish.'[21] For example, human unrighteousness *shows* the righteousness of God (Rom 3:5) and God *demonstrates* his love in Christ's death while we were yet sinners (Rom 5:8) (cf. 2 Cor 7:11).[22] Here, it carries that sense of Paul demonstrating, showing, or establishing himself as a transgressor.

Paul, here, uses *parabatēs*, 'transgressor' rather than 'sinner,' which he has already used and applied to himself in the previous verse. *Parabatēs* means a 'violator, transgressor'[23] and is used for

---

21. See further BDAG 973.
22. *Synistēmi* can also mean 'standing' (Luke 9:32), 'commend' (Rom 16:1; 2 Cor 3:1; 4:2; 5:12; 6:4; 10:12, 18; 12:11), 'hold together' (Col 1:17), or 'put together, form' (2 Pet 3:5).
23. BDAG 759 notes it is used most often for soldiers who are beside the charioteer.

breaking Jewish law (cf. Jas 2:9. 11). In Rom 2:25 transgressing the law renders circumcision uncircumcision, i.e., worthless before God (Rom 2:25, 27). Here, his use is again profoundly ironic. If he reinstates the Jewish law as the means of gaining righteousness (as do the Judaizers), rather than keeping the law, he becomes a transgressor of the 'new law;' the 'law of Christ' (6:2), the 'law of faith' (Rom 3:27), and the 'law of the Spirit of life' that sets people free from the 'law of sin and death' (Rom 8:1). He would then reveal his own transgression, furthering the work he did as a Pharisaic persecutor of the church. This is indeed what the Judaizers are doing. In their zeal, they are reinstating Torah—which to them is commendable. For Paul, they are violating the heart of the one who is the consummation of the law, Jesus the Messiah and Lord. They are revealed as lawbreakers, as would be Paul if he was to do so.

In light of the previous verse, which indicates that the Judaizers are charging Paul with making Christ a servant of sin, it is, in fact, the Judaizers that are servants of sin—they are transgressors of the law of Christ. This is difficult to interpret, but once grasped, is stunningly rhetorical and ironic.

CHAPTER 13

CHAPTER THIRTEEN: DEAD TO THE LAW, ALIVE IN CHRIST, BY GRACE, NOT LAW (2:19–21)

DEAD TO THE LAW TO ALIVE TO GOD (2:19A–B)

Using *gar* here in **Galatians 2:19–20b**, 'Paul sets up both v. 19 and v. 20 as Paul's positive rationale for his claim that to revert to the Mosaic law in living one's Christian life is to nullify the law's own intent (cf. v 18):'[1]

For (*gar*, 1:2) **through** (*dia*, 1:10) **the law** (genitive *nomos*, 2:16) **I** (*egō*, 1:2) **died** (aorist *apothneskō*, 2:19)[2] **to the law** (dative *nomos*), **so that** (*hina*, 1:16) **I might live** (aorist *zaō*, 2:14) **for God** (dative *Theos*, 1:1).

Paul continues in the first person. He lays out why he cannot possibly contemplate rebuilding what is now torn down, a theology based on law. How could he even consider doing so now that he has died to the law through Christ and been granted eternal life with God? By analogy, this is the case for all Jewish Christians. There is no going back, for the ages have turned and the law has had its day to guard Israel. Christ has come. Eternal life with God is in him. In effect, this of course applies to all Christians, so the Galatians must not go under something that, like their former pagan lives (cf. 4:8–12), is dead to them.

---

1. Longenecker, *Galatians*, 91.
2. The verb ἀποθνῄσκω (*apothneskō*) is used twice in Galatians. It compounds *apo*, 'from, away' (1:3) and *thnēskō*, 'die', and is effectively synonymous with *thnēskō*. Paul does not use the latter, but *apothneskō* forty–two times. The two uses are in 2:19 of Paul's spiritual death to sin, and in 2:21 of Christ's actual death.

'Through the law' is difficult. What law? Through the Mosaic law? Hardly, for the law could not bring death to the law. So, although Paul's use of *nomos* is completely dominated by the Jewish Torah, we need to find an alternative.[3] Possibilities include 'the law of faith' (Rom 3:27). This fits nicely with 2:16 where works of the law do not produce righteousness, whereas faith does. In Gal 3:12, he comes close to this, stating that 'the law is not from faith.' Another possibility is 'the law of the Spirit of life' (Rom 8:2) which sets free believers from 'the law of sin and death' (Rom 8:2). A third option is 'the law of Christ' referred to by Paul in 6:2: 'bear one another's burdens, and so fulfill *the law of Christ.*' Potentially connected to this is Rom 7:4: 'you also have died to the law through the body of Christ.' Some scholars link this to Gal 3:13: 'Christ redeemed us from the curse of the law by becoming a curse for us.'[4] As such, Christ took the curse of the law, and by doing so, believers are released from the obligation to the Torah. In 3:21, Paul states that 'if a law had been given that could give life, then righteousness would indeed be by the law.' One could then say that a 'law' has been given—the law of Christ, the law of faith, or the law of the Spirit of life. These are all, in fact, ways of saying the same thing. Therefore, here, 'law' is ironic in a sense.

Moo notes other options. He and others argue that Paul has in mind his frustration and ultimate failure in living by the law, something reflected in Rom 7:4–14. Paul then is saying in effect,

3. Paul uses *nomos* of law in Galatians in all but three of the thirty-two occasions (2:16, 19, 21; 3:2, 5, 10 [Book of the law], 11, 12, 17, 18, 19, 21, 23, 24; 4:4, 5, 21; 5:3, 4, 14, 18, 23; 6:13). *Nomos* used of Jewish law is dominant in his other letters, especially Romans (Rom 2:12, 13, 14, 15, 17, 18, 20, 23, 25, 26, 27; 3:19, 20, 21, 28, 31; 4:13, 14, 15, 16; 5:13, 20; 6:14, 15; 7:1, 2, 5, 6, 7, 8, 9, 12, 14, 16, 21, 22; 8:3, 4, 7; 9:31; 10:4, 5; 13:8, 10; 1 Cor 9:8, 9 [the law of Moses], 20; 14:21; 15:56; Eph 2:15; Phil 3:5, 6, 9; 1 Tim 1:8, 9). In close relationship to these uses, he also employs it in other ways: 'what kind of *law*?' (3:27), a specific aspect of law, the law of marriage (Rom 7:2, 3), the law of sin (Rom 7:23, 25) contrasted with the law of my mind (Rom 7:23), gentiles who live by the law (Rom 2:14), and the unclear statement in 1 Cor 14:34 which could be the law of the church, the law of love, Paul's law, and the Torah, among other possibilities.

4. See J. L. Martyn, *Galatians: A New Translation and Introduction with Commentary*, AYB 33A (New York: Doubleday, 1997), 257 among others.

'Through my recognition that I could not fulfill the law, I came to understand that I must die to it' (cf. 3:10).[5] However, Romans 7:4–14 better represents Paul's reflection on life under the law *after his conversion*, after he had died to the law. Before his conversion, he was utterly self-confident where the law was concerned (cf. Phil 3:6). He was advancing in Judaism and extremely zealous for Jewish tradition, rather than riddled with angst (1:14). Another alternative is that of Bruce and Dunn, who argue that this refers to Paul's career as a persecutor of the church (1:13–14). 'Through' his faulty passion for the law, he came to see his need to die to it.[6] In my view, 'law' here is most likely 'the law of faith,' 'the law of Christ,' or 'the law of the Spirit of life.' All are creative ways of saying the same kind of thing. Jesus fulfilled the law, and as such, is the law's completion (cf. Rom 10:4). This fits the context and wider emphasis of the letter.

'Died to the law,' however, clearly refers to the Jewish law as a means of gaining righteousness before God. Paul has died to it. 'Died' (*apothnēskō*)[7] is not physical death as in Christ's actual death in 2:21, as Paul lives on in the body. Rather, it is a particular type of death—to the law and its requirements (and to sin and death itself in an ultimate sense). Just as a married woman is released from the law of marriage at her husband's death, 'likewise, my brothers and sisters, you also have died to the law through the body of Christ' (Rom 7:4). Death then is a metaphor for 'release' from the law's requirements (Rom 7:6).

Christ fulfilled all law, died, and rose, and now in him, the law is fulfilled; we are in him, and no such burden remains on us.

5. Moo, *Galatians*, 167–68. He notes in support Lightfoot, Burton, and Mussner.

6. Bruce, *Galatians*, 143; Dunn, *Galatians*, 143.

7. *Apothnēskō* is used by Paul forty–two times overall. It is used of Christ's death: 'for the ungodly … for us' (Rom 5:6–8) and 'for our sins' (1 Cor 15:3, cf. Rom 8:34; 14:9, 15; 1 Cor 8:11; 2 Cor 5:14, 15; 1 Thess 5:10). It is used for Christians who die to the law, sin, and sin's ultimate consequences (destruction) through, with, and in Christ (Rom 5:15; 6:2, 7, 8, 9, 10; 7:6; 2 Cor 5:14; Col 2:29; 3:3; 1 Thess 4:15). Similarly, believers die to themselves and live to the Lord (Rom 14:7–8). It is applied to the human physical death (Rom 7:2, 3; 14:8; 1 Cor 9:15; 15:22, 32; Phil 1:21), and generally (1 Cor 15:36). It is used for spiritual death which is the consequence of sin (Rom 7:10; 8:13). It can also speak figuratively of suffering (1 Cor 15:31; 2 Cor 6:9).

Rather, he lives in us by his Spirit, and we live by the Spirit's impulse, the law engraved on the tablets of human hearts so to speak (Jer 31:33; 2 Cor 3:3), and the law is fulfilled. This is an indicative status and identity statement. As with much of Paul's theology, our challenge is to become what we are—we are justified so that we will be slaves of righteousness, we are holy ones so that we will be holy, and we are free from sin so that we do not sin (and so on). Here, the law is fulfilled—done and dusted.

Now our challenge is to live this out, to become what we are, people who live by the 'law' of the Spirit of life etched on our hearts. Put in other ways as in 3:23–24, believers previously held captive, imprisoned, or tutored under the law are now released by faith *in Christ*. They are redeemed (4:5). They are no longer obligated to keep the law (5:3). They are under grace (5:4). They are governed by the law of love led by the Spirit producing love and other godly virtues from within (5:14, 18, 22). They are under the 'law' of Christ, bearing each other's burdens (6:2).

'*So that* (*hina*) I might live (*zao*) to God' provides the purpose and result of this death to law, 'so that I might live for God.' Paul likes *zao*, using it fifty-nine times. Whereas in 2:14 *zao* refers to a Jewish mode of living (cf. 3:12), here this speaks of new life and eternal life, not in a physical sense, but spiritually—the inward renewal of the heart by the death of Christ through the work of the Spirit. It is eschatological; eternal life has begun now[8] within the renewed human heart through faith (Rom 1:17), which culminates in the completeness of eternal life in bodies and beings completely renewed.

The believer has 'died to law,' and has 'died to sin.' As such, he/she no longer lives in sin, but is '*alive* to God in Christ Jesus,' 'brought from death to *life*,' and 'the life he/she lives he/she *lives* to God.'[9] Similarly, Paul tells the Corinthians in light of Christ's death, 'that those who live might no longer *live* for themselves but *for him* who for their sake died and was raised'—Christ (2 Cor 5:15, cf. Rom 14:7–8; 2 Cor 13:4; Phil 1:21; 1 Thess 5:10; 2 Tim

8. John's theology draws this out most clearly as he repeatedly refers to eternal life as a present status (e.g., John 3:15–16, 36; 5:24, 26; 6:47, 54).
9. See Rom 6:2, 10, 11, 13, cf. Rom 8:13; 2 Cor 4:11; 6:9; 1 Thess 3:8.

3:12). Paul explicates this further in the next verse—while dead to himself, he lives in Christ who is in him, and he lives by faith, not the flesh. This can be redefined as living by faith (3:11) or by the Spirit (5:25, cf. Tit 2:12).[10]

CRUCIFIED WITH CHRIST AND LIVING BY FAITH IN CHRIST
(2:19C–20)

Galatians 2:19c–20 form a unit, one of those many places in Scripture where, in some versions, the verse marker is misplaced. In it, we have one of the great deeply personal Pauline statements of the Christian life. He continues to testify to why he cannot contemplate rebuilding the edifice of law-observance as the basis for salvation, inclusion, perseverance, ethics, and mission:

I have been crucified with (aorist passive *synestauroō*)[11] **Christ** (dative *Christos*, 1:1) **and** (*de*, 1:15) **I** (*egō*, 1:2) **no longer** (*ouketi*)[12] **live** (present *zaō*, 2:14), **but** (*de*, 1:15) **Christ** (*Christos*) **lives** (*zaō*) **in me** (dative *egō*). **And the life** (*hos*, 1:5) **I now** (*nyn*, 1:23) **live** (*zaō*) **in** (*en*, 1:6) **the flesh** (*sarx*, 1:16), **I live** (*zaō*) **by** (*en*, 1:6) **faith** (dative *pistis*, 1:23) **in the Son** (*huios*, 1:16) **of God** (genitive *Theos*),[13] **who** (genitive *ho*, 1:1) **loved** (aorist genitive participle *agapaō*)[14] **me** (*egō*), **and** (*kai*, 1:1) **gave** (aorist active genitive

---

10. On *zaō* see on 2:14.
11. The verb συσταυρόω (*systauroō*) compounds *syn*, 'with' and *stauroō*, crucify, and denotes 'crucified together with.' It is found only in 2:19 of Paul's co-crucifixion with (in) Christ. *Stauroō* is found three times (3:1; 5:24; 6:14)—see on 3:1.
12. The negative adverb *ouketi* is used four times in Galatians. While it can mean 'not,' 'no more,' or 'no further' (BDAG 736), all four uses are temporal, 'no longer:' 'I who live' (2:20); 'comes from the promise' (3:18); 'subject to a *paidagōgos*' (3:25); and 'a slave but a child.' It is important eschatologically speaking of the shift of status of a person in Christ. It refers to what they have shifted from.
13. **Variant:** Some texts, including P46, have *Theou kai Christou* (Son of God *and of Christ*) rather than just 'Son *of God*' (*tou Theou*). However, as Metzger, *Commentary*, 524 notes, 'it can scarcely be regarded as original since Paul nowhere else expressly speaks of God as the object of a Christian's faith.' This is likely an example of scribal error. If not, we have support for the 'faith/faithfulness of Christ' perspective discussed in 2:16 and 3:22.
14. The verb ἀγαπάω (*agapaō*), 'love' is used twice in Galatians; in 2:20 of Christ's love for Paul and in 5:14 in the command to love one another. See also *agapē*, 5:6, 13, 22.

participle *paradidōmi*)[15] **himself** (genitive *heautou*, 1:4) **for** (*hyper*, 1:4) **me** (*egō*).

The verse includes a lot of repetition of terms: Christ language is used five times (Christ twice, Son of God once, plus two pronouns); *zaō*, 'live' (four times), and *egō* (four times, plus four first-person verbs, all with *zaō*). This is profoundly Christological and personal. The emphasis falls on life in Christ.

He begins by stating that he has been crucified with Christ. This is not literal of course, only the two rebels on either side of Christ can claim this 'honor;'[16] although only one of them made the most of the moment (Luke 23:39–43). The very rare verb *systauroō*, 'crucify together with' is used literally for these two men in Matt 27:44; Mark 15:32; and John 19:32. However, in Paul, *systauroō* speaks of Christ's physical death as the means by which Paul's spiritual death for his sins has been dealt with. He is 'in Christ,' and so Christ's death is 'his death,' whereby his and all believers' sins are dealt with for all eternity. So, he writes in its only other use, 'we know that our old self was *crucified with him* in order that the body of sin would be destroyed so that we would no longer be enslaved to sin' (Rom 6:6). Here, he says much the same thing. As one crucified with Christ, one is no longer subject to the law and is free from sin. All consequences are dealt with. The way is paved for resurrection, the Spirit-empowered body, and the fullness of eternal life (a life that had clearly begun now, as this verse shows).

'And I no longer live, but Christ lives in me' is not literal but hyperbolic, for Paul continues to exist as a human person (as the next clause shows). However, while living on, he is 'dead to himself,' crucified with Christ, and now living sustained by the power of Christ within him. The 'Spirit of Christ' lives in him (Rom 8:9, cf. 1 Pet 1:11)—the 'Spirit of Jesus' (Phil 1:19). Paul here

---

15. The verb παραδίδωμι (*paradidōmi*), compounding *para* (from, away from) and *didōmi* (give), literally suggests 'give over,' and is used of something handed over—it is used consistently of Christ's handing over. It's one use in Galatians is 2:19 of Christ the Son of God who gave himself over for Paul (and all humanity).

16. Jacob and John should, of course, have been on those crosses if indeed they had followed through on their bravado in Mark 10:35–40.

is speaking of the reality of Christ living in him by the Spirit. In fact, this is a reference to the Spirit expressed christologically. The interchangeability of ideas (Spirit of Christ, Spirit of God, God within, Christ within, etc.) speaks of the perichoretic nature of the Godhead. So Paul, quickened by Christ dwelling in him by his Spirit, is dead to his corrupted flesh, the law, sin, and its consequences, as he has died with Christ. Now, he is living the inside-out, Christ (Spirit)-empowered life.

'The life I now live in the flesh' refers to his present ongoing existence in his human carcass. He continues to live in a jar of clay (2 Cor 4:7), carrying in his body the death of Christ (2 Cor 4:10), wasting away (2 Cor 4:16), living in weakness (2 Cor 12:9–10), filling up what is lacking in Christ's afflictions (Col 1:24), overcoming sin, and dying every day (1 Cor 15:31). Yet he is sustained by the power of Christ within.

'The life' in Greek is the neuter singular of the pronoun 'the' and so 'the thing.' Here, 'the thing' is clearly 'the life' (an adverbial accusative).[17] While it is subject to death and in and of itself stands in enmity to the Spirit's desires, now he is motivated and empowered not by his carnal desires, but by the power of Christ. With the Spirit bursting through his veins (so to speak), whereas previously he was unable to live to please God, now he has the power to live the Spirit-led life and 'walk not according to the flesh but according to the Spirit' (Rom 8:4), to set his mind 'on the things of the Spirit' and 'experience life and peace' (Rom 8:5–6), and 'to put to death the deeds of the body' (Rom 8:13).

Or, as he will expound in Galatians, he is set free not to 'gratify the desires of the flesh' which oppose the Spirit, and renounce 'the works of the flesh' (5:1, 6, 19–21), and 'walk in the Spirit' (5:16), eat of the fruit of the Spirit (5:22–24), 'live by the Spirit … keep in step with the Spirit' (5:25), fulfill the law of Christ (6:2), and sow to please the Spirit and reap eternal life (6:8).

So, Paul can say 'I live by faith in the Son of God.' As in 2:16, 'by faith which is *in* the Son of God' can be rendered 'in (*en*) the faith/faithfulness which is *of* the Son of God.' As with the

---

17. Robertson, *A Grammar*, 479; Moo, *Galatians*, 171.

discussions on 2:16, this is fiercely debated by subjective and objective proponents. It is difficult to decide grammatically. All the same arguments stand. Is Paul emphasizing Christ's faith/faithfulness demonstrated in his love and self-giving for him? Is Paul speaking of Christ as the object of faith in contrast to the works of the law as the means of gaining right standing before God? Is it both-and? As with the earlier discussion, I support the objective (faith in Christ) view, as Paul's emphasis in Galatians (and Romans and Phil 3) is faith and faith alone. Then again, perhaps Paul is being intentionally ambiguous—he is certainly capable of such brilliance. Whichever is correct, this is a most intriguing debate. Either way, it is by faith that God justifies and decidedly not because of people doing works of the law, or any works for that matter.

'Who loved me' is highly personal. He uses *agapaō* from which we get the substantive *agapē* (5:6, 13, 22).[18] Quite rightly, the verb has pride of place in Christian ethical thought, expressing God's unconditional and merciful self-giving love. It is used of God's love expressed in Christ toward his people.[19] As is evident in 5:14, Paul stresses the second great commandment (Mark 12:31)—believers are urged to emulate God's love for his people with love for each other and all humanity (Rom 13:8, 9; 1 Thess 4:9).[20] Here Paul stresses God's love for him (and by extension all humanity)—'God demonstrates his love in that, while we were yet sinners, Christ died for us' (Rom 5:8).

'Gave himself for me' also personalizes the self-giving of Christ

---

18. Paul does not use *agapētos* (beloved) in this letter, a term he uses in every letter aside from Galatians, 2 Thessalonians, and Titus. This is another indicator of the depth of his feeling of frustration toward them.

19. See especially Rom 8:35–40, *agapaō*, v. 37; Eph 1:6; 2:4; 5:2; Col 3:12; 1 Thess 1:4; 2 Thess 2:13, 16.

20. *Agapaō* is also used rarely in Paul of Christian's love for God (Rom 8:28; 1 Cor 2:9; 8:3) and Christ (Eph 6:24), in the contrast of God's love for Jacob and hatred for Esau (Rom 9:13), the gentiles loved by God (Rom 9:25), God's love for a cheerful giver (2 Cor 9:7), and Paul's love for his churches (2 Cor 11:11; 12:15). Husbands are to emulate Christ's love for the church and their self-love that should lead to love for their wives (Eph 5:25, 33; Col 3:19), believers loving his future coming (2 Tim 4:8), and Demas' love for this world (2 Tim 4:10).

for humanity. As noted in the translation, 'gave' is the compound *paradidōmi* meaning 'give or hand over'; a verb used commonly in the NT of the betrayal, arrest, and handing over of Christ during his final hours.[21] Paul uses *paradidōmi* in this way in 1 Cor 11:23 in the context of the Lord's Supper, of his betrayal and arrest—'the night he was *handed over*.' Elsewhere, he uses *paradidōmi* of Christ's being handed over for 'our trespasses' (Rom 4:25). In Rom 8:32, God is the agent of this, 'who did not spare his own Son but *handed him over* for us.'

Here in 2:20, Christ is the agent of his own handing over—'gave *himself* (*heauton*).' A similar sentiment to this is found in Eph 5:2 where 'Christ loved us and *gave* (aorist *paradidōmi*) *himself* (*heauton*) *up* for us, a fragrant offering and sacrifice to God.'[22] Thus, while it is theologically true that God handed Christ over to die for the world and historically correct that Judas, Jewish leaders, and Pilate handed Jesus over to die, here we have Christ willingly giving himself up to save the world; here, to

---

21. See Matt 10:4; 17:22; 20:18, 19; 26:2, 14, 16, 21, 23, 24, 25, 45, 46, 48; 27:2, 3, 4, 18, 26; Mark 3:19; 9:31; 10:33; Mark 14:10, 11, 18, 21, 41, 42, 44; 15:1, 10, 15; Luke 9:44; 12:58; 18:32; 20:20; 21:16; 22:4, 6, 21, 22, 48; 23:25; 24:7, 20; John 6:64, 71; 12:4; 13:2, 11, 21; 18:2, 5, 30, 35, 36; 19:11, 16; 21:20; Acts 3:13.

22. In Paul, see also Eph 5:25. Paul also uses it of his giving his body over that he may boast (1 Cor 13:3); he and other missionaries being given over to death (2 Cor 4:11); of God giving over people to sin due to their idolatry (Rom 1:24, 26, 28); people giving themselves over to sensuality (Eph 4:19); of the handing on of Christian teaching and traditions (Rom 6:17; 1 Cor 11:2, 23; 15:3); of handing someone over to Satan for the destruction of the flesh and salvation of the spirit (1 Cor 5:5) or to be taught not to blaspheme (1 Tim 1:20); and of Christ handing over everything to God (1 Cor 15:24). In the wider NT, it is used of the arrest of John the Baptist (Matt 4:12; Mark 1:14); Christians being arrested and handed over (Matt 10:17, 19, 21; 24:9, 10; Mark 13:9, 11, 12; Luke 21:12, 16; Acts 8:3; 12:4; 21:11; 22:4; 27:1; 28:17); God handing all things over to, entrusting to, Christ (Matt 11:27; 10:22), a master who entrusts his property to his servants (Matt 25:14, 20, 22), of Jesus entrusting himself to God (1 Pet 2:23); ripe fruit ready for harvest and handing over (Mark 4:29); traditions handed over, handed down (Mark 7:13; Acts 6:14), including the Christian word (Luke 1:2) or the Jerusalem decree (Acts 16:4, cf. 2 Pet 2:21; Jude 3); Satan believing all authority and glory has been given to him (Luke 4:6); Jesus handing over his spirit to God as his final breath (John 19:30); God handing idolatrous humanity over to deeper sin (Acts 7:42); someone commended (handed over) to the grace of God (Acts 14:26; 15:40); and of risking oneself, handing oneself over to danger (Acts 15:26); and God handing sinful angels over to hell (2 Pet 2:4).

save Paul in particular! We can all say the same thing as Paul here, hallelujah!

The use of the reflexive pronoun 'himself' (*heautou*) of Christ calls to mind other instances where Christ acts as the active agent, demonstrating his willful self-giving.[23] In Romans 15:3, for example, 'Christ did not please *himself*' but received the reproaches of humanity. Christ reconciles the believers and the world *to himself* (2 Cor 5:18–19). Jesus '*gave himself* as a ransom for all' (1 Tim 2:6) and '*gave himself* to redeem us from all lawlessness' (Tit 2:14). The supreme examples are Phil 2:7, 8 where Jesus 'emptied *himself*' and 'humbled *himself*' in taking the form of a slave, a human, fully obedient to the point of dying on a cross (s.a. Eph 5:2, above, cf. Eph 5:25, 28, 33).[24] One of the clearest examples is in Gal 1:4, where 'Christ *gave himself* for our sins to deliver us from the present age.' We know we are truly loved when we realize what Christ has done for us.

UPHOLDING GRACE FOR CHRIST DIED TO DECLARE SINNERS RIGHTEOUS (2:21)

In *Galatians 2:21*, Paul concludes this section:
I do not (*ou*, see 1:1) **abolish** (present *atheteō*)[25] **the grace** (*charis*, 1:3) **of God** (genitive *Theos*, 1:3). **For** (*gar*, 1:10) **if** (*ei*,

---

23. See also in Hebrews, Jesus 'did not exalt *himself* to be made a high priest' but was appointed Son by (Heb 5:5). As the High Priest, 'he offered up *himself*' (Heb 7:27) and 'offered *himself* without blemish to God' (Heb 9:14, cf. Heb 9:25. See also Luke 9:25; 12:21; 14:26; 16:9; Rom 6:13, 16; 12:16, 10; 16:4, 18; 1 Cor 14:4; Gal 6:8; Phil 2:12; 1 Thess 2:8; 2 Thess 3:9).

24. This calls to mind those NT instances where believers are to act in emulation of the pattern of self-giving Christ demonstrated, such as 1 Cor 10:24 where Paul writes: 'Let no one seek his/her own good, but the good of the other.' In Philippians 2:3–4 believers are to 'do nothing from selfish ambition or conceit, but in humility consider others above *yourselves*. Let each of you look not only to *your own* interests but also to the interests of others' (cf. Phil 2:21). See also 'deny *him/herself* and take up his/her cross and follow me' (Matt 16:24; Mark 8:34), 'bear *his/her* own cross' (Luke 14:27); expressions urging believers to 'humble *him/herself* like a child' (Matt 18:4), 'whoever exalts her/*himself* will be humbled, and whoever humbles *him/herself* will be exalted (Matt 23:12; Luke 14:11; 18:14), 'love your neighbor as *oneself*' (Mark 12:33).

25. The verb ἀθετέω (*atheteō*) is found twice in Galatians. First, in 2:21, it refers to Paul who does not 'nullify, abolish, render void' the grace of God. The second use is 3:15 of

1:7) **righteousness** (*dikaiosynē*)²⁶ **[is] through** (*dia*, 1:1) **the law** (genitive *nomos*, 2:16), **therefore** (*ara*),²⁷ **Christ** (*Christos*, 1:1) **died** (*apothnēskō*) **for nothing** (accusative²⁸ *dōrean*).²⁹

In saying 'I do not abolish the grace of God,' Paul distinguishes himself from the Judaizers. The essential contrast in Galatians concerns how a person must respond to the gospel; is it through justification by law-observance or through faith alone? As he did earlier in 1:6, Paul here indicates that there is a deeper abandonment that comes from seeking justification through the law; desertion of the 'grace of God.' The Judaizers are preaching a different gospel (in reality a non-gospel), calling the Galatians to desert 'the one who called you in the *grace* of Christ.'

Judaizers are arguing justification requires more than faith. For them, it requires faith plus law-observance and particularly participation in Jewish boundary markers (esp. circumcision). Paul is countering, 'no way!' It is by faith in Christ alone. To abandon faith is to abandon grace. To relinquish grace is to reject

the general principle that no one 'annuls' a covenant once it is ratified (cf. 1 Cor 1:19; 1 Thess 4:8; 1 Tim 5:12).

26. Paul uses the noun δικαιοσύνη (*dikaiosyne*), 'righteousness,' four times. In each case, it relates to 'righteousness' through grace—Paul (2:21), by faith—Abraham (3:6), and not by law (3:21). In 5:5 it is in the future tense in reference to believers who 'eagerly wait for the hope of *righteousness*.' See also *dikaioō*, 2:16 (used eight times).

27. The conjunction ἄρα (*ara*) is a marker of inference based on the preceding, 'so, then, consequently, you see,' an expression of result, 'then, as a result, consequently,' or expresses something tentative, 'perhaps, conceivably' (BDAG 127). It is used five times in Galatians in 2:21: 'so then Christ died for no purpose;' 3:7: 'know then that it is those from faith who are the children of Abraham;' 3:29: 'and if you are of Christ, then you are Abraham's offspring;' 5:11: 'consequently the offense of the cross is removed;' and 6:10: 'so then, as we have opportunity, let us do good to everyone.' It differs from ἆρα in 2:17 although its transliteration is the same.

28. Wallace, *Greek Grammar*, 200 sees δωρεάν (*dōrean*, 'for no purpose') as an accusative of manner (adverbial accusative) where '[t]he accusative substantive functions semantically like an adverb in that it *qualifies* the action of the verb rather than indicating *quantity* or extent of the verbal action. It frequently acts as an adverb of manner, though not always (hence, the alternative category title is really a subcategory, although the most frequently used one). Apart from the occurrence with certain words, this usage is not common.'

29. The adverb δωρεάν (*dōrean*) is found only once in Galatians, in 2:21 where it does not have its more common sense of 'as a gift, freely' (Rom 3:24; 2 Cor 11:7; 2 Thess 3:8), but 'to no purpose, in vain, for nothing.'

Christ and his Father God. Justification and inclusion in the people of God are free gifts granted at the moment of belief. At that moment, a person experiences incorporation into Christ, receipt of the Spirit (an anointing, a seal, and a deposit [2 Cor 1:21–22; Eph 1:14]), redemption, justification, reconciliation, adoption into Christ's family, forgiveness, and so on. This is the grace of God offered to all humanity in and through Christ.

The verb *atheteō* is linked to *tithēmi*, which can have the sense of 'establish;' hence, with the negating alpha-prefix, it carries the sense of 'disestablish'—to 'reject something as invalid, declare invalid, nullify.'[30] Here it can have the sense of 'reject' the grace of God, with the term in the NT commonly having the sense 'reject' as in rejecting a commandment of God (Mark 7:9; Luke 7:30), to reject Jesus or his emissaries (Luke 10:16; John 12:48), or to reject authority (Jude 8). Paul uses it of God nullifying the intelligence of the intelligent (1 Cor 1:19) and of disregarding a command of Paul (1 Thess 4:8). His other use in Galatians is of (not) annulling a legal covenant once it is ratified (3:15).[31] In 1 Timothy 5:12, he speaks of widows who are led astray from Christ by passions and so 'have *abandoned* their former faith' (1 Tim 5:12). The writer of Hebrews employs it of those who were killed for setting aside the law of Moses (Heb 10:28). Here then, it has the sense of 'reject, annul, or abandon' the grace of God.

The particular construct 'grace of God' is not common in the NT (nineteen times). Luke uses it four times in Acts. Two are particularly significant for this context in Galatians (cf. Acts 14:26; 20:24). First, and significantly, it is the 'the grace of God' that Barnabas observed functioning in the new uncircumcised believers in Syrian Antioch (Acts 11:23). Second, Paul and Barnabas urge the Pisidian Antiochian believers to 'continue in the grace of God' (Acts 13:43). This is just what Paul is urging the Galatians to do here. Clearly, they failed to heed this injunction fully after Paul and Barnabas moved on.

In Romans 5:15, Paul links the 'grace of God' to 'the free gift

---

30. BDAG 24.

31. Also used by Mark for breaking an oath (Mark 6:26).

by grace of that one man Jesus Christ.'[32] He is concerned that the Galatians have received 'the grace of God in vain,' as he says in 2 Cor 6:1 to the wayward Corinthians (cf. Heb 12:15).[33] Here, as in Col 1:6, it is essentially a synonym for 'the gospel;' or, as in Tit 2:11, for Christ himself—I do not abandon the gospel, I do not abandon Christ. For, to resort to law-observance is to do both. Why would one do this? God, by his grace, has gifted us justification and inclusion. Only a foolish one would do so. This sets the scene for what follows in 3:1.

32. See also 1 Cor 1:4, of 'the grace of God' granted to the Corinthian church, which is likely inclusive both of salvation and their extraordinary spiritual giftedness. He uses the phrase in relation to his own ministry as granted 'by the grace of God' (1 Cor 3:10; 15:10). He tells the Corinthians he acted toward them 'by the grace of God'—with integrity in relation to the gospel (2 Cor 1:12). He also uses it in relation to financial generosity toward the Jerusalem Collection (2 Cor 8:1; 9:14).

33. As with Paul in Galatians, the writer of Hebrews is concerned in Heb 12:15 that his readers fail 'to obtain the grace of God,' and so speaks of the salvation that comes from grace. He also uses it of Christ's death 'by the grace of God' (Heb 2:9). 1 Peter 5:12 also speaks of the letter as 'the true grace of God' in which the readers are to 'stand firm.'

CHAPTER 14

CHAPTER FOURTEEN: REMEMBER THE SPIRIT WAS RECEIVED BY FAITH, NOT LAW (3:1–5)

Paul now moves away from talking in the first person and speaking of his personal refusal to rebuild the edifice of the Jewish Torah and to live out of the grace of God by faith in Christ. He now shifts to challenge the Galatians directly. He speaks strongly, twice calling them 'foolish.' He reminds them of his preaching of the cross. He asks them a series of rhetorical questions concerning who has bewitched them after having Christ crucified portrayed to them through the apostolic preaching? Two questions focus on the basis on which they received the Spirit and experienced miracles. He asks them whether they really think that they can be completed through their fallen flesh. He challenges them as to why they suffered so much (at the hands of Jewish persecutors) if it was all in vain.

The emphasis is on their experience of the Spirit, who came to them and filled them, not on the basis of submitting to the Torah and its works, but through their believing the message of the cross preached to them by Paul and his team. The implication is abundantly clear—do not be so stupid as to yield to those who bewitch you and accept circumcision and Torah observation; this is defunct. Rather, continue to live by faith, for faith alone suffices.

THE FOOLISHNESS AND BEWITCHING OF THE GALATIANS (3:1)

In *Galatians 3:1*, Paul states:

O (ō)[1] **foolish** (*anoētos*)[2] **Galatians**[3] (plural *Galatēs*).[4] **Who** (*tis*)[5] **has bewitched**[6] (aorist *baskainō*)[7] **you** (plural *sy*)—**to whom** (plural *ho*, 1:5) **Jesus** (*Iēsous*, 1:1) **Christ** (*Christos*, 1:1) **was before** (*kata*, 1:4) **your eyes** (accusative plural *ophthalmos*)[8] **portrayed**[9] (aorist passive *prographō*)[10] **as having been crucified** (aorist passive *stauroō*)?[11]

The shift of tone is stark, Paul moving from 'we Jewish Christians' which form the subject of 2:15–16, to the first person

1. The interjection ὦ (*hō*) carries the sense of the English 'O! Oh!' Paul uses it once in Galatians 3:1, '*O foolish Galatians!*' Elsewhere, '*O man!*' in diatribe (Rom 2:1, 3; 9:20), or in appeal, '*O man of God*' or '*O Timothy*' (1 Tim 6:11, 20). Otherwise, 'Oh!' in a cry of praise, a doxology (Rom 11:33).

2. The adjective ἀνόητος (*anoētos*) is linked to the terms of intellect, *nous*, 'mind,' *noeō*, 'think,' and is antithetical to wisdom or knowledge, i.e., 'ignorant, foolish, dumb, stupid.' He uses it twice in his direct appeal of 3:1, 3 (cf. Rom 1:14; 1 Tim 6:9; Tit 3:3).

3. Here, the nominative of address is used, a vocative nominative—Γαλάται (*Galatai*, Galatians). Here it is used with Ὦ (*ō*, Oh!). 'Here the presence of the particle ὦ is used in contexts where deep emotion is to be found.' See Wallace, *Greek Grammar*, 55, 68.

4. There is only one use of Γαλάτης (*Galatēs*), 'Galatian,' in 3:1, in the plural, as the object of Paul's interjectory address describing them as foolish. This is a *hapax legomenon*, the only use in the NT.

5. The interrogative pronoun τίς (*tis*) is used five times in the letter. In the masculine tis, 'who' (3:1; 5:7), the neuter indicates 'why' (3:19; 5:11) or 'what' (4:30).

6. **Variant:** The Textus Receptus follows a range of texts including C Dc K L P and Ψ and others adding *tē alētheia mē peithesthai*, 'from obeying the truth' which is found in 5:7. The better earlier manuscripts do not include this, and it is to be rejected.

7. The verb *baskainō* is found once in the NT, a *hapax legomenon*, in 3:1, 'who has *bewitched* you?' Otherwise, it is rare.

8. The noun ὀφθαλμός (*ophthalmos*), 'eye' (related to Eng. 'ophthalmology,' etc.), is used twice in Galatians. In 3:1, Christ being portrayed *kat' ophthalmos*, 'according to the eyes,' indicating 'publicly' or 'before your eyes;' and 4:15 of Paul's very eyes, which the Galatians wanted to replace with their own.

9. **Variant:** Some mss (D E F G K L) followed by Textus Receptus adds *en hymin* to 'portrayed,' yielding 'portrayed among you' or 'portrayed as crucified among you.' However, the support for deleting *en hymin* is stronger and the words were likely added to clarify meaning as some were confusing the idea that the Galatians actually saw Jesus' crucifixion. Interestingly, many students make this mistake in their essays—watch that one!

10. The verb *prographō* compounds *pro* (before) and *graphō* (write, inscribe), and yields 'written before,' and in 3:1, its only use in Galatians (cf. Rom 15:4; Eph 3:3; Jude 4), it has the sense of 'portrayed.'

11. The verb σταυρόω (*stauroō*), which speaks of being crucified is used thrice; first, of the preaching of the cross in which Christ is presented as the crucified Messiah (3:1). The second and third uses are of the flesh of believers and 'the world' crucified in Christ (5:24; 6:14).

singular 'I' in 2:17–21, and to 'you'—directly addressing the Galatians. He names them directly as 'Galatians,' indicating the addressees of the letter. As discussed in the Introduction, this can either be the whole province of Galatia, the region of north Galatia, or as is far more likely, those in the south Galatian churches Paul and Barnabas planted in Pamphylia, Pisidia, and Lycaonia. This is the only use of the term in the LXX or NT. Elsewhere Paul speaks in such direct terms to the 'Corinthians' as a collective (2 Cor 6:11). Here, the intent is to challenge them.

'O' is an interjectory particle used seventeen times across the NT, sometimes with a sense of positivity (Matt 15:28; Acts 1:1), or neutrally (Acts 18:14). Paul uses the term elsewhere in diatribe (Rom 2:1, 3; 9:20), praise (Rom 11:33), and for an injunction (1 Tim 6:11, 20). Here, it is used in the lead-in to a rebuke. Jacob uses it this way, 'O vacuous person!' (Jas 2:20). Jesus cries out to Israel, 'O faithless and twisted generation ...' (Mark 9:19, and parr.). In a manner similar to Paul here, Jesus says to the Emmaus Road travelers, 'O foolish ones (ō anoētai), and slow of heart to believe ...' (cf. Acts 13:10; 27:21). Here then, it introduces a rebuke.

'Foolish' (anoētos) is blunt rebuke. The adjective is part of a wide range of terms based on noeō, nous, referring to the mind and cognition. It has a wide semantic range depending on context and often is active, meaning 'unwise,' 'irrational,' 'foolish,' 'both intellectually and ethically, of persons lacking in understanding or judgment.'[12]

In Wisdom Literature, it is used of one characterized by folly (Prov 15:21), the foolish (Sir 42:8), and a fool (Prov 17:28; Sir 21:19). It is rare in the NT (six times), used by Paul of 'the foolish' in contrast to the 'wise' (Rom 1:14), those seeking riches being trapped in senseless desires (1 Tim 6:9), and of the former state of believers as foolish (Tit 3:3). As noted above, Jesus uses it to address the Emmaus Road travelers who cannot grasp a suffering Messiah (Luke 24:25). The label is caustic and to the point, a term that we find a bit distasteful today. However, it grasps the

12. J. Behm, 'ἀνόητος,' in TDNT 4:961.

futility of the Galatians in their flirtation with the Judaizers. They are not 'foolish' ontologically, for they are also 'brothers and sisters,' but 'they have become ἀνόητοι with respect to the Pauline gospel.'[13]

Paul poses his first question. In many English translations it is shortened to 'Who has bewitched you?' However, in the Greek, it runs through to the end of the verse: Who has bewitched (baskainō) you—to whom Jesus Christ was before your eyes (kat ophthalmos) portrayed (prographō) as having been crucified (stauroō)?' This is one of two rhetorical questions in Galatians where the implied answer is the Judaizers. The other is Gal 5:7; 'who hindered you from obeying the truth?' Again, we see Paul's determination not to name the Judaizers—they are not worthy of being named.

'Bewitched' is a term only found here in the NT, baskainō.[14] It has the senses 'to envy' (e.g., Ign. Rom. 3.1), 'to revile,' or 'bewitch.' The latter idea is linked to witchcraft or magic, especially 'exercised through hostile looks or words'—'harmful magic' and can convey the notion of 'the evil eye'[15] or demonic forces. Paul may then be hinting at the Judaizers being complicit with demonic forces deceiving the Galatians through their creative but false words, proclaiming a Judaizing gospel. As Delling says, '[t]he dangerous Feature is that the Galatians have willingly yielded to these magicians and their influence without realising to what powers of Falsehood they were surrendering.'[16] The term is also likely chosen intentionally to play on 'according to eyes' which follows. As Christ has been portrayed before them as crucified, they should not be diverted by the 'evil eye' of the Judaizers. Justification is through Christ's vicarious, sacrificial death. They must 'turn their eyes on Jesus' and not be bewitched by the sorcery of the Judaizers.

---

13. See Horst Robert Balz and Gerhard Schneider, 'βασκαίνω,' in *EDNT* 1:208.
14. In the LXX it is used of someone who *begrudges* food to another (Deut 28:54, 56), someone who *begrudges* or looks disapprovingly on oneself (Sir 14:6), or upon others (Sir 14:8).
15. BDAG 171 notes the meaning 'to exert an influence through the eye.'
16. See for these ideas especially G. Delling, 'βασκαίνω,' in *TDNT* 1:595.

In the remainder of the question, Paul describes his proclamation while he was among them as the portrayal of Christ crucified before their eyes. This is not literal, as if some of the Galatians were in Jerusalem and saw Jesus crucified. Rather, this speaks of the focus of his preaching, drawn on more in 1 Corinthians as he combats the deficient Christology of the Corinthians. The Corinthians' problem was not so much a false understanding of justification but that they did not understand the function of the cross as a portrayal of the ethical and ecclesiological life required of a believer—cruciformity.

In his argument combatting Corinthian disunity, he emphasizes Christ as the basis of unity and refers to his preaching of the cross among them. Christ sent him not to baptize, but to preach the gospel, and not with wisdom of speech, lest the cross is emptied of its power to generate faith and bring justification (1 Cor 1:17). The message of the cross is the power of God for those who are being saved (1 Cor 1:18). Its message of a crucified divine Son and Lord is foolishness, but through this message, God was pleased 'to save those who believe' (1 Cor 1:21). He preaches 'Christ crucified,' which causes Jews to stumble and is blithering nonsense to unbelieving gentiles (1 Cor 1:22). These Judaizers are playing this out, not satisfied with a crucified Messiah as the basis for justification, and demanding they yield to Jewish legal boundary markers and come under the law. The 'wisdom of God' is the message of the cross (1 Cor 1:24). This is the power that converts (1 Cor 1:25). It is also the power that sustains, where the respondent continues to stand in faith. Through this message, God called the 'foolish,' 'weak,' 'lowly' Corinthian nobodies and is forming them into his body and temple (1 Cor 1:26–28). Similarly, he did so on Paul's missionary journeys in Galatia (Acts 13–14).

Christ then is God's wisdom and the basis of boasting—not circumcision, law, Moses, or anything that has been completed in Christ (1 Cor 1:29–31). When in Corinth, Paul purposefully refused to preach anything other than Christ and him Christ crucified, in content, and in the form he adopted (weakness, fear, trembling), to ensure that what converted the Corinthians was

God's power and not Paul or his rhetoric (1 Cor 2:1–5). Similarly, in Galatia, we read here that he portrayed before their eyes Jesus Christ crucified, and as it was heard with faith, God liberated to them the Spirit (3:2, 5). Paul is urgent; do not relinquish Christ and Christ crucified, for to do so is to empty the cross of any soteriological value.

The precise wording of Gal 3:1c is intriguing. 'Before your very eyes' is literally 'according to eyes.' As noted earlier in the verse, the use of *ophthalmos* (eyes) calls to mind the 'evil eye.' Paul did not bewitch them, but God converted them through the message of the cross.

Prographō (*pro*, 'before' plus *graphō*, write, portray) means 'write before' in a literal sense elsewhere in the NT, including the OT writings (Rom 15:4), earlier writing in a letter (Eph 3:3), and of people inscribed for condemnation in the past (Jude 4). Here it has two possibilities. It can imply 'public promulgation' as it was used widely for published notices or placards. So, it can here mean, 'before whose eyes Jesus Christ has been set as the Crucified like a posted proclamation.'[17] The ESV thus has 'Jesus was publicly portrayed as crucified.' Alternatively, it can mean 'depicted before your eyes,' speaking of Paul's proclamation of a crucified Messiah as vividly as possible. Although *prographō* is not used in this sense in wider literature, *graphō* is often used 'to draw' and 'to paint,' and so this is also possible.

'Crucified' is the perfect passive of *stauroō*. In 2:19, Paul used *systauroō* (*syn*, 'with' plus *stauroō*, 'crucify,' so 'crucify together with'), of his being co-crucified with and in Christ. Here, he uses the basic verb *stauroō*, a verb used commonly in the NT of Christ's crucifixion (forty-six times).[18]

Paul uses it eight times, ironically of himself as one not crucified (Christ is) (1 Cor 1:13), and of Christ who was crucified (1 Cor 2:8), and in weakness (2 Cor 13:4). In 1 Cor 1:23, 'Christ crucified' is central to Paul's proclamation—'we herald Christ

---

17. G. Schrenk, 'προγρα´φω, in *TDNT* 1:771.

18. Outside of Paul *stauroō* is used frequently: Matt 20:19; 26:2; 27:22, 23, 26, 31, 35, 38; 28:5; Mark 15:13, 14, 15, 20, 24, 25, 27; 16:6; Luke 23:21, 23, 33; 24:7, 20; 23:21; John 19:6, 10, 15, 16, 18, 29, 23, 41; Acts 2:36; 4:10; Rev 11:8 (see also Matt 23:34).

crucified' (1 Cor 1:23). Similarly, 'I decided to know nothing among you except Jesus Christ, and him *crucified*' (1 Cor 2:2). In Galatians, this is the first use and speaks of Christ's crucifixion, which as in 1 Cor 1:23 and 2:2, forms the basis of his preaching. He uses it again in 5:24 of believers who 'have *crucified* the flesh with its passions and desires and in 6:13 of his boasting of the cross 'by which the world has been *crucified* to me, and I to the world.' These tease out the implications of co-crucifixion in and with Christ (2:20). This here indicates Paul's emphasis on the cross in his preaching. It is by Jesus' death on the cross that the problem of sin and its consequences are dealt with.

THE SPIRIT RECEIVED BY FAITH AND NOT WORKS (3:2)

In *Galatians 3:2*, Paul, after a preamble, directs a second question to the Galatians:

This thing (neuter *houtos*, 2:10) **only** (*monon*, 1:23) **I wish** (*thelō*, 1:7) **to learn** (infinitive *manthanō*)[19] **from** (*apo*, 1:1) **you** (plural genitive *sy*, 1:3): **did you receive** (aorist *lambanō*, 2:6) **the Spirit** (*pneuma*)[20] **from** (*ek*), 1:1) **works** (plural genitive *ergon*, 2:16) **of the law** (genitive *nomos*, 2:16) **or** (*hē*, 1:8) **from** (*ek*) **hearing** (genitive *akoē*)[21] **with faith** (genitive *pistis*, 1:23)?

Paul now emphasizes their experience of receiving the Spirit of God. This is the first reference to the Spirit in Galatians, but it is a very important theme (eighteen times). It dominates this section, referenced three times (cf. vv. 3, 5), indicating that their experience of the Spirit is the key basis for the argument here. He speaks of the promise of the Spirit in 3:14, emphasizing

---

19. The verb μανθάνω (*manthanō*), 'learn,' is used once in Galatians in 3:2 in Paul's inquiry to learn from the Galatians on what basis did they receive the Spirit.

20. Galatians 3:2 is the first instance of *pneuma* in Galatians. It is found eighteen times, once it clearly means the spirit of the Galatians (their 'human' spirit) (6:18). In 6:1, it can either be a 'spirit of gentleness' or the 'Spirit of gentleness.' The other sixteen uses all refer to the Holy Spirit (3:2, 3, 5, 14; 4:6, 29; 5:5, 16, 17, 18. 22, 25; 6:8). It is contrasted with flesh and law, with believers called to live by the Spirit.

21. The noun *akoē* can mean the faculty of hearing, the act of listening, the ear, or what is heard. It is found twice in Galatians in 3:2 and 3:5, both times recalling the Galatians' hearing of the gospel and responding to it with faith ('hearing with faith').

the fulfillment of Jewish hope seen in Pentecost and subsequent Spirit-reception among God's people.

In 4:6, it is the Spirit of 'his Son' who is sent into the human heart (*kardia*). This Spirit generates familial intimacy with God and so believers cry out, 'Abba! Father!' In 4:29, believers are 'born according to the Spirit' and receive persecution from those who are 'born according to the flesh.' In Galatians 5, the Spirit generates hope through faith (5:5) and is the guide for Christian ethics and behavior through Spirit-fruit (5:16–25). In 6:1, *pneuma* can refer to 'the Spirit of gentleness' by which one must restore the sinful other (alternatively a spirit of gentleness, cf. 6:18—'your spirit'). Believers are to sow to this Spirit, and from the Spirit will yield eternal life (6:8).

Part a of the verse serves to emphasize the intent of the question. Paul cleverly compels them to focus their attention on what is being asked. 'This thing' is specified in what follows—which is it? Did they receive Spirit as a result of law-observance or because they believed the gospel? There is some irony in 'I wish to learn from you,' as he has labeled them 'foolish,' and this forces them to think through their 'foolish position.' He wants them to explain their experience of receiving the Spirit. Was it by law? Was it by faith? We can ask the same question, and the answer is, on account of our faith.

The question itself is then specified with what appears to be a straightforward one-or-other alternative. The basis of the question is their experience of receiving the Spirit in Paul's initial evangelization of the region. Luke alludes to this event in the lives of the Christians of Pisidian Antioch in Acts 13:52: 'and the disciples were filled with joy and *the Holy Spirit.*' Interestingly, there is nothing about tongues here; the only manifestation is joy. This shows that tongues are not a necessary experience of receiving the Spirit.[22]

---

22. This is the case in Acts where the gift of tongues is mentioned at Pentecost (Acts 2:4), the conversion of Cornelius' family (Acts 10:46), and Ephesus (Acts 19:6) but not at the outpourings on the Jerusalem church (Acts 4:31), Samaria (Acts 8:17–18), Paul (Acts 9:17–18), nor is it referenced in the evangelization of Galatia, Macedonia, and Greece (Acts 13–14; 16–18).

Apart from this, unlike other accounts in Acts, including
Pentecost (Acts 2:1–4), again in Jerusalem (Acts 4:31), Samaria
(Acts 8:17), Paul (Acts 9:17–18), Cornelius (Acts 10:44–46), and
Ephesus (Acts 19:6), Luke does not give any detail to this among
the other Galatians on Paul's first Antiochian missionary
journey. However, we can surmise that as Paul preached through
the cities of the region, as in these other situations, new believers
had various experiences of the Spirit. Indeed, this passage
confirms that this is so, despite Luke's lack of detail.

Paul is here asking them to cast their minds back to these
experiences and ask upon what basis they received the Spirit.
Remember when you first experienced the Spirit? Was it on the
basis of submitting to the Torah and its boundary markers? Or
was it through believing in the message? The implied answer is
clearly the latter—faith. As in the Cornelius account, where the
Spirit fell on the uncircumcised gentile family (Acts 10:44–46),
they experienced the Spirit through faith. Likely, as in the
accounts of the coming of the Spirit in Acts, as Paul and Barnabas
laid hands on them, or spontaneously, alongside the joy Luke
mentions (Acts 13:52), they had other experiences such as some
speaking in tongues (Acts 2:3–4; 10:46; 19:6), praise (Acts 10:46),
prophecy (Acts 19:6), healing (Acts 9:18), mission zeal (Acts
2:14–41; 3:1–26; Chs. 4–5), strong winds (Acts 2:2), tongues of
fire (Acts 2:3), rooms shaken (Acts 4:31), and more.

As noted earlier concerning 2:16, 'works of the law' can be
boundary markers in particular (esp. circumcision), or legal
observance in a more general sense. Likely, the latter is correct,
but the boundary markers have some priority, for it is these that
are at stake for the Judaizers who believe that one is included in
God's people through them.

The construct 'hearing with faith' is a slippery genitive,
literally, 'hearing of faith.' What this means is disputed. First,
what faith? Whose faith? We return then to the question of 2:16:
is it the faith/faithfulness of Christ? If so, we have here the notion
of hearing of the faith or faithfulness of Christ. Another
possibility is that faith here is being used in the same sense as in
1:23 (preaching the faith) with faith equivalent to the gospel, i.e.,

'hearing the gospel.' So, the receipt of the Spirit is connected with their hearing of the gospel.

However, the issue in Galatians is *what a person must 'do'* to be saved, included in God's people, and remain in that status. For the Judaizers, faith is not enough; they must yield to the law and especially its covenantal boundary markers (esp. circumcision). Throughout the letter, Paul is countering such claims. His response is, *mē genoito!* *Anathema!* It is by faith alone! Hence, the presenting issue is the response of people to the gospel. That it is the believers' response in mind rather than Christ's faith is confirmed in what follows as Paul contrasts the Spirit with the flesh, which refers to the Galatians seeking to complete their God's salvation through their own willful response.

A key to understanding this text is Rom 10:14–17. Here, Paul asks a series of rhetorical questions concerning the Jews; have they heard the gospel? If not, they are not responsible before God. The answer Paul gives is, 'yes!' (Rom 10:18–21), as the apostles and other disciples had preached Christ to them. They *had* heard the message. But they were not responding with faith and obedience to the gospel. Despite the loveliness of the feet of those who preached the good news to them, they are like Israel at the time of Isaiah that did not believe the message (Isa 52:7; 53:1). Then in v. 17, 'therefore, faith (*pistis*) [comes] from hearing (*akoē*), and hearing through the word of Christ.' Faith then is generated through the hearing of the proclamation of the gospel of Christ.

This stresses the importance of evangelism—it is by the preaching of the gospel that faith is generated. Hence, we must continue to share the message of God so that people can be justified by faith and receive the Spirit.

Here, we have the same kind of notion. The faith spoken of is the Galatians' response to the hearing of the gospel. As they heard it, faith was generated in them. The genitive then is not so much one of origin, source, or production (faith produced by hearing), as hearing itself does not generate faith, God does this by his Spirit. However, it is close to this idea as it is *through* the hearing of the message of the gospel that faith is generated within the spirit of the believer as the person yields to the work of the Spirit through the spoken word. The hearing is the means by which the Spirit does his work.[23]

As faith is birthed, the Spirit of God floods the person, pours love into their hearts, and testifies to the spirit of that person that they are children of God (Rom 5:5; 8:16). The person is anointed—signed and sealed to be delivered for redemption (2 Cor 1:21–22; Eph 4:30). As Galatians 3:15 suggests, they have received the promise of the Spirit through their faith. Again, in 4:6, at the moment of faith, God sent the Spirit of his Son into their hearts, crying 'Abba! Father!' Further, in 4:29, they have been born anew according to the Spirit.

The process in mind is nicely illustrated in Eph 1:13–14, where Paul describes the conversion of the Ephesians: 'in him you also [were] when you *heard* the word of truth, the gospel of your salvation. In him also you *believed* and were *sealed* with the promised Holy *Spirit.*' The Ephesians heard the gospel. They believed it. They were sealed. The Galatians had this same experience. They heard the gospel and received it with faith. They received the Spirit. They did not do so by becoming Jews through Torah submission. They did so through faith and faith alone. Paul is calling them to recall this. It was not by law, but by faith, so, *'Do not yield to the Judaizers!'* He will reemphasize this in v. 5.

START BY THE SPIRIT, FINISH BY THE SPIRIT (3:3)

In *Galatians 3:3*, Paul continues with his third and fourth

---

23. We get a further sense of this in 1 Cor 2:1–5 where Paul chooses to preach the gospel without the flowery dynamic and *pathos*-inducing rhetoric popular in his day. He chooses to preach the gospel focusing on Christ and Christ crucified with clarity embodying the gospel itself in his approach—simple, unadorned, and to the point that neither his dynamic delivery nor presence gets in the way. This is so that the power of God in the gospel itself does the converting. See Mark J. Keown, 'Preaching Christ Crucified: Cruciformity in Content and Delivery,' in *Text Messages: Preaching God's Word in a Smartphone World*, ed. John Tucker (Eugene, Oreg.: Wipf and Stock, 2017), 217–29.

questions, the first leading into the second (alternatively, it could be one long question):

Are you (*eimi*; 1:7) **so** (*houtos*, 1:6) **foolish** (*anoētos*, 3:1); **having begun** (*enarchomai*)[24] *with the Spirit* (dative *pneuma*, 3:2), **[are you] now** (*nyn*, 1:23) **being completed** (*epiteleō*)[25] **by the flesh** (dative *sarx*, 1:16)?

Part a of the verse continues the themes of verses 1 and 2. Again, using *anoetos*, 'foolish,' he challenges their mindset, asking them whether they are imbeciles. The adverb *houtōs* can go with the previous sentence—'in this way are you foolish?' However, that makes little sense, as the previous sentence was a question. Alternatively, it can go with what follows, 'you are foolish *in this way* …). The best option is to see it as 'a marker of relatively high degree,' and so translate it 'so,'[26] with *houtōs* modifying *anoētoi este*: 'are you *so* foolish?' Paul is questioning their capacity for false thinking. 'Can it be that you are so foolish?'[27]

The second question draws out what Paul has in mind. 'Having begun with the Spirit, are you now being completed in the flesh?' Paul here is thinking of the beginning of Christian life and its culmination using two verbs, *enarchomai* (begin) and *epiteleō* (complete, perfect, mature). Paul uses the same two verbs in Phil 1:6: 'he who began (*enarchomai*) a good work in you, will bring it completion (*epiteleō*) at the day of Jesus Christ.'[28]

The contrast of Spirit and flesh is one of the dominant Pauline

---

24. The only use of the verb ἐνάρχομαι (*enarchomai*) is in 3:3, speaking of the beginning of a person's Christian life. It is contrasted with its completion. The only other use is in Phil 1:6.

25. The verb ἐπιτελέω (*epiteleō*) is found once in the letter, in 3:3, speaking of completion in contrast with the beginning of the Christian life. The same contrast is found in Phil 1:6. The verb is also used by Paul (15:28; 2 Cor 7:1; 8:6, 11) and the author of Hebrews (Heb 8:5; 9:6; 1 Pet 5:9).

26. See BDAG 742; 'οὕτως,' in *EDNT* 2:549.

27. BDAG 742.

28. Whereas the first verb *enarchomai* is found only this one other time in the NT, Paul employs *epiteleō* more often including the completion of a mission (Jerusalem Collection) (Rom 15:28; 2 Cor 8:6, 11) or the completion of holiness (2 Cor 7:1). The writer of Hebrews uses it for the completion of the erection of the tabernacle or for fully carrying out ritual duties involved in Tabernacle worship (Heb 8:5; 9:6). It is found once in 1 Pet 5:9 of completely enduring suffering (1 Pet 5:9).

motifs. The contrast is struck in Genesis 6:3, where, due to human depravity, the Lord spoke, 'My *Spirit* (*rûaḥ*, LXX *pneuma*) shall not abide in humankind forever, for he is *flesh*: his days shall be 120 years.' Here, humanity in its fleshly state is corrupted and subject to death. John strikes a similar distinction noting that what is born of the flesh is flesh, whereas what is born of Spirit is spirit (John 3:6). For John's Jesus, 'it is the *Spirit* who gives life; the *flesh* is no help at all' (John 6:63).

However, it is Paul who develops the contrast of the Spirit and flesh, speaking of two ways of being and doing. A believer has received the Spirit and is to live according to the Spirit. The unbeliever cannot do so and lives according to the flesh (Rom 8:4). The believer who has received the Spirit (Rom 8:9) must not lapse back into fleshly carnal living (1 Cor 3:1–4), with minds set on the desires of the flesh, but must live by the impulses of the Spirit (Rom 8:5). Doing so yields life and peace, but the converse produces death, both physical and eternal (if one does not believe in God and his Son, see Rom 8:6, 13). The antithesis will feature in Gal 4:29 of the births of Ishmael (according to the flesh) and Isaac (according to the Spirit), and especially in Paul's ethical teaching in Chs. 5–6 (further below).

Here, in Galatians 3:3, the genesis of the Christian life is 'in the Spirit.' This refers back to 3:2, where the Spirit was received through believing the message. Paul's view is that the Galatians must continue their Christian lives in the same way, by the Spirit. To do so, they are to live by faith, eagerly awaiting the hope of righteousness *through the Spirit* (5:5). They are to 'walk in the Spirit' and are not to 'gratify the desires of the flesh' as 'what the flesh desires is opposed to the Spirit, and what the Spirit desires is opposed to the flesh.' The two impulses stand in opposition (5:16–17). They then are to be 'led by the Spirit' and not be subject to the law (5:18). They are to live by the Spirit who will bud fruit on the branches of their lives (5:22). They are to be guided by the Spirit living lives led by his inner unction (5:25). Their whole beings are to be dedicated to sowing to the Spirit so that they reap eternal life (6:8).

However, in yielding to the Judaizers, the Galatians are seeking to complete their Christian lives by yielding to the law. Paul describes this as seeking completion through the flesh. For Paul, the flesh stands in antithetical opposition to the Spirit. It speaks of the frailty and failure of humanity to please God. Subject to sin, humanity simply cannot defeat sin's power, is under its thralldom, and so is unable to not sin. As such, humanity is in its flesh, in a weakened state, decaying and destined to death, and sin's ultimate consequence, eternal destruction. To seek to live by law is to rely on one's own ability to please God through the flesh. In our Adamic state, this is implausible.

The inheritance of eternal life can only be granted to the perfected, the one free of sin, for sin must be extinguished. After all, why would God allow sin an eternity in which to flourish and wreak havoc? So, God has solved the problem by sending the sinless one to die in our place, to take our sin and extinguish it, to take upon himself our destruction in crucifixion, and to die our death. We must simply place our faith in him, and his death becomes ours. We can, thus, say as did Paul, 'I am crucified with Christ.' We are then declared righteous. We are declared holy in Christ. We are reconciled to God. We receive the Spirit of sonship. We are adopted. All these salvation ideas are generated through the simple response of faith. We need 'do' no more than believe. We then are free to live by the Spirit who fills us and flows through our every part. This the Galatians did at the beginning.

Sadly, now they are being bewitched by the Judaizers to turn to the law, to rely on their flesh, which is an impossibility! Nein! No way, Jose! As Paul himself says in Philippians 3, after declaring that if anyone has a claim according to the flesh, it is he himself. He lists his brilliant Jewish CV. He then declares it *skybalon*! Feces! The Galatians must complete their Christian lives by walking by faith in the power of the Spirit. There is no other way.

OUR SUFFERING IS NOT IN VAIN (3:4)

Another question (the fifth) is then asked in **Galatians 3:4**
   Did you suffer (aorist *paschō*)[29] **so much** (neuter *tosoutos*)[30] **in**

vain (dative *eikē*)?[31] **If** (*ei*, 1:7) **indeed** (*ge*),[32] **[it is] even** (*kai*, 1:1) **in vain** (dative *eikē*)?

The meaning of *paschō* is disputed. It can either refer to their 'experiences' which would be the many spiritual experiences they have had. Alternatively, it signifies their suffering. The strongest evidence in support of 'experienced' here is the context—the verse is sandwiched between references to the Spirit's work among the Galatians.

However, there are very strong reasons to reject experience here and run with 'suffer.' First, in the LXX and Pseudepigrapha, aside from Let. Aris. 214 and T. Ab. (A) 7.1 where it can possibly indicate 'experience' and Ezek 16:5 where the verb *paschō* appears to mean 'do,' every use is of suffering.[33] The same goes for the Apostolic Fathers, where all have the explicit meaning 'suffering' except 2 Clem 7:5, where it seems to have the meaning 'think.' Most commonly, it is used of Christ's sufferings.[34]

In the NT, the pattern continues. Outside of Paul, it is used

29. The verb πάσχω (*paschō*), which can mean 'suffer' or 'experience' is found once in Galatians, in 3:4. The term is used six other times in Paul, all in reference to suffering, and so should be translated this way here (1 Cor 12:26; 2 Cor 1:6; Phil 1:29; 1 Thess 2:14; 2 Thess 1:5; 1 Tim 1:12). See also the related *pathēma* in 5:24.

30. Galatians 3:4 is the only use of τοσοῦτος (*tosoutos*) in the epistle, and Paul only uses it once elsewhere, in 1 Cor 14:10—'there are no doubt *many* different languages in the world.' It can indicate 'many' or a high degree, 'so much, so great,' as here. Either it refers to their experience of 'so many things' or 'such great suffering.'

31. The noun *eikē*, which in the NT (only in Paul) can mean, 'without cause,' 'to no purpose,' 'without due consideration,' or 'to no avail, in vain' (BDAG 281), is used only in the latter sense in the three uses in Galatians. Twice in 3:4, it refers to the Galatians suffering 'in vain' or 'without cause.' In 4:11 it has the sense, 'in vain'—if the Galatians Judaize, his effort among them is to no avail.

32. The particle *ge* is found once in Galatians, with *ei*, producing 'if indeed,' in 3:4. 'Γέ is an enclitic particle that serves to emphasize the word with which it is joined' ('γέ', in *EDNT* 1:239). It is found six times in this form, εἴ γε, yielding 'if indeed' (Rom 5:6; 2 Cor 5:3; Gal 3:4; Eph 3:2; 4:21; Col 1:23).

33. See Wis 12:27; 18:1, 11, 19; 19:13; Sir 38:16; Esth 9:26; Amos 6:6; Zech 11:5; Ep Jer 33; 2 Macc 6:30; 7:18, 32; 9:28; 4 Macc 10:10; 13:17; 14:9; Sib. Or. 1.290; 3.529, 452; 7.16; 8.250, 324; 11.282; 14.209. 350; T. Reu. 3.8; 4.1; T. Sim. 4.3; T. Gad. 5.11; T. Benj. 7.4; T. Job 47.7; T, Sol. 11.6; 12.3; 18.21, 31, 35; Jos. Asen. 7.4; 24.1). Even in the case of the exceptions, suffering may still be in mind.

34. See *1 Clem.* 6. 1, 2; 45:5; *2 Clem.* 1.2; 7.5; Ign. *Trall.* 4.2; 10.1; Ign. *Rom.* 4.3; 8.3; Ign. *Smyrn.* 2.1; 6.2; Ign. *Pol.* 7.1; 8.2, 3; 17.2; *Barn.* 5.5, 13; 6.7, 9; 7.2, 5, 10, 11; 12.2, 5;

of other people (often Christians) suffering.[35] *Paschō* is often employed of Christ's sufferings.[36] In Paul's other six mentions, it always refers to Christian suffering.[37] Not once in the NT in other uses does it mean 'experience.' As such, it should be read as suffering here.

So then, Paul here is asking the Galatians whether they have suffered so greatly for nothing. What this suffering constitutes is not completely clear. Acts 13–14 gives some evidence of persecution against the churches planted on Paul's mission. After an initially positive reception, the Jewish response was strong as they contradicted (*antilegō*) and slandered (*blasphēmeō*) Paul and Barnabas (Acts 13:45). They aroused (*paratrynō*) pious women and leaders of Pisidian Antioch to persecute (*diōgmos*) Paul and Barnabas and drove them (*ekballō*) from the district (Acts 13:50). Again, in Iconium, unbelieving Jews with the support of gentiles mistreated (*hybrizō*) and sought to stone (*lithobeleō*) the disciples (Acts 14:1–5). Again, in Lystra, after a healing and the crowds divinizing the apostles, Jews from Pisidian Antioch and Iconium incited the crowds, and Paul was stoned and dragged from the city as if dead (Acts 14:19). The primary antagonists appear to be the Jews who resisted the proclamation of Jesus as Christ, Son of God, savior, and Lord.

Aside from this text, there are few indications of the ongoing persecution of the Galatians. However, in 4:29, it is hinted that the church is suffering from those born according to the flesh, which in the context of the Judaizing heresy, may indicate ongoing Jewish persecution. Further, in 6:12, Paul appears to suggest that the Judaizers in their desire that the Galatians are circumcised are, in part at least, motivated by a desire to escape persecution. If so, again the source would be Jews. While the

---

Herm. *Vis.* 3.1.9; 3.2.1; 3.5.2; Herm. *Sim.* 6.3.4; 6.3.6; 6.5.4; 6.5.6; 8.3.6; 8.3.7; 8.10.4; 9.28.2; 9.28.3; 9.28.4; 9.28.5; 9.28.6.

35. See Matt 17:15; 27:19; Mark 5:26; Luke 13:2; Acts 3:18; 9:16; 28:5; 1 Pet 2:19, 20; 3:14, 17; 4:1, 15, 19; 5:10; Rev 2:10.

36. Matt 16:21; 17:12; Mark 8:31; Luke 9:22; 17:25; 22:15; 24:26, 46; Acts 1:3; 3:18; 17:3; Heb 2:18; 5:8; 9:26; 13:12; 1 Pet 2:21, 23; 3:18; 4:1.

37. See 1 Cor 12:26; 2 Cor 1:6; Phil 1:29; 1 Thess 2:14; 2 Thess 1:5; 2 Tim 1:12.

evidence is sparing, it is likely that the opposition encountered in the initial evangelization of the region continued, with the Jews opposing the nascent Christian movement.

Their suffering of persecution would be in vain if the Galatians deserted the gospel of grace and faith for a Judaizing gospel. They would no longer be relying on the Spirit but on the flesh. The term for 'vain' is *eikē*, a word used in the NT only by Paul. Its 'basic meaning is "at random," "with no plan or goal," "for no objective reason." It thus comes to mean "without true right," and the further senses of "in vain," "moderately" and "simply" must also be considered.'[38]

Elsewhere he uses it to warn the Corinthians that to fall from faith in a resurrected Christ is to 'believe in vain' (1 Cor 15:2). Later in Gal 4:11, he uses the term of his fear that his work among the Galatians will be in vain.[39] Here, it refers to their suffering 'in vain.' As their suffering has been mainly at the hands of Jews, if the Judaizers are right, it has been utterly meaningless. They should have been circumcised at the time by Paul and Barnabas, and the Jews would not have persecuted them. If they now Judaize, they render empty their suffering.

The final clause is cryptic, 'if indeed it is even in vain.' Introduced by *ei*, it is a conditional clause. The Greek particle *ge* 'serves to focus the attention on a single idea, and place it, as it were, in the limelight'—hence, 'indeed.'[40] *Kai* here is adverbial, and adds intensity, so 'really.' There is no apodosis to the conditional clause, it is unresolved. This leaves the intent intentionally open. As such, it can be read as a reinforcement of the warning, 'unless all this, indeed, is in vain.' Alternatively, it is hopeful, 'if indeed [as I cannot believe] it has been in vain.'[41] Likely, it is open intentionally—the response of the Galatians will decide this. If they back off their flirtation with the Judaizers, it will not be. If they do not, it will be. As many commentators

---

38. F. Büchsel, 'εἰκῇ,' in *TDNT* 2:380.
39. Paul's other two uses are in Rom 13:4 of the state not bearing the sword in vain, and in Col 2:18, of heretics puffed up without cause.
40. BDAG 190. *Ei ge* is used five times, all in Paul: 2 Cor 5:3; Eph 3:2; 4:21; Col 1:23.
41. Moo, *Galatians*, 186.

suggest, while open, it expresses Paul's hope. So, Lightfoot writes, 'The Apostle hopes better things of his converts. Εἴ γε leaves a loophole of doubt, and καί widens this.'[42]

THE SPIRIT AND MIRACLES BY FAITH AND NOT WORKS (3:5)

In *Galatians 3:5*, Paul returns to the theme of the Spirit from v. 2 with a sixth question:

Therefore (*oun*),[43] **does the one** (*ho*, 1:1) **who supplies** (present participle *epichorēgeō*)[44] **the** (*ho*) **Spirit** (*pneuma*, 3:2) **to you** (dative plural *sy*, 1:3) **and** (*kai*, 1:1) **[who] works** (*energeō*, 2:8) **miracles** (plural *dynamis*)[45] **among** (*en*, 1:6) **you** (dative plural *sy*) **[do so] from** (*ek*, 1:1) **works** (plural *ergon*, 2:16) **of the law** (genitive *nomos*, 2:16) **or** (*ē*, 1:8) **from** (*ek*) **hearing** (*akoē*, 3:2) **with faith** (*pistis*, 1:23)?

Paul links this to the previous sentence with the inferential *oun*, 'therefore, so then …' The intent is the same as v. 2, although there are differences. God is described as 'the one who supplies

42. Lightfoot, *Galatians*, 131.
43. The conjunction οὖν (*oun*) can be inferential meaning 'so therefore, consequently, accordingly, then,' is a marker of the continuation of a narrative, 'so, now, then,' has the sense 'certainly, really, to be sure,' or an adversative, 'but, however' (BDAG 737). It is used six times in Galatians. In 3:5 it builds off Paul's rhetorical questions, 'therefore,' 'so then,' leading into a question akin to 3:2. Again, in 5:1, it has the sense 'therefore,' '*Therefore*, stand firm …' Similarly, in 3:19 it is inferential, 'so then, why the law?' as it is in 6:10, 'therefore then, as we have opportunity …' In 3:21, it has the meaning 'then,' 'Is the law *then* contrary …; similarly, in 4:15, 'What *then* has become …'
44. The interesting verb ἐπιχορηγέω (*epichorēgeō*) compounds *epi* (upon) and *chorēgeō* ('chorus leader,' cf. Eng. 'chorus'). It can have the meaning of 'convey as a gift, give, grant' or 'provide (at one's own expense), supply, furnish' (BDAG 387). Elsewhere, it is used twice by Paul for the supply of seeds (2 Cor 9:10) and the supply of body parts (Col 2:19). Peter uses it twice: to add virtues (2 Pet 1:5), and the provision of a way into eternity (2 Pet 1:11). The associated noun, *epichorēgia*, 'assistance, support,' is used twice for the help or supply of the Spirit (Phil 1:19) and the supporting ligaments of the body (Eph 4:16). Here, in Gal 3:5, the only use in the letter, it carries the meaning 'supply.'
45. The plural of *dynamis*, 'power,' is used across the NT of 'miracles,' i.e., 'powerful acts.' This is most common in the Synoptics and Acts where it is used fourteen times in this way. Paul uses *dynameis* of spiritual powers (Rom 8:38) and as here, of miracles in 1 Cor 12:28, 29. The only other NT usage is Heb 6:5.

the Spirit to you and works miracles among you.' The verb for supply is *epichorēgeo*, which is rare. In wider sources, it is used for financial support (Dionysius of Halicarnassus, *Ant. rom.* 4.69.1; Strabo, *Geogr.* 11.14.16). It is found thrice in the LXX of a wife who 'supports' her husband (Sir 25:22), to establish a gymnasium (2 Macc 4:9), and feeding people (1 En. 7.3). In its other four uses in the NT, it is applied to God, who supplies seed to a sower and similarly financial reward to generous Christians (2 Cor 9:10). In Col 2:19, it speaks of the nourishment of the body of Christ by God (Col 2:19). Peter employs it of believers seeking to support faith with goodness and other virtue (2 Pet 1:5) and God supplying entry into eternity (2 Pet 1:11). The cognate noun *epichorēgia* is used of the help or supply of the Spirit in Phil 1:19. In Eph 4:16, *epichorēgia* is used physically for supporting ligaments. Here then, God supplies the Spirit to the Galatians.

He also works miracles, *dynameis*. The plural of *dynamis*, which literally means 'powers,' is used across the NT of miracles—'deeds of power.'[46] These God worked (*energeo*) among them (cf. 2:8).[47] This reference to miracles indicates that the miraculous was another aspect of the early mission. No doubt through prayer and the laying on of hands, God did marvelous signs among the Galatians. There are some indicators of such things in Acts 13–14. In Acts 14:3, Luke summarizes Paul and Barnabas' ministry in Iconium, including the Lord 'granting *signs and wonders* to be done by their hands.' Most notable is the dramatic city-impacting healing of the man crippled from birth in Lystra through Paul's word (Acts 14:8–10). There is also the possible healing or resurrection of Paul himself after stoning

---

46. See Rom 8:38; 1 Cor 12:28, 29, cf. Matt 7:22; 11:20, 21, 23; 13:54; Mark 6:2; Luke 10:13; Acts 8:13; 19:11.

47. Paul uses *energeo* eighteen times, always of something working in and through another whether it be: 1) Sinful passions working in the body (Rom 7:5); 2) death working in people (2 Cor 4:12); 3) faith working out in love (5:6); 4) Satan at work in the disobedient (Eph 2:2); or as here, 5) mystery of lawlessness (2 Thess 2:7); 6) God's word working in believers (1 Thess 2:13); 7) God by his Spirit working in people including gifts (1 Cor 12:6, 11), comfort (2 Cor 1:6), various ministries (Gal 2:8; Col 1:29), miracles (Gal 3:5), all things in the cosmos (Eph 1:11), resurrection (Eph 1:20), beyond what we can ask or imagine (Eph 3:20), and salvation (Phil 2:13).

(Acts 14:19–20). While Luke does not mention any others, it is likely that such things were part and parcel of the ministry of the gospel in the first phase.[48] As with the ministry of Christ, healing sits alongside proclamation and caring for the needy (esp. feeding the poor) as constitutive of Christian mission. While one may repudiate the way healing is utilized in some parts of the church and the false claims and expectations some make and have, as in the case of Christ's mission, the offer of prayer for God's healing touch is essential to holistic Christian witness.

The final part of the verse includes the same antithetical options as v. 2, 'from works of the law, or hearing with faith.' As in v. 2, the implied answer is the latter. It was on the basis of their response of faith that God acted. We see this in Acts 14:9 where Paul looked intently at the crippled man and saw 'that he had faith' and acted. The connection between faith and the miracle is clear in this instant.

This shows the common link in the NT between faith and miracles, especially in the Synoptic Gospels. This leads some to argue that faith determines whether miracles happen, leading to hyper-faith thinking whereby the lack of a miracle is due to a failure of faith. However, on closer inspection, faith is not always mentioned in healing accounts. Indeed, not one of John's miracles speaks of the faith of the recipient. Furthermore, we cannot say Jesus did not have faith in the Garden of Gethsemane when his prayer was not answered (Mark 14:32–42). Similarly, Paul had no deficiency of faith when God did not remove his fleshly thorn (2 Cor 12:7–10). Sometimes God acts, sometimes he does not. So, we must not overstate the role of faith. On the other hand, faith is clearly a factor that moves God to act.

The converse of God acting in giving the Spirit and faith is then affirmed. God did not gift the Spirit and do miracles because of their Judaizing. The overall implication is clear: don't Judaize, for to do so, is to abandon faith and Christ-sufficiency. To do so violates the gospel and takes them back into bondage.

---

48. Compare Rom 15:19a; 2 Cor 12:12; Acts 2:43; 3:1–10; 4:9, 14, 22, 30; 5:12–16; 8:6, 7, 13; 15:12; 28:8.

CHAPTER 15

CHAPTER FIFTEEN: CHILDREN OF ABRAHAM BY FAITH (3:6–9)

Although *kathōs* appears to link this section to the previous and implies continuity, this is a new section introducing a new phase in Paul's argument—Abraham and faith—something that will carry through this whole chapter and in the Hagar/Sarah allegory at the end of Gal 4. Paul's point is to argue from the Jewish Scriptures that the principle of justification by faith he is espousing in the face of justification through works of the law is etched into Israel's story. Indeed, it is found in the Torah and from its foundation in Abraham. As such, he seeks to out-Judaize the Judaizers, who are likely arguing from Genesis 17 that circumcision is the essential boundary marker of Judaism, and so it should be for Christianity. Paul demonstrates that the promise of blessing and faith precede this.

ABRAHAM JUSTIFIED BY FAITH AND NOT LAW (3:6)

He begins in *Galatians 3:6*:

As (*kathōs*, 2:7) 'Abraham (*Abraam*)[1] believed (aorist *pisteuō*, 2:7) in God (dative *Theos*, 1:1), and (*kai* 1:1) it was credited (aorist *logizomai*)[2] to him (dative *autos*, 1:1) as (*eis*, 1:5) righteousness (*dikaiosynē*, 2:21).'

The introductory *kathōs* points forward to what follows. Verse

1. The name Ἀβραάμ (*Abraam*) features nine times in Galatians, eight in Ch. 3 (3:6, 7, 8, 9, 14, 16, 18, 29) and once in Ch. 4 (4:22). Clearly, this is the historical figure from Israel's story, Abraham (esp. Gen 12–25).
2. The verb λογίζομαι (*logizomai*) is found once in Galatians, in 3:6, of Abraham to whom was credited righteousness on the basis of faith. The term was used in accounting meaning it has that sense of calculated thought.

6 provides the comparison, and verse 7 draws it out. Just as Abraham's faith was credited to him as righteousness, know then that those who believe (as did Abraham) are children of God. This comparison is then explicated. The implication is that just as Abraham was justified by faith, so it is with all believers, Jewish or otherwise. Hence, do not Judaize, for to do so is to repudiate faith.

The name Abraham invokes Israel's genesis as a nation. It was he who God called out of the nations of the world to go to the land he would show him. He promised him blessings and greatness and that the nations would be blessed through him (Gen 12:1–3). Abraham obeyed, and his life story dominates Gen 12–25. The story of Israel is the story of his family, for Israel was his grandson Jacob, renamed after wrestling with God (Gen 32:22–32). With Abraham, God made a covenant (Gen 15:1–20). The core sign of the covenant community was circumcision of all males (Gen 17:1–27). So, we can see how the Abraham narrative lies at the heart of the Judaizing issue.

This text cites Gen 15:6 from the LXX: 'Abraham believed (see on 2:7, 16) God, and it was credited[3] to him as righteousness'[4] (cf. Rom 4:3, 9; Jas 2:3). Abraham's faith is also mentioned in Neh 9:8: 'you found his heart faithful before you' [2 Esd 19:8].

Genesis 15:6 is the first reference to faith in the biblical narrative, and for Paul, it is paradigmatic. This verse lies in the passage in which the covenant with Abraham was established. It came with the promise of multiple offspring, as many as the stars in the sky (Gen 15:5).

---

3. The Greek *logizomai* is one of the thinking terms in the NT, where it has the sense of calculated careful thought or consideration (John 11:50; Rom 2:3; 3:28; 6:11; 8:18; 14:14; 1 Cor 4:1; 13:5, 11; 2 Cor 3:5; 10:2, 7, 11; 11:5; 12:6; Phil 3:6; 4:8; Heb 11:19; 1 Pet 5:12). However, it has its origins in accounting and here has the sense of God crediting to Paul's account the status of righteousness (cf. Rom 2:26; 4:3, 4, 5, 6, 9, 10, 11, 22, 23, 24). Similarly, elsewhere, it is used of Jesus being 'counted among the lawless' (Luke 22:37), the Lord 'will not reckon sin' (Rom 4:8, cf. 2 Cor 5:19), 'we are reckoned as sheep to be slaughtered' (Rom 8:36), and 'the children of the promise are reckoned as descendants' (Rom 9:8) (cf. 2 Tim 4:16).
4. Wallace, *Greek Grammar*, 47 notes that εἰς δικαιοσύνην (*eis dikaiosynē*) here functions as a predicative nominative to the verb *logizomai*.

The text is also cited in Romans 4, where Paul gives more detail concerning the relationship of Abraham's faith to Christian faith. As he was justified by faith and not works, he has no basis for boasting before God (Rom 4:1–2). The blessedness he has from God is for both the circumcised and uncircumcised, the Jew and gentile (Rom 4:9). He received the blessing of God before his circumcision, i.e., when he was a gentile (Rom 4:10–11). He is thus the father of all, gentile or Jew (Rom 4:12). The promise comes to him and his descendants through faith (Rom 4:13). It is not granted on the basis of law, for otherwise 'faith is null and the promise is void' (Rom 4:14).

The law does not bring righteousness, but wrath and awareness of transgression (Rom 4:15). Righteousness depends on faith as in the case of Abraham (Rom 4:16). The kind of faith required is a faith like that of Abraham who trusted in the promise of God that he would have many offspring, no matter how bleak things looked (Rom 4:16–21, cf. Heb 11:8, 17–19). He believed 'that God was able to do what he had promised' (Rom 4:21).

The words in Gen 15 cited in both Galatians and Romans, 'it was counted to him,' apply to those who hear the gospel of Christ (Rom 4:23). Paul concludes by stating, 'It will be counted to us who believe in him who raised from the dead Jesus our Lord, who was delivered up for our trespasses and raised for our justification' (Rom 4:24–25). As such, 'having been justified by faith, we have peace with God through our Lord Jesus Christ' (Rom 5:1).

In this chapter, he will state similar things. 'Those who believe are children of Abraham' (3:7). 'Those who believe are blessed with Abraham who believed' (3:9). Through Christ Jesus, the blessing of Abraham has come to the gentiles who have received the Spirit (3:16). If a person belongs to Christ (by faith), they are Abraham's offspring and heirs to the promise (3:29).

This verse has monumental significance for understanding the salvation story. Now a Christian, Paul has thought through Israel's narrative and recognizes that righteousness before God has always and ever will be, based on faith and faith alone. This faith principle precedes the law and continues in the Christ-story. True Israel then is not those born by human descent from Abraham but is humanity who believes in God (see 6:10, 16). This faith principle applies before Christ in the likes of Noah and Enoch (see Heb 11). It remains is true now. Israel then pre-exists the nation in those of faith. It continues in the people of God forming in Christ.

THOSE WHO BELIEVE ARE THE CHILDREN OF ABRAHAM (3:7)

Galatians 3:7 draws out the comparison with Abraham in v. 6:

So then (*ara*, 2:21), **know** (present imperative *ginōskō*, 2:9) **that** (*hoti*, 1:6) **[it is] those** (masculine plural nominative *ho*, 1:1) **from** (*ek*, 1:1) **faith** (*pistis*, 1:23) **who**[5] (plural *houtos*, 2:10) **are** (present *eimi*, 1:7) **the children** (plural *huios*, 1:16) **of Abraham** (genitive *Abraam*, 3:6).

As in 2:21, *ara* leads into an inference from the citation of Gen 15:6, 'so then, consequently.' 'Know' here can be the indicative of *ginōskō*, 'you know that …' However, almost certainly, it is imperative with Paul telling the Galatians what they should already know. This is the second imperative directed at the Galatians after *idou*, 'behold,' in 1:20. Paul here is addressing their foolishness in direct terms, telling them what they should know as believers. The placement of the verb first gives the command prominence.

'Those from (*ek*) faith' introduces the second use of 'from faith' (*ek pisteōs*), a device used nine times in Galatians and usually contrasted with 'from works of the law' or 'the law' (see on 2:16, cf. 3:8, 9, 11, 12, 22, 24; 5:5).

'Those from faith' are not those who are 'from the faith/faithfulness of Christ,' but those who respond to God with faith. Those people (*houtoi*) that do believe are 'sons of Abraham.' While couched in the masculine, this is inclusive of men and women, hence 'children' is a better translation. While the focus is the Galatians, drawing Paul's theology together (and that of the

---

5. Literally: 'these people.'

writer of Hebrews in particular), this includes all humanity that has faith in God like Abraham.[6]

Clearly, this includes people of Israel's history. It likely includes those who lived before Jesus who are defined as righteous such as Noah, although faith is not attributed to him by Paul (Gen 6:9; 7:1, cf. Heb 11:7). People who called on the name of the Lord from Gen 4:26 on would be included (cf. Rom 10:13) as would those who walked with God like Enoch and Noah (Gen 5:22, 24; 6:9). It would include those born of Abrahamic descent who had a true faith in God like Moses (Num 12:7), David (Ps 27:13), and other Psalmists (Ps 116:10; 119:66).[7] It likely includes others from beyond Israel who had faith in God, as did Abraham the wandering Aramean (Deut 26:5), such as Melchizedek (Gen 14:18; Ps 110:4; Heb 5:6, 10; 6:20; 7:1, 10, 11, 15, 17)[8] and the Ninevites who accepted Jonah's words (Jonah 3:5).

Hebrews has the same kind of idea in Heb 11 which includes a list of OT figures whom the writer considers people of faith. A number predate Abraham and circumcision, including Abel, Enoch, Noah, and Abraham. Abraham is commended (Heb 6:13–15; 11:8, 17–19) as are his direct descendants Isaac, Jacob, Sarah, Joseph, Moses, Rahab (despite being a prostitute and gentile), Gideon, Barak, Samson, Jephthah, David, Samuel, and the prophets. These people are 'commended for their faith' (Heb 11:39, NET).

---

6. God determines what faith is sufficient. See 2:16 on this, a faith that includes *notitia*—intellectual belief in God as revealed to the respondent; *assensus*—a yielding 'yes' to this God; and *fiducia*—trusting this God' *affinitas*—a deep relational awareness of God.

7. Compare Exod 14:31; 2 Kings 17:14; 2 Chron 20:20; Ps 78:22, 32, 37; 106:12, 24; Jer 40:14; Hab 2:4.

8. Neither faith nor righteousness is attributed to Melchizedek. However, in Gen 14:21–22 he is a 'priest of God Most High,' pronounces a blessing over Abraham, praising God who he describes as 'Creator of heaven and earth,' and 'God Most High.' Abraham, the man of faith, tithed to him—which for the author of Hebrews, speaks of his superiority to Abraham (Heb 7:1–10). He also fought with Abraham to deliver Lot from evil hands. In Ps 110:4, it is foretold that the Messiah will be a priest of his order. For the author of Hebrews, Jesus fulfils this. As such, it is pretty clear, he was a man of faith, despite not being an Israelite. There is also no reference to his circumcision.

Clearly, for the Galatians, the faith in mind is faith in Christ, who was portrayed as crucified before their very eyes and in whom they believed. God, in his wisdom, has fully and finally revealed himself in Christ (Heb 1:1–4). Once the gospel of Christ is proclaimed and heard, righteousness is credited on the basis of a faith relationship with the Son of God and his Father. Clearly, then the people of faith do not include Judaizers. They have not embraced grace and faith as all that is required. They continue to preach a false compromised gospel, which is not the gospel at all (cf. 1:7–8; 2 Cor 11:4). It is hardly surprising that Paul repudiates them as 'dogs, evil workers, and mutilators of the flesh' in Phil 3:2.

Both Judaizers and Paul recognize that descent from Abraham is not premised only on genetics. For the Judaizers, one must be circumcised. Circumcision happened on the eighth day for a Jewish boy. For a proselyte, this was part of the conversion process. So, for those Judaizers who do recognize Jesus as Messiah, a person believing in Christ is a great first step. However, it is not enough; 'wait there's more.' That person, if a male, must *also* be circumcised. Male or female, they must yield to the core legal requirements of the Torah including Sabbath observance, festivals, purity, food laws, and so on. Not so for Paul. Faith is enough. It always has been since the time of Abel. It always will be until Christ returns and faith is supplanted by full knowledge. Those who believe in God *are* (present tense) sons and daughters of Abraham. This is a present reality. As such, they are members of God's covenant people alongside all humanity with a saving faith in God the Father from history.

This has important implications for those born into Christian homes. The faith of their parent(s) is important, but once the child is able to hear and understand the gospel, righteousness is conferred on the basis of the child's faith, not that of the parents.

'Children of Abraham' is a glorious covenantal concept. It is effectively synonymous with being 'children of God.' Kinship is Paul's favored way of describing the church. God is Father. The father of faith is Abraham. Jesus is the Son. Believers are siblings, joint heirs of their Savior, Lord, and big brother, Jesus. He is

King. We are princes and princesses alongside our sovereign King. There is no next in line to the throne, for the throne is filled. Amazingly, we are in him and he in us. We are then royalty. This truth, however, should not lead to arrogance and a desire to dominate the world. Sadly, for too much of Christian history, it has. Rather, it should inspire us to take up our towels (John 13:1–15) and crosses (Mark 8:34) and join our brother Paul in his mission for the redemption of the world. We will suffer as he did, but to do so in Christ's service is our greatest honor (cf. Phil 2:29–30, cf. 1 Pet 4:12–16). We do so by the power of the Spirit imparted to us on the basis of faith! Our first call then is to continue to believe, without compromise. For it is faith that unites us with Christ. Believing sincerely sees us anointed and sealed by the Spirit and incorporated into God's family. This is the family of Abraham. This truth, we, like the Galatians, must *know*!

THE PRIOR PREACHING OF THE GOSPEL TO ABRAHAM (3:8)

In *Galatians 3:8*, Paul continues to draw out of the story of Abraham, connecting him to the gospel he preached and introducing the critical theme of the blessing of the gentiles that would come through the patriach:

And (*de*, 1:15) **the Scripture** (*graphē*),[9] **having foreseen** (aorist passive *prooraō*)[10] **that** (*hoti*, 1:6) **God** (*Theos*, 1:1) **would justify** (present *dikaioō*, 2:16) **the gentiles** (plural *ethnos*) **from** (*ek*, 1:1) **faith** (*pistis*, 1:23), **preached the gospel beforehand** (*proeuangelizomai*)[11] **to Abraham** (dative *Abraam*, 3:6) **[saying]**

---

9. The noun *graphē*, 'Scripture,' is found three times in Galatians, always of the OT Scripture or a particular OT text: 3:8, 22; 4:30.
10. The verb προοράω (*prooraō*) compounds *pro* (before) and *horaō* (see) and implies 'see beforehand.' It is used once in Galatians and in the NT (*hapax legomenon*), of the Scripture foreseeing that God would justify the gentiles by faith. It is found rarely across most Jewish Greek comparative literature but not uncommonly in the Greek Classics and Josephus.
11. The verb προευαγγελίζομαι (*proeuangelizomai*) compounds *pro* (before) and *euangelizomai* (preach the gospel) and so yields 'preach the gospel beforehand.' It is found only in Gal 3:8 in the NT (a hapax *legomenon*), and in the unique sense that the

that (*hoti*), **in** (*en*) **you** (dative *sy*) **all** (*panta*) **the nations** (plural *ethnos*) **shall be blessed** (future passive *eneulogeō*)[12] ...

This verse continues the thought with *de*, which here is continuous (and) rather than adversative (but). Paul then personifies the Scripture as a prophet who saw into the future to the justification of the gentiles by faith and preached the gospel to Abraham, despite being written after Abraham's death.

In the first part of the verse, 'the Scripture' (*graphē*) is possibly the whole OT rather than a specific text. Such a use of *graphē* is common in Paul[13] and the wider NT.[14] However, texts Paul is using in his argument for justification by faith and especially Gen 15:6 spring to mind (cf. Hab 2:4).[15]

The Scripture looks forward (metaphorically) to the day that the nations would be justified by (*ek*) faith—the third use of *ek pisteōs* in Galatians (see further 2:16; 3:7, 9, 11, 12, 22, 24; 5:5). This is clearly coming to pass. As such, while the law has no power to save, and one does not have to do its works, it still holds within its writings the prophetic anticipation of justification by faith. So, Paul can say in Rom 1:2 that the gospel 'he promised beforehand *through his prophets in the holy Scriptures*.' Or, in Rom

---

Scripture preaches to Abraham (despite being written after his death) that in him all the nations will be blessed. It is extremely rare, used only by Philo in Jewish Greek comparative literature (see further in commentary and notes).

12. The verb ἐνευλογέω (*eneulogeō*) is found only once in Galatians in 3:8 of all the nations being blessed in Abraham. The only other NT use is in Acts 3:25 where is has the same sense. See also its only LXX uses in Gen 18:18; 22:18; 26:4; 28:14, where it is also used of the Abrahamic blessing. See also *eulogeō*, next verse and note.

13. See Rom 1:2; 15:4; 1 Cor 15:3, 4; 2 Tim 3:16.

14. See Matt 22:29; 26:54; Mark 12:24; Mark 14:49; Luke 24:47, 32, 45; Acts 17:2, 11; 18:24, 28; 2 Pet 1:20; 3:16.

15. Otherwise, Paul uses *graphē* of the prophetic Scriptures (Rom 16:26); specific texts, Gen 15:6 (Rom 4:3); Exod 9:16 (Rom 9:17); Isa 28:16 (Rom 10:11); Gen 21:10 (Gal 4:30); Deut 25:2 (1 Tim 5:18); or a passage (1 Kings 19; Rom 11:2). *Graphē* is used in the wider NT in referencing specific citations from the law: Lev 19:18 (Jas 2:8); the Psalms: Ps 118 (Matt 21:42; Mark 12:10); 69:9 (John 2:22); Isa 61:1–2 and 58:6 (Luke 4:21); Ps 82:6 (John 10:35); Ps 41:9 (John 13:18; 17:12); Ps 22:18 (John 19:24); Ps 69:21 or 22:15 (John 19:28); the scriptures of the prophets (Matt 26:56); a specific passage—Mic 5:2 (John 7:42); Zech 12:10 (John 19:37); Isa 53:7–8 (Acts 8:32, 35); Gen 15:6 (Jas 2:23); Isa 28:16 (1 Pet 2:6); uncertain (John 7:38; Jas 4:5); and multiple passages (Exod 12:46, Num 9:12, and Ps 34:20—John 19:36; John 20:9; Acts 1:16).

3:21–22: 'But now the righteousness of God has been manifested apart from the law, *although the law and the Prophets bear witness to it*—the righteousness of God through faith in Jesus Christ for all who believe (cf. Rom 16:26; 1 Cor 15:3–4). The notion of this is similar to 3:22, where the Scripture has imprisoned all things to sin, 'so that the promise by faith in Jesus Christ might be given to those who believe.' This promise is in mind here in 3:8. Jacob says something similar in Jas 2:23: 'and the Scripture (*graphē*) was fulfilled that says, "Abraham believed God, and it was counted to him as righteousness."'

In the second part of the verse, the Scripture preaches the gospel to Abraham through God's words to Abraham: 'in you all the nations will be blessed.' On the face of it, Gen 12:3 is cited. However, Genesis 12:3 ends with 'all the tribes of the earth' rather than 'all the nations,' and as this chart below shows, Paul could equally have other Genesis texts and one in Sirach in mind.

Gal 3:8	*eneulogēthēsontai*	*en soi*	*panta ta ethnē*
	Will be blessed	in you	all the nations
Gen 12:3	*eneulogēthēsontai*	*en soi*	*pasai hai phylai tēs gēs*
	Will be blessed	in you	all the tribes of the earth
Gen 18:18	*eneulogēthēsontai*	*en autō*	*panta ta ethnē tēs gēs*
	Will be blessed	in him	all the nations of the earth
Gen 22:18	*eneulogēthēsontai*	*en tō spermati sou*	*panta ta ethnē*
	Will be blessed	in your seed	all the nations
Gen 26:4	*eneulogēthēsontai*	*en tō spermati sou*	*panta ta ethnē tēs gēs*
	Will be blessed	in your seed	all the nations of the earth
Gen 28:14	*eneulogēthēsontai*	*en soi*	*pasai hai phylai tēs gēs kai en tō spermati sou*
	Will be blessed	in you	all the tribes of the earth and in your seed
Sir 44:21	*eneulogēthēsontai*		*ethnē en tō spermati autou*
	Will be blessed		a nation in his seed

Alternatively, all such texts could be in mind. What Paul seems to be saying is that this sacred text predicting the blessing of every nation in Abraham looks forward to the same reality cited in the previous part of the text; justification by faith in the one to come from Abraham through whom the world would be blessed. So, the promise from God proclaims the gospel before its time to Abraham.

This introduces the Abrahamic promise to Paul's argument. It was this promise that launched Abraham's life in the God who revealed himself with it. While imperfect, Abraham lived by faith in that promise, through thick and thin. The promise was passed down to his descendants, and for Paul, has found its ultimate fulfillment in the son of Abraham, Jesus Christ. Now, justification by faith is achieved through him. The blessing promised to the nations through and in Abraham has come. The Scriptures are being fulfilled. The Judaizers have it wrong. They have a deficient Christology and 'Abrahamology.' Their hermeneutic is flawed, leading them to a false gospel. They consider law still important for righteous standing before God. It is no longer needed. Its time is over. The promise to the nations has come, and all that is left is to believe.

BELIEVERS ARE BLESSED WITH ABRAHAM (3:9)

In *Galatians 3:9*, Paul draws out the inference of this:
> **so that** (*hōste*, 2:13) **those** (plural *ho*, 1:1) **from** (*ek*, 1:1) **faith** (genitive *pistis*, 1:23) **are being blessed** (present passive *eulogeō*)[16] **with** (*syn*, 1:2) **the faithful one** (dative *pistos*),[17] **Abraham** (dative *Abraam*).'

Hōste links to the previous statement, drawing the inferences that Scripture has foreseen justification by faith and that in Abraham, all the nations shall be blessed—'so that' (see further on *hōste* 2:13).

'Those from (*ek*) faith' for the fourth time in Galatians uses *ek pisteōs* (see further 2:16, also 3:7, 8, 11, 12, 24; 5:5). 'Those' is inclusive of all the people of the world who have responded to God's revelation and to the gospel of Christ with belief. It also includes those who preceded the coming of Christ who had a faith like Abraham (previous verse). In context, the Galatians who received the gospel with faith are in mind. It is those 'from faith' (*ek pisteōs*)[18] who are blessed. The construct is critical to Galatians, Paul arguing that the Christian faith is 'from faith' and not 'works of the law.'

Such people are 'being blessed.' Paul here shifts from the less common *eneulogeō* to *eulogeō*, a standard word for blessing in the

---

16. The only use of εὐλογέω (*eulogeō*), 'bless,' is found in Gal 3:9. It is synonymous with *eneulogeō*, used of the Abrahamic blessing (see previous verse and note).
17. *Pistos*, 'faithful, believing,' is used of Abraham in 3:9. Another of the *pist-* terms, it is connected with pisteuō (see 2:7) and *pistis* (see 1:23) and stresses Abraham's faithfulness, for which was credited righteousness.
18. Nine times in the letter: see 2:16; 3:7, 8, 9, 11, 12, 22, 24; 5:5.

OT (451 times LXX). It is used in the creation narrative of God's blessings on creation (e.g., Gen 1:22), the seventh day (Gen 2:3), and on humanity (Gen 5:2). Aside from Noah and his family, who God blessed in Gen 9:1, Abraham's blessing is the first. It marks the formation of a nation which God would bless, and through whom the nations would be blessed (Gen 12:2–3), reasserted again in Gen 22:17. The term is also used for God's blessings on Sarah—to have a son (Gen 17:16), Ishmael (Gen 17:20), and Isaac (Gen 25:11; 26:3, 12, 24).

In the NT, the term is used diversely of God's favor, praise toward God, the blessing of food, and people blessing others.[19] The idea of blessing from God speaks of his divine favor, particularly seen in protection, provision, progeny, and peace—Shalom. Through Abraham, the nations would be beneficiaries of these things from God as his family. The blessing to Abraham also features in Heb 6:13–15, where Gen 22:17 is cited, 'Surely I will bless you and multiply you.' Abraham is commended for waiting patiently for the promise. The blessing is also echoed in Eph 1:3, where Paul speaks a blessing (praise) to God (*eulogētos*) 'who has blessed us in Christ with every spiritual blessing (*eulogia*) in the heavenly places.' This is the blessing of Abraham flowing through Christ by the Spirit to God's cosmic people.

They are blessed with the faithful one, Abraham. As noted in the translation, 'faithful' is *pistos*, hat carries the sense of one who is faithful, believing, or trusting.[20] Abraham then is the believing

---

19. In the NT, *eulogeō* is used forty–one times: 1) of Jesus blessing food (Matt 14:19; 26:26; Mark 6:41; 8:7; 14:22; Luke 9:16; 24:30; 1 Cor 10:16); 2) of Jesus who comes in the name of the Lord as the 'Blessed One' (Matt 21:9; 23:39; Mark 11:9; Luke 13:35; 19:38; John 12:13, cf. Ps 118:26); 3) eschatological blessing on God's people (Matt 25:34); 4) the blessed coming kingdom (Mark 11:10); 5) women and their children blessed (Luke 1:42); 6) of people blessing God with praise (Luke 1:64; 2:28; 24:53; 1 Cor 14:16; Jas 3:9); 7) of people conveying a blessing on others (Luke 2:34; Heb 11:20, 21); 8) Christians blessing enemies (Luke 6:28; Rom 12:14; 1 Cor 4:12; 1 Pet 3:9); 9) Jesus blessing his people as he departs (Luke 24:50–51); 10) of people blessed by Jesus' coming (Acts 3:26); 11) of God blessing humanity in Christ (Eph 1:3); 12) of the blessing of Abraham by God (3:9; Heb 6:14), and by Melchizedek (Heb 7:1); 13) Abraham blessing Melchizedek (Heb 7:6–7).

20. Compare Acts 10:45; 16:1, 15; Heb 3:2, 5; 1 Pet 5:12; Rev 7:14. Paul uses *pistos*

or faithful one, whose faith was credited as right standing before God, and who is paradigmatic of Christian belief toward God and his Son.

positively of a faithful person or people (1 Cor 4:17; Eph 1:1; 6:21; Col 1:2, 7; 4:7, 9; 1 Tim 1:12; 3:11; 2 Tim 2:2, cf. Rev 2:13). He also applies it to God (or the Lord) who 'is faithful' (1 Cor 1:9; 10:13; 2 Cor 1:18; 1 Thess 5:24; 2 Thess 3:3; 2 Tim 2:13, cf. Heb 10:23; 11:11; 1 Pet 4:19; 1 John 1:9). Otherwise, it is used of Jesus who is faithful (Heb 3:2; Rev 1:5; 3:14; Rev 19:11); the faithful servant in parables (Matt 24:45; 25:21, 23; Luke 12:42; 19:17) pointing to the ideal of the Christian who faithfully serves God (Luke 16:10–12; 1 Cor 4:2; 7:25); actively of believe (John 20:27); sure blessings (Acts 13:34); believer(s) (2 Cor 6:15; 1 Tim 4:3, 10, 13; 5:16; 6:2; Tit 1:6; 1 Pet 1:21); trustworthy sayings (1 Tim 1:15; 3:1; 4:9; 2 Tim 2:11; Tit 3:8); the trustworthy word (Tit 1:9, cf. Rev 21:5; 22:6); the trustworthy high priest (Heb 2:17); a faithful thing (3 John 5); and 'be faithful' (Rev 2:10). If the subjective interpretation is correct, the *pistis Christou* sayings speak of Jesus' faithfulness (Gal 2:16; 3:22, etc.).

CHAPTER SIXTEEN: REDEEMED BY CHRIST FROM THE CURSE OF THE LAW (3:10–14)

Still dealing with the overall question of justification of faith versus justification through works of the law, Paul now shifts to the means by which the blessing of Abraham is coming to the world—it is not through observance of the works of the law, but it is through faith in Christ who has become the curse of God to redeem fallen humankind from the law which curses. The blessing is not received through works of the law for those who rely on them—they are under a curse. This is because law observance must be total and complete to receive the blessing of Abraham by it. Otherwise, they are under a curse, the curse of sin.

As such, no one can be justified by God through the law. Rather, as Habakkuk 2:4 says, it is by faith, which the law is not. The law is premised on 'doing,' and no one other than Christ has done or can do so. Christ has redeemed all humanity from the curse of the law by becoming the curse through the cross. As a result, the blessings promised to Abraham for the nations has come, and now they have received the Spirit *through believing* (and so not through doing the works of the law). The implication for the Galatians is obvious. Do not yield to the Judaizers' demands, for to do so will mean that they are shifting from Christ-reliance to law and self-reliance, and on this basis, they will fail. The cross has dealt with this, and all they must continue to do is believe.

ALL THOSE SEEKING JUSTIFICATION BY OBSERVING THE LAW
ARE ACCURSED (3:10)

Galatians 3:10 is linked to 3:9 by *gar*, which is explanatory, as
Paul continues relentlessly dealing with the Judaizers and the
Galatians who are potentially being swayed by them. However,
there is also a shift of thought to the role of the law and Christ in
bringing the Abrahamic blessing. So, this is a sub-section of the
overall argument. Paul writes,

For (*gar*, 1:10) **as many as** (plural *hosos*)[1] **are** (present *eimi*,
1:7) **[relying] on** (*ek*, 1:1) **works** (plural *ergon*, 2:16) **of the law**
(genitive *nomos*, 2:16), **are** (present *eimi*) **under** (*hypo*, 1:11) **a
curse** (*katara*).[2] **For** (*gar*) **it is written** (perfect passive *graptō*),[3]
'(*hoti*, 1:6)[4] **cursed** (*epikrataratos*)[5] **[is] anyone** (*pas*, 1:2) **who**
(plural *hos*, 1:5) **[does] not** (*ou*, 1:1) **abide by** (present *emmenō*)[6]
everything (*pas*) **that** (plural dative *ho*, 1:1) **is written** (perfect
passive participle *graptō*) **in** (*en*, 1:6) **the book** (*biblion*)[7] **of the
law** (genitive *nomos*), **[and] do** (aorist infinitive *poieō*, 2:10) **these
things** (neuter plural *autos*, 1:1).'

Here the problem of law Is laid out. 'All' or 'as many as' rely on

---

1. Paul uses ὅσος (*hosos*), which means 'as many as,' or 'all,' five times in Galatians (3:10, 27; 4:1; 6:12, 16).
2. The noun κατάρα (*katara*), 'curse,' is used three times, once in 3:10 and twice in 3:13. It speaks of the curse of the law and Christ taking this curse upon himself. Otherwise, it is only used three times in the NT, of cursed ground (Heb 6:8), verbal cursing (and blessing) (Jas 3:10), and in an imprecation on false teachers, 'accursed children' (2 Pet 2:14).
3. The verb *graphō*, 'write,' is used seven times in Galatians; three times in the form *gegraptai*, 'it is (or has been) written' introducing OT quotes or allusions (Gal 3:10, 13; 4:22). It is also used regarding Paul writing the letter (Gal 1:20; 6:11) and what is written in the book of the law (Gal 3:10).
4. The *hoti* is not translated as it is a marker of discourse and so functions as an initial speech mark.
5. The adjective ἐπικατάρατος (*epikataros*) means 'accursed, cursed,' and is used twice in Gal 3:10 and 3:13. These are the only two uses in the NT.
6. The verb ἐμμένω (*emmenō*) is rare in the NT. It can be temporal, 'remain, stay' (Acts 28:30), or 'to persist in a state or enterprise, persevere in, stand in,' (BDAG 322), so 'abide' (cf. *menō*). It is used once in this sense in 3:10 of abiding by everything written in the book of the law. See also Acts 14:22; Heb 8:9.
7. The standard noun for book or writing, *biblion*, is used once in Gal 3:10—'*book* of the law.'

(literally, 'are from') works of the law (and not faith), are under a curse. Curse is the counter to blessing—a means through which harm or ill effects is conveyed, often from a supernatural or divine source. In the OT, the language is particularly associated with the blessings and curses of the covenant (Deut 28).

In the NT, *katara* is used only six times, three times in this passage (cf. Heb 6:8; Jas 3:10; 2 Pet 2:14).[8] The specific curse in mind is outlined in what follows, a curse that flows from the failure of those who seek righteousness through the law to fulfill the works of the law. 'Works of the law' here is particularly the boundary markers of Judaism, especially circumcision (see on 2:16).

The cause (*gar*, 'for') of this accursed state is given in a version of Deuteronomy 27:26. Paul introduces the OT text with *gegraptai*, the perfect passive of *graphō* (see on 3:10)—the dominant way of introducing an OT text in the NT. Paul uses it thirty times to introduce OT texts, including four times in Galatians (3:10, 13; 4:22, 27).[9] The perfect tense speaks of its stative function of something written in the past but with an

---

8. The term *katara* is used forty-five times in the LXX of people cursing—verbally conveying harm—toward others (Gen 27:12, 13; Num 23:25; Deut 23:9; Judg 9:57; 2 Sam 16:12; 1 Kings 2:8; Ps 108:17, 18 [Eng. 109:17, 18]; Job 31:30; Sir 3:9; 29:6). In Deuteronomy, blessings and curses are associated with being obedient to the covenant (Deut 11:26–29; 27:11–13; 28:1–45 cf. Deut 29:27; 30:1, 19; Mal 2:2; Jer 36:22; Dan 9:11), the curses being the converse to the blessings: insecurity, poverty, barrenness, invasion, and so on (cf. Josh 9:7). It is also used to describe a devastated place becoming an object of cursing (2 Kings 22:19; Prov 3:33; Zech 8:13; Isa 64:10; Jer 24:9; 33:6; 51:8, 12), and an accursed memory (Sir 23:26). See also Sir 41:9; 41:10; Isa 65:23.

9. Matthew uses it this way nine times, Mark seven, Luke fourteen (Luke-Acts), Paul thirty times (also 1 Cor 4:6), John uses it four times but not as an introductory formula (John, 1–3 John, Rev), Hebrews once, and 1 Peter once. Paul's uses are Rom 1:17 (Hab 2:4); 2:24 (Isa 52:5); 3:4 (Ps 51:4, LXX); 3:10 where it introduces a string of texts (Ps 14:1–3; 5:9; 140:3; 10:7; Prov 1:16 Isa 59:7, 8; Ps 36:1); 4:17 (Gen 17:5); 8:36 (Ps 44:22); 9:13 (Mal 1:2–3), 33 (Ps 28:16); 10:15 (Isa 52:7); 11:8 where it introduces two texts (Isa 29:10; Deut 29:4), 26 (Isa 59:20–21); 12:19 (Deut 32:35); 14:11 (Isa 45:23); 15:3 (Ps 69:9), 9 where it introduces four texts (2 Sam 22:50/Ps. 18:49; Deut 32:43; Ps 117:1; Isa 11:1); 15:21 (Isa 52:15); 1 Cor 1:19 (Isa 29:14); 1:31 (Jer 9:23–24); 2:9 (Isa 64:4); 3:19 (Job 5:13); 9:9 (Deut 25:4); 10:7 (Exod 32:6); 14:21 (Isa 28:11–12); 15:45 (Gen 2:7); 2 Cor 8:15 (Exod 16:18); 9:9 (Ps 112:9). Paul also uses it in 1 Cor 4:6

ongoing state of present effect. For Paul and the other NT writers, the passive speaks not merely of the human writers, but the God who wrote the Scriptures by his Spirit through human agency. Below are the two texts from the LXX and Paul.

Deut 27:26: *epikataratos pas **anthrōpos**, hos ouk emmenei **en pasin tois logois** tou nomou **toutou** tou poiēsai **autous**,* 'cursed be any person, who does not abide in all the words of this law and does them.'

Gal 3:10: *epikataratos pas **hos** ouk emmenei en pasin tois **gegrammenois en tō bibliō** tou nomou tou poiēsai **auta**.* 'Cursed be anyone who does not abide in all which is written in the book of the law and does them.'

The highlights above reveal some differences; however, the overall effect is the same. In Deuteronomy, the text comes at the end of twelve curses that Moses invokes which must be cited by the Levites on Mount Ebal. The verse is the final summative curse (cf. Ps 118:21 [119:21]). It is also referenced in Jer 11:3, where Jeremiah warns Israel of forthcoming exile.[10] 'The book of the law' refers specifically to the Torah, rather than the whole OT.

Paul takes the passage literally here. Those who place their reliance on works of the law for righteousness before God and inclusion in God's people must continually abide in *all* that is written in the book of the law and do its commands. So, yielding

---

of all that is written—the whole OT. He does not use it in Eph, Phil, Col, 1 Thess, 2 Thess, the Pastorals, or Philemon.

10. Paul uses a different term, *epikataros* which compounds *epi* (upon) and *kataros* (curse) and invokes a divine curse. It is used of the curse on the serpent (Gen 3:14) and the land (Gen 3:17) in the Fall narrative; the curse on Cain (Gen 4:11) and Canaan (Gen 9:25); those who curse Isaac (Gen 27:29); and the anger of Simeon and Levi (Gen 49:7). It recurs through the twelve curses of Deut 27:15–26 as a result of sins like idolatry, dishonoring parents, shifting borders, misleading the blind, injustice to the marginalized, sexual immorality (three curses), striking one's neighbor, and killing the innocent. Through Deut 28:16–19, it is used six times reserved for disobedient Israel in the city, the country, in provision, with barrenness, and going out or in. It is invoked upon one who rebuilds Jericho (Josh 6:29) and the Gibeonites (Josh 9:28). It is a favorite of Jeremiah (Jer 17:5; 20:14, 15; 31:10). See also Judg 5:23; 21:18; 1 Sam 14:24, 28; 26:19; Prov 24:39; Wis 3:12; 14:8; Tob 13:12; Mal 1:14; Isa 65:20; 4 Macc 2:19.

to the Judaizers takes the Galatians into a state where to please God by the law, they must do everything in it. The Torah is full of precepts. Paul knows fulfilling them is an impossibility because all humanity, Jew and gentile alike, are under sin, and cannot achieve right standing through the law. Even if a person who came to Christ could do so, they would remain sinful as prior to their life in Christ, they sinned. The law does not liberate people from sin, it makes them more aware of sin and their failure. It is simply impossible for a person to be justified by law.

The Scriptures, which predict salvation, serve to imprison people under sin (3:22, 23, cf. Rom 3:9, 19–20, 23). This is indeed why Jesus came. To set free Israel from its bondage to law and sin and to set the world free from sin. So, while indeed the issue in Galatians is boundary markers and especially circumcision, to accede to the Judaizers means the Galatians who yield to them walk back into captivity—not to their pagan demonic religious pasts, but to the law. This is because they are incapable of full observance of its precepts. The same goes for anyone who converts from Christianity to Judaism or who seeks to do the law for justification and inclusion in God's people.

THE RIGHTEOUS WILL LIVE BY FAITH AND NOT LAW (3:11)

In *Galatians 3:11,* he continues:

And (*de*, 1:15) **[it is] evident** (*dēlos*)[11] **that** (*hoti*, 1:6) **no one** (*oudeis*, 2:6) **is being justified** (present passive indicative *dikaioō*, 2:16) **before** (*para*, 1:8) **God** (*Theos*, 1:1) **by** (*en*, 1:6) **the law** (dative *nomos*, 2:16), **for** (*hoti*) 'the righteous one (*dikaios*, 3:11) **from** (*ek*, 1:1) **faith** (*pistis*, 1:23) **will live** (future *zaō*, 2:14).'

The beginning of the verse, *hote de*, is awkward. It can carry the sense 'and that,' 'but that,' 'and because,' or 'but because.' While some argue it is adversative,[12] here it is likely consecutive restating in a different way the general principle he is working

---

11. The adjective δῆλος (*dēlos*) is found only in Gal 3:11, in the sense of something clear or evident; namely, that one cannot be justified by the law. The only other use in Paul is 1 Cor 15:27.

12. Longenecker, *Galatians*, 118.

with—no one can be justified by the law. As a result, some translations use 'now' (e.g., ESV, NRSV, NET). The NIV simply begins 'clearly' and drops the connective.[13] I prefer to retain the sense of *de*, 'and,' keeping continuity and drawing out the impact of *hoti* with *dēlos*, 'it is evident that …'

As noted in the translation, 'it is evident' uses *dēlos* (1 Cor 15:27) that speaks of something evident or clear; here, what is evident is that a person cannot be justified by the law.[14] 'By the law' here uses *en* (in) and can be 'in the sphere of the law,' i.e., Judaism. However, it more likely is instrumental—'by' or 'by means of the law.'[15] The verb *dikaioō* here is present passive. The passive speaks of the agency of declaration of righteousness by God, and the present speaks of something timeless.[16] 'Before God' uses *para tō Theō*, and means in the sight of God, speaking of judgment (cf. Rom 2:13).[17] 'No one' is emphatic and absolute, speaking of all humankind. Aside from the Lord himself, no human can be justified by the law. It is and always has been faith, as he will now argue in his reason below.

The reason given for the premise that no one can be justified by law is a citation from another biblical text. Unusually, Paul does not use *gegraptai* (as it is written) (cf. 3:10, 13; 4:22, 27). The making of a direct link to the prophetic text is likely because it is well known to the Galatians. This is likely because Paul has taught it amongst them. The text is from the Prophets, Habakkuk 2:4b. Having argued from the Torah (Gen 15:6), he strengthens his argument for justification by faith from the Prophets. Notably, in Rom 4:6–8 he will strengthen it further with a citation from Ps 32:1–2. Habakkuk 2:4 is cited in the NT three times, including here, in Romans 1:17, and by the writer of Hebrews in Heb 10:38. By using Hab 2:4 alongside Gen 15:6, Paul

---

13. Also, Longenecker, *Galatians*, 118.
14. See the discussion in Moo, *Galatians*, 205 on various ways of dealing with the second *hoti*. He agrees that it is causal.
15. Similarly, Moo, *Galatians*, 205.
16. Moo, *Galatians*, 205.
17. See BDAG 757 meaning 2 in which *para* carries the meaning 'in the sight of the judgment of someone,' which here is God in judgment. On *para tō Theō*, see Mark 10:27; Luke 1:30; 18:27; Rom 2:11, 13; 3:19; Jas 1:27.

draws on a second part of the OT to stress that the Scriptures endorse his argument.

Hab 2:4 LXX
Ho de dikaios ek pisteōs mou zēsetai
and the righteous from my faithfulness shall live
Hab 2:4 MT
but the righteous by his faith shall live
Gal 3:11
ho   dikaios ek pisteōs zēsetai
The righteous from faith shall live
Rom 1:17
ho de dikaios ek pisteōs zēsetai
The righteous from faith shall live
Heb 10:38
ho de dikaios mou ek pisteōs zēsetai
And my righteous one from faith shall live

Aside from the presence of *de* in Rom 1:17, the citations in Romans and Galatians are identical. The MT is ambiguous, with the righteous one living by 'his' faith. Here *pistis* can be the person's faith/faithfulness or that of God. The LXX deals with this issue by rendering 'his faith' as 'my faithfulness,' clarifying that it is Yahweh's fidelity, which is the basis of righteousness. Hebrews transfers the pronoun 'my' to the 'righteous one' speaking of the person who is righteous. Paul drops 'my' and 'his' and states that the righteous one shall live by faith or the righteous by faith shall live.

There is much scholarship discussing whether Paul is thinking in the Lutheran preference, 'the one who is righteous by faith, shall live,' emphasizing conversion, with *ek pisteōs* (by faith)[18] modifying *dikaios* (the righteous).[19] Alternatively, it can have the sense 'the righteous one shall live by faith' stressing ongoing Christian life, with *ek pisteōs* (from faith) modifying *zēsetai* (will

---

18. This is the fifth use of *ek pisteōs*, 'from faith,' in Galatians, all but two in this chapter (see further 2:16, also 3:7, 8, 9, 12, 22, 24; 5:5). As in cases, the faith in mind is a human response, not Jesus'.

19. Bruce, *Galatians*, 161; Morris, *Galatians*, 104; Moo, *Galatians*, 206.

live).[20] Another possibility is that 'by faith' modifies both the verb 'will live' and 'the righteous one.'[21]

The latter seems by far the best option. Indeed, from a theological perspective and consideration of the letter, this seems a redundant question. As evident through the letter, Paul is vigorously defending the premise that one is justified by faith and only faith (entry into God's righteous covenant people, salvation, redemption, adoption, and sanctification, etc.). Equally importantly, for the already Christ-believing Galatians, they remain in this righteous status before God *by faith,* and one lives life by faith, with faithfulness (cf. 5:22). Life now is 'faith working through love' (5:6). That entry and ongoing life is by faith is the main argument of Galatians—the Judaizers are saying faith is not enough. The Galatians must go further and add works of the law to faith. Hence, the saying is likely intentionally ambiguous with 'by faith' modifying entry and ongoing life. The sentence encompasses both aspects of theology—initial justification and the ongoing status of righteousness; both of which, are by faith.

Whose faith is in mind? In the LXX, it is God's faithfulness that justifies. Paul may have this in mind in his citations—the righteous shall live through God's faithfulness, not one's own. One can push this to Jesus' faith/faithfulness—the righteous shall live through the faithfulness of Christ.[22] As argued throughout this commentary, the debate in Galatians is about what a person has to do to be justified. This issue is seen in what flanks this verse which focuses on a person 'doing' the things written in the law (vv. 10. 12). Paul's answer is that there is a human response, and it is faith and faith alone. So, the faith here is not God's or

---

20. This is defended on the basis of the original context of Hab. 2:4b which is a call to Israel in difficult times to 'live' in dependence on God's faithfulness. See for example H. C. C. Cavallin, "'The Righteous Shall Live by Faith:' A Decisive Argument for the Traditional Interpretation,' *ST* 32 (1978): 33–43.

21. Dunn, *Galatians,* 174; Martyn, *Galatians,* 314.

22. See for example G. Howard, *Paul: Crisis in Galatia; A Study in Early Christian Theology* (SSNTM 35; Cambridge: Cambridge University Press, 1979), 63–64. Some think it is both Christ's faithfulness and human faith—e.g., Richard B. Hays, 'Galatians,' in *The New Interpreter's Bible* XI (Nashville, TN: Abingdon, 2002), 138–41; Martyn, *Galatians,* 1997.

Christ's, but people's response to the hearing of the gospel. If it is 'with faith,' they live by the power of the Spirit (3:2, 5).

Grace is the Godward side of justification—by the gospel of grace expressed in Christ, people are called by God. He offers them the status of righteousness. As discussed on 2:16, the faith in mind is cognitive (*notitia*), assent (*assensus*), trust (*fiducia*), and relationship with God (*affinitas*). It is enabled by God. Such faith is the basis of God justifying a human being. Consequently, one is not justified by doing law; one is justified by one's response of faith. One remains justified by one's ongoing response of faith.

It is notable here that the status of righteousness is paralleled with 'live.' 'Live' here is not merely present Christian life (important though this is), but the status of *eternal* life. Eternal life begins at the point of faith. Eternal life is born as the Spirit enters the human heart, and God's transformation begins. It will be consummated at the transformation of the body from perishability to imperishability, from mortality to immortality (1 Cor 15:53–54). The paralleling of righteous status and life here again shows the versatility of Paul's metaphors. One could parallel righteousness with adoption, reconciliation, redemption, sanctification, regeneration, and other metaphors used in Paul and the NT.

THE LAW IS NOT FAITH (3:12)

In *Galatians 3:12* Paul contrasts the law with the principle he has been highlighting through the letter, 'from faith:'

But (*de*, 1:15) **the law** (*nomos*, 2:16) **is** (*eimi*, 1:7) **not** (*ou*, 1:1) **from** (*ek*, 1:1) **faith** (*pistis*, 1:23), **but** (*alla*, 1:1) **the one who does** (aorist participle *poieō*, 2:10) **these things** (neuter plural *autos*, 1:1) **will live** (future *zaō*, 2:14) **by** (*en*, 1:6) **them** (dative plural *autos*).

'The law is not from (*ek*) faith'[23] does not suggest that there is no reference to faith in the law, that faith as a justification-principle is not even endorsed by or in the law (e.g., Gen 15:6),

---

23. This is the sixth use of *ek pisteōs* in Galatians (see further 2:16, also 3:7, 8, 9, 11, 22, 24; 5:5).

that Moses had no faith as he received the law or anything of the sort. Rather, it refers to the law as a system. It has no capacity to generate faith and justification. From that point of view, although the law has a critical function (which Paul will come to below), it does not bring faith. From the perspective of faith generation and producing eternal life, it is defunct. Paul has already made plain that justification is *ek pisteōs*, from faith. This has come in Christ. So, for the Galatians to contemplate Judaizing opens up the horrendous thought that they fall away from faith to law-reliance—which is self-reliance, and implausible.

The law demands that 'the one who does these things will live by them.' 'The one' in mind is the Jew or Judaizer that opts for the Jewish system against the faith that has come in Christ. 'Live' then speaks not merely of living in the present, although this is supposed, but living eternally. 'Does' is defined by the previous verse, which demands constant abiding in them and flawless observance of the law for eternal life. Again, this is implausible. One will 'live in them' but not see eternal life for only faith can see one included in Christ and receive the promised seal of the Spirit and live eternally.

While 'by them' is literally 'in them,' Paul is thinking of means here. To Judaize places one into the system that requires living by the precepts of the law every moment of every day, 168 hours a week, fifty-two weeks a year, until death. Achieving this is a fanciful concept. It is likely Paul did not hold this perspective on the law as a Jew. Rather, he saw the law as something to be done with great diligence. He says in Phil 3:6 that under the law, he was blameless. He was a Pharisee, a member of the most legally observant sect of Judaism. He was advancing in Judaism beyond others his own age. Now that Christ has come, in a most unexpected way, as a crucified Messiah, he has reworked his understanding. He recognizes that living by the law is an unattainable goal for all humanity, the Jew included. He works this out most clearly in Romans 7, speaking of the cognitive dissonance the law creates in the Jew and Judaizer. One knows what one must do, but one cannot do it. Thankfully, God has acted in Christ, rescuing Paul from his body of death, the law of the Spirit of life set him free from the law of sin and death, to which all are captive.

Now he has a reworked soteriology, recognizing that justification was never from the law. The law serves to imprison people to sin and to recognize their desperate need for grace and faith. As he looks over Israel's story, he sees that it has, in fact, always been faith, for faith precedes the law, especially in the life of Abraham, who was 'justified by faith.' The very thing that disqualified Jesus when he was a law-observant Jew, his crucifixion, is the key that opens the way to faith. He will explain this further in what follows. What matters for the Galatians is that they hear loud and clear—do not yield to the Judaizers or you will enter that now-defunct religious system and be lost to faith and so to God.

CHRIST CRUCIFIED, THE CURSE OF THE LAW (3:13)

Galatians 3:13 tells of how God has once for all dealt with the curse that the law brings upon all who seek to live through its precepts—through Christ:

Christ (*Christos*, 1:1) **redeemed** (*exagorazō*)[24] **us** (accusative plural *egō*, 1:2) **from** (*ek*, 1:1) **the curse** (*katara*, 3:10) **of the law** (genitive *nomos*, 2:16) **by becoming** (aorist middle participle *ginomai*, 2:17) **for** (*hyper*, 1:4) **us** (plural genitive *egō*) **a curse** (*katara*); **as it is written** (perfect passive *graphō*, 3:10), '**Cursed** (*epikataros*, 3:10) **[is] everyone** (*pas*, 1:2) **who** (*ho*, 1:1) **is hanged** (*kremannymi*)[25] **on** (*epi*, 3:13) **a tree** (*xylon*)!'[26]

The first question is who Paul has in mind with 'us.' Many

---

24. The verb ἐξαγοράζω (*exagorazō*) compounds *ek*, 'out of' and the commercial term *agorazō*, 'buy, purchase,' and speaks of 'buy out of, redeem, deliver.' Paul is the only NT writer who uses this term, twice in Galatians of Christ redeeming people from the curse of the law (Gal 3:13; 4:5), and otherwise of 'redeeming the time' (Eph 5:16; Col 4:5).

25. The verb κρεμάννυμι (*kremannymi*) is found once in Galatians, of someone hanged on a tree (Christ being the one in mind). It is not widely used in the NT aside from this use, six times including those crucified (Luke 23:39) including Christ (Acts 5:30; 10:39); a millstone hung on a neck (Matt 18:6), the law and the prophets hanging on

argue these are just Jews. Others consider this general. In my view, the text functions at two levels. In a literal sense, 'us' is Jews, as gentiles were not under the law before Jesus came, and it became a curse for Israel. Paul also (in v. 14) distinguishes 'us' from 'the gentiles' to whom the blessings of Abraham have come in Jesus. However, the text becomes inclusive rhetorically when read by the Galatians who are considering submitting to the Judaizers and Torah. Jesus became a curse for all humanity not just for Jews. The gentiles are being lured into law observance, and the argument is directed at them—they are redeemed from the need to come under the law. So, I would argue that the 'we' is at a surface literal level, Israel under the law. Yet, when it is read in the light of the Galatian controversy, it becomes universalized and applies to all humanity.

The term for redeemed here is not one of the usual *lytr-* terms,[27] but *exagorazō* (*ek* plus *agorazō*), which literally implies 'bought out of' (cf. Rev 14:3, 4, both, *agorazō*). The term is used only by Paul here and in 4:5 of redemption from the law; otherwise, it is used of redeeming the time or making the most of an opportunity (Eph 3:13; Col 4:5, cf. Dan 2:8). It is a parallel idea, drawing on the notion of redemption in Israel's story. Here, it has the sense of 'purchase out of' or 'redeem' from the law.

'Us' can be all humanity, or as is more likely in context, Jews who lived their life under the law but are now purchased out from its rule. Still, as has been noted, even if Jews are in view, all people are now implicated including those who might join Jews under the law. They are now under the rule of Christ. The

---

the two great commandments (Matt 22:40), and a snake hanging off a hand (Acts 28:4).

26. The Greek ξύλον (*xylon*), meaning 'tree, wood, or cross,' is used once in Galatians of a tree or cross on which someone hangs. In context, Christ is in mind. Paul's only other use is in 1 Cor 3:12 of wood which burns in fire.

27. Such *lytr*-terms include *lytrōsis*, 'redemption' (Luke 1:68; 2:38; Heb 9:12); *apolytrōsis*, 'redemption;' (Rom 3:24; 8:23; 1 Cor 1:30; Eph 1:7; 4:30; Col 1:14); and the verb *lytroō* (Luke 24:21; Tit 2:14; 1 Pet 1:18). Another term is *ruomai*, 'deliver, rescue,' used by Paul twelve times (Rom 7:24; 11:26; 15:31; 2 Cor 1:10; Col 1:13; 1 Thess 1:10; 2 Thess 3:2; 2 Tim 3:11; 4:17, 18). In 1:4 he uses *exaireō*, 'deliver, rescue' (cf. Acts 7:10, 34; 12:11; 23:27; 26:17, see further 1:4).

curse of the law' has been discussed above, the curse of failing to be able to complete it and so failing to gain righteousness by law before God. Jews then are left in their sinful state. Only faith suffices. If one is reliant on law, one remains in sin and death, and the consequence is destruction.

Jesus overcame the curse of the law[28] by becoming[29] a curse. 'For us' (hyper ēmōn) has a clear substitutionary aspect here; Christ died on our behalf, in our place (cf. 2 Cor 5:14; John 11:50). This is soteriologically significant; in dying, he took the curse of the law for us.[30] As noted above earlier in this discussion, 'us' here includes Jews who are set free from the curse through Jesus becoming the curse for us. However, it goes further and includes all humanity.

Jesus taking the curse is a big concept. First, the context explains that this refers to the cross upon which Jesus died. Such a death was a sign of divine accursedness. Paul cites an OT text in support. As in 3:10; 4:22, and 4:27, he uses gegraptai, the perfect passive of graphō (see on 3:10); the dominant way of introducing an OT text in the NT, used by Paul thirty times including. The verb speaks of the present power of the Scriptures written in the past; they are infused with God's power by the Spirit. The citation is a variation of Deut 21:23.

Deut 21:23	kekatēramenos[31] hypo Theou pas	**kremamenos epi xylon**
Gal 3:13	epitataratos pas ho	**kremamenos epi xylon**

As such, for a law-abiding Jew, Jesus is cursed by God in his death on the cross—here described in terms of Deut 21:23 as a xylon, a tree.[32]

The verb for hanged is kremannymi is found through the OT

---

28. This may be a genitive of production, 'the curse produced by the law' (Wallace, Greek Grammar, 105).

29. The verb ginomai is common. This is the first use with the sense 'become, became' in Galatians (see 3:13; 4:12, 16; 5:26). See further on the verb in 2:17.

30. Wallace, Greek Grammar, 387.

31. The perfect passive of kataraomai, another term associated with katara.

32. See Acts 5:30; 10:39; 13:29; 1 Pet 2:24. Xylon can mean a wooden club (Matt 26:47, 55; Mark 14:43, 48; Luke 22:52), wood (Luke 23:31; 1 Cor 3:12; Rev 18:12) or wooden

as a typical ANE punishment. So Pharaoh hanged the baker on a pole (Gen 40:19, 22; 41:13), Joshua hanged the Canaanite leaders (Josh 8:29; 10:26), David hanged his enemies (2 Sam 4:12), and Mordecai and Haman's sons were hanged.[33] It is found of Absalom, who was hanged on a tree (2 Kings 18:9–10).[34] In Deut 21:22–23, a person is sentenced to be hanged by judicial decision and is hanged on a tree. The deceased cannot stay hung up overnight but must be buried. Such a person is cursed.[35]

In the NT, as mentioned in the translation, it can be used of things hanging from something (Matt 18:6; Acts 28:4; Matt 22:40), and so refers to people being hung up in crucifixion.[36] In Jewish thought, such a person is accursed.

This is so for Paul. Jesus *is* cursed on the cross, but for him, it is a vicarious cursing of an innocent Jesus for the world. In being nailed to a tree, and so being cursed, Jesus took humanity's curse upon himself in his accursed state, and redeemed people from the curse of the law. This is another way of expressing the vicarious power of Christ.

It is 'for us' (*hyper ēmōn*) as in 1:4, 'he gave himself *for our* sins to deliver us from the present evil age;' or 2:20, 'the Son of God, who loved me and gave himself *for me*.' 'Us' here can be all humanity, and in a sense is, but is in particular Jewish Christians who live under the law. They are set free from the failure of achieving righteousness through law because of their sin and fallen flesh. They are redeemed, as was Israel from Egypt. Jesus' death is accursed, taking the curse of the law upon himself—he who had no sin (2 Cor 5:21)—and breaking its power.

Now, all that is required is to believe in the accursed one who has carried the curse with him to death. He arose, and so the

---

stocks (Acts 16:24). It is also used for the Tree of life (Rev 2:7; 22:2, 14, 19); the cross in a theological sense, being this tree, from which one must eat (cf. John 6:25–58).

33. See Esth 6:4; 8:7; 9:13, 14, 25. For others, see 1 Macc 1:61; 1 Esd 6:31; Lam 5:12.

34. *Kremannymi* is used of hanging up shields (Song 4:4) and figuratively of a life hanging in doubt (Deut 28:66, s.a., Jdt 8:24), to hang in there (1 Macc 1:62; 2 Macc 6:10).

35. Wallace, *Greek Grammar*, 523–33 sees the present participle of κρεμάννυμι as a gnomic present. Such a present is something customary, a 'general timeless fact.' It is atemporal. It is often used for something proverbial as in this case.

36. Of Jesus' crucifixion, see Luke 23:39; Acts 5:30; 10:39; Gal 3:13.

curse of the law is utterly broken. It must not be reinstated by yielding to the Judaizer demands. To yield is to repudiate the Accursed One and place oneself under the curse of the law, and so be imprisoned to sin, death, and destruction.

THE ABRAHAMIC BLESSING AND THE SPIRIT IS RECEIVED IN CHRIST (3:14)

Galatians 3:14 includes two *hina* clauses:

So that (*hina*, 1:16) the blessing (*eulogia*)[37] of Abraham (genitive *Abraam*, 3:6) might come (aorist middle subjunctive *ginomai*, 2:17) to (*eis*, 1:5) the nations (plural *ethnos*, 1:16) in (*en*, 1:6) Christ (dative *Christos*, 1:1) Jesus (dative *Iēsous*, 1:1), so that (*hina*) we might receive (aorist subjunctive *lambanō*, 2:6) the promise[38] (*epangelia*)[39] of the Spirit (genitive *pneumatos*, 3:2) through (*dia*, 1:1) faith (genitive *pistis*, 1:23).

The two *hina* clauses can be sequential, the first drawing out the implications of Christ taking the curse of humanity on the cross, and the second drawing out the consequences of the blessing coming to the nations. However, it is better to read them as two consequences of Christ taking the curse—they are two bullet points drawing inferences from Christ's vicarious accursedness. As Moo notes, *hina* is most often purposive and sometimes speaks of result; however, here, both purpose and result are expressed.[40]

The first purpose/result is that the blessing to the nations through his seed promised to Abraham (Gen 12:3), has come to pass in Christ. This is seen in the conversion of the Galatians

---

37. There is only one use of εὐλογία (*eulogia*), 'blessing,' in Galatians in 3:14, of the Abrahamic promise. It is another of the *eulog-* terms in the letter. It literally means 'good word,' and so a word of blessing (Eng. 'eulogy').

38. **Variant**: In place of the Greek for promise (*epangelia*) some texts have *eulogia* (blessing) as in the previous clause. These include P46 and other variant texts. This could be a scribal error, and the quality of the support for *epangelia* is superior.

39. A Greek noun for promise, ἐπαγγελία (*epangelia*), recurs ten times in Galatians, all in Gal 3–4 including the promise of the Spirit (3:14), the Abrahamic promises (3:16, 18, 29; 4:23, 28), a covenantal promise in principle (3:17, 18), the promises of God (3:21), the promise from faith in Jesus Christ given to believers (3:22).

40. Moo, *Galatians*, 214.

and many others around the Mediterranean region through the
ministry of Paul and others. The Galatians are recipients of the
blessings of Abraham in Christ—implication: do not submit to
works of the law!

The second purpose/result clause is that believers, Jew and
gentile (we), are receiving the promise of the Spirit through faith.
The promise of the Spirit calls to mind the Jewish dream that
God would not merely send his Spirit in power upon key figures
in a temporary way,[41] but would pour out his Spirit on his
Messiah (Isa 11:2; 61:1, cf. Isa 42:1) and all Israel at the
culmination of the age.[42] Now the promise has come, by faith
(3:2, 5).

---

41. See e.g., Num 24:2; 27:8; Deut 34:9; Judg 3:10; 6:34; 11:29; 13:25; 14:6, 19; 15:14; 1
   Sam 10:6, 10; 11:6; 16:13–14; 19:10, 23; 2 Kings 2:16; 1 Chron 12:18; 2 Chron 16:1;
   20:15; 24:20; Neh 9:30; Ps 51:1; Ezek 2:2; 3:12, 14, 24; 8:3; 11:1, 5, 24; 43:5; Mic 3:8.
42. See e.g., Num 11:17, 25–29; Neh 9:20 [2 Esd 19:20]; Ps 104:30; Isa 32:15; 44:3; 59:21;
   63:14; Ezek 11:19; 18:31; 36:26–27; 37:1–29; 39:29; Joel 2:28–29.

CHAPTER SEVENTEEN: THE ABRAHAMIC PROMISE FULFILLED THROUGH CHRIST NOT LAW (3:15–18)

The lack of a connective indicates a new sub-section of Paul's argument against justification through law-observance. He works from the perspective of a human covenantal agreement, which cannot be revoked once ratified. He then applies this to the Abrahamic covenant in which promises were made to Abraham and 'his offspring,' singular. Paul then states that this is fulfilled in Abraham's descendant—Christ.

On the other hand, the law came some four centuries after the Abrahamic Covenant. It does not annul the former covenant and void the promise, the promise still stands. It will come to his singular offspring, Christ. However, if as the Judaizers are arguing, the inheritance promised to Abraham and his offspring Christ does come through the law, then it is not based on the covenantal promise—even though it has not been annulled. In other words, they are the people revoking the Abrahamic Covenant and placing law as the means of receiving the promise, not Christ. In that they are saying that Paul is violating the Abrahamic covenant by not requiring circumcision, Paul has turned their argument on its head. There is no need for circumcision. Galatians! Don't do it!

A HUMAN-MADE COVENANT OR WILL CANNOT BE REVOKED (3:15)

He begins in *Galatians 3:15*:

Brothers and sisters (plural *adelphos*, 1:1), **let me speak** (*legō*, 1:9) **concerning** (*kata*, 1:4) **a human [example]** (*anthrōpos*, 1:1);

likewise (*homōs*)[1] **when a human** (genitive *anthrōpos*) **covenant** (*diathēkē*)[2] **has been ratified** (perfect passive participle *kyroō*),[3] **no one** (*oudeis*, 2:6) **sets it aside** (*atheteō*, 2:21) **or** (*ē*, 1:8) **adds to it** (present *epidiatassomai*).[4]

As noted above, there is no connective in Gal 3:15 (asyndeton, see 2:6). Paul, for the first time since 1:11, addresses them with his customary term of address that stresses kinship in God—'brothers and sisters' (it is inclusive as always, see on 1:11). This could suggest a new section, but there is continuity, albeit a new phase in the argument. His use reminds us that he is writing to Christians and is not accusing them of complete abandonment of the faith (yet). He is speaking as one brother to a sibling urging them to do the right thing.

He gives a human example, speaking 'according to a human' way of thinking. Using *diathēkē* in its broader sense of a 'last will and testament' (cf. Heb 9:16–17), he states the legal truth that when people sign a will, it is legally ratified (*kyroō*).

The verb *kyroō* is a legal term and can mean 'to enforce,' 'to confirm,' or 'to validate.' In the LXX, it is used for the signing over of property (Gen 23:20; Lev 25:30), and King Darius signing

1. The adverb ὅμως (*homōs*) is found only three times in the NT, once in Galatians (3:15). It carries the meaning 'all the same, nevertheless, yet' (BDAG 710). This is the sense in the only non-Pauline use in John 12:42 where it means 'nevertheless.' However, in 3:15 and 1 Cor 14:7 it is more like the older ὁμῶς (*homōs*) and has the sense 'likewise' and used in a comparison (BDAG 710).
2. The noun διαθήκη (*diathēkē*) is used three times in Galatians in 3:15, 17, and 4:24. In 3:15 it is used in the sense of a legal will, which cannot be supplemented or revoked upon death. In 3:17 it is used of the Abrahamic covenant. In 4:24 it is used of the two covenants; Sarah and Hagar, who represent the Abrahamic and Sinai covenants.
3. The only reference to κυρόω (*kyroō*) in Galatians is found in 3:14 of the ratification of a will. Its only other NT use is 2 Cor 2:8 of the Corinthians 'reaffirming,' or 'ratifying,' their love for the repentant sinner. The related *prokyroō* is found in 3:17 of the ratification of the Abrahamic covenant. The antonym *akyroō*, 'annul, revoke,' is found in 3:17.
4. The verb ἐπιδιατάσσομαι (*epidiatassomai*) compounds *epi* (upon) and the middle of *diatassō* (make arrangements, give instructions) and so literally to 'make upon' or 'make further,' i.e., 'to add,' is found once in Galatians and the NT (*hapax legomenon*). It signifies to add something, here, the codicil to a will (BDAG 370). It is extremely rare, not found in the LXX, Pseudepigrapha, Josephus, Philo, or in a Logos Perseus word search.

the document that led to Daniel being thrown to the lions (Dan 9:6). Here, it speaks of a 'will which has come into force.'[5]

When a legal will comes into play, no one can simply 'declare it invalid,' 'nullify it,' or 'ignore it' (*atheteō*). The verb was used in 2:21 of nullifying the grace of God (which Paul does not do).[6] The second verb *epidiatassomai* means to add to, and so to add something to a will, i.e., a codicil (a legal instrument made to modify an earlier will). In sum, a will cannot simply be set aside or added to (or if this is done, it violates the law).

Of course, this holds true in our society today. Once ratified, unless revoked, a legal will holds true—as anyone who has been part of a dispute over a will knows from bitter experience. The comparison will be drawn out in the verses that follow, namely, that the covenant with Abraham has not been annulled or added to by the Mosaic Covenant. The promise remains (esp. vv. 17–18).

CHRIST, THE SEED OF ABRAHAM (3:16)

In *Galatians 3:16*, Paul returns to the theme of the Abrahamic covenant and promises:

And (*de*, 1:15) **the promises** (*epangelia*, 3:14) **were said** (aorist passive *eipon*, 2:14) **to Abraham** (dative *Abraam*, 3:6) **and** (*kai*, 1:1) **his** (genitive *autos*, 1:1) **seed** (dative *sperma*).[7] **It does not** (*ou*, 1:1) **say** (*legō*, 1:9),[8] '**And** (*kai*, 1:1) **to offsprings** (plural dative *sperma*),' **as** (*hōs*, 1:9) **upon** (*epi*, 3:13) **many** (genitive plural neuter *polus*,

---

5. See J. Behm, 'κυρόω,' in *TDNT* 3:110. The only other NT use is in 2 Cor 2:8 where Paul begs the Corinthians to *reaffirm* their love for the sinner.

6. BDAG 24 gives these meanings for *atheteō*. Elsewhere it is used of breaking an oath (Mark 6:26), violating a command or purpose of God (Mark 7:9; Luke 7:30), rejecting someone (Luke 10:16; John 12:48), God thwarting the discernment of the discerning (1 Cor 1:19), nullifying the grace of God (Gal 2:21), disregarding an instruction of Paul (1 Thess 4:8), abandoning former faith (1 Tim 5:12), setting aside the law of Moses (Heb 10:28), or to reject authority (Jude 8). It is always negative.

7. The noun σπέρμα (*sperma*) is use five times in Galatians, all of Abraham's descendent(s) (3:16, 19, 29).

8. Wallace, *Greek Grammar*, 532–33 sees the introductory formula as a perfective present whereby the 'present tense may be used to emphasize that the results of a past action are still continuing. This usage is not very common.'

1:14), but (*alla*, 1:1) as (*hōs*) upon (*epi*) one (*heis*).[9] 'And (*kai*) to your (genitive *sy*, 1:3) offspring (*sperma*),' who (*hos*)[10] is (*estin*, 1:7) Christ (*Christos*, 1:1).

The covenant relationship with Abraham involved God making promises to Abraham. The promises sprinkle Genesis:

To Abraham

I will make you a great nation, and I will bless you and make your name great, so that you will be a blessing. I will bless those who bless you, and him who dishonors you I will curse, and in you all the families of the earth shall be blessed (Gen 12:2–3, ESV).

To your offspring (singular *sperma*) I will give this land (Gen 12:7).

Lift up your eyes and look from the place where you are, northward and southward and eastward and westward, for all the land that you see I will give to you and to your offspring forever. I will make your offspring as the dust of the earth, so that if one can count the dust of the earth, your offspring also can be counted. Arise, walk through the length and the breadth of the land, for I will give it to you. (Gen 13:14–18).

Fear not, Abram, I am your shield; your reward shall be very great ... This man shall not be your heir; your very own son shall be your heir ... Look toward heaven, and number the stars, if you are able to number them ... So shall your offspring be ... I am the Lord who brought you out from Ur of the Chaldeans to give you this land to possess ... Know for certain that your offspring will be sojourners in a land that is not theirs and will be servants there, and they will be afflicted for four hundred years. But I will bring judgment on the nation that they serve, and afterward they

9. The number one, εἷς (*heis*) is found eight times in Galatians: one offspring of Abraham (3:16); a mediator not denoting one, but God is who is one (3:20); being one in Christ (3:28); one son by Hagar and one by Sarah (4:22), and one from Mt Sinai (4:24); and one message (5:14).

10. If we follow Greek 101, one might expect the article here to be neuter in line with the neuter σπέρμα (*sperma*). However, the masculine here 'occurs when the focus of the discourse is on the predicate nominative: the dominant gender reveals the dominant idea of the passage.' (Wallace, *Greek Grammar*, 338). Here, the dominant gender is decided by Χριστός (*Christos*), which is masculine.

shall come out with great possessions. As for you, you shall go to your fathers in peace; you shall be buried in a good old age. And they shall come back here in the fourth generation, for the iniquity of the Amorites is not yet complete (Gen 15:4–16).

I am God Almighty; walk before me, and be blameless, that I may make my covenant between me and you, and may multiply you greatly … Behold, my covenant is with you, and you shall be the father of a multitude of nations. No longer shall your name be called Abram (exalted father), but your name shall be Abraham (father of a multitude) for I have made you the father of a multitude of nations. I will make you exceedingly fruitful, and I will make you into nations, and kings shall come from you. And I will establish my covenant between me and you and your offspring after you throughout their generations for an everlasting covenant, to be God to you and to your offspring after you. And I will give to you and to your offspring after you the land of your sojournings, all the land of Canaan, for an everlasting possession, and I will be their God … As for you, you shall keep my covenant, you and your offspring after you throughout their generations. This is my covenant, which you shall keep, between me and you and your offspring after you: Every male among you shall be circumcised. You shall be circumcised in the flesh of your foreskins, and it shall be a sign of the covenant between me and you. He who is eight days old among you shall be circumcised. Every male throughout your generations, whether born in your house or bought with your money from any foreigner who is not of your offspring, both he who is born in your house and he who is bought with your money, shall surely be circumcised. So shall my covenant be in your flesh an everlasting covenant. Any uncircumcised male who is not circumcised in the flesh of his foreskin shall be cut off from his people; he has broken my covenant … As for Sarai your wife, you shall not call her name Sarai, but Sarah shall be her name. I will bless her, and moreover, I will give you a son by her. I will bless her, and she shall become nations; kings of peoples shall come from her … No, but Sarah your wife shall bear you a son, and you shall call his name Isaac. I will establish my covenant with him as an everlasting covenant for his offspring after him. As for Ishmael, I have heard you; behold, I have blessed him and will make him fruitful and multiply him greatly. He shall father twelve princes, and I will make him into a great nation. But I will establish my covenant with Isaac, whom Sarah shall bear to you at this time next year. (Gen 17:1–17).

Where is Sarah your wife? … I will surely return to you about this time next year, and Sarah your wife shall have a son … Why did Sarah laugh and say, 'Shall I indeed bear a child, now that I am old?' Is anything too hard for the Lord? At the appointed time I will return to you, about this time next year, and Sarah shall have a son. (Gen 18:9–14).

Shall I hide from Abraham what I am about to do, seeing that Abraham shall surely become a great and mighty nation, and all the nations of the earth shall be blessed in him? For I have chosen him, that he may command his children and his household after him to keep the way of the Lord by doing righteousness and justice, so that the Lord may bring to Abraham what he has promised him. (Gen 18:17–19).

By myself I have sworn, declares the Lord, because you have done this and have not withheld your son, your only son, I will surely bless you, and I will surely multiply your offspring as the stars of heaven and as the sand that is on the seashore. And your offspring shall possess the gate of his enemies, and in your offspring shall all the nations of the earth be blessed, because you have obeyed my voice. (Gen 22:16–18).

These can be summed up as: 1) God will make Abraham a great nation (Israel); 2) Abraham will be a blessing to the nations; 3) The land will be given to them in the fourth generation; 4) A son will be born to Sarai and then a multiplicity of offspring; 5) Abraham will be the father of a multitude of nations from which kings will come—both from Ishmael and Isaac; 6) An everlasting covenant to be his God and that of his offspring.

These promises are conveyed to his 'seed,' Isaac, and Jacob:

To Isaac

Do not go down to Egypt; dwell in the land of which I shall tell you. Sojourn in this land, and I will be with you and will bless you, for to you and to your offspring I will give all these lands, and I will establish the oath that I swore to Abraham your father. I will multiply your offspring as the stars of heaven and will give to your offspring all these lands. And in your offspring all the nations of the earth shall be blessed, because Abraham obeyed my voice and kept my charge, my commandments, my statutes, and my laws. (Gen 26:2–5).

I am the God of Abraham your father. Fear not, for I am with you and will bless you and multiply your offspring for my servant Abraham's sake. (Gen 26:25).

Stressed in these promises are: 1) The land; 2) The covenant; 3) A multiplicity of descendants; 4) The nations blessed through his offspring.

To Jacob

I am the Lord, the God of Abraham your father and the God of Isaac. The land on which you lie I will give to you and to your offspring. Your offspring shall be like the dust of the earth, and you shall spread abroad to the west and to the east and to the north and to the south, and in you and your offspring shall all the families of the earth be blessed. Behold, I am with you and will keep you wherever you go, and will bring you back to this land. For I will not leave you until I have done what I have promised you. (Gen 28:13–15).

I am God Almighty: be fruitful and multiply. A nation and a company of nations shall come from you, and kings shall come from your own body. The land that I gave to Abraham and Isaac I will give to you, and I will give the land to your offspring after you. (Gen 35:11–12).

In these, the focus is on four elements: 1) The same God of Abraham and Isaac; 2) The land; 3) Multiple descendants and nations from him including kings; 4) These will spread geographically widely.

What Paul has in mind in the promises is not explicitly stated, but the emphasis falls on the seed through whom the promises will be fulfilled. Reading between the lines, the stress appears not to be on the land (which is not mentioned), the greatness of Abraham (which is assumed), but on the covenant (which is being fulfilled in Christ); the blessing to the nations through Abraham and a multiplicity of descendants who will become children and heirs of Abraham through this seed (who is, of course, Christ) (3:29). This blessing is coming through the righteousness by faith which justifies the ungodly as it did Abraham himself.

Paul goes on and does some exegesis of the text. He notes that the promise to Abraham and his seed (offspring) is in the singular, not the plural. Hence, the inheritance promise to Abraham is conveyed to one descendant, not to the many. In the first instance, Isaac might be in mind. However, Paul is clear; the offspring is Christ. The Greek for offspring is *sperma* (cf. Eng. 'sperm,' cf. Lev 15:6),[11] which can mean a literal vegetation seed (Gen 1:11, 12, 29). It is also used of human descendants, with the first use in this sense in Gen 3:15, the so-called protoevangelium, where it is predicted that one of Eve's descendants will strike the heel of the serpent (Gen 3:15). Theologically, this is coming to pass through the descendant of Abraham—Christ.

The term comes up frequently through the promises noted above. While Abraham will have a multiplicity of descendants[12] and they will be aliens in Egypt (Gen 15:13), in Gen 12:3 it is promised 'to your offspring (*sperma* singular) I will give this land.'[13] Further, God will establish his covenant between himself and Abraham and 'your offspring (singular *sperma*) after you throughout the generations, for an everlasting covenant, to be God to you and to your offspring (singular *sperma*) after you' (Gen 17:7, cf. 17:9, 10, 19). The blessing to the earth will also come through one offspring (Gen 22:18; 26:4; 28:14). As noted above, in later Jewish thought, this promise involves his inheriting the whole world (Sir 44:21). Consistent throughout these texts is the use of the singular, which Paul is grabbing here for his argument.[14]

11. *Sperma* relates to the male semen which must not be spilled.
12. Gen 13:16; 15:5; 16:10; 22:17; 26:4, 24; 28:14; 32:13; Josh 24:3; Dan 3:35 LXX.
13. Similarly, see Gen 13:15, 17; 15:18 [LXX]; 17:8; 24:7; 26:3, 4; 28:4, 13; 35:12; 48:4; Exod 33:1; Deut 11:9; 34:4; 2 Chron 20:7.
14. Three ideas, covenant, land, and promise are found in the LXX of Neh 9:8 (2 Esdr. 19:8).

Embedded in these texts is the expectation that every male offspring and even slaves are to be circumcised on the eighth day (e.g., Gen 17:10, 12). It is through Isaac that this offspring (singular *sperma*) will be named for Abraham, and not Ishmael (Gen 21:12), although he too will become a great nation (Gen 21:13). His line is not the line of promise. Now that Christ has come, his line (by faith) is the line to whom the promise flows. For Paul, it does not follow that every gentile convert must then be circumcised now that Christ has come. They are in the circumcised one, and Christ's physical circumcision suffices. What counts is their hearts circumcised by faith (Deut 10:16; 30:6; Jer 4:4; Rom 2:25–29).

Later, at the inauguration of the Davidic covenantal relationship, God similarly promises after David's death to 'raise up your offspring (singular *sperma*, LXX) after you, who shall come forth from your body, and I will establish his kingdom' (2 Sam 7:12, cf. 1 Chron 17:11). While this is Solomon in the first instance, it points forward to the coming of the seed of David (and Eve and Adam, and Abraham and Sarah)—Christ (cf. 2 Sam 22:51). This promise is an everlasting one,[15] and after the fall of the Davidic monarchy, it is Christ who fulfills this.

Another interesting connection to the Abrahamic promise and 'seed' is Deutero-Isaiah. Isaiah addresses Israel as 'the offspring of Abraham, my friend' who God gathered from the ends of the earth (Isa 41:8). This offspring scattered in exile will be gathered from the east and west (Isa 43:5). This is occurring in Christ. Equally interestingly, God will pour his Spirit out upon Jacob's (and Abraham's) descendants (Isa 44:3, cf. Gal 3:2, 5). Ultimately, all the seed of Israel shall triumph and glory (Isa 45:25). Isaiah's Servant 'shall see his offspring and shall prolong his life' (Isa 53:10). Israel will expand (Isa 54:3). The descendants will be known throughout the nations and seen as blessed (Isa 61:9). In Isa 65–66 which includes a vision of the new heavens and new earth, God 'will bring forth seed of Abraham' (Isa 65:9), they will be blessed (Isa 65:23), and they shall remain (Isa 66:22).

---

15. See 1 Kings 2:33; Ps 17:11 (Eng. 18:50); 88:5, 30, 37 (Eng. 89:4, 19, 36).

For Paul, these things Isaiah refers to—the gathering of people, the outpouring of the Spirit, and the offspring of Abraham—are occurring in Christ.

Paul's argument is hermeneutically dynamic. He takes a specific grammatical point (the singular) and forms a whole argument around it. This can seem a bit strange, but it leads to what follows that in this one seed are many who are also 'the seed of Abraham.' The singular points to the wider reality of the corporate who are 'in' this seed.

THE LAW DOES NOT ANNUL THE ABRAHAMIC COVENANTAL PROMISES (3:17)

In *Galatians 3:17*, Paul draws out his analogy with the general statement concerning wills in 3:15 with regard to the Abrahamic covenant and the law. His overall point is clear; the giving of the law did not revoke the Abrahamic Covenant:

And (*de*, 1:15) **this** (neuter *outos*, 2:10) **[is what] I am saying** (*legō*, 1:9), **the law** (*nomos*) **that** (*ho*) **came** (perfect active participle *ginomai*) **four hundred** (*tetrakosioi*) **and** (*kai*) **thirty** (*triakonta*) **years** (*etos*) **later** (*meta*), **[does] not** (*ouk*) **revoke** (*akyroō*) **a covenant** (*diathēkē*, 3:15) **previously ratified** (*prokyroō*)[16] **by** (*hypo*, 1:11) **God** (genitive *Theos*),[17] **so as to** (*eis*) **abolish** (*katargeō*)[18] **the promise** (*epangelia*, 3:14).

---

16. There is one use of προκυρόω (*prokyroō*) in Galatians. It compounds *pro* (before) and *kyroō* (ratify, see 3:15). It speaks of the ratification of the Abrahamic covenant by God.

17. **Variant:** After God (*Theou*) a range of texts including Dgr Ggr Ivid K 0176 88 614 2127 2495 and others add *eis Christon* ('in Christ'). The support for the shorter text is much stronger (P46 ℵ A B C P Ψ 33 81 1739, etc.) and it is added for clarification.

18. The verb καταργέω (*katargeō*) compounds *kata* (according to, against) and *argeō* (to stop doing something, slack off, become idle, BDAG 128). The compound yields *katargeō* which has the strict sense 'according to idleness or inoperativeness.' However, it is a flexible term which aside from Luke 13:7 (depleting soil) and Heb 2:14 (destroy) is found only in Paul. It is used three times in Galatians. In 3:17 it has the meaning 'nullify' or 'abolish'—the law given subsequent to the Abrahamic Covenant does not nullify or abolish the promise. Second, in 5:4, it means 'cut off or severed from Christ,' if one submits to circumcision and law. The third use in 5:11, where the offense of the cross is rendered obsolete if Paul is preaching circumcision as accused.

The introductory words render literally, 'and this I say.' They introduce what follows in which Paul clarifies his analogy between wills and the Abrahamic covenant and its promises and the law.

The English versions rearrange the Greek which begins 'a covenant previously ratified by God.' *Diathēkē*, 'covenant,' is found 344 times in the LXX and translates בְּרִית (*berîṯ*)—meaning a treaty or agreement between two parties with the relationships of the two parties varying according to context.[19] Some are found in the OT between human parties, such as between Abraham and Isaac with Abimelech of Gerar (Gen 21:27, 32; 26:28), Jacob and Laban (Gen 31:44), Israel and the Gibeonites (Josh 9:12–22), David and Jonathan (1 Sam 23:18), and Israel and Assyria (Hos 12:1).

In the OT, such agreements between God and humanity are made including:[20]

1. **Adamic Covenant**: There is no mention of an Adamic covenant in Genesis, but in Hosea 6:7 the prophet speaks of Israel transgressing the covenant like Adam (cf. Sir 17:12). He and Eve were commissioned as God's image-bearers (Gen 1:26–30) to rule over the world. They failed and were shut out of the garden (3:22–24). Jesus is the New Adam who does not fail but resists temptation and dies to restore humankind to the relationship shattered in Eden (Rom 5:17).
2. **Noahic Covenant**: God's promise to save Noah's family, never to flood the world destroying all flesh and the earth again, with the rainbow as the sign of the everlasting covenant (Gen 6:18; 9:9–16).

---

19. DBL Hebrew 1382.
20. See also the salt of the covenant (Lev 2:13) and covenant of salt (Num 18:19). Also, a covenant of peace and perpetual priesthood with Phinehas for his zeal (Num 25:11–13), a covenant of life and well-being with Levi which was being corrupted (Mal 2:4, 5, 10). A covenant with death (Isa 28:15) which will be annulled (Isa 28:18). A covenant of peace (Isa 54:10). The judgment of the exile was due to the breaking of the Mosaic Covenantal conditions, the law (Hos 8:1; Isa 24:5; Jer 11:10; 22:9; Ezek 16:59).

3. **Abrahamic Covenant**: God's promise to Abraham and his descendants through Isaac to be his God, to give his family the land (Gen 15:18), a multiplicity of descendants including nations and kings, a new name from Abram (exalted ancestor) to Abraham (ancestor of a multitude) (Gen 17:2–8), with the sign of the covenant being circumcision (Gen 17:9–14, 19; Exod 2:24; 6:4–5). Aspects are restated in Exod 34:10 (cf. Lev 26:42).

4. **Sinai Covenant**: A continuation of the Abrahamic covenant at Sinai and the giving of the law (Gen 19:5; 23:2 [LXX]; 34:27, 28), the book of the covenant (Exod 24:7), ratified by the blood of the covenant from sacrifices (Exod 24:8), and the ark of the covenant with the documents (Exod 27:21; 31:7; 39:15). An exclusive covenant—no other gods (Exod 23:32), or with the inhabitants of the land (Exod 34:12, 15). An eternal covenant (Exod 31:16). This included the Sabbath (Lev 24:8), and blessing for keeping the covenant, curses for failure.[21]

5. **Davidic Covenant**: God's promise to David of kingship with a descendant ruling eternally.[22] This is a messianic covenant fulfilled in Christ.

6. **Servant Covenant**: God's promise to give the Servant (Christ) as 'a covenant to the people, a light to the nations, to open the eyes that are blind, to bring out the prisoners from the dungeon, from the prison those who sit in darkness' (Isa 42:6, cf. LXX 49:6, 8).

7. **Spirit Covenant**: God's promise of the giving of the Spirit (Isa 59:21).

8. **Renewed/New Covenant**: The law written on human hearts, God being their God, all knowing God without being taught, and forgiveness.[23]

---

21. See Lev 26:18, 25, 42, 44, 45. See also through Deuteronomy (Deut 4:13, 23; 31; 5:2, 3; 7:2, 9, 12; 8:18; 9:5, 9, 11; 10:8; 17:2; 29:1, 9, 12, 14; 29:20 [LXX]; 29:21, 25; 31:9, 16, 20; 31:25, 26; 33:9) and restated later in the land (Josh 24:25).
22. See 2 Sam 23:5; Ps 88:4, 29, 35, 40 [Eng. 89:3, 28, 34, 39]; Isa 55:3, cf. 2 Sam 7:4–17.

Each of these covenants is not a revocation of earlier covenants. There is a development of the relationship between God and his people. The Adamic covenant was violated, but in Christ the New Adam is established, and so one can say it is renewed in the New Covenant. The Noahic covenant remains in force today. The Abrahamic Covenant is the basis for all future covenants. Sinai ratified this, and the law was given as a basis for the relationship. The Davidic Covenant provided leadership for God's covenant people and looked forward to the fulfillment of the Abrahamic covenant through Jesus the Christ, the descendant of Abraham and David. The future covenants of the Servant and the renewed/new covenant of Jeremiah are one and speak of the renewal of the Abrahamic Covenant, being fulfilled now through the work of Christ.

The covenant in mind here is the Abrahamic Covenant established between God and Abraham. The Sinai covenant does not annul the Abrahamic Covenant. It is the same God and same people (children of Abraham) who meet, and God lays down the humanward terms of their relationship, the law.

Paul notes that the law came[24] 430 years after Abraham. This is drawn from Exodus 12:40–41 where we read that 'the time the people of Israel lived in Egypt was 430 years' after which they were led out. This would indicate either ca. 1870/80–1440/50 BC or ca. 1750–1250 BC).[25] The giving of the law speaks of God giving the law to Moses on Mt Sinai (Exod 19–32).

This law was not given to revoke the earlier covenant, which

---

23. See Jer 38:31–44 [Eng. 31:31–34], cf. Jer 27:5; 39:40; Isa 61:8–9; Ezek 16:60, 62; 37:26; 44:7.

24. See on *ginomai* 2:17. Here it has the sense 'came,' i.e., came to pass, into being (see also 3:18, 19).

25. Two dates are proposed for the Exodus: It occurred in the fifteenth Century BC, based on 480 years from Exodus to Solomon whose reign began 960–970 BC. If this is correct, then the Exodus is around 1440–1450 BC. This would place the entry to Egypt around 1870–1800 BC. Some archaeological findings are cited to support this. The later date is during the thirteenth century BC based on mention of the 'city of Rameses' in Exod 11:1 which suggests Rameses II. Again, archaeological evidence is cited and evidence of the conquest. If so, entry into the land is in the mid-late seventeenth century BC. See the brief discussion in A. Chadwick Thornhill, 'Exodus,' in *LBD*.

stands. The term for annul is *katargeō*, a verb which in the NT is primarily Pauline.[26] Paul's use includes nullifying something, whether it be God's faithfulness (Rom 3:3), the law by faith (Rom 3:31), or the Abrahamic promise (Rom 4:14). Another angle is people being discharged from the law in Christ (Rom 7:2, 6). In Ephesians 2:15, Christ has abolished the law. At times it has the sense of reducing something to nothing (1 Cor 1:28), something like tongues, prophecies, or what is partial, childhood coming to an end (1 Cor 13:8, 10, 11), and of the glory in the law (2 Cor 3:7, 11, 12, 14). As in Heb 2:14, it can have the sense of 'destroy' as in the body of sin destroyed in Christ (Rom 6:6), the rulers of this age at the consummation (1 Cor 2:6; 15:24), the stomach and food (1 Cor 6:13), death (1 Cor 15:26; 2 Tim 1:10), and the man of lawlessness (2 Thess 2:8).

Three times *katargeō* is employed in Galatians. In 5:2, it has the sense of 'cut off, severed' of the state of the Galatian who submits to the Judaizers' demand for circumcision—they are cut off from Christ. In 5:11, it speaks of the offense of the cross rendered obsolete if Paul is elsewhere preaching circumcision. Here, it is used in the same sense as Rom 4:14—the law does not annul, nullify, bring to anything, or supersede the Abrahamic promise. Rather than nullify the Abrahamic promise, the law gives terms for that same covenant relationship, which continues on for Paul, through the Davidic Covenant, to Christ, and now the covenant people are forming in him, the seed of Abraham.

THE INHERITANCE COMES THROUGH GOD'S PROMISE (3:18)

In *Galatians 3:18*, Paul continues with a conditional statement based on the false premise that the promise came from the law. He follows with a statement repudiating the false premise established. The Judaizers are not likely stating this directly, but Paul is exposing the logic of their position which requires legal observance alongside faith in Christ for justification:

For (*gar*, 1:10) **if** (*ei*, 1:7) **the inheritance** (*klēronomia*)[27] **[comes]**

---

26. Luke uses it once of the nutrients of soil being used up (Luke 13:7). In Hebrews 2:14 it has the sense of 'destroy'—death destroyed through Christ.

from (*ek*, 1:1) **the law** (*nomos*, 2:16), **[it is] no longer** (*ouketi*, 2:20) **from** (*ek*) **promise** (*epangelia*, 3:14). **But** (*de*, 1:15), **through** (*dia*, 1:1) **a promise** (*epangelia*), **God** (*Theos*, 1:1) **gave** (perfect[28] *charizomai*)[29] **[it] to Abraham** (dative *Abraam*, 3:6).

The *gar* is explanatory, 'for.' The protasis of the conditional sentence states 'if the inheritance comes from the law.' The condition is first-class, with the present of the verb *eimi*, 'is,' or *ginomai*, 'comes' assumed, hence, a statement assumed to be true for the sake of argument (see on 1:9). Of course, for Paul, it is decidedly not true. 'Inheritance' is *klēronomia*, used in the wider NT literally of an inheritance (Luke 12:13), in the Parable of the Tenants of the inheritance of the son who is promptly killed (Matt 21:38; Mark 12:7; Luke 20:14), of the land promised Abraham (Acts 7:5; Heb 11:8), and of an eternal inheritance that awaits believers (Acts 20:32; Heb 9:15; 1 Pet 1:4). Paul uses it in the same latter way of the glorious, eschatological inheritance the faithful receive (Eph 1:14, 18; 5:5; Col 3:24).

It is not immediately apparent what Paul has in mind regarding inheritance here. In the OT promises referred to above, the inheritance would include many descendants, nations, and kingship; the land; the nations blessed through Abraham. However, in Rom 4:13, Paul speaks of Abraham as 'heir of the world,' which is likely what Paul has in mind here in Galatians. Moo says of Rom 4:13:

This language does not exactly match any promise to Abraham found in the OT but succinctly summarizes the three key provisions of the promise as it unfolds in Genesis: that Abraham would have an immense number of descendants, embracing "many nations" (Gen. 12:2; 13:16; 15:5; 17:4–6, 16–20; 22:17),

---

27. The noun κληρονομία (*klēronomia*), signifying 'inheritance,' is found once in Galatians in 3:18 where it speaks the promises to Abraham. See also the associated verb *klēronomeō*, 4:30.

28. Wallace, *Greek Grammar*, 581 notes that the perfect tense of κεχάρισται (*kecharistai*) here is the perfect of allegory where '[t]he perfect tense can be used to refer to an OT event in such a way that the event is viewed in terms of its allegorical or applicational value. This usage is rare, though the author of Hebrews is particularly fond of it.'

29. The verb χαρίζομαι (*charizomai*), 'give freely, give by grace,' is used once in 3:18 of the gift of inheritance promised Abraham.

that he would possess "the land" (Gen. 13:15–17; 15:12–21; 17:8), and that he would be the medium of blessing to "all the peoples of the earth" (Gen. 12:3; 18:18; 22:18). Particularly noteworthy is the promise in Gen. 22:17b that Abraham's seed would "possess the gate of their enemies." Later in the OT, there are indications that the promise of the land had come to embrace the entire world (cf. Isa. 55:3–5), and many Jewish texts speak of Israel's inheritance in similar terms.[30] Against this background—to which we can add Jesus' beatitude, "Blessed are the gentle, for they shall inherit the earth"—Paul probably refers generally to all that God promised his people.[31]

This promise of inheritance was granted prior to the coming of the law as a gift (*charizomai*) and a promise. The verb *charizomai* is a verbal form of *charis*, grace, and speaks of a gift of grace or freely given. He uses it for God giving all things to redeemed humanity, which in a sense speaks of the same inheritance promised Abraham and his God's people of faith (Rom 8:32, cf. 1 Cor 2:12).[32]

30. Moo cites here Sir. 44:21: 'and give them an inheritance from sea to sea and from the Euphrates *to the ends of the earth*' (NRSV); Jub. 22:14: Abraham to Jacob—'May he strengthen you and bless you, and may you *inherit all of the earth*;' Jub. 32:19: 'And I shall give to your seed *all of the land under heaven* and they will rule in *all nations* as they have desired. And after this *all of the earth will be gathered together and they will inherit it forever*;' 2 Bar. 14:13: 'Therefore, they leave this world without fear and are confident of *the world which you have promised to them* with an expectation full of joy;' and 51:3: 'so that they may acquire and receive the undying world which is promised to them.' (Citations all from Charlesworth, aside from Sirach).

31. Douglas J. Moo, *The Epistle to the Romans*, NICNT (Grand Rapids, MI: Eerdmans, 1996), 273.

32. Paul also uses it of God giving the Philippians the gift of suffering along with believing (Phil 1:29), giving Jesus the name above every name (Phil 2:9), of his being graciously given to Philemon (Phlm 22), or to forgive sin (2 Cor 2:7, 10; 12:13; Col 2:13; Col 3:13).

CHAPTER EIGHTEEN: THE LAW'S FUNCTION TO PREPARE FOR JUSTIFICATION BY FAITH IN CHRIST (3:19–24)

Paul now shifts from the Abrahamic promise of an inheritance based on gift and promise to the function of the law. If the blessings promised Abraham are not granted on the basis of law, what is its function? For the Judaizers, it remains active as a basis for salvation, perseverance, ecclesiology (inclusion), ethics, and mission (a Judaizing gospel). For Paul, this has been repudiated. So, the question is begged, what is the place and function of the law for the new covenant community? Paul shifts into diatribe here, posing rhetorical questions anticipated from an interlocutor and then responding. In vv. 19–22, he asks two such questions: 'Why then the law?' And 'Is the law then contrary to the promises of God?'

WHY THE LAW? (3:19)

In *Galatians 3:19*, he asks the first and responds in 3:19b–20:
   Why (neuter *tis*, 3:1) **then** (*oun*, 3:5) **the law** (*nomos*, 2:16)? **It was added**[1] (aorist passive *prostithēmi*)[2] **on account** (*charin*)[3] of

---

1. **Variant**: There are a range of variant readings of the Greek *nomos; tōn parabaseōn charin prosetethē* (the law on account of transgressions was added). D* reads, 'It was established on account of traditions.' F G and others read, 'Why then the law of actions? It was established until …' P46 reads, 'Why then the law of actions?' and omits what follows completely. However, the NA28 text is well attested (e.g., ℵ A B C Ψ, etc.).
2. The verb προστίθημι (*prostithēmi*) means 'add' and is used once in Gal 3:18, 'it [law] was added because of transgressions.' Now that transgressions are dealt with in Christ, it is no longer necessary.

transgressions (genitive plural *parabasis*),[4] **until** (*achri*)[5] **which time** (genitive *hos*, 1:5) **the offspring** (*sperma*, 3:16) **might come** (aorist subjunctive[6] *ginomai*, 1:21) **to whom** (dative *hos*) **it has been promised** (perfect passive *epangellomai*),[7] **having been ordered** (aorist passive participle *diatassō*)[8] **through** (*dia*, 1:1) **angels** (genitive *angelos*, 1:8) **by** (*en*, 1:6) **the hand** (*cheir*)[9] **of a mediator** (*mesitēs*).[10]

The first part of the verse poses the question: 'Why then the law?' What is its purpose, if it is not to bring forth the promises to Abraham and his descendants? Paul answers his own question.

It was added[11] on account of transgressions. *Charin* here is not

---

3. The preposition χάριν (*charin*) is found only in Gal 3:18 meaning 'because, on account of, for the sake of.' Here, on 'account of transgressions.'

4. The noun παράβασις (*parabasis*) is found once in Galatians, in 3:19, of transgressions or sin. It is rare in the NT, with seven occurrences—five in Paul (Rom 2:23; 4:15; 5:14; 1 Tim 2:14) and twice in Hebrews (Heb 2:2; 9:15).

5. The preposition ἄχρι (*achri*) is used twice in Galatians (3:19; 4:2), both times meaning 'until.'

6. Wallace, *Greek Grammar*, 479 notes that '[t]he subjunctive is frequently used after a *temporal adverb* (or *improper preposition*) meaning *until* (e.g., ἕως, ἄχρι, μέχρι), or after the temporal conjunction ὅταν with the meaning, *whenever*. It indicates a future contingency from the perspective of the time of the main verb.' Here, this makes sense because of the uncertainty of the time when the offspring would come (from the point of view of the past when the law was given).

7. The verb ἐπαγγέλλομαι (*epangellomai*), promise, is used once in Galatians 3:19 of the offspring promised to Abraham (Christ).

8. The verb διατάσσω (*diatassō*) features once in Gal 3:19. It compounds *dia* (through, because) and *tassō*, (arrange, put in place, determine, fix, appoint) and here indicates 'put in place' or 'ordered' (BDAG 237).

9. The noun *cheir*, 'hand,' is found twice; first in 3:19 of Moses, as a mediator, receiving in his hand the law from God, and in 6:11, of Paul writing large letters with his own hand, marking the genuineness of the letter.

10. The only two uses of *mesitēs*, 'mediator' or 'intermediary' come in 3:19–20 where it refers first to Moses (implied) as the mediator at the giving of the law from angels and of an intermediary, implying more than one in contrast to God, who is one (see also 1 Tim 2:5; Heb 6:8; 9:15; 12:24).

11. 'Added' is the verb *prostithēmi* used across the NT of something added: time (Matt 6:27; Luke 12:25), God's provision (Matt 6:33; Mark 4:24; Luke 12:31), adding an imprisonment (Luke 3:20), faith (Luke 17:5), a servant (Luke 20:11, 12), people added to the Lord (Acts 2:41, 47; 5:14; 11:24), added to one's deceased fathers in the grave (Acts 13:36). It can also mean 'again' of telling a parable (Luke 19:11), to proceed (Acts 12:3), or further (Heb 12:19).

'grace' as rudimentary Greek would suppose, but a preposition which usually comes after the word it governs and can indicate consequence, 'therefore;' or, it indicates a causal relationship, 'because, for this reason' (Eph 3:1, 14; Tit 1:5), or 'for' (1 Tim 5:14).' Here it is causal, but its exact nuance is disputed.[12]

First, *charin* can be causal in a specific sense; the law was introduced to give people the awareness of their transgressions. So, Calvin writes, 'the law was added *because* of the need to reveal to people their sins.'[13] This view relies on Rom 3:20b: 'through the law, we become conscious of sin.'

Second, *charin* may have the sense 'because of' but with a more general intent: '[t]he law was given because of the need to deal with sins.'[14] This then can be negative, the law giving the means by which sin can be punished.[15] Alternatively, it can be positive; the law is helping keep transgressions under control or possibly dealing with them through Israel's atonement system.[16]

The third possibility is that *charin* here means 'for the sake of' and so refers to the way law provokes sin. For example, Betz writes 'the law was added for the sake of causing sins.'[17] This idea draws on Rom 7:5, where sinful passions are aroused by the law. The final idea again takes *charin* as 'for the sake of,' and refers to the law's function of demonstrating the seriousness of sin and its ultimate nature. Witherington, for example, suggests

that what Paul means is that the law turns sin, which certainly already existed before and apart from the law, into transgression of the law. That is, the law makes it quite clear that every sin is a sin against God.[18]

The law does not increase the number of sins but the

---

12. See also Moo, *Galatians*, 233–34.
13. John Calvin, Commentaries on the Epistles of Paul to the Galatians and Ephesians (Edinburgh: Thomas Clark, 1854), 64.
14. Longenecker, *Galatians*, 138.
15. F. Thielman, From Plight to Solution: A Jewish Framework for Understanding Paul's View of the law in Galatians and Romans, NovTSup 61 (Leiden: Brill, 1989), 74–75.
16. For example, Dunn, *Galatians*, 189–90. See Moo, *Galatians*, 233 for others.
17. H. D. Betz, Galatians: A Commentary on Paul's Letter to the Churches in Galatia, Hermeneia (Minneapolis: Fortress, 1979), 164–65.
18. Witherington, *Grace*, 255–56. See also BDAG 1709.

responsibility for sin.[19] This idea draws from Romans 5:20a that 'the law was brought in so that the trespass might increase.'[20]

My view is that these ideas are not necessarily mutually exclusive, and the text seems to be inclusive of all—Paul is being general here. The law reveals people's sense of consciousness of sin; it does give guidelines for avoidance for sin (if not the power) and does provide a temporary solution for atonement (Israel's sacrificial system); it does provoke sin, not increasing the number, but awareness of sin. Finally, it does make sin more than just sin. It is the transgression of God's law and so a violation of his expectations for his image-bearers. In what follows, the law cannot bring life, and justification is not achieved through the law; it is received through Christ. It serves to imprison people, holding them captive. It is a guardian that is no longer needed. People are redeemed from captivity to the law. They are free from it. Life is now by the Spirit who generates the fruit of love by which the whole law is fulfilled.

The term for transgressions is *parabasis*, compounding *para* (beside) and *basis* (foot), and thus has the sense of overstepping or 'deviating from an established boundary or norm.'[21] It is not a commonly used term in the Greek world or for sin in Jewish Greek literature. In the NT, five of its seven uses are in Paul who uses it of 'transgressing the law' (Rom 2:23), the transgression of Adam (Rom 5:14), and of Eve as a transgressor (1 Tim 2:14) (cf. Heb 2:2; 9:15). In Rom 4:15, he writes, 'where there is no law, there is no transgression.' Hence, the law serves positively to reveal the boundaries Israel was not to cross over. However, due to human frailty, the law could not deal with transgressions in the sense of enabling people to overcome sin's power; rather, it reveals sin and so human need and struggle (cf. Rom 7).

'Until the offspring might come' refers to the coming of the seed of Abraham, Jesus (vv. 16–17). Jesus' physical descent from Abraham is confirmed in both Matthew and Luke's genealogies

---

19. Witherington, *Grace*, 255–56.
20. Moo, *Galatians*, 234.
21. BDAG 758.

(Matt 1:1; Luke 3:34). 'To whom the promise had been made' refers to Abraham, the recipient of the promises noted above.

'And it was put into place through angels by the hand of a mediator' speaks of Moses as a mediator between God and Israel at the giving of the law. 'Put into place' is *diatassō*, which is military terminology, and the implied agency here is God—'ordered [by God] through angels.'[22] The giving of the law to Moses' hand is referred to in Exod 32:15 where he came down the mountain with the tablets of the law engraved by God in hand. He then threw them down and broke them (Exod 32:19). He later returned, and he rewrote them (Exod 34:28). The involvement of angels is not mentioned in these accounts. However, in later Jewish tradition, this is found.

The idea that angels were involved in the giving of the law is not explicit in the Hebrew OT but is found in Deut 33:2 (LXX), other Jewish traditions (Jub. 1:27–2:1; Philo, *Somn.* 1.143; Josephus, *Ant.* 15.136), and in the NT (Acts 7:38, 53; Heb. 2:2).[23] Reference to angels is not necessarily a repudiation of the law as second rate, for it is still God who gave it to Moses through his angels. However, in 1:8, Paul writes to the Galatians that even if an angel brings a gospel that differs from the message that he and Barnabas preached amongst them, they should repudiate it. Hence, there is the suggestion of the superiority of the coming of the gospel of Christ as compared with the giving of the law. He is perhaps ironic in 4:14 when he says that they received Paul 'as an angel of God,' but now are rejecting his gospel despite this.

ONE MEDIATOR, ONE GOD (3:20)

Paul, in *Galatians 3:20*, continues with the theme of a mediator or intermediary:

But (*de*, 1:15) **the mediator** (*mesitēs*, 3:19) **is** (*estin*, 1:7) **not** (*ou*, 1:1) **one** (*heis*, 3:16), **but** (*de*) **God** (*Theos*) **is** (*estin*) **one** (*heis*).

This verse is highly debated with little consensus. What is clear is that Paul is contrasting the work of a mediator (who is not one)

22. BDAG 238.
23. Moo, *Galatians*, 235.

with God (who is one). Beyond this, there is a range of ideas. Moo proposes three categories:

1. The contrast is between the many angels and God. Moses is the one mediator and the mediator on behalf of many angels, and so not on behalf of God.[24] However, this puts a distance between God and the law that is unlikely.
2. The contrast is between the two parties involved in a mediation and God, who is one (of course, it may include the angels too). The mediator is generally taken to be other than Moses.[25] It requires two parties for the law to function. The promise involves one.
3. Some take 'one' in v. 16 (anaphora)[26] as one people of God rather than Christ, and so here, Moses is not the mediator through whom one people of God is formed.[27] This is unlikely as in v. 16, the one is explicitly Christ who is the offspring in mind.

Moo rightly comments:

On the whole, then, the second general approach to this verse offers the fewest difficulties. The very existence of a mediator in the giving of the law implies an involvement on the human side that stands in contrast to the gift-character of the promise, suggested (albeit very remotely) by the confession that God is one.[28]

Aside from the point that Paul is making, which is somewhat blurred, we have another reference to the essential oneness of

---

24. For example, Martyn, 365–70.
25. For example, Longenecker, *Galatians*, 142.
26. Anaphora is '[a] reference back to a previous context by the repetition or the inclusion of a word or phrase (ἀναφορά [anaphora], "a carrying back"). The anaphoric article, for example, points back to something stated or implied in a previous context. In rhetoric, anaphora occurs when successive clauses begin with the same word or group of words. See Romans 3:22, 24–25. It is also known as epanadiplosis and epanaphora. The opposite of anaphora is cataphora, in which the reference is forward.' See *PDSNTG* 18.
27. N. T. Wright, *The Climax of the Covenant* (Minneapolis: Fortress, 1992), 157–74.
28. Moo, *Galatians*, 237.

God. This is something Paul stresses elsewhere. Although he can speak of the deity of Christ, he preserves the utter Oneness of God[29]—hence, the Trinity. At a stretch, this may also be a veiled reference to Christ's divinity. God is one, he is the mediator, yet implied is that he is God.

THE LAW CANNOT BRING LIFE (3:21)

Paul asks his second interlocutory question in the first part of *Galatians 3:21*, and then answers it in the remainder of the verse and v. 22:

So then (*oun*, 3:5), [is] the law (*nomos*, 2:16) according to (*kata*, 1:4) the promise (*epangelia*) 3:14) of God[30] (genitive of *Theos*, 1:1)? May (*mē*, 1:7) it never be (optative *ginomai*, 2:17)! For (*gar*, 1:10) if (*ei*, 1:7) a law (*nomos*, 2:16) has been given (aorist passive *didōmi*, 1:4) that is able (middle participle *dynamai*)[31] to give life (aorist infinitive[32] *zōopoieō*),[33] righteousness (*dikaiosynē*, 2:21) would (*an*, 1:10) be (imperfect *eimi*, 1:7) from (*ek*, 1:1) the law (*nomos*).

The question links the law with the Abrahamic promise, which Paul has been discussing in the previous verses. While circumcision is expected (Gen 17), the Abrahamic covenant

---

29. Rom 3:30; 1 Cor 8:4; Eph 4:6; 1 Tim 2:5.
30. **Variant**: The majority of witnesses include 'of God' (*tou Theou*). However, some do not include them (P46 B, etc.). The shorter reading is enticing and *tou Theou* would be a natural addition. However, it may be due to accidental scribal omission. Its disputed nature is indicated in Metzger, *Textual Commentary*, 526 who gives it a {C} rating.
31. The verb δύναμαι (*dynamai*), 'able, can,' is found once in Galatians; in 3:21 of the ability of the law to bring life—if it *could*, then logically, righteousness would be gained in this way. For Paul, it cannot. Therefore, there is the need for Christ.
32. The infinitive ζωοποιῆσαι (*zōopoiēsai*, 'to make alive') is here complementary, functioning to support the main verb ἐδόθη (*edothē*, given). See Wallace, *Greek Grammar*, 598.
33. The only use of the verb ζωοποιέω (*zōopoieō*) is found in 3:21. It compounds life (*zoē*) and the common verb *poieō* (make, create), and so implies 'make life,' here, eternal life. It is not common in the NT with Paul using it of God's ability to give life to the dead (Rom 4:17), making bodies alive through resurrection (Rom 8:11) in Christ (1 Cor 15:22), as with a seed (1 Cor 15:36) through Christ the life-giving Spirit (1 Cor 15:45, cf. 2 Cor 3:6).

involves God promising and giving Abraham the blessings. Is the giving of the law also according to the promise?

For Paul, this an absolute non-possibility. Paul uses his characteristic *mē genoito*, 'may it never be, absolutely not!'—something he rules out with a prayer wish (see further on 2:17). He draws out what he is saying with a first-class conditional sentence where the protasis gives a premise for the sake of argument and, in the apodosis, draws out the conclusion if it were true (see on 1:9). The assumption of truth states that if a law had been given (at Sinai) that was able to give eternal life (something Paul refutes), then justification/righteousness would be from the law. The giving of the law recalls Moses on Sinai.

'Give life' is an interesting verb compounding *zoē* (life) and *poieō* (make, do, create), yielding 'make alive.' It is only rarely found across wider Greek sources and is not found in the Pseudepigrapha, Philo, or Josephus. In the LXX, it is used for saving a life (Judg 21:14), of wisdom that gives true life (Eccles 7:13), and of God who gives both death and life (2 Kings 5:7, cf. Job 36:6), who revives the Psalmist (Ps 70:20 [Eng. 71:20]), and the creation (Neh 9:6 [2 Esd 19:6]).

Seven of the eleven uses in the NT are in Paul. Otherwise, it is found in John's writings of God, Christ, and the Spirit who raises the dead and gives eternal life (John 5:21; 6:63). Peter uses it once for Christ's resurrection (1 Pet 3:18). Paul employs it of God who through Christ by the Spirit gives life to the dead creationally and eternal life soteriologically.[34] It is thus creation language—God, in his renewed creation is undoing death's sting and gifting eternal life. This is through Christ, not law, which is impotent to stop death. In fact, it serves to reveal the infection of a person by sin and even excites sin. Only Christ can resolve that problem. It is thus resurrection language—faith in Christ brings resurrection life in Christ by the Spirit. The law cannot do so as is proven in history. It had a temporary role, and this is now complete.

---

34. Rom 4:17; 8:11; 1 Cor 15:22, 45; 2 Cor 3:6, cf. 1 Cor 15:36.

The Promise Given to Sin's Prisoners by Faith in Christ (3:22)

Paul continues in *Galatians 3:22* explaining the way in which law fails to liberate people into righteousness:

But (*alla*, 1:1) the Scripture (*graphē*, 3:8) imprisoned (*synkleiō*)[35] all things and people (neuter *pas*, 1:2) under (*hypo*, 1:11) sin (*hamartia*, 1:4), so that (*hina*, 1:16) the promise (*epangelia*, 3:14) from (*ek*, 1:1) faith (*pistis*, 1:23) in Jesus (genitive *Iēsous*, 1:1) Christ (genitive *Christos*, 1:1) might be given (aorist passive subjunctive *didōmi*) to believers (dative present participle *pistis*, 1:4).

Paul shifts from the law to the Scriptures (*ē graphē*), here in a general sense, something he commonly does.[36] The effect is the same; all parts of Israel's Scriptures have the same effect.

'Imprisoned' is the verb *synkleinō* used four times in the NT. The verb is a powerful one, used often in Jewish Greek writings of military settings where enemies are trapped or confined,[37] a city or region is closed off, besieged, or hemmed in,[38] being confined to death (Ps 77:50 [Eng. 78:50] or the sword (Ps 77:62 [Eng. 78:62], or the imprisoning of demons (T. Sol. 1:7; 22:15).[39]

Aside from Paul, the only NT usage is by Luke of the netting of fish (Luke 5:6). Paul uses it one time outside this Galatians passage; in Romans 11:32, where Paul states that God has

---

35. The verb συγκλείω (*synkleiō*) compounds *syn* (together, with) with *kleiō* which means 'shut, lock, bar, close,' a verb Paul does not use at all. *Synkleiō* is found once in Romans of God imprisoning all people under disobedience (Rom 11:32). It is found twice in Galatians 3:22–23 of Scripture being God's agent to imprison humanity under sin's power, and of Jews being both imprisoned and guarded by the law.

36. See Rom 1:2; 15:4; 1 Cor 15:3, 4; Gal 3:8; 2 Tim 3:16; see further 3:8, cf. 4:30.

37. See Ps 30:9 [Eng. 31:10]; Ps 34:3 [Eng. 35:3]; Amos 1:6, 9; Obad 14; 1 Macc 6:18.

38. See Josh 6:1; Jer 13:19; 21:4; 21:9; Ezek 4:3; 1 Macc 3:18; 4:31; 6:49; 11:65; 15:25.

39. Also of people confined (Job 3:23), shut off roads (Judith 5:1), people shut out (Judith 13:1), leaders shut in to consider something (1 Esd 9:16), to close the womb (Gen 16:2; 20:18; 1 Sam 1:6; Job 3:10), the wilderness trapping Israel (Exod 14:3), overlaying something with gold (1 Kings 6:20; 7:35; 10:21; 11:27; 2 Kings 24:14, 16), close mouths (Ps 16:10 [Eng. 17:10]), steps hampered (Prov 4:12), almsgiving stored up (Sir 29:12), or shutting a building, door, or gate (Tob 8:4; Mal 1:10; Isa 45:1; 2 Macc 1:15; 12:7).

imprisoned all people (masculine *pas*) in disobedience. This verse bears similarity to this passage where the agency of God is the Scripture or law, which has imprisoned all under sin (s.a. in v. 23).

The translation 'all things and people' is an attempt to capture the neuter of *pas* here. Unlike Rom 11:32 which, being masculine, clearly has people in mind; here, it is broader, speaking of the subjection of the *whole cosmos* to the power of sin and its consequences; decay, death, and wrath leading to destruction (cf. Rom 8:19–23; 1 Cor 15:26). The sin of Adam in Paul's thought had cosmic effects—not just causing death in humanity (Rom 5:12, 21), but the cause of all suffering and death, including the devastation of the natural order.

Sin was discussed in 1:4 more fully, but here speaks of sin as a personified sovereign power that dominates humanity, stinging her (1 Cor 15:56) so that humanity is corrupted, marred, and infected, and sin's poison causes humanity's essential problem. People cannot escape their bondage or enslavement to sin as it infects every aspect of human life, individual and corporate (cf. Rom 6:6). This infection has marred the whole world. Humanity and all creation are thus in bondage under sin's dominion (cf. Rom 3:9).

For Paul, the wonder of Christ's work is that he who knew no sin was made sin for humanity so that believers may become the righteousness of God (2 Cor 5:21). Now the problem of sin is dealt with; the crucified and raised Christ having died 'for our sin' (1 Cor 15:3) and now the antidote for sin's sting. So, where faith in him is found, people are set free from sin's enslavement (Rom 6:7). In Christ, people have died to sin and are alive (by the Spirit) to God in Christ (Rom 6:11). Though once dead in sins and transgressions, now they are saved (Eph 2:1–9) and forgiven (Col 1:14). This death in Christ is the basis of Pauline ethics—believers are not to allow themselves to let sin continue its dominion over them (Rom 6:12, 13). They are not under the law, but grace (Rom 6:14).

However, by yielding to the Judaizers, the law comes into effect for these gentiles, and they are again under sin. They then have a choice—either live under sin or in the righteousness they have in Christ (Rom 6:16–21). If they do, the gift of God is eternal life and not sin's wages, death (Rom 6:23).

The law itself is not corrupt in any way. It is good (Rom 7:12). But it makes sin known and excites sin and creates a painful cognitive dissonance whereby one knows what one ought to do in mind but cannot do it (Rom 7:7–23). The *euangelion* is that God has sent Christ and set Paul and all Jews free from this effect of the law (Rom 7:25–8:3). The recently converted gentiles now saved in Christ must not yield to the law again by submitting to circumcision and other requirements of the Judaizers. To do so takes them from grace to law and so subjugates them to sin again. It brings in the law as a means to empower sin in the flesh (1 Cor 15:56). They must live by the Spirit (Rom 8:5–17) as he will stress in Gal 5–6. Jesus gave himself for humanity's sins and set them free from the present evil age—to which they must not return (Gal 1:4).

The second part of the verse is a *hina* purpose clause (see further 1:16) explaining why the Scripture has imprisoned all things under sin. 'The promise from faith' summarizes the ultimate outcome of the Abrahamic promise—resurrection, eternal life, the restoration of all things, and the inheritance of the world.

'From (*ek*)[40] faith in Jesus Christ' has all the same questions discussed in 2:16. As argued there, this should be taken as an objective genitive (faith in Jesus Christ), compelling though the argument for a subjective is (faith/faithfulness of Jesus Christ). The whole point of Galatians is that what is required is faith and not anything additional; in context, works of the law and particularly circumcision. The repetition of faith language then is not a tautology but is emphatic.

So then, Abraham as a model of faith in Galatians does not correlate to Jesus' faith or faithfulness, but faith directed toward God as the object. Similarly, here, Jesus Christ is the object of faith. Where such faith is found in the heart of the believer, the

40. The seventh use of *ek pisteōs* ('from faith' as opposed to 'from the works of the law/the law') in Galatians, stressing its thematic importance (see 2:16, also 3:7, 8, 9, 11, 12, 24; 5:5).

promises to Abraham and indeed all the promises the gospel offers, kick into play for the one with faith. We join Abraham as heirs of the world, in the Son, who is The Heir of the world. As we live the cruciform life in the present, we will suffer; it is unavoidable as the path to glory (Rom 8:17). However, perseverance in faith will see us through. God makes this possible through the power of the Spirit. The Galatians are being diverted from 'justification by faith' to 'justification by the law;' this must not be because it is an impossibility and ends in destruction.

The second reference to faith is the participle *tous pisteuousin*, the present participle of *pisteuō* indicating 'the ones who believe, believers.' The participle is present, and so this speaks of ongoing belief. Such participles are used commonly in soteriological contexts in the NT. This is because the NT writers 'by and large saw continual belief as a necessary condition of salvation.'[41]

HELD UNDER THE LAW UNTIL FAITH REVEALED (3:23)

In *Galatians 3:23*, linked with a consecutive *de* which has more the sense of 'now,' or 'further to the point,' Paul again states the role of the law:

Now (*de*, 1:17) **before** (*pro*, 1:15) **faith** (*pistis*, 1:23) **came** (aorist infinitive[42] *erchomai*, 1:21), **we were held under custody** (imperfect *phroureō*)[43] **under** (*hypo* 1:11) **the law** (*nomos*, 2:16),

41. Wallace, *Greek Grammar*, 620. He notes this participle is both gnomic and continuous. *Gnomic* means it is related to a wisdom saying, a maxim, something aphoristic, a timeless truth, and omnitemporal (*PDSNTG* 63). Wallace notes the present participle is used forty-three times, mostly in soteriological contexts (John 1:12; 3:15, 16, 18; 3:36; 6:35, 47, 64; 7:38; 11:25; 12:46; Acts 2:44; 10:43; 13:39; Rom 1:16; 3:22; 4:11, 24; 9:33; 10:4, 11; 1 Cor 1:21; 14:22 [*bis*]; Gal 3:22; Eph 1:19; 1 Thess 1:7; 2:10, 13; 1 Pet 2:6, 7; 1 John 5:1, 5, 10, 13). Wallace adds that the promise of salvation comes with the present participle *ho pisteuōn* and almost never the aorist *ho pisteusas*, which would highlight the moment of belief. The closest parallels are John 7:39; Heb 4:3; and the interpolated Mark 16:16.

42. As noted concerning 2:12, *pro* plus the infinitive forms a 'before' temporal structure. This clause is an example of a participle in the fourth attributive position (Πρὸ τοῦ δὲ ἐλθεῖν). If it is attributive, it modifies a substantive. Here, it modifies τὴν πίστιν (*tēn pistin*, the faith). See Wallace, *Greek Grammar*, 618.

imprisoned (*sunkleiō*, 3:22) **until** (*eis*, 1:5) **the coming** (participle *mellō*)[44] **faith** (*pistis*) **would be revealed** (aorist passive infinitive *apokalyptō*, 1:16).

'Before faith' does not mean before there was faith, or before faith existed as a means of salvation. Looking back from his new perspective in Christ, Paul now acknowledges that it is and always has been faith that brought justification. So, while he does not ponder the righteousness of the likes of Abel, Melchizedek, Noah, and other pre-Abraham figures, by analogy, we can surmise he sees them as people 'justified by faith.' Further, faith justified Abraham (Gen 15:6). What he means is that before faith was revealed in Christ, it was still the means of justification. Theologically, this was achieved in Christ despite Christ not yet having come. A person's faith leads God to declare at the final judgment, 'Righteous!' This is so because they believed in God and Jesus died for them. Christ's death works across all of history saving all with faith—a cosmic and timeless event, actioned within time.[45]

Paul now knows this from his experience of meeting Christ on the Damascus Road and working through his understanding of the gospel. Law has had its day. It was good while it lasted, but it has now completed its work of holding Israel in custody. This imprisoning was both positive and negative. On the one hand, it

---

43. The verb φρουρέω (*phoureō*) is found once in Galatians, in 3:23. It means 'guard' in the other three uses in the NT (2 Cor 11:32; Phil 4:7; 1 Pet 1:5). Here it can have this sense of being held in custody (BDAG 1067).

44. The verb μέλλω (*mellō*) is used only once in Galatians, in 3:23, in the sense of something, here faith, 'coming.' Aside from this Paul uses the verb thirteen other times. It always has a futuristic sense including 'will be' (Rom 4:24), 'you *will*' (Rom 8:13), '*will*' suffer (1 Thess 3:4), '*will* believe' (1 Tim 1:16), something to come (Rom 5:14), something that 'is to be' revealed (Rom 8:18), 'things to *come*' (Rom 8:38; Col 2:17), 'the *future*' (1 Cor 3:22; 1 Tim 6:19), and future judgment (2 Tim 4:1). In 3:23, it modifies *pistin*, so 'coming faith' (which has now come), the one to come (Eph 1:21).

45. See, e.g., Arthur Walkington Pink, *The Arthur Pink Anthology* (Bellingham, WA: Logos Bible Software, 2005), 'Chapter 3.' He rightly states, 'From Abel onwards, God has dealt with sinners in sovereign grace, and according to the merits of Christ's redemptive work—which was retroactive in its value and efficacy (Romans 3:25; 1 Peter 1:19, 20).' He mentions Noah (Gen 6:8), Abraham (Gal 3:8), Jacob (Gen 49:18), the Hebrews list (Heb 11), Job (Job 19:25, 26), and others.

protected her and set her apart. On the other, it became a hideous monster causing Israel to get lost in minutiae and separating her from the world.

Paul uses another term that speaks of imprisonment and custody under the law, *phoureō*. *Phoureō* is used in 2 Cor 11:32 to describe the governor of King Aretas guarding the city of Damascus to arrest Paul. In Phil 4:7, it speaks of God guarding the hearts and minds of believers. The only non-Pauline NT use is in 1 Pet 1:5, where believers are being guarded through faith by God's power.[46]

Here then, it speaks of the role of the law as guarding or holding Israel in custody. The law then is effectively personified as a prison guard—'*Nomos* (or *Torah*) the Prison Guard.' The verb is imperfect, speaking here of the period of time of Israel's imprisonment to the law, begun at the law's giving to Moses at Sinai through angels, and completed (or so it should be) now that Christ has come. Sadly, Israel has not grasped what the gospel means for her. Messiah has come. Faith is all that is required. The walls of enmity are down. The Galatians must not join resistant faithless Israel as the Judaizers falsely demand.

'Under the law' is used only in Galatians. Clearly, *nomos* here is the Torah. The preposition *hypo* is discussed regarding 1:11. In Galatians, it is used in two main ways. First, with the genitive of agency it is rendered 'by' (1:11; 3:17; 4:9). Second, with the accusative, it always means 'under.' This can have the sense of 'under the control of, under obligation to.'[47] This is the sense *hypo* is used in Galatians. Elsewhere it speaks of people '*under* a curse' (3:10), '*under* a guardian' (3:25) or 'guardians' (4:2), and '*under* the elementary powers' (*stoicheia*) (4:3). Each of the accusative uses refers to the law in some way. Here, he is explicit '*under* the law.' He will use this construct again in 4:4 of Christ 'born *under* the law,' indicating he is born into a political, economic, and religious

---

46. It is used twice in the LXX, of those who guard the city (1 Esd 5:46; cf. 2 Cor 11:32), and those shut up in prison (Wis 17:16). Josephus uses it a lot, fifty-one times, almost always of something being guarded, e.g., a village (*Ant.* 13.29) or a citadel (*Ant.* 13.39).

47. See BDAG 1036 which distinguishes between 'under' and 'under the control of,' when in reality, they are nuances of the same sense.

system governed by the Torah and the Priests who enforce it. In 4:5, Jesus came to redeem those held captive 'under the law,' which speaks of Jesus releasing believing Israel from the tyranny of the law. In 4:21, he refers to those who 'want to be *under* the law'—those who like the Judaizers want to yield to the demands of the Torah. Finally, in 5:18, he tells the Galatians that if they are 'led by the Spirit,' they 'are not *under* law.'

As such, the phrase speaks of those who are governed by Torah not just for life, but for seeking righteousness before God. We can recognize this in Islamic nations under Sharia law. In such nations, there is no separation of mosque and state; rather, the whole political, economic, religious, and social system is set up on the basis of Islamic law. In Paul's days, the world was governed by such systems, whether it is Judaism with Torah, the Roman world with its polytheistic philosophical undergirding, or other nations with their religious worldviews.

In Christendom, Christianity was the religious undergirding of the national identities of many European nations exported in Colonialism. We live in a different context where secularism means that traditional religions are pushed to the side of the life of the State. What has happened, of course, is that a new 'religion' has emerged which is a blend of ideas from Christianity, philosophy, science, and other religious traditions. We can call it some kind of social liberalism, humanism, or whatever. Jesus came to redeem all humanity from all such systems beginning with Judaism.

Getting back to Galatians, those living under the Torah are held captive under the law. The verb here is again *synkleiō*, used in the previous verse, speaking of Israel's imprisonment under the law. What is a good law gifted by God to Israel as the basis for a religion that was from its inception based on grace and faith, but has now become a tool of oppression.

Religion as a tool of oppression is common in nations where priests (or Imams, Pujari, etc.), temple(s) (or Mosque, church) and ruler(s) work together. Religion, however good, becomes a tool of domination. So, it is with the Torah. 'We' who were held captive here strictly speaking is Israel. However, rhetorically it speaks to the Galatians, urging them not to return to that same kind of captivity.

Now is the salvation era of faith, the salvation era of law is complete. The law's role in guiding and protecting Israel is over. Now all the law does is reveal people's desperate need for justification. Faith has now come. All peoples are now justified by faith. For Paul, justification by faith is how it has always been. Now it is clarified, revealed, and made known. Christ is everything. He is the faithful one (although, as I have argued, this is not Paul's point in the genitive), and he has completed the works of the law (cf. Heb 3:2). Believers of all ethnicities are in him, and the law is completed and fulfilled. They do not need to be legalistic pedants concerned to ensure that they do not break a jot or tittle of the law (cf. Matt 23). By faith, they can live the life of the Spirit in complete confidence, a life shaped by faith, hope, and love.

The use of the verb *apokalyptō* recalls Paul's experience of revelation in 1:16 of the moment when God 'revealed his Son to me.' It was then that the pieces of the jigsaw dropped into place. In this aha moment, Paul experienced not only the revelation of the Son but also the gospel of the Son (1:12). It is by faith, not by works of the law. He is thus free from the law. This is not freedom free to sin, but freedom to live life in the Spirit with the law inscribed on his heart (Rom 2:15; 2 Cor 3:2; Jer 31:33). The Galatians are similarly free, having experienced the Spirit and miracles by faith (3:2, 5). They must not yield to a new master, even if it is God's good, holy, and righteous law. They must yield to the righteousness that is by faith.

THE LAW AS TUTOR UNTIL CHRIST AND FAITH (3:24)

In *Galatians 3:24*, Paul concludes his assessment of the law with a summary statement:

so then (*hōste*, 2:13), **the law** (*nomos*, 2:16) **has become** (perfect *ginomai*, 2:17) **our** (genitive plural *egō*, 1:2) **guardian** (*paidagōgos*)[48] **until** (*eis*, 1:5) **Christ** (*Christos*, 1:1), **so that** (*hina*,

1:16) **we may be justified** (second person aorist passive *dikaioō*, 2:16) **by** (*ek*, 1:1) **faith** (genitive *pistis*, 1:23).

Paul draws his ideas together with the inferential conjunction *hōste*, 'so then, therefore.' 'Our' here is Israel under the law that functioned as her guardian.

'The law has become our guardian' introduces a fresh idea, the law as a *paidagōgos*, a 'tutor,' 'guardian,' 'disciplinarian,' 'superintendent,' or 'pedagogue.' The term is not widely used in the comparative Jewish Greek literature, absent completely from the LXX or the OT Pseudepigrapha.

Josephus employs it in a range of ways including Cain as Abel's pedagogue or brother (*Ant.* 1.56), those who bought up Ahab's children (*Ant.* 9.125), Nebuchadnezzar's aides who took Daniel and the others under their wing (*Ant.* 10.186), the pedagogue of Tiberius Caesar's grandson (*Ant.* 18.212), Nero's tutor Burrhus (*Ant.* 20.183), and a pedagogue at the service of Josephus (*Life* 429).

Philo's use helps us understand their role. He speaks of their expense (Philo, *Spec.* 2.233), their shaping the boy ethically (mostly negatively for Philo),[49] correcting and punishing them (*Migr.* 116), beating them (*Det.* 145), of boys hating their pedagogues (*Sacr.* 51), and of pedagogues of Gaius Caligula (*Legat.* 26, 27, 53).

As discussed in the translation notes, Paul is the only NT writer who employs the term, here, and in 1 Cor 4:15, where he is the father and those who nurture the Corinthians in his absence are their tutors. Invoking the father image enables him to exert his authority. Here, having personified the law as a jailor, he now personifies the law as a guardian, tutor, or pedagogue, over Israel—*Nomos* (or *Torah*) the guardian or tutor.

Schneider notes that the pedagogue is commonly referenced

---

48. The noun παιδαγωγός (*paidagōgos*) is used twice in Galatians, in consecutive verses, 3:24 and 25. It is a technical term for a tutor or pedagogue who served as a mentor for the elite Roman young man. Here, the law is likened to the *paidagōgos*. The other use is 1 Cor 4:15 of the Corinthians having many pedagogues but only one father, Paul. He has authority and they should yield to him.

49. See *Sacr.* 15; *Her.* 295; *Mut.* 217; *Virt.* 178; *Flacc.* 15.

in Euripides and Herodotus in the fifth-century BC and literally means 'child-leader.' Plato notes that the pedagogue was usually a slave whose role differed from the schoolteacher (Plato, *Lys*, 208c).[50] He took charge of the boy's education regarding courtesy, table manners, and general conduct from about six to sixteen. He functioned as a supervisor or disciplinarian. As noted in Philo above, he was often viewed negatively.[51]

Paul's uses here and in 1 Cor 4 may be seen negatively.[52] However, this is not likely as Paul does not have an issue with Israel and her law before the coming of Christ. Rather, the law functioned positively to guide Israel in its worship and life. However, negatively, it revealed her disobedience and need for a 'father.'

'Until Christ' refers to the present state of affairs for Paul, Israel, and the Galatians. Using the analogy, while the 'father' himself has not come, he has acted in sending his Son to rule on his behalf as sovereign Lord. As such, the tutor's job is done. He is redundant. Now, Israel can come to maturity and know God by his Spirit. For the Galatians to yield to Judaizers and come under law places them back in the care of a tutor who has since been fired, rather than the Father by his Son. They must not do so.

The final *hina* purpose clause draws thoughts back to the central thesis of the letter, justification by faith. Paul uses the inclusive 'we,' which includes all Jews who previously were seeking justification by the law and all gentiles, including the Galatians. Christ has come, faith is revealed, and so in Christ, 'we may be justified by (*ek*) faith' (see especially 2:16).[53] Faith is the only means of gaining right standing before God.

Jews in Paul's time, Paul the pre-Christian Pharisee included, were seeking justification through the law. The Judaizers

---

50. Plato writes, 'But someone controls you? Yes, he said, my tutor (*paidagōgos*) here. Is he *a slave*? Why, certainly; he belongs to us, he said. What a strange thing, I exclaimed; a free man controlled by a slave! But how does this tutor actually exert his control over you? By taking me to school, I suppose, he replied.'

51. G. Schneider, 'παιδαγωγός,' in *EDNT* 3:2–3.

52. Schneider, 'παιδαγωγός,' 3.

53. The eighth use of *ek pisteōs*, 'from faith' (see 2:16 especially, also 3:7, 8, 9, 11, 12, 22; 5:5).

continued this, unable to accept the amazing grace that is in the gospel, that Jesus has done it all, and all we must do is yield with active trust and belief. They want more. They want the Galatians to be circumcised and yield to the core tenets of Jewish law-observance. They must not do so for this would thrust them under the law, and they would be required to do everything written in the book of the law for righteousness, and this is impossible, Jesus aside. Rather, they must place their trust in Jesus Christ as Savior and Lord and live by faith. Then his works suffice, and they are justified, clothed in Christ, their lives are hidden in his righteousness (Col 3:3). They are justified! Righteous! Acquitted! Not guilty! Pardoned! *Gerechtfertigt!*

CHAPTER NINETEEN: THE INCLUSION, UNITY, AND EQUALITY OF ALL BELIEVERS IN CHRIST (3:25–29)

NO LONGER UNDER THE LAW AS TUTOR (3:25)

Paul now makes a concluding statement again interpreting the law as a guardian (*paidagōgos*), *Nomos*, who tutored Israel from Sinai up to the time of faith in Christ. He then draws out the consequence of this; believers are no longer under the guardian *Torah* but are in *Christ Jesus*, God's Son and appointed heir of all things, and so are God's children through faith (and so not the law, implied). He links status to the primary Christian initiation; baptism—those baptized into Christ have 'put on Christ.' Christ is their skin so to speak! This image has extreme counter-cultural, social implications—the breaking down of social boundaries including racial, social status, and gender in the first-century setting and for all time where the Christian movement spreads. He then brings it back to Abraham—if one belongs to Christ, then they are descendants of Abraham and heirs based on God's promise.

In *Galatians 3:25*, Paul concludes the theological argument concerning Abraham, promise, faith, and law. This perspective will become the basis for his radical anthropology, ecclesiology, and sociology in 3:28. He writes:

but (*de*, 1:5) **[now] faith** (*pistis*, 1:23) **has come** (aorist *erchomai*, 1:21), **we are** (first-person plural *eimi*, 1:7) **no longer** (*ouketi*, 2:20) **under** (*hypo*, 1:11) **a guardian** (*paidagōgos*, 3:24).

He mentioned the coming of faith in 3:23, speaking of before faith came. Now it has come, in Christ. What was always the case, that one is justified by faith (as in Abraham, Gen 15:6), has now been revealed fully in Christ's coming. Faith in Christ suffices.

'We are no longer under a *paidagōgos*,' i.e., *Nomos/Torah/law*. Here, 'we,' is first of all Jews who were under the law which functioned as a guardian but is now no longer under the law. However, functionally and rhetorically, it speaks at two levels (as in 3:13–14) of all Christians, Jew or gentile. It is what Paul wants for all Jews and all humanity. The universalization is seen in the next verse where '*you* are all children of God' and so in no need of submitting to the law, the *paidagōgos*.

God forbid that the Galatians subordinate themselves to *Nomos*, who will become to them a prison guard and tutor leading them astray. *Nomos*, where believers are concerned, is now unemployed, no longer required. We are in Christ, and so complete and in no need of a tutor. *Nomos* is inscribed on the heart by the Spirit and so is not required. As he will go on to say, the Son has come, and we are children of God, imbued with the Spirit, and so we can grow to the fullness of maturity, not through the law, but through the Christ-life by the Spirit. We have 'outgrown' *Nomos*. We are no longer infants (*nēpios*, 4:1, 3) who are under a tutor but have come of age, taken up the toga, who is Christ, in whom we have been clothed. We who believe are now sons (and daughters), heirs who are fully mature (at least in a status sense—we must seek to embody this maturity by the Spirit).

ALL CHILDREN OF GOD BY FAITH IN CHRIST (3:26)

In *Galatians 3:26* Paul begins to draw out the implications of his perspective on the law:

For (*gar*, 1:10) **you are** (second person *eimi*, 1:7) **all** (*pas*, 1:2) **children** (*huios*, 1:16) **of God** (genitive *Theos*, 1:1) **in** (*en*, 1:6) **Christ** (*Christos*, 1:1) **Jesus** (*Iēsous*, 1:1) **through** (*dia*, 1:1) **faith** (genitive *pistis*, 1:23).

The implication is drawn out here for the Galatians ('you') who form a sub-group of the 'we' in the previous verse. They too are children of God by faith in Christ Jesus.

The term translated 'all' (*pantes*) is placed first for prominence. In context, it is clearly inclusive of both Jewish and gentile believers, men and women, slaves and free, as v. 28 makes clear. 'All' (*pantes*) here is not universalistic as the verb *estin* is second person and directed to the Galatians and includes all of them (and any other readers) who have 'faith in Christ Jesus.' The verb 'are' (*estin*) is present tense, indicating that this is a current status made possible through faith in Christ Jesus. As such, they *are* already God's children and do not need anything additional like circumcision. They are 'in,' so to speak.

'Children' is the masculine *huios* rather than the more general *teknon* (cf. 4:19, 28, 31). However, the mention of 'female' in v. 28 indicates we should read 'sons' here inclusively as 'children,' as with the children of Abraham (3:7) and other references to believers' divine childship (4:6, 7).[1]

'Children of God' understood against the background is an extraordinary statement of status. In the Greek world, *huios* is used for sons of Zeus (e.g., Homer, *Il.* 5.683) and other gods (Homer, *Il.* 13.345), including the Olympian family dynasty. The gods mated with mortals and birthed the likes of Dionysius or Heracles. In Hellenistic Greek, especially in eastern rulers such as Egypt, rulers were regarded as 'sons of god,' e.g., 'sons of Helios,' 'sons of Zeus.' For example, Alexander the Great was called 'son of Ammon,' another name for Zeus. After 331 BC, later Greek gods like the Ptolemy's took the title. The Latin *Divi filius* is taken in this way of Augustus. Some great figures like the Spartan general Lysander, Pythagoras, and Plato were regarded as sons of the divine. In Jewish thought, divine sonship is applied to angels,[2] Israel in a corporate sense,[3] and the king.[4]

Earlier, Paul noted that Christ is Son of God who was revealed to him by God on the Damascus Road (1:15), and in whom he now lives his life (2:20, cf. 4:4). Here, the title is applied to all who believe. They are children of Abraham (3:7; 4:28) and Sarah

1. Paul also uses *nēpios*, of a young child in 4:1, 3—again, it is inclusive.
2. See, e.g., Gen 6:2, 4; Job 1:6; 2:1; 38:7; Dan 3:25.
3. See Exod 4:22–23; Hos 11:1; Mal 2:10.
4. See 2 Sam 7:14; Ps 2:7; 89:26–27.

(4:31), children of Paul (4:19), and here, children of God. This attribution is a stunning statement indicating that children are part of God's family into which they are adopted with full familial rights (4:6) and recipients of God's Spirit (4:7). As children of God, they receive a status only conferred on the divine, royalty, and super-citizens in the Greco-Roman setting. Where Israel is concerned, they are afforded the status of the whole nation as God's elect, and most importantly, children of God alongside the Messiah King and Son.

The text can read 'for you are all children of God through faith in Christ Jesus' (KJV). Alternatively, it can be taken as 'for you are all children of God in Christ Jesus through faith.' In the former, Christ Jesus is the object of the faith. In the latter, 'in Christ Jesus' is absolute and modifies children of God. The Greek order favors taking it in the former manner as retained in this translation.[5] If this is correct, then it is clear that the object of faith is Christ. It may also lend support to taking genitive constructs *pistis Christou* subjectively as Christ's faith or faithfulness. However, most take it in the second way, arguing that *en* is not often used to introduce the object of faith found mainly in the disputed Paulines.[6]

'In Christ Jesus' gives the context for which these Galatians have this honor. However, while in Christ, each Galatian retains her or his individuality. Yet, while individuals in Christ, it also speaks of their joint eschatological, soteriological, familial, and ecclesiological status. They are now a part of God's eternal people. They are all saved by this Christ. They are part of God's family, his church. Their status is derivative of Christ's status as the Son. It is through faith.

If we should take *pistis Christou* constructs in 2:16 and 3:22 subjectively, then this may here refer to the faithfulness or faith of Christ—the Galatians (and all believers) are the children of God through the faith/faithfulness of Christ. Yet, as has been consistently argued in this commentary, this is the faith of the

5. Morris, *Galatians*, 120.
6. See Eph 1:15; Col 1:4; 1 Tim 1:14; 3:13; 2 Tim. 1:13. Moo, *Galatians*, 250.

person directed toward God and his Son Christ. Indeed, as argued on 2:16, if we take *pistis Christou* subjectively, every such faith statement in Paul faces the same dilemma unless it clearly states who the object is. The whole point of Galatians is to reinforce that one is justified by faith and not by law (or any other thing for that matter).

ALL BAPTIZED INTO CHRIST ARE CLOTHED IN HIM (3:27)

In *Galatians 3:27*, Paul continues in the second person, linking the Galatians' incorporation into the family of God with baptism:

For (*gar*, 1:10) **as many** (personal *hosos*, 3:10) **[of] you who have been baptized** (second person aorist passive *baptizō*)[7] **into** (*eis*, 1:5) **Christ** (*Christos*, 1:1), **have put on** (second person aorist middle *endyō*)[8] **Christ** (*Christos*).

Gar, 'for,' is more explanatory than causal leading to Paul further explaining why justification and incorporation into God's family is by faith. 'As many as' effectively means 'all' (see 3:10). 'Who have been baptized' uses *baptizō*. Here, it is unclear whether Paul has in mind water or Spirit baptism, with both ideas having support in contemporary scholarship.[9]

Other references to baptism in Paul can lead us in either direction. In support of water baptism, which remains the dominant view, there is a clear similarity with Romans 6:3.[10] Most likely, Rom 6:3 concerns water baptism, it being a visual demonstration of the death, burial, and resurrection of the

---

7. The verb βαπτίζω (*baptizō*) meaning 'to baptize' is found once in Galatians 3:27. Paul also refers to baptism in Rom 6:3; 1 Cor 1:13, 14, 15, 16, 17; 10:2; 12:13; 15:29.
8. The only reference to the verb ἐνδύω (*endyō*) in Galatians is 3:27. It can mean 'to put clothing or apparel on someone, dress, clothe' or 'to put any kind of thing on oneself, clothe oneself in, put on, wear' (BDAG 333–34).
9. For Spirit baptism, e.g., Dunn, *Galatians*, 203; Witherington, *Grace*, 276–77. For water baptism, the dominant position, see Moo, *Galatians*, 251; William Hendriksen and Simon J. Kistemaker, *Exposition of Galatians*, NTC 8 (Grand Rapids: Baker Book House, 1953–2001), 149; Longenecker, *Galatians*, 155; George, *Galatians*, 275–82; Ronald Y. K. Fung, *The Epistle to the Galatians*, NICNT (Grand Rapids, MI: Eerdmans, 1988), 172–75; Bruce, *Galatians*, 185–86.
10. This can be seen by comparing the transliterated Greek below. Gal 3:27a: *hosoi gar eis Christon ebaptisthēte.* Romans 6:3a: *hosoi ebaptisthēmen eis Christon.*

believer which identifies them with Christ's work. However, as with this text in Galatians, it may be that Paul considers the baptism into Christ a prior event at the moment of faith whereby the Spirit baptizes the person. This prior work of God is enacted in water baptism (for the same reasons argued on Gal 3:27 below). Similarly, the imagery of Col 2:12 of burial and resurrection suggests water baptism is in mind. In 1 Cor 1:13–17, Paul refers to the water baptism of the Corinthians.[11]

1 Corinthians 12:13 speaks of Spirit baptism—'for in one Spirit we were all baptized into one body—Jews or Greeks, slaves or free—and all were made to drink of one Spirit.'

Here in Galatians, although on the face of it, it seems obvious to see it in the same sense as Rom 6:3, there are problems with seeing this as water baptism. Most importantly, Paul has made crystal clear that it is faith and faith alone that sees a person incorporated into Christ, as argued through Galatians to this point (esp. 2:16, 20; 3:2–14, 22–26). Boundary markers such as circumcision are not required for incorporation. It would be rather strange for Paul to now introduce water baptism as a Christian boundary marker. Furthermore, faith is directly linked to the receipt of the Spirit in Galatians (see 3:2, 5).

As such, it is likely Spirit-baptism that is in mind first and foremost. For Paul, people are 'baptized by the Spirit' in Christ at the moment of faith. The anointing of the Anointed One (Christ, Messiah) is conveyed to the believer, who is sealed for redemption by the Spirit, who is a deposit guaranteeing eternal life (2 Cor 1:21–22; Eph 1:13–14). However, the evidence of the NT is that those who came to faith were baptized very quickly and the two events are not separated as they often are in modern Christian practice.[12] Water baptism dramatically symbolizes what happens at the moment of faith and Spirit reception.

11. Of little value for this article is 1 Cor 10:2 (baptism into Moses) and 1 Cor 15:29 speaks of the Corinthians baptizing people on behalf of the dead, a minefield for critical speculation.

12. See, e.g., Acts 2:28; 8:12, 36; 9:18; 10:48; 16:15, 33. It should be noted, however, that these references may telescope a longer period. Further, the other writings of the NT do not indicate immediate baptism.

Further, it is likely that faith, Spirit reception, and water baptism were all closely linked, and so the debate may be an anachronism based on the church's later practice. So, while strictly speaking, Spirit baptism fits the context better, perhaps baptism as a whole is in mind with the two so closely linked.

Whatever baptism is in mind, the believer is 'baptized into Christ' speaking of the mystical union a believer has with his/her Savior and Lord. This baptism is an individual experience but becomes ecclesiological; all believers are fused together as one people into Christ (something Paul will draw out in the next sentence). They are built together into one Temple of the Spirit (1 Cor 3:16; 6:19; Eph 2:19–22). The 'you' here focuses on the Galatians who are baptized into Christ as his children, and they are clothed in Christ. However, this, of course, functions at two levels in a kind of reverse way the 'we' did earlier in vv. 13–14, 23–25. Whereas the 'we' was primarily the Jews, it had a rhetorical impact on the Galatians who must not go back into enslavement to the law. Here, the 'you' speaks of the Galatians, but of course includes all Christians, Jew or gentile.

The one baptized into Christ by the Spirit through faith has 'put on Christ.' The verb *endyō* is used of the putting on of clothes.[13] At times it is used figuratively as being clothed in power from on high (Luke 24:49) or the perishable body putting on the imperishable (1 Cor 15:53, 54). Paul also uses it figuratively in Rom 13:12, encouraging the Roman Christians to 'put on the armor of light' and in Rom 13:14 to 'put on the Lord Jesus Christ' speaking of Christians clothing themselves with the attitude and ethical values of Christ and repudiating fleshly desires. Similarly, in Eph 4:24, believers are to put on the new person, created in the likeness of God (Col 3:11), while in Eph 6:11, they are to put on the full armor of God including putting on righteousness (also 1 Thess 5:8). In Col 3:11–12 they put on the new self and a range of Christlike virtues.

Whereas in Rom 13:14, clothing oneself in Christ is in the

---

13. See Matt 6:25; 22:11; 27:31; Mark 1:6; 6:9; 15:20; Luke 8:27; 12:22; 15:22; Acts 12:21; Rev 1:13; 15:6; 19:14.

imperative mood; here, it is an indicative reality. One who is baptized into Christ is clothed in Christ. This motif is clearly figurative, speaking of the believers' in-Christ status. It is another way of stating this reality, with the metaphor of clothing. It is soteriological—one is saved in Christ. It is eschatological, becoming a part of God's eternal community. It is familial, being adopted into God's family. It is ecclesiological, a part of God's people. It is pneumatological, anointed by the Spirit in the anointed one, and bound together with others in God's household. It is missional, the believer clothed (as Christ was) in armor as they live in unity and serve Christ in the world.

SOCIAL BARRIERS SUBSUMED IN UNITY IN CHRIST (3:28)

Paul does not use a connective in *Galatians 3:28* (asyndeton, see 2:6). However, he is clearly drawing out the ecclesiological implications of their status as those baptized into Christ and clothed in him:

There is (*eni*)[14] neither (*ou*, 1:1) Jew (*Ioudaios*, 1:14) nor (*oude*, 1:1) Greek (*Hellēn*, 2:3), neither (*ou*) is there (*eni*) slave (*doulos*, 1:10) nor (*oude*) free (*eleutheros*),[15] neither (*ou*) male (*arsēn*)[16] and (*kai*, 1:1) female (*thēlys*).[17] For (*gar*, 1:10) all (*pas*, 1:2) are (*eimi*, 1:7) one (*heis*, 3:16) in (*en*, 1:6) Christ (*Christ*, 1:1) Jesus[18] (*Iēsous*, 1:1).

---

14. The verb ἔνι (*eni*) stands for *enestin* and means 'to be or exist in a certain context' and so is translated as 'there is.' It is used in 3:28 three times: '*there is* neither Jew nor ... *there is* neither slave ... *there is* neither male ...' It is uncommon, only used elsewhere in the NT in 1 Cor 6:5; Col 3:11; and Jas 1:17.
15. The noun ἐλεύθερος (*eleutheros*) meaning 'free person' is found six times in Galatians—once in the contrast between slave and free in 3:28 and five times of Sarah the free woman (4:22, 23, 26, 30, 31).
16. The common Greek noun for 'man, husband,' ἄρσην (*arsēn*), is used once in Galatians 3:28 in the contrast of man and woman.
17. The usual Greek word for woman or wife, θῆλυς (*thēlys*), is used once in Galatians in the contrast, 'neither male and female,' in 3:28.
18. **Variant:** The words 'one in Christ' (*eis este en Christō*) have excellent support (2א B C D Ψ etc.). A number of other readings have arisen replacing *eis* with *en* ('are in in Christ Jesus'), which is clearly an error. P46 and A include 'you belong to Christ Jesus' which is likely an assimilation to 3:29 (so Metzger, *Textual Commentary*, 526).

The verse is neatly structured in Greek as this transliteration shows, with three sentences, of which the first two have an identical structure, and the third very similar with the only difference the shift from *oude* to *kai* (further on this below).

ouk eni Ioudaios	*oude*	*Hellēn*
ouk eni doulos	*oude*	*eleutheros*
ouk eni arsen	*kai*	*thēly*

The verse then concludes with a statement of the unity of all these people in Christ. The absence of a connective does not necessarily indicate a shift of thought or a new section. Rather, the asyndeton (see 2:6), along with the first placement of the negation *ouk*, draws the readers' attention and suggests Paul wants to emphasize to them what follows.

The three couplets combine to paint a picture of the unified people of God in which social boundaries and power structures essential to the first-century world are broken down—ethnicity (Jew over gentile/gentile over Jew),[19] social status (free over slave), and gender (male over female). This verse is one of the most important passages in Scripture for understanding the social and political (power) implications of the gospel.

'Neither Jew nor Greek' speaks of the classical, ethnic boundary from the perspective of a Jew. The Romans, who considered themselves one with the Greeks, saw the world differently, dividing it primarily between Greeks (including Greeks and Romans) and Barbarians (cf. Rom 1:14). The Jews saw the world through a Jew-gentile lens. Jewish self-identity is based on their covenantal relationship with God and adherence to the law, especially its boundary markers, circumcision, Sabbath, festivals, food laws, and purity regulations.

One became a Jew in a formal sense first through descent from a Jew. Alternatively, one converted to Judaism formerly[20] by

---

19. 'Greek' here is essentially parallel to 'gentile.' The Jew-gentile power structure varied depending on perspective. Politically, Greek (inclusive of Roman) dominated Jew. However, religiously, due to Israel's exclusive theology, Jew dominated gentile (from a Jewish perspective).

becoming a proselyte (one who has arrived at)—a person who then gains the legal status of a Jew by birth (cf. Lev 18:26; 19:23–34; Num 15:14–16). Burns notes that proselytes were required to integrate into their local Jewish communities and 'commit to complete observance of the traditional Jewish law and cult.'[21] Circumcision was obligatory for a male (e.g., Josephus, *Ant.* 20.38–48).[22] A good example is Achior who converts in Judith 14:10: 'When Achior saw all that the God of Israel had done, he believed firmly in God. So, he was circumcised and joined the house of Israel, remaining so to this day.'

Where women are concerned, they were also required to submit to Jewish custom (aside from circumcision). Burns suggests marriage to a Jewish man was the initial, visible symbol and 'demonstrative rejection of her native religion' (Jos. Asen. 10.10–13). Ultimately, rabbis introduced a kind of penitential baptism for men and women.[23]

So, it was quite a thing to become a Jew. It remains so today. I know a woman who has been trying to become an Orthodox Jew for over twenty years. She is married to a Jewish man who will not agree to limit his driving on the Sabbath. So, she is blocked. Very tough!

With all this in mind, Jewish attitudes to gentiles tended to be separatist. Gilbert argues six issues dominated Jewish attitudes of separation. First, there was concern over gentile polytheistic idolatry with many in rabbinic Judaism advocating avoidance of

---

20. J. E. Burns, "Conversion and Proselytism," in *EDEJ* 484–86 distinguishes between informal and formal conversion. He notes some scholars see informal conversion to Judaism loosely defined as gentile adoption of Jewish practices and rituals such as recognizing Yahweh as a god or God, rejecting polytheism for Jewish monotheism, and showing favor to Jewish acquaintances. Burns, however, notes that 'Jewish law made no distinction between those gentiles who were favorably disposed to Jews and those who were not' (p. 484).

21. Burns, 'Conversion,' 484.

22. In this passage Izatus, king of the Parthian client kingdom of Adiabene (*ca.* AD 1–55), becomes a proselyte embracing Jewish customs entirely and wishes to be circumcised. He is talked out of it for political reasons until a Jew named Eleazer persuades him of its imperative on the basis of the Mosaic law and injuring God by not doing so. See also *Ant.* 13.257–58, 319.

23. Burns, *Conversion*, 484–85.

association with gentile religious practices (something difficult where religion and wider life were fused). So, a Jew could not drink gentile wine or pick up an object in front of an idol!

Second, while some writers show respect for gentile gods and religion,[24] gentile religious practice in the postexilic period was repudiated as false (cf. Isa 45:5) and mocked as ignorant, perverse, and immoral (see esp. Wis and Sib. Or.).

Third, Jewish and gentile interaction was one of tolerance and respect (Exod 22:20; Num 15:15–16). However, no gentile could participate in Passover (Exod 12:43), and Israelites could gain interest from loans to gentiles but not Jews (Deut 23:20–21). They also tended to live separate lives in ethnic enclaves based on the synagogue for fear of becoming compromised. Intermarriage was forbidden, and endogamy[25] practiced.[26] While many Jews were educated in the gymnasium, went to the theater and bathhouses, and did business among gentiles, there was a tendency to refuse to eat with gentiles (important in 2:11–14) (Jub. 22:16; 3 Macc. 3:3–7).

While acknowledging contact was required and unavoidable, rabbis generally urged *amixia* (not mixing) with gentiles (*Exod. Rab.* 31.1). Gentiles who wished to convert and God-fearers like Cornelius and Lydia (Acts 10:2; 16:14) were welcomed to the synagogue and festival activities and honored for any contributions made, but there was little centrifugal missionary activity.[27]

A fourth issue was the gentile presence in the land and the repudiation of idolatry on its soil, an issue that catalyzed Josiah's reform and the Maccabean Revolt. Participation in the Temple, even in the 'Court of the gentiles,' was restrictive.[28]

---

24. See, e.g., Exod 22:27 LXX; Philo, *Spec. Leg.* 1.53; Mos. 2.205.

25. Endogamy is the practice of marrying within an exclusive social group.

26. See e.g., Exod 34:16; Ezra 9–10; Tob 4:12; Jub. 30:7–17; T. Levi 9:10; Philo, *Spec. Leg.* 3:29.

27. Matthew 23:15 is seen as an exception and its meaning is disputed. It can mean some missionary activity or the conversion of God-fearers to full proselytes. See R. Riesner., 'A Pre-Christian Jewish Mission,' in *The Mission of the Early Church to Jews and gentiles*, ed. J. Ådna and H. Kvalbein, WUNT 127 (Tübingen: Mohr Siebeck, 2000), 211–50.

390 MARK J. KEOWN

Ritual purity concerns were also important. This fifth factor links to a range of biblical texts whereby a Jew could become contaminated. Contact with gentile corpses or gentile contact with Jewish corpses could lead to impurity being transmitted (Num 19; 31, cf. The Good Samaritan). Their idolatry meant they were morally impure (Jub. 22:17–22). In rabbinic thought, gentiles cause defilement as does a person with a genital discharge or a woman in mensuration (t. Zab. 2.1; m. 'Abod. Zar. 3.6).

The final issue is judgment with some texts speaking of the gentiles coming to acknowledge God.[29] Other texts are negative about the eternal fate of the gentiles (see Jubilees; Testament of Abraham). Rabbis differed on their perspective with some repudiating gentile salvation, and others being more open (m. Sanh. 10:2).[30]

Bohak considers gentile attitudes toward Jews in the same period. He notes intellectual discussions such as Plutarch arguing that the Jewish God is the same as Bacchus (Dionysius) (Quaest. Conv. 4.6). He notes Tacitus' discussion of wildly different and ludicrous accounts of the Exodus including stating that 'the Jews regard as profane everything we hold sacred; on the other hand, they permit all that we abhor' (Tacitus. Hist. 5.2–4), and 'the other customs of the Jews are base and abominable, and owe their persistence to their depravity' (Hist. 5.5). He speaks of their 'hate and enmity' toward other people (Hist. 5.5). Bohak notes that some Jews could gain good status if they abandoned Judaism (e.g., 3 Macc 1:3; Josephus, Ant. 20.100; Life 16). There were also a few rare Jews loyal to tradition who gained prominence, e.g., Herod and Philo's brother, Alexander, of Alexandria (Josephus, Ant. 20.100).

Where the general public is concerned, there were two tendencies: mockery and animosity, otherwise, attraction and even conversion. Things ridiculed included versions of the Exodus (e.g., Tacitus above), claims they worshiped a donkey,

28. See Josephus, J.W. 5.194, cf. Ezek 44:5–9; 4QFlorilegium; J.W. 2.409–17.
29. See Isa 56:6–7; 66:23; Mic 4; Zech 14; Tob 14:6; Sir 36; T. Levi 14:4; Pss. Sol. 17:34.
30. See G. Gilbert, 'Jewish Attitudes toward gentiles,' in EDEJ 670–73.

circumcision, food laws (especially attitudes to pork), the Sabbath (a sign of laziness), a refusal to say God's name, being degenerate, effeminate, and superstitious (e.g., Philo, *Legat.* 353, 361–362). There were also examples of violence against Jews such as the Alexandrian anti-Jewish riot in AD 38 (Philo, *Flacc,* 55–72; *Legat.* 120–31), the celebration of the Roman destruction of Jewish Communities of Egypt in AD 115–117 (CPJ 2:450). The expulsions of Jews from Rome, especially by Claudius in AD 49, is also worthy of mention.[31]

The positive tendency saw some holding admiration for Jewish culture as we see with the God-worshipers or fearers in the NT[32] and proselytes like Nicolaus.[33] Josephus also records the conversion of the royal house of Abiadene (Josephus, *Ant.* 20.17–96). Gentile conversion was an aspect of interest among some Romans in Oriental philosophies. Large numbers of gentiles were attracted to the Synagogue, and some followed Jewish customs. The Jewish war in the late AD 60s did nothing, however, to improve relations. While this postdates Galatians, at the time of writing, Jewish nationalism was on the rise. Their main problem was separationism which manifested as a refusal to participate in aspects of gentile life and so they were seen as 'haughty and aloof.' The rise of Christianity after Galatians also bought Jewish culture into greater visibility.[34]

With all this in mind, Paul's statement is astonishing, especially when one considers Paul was a Pharisee and a former zealous nationalist who, until his conversion, no doubt enforced Jewish separatism from gentiles with some passion. Now the two people are one, bound together in Christ, clothed in him, still Jew and Greek, but united in a common culture of faith, hope, and love.

The second couplet, 'neither slave nor free,' is equally

---

31. There were expulsions of Jews from Rome in AD 139 for aggressive proselytizing (Valerius Maximus, *Fact. ac dict.* 1.3.2); by Tiberius in AD 19 for the same reason (Josephus, *Ant.* 18.81–84; Tacitus, *Ann.* 2.85.5; Suetonius, *Tib.* 36; Dio Cassius, *Hist.* 57.18.5); and the Claudian Edict, which was due to the infighting over *Chrestus*, who is almost certainly Christ (Suetonius, *Claud.* 25.4; Acts 18:1–2).

32. See Acts 10:2; 13:50; 16:14; 17:4; 18:7.

33. See, e.g., Acts 1:11; 6:5; 13:43.

34. See G. Bohak, 'Gentile Attitudes toward Jews and Judaism,' in *EDEJ* 668–70.

remarkable. As with all the Roman world, one of its central social divisions was the divide between the freed people and slaves (s.a. on slavery, 1:10). Freedom was highly valued while slavery was a repudiated status. The number of slaves is disputed with estimates between fifteen to thirty-three percent of the population in urban areas.[35] While it is true many slaves could gain good positions and wealth,[36] most did menial work and were on struggle-street and part of a repudiated status. Despite some scholars claiming the contrary, most slaves never gained their freedom (manumission).[37]

Paul's statement is remarkable. While he never repudiates the institution of slavery, this text, combined with Phlm 16 and Eph 6:9, points to a vision for a church in which if slavery exists, it is subordinated to *agapē, koinōnia, unity*, and a humble cruciform servitude toward the other in Christ. The seeds for the Wilberforce revolution are more than established in Paul. His argument is that slaves and freedpeople alike are in Christ and clothed with him. As such, their identity is one of equality of status whatever one's rank in the world.

The final couplet differs grammatically. Rather than 'neither slave *nor* (*oude*) free,' it says, 'neither male (*arsen*) *and* (*kai*) female (*thēly*).' This construct likely draws the reader back to Genesis 1:27 in the LXX: 'and God made humankind, according to the image of God he made him, *male* (*arsēn*) *and female* (*thēly*) he made them.' As such, Paul is making the remarkable statement that the distinctiveness of male and female etched into creation and humanity's image-bearing is swept up into Christ and 'clothed' in him. This subsuming of gender in Christ does not mean a rejection of gender difference which is endorsed or celebrated,

---

35. Harrill, 'Slavery,' 1124–27.
36. Harrill, 'Slavery,' 1125–26 notes that some could be in the imperial household (e.g., Phil 4:22) and could gain positions as doctors, architects, artisans, retailers, cooks, barbers, artists, thespians, magicians, prophets (e.g., Acts 16:16–24), teachers, professional poets, and philosophers.
37. Harrill, 'Slavery, 1126 notes that the idea they automatically gained their freedom after six years is based on faulty evidence.

but that Christian identity is primarily defined by in-Christness rather than gender.

In Paul's world, as it is in many of today's cultures, generally speaking, society was patriarchal with women subordinate to men in most spheres of life outside of the raising of children (although tutors were used for boys), midwifery, and other specifically women's concerns. Kroeger notes that Jewish women had differing degrees of freedom. Philo of Alexandria was radical, arguing that unmarried Jewish women should only go to the door of the women's quarters while married women could be carried on a litter as far as the front door or to the synagogue for prayer.[38]

Jewish women were expected to be virgins until married soon after menstruation. She could not divorce but was often divorced by her husband. Typical work was domestic—cooking, laundry, spinning, weaving, sewing, getting water, firewood, selling produce, caring for animals, midwifery, nursing, and professional mourning. Some were involved in the occult.

Synagogues required ten attending men (Philippi did not have one, cf. Acts 16:13), and women could attend but not as members. There is evidence that women had leadership roles in some synagogues. Women could not carry their children outside on the Sabbath, and so often did not attend. Women were required to maintain a kosher home and keep purity laws (including menstruation).

There were also situations where Jewish women were 'unclean,' particularly after childbirth and during menstruation (Lev 12:1–8; 15:19–23), or when suffering from a bodily discharge (Lev 15:25–28). It could be that the Judaizers were seeking to impose such rules on the women in the church. The emphasis on circumcision also effectively marginalizes women as it has nothing to do with them.

Greek women were more secluded with lower-class women expected to leave homes to get water from wells and fountains

38. Catherine C. Kroeger, 'Women in Greco-Roman World and Judaism,' in *DNTB* 1276 (to whom I am indebted for the material in this section).

and to trade in the agora. They were married very young, and many died in childbirth (av. age. 37). They were often defined sexually,[39] and wives, generally speaking, were neglected socially and sexually. Many were involved in sacral prostitution. Exposed girls often became slaves and were sexual partners or things like musicians to entertain men at symposia. They tended to be housed in women's quarters, which were small, dark, and cramped.

In the fifth century BC, Athenian women citizens were not to show faces in windows or doors. By the first century, there was more freedom in some instances; however, in many places like Tarsus (Paul's home city), old patterns persisted, and women were heavily veiled (as in some Islamic settings). Women were seen as less virtuous and intelligent and lived restricted lives.

In many households, women lived in women's quarters and did not converse, sleep, or eat with men. Fathers decided the fate of newborns—exposure or life, and girls were more discarded than boys. Mothers raised boys to age seven, and then they were raised by men often with tutors (paidagōgos, cf. 3:24–25) until they came of age. Boys ate better than girls. Women citizens did not converse with men outside the family, so situations like Paul and Lydia in Philippi (Acts 16:11–15), Jesus and the Samaritan woman (John 4:7–30), and him with the Syro-Phoenician woman (Mark 7:24–30) are somewhat remarkable.

Women engaged in a range of work including shepherding, selling goods, working with wool, washing clothes, acting as scribes, and hairdressing. At the Women's Market, some were in retail selling oil, salt, honey, sesame seed, flowers, perfume, dyes, shoes, and textiles. Within the home were wet nurses, matrons, nannies, and ladies' maids. Some were entertainers including flute players, dancers, acrobats, jugglers, harpists, and singers.

---

39. Kroeger, 'Women,' 1278 notes that Greek women were defined by their sexual function: 'courtesans for companionship, concubines for the daily pleasure of the master of the house and wives to bear legitimate children and keep the house.' The courtesans (hetaera) were often chosen for their intelligence and wit. They were particularly common in Corinth.

Some learned to read. Some female painters, poets, and philosophers were important. Some wrote novels.

Women were often denied participation in Greek religious practices like sacrifices and entry to temples or prayer. Women often worshiped different gods on specific days and in sanctuaries. Some cults gave an opportunity for leadership, e.g., Fates and Furies had female officials, the oracular sibyls, the high Artemis priestess in Ephesus, and the Oracle of Delphi. Lower-status women and slaves had fewer religious opportunities than others. Some cults included drugs and alcohol (Dionysus) and were enjoyed by some. Debauched behavior in religious celebrations was one outlet. Funerals and religious occasions were one of the few times they could leave home. Otherwise, they were basically imprisoned in homes.

Roman women experienced greater freedom than Greeks with more respect and a higher place in society. Roman farms had matrons. Girls were married at fourteen, in arranged marriages. The day before a virgin married, her hymen was broken on the phallus of the god Priapus[40] or Mutunus Tutunus.[41] Husbands and wives lived separate lives.

In the cities, women lived in three-storied buildings with little to do. They were bound to a male protector or tutor (father or husband in some instances) who would give consent for some trade. The ultimate power (*patria protestas*) lay with the leading family male. Many girls were prostitutes who lived in lower-class brothels (*lypanara* = wolf dens) or were higher-class courtesans who were used by the upper class. They were discarded as they aged, and many died of starvation.

Women worked in the textile industry including Priscilla

---

40. Priapus was the son of Aphrodite (or Chione) and Dionysus and a minor fertility god who was marked by his oversized penis ('Priapus,' *Wikipedia*, https://en.wikipedia.org/wiki/Priapus). Green, *The Letters*, 35 notes that 'the image of Priapus was an enlarged phallus with a small, grotesque body attached.'

41. Mutunus Tutunus (also Mutuunus Tunuutus or Mutinus Titunus) was a Roman phallic marriage god like Priapus. He was portrayed in a manner similar to Priapus. The practice of young virgins sitting on the phallus in preparation for marriage was repudiated by early Christian apologists like Arnobius. See 'Mutunus Tutunus,' *Wikipedia*, https://en.wikipedia.org/wiki/Mutunus_Tutunus#cite_note-1.

(tents) and Lydia (purple cloth). Others worked in wool, which was even considered aristocratic work. Others did similar work to the Greek women (above). Some were independent entrepreneurs, innkeepers, barmaids, waitresses (tavern work), actresses, musicians, gymnasts (theatre), and even gladiators. Slave women did domestic work. Many went to the arena to wash violent combat.

Elite women were involved in athletics, literature, academia, the theater, games like draughts and knucklebones, and looking good. Such noble women participated in the worship of Roman gods. The Vestal Virgins were held responsible for Rome. The consul's wife led the annual worship of the Good Goddess. Many women were priests including in Asia (in which is Galatia). Many lower-status women were engaged in the occult, spells, curses, and magic. Worship of eastern gods was attractive, especially Dionysus, Sabizios, Cybele, Isis, and Demeter. These religions gave more personal satisfaction, and it is not surprising that Christianity was received well among women.[42]

In light of the above analysis, Paul's statement is equally as astonishing as his changed perspective concerning ethnicity and social status. Men and women alike are one in Christ; the boundaries shattered. Gender is no longer the basis for status differentiation. Men and women are both baptized in Christ, and there is no case for any discrimination in our church communities. They both stand righteous before God by faith in Christ. There is no ground for prejudice on the basis of gender in the Christian church.

This verse provides the foundation for the transformation of society Christianity brings (when rightly understood and applied). The church continues to struggle to grasp its implications. Generally speaking, Christians understand that there should be no racial preference in the church as in apartheid or American racial divisions. There is no basis for preference. Christian churches should be without prejudice, explicit or

---

42. For the material in this section, I am indebted to the excellent article by Kroeger, 'Women,' 1276–80.

implicit. There is no dominant culture other than the culture of the gospel—faith, hope, and love (the fruit of the Spirit).

Our problem in this area today is not usually explicit racism but ethnic bias. Often the people of the dominant culture in a church cannot see ways in which they ask newcomers to fit into their culture, allow leadership positions to be dominated by their own kind of people, and have expectations of the 'way things are done around here.' A deep understanding of Paul's thought here leads us to a much more integrated cultural experience where culture is celebrated, all cultures are critiqued by the gospel, and the culture of the gospel binds people of diversity together. Mono-ethnic churches are problematic here, and their very existence is questionable in the light of the gospel.

It took western civilization about seventeen centuries to really question the institution of slavery. Thankfully, slavery is now repudiated in our culture. However, it is still a major global issue, and we must continue the fight. The other concern is the increasing gap between rich and poor, which is not slavery in the technical sense of the word, but enslavement within an economic system that favors a few. We need to resist this and seek to ensure that there is an equitable distribution of wealth (cf. 2 Cor 8:13).

Gender discrimination is still a major issue in our churches. Some denominations bar women from leadership on the basis of a couple of Pauline texts. However, in my view, these are most likely context-relevant moments rather than general statements for all time in all churches.[43] Women are as capable as men and must be free to take up the call of God and use their gifts for him. We must not respond to the disintegration of the morality of western civilization by resorting to a new conservatism that repeats the mistakes of our sexist past.

Finally, some use Gal 3:28 in contemporary debates over

---

43. 1 Corinthians 14:34–35 should be read as a response to women's participation in the chaotic worship of Corinth highlighted in 1 Cor 14:1–33 (cf. 1 Cor 11:1–16). 1 Timothy 2:8–15 is likely a response to women in the Ephesus church involved in the problem of false teachers and where they were dominating men. There are no limitations on women in the other Paulines, rather, those who are spiritually gifted are to be encouraged to use their gifts in love (Rom 12:4–8; 1 Cor 13:1–3).

sexuality, effectively arguing Paul would say today 'neither gay nor straight,' or something similar. We simply cannot absolutely know what Paul would say today. However, what we can say is that the Paul of the NT would decidedly *never* say such a thing. For him as for Jesus,[44] heterosexuality is the basis for human life laid down in creation (Rom 1:19–28). Heterosexual marriage is the only context in which people should engage in sexual intercourse (Rom 1:19–28; 1 Cor 6:12–20). He explicitly repudiates homosexual acts by men and women as idolatry, shameless, and contrary to created nature (Rom 1:19–27; 1 Cor 6:9–10). He endorses marriage (1 Cor 7) and urges marriages of mutual service and *agapē* (Eph 5:21–31). To argue that we can add to this text such an idea flies in the face of the whole biblical narrative, and I argue God's people should resist it with respect, humility, and grace.

THOSE OF CHRIST ARE ABRAHAM'S CHILDREN AND HEIRS TO THE PROMISE (3:29)

In *Galatians 3:29*, Paul links belonging to Christ to the dominant theme of the chapter: Christian descent from Abraham, inheritance, and the Abrahamic promise:

And (*de*, 1:15) if (*ei*, 1:7) **you** (plural *sy*, 1:3) [**belong to**] **Christ** (genitive *Christos*, 1:1), **then** (*ara*, 2:21) **you are** (*eimi*, 1:7) **offspring** (*sperma*, 3:15) **of** (genitive *ho*,[45] 1:1) **Abraham** (genitive *Abraam*, 3:6), **heirs** (plural *klēronomos*)[46] **according** (*kata*, 1:4) **to promise** (*epangelia*, 3:14).

The *de* here is continuous rather than adversative, hence 'and.' Paul again uses a conditional sentence with *ei*, the ninth thus far in the letter (cf. 1:7, 9, 10; 2:1, 17, 18, 21; 3:4, 21). Here,

44. See e.g., Matt 5:29–30; 15:19; 19:1–12, 18; Mark 7:21–23; 10:1–12; Luke 16:18–20, s.a., John 7:53–8:11.

45. The genitive article (ἄρα τοῦ Ἀβραὰμ σπέρμα, *ara tou Abraham sperma*) is used to indicate the case of the indeclinable noun Abraam. See Wallace, *Greek Grammar*, 240).

46. The noun κληρονόμος (*klēronomos*) is found three times in Galatians each time meaning heirs—heirs according to the Abrahamic promise (3:29); an heir in a general sense (4:1); and 'an heir through God' (4:7). See also *klēronomia*, 'inheritance' in 3:18 and *klēronomeō*, 'inherit' in 4:30.

the protasis lacks a verb, with the present of *eimi* (to be) likely, 'are.' The sentence is a first-class condition, true for the sake of argument (and for Paul actually true) (see on 1:9). The genitive 'of Christ' here does not mean 'of the faith of Christ,' but 'of Christ' in the sense of 'belonging to,' 'a part of,' equivalent to 'in Christ.' It is not so much possession as this could sound like a new slavery that is repudiated in the previous verse, although one might say there is willing enslavement to Christ. Here it expresses *agapē* based belonging and inclusion.

The apodosis is launched by *ara*, which is a conjunction drawing out the consequence of this belonging to Christ, 'then, therefore, so then, consequently.' 'You are offspring' uses the second person of the verb 'to be,' *eimi*, and expresses a present state of being—you 'are.' 'You' at one level would appear to be the Galatians. However, clearly what follows is for all Christians, so it is inclusive of the believing Galatians who are in Christ, baptized into him, and are of him. This status of being of Christ and Abraham's seed indicates that nothing further is required, e.g., circumcision. They are in!

Abraham's seed was well discussed in the previous references to the notion (3:16, 19). Here, *sperma* is singular, a corporate term. Christ is *the* seed of Abraham. Believers are *en Christō*. Thus, they are in a corporate sense the seed of Abraham, which speaks implicitly of the 'body of Christ.' Within Christ, there is no room for church divisions over race, social status, and gender.

The final clause draws out the consequence of this status of the church as the offspring of Abraham. They are heirs according to the promise. As discussed concerning 3:14, the promise is all that God promised Abraham and explained in Paul's theology, including eternal life and the renewed cosmos as an inheritance. The nations are being blessed through Abraham, specifically through his seed, a descendant of Abraham, Isaac, and Jacob. The regions of Pisidia, Lycaonia, and the centers of Perga, Antioch, Iconium, Lystra, Derbe, and wherever else the gospel has now spread in Galatia are being blessed (and so we too experience this blessing wherever we are, every minute of every day). The inheritance promised Abraham has come to them. They are people of Israel, being reconstituted in Abraham, gentiles of faith being grafted into the historic people of faith from Abel to Christ. The inheritance is jointly shared by all members of the church in which there is no status variation. Hallelujah!

For us in NZ or wherever we are reading this, the truth is the same. If we just believe in Jesus as Lord and savior, we belong to Christ. We are children of Abraham. We are in Israel, grafted into the Olive Tree. We are God's people. We are the circumcision, within the circumcised one. We are within the body of Christ. We are recipients of the inheritance promised to Abraham. We have eternal life. We will inherit the earth. In the meantime, even where Christ is preached and rejected, blessing flows from God to the nations as they are transformed by the presence of God's people in them (like salt, yeast, and light working into food, dough, and darkness, cf. Matt 5:13–16).

Yet, we must go through suffering to get to experience the fullness of blessing (Rom 8:17). Whatever miseries we face, whatever 'demons' haunt us, whatever rejection we feel, whatever our sense of abandonment, whatever we are presently dealing with, and whatever our future, this is our truth. We are safe in Christ and destined for glory. So, in the meantime, we press on with crosses slung over our backs and joy in our hearts to take hold of what is promised (Phil 3:14–15).

CHAPTER TWENTY: NO LONGER SLAVES BUT REDEEMED CHILDREN AND HEIRS (4:1–7)

BEFORE COMING OF AGE, A CHILD IS EFFECTIVELY A SLAVE (4:1)

This section continues from the previous with *de*, 'and.' Paul picks up the notion of inheritance, comparing the shift of status that occurs for a Jew in Christ from that of a slave to an heir. Such a shift was not uncommon in the Roman world. For example, Diocletian was a slave who became emperor.[1]

An heir while a child is effectively in the same place as a slave, an owner of all things in a proleptic sense, but not yet able to have access to it. Rather, he is under guardians and household managers put in place by the father until he comes of age. The point of this imagery becomes clear in v. 3, with 'we' (here likely Jews are in mind first and foremost, but also all Christians as vv. 6–8 will show) as children yet to come of age, are enslaved to the *stoicheia* (the elemental principles of the world). They were held captive to the law, and the Galatians to the religions and spiritual forces of their context.

The turning point in the section is v. 4. Here Paul describes how the turning of the ages has come in the fullness of time and how God has sent forth his Son Jesus Christ the Lord, born of a woman as a human, born under the law as a Jew, to redeem those born under the law. The purpose is that they may now be

---

1. Although not a slave, Caesar Augustus—the paradigm of the great Roman emperor, who brought peace to the region—was initially a slave. He was the grandnephew of Julius Caesar who adopted him and became emperor.

legally adopted as children. Having been adopted and now with
the full status of children, God has sent his Spirit into the hearts
of these believers by which they cry out, as did Jesus, 'Abba!
Father!' They are fully-fledged family members, no longer in the
status of slaves or children yet to come of age; they are children
with full inheritance rights through God.

In *Galatians 4:1*, Paul switches to speaking in human terms
describing the status of an heir before their coming of age:

And (*de*, 1:15) **I say** (*legō*, 1:9), **for** (*epi*, 3:13) **as long as** (*hosos*,
3:10) **the time** (*chronos*)[2] **the heir** (*klēronomos*, 3:29) **is** (present
eimi)[3] **an infant** (*nēpios*),[4] **[he is] no** (*ouden*, 2:6) **different**
(*diapherō*, 2:6) **to a slave**[5] (*doulos*, 1:10), **although he is** (present
participle *eimi*, 1:7) **master** (*kyrios*, 1:3) **of all** (*pas*, 1:2).

'And I say' sounds awkward and has the sense 'and this is what
I am saying.' *Kairos* in classical Greek thought has the sense of a
'point in time, moment, instant.'[6] It is 'the moment determined by
fate, though this is also a moment that should be both recognized
and grasped by a person, a moment demanding a decision.'[7] Paul
uses it in Galatians 4:10 of 'seasons' (festivals) and of reaping in
'due season' (6:9, 10). Conversely, *chronos*, used here, carries the

---

2. One of the two standard words for time in Greek thought, χρόνος (*chronos*, cf. *kairos*),
is found twice in Galatians. In 4:1, 'for as long as the time the heir is an infant,' refers
to the time of infancy before adulthood. The second is in 4:4 of 'the fullness of time.' It
can have the sense of a section of time, as in 4:1, a section of a lifespan. It can also
mean a point in time, as in 4:4. *Chronos* was the subject of much philosophical
discussion. See G. Delling, 'χρόνος,' in *TDNT* 9.581–85.

3. Wallace, *Greek Grammar*, 308 notes that the clause ὁ κληρονόμος νήπιός (*ho klēronomos
nēpios*, the heir is a child), is an example of an article-noun-adjective construct.
Wallace notes, '[h]ere, the emphasis seems to be either equally placed on noun and
adjective or is slightly heavier on the noun.'

4. The noun νήπιος (*nēpios*) refers to a child in the infant stages before adulthood. It is
found in 4:1, 3 of a child before maturity and inheritance, and of humanity as infants
enslaved by elemental spirits.

5. This is a genitive of comparison where '[t]he genitive substantive, almost always after
a comparative *adjective*, is used to indicate comparison. The genitive, then, is the
standard against which the comparison is made (i.e., in "X is greater than Y," the gen.
is the Y). This usage is relatively common.' Sometimes *diapherō* is used instead of the
comparative adjective as in Matt 10:31 as here. See Wallace, *Greek Grammar*, 111.

6. J. Baumgarten, 'καιρός,' in *EDNT* 2:232.

7. H. Hübner, 'χρόνος,' in *EDNT* 3:488.

sense of a period, a section of time, and is dominant in Greek philosophy, and is also an important deity.[8] In the NT, the terms no longer carry that same absolute force and distinction, but here *chronos* refers to a period of time.

The construction, *eph hoson chronon*, is rendered literally above, 'for as long as the time.' It can be simplified in English (as in most translations) to 'as long as.' Then Paul draws on the common understanding of the son (assumed in the culture at the time) in a home who is in position as the family heir but is yet to come of age. Longenecker summarizes Paul's point neatly:

The picture he draws is of a boy in a home of wealth and standing who is legally the heir (*ho klēronomos*) and so the "young master" (*kyrios*, lit. "lord" or "owner") of the family estate, but who is still a minor (*nēpios*) and so lives under rules very much like a slave (*doulos*). The picture is that of a family, and so is a pleasant one overall—certainly not a bad situation per se, but one only judged to be an inferior relationship in comparison to adulthood.[9]

The slave, of course, has no inheritance. 'Infant' is the term *nēpios* (cf. Eng. 'nappy'), which differs from *huios* (son or child, 1:16) and *teknon* (child, 4:19) by referring to a young child.[10] It here carries the sense of one not yet of legal age, a minor.[11] Paul uses the term elsewhere, including in 1 Cor 13:11, where he contrasts life in this age (infancy) with the fullness of life in the eschaton (adulthood). Here he uses it to contrast life before Christ when Jews are under the law, under the elemental spirits

8. See especially Plato, *Tim.* 37–41 in which God is eternal and created 'time.' *Chronos* created days, nights, months, and years when he created heaven. He denies the real existence of 'was' and 'will be' for 'is' alone is rightly applicable. 'Was' and 'is' relate to 'becoming' which proceeds in time, they are motions. Time and heaven co-exist. The sun, moon, five planets, and other revolving stars. From the sun come night and day, years. Chronos is a god, who with Rhea bore Zeus and Hera, the supreme god-couple.

9. Longenecker, *Galatians*, 162 with the Greek transliterated.

10. It is used fifteen times in the NT. Paul also uses it of Jews who claim to be the teacher of 'infants' (Rom 2:20), of the Corinthians as 'infants in Christ' (1 Cor 3:1), of mature Christians who are no longer 'infants' deceived by false teaching (Eph 4:14), and of nursing the Thessalonians as infants in his mission (1 Thess 2:7). See also Matt 11:25; 21:16; Luke 10:21; 5:13.

11. BDAG 671.

of the world (*stoicheia*, 4:3). While yet to come of age, as the next verse makes clear, the *nēpios* is under guardians and managers put in place (see v. 2). Boys came of age between fourteen and sixteen and if from a citizen's family, were registered on the list. Stamps notes that:

> ... at the feast of the *Liberalia* on March 17, a young man and his friends would ceremoniously exchange their *toga praetexta* (white with purple hem) for the *toga pura* (all white), which was a public sign of adulthood. Sometimes this transition period included shaving the boy's first beard and keeping the shavings in a shrine (*depositio barbae*).[12]

We also have in this verse the non-christological use of *kyrios*, often used of God or Jesus (Lord); here it refers to the master of the home and slaves.[13]

UNDER FAMILY GUARDIANS AND MANAGERS (4:2)

Paul continues the analogy in *Galatians 4:2*:

but (*alla*, 1:1) **he is** (present *eimi*) **under** (*hypo*, 1:11) **guardians** (plural *epitropos*)[14] **and** (*kai*, 1:1) **managers** (plural *oikonomos*)[15] **until** (*achri*, 3:19) **the day appointed** (*prothesmia*)[16] **by the Father** (genitive *patēr*, 1:1).

The son and heir, while still a child, is under those in the

---

12. D. L. Stamps, 'Children in Late Antiquity,' in *DBNT* 198–99.
13. On slaves see 1:10; 3:28.
14. The noun ἐπίτροπος (*epitropos*) compounds *epi* (upon, on, over) with *tropos* (manner, kind, customs, ways, kind of life, behavior, etc.) and so yields the sense of one who oversees something or someone's development. It is found once in Paul; in 4:2, of the household managers who care for the children. It is twice else used in the NT, of a vineyard manager (Matt 20:8) and Chuza who is Herod's household manager.
15. The noun οἰκονόμος (*oikonomos*) is found once in Galatians 4:2 of those who manage children. It is used to describe household managers, treasurers, or administrators (see BDAG 698). Paul's other use is 1 Cor 4:2 of those who manage a home and of elders (*episkopos*) who are God's managers or stewards.
16. The noun προθεσμία (*prosthesmia*) compounds *pros* (to, toward) and *thesmios* (laws, customs, rites, fixed, settled, fitting). It is found only in the NT in Gal 4:2 (*hapax legomenon*) and speaks of an appointed day or fixed time. In 4:2 this is the time of coming of age fixed by the father. This figuratively parallels Christ's coming in the fullness of time in v. 3.

household employed to care for him. The two terms Paul uses here are non-specific and speak of all those who care for a boy yet to come of age. Some consider that they parallel *paidagōgos* from 3:24;[17] however, the use of two terms and plural suggest Paul has in mind a wider range of carers of a son before he comes of age including the *paidagōgos*. With that said, the impact is the same.

The first term *epitropos* is used three times in the LXX of a significant administrator of a King (2 Macc 11:1; 13:2; 14:2). In the NT, Chuza is in this position in relation to Herod (Luke 8:3). In Matt 20:8, it is used of the manager of a vineyard, who is analogous to a royal figure appointed to govern God's vineyard, Israel. Josephus uses *epitropos* of people in a range of significant political positions under a king. Examples include a King's steward (*Ant.* 7.267), those in financial management (*Ant.* 7.369; 8.59), a governor (*Ant.* 9.247), a procurator (*Ant.* 15.65), and significant rulers of a kingdom (*Ant.* 10.5; 11.61).

The second term, *oikonomos*, is linked to *oikos* (household) and refers to a significant leader in a home, literally or more broadly. In the LXX, it is someone overseeing the king's palace, i.e., his household,[18] and other significant but subordinate political officers.[19] It has a similar sense in the Gospels where it is employed of managers in parables (Luke 12:42; 16:1, 3, 8), and by Peter of Christians as administrators of God's grace (1 Pet 4:10). Paul uses it of Epaphras, who was a significant Corinthian administrator (Rom 16:23), of Christian leaders as administrators of God's household who need be faithful (1 Cor 4:1–2), and elders (Tit 1:7).

A Roman boy was under the *tutela impuberis* ('guardianship of a minor') or *tutela testamentaria* ('guardianship established by testament').[20] He was governed by a range of carers including a wet nurse until weaned at eighteen to twenty-four months, a

17. For example, Longenecker, *Galatians*, 162: 'There can be no doubt that they are meant to be synonymous with παιδαγωγὸς ("supervisory guardian").'
18. See 1 Kings 4:6; 16:9; 18:3; 2 Kings 18:18, 37; 19:2; Isa 36:3, 22; 37:2.
19. See 1 Esd 4:47, 49; 8:64; Esth 1:8; 8:9.
20. Longenecker, *Galatians*, 163.

tutor or *paidagōgos* until the coming of age (see 3:24), teachers at schools from age seven to twelve, the *grammaticus* in the home from twelve to sixteen who taught language, literature, music, philosophy and basic rhetoric, and then the *rhetor* at the rhetorical school who focused on literature, language, and rhetoric. The very elite studied around age eighteen at a foreign academy. Some were instructed at the gymnasium, which often included sexual relationships with the teacher.[21]

However, Longenecker is right to say, 'that Paul, being more interested in application than precise legal details, made the specifics of his illustration conform to his purpose.'[22]

The date set by the father will refer to the birthday and festival of *Liberalia* referred to above. More significantly, it points forward to the point of time God chose to send his Son into the world for its redemption—'the fullness of time' (v. 4).

FORMERLY ENSLAVED TO THE BASIC POWERS (4:3)

In *Galatians 4:3*, Paul draws out the point of his analogy:
Similarly (houtōs. 1:6), **we** (plural *sy*, 1:2) **also** (kai, 1:1), **when** (hote, 1:15) **we were** (second person plural *eimi*, 2:7) **infants** (nēpios, 4:1), **were** (imperfect *eimi*) **enslaved** (perfect passive participle[23] *douloō*, 4:3)[24] **under** (hypo, 1:11) **the basic powers** (plural *stoicheion*, 4:3)[25] **of the world** (genitive *kosmos*).[26]

---

21. Stamps, 'Children,' 197–99.
22. Longenecker, *Galatians*, 164 notes various views of the preciseness of Paul's terms in Greek, Roman, or Jewish contexts. He is right to say that Paul's intent is broader and not every aspect of the analogy important.
23. The clause ἤμεθα δεδουλωμένοι (ēmetha dedoulōmenoi), 'we were enslaved' is periphrastic. See the notes on 1:22 for the periphrastic.
24. The verb δουλόω (douloō), which is related to *doulos* (slave), means 'enslave' and is used once in 4:3, of those who, before Christ, were enslaved to the elemental principles (stoicheia).
25. The noun στοιχεῖον (stoicheion) is slippery, speaking of the elemental principles of a range of things like the world itself (the elements, so 2 Pet 3:10, 12), music, religion, philosophy, and spiritual forces. It is used twice in Galatians. In 4:3, it is either a description of the law (if 'we' is Jewish Christians), or all religious and philosophical basic ideas which enslave all humanity (if 'we' is general)—as used in 4:9. Paul uses the term in Col 2:8 of elemental ideas/spirits of the world/universe to which the

This verse must be interpreted with consideration of the preceding. There are issues here. First, who is the 'we' Paul has in mind? As with the uses of 'we' in 3:13–14, 23–25, at one level, it would seem to obviously refer to the Jews (in contrast to 'you,' the Galatians), a view defended by many.[27] However, as noted concerning these earlier verses, 'we' and 'you' function at two levels throughout the passage.[28] On the one hand, 'we' who are under guardians and managers (like the law as *paidagōgos*), would seem to speak of Jews. However, the plural 'guardians and managers' seems strange. Further, in 3:13–29, while there is a 'we-you'/Jewish Christian-Galatian antithesis, it is not quite absolute. So, 3:14, the blessing of Abraham comes to the gentiles, 'so that *we* might receive the promised Spirit through faith'—the 'we' of 3:14 here is universal. As noted concerning 3:13, 23–25, while the 'we' applies first to Jews, it speaks of something greater to the Galatians—they too are free from the law (which they were never under), and so must not yield to it. Similarly, when Paul uses 'you' in 3:26–29, while he is directly addressing the Galatians, all believers are in mind. All are children of God through faith, all who are 'baptized into Christ have put on Christ,' and '*all* are one in Christ Jesus,' including Jew and Greek.

Colossians died (2:20). See also Heb 5:12. I have chosen the translation 'elemental powers' as 4:9 indicates that Paul considers demonic forces to be active in the subjugation of the Galatians. He likens coming under the law to be similar. Hence, he is thinking of law in 4:3 not just merely in terms of a false philosophy or ideology, but a power that enslaves. He may have in mind demonic forces using what is good (the law, Rom 7:12) to subjugate people. We see this in the Temptation where Satan distorts Scripture against Christ (Matt 4:1–11 and par.). Similarly, the Judaizers in the backdrop of this letter are using biblical texts to impose the law. Alternatively, the law itself acts as a power that excites sin and enslaves.

26. The noun κόσμος (*kosmos*), 'world, universe,' is used three times in Galatians: of people's enslavement to elemental principles of the world (in its fallenness) (4:3), and of the world crucified to Paul in Christ, and he to the world (6:14).

27. Longenecker, *Galatians*, 190; Bruce, *Galatians*, 193 (primarily).

28. Similarly, Moo, *Galatians*, 260 notes that 'it is very difficult to find any consistent pattern in Paul's use of pronouns in Galatians; rhetorical concerns and context seem to be the more important issues. In this case, Paul's application of the situation he describes to the Galatian Christians in 4:8 makes it likely that the ἡμεῖς refers to Christians generally.'

So, as we come to the 'we' in 4:3, on one level, Jews are in mind, but in fact, it is universal.

This inclusiveness is seen in 4:8–9 where he asks the Galatians (you) who were previously enslaved to false deities but are now God's children how they can countenance turning back 'to the elementary principles' (*stoicheia*). This use makes no sense if they were previously not under *stoicheia*, albeit different manifestations of the *stoicheia* than the Jews. Hence, here Paul seems to be speaking of the common human experience of all cultures being enslaved to *stoicheia* in their philosophical and religious systems. The Jews are under the law. The gentiles are under their wide range of philosophical and religious ideas and the spiritual forces behind them (below). This verse may give some insight into Paul's view of other religions before Christ's coming. While they are incomplete and flawed, they still have a function as did the law for the Jews.[29]

'When we were infants' refers to vv. 1–2, where Paul used the analogy of a child before coming of age and under those appointed to care for him. Israel under the law were infants under the 'care' of the law, a *paidagōgos* (tutor) and multiple *epitropoi* (guardians) and *oikonomoi* (managers). Similarly, the pagan world was under a range of powers governing them until the coming of Christ who redeemed them.

As infants, they 'were enslaved under the basic principles (*stoicheia*) of the world.' In Jewish Greek literature, the term *stoicheion* is used of the elements from which the world and people are made (Wis 7:17; 19:18; 4 Macc 12:13).[30] This use is found in Josephus (*Ant.* 3.183; *J.W.* 1.377; 6.47) and often in Philo (e.g., *Opif.* 38),[31] It is commonly utilized in the Sibylline Oracles

---

29. Hence, we can read the sermons of Paul in Lystra and Athens and see him draw on Greco-Roman theological and anthropological ideas and build his messages on them (Acts 14:15–17; 17:22–31).

30. In classical thought, the four elements are earth, wind, fire, and aether. Aether fills the region of the universe above the terrestrial sphere.

31. Philo uses the term commonly of the four elements—earth, water, air, fire: *Opif.* 52; 131, 146; *Cher.* 127; *Det.* 7, 8; *Gig.* 22; *Plant.* 10; *Her.* 134, 140, 152; 197, 209, 226, 227 (out of which the Tabernacle utensils are made and symbolize); *Somn.* 1.21, 212; *Abr.* 162 (whether there is a fifth of which the celestial bodies are made); *Mos.* 1.96, 97, 155,

of the elements the world, which is made from more than four such things (Sib. Or. Pro. 102)—air, earth, sea, light, vault of heaven, days, and nights.[32]

A second use not found in the LXX but in the Pseudepigrapha and especially in Philo is of language in such things as letters of the alphabet,[33] syllables of a word (Sib. Or. 12.165), a mark on the forehead (T. Sol. 17.4), elements of grammar and numbers (Philo, *Opif.* 126, 127; *Leg.* 1.14).[34] Philo also uses it of philosophical principles (Philo, *Det.* 7), (*Her.* 210), and the divine elements from which the soul is formed (*Deus* 46). The other use is of spiritual beings (demons, gods) who are also astral bodies (T. Sol. 8.2; 15.5; 18.1, 2 [first to third-century AD]; T. Adam 1.3 [second to fifth-century AD]).

Outside of Paul, it is found in Heb 5:12 of the 'elementary teachings' of God's oracles—the basics of the faith. Peter uses it of the basic elements of the cosmos that will be destroyed by fire, a use similar to the first common Jewish Greek mentioned above (2 Pet 3:10, 12). In Paul, outside of Galatians, the term is used only in Colossians 2:8, 20 of 'the *stoicheia* of the world (*kosmos*)' which the Colossians died to in Christ. In Colossians 2:8, it refers to a heresy which includes philosophical ideas, empty deceit, and human traditions. These include the legal demands of the law which is now nailed to the cross (Col 2:14). To such things the Colossians have died, a similar idea to Gal 4:8–9—the Galatians and all Christians are set free from enslavement to *stoicheia*.

Here, in 4:3, 8, in a similar way, the law and the religious and philosophical traditions of the Galatians before their conversion, appear to be in mind. Hence, it speaks of ideas of a particular

---

156, 216; 2.53, 65, 88, 121, 148, 154, 251, 267, 286; *Decal.* 31; *Spec.* 1.208, 266, 294, 328; 2.151, 255; *Virt.* 73; *Praem.* 44; *Contempl.* 3, 4; *Aet.* 6, 29, 61, 74, 78, 82, 90, 103, 107, 109, 111, 116, 123, 144; *Flacc.* 125; *Legat.* 80; *Prov.* 2.45, 53.

32. See Sib. Or. 2.206–207, cf. Sib. Or. 3.80; 8.337, 447.

33. See Sib. Or. 5.15; 11.142, 154, 190, 196; 12.16, 97, 238, 271; 14.183; Apoc. Dan. 3.12. These are usually of a specific numbered letter (e.g., first, third) referring to a King or historical figure whose name starts with it (Augustus, Alexander, Adam, Aenus, Philip, Galba, Pertinax, Alexander Severus, Constantine).

34. See also Philo, *Leg.* 3.121; *Sacr.* 74; *Agr.* 136; *Her.* 190, 282; *Cong.* 150; *Mut.* 61, 77; *Abr.* 81; *Aet.* 113; *Flacc.* 55.

culture that are revealed in and through Christ. Some find here spiritual powers, reflected in the NIV translation 'elemental spiritual forces of the world,' (cf. ESV, 'elemental spirits' in Col 2:8, 20). A spiritual interpretation finds support in the Pseudepigrapha (above), although these writings postdate the NT and leave us unsure whether *stoicheion* was used in this way at this time. Furthermore, seeing spirits as an aspect of *stoicheia* fits the worldview of the Roman world. In addition, Paul elsewhere on occasion refers to Satan and evil spirits.[35] There is no doubt he recognizes them as a factor as they work spiritually in the world of human life, corrupting, deceiving, binding, and destroying.

The strongest argument for seeing here some kind of spiritual power as an element of Paul's thought is the repeated use in 4:8–9. Here, he speaks of the Galatian's enslavement to false gods. As they are now walking in relationship with God, how is it that they would turn back to the weak and beggarly *stoicheia*?

Finally, a first-century worldview, and that of many non-western nations today, does not hold to the sacred-secular divide westerners are used to. Religion and life are totally enmeshed. Everything is religious. Hence, we cannot separate ideology from religion. This non-dualistic perspective is best understood today as we consider Islamic nations where there is no separation of church and state.

As such, while we can say that here in 4:3, the emphasis is on the law, it also involves other ideological, religious, and philosophical ideas that bind people. In this sense, the *stoicheia* are the religious and philosophical ideologies, ideas, and legal requirements from the religion of Israel and found throughout all cultures of the world and manifest in different ways. Still, the spiritual dimension is there at least in the conceptual background. Conversely, in 4:9, the spiritual power aspect of *stoicheia* is in the foreground while the ideological dimension is less overt. Still, both are in mind. Hence, I have translated *stoicheia* here as 'elemental powers.' The law although

---

35. See for example Rom 16:20; 1 Cor 5:5; 7:5; 10:20, 21; 2 Cor 2:11; 11:14; 12:7; Eph 2:2; 4:27; 6:10–17; 1 Thess 2:18; 2 Thess 2:9; 1 Tim 1:20; 3:6, 7; 4:1; 5:15; 2 Tim 2:26. Other passages like Romans 8:38–39 may also refer to spiritual powers.

good, holy, and righteous, in the hands of Satan and his emissaries, is a power that serves to enslave people. It is thus a power.

So, Paul's point is that prior to their conversions, Christians are held captive to false ideologies and spiritual powers. This subjugation to elemental powers is true in our context. We are all born into cultural settings with assumed preset accepted ideas, good and bad. While in western countries, spiritual beings are things of fantasy books and movies, they work their power in and through these ideological systems.

In my NZ context, these ideologies have shifted markedly in the last fifty years. Whereas in the mid-twentieth century, these might include such things as the importance of heterosexual marriage, family, work, community voluntarism, largely national isolationism, rugby, racing, and beer, all wrapped up in eurocentrism; these have shifted. We still value education, health, justice, democracy, egalitarianism, and to a large extent, compassion. However, there have been radical shifts in the direction of individual freedom, consumerism, feminism, freedom of sexual orientation, gender fluidity, tolerance, multiculturalism, globalism, and radical changes in life from science and technology. While many of these have aspects consistent with the gospel and have brought many gains, we need to dwell deep in the gospel and identify the *stoicheia* to which we are enslaved and in Christ, by his Spirit, find God's freedom.

We must also examine our church traditions which can easily move from grace to being dominated by law. Satan corrupts God's people, and what are good doctrines and laws can become *stoicheia* which enslave. This can happen in any church but is especially problematic with longstanding denominations with much church law (e.g., my own Presbyterian heritage).

We need to ensure that we are being shaped by the gospel and not the assumed *stoicheia*, whatever our culture. We must recognize the 'wisdom of the world' (1 Cor 1:20; 3:19), the 'spirit of the world' (1 Cor 2:12) and not be conformed to it. Rather, we must be transformed with renewed minds living out of the wisdom of God, presenting ourselves as living sacrifices, and emulating the pattern of Christ in the world (Rom 12:1–2).

One final comment on this verse involves Paul's use of *kosmos*, 'world.' The term can mean 'universe' in Greek philosophical thought, and so if we read *stoicheion* as spiritual beings, it can have that wider sense. Here it more likely means 'the world.' This is the geographical world that God created (Rom 1:20; Eph 1:4), in which humanity lives, that is full of languages, sounds (1 Cor 14:10), and people—the foolish, the wise, the weak, the strong, the low, and despised (1 Cor 1:27–28), and the immoral and sinful (1 Cor 5:10). This is the world into which we brought nothing, and from which we will take the same (1 Tim 6:7).

This is a cosmos invaded by sin and death (Rom 5:12, 13) and false idols which are really non-existent (1 Cor 8:4),is ruled falsely by demons (Eph 2:2), that is full of grief producing death (2 Cor 7:10), that has its own false wisdom (1 Cor 1:20; 3:19), is enslaved to its false ideologies (Gal 4:3; Col 2:8, 20), that does not know God (1 Cor 1:21), and that sucks our attention and worries (1 Cor 7:33, 34).

Yet, this is the world into which Jesus came to save sinners (1 Tim 1:15), and in which he is believed in (1 Tim 3:16), and that is now passing away as Christ's power is working in it to transform it (1 Cor 7:31). This is the world that God and his people will judge (Rom 3:6, 19; 1 Cor 6:2) and condemn (1 Cor 11:32), in which God is present even in its fallenness (Eph 2:12), and to which believers are crucified (Gal 6:14).

This world is and will be reconciled (Rom 11:12; 2 Cor 5:19); this is the world that will be healed and believers will inherit (Rom 4:13; 11:12; 1 Cor 3:22), in which God's children are to shine (Phil 2:15), in which the gospel is proclaimed (Rom 1:8; 2 Cor 1:12), and in which the gospel is spreading (Col 1:6) even if it repudiates God's missionaries (1 Cor 4:9, 13).

THE SON SENT, OF A WOMAN, UNDER THE LAW (4:4)

In *Galatians 4:4*, Paul turns from the state of enslavement to liberation in Christ:

But (*de*, 1:15) **when** (*hote*, 1:15) **the fullness** (*plērōma*)[36] **of time** (genitive *chronos*, 4:1) **came** (aorist *erchomai*, 1:21), **God** (*Theos*, 1:1) **sent** (*exapostellō*)[37] **his** (genitive *autos*, 1:1) **son** (*huios*, 1:16), **born** (*ginomai*, 2:17) **from** (*ek*, 1:1) **a woman** (*gynē*),[38] **born** (*ginomai*) **under** (*hypo*, 1:11) **the law** (*nomos*, 2:16).

'But when' (*hote de*) is used in 1:15 in the context of Paul's life in which he was greatly advancing in Judaism and God intervened in his life to reveal to him his Son Jesus (cf. 2:11, 12). It has the same power as *nyni de* ('but now'), *de* here carrying strong adversative force (see further 1:15).

'The fullness of time' uses *chronos* from 4:1, where it speaks of the period when an heir is an infant. Thus, while the world was in its infancy, at the right time, God sent his Son. 'Fullness' is also used of time in Eph 1:10, with *kairos*, where God's plan is to unite everything in heaven and earth in him.

'The fullness of time' corresponds to *prosthesmias* in 4:2, the date set by the Father for the child's coming of age.[39] Fullness speaks of completeness.[40] Here it is the culmination of a period of time (which has come to completion [fullness]), and so speaks

---

36. The noun πλήρωμα (*plērōma*) is found once in Galatians, in 4:4, temporally, of 'the fullness of time'—which speaks of God's oversight of time and his choice of the moment to introduce his Son into the world to save it.

37. The verb ἐξαποστέλλω compounds *ek* (from) and *apostellō* (send) which is found twice in Galatians in one section, 4:4, 6. While it means 'sent from' here it is used synonymously with *apostellō*. In 4:4 it is of the sending of God's Son, and in 4:6 of the sending of the Spirit of his Son into the hearts of believers. These are Paul's only two uses of the term. Otherwise, it is used ten times in the NT and once in the shorter longer ending of Mark.

38. The noun γυνή (*gynē*) is the common Greek term for 'woman' or 'wife.' It is used once in Gal 4:4 of the woman who gave birth to Christ, Mary. It can hardly here mean 'wife,' otherwise we are into Greek religions which have gods and goddesses producing offspring.

39. Bruce, *Galatians*, 194.

40. Outside of Paul, *plērōma* is used of a patch which *fills* the rip in a cloth (Matt 9:16; Mark 2:21), a full basket (Mark 8:20), and in John of Christ's fullness, which we have received, and from this, grace upon grace, the Spirit (John 1:16). Paul uses *plērōma* of the fullness of all the gentiles who will come into Christ (Rom 11:12, 25), the fullness of blessing in of Christ (Rom 15:29), the fullness of things in the earth which belong to God (1 Cor 10:26), the fullness of Christ which fills all things (Eph 1:23), and of believers filled with the fullness of God (Eph 3:19) as was Christ (Col 1:19; 2:9),

of a point in time. 'The πλήρωμα τοῦ χρόνου [fullness of time] is *the* καιρός [time] of world history. But the χρόνος [time] here is not in itself the καιρός, but only in that it has come to fullness.'[41]

So, 'fullness' here has the sense of the completion of a period of time, an age, so to speak, with the eschatological age beginning in the coming of Christ. It is the 'turning of the ages' we have the end of one eon and the launch of another—the line between two epochs. The phrase speaks of God as sovereign over time, acting out his will in history. It is eschatological, God setting in motion his purposes to save his world and bring it to its consummation in the sending of his Son.

Galatians 4:4b–5 is a well-recognized chiastic structure with other interesting symmetry:

A1   God sent (**exapostellō**) his Son (**huios**)
    B1   Born (**ginomai**) from a woman, born (**ginomai**) **under the law**
    B2   In order to (**hina**) redeem (**exagorazō**) those **under the law**
A2   So that (**hina**) they might receive adoption (**huiothesia**).

The chiasm is seen in the repetition of *huio-* language in A and A' and the repetition of 'under the law' in B and B'. There are also repetitions of *ex-* language, *ginomai* (born), and *hina*. The poetic dimensions suggest this could be something used in worship—something creedal or hymnic.

The first part of the chiasm speaks of God sending his Son. Paul uses *exapostellō* rather than the more usual terms for send, *pempō* and *apostellō* (cf. apostle), the term compounding *ek* (from) with the latter term and so meaning 'send out, away.' However, it is used here with the same meaning as *apostellō*. Paul uses it twice, here of the sending of Christ by God, and in 4:6 of the sending of the Spirit into the hearts of believers.[42]

Otherwise, he uses it of 'fulfil;' love fulfils the law (Rom 13:10) and of believers reaching maturity of 'the measure of the *full* stature of Christ' (Eph 4:13).

41. Hübner, 'χρόνος,' 3.488.

42. Otherwise *apostellō* is a Lukan term used of someone sent away empty-handed (Luke 1:53; 20:10, 11), Jacob sending his sons to get food from Egypt (Acts 7:12), Paul being sent to Tarsus from Caesarea (Acts 9:30) and from Berea to the coast (Acts 17:14),

The use of *apostellō* language calls to mind Paul's apostleship; he is sent through God and Jesus (1:1). There is a subtle plug here for Paul's authority. Similarly, God sent the apostles of Jerusalem (1:17, 19)—Paul is sent as they are (2:7–9). This same God also sent Jesus and the Spirit. For Paul, the sending of Christ, here again, called 'his Son,' is an apostolic act of God. God is a sending God, as John emphasizes.

This second part of the chiasm is an example of parallelism:

A1 born   (*genomenon*) from a woman
A2 born   (*genomenon*) under the law

'Born of a woman' uses the aorist middle participle of the common *ginomai* (668 times in the NT), which more often means 'come, become, be' (see 2:17), but here is used in the sense of 'born.' Similarly, in Rom 1:3, Christ 'has been *born* (*ginomai*) from the seed of David according to the flesh') and in Phil 2:7 Christ 'has been *born* (*ginomai*) in human likeness.'

Here he is 'born of a woman,' using *gynē*, the common Greek term for a 'woman.' The woman in mind is clearly Mary, although she is not named. This verse is one of the few references to Jesus' birth in Paul, his emphasis being Jesus' sacrificial death and resurrection. Earlier, Paul referred to his own mother's womb from which he was set apart (1:14). Here it is Jesus' mother. Later, Paul himself will identify himself as the mother of the Galatians (4:18–19). Similarly, Sarah is 'our mother' (4:26). We have an implicit reference to women of great importance in Christian history.

'Born under the law' repeats the same verb in parallel (see above). The clause does not speak of Jesus being under the curse of the law [43] but speaks of Jesus being born into Judaism and subjugation to the law of Moses.[44] This submission is seen from

Barnabas sent to Antioch from Jerusalem (Acts 11:22), God sending an angel (Acts 12:11), the message of salvation (Acts 13:26), and Christ sending Paul to the gentiles (Acts 22:21). It is found in the much later shorter longer ending of Mark of Christ sending out the disciples in mission (Mark 16:8).

43. In-Gyu Hong, "Being 'under the law' in Galatians," *ERT* 26 (2002): 360–70; T. A. *The Curse of the law and the Crisis in Galatia: Reassessing the Purpose of Galatians*, WUNT 225 (Tübingen: Mohr Siebeck, 2007), 35–36.
44. Moo, *Galatians*, 266.

the start in his circumcision on the eighth day, an event recorded by Luke 2:21. Furthermore, Jesus participated in synagogue worship (e.g., Luke 4:15–30), attended festivals,[45] and celebrated the Sabbath (e.g., Mark 1:21). Christ's birth under the law and his submission to it is critical for his role as savior. Although Paul does not state that Jesus lived a fully perfect life under the law, it is implied in his view of Jesus as sinless—one who 'knew no sin' (2 Cor 5:21). As such, he qualifies for justification on the basis of the law. Whereas we are sinners and lawbreakers, he is not. We are in him. His obedience becomes our obedience. So, we are justified under both the law and by grace—in him.

REDEEMED AND ADOPTED (4:5)

Galatians 4:5 should not be separated from 4:4, as the *hina* clause stands in parallel to part B of the chiasm in v. 4b, although this can be read as two purpose/result clauses flowing from born under the law (kind of like two bullet points). Rather, they are consecutive with the first *hina* clause giving both the result and purpose of God's sending of his Son and his birth to a woman under the law. This is then followed by a second *hina* clause giving the overall consequence which stands in parallel to 'God sent his Son.' This is clear because of the chiastic structure:

in order to (*hina*, 1:16) **redeem** (*exagorazō*, 3:13) **those** (plural *ho*, 1:1) **under** (*hypo*, 1:11) **the law** (*nomos*, 2:16), **so that** (*hina*) **we might receive** (second person plural subjunctive *apolambanō*)[46] **adoption** (*huiothesia*).[47]

---

45. E.g., John 2:13; 4:45; 5:1; 7:10; 10:22; 11:55.

46. The verb ἀπολαμβάνω compounds *apo*, 'from' and *lambanō*, 'receive,' and so yields the idea of receiving something from a source (it can also mean 'recover, get back' or 'take away'). In Paul, God is the source in its three uses. It is not common, found once in Galatians, in 4:5, of believers receiving adoption as God's children. It is only used twice else in Paul; in Rom 1:27 of indecent men receiving a penalty for their sin and in Col 3:24 of believers receiving an inheritance from God for their work.

47. The noun υἱοθεσία (*huiothesia*) compounds *huios*, 'son' and *thesis*, 'position' (cf. English thesis), yielding the '*position* of a son;' in other words, legally a son—'adoption.' The term in the NT is Pauline with Paul using it four times elsewhere (Rom 8:15, 23; 9:4; Eph 1:5).

The first *hina* clause parallels 'born of a woman, born under the law,' repeating the phrase 'under the law.' *Hina* can signify a purpose or a result clause, and here it is purposive—with the purpose of redeeming those under the law.' This clause gives a clear statement of God's missional purpose. He sent his Son to become human living under Jewish law to redeem Israel, his people. Such an emphasis is very Matthean as Matthew stresses Jesus' mission to the 'lost sheep of Israel' (Matt 10:6; 15:24). Similarly, as Paul says in Rom 15:8, 'Christ became a servant to the circumcised.' Earlier in 3:13–14, Paul wrote similarly:

Christ redeemed (*exagorazō*) us from the curse *of the law* by becoming for us a curse; as it is written "Cursed [is] everyone who is hanged on a tree, *so that* (*hina*) the blessing of Abraham might come to the nations in Christ Jesus, *so that* (*hina*) we might receive the promise of the Spirit through faith.

The upshot is that God sent his son to redeem Israel. That is, to set them free from enslavement to the law as he formerly set Israel free from Egypt and Babylon (on redeem, see 3:13). Here, it is redemption from enslavement to the law. In this enslavement, Israel was held in check by the law, imprisoned, tutored, guarded, and managed by it; yet they were not bought into salvation through it. The law has no latent power to save. Only God can save, and his salvation is by grace through faith.

The tragedy of the salvation story is that Israel, in the main, rejected Jesus. They heard the gospel, but, unlike the Galatians (3:2, 5), the word was not heard with faith (Rom 10:14–17). However, as is the case in salvation history, a remnant has heard the word and responded by faith, having been chosen by grace (Rom 11:5). This remnant includes Paul, Barnabas, and those other Jews who believe in Jesus, like the 'brothers and sisters' in Antioch (1:2), Peter, Jacob, John, and the other believers in Jerusalem. They are the redeemed. The Judaizers are acting on behalf of their former slave-master, the law, seeking to return them to Egypt, to Babylon. They must not allow themselves to return willingly. They are then kind of like Israel in the wilderness considering returning to Egypt. Even worse, they are like Israel already in the land (justified by faith), and yet wanting to return to slavery in Egypt! They must not.

The second *hina* clause stands in chiastic parallel to 4:4b: God sent his Son—'so that (*hina*) we might receive adoption (*huiothesia*).' It speaks of the result (rather than purpose) of the redemption of those under the law. 'We' here would naturally include the Jews, who were under the law, but are now redeemed. But, as throughout Galatians, 'we' is slippery, here; it clearly refers to at least Jews, but also to 'all' who God adopts as his children (cf. 3:26—'you are *all* sons (children) of God.' It rhetorically reminds the Galatians that this is also their own status in Christ, and so they must not contemplate joining the Judaizers.[48]

The Greek *huiothesia* compounds *huios* (son, child) with *thesis* (placing) (cf. Eng. 'thesis'). In Greek thought, it means 'adoption as a child.'[49] The term is absent from Jewish Greek literature, so it is a decidedly Greek thought. In fifth-century Greek culture, adoption was permitted and took place in the Agora before the assembled citizens and Tribune. Sometimes, it was to deal with the problem of having no heir. The adopted son is presented to the family and inscribed in city records. Often a will was also created, and the adoptee agreed to care for the parent so that they retained their name, and the family was maintained. Adoption by a deity was rarely used in Greek religious thought. However, Heracles Zeus persuaded his wife Hera to adopt him, and she took him and let him slip to earth under her robes, mimicking natural birth, and so he was legitimized.

---

48. See the discussion in Moo, *Galatians*, 266–67 who notes the differing views. The majority view is that both clauses refer to all believers, however, it can hardly be said that redeeming those under the law includes gentiles (see for example Bruce, *Galatians*, 197; Moo, *Galatians*, 266–67 who see this as general). Some consider that in the 'we' in the second part only includes the adoption of Jews as sons by faith, i.e., Jewish Christians (e.g., Longenecker, *Galatians*, 172; Witherington, *Grace*, 288–89). Some think it shifts to purely gentile Christians, which is very unlikely (e.g., Frank J. Matera, *Galatians*, SP [Collegeville, MN: Liturgical Press, 1992], 156; Hays, 'Galatians,' 284). Others, as I do here, consider that while the first part refers to Jews, the second 'we' refers to all believers (Betz, *Galatians*, 208; Dunn, *Galatians*, 216–17).
49. P. W. von Martitz, 'υἱοθεσία,' in *TDNT* 8:397.

In the NT, it speaks not of natural sonship (as in the case of Jesus), but humans adopted by God's sovereign act. Paul uses it once of Jewish adoption,[50] Israel adopted as God's children by covenant relationship. Twice else in Romans he uses the term. In Rom 8:15 as here, it is linked with the receipt of the Spirit—'you received a Spirit of adoption in which we cry out, "Abba, Father".' The receipt of the Spirit sees the person adopted legally, sealed as it were by the Spirit, guaranteeing redemption (cf. 2 Cor 1:20–21). In Rom 8:23, adoption is in the future, speaking of the final ratification of this adoption at the resurrection, 'the redemption of our bodies.' In the meantime, the Christian experience is longing and inward groaning.

Other than 4:5, the only other use of *huiothesia* is in Eph 1:5 of Christians being predestined for adoption as God's children through Christ Jesus in accordance with God's love, pleasure, and will. This refers to both present state of adoption as God's children and the future consummation of this. Moo rightly says of this adoption: 'In claiming that Christians enjoy υἱοθεσία, then, Paul is claiming not only that we believers become his adopted children, with all the rights and privileges pertaining to that status, but also that we have become his people, inheriting the status and blessings promised to his people Israel.'[51]

Here in Galatians 4:5, adoption coincides with liberation from the law.[52] As such, how can the Galatians Christians, Jew or Greek, consider going under the law which only serves to enslave? As in Rom 8, it is linked to the receipt of the Spirit and the familial cry, 'Abba, Father.' It speaks of redemption from the status of being a slave to one of being God's son or daughter.

This verse is a magnificent statement of our identity and status in God. We are his children; he is our Dad. He has poured love into our hearts by his Spirit, and we are signed and sealed to be delivered for final transformation at the culmination of the ages. Finally, we are heirs—this world is to be ours, to be shared, enjoyed, and further developed in love. Glory be to God. Amen.

---

50. See Rom 9:4, cf. Exod 4:22; Jer 31:20 (38:20 LXX).
51. Moo, *Galatians*, 268.
52. See also the discussion in E. Schweizer, 'υἱοθεσία,' in *TDNT* 8:399.

THE SPIRIT SENT, THE CRY 'ABBA FATHER' (4:6)

In *Galatians 4:6*, Paul continues drawing out the implications of our divine son/daughtership:

And (*de*, 1:15) **because** (*hoti*, 1:6) **you are** (second person present *eimi*, 1:7) **sons and daughters** (plural *huios*, 1:16), **God** (*Theos*, 1:1) **sent** (*exapostellō*, 4:4) **the Spirit** (*pneuma*, 3:2) **of his** (genitive *autos*, 1:1) **Son** (*huios*, 1:16) **into** (*eis*, 1:16) **our** (plural genitive *sy*, 1:2)[53] **hearts** (plural *kardia*)[54] **crying** (*krazō*),[55] **'Abba** (*abba*)[56] **Father** (*patēr*, 1:1).'

The *de* is consecutive, 'and,' rather than adversative, 'but.' The *hoti* with it is causal, 'because …'[57] The causal *hoti* helps resolve dilemmas concerning who is in mind with the pronouns 'we' and 'you.' If we take 'you' as the gentile Galatians and the 'we' as Jews, we end up with Paul saying that because the Galatians are children, God sent the Spirit into Jewish hearts. Clearly, this is flawed. As such, as argued below, the 'we-you' antithesis is not sharp but focuses on a particular group within the collective (whether the Galatians—'you,' and the Jews—'we').

'You are sons' sees Paul turn from the inclusive 'we' to target the Galatians more particularly, 'you.' As with 'we' in the previous verse, 'you' is a little uncertain. Clearly, the Galatians are in mind, but what he says applies to all believers. This generality is seen

53. **Variant:** Some witnesses prefer 'your' (*hymōn*) rather than 'our' (*hēmōn*). This is a natural adjustment to the 'you are sons and daughters' in the first part of the verse. However, the strength of support of 'our' (P46 ℵ A B C D* F G 1739 etc.) outweighs 'your' (D2 Ψ etc.). 'Our' is also the more difficult reading.
54. There is one reference in Galatians to the common noun καρδία (*kardia*), 'heart,' in 4:6 of God sending the Spirit of Christ into the hearts of believers (fifty–two times in Paul). It of course includes more than the affections as we might use it in common Christian parlance but is the seat of the mind and affections.
55. The verb κράζω (*krazō*) is found once in Galatians, in 4:6. It implies 'cry out' loudly, which we as God's children can do, crying 'Abba, Father.' Otherwise, it is only found thrice in Paul—very similarly in Rom 8:15 and in Rom 9:27 of Isaiah crying out concerning Israel.
56. One of the few examples of Aramaic carrying over into the Greek NT (e.g., *amēn*), ἀββά (*Abba*) means 'father,' and is a term of affection. It is found once in Gal 4:6. Paul uses it only elsewhere in Rom 8:15 in a similar way. The one other use is Jesus' cry in the Garden of Gethsemane, Mark 14:36.
57. Wallace, *Greek Grammar*, 461.

in the shift from 'you' here to 'into *our* hearts,' indicating that while focusing on the Galatians, he is thinking of all believers. The verb 'to be' is a second person present and so speaks of a present state of affairs—a status, a state of being. The Galatians are now God's children. They do not have to wait for the final judgment. They are now adopted. This status is the starting point of 'self-identity'—I am a child of God. One could perhaps add, 'with whom he is well pleased,' as God said to Jesus at his baptism before his ministry began. So, it is with us. Our adoption should spur us on to action that pleases the God who makes us his kids.

Because believers have this status as God's children, God sent his Spirit into the hearts of his children (see comments on 'our' above). Whereas in v. 4 God sent his Son, here, he sends his Spirit. Paul uses the same verb *exapostellō*, discussed on v. 4. It effectively means the same as the more common Greek terms for 'sending,' *pempō* and *apostellō* (it is a compound of the latter). This sentence speaks of God as a sending God. He sent his Son (v. 4). He sends his Spirit (here). The notion of the Spirit being sent is found twice in John of the Father sending the Paraclete (helper, comforter, advocate) in Christ's name, and of Christ sending the Spirit who proceeds from the Father (John 14:26; 15:16). Peter also speaks of the Spirit sent from heaven (1 Pet 1:12). God also sent Paul as his *apostolos* (1:1) as he sent the other *apostoloi*, Peter, John, and Jacob. The Spirit sends others into mission, including Paul (Acts 13:4). God as a sending God, is a great Johannine theme,[58] but it is not absent from Paul. Paul also often sends emissaries, especially Timothy (e.g., Phil 2:19). He sends letters (like Galatians). Central to mission is sending, and God is the sender. Jesus, as God's appointed King, also sends apostles. As his people whom he sent, we as leaders emulate him, sending others into the mission field.

The Spirit is described as the 'Spirit of his Son,' linking this with the sending of the Son born of a woman under the law in 4:4. The Spirit of this One, who was conceived (by the Spirit), was

---

58. The language of sending is used of John (e.g., John 1:6), Jesus (e.g., 3:16), disciples (e.g., 4:48), and the Spirit (e.g., 14:26).

born, died, and rose again, and sits at God's right hand, has now been shared abroad to his people by faith, to God's children. The Spirit features in Ch. 3 where Paul asked the Galatians whether they had received the Spirit from works of the law or faith—answer, faith! (3:2, 5, 14). As such, they must not seek to complete their justification by the flesh, for the weakness of the flesh, subject to sin and death, is not able to do this. They began by the Spirit and must continue to do this (3:3). To receive the fullness of the Abrahamic blessing, they must continue in faith (3:14).

Here, Paul describes the Spirit as the 'Spirit of his Son,' *pneuma* not referring to the spirit of Jesus that animated his life (e.g., Luke 23:46), but another way of describing the Holy Spirit. The most common way of describing the Spirit in the NT is 'the Spirit' (some 105 times). The second most common is the Holy Spirit (ninety times),[59] found in Paul sixteen times, but not in Galatians. Other constructs are used, commonly including God, e.g., 'the Spirit of God.'[60] Outside of Paul, there is a similar close association of the Spirit and Christ. Luke calls the Spirit 'the Spirit of Jesus' (Acts 16:7) and Peter similarly labels him as 'the Spirit of Christ' (1 Pet 1:11). Paul in Rom 8:9 describes the Spirit as both the Spirit of God and the Spirit of Christ and in Phil 1:19 'the Spirit of Jesus Christ.' In 2 Cor 3:17–18, he draws the Spirit and Christ together describing the Spirit as 'the Spirit of the Lord,' stating that 'the Lord is the Spirit,' and speaking of 'the Lord who is the Spirit.' This passage draws Christ and the

---

59. See also, 'Spirit of holiness' (Rom 1:4). The Holy Spirit as a descriptor speaks of the character of the Spirit as other, pure, consecrated and the Spirit's function within people to sanctify them. First, as a status—'holy ones' or 'saints,' people set apart by God for his purposes. Second, in the process of sanctification, the Spirit as the internal power transforming the believer to be more and more like Christ, the image of God, full of the fruit of the Spirit (cf. 2 Thess 2:13).

60. Outside of Paul these include the Spirit of your Father, the Spirit of the Lord, the Spirit of truth, the Spirit of life, the Spirit of grace, and the Spirit of glory and God. Paul uses 'the Spirit of holiness' (Rom 1:4), 'the Spirit of adoption' (Rom 8:15), and the Spirit of wisdom (Eph 1:17). He often uses 'the Spirit of God' (Rom 8:9; 15:19; 1 Cor 2:14; 6:11; 7:40; 12:3; 2 Cor 3:3; Phil 3:3); similarly, the Spirit of him who raised Jesus from the dead (Rom 8:11).

Spirit closely together, not to identify them as the same Being, but that their work coincides. The Spirit continues the work of Jesus Christ Lord on earth.

'Into our hearts' uses *kardia* (cf. Eng. 'cardiac'). In much popular Christianity, the 'heart' as the seat of our emotions stands distinct from the 'mind' as the center of our thought. However, in Paul's fifty-two uses of *kardia*, his use is fluid. At times it stresses the mind even more than the emotions—the heart darkened in understanding (Rom 1:21) and veiled (2 Cor 3:15). The heart is where one's internal voice speaks (Rom 10:6). It can be the center of desire (Rom 1:24; 10:1), of emotional pain (Rom 9:2; 2 Cor 2:4), and of love-based relationship.[61] It is capable of being encouraged (Eph 6:22; Col 2:2; 4:8; 2 Thess 2:17) and strengthened (1 Thess 3:13). At times it is the center of the being where wrath is stored (Rom 2:5), where secrets are held (1 Cor 14:25), which God searches by his Spirit (Rom 8:27), and which prophecy can disclose (1 Cor 14:25).

The heart is where the law is written (Rom 2:15; 2 Cor 3:2–3) and which is circumcised where there is faith (Rom 2:29). The light of God shines on its darkened state and imparts the knowledge of Christ (2 Cor 4:6). It is personified as a being with eyes enlightened by God (Eph 1:18). It is the center of our conviction (Rom 6:17; 1 Cor 7:37; 2 Cor 9:7), belief (Rom 10:8, 9, 10), and eagerness (2 Cor 8:16). God tests the heart, i.e., its resolve and purposes (1 Thess 2:4), and he directs it (2 Thess 3:5). It is to be pure (1 Tim 1:5; 2 Tim 2:22). It is capable of being deceived (Rom 16:18) and can be hardened to reject God and live in alienation from God (Eph 4:18). It is the center of our imaginations (1 Cor 2:9), where purposes are formed (1 Cor 4:5), and which must not be divided (Eph 6:5). The heart is capable of singing praise with gratitude (Eph 5:19; Col 3:16).

At times it is the inner person in contrast to external appearances, the internal being the true person (2 Cor 5:12). It must be guarded along with the mind through prayer so that believers can experience God's peace (Phil 4:7), a peace that one

---

61. See 2 Cor 6:11; 7:3; Phil 1:7; 1 Thess 2:17.

must yield to (Col 3:15). As such, we cannot simply say that the heart is that part of us other than our minds. While the mind is at times distinguished from the heart, the heart is our whole inner being or one portion or aspect of it.

Elsewhere, Paul speaks of the heart as the internal receptacle of the Spirit. So, in Rom 5:5: 'God's love has been poured into *our hearts* through the Holy Spirit which has been given to us.' In 2 Cor 1:22, God anoints believers and places his 'seal on us and *gives us the Spirit in our hearts* as a deposit.' In Eph 3:17, although the Spirit is not explicitly mentioned, the idea of Christ dwelling in the hearts through faith implicitly refers to the Spirit.

Where receipt of the Spirit is concerned, the heart is our whole inner being, into which the Spirit is poured, imparting love, sealing us for redemption, God's own self in our inner selves melding us with him and working his transformation. Our call is to yield to the Spirit. In Gal 5–6, rather than the law in our fallen flesh, the Spirit will be the key to Paul's ethics. Our call in Christ is to live lives fully submissive to the Spirit's gentle nudging.

In 'crying Abba Father,' the term for 'cry' is *krazō*, which refers to a loud cry or a shout with real gusto. Paul only uses it three times, twice of crying 'Abba, Father' (Rom 8:15) and Isaiah's cry cited in Rom 9:27–28 (Isa 10:22–23). In Rom 8:15, the believer, having received a Spirit of adoption rather than one of 'slavery and fear' cries 'Abba, Father.' Here, the Spirit entering the human heart cries the words.

The words cried are those used in the prayer of Jesus in Mark's Gethsemane account (Mark 14:36). Abba is a Greek rendering of the Aramaic אַבָּא, *Abba*, one of the few Aramaic words found in the NT. 'Father' (*patēr*) gives the Greek equivalent. The Greek term is found only in the three NT references in Jewish or Christian Greek literature or wider Greek sources. The term is not used of God in Jewish thought except rarely in the form 'our Father' in two Jewish prayers.[62]

The address 'O Father' is found once in the Greek document Wisdom 14:3. It is, however, used in wider thought of one's

62. H. -W. Kuhn, 'ἀββά,' in *EDNT* 1:1–2

father, where it is used as a nursery term by children. It thus carries the nuance, 'Daddy.'[63] Its use in early Christian writings is intriguing. Kittel notes that in using this term, Jesus 'applies to God a term which must have sounded familiar and disrespectful to His contemporaries because it is [*sic.*] used in everyday life of the family. In other words, He uses the simple "speech of the child to its father."'[64] Paul's use may call to mind its presence in Christian worship, perhaps from the Lord's Prayer. Kittel goes on, 'Jewish usage shows how this Father-child relationship to God far surpasses any possibilities of intimacy assumed in Judaism, introducing indeed something which is wholly new.'[65] Elsewhere in the NT, God is directly addressed as 'Father,' but only in these three instances is the Aramaic retained.[66]

NO LONGER A SLAVE BUT A CHILD AND HEIR (4:7)

Galatians 4:7 completes the unit:

Therefore (*hōste*, 2:13), **you are** (second person *eimi*, 1:7) **no longer** (*ouketi*, 2:20) **a slave** (*doulos*, 1:10) **but** (*alla*, 1:1) **a son or daughter** (*huios*, 1:16), **and** (*kai*, 1:1) **if** (*ei*, 1:7) **[you are] a son or daughter** (*huios*), **then [you are] also** (*kai*, 1:1) **a heir** (*klēronomos*, 3:29) **through** (*dia*, 1:1) **God** (genitive *Theos*, 1:1).[67]

---

63. Kuhn, 'ἀββά,' 1 also notes by NT times it was used by all children and even for old men.

64. G. Kittel, 'ἀββά,' in *TDNT* 1:5–6.

65. Kittel, 'ἀββά,' 6.

66. Including the so-called 'Lord's Prayer (Matt 6:9; Luke 11:2) and elsewhere on the lips of Jesus (Matt 11:25, 26; Luke 10:21, 22; 23:34, 46; John 12:28; 17:1, 5, 11, 21, 24, 25). See also the Gethsemane parallels, Matt 26:39, 42; Luke 22:42 (cf. Mark 11:25; Luke 11:13; 15:1; John 14:16; 16:23, 26). Paul prays to the Father on occasion as in 1:4–5 (2 Cor 1:3; 11:31; Eph 1:3; 3:14; Phil 4:20, cf. Rom 15:6; Eph 2:18; 4:6; 5:20; Col 1:3, 12; 3:17; 2 Thess 2:16). See also Jas 3:9; 1 Pet 1:3. However, none use Abba. We can assume where 'Father' is found on Jesus' lips in prayer, it was originally the Aramaic *Abba*.

67. **Variant:** 'Through God' (*dia Theou*) has good support (P46 ℵ* A B C* 33 1739, etc.). However, there are a range of alternatives including: 'through Christ' (*dia Christou* or *dia Isou Christou*); 'of God' (*Theou*); 'of God and through Christ' (*theou dia Christou*); 'of God through Jesus Christ' (*Theou dia Iēsou Christou*); and 'on the one hand of God, and on the other hand co-heirs of Christ' (*men Theou, synkleronomous de Christou,*' cf. Rom 8:17). Metzger, *Textual Commentary*, 526–27 argues that the unusual *klēronomos dia*

Paul draws out the consequences of believers being redeemed from enslavement to the law, being adopted as God's children, and receiving the Spirit. 'You' strictly speaking, refers to the Galatians (as opposed to the 'we'). However, as throughout Galatians, the pronoun emphasizes the Galatians but is true of all believers—they (and all Christ-believers) are no longer slaves but sons or daughters of God. They are thus not enslaved to elemental principles or spirits. They are no longer subject to the law. If they are his children, then they are heirs through God.

The term 'heir' is *klēronomos* which was used in 3:29 of believers as heirs of the promise of Abraham. This promise is effectively the promise of the world as inheritance, for Abraham is heir to the world (Rom 4:13, cf. Heb 6:12). In Titus 3:7, believers are heirs 'according to the hope of eternal life'—ongoing eternal existence without suffering in a fully healed world.[68] Similarly, Heb 1:14 speaks of believers inheriting salvation (Heb 1:14). In Heb 1:2, Jesus is 'heir of all things,' and in this, we participate (cf. Heb 6:17; 11:7). Jacob speaks of believers as 'heirs of the kingdom' (Jas 2:5, cf. Matt 19:29). In Matthew 5:5, the meek shall 'inherit the earth' (Matt 5:5). A restored cosmos is the kingdom prepared from the foundation of the world (Matt 25:34, cf. Matt 19:28).

In Romans 8:17, believers must experience suffering en route to the glory that awaits them. But this glory is assured for those who persevere in faith. What a privilege to imagine that this world is ours to inherit after our time of service as God's children working for the redemption of our fellow human sojourners! As will be discussed when considering 5:20, those who do not walk in faith but yield to the works of the flesh will fail to inherit this kingdom (cf. 1 Cor 6:9–10).

Theous (heirs through God) is most likely the original not merely because of early attestation, but because it accounts for the other readings.

68. Cf. 1 Cor 15:50; Mark 10:17; Luke 10:25; 18:18; Rev 21:7.

CHAPTER TWENTY-ONE: DO NOT RETURN TO SLAVERY (4:8–11)

Paul now more directly addresses the Galatians. He reminds them of their former life as polytheistic pagans, worshiping and conforming their lives to their many deities. Now, they are walking in relationship with God. As such, he asks them how they can envisage placing themselves under bondage again to the false ideologies and spiritual powers of the world. In verse 10, we get a hint of one of the aspects of the influence of the Judaizers, as the Galatians observe Jewish calendric requirements. In v. 11, Paul speaks of his own concerns in the face of their response—fear that his great efforts to bring Christ to them have been in vain.

THE GALATIANS' PRIOR ENSLAVEMENT TO NON-GODS (4:8)

In *Galatians 4:8* he begins reminding them of their former lives:
But (*alla*, 1:1) **on the one hand** (*men*),[1] **formerly** (*tote*)[2] **when you did not know** (perfect participle *oida*, 2:16) God (*Theos*, 1:1), **you were enslaved** (aorist *douloō*, 4:8) **to those** (dative plural *ho*, 1:10 **[that] by nature** (dative *physis*, 2:15) **are** (present participle *eimi*, 1:7) **not** (*mē*, 1:7) **gods** (plural dative[3] *Theos*).

1. The affirmative particle μέν (*men*) is found three times in Galatians. In 4:8–9, 23 with *de* in a 'on the one hand' (*men*) ... 'on the other hand' (*de*) construct. In Gal 4:24 the 'one the one hand ... on the other hand' is spaced out over three verses with 'on the one hand' speaking of Hagar, and 'on the other hand' of Sarah in v. 26.
2. The adverb τότε (*tote*) refers to earlier time, 'then, in that time, formerly.' It is found three times in Galatians. In 4:8 it speaks of the former time when the Galatians were pagans worshipping idols. In Galatians 4:29, it refers to the time of Ishmael and Isaac. It is consequential in 6:4, carrying the sense 'so then.'
3. The dative θεοῖς (*theios*) is a predicative dative whereby '[t]he dative substantive makes

'But' (*alla*) strikes a strong contrast between the former statement of the Galatians' divine childship and inheritance rights with their former lives in pagan idolatry. Paul here uses *men*, which with *de* in the next verse, forms an 'on the one hand … on the other hand' contrast between the former state of the Galatians and their present status, which is restated in v. 9 regarding knowledge of God.

'Formerly' is *tote*, an adverb of time, which here, as in Rom 6:21, speaks of the Galatians' former state, 'then, in that time.' In 4:29, Paul will use it for a person's past situation 'in that time.' In 6:4, he applies it to the outcome of the present action of self-testing.[4] Here, the emphasis is on what they were before coming to Christ and leads onto Paul challenging them as to how they can even consider returning to such a state.

'Not knowing God' speaks of their pagan idolatrous state in which as polytheists, they worshiped a plethora of gods. The Galatians were clearly mainly a gentile community of Christ believers. Both Romans, Greeks, and local Asians worshiped a range of gods.[5] In Acts, we read, for example, of the attempt to deify Barnabas as Zeus and Paul as Hermes. There was also a temple of Zeus at the entrance of the city. The temple priest sought to make sacrifices of oxen and place garlands of flowers

---

an assertion about another dative substantive, much like a predicate nominative does. The difference, however, is that with the predicate dative, the equative verb is a participle (in the dative case) rather than a finite verb. This category is quite rare.' (Wallace, *Greek Grammar*, 152). Here the participle is οὖσιν (*ousin*, 'were').

4. Overall *tote* is found twelve times in Paul. Elsewhere, *tote* is used by Paul of a future time to come—'when' (1 Cor 16:2), as in 6:4 consequentially of an outcome from a present situation—'then …' (2 Cor 12:10), and eschatologically of the future age—'then' (1 Cor 4:5; 13:12; 15:28, 54).

5. On Roman deities see: 'List of Roman Deities,' in *Wikipedia*, https://en.wikipedia.org/wiki/List_of_Roman_deities; 'Roman God's List,' in *Wikipedia*, http://www.talesbeyondbelief.com/roman-gods/roman-gods-list.htm. On Greek deities: 'List of Greek Gods and Goddesses,' http://www.gods-and-monsters.com/list-of-greek-gods-goddesses.html; 'List of Greek Mythological Figures,' in *Wikipedia*, https://en.wikipedia.org/wiki/List_of_Greek_mythological_figures; 'Greek Gods,' http://www.theoi.com/greek-mythology/greek-gods.html; on Asian gods see 'Asia Minor,' http://www.sacred-texts.com/cla/orrp/orrp07.htm. See also D. E. Aune, 'Religion, Greco-Roman,' *DNTB* 918–25.

on the apostolic pair (Acts 14:12–18). Roman myth and archaeology support that Zeus and Hermes were worshiped in Lystra.[6] The Imperial Cult was of great significance with some buildings dedicated to the Emperor. The main god of Pisidian Antioch was Mên Askaênos, and in the mid-second century BC, an Ionic temple was built at the extramural sanctuary.[7] He is basically the Persian moon god Mao, as Anaitis is the Persian Anahita (and Artemis). Mên Askaênos was later identified with Attis (below). There was also an impressive sanctuary to the god near Pisidian Antioch.[8] The city also boasts a Temple to Augustus. Iconium is also associated with Greek myth as it was there that Perseus supposedly beheaded Gorgon Medusa (Hesiod, *Theog.* 270). Tradition links the name of the city based on the Greek *eikōn* (image) to this event.[9]

In the important center Ancyra to the north of the churches involved (assuming the South Galatia hypothesis), there was a temple to Augustus and the goddess Roma built between 10 BC and AD 20. It contains an inscription with Augustus' achievements. The remains of a similar temple dedicated to Augustus is found in Pessinous.

In Pessinous, there is also a temple of Cybele (or Agdistis). She is the Hittite mother of the gods of the Anatolian pantheon. The high priest was called Attis. Legend has it, Agdistis (Cybele) was a bisexual monster trapped by Bacchus and castrated. Attis then castrated himself. The goddess was worshiped by devotees called

6. Witherington, *Acts*, 421–23 notes that the encounter calls to mind Ovid (43 BC—17 AD) in *Metamorphosis* 8.626 who recounts a story set in the region of Phyrgia or Lycaonia which refers to Jupiter (Zeus) taking the guise of a man and with Mercury or Hermes came to a thousand homes seeking rest. They came to an old poor couple Baucis and Philemon who offered Zeus rest and the mixing bowl kept refilling. The gods made themselves known to the couple and saved them while they flooded the area. When asked by the gods for anything they wanted for their generosity, they asked the gods to guard the temple and that they might die together. He notes too that near Lystra statues and altars dedicated to Zeus and Hermes have been discovered. The images of Zeus and Hermes make sense of their identification with Barnabas (an older bearded man) and Paul (a younger man perhaps in his forties).
7. S. Mitchell, 'Antioch,' in *AYBD* 1:264.
8. J. A. Egger, 'Galatia,' in *LBD*.
9. W. Ward Gasque, 'Iconium,' in *AYBD* 3:357.

Galli, who engaged in orgiastic dancing and castrated themselves in their ecstasy. This revelry occurred on the *Dies sanguinis,* the 'day of blood,' March 24 (also Bellona's Day).[10] The devotees put on mostly yellow women's clothing, headgear, earrings and other pendants, and wore make-up. Roman citizens were not permitted to do this. During the remembrance for Attis (15–28 March), they went into ecstatic trances dancing and flagellating themselves.[11] They sprinkled their blood on the Cybele statues and temple. Some even emasculated themselves. This practice of castration may be connected to Paul's statement of emasculation in Gal 5:12.[12] These Galli were wanderers who begged and received money in exchange for oracles.

The ritual was linked to Bellona's Day, where the Roman devotees of the war-goddess Bellona mutilated their arms and legs and drank their own blood to placate the goddess and fire themselves up for war. Such behavior was painful of course. To assist in their self-mutilation, devotees ate Ballonaria plant (Solanum) seeds. These supposedly invoked hallucinations enabling them 'to prophesy.' On the 25 March, the Hilaria was celebrated which involved some serious partying in honoring the goddess. March 26 was a day of rest. On March 27, the image of the deity was bathed in a river.[13] A huge monument stands to the goddess on the slopes of Mount Sipylus.[14] Throughout Asia Minor, there are many carved rock facades, niches, and thrones, on which the statue sat. She was often flanked by lions, in a long garment, often bare-breasted and flanked by musicians, and wearing a cylindrical crown.

Another goddess worshiped was Ma of Comana (mother) who was distinct from Cybele and identified with the war goddess Bellona. The Encyclopedia Britannica notes that:

Asia Minor shows a remarkable continuity in its worship.

10. 'Dies sanguinis,' in *Wikipedia,* https://en.wikipedia.org/wiki/Dies_sanguinis.
11. 'Galli,' in *Wikipedia,* https://en.wikipedia.org/wiki/Galli.
12. Egger, 'Galatia.'
13. 'Dies sanguinis,' *Wikipedia.*
14. *Encyclopedia Britannica Online,* s. v. 'Anatolian religion,' accessed August 06, 2016, https://www.britannica.com/topic/Anatolian-religion.

From the Neolithic Period, for 6,000 years, the population venerated a divine pair, mother goddess and weather god, the former in association with the lion, the latter with the bull; a divine son, associated with the panther; and a god of hunting whose symbolic animal was the stag. To the ancients, for whom the essence of a thing lay in its name, this continuity was less obvious than it is today. The many names under which the deities were known at different times and places appear to us of less significance, in a religious sense, than the constancy of the types.[15]

Clearly, like most cultures of the time, those in Galatia were polytheists who worshiped gods and goddesses galore. For Paul and Jews in general, these pagans did not know 'the God,' Yahweh, who they now know in and through Jesus Christ, his Son. In this time, they were enslaved (*douloō*) to these gods.

'Enslaved' is the verb associated with *doulos*, 'slave,' which has featured in Galatians in 1:10 of Paul as a slave of Christ, in 3:28 of the church in which there is neither slave nor free; in 4:1, of a child before coming of age is no different in status to a slave in the family; and in 4:7, of believers no longer being 'a slave' but a child and heir of God (cf. *paidiskēs*, 'female slave,' 4:22, 23, 30, 31). Here, while not knowing the God of Israel, they were enslaved to their deities.

Paul qualifies this with a caveat: '[that] by nature (*physis*) are not gods' (on *physis*, see 2:15). Here *physis* (cf. physical) speaks of their ontology. While they were worshiped as gods, for Paul and other Jews, they are not in their very nature God in any sense of the term. However, they are worshiped as such. Along with all Jews and Christians (and Muslims), Paul was convinced that there is one God, as Paul states in 2:20.[16] For him, at best, they are lesser fallen sinful spiritual beings, demons, which, as Paul says in 1 Cor 10:20–21, are behind idols.

---

15. See further on the ranges of gods in the region 'Anatolian Religion' (EBO).
16. See Rom 3:30; 1 Cor 8:4, 6; Eph 4:6; 1 Tim 2:5.

NOW KNOWING GOD AND KNOWN BY GOD (4:9)

In *Galatians 4:9,* using the coordinate *de,* 'on the other hand,' 4:9 Paul speaks of their present state:

But on the other hand (*de,* 1:15), **now** (*nyn,* 1:23) **that you have come to know** (participle *ginōskō,* 2:9) **God** (*Theos,* 1:1), **and** (*de*) **even more** (*mallon*),[17] **are known** (aorist passive *ginōskō*) **by** (*hypo,* 1:11) **God** (*Theos*), **how** (*pōs,* 2:14) **can you turn back** (*epistrephō*)[18] **again** (*palin,* 1:9) **to** (*epi,* 3:13) **the weak** (*asthenēs*)[19] **and** (*kai,* 1:1) **beggarly** (*ptōchos,* 2:10) **elemental spirits** (plural *stoicheion,* 4:3), **to which** (dative plural *hos,* 1:5) **you**

17. The adverb μᾶλλον (*mallon*) is used twice in Galatians. It can mean 'rather, more.' In 4:9, while some translate it 'rather,' this would suggest that the Galatians do not in actual fact know God but are known by God. This seems to distort Paul's point which is that they have come to know God, but more, they are known by him. Again, it has the meaning 'more' in 4:27; 'that the many children of the desolate one are *more* than those of the one who has a husband.'

18. The verb ἐπιστρέφω (*epistrephō*) compounds *epi* (upon) and *strephō* (turn) and carries the meaning 'turn back, return.' It is used once in Gal 4:9, where it speaks of the Galatians returning or turning back to submission to the *stoicheia*—weak and beggarly powers. In this context, this occurs through coming under the Torah, which is effectively identical to their former submission to the elemental powers of their former lives as pagans. This is a dramatic paralleling of Judaism-outside-of-Christ with pagan religion now that Christ has come. This does not mean Paul considers Judaism leading to the coming of Christ as a pagan religion. Rather, now that Christ has come, in rejection of Christ, Judaism is effectively a 'pagan' religion. For Paul, Judaism goes on, but in Christ and in Christ alone. This is an astonishing statement from a Jewish Pharisee.

19. The adjective ἀσθενής (*asthenēs*) can mean 'sick,' however, in its one use in Gal 4:9, clearly has the sense of 'weak.' Here, it is partnered with 'poorly' or 'beggarly' as a descriptor of the elemental powers. In contrast to the one omnipotent God, the *stoicheia* are pathetic. Yet, they are capable of enslaving a human, as they formerly did the Galatians through their pagan worship, the Jews under the law, and the Judaizers. This kind of subjugation is seen today in religions and philosophies which capture the souls of people. This can happen with 'Christian' cults and even in orthodox denominations as they veer from the gospel or get stuck in traditions that violate the freedom of the gospel. See also *astheneia* in 4:13 of Paul's weakness (sickness) of the flesh.

over (*anōthen*)[20] **again** (*palin*) **want** (second person present *thelō*, 1:7) **to be enslaved** (*douloō*, 4:8)?

The contrast with the Galatians' past enslavement to their 'gods' (which are, in reality, not gods at all) is their relationship with God. This God, the one God, they have come to know. The verb *ginōskō* in contrast to other Greek terms of knowledge like *dokeō* (2:2, 6, 9), which stresses subjective knowledge and *aisthsnomai* which refers to sensory knowledge (and so untrustworthy to Greek thought), refers to something concrete and known through experience. The verb is an aorist participle, perhaps stressing their coming into that awareness–an ingressive aorist.

In their conversion experience, the Galatians have come to know God. They have encountered him and have experienced him. By faith, they have come to know the power of his Spirit as they heard the gospel of a crucified Messiah with faith. They have experienced his power working miracles among them. They have seen the power of God break down historical enmities. They are like so many of us in God's church, who have experienced God's salvation power, and despite tests and seductions, simply cannot deny God. We cannot explain this knowledge other than to acknowledge it. We know because we know (cf. Rom 8:16).

But Paul goes a step further, 'wait, there's more!' He adds 'and even more (*mallon*), you are known (aorist passive *ginōskō*) by (*hypo*) God.' *De* here can be adversative 'but' or 'and.' The consecutive sense fits better here as Paul is speaking of an additional element of their relationship with God. *Mallon* can be 'rather' or 'more' here. While some translations opt for 'rather,' this is problematic as it suggests that their knowledge of God is inconsequential. However, their knowledge of God through

---

20. The adverb ἄνωθεν (*anōthen*) can mean 'again' or 'above' (see its use in John 3:3, 5 where it means 'from above' but is heard by a confused Nicodemus as 'again'—strangely, 'being born again' has become almost a technical term for a 'real Christian,' which amusingly messes up the intent of John 3). Anyway, it occurs once in Gal 4:9 paired with the more usual Greek term for 'again,' *palin*. The pairing of the two synonyms is emphatic giving the sense of 'over again' ('over' capturing the idea of 'above' in *anōthen*). 'Really Galatians—not *again*!' Fools! (3:1).

faith is critical and as wonderful as the omniscience of God. After all, we know God because God chooses to make himself known by revelation. When we consider how amazing God is—the One who created all that we know, who guides history, and who is the architect of salvation history—what a glorious thing it is to say, 'I know God.' In fact, this lies at the heart of the whole letter, which affirms faith as the human response to God's grace that brings justification. So *mallon* here has the sense of 'more,' or better, 'even more!'

The great thing about salvation is that not only can we know God, but God knows us fully; something that is both wonderful and scary. It creates fear in us if we are given over to sin, no matter how secret. For this God knows our hearts.[21] However, the Galatians (and we) are his children, so believers have no need to fear the one to whom they cry, 'Abba, Father.' He might discipline us as a good parent does (Heb 12:7–11), but his perfect love drives out all fear (1 John 4:18).

Still, it is glorious to think that the one who formed the cosmos, the architect of salvation, who saved us through self-giving, emptying, humbling, and the horror of crucifixion, knows us! God, of course, knows all people. This knowledge runs deeper; he knows us and loves us. He knows us and accepts us. He knows us and if we yield in faith, he adopts us.

This use of *ginōskō* (know) has something of the Hebrew יד״ (*yā·dă'*) in mind, a term used of sexual relationships, the most intimate of human bonding.[22] God similarly knows us in binding himself to us and we to him by his Spirit (cf. Acts 15:8; 1 John 3:24). This calls to mind David's song in Ps 139:

O LORD, you have searched me and known me! You know when I sit down and when I rise up; you discern my thoughts from afar. You search out my path and my lying down and are acquainted with all my ways. Even before a word is on my tongue, behold, O Lord, you know it altogether. You hem me in,

---

21. Cf. 1 Cor 2:10; 3:13; 4:5; 14:25; 1 Sam 16:7; 1 Chron 28:9; Prov 21:2; Luke 16:15; Acts 15:8; Heb 4:12–13.

22. Ludwig Koehler et al., *The Hebrew and Aramaic Lexicon of the Old Testament* (Leiden: E.J. Brill, 1994–2000), 391.

behind and before, and lay your hand upon me. Such knowledge is too wonderful for me; it is high; I cannot attain it.' (Ps 139:1–6, ESV).

It also calls to mind 1 Cor 13:12 where Paul speaks of seeing God and his ways in a mirror dimly, or as in a riddle. He compares knowledge of God and his ways in the present with what is to come: 'now I know in part; then I shall know fully, even as *I am fully known*.' While it is glorious that we know God, even greater is that he knows us! This is the language of the wonderful intimacy of people with God that lies at the heart of the Christian faith. How indescribably sensational! 'For from him and through him and to him are all things. To him be glory forever —Amen' (Rom 11:36).

In light of this mutual knowing, Paul asks, 'how can you turn back (*epistrephō*) again (*palin*) to the weak and beggarly elemental powers (*stoicheia*, 4:3), to which you over (*palin anōthen*) want to be enslaved (*douloō*)?' Paul again uses the plural of *stoicheion*. As discussed above on 4:3, these are both spiritual forces and the ideologies they promote and inhabit that enslave humanity. Here, particularly in mind, are the false gods of the Galatian world, which formerly dominated their thinking. They are enslaved to the expectations of these religions, the cultures of their people who worship them, and the demons working in and through these false religions.

In describing the *stoicheia*, Paul uses two adjectives (weak and beggarly). The first translated 'weak' is *asthenēs*—a term related to *astheneia* used in 4:13 of Paul's *weakness* of the flesh (sickness). The term can mean 'sick, weakened by disease' (Matt 25:43, 44; Luke 9:2; 10:9; Acts 4:9; 5:15, 16; 1 Cor 11:30). However, here in Gal 4:9, it carries the sense of 'weak.' This sense is used of the flesh which is weak, despite the willingness of the spirit (Matt 26:41; 14:38), women being physically weaker than men (1 Pet 3:7), the human in a fleshly state who is too weak to resist sin (Rom 5:6), the weak who are a precious part of God's churches (1 Cor 1:25, 27; 9:22; 12:22; 1 Thess 5:14), a weak conscience (1 Cor 8:7, 9, 10), and Paul's supposedly weak bodily presence (2 Cor 10:10). These powers, then, are weak.

Here, it describes the *stoicheia*, which as discussed, includes the law, pagan religions, and the spiritual forces working in and through them. Where the law is concerned, elsewhere, the writer of Hebrews describes the former commandments of the law as 'weak and useless' (Heb 7:18). The law, while holy, righteous, and good (Rom 7:12), has no power to generate obedience. It is merely writing on paper (or a stone or scroll). Humans, in their weakened fleshly state (Rom 5:6), are unable to generate the ability to 'do the law.' At best, they do so in part and experience cognitive dissonance—they want to do it but cannot (Rom 7:13–25).

The pagan religions are beset with the same problem. While to various degrees they ask for their devotees to act in obedience, they provide no power to do so. In contemporary terms, we can think of Buddhism with its eight-fold path or Islam with its five pillars. Or we might think of communism or the contemporary religion of western social liberalism, with its demands for tolerance (apart from exclusive religions), ecological concern, social justice (in various ways), and so on. None of the adherents to these religions can reach their lofty expectations, despite their zealotry.

Where demons are concerned, the use of 'weak' is somewhat ironic. They certainly are not weak at one level, enslaving people to their power through false ideologies and structures associated with their idolatry. However, in comparison to God, Father, Son, and Spirit, they are weak and pathetic. They have no power, except for the opportunity and control we give them. They have no capacity to generate eternal life and enable transformation into Christlikeness and the defeat of sin. Even the so-called 'foolishness of God' is stronger than any human or demonic 'wisdom' (1 Cor 1:25). Because of Christ's death and our participation in it through faith, it is the Spirit of God who brings freedom from *stoicheia* and the capacity to live the life of God. How can the Galatians even contemplate 'going back?'

The second adjective is the term *ptōchos* (2:10) used most commonly in the NT for the materially poor as in 2:10,[23] or those poor in spirit (Matt 5:3). The original sense of the term was 'begging'[24] and so adjectivally and can be translated 'beggarly' or 'poorly.' Together, the adjectives write off the *stoicheia* as unworthy of the attention of the Galatians.

'To which you over again want to be enslaved' again uses the verb *douleuō*, used in the previous verse of the Galatians' former subjugation to the *stoicheia* in their pagan state. Here, as they yield to the Judaizers, they threaten to be subjugated again. To do so is preposterous considering that they now live in the freedom of the Spirit.

Paul also here uses the emphatic construction *palin anōthen*. *Anōthen* can mean 'again' or 'above' as students of John's Gospel know from John 3:3—'born again' or 'born from above.' Here then, it can be translated 'again again' or 'again above' with the latter in mind, 'over again.' Its use stresses Paul's disdain.

The verb, 'you want,' is *thelō*, which is used in Galatians nine times (see for detail 1:7). Through Galatians, the verb *thelō* is used on occasion of Paul's desires—to know something from the Galatians (3:2), to be present with them (4:2). Most often in the letter, it refers to the active will of the Judaizers, who want to distort the gospel (1:7), to shut out the Galatians (4:17), and to make a good showing in the flesh (6:12) by having the Galatians circumcised (6:13). Here, its use balances those concerning the Judaizers. It speaks of the Galatian's willing volition in their subjugation. They are complicit in yielding. The use of *thelō* in 5:17 is related. There it speaks of the Spirit's power to keep the Galatians (and all Christians) from doing the sinful things that they *wish* to do. It is the Spirit that will enable them to resist the Judaizers if they yield to his unction and the will of God. As noted on 1:4, this is part of the battle of wills that is going on in Galatians. Will the Galatians hear the will of God and through their wills, yield? Or will they allow the false desires of the Judaizers draw them away from the gospel of Christ?

23. Cf. Matt 11:5; 19:21; 26:9, 11; 10:21; 12:42, 43; 14:5, 7; Luke 4:18; 6:20; 7:22; 14:13, 21; 16:20, 22; 18:22; 19:8; 21:3; John 12:5, 6, 8; 13:29; Rom 15:26; 2 Cor 6:10; Jas 2:2, 5, 6; Rev 13:16.
24. BDAG 896.

OBSESSED WITH THE JEWISH CALENDAR (4:10)

In *Galatians 4:10*, Paul gives another crucial reference to what
the Judaizers were drawing the Galatians into:

you observe (*paratēreō*)[25] **days** (*hēmera*, 1:18) **and** (*kai*, 1:1)
months (*mēn*)[26] **and** (*kai*) **special times** (*kairos*, 4:10) **and** (*kai*)
years (*eniautos*).[27]

'You' is specifically the Galatians here, as it is they who are
being drawn into Jewish calendric observation. 'Observe' means
to 'closely keep,' the verb otherwise used in the NT of the Jewish
leaders keeping close watch over Jesus (Mark 3:2; Luke 6:7; 14:1;
20:20) and the Damascus city officials watching the city gates
closely to ensure Paul did not escape (Acts 9:24). It is used by
Josephus of observing laws such as the Sabbath and food laws
(e.g., Josephus, *Ant.* 3.91; 11.294; 13.234; 14.264; *Ag. Ap.* 2.282).[28]
The present tense speaks of present and continuing observance.
What is observed is fourfold. 'Days' likely refers to Sabbaths and
other key days in Israel's calendar, e.g., the Day of Atonement,
Yom Kippur (Lev 23:27–28), the day of Pentecost (Acts 2:1), and
'the day of firstfruits' (Num 28:26). Dunn notes that the Sabbath
is of particular importance here:

Already before the Maccabean crisis 'violating the sabbath'
ranked with 'eating unclean food' as the two chief marks of

---

25. The verb παρατηρέω (*paratēreō*) compounds *para* (beside) and *tēreō* (keep) and literally
connotes 'keep beside' or 'alongside' something. It is used once in Galatians, in 4:10. It
means to 'watch closely' or 'closely observe' and the latter use is in mind here—they
are carefully observing days, months, seasons, and years. This is another aspect of the
Judaizing concern—submission to Jewish calendric protocols. This is Paul's only use.
Otherwise, it is used in the NT literally of people closely observing others—Jewish
leaders observing Jesus (Mark 3:2; Luke 6:7; 14:1; 20:20) and the Damascus city
officials watching to see if Paul sought to escape (Acts 9:24).
26. The only reference to μήν (*mēn*), 'month' is found in Gal 4:10 of the Galatian's
concern to keep new moon festivals which happened at the beginning of the month
(cf. Col 2:16). (cf. the English, *menstruate*).
27. The noun ἐνιαυτός (*eniatos*), in Classical Greek meant any cyclic period of time
whereas *etos* was fixed in meaning, 'year' (see on *etos*, 1:18). The only use in the letter is
in 4:10 of the Galatian concern to keep yearly events. The translation 'year' is
appropriate as it is likely that the Jewish annual events are in mind.
28. Philo customarily uses it in injunctions to the reader to observe something in the
biblical text (e.g., *Leg.* 3.61, 147; *Sacr.* 98).

covenant disloyalty according to Josephus (*Ant.* xi.346). The increasingly elaborate halakah that is attested in *Jubilees* (ii.17–33; 1.6–13), in the Damascus document of Qumran (CD x.14–xi.18), and in the Gospels (Mark 2:23–3:5 pars), indicates the importance of the Sabbath as a test of covenant righteousness within the factionalism of late second-Temple Judaism. Within the diaspora the unusual religious practice of having one day in seven as a day of rest was no doubt one of the factors which attracted sympathetic gentiles to Judaism (Philo, *Mos.* ii.21; Josephus, *Ap.* ii.282; Juvenal, *Satires* xiv.96; see further my *Romans* 805–6).

The four categories recall Gen 1:14: 'and let them [the two lights] be for signs and for seasons (*kairos*) and for days (*hēmera*) and years (*eniautos*).' It is likely that the Judaizers see the core elements of the Jewish calendar as rooted in creation and, as such, essential to all who name Yahweh as God. However, for Paul, any notion of the Jewish calendar is fulfilled in Christ. In Romans 14:5, he speaks of differences among Christians concerning the importance of 'days,' urging each believer to live out of their particular belief concerning such non-essentials and not to judge the other.

In Col 2:16, he counsels the Colossians to reject judgmentalism of what people eat and drink and concerning 'a festival or a new moon or a Sabbath.' Such things he considers a 'shadow of things to come' which have an appearance of wisdom but reflect self-made religion—they have 'no value in stopping the indulgence of the flesh' (Col 2:17–23). Here, his implied message is similar. These are things from their time under the law and now are of limited value. In the Galatian context, they reflect their rejection of grace and faith and yielding to law as a basis for righteousness before God. As such, they are to be repudiated.

As in Col 2:16, 'months' may refer to the Jewish new-moon festival (Gk. *neomēnia*, *neo*, 'new' plus *mēn*, 'moon'). The Jewish year begins in the month of Nissan (March–April), the month of Exodus and Passover (Exod 12:2). On the first day of every month, a prescribed sacrifice was made.[29] It is sometimes paired with Sabbaths in Jewish writings.[30] Dunn notes that the moon was considered one of the 'elemental forces' (*stoicheia*) in pagan thought; there may be a play on ideas here.[31]

'Special times' is the Greek *kairos*, 'time.' As noted on 4:1, Classical Greek saw *chronos* as a period or section of time and was dominant in Greek philosophy, whereas *kairos* refers to a point in time, a moment, or instant. However, this distinction does not hold in the NT. *Kairos* will be used figuratively in 6:9, 10 of harvest time. Here, it is likely the appointed feasts of Israel. While it is not completely clear which of these were celebrated at the time of Paul, these included New Moon feasts (see above), three pilgrimage festivals (Passover/Unleavened Bread, Weeks, and Booths [Tabernacles]), a festival of trumpet blasts, and the Day of Atonement. Of particular importance were the three pilgrimage festivals, which drew enormous crowds, including from the Diaspora.[32] Falk notes,

The pilgrimage festivals especially were occasions of great joy, drawing large crowds even from throughout the Diaspora ... They provided the only occasions for assembly of all Israel and thus nurtured a sense of identity and common values ... They also provided a focus for national aspirations and opportunities to discuss issues and make resolutions affecting Jewish communities ... These included occasions for complaints and appeals to the governor ..., and anger frequently flared into violent protest. Because of the large crowds, during the early Roman period troops were on high alert (Matt. 26:5; [Josephus,] *Ant.* 20.107), and occasional confrontations cost thousands of lives ... There is less evidence about how the festivals were observed in communities at a distance from Jerusalem (Galilee, Diaspora) by those unable to make the pilgrimage, but there are hints of festive meals and assemblies (e.g., *Ant.* 14.213–16, 241–42, 257–61), which probably included Torah readings, prayer, and singing or reciting Psalms.[33]

---

29. See Num 10:10; 28:11–15; 29:6; 1 Chron 23:31; Ezra 3:5; Ps 81:3; Isa 1:13; 66:23; Ezek 46:1, 6; Josephus, *Ant.* 3.237; Philo, *Spec.* 2.41.
30. See 2 Kings 4:23; Isa 1:13; 66:23; Ezek 46:1; Amos 8:5.
31. Dunn, *Galatians*, 227.
32. See, e.g., Josephus, J.W. 6.422–426; Philo, *Spec.* 1.69–70; Acts 2:5–11.

It is likely that the Judaizers were passionate about the Christians participating in Jewish feasts. They were perhaps encouraged to pilgrim to Jerusalem for the three pilgrimage feasts, and if not, to participate in their local synagogue celebrations. With the rise of nationalism (eventually leading to the Jewish revolt) at the time, the pressure may have been intense.

The final category is 'years' (*eniautos*). In Classical Greek, *eniautos* differed from *etos* with the latter referring strictly to a 'year' and *eniautos* a fixed cyclic period. However, by the time of the NT, Koine did not hold the distinction, with both terms meaning a year. While Paul is somewhat vague in his language, he is not here referring to pagan celebrations.[34] However, he may be regarding Jewish celebrations on the same level now that Christ has come. *Eniautos* here could refer to the Sabbath Year of agricultural rest which was to be celebrated every seventh year (Lev 25:1–7) and the Year of Jubilee where the fiftieth year was a year of rest, restoration, and liberty (Lev 25:8–22, cf. Luke 4:19).[35] Of note here is Jubilees 2:9: 'And the Lord set the sun as a great sign upon the earth for days, Sabbaths, months, feast (days), years, Sabbaths of years, jubilees, and for all the appointed times of the years.'[36]

As Christ is the completion of all that Judaism holds, now the Galatians are to be concerned not about pleasing God through calendric observance, but through faith. These things may have value (and even be practically beneficial), but they do not bring righteousness.

This verse and others referred to above have interesting implications for contemporary Christians who differ over the importance of the Christian calendar. Reading between the lines of Paul's thoughts, it would seem Paul would have no problem

---

33. D. K. Falk, 'Festivals and Holy Days' in *EDEJ*, 636. See the whole article for detail (pp. 636–45).

34. Betz, *Galatians*, 217–18.

35. Moo, *Galatians*, 278. However, Dunn, *Galatians*, 228 rejects the Sabbatical Year as a possibility as it was mainly a Palestinian idea. Yet, he notes that it was in a sense observed in Qumran (1Qx.6–8).

36. Moo, *Galatians*, 278.

with people following a Christian calendar as long as they do so with the right attitude. Critically, they recognize that their justification is by grace through faith and not through observing Lent, Easter, Pentecost, and Advent, etc. Rather, they are to be observed as acts of people who already know they are righteous by faith and to enhance their remembrance of Christ's work for humanity and their relationship with God. Other Christians will find little is gained through such observance, and they are not to be judged for this. Rather, each is to live out their righteous status as they feel led by Christ and in their desire to please the God who has gifted them with salvation.

Finally, they should not judge the other. Those who find value in the Christian calendar should do so without judging those who do not. Conversely, those who find such things of little spiritual value should not stand in judgment over others that do. Neither side must create a law concerning such things (e.g., give up something for Lent). Contrariwise, one must not create a law that says if one does keep the Christian calendar, one is displeasing God. Such a judgment cannot be assumed. If something is done on the basis of faith and is not tied to inclusion or salvation, it is a good thing. What matters from both parties is the knowledge that faith is the only human response that justifies people before God.

HAVE I LABORED IN VAIN? (4:11)

Returning to Paul's letter, in *Galatians 4:11*, Paul states his concern over the Galatians yielding to the Judaizers' demands for the Galatian gentile Christians to observe the Judaic calendar:

I fear (present middle *phobeō*, 2:12) **for you** (accusative plural *sy*, 1:3), **lest** (*mē*, 1:7, *pōs*, 2:2) **I have labored** (perfect *kopiaō*)[37] **for** (*eis*, 1:5) **you** (accusative plural *sy*) **in vain** (*eikē*, 3:4).

While the term for vain differs and the chosen metaphor shifts from athletics to the world of work, this verse recalls 2:2 where

---

37. The verb κοπιάω (*kopiaō*) is found once in Galatians. It speaks of hard toil and is used as often by Paul, of missional effort—in 4:11 of his missionary toil to win the Galatians to Christ and to see them persevere.

Paul speaks of his visit to Jerusalem to set the gospel before the Jerusalem leaders to 'make sure I was not running or had not run in vain.' Whereas in 2:2 the issue is his own ministry—is he preaching the right gospel? Here, the issue is the Galatians themselves. This clause then recalls 3:4 where Paul asks the Galatians—who were seeking to complete their justification through the flesh (law) and not the Spirit—whether they had experienced suffering 'in vain (eikē) if indeed it was in vain (eikē).'

The shift from the second person to the first person redirects the Galatians to Paul's own concern. The term for 'fear,' phobeō, is used in 2:12, of Peter's fear of the circumcision party that led to his withdrawal from table fellowship with the gentile believers. Here, it is Paul's fear. As noted concerning 2:12, the verb has a wide range[38] and here speaks of more than deep concern as their eschatological futures are at stake, a fear then that may verge on bewildered terror. While it can be passive, here, it is the middle voice which in general indicates that 'the subject *performs* or *experiences the action* expressed by the verb in such a way that *emphasizes the subject's participation*.'[39] The emphasis is enhanced by the first placement of the verb.

Paul twice uses the plural accusative *hymas* emphasizing the Galatians in relation to himself. I have sought to retain this in the translation, although a number of translations elide the two uses into one. For example, ESV: 'I am afraid I may have labored over *you* in vain.' However, the repetition of 'for you' speaks of the basis for Paul's fear—he is desperately afraid his converts may abandon Christ. The blending of *mē* with *pōs* as in 2:2 yields 'lest,'[40] here, with the sense, 'because of the possibility that,' which can be simplified to 'that'—'I am afraid that ...' (see further on *mē pōs* 2:2).

'Labored' is *kopiaō*, a verb that literally speaks of being bone-tired or weary (Matt 11:28; John 4:6; Rev 2:3). More often it means 'to exert oneself physically, mentally, or spiritually, work hard, toil, strive, struggle'[41]—to do that which makes one bone-

---

38. See BDAG. 1060.
39. Wallace, *Grammar*, 414.
40. BDAG 1062.

weary! (Including studying theology or ministry, although there are many much harder lives in the world!). It can be used of laboring in work,[42] and Paul sometimes uses it particularly of his tentmaking work (1 Cor 4:12). Somewhat often it is employed in the wider NT (John 4:38) and in Paul for laboring in ministry.[43] As noted discussing 2:2, Paul uses the same kind of language in Phil 2:16 of his concern for the Philippians that they live holy lives and hold forth (or fast) to the word of life, 'so that on the day of Christ it may be a boast to me that I did not run in vain or labor in vain.' Here, he uses the perfect tense of *kopiaō*, referring to the present effects of his initial work for the salvation of the Galatians (for you).

'In vain' uses *eikē* which, as discussed in 3:4, is a strictly Pauline term in the NT and has the sense 'to no avail.' Paul is concerned that he has labored over the Galatians for no result. This clause is the language of falling away from the faith. There is a Christian school of thought that one cannot fall away from faith, and that if one does, one's faith was not genuine or saving in the first instance. This verse would appear to support the idea that one can indeed fall away from faith. The Galatians clearly began with hearing, with faith (3:2). They received the Spirit by that faith, indicating it was genuine (3:3, 4). However, they have become seduced by the Judaizers and turning from faith to justification by works of the law, through the flesh.

'In vain' here and in other Pauline texts seems to indicate that their initial faith and Paul's work to bring them to Christ is for naught. 1 Corinthians 15:2 is similar—'otherwise *you have believed* (aorist) in vain.' The Corinthians certainly believed, were called by God through Paul's preaching, believed in him, and were granted the status of God's people and received the Spirit (1 Cor 1:17–2:9). However, with some of them moving away from faith in a resurrected Messiah, they are in danger of their initial faith counting for nothing. Similarly, if there is no resurrection

---

41. BDAG 558.

42. Luke 5:5; 12:27; Eph 4:28; 2 Tim 2:6.

43. See Rom 16:6; 1 Cor 15:10; 16:16, 12; Col 1:29; 1 Thess 5:12; 1 Tim 4:10; 5:17, cf. Acts 20:35.

of Christ, Christian preaching is 'in vain,' and the Corinthians' faith is similarly 'in vain' (1 Cor 15:14). Conversely, God's grace toward Paul is not 'in vain' (1 Cor 15:10) and if the Corinthians persevere in trusting in a resurrected Messiah (bodily resurrection), their labor in the Lord will not be in vain but will reap a glorious reward (1 Cor 15:57–58).

In 2 Corinthians, Paul appeals to the Corinthians not to 'receive the grace of God in vain' (2 Cor 6:1). Clearly, they have received the grace of God but are in danger of receiving it for no eternal gain. So as today is the ever-present day of salvation, they must again be reconciled to God (2 Cor 5:20; 6:2).

In Phil 2:16, his concern for the Philippians is that they continue to be engaged in the mission of the gospel so that he did not run or labor over them in vain. He writes to the Thessalonians reminding them that his visit to them was not 'in vain' (1 Thess 2:1) as some believed. However, he writes the letter concerned that his 'labor would be in vain' if they were tempted away from faith in Christ (perhaps by Judaizers or Jews, who were very active in Thessalonica) (1 Thess 3:5, cf. Acts 17).

Returning to Galatians, earlier in the letter, Paul laid his gospel out to ensure that he 'was not running or had not run in vain' (2:2). In 3:4, he asks the Galatians who believed and received the Spirit (3:2, 5), whether they suffered so much 'in vain.' In what follows, he will remind them again of the time of their conversion as they received a sick Paul as an angel, caring for him, and honoring him. He will urge them to persevere and not be diverted by the Judaizers. Unless Paul is being hypothetical, rhetorical, hyperbolic, or deceitful,[44] one is hard-pressed to find exegetical paths away from the seemingly clear conclusion: Paul held that a person could have an initial faith in Jesus, receive the Spirit, and yet all this be in vain if that person should turn away from the grace and faith found in the gospel. This is why

44. The first three options are possible. But if so, it opens up a whole can of worms with all of Paul's teaching. When is he being hypothetical? Hyperbolic? For example, is he being so concerning the state of people engaging in sin in 5:19–21? Does he really believe in eternal destruction? Will we really receive eternal life? Such a hermeneutic must be very clear to be considered.

he is writing with such passion. His concern is for the Galatians' eternal state. Still, the debate goes on.

CHAPTER TWENTY-TWO: REMEMBER
YOUR CONVERSION (4:12–20)

As there is no connective (asyndeton, see 2:6), Paul here begins a new section. As is common, he does so with the affectionate 'brothers and sisters.' In vv. 12–14, he directly urges the Galatians to emulate his example of perseverance in faith in Jesus Christ and, by implication, not to yield to a false Judaizing gospel. He does so with a brief narratio of his time among them (recalling 1:11–2:14).

In the earlier narrative, asserting his apostolic authority and the veracity of his gospel, Paul reminded the Galatians of his life from his time as a Christian-persecuting Pharisee, through his call, his mission trips to Arabia, Jerusalem (cf. Acts 9:26–30), Cilicia and Syria (Acts 9:30; 11:25–26), and again to Jerusalem (Acts 11:29–30). He recalls Peter and the Judaizers coming to Syrian Antioch where Paul and Peter clashed; likely, sometime after Peter escaped Jerusalem to Caesarea Maritima when his life was threatened (Acts 12:1–19, c. 48). The portion of his life he recalls here is when Paul and Barnabas came to the south Galatian region to evangelize the region (Acts 13–14), sometime after he came to Galatia (ca. 47–48) and returned to Antioch, but before the Jerusalem Council in AD 49.

Using the second person 'you,' he reminds them of their knowledge of his visit to them to preach Christ. Despite his being ill and a trial to them, they did him no wrong, not rejecting him, but honoring him. They received him as an angel as he preached the gospel to them, even as Jesus himself. In v. 15, he then turns to rhetorical questions, recalling 3:1–5. In light of this wonderful time, he asks what has become of their blessed state of being and mind, a state in which they were prepared to rip their own eyes out to help him.

This passage *perhaps* gives us a vital clue as to Paul's condition—an eye problem. He enquires whether he is now their enemy for preaching the truth of the gospel. In v. 17, using a chiasm, he speaks of the Judaizers as 'them.' They make a big deal of the Judaizers, but their purposes are false. They want to shut out the Galatians so that the Galatians will make a big deal of them. He thus questions their motives—it is about their honor and not the gospel.

In vv. 18–20, as their mother in the faith, Paul speaks of his deep yearning for the Galatians. They have turned from Christ, and he is desperate that they are 'born again' into the faith they began with so that Christ is formed in them again. He finishes with a statement of his desire to be with them that he could speak more gently and that he is at a loss concerning them. One can feel the beating heart of an evangelist-pastor who is seeing his converts turn away. Like a mother protecting her children, Paul is in damage control, desperate that they again return to Christ.

Another aspect of this situation is worth noting. Jewish law considered people who are diseased unclean and often disease was associated with sin (Lev 13–14). It could be that Paul's ailment was causing the Judaizers to argue that he is not righteous and is unclean. By reminding them of their warm welcome of Paul in his illness, they heard the gospel and were saved. He can hardly be unclean and a 'sinner' as a result.

BECOME AS I AM (4:12)

In *Galatians 4:12*, Paul begins this section, directly asking them to emulate his example:

Because (*hoti*, 1:6) **I also** (*kagō*)[1] **[became] as** (*ōs*, 1:1) **you** (plural *sy*, 1:3), **brothers and sisters** (vocative plural *adelphos*, 1:2), **I beg** (*deomai*)[2] **you** (plural *sy*) **[to] be** (present middle imperative

---

1. The crasis κἀγώ (*kagō*) compounds *kai* (and, also) and *egō* (I) yielding 'and I' or 'I also.' Paul uses it twice in Galatians: 1) 4:12: '*I also* have become as you are;' 2) 6:14: 'the world has been crucified to me, *and I* to the world.'

ginomai, 2:17) **as** (*ōs*) **I** (*egō*, 1:2) **[am]**! **You did me** (*egō*) **no** (*ouden*, 2:6) **wrong** (*adikeō*).[3]

The order of the English translation of the first part of the verse differs from the Greek which reads: 'Be as I [am], because I am also as you, brothers and sisters, I plead with you.' 'Be as I am' uses *ginomai* placed first for prominence and could be translated as 'become' (see on *ginomai*, 2:17). The verb is an imperative, and remarkably only the third imperative directed to the Galatians (after *idou*, 1:20; and 'know' in 3:7). As noted regarding 1:8, Paul uses imperatives sparingly, and in Galatians where direct appeals to readers are concerned, they are clustered between this appeal and 6:17.[4]

While Paul does not here use *mimēsis* language, this is one of his customary appeals and references to his converts seeking or endorsing emulation of his example.[5] These appeals feel awkward to many contemporary Christians who see them as arrogant and presumptuous and out of keeping with Christian

---

2. The verb δέομαι (*deomai*) has the sense of 'plead, beg' and is often used in prayers pleading with God for his action (in Paul see Rom 1:10; 1 Thess 3:10). It's one use in Galatians if for Paul's fervent appeal to the Galatians to become as he is in 4:12 (cf. 2 Cor 5:20; 8:4; 10:2).

3. The verb ἀδικέω (*adikeō*) is one of Paul's *dik*- language terms with a courthouse background. It speaks of wronging, mistreating, or injuring someone. Paul uses it once in Galatians 4:12 of the Galatians doing no wrong or harm to him when he came to them sick and preached the gospel.

4. He uses two imperatives in 1:8, 9: '*let him be* accursed,' s.a., 1:20; 3:7. Aside from those used in citations, he will use imperatives another thirteen imperatives in the remainder of Ch. 4 through Ch. 6: 'tell me' (4:21); 'stand firm' (5:1), 'do not submit again' (5:1), 'become slaves of one another' (5:13), 'watch that you care for one another' (5:15), 'live by the Spirit,' 5:16), 'restore one another gently' (6:1), 'bear one another's burdens' (6:2), 'test his or her own work' (6:4), 'share with their teachers in all good things' (6:6), 'do not be deceived' (6:7), 'see what large letters …' (6:11), and 'let no one make trouble for me' (6:17). The imperatives in 4:27 are found in the citation of Isa 54:1 and only implicitly speak of the Galatians' rejoicing and breaking forth and crying aloud that people are coming to Christ. The imperative of 4:30, while speaking of Sarah's words to Abraham in Gen 21:10, becomes an appeal from Paul to the Galatians to expel the Judaizers. There are also hortatory (let us) subjunctives that function as inclusive imperatives in 5:25, 26; 6:10. A command, a cohortative (command or volitive) indicative is used in 5:14, 'love your neighbor.'

5. Cf. 1 Cor 4:15; 11:1; 1 Thess 1:6; 2 Thess 3:9; Phil 3:17; 4:9, cf. 1 Thess 2:14; Eph 5:1.

humility. However, this is an anachronistic understanding. In Paul's world, life was passed on from person to person primarily through example—father to son, mother to daughter, rabbi to disciple, philosopher to student, priest to initiate, and so on. While the elite would learn to read, in this age, scrolls were expensive and rare. They had nothing like the media we have today. Life was passed on through observation and learning from others. It was a world of apprenticing and mentoring. So, Paul is simply stating the obvious as their church planter and teacher.

Further, Paul's imitation is premised on his own emulation of Christ and particularly Christ crucified as a pattern for life. The key text is 1 Cor 11:1, 'imitate me as I imitate Christ.' Paul had not known the human Christ but had met him in his resurrected state and pondered deeply on the mystery of a crucified Messiah (1:11–15). This experience shapes his understanding of how to live, out of the pattern of the cross—self-emptying, self-humbling, selflessness, other-centeredness, sacrifice, suffering, and service on behalf of the other, whatever the cost. No doubt in his times with Peter, Jacob, John, Barnabas, John Mark, and others in Jerusalem (1:18–2:10), he heard more of the life of Jesus and learned of Jesus' whole life of service and suffering. Later he would learn even more through his traveling companion Luke. Called to be the apostle to the gentiles, as he deeply meditated on the story of God and his Son who came as Servant, his life pattern was shaped. As such, it makes perfect sense that Paul would frequently appeal to his converts to 'be as I am.'

While we find this idea of being a role model difficult and potentially arrogant, contemporary Christian leaders need to own the challenge to be people worthy of emulation. After all, people learn by observation anyway, and invariably, Christian leaders form communities in their own image. With that the case, we need to take this seriously and seek to be people worthy of Christ in this regard, albeit authentic and acknowledging our weaknesses and flaws.

'Be as I [am]' here likely refers not to total emulation of Paul's life in its every part, but his reliance on faith for justification and his rejection of the 'gospel' of the Judaizers. They are to join in his rejection of them and their false teaching.

'Because I also became as you' in Greek has no verb. The aorist of *ginomai* seems appropriate, speaking of Paul's becoming as the Galatians referring to Paul's time among them on his journey when he entered into their life (Acts 13–14). He did not come as a Judaizer imposing Jewish culture upon them—circumcision, eating protocols, and concern for the Jewish calendar. Rather, he came and preached the gospel of grace. Through his preaching, Christ has called them through the gospel and their response of faith. As essential to his mission practice, he did what he did among all the Greeks. Although Paul was free to live by any non-sinful cultural protocols he wants, he emulated the Christ—who came to earth as the ultimate Servant—and made himself a servant to them, so that he might win more of them to Christ. While with Jews, he 'became as a Jew, in order to win Jews,' and 'to those under the law' he 'became as one under the law ... that he 'might win those under the law'—despite not being under the law himself.

Conversely, when among 'those outside the law' (including the Galatian gentiles), he 'became as one outside the law' ... that he 'might win those outside the law'—this because he is not outside the law of God (he is in Christ who has fulfilled it) but under the law *of Christ*. Indeed, as was his missionary practice, he became 'all things to all people, that by all means, he might save some' (1 Cor 9:19–22). Of course, this applies to the non-essentials of the gospel, things like whether one is circumcised or not, whether one eats this or that food, whether one likes to follow a faith calendar or not, or whether one washes one's hands before eating as did Jews. Today we might add drinking alcohol in moderation, preferring this or that music, or following the church calendar. Such things are neither here nor there where the essence of the gospel is concerned.

As such, when in Galatia, Paul ate with the Galatians (even food sacrificed to idols, 1 Cor 8), lived by the flow of Galatian life, hung out with them in their homes, and lived as a Galatian. He did not participate with them in the fatally compromised aspects of their life like sexual immorality, drunkenness, debauchery, attendance at the pagan temple worship, factionalism, concern for status and honor at all costs, and so on (cf. 5:19–21). However, where the culture was concerned, he was one with them. He did not withdraw from table fellowship for concern that he might offend other Jewish Christians (2:11–14). He was one with them, living out his mantra, a Jew living as a Greek, a free man who is a friend and equal with slaves, a male on a par with females (3:28).

Now some of the Galatians are being seduced into separation on the basis of culture. They are being drawn into an exclusive mode of being, where one must live as a Jew which gains them nothing before God, for faith justifies them. Hideously, it separates them from others who are not Jewish in culture within the Christian community. It thus tears the community apart, introduces status and rank on the basis of culture and gender (only males can be circumcised), and breaks up the body of Christ. Jesus came to end all such enmities, to build a Temple of God—one people without dividing walls of hostility (cf. Eph 2:14). Paul has modeled this; they must emulate him and back off such *skybala* (Phil 3:8, translation 'shite').

The use of 'brothers and sisters' is important here.[6] As previously discussed, the vocative plural of *adelphos* is Paul's customary term of address in his letters. It is inclusive, the masculine also encompassing the women in the churches. It expresses unity, familial intimacy, and Paul's love. It is one key aspect of the church as the Household of God or faith in which God is the Father, Jesus the Son, and our big Brother, and we God's children and brothers and sisters together (see further on 1:2, cf. 6:10). While Paul has expressed concern that he has labored over them in vain, this is not yet the case. They are still *whanau*,[7] family, and siblings in Christ. But the family is in danger of coming apart, and if they continue down the Judaizing track, some will be lost. But they are not there yet. They are still

---

6. Cf. 11; 3:15; 4:28, 31; 5:11, 13; 6:1, 18.
7. The NZ Māori word for 'family.'

God's children and family together with Paul and the brothers and sisters with him in Antioch (and the world).

The verb 'I beg' is *deomai*, which is often used in Paul and elsewhere in the NT (especially Luke) as a term for prayer directed toward God.[8] It has the sense of 'plead or beg' another person to do something. Luke uses it this way of people pleading with Jesus and the disciples to heal them (Luke 5:22; 9:38; 9:30), the demons in the demoniac pleading with Jesus not to torment them (Luke 8:28, 38), the Ethiopian Eunuch pleading with Philip to explain Isa 53 (Acts 8:34), and Paul pleading to be allowed to speak to people at the Temple and for Agrippa II to listen to him (Acts 21:39; 26:3).

Paul uses it three times in 2 Corinthians in this manner, imploring the Corinthians 'to be reconciled to God' (2 Cor 5:20), of the poor Macedonians pleading to be able to contribute to the Jerusalem Collection (2 Cor 8:4), and of Paul begging the Corinthians that they respond so that he would not have to assert his authority when he comes to them (2 Cor 10:2). Here, Paul uses it in this latter sense; he is pleading with or begging the Galatians to heed his appeal and become as he is—living in the freedom of the gospel. It thus is a powerful term of appeal—Paul is on his knees, begging them! This is the love of a parent for their wayward children, imploring them to get off the wrong track and out of bad relationships that can only end in trouble or disaster.

The final clause of the verse should be placed with the next verse as it leads into a brief narration of Paul's time with them, a section that runs through to v. 14. He states, 'you did me no wrong (*adikeō*).' The verb *adikeō* is from the *dik*-range of terms that includes *dikaiosynē* (righteousness, justice), *dikaioō* (justify, declare righteous), and *dikaios* (righteous, just), among others. It is thus legal language. It carries a range of nuances, including the doing of wrong toward another person. It speaks of something unjust and harmful. So, in Matt 20:13, in the parable of the vineyard, the employer responds to the workers' complaints of

---

8. *Deomai* is found twenty-two times in the NT, mostly for prayer—'I pray earnestly' (Matt 9:38; Luke 10:2; 21:36; 22:32; Acts 4:31; 8:22, 24; 10:2; Rom 1:10; 2 Thess 3:10).

underpayment, 'friend I am *doing you no wrong*,' as you agreed to the deal. Luke records Paul stating to the Roman Governor Festus, 'to the Jews I have *done no wrong*' (Acts 25:10, cf. 25:11).

Paul uses it in his letters to describe the Corinthians who suffer pain from each other rather than go to the courts over trivial matters and further wronging each other (1 Cor 6:7, 8). In 2 Cor 7:2, Paul asks the Corinthians to open their hearts to him and his team, for 'we have wronged no one' (cf. 2 Cor 7:12). He tells Philemon he will recompense him for any wrong that Onesimus has done (Phlm 18).[9] Here then he endorses the Galatian treatment of him while among them on his mission. They did not harm him, wrong him, or act unjustly toward him.

PAUL FIRST PREACHED IN GALATIA BECAUSE OF ILLNESS (4:13)

Paul continues the narrative he began in the final clause of v. 12 through vv. 13 and 14. *In Galatians 4:13*, he speaks of their knowledge of his visit to them:

And (*de*, 1:15) **you know** (second person perfect *oida*; 2:16) **that** (*hoti*, 1:6) **[it was] because** (*dia*, 1:1) **of weakness** (*astheneia*)[10] **of the flesh** (genitive *sarx*, 1:16) **[that] I first** (*proteros*)[11] **preached the gospel** (*euangelizomai*, 1:18) **to you** (dative *sy*, 1:3).

The *de* is consecutive, meaning 'and,' rather than 'but.' 'You know' uses *oida*, which speaks of concrete agreed knowledge (see on 2:16). It is in first position giving it prominence. Here, it speaks of the Galatians' shared knowledge, gained when Paul was among them. The 'you' of course targets the Galatians but is also

---

9. See also in Acts 7:24 where Moses killed the Egyptian when he saw him wronging the slave (cf. Acts 7:26, 27). It is also used of God repaying wrongdoers for their wrongdoing (Col 3:25, cf. 2 Pet 2:13). *Adikeō* can also mean to 'harm' or 'hurt' (Luke 10:19; Rev 2:11; 6:6; 7:2, 3; 9:4, 10, 19; 11:5) and of evildoers (Rev 22:11).

10. The noun ἀσθένεια (*astheneia*) is used once in Galatians (4:13). It is related to *asthenēs* used in 4:9 of the weak elemental powers,' *astheneia* meaning 'weakness,' or as it is used in Galatians, 'sickness' of the flesh.

11. The adverb πρότερος (*proteros*) means 'first,' and is used once in Galatians 4:13 of Paul first preaching the gospel among the Galatians because of sickness.

something Paul knows—he could have used 'we.' The emphasis is on *their* knowledge with Paul subtly urging them to remember what they know. One can imagine hearers recalling those days as they hear these words read. The content of the knowledge is signaled by the *hoti*, 'that,' a marker of discourse content. The verb 'it was,' the imperfect of *eimi*, is implied.

'Because of the weakness of the flesh that I first preached the gospel to you (on *euangelizomai*, see 1:18)' recalls Paul's coming to Galatia. 'Weakness of the flesh' uses *astheneia*. The term is used twenty-four times in the NT of physical sickness.[12] However, Paul also uses it of human weakness,[13] of Christ who was crucified in weakness (2 Cor 13:4), and of the human propensity to sin due to 'weakness of the flesh'—*sarx* speaking of humanity in its fallen, sinful state (Rom 6:19, cf. Rom 8:26) and subjection to death (1 Cor 15:43).

Here then 'weakness of flesh' can either speak of some struggle with sin or illness. Most likely, the latter is in mind. Paul may, however, have used 'flesh' (*sarx*) intentionally to highlight the human problem—we are weakened in a fleshly state and subject to sickness and death. Only God can redeem us from this and grant us eternal life. He has done so in Christ. In rejecting the gospel, the Galatians are in danger of being again subject to flesh as they were in their pre-conversion state.

Paul's illness is unclear. Some take both references to refer to opposition, but this seems stretched—the language of 'flesh' would seem to refer to a bodily issue. The issue could be caused by opponents through persecution and physical beatings.[14] However, how such things might have affected his eyes is unclear. It may be the same problem as the 'thorn in the flesh' from 2 Cor 12:7, although this is not certain. Yet, the commonness of language (weakness of the flesh/thorn in the flesh) would make it likely.

Most see this as a bodily condition, which makes sense of the common use of *astheneia* for illness and *sarx*, 'flesh.' Ramsay

---

12. See Matt 8:17; Luke 5:15; 8:2; 13:11, 12; John 5:5; 11:4; Acts 28:9; 1 Tim 5:23.
13. See 1 Cor 2:3; 2 Cor 11:30; 12:5, 9, 10, cf. Heb 4:15; 5:2; 7:28; 11:34.
14. Hays, 'Galatians,' 293–94.

famously argued Paul got chronic malaria fever when he landed in Asia Minor, so he left the south and went north into the mountains of Pisidian Antioch. Ramsay argues that malaria created 'distressing and prostrating paroxysms' and pain 'like a red-hot bar thrust through the forehead,' which debilitated Paul whenever he exerted himself and was seen by others.[15] However, as Witherington notes, 'oozing or red and encrusted eyes or even the side effects associated with ophthalmia (squinting, rubbing of eyes, etc.) were far more likely to create an immediate visual impact than malaria would have.'[16]

The vivid and horrid idea of the Galatians digging out their eyes and giving them to Paul in verse 15 gives us the best clue to Paul's condition. While this can mean that they wanted to tear out their eyes due to Paul's horrific condition (cf. 2 Cor 10:10), that they wished to give them *to Paul* rules this out.[17] Witherington argues persuasively that the best view is that: 'Paul had, at least periodically, eye problems of some sort, which hampered his travel, and as an orator damaged his *ethos*.'[18] In addition to the eye-gouging and the language, 'weakness of the flesh,' he rightly deduces that the visibility of the problem indicates that it was outside the area of the toga—'on the head and neck, the hands, the lower legs, or the feet.'[19] The reference to 'large letters' in 5:11 may also point to an eye impairment. The presence of the physician Luke with Paul may indicate an ongoing issue (see the 'we-passages' in Acts;[20] Col 4:14). Paul's blinding at his conversion may have triggered such problems (Acts 9:8–19). When Paul speaks of his vision in 2 Cor 12:1–7, he does not mention seeing things but hearing them and then speaks of his weakness.[21] An ongoing eye issue would seem to be the best read on the evidence.

---

15. Ramsay, *St. Paul the Traveller*, 94–97.
16. Witherington, *Grace*, 310 n. 39.
17. Similarly, Moo, *Galatians*, 283; Dunn, *Galatians*, 236.
18. Witherington, *Grace*, 310.
19. Witherington, *Grace*, 309.
20. See Acts 16:10–17; 20:5–16; 21:1–18; 27:1–28:16.
21. Witherington, *Grace*, 308–10.

When this proclamation of the gospel occurred is also tricky. The term *proteros* is a little vague. It can mean simply mean 'earlier, formerly, before.'[22] At times, 'first' fits the context better (2 Cor 1:15; Heb 7:27).[23] Here, it can simply refer to 'earlier;' a former time when Paul preached to them. However, equally, it could refer to the first time.

At the time of Paul, 'Galatia covered a large territory that included ethnic Galatia as well as parts of Phrygia, Pisidia, Lycaonia, and other regions in southern Asia Minor.'[24] If the letter is directed to North Galatia, sometime during his second Antiochian mission, he traveled into this area as a result of sickness. Luke mentions him passing through Galatia in Acts 16:6, which could be the occasion for the preaching (cf. Acts 18:23). However, as argued in the Introduction, this is unlikely for a range of reasons. Luke records that on the second Antiochian missionary journey Paul delivered the decisions of the Jerusalem Council to the cities he visited (Acts 16:4). While he did pass through Galatia, he was not diverted north or south but went to Macedonia (Acts 16:6–10).

This event would seem better placed earlier and refers to Paul and Barnabas' mission to the South Galatian cities of Phrygia, Pisidia, and Lycaonia (Acts 13–14). On this journey, Paul, Barnabas, and John Mark traveled through Cyprus and entered the Galatian region at Perga in Pamphylia. There is no reference to Paul preaching in Acts, so we are left to wonder whether he preached in this city. Luke records he traveled 200km inland from Perga to Antioch in Pisidia and engaged in preaching in the synagogue. However, there is no reference to sickness in Perga, Antioch, or between (or for that matter in Acts 16 and 18). Hence, we are left to speculate on what happened. It is possible that he needed treatment in either Perga, Antioch, or somewhere on the 200km journey inland between the two centers. As he was treated, perhaps he shared Christ with those who cared for him.

---

22. See, John 6:62; 7:50; 9:8; Eph 4:22; 1 Tim 1:13; Heb 4:6, 32; 1 Pet 1:14. See also BDAG 888–889.
23. See also LSJ 1534–35 for the range of the term.
24. Egger, 'Galatia,' in *LBD*.

We simply have no idea. Aside from it perhaps being something to do with his eyesight, we have no idea what he received treatment for.

Whatever the circumstances, we see here the sovereignty of God in evangelism. Paul's illness, whatever it was, seems to be a real problem. Perhaps it was this illness that caused John Mark to desert Paul and Barnabas? Whatever the issue, God worked in the circumstances of Paul's suffering to bring salvation to the Galatians. Throughout Scripture, God turns seemingly disastrous situations into opportunities. One thinks of Joseph sold as a slave by his brothers, yet he ended up saving Israel—what was intended as evil God meant for good (Gen 50:19–20). Similarly, when Paul himself launched his assault on the Jerusalem church, the persecution caused the gospel to spread (Acts 8:4–5; 11:19). Again, when Paul was imprisoned in Rome, it had the effect of the gospel spreading among Nero's guards and inner circle (Phil 1:12–14; 4:22). Supremely, when Jesus was brutally assassinated on a cross by the Roman leadership at the instigation of the Jewish leaders, the people of the world are able to be saved. God is at work in the messiness of life, turning ashes into beauty (Isa 61:3). This is Rom 8:28 at work.

I remember one time my wife had a cycling accident and ended up in a hospital getting a knee reconstruction. While there, we met an older woman with more serious issues. We shared our stories together. A few months later, I got a call. She had tracked me down in my pastorate. She asked that I come and see her. I did. Facing her imminent death, she asked me what would happen to her when she died. I shared the gospel of grace with her. She responded by yielding her life to God. She died a week or so later. I got to share at her funeral, and the gospel went out to all her friends and family. My wife's bike accident was horrific (thankfully, she recovered). Yet, through it all, God worked to save this precious soul. Another of her friends who attended the funeral out of the blue rang me to talk about a serious life of sin. He gave his life to Jesus by phone and was delivered from sin. God is glorious.

WELCOMED AS CHRIST JESUS HIMSELF (4:14)

Galatians 4:14 continues the narrative of v. 13 linked with *kai*, 'and:'

And (*kai*, 1:1) **you did not** (*ou*, 1:1) **despise** (second person aorist *exoutheneō*)[25] **or** (*oude*, 1:1) **repudiate**[26] (second person aorist *ekptuō*)[27] **your** (genitive plural *sy*, 1:3)[28] **trial** (*peirasmos*)[29] **caused by** (*en*, 1:6) [the condition of] **my** (genitive *egō*, 1:2) **flesh** (*sarx*, 1:16), **but** (*alla*, 1:1) **you received me** (aorist middle *dechomai*)[30] **as** (*ōs*, 1:1) **an**[31] **angel** (*angelos*, 1:8) **of God** (genitive *Theos*, 1:1), **as** (*ōs*) **Christ** (accusative *Christos*, 1:1) **Jesus** (accusative *Iēsous*, 1:1).

This verse focuses on the welcome afforded Paul by the

25. The verb ἐξουθενέω (*exoutheneō*) is found once in Galatians 4:14 of the Galatians who, despite Paul's sickness, did not scorn or despise it or him.

26. **Variant**: the verb *ekptuō* (below) is excluded from P46. However, it is found in other texts, and this is likely a scribal error.

27. The verb ἐκπτύω (*ekptuō*) compounds *ek* (from) and *ptuō* (spit) and yields 'spit out,' and so suggests 'despise' someone, 'repudiate,' or 'treat someone with contempt.' It is an onomatopoeia which can easily be demonstrated by pronouncing it by highlighting the k with the pt sound. It is synonymous with *exoutheneō*. It is a hapax *legomenon*, found only here in the NT.

28. **Variant**: The phrase *ton peirasmos hymōn*, 'your testing' is well attested, so it is likely original. Some texts replace *hymōn* with *mou* (my testing) or *mou ton* or simply *ton* which has the same effect of shifting the trial from the Galatians to Paul. However, this removes the key element of the verse; namely, that Paul's suffering was a trial not only to him (by implication), but to the Galatians!

29. The noun *peirasmos* means 'test' or 'temptation' and is found once in 4:14 in the sense of trial—Paul's illness being a trial to the Galatians. It is rare in Paul with his other three uses carrying the meaning of temptation (1 Cor 10:13; 1 Tim 6:9).

30. The verb δέχομαι (*dechomai*) means 'welcome, receive' and is only found once in Galatians, of the Galatians welcoming Paul despite his illness (4:14). Wallace, *Greek Grammar*, 421 notes, 'Although δέχομαι never occurs as an active, it should not be treated as a deponent verb. The lexical notion of receiving, welcoming connotes a special interest on the part of the subject.' This is significant because it emphasizes the person's involvement in welcome (cf. the middle voice).

31. Wallace, *Greek Grammar*, 252 argues that ὡς ἄγγελον θεοῦ (*hōs angelon Theou*) should be '*the* angel of the Lord' rather than '*an* angel of the Lord' as in the OT. While I agree that the article is not required and it can be translated as 'the angel of the Lord,' doing so seems strange here in Gal 4:14 when Paul could be any one of the myriads of angels (Gabriel? Michael). So, the Galatians welcome him as 'an' angel, not 'the' angel of the Lord—which would imply there is one particular angel in mind.

Galatians in which they did him no wrong (v. 13). Paul's illness is not defined in its own right, but in terms of the trouble it caused the Galatians—'your trial.' The term for trial, *peirasmos*, can mean 'temptation' from sin,[32] but often has the broader sense of 'trial, testing.'[33] While sometimes it is difficult to choose between the two meanings (Luke 8:13; 1 Cor 10:13), here, it is clearly the latter meaning that is in mind. In describing his illness as a trial for the Galatians (whatever the ailment was), Paul shows that it was not an easy thing to deal with.

'You did not despise or repudiate me' uses two similar-sounding verbs, *exoutheneō*, and *ekptuō* (assonance). *Exoutheneō* recurs in the NT eleven times, only in the writings of Luke and Paul. It carries the meaning 'despise' or 'disdain.'[34] Luke uses it of the contemptuous treatment of the righteous who are being marginalized by the seemingly righteous (Luke 18:9). He applies it to Herod and his soldiers' maltreatment of Christ (Luke 23:11), fulfilling the prediction that the Messiah will be a stone rejected by the builders (Acts 4:11). Paul repudiates the attitude, urging the Romans not to despise other Christians with differing views on what one can or cannot eat (Rom 14:3) and other non-essential matters of faith (Rom 14:10). Many of the Corinthians were from those classes of society that are despised, like slaves (1 Cor 1:28; 6:4). Timothy is not to be despised when he comes to Corinth (1 Cor 16:11), while Paul's speech was treated with contempt (2 Cor 10:10). Prophecies are not to be despised (1 Thess 5:20). The Galatians did not so treat Paul.

The second verb is an *hapax legomenon*, this being its only NT use. While P46 does not include it, this is a scribal anomaly; it is present in other mss and witnesses. The term compounds *ek* (from, 1:1) and *ptuō* (spit, cf. Mark 8:23; John 9:6) giving the literal sense of 'spit out.' It is onomatopoeia with the sound of the term sounding like spitting. It is also a vulgar term. As in many cultures, spitting was a mark of contempt.

In the first-century setting (and in some contemporary non-

32. See Matt 6:13; 26:41; Mark 14:38; Luke 11:4; 22:40, 46; 1 Tim 6:9.
33. See Luke 22:28; Acts 20:19; Heb 3:8; Jas 1:2, 12; 1 Pet 1:6; 4:12; 2 Pet 2:9; Rev 3:10.
34. BDAG 352.

western ones), spitting was also a means of warding off evil spirits. So, for example, the herder Damoctas spat three times on his chest to avoid the evil eye (Theocrates 6.39).[35] It was also used to ward off disease.[36] The use calls to mind *baskainō* in 3:1—'bewitched.' The Galatians did not repudiate Paul, despite his sickness, and the trial it was to them. They did not treat him as an evil spirit, or with contempt spit him out, so to speak (cf. Rev 3:16).

Rather, they welcomed him into their midst. 'Welcomed' is *dechomai*, a term associated with hospitality, a vital aspect of ancient cultures. It is a strong verb, emphasizing the welcoming agent's hospitality.[37] *Dechomai* is used in the Synoptics of welcoming disciples and the gospel. Where this does not occur, one must shake off the dust of those who reject them.[38]

The importance of hospitality is seen in Jacob and John's desire to demolish the Samaritan town where its inhabitants did not welcome Jesus (Luke 9:51–53). Similarly, Rahab is commended by the writer of Hebrews for welcoming the spies into Jericho (Heb 11:31). Paul uses it of the Colossians welcoming John Mark (Col 4:10).[39] The Galatians did not despise or repudiate Paul, despite his condition and the trial it caused them. Rather, they welcomed him.

'As an angel of God' contrasts with the idea of spitting out toward Paul, treating him as some kind of evil messenger. Rather, they received him as an angel of God. There is some irony here, of course, as earlier he repudiates any angel or person (even himself) who preaches a different gospel (1:8). He mentions too

---

35. See BDAG 309.
36. H. Schlier, 'ἐκπτύω,' in *TDNT* 2:448.
37. See Wallace, *Greek Grammar*, 421. See further the associated note on the verb in the translation.
38. See, e.g., Matt 10:14, 40–41; 18:5; Mark 6:11; 9:37; 10:15; Luke 9:5, 48; 10:8, 10.
39. Otherwise, Paul uses *dechomai* of people receiving (or not) spiritual gifts (1 Cor 2:14), the Corinthians accepting the grace of God in vain (2 Cor 6:1), receiving Titus (2 Cor 7:15), Paul's appeal for financial gifts for Jerusalem (2 Cor 8:17, cf. Phil 4:18), accepting Paul as a fool (2 Cor 11:16), of the acceptance of the gospel (2 Cor 11:4; 1 Thess 1:6; 2:13, cf. 2 Thess 2:10; Jas 1:21), and receiving the helmet of salvation (Eph 6:17).

that the law was delivered to Moses by angels (3:19). The Galatians then recognized that Paul was a genuine messenger sent from God with their salvation. Thus, it is ludicrous that they should now reject that he is a sent one—an apostle—in favor of the Judaizing heretics.

'As Christ Jesus' goes further—in their welcome of Paul and his message, they received him as Jesus Christ himself come to Galatia to preach God's message. To invoke Christ in this way is the highest possible commendation. The point of this is to remind them of their common experience. They welcomed Paul and his message as if Jesus himself was amongst them. They paid him great honor as a mouthpiece from God. They received the gospel he preached. This verse leads into v. 15 where he will ask how it can be that they have rejected the gospel and, by implication, its messenger Paul.

THEIR PREPAREDNESS TO GIVE PAUL THEIR EYES (4:15)

In *Galatians 4:15*, having narrated their first experiences together, Paul asks the first question of the section, and follows it up with a personal testimony of the extent of their warm receipt of him:

Where (*pou*)[40] **then** (*oun*, 3:5) **[is] your** (genitive plural *sy*, 1:3) **blessedness** (*makarismos*)?[41] **For** (*gar*, 1:10) **I testify** (*martyreō*)[42] **to you** (dative plural *sy*) **that** (*hoti*, 1:6) **if** (*ei*, 1:7) **possible** (*dynatos*),[43] **you would have dug out** (*exoryssō*)[44] **your** (genitive plural *sy*)

---

40. The only reference to the interrogative adverb ποῦ (*pou*), 'where' is here in 4:15: '*where* then is your blessedness?'

41. The noun μακαρισμός (*makarismos*), 'blessedness' is found once in Galatians, in 4:15, of the state of the Galatians when they received Paul.

42. The verb μαρτυρέω (*martyreō*), 'I witness, testify' is found once in 4:15 of Paul's testimony that the Galatians were prepared to rip out their eyes for his sake on his first visit to them.

43. The adjective δυνατός (*dynatos*) means 'able, possible,' and is used once in Galatians of the Galatian Christians who 'if *possible*' would have given their very eyes for Paul.

44. The only reference to the verb *exoryssō* in Galatians is 4:15. The term compounds *ek* (from) and *oryssō*, 'dig' (Matt 21:33; 25:18; Mark 12:1) and so 'dig out.' It is used in Paul's testimony that the Galatians would have 'dug out' their eyes for him. It means

eyes (plural *ophthalmos*, 3:1) **to give** (aorist infinitive *didōmi*, 1:4) **[them] to me** (dative *egō*, 1:2)!

Paul asks what has become of the Galatians' state of blessedness. The term blessedness is *makarismos*, one of the *makar–* terms that refer to the state of being blessed in the sight of God (e.g., *makarios*, e.g., the Beatitudes). The *eulogeō* terms tend to speak of God's blessing toward humanity (e.g., Gen 12:2). *Eulogia*, for example, is used in 3:14 of the blessing of Abraham that has come to the gentiles in Christ. *Makar–* language is generally used for the state of being blessed.

Makarismos is rarer than *makarios*, found in the NT three times—all in Paul. The other two uses are in Romans of blessedness that comes to those to whom God grants righteousness apart from works (Rom 4:6)—a blessedness for the circumcised and uncircumcised (Rom 4:9).[45] Here, it can mean their state of blessedness before God or toward Paul. In the wider context of Galatians, the former would seem appropriate (cf. Rom 4). They received Paul as Jesus Christ and believed the gospel (cf. 3:2–5). They experienced the joys of salvation and inclusion in the people of Abraham.[46]

However, the immediate context emphasizes their wonderful reception of Paul, and their blessedness toward him (their relationship with Paul flanks the saying).[47] A shift from a joyous relationship to enmity is affirmed in v. 16 where Paul asks whether he has become their enemy. However, the two possible ideas of God's blessing and blessing toward Paul are intertwined. As they received Paul as an angel, even as Jesus, they received with faith the message he preached, and were converted, the Spirit poured into them. With Paul, they experienced wonderful blessings, not through the Judaizers or law-observance.

---

to extract something by force, the only other use is in Mark 2:4 of ripping a hole in the roof to lower the crippled man to Jesus for healing.

45. The term *makarismos* is rare in wider sources, see e.g., Sib. Or. 13:117 (things being so bad it was a blessing going from the living to the dead); Josephus, *J.W.* 6.213 (in a famine being dead was a state of blessedness); Philo, *Somn.* 2.35 (a name Asser meaning 'blessed').

46. Dunn, *Galatians*, 235.

47. Moo, *Galatians*, 285–286, Hays, 'Galatians,' 294.

However, more importantly, they became God's children and experienced God's favor. As such, the use of the term is double layered with the most apparent meaning being their blessing of Paul, but even more the blessed state they were thus in.

In the second part of the verse, as if standing in a court or writing an affidavit, Paul testifies to the extent of the Galatians' concern for Paul on the basis of his experience of it. He uses the verb *martyreō*, a verb found commonly in the NT (seventy-six times, esp. John, and to a lesser extent Luke and Hebrews), but sparingly by Paul (eight times). Paul uses it on three other occasions in the sense of giving witness to something relevant to his argument (Rom 10:2; 2 Cor 8:3; Col 4:13)'[48] Here, he gives witness to the Galatians of their treatment of him.

Specifically, that 'if possible, you would have dug out your eyes to give to me.' As noted above on v. 13, this gives us a clue as to Paul's condition—some kind of recurring eye complaint. 'If possible,' speaks of the stupidity of such an act, for all it achieves is self-blindness. Even today, while we can remove parts of the eye and transplant them (e.g., retina) and are close to being able to transplant the whole eye, this would not be achieved by the gouging out of one's eyes!

The term for 'dig' is *exoryssō*, a verb that compounds *ek* (from) and *oryssō*, 'dig.' The latter term is used for digging a winepress (Matt 21:33; Mark 12:1) and digging a hole to bury a coin (Matt 25:18). *Exoryssō* is used once else, of men digging out a hole in a roof to lower a disabled man to Jesus for healing (Mark 2:4, cf. Josephus, *J.W.* 7.379 of the destruction of the temple foundations). The image of gouging out eyes is also found in 1 Sam 11:2 where the Ammonite Nahash offers to make a treaty with Jabesh-Gilead if the men of Jabesh gouged out their right eyes (cf. Josephus, *Ant.* 6.71). As a result, Saul plundered the Ammonites.

Here, the Galatians are prepared to gouge out their eyes for

---

48. Paul's other uses include the law and Prophets bearing witness to righteousness by faith (Rom 3:21), sharing the gospel of Christ's resurrection as giving witness (1 Cor 15:15), having a good reputation (witness) (1 Tim 5:10), and Christ's testimony before Pilate (1 Tim 6:13).

Paul. This has some resonances with the common Jewish idea (the *lex talionis*, 'the law of retaliation'), 'an eye for an eye.' This law lay at the heart of the Jewish understanding of just retribution for harm done (Exod 21:24; Lev 24:20; Deut 19:21). In the Sermon on the Mount, however, Jesus urges disciples not to live by this command but to respond to those who harm them with non-violence, generosity, love, and prayer (Matt 5:38–46). Here, Paul may have this command in the back of his mind, as he commends them for their desire to exchange an eye for an eye in the positive sense of healing.

This verse is another example of Paul's preparedness to use strong language and vivid ideas. In v. 14, he used a vulgar term for spitting. He will later state his wish that the Judaizers would castrate themselves! In Phil 3:2, he speaks of Judaizers as dogs, evil workers, and mutilators of the flesh (like Ba'al prophets and pagans who self-mutilate). He takes the claims of his former life in Phil 3:5–6 and deems them excrement (Phil 3:8). Paul is not afraid to state things as they are.

'To give to me' uses *didōmi*, 'give' (see on 1:4) and speaks of grace—they were so concerned about Paul's state that they wanted to give him their own eyes. The verb exemplifies their state of blessedness—rather than repudiate Paul despite his sorry state, full of the grace of the gospel, they were prepared to blind themselves for Paul's healing. That they were prepared to give their eyes to Paul rules out the Galatians repudiating Paul, the converse is the case.

AM I NOW YOUR ENEMY? (4:16)

In *Galatians 4:16*, Paul asks a second question in this section:
So then (*ōste*, 2:13), **have I become** (perfect *ginomai*, 2:17) **your** (genitive plural *sy*, 1:3) **enemy** (*echthros*)[49] **in telling the truth** (present participle *alētheuō*)[50] **to you** (dative plural *sy*)?

The inferential conjunction *ōste* (see further 2:13) here has the

49. The noun ἐχθρὸς (*echthros*) is found in 4:16 only. The term means 'enemy.' Otherwise, Paul uses it eight times. It is related to *echthra*, 'enmity' used in the vice list in 5:20.
50. The verb *alētheuō*, 'tell the truth,' is used only once in Galatians 4:16 of Paul's telling

sense 'how is it then ...' 'so how is it then ...' In light of your former love for me, how on earth have things changed so much that I am now your enemy for telling the truth to you?

'Have I become' uses *ginomai*, used three times in the letter in the form *mē genoito* (may it not be, come to pass) (2:17; 3:21; 6:14). Here, in the perfect tense, it refers to their state of mind toward Paul. Paul is asking whether in the period since they welcomed him as an angel or Jesus Christ and were prepared to rip out their eyes for him, they have somehow shifted their view of him to see him as an enemy.

Clearly, for Paul, the Galatians are not his enemies—they are his brothers and sisters whom he led to Christ and loves as a mother (see v. 19). The question is, has their view of Paul shifted from love to enmity. Paul uses the standard Koine term for 'enemy,' a term that comes from the root idea 'hated' and speaks of someone who is repudiated as an opponent or adversary.[51]

'For telling the truth to you' uses the present participle of *alētheuō*, 'to be truthful, to tell the truth.' It is only used twice in the NT with the other use in Eph 4:15—'rather, speaking the truth in love ...' Here, it refers to Paul's sharing the gospel with them, the truth commonly associated with the gospel. In Eph 1:13, Paul describes the gospel as 'the word of truth, the gospel of your salvation (cf. Col 1:5). This close connection between gospel

---

the truth to the Galatians. The only other use is Eph 4:15 where the body of Christ is built up through 'speaking the truth in love.' See also the noun *alētheia* (2:4, 14; 5:7).

51. See W. Foerster, 'ἐχθρός,' in *TDNT* 2:811. In the wider NT, it is used of any enemy whom one is to love and not hate (Matt 5:43–44; Luke 6:27, 35) including from within one's own household (Matt 10:36), the ultimate adversary—Satan (Matt 13:25, 28, 39; Luke 10:19) who God will subjugate under Jesus' feet (Matt 22:44; Mark 12:36; Luke 20:43; Acts 2:35; Heb 1:13; 10:13, cf. Ps 110:1), whom God saved Israel from (Luke 1:71, 74),—enemies in parables (Luke 19:27), Israel's enemies (Rome) (Luke 19:43), Elymas in Cyprus who opposed Paul (Acts 13:10), friends of the world who are enemies of God (Jas 4:4), and enemies of the two prophets (Rev 11:5, 12). Paul uses it of humans in their fallen state as enemies of God (Rom 5:10; Col 1:21) including Jews who reject Christ before God (Rom 11:28), all God's enemies who will be subjugated including death (1 Cor 15:25–26, Ps 110:1), enemies one should feed (Rom 12:20), enemies of the cross (Phil 3:18), and the lazy who are not to be regarded as an enemy but warned as a brother (2 Thess 3:15).

and truth is reflected in 2:5 where Paul lays his gospel before the Jerusalem pillars 'so that *the truth of the gospel* might remain for you.' Similarly, in 2:14, Peter is challenged by Paul for his conduct out of step with *the truth of the gospel*.' Here in 4:16, it speaks of his initial gospel and Paul's teaching in the letter.[52]

The idea of 'truth' shows Paul's confidence in his gospel and also reminds them that there is one true gospel, and that is what they heard from Paul. He is reasserting this in the letter. The Judaizers have diverted the Galatians from a positive reception and esteem of Paul, causing them to see him as an enemy who preaches a false gospel. Paul is countering—the converse is the case! It is the Judaizers who are their enemies—perverting the gospel and misleading them. This verse demonstrates that the issue was not simply doctrine but included a rejection of Paul himself. One senses his pain as he writes these words.

THEY ZEALOUSLY SEEK YOU AND YOUR ZEAL (4:17)

In *Galatians 4:17*, Paul speaks of the motives of the Judaizers:
They are zealous [for] you (third-person present plural *zēloō*),[53] **not** (*ou*, 1:1) **commendably** (*kalōs*),[54] **but** (*alla*, 1:1) **they want** (present plural *thelō*, 1:7) **to exclude** (aorist infinitive *ekkleiō*)[55] **you** (plural *sy*), **so that** (*hina*, 1:16) **you are zealous** (second person plural *zēloō*) **for them** (plural *autos*, 1:1).

---

52. Those who date Galatians later like Lightfoot suggest this could refer to warnings given on earlier trips, e.g., Acts 18:23 (Lightfoot, *Galatians*, 176).

53. The verb *zēloō*, 'be zealous, strive, desire, be jealous,' is used thrice in Galatians, twice in 4:17 of the Judaizers being zealous for the Galatians so that they would be the same for them. In 4:18, Paul confirms the principle that being zealous is good, if for a good purpose. In 5:20, he uses the associated noun, *zēlos*, negatively of jealousy. Otherwise, the term can connote a positive zeal.

54. The adverb καλῶς (*kalōs*) meaning 'fitly, well, appropriately, commendably' and so on, is used twice. The first use is 4:17, where it is negated of the Judaizers who make a big deal of the Galatians for 'no good purpose.' In 5:7, it is used positively of the Galatians 'running well' in their Christian lives, only to be hindered by the Judaizers who are cutting in on them. The adverb is linked to the adjective *kalos*, 'good, well' used in 4:18 and 6:9.

55. The one use of ἐκκλείω (*ekkleiō*) is in 4:17. The term compounds *ek* (from) and *kleiō* (shut, lock, bar), a term not found in Paul. The compound speaks of being 'shut out'

This verse is clearly a chiasm:

A1   *They* are *zealous* (*zēloō*), for *you* not commendably,

   B   but they want to exclude you,

A2   So that *you* are *zealous* (*zēloō*) for *them*.

The chiasm is seen in the repetition of *zēloō* in A and A' and the inversion of the direction of the zeal; for you—for them. The verb *zēloō* used twice here and once in the next verse, speaks of zeal or jealousy for the other. It can be a positive attribute, where one is zealous of a good attribute (1 Cor 12:31; 14:1, 39) or zealous for someone out of love (2 Cor 11:2). Otherwise, it is negative, someone zealous after something false or jealous of another in a sinful sense (Acts 7:9; 17:5; 1 Cor 13:4; Jas 4:2). It then carries the idea of passion for something or someone, whether positive or negative.

The first use speaks of the Judaizers' passion for the Galatians. They are perhaps influenced by the zealot tradition of Israel, as was Paul in his pre-conversion state. They were seeking to emulate the role models of zeal from Israel's tradition. Of special note is Phinehas, the grandson of Aaron, who rose up and dealt with Ba'al worshipers in the wilderness (Num 25:11, 13). The language is used concerning Phinehas in later Jewish writings in which he is a prototype of zeal for Yahweh.[56]

Similarly, *zēloō* is used for Elijah, who rose up and destroyed the Ba'al prophets (1 Kings 19:10, 14; 1 Macc 2:58). The term is used with regard to the Maccabees who were believed to stand in this tradition upholding the name of God and his holy law (1 Macc 2:24, 26, 27, 50).[57] His opponents likely saw Paul as a

and this is what Paul believes the Judaizers are wanting to do to the Galatians—in their zeal to bring them under the law, they are willing to shut them out of Christ.

56. See Sir 45:23; 1 Macc 2:54, cf. 1 Macc 2:26; 4 Macc 18:12.

57. See also 2 Sam 21:2; 2 Kings 10:16, 18; Judith 9:4. *Zēloō* is also used of God's zeal for his name (Ezek 39:25), his people, and land (Deut 32:19; Josh 24:19; Isa 11:11, 13; Joel 2:18; Zech 1:14; 8:2). It is used negatively of jealousy, as in the case of Joseph's brothers (Gen 37:11, see also Gen 26:14; 30:1; Num 11:29; Ps 72:3 [Eng. 73:3]; Prov 3:21; 4:14; 23:17; 24:1; Sir 9:1, 11; 37:10; 45:18, cf. Wis 1:12; Ezek 31:9). It can also be used positively of a jealous or zealous love for another (see also Num 5:14, 30), positive envy of the busyness of the ant (Prov 6:6), and zeal for good (Sir 51:18) (cf. 2 Macc 4:16).

turncoat or a compromiser, prepared to compromise the law to win converts.

'Not commendably' translates the awkward Greek *ou kalōs*. The adverb *kalōs* speaks of something 'done well, good, rightly, commendably.' Paul uses it twelve times of something true (Rom 11:20), yielding easily (2 Cor 11:4), and most often of doing something well including marry (1 Cor 7:37, 38), give thanks (1 Cor 14:17), contribute financially to Paul (Phil 4:14), manage a household (1 Tim 3:4, 12), serving (1 Tim 3:13), or leading (1 Tim 5:17). In 5:7, he uses it of the Galatians 'running well' but now being put off their stride by the Judaizers. It can also have the sense of acting commendably or honorably (Heb 13:18).

Here, it can go in the direction of motive and/or their alignment with the gospel. If motivation is in mind, while noble in their zeal and commitment to the Galatians, they are acting dishonorably. If the gospel is in mind, they are zealous, but their zeal is misguided, as despite their zeal, they are acting out of step with the gospel. 'They have a zeal (*zēlos*) for God, but not according to knowledge' (Rom 10:1). They have the kind of zeal (*zēlos*) Paul had as a persecutor of the church (Phil 3:6). They are pouring their attention on the Galatians, perhaps alluring them with the attention, but they are doing so with a false gospel. As noted in the notes, it is linked to *kalos* (good) in v. 18.

In part two of the verse, B, the center of the chiasm, Paul states what they *are* doing. 'But' is *alla*, striking its usual strong contrast (see on 1:1). 'Want' is *thelō*, speaking of their will and desire (see on 1:7). Here, it speaks of the will of the Judaizers, which is counter to the will of God and that of Paul (see on 1:4, 7).

'To shut you out' is *ekkleiō*, another compound verb that blends *ek* (from) and *kleiō* meaning to 'shut, lock, bar' passage.[58] It thus has the sense 'shut out from.' What is in mind is exclusion from God's people, the *ekklēsia* (note the similarity of terms) into

---

58. The verb *kleiō* is used of shutting a door to pray (Matt 6:6), a locked house (Luke 11:7; John 20:19, 26), prison (Acts 5:23), or temple (Acts 21:30), locking people out of the kingdom (Matt 23:13; 25:10 [wedding banquet]; Rev 3:7, 8), the heavens shut so there is no rain (Luke 4:25; Rev 11:6), shut up affections (1 John 3:17), a locked abyss (Rev 20:3), and the final eschatological kingdom with open doors (Rev 21:25).

which they have been called. The Judaizers claim to be including them by enforcing Mosaic expectations, where in fact, they are shutting out the Galatians. Or better, they are shutting them in Judaism without Jesus, imprisoning them in the jail of the law and sin, and part of a false Judaism which has had its day and is now as defunct as a pagan religion (see on 4:8–9).

The final *hina* purpose clause (see on *hina*, 1:16) and part A' of the chiasm reverses the flow of zeal in part A. According to Paul, their purpose is that the Galatians become 'zealous for them' and their cause—promoting a gospel which urges faith in Jesus plus Torah observance. In so doing, Paul becomes their enemy. This clause speaks of the mission of the Judaizers to make converts from among the Galatians and beyond, and some of Paul's converts taking up their gospel and propounding it. Perhaps they are wanting the Galatians to join them with the zeal of Phinehas in traveling the Christian churches seeking to fully convert those gentiles who have become Christians and remain in an uncircumcised state.

THE GOODNESS OF APPROPRIATE ZEAL (4:18)

In *Galatians 4:18*, Paul continues with the theme of zeal, *zēlos*, and *kal-* language (*kalōs* above, *kalos* here):

And (*de*, 1:15) **[it is] always** (*pantote*)[59] **good** (*kalos*)[60] **to be zealous** (aorist passive *zēloō*, 4:17) **in** (*en*, 1:6) **[doing] good** (*kalos*) **and** (kai, 1:1) **not** (*mē*, 1:7) **only** (monon, 1:23) **in** (*en*) **my**

---

59. The adverb πάντοτε (*pantote*), compounds *pas* (all) and *tote*, itself an adverb of time (at that time, then), and so giving the meaning 'at all times, always.' While it is common, 4:18 is the only use in Galatians. Paul often uses it in relation to prayer.

60. The adjective καλός (*kalos*) is found three times in Galatians, twice in Gal 4:18—'it is always good to be zealous for good.' The third use is in 6:9—'do not become weary of doing good.'

(accusative *egō*, 1:2) **presence** (*pareimi*)[61] **with** (*pros*, 1:17) **you** (accusative plural *sy*, 1:3).

Paul qualifies what he has just said, ensuring that the Galatians understand that zeal for something consistent with God and the gospel is always a good thing. The problem then with the Judaizers is not their zeal, but what they are zealous for.

The term *kalos*, 'good,' is related to *kalōs* above (right, good, commendable) and Paul's use of the two terms is not accidental. *Kalos*, 'good' is more common, found 101 times in the NT. Forty-one of its uses are in Paul in the moral sense of doing what is or is not right. For example, in Rom 12:17, he urges the Romans to 'consider doing what is *right* before all people.' In 2 Cor 8:21, he says, 'we aim to do what is *right* not only before the Lord but also before people.' In 1 Thess 5:21, believers are to 'hold fast to what is *good*.' Later in the letter, in 6:9, he will state, 'and let us not grow weary in *doing good*,'[62] so that Christians may reap an eternal harvest.

Here, the emphasis is on being zealous for what is good. That which is good is what is consistent with the gospel and its ethic. Things like circumcision, eating protocols, and calendric observance are not what matters. What matters is a love that flows from faith (5:6) and the fruit of the Spirit. Doing such things is *always* (*pantote*) good. *Pantote* is a compound of *pas* (all) and *tote* (then, at that time) and so speaks of 'at all times.' This use calls to mind 1 Cor 15:58: '*always* abounding in the work of the Lord.' Similarly, in 1 Thess 5:15 there is a synonymous Greek word for 'good:' 'always seek to do good to one another to and to all people.'[63]

Zeal is a dangerous thing if it is falsely applied. We have seen

---

61. The verb πάρειμι (*pareimi*) compounds *para* (with) and *eimi* (to be), and so yields the idea of one being with the other, hence the meaning 'present, presence.' It is found twice in Galatians of Paul's hypothetical presence with the Galatians (4:18) and his actual desire to be so (4:20). It is a stative verb with a transitive preposition (*pros*). See further on 1:18.

62. See also Rom 7:16, 18, 21; 14:21; 1 Cor 5:6; 7:1, 8, 26; 9:15; 2 Cor 13:7; 1 Tim 1:8, 18; 2:3; 3:1, 7, 13; 4:4, 6; 5:10, 25; 6:12, 13, 18, 19; 2 Tim 1:14; 2:3; 4:7; Tit 2:7, 14; 3:8, 14.

63. Paul often uses *pantote* in terms of prayer (Rom 1:10; 1 Cor 1:4; Eph 5:20; Phil 1:4; Col 1:3; 4:12; 1 Thess 1:2; 2 Thess 1:3, 11; 2:13; Phlm 4). See also 'we are always of good

this in history with world wars sparked by people with maniacal zeal built on false ideologies (e.g., Hitler). In our present world, extreme forms of religious zealotry create international conflict (e.g., Jihadism). Indeed, passion can take any ideology and violate human relations.

'Not only (*monon*, see on 1:23) in my presence (*pareimi*) with you' speaks of the Galatians being faithful in good works (as an outworking of justification by faith) in all situations, whether Paul is there or not.[64] Currently, he is absent from them, in Antioch (or perhaps Ephesus for a late dating of the letter).

In v. 20, he will use the same verb *pareimi*[65] of his wish to be there with them. Like a parent who has left the kids for the holidays (note the mother metaphor in what follows), Paul wants the kids to play nicely (cf. Phil 1:27; 2:12). They are not doing so but are hanging out with the wrong crowd allowing them to lead them astray. If they do behave, they will not welcome in the false teachers but will shut them out, for that would be the 'right' thing to do.

There is no connective (asyndeton, see 2:6) in **Galatians 4:19**, which adds emphasis to what follows:

IN BIRTH PANGS AGAIN UNTIL CHRIST IS FORMED (4:19)

My (genitive *ego*, 1:2) **children** (plural *teknon*),[66] **for whom** (masculine[67] accusative plural *hos*, 1:5) **I again** (*palin*, 1:9) **have**

---

courage' (2 Cor 5:6), and 'rejoice in the Lord always' (Phil 4:4; 1 Thess 5:16). See also 2 Cor 2:14; 4:10; 9:8; Phil 1:20; 2:12; Col 4:6; 1 Thess 2:16; 3:6; 4:17; 2 Tim 3:7.

64. This is a good example of the iterative present whereby '[t]he present tense may be used to describe an event that *repeatedly* happens.' (See Wallace, *Greek Grammar*, 520).

65. The verb compounds *para*, 'with, alongside,' with *eimi*, 'be' and so produces 'be with, here, present, come, coming.' Paul uses it of his presence or otherwise with his congregations (1 Cor 5:3; 10:2, 11; 11:9; 13:2, 10, cf. Col 1:6). See also Matt 26:50; Luke 13:1; John 7:6; 11:28; Acts 10:21, 33; 12:20; 17:6; 24:19; Heb 12:11; 13:5; 2 Pet 1:9, 12; Rev 17:8.

66. The general term for a child, τέκνον (*technon*), is used five times in Galatians—4:19, 25, 27, 28, 31. At other points Paul uses *huios* (son, 1:15; 3:26) in an inclusive manner, and *nēpios* (see 4:1).

67. Keen Greek readers will note that the relative pronoun οὓς (*ous*) is masculine while τέκνα (*tekna*) is neuter which is unusual. Wallace, *Greek Grammar*, 337 notes that often

birth pangs (*ōdinō*)[68] **until** (*mechri*)[69] **which time** (genitive *hos*)[70] **Christ** (*Christos*, 1:1) **has been formed** (aorist passive subjunctive *morphoō*) **in** (*en*, 1:6) **you** (dative plural *sy*, 1:3).

Paul addresses them for the first time other than 'brothers and sisters' or 'O foolish Galatians.' 'My children' uses the plural of *technon*, a standard neuter term for a child—inclusive of male or female. This is the first use of the noun in the letter as usually he prefers *huios* (son, inclusive) or *nēpios*. A similar appeal is made in 1 Cor 4:14, although he adds 'beloved'—'my *beloved* children' (cf. 1 Tim 2:1; 1 John 2:11). Strangely, some translations opt for 'my little children' (ESV, NRSV) or 'my dear children' (NIV). Neither seems appropriate. The clause is simply 'my children,' with *technon* a term for a child up until the coming of age, and the term 'beloved' is not attached here. These are overly interpretative, and as in the NET Bible, it should be translated 'my children.'

However, the address 'my children'[71] is somewhat ambiguous. Clearly, he chooses it because of the family motif in this section. At one level, it is intimate and affectionate, Paul speaking as a parent who loves his children. It is also potentially demeaning, as he is addressing the Galatians as immature Christians, not fully

'relative pronouns do not follow the basic rules of agreement. Sometimes the gender of the RP does not match that of the antecedent, usually because of sense agreement superseding syntactical agreement (*constructio ad sensum*).' He goes on, 'To make matters more difficult, the relation of the RP to its antecedent is sometimes complicated: the antecedent may be lacking, or the relative phrase may be adverbial and thus not refer to a noun or other substantive. As with the demonstratives, the discovery of these syntactical "glitches" occasionally yields a point of exegetical value as well.' Here, in a patriarchal context where the masculine is used inclusively for a group, the masculine seems natural to describe the Galatians.

68. The verb ὠδίνω (*hōdinō*) is found twice in Galatians, of Paul's 'travail, birth pangs' that Christ is formed in the Galatians, and in 4:27 of Sarah who is to rejoice that she is in labor. The only other NT use is Rev 12:2.

69. The preposition μέχρι (*mechri*) means 'until' and is used once in Gal 4:19 of Paul's deep travail *until* Christ is formed in the Galatians.

70. Sometimes the relative pronoun, here *hos*, is used as an indicator of time. It sits with *mechri* here giving the sense 'until which time.' See BDAG 727. Hence, I have not emboldened it as it is redundant to the English translation.

71. There is no need to translate it 'my little children' as do the ESV as *technon* is used of a child up to the coming of age.

formed. In the Roman world, being a child was not something to be esteemed; rather, it meant one is immature and not yet come of age. However, we do not need to decide which of these Paul intends as both angles are likely in mind. Yes, Paul loves them and is deeply concerned for them as a mother with a child (see what follows). Equally, they are not yet mature, allowing themselves to be blown hither and thither by the waves and winds of false teaching (cf. Eph 4:24). They need to grow up, recognize the threat to the gospel, and instead of yielding to the Judaizers, repudiate their message.

In what follows, Paul uses a feminine image of his ministry. Considering so many people falsely think Paul is sexist, somewhat surprisingly, using feminine motifs of his ministry is not unusual for Paul. In 1 Cor 3:1–2, he speaks as a mother who feeds the Corinthians with milk, not solid food. In 1 Thess 2:7, he uses the mother image of his caring for the Thessalonians with gentle affection. He balances this with the use of the father image (1 Cor 4:15; Phil 2:22).

The verb *ōdinō* speaks of the travail of giving birth.[72] This meaning is seen in the only non-Pauline use in the NT, in Rev 12:2, where the woman clothed with the sun standing upon the moon who is adorned with a crown of twelve stars is crying out in the pains of childbirth. The associated verb formed with the suffix *syn*, *synōdinō*, is also used in Rom 8:22 of the whole of creation groaning as in the pains of childbirth up until the present. As in Rev 12:2, in Gal 4:27, *hōdinō* will again be used for the barren woman who has not been in the birth pains of labor but is now to rejoice for she will have many children (*tekna*). Here then, like Mary (4:4) and Sarah (4:27), Paul is again (*palin*) in the pains of childbirth for the Galatians. In their repudiation of the

---

72. In the LXX, it is used metaphorically of conceiving an attitude, like evil (Ps 7:15), and literally of a mother in the pains of labor (Song 8:5; Sir 19:11; 31:5; 48:19). It is also used figuratively in the Prophets of Zion as a woman in labor as Israel is taken to Babylon (Mic 4:10, cf. Isa 23:4; 54:1; 66:7, 8; Jer 4:3), of Israel's birth (Isa 26:7; 45:10), of mountains writhing as if in the pains of childbirth (Hab 3:10), Sarah's birth of the nation (Isa 51:2, cf. Isa 23:4; Jer 29:23). It is used for stars travailing in battle (Sib. Or. 5.514). Philo uses it of the earth producing life (*Opif.* 43).

gospel of grace through faith, they are in a dangerous place and need to be 'born again' so to speak.

'Until Christ has been formed in you' brings to the fore Paul's cruciform theology.[73] The verb *morphoō* is an *hapax legomenon*, found only here in the NT. However, elsewhere Paul uses *morph*–language, especially in Philippians.

In Phil 2:6–11, Jesus Christ was in the 'form (*morphē*) of God'—speaking of his ontology as God pre-existent. Jesus repudiated using violent force or self-arrogation (*harpagmos*) in any way to claim his essential equality with God and dominate the world. Rather, he took the path never traveled, and as the world's sovereign, he emptied himself. This self-emptying does not mean that he in any sense ceased to be God whose form he retained, but that he poured himself out for the world. Still God, he took the form of a slave among us in human form. He showed us what God is really like and what true humanity can be. In a world where humility is weakness, he voluntarily humbled himself to the point of death, even the most heinous and dishonorable of deaths, on a cross from where he cried out his sense of God-abandonment (Mark 15:34; Ps 22:1).

Having died, he was raised from the dead by God and is exalted by God to the fullness of his glory, granted the name above all names, and to whom every knee will bow. He is God the Son. He is Lord. He is our everything.

Believers, when justified by faith, are declared righteous in God's sight, included in Christ, filled with the Spirit, and so begins a journey of transformation. They are formed into Christ (*symmorphos*), the image of God, from one degree of glory to another (Rom 8:29; 2 Cor 3:18; Col 1:15). We become more and more like him as we submit to him; he dwells in us by his Spirit—the Spirit of God and of Christ (Rom 8:9). We are conformed to his likeness, experiencing his life of suffering and

---

73. On Paul's cruciformity see Michael Gorman, Inhabiting the Crucified God: Kenosis, Justification, and Theosis in Paul's Narrative Soteriology (Grand Rapids: Eerdmans, 2009); Cruciformity: Paul's Narrative Spirituality of the Cross (Grand Rapids: Eerdmans, 2001); Becoming the Gospel: Paul, Participation, and Mission (Grand Rapids: Eerdmans, 2015); and Gorman's other writings.

death. We delight in this, wanting to know the fellowship of sharing in his sufferings, morphing to be like him (*symmorphizō*) in his death (Phil 3:10). Believers are able to go through this and be changed to be more and more like him because of the burning cauldron of his presence in our hearts—the Spirit.

Ultimately, having lived the life of faith, we will die and experience the fullness of bodily transformation. Our bodies of humiliation, riddled with sin and death, will be transformed in the twinkling of an eye (*metaschēmatizō, symmorphos,* Phil 3:21) to be like Christ's glorious body—indestructible and immortal (Phil 3:20–21; 1 Cor 15:50–54). Our final enemy will be defeated by the one who went through death into life and in whom we are bound (1 Cor 15:56). We will then no longer be flesh and blood but will have bodies animated utterly and completely by the Spirit. We will then be with God forever (1 Thess 4:17; Phil 1:19–24). Just as we experience resurrection, so the world and universe will be set free from its bondage to death and decay, experiencing the full freedom of the people of God (Rom 8:19–23).

The Galatians have begun this journey, becoming believers as they heard Paul and Barnabas preach the gospel, and receiving the Spirit (3:2–5). They have embarked on the cruciform Christian life—humility, selflessness, service, sacrifice, suffering, love, and even death, for the sake of the world. They know what it is to live in the experience of the cross, empowered by the Holy Spirit, one eye over the shoulder remembering the earthly Jesus, the other eye ahead fixed upon Jesus the exalted Lord, as they press on to win the prize for which they have been called heavenward (Phil 3:12–14).

However, they are now being diverted by Judaizers who are saying Jesus and faith are not enough. They are being seduced to abandon reliance on Christ and to come under law instead. To forsake faith is a disaster, as no flesh can be justified before God by doing the law. One must do it all to make it on this basis. To do so is implausible. If it were possible, Christ would not have needed to come. As it is, he did come, and he lived the law, and the law is complete in him, and all that remains is the 'law' of Christ.

If the Galatians turn back now as they are threatening to do, this will have the effect of abortion or infanticide—killing them, making them sinners again before a glorious, righteous God rather than his beloved children. This God must ultimately act to cleanse his world of all sin, evil, and wrongdoing. If they are in this state, relying on law-observance, trusting in the flesh, they will be lost.

These young Christians are becoming deformed, or rather, conformed to the false patterns of this world (Rom 12:2), and will ultimately die if they do not turn back to grace, faith, and reliance on the Spirit. In light of God's grace, they must repent and offer their bodies as living sacrifices as their spiritual act of worship again (Rom 12:1).

Paul, the church planter and pastor, is like a mother at the bedsides of her children who are sick with a hideous fatal disease. They are being infected or poisoned by the false theology of the Judaizers which brings them out of Christ and under the law, and so sin's potent hold of them is reinstated. They are going back into the prison of sin, under its power. The law will take up its place as a prison-keeper, as a tutor, ruler, and manager, and take a grip on their lives. They will be swept up into the self-reliance and legalism which is the inevitable end of such a journey. Having taken Jesus the ultimate antidote previously, they are now falling prey to death's sting of sin, to sin's poison which destroys, and to sin's power—the law (1 Cor 15:55–56).

'Where is your sting?' has become, 'in your veins and you will die!' The death that was swallowed up in God's victory in Christ, has been released from the maw and is now in danger of again consuming them (1 Cor 15:54). They are on the precipice, so to speak, in danger of being consumed and destroyed not only by their own attitudes as they disintegrate (5:15, 26), but for all eternity.

So Paul is in travail and prayer for them, pleading with God and by letter with them that they repudiate this false notion of law-observance as a means of righteousness, whether to get in or stay in. He yearns that they return to Jesus to again experience his forgiveness and heart-cleansing, the power of his Spirit, and to continue the journey of being transformed more and more into the image of the Son, their God.

PAUL'S YEARNING AND PERPLEXITY (4:20)

Paul's appeal in this section ends in *Galatians 4:20* with a final statement of his desire and frustration:

And (*de*, 1:15) **I wish** (imperfect *thelō*, 1:13) **to be present** (*pareimi*, 4:18)[74] **with** (*pros*, 1:17) **you** (plural *sy*, 1:3) **now** (*arti*, 1:9) **and** (*kai*, 1:1) **change** (*allassō*)[75] **my** (genitive *egō*) **tone** (*phōnē*),[76] **because** (*hoti*, 1:6) **I am perplexed** (*aporeō*)[77] **at** (*en*, 1:6) **you** (dative plural *sy*).

The *de* does not introduce a contrast but a continuation of Paul's feelings toward the Galatians—hence, 'and.' 'I wish' uses *thelō* (see 1:13), Paul expressing his desire, his want, his wish. As noted on 1:4 and 1:7, this fits in with the battle for the Galatians in the letter. Will they yield to God's will, or the demonic perspective of the Judaizers? Picking up the metaphor in the previous verse, this is the desire of a mother who wants desperately to get home and be with her children. The verb is imperfect, likely a voluntative of tendential imperfect, which speaks of something desired but not carried out.[78] The placement of the verb gives it prominence.

'To be present' is the same verb used in v. 18 where he speaks of the Galatians being zealous whether or not Paul is with them;

---

74. As in 1:18; 2:5; 4:18 we have a stative verb (παρεῖναι, *pareinai*) with a transitive preposition (πρὸς, *pros*). See further on 1:18.
75. The verb ἀλλάσσω (*allassō*) meaning 'change' is found once in Galatians in 4:20 where Paul speaks of changing his tone toward the Galatians.
76. The noun φωνή (*phōnē*) means 'voice,' or, as in its one use in Galatians 4:20, 'tone.'
77. The verb ἀπορέω (*aporeō*) is found once in Galatians, in 4:20. It speaks of being 'perplexed' or 'uncertain' at a loss over something. It speaks of Paul's frustration concerning the Galatians flirtation with the Judaizers.
78. See Wallace, *Greek Grammar*, 551. This differs from his earlier view that this is a customary or general imperfect speaking of a state that has continued for some time into the present. On this imperfect see Wallace, *Grammar*, 548.

this time, Paul is expressing his desire to visit the Galatians. He will fulfill this after the Jerusalem Council, which came soon after Galatians was written and he and Barnabas fell out over John Mark. After this rupture of relationship, Paul and Silas traveled through the Galatian churches with the Jerusalem Council letter that reinforced the message of Galatians (Acts 15:41).

His desire to come and be present is so that he can 'change his tone.' 'Change' is the verb *allassō*, used only six times in the NT. It is used outside of Paul twice. First, it is applied to Stephen supposedly saying that Jesus 'will change the customs that Moses handed on to us' (Acts 6:14). Second, it is used of the clothing of the universe being changed in the consummation (Heb 1:12). Paul's other uses include idolatrous humanity that 'exchanged' the glory of God for idols and of the transformation of the body at the resurrection (1 Cor 15:51, 52). It thus connotes a transformation or change.

Here, Paul wants to change his *phōnē*. *Phōnē* is a common noun (139 times in the NT) usually meaning 'voice' (cf. Eng. 'phone') but sometimes meaning 'shout,'[79] sound,[80] or language (1 Cor 14:10). Here it carries the sense of the tone of voice. This mention of tone suggests that Paul is aware that his letter is strong and to the point. Whereas, if he was among them, he could speak with them more gently and reasonably, dialoguing with them over the contentious issues and resolving them.

'Because I am perplexed at you' uses *aporeō*, which is rare in the NT (six times). *Aporeō* commonly speaks of being 'perplexed' as Herod was with John the Baptist (Mark 6:20), the women were at the empty tomb (Luke 24:4), the disciples were at Jesus' prediction that one would betray him (John 13:22), and Festus' quandary over what to do with Paul (Acts 25:20). Paul's one other use is 2 Cor 4:8 of his struggles as an apostle. Here, it speaks of his consternation and confusion over his children in Galatia. He

---

79. See, e.g., Mark 15:37; Luke 23:23; 1 Thess 4:16.
80. See, e.g., Luke 1:44; John 3:8; 1 Cor 14:7, 8; Rev 19:6.

is 'at a loss' concerning them.[81] The dative is causal, 'because of you.'

81. BDAG 119: 'to be in a confused state of mind, be at a loss, be in doubt, be uncertain.'

CHAPTER TWENTY-THREE: BE CHILDREN OF SARAH, NOT HAGAR (4:21–4:31)

THE HAGAR AND SARAH ALLEGORY

This is one of the most interesting passages in Galatians and all of Paul, calling to mind 1 Cor 10:1–5. Here, returning to the theme of Abraham and his family from Galatians 3, Paul delves into the law to seek to convince the Galatians, and perhaps the Judaizers who hear this letter read (those who desire to be under the law), to persevere in faith.

Through the passage, Paul draws on the story of the birth of Abraham's two sons, one to Hagar, the slave woman (Gen 16:1–16), and one to Sarah the free woman (Gen 21:1–7). He allegorizes Hagar and Sarah, Isaac and Ishmael, in terms of the gospel he is defending against that of the Judaizers. He picks up the notion of Hagar as the 'slave' and Sarah as 'the free woman.' As a slave, he argues, Hagar's son Ishmael is born according to the flesh. Whereas Sarah's son Isaac is born according to the promise of God of a son to her and Abraham.[1] The two women represent two covenants. Hagar corresponds to Mount Sinai in Arabia (cf. 1:17), whose children are born into slavery to the law. She also represents the earthly Jerusalem.

In vv. 27 Paul cites Isaiah 54, which speaks of Israel from the perspective of a barren woman (like Sarah) who will rejoice because she will have many children—as Isa 54 unfolds, these

---

1. See Gen 17:15–21, cf. Gen 15:4–5; 16:2–6; 18:9–9–15.

children are from the nations as Israel extends the place of her tent with her offspring possessing the nations.

In verses 28–31, Paul turns his attention directly to the Galatians, telling them that they are, like Isaac, children of the promise of Abraham and Sarah. He recalls Ishmael's persecution of Isaac, perhaps indicating Ishmael's mockery of Sarah (Gen 21:9) and historical enmity between the sons' descendants. Now, the Judaizers are doing the same to the Galatians; they are children of slavery mocking the children of promise.

Verse 30 quotes Gen 21:10 where Sarah demanded that Abraham cast out Hagar and Ishmael so that they will have no claim of an inheritance from Abraham. The quote is a direct statement to the Galatians to 'cast out' the Judaizers and any who yield to their false gospel. He concludes in v. 31 by reminding the Galatians that believers in Christ are not children of slavery (Hagar, the Mosaic Covenant, the law), but are children of the freewoman (Sarah, the Abrahamic Covenant and promise, and faith).

Scholars debate whether this passage should be viewed as a scriptural argumentation after the more direct teaching of 4:8–20[2] or a continuation of the previous passage.[3] As Moo rightly notes, this is a redundant argument, as Paul mixes argument from Scripture with the appeal. This passage differs from his earlier use of OT passages—which was more of a proof-text and exegetical approach (Gal 3:6–14)—to what Paul himself calls an allegorical interpretation of Gen 16–21 (v. 24).

Scholars also discuss whether Paul is defending himself and his gospel from texts used by the Judaizers, with some arguing that he is.[4] Some are unconvinced, suggesting this is Paul's innovation as it serves to continue his arguments in Gal 3:7–29, especially concerning who are the children of Abraham (God/Christ believers) and on what basis (faith).[5] One cannot know for sure, but it makes sense that Paul would be directly challenging the

2. Witherington, *Grace*, 321.

3. Longenecker, *Galatians*, 199.

4. Longenecker, *Galatians*, 207–208; Dunn, *Galatians*, 243; Hays, 'Galatians,' 300; Moo, *Galatians*, 293.

interpretation of the Judaizers, particularly concerning descent from Abraham and the need for circumcision in Gen 17. He has already drawn on Gen 15:6 which follows immediately after the first promise to Abraham of an heir. By drawing on the account of the birth of the two sons of Abraham, he challenges the Judaizers' interpretation of Genesis and its importance. As Moo notes, the slave/free contrast is dominant in the section.[6]

Paul's exegetical approach here is creative. He describes what he is doing as 'speaking allegorically.' The Greek term *allēgoreō* compounds *allos* (other) and *agoreuō* (speak), yielding the idea of 'speak with another meaning,' which could mean a typology, analogy, or an allegory as we might define them today.

Scholars also debate where this passage falls. Some argue it is a typological reading of the OT.[7] A typology differs from a symbol or allegory, as it is 'a representation of an actual, historical reference.' Biblical typology 'deals with the parallels between actual, historical (usually OT) figures or events in salvation history and their later, analogous fulfillment.'[8] Usually, in typology, an OT person (type) is identified with a New Testament person (antitype). Some argue that Paul here does not strictly do this, identifying Sarah and Hagar with institutions (covenants) or places (Mount Sinai, Jerusalem). They prefer to see this as an allegory.[9]

However, this distinction is too fine, and Paul is using both ideas paralleling Hagar and Sarah with people (Hagar: Judaizers and their adherents, Israel in rejection of Christ enslaved to law; Sarah: believers), covenants (Hagar: Sinai; Sarah: Abrahamic), and places (Hagar: Jerusalem; Sarah: Jerusalem above). As such,

---

5. Francis Watson, *Paul and the Hermeneutics of Faith*. CS (Edinburgh: T&T Clark, 2004), 207.
6. Moo, *Galatians*, 393.
7. E.g., Bruce, *Galatians*, 217.
8. For this definition see *PDTT* 117. Such an approach was one of the four basic ways of interpretation in the Middle Ages, the others being literal, analogical, and spiritual.
9. E.g., Richard B. Hays, *Echoes of Scripture in the Letters of Paul* (New Haven: Yale University Press, 1989), 116; Longenecker, *Galatians*, 209, Witherington, *Grace*, 322–23; Dunn, *Galatians*, 247–48.

Paul is using a mixture of the two[10] and likely did not distinguish between them as we might today.

Whatever category we place this passage in, Paul is creatively drawing meaning from the OT texts to the current situation. He is reading the OT texts in Genesis and Isa 54 back through the lens of Christ, and the gospel revealed to him. As Moo says,

Paul knows that Christ is the climax of salvation history and that access to Christ is given by faith (alone!) and through the eschatological gift of the Spirit (see esp. 3:1–5; 5:5). It is therefore by faith in Christ that the "many children" Isaiah has promised to eschatological Zion/Jerusalem have been born.[11]

Paul takes a story that is special to both himself and the Judaizers, one which he believes in historically, and (reading it Christologically) finds an analogy, typology, or allegory that speaks into his situation. For Paul, God speaks through these Scriptures into all situations and times. While some contemporary Christians may have reservations about his approach, it is governed by sound theology and, no doubt for Paul, the leading of the Spirit in biblical interpretation.

This seems an appropriate point to share something of my own experiences in reading Scripture. Before entering formal theological education, I sat under the preaching of an outstanding orator who had limited theological instruction. I loved his preaching. He made amazing connections. I especially remember a great sermon in which he drew together the Tree of Life in Eden and Revelation with Jesus' death 'on a tree' in Acts. He was a man gripped by the Spirit with a solid theology. When I entered formal theological education, I began to become very critical of his ministry as he seemed to find typological and allegorical connections that felt spurious. Yet, when studying Paul and finding passages like 1 Cor 10:1–4 and this one in Galatians, I recognize that his approach is similar to such passages. The preacher's gospel was the true gospel of salvation by faith in Christ. There were points of disagreement, the sort

---

10. E.g., Betz, *Galatians*, 239; Martyn, *Galatians*, 436. Others use a different term altogether, e.g., Fung, *Galatians*, 218 who uses 'analogy.'

11. Moo, *Galatians*, 294.

that good evangelicals have. He is, in fact, one of the finest preachers in NZ, albeit in the twilight of his service.

I have come to realize that while it is good to follow the basic approach to preaching taught in most evangelical seminaries—understand the text in context and apply judiciously—there is space for God to speak through those with a more imaginative approach to Scripture. In fact, sometimes exposition can be downright lacking in imagination.

On the other hand, preachers can become so imaginative that the gospel itself is violated, making connections that begin to cut into the meat of God's message. Paul, in the main, does not use Scripture as he does in this passage. Furthermore, he is likely responding to the Judaizers' use of the OT in the service of the gospel. As such, I would still advise preachers to follow the basics pretty closely—exegete well and apply judiciously.

We also need to remember that Paul was a well-trained exegete and seasoned preacher at the time of writing. He had spent years in the Scriptures, had been trained in exegesis and preaching under Gamaliel, and had a long career of preaching and teaching in Synagogues as a Jew, and in Synagogues, in public, in lecture halls, and churches as a Christian. He knew how to handle the word of truth, perhaps better than any man who has ever lived. After all, Paul wrote a large portion of the Christian Scriptures and has shaped western theology and thinking in many ways.

Like Paul, we must continue to do our homework, study hard, and learn the basic principles of preaching from context and applying well. We need to sit under the teaching and in the writings of those who are seasoned interpreters and preachers. Yet, we must leave room for the Spirit to move in the life of a preacher with a sound understanding of the gospel and use the Scriptures in different ways. The Scriptures are God-breathed (2 Tim 3:16) and the sword of the Spirit (Eph 6:17; Heb 4:11–12), and as we sit dwelling in them with the Spirit in and around us and speaking through others, we should expect to be led to some amazing creative connections. However, such moments as these should perhaps not become dominant as a means of interpretation, for this can lead people to turn Scripture into a playground for their own fancies. Such passages as these remind us that God speaks to his preachers, and sometimes he speaks in strange ways. This passage endorses the gospel, and we should let it speak loud and clear because the undergirding theology is magnificent.

The table below draws out the parallels drawn. Through Gen 21:10, there is an indirect charge to expel from the church those who are espousing and adopting a Judaizing theology and praxis. As he will say in 5:1, the Galatians must stand firm in the freedom of the gospel and not become subject to the Judaizers and their heretical teachings.

Sarah	Hagar
Free woman	Slave woman
Isaac	Ishmael
Born of Promise	Born of Flesh
Abrahamic Covenant	Sinai Covenant
Jerusalem Above	Sinai/Jerusalem
God's people	Judaism/Judaizers
Persecuted	Persecutor
Included	Excluded
Inheritance	No inheritance
Free	Slaves

ARE YOU REALLY LISTENING TO THE LAW? (4:21)

In *Galatians 4:21*, Paul begins with a question directed to those who are considering the Judaizing theology:

Tell (second person imperative plural *legō*, 1:9) **me** (dative *egō*, 1:2), **those** (plural *ho*, 1:1) **wanting** (second person plural *thelō*, 1:7) **to be** (infinitive *eimi*, 1:7) **under** (*hypo*, 1:11) **the law** (*nomos*), **are you not** (*ou*) **listening** (*akouō*, 1:13) **to the law** (accusative *nomos*, 2:16)?

'Tell' is *legō*, one of the standard Koine words for speaking, used seven times in Galatians of Paul's speech in the letter.[12] The

verb is a second person imperative, only the fourth time in the
letter Paul has used the imperative to appeal for a response from
the Galatians.[13] The use of the imperative speaks of the urgency
of the appeal.

Through his written words, Paul is challenging those who are
being seduced by the Judaizers to respond. 'Those wanting to be
under the law' uses *thelō*, 'I want, will, wish,' which is elsewhere
used of the will of the Judaizers,[14] Paul's wishes (3:2; 4:20), and as
here, of the will of some in the Galatian community (4:9; 5:17).
The associated noun *thelēma* is used in 1:4 of God's will that Jesus
would give himself up to death to deliver us from sin. Again,
we have the clash of wills the letter is premised on. Here, it is
a specific group among them—those wanting to be under the
law. Will the Galatians yield to their will, or that of God (see
further 1:4, 7)? The verb speaks of the human will that is involved
in decisions concerning faith matters. In so doing, those of the
Judaizers' perspective want to be severed from Christ, which is
eternally fatal.

Those who wish to be under the law would include any
Judaizers within the orb of the community, and those who are
being seduced to their way of thinking and desiring to yield to
their demands. At an even broader level, it is those who remain
in the Jewish system and reject Jesus (for whom Paul weeps,
Rom 9:2–3; 10:1). They remain yielded to the Torah, the Temple,
the priests, and the Pharisees—of which Paul was once one. He
yearns for them to hear the words of this liberated Pharisee and
recognize that Jesus is their Messiah, and yield to faith. Here,
his beloved converts, who have been liberated from the tyranny
of their former lives lived in submission to the *stoicheia* of Asia
Minor and Rome, are turning back to tyranny. Little wonder
Paul is horrified.

'Under the law' recalls 3:23 where Paul uses the phrase 'under
(*hypo*) the law' of Israel before faith came, when they were
'imprisoned until the coming faith would be revealed' and under

12. See 1:9; 3:15, 17; 4:1, 21; 5:2, 16, see further on 1:9.
13. Cf. 1:20; 3:7; 4:12, 30; 5:1, 13, 15, 16; 6:1, 2, 4, 6, 7, 11, 17, see further on 1:8; 4:12.
14. See 3:2; 4:17; 6:12, 13.

the law as a *paidagōgos*. It is the state that Jesus was born into (4:4) to 'redeem those *under* the law.' In a cosmic prison break, he broke them free from its tyranny. *Hypo* with the accusative (under) is used of being '*under* a curse' (3:10), '*under* a guardian' (3:25) or 'guardians' (4:2), and '*under* the elementary powers' (*stoicheia*) (4:3). Jesus was 'born *under* the law' (4:4) to redeem those held captive '*under* the law' (4:5). The Galatians and all Christians are to be led by the Spirit and 'not *under* the law' (5:18).

It speaks then of submitting to the rule of the Torah, which is oppression. While the religion is different than their own pagan religions from before their conversion, it is a return to a similar tool of oppression, a return to the pre-conversion state of separation from God.

'Are you not listening to the law' uses the verb *akouō*, an extremely common Greek word for hearing. Elsewhere in Galatians, it has the sense of people 'hearing' about something like Paul's persecution (1:13) and his conversion (1:23). Sometimes, as in the Hebrew term for hearing (שָׁמַע, *šā·mǎ*), the term has a deeper sense of listening, understanding, and obeying—heeding. We see this in texts like Deut 4:1—'And now, O Israel, *listen* to the statutes and the rules that I am teaching you, and do them, that you may live, and go in and take possession of the land that the LORD, the God of your fathers, is giving you.' It is used in the Shema, a term based on the Hebrew term *šā·mǎ*—'*Hear*, O Israel, The Lord our God, the Lord is one. You shall love the Lord your God with all your heart and with all your soul and with all your might' (Deut 6:4–5). This is for Jesus the greatest commandment of all (Mark 12:29–30 and parr.). Here the Greek *akouō* carries this power of hearing and heeding. Paul is challenging those who claim to 'listen' to the law and confess the Shema to really listen, understand, and yield to it. He will now deeply delve into the law to challenge them.

ABRAHAM'S TWO SONS (4:22)

In *Galatians 4:22*, Paul writes:

For (*gar*, 1:10), **as it is written** (perfect *graphō*, 1:20), that[15] (*hoti* 1:6) **Abraham** (*Abraam*, 3:6) **had** (*echō*, 2:4) **two** (*duo*)[16] **sons** (plural *huios*, 1:16), **one** (*heis*, 3:16) **from** (*ek*, 1:1) **the slave-woman** (*paidiskē*)[17] **and** (*kai*, 1:1) **one** (*heis*) **from** (*ek*) **the free woman** (feminine *eleutheros*, 3:28).

As in 3:10, 13; 4:27, Paul introduces an OT citation with *gegraptai*, 'it is written,' speaking of the present power of the text scribed centuries earlier (for the Jews, by Moses). 'Abraham had two sons' speaks of Isaac and Ishmael. Concerning the two women, Paul draws a contrast between the free (citizen) and the slave. As discussed concerning 1:10 and 3:28, slavery and freedom are big issues in Roman culture. To be free and a citizen was coveted as a status. To be a slave was repudiated as it meant the loss of one of the greatest of all Roman values, freedom. Paul here uses the duality not of literal freedom and slavery, but of freedom from sin and its consequences (death, destruction) and slavery to sin which is exacerbated by enslavement to law. The two women represent these two contrasting ideas.

'One from the slave-woman' uses *paidiskē*, found only in this passage in the NT, but commonly in the LXX (eighty-seven times), where it is used of female slaves who were often attendants to prominent women.[18] It is used of Hagar.[19] She was

15. This word is not highlighted, as it is not included in the translation. The *hoti* functions like a speech mark signaling the oral discourse that follows.

16. The number δύο (*duo*), 'two' is used twice in Galatians, of Abraham's '*two* sons' (4:22) which symbolically refer to '*two* covenants' (4:24).

17. The noun παιδίσκη (*paidiskē*) meaning 'female slave' is found five times in Paul, all in Galatians. Here it refers to Hagar, slave of Abraham and Sarah (Gal 4:22, 23, 30, 31).

18. E.g., Gen 12:16; 20:14, 17; 29:24; 30:4, 5, 7, 9, 10, 12, 18, 43. See also Exod 20:10; 21:12; Lev 25:6; Deut 5:14, where the *paidiskē* was not to work on the Sabbath; Exod 20:17; Deut 5:21, where one was not to covet the neighbor's *paidiskē*; Exod 21:20, where a slave owner who strikes a *paidiskē* is to be punished, and in Exod 21:32, any ox that gores a *paidiskē* is to be stoned. In Lev 25:44, Israel is not to enslave their own but gain slave-women from the nations. In Deut 12:12, 18; 16:11, 14, they are to worship Yahweh including feasts. They are to be released every seven years (Deut 15:17, cf. Jer 41:9–11). Abimelech, who sought to establish himself as king, was the son of a slave woman (Judg 9:18). It can also mean 'young woman' (Ruth 4:12). The *paidiskē* washed the feet of the elite (1 Sam 25:41, cf. John 13:1–15) and served kings (2 Sam 6:20). Having multiple *paidiskai* was a sign of wealth (Eccl 2:7; Jdt 8:7). Amos rebuked Israel's men for having sex with the same *paidiskē*.

19. See Gen 16:1, 2, 3, 5, 6, 8; 21:10, 12, 13; 25:12.

an Egyptian who likely joined Abraham and Sarah (Sarai) when
they were in Egypt due to a famine (Gen 12:10) and for a short
time became a part of the royal household (because of the
pretense that she was Abraham's sister) (Gen 12:10–13:1).

In Genesis 16, due to her barrenness, Sarah encouraged
Abraham to sleep with Hagar to ensure he had an heir. As a slave,
Hagar did not have much choice and probably embraced the
idea as it would give her status in the family, and her son could
become Abraham's heir. The maintenance of a family through
a male heir was critical in the ancient world. Abraham sleeping
with Hagar backfired on Sarah, who became deeply mortified
when Hagar fell pregnant, and she treated her harshly causing
her slave to run away (Gen 16:5–6). After God's promise to Hagar
that her descendants through her son would be greatly
multiplied, she returned and gave birth to Ishmael (Gen
16:7–16). Ultimately, after the birth of Isaac, Hagar and Ishmael
were cast out at Sarah's beckoning (Gen 21:8–21).

'One from the free woman' speaks of the birth of Isaac. As
discussed concerning 3:16 in particular, the Genesis account of
Abraham pivots around the promise of a legitimate heir rather
than Eliezer of Damascus (Gen 15:2). In Gen 15:4, Abraham's
son as the heir is promised, and many other offspring. As noted
above, in Gen 16, Sarah seeks to resolve the problem of her
barrenness with Hagar. The promise of a son to Abraham is
restated in Gen 17 with the promise of a multitude of
descendants (17:3–6) with the promise Isaac specified (17:19).
In Gen 18, the three visitors restate the promise despite Sarah's
laughing at the idea. After the destruction of Sodom, Lot's
deliverance, and a sojourn in Gerar with Abimelech, Sarah
conceived and bore Isaac (21:1–7). He was thus the legitimate
heir of the 'free woman,' Abraham and Sarah's firstborn son.

ONE SON ACCORDING TO THE FLESH, ONE THROUGH A PROMISE (4:23)

In *Galatians 4:23*, Paul continues, drawing meaning from the
story for the situation in Galatia:

But (*alla*, 1:1), **on the one hand** (*men*, 4:8),[20] **the one** (*ho*,[21] 1:1) **from** (*ek*, 1:1) **the slave-woman** (*paidiskē*, 4:22) **has been born** (perfect[22] passive *gennaō*)[23] **according** (*kata*, 1:4) **to the flesh** (*sarx*, 1:16). **But on the other hand** (*de*, 1:15), **the one** (*ho*) **from** (*ek*) **the free woman** (feminine *eleutheros*, 3:28) **[is born] through** (*dia*, 1:1) **a promise** (*epangelia*, 3:14).

'But' is *alla* which here does not so much contrast with what came previously, but instead draws out the figurative from the literal. So, while one might translate it 'yet, but,' it speaks of another level in the OT account. As in 4:8–9, Paul uses a *men ... de* (on the one hand ... on the other hand) construct to show the contrast between two things—here, the figurative meaning he will draw from the Hagar and Sarah accounts. 'The one from the slave-woman' is Ishmael born to Hagar, as in 4:29. He is born 'according to the flesh.'

The verb *gennaō*, in a literal sense, speaks of someone being physically born (Rom 9:11). It is used in this way in Acts 7:8 of Abraham begetting or becoming the father of Isaac (Acts 7:8) and in Hebrews of descendants born to him (Heb 11:12).[24] It can connote spiritual birth,[25] as when Paul begat or became the

---

20. In this verse, we have an example of alternative personal pronoun use with *men ... de*. See Wallace, *Greek Grammar*, 212. Here, 'the nominal content is to be supplied from the context.'

21. Wallace, *Greek Grammar*, 225 sees here in the articles ἕνα ἐκ **τῆς** παιδίσκης καὶ ἕνα ἐκ **τῆς** ἐλευθέρας the 'well known' (or 'celebrity' or 'familiar')' use of the article. Here, the two women are well known in the biblical narrative.

22. As in 3:18, according to Wallace, the perfect γεγέννηται is a perfect of allegory where an OT event is viewed in terms of its allegorical value. See further on 3:18.

23. The verb γεννάω (*gennaō*) is used three times in Galatians, all in Ch. 4 of Hagar's son '*born* according to the flesh' (4:23), Hagar '*bearing children* for slavery' (4:24), and again of Hagar's son who was '*born* according to the flesh' and who persecuted the child from the promise/Spirit (4:29).

24. It is used forty times alone in the Matthean genealogy in the sense of 'begat,' is the 'father of' (Matt 1:1–18), and of Jesus' birth (Matt 1:20; 2:1, 4; John 18:37). See also Matt 19:12; Mark 14:21; Luke 1:13, 35, 57; 23:29; John 8:41; 9:2, 19, 20, 32, 34; 16:21; Acts 2:8; 7:20, 29; 22:3, 28; Heb 11:23; 2 Pet 2:12).

25. Luke and the author of Hebrews employ it in a citation of Ps 2:7 of Jesus' resurrection (Acts 13:33; Heb 1:5; 5:5). John uses it of those born from people in contrast with those who are born from God (John 1:12–13); those who are 'born from above' (John 3:3, 5, 7), something that Nicodemus cannot understand (John 3:4). He strikes a

father of the Corinthians and Onesimus through preaching the gospel to them and their response of faith (1 Cor 4:15; Phlm 10). He also employs it figuratively of false teachings who 'beget' or 'breed' quarrels (2 Tim 2:23). Here in 4:23, it refers to the two boys, Ishmael and Isaac, the firstborn of the flesh, and the second through the promise.

In 4:24, he uses the perfect tense, indicating that 'the OT event … still retains its (exemplary) meaning.'[26] Here it is employed spiritually, with Hagar's children, born of the flesh, born into slavery. She corresponds to Mt Sinai and the giving of the law (4:25) and Jerusalem, the heartland of Judaism, and she bears (gennaō) children for slavery.

Here, Hagar is allegorized as the mother of those who are in slavery to the law and who have rejected Christ. This is a powerful statement, as Hagar and Ishmael represent gentile nations that have traditionally contended with Israel. So, in adopting this analogy, Paul does something similar to Jesus making a Samaritan, Canaanite, or Roman a prototype of faith and service (cf. Mark 7:24–30; Luke 7:1–10; 10:25–36; 17:11–19). Israel is paralleled with Hagar and Ishmael's descendants—Israel's enemies.

'According[27] to the flesh' (sarx) is contrasted in this verse with 'through[28] the promise,' and in v. 29 with 'the Spirit.' The contrast is with the 'one born from the free woman' which clearly means Isaac who was born from Sarah. The promise is clearly the Abrahamic promise, which (as discussed regarding 3:16–29) refers to the promises to Abraham of the nations being blessed

---

contrast between what is 'born of the flesh,' which is flesh, and what is born of the Spirit, which is spirit (John 3:6). To be born from above is to be born of the Spirit (John 3:8). Being born of God is a critical theme in 1 John (1 John 2:29; 3:9; 4:7; 5:1, 4, 18).

26. Moo, Galatians, 298.
27. Kata with the accusative here speaks of in accordance with, according to. See BDAG 512 meaning B. 5.
28. Dia with the genitive here is difficult. It can have the sense of 'attendant circumstances,' Isaac born 'in conjunction with' or 'as a result of' the promise. It can also be instrumental, 'by, via, through.' See Moo, Galatians, 298; BDAG 224, meaning A. 3.

and becoming his inheritance. This promise is fulfilled in the 'seed' of Abraham, Jesus, through whom these promises have come. Through God and not merely human design and conception, Isaac was born.

The use of *sarx* here is intriguing. On one level, both boys were born 'from the flesh,' conceived in Hagar and Sarah with Abraham's sperm. They are fleshly beings. Yet, for Paul, only Ishmael is born 'from the flesh.' He is thus not using 'flesh' in the basic sense of being human or an animal. At one level, it speaks of Ishmael's conception and birth purely from a human point of view—engineered not by God but by people.[29]

Sarx in Paul also often has that sense of fallenness and corruption through sin. There is thus a double layer to this. Hagar's relationship with Abraham is sexually immoral from the perspective of biblical sexual ethics. Hence, Ishmael is born of sexual immorality. However, more importantly, he is not born into the line of promise, and it is what he and his mother represent to Paul that is fleshly, in antipathy to the promise and Spirit. As he outlines in the following verses, they represent those who yield to law and not the Spirit in Galatia. It is Judaism in rejection of Christ as Messiah, Lord, and divine Son, and the Judaizers that are in view. They rely on law, and so rely on self, their flesh, to please God (see esp. Phil 3:4–9). Pleasing God is implausible for they are fallen and while their minds may desire to please God through the law, they cannot do so (see esp. Rom 7:13–25; 8:8).[30]

TWO WOMEN AS TWO COVENANTS (4:24)

Paul in *Galatians 4:24*, begins the allegory/analogy/typology proper. He states:

These things (plural neuter *hostis*, 2:4) **are** (present *eimi*, 1:7) **being taken allegorically** (present passive *allēgoreō*)[31]—**for** (*gar,*

---

29. Moo, *Galatians*, 298.
30. Similarly, see Dunn, *Galatians*, 246–47.
31. The only use of ἀλληγορέω (*allēgoreō*) in the NT (cf. Eng. 'allegory,' 'allegorical') is in Gal 4:24 (*hapax legomenon*). The verb compounds *allos* (other, another) with *agoreuō*

1:10) **these women** (plural feminine *houtos*, 2:10)[32] **are** (present *eimi*) **two** (*duo*, 4:22) **covenants** (plural *diathēkē*, 3:15)—**on the one hand** (*men*, 4:8), **one** (*eis*, 3:16) **from** (*apo*, 1:1) **Mount** (*oros*)[33] **Sinai** (*Sina*)[34] **[who] bore** (*gennaō*, 4:23) **[children] for** (*eis*, 1:5) **slavery** (*douleia*),[35] **which** (singular feminine *hostis*) **is** (*eimi*) **Hagar** (*Hagar*),[36] …

'These things' is the neuter plural of *hostis*, *hatina*, and refers to the two births mentioned in 4:23. 'Being taken allegorically' uses *allēgoreō*, from which we get the English allegory, allegorical. It compounds *allos* (other, another) with *agoreuō*, 'speak,' and so yields 'to speak in another way' of something.

In wider Greek sources, it is occasionally used. For example, Plutarch uses it when speaking of something indirectly or by analogy (e.g., Plutarch, *De esu* 1.7). He also critiques as frivolous those who allegorize the body as Hades and the soul within the body as deranged and inebriate (Plutarch, *Is. Os.* 28). He also employs it of gods like Hera representing air (Plutarch, *Is. Os.* 32).

Allēgoreō is not found in the LXX, used once by Josephus of God's manner of speaking some things through allegory, in contrast to other things spoken widely and enigmatically. It is commonly used by Philo, who takes OT ideas and allegorizes them. For example, he takes an idea like God creating a helper for Adam (Eve), likening it to the creation of the passions as a helper for the mind (*Leg.* 2.5). Philo also uses it of the mind, which he likens to a field that produces vegetation (*Leg.* 2.10),

(speak), and yields 'to speak in another way' of something. It means to 'use analogy or likeness to express something, speak allegorically' (BDAG 46).

32. Wallace, *Greek Grammar*, 326 notes that with the personal pronoun οὗτος (*houstos*, here in the form *autai*) here one has to consider the context clearly to discern the antecedent. This one is not difficult; it is the two women.

33. The only references to ὄρος (*oros*) in Galatians are in 4:24, 25 of *Mount* Sinai.

34. The place Σινᾶ (*Sina*), 'Sinai,' occurs twice in Galatians, 4:24, 25. Otherwise, it is mentioned in Acts 7:30, 38 of Moses and the burning bush.

35. The noun δουλεία (*douleia*) recurs in Gal 4:24 and 5:1 and speaks of the state of being a slave (*doulos*). It is used first for Hagar's descendants and then regarding slavery to law, from which Christ has set believers free.

36. The name Hagar is mentioned twice in Gal 4:24, 25, in Paul's allegorization of the story of Hagar and Sarah and their two children. These are the only two mentions in the NT.

a house as the soul (Leg. 3.238), Cain building his doctrine as a city (*Post.* 51), the camp of Israel as the body (*Ebr.* 99), 'you shall walk after the Lord your God' (Deut 13:4) as an allegory for the soul following divine law (*Migr.* 131), and the five daughters of Salpaad allegorically speaking of the five senses (*Migr.* 205).[37]

Philo's use of the term and appropriation of OT texts in an allegorical manner, suggests what Paul does in Galatians 4 is not unusual. However, Philo allegorizes OT texts in relation to his Jewish neo-Platonic worldview, whereas Paul does so in his law-free gospel. In what follows, the two women Hagar and Sarah are allegorized regarding the contrast between slavery and freedom, Sinai/Jerusalem and the Jerusalem above, flesh and Spirit, no inheritance and inheritance, and Israel and the people of God (although more implicitly in the last case). The contrast is between Judaism-in-rejection-of-Christ and the Judaizers who corrupt Christ with the law, and the Christian movement which advocates grace, faith, and freedom in Christ.

First, the women represent two covenants. The first is Mount Sinai.[38] In the next verse, Paul describes it as Sinai of Arabia. Arabia, as discussed on 1:17, is all or part of the Sinai Peninsula south of Damascus. Paul's statement indicates that the mountain is found there. Scholars debate where it is exactly. The options for Mount Sinai include the traditional site *Jebel Musa* (Mount Moses) toward the southern tip of the Sinai Peninsula which fits with an eleven-day journey to Kadesh-Barnea (Deut 1:2).

Others reject this as it seems a strange detour from the route of the Exodus. Another nearby mountain, *Ras es-Safsafeh*, is also considered but suffers from the same problem as Jebel Musa. More northern mountains, *Jebel Helal and Har Karkom*, are closer to Kadesh-Barnea and fit with a more northerly route of the Exodus. A range of other locations has also been proposed including mountains in Midian east of the Gulf of Aqaba, *Al*

---

37. See also *Leg.* 3.4, 60; *Cher.* 25; *Agr.* 27, 157; *Mut.* 67; *Somn.* 1.67; 2.31, 207; *Abr.* 99; *Ios.* 28; *Decal.* 101; *Spec.* 1.269; 2.29; *Praem.* 125, 158; *Contempl.* 28, 29.

38. According to J. T. Swann, 'Sinai,' in *LBD*, the etymology of the name Sinai (סיני, syny) is uncertain but likely derives from 'Sin'—the moon god worshiped by desert nomads. He notes that Horeb is more specific, and Sinai is the general regional term.

Manifa, near the Wadi al-Hrob, and *Jebel Katerina* or *Jebel Serbel* south of *Jebel Musa*.[39]

Reference to Sinai speaks of the covenant established between God and Moses on behalf of Israel on the Mountain after the Exodus from Egypt.[40] In that Theophanic encounter, the law was given to Moses, and this forms the basis of the dispute in Galatia.[41] In Judges 5:5, God is known as 'the One of Sinai,' before whom the mountains quake (cf. Ps 68:8). To this mountain, God came with myriads of mighty angels (Ps 68:17). The mountain also symbolizes Israel's idolatry as it was by the mountain that they built the golden calf and bowed in worship to it (Exod 32:1–35; Ps 106:19). Central to this is the law on the two tablets of stone placed in the Ark (1 Kings 8:9; 2 Chron 5:10). Sinai was also known as Horeb and is a critical place in Israel's history including Moses' encounter with God at the burning bush (Exod 3:1–17; Acts 7:30, 38) and Elijah's experience of God who was found in the vibrant silence (1 King 19:8).

This covenant 'gives birth for slavery.' At one level, this speaks of the slave status of Ishmael the son of the slave woman Hagar. Until Isaac came along, Ishmael was the heir to Abraham. As such, Paul is saying something deeper and shocking from a Jewish point of view. The Sinai covenant was premised on Israel being slaves in Egypt, being released from bondage by God, and then becoming God's very own people. Paul, no doubt, saw it this way before his conversion. Yet, now that Christ has come, Paul has come to a new way of thinking concerning the Sinai Covenant and the law. The law, a wonderfully good gift from God for a people released from slavery, now serves to enslave Israel, painfully making her aware of the sin that imprisons all humanity. Hagar then represents the function of the Sinai Covenant and law to do this. It produces enslavement. Only faith can release a person from this slavery.

---

39. See Swann, 'Sinai.'

40. See Exod 19:1–34:35; Deut 5:2: 'the Lord our God made a covenant with us on Horeb,' cf. Deut 29:1.

41. Cf. Lev 7:38; 25:1; 26:46; 27:34; Num 1:1; 3:1, 14; 9:1; 28:6; Deut 1:19; 4:10, 15; Neh 9:13; Mal 4:4.

HAGAR REPRESENTS MT SINAI, PRESENT JERUSALEM, AND SLAVERY TO LAW (4:25)

In *Galatians 4:25*, Paul continues:
and (*de*, 1:15) **Hagar** (*Hagar*, 4:24) **is** (present *eimi*) **Mount** (*oros*, 4:24) **Sinai** (*Sina*, 4:24) **in** (*en*, 1:6) **Arabia** (*Arabia*, 1:17).[42] **And** (*de*) **she corresponds to** (*systoicheō*)[43] **Jerusalem** (*Ierousalēm*)[44] **in the** (dative *ho*, 1:1) **present** (*nyn*, 1:23), **for** (*gar*, 1:10) **she is a slave** (present *douleuō*, 4:8) **with** (*meta*, 1:18) **her** (feminine *autos*, 1:1) **children** (plural *technon*, 4:19).

The conjunction *de* is repeated twice, and both uses are consecutive, 'and,' as Paul continues unlocking his allegorical reading of Hagar and her children. Again, he mentions that she corresponds to Mount Sinai, this time placing it in Arabia, somewhere in the Sinai Peninsula (see on 4:24).[45]

The second part of the verse begins with the verb *systoicheō* placed first for prominence. The verb is a compound of *syn* (with)

42. **Variant**: There are a range of variants to begin this verse and it is heavily disputed—given only a {C} rating by Metzger, *Textual Commentary*, 527. 1) *de Hagar Sina* (and Hagar Sinai); 2) *gar Hagar Sina* (for Hagar is Sinai); 3) *de Sina* (and Sinai); 4) *gar Sina* (for Sinai). *De* has better support than *gar*. Overall, while there is good support for *de Sina*, including P46. However, the first option, *de Hagar Sina*, has the best attestation. Metzger argues that after *gar* was used to replace *de* in some witnesses, *gar Hagar* led to accidental omissions.

43. The only reference to συστοιχέω (*systoicheō*) is in 4:25. The verb compounds *syn* (with) and *stoicheō* (be drawn in a line, to agree with, follow, conform). *Stoicheō* and related words are military terms literally speaking of marching in line and rank. With the prefix *syn* it speaks of marching together in line with. It is found figuratively in the NT in 5:25 (keep in step with the Spirit) and 6:16 (follow this rule) (cf. Phil 3:16; Rom 4:12; Acts 21:24).

44. The second term for Jerusalem is Ἰερουσαλήμ (*Ierousalēm*) is found in 4:25, 26. The other is Ἱεροσόλυμα *Hierousalyma* used in 1:17, 18; 2:1. *Ierousalēm* is used in secular Greek whereas *Ierousalyma* is a Hebraizing form of the name. See also on 1:17.

45. Moo, *Galatians*, 302 translates this 'now the Hagar Sinai mountain is in Arabia' following the order of the Greek. While taking *estin* between 'Hagar' and 'Sinai Mountain' is strongly supported in translations, he argues that Paul usually aligns OT realities with NT counterparts, there is a redundant repetition from the previous verse, the neuter article (to) does not focus on Hagar (the word Hagar) but goes with *oros*, the 'Hagar Sinai mountain' (Hagar and Sinai are adjectives). Finally, he considers that the Galatians would not grasp this esoteric idea and Arabia then lacks explanation. He thus takes the second *de* as 'but she corresponds to present-day Jerusalem.' The meaning is not particularly affected either way.

and *stoicheō*. *Stoicheō* recalls *stoicheia* (4:3, 9). *Systoicheō* is found five times in the NT, and twice in Galatians. *Stoicheō* means to be in a *stoichos*, 'a rank of series, to belong to a series,' and is particularly used in military situations. It can mean 'agree,' 'be in agreement,' or 'be in harmony.'[46] Twice it is used in Galatians of 'keeping in step with the Spirit' (5:25) and of the rule that circumcision is irrelevant while a new creation is everything.[47]

Systoichos itself means 'to be in a series with, to be in the same ranks.' As with *stoicheō*, it is a military term, used to describe armies rapidly advancing in line or rank (e.g., Polybius, *Hist.* 10.23.7). The related noun *systoichos*, 'belonging to a series,' is commonly used in logic of things related or antithetical. Here, Paul establishes a series of correlating ideas; Hagar—Mt Sinai—Jerusalem—and so law observance as a means of gaining righteous status before God.

'Jerusalem in the present' is the city of Jerusalem, the center of Israel in every way, including religion. All 141 references to Jerusalem refer to this city, aside from the 'Jerusalem above' in the following verse, Heb 12:22, and Rev 3:12; 21:2, 3. Paul mentions Jerusalem ten times in his letters. Aside from this use, all refer to the geographical city as in 1:17, 18; 2:1, and the previous verse.[48]

The focus of the earthly Jerusalem is, of course, the Temple on Mt Zion. While there were distinctives among the various groups concerning legal observance, the basis for Israel's life was and remains the Torah. Jerusalem reflects then the cult of Judaism, including Jews who have rejected Jesus as Christ, Lord, and Son of God, and Judaizers who wish to compromise the gospel of grace and faith to Torah observance. This effectively turns Christianity into Judaism, albeit believing in Jesus as the Christ. It is no longer Christianity because the fullness of Christ's effective work of salvation is not affirmed. One has to do more than believe and so, the cross is rendered inadequate. As such, a Judaizing faith is analogous to contemporary variants like

---

46. See G. Delling, 'στοιχέω,' in *TDNT* 7:666–667.
47. See 6:12, cf. Rom 4:12; Phil 3:12; Acts 21:24, see further 5:25.
48. See Rom 15:19, 25, 26, 31; 1 Cor 16:3.

Mormonism and Jehovah's Witnesses. It parallels Protestant Liberalism which reduces Jesus to a dead teacher, or Islam, which considers Jesus a prophet.

There are ironies concerning the final clause that refers to Hagar being in slavery with her children. First, it speaks of the status of Hagar, Abraham's slave-woman, who was with Ishmael and any other children she had. When she left Abraham, she and her family grew, and there is no indication of ongoing slavery (cf. Gen 25:12–18). As such, she was not in slavery anymore.

A second level is historical where there is some irony in this description of Jerusalem. Jerusalem was taken by David around 1010 BC. It was in the hands of Israel/Judah until the Babylonian Exile after which, aside from the (approximately hundred-year) Maccabean period, it was under foreign rule. At the time of Galatians, Jerusalem was under Rome, it was in a sense enslaved (although in John 8:33 Jesus' debating partners repudiate any notion of being enslaved to anyone). However, the slavery Paul is talking about is not to Rome, but to the law, sin, and its deadly consequences.

Regarding the Hagar-Sarah analogy, Paul is drawing on the ideas mentioned earlier in Gal 4. Jerusalem, bound as it is to the Torah, is in slavery as are her children—enslaved to the law. The verb *douleuō*, 'to be a slave, to serve as a slave,' is used in 4:8 of the Galatian's enslavement to the elemental powers—their pre-conversion religions, ideologies, and demonic powers. In 4:9, *douleuō* is again used in a question. He asks them how on earth they can contemplate returning to such enslavement by submitting to Torah.[49] Another related verb *douloō*, 'to enslave' is used in 4:3 to make this very point—Israel (Paul included) was in slavery to the law (as are all peoples to their religious and philosophical worldviews). As such, Israel's religion now that Christ has come functions in a way that correlates with pagan religion.

Jesus, born under the law, came to redeem Israel from the law

---

49. The verb *douleuō* will also be used in 5:13 of the Galatians becoming slaves of each other voluntarily through love.

(4:5), that they may be adopted as God's free children. Sadly (cf. Rom 9:2; 10:1), Judaism-in-rejection-of-Christ and the Judaizers remain enslaved to the law despite Christ coming to set them free. They have heard the gospel as God as held his hands out to them but as a disobedient and contrary people, they have rejected it (Rom 10:14–21). In the case of the Judaizers, they have heard the gospel, and have chosen to syncretize it to aspects of Judaism that render the gospel defunct. While Paul's target here is undoubtedly the Judaizers, all of Judaism in rejection of Christ is in view. They are to be rejected by the Galatians.

OUR MOTHER: THE FREE JERUSALEM ABOVE (4:26)

In *Galatians 4:26*, Paul contrasts the earthly Jerusalem with the Jerusalem above:

But (*de*, 1:15) **the Jerusalem** (*Ierousalēm*, 4:26) **above** (*anō*)[50] **is** (present *eimi*, 1:7) **free** (feminine *eleutheros*, 3:28). **She** (feminine *hostis*, 2:4) **is** (present *eimi*) **our**[51] (plural *egō*, 1:2) **mother** (*mētēr*, 1:15).

Whereas in the previous verse where *de* was consecutive, here it is adversative, 'but,' striking a contrast between Hagar and Sarah (although she is unnamed) and what they represent.

As noted above, all Paul's other references to Jerusalem refer to the geographical entity in Israel. Paul now introduces a new and contrasting concept—'the Jerusalem above' (*anō*). The adverb *anō* is used by John of Jesus' point of origin—'you are from below, I am from *above*; you are of this world, I am not of this world.'[52] In Johannine theology, one must be 'born from above' (*anōthen*) (John 3:3, 7).

---

50. The adverb ἄνω (*anō*), 'above' features once in Galatians of the Jerusalem 'above' (cf. Phil 3:14; Col 3:1, 2).

51. Variant: Some versions have 'all,' (*pantōn*)—'she is the mother of us all' (2א A C3 K L, etc.). However, the present text is well attested (P46 א* B C* D F G Ψ 33 1739, etc.). Further, the shorter reading is to be preferred.

52. The adverb *anō* is only found nine times in the NT. John also uses it of filling a jar to the *brim* (its most above point) (John 2:7), and of Jesus looking 'upward' (John 11:41). Luke uses it once in Acts of 'signs in the heaven *above*' (Acts 2:19). The writer of Hebrews uses it of a root of bitterness springing *up* (Heb 12:15).

The idea of 'being born again from above' has some resemblances with being children of the free woman who is the Jerusalem above. Elsewhere Paul employs the idea of heaven above with *anō*, 'upward.' In Phil 3:14, he presses on to win the prize of 'the *upward* call of God in Christ Jesus,' speaking of God's call to him from the heavenlies. In Col 3:1–2 believers are to seek and place their minds on the things above. 'Above' is 'where Christ is, seated at the right hand of God.'

Here it is 'the Jerusalem above,' which picks up the recurring Jewish eschatological idea of a renewed Jerusalem. As Longenecker discusses, the 'heavenly Jerusalem' is anticipated in some texts in the Jewish Scriptures.[53] In apocalyptic writings it is more thoroughly developed.[54] Here, the Jerusalem above speaks of heaven, the celestial city, from where Jesus was sent to redeem humanity (4:4–5) and from whence he will return (Phil 3:20). It is where God dwells, and Jesus rules as Lord, enthroned at God's right hand (Col 3:1). It is the abode of other celestial beings such as angels who are sent by God to do things like delivering the law to Moses (3:19). From this Jerusalem above, God sent his Son and Spirit (4:4, 6), and in this Jerusalem believing and perfected humans approach God and will live eternally (on earth as heaven descends to it, Rev 21–22).

The notion is found in Heb 12:22–24, where it is described as the *heavenly Zion*. To this place, believers have come. It is referred to as 'Mount Zion,' 'the city of the living God,' where there are 'innumerable angels in festal gathering,' 'the assembly of the firstborn who are enrolled in heaven,' 'God, the judge of all,' 'the spirits of the righteous made perfect,' and 'Jesus, the mediator of a new covenant.'

Similarly, in Rev 3:12, John refers to the 'new Jerusalem' which descends from God out of heaven. It is again mentioned in Rev 21:2 as 'the new Jerusalem, coming down out of heaven from

53. See, e.g., Ps 87:3; Isa 54:1–3; Ezek 40–48; Sir 36:13–22; Tob 13.
54. See 1 En. 53:6; 90:28–29; 2 En. 55:2; Pss. Sol. 17:33; 4 Ezra 7:26; 8:52; 10:25–28; 2 Apoc. Bar. 4.2–6; 32.2; 59.4; 1QM 12.1–2; 4QShirShab. Longenecker, *Galatians*, 214 also notes the idea is found in rabbinic thought, e.g., *b. Ta'an.* 5a; *b.Ḥag.* 12b; *Gen. Rab.* 55.7; 69.7; *Num. Rab.* 4.13; *Midr. Pss.* 30.1; 122.4; *Cant. Rab.* 3.10; 4.4; *Pesiq. R.* 40.6.

God, prepared as a bride for her husband.' In Rev 21:10–22:5 it descends and is vividly described.

'Is free' refers to the status of this city. The notion of a free city (*civitas libera, urbs liberae condicionis*; Greek: *eleuthera kai autonomos polis*) was applied to cities that were afforded the freedom to self-govern during both the Hellenistic and Roman periods. They usually had an exemption from taxation, freedom from having Roman troops inside the city walls, freedom to govern by local custom rather than Roman civic forms, could mint their own coins, and had oversight of their judiciary. They remained under the oversight of the King of Emperor through his *epistates* or curator. Some were also able to produce their own coins. Examples under Rome include at various times, Seleucia, Tarsus, Nicopolis, Thessalonica, Skotussa, Rhodes, and Athens.[55]

Of course, for Paul, 'the Jerusalem above' is free to a completely different level. It is free from all corruption, sin, and death. It is from this Jerusalem that freedom is conferred as a status on its citizens. From this Jerusalem has come Jesus who died to set people free, and from this Jerusalem, he will return as Savior for the final and complete redemption of believers' bodies (Phil 3:20–21). In this city is the 'book of life' in which are inscribed the names of all its citizens by faith (Phil 4:3, cf. Phil 3:9).

'She is our mother' uses *mētēr*. In 1:17, it refers to Paul's biological mother in whose womb Paul was set apart. It also recalls 4:4 where Jesus was 'born of a woman' to liberate humanity trapped by the elemental powers. Paul also uses the analogy of himself as a mother in 4:18–20, yearning for the Galatians as a mother for her children.

The sentence 'she is our mother' is loaded regarding the analogy. At one level, this refers implicitly to Sarah, the free woman. Her son Isaac is the child of promise with the rights of inheritance. At another level, from her (and Mary, 4:4) came

55. Gene L. Green, *The Letters to the Thessalonian*, PNTC (Grand Rapids, MI; Leicester, England: Eerdmans; Apollos, 2002), 18–19; M. S. Guyer, 'Thessalonian,' in *LBD*; 'Free City (classical antiquity),' *Wikipedia*, https://en.wikipedia.org/wiki/Free_city_(classical_antiquity).

'the seed of Abraham,' Jesus, who sets people free from law and sin. More profoundly, he symbolizes the Jerusalem above which is the mother of all who believe. Of course, it is the God in heaven who is really the source of the status of free children, and so it almost picks up the idea of God as a mother. This family includes every genuine God-believer who despite never hearing the gospel of Christ, has faith in God (such as Abraham, Gen 15:6). It includes every human who hears the gospel of Christ and submits with faith, such as Paul and the Galatians. They are descendants of Sarah, the woman of faith, and are people of the celestial city of 'Jerusalem.' This verse speaks in a roundabout way of heavenly citizenship (Phil 3:20–21; Eph 2:19–22).

JOY AT THE MANY CHILDREN OF THE BARREN WOMAN (4:27)

Galatians 4:27 is a citation of a text from Isa 54:1:

For (*gar*, 1:10) **it is written** (perfect passive *graphō*, 1:20), 'Rejoice (aorist passive imperative *euphainō*),[56] **barren woman** (*speira*) [57] **who** (feminine *ho*) **[is] not** (*ou*, 1:1) **giving birth** (present participle *tiktō*),[58] **break forth** (aorist imperative *rēssō*)[59] **and** (kai, 1:1) **cry out** (aorist imperative *boaō*),[60] **she** (feminine *ho*) **[who is] without** (*ou*) **birth pangs** (present participle *ōdinō*, 4:19), **because** (*hoti*, 1:6) **many** (neuter plural *polys*, 1:14) **[are]**

---

56. The verb εὐφραίνω (*euphrainō*) means 'to be glad' and is found once in Galatians, in 4:27, of the barren woman rejoicing at her children (cf. Sarah). Paul uses it also in Rom 15:10 and 2 Cor 2:2.

57. The noun στεῖρα (*speira*), 'barren or childless one,' is used once in Galatians in 4:27 of the rejoicing barren woman who now has children (cf. Sarah). This is Paul's only use of the term.

58. The only use of the verb τίκτω (*tiktō*), 'give birth,' is found in 4:27, of the barren woman breaking forth into celebration. As with *speira*, this is Paul's only use of the term.

59. The verb ῥήσσω (*rēssō*) features only in 4:27 in Paul's writings. It means to 'break forth,' used for the woman who breaks forth into joyous shouting as she has many children.

60. Another verb exclusive to 4:27 in Paul's writings is βοάω (*boaō*), 'cry out,' used of the woman who cries out with joy at her many children. It features of John the Baptist *crying out* in the wilderness (Matt 3:3; Mark 1:3) and Jesus crying out from the cross (Mark 15:34).

the children (plural *technon*) **of the desolate woman** (genitive feminine *erēmos*),[61] **more** (*mallon*, 4:9) **than** (*hē*, 1:8) **the woman** (genitive feminine *ho*) **having** (present participle *echō*, 2:4) **a husband** (*andros*).'[62]

As is common in Romans, 1–2 Corinthians, and this letter, the citation, is introduced by *gegraptai*, the perfect passive of *graphō*, speaking of a text written long past that remains active and is speaking to Paul with fresh power (see 3:10).

It is an exact replication of the LXX of Isa 54:1. Isaiah 54 begins with these words that speak of Israel's rejoicing that she will have many children. She is to enlarge her dwellings right and left as 'your offspring will possess the nations.' Through the passage, Israel is likened to a barren woman, a shamed woman, a widow, a wife deserted and grieved. Israel will be gathered after God's anger is complete. As after Noah's flood, God will remove his anger, Israel will experience God's love and compassion, and his covenant will not be removed (Isa 54:10).

The specific verse likens Israel to the likes of Sarah (Gen 11:30), Rebecca (Gen 25:21), Rachel (Gen 29:31), Zorah's wife (Judg 13:3), and Hannah (1 Sam 2). Here, for Paul, it is not historical Israel at the time of the exile which will be restored and re-peopled, but the people of God in Christ. The Jerusalem above, through people believing the gospel, is giving birth to a multitude of children. The text then calls to mind Israel's tradition of God bringing heirs through the line of promise from Abraham, restoring Israel from Babylon, and bringing people from the nations into God's people in the eschatological future. In Paul's view, this ingathering is coming to pass in the Christ-movement.

'Rejoice' is *euphrainō*, a relatively uncommon verb (cf. *chairō*) that is used of celebration in situations like the return of the Prodigal Son.[63] In Revelation 12:12, the heavens and its

---

61. The adjective ἔρημος (*erēmos*) is found only in Gal 4:27 which usually has the literal sense of 'wilderness' or 'desert' is employed of 'the desolate one' in the sense of a childless woman (BDAG 391).

62. The only use of *anēr*, 'man, husband,' in Galatians, is in 4:27 of the woman who has a husband, who does not have as many children as the once desolate woman.

inhabitants are to rejoice that God's martyrs have conquered, and in Rev 18:20, the saints, apostles, and prophets rejoice at God's judgment. Paul uses it twice else, of his own joy (2 Cor 2:2), and as here, in a citation from Deut 32:43 of the gentiles rejoicing with God's people (Rom 15:10). Here, the verb is imperative; she is to rejoice.

The one who is to rejoice is the barren woman (*speira*) who does not give birth (*tiktō*). Aside from the women of promise in the OT, *speira* calls to mind Elizabeth who was barren until the birth of John the Baptist (Luke 1:7, 36, cf. 23:29). It is also used of Sarah in Hebrews (Heb 11:11). *Tiktō* is used through the NT of women giving birth, including Elizabeth (Luke 1:57) and Mary giving birth to Jesus.[64] Here, the woman giving birth is a little vague. At one level, it is Sarah. At another, it is the heaven above (previous verse), which is, in reality, God. He does this through the work of his Son born of Mary (4:4). He continues this work by his Spirit through his servant Paul (who 'mothered' the Galatians) (4:18–19).

The second line of the citation describes the woman as the one 'without birth pangs.' 'Birth pangs' translates *ōdinō*, a verb discussed on 4:19 which refers to the suffering a woman experiences in giving birth (cf. Rom 8:22; Rev 12:2). In 4:19, Paul uses it of his own pain at the Galatians' acceptance of a Judaizing gospel which had the potential to cause them to fall away. Here, it is applied to the woman who is barren. This woman now, however, is to 'break forth (*rēssō*) and cry out (*boaō*).'

Rēssō is a strong verb meaning 'tear, break, and burst' which is used for animals tearing apart their prey (Matt 7:6), new wine bursting out of old wineskins (Mark 2:22; Luke 5:37), and a demon seizing a boy and throwing him on the ground (Mark 9:18; Luke 9:42).[65] The second verb is *boaō*, another strong verb

---

63. See Luke 15:23, 24, 29, 32, cf. Luke 12:19; 16:19; Acts 2:26; 7:41; Rev 11:10.
64. See Matt 1:21, 23, 25; 2:2; Luke 1:31; 2:6, 7, 11; Rev 12:2, 4, 5, 13, cf. Gal 4:4. See also its use generally in John 16:21. *Tiktō* is also used figuratively of desire giving birth to sin (Jas 1:15), and of land giving forth a crop as faith gives birth to righteous living (Heb 6:7).
65. BDAG 904–905.

meaning to 'cry out,' as in John the Baptist in the wilderness,[66] Jesus in abandonment from the cross (Mark 15:34), desperate people calling to Jesus for healing (Luke 9:38; 18:38), people crying to God for justice (Luke 18:7), demons crying out (Acts 8:7), and crowds crying out before town authorities (Acts 17:6; 25:24).

The two imperative verbs combine to give a picture of a woman in the pains of childbirth crying out with some violence.[67] While I have not experienced such pain, I have given witness to this on three occasions, and it is intense. In a culture where barrenness is repudiated and childbirth a sign of blessing, this is equally a cry of pain and joy. In context, the latter is more in mind, as it parallels 'rejoice' in line one. Heaven is crying out as she is birthing children of God from across the world (cf. Luke 15:7).

The third and fourth lines of the citation are introduced by a causal *hoti* (see on 1:6) and so give the reason for this rejoicing and crying out. The reason is that 'many are the children of the desolate woman.' The desolate woman is at one level, Sarah, who was barren and desperate to have a child with her husband, Abraham.

She is vividly described as the *erēmos*, which literally speaks of the wilderness or desert—a harsh dry, relatively lifeless environment known well in the hot Middle East. Applied to a woman, it speaks of a barren womb unable to produce life. Yet, 'many' are her children. Indeed, they are 'more than the woman having a husband.' This does not compare Sarah and Hagar per se, but who and what they represent. Hagar represents Jerusalem (Judaism). While it has produced descendants of Abraham by faith through the centuries, in its rejection of God's Messiah, it now produces none. It is God through Christ who is doing this. It thus refers to a multitude of children born to God from the nations. God from 'the Jerusalem above,' through his Son and

---

66. See Matt 3:3; Mark 1:3; Luke 3:4; John 1:23.

67. The three imperative verbs in this verse implicitly speak of Christians rejoicing and crying out loudly and joyfully that more people are being liberated from bondage of slavery to freedom in Christ.

by the Spirit, is birthing hundreds and thousands of sons and daughters across the world through Paul, his team, and others who are sharing Christ. Hagar, Sinai, and Jerusalem have run their course outside of Christ.

CHILDREN OF PROMISE (4:28)

In *Galatians 4:28*, Paul directly addresses the Galatians, asserting their identity:

But (*de*, 1:15), **you**[68] (plural *sy*, 1:3), **brothers and sisters** (vocative plural *adelphos*, 1:2), **like** (*kata*, 1:4) **Isaac** (*Isaak*),[69] **are** (present *eimi*, 1:7) **children** (*technon*, 4:19) **of promise** (genitive *epangelia*, 3:14).

Paul brings home the analogy to his converts. 'You' is the Galatians but includes all who believe in Christ as Lord and Savior. 'Brothers and sisters is not merely an inclusive epistolary address, as is customary in Paul across his letters,[70] but builds on the motif of family and descendants of God through the passage. The Galatians are part of these 'many' children coming from the barren woman (Sarah). They are family with Paul and 'all the brothers and sisters with him' who are behind the production of the letter. They have become children of God by faith in Christ. They are descendants of 'the free woman' Sarah, and not Hagar and all she represents. By implication, Paul is pushing them—how then can you contemplate yielding to the Judaizers?

'Are' is the present tense of *eimi*, speaking of their present status as children of the promise. Nothing needs to be added to their faith—they are God's children. 'Children of the promise' invokes the use of promise language in Galatians 3, speaking of God's promises to Abraham that the nations would be blessed.

---

68. **Variant**: Some versions begin the verse 'and, brothers and sisters, *you are* (*esmen*) like Isaac, children of promise' (א A C D2 K L P Ψ, etc.). However, the shorter reading is well attested (P46 B D* F G 33 1739, etc.) and to be preferred. The verb 'to be' is implied. A scribe likely added it for clarification.

69. The only direct reference to Abraham and Sarah's son Ἰσαάκ (*Isaak*) is in 4:28, where the Galatians are told by Paul that they are children of the promise made to Abraham as is Isaac.

70. Cf. 1:11; 3:15; 4:12, 31; 5:11, 13; 6:1, 18.

Indeed, the nations will be his! (Rom 4:13). Through Abraham's free son and heir, Isaac, came the righteous line—his son being Jacob, and renamed Israel. From his line came the 'seed of Abraham,' Jesus. Through Jesus, faith has come, and through the proclamation of the gospel, thousands and ultimately billions are coming into God's enormous cosmic *whanau*. This inclusion does not come about through yielding to Torah, entering through circumcision, and upholding its many requirements like Sabbath, kosher food, ritual purity, the Jewish calendar, and the hundreds of other requirements. It came about by faith.

No, just as Isaac is a child of promise through the work of God making the impossible possible by his power, the Galatians are children of the promise by faith in accordance with (*kata*) Isaac. This people of God includes slave and free, male and female, and the circumcised and the uncircumcised among them.

THE PERSECUTION OF THE CHILDREN BY THE SPIRIT (4:29)

In *Galatians 4:29* Paul returns to the OT narrative for a further analogical component in his allegorization:

But (*alla*, 1:1) **just as** (*hōsper*)[71] **at that time** (*tote*, 4:8) **the one** (masculine *ho*, 1:1) **born** (aorist passive participle *gennaō*, 4:23) **according to** (*kata*, 1:4) **the flesh** (*sarx*, 1:16) **persecuted** (*diōkō*, 1:13) **[the one born]**[72] (masculine *ho*) **according to** (*kata*) **the Spirit** (*pneuma*, 3:2), **so** (*houtōs*) **also** (*kai*, 1:1) **[it is] now** (*nyn*, 1:23).

But (*alla*) strikes a strong contrast between the status of the Galatians and their treatment. Paul draws on the narrative of Ishmael and Isaac. He uses a standard *hōsper ... houtōs*, 'just as ... so ...' comparative sentence with *hōsper* introducing the protasis (just as ...) and *houtōs* the apodosis (so also ...). The protasis

---

71. The conjunction ὥσπερ (*hōsper*) is found once in Galatians. It is often used with *houtōs* in a comparison: *hōsper ... houtōs* signifying '(just) as ... so ...' *Hōsper* introduces the protasis and *houtōs* the apodosis. This is found in the only use of *hōsper* in Galatians in 4:29: 'but *just as* (*hōsper*) at that time the one born according to the flesh persecuted the one born according to the Spirit, so (*houtōs*) also now.'

72. The verb *gennaō* (born) governs both *kata* (according to) clauses.

speaks of the time when the one born of the flesh (Ishmael) persecuted the one born according to the Spirit (Isaac).

This persecution refers to Genesis 21:9 where after the birth of Isaac, Sarah observed Ishmael (the son of Hagar the Egyptian), laughing. The Hebrew for laughing is צָחַק (ṣā·ḥăq) which often carries the sense of mocking or reviling someone.[73] One can argue that there is selective exegesis here, for as much as Ishmael persecuted Isaac, Sarah persecuted Hagar, treating her rather unjustly (Gen 16:6), and expelling her from the family (see next verse). However, Paul does not draw on this point here—rather the sequence of the Genesis narrative moves from Ishmael's mockery of Isaac to the expulsion of Hagar and her son.

Whereas in 4:23, the two sons were contrasted as one born according to the flesh and the other according to the promise, here 'according to the flesh' is contrasted with 'according to the Spirit.' At one level, this suggests Paul believes that the birth of Isaac was a miracle enabled by the Spirit, whereas the birth of Ishmael was a purely 'natural' conception. The conception of Isaac was something more than this, with God enabling their aged bodies to form a baby through his Spirit. Considering 4:4, there is more than a vague possibility that the virgin conception is in the back of Paul's mind as he writes this.

At a deeper level, the flesh-Spirit antithesis strikes at the heart of the Judaizing controversy. For Paul, law observance brings the flesh into play as an agent of righteousness. This avails nothing as the flesh is fallen. Conversely, the gospel is a matter of the Spirit. As faith is born, the Spirit is poured into the hearts of believers, and they experience their adoption as God's children, the Spirit crying out 'Abba, Father' (3:2–5; 4:3–7). In Johannine terms, they are born from above (John 3:3, 5). They are no longer slaves of law or any of the other *stoicheia* but are God's children. As such, by describing Isaac as one born according to the Spirit, he draws in this antithesis.

Persecute is *diōkō*, used by Paul in Gal 1:13 and 1:23 of his own persecution of the children of Sarah, those who are children

---

73. *DBL* Hebrew 7464.

of promise like Isaac. He himself functioned as Ishmael to Isaac, hunting Christians to punish and imprison them, force them to blaspheme, and put them to death (cf. Phil 3:6; 1 Tim 1:13).[74]

'So also it is now' speaks of this ongoing problem. There is evidence through Acts of the ongoing persecution of the Christian movement from Jews. By the time of the writing of Galatians, Paul himself had experienced this from his own people regularly. This persecution includes death plots in Damascus (Acts 9:23–25) and Jerusalem (Acts 9:29), the Jewish magician Elymas' (Bar-Jesus) opposition in Cyprus (Acts 13:8), opposition and expulsion from Pisidian Antioch (Acts 13:45, 49–52), an attempt at stoning him in Iconium (Acts 14:5–6), and an actual stoning in Lystra (Acts 14:19; 2 Cor 11:25). Within a few years of writing Galatians, he speaks of the Jews who persecuted him, seeking to hinder him from preaching the gospel to the gentiles (1 Thess 2:14–16). By the mid-fifties, when he wrote 2 Corinthians, he had received five whippings of thirty-nine lashes from the Jews (2 Cor 11:24). He had often been endangered by his people (2 Cor 11:26).

No doubt, it was not just Paul who experienced such treatment. With the rising tide of nationalism at the time leading toward the rebellion against Rome, a movement like Christianity which did not uphold the core boundary markers of Judaism, was particularly vulnerable. It may be that the Judaizers were seeking to alleviate this persecution in their zeal for circumcision. What is clear is that the Galatian readers of the letter were experiencing significant opposition from Jews, similar to what Paul had received while there. The Judaizers themselves may have been participating in the persecution of the uncircumcised gentile believers.

CAST OUT THOSE WHO ENSLAVE BY LAW (4:30)

In *Galatians 4:30*, using another citation from the Genesis

---

74. Cf. Acts 7:53–8:4; 9:1–5; 22:4–5; 26:10–11.

narrative (Gen 21:10), Paul effectively tells the Galatian Christians to expel the Judaizers from the church:

But (*alla*, 1:1) **what** (neuter *tis*, 3:1) **[do] the Scriptures** (*graphē*, 3:8) **say** (present *legō*, 1:9)? '**Cast out** (*ekballō*)[75] **the slave-woman** (*paidiskē*, 4:22) **and** (*kai*, 1:1) **her** (feminine *autos*, 1:1) **son** (*huios*, 1:16), **for** (*gar*, 1:10) **the son** (*huios*) **of the slave-woman** (genitive *paidiskē*) **will never** (*ou*, 1:1, *mē*, 1:7) **inherit** (future *klēronomeō*)[76] **[the promises] with** (*meta*, 1:18) **the son** (genitive *huios*, 1:16) **of the free woman** (feminine *eleutheros*, 3:28).'

Paul introduces the OT text without using the perfect passive of *graphō*, *gegraptai*, 'it is written' (3:10, 13; 4:22, 27). Rather, he uses the cognate noun *graphē* with a question: 'But what do the Scriptures (*graphē*) say?' The question invites the Galatians to consider the Scripture, which he will now state.

'Cast out' uses the imperative of *ekballō* which compounds *ek* (from) and *ballō* (throw, drive out, expel), yielding a word with some strength and force, 'cast out.' This is Paul's only use of the term. In the LXX it is used of expulsion including Adam being driven out of Eden (Gen 3:24), Cain driven from the soil (Gen 4:14), Pharaoh driving Moses from his presence (Exod 10:11), and expelling Israel from Egypt,[77] the peoples of Canaan driven out in the conquest,[78] others driven out of situations,[79] casting

---

75. The verb ἐκβάλλω (*ekballō*) compounds *ek* (from) and *ballō* (throw, drive out, expel) and so has the sense in its one Galatians use of 'cast out' (4:30). It looks back to the expulsion of Hagar and Ishmael from Abraham's household and by analogy speaks of the Galatians expelling the Judaizers, whoever they are (cf. v. 10). This is Paul's only use of the term. It is often used concerning the expulsion of demons and as the notes on the verse in the commentary show, it is a powerful term for expulsion.

76. The verb κληρονομέω (*klēronomeō*) means 'inherit' and is used twice in Galatians. In 4:30, it is employed of the slave women's children never inheriting with the son of the freewoman. The other use is 5:21 where those who do works of the flesh will never inherit the kingdom of God. See also *klēronomia*, 'inheritance' in 3:18, and *klēronomos*, 'heir' in 3:29.

77. See Exod 6:1; 11:1; 12:33, 39; Jdt 5:8, 12.

78. See Exod 23:28, 29, 30, 31; 33:2; 34:11, 24; Num 21:32; 22:6, 11; Deut 11:23; 29:28; 33:27; Josh 24:18; Judg 6:9; 2 Sam 7:23; 1 Chron 17:21; Ps 77:55 [Eng. 78:55]; 79:9 [Eng. 80:8]; Jdt 5:14, 16.

79. See Judg 9:41; 11:2, 7; 1 Sam 26:19; 1 Kings 2:27; 2 Kings 16:6; 2 Chron 11:16, LXX; 2 Chron 13:19; Ps 108:10 [Eng. 109:10]; Bel 14; 1 Macc 13:11.

out idols (2 Chron 15:8; Isa 2:20), the Assyrians seeking to exile Israel (2 Chron 20:11), expelling unclean things from the Temple (2 Chron 29:5, 16), Israel driven into exile (Hos 9:15; Zech 7:14) like a lion with its prey,[80] to remove troops from a city (1 Macc 11:41, 66), and expelling people from a city or temple (1 Macc 13:47, 50).[81]

Outside of Paul, while in the NT *ekballō* on occasion is used in a softer sense,[82] most often, it speaks of being cast out with some force and even violence. Its uses include the casting out of demons (e.g., Matt 7:22; 8:16, 31; 9:33, 34; 10:1, 8; 12:24, 26, 27, 28; 17:19; Mark 1:34, 39; 3:15; 3:22, 23; 6:13; 7:26; 9:18, 28, 38; Luke 9:40, 49; 11:14, 15, 18, 19, 20; 13:32); of Satan (John 12:31) or people thrown into eternal torment (Matt 8:12; 22:13; 25:30; Luke 13:28); excrement expelled from the anus (Matt 15:17); Jesus driving people from the Temple (Matt 21:12 and parr.; John 2:15); the tenants throwing the Son from the vineyard to kill him (Matt 21:39 and parr.), the Spirit thrusting Jesus into the wilderness to face Satan (Mark 1:12); and the Nazareth crowd driving Jesus to a hill to throw him off (Luke 4:29). *Ekballō* is also used for the expulsion of people from a community such as a man with restored sight cast out of the synagogue (John 9:34, 35),

---

80. See Isa 5:29; 22:17; Jer 12:14, 15; 22:28.
81. *Ekballō* is also used of shepherds driving women away (Exod 2:17), people cast out from God's presence (Exod 23:18, LXX), casting things in sacrifice (Lev 1:16), throwing out impure things (Lev 14:40), a woman divorced from her husband (Lev 21:7; 21:14; 22:13; 30:10; Sir 7:36; Ezek 44:22), a boundary line (John 15:8), blocking someone from serving (2 Chron 11:14), to bring out a woman to put to death (2 Chron 23:14), removing foreign wives (1 Esd 8:90; 9:20; Ezra 10:3), and casting someone out (Ps 16:11 [Eng. 17:11]). Positively, it is used of setting someone free (Ps 43:3 [Eng. 44:2]), casting away God's words (Ps 49:17 [Eng. 50:17], drive out a scoffer (Prov 22:10), drive out a mistress (Prov 24:58), a man driven from his home by his wife's nagging (Prov 27:15) or a woman driven out by slander (Sir 28:15), a time to cast out (Eccl 3:6), drive a confession from a mouth (Job 22:22), drive out a dying groan (Job 24:12), a person driven out (Wis 19:3), throwing out slander (Sir 28:9), Jonah being thrown into the sea (Jon 1:15) and spat out of a fish (Jon 2:11), to drive out someone's teeth (Lam 3:16), an ambush (1 Macc 11:68), to send troops (1 Macc 12:27), and to remove uncleanness (1 Macc 13:48).
82. Some uses of *ekballō* include bringing out treasure (Matt 12:35; 13:52), Jesus bringing justice to victory (Matt 12:20), taking out coins (Luke 10:35), Rahab sending messengers another way (Jas 2:25), and not measuring a part of the temple (Rev 11:2).

Stephen from Jerusalem to be stoned to death while Paul looked on (Acts 7:58), of Paul and Barnabas from Pisidian Antioch (Acts 13:50), and Paul and his team expelled from Philippi (Acts 16:37). It is also used for Demetrius's expulsion of people from the church (3 John 10).[83]

Here, from Gen 21:10, it is an imperative that refers back to Sarah's words to Abraham. Here, this imperative becomes Paul's command to the Galatians to cast out or expel the slave woman and her son. As noted, Paul uses the imperative in commanding the Galatians sparingly in chapters 1–3 (1:20; 3:7, cf. 1:8, 9). In chapters 4–6 he uses them more frequently as he is more direct with the Galatians (see further on 1:8).

This particular imperative is most interesting as it has a double edge. At a surface level, it speaks of the expulsion of Hagar and Ishmael by Abraham at Sarah's behest. Here, it speaks of removing the Judaizers and their influence over the Galatians to yield to Jewish legal expectations. They are to be expelled from the community.

There is a remarkable call to inclusion and unity in Jesus' teaching and Paul. Jesus was the friend of sinners and was unafraid to enter into a relationship with the repudiated and marginalized. Paul is very committed to the inclusion of people in the ecclesia. He rejects marginalization and stratification on the basis of gender, race, or status (3:28; Eph 2:11–21). He strongly critiques the Corinthians for their disunity, especially at the Lord's Supper (1 Cor 1:10–4:21; 11:17–34).

Yet, texts like this show us that Paul did not hold to inclusion no matter what. There are times to expel a person who is corrupting the church. So, in 1 Cor 5:1–13, he urges the expulsion of a man who is arrogantly involved in flagrant sexual misconduct. Here and in 1 Tim 1:18–20, he urges expulsion of

---

83. *Ekballō* is also used of taking a speck or log from an eye (Matt 7:4, 5 and parr.), removing a crowd from a room (Matt 9:25 and parr.; Acts 9:40), Jesus thrusting workers into the harvest field (Matt 9:38; Luke 10:2) and sending people away (Mark 1:43), gouging out one's eye if it causes sin (Mark 9:47), to repudiate a person's name (Luke 6:22), Jesus never casting out his own (John 6:37) but sending them out (John 10:4), and throwing grain off a ship (Acts 27:38).

people whose teaching violates the essence of the gospel. In Titus
3:9–11, he urges that when someone is extremely contentious,
they are to be given two warnings and if not heeded, they are to
have nothing more to do with that person.

Such people corrupt the church either ethically, theologically,
or relationally. Their poison seeps through the church like yeast
through the dough (cf. 5:9). For the good of the church and the
work of the gospel, they are to be expelled. In 1 Cor 5:5 and
1 Tim 1:20, we have hints that Paul's purposes are not that the
person cannot be saved; his hope is that they will be. Indeed,
no doubt, repentance and re-inclusion is an open path if one is
expelled. As Paul himself says, if a branch of the olive tree is cut
off through unbelief, it can be regrafted in (Rom 11:20, 24). These
examples remind us that inclusion is not at the cost of the gospel
itself. Our unity is in Christ. When someone violates the gospel
and corrupting others, there is a time for ex-communication. As
with Matt 18 and Tit 3 mentioned above, this will come after
a genuine process of warnings. The path to re-entry will also
always be open for the truly repentant.

The reason Paul gives (for, *gar*) is that the son of the slave
woman will never (*ou gar mē*) inherit with the son of the
freewoman. The construct ou *gar mē* is emphatic, the
combination of the two negating terms (*ou, mē*), both meaning
'no,' giving a reinforced negation[84]—the sons will *absolutely never*
inherit with the son of the freewoman.

In regards to the analogy, Ishmael will not inherit with
Isaac—only Isaac will receive an inheritance as Abraham's heir.
Applied to the Galatian situation, those who persist with law-
observance for the gaining of the status of righteous despite the
grace of the gospel of Christ, are not heirs to the Abrahamic
promise. They are thus to be cast out. The heirs will inherit with
'the son of the freewoman,'—here, Christ.

Inheritance calls to mind Rom 8:17, where Christians are

---

84. BDAG 646. Often it is used with the subjunctive. Examples in Paul include Rom
4:8—'blessed is the person against whom the Lord will *never* count his/her sin;' 1 Cor
8:13—'I will *never* eat meat.' Here it is used with the future indicative, the only time in
this form in Paul. See further examples in BDAG 646, meaning 4.

children of God and fellow heirs with Christ. The strong negation used here states emphatically that for Paul, any Jew who has heard the gospel of Christ and has rejected Jesus as Messiah, God's Son, Lord, and Savior, or any person who believes law-observance (or any other works for that matter) is essential to salvation (whether alongside faith in Christ or not), will not inherit eternal life.

Judaism reaches a critical turning point when Christ came to God's chosen people. From that point on, salvation is in him alone. All the promises of God and expectations of the law are brought together in him. Everything that makes Judaism what it is has been swept up into Christ. He is the creator, he is the Temple, he is the final complete sacrifice, he is Zion, he is Israel, he is Jerusalem, he is the Land, he is the High Priest, he is the law, and he is the only means of justification, redemption, adoption, reconciliation, sanctification; salvation. His people, in continuity with God's people of faith from time immemorial, are God's people. There is no other way. This verse is a serious warning to all forms of Christian faith that privilege the law in any sense, argue for works for redemption, and even extreme forms of Zionism that envisage different paths of salvation for Jew and Gentile or consider God favors Jews over other races in any way—God does not show favoritism (2:6, cf. Rom 2:11; Acts 10:34).

CHILDREN OF THE FREE WOMEN (4:31)

Galatians 4:31 concludes the section:

Therefore (*dio*),[85] **brothers and sisters** (vocative *adelphos*, 1:2), **we are** (second-person plural *eimi*, 1:7) **not** (*ou*, 1:1) **children** (plural *technon*, 4:19) **of the slave-woman** (genitive *paidiskē*, 4:22) **but** (*alla*, 1:1) **of the free woman** (plural *eleutheros*, 3:28).

'Therefore' is *dio*, bringing Paul's argument to a head—'so then …' Again, the Galatians are 'brothers and sisters,' speaking of

---

85. The logical and inferential conjunction διό (*dio*) connotes 'therefore, so then,' and is used only in Gal 4:31 to conclude Paul's allegorization of Hagar and Sarah as he draws it to a conclusion concerning the status of him and the Galatians (we).

familial unity. They are with Paul, part of the same family, despite the Judaizers. 'We are' is inclusive of Paul and those with him, and the Galatians. It is indeed inclusive of every person in the world who believes in Jesus Christ and lives out of his grace by faith.

'Not children of the slave-woman' means that they are not descendants of the Judaistic system of law observance. This passage shows Paul's remarkable transformation. He lived his life as a zealot for this system (1:13–14). Now, he is no longer a child of the Jewish system. Or better, he considers that the Jewish system *continues in Jesus* and not in the now-defunct Judaism-in-rejection-of-Jesus or the Judaizing version that diminishes his significance. Everything in his Christian world is shaped by Christ and not the Torah which is consummated and fulfilled in him. The Judaizers are children of this now-false system, children of Hagar, Mt Sinai, Jerusalem, and Torah. Conversely, Paul and the Galatians are children of the freewoman. They are descendants of Sarah, recipients of the promise. They are children of the Jerusalem above. She is their mother. They are co-heirs with Christ in the inheritance promised Abraham—the world (Rom 4:13). In 5:1, he will build on this directly urging the Galatians to remain in this status.

CHAPTER 24

CHAPTER TWENTY-FOUR: A FINAL APPEAL: DO NOT ACCEPT CIRCUMCISION (5:1–6)

There is no connective (asyndeton, see 2:6), so this indicates a new section.[1] In v. 1, Paul shifts his tone from the analogy, again getting direct with the Galatians. He draws on the previous contrast between freedom and slavery. The Galatians are free in Christ, free from law observance, sin, and eternal death. They have been set free to embrace this freedom fully. As such, they are to stand firm in this status refusing the Judaizers, repudiating their demand that they yield to Torah observance.

In v. 2, Paul focuses on circumcision, which is likely the dominant legal issue from the Judaizers' perspective. They are demanding that new converts be circumcised. Paul tells them that if they do yield and accept circumcision as a basis for righteousness before God, Christ is no longer advantageous to them (v. 3). If they do, they enter the Torah system and are then obligated to keep the whole law. Paul is absolute; if they do, they are severing themselves from Christ. They have fallen from grace (v. 4). Rather, they must continue to live in the Spirit by faith with an eager hope of the final verdict of righteousness (v. 5).

In v. 6, whether one is circumcised or not is neither here nor there; what counts is faith working itself out with love—anticipating the direction he will take them in 5:13–6:9. In v. 7, Paul employs the athletic metaphor; they were running the Christian race well. He asks, who is hindering their progress in obedience? Logically, the answer is the Judaizers. Their persuasion is not from God who called them by his grace (v. 8).

---

1. As most translations show. However, the NRSV attaches 5:1 to the previous section.

In v. 9, he shifts to a baking metaphor. In the ancient world, this is a feminine motif that also recalls the Passover; a little yeast leavens a lump—implication: they must not let the Judaizers infect the church with their yeast. Rather, the Judaizers must be expelled (cf. 4:30). In v. 10, Paul expresses his confidence that they will accept his point of view, with the one causing them trouble bearing the penalty of expulsion.

In v. 11, we get a sense of another of the Judaizers' critiques. They are saying that Paul elsewhere preaches circumcision, whereas, among the Galatians, he did not. Paul repudiates this telling them that if he is indeed doing this, he would not continue to be persecuted as he is. If he preaches circumcision, the offense of a crucified Messiah does not hold—for his death would be unnecessary. Paul would be a Judaizer, and law-observance for righteousness would be possible. It is not.

In v. 12, with a play on the idea of the removal of the foreskin and the tradition of the Galli, he wishes that the Judaizers would castrate themselves. The overall thrust is to repudiate the Judaizers who want them to be circumcised and to persevere in the freedom of the gospel.

STAND FIRM IN YOUR FREEDOM IN CHRIST (5:1)

In *Galatians 5:1*, without a connective like *gar*, *oun* (see variant), or *de*, Paul begins his final appeal:

For[2] **freedom** (dative *eleuthera*, 2:4), **Christ** (*Christos*, 1:1) **set us** (plural accusative *egō*, 1:2) **free** (*eleutheroō*);[3] **therefore** (*oun*, 3:5), **stand firm** (second person imperative *stēkō*)[4] **and** (*kai*, 1:1)

---

2. **Variant**: Some mss include *oun*, 'so then, therefore,' connecting this to the previous section (D 104 1505 2464 syhmg). There is a range of other variants. Metzger accepts the reading used in the text (ℵ* A B P 33 etc.), as it 'seems to account best for the origin of the others. The apostle's abrupt introduction of exhortations was softened by inserting the relative ᾗ before or after ἐλευθερίᾳ, or by transferring οὖν to the preceding clause.' (Metzger, *Textual Commentary*, 528).

3. The verb ἐλευθερόω (*eleutheroō*), 'set free' is only found in 5:1, 'Christ set us free.' It relates to *eleutheria* (2:4) and *eleutheros* (3:28). It speaks in its only use of being freed from law, sin, and death by Christ.

4. The verb *stēkō*, 'stand firm,' is found once in Galatians in Paul's appeal to the Galatians

do not be harnessed (present passive imperative *enechō*)[5] **again** (*palin*) **to a yoke** (dative *zygos*) **of slavery** (dative *douleia*).

As discussed concerning 2:4 and 3:28, freedom is a critical Roman value. For the Greeks and Romans, it was freedom from the status of slavery and being able to determine one's own destiny. One could argue it is similar to contemporary notions of individual freedom in western thought. Paul here speaks not of freedom in this individual self-actualization and autonomous sense, but freedom from the law, sin, and its consequences. Hence, while a person can be a slave by status, or in a state of extreme privation and oppression, if they believe in Jesus, they are free of law, sin, and (ultimate) death. They may be suffering greatly under extreme oppression, but they suffer as God's children and remain free in Christ despite their seeming subjugation. By the Spirit, they can experience God's freedom despite their bondage to political and social forces.

'For freedom' is dative and prominently placed. The dative can be construed as 'for freedom,' speaking of being free to live the life of freedom. Otherwise, it can be translated 'into freedom,' emphasizing the status of being freedpeople in Christ. The appeal that follows supports 'for freedom,' although 'into the status of freedom' is implied.

'Us' refers to all believers in Christ, including Paul, those with him, all believers across the world, and the still-believing Galatians. It can be appropriated for all later Christian readers, us included. Christ here is the redeemer who has set the Galatians free. This redemption recalls 1:3, where Christ 'gave himself for our sins to deliver us from the present evil age.' Jesus has done this. Believers are freed from sin and its handmaiden, the law. They are free from condemnation and the judgment

---

to stand firm in their status of freedom and not yield to the Judaizers (5:1). It has a military and athletic nuance.

5. The verb ἐνέχω (*enechō*) compounds *en*, 'in' and *echō*, 'have, hold' and so 'hold onto.' The passive has the sense of being held fast. It is found once in Galatians with the sense 'do not submit' in Paul's appeal that the Galatians do not again submit themselves to enslavement to the law, sin, and the *stoicheia* (5:1). This is Paul's only use. The only other NT uses are in Mark 6:19 and Luke 11:53 where it has the sense of being hostile toward another (see BDAG 336).

of eternal destruction (Rom 8:1). While they will die physically, they are freed from death for their lives will go on eternally; they are raised at the return of Christ (1 Thess 4:16–18) and will experience the transformation of the body (1 Cor 15:50–58). He is one in whom believers have been crucified and now live in him by his power (2:19–20). He has redeemed believers from under the law (4:5) and from all the nations. He has set them free from the *stoicheia*, the elemental powers (4:8–9).

Part b of the verse uses *oun*, 'therefore,' and so draws out the consequences of being free in Christ. Aside from 1:8, 9, and in citations, for only the fifth time in the letter uses the imperative, directly appealing to his converts stressing urgency[6]—*stekete*, second person plural imperative, 'stand firm.' The imperative of *enechō* is used in the next clause. As noticed regarding 4:12, imperatival commands to the Galatians are found through Chs. 5–6 in particular.

The verb *stēkō* is used in military contexts of armies standing firm in the face of opposition, and for athletics of wrestlers and other athletes resolutely standing against attack. Paul uses it in other appeals for perseverance: '*stand firm* in your faith, be courageous, be strong' (1 Cor 16:13); '*stand firm* in one Spirit' (Phil 1:27); '*stand firm* in the Lord' (Phil 4:1); 'if you continue to *stand firm* in the Lord (1 Thess 3:8);' and '*stand firm* and hold fast to the traditions that you were taught by us' (2 Thess 2:15) (cf. Rom 14:4).[7] Here, they are to stand firm in the status Christ has brought them into—freedom!

'Do not submit' is the imperative (seventh direct imperative in the letter, see above) an unusual verb *enechō*, used three times in the NT. The verb compounds *en* (in, on) and *echō* (hold, have), and so has a sense like, 'hold onto.' The other two uses are in Mark 6:19 and Luke 11:53 of being hostile toward someone, to bear ill-will.'[8] In the LXX, *enechō* is used is found five times of attackers pressing in on someone (holding them in) (Gen 49:23),

---

6. See on 1:8; 3:7; 4:12, 30, cf. 5:13, 15, 16; 6:1, 2, 4, 6, 7, 11, 17.

7. Otherwise in the NT it is used of standing—Jesus' family standing outside (Mark 3:31) and standing to pray (Mark 11:25).

8. BDAG 336.

serving someone food (2 Kings 4:40), and three times of being entangled (Ezek 14:4, 7; 3 Macc 6:10). The passive has the sense of being held fast or entangled by something, here, the yoke of the law. With the image of a yoke, it has the sense of being constrained, bound to, loaded down, or harnessed with something.[9]

The *zygos* is a yoke that was a frame used to control working animals (e.g., Num 19:2; 3 Macc 4:9).[10] Commonly of the time, it is used to describe a burden of oppression.[11] In the NT, Matthew's Jesus uses the imagery of the burden he places on people (Matt 11:29, 30). Paul, in 1 Tim 6:1, uses *zygos* of 'the yoke of slavery' in a real sense, instructing slaves to treat masters with honor. Similar to Paul's use here is Acts 15:10, where Peter, only a year or so after Galatians (as the Judaizing debate is decided), asks why the Judaizers are 'putting God to the test by placing on the neck of the disciples a *yoke* that neither our ancestors nor we have been able to bear.' Like Paul here, with the Cornelius' event and perhaps with the clash with Paul in mind, Peter argues against the burden of the law being placed on gentile converts.

'Of slavery' uses *douleia* found in 4:24 of the state of being enslaved to another. Here then, the Galatians are not to yield to the demands of the Judaizers to come under Torah, particularly through the boundary marker of circumcision.

CIRCUMCISION ANNULLS PROFIT FROM CHRIST (5:2)

In *Galatians 5:2*, with a very personal appeal, Paul gets to the heart of the Judaizers' demand:

Behold (*ide*),[12] **I** (*egō*, 1:2), **Paul** (*Paulos*, 1:1), **say** (*legō*, 1:9) **to**

---

9. Similarly, see BDAG 336.
10. The *zygos* can also be a scale (Prov 11:1; Job 31:6; Amos 8:5; Hos 12:7; Isa 40:12; Ezek 5:1; Rev 6:5). It is also used for the burden of the tongue (Sir 28:19, 20). It can be used positively of wisdom, to which a person should willingly yoke oneself (Sir 51:26).
11. See, e.g., Gen 27:40; 2 Chron 10:4, 9–11, 14; Sir 40:1; Isa 9:4; 14:25; 47:6; Jer 2:20; 34:6; Ezek 34:27; 1 Macc 8:18; 3 Macc 4:9.
12. The particle ἴδε (*ide*), is the imperative of εἶδον (*eidon*), and means 'look, see, pay attention, take note' (BDAG 466). It is found once in Galatians, in 5:2, in Paul's appeal not to accept circumcision.

you (dative plural *sy*, 1:3) **that** (*hoti*, 1:6) **if** (*ean*, 1:8) **you are circumcised** (present passive subjunctive *peritemnō*, 2:3), **Christ** (*Christos*, 1:1) **will not benefit** (future *ōpheleō*)[13] you (plural *sy*).[14]

Behold is *ide*, a particle which is the imperative of *eidon*, meaning 'look, see, pay attention, take note.' Like the related *idou*, it is found quite commonly in the NT (twenty-nine times), especially in John (fifteen times). Paul uses it only twice. First, he employs it in Rom 11:22 where he urges the Romans to 'therefore, *take note* of the kindness and severity of God.' The second use is this one, where it has the sense of 'take note, pay attention, listen,' with an emphasis on what he will then say concerning circumcision.

'I, Paul,' uses Paul's name for the second time in the letter (1:1). It again reinforces his authorship and the very personally direct nature of the letter. The construct is emphatic, drawing attention to himself and what he is saying.[15] With *ide*, there is a strong call to the Galatians to take note of what Paul is saying.

'Say to you that' introduces the content to which Paul wants to draw attention. 'You' is the Galatians as opposed to Paul and those with him. The shift from the first-person plural to the second-person plural focuses Paul's words on the Galatians markedly.

The content is introduced by *ean* with the subjunctive indicating a third-class conditional statement that speaks of something uncertain in likelihood (see on 1:8). 'If any of you are circumcised' in the protasis speaks of the desire of the Judaizers to force new gentile converts to undergo circumcision. This strikes at the heart of the Judaizing issue. They cannot accept that faith is enough. Likely building on their view of Israel's story and the importance of circumcision as a boundary marker (esp. Gen 17), they have not fully accepted that belief in Christ is sufficient to place a convert in a state of righteousness. It could

---

13. The verb ὠφελέω (*ōpheleō*), 'gain, benefit, profit' is found once in Galatians, in 5:2 of circumcision being of no value to the Galatians in the eschaton (future).

14. See BDAG 466.

15. See also 1 Cor 16:21; 2 Cor 10:1; Eph 3:1; Col 1:23; 4:18; 1 Thess 2:18; 2 Thess 3:17; Phlm 9, 19.

be connected with their sense of nationalism which was on the rise in the period leading to the Jewish war. It could also be a response to persecution from other Jews who are repulsed by the idea of gentiles being recognized as God's people without submitting to the Jewish boundary markers.

As said consistently in this work, this is an issue with immense implications. It affects the question of perseverance—one is sustained in God's people by faith and faith alone. Nothing more is needed whether it be circumcision or obeisance to any law or works. This truth has implications for salvation—one gets in and stays in by faith. It has missiological ramifications—the gospel one preaches is one of grace and faith without any need for law or works in any sense. It has massive implications concerning ecclesiology, culture, status, and gender. Circumcision is a Jewish entry marker. As such, Judaizing is to become a Jew. Making circumcision essential is to privilege one race and culture over another. It creates a status disparity between the circumcised and uncircumcised. It privileges men, for men only can be circumcised, and reinforces the ancient idea that one's faith is defined by the man to whom one is subordinate. It thus creates the potential for racism, ethnocentrism, sexism, and privilege on the basis of status.

The apodosis to the conditional statement draws out the implications of being circumcised—'Christ will not benefit (future ōpheleō) you.' 'Benefit' is ōpheleō, used fifteen times in the NT. It is an accounting term speaking of material profit (Matt 15:5; Mark 7:11). It is also used concerning political gain (Matt 27:24; John 12:19), improvement in health (Mark 5:26), and by Paul for the edification that comes from easily understandable speech in the church (1 Cor 14:6).

On occasion, it is used figuratively with regard to eschatological profit to which gaining the whole world (in a material sense) is contrasted (Matt 16:26; Mark 8:36; Luke 9:25). Similarly, John contrasts the Spirit who gives life with 'the flesh that profits nothing' (John 6:63). Again, the writer of Hebrews recognizes that hearing the gospel without faith gains the hearer no benefit (Heb 4:2). Hebrews also speaks of the lack of benefit gained by eating particular foods rather than grace (Heb 13:9).

Paul also uses *ōpheleō* of circumcision in Rom 2:25, telling his Jewish interlocutor that 'circumcision is, on the one hand, *profitable* if you obey the law.' As he argues in Rom 1:18–3:20 and in Gal 3:10–14, this is implausible because all are incapable of full obedience to the law. As he goes on to say in Rom 2:25b, 'but on the other hand, if you break the law, your circumcision has become uncircumcision.' He also uses it of eschatological gain in 1 Cor 13:3, where he gains nothing from loveless sacrificial acts. So here, in the future tense, it has the eschatological profit before God. This gain has a present dimension of life in the Spirit, who is received from God when the gospel is heard with faith (3:2, 5). More importantly, it speaks of eternal life which is lost if one is circumcised.

The circumcision referred to here is where it is demanded as a condition of salvation/justification and inclusion in God's people and the church. It is circumcision as espoused in the Scriptures (Gen 17; Lev 12:3). In many cultures today, circumcision is a part of life. I learned this in the Cook Islands as a boy in the 1970s. One of the worst insults one can give is to describe another male as uncircumcised, indicating how basic circumcision was to the Cook Island culture at this time. Strangely, this was an expectation of the missionaries who clearly did not understand Paul's theology. Nevertheless, where circumcision is practiced culturally and without being a soteriological demand, it is neither here nor there (aside from any medical benefits or lack thereof). Hence, a contemporary circumcised believer in Christ reading the NT need not be concerned that they are in a precarious place before God—now expected to obey the whole law. Similarly, one who is not circumcised should not be concerned. What matters is faith working out in love (v. 6), or, as in 6:15, a new creation. However, if someone demands that a believer must be circumcised to be righteous before God in any sense, this is repugnant. It is this that Paul is dealing with here.

CIRCUMCISION CREATES AN OBLIGATION TO KEEP THE ENTIRE LAW (5:3)

In *Galatians 5:3*, Paul goes on drawing out the implications of a gentile believer in Galatia yielding to the Judaizing demands:

And (*de*, 1:15) **I testify** (*martyromai*)[16] **again** (*palin*, 1:9) **that** (*hoti*, 1:6) **every** (*pas*, 1:2) **man** (*anthrōpos*, 1:1) **who is circumcised** (present passive *peritemnō*, 2:3) **is** (*eimi*, 1:7) **obligated** (*opheiletēs*)[17] **to do** (aorist infinitive *poieō*, 2:10) **the whole** (*holos*)[18] **law** (*nomos*, 2:16).

The *de* is consecutive, 'and,' with Paul continuing his direct appeal. 'I testify' brings back the first person, this time singular, a shift from the second person plural appeal of v. 3. Paul adds to the deeply personal 'I, Paul' to emphasize Paul's passionate appeal.

'I testify' uses *martyromai*, a legal term speaking here of a forensic rhetorical argument, Paul interpreting the law. Unlike the more common *martyreō*, 'I testify, give witness,' *martyromai* is rarer in the NT. The term has the original meaning 'to invoke someone as a witness about something' including the gods (Plato, *Phileb.* 12b) or another person (Aeschylus, *Eum.* 643). However, it became a general term for making 'a solemn declaration about' something as Paul does here.[19]

The verb is only used by Paul either in Acts or the letters. In Acts, it is found twice, both on the lips of Paul where he gives witness to the Ephesian elders that he is not responsible for their blood (Acts 20:26), and before Herod Agrippa II, that he is testifying to what is in the law and Prophets to small and

---

16. The verb μαρτύρομαι (*martyromai*) is passive or middle of *martyreō*. It stands as a verb in its own right. It is used once in Gal 5:2 and only twice else in Paul (Eph 4:17; 1 Thess 2:12). The term means to give witness or testify. In 5:2, it is part of Paul's personal testimony that if a person is circumcised, they must do the whole law.

17. The noun ὀφειλέτης (*opheiltetēs*) means 'one under obligation' and is found in 5:3 of the circumcised Christian should do the whole law (see also in Paul, Rom 1:14; 8:12; 15:27).

18. The adjective ὅλος (*holos*), 'whole, entire' is used twice in the letter, in 5:3, of the obligation of the circumcised to do the whole law, and in 5:9, of yeast leavening the 'whole batch of dough.'

19. H. Strathmann, 'μαρτύρομαι,' in *TDNT* 4:510.

great (Acts 26:22). In the letters, it is used in Eph 4:17 to his readers that they must no longer live in gentile sin. In 1 Thess 2:12, he solemnly declares that the Thessalonians should lead lives worthy of God. Here, it is Paul's solemn testimony and declaration concerning circumcision and the law. 'I testify *again (palin)*,' recalls 1:9 ('so now I say *again*') where Paul repeats his imprecation against false teachers. 'Again' could refer to 3:10 where the connection between circumcision and fulfilling the whole law is implied. More likely, 'again,' recalls earlier times when Paul stressed to the Galatians that submission to circumcision at the behest of Jews or Judaizers leads to the requirement of complete fulfillment of the law. A similar example is Phil 3:1 where Paul refers to earlier warnings of Judaizers and then restates it in Phil 3:2. Similarly, in Phil 3:18 he refers to telling the Philippians many times of 'the enemies of the cross.'

The content of his declaration tells the Galatians that if any man (*panti anthrōpō*) has been circumcised, they are obligated to keep the whole law. 'Obligated' is *opheiletēs* which is another accounting term speaking of material debt (Matt 18:24; Rom 15:27). It is also applied to spiritual debt, whether it is Paul's spiritual indebtedness to preach the gospel to all peoples (Rom 1:14), spiritual offense or sin (Matt 6:12; Luke 13:4), or indebtedness to the Spirit (Rom 8:12). Here it speaks of indebtedness to do the whole law.

The whole law parallels *ho pas nomos* (the whole law) in 5:14, which is summed up in the love command of Lev 18:19. Jacob uses the same construct as here (*holon ton nomon*) in Jas 2:10 affirming the same point Paul is making here: 'whoever keeps the *whole* law but fails in one point has become accountable for all of it.' He and Paul are on the same page on this one. Paul's point here is similar to 3:10:

For as many as are [relying] on works of the law, are under a curse. For it is written, 'Cursed be anyone who [does] not abide by *everything* which is written in the book of the law, [and] do (*poieō*) these things' (citing Deut 27:26).

For Paul, to submit to Jewish legal entry protocols, supremely circumcision, and to yield to other requirements (ritual cleansing, Sabbath, Kosher food, other calendric expectations, table fellowship, etc.), takes one into a religious system that is loaded with expectations. The overriding requirement is that the circumcised person must seek to complete every requirement of the law 24/7—something that for Paul is utterly inconceivable other than Christ. The good news for all humanity is that Christ, born under the law, has taken the curse of the law upon himself in his accursed state on the cross, and has redeemed all under the law from the law. Hence, a gentile does not need to yield to Torah protocols again. Rather, they believe in Jesus, who gives them his Spirit, and by the Spirit, they live out their faith through love. Through this life of faith-generating and Spirit-empowering love, the whole law is fulfilled (5:14).

CIRCUMCISION MEANS ALIENATION FROM CHRIST AND GRACE (5:4)

In *Galatians 5:4*, he goes on to draw out an even more dramatic outcome of yielding to the Judaizers:

You have been separated (aorist passive *katargeō*, 3:17) **from** (*apo*, 1:1) **Christ** (genitive *Christos*, 1:1), **those** (plural *hostis*, 2:4) **[of] you [who are seeking] to be justified** (present passive *dikaioō*, 2:16) **by** (*en*, 1:6) **the law** (*nomos*, 2:16)—**you have fallen** (*ekpiptō*) [20] **from grace** (genitive *charis*, 1:3).

We have a neat chiasm here:

A **you have** been separated from Christ

    B those [of] you [seeking] to be justified by the law,

A2 **you have** fallen from grace.

In the chiasm, 'you have' is repeated, 'separated' parallels 'fallen,' and Christ parallels 'grace.' In A the verb is placed first, and in A' it is last—neatly balancing the verse.

---

20. The verb ἐκπίπτω (*ekpiptō*) compounds *ek* (from) and *piptō* (fall) giving the literal meaning 'fall from.' This literal meaning is found in the one use in Galatians 5:4—those who Judaize have 'fallen from grace.' Paul's only other use is Rom 9:6 where 'God's word has not failed (or fallen).' It is Israel who failed by resisting God's revelation in Christ.

Paul shifts from the first-person singular to the second-person plural, as in v. 2, directly addressing the Galatians and any Judaizers who are present to hear or read Galatians. However, unlike v. 4, this is hypothetical in that it has likely not occurred yet. However, if they do go with the Judaizers, then it will become actual. Paul is asking the Galatians whether they will continue to be a part of the Christian community premised on Christ and grace, or, whether they will join those severed from Christ and fallen from grace.

While the focus is challenging the Galatians and Judaizers, 'you' refers to the state of every person who is not a believer in Christ—they are not part of the Christ-people. 'Being justified' is a true conative present speaking of something in progress but not complete—something attempted. Wallace comments 'Paul is not declaring that they are being justified by the law, but that they think they are (or they are trying to be), though their attempt can only end in failure' (cf. 6:12)[21]

The verb *katargeō* is prominently placed to further highlight Paul's statement as if such an emphasis is required. As discussed on 3:17, *katargeō* is a term favored by Paul (twenty-five of the NT's twenty-seven uses). In 3:17, it has the sense of 'nullify, annul, render obsolete' (of the law not doing so to the Abrahamic promise). In 5:11, the offense of the cross is annulled if Paul preaches circumcision. Here, it has the sense of being cut off or severed from Christ. Whereas believers are discharged from the law in Christ (Rom 7:2, 6), to submit to Torah is to sever oneself from Christ. One can argue this has the subtle sense of being destroyed as the term is commonly used in this way.[22] It is thus a strong warning. As justification is found in Christ alone, by faith, this is a terrible situation to be in. This is one of the many verses in Paul that are fatal to the 'once saved always saved' theology. One cannot be joined to Christ unless one has faith. Hence, this is a warning to those joined to Christ by faith that if they yield to the Judaizers, this soteriological connection is severed. This

21. Wallace, *Greek Grammar*, 534–35.
22. See Rom 6:6; 1 Cor 2:6; 15:24; 2 Thess 2:8; 2 Tim 1:10, cf. Heb 2:14.

also repudiates theological perspectives that claim all humanity is in Christ per se but must come to recognize this. One is either in Christ or severed from him. One cannot simultaneously be in Christ and yet severed from him. The relationship is annulled.

A second parallel consequence is then given to those who are seeking to be justified by the law. This would include any Judaizers who are hearing the letter read and any Galatians who are being drawn to their false doctrine. 'You have fallen from grace' uses *ekpiptō*, which blends *ek* (from) and *piptō* (fall) literally connoting 'fall from'—as in chains falling from wrists (Acts 12:7) or a flower from a plant (Jas 1:11; 1 Pet 1:24). Paul uses the term once elsewhere of God's word (not) failing (Rom 9:6).[23] Peter uses the term *ekpiptō* warning his readers that they will 'fall away from your own secure position [in Christ]' (2 Pet 3:17). Paul's warning here is that they fall away from grace.

Grace here recalls 'the grace of Christ' in which God called the Galatians by the gospel. This gospel and grace they are deserting (1:6, cf. 1:3, 15; 2:9; 6:18). This here calls to mind 2:21 where Paul does 'not nullify the grace of God,' otherwise, if justification is through the law, Christ died for nothing. Unlike Paul, the Galatians are in danger of falling away from grace. Grace emphasizes the Godward side of the justification event—justification is a gift to an undeserving sinner from God who eternally demonstrates steadfast love. As with the warning that the Galatians can be severed from Christ, this speaks of the loss of a status they currently have. It thus speaks of their potentially falling away from God's grace, which leaves them as fleshly sinners standing before a righteous God, King, and Judge. This leaves them in a precarious state, the end of which is destruction. One is either in grace or in the flesh. As with the first part of the verse, being in Christ is being in a state of grace. One cannot be in grace and fallen from grace simultaneously.

---

23. It is also used nautically of ships running aground (Acts 27:17, 26, 29) and being set adrift (Acts 27:32).

THROUGH THE SPIRIT AND BY FAITH, WE HOPEFULLY AWAIT
RIGHTEOUSNESS (5:5)

In *Galatians 5:5* Paul shifts tone from warning to optimism concerning the future of the Galatians:

For (*gar*, 1:10) **we** (plural *egō*, 1:2), **by the Spirit** (dative *pneuma*, 3:2), **from** (*ek*, 1:1) **faith** (genitive *pistis*, 1:23), **eagerly await** (present middle *apekdechomai*)[24] **the hope** (*elpis*)[25] **of righteousness** (genitive *dikaiosynē*, 2:21).

The *gar* is causal, 'for,' the verse giving the reason one is severed from Christ. There is a noticeable shift from the second person 'you' to the first-person plural 'we.' 'We' is inclusive of all Christians and not just Paul and those with him.[26] This group includes the Galatians who are yet to yield to the Judaizers; those Paul is seeking to persuade not to do so. The 'we' then is invitational, Paul seeking to draw the Galatians to recognize the Spirit within them and join with Paul and others in awaiting the consummation of all things.

Paul in 5:5–6 uses his familiar triad of faith, hope, and love, perhaps made most famous through 1 Cor 13:13—'but now, three things remain; faith, hope, and love.' Similarly, in 1 Thess 1:3, Paul remembers before God the Thessalonians' 'work of faith and labor of love and steadfastness of hope in our Lord Jesus Christ' (1 Thess 1:3, cf. Rom 5:2–5; 1 Thess 5:8).

Paul again links faith with the Spirit (3:2, 5, 14). 'From (*ek*) faith' is used for the last time in the letter, recalling its seven-fold use in Ch. 3 (3:7, 8, 9, 11, 12, 22, 24) and introduction in 2:16. Throughout, 'from faith' is contrasted with 'from the works of the law/the law.' Faith here is not Christ's faith or faithfulness. As throughout Galatians, it is Paul's governing word for the God-

24. The verb ἀπεκδέχομαι (*apekdechomai*) compounds *apek* (away from) and *dechomai* (receive, welcome) and is used exclusively in the NT of eager eschatological expectations. This is the meaning in Gal 5:5 where 'the hope of righteousness' refers to the conferral of final justification by God the King and Judge.
25. The noun ἐλπίς (*elpis*) means 'hope.' It is found once in Galatians 5:5 of 'the hope of righteousness' which those who have received the Spirit by faith eagerly expect.
26. Strangely, Wallace, *Greek Grammar*, 399, sees this as a *debatable* example of the inclusive 'we.' This would seem to be one if those times where 'we' is inclusive of everyone with the Spirit who awaits Christ's coming.

required human response to God's message. When faith is born in the human heart, the Spirit is poured into that heart, and the believer is fused to God in the most intimate of relationships (see esp. 3:2, 5). At that moment of faith, one is justified before God and receives the Spirit. This is not a subsequent moment sometime later, but the actual moment of conversion.

'By the Spirit' translates the dative. This can mean 'in the Spirit,' the sphere in which the believer now lives. Or, as translated, it speaks of the empowering presence of the Spirit to generate the Spirit-fruit of hope.

Faith (or faithfulness) and hope are at times connected in the OT (Ezra 10:2; Isa 38:2). The writer of Hebrews joins the two notions (Heb 10:23; 11:1), as does Peter (1 Pet 1:21). Paul joins them in Rom 5:2, 'through him we have also obtained access by faith into this grace in which we stand, and we rejoice in the hope of the glory of God' (cf. 1 Cor 13:13). In Col 1:23, the Colossians will be presented holy before God if they continue in the faith, stable and steadfast, not shifting from the hope of the gospel (cf. 1 Cor 13:13 above; 2 Cor 10:15; 1 Thess 5:8). No doubt such words could be written to the Galatians. Faith is belief and trust in the God who is faithful. Hope is the future anticipation that is generated from faith—because we can trust in God in the present, we can have positive hope in all circumstances and for our ultimate future. The Spirit's presence by faith in our hearts generates this sense of confidence. The Spirit sustains believers in all situations, no matter how dire. The Spirit also seals us and produces a longing and hope for the final redemption.

The specific word for hope, *elpis*, is found fifty-three times in the NT, although very surprisingly, *elpis* is not in the Gospels. Outside of Paul, *elpis* is commonly used of eschatological hope generally,[27] or more specifically of resurrection.[28] Paul also utilizes *elpis* commonly of future eschatological hope—'the hope of the glory of God' (Rom 5:2; Col 1:27), 'the hope laid up for you

27. See Acts 28:20; Heb 3:6; 6:11, 18; 7:19; 10:23.
28. See Acts 2:26; 23:6; 24:15; 26:6, 7; 1 Pet 1:3, 21; s.a., the hope of material gain (Acts 16:19), being saved at sea (Acts 27:20), the presence of the Spirit giving hope (1 Pet 3:15), and generally of hope in Christ (1 John 3:3).

in heaven' (Col 1:5), 'the hope of salvation' (1 Thess 5:8), 'the hope of eternal life' (Tit 1:2; 3:7), and the hope of Christ's return (Tit 2:13, cf. 2 Cor 3:12; Eph 1:18; 4:4; Phil 1:20; Col 1:23). This hope creation itself feels (Rom 8:20).

For Paul, this hope is the outcome of the character and endurance produced in suffering (Rom 5:4). The key is the Spirit, who pours love and hope into the human heart (Rom 5:5) so that God, by his Spirit, fills believers with joy and peace in faith and abundant hope (Rom 15:13, cf. 2 Thess 2:16). Thus, Paul can say that believers are saved into an eschatological hope for that which is not yet seen (Rom 8:24). Believers are to rejoice in this hope (Rom 12:12), a hope encouraged by the Scriptures (Rom 15:4).[29]

Here it is 'the hope of righteousness.' While believers are presently justified by faith, righteousness here speaks of the final declaration of righteousness before God at the judgment. This hope is effectively equivalent to the 'hope of salvation' (1 Thess 5:8). If people place their reliance on law, they will be in the place of all unbelievers with no eschatological hope (Eph 2:12, cf. 1 Thess 4:13). They are to emulate the likes of the Thessalonians and continue with a steadfastness of hope in Christ (1 Thess 1:3).

This righteousness the believer 'eagerly awaits' (apekdechomai). The verb apekdechomai is rare, not found in the LXX,[30] and is used in the NT exclusively concerning eschatological hope. The verb speaks of creation's yearning or eager longing for the revelation of God's children (Rom 8:19). It is used in the same context of Christians longing for their final adoption as children of God (Rom 8:23, 25). Elsewhere, Paul utilizes it of longing for the revelation of Christ at his return (1 Cor 1:7, cf. Heb 9:28) as Savior (Phil 3:20). Here, it is the final state of righteousness for which believers yearn. This hope is central to being in Christ.

29. Paul also uses it of Abraham's hope of an heir (Rom 4:18), a farmer's hope of a harvest (1 Cor 9:10), his hopes for the Corinthians (2 Cor 1:7; 10:15), the Thessalonians as hope (1 Thess 2:19), and Christ Jesus our hope (1 Tim 1:1).
30. The term apekdechomai is used once in the Testament of Abraham (A) 16.3 of the demon death awaiting God's command. In 1 Pet 3:20, it is used of God's eager waiting for Noah's building of the ark.

The Galatians who are being seduced by the Judaizers are in danger of never hearing this eschatological declaration of righteousness. If they yield, they will stand before God on the basis of law observance and will fall short. Thus, they must persevere in faith. If so, they will be declared righteous and live eternally with God, Christ, and his people.

WHAT COUNTS IS NOT CIRCUMCISION BUT FAITH WORKING THROUGH LOVE (5:6)

In *Galatians 5:6*, Paul concludes this part of his argument:

For (*gar*, 1:10) in (*en*, 1:6) Christ (*Christos*, 1:1) Jesus (*Iēsous*, 1:1), neither (*oute*, 1:12) circumcision (*peritomē*, 2:7) nor (*oute*) uncircumcision (*akrobystia*, 2:7) produces (*ischyō*)[31] anything (neuter *tis*, 1:7), but [what does is] faith (*pistis*, 1:23) working (*energeō*, 2:8) through (*dia*, 1:1) love (*agapē*).[32]

The *gar* is a marker of clarification of Paul's argument, 'for, you see.'[33] 'In Christ Jesus' speaks of the status of believers. They are included in Christ. His righteousness clothes them, and they are thus justified. It speaks not only of individuals, but a people in Christ, bound together from all cultures, male and female, and every stratum of society.

This verse has connections to 1 Cor 7:17–24. Paul tells the Corinthians to remain in the social state they were in at conversion, seeing it as God's call. If a person is circumcised prior to conversion, they should not seek to remove the marks of circumcision (epispasm). If a person was uncircumcised, they should not seek circumcision. This is because 'circumcision is nothing and uncircumcision is nothing.' The Greek shows the similarity to this verse:

31. The verb ἰσχύω (*ischyō*) has the basic meaning of 'have power' and so speaks of being able to do or produce something. It can have the sense of good health (strength), being well. The only use in Galatians is 5:6 where the respective states of circumcision or uncircumcision produce or do nothing; what does, is faith working through love.
32. The noun ἀγάπη (*agapē*) is found three times in Galatians: 'faith working through *love*' (5:6), 'through *love* serve one another' (5:13), and as the first listed fruit of the Spirit (5:22). See also the verb *agapaō* in 2:20 and 5:14.
33. BDAG 189 meaning 2.

1 Cor 7:19

*he **peritome** ouden estin kai hē **akrobystian** ouden estin, alla tērēsis entolōn Theou*

circumcision nothing is and **uncircumcision** nothing is, but observance of God's commandments

Gal 5:6

*en gar Christō Iēsous **oute peritomē ti** ischuei **oute akrobystia** alla pistis di agapēs energoumenē*

in for Christ Jesus **neither circumcision anything** produces **nor uncircumcision but** faith through love working

The similarity shows that we have a Pauline saying here. In 1 Corinthians 7, the emphasis is obedience to God's commandments. Here, this is not the Torah, but the command to yield to God's reign with faith and exercise that faith with love and other virtues (esp. 1 Cor 13).

This verse is also very similar to 6:15 as can be seen by this transliteration with emboldened points of agreement:

Gal 5:6

*en gar Christō Iēsous **oute peritomē ti** ischuei **oute akrobystia alla** pistis di agapēs energoumenē*

in for Christ Jesus **neither circumcision anything** produces **nor uncircumcision but** faith through love working

Gal 6:15

*oute gar **peritomē ti** estin **oute akrobystia alla** kainē ktisis*

neither for **circumcision anything** is **nor uncircumcision but** a new creation

Both use the postpositive *gar*, merely to introduce what follows. 'In Christ' is only mentioned in 5:6, but it can be assumed in 6:15. The construction 'neither circumcision ... nor uncircumcision' is repeated, as is the strong contrasting conjunction *alla*, 'but.' The verbs differ with 5:6 making the point that the state of one's foreskin *produces* nothing, whereas 6:15 avers that it *is* nothing. This verse then speaks of what is produced by a person's state with regards to circumcision, whereas 6:15 speaks of what it actually is, its ontology—it *is* nothing. The concluding clauses differ. In 6:16, Paul pronounces a blessing on all who follow a rule. The double use of 'neither circumcision nor uncircumcision is anything' suggests that this is the rule. Further, 'faith through love working and 'a new creation' are understandably linked. The new creation being produced by God through faith lives out of love expressed in service of God and others.

'Circumcision' speaks of Jews, and by extension, anyone who is circumcised in any other cultural or religious setting. 'Uncircumcision' refers to the swathes of gentiles throughout the world who have not undergone the removal of the foreskin and, in many cases, repudiate the idea as barbarism. It also speaks of every woman outside of cultures where women are circumcised. Paul uses the verb *ischyō*, which has the sense 'to be able or capacity, capacity, power, strength, be healthy.'[34] Here it is negated by *oute* (neither ... nor) referring to the truth that the physical state of circumcision or uncircumcision achieves nothing. While circumcision is a sign of the Abrahamic covenant, it is faith that brings justification and releases the Spirit of God into the life of the believer. Being circumcised is neither here nor there. It produces nothing. There is no ethical value in circumcision. It is the Spirit that brings transformation, not the foreskin or lack thereof. There is no need for a gentile believer in Jesus undergoing circumcision or submitting to other Jewish laws.

The second part of the verse is introduced with *alla*, 'but, on the contrary,' introducing a contrast between the inability of circumcision and the power of faith and love. 'Faith' is *pistis*, used throughout Galatians of the human response of yielding to God and his Son—mind, will, assent, and relationship (see 2:16). The verb for working, *energeō*, was used in 2:8 of God's power working in Peter and Paul's apostolic ministries and in 3:5 of his working miracles among the Galatians. Here, faith is the power working in believers which is the language of the faith-unleashed Spirit in believers.

The *dia* in 'working *through* love' has the sense of instrumentality whereby something is achieved, 'efficient cause

---

34. W. Grundmann, 'ἰσχύω,' in *TDNT* 3:397.

via.'[35] This is not a soteriological statement, as throughout
Galatians, justification is 'by faith.' This speaks of what matters
once one believes, once one is justified by faith. What matters
and is effective is faith expressed through the ethic of love.

This is the first use of *agapē* in Galatians. Earlier Paul uses
the verb *agapaō* of his own experience of being loved by Christ
(2:20). Here, it is believers who are to express love toward others.
Love will feature in what follows; believers serving one another
through (*dia*) *agapē* (5:13), in the law that sums up all law, '*love
your neighbor as yourself*,' and as a fruit generated in the
Christian life by the Spirit (5:22). The clause, *dia agapēs*,
anticipates *dia tēs agapēs* in 5:13. What matters in the Christian
life after faith is loving service of others. It is the emulation of
God (Rom 5:8; 8:35–40) and the Son of God who loved Paul and
gave himself for him (and all people) (2:20). If the Galatians are to
add anything to faith, not that anything is required for righteous
status, it is love generated by faith and the Spirit.

Faith and love are not uncommonly linked in the Scriptures. In
Gen 24:47,[36] Isaac's prayer is based on God who has not 'forsaken
his *steadfast love* (חֶסֶד (*ḥĕ·sĕḏ*) and his *faithfulness* (אֱמֶת (*'ĕmĕṯ*)' (Gen
24:49; 32:10). Similarly, in Exod 34:6, God is 'merciful and
gracious, slow to anger, and abounding in *steadfast love* and
faithfulness.' In Ps 36:5, put to song by Third Day, 'Your *Love*,
O Lord, reaches to the heavens. Your *faithfulness* stretches to
the skies.'[37] Beautiful are the words, '*steadfast love* and *faithfulness*
meet; righteousness and peace kiss each other' (Ps 85:10). In
these texts and others,[38] love and faithfulness are attributes of
God. The Christian in living faith working through love,
emulates the character of God and his Son. In 1 Kings 3:6, God
has shown David steadfast love 'because he walked before you in

---

35. BDAG 224.
36. The citations in this paragraph are from the ESV.
37. 'Your Love O Lord,' 1999 New Spring, Vandura 2500 Songs: Crossroad Distributors
Pty. Ltd.
38. See Deut 7:9; 2 Sam 2:6; 15:20; Ps 25:10; 40:10–11; 57:3, 10; 61:7; 69:13; 89:15; 88:11;
89:1, 2, 14, 24, 33, 49; 92:2; 98:3; 100:5; 108:4; 115:1; 117:2; 138:2; Isa 61:18; Jer 31:3;
Mic 7:20.

faithfulness,' speaking of God's love for the faithful (1 Kings 3:6, cf. Ps 26:3).[39]

Now that Christ has come, the ḥĕ·sĕḏ of God has been poured into the human heart and forms the basis of ethics for the faithful (Rom 5:5). Yet even this is not new. In Prov 3:3, the teacher says to his son, 'Let not *steadfast love* and *faithfulness* forsake you; bind them around your neck; write them on the tablet of your heart.'[40] Hosea rebukes Israel because 'there is no *faithfulness* or *steadfast love*, and no knowledge of God in the land' (Hos 4:1).

Aside from texts that speak of the triad, faith, hope, and love (above), Paul links faith and love often. In 1 Cor 13:2, even if Paul has a supreme faith that enables the removal of mountains, without love, he is nothing (1 Cor 13:2, cf. 2 Cor 8:7). In Eph 1:15, he gives thanks to God because of the Ephesians' faith in Jesus and their love toward their fellow believers (s.a. Col 1:4; Phlm 5). He prays in Eph 3:17 that Christ may dwell in the Ephesians' hearts through faith, firmly rooted and grounded in love (s.a. Eph 6:23). He delights in the Thessalonians' faith and love in 1 Thess 3:6, while in 2 Thess 1:3, he expresses gratitude that both are virtues that are growing abundantly and increasing (2 Thess 1:3).[41] In Gal 2:20, the two are linked with Paul living in the flesh 'by faith in the Son of God, who loved me.' In 5:22, both love and *pistis* (faith, faithfulness) are mentioned in the fruit of the Spirit.[42]

---

39. In Ps 31:23 it is love for God who preserved the faithful.

40. Cf. Prov 14:22; 16:6; 20:6; 20:28.

41. See also 1 Tim 1:5, 14; 2:15; 4:12; 6:11; 2 Tim 1:13; 2:22; 3:10; Tit 2:2; 3:15, cf. Jas 2:5; Rev 1:5; 2:19.

42. Hope is also linked to love in the Scriptures. For example, Ps 33:18: 'Behold, the eye of the Lord is on those who fear him, on those who hope in his steadfast love' (Ps 33:22; 130:7; 147:11; Jonah 2:8). In Paul, see Rom 5:5; 1 Cor 13:7; 2 Thess 2:16.

CHAPTER 25

CHAPTER TWENTY-FIVE: GET BACK IN THE RACE (5:7–12)

WHO CUT IN ON YOU? (5:7)

In *Galatians 5:7*, Paul returns to the second person plural appeal, beginning with a rhetorical question:

You were running (second person plural imperfect *trechō*, 2:2) **well** (*kalōs*, 4:17). **Who** (*tis*, 3:1) **cut in on** (aorist *enkoptō*)[1] **you** (plural *sy*, 1:3) **[to keep you] from obeying** (infinitive *peithō*, 1:10) **the truth** (dative *alētheia*, 2:5)?

The verse begins, 'You were running well.' Again employing the athletic metaphor deployed in 2:2 (see further on 2:2 and below), Paul commends the Galatians for the quality of their Christian lives (running) up until this Judaizing disruption. However, something has changed. Their race has been disrupted.

Part b of the letter is a question. As throughout the letter, Paul does not name the Judaizers. Rather, recalling 3:1, rhetorically he asks who these people are who have cut in on them. The answer is clear to the Galatians—those preaching the 'gospel' of law observance as essential to righteousness and inclusion. As in 2:2 where he utilized it concerning his own ministry as a race

---

1. The verb ἐγκόπτω (*enkoptō*) compounds *en* (in) *koptō* (cut off). It is used once in Gal 5:7. It can be translated in the more literal sense, 'Who cut in on you,' thinking of a race when someone cuts off a runner (NIV). Or in the less literal 'Who hindered you.' The term is not common in the NT, used elsewhere by Paul of hindrances to his travel plans in Rom 15:22 (his passion for planting churches in unreached territories), and of Satan hindering his plan to return to Thessalonica (1 Thess 2:18). There is a play on ideas here with 'cut in' perhaps hinting at the Judaizers who wish to circumcise the Galatians—cutting in on the penis.

which he hopes is not in vain, Paul uses the athletic metaphor (see further 2:2). This time, he applies it to the Galatians.

Here, Paul anticipates the sense of 1 Cor 9:24–27 where Paul urges the Corinthians to run on with purpose and discipline that they may obtain the prize of the imperishable wreath of eternal life, exercising self-control. Like good boxers, they are not to punch the air but with accuracy to win the 'fight.' Similarly, in Phil 3:12–14, the Philippians, gripped by Christ, are to continue to leave the past behind and stretch forward pursuing the goal to make their own that which God is calling them upward, eternal life with Christ. It also parallels Heb 12:1–2 where the recipients of the letter, surrounded as they are by the mighty saints of history, angelic beings, and God himself, must leave behind all hindrances and run with perseverance the race set before them with eyes fixed on Jesus.

Here, he asks who has cut in on them. As noted in the translation, *enkoptō* yields something like the NIV translation, 'Who cut in on you?' Other translations take it in a transferred manner, 'Who hindered you?' The former is to be preferred as there is a play on the term *koptō*, 'cut' in Gal 5. The idea of cutting does not just invoke the athletic metaphor but calls to mind circumcision. In a literal sense, the Judaizers are seeking to cut in on their penises, removing the foreskin. In a running sense, they are cutting in on the Galatians (below). Later, Paul will exclaim that he wishes they would cut off their offending members (*apokoptō*), which itself is a play on ideas (see 5:12). So, retaining 'cut in on you' allows English readers to discern the play on cutting in the passage.

The term used here, *enkoptō*, is used five times in the NT, twice outside of Paul—of detaining someone by a speech (Acts 24:4) and of prayers being hindered (1 Pet 3:7). Paul employs it twice else of his being hindered in his travel plans—his desire to come to Rome being hindered by his mission purposes (Rom 15:22) and Satan hindering his desire to return to Thessalonica (1 Thess 2:18). As such, it has the general sense of being hindered. Where the Galatians are concerned, things that thwart their Christian lives. The Judaizers then are being likened to illegal athletes who have entered the race falsely. We can find some limited analogies from the current world of sport, such as those on performance-enhancing drugs or who affect an outcome for financial gain. In fact, they have illegally entered themselves and will not win the prize with their false Judaizing theology. Perhaps they are like those who tried to cut down runners in the women's marathon at the Rio Olympics, as someone also did to the famed Brazilian runner Vanderlei de Lima. He was heading for gold at the 2004 Olympics only to be tackled by a priest who was later defrocked. However, he ran on winning bronze. He was rewarded with the honor of lighting the Olympic torch in Rio.

The image here is of athletes circling the stadium in a group and a runner cutting in on another athlete causing that athlete to stumble or even fall. As I was writing this, it was just after the 2016 Rio Olympics where the NZ athlete Nikki Hamblin and American Abby D'Agostino fell in the 5000-meter heats. Nikki, who at that time ran at the same NZ athletics club as two of my daughters, was helped up by Abby. Nikki, in turn, helped Abby to continue with a leg injury. They ran to the line to the cheers of the crowds. Both were rewarded with a place in the final and a fair play Olympic award.

The Galatians are being hindered as these two were by other runners (or themselves for that matter). These runners are cutting in on them and causing them to stumble. Paul is urging them to get up and keep going. They are to return to the quality of running they showed earlier. They have become like an athlete who started well in their careers, training hard, and winning some events. They then became distracted by the opportunities that came along to cheat or gain financially by manipulating the result. Their performances fade away, and they end up with disappointing careers. Or someone who begins the race with great energy and passion but cannot sustain the effort and pull out. The Galatians are to run on consistently, not distracted by false teachers.

'From obeying the truth' uses *peithō*, employed in 1:10. This is the first use of *pei–* terms in the next verses in which Paul plays on the idea of obedience and persuasion as he repudiates the Judaizers (see *peismonē* in 5:8, *peithō* in v. 10). The verb has a range of meanings, including convince, persuade, appeal to, cajole, mislead, win over, strive to please (1:10), conciliate, pacify, set at ease, to have confidence, trust, be convinced, certain, persuade, and believe. Here, it has the less common sense of 'obey' (cf. Rom 2:8; Heb 13:17; Jas 3:3).[2] In the verse that follows, Paul employs the related *peismonē*, 'persuasion,' stating that the Judaizing persuasion upon them is not from God. Hence, *peithō* here has the nuance, 'disobey by becoming convinced by an alternative,' or 'they persuaded you not to obey the truth.'

'The truth' recalls 2:5, 14, 'the truth of the gospel.' Rather than obey the laws of the 'sport,' the Galatians are being persuaded to ignore the rules. They are in danger of disqualification and being stripped of any prize. One can think of a myriad of examples of such things in contemporary sport.

THIS PERSUASION IS NOT FROM GOD (5:8)

In *Galatians 5:8*, the rhetorical question is followed up with a clear statement that what the Galatians are hearing from the Judaizers is not from God:

The persuasion (*peismonē*)[3] **[is] not** (*ou*, 1:1) **from** (*ek*, 1:1) **the One calling** (*kaleō*, 1:6) **you** (plural *sy*, 1:3).

The verse begins with a very rare term, *peismonē*, 'persuasion,' the second *pei–* term in four verses (*peithō*, vv. 7, 10). It picks up the sense of *peithesthai*, the final term in the previous verse. The Galatians are disobeying the truth, persuaded by the Judaizers. *Peismonē* is exceedingly rare. As noted, this is the first use found in Greek literature. Ignatius uses the term in *Rom.* 3:3: 'The Work [Christianity] is not a matter of *persuasive rhetoric* (*peismonē*); rather, Christianity is greatest when it is hated by the world.' Here it can mean 'the persuasion' of the Judaizers[4] or 'the

---

2. BDAG 791–92.

3. The noun πεισμονή (*peismonē*) is a hapax *legomenon*—5:8 the only use in the NT. It is not found in any Greek comparative literature, except *Ign. Rom.* 3:3 where it is used to describe persuasive rhetoric. In Galatians 5:8, it speaks of the persuasion of the Judaizers.

disobedience' of the Galatians.[5] Most likely, it is the former that is in mind. The persuasion comes from the Judaizers, who are not spokespeople for the God who called the Galatians through the gospel.

'From the one calling you' uses *kaleō*, 'call,' used in 1:6 where Paul speaks of the Galatian's desertion of 'the One who called you in the grace of Christ' through the Judaizers. This verse reaches back to this and clearly, refers to God the Father. In 1:15, this God set Paul apart from his mother's womb and called him by his grace. In 5:13, Paul will use *kaleō* again of the Galatians being 'called to freedom.' The use of *peismonē* may indicate that the Judaizers were seeking to persuade the Galatians with persuasive rhetoric, using impressive argumentation and delivery to convince the Galatians to yield to a gospel inclusive of law-observance. Paul is emphatic; this persuasion is not from God. Hence, they should repudiate it as false and send the Judaizers packing. Using the sporting analogy, they should be ordered off, red-carded, disqualified, or ejected from the game. They are cheats and frauds.

A LITTLE FALSE TEACHING CORRUPTS THE WHOLE CHURCH
(5:9)

In *Galatians 5:9*, Paul uses an analogy he uses elsewhere, drawn from baking and the Passover remembrance:

4. Moo, *Galatians*, 333; Dunn, *Galatians*, 275.
5. R. Bultmann, 'πεισμονή,' in *TDNT* 6:9; Lightfoot, *Galatians*, 206.

A little (feminine *mikros*)[6] **yeast**[7] (*zymē*)[8] **leavens** (*zymoō*)[9] **the whole** (neuter *holos*, 5:3) **batch of dough** (*phyama*).[10]

This verse is a maxim Paul also uses in 1 Cor 5:7.[11] It recalls the Passover whereby Israel removes all *zymē* or yeast from their homes so that they do not eat it for seven days—the Feast of Unleavened Bread.[12] The rationale is that Israel fled Egypt in the Exodus before they had time to leaven (*zymoō*) the bread (Exod 12:34, 39; Lev 6:17). It is also forbidden that sacrifices, including grain offerings, are made with anything that has been leavened.[13] Conversely, in the Feast of Weeks, the people are to bring two loaves of bread leavened with yeast (Lev 23:17). The noun *phyama* can mean a kneading bowl (Exod 8:3; 12:34; Rom 9:21) or the dough itself, as here (Num 15:20, 21; Rom 11:16). Philo employs the idea of yeast figuratively, suggesting that leaven is forbidden because it puffs up bread and symbolizes human pridefulness (*Spec.* 1.292–293).

In the NT, leaven is utilized by Jesus in parables of the penetration of the kingdom (Matt 13:33; Luke 13:21). He also employs it as Paul does here in warnings against the leaven (false teaching) of the Jewish leaders.[14] As such, yeast is an ideal

---

6. The adjective μικρός (*mikros*) means 'small, little' and is used once in Galatians of a little or small amount of dough.

7. **VARIANT**: Some western manuscripts prefer *doloi* (deceit) to *zymoi* (yeast) (D* itd vg goth Marcion Marius Victorinus Ambrosiaster al). The same is found in 1 Cor 5:6. These are late and clearly secondary.

8. The noun *zymē* means leaven or yeast, used once in 5:9. It speaks non-literally of the false teaching of the Judaizers.

9. The verb associated with *zymē*, 'leaven, yeast,' is *zymoō* used in 5:9. It speaks of leavening dough to make bread. It recalls the practice of leavening bread and the Passover and the Feast of Unleavened Bread where Israel does not use yeast during the period of the festival. It is used symbolically of evil infecting God's people (cf. 1 Cor 5, sexual immorality). In context, it speaks of the way that the false teaching of the Judaizers penetrates the church, corrupting its life.

10. The third term in Paul's analogy concerning the false teaching of the Judaizers penetrating the church is the noun φύραμα (*phyrama*), which in 5:9 speaks of the batch of dough which is leavened by a little yeast. In the analogy, it speaks of the church.

11. Similarly, Moo, *Galatians*, 334.

12. See Exod 12:15, 19; 13:3, 7; Deut 16:3, 4.

13. See Exod 23:18; 34:25; Lev 2:11; Num 6:15–19; 2 Kings 23:9.

metaphor for something evil (sexual immorality, pride, Judaizing) that penetrates a collective (e.g., the church).

As noted above, Paul employs the metaphor in 1 Cor 5:6–8 stating the same maxim and urging the Corinthians to clean out the yeast so that they be a new batch of dough as Christ is their Passover lamb. They are not to be leavened with malice and evil but with sincerity and truth. Here the yeast in mind is the false teaching of the Judaizers or the Judaizers themselves. The Galatians are to repudiate their teaching and cast them out (4:30, cf. 1 Cor 5).

PAUL'S CONFIDENCE IN THE GALATIANS AND THE JUDAIZERS WILL PAY (5:10)

In *Galatians 5:10*, he states his confidence that the Galatians will heed him and will not fall to the Judaizers:

I (*egō*, 1:2) **am confident** (perfect *peithō*, 1:10) **in** (*en*, 1:6) **the Lord** (dative *kyrios*, 1:3) **for** (*eis*, 1:5) **you** (plural *sy*, 1:3) **that** (*hoti*, 1:6) **you will think** (second person future *phroneō*)[15] **no** (neuter *oudeis*, 2:6) **other thing** (*allos*, 1:7). **But** (*de*, 1:15), **the one troubling** (*tarassō*, 1:6) **you** (plural *sy*) **will bear** (future *bastazō*)[16]

---

14. See Matt 16:6, 11, 12; Mark 8:15; Luke 12:1.
15. The cognitive verb φρονέω (*phroneō*) is used once in Galatians concerning Paul's confidence that the Galatians will come to no other mindset than that which he has urged of them—they will repudiate the Judaizing 'gospel' and the Judaizers themselves (5:10).
16. The verb βαστάζω (*bastazō*) is used four times in Gal 5–6. It has the sense of 'bearing' or 'carrying' something. In 5:10, the Judaizing offender will bear the penalty, judgment, and condemnation for their false teaching. In 6:2, believers are to bear one another's burdens and fulfill the law of Christ. In 6:5, each Galatian must bear his or her own load. And in 6:17, Paul bears in his body the marks of Jesus.

the penalty (*krima*),[17] whoever (*hostis*, 2:4)[18] that person may (*ean*, 1:8) be (present subjunctive *eimi*, 1:7).

Up to this point, Paul has warned the Judaizers of the consequences of the Judaizing 'gospel.' If they yield to them, they will be severed from Christ, who will be of no benefit to them; they will have fallen from grace (5:2, 4). Here Paul expresses his confidence in the Lord that they will not go down this path.

'Confident' is the perfect of *peithō*, the third use of the verb in Galatians. In 1:10, it has the sense of seeking to please others, whereas, in 5:7, it speaks of disobedience to the truth (cf. Rom 2:8). This then is the second use of *peithō* and the third use of a *pei–* term in this section (*peismonē*, v. 8).

Paul's use of *peithō* here is more in line with his characteristic use of the term in the perfect tense of his state of solid confidence that something will happen. In the perfect, it speaks of being persuaded and convinced of something. It does not speak of absolute certainty, but a very confident expectation.[19] Where it is a confidence in the Lord, as here, it speaks of something he has come to in prayer and a sense of conviction.

Other examples include Paul's confidence that nothing can separate believers from the love of God in Christ (Rom 8:38). He is also being 'persuaded *in the Lord* that nothing is unclean' (Rom

---

17. The noun *krima* is used once in Galatians, of the penalty the Judaizer will bear for their corrupting teaching (5:10).

18. Wallace, *Greek Grammar*, 478 notes that: 'The subjunctive is frequently used after ὅστις (ἄν/ἐάν) or ὅς (δ') ἄν. The construction normally indicates a generic (or sometimes an uncertain) subject (but cf. Luke 9:4; John 1:33; Rom 9:15; 2 Cor 11:21); hence, the particle of contingency and the need for a subjunctive. The construction is roughly the *equivalent of a third-class or fifth-class condition*. (The difference is that in indefinite relative clauses the element of contingency is not that of time but of person.) Hence, the subjunctive is often translated like an indicative since the potential element belongs to the subject rather than the verb.' Here, the person is uncertain or unspecified and so Paul employs the subjunctive.

19. *Peithō* is also used by Paul of the assurance of others, e.g., 'you are *confident* that you yourself are a guide to the blind' (Rom 2:19). It has the sense of relying on God rather than oneself (2 Cor 1:9). He uses it of persuading others (2 Cor 5:11); of people being confident that they are in Christ (2 Cor 10:7); of Roman Christians becoming confident to be proactive in evangelism by Christ through Paul's courage (Phil 1:14); of confidence in the flesh (Phil 3:3); and of his confidence that the faith dwells in Timothy (2 Tim 1:5).

14:14) and his conviction that God will guard the faith in Paul to the end (2 Tim 1:12). In Philippians, he is confident that God will complete the good work in the Philippians (Phil 1:6), and that he will be released from prison and come to Philippi (Phil 1:25). This is a confidence that he has *in the Lord* (Phil 2:24).

It is also used of his confidence that the readers of his letters will respond to Paul's appeal. For example, Paul is confident of Philemon's obedience (Phlm 21). He is persuaded that the Romans are full of goodness and capable of instructing one another (Rom 15:14). He is confident in the Corinthians (2 Cor 2:3) and the Thessalonians that they will do what he is commanding in the letter (2 Thess 3:4).

In these statements of confidence in his readers, Paul is also appealing to them to do this very thing—it is both an expression of confidence and an appeal. 'In the Lord' speaks both of the basis for Paul's confidence, but also subtly draws them into obedience to Christ (who is the Lord in this case). Having just said that the Judaizing persuasion is not from God, they are subtly urged to do what Paul is confident they will do.

'That you will *think* nothing other' uses *phroneō*, a term used in philosophy and one of the cardinal virtues (*phronesis*, 'practical virtue, wisdom') of a frame of mind or mindset. Outside of Paul, it is used three times, twice of a mindset shaped by God or by a human perspective (Matt 16:23; Mark 8:33) and of Paul's mindset (Act 28:22). Paul employs the term twenty times. Nine of the uses are in Romans where he contrasts a mindset based on the desires of the flesh with that of the Spirit (the latter to be cultivated) (Rom 8:5), an arrogant mindset (which he repudiates) (Rom 11:20; 12:3, 16), a mindset concerning oneself which is realistic (Rom 12:3), being of the same mind together (Rom 12:16; 15:5), and a specific belief in the importance of a particular day (Rom 14:6).

In the Corinthian letters, he contrasts a childish mindset with adulthood (1 Cor 13:11) and having a harmonious mindset (2 Cor 13:11). The term recurs ten times in Philippians, one of the key themes of the letter. Central to the use in Philippians is 2:5 where Paul urges the Philippians to have a cruciform *phronesis*—a mind shaped like that of Christ who, while God in form and status, took on the form of a slave in his life and died the most humiliating of deaths on a cross (2:6–9). *Phroneō* is used in the letter of Paul's Christ-like attitude (1:7) and in his urgings that they are like-minded and unified in thought (2:2; 4:2), emulating him and Christ (3:15), and continuing their sacrificial attitude toward Paul in sending him financial gifts (4:10) rather than the earthly mindsets of false teachers (3:19).

He also uses it in Colossians appealing to them to set their minds on things above and not earthly things (Col 3:2). Here, Paul is confident in Christ that they will take on the mindset he has urged them through the letter—that they repudiate the false gospel of the Judaizers, expel the Judaizers, trust in God by faith and not works of the law, and live by the Spirit.

The *de* in part b of the verse is consecutive, 'and.' Here, Paul explains one aspect of the mindset he wants from them. Namely, that the one troubling them bears the penalty for his discretion. 'The one troubling you' uses the verb *tarassō* also found in 1:7 of the Judaizers troubling the Galatians. As discussed in that context, the verb *tarassō* speaks of a very real disturbance as when the disciples saw Jesus approaching them on the water, seemingly as a phantasm (Mark 6:50), and Jesus' deep grief over his forthcoming trial (John 12:27; 13:21). Here, the singular does not indicate one person causing the disturbance, as the plural is used in 1:7. Rather, the point is that whoever is disturbing the Galatians, they must pay the price.

Paul uses two terms found twenty-seven times in the NT to state the price the one who is troubling the Galatians must pay. The verb *bastazō* is found here for the first time of four uses in Galatians 5–6, the verb meaning to 'carry or bear a burden.'[20] His

---

20. Outside of Paul *bastazō* is used of carrying Jesus' sandals (Matt 3:11), Jesus bearing human diseases on the cross (Matt 8:17), the burden of hard labor (Matt 20:12), carrying a jar of water (Mark 14:13; Luke 22:10), carrying a funeral bier (Luke 7:14) or a dead body (John 20:15), carrying a money bag (Luke 10:4; John 12:6), bearing a child (Luke 11:27), carrying a cross (Luke 14:27; John 19:17), picking up stones (John 10:31), bearing hard teaching (John 16:12), a lame man carried to a place (Acts 3:2), carrying Jesus' name to the gentiles (Acts 9:15), bearing the cost of the law (Acts

other uses are of the root of the olive tree supporting the whole (Rom 11:18) and of the strong bearing with the failings of the weak (Rom 15:1).

In 6:2, the Galatians are to 'bear one another's burdens (*barē*)' while in 6:5, each Galatian is to bear his/her own load (*phortion*). As we will see in 6:2 and 5, the tenses of the verb 'bear' nuances these statements. In 6:17, Paul again uses it of his bearing in his body the marks of Jesus—his scars and pains due to his participation in Christ and his mission. Here then, it means the Judaizers, whoever they are, bearing the consequences of their false teaching.

Krima is a legal term Paul uses twelve times. Non-Pauline uses include judgment from God which reciprocates our judging of others (Matt 7:2), a legal sentence as in a death sentence (Luke 23:40; 24:20), another legal decision (Acts 24:25), God's judgment on believers (Jas 3:1; 1 Pet 4:17), God's judgment of all (Rev 20:4), and eternal judgment (John 9:39; Heb 6:2) or condemnation.[21] Paul uses it regarding the legal judgment of the State on God's behalf (Rom 13:2), civil lawsuits (1 Cor 6:7), God's judgment (Rom 11:33; 1 Cor 11:29, 34), and especially of eternal judgment/condemnation.[22] Here it speaks of the judgment of the Judaizers in the community.

Judgment has previously been intimated through the image of Abraham casting out Hagar and Ishmael in 4:30. Hence, these people are to be 'cast out.'[23] The yeast of false teaching must be removed before it works through the whole batch of dough—the church. The following two verses use the language of removal and cutting off, both with irony against the backdrop of these false teachers being cast out from the church.

The clause may also have the nuance of eternal judgment—these Judaizers will pay the price of being eternally shut out from God's people and destroyed. Some take it this way,

15:10), Paul carried by soldiers (Acts 21:35), putting up with evil people (Rev 2:2), bearing up under persecution (Rev 2:3), and a woman carried by a beast (Rev 17:7).
21. See Mark 12:40; Luke 20:47; 2 Pet 2:3; Jude 4; Rev 17:1; 18:20.
22. See Rom 2:2, 3; 3:8; 5:16; 1 Tim 3:16, 5:12.
23. Longenecker, *Galatians*, 232; Hays, 'Galatians,' 315.

not seeing here the community expelling the offenders, but God
doing so in present judgment[24] or at the final judgment.[25]

Scholars tend to choose between the ideas of casting out of the
church and eternal judgment. However, the two are not mutually
exclusive and are likely flipsides of Paul's irony. The casting out
of the church in the present anticipates their ultimate destruction
if they do not turn from the Judaizing 'gospel' to the gospel
of grace. Elsewhere where Paul speaks of expulsion from the
church, his hope is soteriological, and there is no need to think
otherwise here (1 Cor 5:5, cf. Rom 11:20, 24). The expulsion from
the church is for the community's good, as their presence will
corrupt the church as the yeast metaphor indicates. The effect of
the Judaizing 'gospel' is terminal and would render Christianity
a small Jewish sect at best. God's purpose is for the whole world
to be able to come to Christ without the burden of the law. As
such, they must excommunicate people if they are unrepentant.
Ultimately, he will deal with them in the present and the future
with eternal condemnation.

'Whoever that person may be'[26] is another example of Paul
refusing to name the offenders. While it is singular, this does
not mean there is one offender (cf. 1:7 [some people]; 5:12 [those
disturbing you]). Rather, it speaks of the same penalty whoever
the person(s) is/are. The Galatians are to discern these people
and deal with them. It matters not what credentials they have,
whether they are 'elders' of the church, whether they walked
with Jesus, or are friends of the Jerusalem pillars. It is of no
consequence whether they are rich or poor, male or female, slave
or free, Jew or Greek. Their treatment is to be the same. God
does not show favoritism, and neither should the Galatians (cf.
2:6). God will judge them and all people not on the basis of such

24. E.g., Dunn, *Galatians*, 277.
25. E.g., Moo, *Galatians*, 335 who says, 'This is almost certainly what God intends.'
26. Usually, *ean* introduces a third-class conditional sentence that has a sense of
    uncertainty. Here it is used to connote the uncertainty of the person that this might
    be. *Hostis* is first used in 2:4 and means 'whoever' (see esp. 2:4, also 4:24, 26; 5:4, 19).
    While it is masculine, it could include women. The sense of uncertainty is also
    contained in the subjunctive of eimi, *ē*.

things as their culture, gender, or status, but by their response and work for him. So, the community must expel them. Further, God will show no mercy on the basis of human claims on the Day. If any of these people continue to preach a gospel that distorts God's grace and faith, they will face his judgment without partiality.

This discussion above has huge consequences for contemporary church life. Where the gospel is being compromised and the false ideas spreading like yeast, they must be dealt with. Just as Israel had to remove all yeast from their homes at Passover, so must the yeast be removed from the church. We live in a church infected with a whole range of false ideas and behaviors which have permeated the western church. The church has failed in many cases to deal with it, preferring the path of acceptance and love. We are paying the price with weak and insipid faith in many instances.

I am part of the Presbyterian denomination in NZ and our historical acceptance of ministers who have denied the existence of God and the resurrection, see the Bible as merely another book, who openly advocate the violation of sexual ethics, and so on, has seen the church almost fatally compromised.

On the flip side, some churches have drawn the line at the wrong places and so excommunicate and shut out for the wrong reasons. I remember a friend who sold me his guitar. He and his wife worshiped in a big local church. His wife had left him for another man. She divorced him. He was devastated. Rather than support him, the church expelled him as he was a divorcee. I was horrified. He sold me his guitar because his faith was deeply wounded. These things are not easy. The baseline is that the church knows its gospel, and this is drawn from the story of Scripture. When new ideas come along, they are to be put up against Scripture and the gospel. Is it of the essence of the faith? Is it a fresh take we need to recognize (e.g., slavery and in my opinion, gender equality of opportunity in the church)? Is it a violation of the gospel?

Working through such things takes time. The church took a while to sort through the Judaizing issue. They went through a crisis because of Judaizers who traveled the churches arguing that the Pauline gospel is not the gospel. They put their case. The church worked it through over the early days of the church and at the Jerusalem Council came to a resolution. The Judaizers remained active as seen in Phil 2 and Col 2. However, the gospel was affirmed and to this day, the Judaizing 'gospel' holds only very limited sway. The process cannot be circumvented but must take its course. There is great pain in such processes, as some have their views rejected and are marginalized, and inevitably small mistakes will be made. This is a critical aspect of the cost of the gospel whereby we who are entrusted with it must show tough (genuine) love and preserve the gospel. While individuals and groups must sometimes be marginalized, this is so that God's church must be protected. This is deeply challenging in a world where ideas swirl as never before through our electronic media.

God have mercy on us, and may you, our God, by your power ensure that your gospel ever triumphs. Help us to see clearly in each situation what it is that you want us to do. Help us to make the tough calls but with grace and with the door of repentance always open. God, hear my cry. To you be glory forever, amen.

PAUL'S PERSECUTION SHOWS HE DOES NOT PREACH CIRCUMCISION (5:11)

Galatians 5:11 is one of the most interesting and challenging verses in Galatians as it seems to run counter to all Paul is saying. Likely, this is because it gives us a critical insight into one of the arguments of the Galatians:

But (*de*, 1:15) **if** (*ei*, 1:7) **I** (*egō*, 1:1), **brothers and sisters** (vocative plural *adelphos*, 1:2), **am still** (*eti*, 1:10) **preaching** (present *kēryssō*, 2:2) **circumcision** (*peritomē*, 2:7), **why** (neuter *tis*, 1:7) **am I still** (*eti*) **being persecuted** (present passive *diōkō*, 1:13)? **Therefore** (*ara*, 2:17), **the scandal** (*skandalon*)[27] **of the**

---

27. The noun σκάνδαλον (*skandalon*, cf. Eng. 'scandal'), was used for a trap, an enticement or temptation to sin enticement, or something causes revulsion or disapproval (BDAG 926). It is found once in Galatians in 5:11 of 'the scandal/offense of the cross' which is removed when circumcision is preached (as per the Judaizers, and not Paul).

cross (genitive *stauros*)[28] **is being annulled** (perfect passive *katargeō*, 3:17).

The first part of the verse is launched by *ei* (if) with the present indicative, and so is an 'if ... then' first-class conditional sentence in the form of a question (see on 1:9)—this type of statement assumes something is true for the sake of argument. The protasis introduces the thing assumed true; that Paul currently preaches (present tense) circumcision.

Again, Paul shifts to the first person singular (cf. 5:2–3) after moving between the second- and third-person plural through vv. 4–6 and addressing the Galatians directly concerning the Judaizers in vv. 7–10. His language is emphatic. He places *egō*, 'I' at the beginning of the sentence as the subject of the seventh word, the first-person verb *kēryssō*, 'preach.' The *de* can be consecutive, 'and,' or strikes a contrast, 'but,' or as some translations have it, 'now.'

'If I am still preaching circumcision' comes as a surprise, as clearly, Paul is not preaching circumcision—he opposes it where gentile converts are concerned. One explanation is that Paul is thinking of his pre-Christian life as a Jew, but if that is the case, it is hard to see why he would introduce it into his rhetoric *at this point*.[29]

As such, this can only be explained as an argument being used by his Judaizing opponents. They are likely claiming that Paul preaches circumcision. Obviously, in light of the content of the letter thus far, Paul did not do so while in Galatia. He argues that they received the Spirit through faith and not works of the law. Joining the dots, it is likely that they argue that Paul elsewhere preached circumcision and did not do so in Galatia. They may argue he is trying to make the gospel easy so he can win more converts by repudiating this as a fatal compromise of God's covenantal relationship established through Abraham and ratified by circumcision.

They may perhaps argue from the example of Timothy, whom

---

28. The noun σταυρός (*stauros*) means the cross and is used three times (5:11; 6:12, 14).
29. Longenecker, *Galatians*, 233. This also would define Paul's pre-Christian ministry as 'preaching circumcision' which hardly seems to fit.

he did circumcise while in the Galatian region (Acts 16:3),[30] although this postdates Galatians.[31] However, there may be other examples like this, and they may contend that Paul is inconsistent concerning circumcision, being pro-circumcision where Jews are concerned and not so with gentiles. Timothy is an interesting case in point, as he is half Jew and half Greek whereas Titus was not circumcised (2:3). Perhaps they are arguing Paul vacillates concerning the gospel. They may simply not understand Paul's missiology which is fluid where the gospel and culture are concerned (cf. 1 Cor 9:19–23). Timothy was circumcised because he had a Jewish mother, and so ethnically, he was a Jew. If circumcised, Timothy could participate in the mission in the Synagogue as Jew to the Jews. Titus was not a Jew and so did not require circumcision. He did not need to become what he was not (cf. 1 Cor 7:18–19). Perhaps they are arguing that Paul was weak in allowing the gospel to be compromised in Galatia because of his desire to win more to Christ. Or they are simply lying to help their cause.

Whichever is the best explanation, Paul in the apodosis responds not with *mē genoito* (may it never be!—see 2:17), but with a rhetorical question: 'why am I still being persecuted?' Here, he uses *diōkō*, a hunting term that can mean 'pursue' positively or negatively. Here, as elsewhere in its uses in Galatians, it is negative, 'pursue' with the intent of causing harm, 'persecute.' There is some irony here, of course, for Paul himself was formerly the persecutor (1:12, 23) and now is the persecuted (cf. 6:12). He, like the Christian church, the children of Isaac, are being persecuted particularly by Israel (cf. 4:29). The Galatians are well aware of Paul's maltreatment by the Jews on his first Antiochian mission including contradiction and slander (Acts 13:45), being driven from the region of Pisidian Antioch (Acts 13:50), maltreatment and an attempted stoning in Iconium (Acts 14:1–5), and his actual stoning in Lystra (Acts 14:19) (s.a. on 3:4, cf. 1 Thess 2:14–16; 2 Cor 11:23–27). They know Paul is

30. Hays, 'Galatians,' 316.
31. Rightly, Moo, *Galatians*, 336.

being persecuted by Jews for his perspectives. If he still endorsed circumcision, why would this still be the case?

The final part of the verse speaks of the effect of preaching circumcision assuming was preaching it: 'therefore (*ara*), the scandal (*skandalon*) of the cross (*stauros*) is being annulled (*katargeō*).' The *ara* introduces the consequence of preaching circumcision, something Paul does not do as an apostle, whereas the Judaizers are doing so.

The term *skandalon* is found fifteen times in the NT. It can have the sense of something that causes someone to stumble in sin—a temptation,[32] a snare or trap (Rom 11:9), or an obstacle or hindrance.[33] Citing Isa 28:16, Paul uses the term in Rom 9:33 of Christ being laid in Zion as 'a stone of stumbling, and a rock of *offense*.' He uses it again in 1 Cor 1:23: 'we preach Christ crucified, *a stumbling stone* to Jews and foolishness to the gentiles.' Ignatius in the early second century took up these words in his letter to the Ephesians: 'My spirit is a humble sacrifice for the cross, which is *a stumbling block to unbelievers*, but salvation and eternal life to us' (Ign. *Eph.* 18.1, Holmes).

This all speaks of the offense of the cross to Jewish sensitivities, the idea of a crucified Messiah being ridiculous. The Messiah would instead come in triumph and crush God's enemies (Pss. Sol. 17:21–46).[34] Jesus simply cannot be the

---

32. See Matt 13:41; 18:7; 17:1; 1 John 2:20.

33. See Matt 16:23; Rom 14:13; 16:17; Rev 2:14.

34. Some clips from Pss. Sol. 17 make this clear: 'See, O Lord, and raise up for them their king, the son of David, to rule over your servant Israel in the time known to you, O God. Undergird him with the strength to destroy the unrighteous rulers, to purge Jerusalem from gentiles who trample her to destruction; in wisdom and in righteousness to drive out the sinners from the inheritance; to smash the arrogance of sinners like a potter's jar; o shatter all their substance with an iron rod; to destroy the unlawful nations with the word of his mouth; At his warning the nations will flee from his presence; and he will condemn sinners by the thoughts of their hearts. He will gather a holy people whom he will lead in righteousness; and he will judge the tribes of the people that have been made holy by the Lord their God. He will not tolerate unrighteousness (even) to pause among them, and any person who knows wickedness shall not live with them ... He will distribute them upon the land according to their tribes; the alien and the foreigner will no longer live near them. He will judge peoples and nations in the wisdom of his righteousness. And he will have

Messiah, for 'cursed is anyone hung on a tree' (3:13; Deut 21:23). This contempt is echoed at Qumran, where, in the Temple Scroll, the curse includes those hung on a tree while still alive, including crucifixion (11QT 64:7–13, cf. Pesher Nahum [4QpNa]; 4Q448).[35] In the second century, Jews wrote off Christian claims that Jesus is the Christ on the basis of Deut 21:23. Trypho is quoted by Justin Martyr as saying:

But whether Christ should be so shamefully crucified, this we are in doubt about. For whosoever is crucified is said in the law to be accursed, so that I am exceedingly incredulous on this point. It is quite clear, indeed, that the Scriptures announce that Christ had to suffer; but we wish to learn if you can prove it to us whether it was by the suffering cursed in the law (Justin Martyr, *Dial.* 89.2).[36]

Although the mode of crucifixion varied, it was practiced among a wide range of ancient cultures, including the Persians, Assyrians, Indians, Scythians, Taurians, Thracians, Celts, Germans, Britons, Numidians, the Carthaginians, and the Greeks and Macedonians who picked it up from the Persians.[37] Alexander 'the Great' used crucifixion, once nailing 2,000 Tyrians up.[38]

Crucifixion was used widely by the Romans who took it over from the Carthaginians they defeated.[39] They used various modes and usually flogged the victim (as with Jesus). The victim

---

gentile nations serving him under his yoke, and he will glorify the Lord in (a place) prominent (above) the whole earth. And he will purge Jerusalem (and make it) holy as it was even from the beginning, (for) nations to come from the ends of the earth to see his glory, to bring as gifts her children who had been driven out, and to see the glory of the Lord with which God has glorified her. And he will be a righteous king over them, taught by God. There will be no unrighteousness among them in his days, for all shall be holy, and their king shall be the Lord Messiah.' (Charlesworth).

35. See D. A. Finney, 'Crucifixion,' in *LBD.*

36. Justin Martyr. 'Dialogue of Justin with Trypho, a Jew,' in *The Apostolic Fathers with Justin Martyr and Irenaeus,* ed. Alexander Roberts, James Donaldson, and A. Cleveland Coxe. Vol. 1. The Ante-Nicene Fathers (Buffalo, NY: Christian Literature Company, 1885), 244 (ANF1).

37. See M. Hengel, *Crucifixion* (Philadelphia, PA: Fortress, 1977), 22.

38. See Finney, 'Crucifixion.'

39. Hengel, *Crucifixion,* 23.

usually carried the patibulum (crossbar) to the crucifixion site (as with Jesus). They were most often crucified naked, deepening their humiliation. The site was usually beside a busy road to increase the possibility of it being seen and to warn those watching that this is their fate if they mess with Rome. One of its main purposes was to strike fear into the hearts of those who might think to challenge the imperial power. The victim's families were also often abused or even killed at the same time. While citizens were sometimes crucified, it was especially used for slaves and rebels. Often the victim was left on the cross to be eaten by animals. Sometimes the deceased victim was taken down and abused. At other times, the person was buried by family, or, as in the case of Jesus, a wealthy disciple.[40]

This text speaks of the offense of the cross and not merely Jewish distaste. Crucifixion was generally reviled. The cross was labeled: an 'infamous stake,' 'criminal wood,' and 'most evil.'[41] Josephus writes in *J.W.* 7.203 of Eleazer who was captured by the Romans and sentenced to crucifixion which he describes as 'a most miserable death.' Cicero saw it as 'the cruelest and most terrible punishment.'[42] Origen cites the anti-Christian Celsus as saying of Jesus that he was 'shamefully bound, and disgracefully punished, and very recently was most contumeliously treated before the eyes of all men.'[43] Lucian of Samosata in the second century rejected Jesus as a 'crucified sophist' (Lucian, *Peregr.* 11–13). The humiliation of the cross is referenced in Heb 12:2: 'looking to Jesus, the founder and perfecter of our faith, who for the joy that was set before him *endured the cross, despising the shame*, and is seated at the right hand of the throne of God' (ESV).

Just as the cross is offensive to us as we watch recent examples of ISIS putting people to death by crucifixion, it was offensive

40. See further on these details Finney, 'Crucifixion.'
41. See Finney, 'Crucifixion,' also Hengel, *Crucifixion*, 7–8.
42. Finney, 'Crucifixion.' Citation from Cicero, *Verr.* 2.5.165.
43. Origen, 'Origen against Celsus,' in *Fathers of the Third Century: Tertullian, Part Fourth; Minucius Felix; Commodian; Origen, Parts First and Second*, ed. Alexander Roberts, James Donaldson, and A. Cleveland Coxe, trans. Frederick Crombie, Vol. 4 The Ante-Nicene Fathers (Buffalo, NY: Christian Literature Company, 1885), 577.

in the ancient world. For the Jews, this offense was not merely repugnance of its gross violence, but it spoke of a person being accursed before God. It is a theological oxymoron to say, 'crucified Messiah.' Yet for Paul, this is Christ's glory. Later, in 6:14, he will repudiate the boasting of the Judaizers in the flesh of the Galatians, stating that he will boast of nothing other than 'the cross of our Lord Jesus Christ.'

Katargeō is the verb used to describe the consequence of the offense of the cross. As discussed concerning 3:17, the verb is mainly used by Paul, including three times in Galatians. In 3:17, it carries the meaning to annul a covenant. In 5:2, it is used of the Galatians being cut off or severed from Christ if they accede to the Judaizers. Here, it speaks of the abolition of the offense of the cross. This is because Christ is not required; circumcision is all that matters. Justification could then be achieved through the law. Christianity would then effectively be Judaism.

The offense of the cross is critical to the Christian message. Humanity is held captive under sin's curse which the law (although good in itself) served. Christ took this curse on the cross by becoming an offense to the world. While sinless in his life, he took the curse of sin, died, and rose from the dead. If we believe in him, we are free from the consequences of sin. So, through the offense of the cross, we are declared righteous. The cross cannot be annulled, or Christianity is rendered obsolete. The Judaizers and Jews in rejection of Jesus cannot grasp this. The Judaizers are part way there but have not fully worked through the radical consequences of Christ's life, death, and resurrection. Paul the Christian did not preach circumcision because it would render naught the beautiful, profound, and soteriologically necessary offense of the cross. Circumcision of the penis does not just remove the foreskin; it severs Christian soteriology and circumcision of the heart, which is what really matters.

OH THAT THEY WOULD CASTRATE THEMSELVES (5:12)

In *Galatians 5:12*, Paul makes one of his most blunt, powerful, and for many moderns, disturbing, statements in the letter concerning the Judaizers:

O that (*ophelon*)[44] **those throwing you** (plural *sy*) **into turmoil** (present participle[45] *anastatoō*)[46] **would also** (*kai*, 1:1) **have their penises cut off** (future middle *apokoptō*).[47]

While this verse on one level is offensive to modern western thinking, it is full of deep meaning. 'O that' translates *ophelon*, an interjection expressing a present time wish meaning 'would that, O that.'[48] It was used only four times in the NT, three times by Paul. The non-Pauline use is Rev 3:15 where John's Jesus in full awareness of the insipid works of the Laodiceans exclaims, '*would that* you were either cold or hot!' Elsewhere, Paul uses it in exclamations to the difficult Corinthians; '*would that* you did reign' (1 Cor 4:8) and 'O *that* you would bear with me in a little foolishness' (2 Cor 11:1). Here then, it expresses Paul's wish for the Judaizers.

Earlier, Paul has spoken of the Judaizers as those who trouble the Galatians (1:7; 5:10), *tarassō* a verb of significant strength. Here, he uses a term that is even more powerful, *anastatoō*. It is used only twice else in the NT both times in Acts. First, it is employed of people who drag Jason and other believers before

---

44. The interjection *ophelon* is 'an expression of a wish that something had taken place or would take place, *o that, would that* with the imperfect to express present time' (BDAG 743). Its only use in Galatians is in 5:12—'O that' the Judaizers would emasculate themselves. It is rare in the NT also used by Paul in 1 Cor 4:8 and 2 Cor 11:1. Its only other use is Rev 3:15.

45. This is a nice example of a participle with an article (**oi** ἀναστατοῦντες) indicating that the article substantivizes the verb, '**the ones** troubling you.' See Wallace, *Greek Grammar*, 231.

46. The verb ἀναστατόω (*anastatoō*) is rare in the NT (three times) and is used once in Galatians and all Paul's extant writings as a substantive participle—'those unsettling/ disturbing/ you.' It has the sense of real political agitation used in Luke's writings in the context of a riot (Acts 17:6) and a revolt (Acts 21:38). Hence, some translate it 'these agitators.'

47. The verb ἀποκόπτω (*apokoptō*) is found once in Paul's letters. It compounds *apo* (from) and *koptō* (cut) and so 'to cut from' is its basic meaning. In 5:12, it means to make someone a eunuch through castration or emasculation—something Paul wishes of the Judaizers. It recalls *enkoptō* in 5:7—who cut in on you?

48. The interjection is in the imperfect tense which speaks of the present time; see BDAG 743.

the Thessalonica city authorities crying out that they are *disturbing* the world' (Acts 17:6). The second use is from the Roman tribune who asks Paul if he is the Egyptian who led 4000 Sicarii (ruthless political assassins) in a political revolt. The LXX of Daniel 7:23 employs it of the fourth beast who will 'devour the whole earth, and *throw it into turmoil*, and grind it to pieces.'

To capture the revolutionary force of the term, some translate it 'those agitators' (NIV, NET). However, it becomes difficult to work 'you' into this rendering of the clause and so other translations prefer 'those who unsettle you' (ESV, NRSV). Either way, the force is powerful. These people are turning the world of the Galatians upside down, troubling them, agitating among them, unsettling them, and throwing them into turmoil (as I have translated it).

The content of Paul's wish for these theological agitators is that they would literally 'cut from themselves' or 'cut themselves from.' The verb is a second *koptō* term in the chapter. *Enkoptō* was used in 5:7 when Paul asked the Galatians 'who cut in on you?' As noted in the discussion in 5:7, *enkoptō* is multilayered. At one level, it is an athletic image, Paul envisaging the Galatians' Christian lives as a race, with the Judaizers muscling in on them as they run toward the prize of eternal glory. At another level, it plays on the idea of circumcision. The Judaizers are seeking to cut in on the Galatians' foreskins to bring them into a place of righteousness before God.

Here in 5:12, he uses *apokoptō*, compounding *apo*, 'from' and *koptō*, 'cut.' This clause is also multilayered. In regards to the athletic image, he could be saying he wishes they would cut themselves off from the race—withdrawing so to speak. To do so would mean that they would cut themselves off from the Galatians and the whole Christian church and go back to Judaism without Christ that they are effectively espousing.[49]

However, there is another deeper layer here. The verb *apokoptō* in a literal sense[50] means to 'cut off, 'strike off, or break' in a

---

49. Some including Erasmus and Reformers like Calvin and Luther sought to remove the castration angle by seeing this as separation from the community; see G. Stählin, 'ἀποκο´πτω,' in *TDNT* 3:854.

range of ways including cutting off clothing (2 Sam 10:4), cutting down bridges (Plutarch, *Nic.* 26; Josephus, *J.W.* 1.143), branches of trees (Homer, *Od.* 23.195), ropes (Acts 27:32; Dionysius of Halicarnassus, *Ant. rom.* 3.58), an army (Josephus, *J.W.* 4.565), and parts of the body (Herodotus, *Hist.* 6.91, 114; Plutarch, *Caes.* 16).

Where the human body is concerned, *apokoptō* is used for body parts cut off in battle as with beheadings (Josephus, *Ant.* 14.464; *J.W.* 2.246; 4 Macc 15:20), amputations (Josephus, *J.W.* 1.507), and in punishment for crimes. A good example is Judges 1:6 where Bezek had his thumbs and big toes cut off for attempting to escape. Similarly, Israel is warned by Ezekiel that Babylon will 'cut off your noses and your ears' for their sin (Ezek 23:25). In Deut 25:11, if a woman seizes a man's privates in a fight, she has her hand cut off. The command an eye for an eye and a tooth for a tooth implies a similar 'cutting off.'[51] In the NT, the term features in Jesus' brutal (but not literal) command that a believer should cut off a hand or foot if it causes them to sin, to ensure entering eternal life (Mark 9:43, 45). John uses it to describe Peter's cutting off of the ear of Malchus—the servant of the high priest (John 18:10, 26).

The verb *apokoptō* is also used for emasculation or castration, the cutting off of the penis. Emasculation is found in Deut 23:1 with the consequence being that the castrated person (a eunuch) cannot worship in the gathered community (s.a. Philo, *Ebr.* 213; *Spec.* 1.325; *Leg.* 3.8). Here, it is in the future middle. The middle is a causative direct middle whereby the subject has something done for or to himself. Here then, Paul wishes that the Judaizers would have themselves castrated.[52]

By using the term here, Paul is yet again employing irony.

50. It can have the figurative sense of mourn, take away hope or some other thing, interrupt a writing, or omit something from it. See further Stählin, 'ἀποκόπτω,' 3.852. Examples in Josephus include *J.W.* 1.299 where pretenses are cut off and *J.W.* 1.481 where hope is cut off. Philo tends to use it ethically for such things as cutting off falsehood (Philo, *Leg.* 3.127), passions (*Leg.* 3.130), and pride (*Ebr.* 39).

51. See, e.g., Exod 21:24; Lev 24:20; Deut 19:21, cf. 2 Sam 4:12). See Stählin, 'ἀποκόπτω,' 853. See also Josephus, *Life* 147, 177; *J.W.* 2.642, 644.

52. See further Wallace, *Greek Grammar*, 424. Alternatively, it is a permissive middle, although this is unlikely (see Wallace, *Greek Grammar*, 427).

He wishes these circumcisers who believe new converts need circumcision to be a part of God's people would not only circumcise, but also (*kai*) butcher themselves by removing their penises, and so themselves be shut out from worship (Deut 23:2).[53]

With all this in mind, most translate it 'emasculate themselves' (ESV, NIV), 'castrate themselves' (NET, NRSV), or 'cut off much more' (CEV). Some prefer the more general, 'mutilate themselves' (RSV, NASB95). It is likely that Paul does have castration in mind. Rather than merely cut off the foreskins of men to supposedly bring them into a right relationship with God, he wishes they would cut off their own penises completely. He wishes they would make themselves eunuchs. His words call to mind Phil 3:2–3 where, with a play on words, Paul states that whereas Christians are the circumcision (*peritomē*), the Judaizers are mutilators (*katatomē*). Their circumcision is brutality and nothing better than an expression of pagan worship.

For the Galatians, there is yet another angle to this astonishing statement. The goddess Cybele held pride of place as the mother fertility goddess in the Anatolian pantheon. Polhill notes that the Artemis Temple in Ephesus was dedicated to the same goddess.[54] Her devotees, the *Galli*, were reputed to have castrated themselves while in ecstatic worship (see further 4:8). These Eunuch priests participated in the cult. The center for this was Pessinus, which is north of the area Paul evangelized on his first Antiochian mission, and this reference could support the North Galatian theory (see Introduction). However, such a tradition would be well known among all the Galatians and the influence of the cult no doubt spread through the region.

---

53. Stählin, 'ἀποκο´πτω,' 853 notes reasons for this prohibition: 1) It offends God as the body is given by Creator God; 2) It offends monotheism and the covenant imitating heathen customs; 3) It offends purity of worship as only those who are without blemish can worship God. So, an animal with damaged testicles cannot be used in sacrifice (Lev 22:24). There are also notes of hope for eunuchs though, such as Isa 56:4.

54. J. B. Polhill, *Paul and His Letters* (Nashville, TN: Broadman & Holman, 1999), 138. He suggests that the Galatians' interest in circumcision could be stimulated by this tradition.

As such, as in Phil 3:2–3, Paul is likening their behavior to pagan brutality in the name of worship. As with 4:8–9, now that Christ has come, Judaism-without-Jesus or Christianity-fatally-syncretized-with-the law is akin to pagan religion. True Judaism, birthed in Abel, covenanted in Abraham, and found where there is salvation faith in the living God, now continues in Christ.

Such a saying in Paul also reminds us that although he repudiates crude language,[55] on a rare occasion, he is unafraid to speak with some degree of what we might call crudeness to make a point. For example, he writes off his former life as excrement (*skybala*, Phil 3:8). He labels Judaizers dogs, evil workers, and mutilators (Phil 3:3), and other false teachers are emissaries of Satan (2 Cor 11:13–14). Earlier in Galatians, he used *enkoptō* to speak of cutting in with double meaning. Here he alludes to the *Galli*. Jesus also said things that were very cutting, especially in Matt 23 about the Jewish leaders. This type of language can be difficult to handle but demonstrates that while this does not give us an excuse to use crude language as a rule, for rhetorical purposes, one may choose to do so.[56] A wise preacher, as in the case of Paul, will only do so very infrequently (if at all), and only for a very good reason. Overused, the impact of crass language is lost, with the preacher losing the trust of people who rightly recognize that aside from extreme exceptions, a Christian should seek to use language that edifies God and others.

---

55. See Eph 4:29; 5:4; Col 3:8, cf. Matt 12:34.
56. A celebrated example is Tony Campolo who said, 'I have three things I'd like to say today. First, while you were sleeping last night, 30,000 kids died of starvation or diseases related to malnutrition. Second, most of you don't give a shit. What's worse is that you're more upset with the fact that I said shit than the fact that 30,000 kids died last night' (Source: 'Tony Campolo>Quotes>Quotable Quote,' http://www.goodreads.com/quotes/867293-i-have-three-things-i-d-like-to-say-today-first).

PART FIVE: HOW THEN TO LIVE? FREEDOM, LOVE, BY THE SPIRIT (5:13–6:10)

CHAPTER TWENTY-SIX: THE FREEDOM
TO LOVE! (5:13–15)

While this section forms a part of the body of the letter, there is a shift from a direct appeal to ethics and how to live. If one is not to live ethically out of the law of Moses, then what is the basis and outworking of Christian ethics? Paul focuses on the Spirit as the empowering presence of God in believers by which they are to live. Love is the dominant virtue that flows from a Spirit-empowered life. Corrupted by sin and the passions of the flesh, humans find it impossible to please God in their ethical lives. Further, the law has no internal power to enable a person to live a life that pleases God. The law stands as a set of propositional goals that are elusive. They draw us to them, but we fail repeatedly. Law easily becomes a burden and the basis of judgmentalism. This can be self-recrimination where we castigate ourselves for our failure and drive ourselves harder and harder to please God. This can be a tendency to judge others severely too.

Such a litigious life lacks joy and peace, as we are never satisfied, grimly seeking to do the right thing to please ourselves and others. Such a life is expressed in extreme movements, whether angry left-wing social liberals, right-wing zealots, biblical conservatives railing against sin, extreme Islam; indeed, in any situation where ideology becomes a litigious tool of judgment. There is no freedom in such a life, only an existence governed by unreachable expectations, oughts/ought nots, and shoulds/should nots, and leaving behind more guilt and shame than the freedom of the gospel.

Paul's answer is the freedom of the Spirit and faith expressed in love and a range of other Spirit-produced attitudes. The key is knowing one's status in Christ as free from law! This freedom is not emancipation into sinfulness; may it never be! Rather, it is a freedom to be able to live the life God desires for us, and more and more, as we practice a life of yielding to God's internal gentle urgings. By the Spirit, one is empowered to repudiate and overcome the works of the flesh which entice us due to our corrupted passions—usually, this is something God-given which is distorted by the sin that warps us.

Paul reaches into the law itself for a governing relational and ethical law—Lev 19:18—'love your neighbor as yourself.' All law is fulfilled if we live out of this governing precept. It is by the Spirit that this is lived. So, he urges the Galatians to walk by the Spirit, keep in step with the Spirit, and so on—yielding to his impulses to the goodness that pulses in us as we are in Christ. He encourages the Galatians concerning how to treat each other—restoring gently those who sin, taking care not to sin, bearing each other's burdens, avoiding arrogance, each person testing him or herself, each bearing their own loads, sharing with each other, and sowing to please the Spirit. This is the life of a new creation.

Paul's answer to law-observance is to live by the internal power of the Spirit out of love. This is one of the most glorious passages in Scripture which serves as a guide to what it means to live as a Christian each day.

FREEDOM TO SERVE ONE ANOTHER IN LOVE (5:13)

Paul continues with the theme of freedom, picked up again from 5:1 and a theme that has been important through the letter thus far.[1] The contrast between freedom and slavery was central to the Hagar-Sarah allegory in the previous passage, and in this light, 'freedom' here must be understood. This is freedom from the law and its expectations. Freedom wrongly understood can lead to the misguided belief that if one has faith in Jesus Christ, one is saved, and so one can do anything. This false idea Paul

---

1. See 2:4; 3:28; 4:22, 23, 26, 30, s.a., 5:13.

addresses here. This freedom in Christ is not to lead to fleshly sinfulness, but a freedom to live out of love and service as humans were created to do.

Paul introduces the law in v. 14, not writing it off as irrelevant, but stating that the whole of the Torah and any other law is fulfilled in one saying. This text is itself drawn from the law, showing the ongoing importance of the law for Christian thought—Lev 19:18: 'You shall love your neighbor as yourself.' Then, using the analogy of the Galatians as predatory animals consuming one another, in verse 15, Paul gives us a vivid insight into the way things were going down in Galatia at this time; he warns them that if they continue to battle each other, they will self-destruct. Clearly, and unsurprisingly, with the Judaizers on the loose, this is a set of churches having serious conflicts, and, here, Paul explains how to resolve it.

In *Galatians 5:13*, Paul begins:

For (*gar*, 1:10) **you** (plural *sy*, 1:3) **[are] called** (*kaleō*, 1:6) **to** (*epi*, 3:13) **freedom** (*eleutheria*, 2:4), **brothers and sisters** (vocative plural *adelphos*, 1:2); **only** (*monos*, 1:23), **not** (*mē*, 1:7) **the freedom** (*eleutheria*) **for** (*eis*, 1:5) **[taking] opportunity** (*aphormnē*)[2] **for the flesh** (dative *sarx*, 1:16), **but** (*alla*, 1:1) **through** (*dia*, 1:1) **[the]**[3] **love** (*agapē*, 5:6), **become slaves** (imperative *douloō*, 4:8) **to one another** (dative *allēlōn*).[4]

---

2. The one use of the noun ἀφορμή (*aphormē*) meaning 'occasion, opportunity' (BDAG 158) is in 5:13, where Paul explains to the Galatians that their freedom from the law is not a freedom to please the desires of the flesh. Rather, they should love and serve each other. Otherwise, *aphormē* is rare in the NT used only by Paul six other times (see further the footnotes in the text discussion).

3. Paul uses the article, τῆς ἀγάπης (*tēs agapēs*, the love). This is the Abstract use of the article (the Article with Abstract Nouns). Wallace, *Greek Grammar*, 226 notes: 'Abstract nouns by their very nature focus on a quality. However, when such a noun is articular, that quality is "tightened up," as it were, *defined more closely*, distinguished from other notions. This usage is quite frequent (articular abstract nouns are far more frequent than anarthrous abstracts).' This is also an example of a generic use: 'While the *individualizing* article distinguishes or identifies a particular object belonging to a larger class, the *generic* article distinguishes one class from another. This is somewhat less frequent than the individualizing article (though it still occurs hundreds of times in the NT). It categorizes rather than particularizes.' (Wallace, *Greek Grammar*, 227).

4. The reciprocal pronoun ἀλλήλων (*allēlōn*) (cf. *allos*, other) is a term Paul loves in terms

Having finished dealing with the Judaizers and expressing his wish that they would emasculate themselves, Paul turns again to the Galatians. There is a shift in emphasis from rejecting the 'gospel' of the Judaizers to the way they should be treating each other as children of God. They should live out their freedom in Christ not with sins of the flesh, but through love and mutual slavery.

The *gar* is not so much causal as a marker of clarification, 'for, you see.'[5] 'You' is placed prominently first, Paul beginning the sentence calling the Galatians to attention to what he will say. They are 'called to freedom.'

The verb *kaleō*, 'call,' here is aorist (perfective aspect, here past in context) passive (agent God). It has the same sense as in 1:6 where it is used of the Galatians' call into the grace of Christ by God through Paul's initial preaching and in 1:15 of God's call to Paul by grace through the revelation of God's Son to him.

Here, rather than grace, Paul stresses the theme of freedom (*eleutheria*). This is freedom from the law and its requirements, rather than wholesale freedom to do whatever one wants—an 'if it feels good, do it!' attitude. Or, as the Corinthians might put it, an 'everything is lawful' perspective (1 Cor 6:12; 10:23). Rather, this is freedom from the requirements of the law. Hence, in 2:4, Paul uses *eleutheria* of 'the *freedom* we have in Christ,' on which the Judaizers were spying. In 3:28 and 4:22–31, freedom is contrasted with slavery. Whereas before their conversion to Christ, Jews were enslaved under the law and its requirements, they are now set free from this slavery.

The appeal of the letter to the Galatians is that they do not yield to the demands of the Judaizers to enslave themselves again to the law, for Jesus came to redeem all people from the law (4:5). Paul has warned them that to submit to the Judaizers is to place themselves back in slavery to the elemental powers of the

---

of interpersonal relationships. It is used seven times in Galatians, all in the ethical section: 'serve *one another*' (5:13); 'bite and devour *one another* ... consumed by *one another*' (5:15); the Spirit and flesh are 'opposed to *one another*' (5:17), 'provoking *one another*, envying *one another*' (5:26); 'bear *one another's* burdens' (6:2).

5. BDAG 189.

universe (4:9). Here, then, he urges them to live out the life they are called into, a life of freedom from the law. In broader terms, this is freedom from sin, as the law serves to enslave people in sin rather than release them. It is for freedom that Christ set them free, so live out that freedom! (cf. 5:1).

The Galatians are for the seventh time in the letter addressed with the plural vocative *adelphoi*, which is inclusive of men and women, hence, 'brothers and sisters.'[6] This address reminds them that despite all his warnings and rhetoric, Paul sees them as fellow Christians, members of God's family, brothers and sisters of Christ, children of Abraham, and joint-heirs in Christ. It also carries a sense of intimacy—Paul speaks to them out of brotherly love.

Paul now puts to bed any false ideas the Galatians may have about the freedom he is talking about. Reading between the lines of Paul's letters, it seems that his teaching on grace and freedom was not uncommonly misunderstood in the early churches. We see this particularly in Romans 3:8 where Paul speaks of being slandered by the accusation that he preaches, 'Let us do evil, in order that good may come of it?' Again, in Romans 6, using an interlocutor, Paul asks an anticipated question—'are we to continue in sin so that grace may abound?' (Rom 6:1). And again, 'Are we to sin because we are not under law but under grace?' (Rom 6:15). The first question is not answered, Paul simply states that their condemnation is just. The latter two questions he answers with *mē genoito*, 'may it never be!'

The question is asked by those with a skewed view of grace and freedom. The grace and freedom experienced in Christ are not a license to sin, but freedom from sin. The receipt of grace, rather than giving birth to sinful desires of the flesh, should yield gratitude in a person's life—the person thankful that he or she is accepted by God and is free of sin and its consequences. They are also free from the oppressive burden of a legal demand. They can revel and rejoice in their identity as children of the living God. This freedom and experience of grace then births

---

6. See 1:11; 3:15; 4:12, 28, 31; 5:11, s.a., 6:1, 18.

a desire not to sin, but to please God—to live righteous lives
that honor their redeemer, holy lives that emulate his holiness,
lives overflowing with love, lives of service, sacrifice, humility,
sometimes suffering, and even death. To claim otherwise is to
violate the whole basis of salvation.

It is likely that the Judaizers are making this charge against
Paul, stating that a lawless faith leaves the believer in Christ with
no ethical system, no understanding of right and wrong. They
are likely arguing that the law is required for this so that new
converts know what they can and cannot do as children of God.
They appeal to the Mosaic law as this legal code. Here, Paul will
argue for an ethic based on the Spirit rather than an external
code. He will uphold many of the legal expectations of the law,
but the law itself is not required for the Spirit inscribes the law
on the heart, and the Christian can live the inside-outside life.
It is likely that such false ideas of freedom are found among
the Corinthians who love the slogan 'everything is permissible'
(1 Cor 6:12; 10:23). In 1 Corinthians Paul spills much ink
addressing their false understanding of ethics. Here, Paul
addresses this possible corruption of the freedom one has as a
child of God.

He puts it this way, 'only, not the freedom for an opportunity
for the flesh.' 'Only' is *monos*, used in the neuter (the only thing).[7]
Here it points to the only caveat he wishes to give concerning
freedom, specifically targeted at false ideas of freedom from the
Judaizers.

'Opportunity' is *aphormē*, a word used only by Paul in the NT
seven times. Elsewhere, he uses it an opportunity to boast (2 Cor
5:12; 11:12), of an opportunity for Satan (1 Tim 5:14), and of sin
seizing the opportunity given by the law to deceive and condemn
(Rom 7:8, 11). These latter two verses indicate the problem of the
law—it brings awareness of sin but no power to overcome it. It
leads to self-condemnation at our failure to live up to what we
know we should do (as the whole of Rom 7 describes).

Here, it is using freedom in Christ as an opportunity to allow

---

7. See 1:23; 2:10; 3:2; 4:18; 6:4, 12.

oneself to yield to the desires of the flesh. In 5:19–21, Paul will give an extensive list of such things—our freedom in Christ is not the freedom to let go of self-restraint and do what we feel like at every opportunity. Rather, we live by the Spirit and with his power and unction, resist the desires of the flesh.

The final clause gives the converse with the strong adversative *alla*, 'but,' with the clause telling the Galatians how they are to use their freedom in Christ. 'Through love' uses *dia* instrumentally, giving the means by which something is accomplished or effected—'through.' 'Through *agapē*' speaks of love as the governing ethical attribute of God, Christ, and his followers. Earlier, what matters is not circumcision or uncircumcision, but faith working through love (5:6). Here, he explains what will come through that *agapē*—service to others. Love is the attitude from which this slaving is done (cf. 1 Cor 13:1–3). It is also the shape of the service itself which is love. What love looks like is exegeted in 1 Cor 13:4–7 where Paul uses fifteen verbs to describe *agapē*, seven negative and eight positive:

Love is patient, kind is love. It does not envy. Love is not arrogant, is not puffed-up. It is not crude. It does not seek its own way, is not angry, keeps no record of wrongs. It does not rejoice in wrongdoing, but rejoices with the truth. Love endures in all situations, trusts in all situations, hopes in all situations, and perseveres in all situations.

Here in Gal 5:13, 'through love' has some ambiguity. It can be 'through the attitude of love' or 'through God's love.' The use of the article could indicate '*the* Love' is of God. However, this is a moot point because, for Paul, in Christ, the God of *love* (2 Cor 13:11) has poured *his* love into the hearts of believers by the Spirit (Rom 5:5). This love operates in us. Hence, it is by his love that we express the love that here Paul has in mind. It is the love that comes to life by the work of the Spirit—the head virtue in the list of 5:22.

'Become slaves to one another' uses the *douleuete* which can be either indicative—'through love you are serving one another,' or the imperative, 'through love serve one another.' The imperative is to be preferred because it is clear that the Galatians are not loving one another, but are consuming each other in conflict (5:15, cf. 5:26). This is another of the direct imperatival appeals to the Galatians in the letter (see on 1:8). The present tense speaks of an ongoing attitude of voluntary servitude to one another.

The verb *douloō* is used in 4:8–9 of the Galatians' former enslavement to false gods and the elemental powers. Similarly, Hagar is in slavery with her children to Sinai and Jerusalem (4:25, cf. *katadouloō* 2:4). Jesus has set believers free from all enslavement to false religions, ideologies, and demonic forces, including the law (cf. Rom 6:16). Elsewhere, Christ has set free believers from enslavement to impurity (Rom 6:19), fear (Rom 8:15), pleasures (Tit 3:3, cf. Tit 2:3), and sin (Rom 6:17, 20; 7:25). Now, they have the status of children and not slaves (4:3–7).

However, here as elsewhere, Paul speaks of the Christian life as voluntary enslavement to God (Rom 6:22; 2 1 Thess 1:9; 2 Tim 1:3), to Christ the Lord (Rom 12:11; 16:18, cf. 1 Cor 9:13), to righteousness (Rom 6:18, 19), or in a role like a deacon (1 Tim 3:10, 13; 6:2). Released from bondage to the law, believers serve in a new way by the Spirit and not the law (Rom 7:6). Here, they are to serve as slaves to one another as Onesimus served Paul on Philemon's behalf in prison (Phlm 13, cf. 2 Cor 11:8).

This appeal to be slaves to one another calls to mind Christ, who being in the form of God, took the form of a slave becoming human and giving his life through a slave's death on a cross (Phil 2:6–7). The Galatians are blessed children of God; they are to do the same. This speaks to them all; the free serving those who are in literal slavery, not just the elite being served as they were accustomed to in wider society. The men are to serve the women and not just the converse (cf. Eph 5:21–31). The Jew is to serve the Greek and vice versa. In a society where slaves did the hard work and the free enjoyed status and benefits, this is a counter-cultural command. This service is to be motivated out of love and not any sense of fear or demand. This should be a willing service. This, like Eph 6:5–10 and Philemon, hints at and encourages the end of slavery for all time.

Paul has a particular penchant for the Greek term for 'one another' (*allēlōn*) shown by his forty uses of the term (100 times in the NT). For Paul, it lies at the center of his ethics (below). It is also found elsewhere in an ethical sense. In Heb 10:24, believers are to 'consider how to stir *one another* to love and good works.' Jacob urges believers not to speak evil against one another (Jas 4:11), not to grumble against one another (Jas 5:9), and to confess their sins to one another and pray for each other (Jas 5:16).

Peter urges his Asian recipients to 'love *one* another earnestly from a pure heart' (1 Pet 1:22), 'show hospitality to *one another* without grumbling (1 Pet 4:9), be clothed with humility toward one another (1 Pet 5:5), and greet one another with a kiss of love (1 Pet 5:14).

This 'one-anothering' is also found in John. John speaks of believers having fellowship with one another (1 John 1:7). There is a similar call to mutual service in John 13:14, where, after Jesus had taken on the role of a female slave (cf. 1 Sam 25:41) and washed his disciples' feet, he commands them to wash each other's feet in the same way (John 13:14). Again, in John 13:34–34, Jesus gives a new command, 'love *one another*, just as I have loved you, you are also to love *one another*. By this all people will know that you are my disciples, that you love *one another*.'[8]

Paul uses it in a range of ethical commands including:

1. Being mutually encouraged by one another's faith (Rom 1:12)
2. Individually members of one another in the body of Christ (Rom 12:5; Eph 4:25)
3. Love one another (Rom 12:10), and the one who does, has fulfilled the law (Rom 13:8, s.a. 1 Thess 3:12; 4:9; 2 Thess 1:3)
4. Outdo one another in showing honor (Rom 12:10)
5. Think the same toward one another (without partiality, in unity) (Rom 12:16; 15:5)
6. Let us not pass judgment on one another (Rom 14:13)
7. Pursue peace and the things that bring edification to one another (Rom 14:19)

8. See also John 15:12, 17; 1 John 3:11, 23; 4:7, 11, 12; 2 John 5.

8. Welcome one another (Rom 15:14)
9. Greet one another with a holy kiss (Rom 16:16; 1 Cor 16:20; 2 Cor 13:12)
10. Marriage partners do not deprive one another of intimate relations except for agreed periods of abstinence for prayer (1 Cor 7:5)
11. Wait for one another at meals (1 Cor 11:33)
12. Have the same concern for one another (1 Cor 12:25)
13. Serve one another (Gal 5:13)
14. Bear one another's burdens (6:2)
15. Bearing with one another in love (Eph 4:2; Col 3:13)
16. Be kind to one another, tenderhearted, forgiving one another (Eph 4:32)
17. Submitting to one another (Eph 5:21)
18. In humility consider others above yourself (Phil 2:3)
19. Do not lie to one another (Col 3:9)
20. Encourage one another (1 Thess 4:18; 5:11)
21. Seek to do good to one another and to all people (1 Thess 5:15)

Paul uses the term twice in 5:15 in a negative sense, warning them that if they bite and devour one another, they will be consumed by *one another*. Similarly, in 5:26, inclusively, he urges all Christians not to provoke *one another* and envy *one another*. In 5:17, the Spirit and flesh are opposed to *one another*.[9] Concern for other brothers and sisters lies at the heart of Christian ethics. The motive is to be love. Serving one another is Christianity 101. The summons to serve one another has big implications for us as we engage in church or other contexts with other Christians. We are here to serve our fellow Christians.

Notably, Paul uses the term *douloō* which speaks of voluntary enslavement. A prominent mark of a Christian living by the Spirit is a spirit of serving others with love. This can be as simple

---

9. Paul twice uses *allēlōn* negatively: of being consumed with passion for one another (Rom 1:27) and of hating one another in former lives (Tit 3:3). It is also used for thoughts conflicting with each other (Rom 2:15).

as a gentle hand on the shoulder to the giving of time, support, or money. Our freedom then is the freedom to serve.

It is good to check our attitudes at a time like this. Are we taking an attitude of service with us when we engage with our brothers and sisters in Christ? Are we willing to get our hands dirty when there are things needing to be done, like a working bee at the church, cooking, cleaning, washing the loos, vacuuming, gardening, giving material support to someone who is struggling, helping the leaders, putting away the music gear, putting out the seats, picking someone up for church or to get an important errand done, bearing with the 'extra-grace-required' people, and so on? Are we available to go the extra mile during the week as we hear of our fellow Christians in need?

These attitudes must be practiced, so serving is a part of our lives in all spheres of life. In this, we emulate Jesus who did not come to be served, but to serve. Little wonder he taught his disciples that the path to greatness in the kingdom is being a slave of all.[10] Even if we fail to understand most of the gospel but simply believe in the Jesus of Scripture knowing that it is by grace through faith that we are saved, and then resolve to commit our lives to serve our brothers and sisters in Christ and all we meet in the journey of life, we will know God's delight in our lives.

NEIGHBORLY LOVE AS THE SUM OF ALL LAW (5:14)

In *Galatians 5:14*, Paul gives the reason for his previous appeal to serve one another through love:

For (*gar*, 1:10) the (*ho*, 1:6) **whole** (*pas*, 1:2) **law** (*nomos*, 2:16) **has been fulfilled** (perfect passive *plēroō*)[11] **in** (*en*, 1:6) **one** (*heis*, 3:16) **word** (*logos*);[12] **in** (*en*) **the statement** (*ho*,[13] 1:1), '**love**

10. See Matt 20:26–27; 23:11–12; Mark 9:35; 10:43–44; Luke 22:26.
11. The verb πληρόω (*plēroō*) is found once in Galatians. Its basic meaning is 'fill' but is used in another commonsense way in 5:14, 'fulfill,' of the statement 'love your neighbor as yourself' (Lev 19:18)—which fulfills the whole law.
12. The noun *logos*, which means 'word' and a whole range of other ideas like account, message, statement, etc. is used twice in Galatians. In 5:14, it is used of a statement—the one statement that sums the law—'love your neighbor as yourself'

(agapaō) **your** (genitive *sy*, 1:2) **neighbor** *(plēsion)*[14] **as** *(hōs*, 1:9) **yourself** *(seauton)*.'[15]

Gar here is causal, 'for,' Paul giving the theological basis for the previous appeal to serve. 'The whole law' is found in Deut 4:8: 'and what other great nation has for itself ordinances and just judgments according *to this whole law* that I am delivering to you today' (LXX). For Israel, Moses here speaks of the whole law given to Moses on Sinai, which Deuteronomy will delineate.

Here, in Paul, it speaks of every possible understanding of the Torah, including any rabbinic developments such as the oral law (which of course were formerly very important to Rabbi Paul). While the Torah lies at its center, it speaks of the laws of Judaism in its fullest sense. It is parallel to *holon ton nomon* in 5:3—'every man who is circumcised is obligated to keep *the whole law*.' It also recalls his use of the OT in 3:10 and 12 to make this point (Deut 27:26; Lev 18:5). Here, the whole or entire law is summed up in one commandment. This demonstrates that for Paul, love is the overriding basis and reason for the law. All laws are created to serve this one thing.

'Has been fulfilled' uses the verb *plēroō*, a verb that has the basic root meaning of 'fill,' a meaning Paul uses often.[16] It is also commonly used for the fulfillment of the Scriptures, especially in

---

(Lev 19:18). In 6:6, *logos* is used in the sense of teaching, which is taught by particular members of the church, with whom all good things should be shared by the student.

13. The neuter article introduces the 'whole law' (ὁ γὰρ πᾶς νόμος, *ho gar pas nomos*) while the second article (ἐν τῷ, *en tō*) is likely resumptive. Also, see Rom 13:8. See Wallace, *Greek Grammar*, 238.

14. The noun πλησίον *(plēsion)* is used once in Galatians 5:14 in the citation from Lev 19:18: 'love your *neighbor* as yourself.'

15. The reciprocal pronoun σεαυτοῦ *(seautou)* is formed from *sy* (you) and *autos* (him, her, it) and speaks of yourself. It is found only in 5:14 in the Lev 19:18 citation—'as yourself.'

16. Paul uses *plēroō* in the sense of fill or full of vice (Rom 1:29); God filling people with joy and hope in faith (Rom 15:13); the Romans filled with all knowledge and ability to instruct one another (Rom 15:14); Paul filled with comfort (2 Cor 7:4); Christ filling all things (Eph 1:23; 4:10); people filled with the knowledge of God (Eph 3:19) or of his will (Col 1:9), filled with the Spirit (Eph 5:18) or in him (Col 2:10), and the Philippians filled with the fruit of righteousness (Phil 1:11). It can also carry the meaning 'complete,' including complete obedience (2 Cor 10:6), and completing Paul's joy (Phil 2:2; 2 Tim 1:4).

Matthew.[17] Here, the entire Jewish legal system is summed up or fulfilled in one command, the command to love one's neighbor. Elsewhere, Paul speaks of the righteous requirements of the law fulfilled in believers who walk according to the Spirit rather than the flesh (Rom 8:4). In a similar vein to this verse, in Rom 13:8 he writes, 'the one who loves another has fulfilled the law.' As such, living by the Spirit with neighborly love is the completion of the law. There is no need to be circumcised and come under the law; rather, they are to live by the Spirit serving through love.

The grammar of this verse is interesting. 'In one word' uses *logos* in the sense of a 'statement'—in one statement or saying.[18] Paul uses *logos* in a similar way in Rom 13:9, where, as here, all commandments are summed up in this word—'you shall love your neighbor as yourself.'

17. See Matt 1:22; 2:15, 17, 23; 3:15; 4:14; 5:17; 8:17; 12:17; 13:35; 21:4; 26:54, 56; 27:9 (fourteen times); Mark 14:49; Luke 4:21; 24:44; Acts 1:16; 3:18; 13:27; John 12:38; 13:18; 15:25; 17:12; 19:24, 36; Jas 2:23. It is also used of time fulfilled (Mark 1:15; Luke 21:24), an angelic prediction coming to fulfillment (Luke 1:20), and a saying of Jesus fulfilled (John 18:9, 32). Paul uses it for fulfillment in other ways including the fulfillment of his gospel mission (Rom 15:19) or making the word fully known (Col 1:25), Archippus completing his ministry (Col 4:17), having one's material needs fulfilled (supplied) (Phil 4:18, 19), and God fulfilling Christian plans (2 Thess 1:11).
18. See also for *logos* in the sense of statement(s) in Paul Rom 9:9; 1 Cor 15:54; 1 Thess 4:15; 1 Tim 1:15; 3:1; 1 Tim 4:9; 2:11; Tit 1:9; 3:8, In the wider NT see Matt 7:28; 15:12; 19:1, 1; 26:11; Mark 7:29; 10:22; Luke 1:29; 9:28; John 4:37; 6:60; 15:25; 18:9; 19:8; 21:23). Other uses of *logos* in Paul include a person's words (Rom 3:4; 1 Cor 2:13—taught by the Spirit; 14:19; Eph 5:6; 6:19—given by God; 1 Thess 4:18); and specific words just said (2 Thess 2:2). He frequently uses it of the Christian message as the word of God (Rom 9:6; 14:36; 2 Cor 2:17; 4:2; Col 1:25; 1 Thess 2:13; 1 Tim 4:5; 2 Tim 2:9; Tit 2:5), or 'the word' (Gal 6:6; Phil 1:14; Col 4:3; 1 Thess 1:6; 2 Tim 4:2), or 'of truth' (Eph 1:13; Col 1:5; 2 Tim 2:15), 'of life' (Phil 2:16), 'of Christ' (Col 3:16), 'of the Lord' (1 Thess 1:8; 2 Thess 3:1), 'words of the faith' (1 Tim 4:6), 'words of our Lord Jesus Christ' (1 Tim 6:3), 'his word' (Tit 1:3); of preaching (1 Tim 5:17); of the message—of the cross (1 Cor 1:18); of wisdom and knowledge (1 Cor 12:8); the message Paul preached (1 Cor 15:2; 2 Cor 1:18; 2 Tim 4:15); of reconciliation (2 Cor 5:19); and in a letter (2 Cor 10:11). Other uses include a legal judgment (Rom 9:28); an account given (Rom 14:12); a financial matter (Phil 4:15) or account (Phil 4:17); speech (1 Cor 1:5, 17; 2:1, 4; 4:19, 20; 14:9; 2 Cor 6:7; 8:7; 10:10; 11:6; Eph 4:29; Col 4:6; 1 Thess 1:5; 1 Tim 4:12; 2 Tim 2:17; Tit 2:8), sometimes contrasted with deeds (Rom 15:18; Col 3:17; 2 Thess 2:17); seeming appearance (Col 2:23); something said by word in contrast to a letter (2 Thess 2:2, 15; 3:14); and sound teaching (2 Tim 1:13).

The use of *logos* suggests God as the source, his word, with the term *logos* used in 6:6 of those who share the word in the Galatian churches. There is two dative *en* (in) constructs, it literally reading: 'for the entire law *in* (*en*) *one word* has been fulfilled, in (*en*) the [word] ....' This has the effect of giving prominence to the saying: in this word, in the statement ...

It is notable that Paul does not here use *gegraptai* (as it is written) as he usually does when he cites the OT—'as it is written' (see 3:10, also 3:13; 4:22, 27). Rather, he speaks of the fulfillment of the law in one text. As Paul most often does use *gegraptai*, its absence again focuses the text for special importance.

The citation is familiar to NT readers as the core ethical command in Christian thought. It is drawn from the law, which is critical theologically. By reaching into the Torah for the key ethical command of Christianity, Christ, Paul, Jacob, John, and others indicate the ongoing importance of the law for Christian living. The same can be said for worship, with people called to love God with all that they have—the Shema of Deut 6:4–5.

The essence of the law then has validity for the Christian life. In fact, it is critical. However, the fulfillment of this ethical command does not bring justification. On the converse, one is justified by faith, one receives the Spirit, love poured into the human heart, and by the Spirit, one has renewed power to live the law.

Living the law is summed up in this one statement—love your neighbor as yourself. This summative statement shows us that where ethics is concerned, this is the basic intent and governing rubric for all law. All law is an expression of love, for the purpose of love is to be expressed in love and is love. We fulfill the law when we love the other. We even love God by loving the other.

As such, there is continuity between the life required of Israel by God and by Christians. In a sense, nothing has changed. The law guided Israel regarding God's expectations. This goes on. He is the same God, so a faithful Jew who understood the Torah would live in much the same way as a Christian who believes in the gospel and seeks to live its ethic now. We see this in amazing texts like Mic 6:8 where what the Lord requires is that a person 'do justice, and to *love steadfast love* (ḥĕ·sĕḏ) and to walk humbly with your God?' Or again, Hos 6:6: 'For I desire steadfast *love* and not sacrifice, the knowledge of God rather than burnt offerings.' Indeed, the essential character feature of God in the OT is his ḥĕ·sĕḏ, his steadfast love. For example, Lam 3:23: 'The *steadfast love* of the LORD never ceases; his mercies never come to an end; they are new every morning; great is your faithfulness.'[19]

So, in gifting us his Spirit, he poured his ḥĕ·sĕḏ into us (cf. Rom 5:5), and we are empowered to live this love command. What has changed is that he is working from the inside out, and our call is to yield to the impulses of the Spirit in our relationships with others. We are empowered for this command. This command is a fluid command, and it is not something that can be easily codified; it is shaped to an extent by the situation we find ourselves in. It wants the best for the other. It is patient with the other. It bears with the other. It responds with gentleness and sometimes firmness toward others. It can be strong and lead a person to act with force to protect another. It is very difficult to define, but it puts others first and esteems them above oneself. It is only definable by considering the character of God and his Son.

What Paul shows us is that the Judaizers are misappropriating the law where Christians are concerned. Yes, the law still has validity, especially those core requirements of love. But it is no longer and never has been the basis of justification in any sense. One's status as righteous comes from God by grace through faith. It is not something external we can then codify and seek to conform our lives to. We will fall and fail and live in fear, judgment, and guilt without joy if we seek to live this way. It is a proposition that we can state, but it is lived from the inside out, impelled in every situation by the Spirit to act on behalf of the other. Hence, the law goes on but fulfilled in Christ, written on our hearts, love driving us—if only we will yield.

19. On God's ḥĕ·sĕḏ see also Exod 20:6; 34:6–7; Num 14:18; Deut 5:10; 7:9; 1 Kings 8:23; 1 Chron 16:34; 2 Chron 6:14; Neh 1:5; 9:17, 32; Ps 25:10; 33:5; 36:5–7; 57:10; 85:10; 86:5, 16; 89:1–2, 14; 100:5; 103:8, 11, 17; 106:1; 107:1; 118:1–4, 29; 136:1–26; Isa 54:8, 10; 63:7; Jer 9:24; 31:3; 32:18; 33:11; Joel 2:13.

The word cited is drawn from Lev 19:18. It comes in a chapter that begins with a reminder of God's holiness and core commands such as love for parents, Sabbath observance, a renunciation of idols, and sacrifice protocols (Lev 19:1–8). There are then instructions to leave food in the fields for the poor and sojourner (Lev 19:9–10) and laws mainly concerning the treatment of the other—against a range of things including stealing, injustice, lying (Lev 19:11),[20] the oppression or robbery of a neighbor, paying wages at the end of the day, right treatment of the deaf and blind (Lev 19:13–14), legal injustice and partiality to the poor or great (Lev 19:15), slander or putting a neighbor's life in jeopardy (Lev 19:16), hatred of a brother, lack of openness with a neighbor (Lev 19:17), or vengeance or grudge-bearing toward a fellow Israelite (Lev 19:18a).

Leviticus 19:18 sums up these imperatives concerning behavior toward a fellow Israelite: 'you shall love your neighbor as yourself: I am the Lord.' 'I am the Lord' here tends to suggest that this is an emulation of God who is characterized above all by 'steadfast love.' It is followed by a range of other commands.

Further on in Lev 19:33–34 is written,

when a stranger sojourns with you in your land, you shall not do him wrong. You shall treat the stranger who sojourns with you as the native among you, and you *shall love him as yourself*, for you were strangers in the land of Egypt: I am the Lord your God.

Here, we see the love of neighbor command universalized to all those in the land. It is then an impartial love for all people within the church and outside. The basis for this is that the people of Israel were once slaves and aliens in Egypt and there they were maltreated. As such, they should not emulate Egypt's maltreatment of Israel. Instead, they should show love to all who dwell in the land.

As mentioned above, in the NT, undoubtedly, this command lies at the heart of Christian ethics. In Matthew, Jesus universalizes this saying—completely forbidding hatred toward

---

20. There is also a reminder not to swear by or misuse God's name vain (Lev 19:12) and fear of God (Lev 19:14).

an enemy: stating that it was said 'you shall love your neighbor and hate your enemy' (Matt 5:43); but now Jesus teaches that a Christian must love even enemies and those who harm them (Matt 5:44; Luke 6:27; 35). Jesus asks the Rich Ruler if he has kept this command (Matt 19:19). He claims he has. It turns out he has not, and he cannot count the cost of following through on this belief and selling his possessions and giving to the poor. As in Mark 12:31, it is the second of the great commandments, placed after loving God with all you are and everything you have (Matt 22:39). In Mark, to love one's neighbor as oneself is worth more than all ritual sacrifices (Mark 12:33).

In Luke, Jesus asks a Jewish Scribe how he reads the law, and the scribe validates the same two great commandments. The Scribe seeks clarification of who his neighbor is, and Jesus tells the story of the Good Samaritan to clarify that one's neighbor is anyone in need, even an enemy (Luke 10:25–37).

For Jesus, while Lev 19:18 is focused on the love of one Israelite to another, Jesus interprets it with an eye on Lev 19:33–34 and beyond to mission—one is to love all people as one's neighbor indiscriminately. This love is even to be offered to enemies and those who directly harm us.

While John does not cite the command verbatim, he draws on it when he speaks of Jesus teaching his disciples a new command that, just as he has shown them *agapē*-love, 'you love one another.' This love for one another will be a witness to the world that they are his disciples, i.e., it is the defining mark of being a Jesus follower (John 13:34–35, also John 15:12, 17). This theme of showing love for one another dominates John's epistles; most particularly, 1 John 3:16–17:

By this we know love, that he laid down his life for us, and we ought to lay down our lives for the brothers. But if anyone has the world's goods and sees his brother in need, yet closes his heart against him, how does God's love abide in him? Little children, let us not love in word or talk but in deed and in truth' (ESV).[21]

---

21. See also 1 John 3:11, 23; 4:7, 11, 12; 2 John 5.

In the General Epistles, the love command is critical. Jacob, Christ's earthly half-brother, cites the same command in Jas 2:8, stating that 'you really fulfill the *royal law*' as you live this out. This is likely the 'perfect law of liberty' in Jas 1:25. Similarly, Peter urges his Asian readers to live with purified souls and obedience to the truth with 'sincere brotherly love' and that they 'love one another earnestly from a pure heart' (1 Pet 1:22). Later he writes to do the same since 'love covers over a multitude of sins' (1 Pet 4:8). It is love that holds people together when things go awry. The injunction to greet one another with a brotherly kiss of love is a visual symbol of this deep Christian *agapē koinōnia* (1 Pet 5:14).

Paul cites the Levitical command in Rom 13:9, stating that four of the interpersonal commands drawn from the Ten Commandments (Exod 20:13-17) (adultery, murder, stealing, covetousness)[22] and any other command are summed up in this statement (*logos*). He then states that love does no wrong to a neighbor, and love is 'fulfilling the law.' Believers are in constant debt to love one another (Rom 13:8).

Elsewhere he speaks of love for one another with some frequency. So, in Rom 12:10, the Romans are to be devoted to one another in brotherly and familial love. In Eph 4:2, believers are to 'bear with one another in love.' He prays for the Thessalonians who have been taught to love one another by God (1 Thess 4:9) and who are already loving (1 Thess 3:6), that they yet more 'abound in love for one another and everyone else' (1 Thess 3:12). Gloriously, this prayer is answered, as written a short time later in 2 Thess 1:3, he can say of the Thessalonians that 'the love of every one of you for one another is increasing!' This universalizes the love-imperative in Paul. Just as Israel was to love those they encountered in the land; we are to love all we engage with in the world. A similar universalization is seen as Paul prays for the Philippians who are becoming divided, asking that their love would abound more and more in understanding

---

22. These are drawn from Exod 20:13–17. Paul inverts the order of adultery and murder. He does not include 'false witness' which falls under 'any other commandment.' These may be chosen because they flagrantly violate neighborly love.

and discernment (Phil 1:9). They are to love each other and all people.

Earlier in Galatians, Paul spoke of Jesus' love towards him expressed in self-giving (Gal 2:20). What matters is faith working itself out in love (5:6). In the previous verse (5:13), he has already called for them to 'through love serve one another.' Soon, he will list the fruit of the Spirit with love at its head, the sum of all Spirit-fruit (5:22).

This indicative state of loving then shapes our lives. We are not free in Christ to sin, but to love (cf. 2 Tim 1:13). By the Spirit, this is enabled, with love downloaded from the God who embodies great love (Eph 2:4) into our inner beings (Rom 5:5, also Col 1:8; 2 Tim 1:7). So, we are rooted and established in love (Eph 3:17). Indeed, to be a Christian is to come to know this love of Christ more and more (Eph 3:19).

As the furnace of God's love burns within us, we cannot be separated from it (Rom 8:35–40), and it must overflow with abundance (2 Cor 2:4). As it overflows, love-expressed is fluid and flexible as we respond in each situation with an attitude and resultant actions that serve God and improve the situation of those we meet. It is us emulating God and his Son's love for us that led to our salvation (Rom 5:8). It is the supreme doctrine that governs our love of other Christians—every time we meet a brother or sister, no matter how difficult, it is love that shapes our encounters (Eph 1:15; Col 1:4; Phlm 5).

Love shapes our relationships (Phil 2:1–2), especially toward the weak Christian (Rom 14:15). It can lead to tough love, where we must discipline (1 Cor 4:21). Love builds people and the church up (1 Cor 8:1). As we express the truth to one another (Eph 4:15) and serve with our gifts, the church grows (Eph 4:16). Leaders are to be loved and esteemed (1 Thess 5:13). Indeed, it is love that knits the church together as a beautiful unity before God (Col 2:2). Love forgives and reconciles after division and pain (2 Cor 2:8). By love, we bear with one another in the tough times (Eph 4:2). Without it, as we speak forth, we are merely loud annoying noise (1 Cor 13:2). All gifts are to be expressed through it, and without love, they are worthless and gain us nothing (1

Cor 13:1–3). It is shaped by a range of other attitudes toward the
other that all care for them and want the best for them (1 Cor
13:4–7, above). It is the eternal attribute of the authentic believer
(1 Cor 13:8, 13).

We follow the example of Paul who constantly expresses his
love for his churches.[23] We seek to be examples to one another of
love (1 Tim 4:12). Like Christ and Paul, we gladly pour ourselves
out for others in love (2 Cor 12:15). We are to walk in love as
Christ loved humanity and gave himself up in sacrifice to God
(Eph 5:2). Such self-sacrificial love is the basis of a husband's
treatment of his wife,[24] a wife to her husband (Tit 2:4), and
motherhood (1 Tim 2:15). Older men are to embody love (Tit
2:2). We are to pursue love (1 Cor 14:1; 1 Tim 6:11; 2 Tim
2:22)—a love that comes from a pure heart, a good conscience,
and a sincere faith (1 Tim 1:5). The breastplate guarding our
hearts is faith and love (1 Thess 5:8). Not just some things, but *all*
things are to be done in love (1 Cor 16:14). We are to put on over
everything else that is good, love, the virtue that binds together
our godly attitudes (Col 3:14).

Effectively, to be clothed in Christ is to be clothed in love (cf.
Col 3:9–10). It is from love and with love that we give financially
(2 Cor 8:8, 24, cf. Phlm 7). Love is our motivation for evangelism
(2 Cor 5:14; Phil 1:16). Our gospel witness is governed by
genuine love (2 Cor 6:6).

The specifics of the statement that sums up the law is that
believers shall love one another. Love is *agapaō*, used in 2:20 (see
further on 2:20 for analysis). Here it is not an imperative but a
future indicative (you shall love). However, the future indicative
here is used in the sense of a command, a cohortative (command
or volitive) indicative, as it often does in OT quotations. This
form is sometimes found in classical Greek, but in the LXX and
citations in the NT, its use is due to the literal translation of
the original Hebrew (especially in Matthew). Wallace writes, '[i]ts

23. See, e.g., 2 Cor 2:4; 11:11; Phil 4:1; 2 Tim 3:10.
24. See Eph 5:25, 28, 33; Col 3:19.

force is quite emphatic, in keeping with the combined nature of the indicative mood and future tense.'[25]

'Your neighbor uses *plēsion*, which outside of Paul in the NT is found twelve only times. It once means 'near' (John 4:5). In Acts 7:37, it speaks of fellow Jews and seems to focus on fellow Christians in Jas 4:12. It is found in 'love your neighbor' constructs on seven occasions.[26] Two of the other five flow from an inquiry into the meaning of the law—who is my neighbor? Which man proved to be a neighbor…?' (Luke 10:29, 36). In this passage, Jesus universalizes neighborliness beyond the believing community, as Lev 19:33–34 does for 19:18.

Plēsion is used only five times in Paul, twice in the love-imperative; Rom 13:9 and here. In Rom 13:9–10, there is no limit placed on love, and so it is inclusive of all humanity. Believers are to owe no one anything other than the ongoing debt to love them. The other uses are in Rom 15:2 which restates this imperative, 'let each of us please his neighbor for the good, to build that person up.' This verse helps define love—it is what is for the good of the people we encounter and builds them up. The context is in Christ.

Hence, when we engage with an unbeliever, we are seeking to love them toward Christ. If a believer, we are seeking to build them up in their most holy faith. The other use is Eph 4:25, where Paul exhorts the Ephesians to put away false speech and speak the truth to their neighbor. Again, there is no limit here on who is in mind, and as such, it seems neighbor for Paul is an inclusive term, unlike 'brother,' 'sister,' or 'saint/holy one' which all focus on fellow believers. The imperative to love, of course, does apply to interpersonal relationships and later in 6:10, Paul makes it clear that we should do good to all and especially to those in the household of faith. Galatians 6:10 restates the love command using goodness as a rubric.

Here, the love command especially focuses on interpersonal

25. See further Wallace, *Grammar*, 452. He notes two other examples in Paul, including Rom 7:7; 13:9 (the same as Gal 5:14). See also Matt 4:7, 10; 5:21, 27, 33, 43, 48; 6:5; 19:18; 21:3; 22:37, 39; Mark 9:35; 1 Pet 1:16).
26. See Matt 5:43; 19:19; 22:39; Mark 12:31, 33; Luke 10:27; Jas 2:8.

relationships within the community of faith. This is clear in that it leads into a reference to their internal contention (v. 15, cf. v. 26). However, the love command is general, and all our relationships toward other humans (neighbors) should be governed by love (1 Cor 16:14).

'As yourself' is problematic in societies where self-hate is a common problem. However, here there is an idealization of self-love. One might restate it as 'love your neighbor as you would like to be loved.' Or 'love your neighbor as one should love oneself.' The point is that one should love others with the kind of love and care and a relatively healthy and whole person shows to themselves.

This text is misused to argue we must love ourselves before loving others or even so that we can love others. This is not the point the verse is making. The emphasis in it is not oneself; it is love for the other. One, of course, should love oneself in the sense of self-acceptance and self-respect. And the key to this is not self-actualization through a self-focused mantra or endless self-reflection; rather, it is through knowing who we are before God. We are his image bearers and if we place our trust in him, we are his children he loves with infinite and inseparable affection. Full self-knowing is found in Christ by the Spirit.

Further, it may be true that one cannot fully love others until one loves oneself. Yet, no human fully loves themselves, yet is still called to love one's neighbor. In fact, true self-worth and fulfillment flow from us loving others, for this is what we were created to do, and in doing so, we often find wholeness. What counts is that we hear the clarion call to love others as the basic ethical imperative of our existence.

WATCH YOU DON'T DESTROY ONE ANOTHER (5:15)

In *Galatians 5:15*, Paul continues zeroing in on the personal relationships of the Galatians and again giving us vital and tragic insight into their community life as they negotiate their way through the Judaizing controversy:

But (*de*, 1:15), **if** (*ei*, 1:7) **you bite** (second person present *daknō*)[27] **and** (*kai*, 1:1) **devour** (second person present *katesthiō*)[28] **one another** (*allēlōn*, 5:13), **watch** (second person imperative *blepō*)[29] **[that] you are not** (*mē*, 1:7) **consumed** (aorist passive subjunctive *analoō*)[30] **by** (*hypo*, 1:11) **one another** (*allēlōn*).

The *de* is adversative, 'but,' as Paul is drawing a contrast with the law-fulfilling command 'love one another' and the Galatian's treatment of one another. The language is again vivid, Paul drawing on the world of predatory animals to describe the Galatians' behavior and to warn them of its consequences. Paul does not use 'one another' in the positive sense he usually does in his ethical teaching but in the negative sense of what a Christian should not do. They are not 'loving one another,' they are 'destroying one another,' which in the Christian life is *anathema* (1:6).

The verbs are descriptive. As noted in the translation, the first verb, *daknō*, is found only here in the NT. It literally means 'bite.' It is used in the LXX mainly of snakes that bite a horse's heels (Gen 49:17) and of snakes and sea-serpents that bite people with devastating effects.[31] Philo uses it regularly of snakes biting,

---

27. The verb δάκνω (*daknō*) is a *hapax legomenon* found only in the NT in 5:15. The term means literally to 'bite,' as in a snake, or figuratively, 'to cause discomfort, harm' (BDAG 211). It is used figuratively of the Galatians destroying each other by biting and devouring (see next footnote).

28. Paul uses the verb κατεσθίω (*katesthiō*) once in Galatians, in 5:15. It compounds *kata*, 'from,' and the common Greek term for eating, *esthiō*. Literally, it connotes to 'eat ravenously, devour, consume, swallow, eat up.' Figuratively, it speaks of destroying or devouring something or someone. In 5:15, like *daknō* (above) it is figurative—devour, destroy.

29. Galatians 5:15 is the only use of the common βλέπω (*blepō*), 'I see.' Paul uses it in the sense of 'watch out' in his warning to take care that they do not destroy themselves with their conflict. Such warnings in the second person plural are found ten times in Paul (see footnotes).

30. The verb ἀναλόω (*analoō*) also comes in the form ἀναˉλιˊσκω (*analiskō*) with synonymous meaning (BDF, §101). It means 'destroy, consume' (BDAG 67). It is used twice in the NT of fire consuming the Samaritans (Luke 9:54). Paul's one use is here in Galatians 5:15 of the Galatians consuming one another in their conflict.

31. See Num 21:6, 8, 9; Eccl 10:8, 11; Amos 5:19; 9:3; Hab 2:7, cf. Sir 21:2. It is also used for something that stings (Tob 11:8). It can have the more neutral sense of 'eat' (Mic 3:5) and is used to describe creditors who devour people financially (Hab 2:7). Josephus uses it once of cutting down cloisters (*J.W.* 6.191).

and sparingly of dogs and people doing the same.[32] In most references, he uses the snake or dog biting as an analogy for the way in which passions of pleasure bite the soul.[33] Here, *daknō* speaks of harsh fighting rather than literal biting. The Galatians are sniping at each other like a cobra striking at its prey. They are like fighting dogs, tearing each other apart (an appropriate analogy considering Paul labels Judaizers 'dogs' and 'flesh mutilators' in Phil 3:3). The use of a term frequently used of snake bites in Jewish Greek literature suggests that Paul sees a demonic influence in their behavior as they are behaving more like Satan than God.

The second verb, *katesthiō*, is also vivid in meaning. It is formed from *kata*, 'from' and the usual Greek term for eating, *esthiō*, a term not found in Galatians but forty-three times elsewhere in Paul. *Katesthiō* is a stronger term than *esthiō*, meaning to 'eat up ravenously, eat up, consume, devour, swallow,' or figuratively, 'devour as if by eating.' The force of the term is found in the LXX where it is used literally of wild animals eating people;[34] locusts, worms, flies, or moths devouring crops and/or people,[35] and other gross images.[36] It is frequently used of war with God, enemies, the sword, or how a forest destroys or consumes people, nations, or cities in war (e.g., Exod 15:7; Lev 26:38; Num 13:33).[37] This destruction is at times likened to wild animals or the new moon devouring Israel (Hos 2:12; 5:7; 13:8). Often it is used of fire which consumes an offering, people, and/or their things

---

32. Philo, *Opif.* 157; *Leg.* 2.77, 81, 84–85, 87, 94, 99; *Agr.* 94–95, 106–107, 109; *Ebr.* 223; *Sobr.* 46; *Somn.* 2.88; *Spec.* 3.103), of a dog bite (*Gig.* 35), and drunk men biting as they fight (*Contempl.* 40).

33. See *Leg.* 2.8, 81, 84–85, 87, 93, 99; *Gig.* 35; *Agr.* 94–95, 98, 106–107, 109; *Ebr.* 223; *Sobr.* 46; *Spec.* 3.103, cf. *Migr.* 110.

34. See Gen 37:20, 33; Lev 26:22.

35. See Exod 10:5, 12, 15; Deut 28:38, 39; 2 Chron 7:13; Ps 77:45 [Eng. 78:45]; 104:35 [Eng. 105:31]; Amos 4:9; Joel 1:4; 2:25; Isa 50:9; Ep Jer 19.

36. Such as a stillborn baby with consumed flesh (Num 12:12), a starving woman eating her afterbirth (Deut 28:57), dogs eating dead people (1 Kings 16:4; 20:23; 2 Kings 9:10, 36), and people eating each other (Zech 11:9).

37. See also Deut 28:51; 2 Sam 2:26; 18:18; Ps 78:7 [Eng. 79:7]; Amos 1:4; Nah 2:14; Zech 11:1, 16; 12:6; Isa 1:7, 20; 9:12; 10:18; Isa 31:8; 61:6; Jer 5:16–17; 8:16; 10:25; 12:12; 26:10, 14; 28:34; 30:16; Ezek 36:13; Dan 7:5, 19, 23.

consumed in fire, often in the context of war—especially in the Prophets.[38]

In the NT, birds consume seeds (Matt 13:4; Mark 4:4; Luke 8:5), rapacious Jewish leaders devour widow's houses (Mark 12:40; Luke 20:47), the prodigal son devouring his father's property (Luke 15:30), zeal for the Temple consumes Jesus (John 2:17 from Ps 69:9), a prophet east a scroll (Rom 10:9–10), a fire consumes enemies (Rev 11:5; Rev 20:9), and a dragon seeks to devour a child (Rev 12:4).

Paul's other use is 2 Cor 11:20 of false teachers who prey upon the Corinthians, a situation like this, where false teachers are attacking his flock. Here then, *katesthiō* is a word that connotes violence. The combination of 'bite' and 'devour' envisage the Galatian Christians at each other's throats, which could even indicate physical violence.

Having described their situation, Paul warns them. 'Watch out' is *blepete*, the common Greek word (131 times NT) for seeing (*blepō*)—here in the second person imperative; the sixth imperative directed at the Galatians in Gal 4–6 (see on 1:8).[39] The present tense speaks of this as an ongoing habit of watchfulness. This imperatival form is found twenty-two times in the NT with

---

38. See, e.g., Lev 9:24; 10:2; Num 11:1; 16:35; 21:28; 26:10; Deut 32:22; Hos 8:14; Amos 1:7, 10, 12, 14. See also Judg 6:21; 9:15, 20; 22:9; 1 Kings 18:38; 2 Kings 1:10, 12, 14; 2 Chron 7:1; Ps 20:10 [21:9]; Ps 77:63 [Eng. 78:63]; Job 1:16; 22:20; Sir 43:21; Amos 2:2, 5; 5:6; 7:4; Joel 1:3; 2:5; Obad 18; Nah 3:13, 15; Isa 29:6; 30:30; 33:11; Jer 5:14; 17:27; 27:32; Lam 2:3; 4:11; Ezek 15:7; 19:14; 20:47; 23:25; 28:18. *Katesthiō* is also applied to consuming up money (Gen 31:15), people eating animals (Gen 31:38), eating up grain (Gen 43:2), or grass (Amos 7:2), of birds that are eating food (Gen 40:17), cows eating each other (Gen 41:4, 20), evil people consuming people as if bread (Ps 13:4 [Eng. 14:4], and zeal consuming a person (cited by Jesus of the Temple) (Ps 68:10 [Eng. 69:9]). In Proverbs, it is used of oppressors whose teeth are swords and knives who devour the poor (Prov 24:37). It is used of death consuming people (Job 18:13), figuratively of one being destroyed by passion as leaves are devoured on a tree (Sir 6:3), the honored devoured (Add Esth A 10), of people devouring rulers (Hos 7:7), strength (Hos 7:9), or grain (Hos 8:7), injustice eating people (Mic 3:3), prophets devoured as with a lion by swords (Jer 2:30), Ezekiel ingesting a scroll (Ezek 3:1), Israel's leaders devouring lives like a lion (Ezek 22:25), consuming fat (Ezek 34:3), mountains consuming fruit (Ezek 36:8), and people consuming the last of food (1 Macc 6:43).

39. See 1:20; 3:7; 4:12, 30; 5:13, 16; 6:1, 2, 4, 6, 7, 11, 17.

the sense 'watch out, beware.' It is found in Jesus' teaching in his warnings against false teachers and teaching,[40] Jewish leaders (Mark 8:15; 12:38), persecution (Mark 13:9), and the second coming (Mark 13:33). Elsewhere, it is used in warnings against turning away from God (Heb 3:12) and in threats of judgment (Acts 13:40; Heb 12:25; 2 John 8). Paul uses *blepete* warning believers not to use their freedom in Christ to lead others to stumble (1 Cor 8:9), not fall from faith (1 Cor 10:12), of judgment (1 Cor 10:18), to live righteously (Eph 5:15), and of false teaching and teachers (Phil 3:2; Col 3:8).

Here he tells them to 'beware' or 'watch out' that they do not consume one another. The verb 'consume' is *analoō*, which also takes the form *analiskō*. The latter form is a third extremely strong verb in this verse. It is used in the LXX in a range of ways. These include its use of consumption, destruction, and devouring: of famine consuming Egypt (Gen 41:30), dead bodies consumed in the wilderness (Num 14:33), the poor consumed by the elite (Prov 24:37), fire devouring pastures, the land, wood, trees, and sacrifices,[41] and people consumed in death (Ezek 5:12).[42] The only other NT usage is in Luke 9:54, where Jacob and John ask Jesus whether he wants them to command fire to come down from heaven to consume or destroy the Samaritans who refused to welcome Jesus and his group into their town. The verb is passive and 'one another' is the agent of destruction.

As such, Paul is warning them that if they continue to tear at each other's throats, they will destroy themselves; they will be consumed. Such contention calls to mind Jesus' teaching that a kingdom divided against itself will be destroyed (Mark 3:24; Matt 12:25; Luke 11:17). Not only are they grappling with the heretical ideas of the Judaizers, but they are ripping themselves apart. Their behavior is in stark contrast to the two previous

---

40. See Matt 24:4; Mark 4:24; 13:5, 23; Luke 8:18; 21:8.

41. See Joel 1:19; 2:3; Ezek 15:4, 5; 19:12; 2 Macc 1:31; 2:10–11.

42. *Analoō* is also used of lawmakers destroyed (Prov 23:28), sacrifices consumed each day (1 Esd 6:29), a harvest destroyed (Isa 32:10), the unclean destroyed in the new heavens and earth (Isa 66:17).

verses which urge them to 'through love be slaves to one another' and to 'love your neighbor as yourself.'

In the forthcoming list of the works of the flesh in 5:19–21 and again in 5:26, he will refer to other aspects which likely characterize their interpersonal relationships: enmity, strife, jealousy, anger, rivalry, dissension, division, envy, conceit, provocation, and so on. These sit alongside other sins of the flesh likely known to them including sexual promiscuity, idolatry, sorcery, and drunkenness, etc. The Galatians must cultivate the fruit of the Spirit and live like those who are in Christ Jesus with their carnal desires crucified in him.

CHAPTER TWENTY-SEVEN: WALK IN THE SPIRIT (5:16–18)

Having warned them of the horrendous consequences of their dissension, Paul turns to urge them to leave behind a fleshly life and live by the Spirit. They are to walk in the Spirit, repudiating the cravings of the flesh that oppose the impulses of the Spirit. They are to be led by the Spirit, as they are not under the law. They are to repudiate the works of the flesh. People who live like this will not inherit God's kingdom and as royalty, they are not to fall prey to them. They are to allow the Spirit's fruit to grow in and through them—supremely love. No law can come against such attributes. As those who are in Christ with crucified flesh, they are to renounce their passions and desires and live by the Spirit, keeping in step with Spirit's leading, refusing to become arrogant, provocative, and full of envy.

This section is Paul's solution to the question raised by his argument that Christians are not under the law. How then, do we live? The key is the Spirit whose power burns gently in us urging us to live the life of God. The Christian life is not reaching for unattainable legal demands, but by yielding to the impulses of the Spirit toward love and goodness.

LIVE BY THE SPIRIT AND YOU WILL NOT GRATIFY CARNAL LUSTS (5:16)

In *Galatians 5:16*, Paul states:

But (*de*, 1:15) **I say** (*legō*, 1:9), **walk** (imperative *peripateō*)[1] **by**

---

1. The verb περιπατέω (*peripateō*) compounds *peri* (about) and *pateō* (walk) and figuratively speaks of a way of living. It is found once in Galatians 5:16, '*walk* by the Spirit,' but is used widely by Paul of the Christian 'walk' or life.

the Spirit (dative[2] *pneuma*, 3:2) **and** (*kai*, 1:1) **you will not carry out** (*teleō*)[3] **the desires** (*epithymia*)[4] **of the flesh** (genitive *sarx*, 1:16).

'But' translates *de*, Paul contrasting their horrendous infighting with the solution. 'I say,' introduces the content.

'Walk' is an imperative of *peripateō*, Paul's favorite term to describe the Christian life as a journey. *Peripateō* is commonly used of literal walking (e.g., Matt 4:18; Mark 5:42; Luke 24:17; John 1:36; Acts 3:6; Rev 2:1). Especially in Paul, *peripateō* is used of a mode of living. Outside of Paul, this use of *peripateō* is rarer (Mark 7:5; Acts 21:21; Heb 13:9; Rev 3:4; 21:24), except in John's letters where he urges them to walk in the light, truth, and obedience, rather than the darkness (1 John 1:6, 7; 2:6, 11; 2 John 4, 6; 3 John 3, 4).

'Walking' (הלך, *hlk*, 'walk') is a motif found in Judaism. It derives from texts which use the word in terms of conduct.[5] The term underlies the prominent Jewish idea of Halakah that concerns 'the application of the Torah to various daily aspects of human

---

2. The dative πνεύματι (*pneumati*, by the Spirit) may be a dative of rule (see on 6:16). A dative of rule 'specifies the rule or code a person follows or the standard of conduct to which he or she conforms.' (Wallace, *Greek Grammar*, 157). However, Wallace rightly notes that it can be a dative of sphere or means and rejects a dative of rule here as *pneuma* does not denote a rule or standard but rather speaks of empowerment.

3. The only use of the verb τελέω (*teleō*) in Galatians is in 5:16. The term is related to *telos*, 'end,' and speaks of something 'finished' or 'completed,' 'accomplished,' 'carried out,' 'performed,' 'fulfilled,' 'kept.' In 5:16, it speaks of carrying out or satisfying the desires of the flesh.

4. The noun ἐπιθυμία (*epithymia*) compounds *epi* (upon) and *thymos* which connotes a violent movement of something like air, water, or people. It can have the internal sense of the movement of spirit, anger, sensibility, the mind, thought, or desire. Paul uses *thymos* five times of God's rage at human sin (Rom 2:8) and in vice lists of human anger. The latter use is found in 5:20 which indicates that one of the presenting issues for the Galatians is fury toward one another (s.a., 2 Cor 12:20; Eph 4:31; Col 3:8). *Epithymia* and the verb *epithymeō* denote the direct impulse towards food, sexual satisfaction etc., and also, desire in general. In Paul, it speaks of the lusts of the flesh which stand against God's will for our lives and control us. Only by being led by the Spirit can we resist. This is the only use in Galatians, but it is found eighteen other times in Paul. See also *makrothymia*, 5:22—'patience' or distant *thymos*.

5. See Exod 16:4; 2 Kings 10:31; Jer 9:12; 26:4; 32:23; 44:10, 23; Pss. 78:10; 119:1; Dan 9:10; Neh 10:30; 2 Chron 6:16. See S. J. Stiles, 'Halakah,' in *LBD*.

conduct. Jesus and the New Testament writers lived in a period of intense halakic discourse and debate.[6] At this time, the Pharisees, in particular, held not only to the OT law but the oral Torah (a dual Torah). The oral Torah was placed alongside the written, purportedly passed down from generation to generation since Moses. This oral code was called the Halakah. After Jerusalem's destruction, the oral Torah formed the basis of the Mishnah and other Jewish texts (the Tosefta, Talmuds, and commentaries).[7]

Unsurprisingly for a Pharisee, by using *peripateō*, Paul invokes this tradition that was no doubt important to some, if not all the Judaizers, especially those who were Pharisees. Soon after Galatians was written, such Judaizing Pharisees feature in Acts 15:5 exhorting Judaizing notions at the Jerusalem Council. Rather than a Halakah based on Torah, whether written or oral, Paul exhorts a pneumatic Halakah. Believers are to 'walk' by the Spirit.

In Paul, *peripateō* is one of his favorite ways of describing the Christian life. He proposes an essential contrast between two modes of living—walking according to the flesh or Spirit (Rom 8:4). It also builds on the idea of running, used of Galatians in 5:7. They are not to be diverted from walking or running in the footsteps of the Spirit by the Judaizers cutting in on them.

To walk by the flesh is to allow one's passions to govern one's behavior. It is living to gratify the desires of the flesh. For Paul, living by Spirit is clearly preferred, the flesh corrupted by sin. Indeed, to come under the Torah, as the Judaizers desire that the Galatians do, is to walk according to the flesh. This is flawed for Paul, as to come under law to gain the status of righteousness requires self-effort. For Paul, this stands in contrast to the life God wants.

So, Paul can say to the Romans, 'as in the day, *walk* honorably, not in reveling and drunkenness, not in immorality and licentiousness, not in strife and jealousy (Rom 13:13). Similarly,

---

6. Stiles, 'Halakah.'
7. See further Stiles, 'Halakah.'

to the Corinthians, he says, 'for where there is jealousy and strife among you, are you *fleshly* and *walking* in a merely human way?' (1 Cor 3:3). To walk in the Spirit is to *walk* in the newness of life (Rom 6:4). Although Christians walk as all people, they do not walk by merely human standards (2 Cor 10:2–3). They are to walk by faith in God even if overwhelmed by what they see and experience (2 Cor 5:7). In Eph 2:1–3, before coming to faith (1:13), people *walk* in sin, following the world and its prince Satan—living in fleshly desires (s.a. Eph 4:17).

To walk in the Spirit is to walk in love (Rom 14:15), a love emulating Christ's sacrificial love for us (Eph 5:2). This is living by the pattern of the cross, which Paul teaches and seeks to embody for his disciples. This life, believers are to imitate (Phil 3:17), rather than take on the lifestyle of libertine enemies of the cross (Phil 3:18). This love expresses itself in good deeds God has prepared for us in advance by his Spirit (Eph 2:10). By God's power, believers live lives worthy of God and his call (Eph 4:1; 1 Thess 2:12), lives that please God, overflowing in good works (Col 1:10; 1 Thess 4:1).

This life is characterized by holiness, justice, mercy, compassion, sexual fidelity, marital faithfulness, and ethical integrity. In other words, they live as children of the light (Eph 5:8) and with godly wisdom (Eph 5:15). As a preacher, it means refusing to walk in fleshly ways such as cunning or deceit but seeking to commend oneself to others in God's sight (2 Cor 4:2; 12:18). This is the 'in Christ' life (Col 2:6), living God's way by the power of the Spirit, renouncing the depravity of our age (Col 3:7). Missionally, it means walking wisely before those outside the church with the hope that Christ draws them by his Spirit (Col 4:5; 1 Thess 4:12). It means not being a burden on others, bludging off charity, and working for one's living (2 Thess 3:6, 11).

Here, the verb is a present imperative, urging walking in the Spirit as their characteristic way of being. This is another of the direct appeals using an imperative that sprinkle Gal 4–6.[8]

---

8. See 4:12, 30; 5:1, 13, 15; 6:1, 2, 4, 6, 7, 11, 17, s.a., 5:14, 26; 6:10.

'By the Spirit' translates the simple dative of
pneuma—pneumati. This notion implicitly speaks of the law of
God 'written' on the heart and the believer living by the Spirit's
impulse. Commonly the dative is seen as a very rare dative of
agency (by, through) whereby the 'dative substantive is used to
indicate the personal agent by whom the action of the verb is
accomplished.'[9] Wallace argues against this on the basis of the
rarity of this kind of dative and because *pneumati* does not here
occur with a passive verb; the dative of agency usually occurring
with the perfect passive whereby the subject of the verb is the
agent.[10] Further, this may indicate a back-reading from later
theological understandings of the Spirit as a direct personal
agent. He argues that the dative is one of means or instrument
whereby the Spirit is the means or agency by which the believer
walks (lives).[11]

A dative of means is to be preferred not only on the grounds
Wallace has articulated but because it preserves the role of the
Christian in their life. *They* walk *by* the Spirit. The Spirit then
is not the active agent but is God's personal presence in the
believer prompting them to live in accordance with God's ways.
The believer then yields or fails to do so, preferring to live the
converse life—by the flesh. Paul here is commanding that they do
so.

What follows is translated by some as an imperative: 'and do
not gratify the desires of the flesh.' However, the verb *telesēte*
is not an imperative but a second person aorist subjunctive
indicating what results from walking in the Spirit, not an
additional command. The verb *teleō* is linked to *telos*, 'end, finish,
consummation, completion,' etc.

Outside of Paul, the verb is used of finishing a speech or
teaching (Matt 7:28; 11:1; 13:53; 19:1; 26:1; Rev 11:7), to
complete a legal requirement (Luke 2:39; Jas 2:8), the completion

---

9. Wallace, *Grammar*, 163.
10. Wallace, *Grammar*, 164.
11. Wallace, *Grammar*, 162 describes this: 'The dative substantive is used to indicate the
    means or instrument by which the verbal action is accomplished.' It is thus translated
    'by means of' or 'with.'

of the mystery of God (Rev 10:7), a mission completed (Matt 10:23), a period of suffering ending (Luke 12:50), the completion of God's wrath or plagues (Rev 15:1, 8), the fulfillment of prophetic hope (Acts 13:29; Rev 17:17), the millennium ending (Rev 20:3, 5, 7), and in Jesus' final cry from the cross, *tetelestai*, 'it is finished' (John 19:30, cf. John 19:28).[12]

Paul employs it once of paying taxes (Rom 13:6, cf. Matt 17:24). Otherwise, he employs it of keeping the law (Rom 2:27), of God's power completed in weakness (2 Cor 12:9), and of his completion of his life and ministry, his race (2 Tim 4:7). The term here suggests 'gratify' (ESV, NRSV, NIV), 'satisfy,'[13] or 'carry out' (NET) the desires of the flesh. It is negated by *ou mē*, which is 'the strongest way to negate something in Greek.'[14] So, if one walks in the Spirit, one will in no way satisfy the flesh.

In contrast with the Spirit, flesh (*sarx*) speaks of humanity in its fallenness, its corruption, and proneness to sin (see further 1:16). As discussed on 3:3, Paul regularly strikes a contrast between Spirit and flesh. His teaching here sits alongside Rom 8:1–17 in which he speaks of the freedom Christians have through the Spirit and how they must live in a way that pleases God by the Spirit and not the flesh that stands in opposition to God.

'Desires' is *epithymia*, which outside of Paul, speaks of desire, whether something positive such as Jesus' desire to eat the Passover with his disciples before his death (Luke 22:15), or negatively, of desires that stand counter to righteousness. In Mark's version of the Parable of the Sower, the 'desire for other things' chokes the effect of the word in the heart (Mark 4:19). *Epithymia* is also employed of Satan's desires (John 8:44), lusts birthed from temptation and which give birth to sin (Jas 1:14–15), sinful desires or passions (1 Pet 1:14; 4:2, 3), and corruption in the world due to lust (2 Pet 1:4).

Similar to Paul here in 5:16, Peter urges his readers to 'abstain from the *desires* of the flesh that wage war against the soul' (1 Pet 2:11). He also speaks of those who indulge the flesh in defiled

---

12. *Teleō* can also mean to make a payment (Matt 17:24).
13. BDAG 997.
14. Wallace, *Greek Grammar*, 468.

lust' (2 Pet 2:10) and the false teachers who entice people with 'licentious desires of the flesh.'[15] John similarly mentions the 'desire of the flesh, the desire of the eyes,' which with the world are passing away (1 John 2:16–17).

Half of the uses of *epithymia* in the NT are in Paul (nineteen of thirty-eight). Aside from Phil 1:23, where Paul uses it of his desire to be with Christ, and in 1 Thess 2:17 of Paul's desire to see the Thessalonians again, each use speaks of the passions or lusts of the body. These are God-given, but because of sin, they are perverted and have become agents of corruption where they are allowed to hold sway. Because of the rejection of God, God has given humanity up to 'the *desires* of their hearts for impurity, to the dishonoring of their bodies within themselves' (Rom 1:24).

The language is used in the tenth of the Ten Commandments—'do not covet' (Exod 20:17). Paul refers to this law, speaking of how awareness of the law does not inhibit sin, but produces it because of his fallenness (Rom 7:7–8). In Ephesians, unbelievers live in the 'the *desires* of our flesh' (Eph 2:3, s.a. 1 Thess 4:5), corrupt and deluded by the *lusts* of the old self (Eph 4:22). They are slaves to passions and pleasures (Tit 3:3). Those who live to please the lusts of the flesh, such as the love of money, like the false teachers of Ephesus, will be destroyed (1 Tim 6:9, s.a. 2 Tim 3:6; 4:3).

However, as believers and servants of righteousness, Christians are not to let sin rule their mortal bodies in obedience to these lusts (Rom 6:12). Similarly, in Rom 13:14, he urges the Romans to 'put on the Lord Jesus Christ and make not provision for the flesh to satisfy its *desires*' (Rom 13:14). In Gal 5:24, he will use the term again stating that 'those who belong to Christ Jesus have crucified the flesh with its passions and *desires*.' Again, in Col 3:5, believers are to put to death *epithymia* alongside a range of other sins. So, Timothy is to shun youthful *epithymia* and pursue righteousness, faith, love, and peace (2 Tim 2:22). Similarly, Paul urges that believers are to 'renounce impiety and

15. See 2 Pet 2:18, s.a., 2 Pet 3:3; Jude 16, 18; Rev 18:14.

worldly *passions*, and in the present age, be self-controlled, righteous, and godly' (Tit 2:12, NRSV).

Galatians 5:16 gives the key to how this is to be done—by the power of the Spirit. The cauldron of God's power that simmers in us continually is the missing ingredient for gaining control of the passions of the flesh. Humanity in its fallen Adamic state may have some ability to control the desires of the flesh, but this is limited and achieved only through grim determination and legalistic observance. There is no latent power in the law to help live it out.

While it can be argued that people have some power to resist, this is weak at best. The power of desire is simply too strong most of the time for us to tame. We are subject to many and various desires and cannot resist. Certainly, no one can overcome them all the time from conception to death. So, we fall prey to these desires. We often succumb to a desire, and it enslaves us. This enslavement happens with sexual desire, as we cannot consistently overcome our desires and we find ourselves seeking to gratify our desire with pleasure. We can say the same of the lust for power, for wealth, for honor, and more. We become addicted, utterly enslaved whether it be to alcohol, drugs, pleasure, sex, money, travel, sport, and more. What are in themselves not bad things become warped, and we are enslaved. We are often forced to live a double life, hiding our sin, held in its grip, terrified of it becoming known. If we do not deal with them, they can become openings for Satan to further distort our desires so that they become compulsive and uncontrollable.

Here we see the solution. Jesus died on the cross and overcame sin. As the writer of Hebrews tells us, he was tempted in every way but was without sin (Heb 4:15). Paul, similarly, speaks of Jesus, who knew no sin becoming sin for humankind so that in him, they can become the righteousness of God (2 Cor 5:21). Where faith is found, his death crucified sin. In his body of death, he consumed our sin. It is dealt with in his death. Because of this, we are holy, clean, and pure before God. Hence, God, who cannot dwell eternally with evil (Ps 5:4), can now live in us for we are purified by the blood of the paschal lamb (1 Cor 5:7).

His presence in us by the Spirit is the power that will enable us to overcome any lust of the flesh if we are prepared to yield to him. Although our status and identity are dead to sin, sin remains active in the world and within us, our flesh fighting for control.

The key to victory is to 'walk in the Spirit.' A critical factor to walking in the Spirit is prayer, cultivating a deep relationship with God so that we grow in our ability to hear his whisperings and impulses. Similarly, God speaks through others in community, so ongoing fellowship with other Christians through whom God can speak, is vital. As we pray, gather, and walk in the Spirit, we hear, we practice obedience, and victory can be won. This submission to the Spirit is not merely 'let go and let God,' but an active yielding that leads to us living disciplined lives of self-control (see the ninth Spirit-fruit in 5:23).

The impulses of the Spirit need not be something specific like a loud voice saying, 'do not touch, do not look,' although such experiences cannot be ruled out. Rather, this speaks of a living relationship with God, whereby he gently prompts us inwardly toward love, holiness, and goodness.

THE ENMITY OF FLESH AND SPIRIT (5:17)

In *Galatians 5:17*, Paul draws out the contrast between the two ethical forces functioning in the life of the believer:

For (*gar*, 1:10) **the flesh** (*sarx*, 1:16) **desires** (present *epithymeō*)[16] **against** (*kata*, 1:4) **the Spirit** (*pneuma*, 3:2), **and** (*de*, 1:15) **the Spirit** (*pneuma*) **is against** (*kata*) **the flesh** (*sarx*), **for** (*gar*) **these things** (neuter plural *houtos*, 2:10) **[are] in opposition** (present middle *antikeimai*)[17] **to one another** (dative *allēlōn*, 5:13); **so that** (*hina*, 1:16), **the things** (neuter plural *hos*, 1:5) **you might** (*ean*, 1:8)

---

16. The verb ἐπιθυμέω (*epithymeō*) is associated with *epithymos* in the previous note. It is formed with *epi* and *thymos* (above) and means to have a strong desire, to long for something, and can specifically refer to sexual desire. It is only used in Galatians in 5:17 of the desire of the flesh which opposes the Spirit. Paul uses it on four other occasions in commands not to covet (Rom 7:7; 13:9), of desiring evil (1 Cor 10:6) or wanting a noble role like being an elder (1 Tim 3:1).

17. The verb ἀντίκειμαι (*antikeimai*) compounds *anti* (against) and *keimai* (lie, recline, exist, be there) and speaks of being in a state of opposition. It features only in Gal 5:17. It

want (present subjunctive *thelō*, 1:7) **[to do], these things** (neuter plural *houtos*) **you are not** (*mē*, 1:7) **doing** (present subjunctive *poieō*, 2:10).

There is neat parallelism here in 5:17a–b, whereby *sarx*, 'flesh,' *kata*, 'against,' and *pneuma*, 'Spirit' are all repeated. The verb *epithymeō*, 'desires' is implied in the second half:

For the flesh desires against the Spirit (*ē gar* **sarx** *epithymei* **kata** *tou* **pneumatos**)

And the Spirit [desires] against the flesh (*to de* **pneuma** *kata* *tēs* **sarkos**).

'For' is *gar*, which here is explanatory—giving a further understanding of the antithesis of Spirit and flesh, and Paul's appeal that the Galatians walk according to the Spirit.

He uses the verb associated with *epithymia* from the previous verse, *epithymeō*. The verb as with the noun compounds *epi* and *thymos* and speaks of desires or lust. Outside of Paul's letters, it is found eleven times, sometimes of a positive longing for something, such as the coming of the Messiah (Matt 13:17; Luke 17:22), people (the prodigal son and Lazarus) longing for food (Luke 15:16; 16:21), and Jesus' longing to have Passover with the disciples (Luke 22:15). It is sometimes negative, as in coveting another's money or clothes (Acts 20:33), or sexual lust (Matt 5:28).

For Paul, aside from 1 Tim 3:1 where *epithymeō* is used for desiring the noble office of eldership, the verb is negative. Twice with the negation *mē*, it translates the tenth command of the Decalogue: 'do not covet' (Rom 7:7; 13:9). Otherwise, it is used of Israel's desire for evil in the wilderness (1 Cor 10:6). Here, the flesh is personified as the subject of the verb and so the flesh and all that it stands for, opposes the Spirit and his desires. This speaks of sin standing in stark enmity to God; not just the Spirit itself, but the things the flesh desires (*tauta* and *ha* in parts c and d of the verse). Fifteen of these things Paul will list in vv. 19–21. One can think of much more. I do every day when I look in

---

means 'enemy,' 'adversary,' or 'opponent' and so speaks of real enmity and opposition. They are opposing forces.

the mirror and see the 'wretched man I am!'—'thanks be to God through Jesus Christ our Lord' that he has rescued 'me from this body of death' (Rom 7:24–25). The impulses of the flesh in all forms are antithetical to the things the Spirit wants to cultivate in our lives.

'Against the Spirit' essentially means against the very essence of the Spirit, who is goodness, purity, and love, and the things that the Spirit wants. Nine of these things are outlined in the famous 'fruit of the Spirit' passage which will soon follow (vv. 22–23). 'Against' translated from *kata* which as discussed on 2:11, is used five times of 'against' in the letter (s.a. 2:11; 3:21; 5:23). It speaks of hostility between the flesh and Spirit.

In part b of the verse, the converse is stated; and the Spirit is against the flesh. This does not mean that the Spirit opposes creatures of flesh, but their impulse to sin.

'For these things are in opposition to one another' uses *antikeimai*, which compounds *anti* (against) and *keimai* which has a range including 'lie,' 'recline,' 'be,' 'appoint,' 'destined,' 'exist.'[18] The compound has the sense of being opposed or an adversary to another. In its two non-Pauline NT uses, it speaks of Jesus' opponents put to shame in debate (Luke 13:17) and of Christ enabling Christians to speak with such wisdom that their adversaries will not be able to withstand and contradict (Luke 21:15).

Paul uses it of his many opponents in Ephesus (1 Cor 16:9) and of the Philippian's opponents, before whom they must not be afraid (Phil 1:28). In 1 Tim 5:14 it is used of Satan, 'the adversary!' In 1 Tim 1:10, with some parallel to his use here in Galatians, he speaks of a range of sins which are 'contrary to sound doctrine.' So here, the verb speaks of the flesh and Spirit being in opposition to each other. They are adversaries.

Here we see another use of 'one another' *allēlōn*, here not in the sense he often uses in his 'one another' ethical statements,

---

18. BDAG 538. *Keimai* is used in Paul of a foundation laid (1 Cor 3:11), a veil that is laid over the heart (2 Cor 3:15), of being appointed for the defense of the gospel (Phil 1:16), of being destined for affliction (1 Thess 3:3), and the law laid down for sinners (1 Tim 1:9).

whether positive (e.g., 'love one another,' 5:13; 'bear one another's burdens, 6:2) or negative (5:26). Rather, it is the Spirit of God and the fallen human flesh as two beings in historical and mortal conflict with *one another*.

The challenge of the Christian life is yielding to the Spirit so that the flesh is mortified and the Spirit gains sway in our lives. With the Spirit, we have God's glorious power in us to enable us to defeat the lusts of the flesh—it is up to us to yield, and by his power, to put in place the habits and practices that will further enable us to do so.

The final clause requires some thought. Some things are clear. The negation *mē* goes with the main verb, *poiēte*, rather than with *thelēte*. Paul again uses *thelō*, 'I will, wish,' a verb often found in the letter as he moves between his own will (3:2; 4:20), the Judaizers' (1:7; 4:17; 6:12, 13), and the Galatians' (4:9, 21). As noted on 1:4 and 7, this forms another moment in the battle for the wills of the Galatians. God through Paul is calling them to his Willed One, Jesus. The Judaizers are summoning them to a false 'gospel.' Who will they yield to?

'These things' (*tauta*) is dependent on *ha* (the things). However, beyond this, the clause is very difficult. First, it is launched by a *hina*, which can lead into a purpose clause, a result clause, is explanatory, or consecutive. A decision on this depends on how what follows is understood. Second, 'the things you might want to do' can be negative—the things of the flesh; positive—the things of the Spirit; or general—the things you want to do per se.

As a consequence, there are three main ways this is construed. First, some take 'the things' (*ha*) as those things people want to do *to please the Spirit* with the *hina* indicating result—they cannot do them because of the flesh.[19] Believers seek to do what the Spirit wants, but because of the flesh, they fall short. For some, this is like a condensed version of Rom 7:14–25.[20] Hence, people want to do good, but the flesh gets in the way. This view has a couple of problems. First, it is not clear Rom 7:14–25 is about the

---

19. Wallace, *Greek Grammar*, 473 takes it as assured result; however, this is disputable.
20. Morris, *Galatians*, 169; George, *Galatians*, 387–88.

Christian experience; more likely, it is Paul the Christian's view looking back to his life under the law. Furthermore, as Galatians repeatedly reminds us, a Christian is not under the law so it must be the Jewish experience that is in mind. Second, some rightly question whether *ean thelēte* (if you want) is an appropriate way of speaking about 'the good things the Christian wants to do.'[21]

A second approach is that those things they wish to do are those that *the flesh wants*, with *hina* a purpose clause. The Spirit then opposes the desires of the flesh so that people will not do them.[22] Some who take it this way see the *hina* as signaling a result imperative clause, 'so that you are not to do whatever you want' (NIV). However, this runs converse to the thinking of the passage, whereby being led by the Spirit enables people to defeat the desires of the flesh.

The third alternative is that 'willing' here speaks of general human will, either toward good or in the direction of evil. The *hina* then is consecutive, 'that,' or it signals a result clause explaining the desire for good or evil that characterizes human existence. So, whatever one wishes to do, whether to please God or to satisfy the flesh, believers cannot do what they want for the Spirit stands against their bad behavior and the flesh against their good. Believers are at the whim of these forces. The implication is that they should do what the Spirit wants. Most contemporary scholars adopt this perspective.[23] It seems the best of three alternatives as it continues the theme of the conflict between the flesh and Spirit—both seeking to stop a person living by the other's impulses. In 5:18 (and 5:16), Paul explains how a person can overcome the desires of the flesh.

LED BY THE SPIRIT AND NOT UNDER THE LAW (5:18)

In *Galatians 5:18*, Paul introduces his pneumatological

---

21. Moo, *Galatians*, 355.
22. Witherington, Galatians, 395; Gordon D. Fee, *God's Empowering Presence: The Holy Spirit in the Letters of Paul* (Peabody: Hendriksen, 1995), 436.
23. See e.g., Moo, *Galatians*, 354–56; Longenecker, *Galatians*, 246; Dunn, *Galatians*, 299.

discussion of the law, which the Judaizers want the Galatians to come under:

But (*de*, 1:15) **if** (*ei*, 1:7) **you are led** (present passive *agō*) **by the Spirit** (dative *pneuma*, 3:2), **you are** (present *eimi*, 1:7) **not** (*ou*, 1:1) **under** (*hypo*, 1:11) **the law** (*nomos*, 2:16).[24]

The *de* is adversative, 'but,' speaking of the state of someone who is led by the Spirit. The verse is in the form of a first-class conditional sentence launched by *ei* with the present passive indicative, assuming in the protasis something true for the sake of argument (see on 1:9)—if you are being led by the Spirit. The verb is the second person plural, so he speaks directly to the Galatians (you). The verb *agō* is here used in its basic sense of 'led,' the passive indicating another agency—the Spirit.

Paul uses the verb *agō* found sixty-nine times.[25] The idea of being led by the Spirit is found of Christ, who is led into the wilderness by the Spirit to face Satan (Luke 4:1). Paul uses it seven times including God's kindness leading a person to repentance (Rom 2:4). He employs it negatively of the false leading of pagan gods (1 Cor 12:2) and, consistently with this passage, of being led astray by various desires (*epithymia*) (2 Tim 3:6). In Rom 8:14, those 'led by the Spirit of God are God's sons and daughters.'[26]

Here, 'led by the Spirit' stands in contrast to being led by the desires of the flesh. It is synonymous with 'walking by the Spirit' in 5:16, the image here of a tramping guide leading someone as they walk. As in 5:16, it speaks of a believer living in a yielded state before God, allowing their lives to be shaped by the Spirit and not carnal desire. It is God going ahead of us and us walking into the life he has for us.

The apodosis draws out the consequence of the Galatians

---

24. The verb ἄγω (*agō*), 'lead,' is found once in Paul's statement 'if you are led by the Spirit, you are not under the law.'

25. In other NT writings *agō* is used of 'lead, led' including people led to face a judiciary or punishment (e.g., Matt 10:18; Mark 13:11; Luke 4:29; 19:27; 22:54; 23:32; John 18:13; Acts 6:12; 25:6), and of leading a donkey (e.g., Matt 21:2, 7) or sheep (Acts 8:32).

26. Paul also uses *agō* in the sense 'bring,' of those Jesus brings with him at his return (1 Thess 4:17) and of Timothy bringing Mark with him to Paul in Rome (2 Tim 4:11).

being led by the Spirit—'then, you are not under the law.' As in other uses of 'under the law' in Galatians, it means the Jewish legal expectations. Here it means one is not 'subject to the rule of the law.'[27] The Jews were held captive under the law from Sinai to Christ (3:23). Faith has come as 'God has sent his Son, born under the law, to redeem those who were under the law' so that they would be children of God who have received the Spirit of adoption.

The Galatians were not under the law prior to Christ but must not allow themselves to be enticed under the law, for they will be in the same hapless state as Israel who rejects her Messiah. Rather, they are to be led by the Spirit as they go about their lives. To go under the law will ignite the passions of the flesh and drive the person further from God and deeper into sin. On the contrary, if they are led by the Spirit, they will find God's life growing in them; they will be transformed from people who live by the works of the flesh to people who overflow with Spirit-fruit.

1. midst are: **sexual immorality** (*porneia*), adultery, theft, slander, false swearing, **drunkenness** (*methē*), **strife** (*eris*), **jealousy** (*zēlos*), grumbling, gossip, **idolatry** (*eidōlolatria*), divination, **and such things** (*kai ta toutois homoia*) they are then workers of such works, and of others that are worse.' (My translation).
2. 1 Enoch 91:6–7: 'Oppression shall recur once more and be carried out upon the earth; every form of oppression, injustice, and iniquity shall infect the world twofold. When sin, oppression, blasphemy, and injustice increase, crime, iniquity, and uncleanliness shall be committed and increase likewise.' (Charlesworth).
3. 2 Enoch 10:4–6: 'This place, Enoch, has been prepared for those who do not glorify God, who practice on the earth the sin which is against nature, which is child corruption in the anus in the manner of Sodom of

---

27. Moo, *Galatians*, 357.

witchcraft, enchantments, divinations, trafficking with demons, who boast about their evil deeds—stealing, lying, insulting, coveting, resentment, fornication, murder and who steal the souls of men secretly, seizing the poor by the throat, taking away their possessions, enriching themselves from the possessions of others, defrauding them; who, when they are able to provide sustenance, bring about the death of the hungry by starvation; and, when they are able to provide clothing, take away the last garment of the naked; who do not acknowledge their Creator, but bow down to idols which have no souls, which can neither see nor hear, vain gods; constructing images, and bowing down to vile things made by hands—for all these this place has been prepared as an eternal reward.' (cf. 2 Enoch 34:1–2). (Charlesworth).

4. 4 Maccabees 1:3: 'If, then, it is evident that reason rules over those emotions that hinder self-control, namely, gluttony and **lust** (*epithymia*), it is also clear that it masters the emotions that hinder one from justice, such as malice, and those that stand in the way of courage, namely **anger** (*thymos*), fear, and pain.' (NRSV).

5. 4 Maccabees 1:26–27: 'In pleasure there exists even a malevolent tendency, which is the most complex of all the emotions. In the soul it is boastfulness, covetousness, thirst for honor, rivalry, and malice; in the body, indiscriminate eating, gluttony, and solitary gormandizing.' (NRSV).

6. 4 Maccabees 2:15: 'It is evident that reason rules even the more violent emotions: lust for power, vainglory, boasting, arrogance, and malice.' (NRSV).

7. 1QS 4:9–11: 'However, to the spirit of deceit belong greed, sluggishness in the service of justice, wickedness, falsehood, pride, haughtiness of heart, dishonesty, trickery, cruelty, much insincerity, impatience, much foolishness, impudent enthusiasm for appalling acts performed in a lustful passion, filthy paths in the service

of impurity, blasphemous tongue, blindness of eyes, hardness of hearing, stiffness of neck, hardness of heart in order to walk in all the paths of darkness and evil cunning.'

Such texts demonstrate that vice lists were common in Jewish thought. However, the Christian Paul shapes his vice lists in relation to his renewed understanding of God, Christ, the Spirit, and the gospel. They are also put together with the context in mind—each list giving vital clues as to the core sinful tendencies of his recipients and the wider milieu. Such texts demonstrate that vice lists were common in Jewish and Christian thought.

As we look at Paul's list in Gal 5:19–21, none of the NT or other lists is quite the same. There are similarities with Mark 7:21–23 (three common terms); 1 Pet 4:2–3 (four common terms plus *epithymia* from the chapter), and Rev 21:8 and 15 (both with three common terms). The largest resemblances with his own lists are with Rom 1:29–31 and 1 Cor 5:10–11, both with five common terms, and 2 Cor 12:20–21 with seven terms in common. Several also state that those who do such things will not inherit the kingdom, including 1 Cor 6:9–10. Ephesians 5:3–5 has five terms in common and includes a statement precluding kingdom inheritance. Of the wider sources, 3 Baruch 8:5 includes five common ideas. With that said, the list here is unique and shaped to the Galatian situation.

CHAPTER 28

CHAPTER TWENTY-EIGHT: WALK AWAY FROM THE WORKS OF THE FLESH (5:19–21)

THE VICE LIST OF GALATIANS 5:19–21

In *Galatians 5:19*, he introduces the list and launches it with three descriptors that target sexually immoral behavior:

And (*de*, 1:15) **the works** (plural *ergon*, 2:16) **of the flesh** (genitive *sarx*, 1:16) **are obvious** (*phaneros*).[1] **These things** (plural neuter *hostis*, 2:4) **are** (present *eimi*, 1:7)**: sexual immorality** (*porneia*),[2] **impurity** (*akatharsia*),[3] **debauchery** (*aselgeia*).[4]

'The *works* of the flesh' uses *ergon*, also used in the construct

---

1. The only reference to the adjective φανερός (*phaneros*) is in 5:19 of works of the flesh which are 'evident,' 'obvious,' or 'apparent.'
2. The standard NT term for sexual immorality, πορνεία (*porneia*) is found once in Galatians at the head of the list of the works of the flesh in 5:19. While the term has its origins in prostitution, it effectively means any sexual activity outside of heterosexual, lawful marriage—whether same-sex, pre-marital sex, adultery, engaging in pornography, masturbation, non-consensual sexual relationships, foreplay outside of marriage, sex with animals, etc. While sexual desire is God-given and essential for the propagation of the species, it is the warping of God's intention expressed especially in Gen 1:27–28 and 2:24. See BADG 693, which states it means '*prostitution, unchastity, fornication,* of every kind of unlawful sexual intercourse' (emphasis theirs).
3. There is one reference in the vice list of 5:19–21 to the noun ἀκαθαρσία (*akatharsia*) which can mean 'rubbish,' but speaks of 'uncleanness,' 'moral corruption,' 'vileness,' or 'immorality.'
4. A third term in the list of 5:19–21 which is only found once in Galatians is ἀσέλγεια (*aselgeia*) which means a 'lack of self-constraint which involves one in conduct that violates all bounds of what is socially acceptable, self-abandonment' (BDAG 141). It speaks of a lack of self-control, and so can be translated as debauchery, licentiousness. As with the two previous terms, sexual immorality is associated with this along with excessive alcohol, revelry, gluttony, and other debauched behavior.

'*works* of the law.' In terms of the enmity of the flesh and Spirit referred to in v. 18, the clause speaks of some of those things that the flesh seeks to excite in people.

'Are obvious' is a little ambiguous and problematic for many today. The term is *phaneros*, placed first for stress. In its nine non-Pauline NT uses, it is used of a person or their name made known (Matt 12:16; Mark 3:12; 6:14; Acts 7:13), the exposing of something secret (Mark 4:22; Luke 8:17). It has the sense of something evident, such as the fact that a miracle has been done (Acts 4:16), or that some are the children of God (1 John 3:10). Paul uses it of a person's outward physical state (Rom 2:28). Otherwise, it indicates something made plain or clear such as a person's work and heart on judgment day (1 Cor 3:13; 14:25), someone seen for who they are (1 Cor 11:19; 1 Tim 4:15), and the reason for Paul's imprisonment made clear (Phil 1:13). Here, his use is comparable to Rom 1:19, where he speaks of God's reality being evident through creation (Rom 1:19). For Paul, the works of the flesh are similarly evident, clear, obvious, or plain to perceive.

From the perspective of many in the gentile world (and many in our world today), such a claim would be disputed, as for many, things like sexual immorality, lust, idolatry, sorcery, and drunkenness were (are) culturally normalized. Paul is thinking as someone steeped in the gospel and Israel's law and story. For a Jewish thinker, these things are evident and obvious. With his understanding of creational heterosexual marital sexuality (Gen 1:27–28; 2:24; 1 Cor 6:16; Eph 5:31), any sexual desire expressed outside of monogamous heterosexual marriage is clearly a work of the flesh. For many in the Greco-Roman world, this would be the same with some moralists endorsing sexual fidelity (see below). His views of sorcery and idolatry would not be so readily evident to those from the gentile world. The use of occult methods, such as divination, was commonplace. As discussed on 4:8, idolatry was an essential aspect of the fabric of the Roman and Asian worlds. However, for a Jew steeped in God's law, any occult activity and idolatry were repudiated, at least at a theological level. Hence, Paul here is speaking from the perspective of his understanding of God and the ethics he desires of humanity.

Implicit here is Paul drawing on the essential goodness of the law (Rom 7:12). Paul's ethics are drawn in great part from his positive view of the law. While Christians are no longer subject to the law (having been redeemed from enslavement to it), the law still reveals God's ethics in many instances. It still reflects the heart of God. Indeed, sin is revealed in the light of the law (Rom 3:20; 7:7–12, cf. Gal 3:19). The law may have no latent power to help a person to please God and be righteous before him by doing it, but it still gives critical insight into God's ideals.

At no point does Paul repudiate the central laws, especially the Decalogue. So, in Rom 13:8, to love one another is to fulfill the law. The love command is the sum of the law. However, this does not render laws such as those mentioned in Rom 13:9 as redundant and worthless—rather, they are aspects of the love law and are to be lived within a love framework. 'You shall not commit adultery' within the framework of the law of love remains active for Paul (cf. 1 Cor 6:9). Similarly, one should not murder (cf. Rom 1:29). Thieving is still repudiated (1 Cor 6:8, 10; Eph 4:28). To covet is still sinful (Rom 1:29; 7:7–8; Eph 5:3, 5; Col 3:5). As such, for Paul, the works of the flesh are evident both from the perspective of the way in which they breed destruction in society, and because God has made known by his revelation what these things are.

Most translations simplify the Greek introduction not translating the last clause *hatina estin*, 'and the works of the flesh are obvious; such things are (*hatina estin*)...' The final clause of 5:19 ('such things are') along with *kai ta homoia toutois* in 5:21 (and the things like these), which comes at the end of the list, reinforces that Paul is being selective. There are many other such things (see the lists above for a few more).

The first mentioned in the list is *porneia*. The term is not widely found in wider Greek sources. Its main use is for prostitution,[5]

---

5. See, e.g., Dionysius of Halicarnassus, *Ant. rom.* 4.24.4; Athenaeus, *Deipn.* 13.595b; Aeschines, *Tim.* 124.

although it can have a wider sense of sexual immorality (e.g., Aeschines, *Tim.* 144). It is often argued that *porneia* does not refer to sexual immorality in a general sense, inclusive of a wide range of sexual immorality. However, this does not bear up under an analysis of the term in Jewish Greek literature. This can be easily demonstrated.

In the LXX, *porneia* is sometimes used in its figurative sense of idolatrous (adulterous) unfaithfulness to God to whom Israel is betrothed.[6] In these uses, unless specified as in Nah 3, the image is not one of prostitution, for which one receives wages, but of marital unfaithfulness—adultery. It is used for adultery (Gen 38:24;[7] Sir 23:23;[8] 26:9[9]), general sexual immorality (Sir 41:17[10]; Tob 4:12;[11] Hos 1:2;[12] 2:2), premarital sexual relations (Tob 8:7[13]), and only occasionally of prostitution (Mic 1:7[14]).

---

6. See Num 14:33; 2 Kings 9:22; Wis 14:12; Hos 4:11, 12; 5:4; 6:10; Isa 47:10; 57:9; Jer 2:20; 3:2; 13:27; Ezek 16:15, 22, 25, 33, 34, 36, 41; 23:7, 8, 11, 14, 17, 18, 19, 27, 29, 35; 43:7, 9, s.a., Nah 3:3–4 of Nineveh.

7. While Tamar poses as a prostitute, the Hebrew text uses זָנָה (zā·nā(h)) which can mean 'prostitute' but in context, Tamar is being rebuked at this point of the discussion for her unfaithfulness without any specifics. She is condemned to be burned to death. She then reveals what she has done. Hence, *porneia* here is general rather than the more specialized meaning found in some contexts—prostitution.

8. Here *porneia* refers to a married woman who becomes pregnant from someone other than her husband. Hence, this is not prostitution but marital infidelity; adultery.

9. In context, this is found in a discussion of a wife who is adulterous and given away by the way she looks at another man.

10. This is a general warning to be ashamed of sexual immorality before one's parents.

11. This is general—'beware, my son, of every kind of *porneia*.' D. Stuart, *Hosea–Jonah* (WBC 31; Dallas: Word, 2002), 26 states: 'The term אשת זנונים cannot mean "a prostitute" or "a prostitute for a wife." "Prostitute" would appear in Hebrew as either זונה or אשה זונה (cf. Josh 2:1; Judg 11:1; etc.). Instead זנונים as a plural abstract refers more to a trait than a profession. The entire sequence of events in chaps. 1–3 demonstrates nothing about Gomer's marital faithfulness. There is no evidence that she was adulterous and none that she was a practicing prostitute.' As such, we should consider this general rather than specific prostitution. Alternatively, she is an adulteress.

12. The Hebrew זְנוּנִים (zenû·nîm) cannot be limited to prostitution as is assumed by many translations and scholars.

13. A marriage not based on *porneia* but with sincerity, i.e., not a shotgun wedding or because a man violated a woman's honor and was forced to marry her.

14. The phrase 'wages of a prostitute' indicate a specific form of *porneia* here, prostitution.

Pseudepigraphal use includes sexual unfaithfulness in a general sense,[15] adultery,[16] incest/adultery (T. Reu. 1.6; T. Jud. 13:3), pre-marital sex (T. Jos. 3.8), general sexual relationships including homosexuality and rape (T. Benj. 9:1), and rarely, prostitution (T. Jud. 12.2).

While Josephus does not use the term, Philo's two uses are of general sexual immorality (rather than prostitution) (Philo, *Mos.* 1.300) and figuratively, of the promiscuity of the soul (in a general non-specifically prostitution sense) (*Spec.* 1.282).

New Testament use beyond Paul includes adultery (Matt 5:32; 19:9;[17] John 8:41[18]), general sexual immorality (Matt 15:19; Mark 7:21;[19] Acts 15:20, 29; 21:25[20]), and idolatry.[21] The use of the term in the Apostolic Fathers is also of general sexual immorality (*Did.* 3:3; 5:1; Herm. *Mand.* 4.1.1; 8.3) or adultery (Herm. *Mand.* 4.1.5).

Paul utilizes *porneia* ten times overall. In 1 Corinthians 5:1, it is used of incest/adultery, a man sleeping with his father's wife, his stepmother (cf. Lev 18:9). The use in 1 Cor 6:14 includes sex with a prostitute but need not be limited to this specific sexual activity any more than we can specify the particular food in mind in this text; rather, the context includes the sexual immorality of Ch. 5 and anything else that the Corinthians are engaging in. Genesis 2:24 is cited, indicating that this sets the basis for Paul's sexual ethic—sexual activity is for those who are in a monogamous

---

15. See 1 En. 10:8; 3 Bar. 4:17; 8:5; T. Reu. 3:3; 4:6, 7, 8, 11; 5:3; 6:1, 4; T. Sim. 5:3, 4; T. Levi 9:9.

16. See 3 Bar. 13:4; T. Reu. 5:5; T. Jud. 14:2, 3; 15:1; 18:2; T. Dan 5:6; T. Benj. 8:2; 10:10; Mart. Asen. Isa. 2:5; 3:28.

17. The context of marriage is specified in both Matt 5:32 and 19:9. The nature of this adultery could include any form of sexual immorality that violates Gen 2:24.

18. 'Born from sexual immorality' here is most likely spiritual adultery; they are not born of God but are idolatrous, seen in their rejection of God's Son.

19. In both Mark 7:21 and Matt 15:19 the command is general without specificity. In a Jewish setting, it would involve anything that violates the premise of Gen 2:24.

20. Acts 21:25 is general and like Mark 7:21 and Matt 15:19, would include any violation of Gen 2:24. It is argued that this is a cultural accommodation for context as are the other requirements of the gentiles. However, unlike the other requirements, the whole Biblical Corpus supports this ban indicating that this is stating a universal expectation.

21. See Rev 2:21; 9:21; 14:8; 17:2, 4; 18:3; 19:2.

heterosexual marriage which is ideally speaking, faithful and loving. It is disputed whether Paul would consider sex within a second marriage was *porneia*. Likely, he would do so in all second marriages other than where a believer is divorced by an unbeliever and so is no longer enslaved (1 Cor 7:15).[22]

Paul's attitude to all sexual activities that violate Gen 2:24 is summed up in 1 Cor 6:18, in exactly the words found in T. Reub. 5:5: 'flee *porneia!*' They are to do as Joseph did in Gen 39:12 (cf. T. Reub. 6:1). Where a Christian is struggling with sexual immorality, he urges marriage (1 Cor 7:2). The term features in other vice lists (2 Cor 12:21; Eph 5:3). In Eph 5:3, it is not to be even mentioned among Christians. Sexual desire must be put to death (Col 3:5) and abstained from (1 Thess 4:3). The term in Gal 5:19 likely heads the list because, as in all the Greco-Roman world, it is a particularly prevalent problem. As in our increasingly liberal world in which we can access porn at will and all manner of sexual opportunities are available, we need to hear Paul loud and clear here. There is no place for sexual immorality in God's people. It is the work of the flesh. It is as Jesus says in Mark 7:21, one of those 'evil things' that defile a person.

Some argue that there is little in the NT concerning homosexuality as a sin. This is simply untrue as every reference to *porneia* includes all manner of sexual immorality that violates God's ideal of monogamous heterosexual marriage, whether it be pedophilia, rape, premarital sex, homosexuality, bestiality, necrophilia, accessing pornography, or any other form of sex one can imagine.

Pornography is a special challenge for our culture. The problem with it is that it objectifies real people and by using them for our pleasure, we denigrate them, their creator, and our

---

22. See the discussion of this in R. E. Ciampa and B. S. Rosner, *The First Letter to the Corinthians*, PNTC (Grand Rapids, MI; Cambridge, U.K.: Eerdmans, 2010), 302 who note that such language in all Jewish and most Greco-Roman divorce certificates indicates that the person is free to marry any person that the divorcee wishes. They state, '[t]hat is, spouses are not stuck in the slavery of a no-man's-land where they have no spouse (because they have been abandoned) and yet are not able to remarry (because they remain married). They are free. They see this then as parallel to Rom 7:2 where a spouse has died.

own bodies. We dehumanize people for the pleasures of the flesh. If we are married or in a serious relationship, we sin against our loved ones. We grieve the Spirit who is in us. We also warp our sexuality as the things that are done become normalized. With such vile material freely available on our devices, one of the greatest challenges today is to discipline ourselves so that we do not look at this stuff.[23] Some argue masturbation is ok for Christians. The problem is not the act but where the mind goes—and this makes it sin. Rather, a Christian, by the Spirit (and if need be, counseling), should seek mastery over the desires of the body and train themselves in sexual purity.

With that said, the Bible is not against sex. Sex is a glorious gift of God for the propagation of the species and to express marital love and union. Within the bounds of God's ideals, it is truly wonderful and beautiful. However, like all desires of the flesh, it always threatens to enslave us, addict us, and drive us into self-hate and despair as we fall prey to carnal desire.

When this happens, we must seek help as with all addictions. We find professional Christian counsel and prayer, and by the Spirit, we can overcome this. We make ourselves accountable to others we trust, and we share our struggles, find grace and forgiveness, and are strengthened as we pray for each and hold each other accountable. There are simply no grounds for the church to move away from the NT sexual ethic. The church grew up in a Greco-Roman world where 'anything goes.' Not for one minute did they yield to the sexual immorality of their world. The world can do what it wants where marriage and sexuality are concerned. God will be its judge. We are to be engaged in this world, but as holy people who live as God wants us to live. The key is the Spirit.

We need also note that over all such things we must apply lavish quantities of grace. Grace drives the gospel. Grace must be our response where believers struggle in these areas. Indeed, we all do from time to time. Such grace is represented in 6:1–3.

---

23. See further Mark J. Keown, 'Porn? Ok or not?' http://drmarkk.blogspot.co.nz/2008/05/porn-ok-or-not.html.

The second term is *akatharsia,* which is not as specifically sexual as *porneia* or *aselgeia* which will follow. The term *katharos* speaks of something clean or pure whether being cleansed of an illness like leprosy (Matt 8:2), cleaning a cup (Matt 23:25), clean (kosher) food (Matt 7:19), the human heart (Matt 23:25; Acts 15:9), cleansed of sin (2 Cor 7:1; 1 John 1:7), and so on.

Akatharsia speaks of the converse state, of uncleanness. This sense is important in OT law, whereby the term is used widely in terms of ritual purity. So, a person must avoid contact with anything that can contaminate them spiritually (Lev 5:3; 7:11), for to participate in religious rituals like sacrifice and tithing requires ritual purity (Lev 7:10; 22:3–5). A man is unclean when he has a discharge (Lev 15:2), a woman during menstruation (Lev 15:24–26, 30–31; 18:19; 2 Sam 11:4; Ezek 22:10), a man who has had sex with his brother's wife (Lev 20:21), or a person who has touched a dead body (Num 19:13). As noted, some of these things may have been promoted by the Judaizers (see the discussions in 3:28; 4:13–14).

Israel's sacrifices made atonement for Israel's impurities (Lev 16:16, 19). Certain foods were considered clean and could be eaten, others not so and they were to be avoided (Lev 20:25; Ezek 4:14). The cleanliness of the temple was the function of the priests and Levites (2 Chron 29:5, 16). The term is used for the pollution of unfaithful kings (1 Esdr 1:40), the gentiles (1 Esdr 1:47; 8:66, 80; Ezra 6:21), and Israel (1 Esdr 8:84; Ezra 9:11; Lam 1:9). It is used for the sinful state of Israel and the Temple by the Prophets.[24]

For this reason, God sent them into exile to purge them of their filth (Ezek 22:15; 24:11). He will restore them, cleansing them of their polluted state (Ezek 36:25, 29). In the vice list of Prov 6:16–17 (referred to earlier in the introduction to this section), seven sins are 'unclean' to God as is the scoffer to all (Prov 24:9). In the Maccabean period, cities were cleansed of uncleanness (1 Macc 13:48; 14:7). The OT tradition speaks then

---

24. See Hos 2:10; Mic 2:10; Nah 3:6; Jer 19:13; 39:34; Ezek 9:9; 36:17; 39:24, cf. Ezek 7:20.

of ritual purity maintained through avoiding contact with those things seen as unclean. This can be passed on. There is also a concern for the internal state.[25]

In the NT, ideas of 'cleanness' and 'uncleanness' shift from the external concern for ritual purity to an internally pure state. In the only non-Pauline NT use of the term, Jesus calls imprecations on the Jewish leaders for their excessive concern for external purity while neglecting the more important issue of the purity of the heart (Matt 23:47). Paul uses it once in a clearly non-sexual way, of impure missional motives, which he repudiates (1 Thess 2:3).

Otherwise, it is used of the impurity of sexual sin whereby people degrade their bodies with one another (Rom 1:24, s.a. 6:19).[26] He further uses the term alongside *porneia* (above) here in Gal 5:19, and in 2 Cor 12:21; Eph 5:3; and Col 3:5. Similarly, in 1 Thess 4:7, after appealing to the Thessalonians to avoid *porneia* (1 Thess 4:3) and lustful passions (1 Thess 4:5), he uses the term—God has called believers to holiness rather than impurity. His other use is Eph 4:19 where it is inclusive of sexual sin but has a broader sense of gentiles who practice 'every kind of impurity.'[27]

Here, flanked by porneia and *akatharsia* is another sexual term, *aselgeia*—the three terms emphatically warning the Galatians against anything that deviates from God's sexual ideals (see above on *porneia*). Such things defile us, and cause us to be unholy and polluted. While the work of Christ declares us holy, we must

25. In the Pseudepigrapha, *akatharsia* is used of impure mouths (slanderous) (1 En. 5:4), sexual impurity (1 En. 10:11; T. Jud. 14:5; T. Jos. 4.6), the impurity of sin in general (1 En. 10:19), Israel's uncleanness leading to exile (T. Levi 15:1), in an abstract descriptive sense (T. Ab (A) 17.13), the corruption of Jerusalem and temple (3 Macc 2:17; Pss. Sol. 8:12, 22), dirty water (Pss. Sol. 8:20), and Israel polluted by gentiles (Pss. Sol. 17.45). Philo employs it of the impurity of vain opinions (*Leg.* 1.52) and passions (*Leg.* 2.29), cleansing a plant (*Plant.* 95, 99, 109) which he interprets ethically, and the soul as an oracle in the midst of human impurity (passions) (*Her.* 113).

26. While Rom 6:19 can be general, the most obvious application of his teaching concerning the members of the body would be sexual. However, he may have in mind other bodily sins like gluttonous eating.

27. The term is used twice in the Apostolic Fathers. Once it speaks of unclean speech (Barn. 10:8), and once of sexual impurity (Barn. 19:4).

aspire to live up to the call of our holiness and 'be holy!' We are to become what we have been declared to be.

The third term is *aselgeia* speaks in the NT of 'licentiousness' or 'debauchery.'[28] BDAG describes it as a 'lack of self-constraint which involves one in conduct that violates all bounds of what is socially acceptable, self-abandonment.'[29] It then goes further than *porneia* which refers to any sexual sin, to a self-abandonment to the physical desires of the flesh. It is found twice in the LXX, once used for the licentious deeds of Ptolemy (3 Macc 2:25), and in the vice list of Wis 14:24–27 (see the introduction of this section) where it sits alongside a range of other sexual vices.

While it is not always sexual for Josephus, used of insolent words (Josephus, *Ant.* 4.151) and excessive violence (*Ant.* 20.112), it is applied to the licentiousness of governors (*Ant.* 8.252), Jezebel (*Ant.* 8.318), Cleopatra (*Ant.* 15.98), Mariamne (*Ant.* 16.185; *J.W.* 1.439) (s.a. *Ant.* 17.110), and women in general (*J.W.* 2.121; 4.562). It is used by Philo of sexual excess (*Mos.* 1.3, 305; *Spec.* 3.23), and similarly in the Pseudepigrapha (Sib. Or. 2.279; 8.381; T. Jud. 23.1).

As such, *aselgeia*, along with *porneia* and *akatharsia*, combine to speak of sexual promiscuity. That is, allowing the sexual desires full reign. The Spirit stands in opposition to this. As such, all who name Jesus as Lord should seek to gain control of their sexuality, expressing it within God's purposes—faithful, loving, heterosexual, and monogamous marriage. Alternatively, one seeks to live the celibate life well. This also applies to those in a marriage situation where for one reason or another, their spouse is unable to have (for health reasons) or is undesirous of sexual relations. While ideally each spouse will want to and seek to satisfy the other (cf. 1 Cor 7:3), true love waits patiently (1 Cor 13:4). Each spousal partner should seek to find ways to cultivate a healthy sexual relationship whereby both are fulfilled. When, for some reason, this is not happening, help is available whether

---

28. H. Goldstein, 'ἀσελ´γεια,' in *EDNT* 1:170.
29. BDAG 141.

medical or counseling. Couples should not hesitate to get help if needed.

In *Galatians 5:20*, Paul continues his list of works of the flesh, shifting from sexuality to two focused on worship, and the verse includes seven (of eight overall) false attitudes and resultant actions that tear apart relationships:

idolatry (*eidōlolatria*),[30] **occult-practices** (*pharmakeia*),[31] **enmities** (plural *echthra*),[32] **strife**[33] (*eris*),[34] **jealousy** (*zēlos*),[35] **fits of rage** (plural *thymos*),[36] **selfish ambition** (*eritheia*),[37]

---

30. The noun εἰδωλολατρία (*eidōlolatria*) means idolatry and is only found in 5:20, the fourth of the fifteen-part vice list of 5:19–21. Otherwise, Paul uses it in 1 Cor 10:14 and Col 3:5, and Peter uses it once in 1 Pet 4:3.

31. The noun φαρμακεία (*pharmakeia*) (English 'pharmacy') is found once in 5:20, the fifth term in the vice list. Its only other use in the NT is Rev 18:23 where the nations are deceived by the sorcery of Babylon. It speaks of sorcery and magic, i.e., occult practices.

32. The noun ἔχθρα (*echthra*) is used only once in Galatians in 5:20, the sixth in Paul's fifteen-word vice list. It is the first of the directly relational terms used. Paul's only other use is Rom 8:7; Eph 2:14, 16. It is related to *echthros*, 'enemy' in 4:16, where Paul asks if he has become an enemy of the Galatians.

33. **VARIANT**: Some witnesses (C D1 F G K L P Ψ 0122 0278 81 104 365 1175 1241 2464 ◊ latt syh co; McionE Irlat Cl) read the plural *ereis* (disputes, strife) rather than the singular *eris*. This is followed by Textus Receptus (see NKJV, 'contentions'). The singular is found in ℵ A B D* 326 614 630 1505 1739 1881 syp. In accord with Paul's use of the singular in vice lists through his corpus, it is to be preferred.

34. The noun ἔρις (*eris*) features only once in 5:20, the second of the social relationship vices, the seventh overall. It is only found in Paul in the NT (nine times). It speaks of strife, discord, contention, quarreling, and is used of Greco-Roman political enmity. It is a core element of the Corinthian factionalism (1 Cor 1:11; 3:3, s.a., Phil 1:15) and features in vice lists like 5:19–21 (s.a., Rom 1:29; 13:13; 2 Cor 12:20; 1 Tim 6:4; Tit 3:9).

35. The noun ζῆλος (*zēlos*) can be a positive term connoting, 'zeal, passion,' for something good, or the negative idea of jealousy. This is the sense in its one use in 5:20 as the third term speaking of broken social relationships, and the eighth term overall. It speaks of the Galatians living in jealousy of each other. *Zēlos* is linked closely with the verb *zēloō* in 4:17–18 where it is used of the Judaizers being zealous for the Galatians to be the same for them. Paul approves of zeal for good, but not false zeal or jealousy for what another has or has achieved. He uses *zēlos* ten times overall.

36. The noun *thymos* speaks of rage or anger. It is used once in Galatians 5:20 in the vice list, the fourth of the terms of social and relational breakdown, and is the ninth overall. Paul uses it four other times, of God's fury at sin and sinners, and as here, in vice lists (2 Cor 12:20; Eph 4:21; Col 3:8). It is linked to *epithymia* ('desires') used in

dissensions (plural *dichostasia*),[38] **factionalism** (plural *hairesis*),[39]
...

There is a marked shift from terms of sexual license to two terms that speak of worship. The first is *eidōlolatria*, 'idolatry,' a term found only found in the OT and NT. As discussed concerning Galatians 4:8, the Asians were worshipers of a vast range of gods. Idolatry was basic to their polytheistic worldview. Paul here sees this as a fleshly work. It violates the first two commands of the Decalogue which demand that Israel worships no other gods before Yahweh, and as God's image bearers on earth (Gen 1:26–27), makes no idols (Exod 20:3–4).

The condemnation of idolatry recurs through the OT and apocryphal writings (e.g., Lev 19:4; 26:1). Israel's failure to renounce idolatry was a core reason for judgment and ultimately exile.[40] Kings were assessed on their willingness to destroy idols and condemned for the converse.[41] Israel's monotheism and repudiation of idolatry stood it in marked contrast to other

---

5:16 and *epithymeō* (to desire) in 5:17. In both instances, 'the desires of the flesh' are in view. Here, one of those, *epithymia*, is the desire to express *thymos* when one feels wronged. See also *makrothymia* in 5:22.

38. The noun ἐριθεία (*eritheia*) can mean strife, contentiousness, or as it is often translated, 'selfish ambition' (BDAG 392). It is only found in Jacob (James) and Paul; for Paul, it features in vice lists (2 Cor 12:20) and is an aspect for which humankind God's wrath (Rom 2:8). As with *eris*, it is a feature of those who are preaching to cause Paul harm in Rome (Phil 1:17) and to be rejected in favor of humility and honoring others above oneself (Phil 2:3). In 5:20, the only use in Galatians, it is the tenth of the vices and the fifth social relationship term.

38. The noun διχοστασία (*dichotasia*) is used once in Galatians. The only other use in the NT is Rom 16:17. The term speaks of 'divisions,' 'disunity,' and 'contention,' and was used in a political sphere. In both Romans and Gal 5:20, it speaks of divisions. It is the eleventh of the vices, the sixth of the social relationship sins, and no doubt, a feature of the conflict in the Galatia churches.

39. The one use of the noun αἵρεσις (*hairesis*) is in Gal 5:20, where it is the twelfth vice listed and the seventh of the eight vices which target social relationships. We get the English term heresy from it. The term speaks of a 'school,' 'party,' 'faction,' or 'opinion,' 'dogma' (BDAG 27). It is only used once by Paul elsewhere in 1 Cor 11:19, where Paul endorses that there must be *haireseis* among the Corinthians to discern who is genuine. Here it is negative, a party spirit or breaking up the church into factions. Luke uses it in Acts of various sects in Judaism (see footnotes 5:20).

40. See Deut 32:21; 1 Kings 16:13; 2 Kings 17:11, 15; 1 Chron 15:8.

41. See, e.g., 1 Kings 15:12; 16:26; 21:26; 2 Kings 21:11, 21; 23:24; 2 Chron 24:18; Isa 2:8;

nations.[42] Idolatry as an idea is frequently mocked in Israel's tradition.[43] Before God, all idols will be destroyed.[44] Idolatry was fundamental to the Maccabean revolt's motivation, Israel's men rising up against idolatrous gentiles and those who joined them in their false worship.[45] Some Jewish writings envisage the gentiles destroying their idols and worshiping God (Tob 14:6).

In the NT, idolatry is also repudiated (Acts 7:41) with the Jerusalem Council letter urging gentile Christians not to eat food polluted by idols (Acts 15:20, 29; 21:25)—something Paul does not endorse in 1 Cor 8.[46] His repudiation of idolatry is seen in Athens when Luke records Paul's deep distress at seeing the city full of idols (Acts 17:16).

In First Corinthians, Paul effectively declares idols the non-existent (1 Cor 8:4; 10:19; 12:2). However, this does not mean that there are no powers functioning in and through pagan religion. Such power is demonic (1 Cor 10:20–22). In parallel with his injunction to flee sexual immorality in 1 Cor 6:18, Christian believers are to 'flee from idolatry' (1 Cor 10:14, cf. 2 Cor 6:16). He views idolatry as the fundamental failure of humanity, an inexcusable rejection of the Creator for the worship of the images of the created. Because of this idolatry, God has given humanity over to sin, whether sexual or otherwise (Rom 1:19–32). For Paul, essential to authentic Christian conversion is the repudiation of all idolatry. Hence, he delights in the Thessalonians who 'turned to God from idols to serve the living and true God' (1 Thess 1:9).

10:11; Jer 8:19; Ezek 6:4–7; 14:3–7; 16:36; 18:5–18; 20:7–8, 16–39; 23:7–49; Hos 8:4; 11:2; Mic 1:7.
42. See, e.g., 1 Sam 31:9; 2 Sam 5:21; 1 Chron 16:26; Ps 96:5; Bel 3, 5.
43. See Ps 97:7; 135:15; Isa 40:19–20; 44:9–20; 45:20; Jer 10:3–9, 14–15; Jer 50:38; 51:17; Hos 13:2; Esth 14:8–10; Wis 14:8–12, 27–30; 15:15; Sir 30:19.
44. See, e.g., Jer 50:2; Ezek 30:13; 36:18, 25; Hab 2:18; Zech 13:2.
45. See e.g., 1 Macc 1:43, 47; 1 Macc 3:48; 13:47; 2 Macc 12:40; 4 Macc 5:2.
46. Paul accepts the eating of idol food in part. Where someone's conscience is offended, he endorses this prohibition for the sake of the 'weaker' brother/sister. However, in principle, while Paul repudiates idolatry and attendance at pagan temple worship, he sees no issue with eating food that comes from idol worship away from the place of worship. See 1 Cor 8, 10.

Three times Paul employs the term *eidōlolatria*. He warns the
Corinthians to 'flee from idolatry (*eidōlotria*) in 1 Cor
10:14—they can eat food sacrificed to idols if no questions of
conscience are raised. However, they must not eat at the Temple
banquets for to do so means fellowship with demons. In Col 3:5,
believers are to avoid greed (*pleonexia*), which for Paul is a form
of idolatry. This is because greed is effectively the satiation of
the fleshly demand for pleasure, which comes at the expense of
the worship of God. The only other NT use is 1 Pet 4:3 where,
in a vice list, Peter exhorts his readers to abstain from 'lawless
idolatry,' which is a feature of the life of the gentiles. With
different language, writing to Christians further to the west in
Asia Minor, full of the same kinds of paganism as Galatia, John
urges his readers to 'keep yourselves from idols' (1 John 5:21).
In Revelation written to the same churches, idolatry is roundly
repudiated (Rev 2:14, 20; 9:20).

Here in the vice list, the reference may be broad and
encompass greed and other comparable attitudes and actions.
It at least refers to compromising worship of God and his Son
for the idols that were in the face of the Galatians day after
day—gods and goddesses they previously worshiped. Such things
are a work of the flesh to be put to death by the power of the
Spirit. Today, we too are under a range of gods which summon us
to their feet. They are not graven images, but through our various
media, we are bombarded by ideologies that seek to excite our
desires and claim our hearts. We are not to bow to them, and
instead give exclusive worship to our Triune God.

The second term in the verse is *pharmakeia* from which we
get the English terms like 'pharmacy.' BDAG suggests it means
here sorcery or magic.[47] In wider Greek sources, *pharmakeia* is
commonly employed of medicines,[48] and sometimes of poisons.[49]

---

47. BDAG 1049. See also *EDNT* 3:417; LSJ 1917.
48. See, e.g., Plutarch, *Alex.* 19.2; 41:4; Diodorus Siculus, *Hist.* 1.97.7; Plato, *Prot.* 354a; Aristotle, *Eud. eth.* 1214b.30–34.
49. See, e.g., Plutarch, *Alex.* 77.1; *Art.* 18.4; Dionysius of Halicarnassus, *Ant. rom.* 4.25.5; 4.79.2; Diodorus Siculus, *Hist.* 4.45.3; Strabo, *Geogr.* 15.1.30.

It is more rarely used of magical enchantments (Strabo, *Geogr.* 1.2.10).[50]

In Jewish Greek sources, it is used mainly to describe sorcery. So, in LXX texts it is always used of the sorcery, witchcraft, or incantations whether of the magicians of Egypt who sought to match Moses' miracles before Pharaoh,[51] of the Canaanites (Wis 12:4) and Babylon (Isa 47:9, 12). In the Pseudepigrapha, in 1 Enoch it refers to the magic the sons of God taught women when they cohabitated with them,[52] to Roman sorcery (Sib. Or. 5:165), and sorcery in Israel under Manasseh (Mart. Ascen. Isa. 2.5). Josephus also employs it once of the use of magical arts to set a snare (*Ant.* 15.47). Josephus and Philo both use it more in line with wider Greek sources of medicines employed by those who are in the magic/medicine business, and so is used for poisoning someone.[53]

The two NT uses align with Jewish Greek use where it does not refer to medicines, but negatively, to magic or sorcery. In Rev 18:23, it is of the sorcery of Babylon which deceives the nations. Here, it speaks of the use of magic or sorcery, something commonplace in the ancient world. This is repudiated by the biblical writers. I have translated it 'occult-practices.'

In our context, it would include astrology, tarot cards, Ouija boards, fortune-telling, curses, spells, voodoo dolls, and so on. This brings into play questions of whether Christians will let their children be exposed to occult ideas in the media, such things as the *Harry Potter* novels, etc. On the one hand, it helps them understand the world and can excite their imaginations. This was my experience with the *Lion, the Witch, and the Wardrobe* by C. S. Lewis and Stephen Donaldson in *The Thomas Covenant Chronicles*. On the other, it arguably exposes them to the occult. Such questions lie beyond the scope of this work, but each Christian should think through such things and live out of their

---

50. It can also be used of paint mixed for art (Plato, *Crat.* 434b).

51. See Exod 7:11, 22; 8:7, 18; Wis 18:13.

52. See 1 En. 7:1; 8:3, cf. Gen 6:1–4; s.a. Sib. Or. 1:96; Jub. 4:15.

53. See Josephus, *J.W.* 1.227, 452, 632; Philo, *Spec.* 3.94, 98; Polybius, *Hist.* 6.13.4.

conscience, and dialogue with other believers about such things in love—seeking truth and healthy community together.

With the next term, Paul slightly shifts gear, beginning his eight terms concerning social relationships. These indicate that there is likely a serious breakdown of community in the Galatian churches (see on 5:13 esp.). The first of the eight terms is *echthra*, which means 'enmity, hatred.'

In the LXX the term is used of enmity between the serpent and the woman (Gen 3:15), personal hatred or enmity,[54] enmity toward God (Mic 2:8; 7:8; Isa 63:10), enmity toward Israel[55] or other nations (Ezek 35:11), and other forms of political enmity.[56]

In the non-Pauline NT, it is used twice. First, *echthra* is used for the end of the political and personal enmity between Pilate and Herod as they dealt with Jesus (Luke 23:12). Second, Jacob speaks of 'friendship with the world as enmity with God'—it speaks of hostility and rejection. Paul too uses it of the flesh's hostility or enmity toward God (Rom 8:7). In Eph 2:14, 16, the dividing wall of hostility/enmity, the historical separation of Jew and gentile, is removed in Christ.

The nature of the enmity Paul has in mind could arguably include enmity toward God as they violate the gospel. As the associated noun *echthros*, 'enemy' is used in 4:16—'have I become your enemy'—this could include enmity toward Paul. The references in Eph 2 bring into play racial enmity, especially between Jews and gentiles, which the Judaizers are intensifying. There may be other enmities at play, along the lines of gender and social status (cf. 3:28). The suggestion of destructive relationships in 5:13 suggests that this includes to some extent their divisions. Some are likely siding with the Judaizers and others are not. All in all, whatever enmity or hostility is in mind, Paul repudiates it.

His teaching here has important ramifications for enmity within the Christian world, whether it be toward people of other

---

54. See Num 35:20, 22; Prov 6:35 LXX; 10:18; 15:17; 25:10 LXX; 26:26; Sir 6:9; 37:2; Jer 9:8.
55. See 1 Esdr 5:49; Mic 7:10; Ezek 35:5; 1 Macc 13:6.
56. See 1 Macc 11:12, 40; 13:17; 2 Macc 4:3; 4 Macc 2:13.

denominations, between followers of theologians (e.g., Arminianism, Calvinism, Barthianism), hostility due to personal relationship breakdown, and so on. The converse is reconciliation. Believers are reconciled to God in Christ (Rom 5:10, 11; 11:15; 2 Cor 5:18–20) as are all things (Col 1:22). Christ's work in us is to fill us with his Spirit of forgiveness and reconciliation and see all such hostilities come to an end (Matt 5:24; Isa 2:4). We are called to reconcile with our enemies and live together by the Spirit's fruit (5:22–24).

This has ramifications in our homes, as a husband and wife lay aside enmities and live together in harmony; similarly, parents with children and children with parents. It has huge implications for the way we respond to a world that is hostile toward us. We are even to love our enemies which speaks of seeking to do all we can not to promote enmity but everything we can to break it down. As Jesus says, 'Blessed are the peacemakers' (Matt 5:9). As Paul says in Rom 12:18, 'If possible, so far as it depends on you, live peaceably with all.'

Of course, in a sense, Paul is promoting a form of enmity in the letter, urging the Galatians to be united without hostility within their communities, and stand strong against the Judaizing 'enemies of the cross' (Phil 3:18). They are to reject their false doctrine, and if need be, expel them. However, while they may do so, they are not to hate them. Christians are not haters, even where enemies are concerned. We are lovers of our enemies (Matt 5:43–44; Luke 6:27, 35). Such love is easier said than done, but we have in Jesus the example par excellence. Rather than employ his divine omnipotence or call down legions of angels to destroy his enemies (Matt 26:53), he cried from the cross 'Father forgive them' (Luke 23:34)—we are to do the same. We leave any punishment to God (Rom 12:19–21). The emphasis here is that enmity, hostility, and hatred within the community are works of the flesh. Such works are to be put to death in us and will be so as we are led by the Spirit (5:16). What will flow will be love, joy, peace, and other fruit of the Spirit. Of course, when the gospel is being violated by false teachers, such love is hard to express. Still, our challenge is to resolve our disputes in a loving and constructive manner.

The second relational term is *eris* carrying the senses of 'rivalry,' 'strife,' 'discord,' 'contention,'[57] 'dispute,' or 'quarrel.'[58] In the Greco-Roman world, *Eris* is the Greek goddess of discord and strife (Lat. *Discordia*) who opposes *Harmonia* (Lat. *Concordia*). Homer equated her with Enyo, the war-goddess (Lat. *Ballona*).[59] In the LXX, it is found only in the Apocryphal Wisdom text Sirach, used of a hasty quarrel which kindles a fire (Sir 28:11), and the strife experienced by the rich, powerful, and sinners (Sir 40:5, 9).[60]

Eris is repudiated in the Pseudepigrapha. In Sib. Or. 2.147 'strife engenders strife,' speaking of how such attitudes escalate. It is associated with Babel (Sib. Or. 3.103; 11.13), the contention among the gods (Sib. Or. 3.119), Roman political turmoil (Sib. Or. 3.379), political strife leading to war (Sib. Or. 5.341), the strife caused by Alexander the Great (Sib. Or. 11.212), and other similar political turmoil.[61] The eschaton will be the end of strife (Sib. Or. 8.120).

In other Pseudepigraphal works, *Eris* is a demon who causes strife (T. Sol. 8.3)—'by making available clubs, pellets, and swords, my implements of war' (T. Sol. 8.6) and with 'Distress' (*zalē*) causes people to lack moderation, to divide into factions, keeps people divided, and sets them against each other (T. Sol. 8.8). The angel Baruchiel is said to oppose Eris. Eris also lies in the Jewish vice list of 3 Baruch 8.5 which, as noted above, has five vices in common with 5:19–21 (cf. 3 Bar. 8.5).

Philo repudiates *eris* as 'the mother of anger' (*Leg.* 3.131), 'a horrid disease' (*Deus.* 97), a negative aspect of drunkenness (*Ebr.* 15), and something that leads to unjust treatment (*Ebr.* 18). Such

---

57. BDAG 392.
58. H, Giesen, 'ἔρις,' in *EDNT* 2:52.
59. See further 'Eris (mythology),' in *Wikipedia*, https://en.wikipedia.org/wiki/Eris_(mythology).
60. In Josephus, it is also used for conflict (e.g., *Ant.* 7.17; 9.240) including political and military contention (*Ant.* 16.194; *J.W.* 1.206; 5.71, 396, 502).
61. See, e.g., Sib. Or. 12.242; 13.77; 14.16, 73, 93, 196, 324; Let. Aris. 250; Jos. Asen. 1.10.

contention is a feature of philosophical life (*Her.* 246, 247; *Mut.* 10). He includes it in a vice list, things that oppose contentment (*Mut.* 95).[62]

As can be seen by the previous analysis, the term is rich speaking of contention, discord, strife, and not of an insignificant 'tiff' kind. Rather, this speaks of real arguments and quarrels. Again, we get a glimpse into the life of the Galatian churches. Coincidentally, I write this a few days after attending a church meeting. The meeting was contentious with a small rump of former leaders arguing strongly against the work of the new team. As one might expect, this was not received well. This led to public debate, shaking heads, vicious looks, angry words, muttered expletives, and so on. Thankfully, there was some reconciliation between the offended/offending parties after the meeting. However, there are still wounds to be healed.

Such contention is not the way God wants us to do business. We must find ways to rise above the sewer of such behavior, no matter how right we think ourselves to be, and speak the truth to one another in love. One solution is to bury such things and not allow the debate. Doing so is not always helpful for it just drives the anger and resentment underground and leads to embittered people who operate out of passive-aggressive political manipulation. Rather, we have to dig deep to find ways to have those hard conversations, but in a spirit of love.

This the Galatians need to do (as in the church referred to above). Where such things are allowed to happen, deep wounds can form and fester. Over time, such churches or denominations will lose their way, lost in the mire of their infighting. Joy will be lost. Grumpiness will take over. Enmity will grow. Strife and discord will be normalized. The mission will be vanquished. The saints will vote with their feet, and there will be progressive decline. The Spirit will be quenched. Satan will rejoice.

Churches that go to this dark place must let the light of the gospel shine on it, and each person examine themselves and seek forgiveness and reconciliation. Where need be, we need to get

---

62. See also *Ebr.* 99; *Mos.* 1.24; *Spec.* 1.108; *Virt.* 115.

help to ensure that we put away our anger and learn to speak the truth in love. Strife and discord are works of the flesh. If we let the Spirit reign, we can have those hard conversations and come out on the other side as one people.

The third term indicating a breakdown of social relationships among the Galatians and the eighth in the list is *zēlos*. The term speaks of 'ardor' or 'zeal,' or as we might say today, passion for something. It can be positive zeal for good or jealousy for someone/something out of love and positive desire, or a negative attitude; jealousy or envy.

In the sense of jealousy for someone loved (cf. Song 8:6), God shows such an attitude toward Israel (e.g., Num 25:11; 2 Kings 19:31; Wis 5:17). This *zēlos* led him to protect Israel, and at times punish her enemies and even Israel herself so that she may return to him.[63]

Zēlos is used in this way of the fury of God's fire of judgment (Heb 10:27). Such a positive *zēlos* is exemplified by Jesus, who, like God, had *zēlos* for God's house as he cleared it, the Temple (John 2:17; Ps 68:10). Phinehas and Elijah are the prototypical Israelites where such positive zeal is found (1 Macc 2:54, 58).

As discussed in 1:14, Paul emulated this attitude (*zēlōtēs*) in his former life as a persecutor of the church (Phil 3:6). Similarly, he is jealous for the Corinthians as a daughter betrothed to Christ (2 Cor 11:2). In 4:17–18, Paul uses the associated verb *zēloō* three times. The first use is of the Judaizers' false zeal for the Galatians so that they will return the favor. He then tells the Galatians that positive zeal for a good purpose is appropriate. Hence, he commends the Corinthians for their zeal for him (2 Cor 7:7, 11) and the Jerusalem Collection (2 Cor 9:2). However, as with the Judaizers, such zeal can lack knowledge and be false (*s.a.* Rom 10:2).

However, here in 5:20, *zēlos* is being used in its negative sense of jealousy. Such jealousy is rejected in the OT (Prov 27:4), where a righteous person must not be jealous of the wicked.[64] In Sirach

---

63. See, e.g., Ps 78:5 [Eng. 79:5]; Zeph 1:18; 3:8; Zech 1:14; 8:2; Isa 9:7; 37:2; Ezek 5:13; 16:42; 36:6.

64. See, e.g., Ps 36:1 [Eng. 37:1]; Prov 24:19, s.a. Eccl 9:6; Job 5:2; Sir 40:5; 1 Macc 8:16.

30:24, jealousy, anger, and anxiety bring on premature old age and shorten life.

Luke employs *zēlos* twice of the envy of opponents of the Christian movement (Acts 5:17; 13:45). Jacob uses similarly, warning his readers against such jealousy (Jas 3:14, 16). Paul repudiates the Corinthians as immature and fleshly for exhibiting *zēlos* and *eris* (strife, see above) (1 Cor 3:3). Always following *eris*, *zēlos* is found in the vice lists of Rom 13:13; 2 Cor 12:20. Its placement after *eris* suggests that Paul closely links strife and the attitude of jealousy. No doubt Paul perceives that jealousy is a part of the Galatian issue. There may be jealousy toward Paul from the Judaizers and among the Galatians, as they vie for status, locked as they are in a society consumed by seeking rank, status, and honor.

Envy is repugnant, a work of the flesh, to be put to death as we walk in the Spirit. Instead, when we see others moving ahead of us in whatever pecking order we find ourselves in, we honor them above ourselves—as we must people who are supposedly 'below' us (Phil 2:3). We are to be driven by pleasing God in whatever situation he has put us in, and not bemoan that we are not further up the ladder of 'success.'

The fourth specifically relational term and the ninth overall is *thymos*, a very common term. *Thymos* has been briefly mentioned in the discussion of *epithymia* in 5:16 (s.a. *epithymeō* in 5:17). It has its origins in *thyō* which speaks of 'the violent movement of air, water, the ground, animals, or people.'[65] It has a range of senses like 'well up,' 'boil,' 'smoke,' 'sacrifice' and elides into 'a. desire, impulse, inclination, b. spirit, c. anger, d. sensibility, e. disposition or mind, f. thought, consideration.'[66]

For the likes of Plato, *thymos* means 'spirit, anger, rage, agitation.'[67] *Thymos* is very common in the LXX (321 times). It mostly speaks of intense anger—fury. Proverbs 20:2 gives a sense of its force: 'a threat of a king does not differ from the fury of a lion' (Gen 27:45). It is often used of the anger of people such as

65. F. Büchsel, 'Θυμός,' in *TDNT* 3:167.
66. Büchsel, 'Θυμός,' 167.
67. Büchsel, 'Θυμός,' 167.

Simeon and Levi toward the Shechemites who raped their sister Dinah (Gen 49:6, s.a. Gen 34:25–29), Moses at Israel's golden calf idolatry leading him to smash the ten commandments tablets (Exod 32:19), a husband who is jealous (Prov 6:34), and the anger of the Maccabean revolters (e.g., 1 Macc 2:24, 44, 49). It is used extremely commonly of God's wrath.[68]

Sirach 30:24, cited above on *zēlos*, reminds us of the danger of an anger problem: 'Jealousy and anger shorten days, and anxiety brings on old age before its time' (LXX). Drunkenness (*methē*), which is also featured here, 'increases the anger of a fool to offense, reducing his strength and adding wounds' (Sir 34:30, LXX). The life of the wealthy is characterized by such things as anger and jealousy (*zēlos*) (Sir 40:5). The wisdom tradition includes methods of dealing with *thymos*. For example, Prov 15:1: 'a soft answer turns away wrath, but a harsh word stirs up anger' (NRSV). Another is Prov 29:11: 'a fool gives full vent to anger, but the wise quietly holds it back' (NRSV). Similarly, Eccl 7:10): 'do not be quick in your spirit to be angry (*thymoō*), for anger (*thymos*) lodges in the breast of fools' (LXX), and Eccl 11:10: 'remove rage from your heart' (LXX).

In the NT, *thymos* is found outside Paul of the synagogue's fury at Jesus' Nazareth sermon, a rage that led to them trying to kill him (Luke 4:28). Similarly, it is used to describe the rage of the rioting Ephesians (Acts 19:28). In Hebrews, it is once employed of the anger of Pharaoh at Israel (Heb 11:27). Ten times it features in Revelation of the wrath of Satan (Rev 12:12), Babylon (Rev 14:8), and God's wrath expressed in earthly suffering and eternal torment.[69] Paul also uses it of God's wrath, expressed in the destruction of those who reject God's truth (Rom 2:8). His other three uses, as here in 5:20, are in ethical teaching that targets human rage which is to be repudiated (2 Cor 12:20). In Eph 4:31,

---

68. See Exod 22:24; Lev 26:24; Num 12:9; Deut 29:23–24, 27–28; Josh 7:26; Judg 2:14; 1 Sam 28:18; 2 Kings 24:3; 2 Chron 34:21; Ezra 8:22; Ps 2:5, 12; Job 19:29; Sir 5:6; Hos 11:9; Mic 5:15; Jonah 3:9; Nah 1:2; Hab 3:12; Zeph 2:2; Isa 1:24; 51:17; Jer 4:8; Bar 1:13; Lam 1:12; Ezek 5:13; Dan 9:16.

69. See Rev 14:10, 19; 15:1, 7; 16:1, 19; 18:3; 19:5.

'all bitterness and *thymos* and anger and rioting and slander are to put away' (s.a. Col 3:8).

Strong anger then is a work of the flesh and to be overcome by the power of a life yielded to the Spirit. No doubt, as the Galatians bite and devour each other, they are at times acting with fierce anger (5:13). This is not acceptable in a Christian context.

This reference to *thymos* as a work of the flesh strikes me personally, as I have since childhood tended to become angry when pressured. Some years ago, recognizing this problem, I went for counseling. It turned out to have its roots in my childhood. Through prayer and counsel, to a large extent, I have been able to deal with this. I am not alone. Many of us have such a problem, particularly men. What men like me tend to do is to allow things that hurt us to build up, and it is released in anger. We need to develop tools to deal with these struggles in a healthier way, expressing our emotions in safe ways, and not resorting to anger. I can say from my own bitter experience (especially in my early days), that anger produces nothing but pain and brokenness.

In our strange, driven world, many of us carry stuff that threatens to break out. You see it as you drive on any busy road, as people vent to each other with words, gestures, tooting horns, and worse. We need to yield to the Spirit who is seeking to cultivate in us love, peace, patience, kindness, gentleness, self-control, and the like. The Galatians desperately need this. We need this in every situation we find ourselves in. I live in a nation where families especially are busted up with domestic violence. Such pain is producing broken, angry young people who will do the same. We need to break the cycle, yield to the Spirit, get help if need be, and become what God wants us to be.

The tenth vice listed and fifth of the relational terms is *eritheia*. The term derives from *eris*, 'strife, contention' (above). As such, some consider it has the same kind of meaning—'strife,' 'contentiousness,' 'rivalries' (ESV), or 'quarrels' (NRSV). Most consider it speaks of 'selfishness' or 'selfish ambition,' mainly on the basis that there is no need to repeat the same idea in vice lists—selfishness (RSV), 'selfish rivalries' (NET), or 'selfish ambition' (NIV).[70] However, Paul will often repeat an idea with a different word in a vice list to reinforce the point. This is seen in this list with three sexual terms with overlapping meanings and the synonyms *zēlos* and *phthonos*, both terms meaning 'envy' or 'jealousy.'

Discerning its meaning is difficult as it is found only in Aristotle's *Politics* twice in the non-Christian Greek corpus. Aristotle uses it first in a discussion on the motives behind political disturbances. In what is effectively a political vice list, he mentions a desire for gain and honor and then lists a range of other reasons for political contention. These include arrogance (*hybris*), fear, dominance, contempt, disproportionate growth in power, along with others such as *eritheia*, putting others down, small-mindedness, and dissimilarity (Aristotle, *Pol.* 1302b.1–5). It is difficult to discern the intent of *eritheia* here, with either meaning possible. His second use favors the first meaning, factiousness. He describes how political institutions take place even without revolutions because of strife (*eritheia*). The only other non-NT uses are in Ignatius' letter to the Philadelphians, where he urges them to do nothing according to *eritheia*, clearly echoing Paul in Phil 2:3.

The NT uses are all in Jacob and Paul. Jacob links it twice to jealousy (*zēlos*) (Jas 3:14, 16). In Jas 3:16, he states that where jealousy and *eritheia* are, there is disorder and every foul practice.' Here, *eritheia* leads to disorder and so can be divisiveness or a desire for one's own way (Jas 3:14). Paul uses the term for those who are from *eritheia* and disobedience to the truth who obey unrighteousness—such people experience God's wrath and fury. In the vice list of 2 Cor 12:20, *eritheia* is listed, as here, after *eris*, *zēlos*, and *thymos*. The other two uses are in Philippians. In Phil 1:17, Paul's opponents are preaching Christ out of *eritheia*, seeking to cause him suffering in prison. Again, he uses *eris* in the same context (Phil 1:16), and so *eritheia* is most likely the attitude that leads to strife and contention—selfish ambition, a desire for

---

70. See the discussion in BDAG 392.

one's own way. In Phil 2:3, the believer is to do nothing out of selfish ambition or empty self-glorification; rather, in humility, and in emulation of Christ (2:5–8), they are to consider more significant than themselves. This text gets to the heart of the meaning of *eritheia* for Paul. It is a concern for one's gain at the expense of the other.

One gets further insight into the mindset of the Galatians. They want things their way. They are about personal progress; who cares who is in the way? They likely seek church office for the wrong reasons. Rather than being motivated to please God and serve him and his people with their gifts, they want places of honor.

This casts our minds back to 1:10 where Paul asks who he is seeking to please, God or people. If the latter, he is not a worthy slave of Christ. By implication, the Judaizers are in fact those who are not such servants. In church decision-making, they are determined to get their way at the expense of others. We need to ensure that we are not functioning out of selfish ambition as we go about the Lord's work. We are not in it for our own glory, but for the glory of God. We must be always prepared to recognize when we are wrong.

The next term (eleventh), the sixth of the relational terms, is *dichostasia*. While not as rare as *eritheia*, the noun is not common. It connotes 'the state of being in factious opposition, dissension.'[71] In wider Greek sources, it speaks of political sedition and dissensions which threaten stability.[72] Strabo states, 'Concord is maintained, where all sedition (*dichostasia*) is removed. They come through greed and indulgence' (*Geogr.* 10.4.16, my translation, cf. 13.2.3).

The one LXX use also speaks of political dissension caused by Antiochus (1 Macc 3:29). The political nature of the term is confirmed in Pseudepigraphal works where it is used for a

71. BDAG 252.
72. See, e.g., Plutarch, *Alex.* 53.4; *Nic.* 11.3; *Comp. Lys. Sull.* 1.2; Dionysius of Halicarnassus, *Ant. rom.* 5.66.4; 5.77.3; Herodotus, *Hist.* 5.75.2). In *Nic.* 11. 3, Plutarch cites a saying 'but in a time of sedition (*dichostasia*), the evil man is held in honor.' This is attributed to Callimachus, an Alexandrian poet and scholar (310–235 B.C.).

political disturbance (Sib. Or. 4.68). Further, it is seen as a demonic attitude with the disruption to people's minds caused by the demon Saphtoreal (T. Sol. 18.16). In the Apostolic Fathers' writings, it is used of church dissensions and is repudiated.[73]

The only other NT use of the term is Rom 16:17 where Paul urges the Romans to watch out for those who cause dissension in the church (who are very likely the same kinds of people as these Judaizers). Here then, it speaks of those who function to disrupt, who are seditious and divisive, causing dissension. *Dichostasia* is a work of the flesh, not the Spirit. As discussed earlier concerning *echthra*, churches can become prey to this type of behavior. We must not function in this way.

The final term in 5:20 (the twelfth term, seventh in the relational string) is *hairesis*, which has some similarities to the previous term. *Hairesis* is reasonably common, especially in wider non-Jewish/Christian Greek sources, where it has a wide range.[74] Schlier notes that the term became especially associated with a doctrine (cf. Eng. 'heresy') or a school of thought. The two ideas are linked, for the school develops around the differences of doctrine from philosopher to philosopher—the *haeresis* of a particular school.[75] This type of meaning is not found in the LXX, where it only means choice.[76] The related notion of heresies or false doctrine is found in the Pseudepigrapha (T. Sol. 8.5; Mart. Ascen. Isa. 3.22) (further below).[77]

Josephus uses *hairesis* in the sense of a party or school of thought, especially of the three 'sects' of Judaism—the Pharisees,

---

73. 1 Clem. 46:5; 51:1; Herm. *Vis.* 3.9.9; Herm. *Sim.* 8.7.5, 10.2.

74. See LSJ 41, which notes meanings including 'to take' as in a town; 'choice' 'election;' 'inclination,' 'purpose, course of action, thought;' a philosophical system, sect, school, faction, party; 'corps;' astrological condition; proposed condition, proposal, commission, freewill offering, and to bid at an auction. It is thus very diverse.

75. H. Schlier, 'αἵρεσις,' in *TDNT* 1:180–81.

76. The choice of Simeon and Levi (Gen 49:5), a freewill offering—an offering of one's choice (Lev 22:18, 21)—and one's free choice to add or remove treaty terms.

77. Can also mean to be of the same mind (Let. Aris. 7).

the Sadducees, and the Essenes, which he describes.[78] Philo too uses it in this way, as in the 'school of the Cynics' (*Plant.* 151).[79]

This use is found in Luke's writings of 'the party of the Sadducees' (Acts 5:17), 'the party of the Pharisees' (Acts 15:5; 26:5), 'the sect of the Nazarenes' (Acts 24:5), and the Christians labeled a sect—'the way' (Acts 24:14; 28:22). Paul's one other use is in 1 Cor 11:19, where he acknowledges the positive aspect of such groups—there must be *haireseis* among the Corinthians to discern who is genuine or not.

Here in Gal 5:20, *hairesis* refers negatively to a partisan spirit. This can be like the Corinthian situation, with the Galatians gathering into sects with differing viewpoints, and seeking to enforce it (cf. 1 Cor 1:10–12). If so, it is likely that the Judaizing school of thought lies at the heart of this. They are gathering supporters and disrupting the life of the church.

The later technical sense of heresy should not be read into this situation. This meaning begins to emerge in the Apostolic Fathers' writings. So, Ignatius writes to the Ephesians that they 'all live in accordance with the truth and that no *heresy* has found a home among you' nor even listened to (Ign. *Eph.* 6.2). Similarly, in *To the Trallians*, Ignatius writes 'partake only in Christian food, and keep away from every strange plant, which is *heresy*' (Ign. *Trall.* 6.1). In the Martyrdom of Polycarp, Polycarp supposedly refuted every heresy (*Mart. Pol.* 23.2) (s.a. Herm. *Sim.* 9.23.5).

Paul's thought is heading in this negative direction as he warns against partisan ideas which conflict with the gospel. The emphasis here is not on the teaching itself (which the whole letter addresses), but on the desire to enforce one's view on others. Hence, it is consistent with the other terms it sits alongside, especially enmity, strife, selfish ambition, and dissensions. As

---

78. See *Ant.* 13.171; *Life* 10, s.a. 13.288, 293; 20:199; *Life* 12, 191, 197; *J.W.* 2.122, 137, 142, 162. For other similar uses see *Ant.* 7.347; 15.6; *J.W.* 2.118. Josephus also uses *hairesis* in the sense of 'choice' (*Ant.* 1.169; 6.71, 91; *J.W.* 1.199), a political choice (Ant. 7.321), and God's choice (Ant. 7.322). He also uses it quite often of taking a city (e.g., *Ant.* 7.160; 12.363).

79. Philo's use is diverse. He uses it of choice (e.g., Philo, *Cher.* 30; *Post.* 78; *Deus.* 49), appoint (*Congr.* 110; *Mos.* 2.177), election (*Mos.* 2.160), among a range of ways.

with all the attitudes here, this is a fleshly desire to divide and conquer. This is repudiated. Rather, in the gospel, God's people live in love, joy, and unity.

Galatians 5:21 includes three further works of the flesh, and then a serious warning of the consequences of continuing in these activities:

envy[80] (*phthonos*),[81] **drunkenness** (plural *methē*),[82] **debauched partying** (*kōmos*),[83] **and** (*kai*, 1:1) **things like** (plural neuter *homoios*)[84] **these** (plural neuter *houtos*, 2:10). **I am warning** (*prolegō*)[85] **you** (dative plural *sy*, 1:3), **just as** (*kathōs*, 2:7) **I warned you previously** (*proeipon*, 1:9) **[about] these things** (plural neuter *ho*, 1:1); **that** (*hoti*, 1:6) **those who practice** (present participle *prassō*)[86] **such things** (*toioutos*)[87] **will not inherit** (future

---

80. **VARIANT:** Some witnesses add *phonoi*, 'murder,' after *phthonos* (A C D F G K L P Ψ 0122 0278 104 365 630 1175 1241 1505 1739 1881 2464 ◊ lat sy(p) bo; (Cyp)). Others only have *phthonos* (P46 ℵ B 33 81 323 945 vgmss sa; McionE Irlat Cl Ambst). Metzger, *Textual Commentary*, 529 prefers *phthonos* alone, although recognizing that the 'the shorter reading may have originated in accidental omission due to homoioteleuton.' The weight of mss and the shorter reading is likely to be preferred with *phonoi* added on the basis of Rom 1:29. Metzger gives it a {C} rating which suggests it is probable but not certain. Homoioteleuton is 'an unintentional error of eyesight committed when copying the biblical text, due to words or lines that end similarly' (*PDSNTG* 68).

81. The noun φθόνος (*phthonos*) is used once in Galatians 5:21, the thirteenth term and eighth and final directly social term. It translates as 'envy.' Paul uses it four times elsewhere including in vice lists (Rom 1:29, s.a., Phil 1:15; 1 Tim 6:4; Tit 3:3). The verb 'to envy' (*phthoneō*) is found in 5:26 indicating this is a significant issue in the church.

82. The noun μέθη (*methē*) (Eng. 'meths') is used once in the vice list of Gal 5:21. It connotes drunkenness (cf. Luke 21:34; Rom 13:13). In Rom 13:13 and 5:21, it is linked to *kōmos* (below) and speaks of the Greco-Roman penchant for debauched parties.

83. The noun κῶμος (*kōmos*) features three times in the NT, twice in Paul—once in Galatians 5:21, the other is with *methē* in Rom 13:13. The only other NT use is in 1 Peter where *kōmos* is again linked to drunkenness, although with different Greek terms. The *kōmos* was originally a procession and a way to honor Dionysus (also Bacchus). This was followed by an orgiastic party.

84. The adjective *homoios* is used once in Galatians, in 5:21, where it is neuter referring to 'like or similar things,' (cf. Eng. *Homo-* terms, *homo* the opposite of *hetero*, 'other') referring to works of the flesh like those he has just listed. This is Paul's only use.

85. The compound verb προλέγω (*prolegō*) blends *pro* (before) and *legō* (I say, tell, see on 1:9) and connotes to say something in advance or before. In Gal 5:21, with the synonym *proeipon*, it speaks of a warning previous and restated. The combination of verbs is emphatic.

klēronomeō, 4:30) **the kingdom** (*basileia*)[88] **of God** (genitive *Theos*, 1:1).

Paul finishes his list of works of the flesh that destroy social cohesion with *phthonos*, 'envy.' It is synonymous with *zēlos* (jealousy) in its negative sense. It is another very common term in wider sources, Josephus, the Pseudepigrapha, and Philo, but less so in the LXX and NT. LSJ notes that it carries the sense of ill-will, malice, and especially envy or jealousy of the good fortune of others. This envy can be grudging.[89]

In the LXX, its use is late, of the jealousy of God (Wis 2:24). In Wis 6:23, *phthonos* cannot be associated with wisdom. Daniel's opponents are described as envious (3 Macc 6:7).[90] In Pseudepigraphal writings, *phthonos* is repudiated. It is not good for mortals (Sib. Or. 3.662). It is listed in the vice list of 3 Bar. 13.4 (see the introduction to these verses previously). The writer of the Testament of Simeon warns readers to 'beware of the spirit of deceit and *envy*. For *envy* dominates the whole of a person's mind and does not permit that one to eat or drink or to do anything good' (T. Sim. 3.1–2). He also warns his readers to 'guard yourself ... from all jealousy (*zēlos*) and *envy*.'[91] In the Testament of Benjamin, *phthonos* is the first of seven great evils (T. Benj. 8.1). Beelzebul and the demon Rhyx Autoth seek to cause it among people (T. Sol. 6.4; 18.38, s.a. Jub. 10.1).

---

86. The verb πράσσω (*prassō*) is found once in Gal 5:21, of those who 'do, practice' the sins of the flesh.

87. The demonstrative pronoun τοιοῦτος is used three times in Galatians. In 5:21 it is neuter referring to 'such things' as the works of the flesh listed; things that are not consistent with the gospel of love. Similarly, the neuter in 5:23 speaks of the 'such things' as the fruit of the Spirit, which are beyond the law in a sense. Finally, in 6:1, it is used in the masculine of 'such a person' as is caught in sin—that person is to be restored with gentleness. Overall, Paul uses it thirty-two times.

88. The one reference in Galatians to the noun (βασιλεία) *basileia* (more common in the Synoptic tradition), is in 5:21 in the formula, 'kingdom of God.' It speaks of God's reign in the future consummated sense. Believers will not inherit eternal life by doing the sins of the flesh.

89. LSJ 1930.

90. In 1 Macc 8:13, somewhat over-optimistically, the writer states that the Roman senate is free of envy and jealousy. Time proved this incorrect.

91. See T. Sim. 4.5, s.a. 3.6; 4.7; 6.2; T. Dan. 2.5; T. Gad 4.5; T. Jos. 1.3.

In the Letter of Aristeas 224, the king asks a dinner guest, 'How could one be free from envy (*phthonos*)?' The answer is given:

First of all, by realizing that God assigns glory and greatness of wealth to kings, each and everyone and that no king is independent. All of them wish to share this glory, but they can not—it is a gift of God.

This answer indicates that in Jewish thought, God is to be honored for what a person has and is, and so envy is unnecessary.

As in Jewish thought, aside from Jas 4:5 where it is used of God's positive jealousy for his people (akin to positive uses of *zēlos*, above), *phthonos* is denounced. It characterizes the Jewish leaders who sought Jesus' death (Matt 27:18; Mark 15:10). Peter urges his readers to put it away with other sins, malice, deceit, hypocrisy, and slander (1 Pet 2:1).

In Philippians, Paul critiques his Christian opponents preaching to cause him pain in prison as being characterized by envy and *eris*—rivalry. They are doing so to bring Paul down and gain status themselves (Phil 1:15). In the vice list of Rom 1, it is one of the characteristics of fallen humanity alongside a range of other vices (Rom 1:29, s.a. Tit 3:3; 1 Tim 6:4). As with the other relational terms, likely jealousy and envy characterize members of the Galatian church and the Judaizers. Such attitudes tear apart relationships. The problem of envy among the Galatians is further indicated by the use of the associated verb *phthoneō* in 5:26—'Let us not become arrogant provoking one another, envying (*phthoneō*) one another.' As said previously in the discussion of *zēlos*, in Christ by the Spirit we are not to envy but admire and celebrate what others do and have in the Lord.

Paul now shifts tack again away from works of the flesh that destroy social cohesion to two further sins associated with the Roman world. Together with the first three terms which focus on sexual immorality, they speak of debauchery. It is clear that the Galatians, perhaps like the Corinthians, were struggling to leave behind their pagan pasts.

The next term (fourteenth overall) is *methē* (cf. Eng. 'meths'). The term is commonplace in non-Jewish Greek writings (1745 times in a Logos Search of the Perseus Greek Classics). This is hardly surprising as '[d]runkenness (Heb. *šikārôn* [Jer 13:13; Ezek 23:33]; Gk. *methē* [Luke 21:34; Rom 13:13; Gal 5:21], *oinophlygia* [1 Pet 4:3]) was a widespread vice in the Ancient Near East.'[92] This was especially the case throughout the current Empire where the wine god Dionysus (Bacchus) was venerated all over the Roman world. In the Jewish world, however, the pious did not agree with it.

While it is encouraged to give strong drink (*methē*) to someone in real pain (Prov 24:74) and such drink was used in Judith's victory (Jdt 13:15), the Jewish attitude to wine is seen in Prov 20:1, where the LXX reads: 'Wine is undisciplined, and strong drink is insolent, and every fool is entangled with such as these' (LES). Similarly, in Sir 34:30: 'Drunkenness increases the anger of a fool to his own hurt, reducing his strength and adding wounds' (LES) (see also Tob 4:15).

The prophets repudiated Israel's drunkenness (Joel 1:5; Hag 1:6), including Israel's leaders, the priests, and prophets (Isa 28:7).[93] As here, *methē* features in the vice lists of the Pseudepigraphal work of Baruch 8:5 and 13:4, alongside other vices listed here (see the Introduction to 5:19–21). In the Testament of Judah, *methē* is linked to Judah's sexual sin (T. Jud. 11.2; 12.6) and readers are warned that it confuses the mind and leads to dirty thoughts, unashamed adultery, and disrespecting others (T. Jud. 14.3–8, s.a. T. Jud. 16.2).

Josephus mentions *methē* in his narrations, not uncommonly noting that people were drunk when defeated implying that it lessened the ability to fight[94] and make good decisions (*Ant.* 1.301; 6.301; 12.188).[95] He also repudiates drunkenness as against God's law (*Ag. Ap.* 2.204) as it is 'against the will of God' and the cause of injury and excess (*Ag. Ap.* 2.195).

---

92. D. F. Watson, 'Wine,' in *DJG* 872.
93. Cf. Jer 28:57; Ezek 23:32; 39:19.
94. See, e.g., *Ant.* 1.177; 7.175; 10.168–169; 13.398; *J.W.* 5.21, 23.
95. In one memorable passage, Josephus records King Darius' speech on wine and how it deceives the mind into doing things like reducing a king to the state of an orphan and in need of a tutor, how it quenches sorrow and suffering, and helps people forget debts, makes them behave improperly and forget friends, and forget the night before. Darius concludes with a positive view of its power (*Ant.* 11.37–42).

Philo's attitude is negative with intoxication causing men 'to act like fools.'[96] In *Planting* 141–148 he considers those who approve of drunkenness against those who do not, concluding it is madness to drink wine in excess although there are times when a wise man will get drunk (*Plant.* 174). He devotes two whole books to the problem (*On Drunkenness, Sobriety*) noting that it is a product of disobedience leading to alienation of mind and folly (*Ebr.* 1). He states, 'sobriety is the cause of exactly as many good things, as drunkenness, on the contrary, is of evils' (*Sobr.* 2, Yonge).

Methē is only used twice else in the NT. In Luke 21:34, Jesus warns his disciples to be on their guard that their hearts are not weighed down with drinking bouts and drunkenness as they await his coming. The other use is in Paul's vice list in Rom 13:13 where it is also paired with *kōmos*—'let us walk honorably as in the day not in carousing and *drunkenness*, not in sexual excess and sensuality.'

Here then, Paul is repudiating drunkenness. Outside of Paul, John the Baptist did not drink at the Lord's specific command (Luke 1:15), while Jesus did and was called a drunkard (Matt 11:19; Luke 7:34). When the wine ran out at Cana, Jesus supplied a huge amount more, despite the drunkenness of the guests (John 2:1–11). Peter also repudiates drunkenness (*oinophlygia*)[97] and drinking parties (*potos*).[98] Paul reviles drunkenness as here and in Rom 13:13 (above).

In 1 Cor 5:11 *methysos* (a term related to *methē* meaning 'drunkard') is listed among those things for which a supposed brother or sister in Christ is to be expelled from the church if that person is unrepentant and continues in the activity. In 1 Cor 6:10, drunkards 'will not inherit the kingdom of God.' We can discern from 1 Corinthians 6:11 that some of the Corinthians were involved in this before conversion, now they should not

---

96. See *Leg.* 3.155, cf. *Leg.* 2.69; *Cher.* 92; *Plant.* 165.

97. *Oinophlygia* uses *oinos* (wine) and *plyō* (bubble up) and speaks of drunkenness. See BDAG 701.

98. *Potos* is a social gathering at which wine was served, a drinking party (BDAG 857), or as a Kiwi might say, a 'piss-up.'

do so for they are saved in Christ. However, some were getting drunk at the Lord's Supper (*methyō*, a verb from the same word group).[99]

The key text in Paul on this issue is Eph 5:18 where he tells the Ephesians: 'do not get *drunk* (*methyō*) on wine which leads to debauchery but be filled with the Spirit.' This is important for Paul, as seen in his expectation that an elder or deacon is not a drunkard (1 Tim 3:3, 8; Tit 1:7). However, Paul does not forbid drinking even urging Timothy to take a little wine for his upset stomach (1 Tim 5:23). The only time Paul urges full sobriety is in Rom 14:21, where one should not drink wine if doing so causes a fellow Christian to fall. As such, Paul urges moderate drinking and where our drinking may cause others to stumble, sobriety.

Some in pastoral ministry choose sobriety because of the widespread problems with alcohol in almost every society. This is to be commended. Others choose to drink moderately, which too is appropriate, unless it causes others to fall. Indeed, Jesus modeled moderated drinking and turned water into wine. Hence, it can hardly be completely rejected. However, what the NT clearly repudiates is drunkenness, as Paul does here.

Let me add another personal story. Before I became a Christian, I was a typical Kiwi young adult heavy drinker. When I became a Christian, I gave up drinking alcohol. At my sports clubs, I did not drink at all. I found that it was hard to have good conversations with the other players who imbibed liberally. One day, a friend was convicted of a bad crime and was marginalized by others. I went to his home and as I entered, he said, 'Oh Mark! So great to see you! Have a beer.' I knew in an instant I should say, 'yes.' So, I accepted, and we had a great chat. He went to prison, but because of that decision, I was able to share Christ with him and a group of us were able to go and minister in the prison. I then realized that moderate drinking can sometimes open up relationships with non-Christians. So, I started having a few drinks again. This led to some sports friends coming to Christ. On the other hand, my younger sister died after a

---

99. On *methyō* see also Matt 24:49; Acts 2:15; 1 Thess 5:7; Rev 17:6.

drinking binge, which was a horrific time of pain for my family. Making decisions on whether to abstain or moderately drink is difficult, and each of us should seek the Lord on this and make our own decisions. We should not judge each other. However, we should all avoid drunkenness.

The final term is *kōmos*. Mare notes that here 'Paul is describing in part the sexual and physical excesses practiced in the polytheistic and secular Roman society.'[100] Translating the term 'orgies,' he adds:

Greek, *kōmoi*, was used in Greek classical writers from Homer on. The word meant 'reveling, carousing,' and was connected with drinking and festival processions in honor of the gods, particularly the Roman god Bacchus, and the Greek Dionysus, the god of wine. Compare the USA festival of Mardi Gras, often celebrated with excessive feasting.[101]

By the time of Paul, the term had become generalized to describe a feast or a banquet with associated excessive drinking, eating, and sexual gratification. *Kōmos* is found twice in the LXX, both negatively. In Wis 14:23, it is repudiated alongside child sacrifice. In 2 Macc 6:3–4, gentile debauchery in the Temple is described:

Harsh and utterly grievous was the onslaught of evil. For the temple was filled with debauchery and reveling (*kōmos*) by the gentiles, who dallied with prostitutes and had intercourse with women within the sacred precincts, and besides brought in things for sacrifice that were unfit.

In Sibylline Oracles 5.317, a woe is pronounced on those who engage in *kōmos*: 'Woe to you, Cibyra, fair city, desist from *revelry* (*kōmos*)' (s.a. Sib. Or. 5.394; 8.118). Philo mentions it negatively (*Cher.* 92). The other two references are in vice lists, Rom 13:13 and 1 Pet 4:3, where they are paired with *methē*, 'drunkenness.' It thus speaks of excessive partying including getting drunk, eating to excess, and engaging in all manner of sexual perversions. Some translate it 'orgies' for this reason (ESV). Others prefer

---

100. W. H. Mare, New Testament Background Commentary: A New Dictionary of Words, Phrases and Situations in Bible Order (Ross-shire, UK: Mentor, 2004), 248.

101. Mare, New Testament Commentary, 299

'carousing'—a drunken revel (NRSV, NET). I have suggested 'debauched partying' to try and capture the senses of excessive food, drink, and sexual activity.

Such debauched behavior in the ancient world is very much like a description of the behavior of many people in our world who get excessively drunk on the weekends (or more often) and party without any concern for their well-being. They drink to excess, and many take drugs (which are now being liberalized in many countries). They often eat gluttonously. They sometimes wind up in one-night stands and engage in all sorts of crazy sexual stuff. They remember little the next day. This targets our youth culture directly and fiercely. And not just youth and young adults, hard-core alcohol use is prevalent in various age groups of many cultures.

Such stuff is of the flesh, allowing its desires full reign, living purely to satisfy our lusts. Such a life is destructive in many ways. It destroys our health. It wrecks relationships. It leads to abortions. It can leave us depressed and in self-hate. It drives us away from God to a dark place of addiction and demonization. By the Spirit, we can leave such a life behind. Many have done so.

I was not the worst person in the world, but as mentioned above, I regularly got smashed at the weekends. I dabbled in recreational drugs. I was often a glutton enjoying a 'pig-out.' I went down this track too far. Thanks be to God that on 1 Jan 1985 I gave up that life. I went back for one stupid night a few months later and learned the hard way that that kind of life was death. It is only by the power of the Spirit that I have overcome all this stuff, although I still drink moderately (see above). It can be done if we trust in him and allow his Spirit to lead us.

'And things like these' uses *homoios*, a term found forty-five times in the NT[102] but is Paul's only use of the term. The adjective

---

102. It is commonly used in Jesus' teaching, especially in parables, where he compares two things. Often it is the kingdom—'the kingdom is like …' (e.g., a grain of mustard, Matt 13:31; or, like yeast, Matt 13:33). He also uses it of comparing his generation (e.g., Matt 11:16). The two Great Commandments are 'like' one another (Matt 22:39). In Revelation it is used in John's attempts to describe his visions; so, John sees 'one like a son of man' (Rev 1:13) who has 'feet like burnished bronze' (Rev 1:15). God on the

means 'of the same nature, similar,'[103] here in the neuter meaning 'like or similar things' (Eng. 'homo'). As such, Paul indicates that although this is one of the longest vice lists in the NT, there are other things he could add. Such things are evident in the vice lists in the Introduction to 5:19–21 above and other NT lists. Anything that violates God's ideals for human relationships could be listed. The reader here is invited to think of other things that can be listed.

The introductory words of Paul's warning that follows are complex in Greek. Paul uses two synonyms *prolegō*, 'tell something before,' in the present tense, and *proeipon*, 'to say before' (1:9).[104] *Prolegō* means 'tell something before;' however, Paul uses it in warnings. So, in 2 Cor 13:2, Paul uses the term together in a warning to the Corinthians: 'I have warned (perfect *proeipon*), and I warn now (present *prolegō*) ...' Similarly, he warned the Thessalonians of impending suffering (1 Thess 3:4). Here then, the awkward construct speaks of former warnings which Paul is now reasserting.

The warning is that those who do such things will not inherit[105] the kingdom of God. Up until this point, Paul has used inheritance-language of the Abrahamic promises (3:18, 29; 4:1, 7, 30). As discussed, this speaks of the inheritance of the world (cf. Rom 4:13). In 4:7, Paul does not specify the inheritance, but this text explains it well.

'The kingdom of God' is widely used as the core of Jesus' message in the Synoptic Gospels. He came to announce the

---

throne is described—'he who sat there had the appearance of jasper and carnelian ...' (Rev 4:3). There is a sea of glass, like crystal (Rev 4:6). The living creatures are like a lion, an ox, like the face of a man, like an eagle (Rev 4:7). The city of God has a wall like clear glass (Rev 21:18), and so on.

103. BDAG 706.
104. *Proeipon* is found only twelve times in the NT of Jesus saying something beforehand (Matt 24:25; Mark 13:23), the Scriptures speaking beforehand (Acts 1:16), a prophet or apostle predicting in the past (Rom 9:29; 2 Pet 3:2; Jude 17), as here, Paul saying something previously (2 Cor 7:3; 13:2; 1 Thess 4:6), something quoted earlier (Heb 4:7).
105. The future is a predictive future indicating 'something will take place or come to pass.' See Wallace, *Greek Grammar*, 568.

kingdom in his ministry; he is God's appointed Messianic Servant King come to set in motion the redemption of the world. His work was to establish God's reign, inviting people to enter the kingdom through repentance and faith (e.g., Mark 1:14–15). The kingdom would grow in the world, penetrating it, as the gospel of the kingdom is preached to all nations (Mark 4:26–32; Matt 13:31–32; 13:10; Matt 24:14).

Luke continues to use the idea in Acts. The kingdom is introduced in Acts 1:3, where Jesus completed his teaching concerning the kingdom. Acts culminates in Paul in Rome proclaiming the kingdom of God (Acts 28:31). Framed by these references, the story of Acts is a narrative of the growth and penetration of the kingdom.

Like John (John 3:3, 5) who prefers 'eternal life' as his governing theological notion, Paul uses the idea sparingly, preferring other ideas to describe God's redemptive work (e.g., righteousness, justification, reconciliation, redemption, 'in Christ,' and so on). On occasion, he does refer to the kingdom, the phrase sometimes popping up in his letters, indicating that he is familiar and comfortable with the idea even if he does prefer other language. So, in Rom 14:17, he states that the kingdom of God is not about eating and drinking but 'righteousness and peace and joy in the Holy Spirit.' In 1 Cor 4:17, the kingdom of God is not about fancy rhetoric but the power of God to convert through a gospel of a crucified Christ. In his resurrection chapter in 1 Cor 15, the kingdom of God will consummate when Jesus has defeated all his enemies, and he hands the cosmos rid of all evil to his Father (1 Cor 15:24).

The kingdom is mentioned twice in Colossians, once 'the kingdom of his beloved Son' in which believers now redeemed and forgiven exist, having been delivered from the dominion of darkness (Col 3:13–14). He mentions his coworkers who work 'for the kingdom of God,' i.e., its proclamation, extension, and penetration (Col 4:11). He mentions the idea twice to the Thessalonians. Believers are called into God's kingdom (1 Thess 2:12) and considered worthy of it, even suffering for it (2 Thess 1:5). Christ's kingdom is the basis for the proclamation of the word in 2 Tim 4:1, and God will bring Paul safely into this heavenly kingdom (2 Tim 4:18). God is the 'king of ages' (1 Tim 1:17), and Christ is 'king of kings' (1 Tim 6:17). God thus exercises his sovereign rule through his appointed world King, Jesus Christ our Lord.

The idea of the kingdom of God is also implicit in the titles of Jesus. He is the Messiah, the Christ, the final Davidic King establishing God's reign, not merely over Israel but the world (some 380 times in Paul). He is the Son of God, a term used of rulers like Caesar and the Davidic King, to whom God has given the world to rule on his behalf (see 1:16) (some ten times in Paul). To God, Jesus will bring this redeemed world (1 Cor 15:24–28). He is the Lord *kyrios*, a term he uses some 250 times of Christ. It was often used of God, of the gods of the wider world, and the Emperor. His use of citizenship language also suggests a kingdom. Believers have their *politeuma* in heaven, with *politeuma* suggesting the center of the kingdom (Phil 3:20). As heavenly citizens, they live worthy of the gospel (Phil 1:27). They are fellow citizens of God's house, which is synonymous with the kingdom (Eph 2:20).

Five times Paul speaks of inheritance of the kingdom. Jesus employs this idea once in the Sheep and Goats Judgment account in Matt 25:34: 'Then the King shall say to those on his right, "Come, you who are blessed by my Father, inherit the kingdom prepared for you since the foundation of the world."' Those who have shown material concern for God's people are welcomed into eternal life.[106]

In the Corinthian correspondence, as here, twice Paul warns the Corinthians. First, in 1 Cor 6:9–11: 'do you not know that the unrighteous will not inherit the kingdom of God.' He then gives a list of such people including the sexually immoral (*porneia*), idolaters (*eidōlolatria*), adulterers, men who engage in

---

106. The Sheep and Goats is commonly read as an injunction to believers to care for those in distress to inherit the kingdom. However, it is about how the people of the nations have treated the brothers of Christ and so speaks of judgment on the basis of receiving those sent with the gospel and by implication the gospel itself. See e.g., D. L. Turner, *Matthew*, BECNT (Grand Rapids: Baker, 200), 603–11.

homosexuality, thieves, the greedy, revilers, and swindlers. Some of the Corinthians were engaged in such things in their past but are now delivered from such things. They must not continue to do them.

Second, in 1 Cor 15:50, the broader statement is made that 'flesh and blood cannot inherit the kingdom of God.' Flesh in its fallen state through sin, must be transformed into immortality and imperishability for entry. For those who have faith in Christ, at his return, this will gloriously happen in the twinkling of an eye.

The other reference is in Eph 5:5, where again, the sexually immoral (*pornos*), impure (*akathartos*), and those who covet who are idolaters (*eidōlolatria*), will have no inheritance in the kingdom of Christ and God. In all but the Ephesians text,[107] the verb *klēronomeō* is used in the future, Paul talking about the final state. Paul wants his converts to be under no illusion, those who do things like those listed in 5:19–21 and other such things will not inherit the kingdom of God at the consummation.

This verse leads to questions about Paul's theology. On the one hand, he is saying one is justified by faith aside from works of the law. Elsewhere, he will state that one is saved by grace through faith, not through works (in a more general sense) (Eph 2:8). Yet, in these passages, he seems to state that where one engages in such works of the flesh, one cannot inherit the kingdom of God. Paul does not tidy this up for us, and we are forced to read between the lines.

Paul is emphatic that one who has a saving faith in Christ and has received the Spirit is justified by faith and will inherit eternal life. While people may sin in some of the ways listed (and others), where this is authentic faith, their status is not affected, as Christ's death is sufficient for all sin.

---

107. The use of the present *echō* (has no inheritance) fits with the more realized eschatology Paul uses in Ephesians whereby the final state is spoken of as a present experience (e.g., saved, seated at the right hand, etc., in 2:4–7). However, the use of the present is to stress the current reality as Paul states Christ's supremacy over the powers. It is likely that Paul is using this hortatively to encourage the Ephesians to recognize this.

However, questions remain. Is Paul saying that if the Galatians persist in such things, there is a point where they disqualify their faith, i.e., do they render faith obsolete because while they verbally state they believe in God and his Son, their repulsive sinful behavior demonstrates to God that they do not believe? Is Paul merely using this list to remind them of the revolting lifestyles of the world and for many, their former states, to remind them not only to believe in Jesus but to yield to the Spirit and put them to death?

Are they hortatory—Paul warning them of what becomes of a person who is not in Christ but living by the flesh so as to encourage them to live their status—people not of the flesh but the Spirit? Is this warning calling them to be what they already are in Christ—people free of sin, so do not be a slave to sin (cf. Rom 6)? Is he simply seeking to show them that such fleshly living is not what God wants, to urge them to live the Christ-life in conformity with God's ethics? Elsewhere, people who continue to do such things are to be expelled (cf. 1 Cor 5). Is he warning the Galatians that those who do so should also be banished, albeit in the hope that they will ultimately be saved and re-integrated into the Christian community and the new creation?

My read on all this is that there may be a point where God says, 'Enough, you say you believe, but your deeds demonstrate you do not. You are a hypocrite.' So, as in James 2, where 'faith without works is dead,' God looks at the heart and sees that while the words and even the actions are there, the faith is not, and so that person perishes (cf. Matt 7:21–23). If so, this is not for us to judge. However, where we are concerned, as Paul warns the Galatians, we should remind those among us who are violating the gospel with fleshly sin that they are in a perilous state. People who do such things will not inherit the kingdom of God. We leave the judgment to God.

CHAPTER TWENTY-NINE: CULTIVATE THE FRUIT OF THE SPIRIT (5:22–26)

After outlining what it means to live by the works of the flesh and implicitly summoning the Galatians not to live by such impulses, Paul turns to the positive attributes that grow in those who live by the Spirit.

EXCURSIS: VIRTUE LISTS

Galatians 5:22–23 Paul counters the vice list with a virtue list. Just as vice lists are found across the milieu, so are virtue lists in which ethically ideal behaviors are encouraged. As noted above, the Greeks and Romans had four cardinal virtues: *phronēsis* (wisdom, prudence, understanding), *sōphrosynē* (moderation, temperance, self-restraint), *dikaiosynē* (justice), and *andreia* (courage).[1]

In some OT and Apocryphal texts, virtue lists are rare, but some are found. These appear in a range of forms such as descriptions of God, of those endowed by God, righteous people, wisdom, and in prophetic appeals for goodness. Here are some examples (terms from Gal 5 highlighted with Greek transliterations; other related terms are highlighted).[2]

1. Exodus 34:6–7: 'The LORD passed before him and proclaimed, "The LORD, the LORD, a God merciful and

---

1. Comparable lists from Greek and Roman writings are mentioned among those listed in the footnotes on the introductory comments on 5:19–21.
2. For these Jewish virtue lists I am indebted to Fitzgerald, 'Virtue/Vice Lists,' 6.858. I have added and deleted a few. See also, e.g., Ex 31:3; 35:31; 1 Kings 10:0; 2 Chron 9:8; Ps 25:6; 33:5; 40:11; 51:1; 69:16; 89:14; 145:8; Jer 9:24; Hos 2:19; Neh 9:17.

gracious, slow to **anger** (*makrothymos*, LXX), and abounding in *steadfast love* and *faithfulness*, keeping steadfast love for thousands, forgiving iniquity and transgression and sin, but who will by no means clear the guilty, visiting the iniquity of the fathers on the children and the children's children, to the third and the fourth generation.'" (ESV).

2. Numbers 14:18: 'The LORD is slow to anger and abounding in *steadfast love*, forgiving iniquity and transgression, but he will by no means clear the guilty, visiting the iniquity of the fathers on the children, to the third and the fourth generation.' (ESV).

3. Ps 86:15: 'But you, O Lord, are a God merciful and gracious, **slow to anger** (*makrothymos*, LXX) and abounding in *steadfast love* and *faithfulness*.' (ESV).

4. Ps 103:8: 'The LORD is merciful and gracious, **slow to anger** (*makrothymos*, LXX) and abounding in *steadfast love*.' (ESV).

5. Jonah 4:2: 'for I knew that you are a gracious God and merciful, **slow to anger** (*makrothymos*, LXX) and abounding in *steadfast love*, and relenting from disaster.' (ESV).

6. Ecclesiastes 2:26: 'For to the one who pleases him God has given wisdom and knowledge and *joy*, but to the sinner he has given the business of gathering and collecting, only to give to one who pleases God.' (ESV).

7. Job 1:1: 'There was a man in the land of Uz whose name was Job, and that man was blameless and upright, one who feared God and turned away from evil.' (ESV).

8. Job 1:8: 'And the LORD said to Satan, "Have you considered my servant Job, that there is none like him on the earth, a blameless and upright man, who fears God and turns away from evil?"' (ESV)

9. Job 2:3: 'And the LORD said to Satan, "Have you considered my servant Job, that there is none like him on the earth, a blameless and upright man, who fears God and turns away from evil? He still holds fast his

integrity, although you incited me against him to destroy him without reason."' (ESV).

10. Hosea 2:19: 'And I will betroth you to me forever. I will betroth you to me in righteousness and in justice, in steadfast love and in mercy. I will betroth you to me in *faithfulness*.' (ESV).

11. Micah 6:6: 'He has told you, O man, what is good; and what does the LORD require of you but to do justice, and to love kindness, and to walk humbly with your God?' (ESV).

12. Wisdom 8:7: 'And if anyone loves righteousness, her labors are virtues; for she teaches self-control and prudence, justice and courage.' (NRSV). Note the use of the four cardinal virtues here.

Virtue lists in the Jewish writings can be found. In the Pseudepigrapha, for example:

1. 2 Enoch 9:1: 'This place, Enoch, has been prepared for the righteous, who suffer every kind of calamity in their life and who afflict their souls, and who avert their eyes from injustice and who carry out righteous judgment who give bread to the hungry, and who cover the naked with clothing, and who lift up the fallen, and who help the injured and the orphans, who walk without a defect before the face of the LORD, and who worship him only—even for them this place has been prepared as an eternal inheritance.' (Charlesworth).

2. 2 Enoch 66:6: 'Walk, my children, in long-suffering, in meekness, honesty, in affliction, in distress, in *faithfulness*, in truth, in hope, in weakness, in derision, in assaults, in temptation, in deprivation, in nakedness.' (Charlesworth).

3. 4 Maccabees 1:18: 'Now the kinds of wisdom are rational judgment, justice, courage, and self-control.' (NRSV). These reflect the Greek cardinal virtues showing the Greek influence on the text.

4. 4 Maccabees 5:22–25: 'You scoff at our philosophy as though living by it were irrational, but it teaches us self-control, so that we master all pleasures and **desires** (*epythymia*), and it also trains us in courage, so that we endure any suffering willingly; it instructs us in justice, so that in all our dealings we act impartially, and it teaches us piety, so that with proper reverence we worship the only living God.' (NRSV). Again, note the cardinal virtues.

5. 4 Maccabees 8:3: 'When the tyrant had given these orders, seven brothers—handsome, modest, noble, and accomplished in every way—were brought before him along with their aged mother.' (NRSV).

In the New Testament, outside of Paul, Fitzgerald notes these three virtue lists:

1. Hebrews 7:26: 'For it was indeed fitting that we should have such a high priest, holy, innocent, unstained, separated from sinners, and exalted above the heavens' (ESV).

2. 1 Peter 3:8–9: 'Finally, all of you, have unity of mind, sympathy, [sibling] love, a tender heart, and a humble mind. Do not repay evil for evil or reviling for reviling, but on the contrary, bless, for to this you were called, that you may obtain a blessing' (ESV, adapted).

3. 2 Peter 1:5–7: 'For this very reason, make every effort to supplement your **faith** (*pistis*) with virtue, and virtue with knowledge, and knowledge with **self-control** (*enkrateia*), and **self-control** with steadfastness, and steadfastness with godliness, and godliness with [sibling] affection, and [sibling] affection with **love** (*agapē*)' (ESV, adapted).

Most virtue lists are found in Paul's paraenesis (all ESV):[3]

---

3. Again, Fitzgerald, 'Virtue/Vice Lists,' 8.858. I have added Rom 12; 1 Cor 13:13; Phil 2; 4; 1 Thess 5.

1. Rom 12:9–21 (Excerpts): 'Let **love** (*agapē*) be genuine ... hold fast to what is good. Love one another with [family] affection. Outdo one another in showing honor. Do not be slothful in zeal, be fervent in spirit, serve the Lord. **Rejoice** in hope, be patient in tribulation, be constant in prayer. Contribute to the needs of the saints and seek to show hospitality. Bless those who persecute you; bless and do not curse them. **Rejoice** with those who **rejoice**, weep with those who weep. Live in harmony with one another. Do not be haughty, but associate with the lowly. Never be wise in your own sight. Repay no one evil for evil, but give thought to do what is honorable in the sight of all. If possible, so far as it depends on you, live **peaceably** with all. Beloved, never avenge yourselves, but leave it to the wrath of God ... Do not be overcome by evil, but overcome evil with good' (ESV, adapted),

2. 1 Cor 13:4–8a. '**Love** (*agapē*) is patient and kind; **love** (*agapē*) does not envy or boast; it is not arrogant or rude. It does not insist on its own way; it is not irritable or resentful; it does not **rejoice** at wrongdoing, but rejoices with the truth. Love bears all things, **believes** all things, hopes all things, endures all things. **Love** (*agapē*) never ends' (ESV).

3. 1 Cor 13:13: 'So now **faith** (*pistis*), hope, and **love** (*agapē*) abide, these three; but the greatest of these is **love** (*agapē*)' (ESV).

4. 2 Corinthians 6:4–7: 'but as servants of God we commend ourselves in every way: by great endurance, in afflictions, hardships, calamities, beatings, imprisonments, riots, labors, sleepless nights, hunger; by purity, knowledge, **patience** (*makrothymia*), **kindness** (*chrēstotēs*), the Holy Spirit, genuine **love** (*agapē*); by truthful speech, and the power of God; with the weapons of righteousness for the right hand and for the left' (ESV).

5. Ephesians 4:1–3: '...walk in a manner worthy of the

calling to which you have been called, with all humility
and **gentleness** (*prautēs*), with **patience** (*makrothymia*),
bearing with one another in **love** (*agapē*), eager to
maintain the unity of the Spirit in the bond of **peace**
(*eirēnē*)' (ESV).

6. Ephesians 4:23–5:9 (Excerpts): 'to be renewed in the
spirit of your minds, and to put on the new self, created
after the likeness of God in true righteousness and
holiness … speak the truth with his neighbor, … but
rather let him labor, doing honest work with his own
hands, so that he may have something to share with
anyone in need … but only such [speech] as is good for
building up, as fits the occasion, that it may give grace to
those who hear. Be **kind** to one another, tenderhearted,
forgiving one another, as God in Christ forgave you.
Therefore be imitators of God, as **beloved** children. And
walk in **love** (*agapē*), as Christ **loved** us and gave himself
up for us, a fragrant offering and sacrifice to God … let
there be thanksgiving … Walk as children of light (for
the fruit of light is found in all that is **good** (*agathēsynē*)
and right and true), and try to discern what is pleasing
to the Lord' (ESV).

7. Philippians 2:1–4: 'So if there is any encouragement in
Christ, any comfort from **love** (*agapē*), any participation
in the Spirit, any affection and sympathy, complete my
joy (*chara*) by being of the same mind, having the same
love (*agapē*), being in full accord and of one mind … in
humility count others more significant than yourselves.
Let each of you look not only to his own interests, but
also to the interests of others' (ESV).

8. Philippians 4:4–9 (Excerpts): '**Rejoice** in the Lord
always; again I will say, **rejoice**. Let your reasonableness
be known to everyone. The Lord is at hand; do not be
anxious about anything, but in everything by prayer and
supplication with thanksgiving let your requests be
made known to God. And the **peace** (*eirēnē*) of God …
whatever is true, whatever is honorable, whatever is

just, whatever is pure, whatever is lovely, whatever is
commendable, if there is any excellence, if there is
anything worthy of praise, think about these things ...
and the God of **peace** ...' (ESV).

9. Colossians 3:12–15 (Excerpts): 'Put on then, as God's
    chosen ones, holy and **beloved**, compassionate hearts,
    kindness (*chrēstotēs*), humility, **meekness** (*prautēs*), and
    patience (*makrothymia*), bearing with one another and, if
    one has a complaint against another, forgiving each
    other; as the Lord has forgiven you, so you also must
    forgive. And above all these put on **love** (*agapē*), which
    binds everything together in perfect harmony. And let
    the **peace** (*eirēnē*) of Christ rule in your hearts, to which
    indeed you were called in one body. And be thankful ...'
    (ESV).

10. 1 Timothy 3:2–7 (Excerpts): 'Therefore an overseer
    must be above reproach, the husband of one wife, sober-
    minded, self-controlled, respectable, hospitable, able to
    teach, not a drunkard, not violent but gentle, not
    quarrelsome, not a lover of money. He must manage his
    own household well, with all dignity keeping his
    children submissive ... He must not be a recent convert
    ... he must be well thought of by outsiders ...' (ESV).

11. 1 Timothy 3:8–12: 'Deacons likewise must be dignified,
    not double-tongued, not addicted to much wine, not
    greedy for dishonest gain. They must hold the mystery
    of the faith with a clear conscience ... blameless. Their
    wives likewise must be dignified, not slanderers, but
    sober-minded, faithful in all things. Let deacons each be
    the husband of one wife, managing their children and
    their own households well' (ESV).

12. 1 Timothy 4:12: 'Let no one despise you for your youth,
    but set the believers an example in speech, in conduct,
    in **love** (*agapē*), in **faith** (*pistis*), in purity' (ESV).

13. 1 Timothy 6:11: 'But as for you, O man of God, flee
    these things. Pursue righteousness, godliness, **faith**
    (*pistis*), **love** (*agapē*), steadfastness, **gentleness**' (ESV).

14. 1 Timothy 6:18: 'As for the rich in this present age ... They are to do good, to be rich in good works, to be generous and ready to share ...' (ESV).
15. 2 Timothy 2:22–25: 'So flee youthful passions and pursue righteousness, **faith** (*pistis*), **love** (*agapē*), and **peace** (*eirēnē*), along with those who call on the Lord from a pure heart ... And the Lord's servant must be ... kind to everyone, able to teach, patiently enduring evil, correcting his opponents with gentleness' (ESV).
16. 2 Timothy 3:10–11b: 'You, however, have followed my teaching, my conduct, my aim in life, my **faith** (*pistis*), my **patience** (*makrothymia*), my **love** (*agapē*), my steadfastness, my persecutions and sufferings ...' (ESV).
17. Titus 1:8: 'He must not be ... but hospitable, a lover of good, self-controlled, upright, holy, and disciplined' (ESV).
18. Titus 2:2–10: '... teach what accords with sound doctrine. Older men are to be sober-minded, dignified, self-controlled, sound in faith, in **love** (*agapē*), and in steadfastness. Older women likewise are to be reverent in behavior, not slanderers or slaves to much wine. They are to teach what is **good**, and so train the young women to **love** their husbands and children, to be self-controlled, pure, working at home, **kind**, and submissive to their own husbands, that the word of God may not be reviled. Likewise, urge the younger men to be **self-controlled**. Show yourself in all respects to be a model of good works, and in your teaching show integrity, dignity, and sound speech that cannot be condemned, so that an opponent may be put to shame, having nothing evil to say about us. Bondservants are to be submissive to their own masters in everything; they are to be well-pleasing, not argumentative, not pilfering, but showing all good **faith** (*pistis*), so that in everything they may adorn the doctrine of God our Savior' (ESV).

As can be seen, from the above list of texts, Paul introduces his virtues without a set form, and each list is different.

THE FRUIT OF THE SPIRIT (5:22–23)

Galatians 5:22 launches the list with the first seven of the virtues which the Spirit yields in the believer's life:

But (*de*, 1:15) **the fruit** (*karpos*)[4] **of the Spirit** (genitive *pneuma*, 3:2) **is** (present *eimi*, 1:7) **love** (*agapē*, 5:6), **joy** (*chara*),[5] **peace** (*eirēnē*, 1:3), **patience** (*makrothymia*),[6] **kindness** (*chrēstotēs*),[7] **goodness** (*agathōsynē*),[8] **faithfulness** (*pistis*, 1:23).

Here, he presents the virtues as 'the fruit (*karpos*) of the Spirit.' The term is used literally for fruit (e.g., an orange) (Gen 1:11, 29), including human 'fruit'—children (Gen 30:2). In some of the OT and particularly the Wisdom literature, 'fruit' is used figuratively and ethically. So, in the LXX, 'the fruit of the ungodly is sin' (Prov 10:16) and 'the fruit of the righteous grows a tree of life' (Prov 11:30). Amos declares to Israel, 'Because you have perverted judgment into wrath, and the *fruit of righteousness* into bitterness,' speaking of Israel's injustice and violation of the ethical requirements of the law (Amos 6:12).[9] *Karpos* in the NT is used of agricultural produce,[10] or descendants (Luke 1:42; Acts

---

4. The common Greek noun for fruit, καρπός (*karpos*), is used once in Galatians 5:22 of the virtues the Spirit bears in the life of a believer.
5. The common noun χαρά (*chara*), meaning 'joy, gladness,' is used once in Galatians 5:22 as the second in the list of the fruit of the Spirit. The related verb *chairō* is absent.
6. The noun μακροθυμία (*makrothymia*) means 'patience,' 'forbearance,' 'long-suffering' and is used once in Galatians as the fourth of the fruit of the Spirit. It compounds *makro* (distant, far away) and *thymos* (anger). *Thymos* is used in the vice list and means 'anger, fits of rage.' Another *thymos* compound, *epithymia* and the verb *epithymeō* are used in 5:16 and 17 of sinful desires.
7. The fifth fruit of the Spirit in 5:22 is χρηστότης (*chrēstotēs*) a noun meaning kindness, goodness, generosity (BDAG 1090). It is only found in Paul on ten occasions.
8. The noun ἀγαθωσύνη (*agathōsynē*) is related to *agathos*, the common Greek term for good, used in 6:6 of sharing good things with teachers and in 6:10 of doing good to all, and especially to believers. Hence, it means goodness, generosity (BDAG 4). The only use is in 5:22 where it is the sixth fruit of the Spirit.
9. See also Prov 12:14; 13:2; 15:6; 18:21; Sir 27:6; 37:22, 23; Hos 10:12–13;14:3; Mic 7:13; Jer 6:19.
10. Matt 21:19; Luke 12:17; Jas 5:7, 18; Rev 22:2. In the fig tree cursing narrative (s.a.,

2:30), but also frequently in an ethical sense. So John the Baptist declared, 'bear fruit in keeping with repentance' (Matt 3:8, s.a. Matt 3:10; Luke 3:8–9).

Jesus employs the motif regularly, speaking of people as trees who produce good or bad fruit and who are known by this fruit (Matt 7:16–20; Luke 6:43–44, cf. 12:33). John's Jesus uses it for ethical fruit such as love for one's neighbor (John 15:2–8, 16). The writer of Hebrews uses it of, 'the peaceful *fruit* of righteousness' that is yielded from those the Father has disciplined (Heb 12:11, cf. Heb 13:15). Jacob speaks of wisdom from above that is 'full of mercy and good *fruit*' (Jas 3:17). Jacob also says that 'the *fruit* of righteousness is sown in peace for those who make peace' (Jas 3:18).

Paul uses *karpos* of missional fruit (converts) (Rom 1:13; Phil 1:22), gain (Rom 6:21), money (Rom 15:28), eschatological reward (Phil 4:17), and agricultural fruit (1 Cor 9:7; 2 Tim 2:6).[11] On three occasions, Paul uses *karpos* of ethical fruit. In Eph 5:9, he speaks of the 'fruit of the light in all goodness and righteousness and truth.' In Phil 1:11, Paul prays that the Philippians will on the Day of Judgment stand before God pure and blameless, 'filled with the fruit of righteousness that comes through Jesus Christ.' As here, this is fruit produced by God in a person's life. Here it is the fruit produced by the Spirit as people 'walk by the Spirit,' 'are led by the Spirit,' 'live by the Spirit,' and 'keep in step with the Spirit' (5:16, 18, 25). The genitive 'fruit of the Spirit' can be an attributive genitive, 'spiritual fruit,'[12] a 'genitive of production,' whereby the Spirit produces these things in a person's life.[13] Alternatively, it is a genitive of source,

---

Mark 11:14), it is symbolic of Israel. Other texts refer to missional fruit—converts and/or growth (e.g., Matt 13:8, 26; 21:34, 41, 43; Mark 4:7, 8, 29; 12:2; Luke 8:8; 13:6–9; 20:10; John 4:36; 12:24).

11. In both of these uses of *karpos*, Paul is using crops as an analogy for the wages of the preacher. So, in a sense, it speaks of money.

12. On this genitive, see Wallace, *Grammar*, 89.

13. On this genitive, see Wallace, *Grammar*, 105 who lists this use in 5:22 in this category. Similarly see Eph 4:3: 'the unity produced by the Spirit;' Eph 5:9: 'the fruit produced by the light.'

whereby the virtues are sourced in the Spirit.[14] Most likely, as Wallace agrees, it is a genitive of production.

The image of fruit speaks of something that is cultivated in those who have received the Spirit. The Spirit, who is shaped by these virtues, is kind of like a fertilizer that generates the growth of these attributes in human lives. Whereas those who have not received the Spirit are defenseless against the desires of the flesh, unable to overcome them, we who believe in Christ have received the Spirit.

If we are believers, as fleshly creatures imbued with the Spirit, we have two impulses working with us at any given time, the desires of the flesh and the promptings of God's Spirit. Our call in the gospel is to yield to the latter and allow the Spirit to shape us, morphing us to be more and more like Jesus. Due to our fallenness and sinfulness, we are all susceptible to the sins of the flesh, each with our own weaknesses. For some, it is pride, for others sexual desire or the love of money and stuff, the desire for power and control, anger, and other such vices. Our challenge is to listen to the Spirit's gentle voice within, through others, through God's word, and resist the desires of the flesh so that the Spirit's fruit can grow in us. This fruit is seen in the context of relationships. Such growth is the primary challenge of Christian ethics.

Discerning any particular structure to the list is difficult. Lightfoot argues that there are three virtues of the mind, three of social relationships, and three of conduct. He says of the list:

The catalogue falls into three groups of three each. The first of these comprises Christian habits of mind in their more general aspect, 'love, joy, peace'; the second gives special qualities affecting a man's intercourse with his neighbour, 'long-suffering, kindness, beneficence'; while the third, again general in character like the first, exhibits the principles which guide a Christian's conduct, 'honesty, gentleness, temperance.'[15]

However, Moo rightly rejects this as unclear but rightly states

---

14. See Wallace, *Grammar*, 109.
15. Lightfoot, *Galatians*, 212.

that '[t]he one significant matter in the sequence is the fact that "love" comes first as the primary and foundational "fruit."'[16]

The first fruit then is *agapē*, discussed concerning 5:6, 14. Defined by the God of love (2 Cor 13:11), *ḥĕ·sĕḏ* (e.g., Exod 34:6), *agapē* is most powerfully demonstrated in the giving of his Son (Rom 5:8; Tit 3:4; Eph 2:4), and Christ's selfless self-giving for the world (Eph 5:1–2; Gal 2:20). *Agapē* is for Paul and the other NT writers, the primary virtue and the heart of Christian ethics.[17] This love is poured into the human heart through the Spirit (Rom 5:5). This love is to be directed to God, as we worship him in humble adoration.[18]

Love for one's neighbor is the sum and fulfillment of all law (5:14; Rom 13:8–10). Love is generated in us by the Spirit (cf. Rom 15:30) and our call 'in Christ' is to put to death the works of the flesh and allow God's love to shape every aspect of our lives as we relate to the other—our attitudes, our speech (Eph 4:15), our actions (1 Cor 16:14), our family life,[19] our church relationships,[20] church life (Eph 4:16), and our mission (2 Cor 5:14; 2 Thess 1:3). Every gift we have is to be used from the motivation of love (1 Cor 13:1–3). Love is our ethic for all eternity (1 Cor 13:13).

As Paul has just said in this passage, what counts is faith working through love, seen in Galatians voluntarily and among those who live joyfully as slaves of one another (5:13). I join Paul in praying for us that our 'love may abound more and more in knowledge and depth of insight' (Phil 1:9; 1 Thess 3:12).

The second fruit is joy (*chara*). The noun *chara*, 'joy' and verbs *chairō*, 'rejoice' and *synchairō*, 'rejoice with,' are found some 140 times in the NT, fifty-four times in Paul.[21] *Chara* means 'to

---

16. Moo, *Galatians*, 364.
17. See, e.g., Mark 12:31 and parr.; John 13:34–35; Jas 2:8; 1 Pet 3:8; 2 Pet 1:7; 1 John 3:16–17.
18. See Rom 8:28; 1 Cor 2:9; 8:3; Eph 6:24.
19. See Eph 5:25, 28, 33; Col 3:19; Tit 2:4.
20. See Eph 4:2; Phil 2:2; Col 3:14; 1 Thess 4:9.
21. Other terms are related including *charis*, 'grace;' *charizomai*, 'give graciously;' *charitoō*, 'show grace;' *acharistos*, 'ungrateful;' *charisma*, 'gift of grace, spiritual gift;' *eucharisteō*, 'give thanks;' *eucharistia*, 'thankful;' and *eucharistos*, 'thanksgiving.'

experience gladness'[22] or joy or delight.[23] While this language has not been used thus far in Galatians, using the synonym *euphainō*, using Isaiah, Paul has spoken of Sarah's rejoicing of exiled Israel's joy. This is now being ultimately fulfilled in the many gentiles coming into Abraham's family through the gospel of faith and promise (Gal 4:27).

For Paul, the kingdom of God is about righteousness, peace, and joy in the Holy Spirit (Rom 14:17)—as here, the Spirit is the source of joy. He prays for the Romans that the God of hope may fill them with joy and peace in faith, again linking this to the Spirit (Rom 15:13). The power of the Spirit enables believers in a severe struggle to remain in a place of abundant joy, not because of the circumstances or even God relieving them of their pain, but because of the power of the Spirit to generate inward delight in God who is with us in our sufferings (2 Cor 8:2; Col 1:11). When he is weak, he rejoices (2 Cor 13:9).

Paul knows God's joy, so he can testify that while at times he is full of sorrow, he rejoices (2 Cor 6:10). He prays with joy even though he is chained in a Roman prison (Phil 1:4). When people are preaching to cause him harm when he faces trial before Caesar Nero, he rejoices because, through God, he will know salvation come what may (Phil 1:18). He goes as far as saying that he rejoices in his sufferings! (Col 1:24). Why? Because in and through afflictions, he is walking the Christ-journey with the Lord, Christ's own body filled with Paul's sufferings on his behalf. Hence, for Paul, it is an honor; it is being conformed to the death of Christ—cruciformity (Phil 3:10). He knows too that it is through our suffering that we are shaped, for from our sufferings come endurance, character, and a hope that does not disappoint—for God's Spirit is in us (Rom 5:3–5, cf. Jas 1:2–5).

One of the core things Paul wants to see in his letter-recipients, who for him are his joy,[24] is a deepening of their experience of joy despite their struggles (Phil 1:25). He yearns for them to rejoice in hope (Rom 12:12), to rejoice with those who rejoice (Rom

---

22. BDAG 1077. Similarly, Louw & Nida, 1:301.
23. LSJ 1976.
24. See Rom 16:19; Phil 4:1; 1 Thess 2:19–10; 3:9; 2 Tim 1:4.

12:12) and that his converts would rejoice with him as he rejoices (Phil 2:18). So, Paul can say, 'Rejoice in the Lord always, and again I say, rejoice' (Phil 4:4, cf. Phil 3:1). For Paul, joy is linked to love, with the one who loves refusing to rejoice in wrongdoing but delighting in the truth (1 Cor 13:6).

In the journey of life, we meet those wonderful saints who always find something to be joyful for, despite their suffering. Often, they are older, mature believers, who are becoming frail, even facing their mortality, having lost loved ones, and facing the trial of failing health and trying circumstances every day. These are those who have grasped what Paul thinks about joy. It is us remembering that even though our struggles are real and deeply trying, God is good. He is with us. He knows our pain—having been mercilessly rejected and crushed, hung on a cross. He is shaping history around us who love him and have been called by him. He is in us by his Spirit, experiencing everything we experience. Imagine that! God, dwelling in the hearts of billions of people in their every moment and feeling what we feel. Wow!

Neither is God capricious nor passive. Rather, he is comforting us. He is strengthening us. He is guiding us. He is with us in every sense of the word. Even our struggles he will use to shape us to be more and more like his Son. And wonderfully, we will experience the fullness of joy when he returns and we are raised from the dead, gloriously transformed, to live forever with him without pain and suffering. We will then know the fullness of his joy. The thing is that we do not have to wait because God's eschaton has come in Christ and is in our hearts. Every minute of every day we have the Spirit in us generating joy, if only we will just allow the Spirit to overflow from us.

Thus, ours is to allow that joy to well up. This is the joy that can lead a person to walk in the door of a church, despite all the pain and struggle, and determine 'I will praise God. I will rejoice in his name.'[25] This is not turning a blind eye to suffering and playing it down. No way! It is real, and it sucks. But it is allowing the Spirit to whisper into our hearts, 'nothing can separate me from

---

25. See e.g., Pss. 31:7; 35:9; Isa 61:10; Hab 3:18; Phil 1:18b; Rev 11:10.

the love of God and his Son Christ Jesus' (cf. Rom 8:35–40) and finding hope and joy in this. What is there left to do but, *pantote chairete*—'rejoice always!' (1 Thess 5:6).[26]

The third great Spirit-fruit is the virtue of 'peace' (*eirēnē*). Peace instantly calls to mind the Hebrew שָׁלוֹם (*šā·lôm*) in Israel's story, which is translated *eirēnē* in the LXX. For Gideon, the Lord himself is peace (Judg 6:24). Shalom is a blessing for Israel if she is faithful to the covenant that is holistic in scope, including an end of war and the removal of predators (Lev 26:6, cf. Ps 29:11). It involves prosperity (Ps 37:11; 71:3) and good health (Ps 37:4). The Aaronic blessing too focuses on peace (Num 6:26). The source of true shalom is God, e.g., 'for he will speak *peace* to his people' (Ps 84:9, NRSV). Conversely, the absence of peace is a sign of covenantal accursedness (e.g., Jer 16:5; Ezek 13:10). The concept is intimately tied to God's character and action toward Israel; his *ḥě·sěḏ* (steadfast love, *agapē*), his *'ěmět* (faithfulness, cf. *pistis*), and his *ṣě·ḏěq* (righteousness, cf. *dikaiosyne*).[27]

For example, the lovely Ps 84:1: 'Steadfast love and faithfulness will meet; righteousness and peace will kiss each other.' So central is peace that the term is the essential Jewish greeting (e.g., Judg 21:13) and farewell—'go in peace' (e.g., 1 Sam 1:17; 2 Kings 5:19). It is used for a good person's final departure—'to go in peace' (e.g., 2 Chron 34:28). The righteous pray for the peace of Jerusalem (Ps 121:6),[28] and the Psalmist cries, 'Shalom be upon Israel' (Ps 124:5; 127:6). The paths of Wisdom are peace (Prov 3:17) and the fear of the Lord, and the crown of wisdom brings peace and wholeness (Sir 1:18).

The eschatological hope of Israel is eternal peace.[29] This peace

---

26. See also Rom 15:32; 1 Cor 7:30; 16:17; 2 Cor 1:24; 2:3; 7:4, 7, 9, 13, 16; 8:2; 13:11; Phil 2:2, 17, 28, 29; 4:10; Col 2:5; 1 Thess 1:6; Phlm 7.

27. The LXX translates *ḥě·sěḏ* as *eleos*, 'mercy' and *'ěmět* as *alētheia*. However, in the NT *agapē* is preferred for God's love and *pistis* often translates *'ěmět* elsewhere.

28. This is the prayer the righteous pray: 'May they prosper who love you. Peace be within your walls, and security within your towers.' The Psalm goes on in vv. 8–9: 'For the sake of my relatives and friends I will say, "Peace be within you." For the sake of the house of the LORD our God, I will seek your good.' (NRSV).

29. See, e.g., 1 Kings 2:33; Hag 2:9; Zech 8:12; 9:10; Isa 14:30; 57:2, 19; 60:17; 66:12; Jer 14:13; 36:11; 40:6; Ezek 34:25.

is tied to the messianic hope (Isa 9:7). The punishment of the Servant will bring peace (Isa 53:5). This eternal covenant will be one of peace (Isa 54:10; Ezek 37:26). The proclamation of the good news of peace is lovely (Isa 52:7; Nah 1:15). In Ps 33:15, the righteous is to 'turn from evil and do good, seek (*zēteō*) peace (*eirēnē*) and pursue (*diōkō*) it.'

In the Gospels and Acts, *eirēnē* is used as a blessing (Matt 10:13), the cessation of war and security (Matt 10:34; Luke 11:21; 12:51; 14:32; Acts 12:20; 24:2), to go in peace healed (Mark 5:34; Luke 7:50; 8:48), the way of peace (Luke 1:79), as a blessing (Luke 2:14; 10:5), to die in peace (Luke 2:29), of a righteous person as a son of peace (Luke 10:6), of God's work in Jesus (Luke 19:38, 42), what Christ gifts the disciples through the Spirit and his word (John 14:27; 16:33), as a greeting (John 20:19, 21, 26), reconciled relationships (Acts 7:26), freedom from persecution (Acts 9:31), the gospel of peace (Acts 10:36), and to be blessed for a journey (Acts 15:33; 16:36).

Other NT uses other than Paul include Melchizedek, 'king of *peace*'—applied to Jesus—(Heb 7:2), a hospitable welcome (Heb 11:31), a warm farewell (Jas 2:16), as something we make every effort to gain (2 Pet 3:14), and cessation of war (Rev 6:4). At times peace is used ethically, as in Heb 12:14: 'strive (*diōkō*) for *peace* with everyone.' Similarly, James 3:18: 'and the fruit (*karpos*) of righteousness is sown in *peace* to all who make peace.' For Peter, the righteous 'seek (*zēteō*) peace and pursue (*diōkō*) it' (1 Pet 3:11).

As with Paul, who characteristically begins his letters with a blessing of peace (usually alongside grace), a number of NT writers use similar greetings.[30] These greetings are prayers for God's people to experience the fullness of God's Shalom.[31] Paul also employs peace in his farewells (Eph 6:23). As for Paul[32] and the writer of Hebrews, God is a 'God of peace' (Heb 13:20). The destiny of the righteous is eternal peace (Rom 2:10).

---

30. See 1 Pet 1:2; 5:14; 2 Pet 1:2; 2 John 3; 3: John 15; Jude 2; Rev 1:4.

31. See 1:3; Rom 1:7; 1 Cor 1:3; 2 Cor 1:2; Eph 1:2; Phil 1:2; Col 1:2; 1 Thess 1:1; 2 Thess 1:2; 1 Tim 1:2; Tit 1:4; Phlm 3, s.a. 2 Thess 3:16.

32. See Rom 15:33; 16:20; 1 Cor 14:33; 2 Cor 13:11; Phil 4:9; 1 Thess 5:23; 1 Tim 1:2; 2 Tim 1:2.

Humanity in its fallen state is characterized by a failure to know the way of peace (Rom 3:17, cf. Isa 59:8; Luke 1:79). This human failure has separated humanity from God. However, through being justified by faith, the enmity is removed with people having peace with God through Christ (Rom 5:1). The work of the Spirit in believers is to generate peace (Rom 8:6; Rom 14:17). By his Spirit, God fills believers with joy, peace, and hope (Rom 15:13). By prayer, the peace of God imparted by the Spirit guards the believer's heart and mind (Phil 4:7).

As such, believers should pursue the things of peace (Rom 14:19). They are called to peace even with a departing spouse (1 Cor 7:15). They should send God's workers on in peace (after a good welcome and hospitality) (1 Cor 16:11). They are to let the peace of Christ rule in their hearts as they live in unity (Col 3:15). Timothy must pursue peace, alongside righteousness, faith, and love (2 Tim 2:22).

Later in Galatians, Paul will give a blessing of peace and mercy upon all who repudiate Judaizers and upon the people of God (6:16). Peace has a special import regarding the Judaizing dispute. In Eph 2:14, 17, Christ is 'our peace' who has broken down the wall of division between Jew and gentile, destroying the rule of the law. Christ 'preached peace' uniting people together in him as one Temple by faith.

By the Spirit, believers are to do all they can to 'maintain the unity of the Spirit in the bond of peace' (Eph 4:3). Peace is also missional—they are to be always ready with the 'gospel *of peace*' to take the good news to others (Eph 6:15). Paul also employs the associated verb *eirēneuō* in Rom 12:18, urging the Romans as much as it depends on them to live at peace with everyone. At Paul's time, the Roman world was in a state of relative peace, established through brutal military might and power (cf. 1 Thess 5:3). Except, only in Christ can the world truly know the fullness of Shalom.

Here, peace first speaks of the Galatians' relationship with God. By faith, they are justified and are reconciled to God. They must not turn from this faith to the Judaizing theology of law-observance. If they do, their state of reconciliation with God is maintained. Second, they must live in unity, putting behind them their infighting (5:13, 19–21), and maintain the bond of peace. Third, as much as it depends on their own capacity, they must continue to live at peace with all and share the gospel of peace with their fellow Galatians. They must not adulterate that gospel to the Judaizers' demands.

The fourth term is *makrothymia*. The term like *epithymia* (desires) and its verb (5:16, 17) is related to *thymos* used in 5:20, where it means extreme anger, rage. It compounds *makros*, 'long, far away, distant' and *thymos*. Literally, then, it has the sense of a lack of *thymos*, hence patience, long-suffering, or forbearance, rather than raging when provoked.

Rare in the LXX; it is used of the wise being quick to hear and patient in answering (Sir 5:11) and God who gives patience to the suffering (Isa 57:15).[33] In the Pseudepigrapha, *makrothymia* is an attribute of God—his long-suffering or patience.[34] It is also desired as an attribute of the godly (T. Dan. 2:1; 6.8). In the Testament of Joseph is written, 'patience is medicine' (T. Jos. 2:7, s.a. T. Jos. 17:2; 18.3). Similarly, 'patience is better than anything' (T. Job. 27:7).

The term is not found in the Gospels and Acts, only in the epistles. The writer of Hebrews uses it of ancient saints whose faithful perseverance Christians should emulate (Heb 6:12; Jas 5:10). Paul also speaks of Christ's patience as an example for believers (1 Tim 1:16). Otherwise, outside of Paul, it is used of God's patience at the time of Noah (1 Pet 3:20) as well as presently—his patience being salvation (2 Pet 3:15).

Likewise, Paul uses it of God's *makrothymia* which leads people to repentance (Rom 2:4) and which endures those destined for destruction (Rom 9:22). Paul's other uses are all in virtue lists, whether his own patience (2 Cor 6:6; 2 Tim 3:10) or as desired Christian virtue (Eph 4:2; Col 3:12). He prays for the Colossians that they would have endurance and patience (Col 1:11). Those

---

33. *Makrothymia* is also applied to a king able to be persuaded by patience (Prov 25:15), in a prayer that God would not be long-suffering with Jeremiah's persecutors (Jer 15:15), and of the Romans' patience in conquering nations (1 Macc 8:4).

34. See Gr. Apoc. Ezra 2:8; T. Gad 4:7; Let. Aris. 188; 2 Bar. 12:4.

engaging in ministry are to do so with 'all patience,' indicating it is a virtue that should be seen in the lives of those in Christian ministry (2 Tim 4:2). The Galatians then are to be patient with one another. In this, they will emulate God and his Son who show patience with humanity.

The fifth term is *chrēstotēs*, which means 'goodness, kindness, generosity.'[35] As with *makrothymia*, in Jewish writings (especially the Psalms), the term is used for God and his treatment of people. So, David sings, 'According to your mercy remember me, on account of your *kindness*, O Lord' (LXX Ps 24:7 [Eng. 25:7]).[36] It is also used for those who do good (Ps 13:1, 3 [Eng. 14:1, 3]), something God's people are urged to do (Ps 36:3 [Eng. 37:3]).

Chrēstotēs is a purely Pauline term in the NT, used of God's kindness (and forbearance) (Rom 2:4; 11:22) demonstrated in Christ (Eph 2:7; Tit 3:4), humanity which lacks goodness (Rom 3:12, cf. Ps 14:1), and as an attribute of the godly (2 Cor 6:6; Col 3:12). It speaks of people emulating God and his Son and treating each other well, with kindness and generosity. To not do so is a work of the flesh (Rom 3:12). As they battle away, the Galatians are challenged to turn from anger and contention to patience and goodness.

The sixth term is *agathōsynē*, from *agathos*, 'good' (6:6, 10), and so means 'goodness, generosity.'[37] It is used sparingly in the LXX of God's goodness (Neh 9:25, 35; 13:31), in Ecclesiastes of pleasure, enjoyment, good things, or prosperity (Ecc 4:8; 5:17; 6:3, 6; 7:15), and elsewhere of people doing well or good, or their goodness (Judg 9:16; 2 Chron 24:16; Eccl 5:10). Conversely, wrongdoers love evil more than good (Ps 51:5 [Eng. 52:3], s.a. Eccl 9:18). In the Pseudepigraphal work Testament of Judah 18:4, the reader is warned that sexual immorality and the love of

---

35. BDAG 1090.
36. See Ps 20:4 [Eng. 21:3]; 30:20 [Eng. 31:19]; 64:12 [65:11]; 67:11 [Eng. 68:10]; 84:13 [Eng. 85:12]; 103:28 [Eng. 104:28]; 105:5 [Eng. 106:5]; 118:65 [Eng. 119:65]; 144:7 [Eng. 145:7]; 1 Esd 5:61). *Chrēstotēs* is also used for God's judgments (Ps 118:68 [Eng. 119:68]). See also in the Pseudepigrapha, Gk. Apoc. Ezra 2.21; Pss. Sol. 5:13–15, 18; 8:28; 9:7; 18:1.
37. BDAG 4.

money deprive the soul of all goodness. Abraham is commended as being righteous in goodness, due to his generous hospitality and love (T. Ab. (A) 1.5). It is thus a virtue in Jewish thought.

In the NT, it is used only by Paul four times. These include his confidence that the Romans are full of goodness (Rom 15:14) and that God would fulfill every resolve for good among the Thessalonians (2 Thess 1:11). As here, in Eph 5:9, *agathōsynē* is found in a virtue list alongside righteousness and truth. The Galatians are to yield to the Spirit, who is sowing goodness in their minds and hearts. They are to let this flow in and through them in their relationships in the church and in mission. This goodness includes sharing with their teachers of the word in all *good things* (*agathos*, 6:6) and doing *good* to all people, especially to those who are believers (again, *agathos*, 6:10).

The seventh in the list is *pistis*, discussed in 1:23. *Pistis* is the term for Paul and John, in particular, that captures the required human response to God—belief, faith, trust (2:16). This faith comes when the word is heard with an open heart (3:2, 5), and the Spirit dwelling in the believer. Such belief is the work of the Spirit who enables this response in a person.

As discussed more fully in 2:16, a saving faith has four dimensions: 1) Intellectual belief in Christ and his the gospel (*notitia*); 2) Assent, a surrendering 'yes' to the call of God through the gospel—which is ongoing (*assensus*); 3) Trust in God and his Son no matter how difficult life may be (*fiducia*); and 4) Walking in relationship with God (*affinitas*). Such faith is enabled by the Spirit.

The message of Galatians is emphatic—the Galatians must continue to 'walk by faith' to remain in that saving relationship with God (cf. 2 Cor 5:7). To yield to the Judaizers is to be 'severed from Christ' and 'to fall from grace' (5:4). However, the Spirit is working in them, calling them not to do this and to persevere in faith. This is the same for us; we believe because of the Spirit's power to enable this faith. We continue to endure in faith because of the Spirit's power.

The term also carries with it the idea of faithfulness toward others relationally, trustworthiness or fidelity. *Pistis* can have this meaning. Jesus shares that the core matters of the law are justice, mercy, and faithfulness (Matt 23:23). Paul speaks of God's covenantal faithfulness (Rom 3:3). As discussed on 2:16, 20; 3:22, some argue *pistis Christou* constructs speak of Christ's faithfulness (cf. Rom 3:22, 26; Phil 3:9). Some texts in the Pastorals may take this meaning.[38]

As the majority of terms in the passage are relational, "faithfulness" may be the intended sense here, as reflected in most translations (ESV, NRSV, NIV, NET) and defended by a majority of commentators.[39] However, it is possible that the two ideas are in mind. Dunn argues that Paul does not make a sharp distinction between 'justifying faith' (2:16; Rom 5:1); 'charismatic faith' (1 Cor 12:9; 13:2), 'faith' as accepting God's grace, and 'faithfulness' as the ongoing response to God's grace.[40] Paul then is speaking of the Galatian's perseverance in faith by the power of the Spirit and live a life full of faith, trustworthiness, and fidelity toward God and others.

In *Galatians 5:23*, Paul brings his list to a conclusion with two further virtues, and then speaks of their relationship to the law: **gentleness** (*prautēs*),[41] **self-control** [42](*enkrateia*)[43]—**against**

---

38. 1 Tim 4:12; 6:11; 2 Tim 2:22; 3:10.
39. E.g., Moo, *Galatians*, 265.
40. Dunn, *Galatians*, 311–12.
41. The noun πραΰτης (*prautēs*) is employed twice in Galatians. It carries the sense 'the quality of not being overly impressed by a sense of one's self-importance, *gentleness, humility, courtesy, considerateness, meekness* in the older favorable sense … and occasionally, other qualities.' (BDAG 861, emphasis theirs). It is used in 5:23 in the list of the fruit of the Spirit. Its other use is in 6:1 where it is used for restoring a person who is caught in a transgression with gentleness. It is only used by Paul in the NT. I have chosen to translate it 'humility' as most translations neglect this possibility.
42. **VARIANT:** Some texts prefer *agneia*, 'purity, chastity' (D* F G it vgcl; Irlat Cyp Ambst). However, this is to be rejected on the basis of the wide attestation without the term. The term was likely added because of concern for sexual immorality in the later church. Some texts include *hypomonē*, 'steadfastness' (Nc 442 463). This too is clearly an interpolation. See also Metzger, *Textual Commentary*, 529.
43. The noun ἐγκράτεια (*enkrateia*) blends *en* (in) and *krateō* which has a range of meanings including 'hold, control, restrain, hold back' (BDAG 564). It thus has that sense of 'hold in,' speaking of 'restraint of one's emotions, impulses, or desires, self-control.' (BDAG 274). It is used once in Galatians 5:23 as the final virtue in Paul's

(*kata*, 1:4) **such things** (plural genitive *toioutos*, 5:21) **there is** (present *eimi*, 1:7) **no** (*ou*, 1:1) **law** (*nomos*, 2:16).

The eighth term in the Spirit-fruit list is *prautēs*. It is not common. In the LXX, it is used nine times. The term can have the meaning 'humility' (Ps 89:10 [Eng. 90:10]; 131:1 [Eng. 13:1]; Sir 3:17). For example, in Sir 10:28, the reader is instructed to 'honor your soul with *humility*, and give it honor according to its worthiness.' Moses is similarly commended for his trust and humility, likely recalling Num 12:3 where he is commended as the humblest man in the world.

Alternatively, it is used of 'gentleness' as in Ps 44:5 (Eng. 45:4) where the king rides as a warrior in victory 'on account of truth and *gentleness*' (*praustēs*). Similarly, in Sir 4:8, the wise person listens to the poor and answers them 'peacefully with *gentleness*.'

Sometimes, the two ideas merge. For example, in Sir 36:28, if there are mercy and *praustēs* upon a wife's tongue, her husband is more fortunate than others. Here, *praustēs* can be humility or gentleness; both ideas seem in mind as what is envisaged in the term is either the attitude that leads to a gentle approach (humility) or the actual gentleness itself.

Three of the eleven NT uses are by Jacob and 1 Peter. In Jas 1:21, believers are to rid themselves of sin and welcome the implanted word with *prautēs* (humility). Similarly, in Jas 3:13, believers are to do their works with a humility of wisdom that is free of jealousy and selfish ambition. Peter speaks of believers responding to questions concerning the faith with reverence and *praustēs* (1 Pet 3:15). Here, the term can mean either humility or gentleness.

The text that governs Paul's understanding of the term is 2 Cor 10:1, where Paul appeals to the Corinthians through the humility/gentleness of Christ. It is there linked to the more common humility (*tapein-*) language. Christians demonstrating *praustēs* are emulating the attitude of Christ. In 1 Cor 4:21, Paul asks the Corinthians whether he should come with a rod or a

---

Spirit-fruit list. It may be that it functions summatively as the basis for the restraint of the works of the flesh and for living by the positive virtues just listed.

spirit of *prautētos*. Here, gentleness is more clearly in mind, in contrast with giving them a caning. Again, gentleness is closer to its meaning in 2 Tim 2:25 and Tit 3:2, which speak of dealing with opponents with gentleness and showing every *graciousness* to all people.

Conversely, the other use in Galatians is 6:1 could refer to humility. Paul instructs the Galatians to restore any who are caught in a transgression with a spirit of *prautēs* while taking care that they themselves are not tempted. Here, humility seems closer to the meaning, although gentleness of approach would naturally be associated with humility of correction. In the virtue lists of Eph 4:2 and Col 3:12, *prautēs* is listed in the virtue list in association with *tapeinophrosynē*, 'humility,' showing how closely the ideas are linked.[44]

As such, it is legitimate to translate *prautēs* either as 'humility' or 'gentleness,' with either translation implying the alternative—being humble in the sight of others would mean to deal with them with gentleness, and conversely being gentle comes from humility. I have chosen to translate it gentleness as the emphasis here is relational and speaks of the way in which people relate to each other. However, readers need to realize that underlying this gentleness is an attitude of humility that mirrors that of Jesus, who humbled himself on behalf of the world in self-giving to the point of death.

The final term is *enkrateia*, which compounds *en* (in) and *krateō* and speaks of something held fast, seized, or controlled.[45]

---

44. The term features in the Apostolic Fathers. It is used for the ideal of a woman demonstrating a desire to be gentle/humble (1 Clem. 21:1). It is paired with *tapein-* (humble) language in 1 Clem. 30:8. It is used as a descriptor of leaders (1 Clem. 61:2). A bishop's *praustēs* is his power—his humility/gentleness, with humility more likely as an accurate translation here (Ign. *Trall*. 3.2). In Ign. *Trall* 4.2, it speaks more of the converse of envy, which would be humility rather than gentleness. Conversely, gentleness would seem appropriate in Ign. *Poly*. 2.1 where one brings troublesome people into submission. Similarly, in Ign. *Poly*. 6.2, gentleness would seem appropriate in the command to 'be, therefore, patient and *gentle* with one another, as God is with you' (s.a., Did. 5.2; Barn 20.2 where patience is paired with the term). In Herm. *Mand*. 2.6 the attitude is clearly gentleness, contrasted with harshness. Yet, in Herm. *Mand*. 12.3.1 it would seem that humility is more clearly in mind as it refers to the underlying attitude that generates gentleness. Similarly, see Diogn. 7.4.

Enkrateia then has the sense of keeping one's control, 'self-restraint,' or 'self-control,' regarding one's emotions.

In the Greco-Roman world, the term is important ethically. Xenophon writes of *enkrateia*: 'Should not every man hold *self-control* (*enkrateia*) to be the foundation of all virtue, and first lay this foundation firmly in his soul?' (Xenophon, *Mem.* 1.5.4).[46] Aristotle sees it as a critical virtue, defining it 'the virtue of the seat of desires according to which, by reason, people *restrain* their desires (*epithymia*) when they are set on base pleasures' (my translation) (Aristotle, *[Virt. vit]*. 1250a.10–14). He also writes, 'for *self-control* is virtue, and through virtue makes people more righteous' (my translation) (Aristotle, *Eud. eth.* 1223b.10–14). Self-control produces serenity in the virtuous man (Plutarch, *Mor.* 7). So Grundmann notes, *enkrateia* speaks of

the ideal of the free and independent man, of the man who is under no control but who freely controls all things and who in self-restraint maintains his freedom in the face of the φαῦλαι ἡδοναί [base pleasures] which would deprive him of it.[47]

Self-control is essential to the life of the righteous Jew in Sirach with a section headed 'the self-controlled life (Sir 18:29c). The first verse in the section reads, 'Do not go after your desires, and restrain yourself from your appetites.' Similarly, in 4 Macc 5:34 is written: 'I will not play false to you, O law that trained me, nor will I renounce you, beloved self-control (*enkrateia*).' (NRSV). Here, we see the intimate link between Jewish law and self-control.[48] Another example is in the *Let. Aris.* 277–278, where the king asks why the majority of people do not recognize virtue. The explanation is given (which is approved by the King):

"Because all men," he said, "have become naturally intemperate, and inclined to pleasures, as a result of which injustice came

45. BDAG 565. *Krateō* is used twice by Paul of the body holding fast to the head (Col 2:19) and the Thessalonians' holding fast to traditions (2 Thess 2:15).
46. Xenophon, *Xenophon in Seven Volumes*, 4, trans. E. C. Marchant (Medford, MA: Harvard University Press, Cambridge, MA; William Heinemann, Ltd., London., 1923).
47. W. Grundmann, 'ἐγκράτεια,' in *TDNT* 2:340–41.
48. See also T. Iss. 2:1 where Rachel preferred self-control over sexual relations with her husband and T. Naph. 8:8 where it speaks of the restraint from sex for the purpose of prayer (cf. 1 Cor 7:3–5).

about and the mass of greed.278 The virtuous disposition, on the other hand, restrains those who are attracted to the rule of pleasure, and commands them to respect *self-control* (*enkrateia*) and justice more highly. God directs all these matters." (Charlesworth).

Josephus, in *Jewish Wars* 2.120, writes of the Essenes, 'They shun pleasures as a vice and regard temperance and control (*epikrateia*) of the passions as a special virtue' (Loeb).

Philo esteems *enkrateia* highly. It suggests ruling over one's passions. He also admires the self-control of the Essene, who never marries and is celibate (*Hypoth.* 11.14).[49] Not unlike Paul in this section of Galatians, but without the emphasis on the Spirit, he speaks of a war between being ruled by one's passions and self-control (*Opif.* 164). The one trained in the mindless passions must practice self-control by force (*Legat.* 3.18). It sits alongside a range of other virtues.[50] When one sees someone allowing themselves to succumb to their passions, one should show that person the true path of self-control (*Det.* 19).

It brings health and strength (*Legat.* 14). Self-restraint brings health and longevity, expels evil, and is the solution for intemperance (*Agr.* 98). He argues that 'philosophy produces self-control over the stomach, self-control over the parts below it, and self-control also over the tongue' (*Congr.* 80, my translation, cf. *Mut.* 229). Such a person moves from 'love of pleasure to self-restraint' (*Abr.* 24) or from intemperance to temperance (*Virt.* 180; *Praem.* 116) and moves among those who are characterized by self-control (*Mos.* 2.185).

He describes the righteous man in *On Dreams* 1.123 as a person of the word who is characterized by self-control (among many other virtues) (s.a. *Somn.* 2.40). He notes that *enkrateia* is beneficial for all matters of life and especially for the governance of the state (*Ios.* 55). It is the opposite of *epithymia*, the passions of the flesh, where one must do everything at one's disposal to acquire for self and state (*Spec.* 1.149, cf. Gal 5:16–17). It is a pure

---

49. The reason is appalling—because women are supposedly selfish, jealous, agitators, and deceptive. Nice! Not!

50. See *Sacr.* 27; *Det.* 72; *Her.* 48; *Ios.* 153; *Mos.* 1.154.

and unblemished virtue that opposes excessive eating, drinking, and self-boasting (*Spec.* 1.150). The law is focused on bringing people to this virtue (*Spec.* 2.195). Finding *enkrateia* is a tough uphill road, but more profitable than any other road (*Spec.* 4.112). The righteous person is preeminent in this along with all other virtues (*Virt.* 127).

In the NT, it is rare, found four times in three verses. In Acts, Paul speaks to Felix of justice, self-control, and the coming judgment, causing Felix to become afraid (Acts 24:25). This reference suggests Paul was talking to some extent about ethics. Peter uses it twice in 2 Pet 1:6 of self-control as something to be added to faith alongside virtue, knowledge, steadfastness, godliness, sibling affection, and love. This reference is Paul's only use. Whereas the Judaizers, like Philo, likely linked *enkrateia* with the law, Paul links it to the Spirit, who enables believers to gain mastery over the flesh, and self-restraint. Self-control must be practiced and become a habit. The Spirit, then, enables resistance.

Paul concludes the section with 'against such things, there is no law.' As at the end of the fifteen-strong works of the flesh list, also using *toioutos*, 'such things' (see v. 21), Paul implies there is a range of other virtues he could add. Possibilities can be discerned from the virtue lists recorded at the beginning of this discussion of the fruit of the Spirit.

Longenecker notes that some four hundred years earlier Aristotle wrote of people who were highly virtuous: 'against (*kata*) such people (*tōn toioutōn*) there is no (*ouk*) law (*nomos*)' (*Pol.* 3.13.1284a). This statement, then, may be a maxim that Paul is appropriating to make his point.[51]

As in Gal 2:11; 3:21; and 5:17, the preposition *kata* means 'against.' 'Against such things, there is no law' suggests that these attitudes and resultant behaviors supersede all law, they fulfill the law, they are the goal of the law, they are the living out of the intent of the law, and they complete the law. This does not mean that they are laws themselves, a new legal code.[52] Rather, in

51. Longenecker, *Galatians*, 263–64.

allowing the Spirit to reign, the law is lived through such virtues. Indeed, a look at the list calls to mind Jesus who walked among us embodying them. They are descriptors of the life of the Son, and so the Father. When we live them, no law is required, for this is being who we were created to be as God's image-bearers. Where people live like this, no laws are required. This will be the life of the eschaton. This is our aspiration in the present.

CHRIST'S PEOPLE HAVE CRUCIFIED THE FLESH (5:24)

In *Galatians 5:24*, Paul returns to the theme of the flesh, and its passions and desires:

And (*de*, 1:15) **those** (plural *ho*, 1:1) **who belong to Christ** (genitive *Christou*, 1:1) **Jesus**[53] (genitive *Iēsous*, 1:1) **have crucified** (aorist *stauroō*) **the flesh** (*sarx*) **with** (*syn*) **[its] passions** (*pathēma*)[54] **and** (*kai*, 1:1) **desires** (plural *epithymia*, 5:16).

The *de* is consecutive here, 'and,' with which Paul is continuing from the virtues generated by the Spirit in the life of the believer to the believer's identity and status.

'Those who belong to Christ Jesus' is literally, 'those of Christ Jesus,' and as in 3:29, speaks of Christians, including Paul, those with him, and the Galatians. Indeed, it includes all who have a saving faith in God and his Son.

'Have crucified the flesh' uses the verb *stauroō* recalling the crucifixion of Christ which Paul proclaimed to the Galatians when they became Christ's people by faith (3:1). There, Christ hung on a cross and became a curse on our behalf (3:13). In

---

52. Longenecker, *Galatians*, 263–64.
53. **VARIANT:** Some witnesses include *Christou* without *Iēsou* (P46 D F G K L 0122* 2 81 104c 365 630 1505 2464 ◊ latt sy). Others include *Christou Iēsou* (א A B C P Ψ 01221 0278 33 104* 1175 1241 1739 1881 l 249 co). This is a split decision as there is strong support either way. While Metzger, *Textual Commentary*, 529 includes it, there is real doubt as to whether *Iēsou* should be added. As meaning is unaffected, I have retained the agreed text with some reservations.
54. The noun *pathēma* is found once in Galatians 5:24 of the passions of the flesh. The term is found only in Paul in the NT used of sinful passions (Rom 7:5) and otherwise, of sufferings (Rom 8:18; 2 Cor 1:5, 6, 7; 3:10; Col 1:24; 2 Tim 3:11). It is related to *paschō*, Gal 3:4.

so doing, he became a crucified savior, an offense to Jews who cannot contemplate that one hung on a tree can be God's redeemer (3:13; 5:11). Sadly, they miss the point. Indeed, Jesus was accursed, but he is so on our behalf so that the curse of sin can be finally dealt with. So, Paul in 2:19 can cry out, 'I have been crucified with (*systauroō*) Christ.' Indeed, he will soon boast of nothing else except the cross of Christ through which he has been crucified to the world and the world to him (6:12, 14).

Here, as in Romans, Paul similarly speaks of our co-crucifixion with Christ. His death has become our death. 'Our old selves have been crucified with him so that the body of sin may be destroyed, and we may no longer be enslaved to sin' (Rom 6:6). While we live on in our fleshly bodies, still subject to sin, in a spiritual sense, our flesh has been killed in Christ. From the perspective of our sinful state, we are dead. We no longer live (Gal 2:20). We are dead to sin and alive to God in Christ Jesus. Now Christ lives in us.

With the mortification of our flesh in Christ, our passions and desires are also destroyed. *Epithymia* is discussed at its first use in 5:16, where it speaks of the desires of the flesh that must be overcome in favor of the fruit of the Spirit.

'Passions' is *pathēma*, linked to *paschō* from 3:4, where it meant 'suffering' (3:4). The term in wider Greek sources is mainly used of 'misfortune,' 'suffering,' and especially that which is experienced rather than learned.[55] In Greek Jewish writings, *pathēma* is mainly confined to Josephus and Philo of unsettled natural phenomena,[56] animal passions (*Mos.* 2.126), suffering and affliction.[57]

The author of Hebrews and Peter employ it of the suffering of Christ[58] and believers (Heb 10:32). Peter also uses it the latter way (1 Pet 5:9), seeing Christian sufferings as participation in those of Christ (1 Pet 4:13).

Seven of Paul's nine uses of *pathēma* are of the suffering of

55. W. Michaelis, 'πάθημα,' in *TDNT* 5:930.
56. See Josephus, *Ant.* 1.155; Philo, *Opif.* 70; *Cher.* 88; *Conf.* 23; *Abr.* 2; *Spec.* 1.210.
57. See Josephus, *Ant.* 2.299; 6.10; 7.325; 8.115; 20.112; Philo, *Gig.* 10.
58. See Heb 2:9, 10; 1 Pet 1:11; 5:1.

Christ in which Christians participate.[59] In Rom 7:5, he employs it of 'sinful passions,' which were aroused by the law among those who were living in the flesh (aside from Christ). This is the sense Paul is using here, the passions of the flesh. It is thus synonymous with *epithymia*.

The implication here is that Christians' flesh and passions are crucified in Christ. As such, they should live by the Spirit and not the works of the flesh. To do the latter is to return to their former state. Rather, they should live out their status as Spirit-people whose flesh has been mortified. They should not contemplate the sins of the flesh such as those of Gal 5:19–21. If they yield to the power of God swirling in their beings, they will be able to do so.

At a practical level, this means that when a person is tempted, they can pray something like, 'This rubbish is dead to me, and I am dead to it. God, by your Spirit, empower me to resist this corruption, show me your way out' (cf. 1 Cor 10:13).

KEEP IN STEP WITH THE SPIRIT (5:25)

Galatians 5:25 moves from Christ's crucifixion to the Spirit, Paul restating what he has said earlier in 5:16 and 18:

If (*ei*, 1:7) **we live** (third-person plural *zaō*, 2:14) **by the Spirit** (dative *pneuma*, 3:2), **let us also** (*kai*, 1:1) **keep in step** (*stoicheō*)[60] **with the Spirit** (dative *pneumati*).

The verse is chiastic and repeats the same word within the same clause (*pneuma*), a rhetorical device termed *epanalepsis*:[61]

   A1   *Ei zēmen* (if we live)

      B1   *pneumati,* (by the Spirit)

---

59. See 2 Cor 1:5; Phil 3:10; Col 1:24, s.a. Rom 8:18; 2 Cor 1:6, 7; 2 Tim 3:11.

60. The verb στοιχέω (*stoicheō*) is a military motif speaking of people marching in rank (see in G. Delling, 'στοιχέω,' in *TDNT* 7.666–67). It thus has the sense of 'agree,' 'follow,' or 'keep in step with.' Luke uses it of following the law (Acts 21:24). Paul uses it twice in Galatians of people keeping in step with the leading of the Spirit (5:25) and of 'following' the rule that sees circumcision as nothing but a new creation as what matters (6:16). It is used in Rom 4:12 for following the faith of Abraham and in Phil 3:16 of keeping in line with what the Philippians have already attained in Christ.

61. *PDSNTG* 51 defines 'epanalepsis' as '[t]he repetition of a word or group of words within the same clause. See Philippians 2:8.'

B2   *pneumati*, (by the Spirit)
A2   *stoichōmen* (let us keep in step)

The sentence is also a first-class condition (*ei* plus indicative) indicating something assumed true for the sake of argument (see on 1:9). In this case, it is true of those who are in Christ and whose flesh is crucified with Christ, i.e., the Galatians and all Christians.

'If we live by the Spirit' speaks of the ideal of the Christian life. It effectively restates 'walk [live] by the Spirit' (5:16). The verb *zaō* is found in 2:14 of Peter's living like a gentile, in 3:11–12 of the righteous who 'live by faith' (Hab 2:4) in contrast to living by law obedience. Paul employs it five times of his life in 2:19–20: 'For through the law, I died, so that I might *live* to God, I have been crucified with Christ. And, it is no longer I who *lives* but it is Christ who *lives* in me. And the life I now *live* in the flesh, I *live* by faith in the Son of God ….' Here, his use of the verb is parallel to living by faith in the Son of God who lives in him by his Spirit.

The second half of the verse uses the third person plural hortatory subjunctive, and so is imperatival.[62] The third person plural is inclusive of Paul and the brothers and sisters with him, the Galatians, and anyone else who names Christ as Lord. The verb is *stoicheō*. As noted, this is a military notion, derived from *stoichos*, 'a rank of series,' 'to belong to a series.' So, it is used to describe soldiers who march in rank. It has a range of other applications such as 'to agree,' 'to be in harmony with,' 'to assent to,' 'to stay in line with what was before,' etc.[63]

In the NT, it is used of living in agreement with the law (Acts 21:24). Paul uses it in Rom 4:12 of following or keeping in step with the example of Abraham. Similarly, in Phil 3:16, it is used of walking in agreement with what has been previously attained by

---

62. Wallace, *Greek Grammar*, 464. He notes '[t]he subjunctive is commonly used to exhort or command oneself and one's associates. This use of the subjunctive is used "to urge someone to unite with the speaker in a course of action upon which he has already decided." Since there is no first-person imperative, the hortatory subjunctive is used to do roughly the same task. Thus, this use of the subjunctive is an exhortation in the *first-person plural*. The typical translation, rather than *we should … is let us.....'*

63. See further in Delling, 'στοιχέω,' 668–69. The term is rare in Greek Jewish literature and its meaning is unclear (Eccl. 11:6; Jub. 3.13).

faith (justification before God). In 6:16, Paul will again use it of marching in agreement; in step with the rule that circumcision is neither here nor there—matters is a new creation. Here, it speaks of living in agreement with or harmony with the guidance of the Spirit. It connects with the idea of being 'led by the Spirit.' Like soldiers in rank, we are to walk in the footsteps of the Spirit who guides us from within, gently urges us to live as Christ would want us.

REMOVE PRIDE, PROVOCATION, AND ENVY (5:26)

The final verse of the chapter, *Galatians 5:26*, picks up the tenor of the vice list of vv. 19–21, effectively giving three more elements that the Galatians and all Christians (us) are to repudiate. The verse contains three words found only here in the NT (*hapax legomena: kenodoxos, prokaleō,* and *pthoneō*). It continues the hortatory nature of v. 25b:

Let us not (*mē*, 1:7) **become** (*ginomai*, 2:17) **arrogant** (plural *kenodoxos*),[64] **provoking** (*prokaleō*)[65] **one another** (*allēlōn*, 5:13), **envying** (*phthoneō*)[66] **one another** (*allēlōn*).

If the previous verse states that those who live in the Spirit should keep in step with the Spirit, this states the converse. 'Become' is *ginomai* which can simply stand in the place of the verb 'to be' (let us not be arrogant), or as a warning not to become so. In light of the tone of the letter, it likely holds together both ideas—let us not be and become more arrogant (see further on *ginomai*, 2:17). As with *stoichōmen* in the previous verse, *ginōmetha* is a hortatory subjunctive urging the Galatians,

---

64. The adjective κενόδοξος (*kenodoxos*) compounds *kenos* (empty) and *doxa* (glory), yielding 'empty/vainglory.' It is a hapax *legomenon*, found only in 5:26. It speaks of seeking self-glory, conceit, arrogant, or boastfulness.

65. The verb προκαλέω (*prokaleō*) which compounds *pro* (before) and *kaleō* (call) means 'provoke, challenge.' It is the second hapax *legomenon* in 5:26.

66. The verb φθονέω (*phthoneō*) means 'to envy,' and is associated with the noun *phthonos* from v. 21 (envy). This is the only use of the verb in the NT. Its use alongside *phthonos* indicates that envy may be a real issue among the Galatians. It is the third hapax *legomenon* in this one verse.

himself, and those with him (and any other readers, like us!), to do this (see also 6:9).

The term I have translated 'arrogant' is the first of the three *hapax legomena* in the verse, a compound noun meaning to seek vain or empty glory. It suggests self-glorification. BDAG describes it thus, 'to having exaggerated self-conceptions, conceited, boastful.'[67]

The term is not used that often, absent from the LXX and Josephus. When Plutarch is speaking about what brings a man to anger, he uses it negatively of the *conceited* man who becomes angry at being maligned (Plutarch, *Cohib. ira* 8). Lucian records a Cynic speaker crying out concerning virtue, asking if anyone dares to call Proteus conceited—the answer being no because Proteus was a hero (Lucian, *Peregr.* 4).[68]

Polybius attributes *kenodoxos* to Polyaratus (Polybius, *Hist.* 27.7.12), an arrogant man of Rhodes who supported Perseus in the second Macedonian War. He was a consummate political manipulator who used money to try and buy the king's help. He ended up fleeing, and ultimately in Rome as a prisoner.[69] Epictetus slams it as a negative feature: 'Let him who claims what belongs not to him be arrogant, be vainglorious (*kenodoxos*), be base, be a slave; let him grieve, let him envy, let him pity; and, in a word, let him lament and be miserable' (Epictetus, *Diatr.* 3.24.43).

In wider Jewish sources, it is only found twice. In the Letter of Aristeas, those who are self-inflated have a love for gold which

---

67. BDAG 539.

68. In Greek mythology, Proteus was a man of the sea and a carer of its animals like seals. He was under Poseidon the sea god. He lived near Pharos (near the Nile's mouth) or Capathus (between Crete and Rhodes). He was a prophet who knew all things. Those wanting knowledge from him had to capture him and tie him up, but he was a shapeshifter and would seek to escape. If he could not escape, he gave an answer to be freed. Lucian goes on to say that Proteus was imprisoned in Syria, renounced 5000 talents in favor of his native land, was banished from Rome, was more conspicuous than the sun, was even a rival to Zeus, and died by fire. See further on Proteus, The Editors of Encyclopaedia Britannica. 'Proteus,' *Encyclopedia Britannica Online*, https://www.britannica.com/topic/Proteus-Greek-mythology.

69. See 'Polyaratus' at http://www.perseus.tufts.edu/hopper/text?doc=Perseus:text:1999.04.0104:entry=polyaratus-bio-1.

does not match the value of the pursuit of culture for the wise (Let. Aris. 8). Philo repudiates the dreamer who is conceited (*Somn.* 2.105). In the Didache, the teacher urges the reader to 'not be a liar, since lying leads to theft. Do not be avaricious or *conceited*, for all these things breed thefts' (Did. 3.5).

This is the only use in the NT and speaks against all forms of arrogance and conceit. The associated noun is found in Phil 2:3: 'do nothing out of selfish ambition nor out of *conceit* (*kenodoxia*).' Rather, the Philippians are to live in humility, considering others above themselves, and be concerned not only for their own interests but for the interests of others. They are to emulate the mindset of Christ who although God in form and status, poured himself out for the world as a slave, humbling himself and being obedient to death on a cross. Hence, rather than arrogance, believers are to be characterized by humility, service, and sacrifice, no matter what the cost.

'Not provoking one another' uses the second *hapax legomenon* in the verses, *prokaleō*. This is a compound verb (*pro*, 'before' plus *kaleō*, 'call' [1:6, 15; 5:6, 13]). The verb at a literal level means 'call before,' and so, it connotes 'call out someone to come forward.'[70] Although it is only used once in the NT, it is widely used in wider Greek sources. LSJ notes that it often has the meaning 'invite, summons,'[71] but is commonly used of a challenge to a fight.[72] So Lucian uses it of a musician calling another out for a flute challenge (Lucian, *Symp.* 20). Josephus uses it of Goliath's challenge to Israel to send someone to take him on (*Ant.* 6.174, 177).[73] Here, in Galatians, it speaks of provoking one another, drawing others into argument and contention. The Galatians are not to treat each other like this; rather, they are to be loving, kind, patient, and gentle toward each other.

The third *hapax legomenon* in the verse is *phthoneō*—'to envy, begrudge.' It is the cognate of *phthonos*, used in 5:21. As discussed, envy is repudiated in wider Greek sources. This verb is common

---

70. BDAG 871.
71. See, e.g., 2 Macc 8:11; Josephus, *Ant.* 1.314; 5.168; Philo, *Leg.* 1.34; *Spec.* 2.234.
72. See, e.g., Homer, *Il.* 13.809; *Od.* 8.142; Xenophon, *Mem.* 2.3.17. See LSJ 1483.
73. See also Josephus, *Ant.* 7.315; *Life* 120, 400, 405; *J.W.* 1.381; 4.44.

in wider Greek writings. In the only references in the LXX, when a person is giving to the poor, the giver should not envy the gift that is given (Tob 4:7, 16).[74] Philo uses the verb in his repudiation of envy. So, when we see a superior athlete, we should not envy that person (*Agr.* 121). Similarly, if one has little, that person should not envy the one with much (*Ios.* 144). In T. Gad 3:3, the hater envies the successful. As noted in the discussion on *phthonos*, in the Testament of Simeon 3.1–3, the readers are warned to watch out for the spirit of deceit and envy, as they consume the mind until they have destroyed the one envied. Conversely, the person who yields to God turns to compassion and sympathy for the person previously envied. This advice would be sage for the Galatians, and for all of us who struggle with envy.

---

74. See also T. Sim. 2:14; 1. Gad 7:2; T. Benj. 4:4; Josephus, *Ant.* 4.235; 6.236; 10.250; 12.190; 13.303; *Life* 85; *Ag. Ap.* 2.209, among other references. It can mean begrudge. So, a woman begrudged giving her milk to another (Gk. Apoc. Ezra 5:2, s.a., 2 Clem. 15.5; Philo, *Agr.* 112).

CHAPTER THIRTY: BEAR ONE ANOTHER'S BURDENS (6:1–6)

The *kai* connects this to the previous section. As such, it is not clear whether this is a new section or a continuation of Paul's teaching on a pneumatological ethic. Aside from *kai*, the use of *pneuma* in v. 1 suggests some continuity. However, there is a shift to supporting each other in vv. 1–2, then returning in vv. 3–4 to focus on oneself in relation to others. As such, I am treating this as a sub-section of the passage beginning in 5:13 and ending in 6:10.

First, Paul directs the Galatians concerning the treatment of anyone who is caught in a sin, such as the ones listed in 5:19–21; they are to restore that person gently. They must do so humbly, watching that they do not also fall into sin. They are to support each other in their struggles, for this fulfills the law of Christ, the law of love. They are to be on their guard against pride and self-deception. Their focus is not on judging others but on testing their own work ensuring that any pride is only in their own work rather than that of others. This is critical because every Christian will stand before God bearing the load of the life lived. Finally, the Galatians are to share all good things with those who teach them the word of God.

LET THE SPIRIT RESTORE SINNERS WITH HUMBLE GENTLENESS (6:1)

Paul begins this section in *Galatians 6:1*:

Brothers and sisters (plural vocative *adelphos*, 1:2), **and** (*kai*) **if** (*ean*, 1:8) **a person** (*anthrōpos*, 1:1) **is caught** (aorist passive subjunctive *prolambanō*)[1] **in** (*en*, 1:6) **any** (neuter *tis*,[2] 1:7) transgression (*paraptōma*),³ [then] you (second person plural *sy*, 1:3) **who are spiritual** (plural *pneumatikos*)⁴ **restore** (present imperative *katartizō*)⁵ **such a person** (*toioutos*, 5:21) **with** (*en*) **the Spirit** (*pneuma*, 3:2) **of gentleness** (*prautēs*, 5:23), **watching** (participle *skopeō*)⁶ **yourself** (*seautou*, 5:14) **that you** (*sy*) **also** (*kai*) **are not** (*mē*, 1:7) **tempted** (aorist passive subjunctive *peirazō*).⁷

So how should a person in the community who falls into the works of the flesh such as those listed in 5:19–21 be treated? Paul answers here—they are to be restored with humility.

As elsewhere in Galatians (and throughout his letters),⁸ he

1. The verb προλαμβάνω (*prolambano*) compounds *pro* (before) and *lambanō* (take, seize) and literally means 'seize/take beforehand.' According to BDAG (p. 872), in the NT it can have the sense 'do something before the usual time, anticipate something,' 'take it upon oneself, undertake,' to take or get a meal, or to 'detect, overtake, surprise.' The latter is assumed by most scholars to be the right meaning in its one use here in Galatians 6:1. However, it is a slippery term in this context.

2. Wallace, *Greek Grammar*, 347: 'The indefinite pronoun (τις, τι) is used to introduce a member of a class without further identification. It is used both substantively (as a true pronoun) and adjectivally. It can be translated *anyone, someone, a certain*, or simply *a(n)*.' The use in 6:1 is adjectival, 'any transgression.'

3. The noun παράπτωμα is used once in 6:1. It compounds *para* (beside) and *ptōma* (fall, cf. *piptō*)—'to fall beside.' It often speaks of slip, error. It then means to fall into sin, 'a violation of moral standards, offense, wrongdoing, sin' (BDAG 770); hence, the translation, 'transgression.' Paul uses it sixteen times overall.

4. The adjective πνευματικός (*pneumatikos*) speaks of someone who is spiritual. In the case of Gal 6:1, its only use in the letter, it speaks of someone imbued with the Spirit. The term is particularly important in the Corinthian correspondence where Paul uses it in terms of those who think of themselves as spiritually elite. Here, it is expressed positively adding to his appeal.

5. The verb καταρτίζω (*katartizō*) speaks of preparing something (Rom 9:22), training someone (e.g., Luke 6:40), restoring something (e.g., fishing nets, Matt 4:21), supplying something (1 Thess 3:10), and creating something (Heb 11:3). It is used once in 6:1 of restoring a sinner who has fallen into transgressions.

6. The verb *skopeō* means to 'pray careful attention to, look (out) for, notice' (BDAG 931). It is used once in Galatians 6:1 in the injunction to the Galatians to watch out that they do not become tempted as they restore the transgressor. Five of the six NT uses are in Paul.

7. The verb πειράζω (*peirazō*) is found once in Galatians. It means 'tempted, tested,' and in 6:1, the latter is in mind. The Galatians are to watch that they do not fall into temptation as they restore the sinful Christian. All seven uses of the verb in the NT are in Paul with the meaning 'tempt' (1 Cor 7:5; 10:13; 1 Thess 3:5) or 'test, examine' (1 Cor 10:9; 2 Cor 13:5).

begins with the vocative plural of *adelphos*, *adelphoi*. As in all these uses, it implies 'brothers and sisters;' the Galatians form a part of God's family, brothers and sisters of Christ and of Paul, members of the family of faith together. They are Christians, and this speaks of inclusion and intimacy.

This is followed by a third-class conditional sentence (*ean* plus subjunctive), 'if … then,' supposing a hypothetical situation (see on 1:8). It is thus non-specific and may imply some in a general sense who are falling into sin and need restoration. *Anthrōpos* is inclusive and suggests a man or woman in sin.

The verb translated 'caught' is *prolambanō*. At a literal level, it compounds *pro* (before) and *lambanō* (take, seize), and so can have the temporal sense of 'seize, grasp, or take before.'

'In any transgression' uses *paraptōma*, which combines *para* (beside) and *ptōma*, a term related to the verb *piptō* (fall) and meaning something fallen.[9] The compound speaks of falling from (beside) a standard. In wider sources it is rare, used by Diodorus Siculus of a military defeat (e.g., Diodorus Siculus, *Hist.* 19.100.3) and Polybius of a false step, slip, or blunder (e.g., Polybius, *Hist.* 9.10.6). Otherwise, it is used for a transgression or trespass—a failure to meet a moral standard.[10] In the LXX and Pseudepigrapha it is employed to describe sins and transgressions with the implication these are committed against God and his law.[11]

In the NT, *paraptōma* is found nineteen times, of which only three are outside of Paul. Two come immediately after the Lord's Prayer (Matt 6:14–15) and in Mark 11:25 of the forgiveness of trespasses. Paul uses it of human trespasses[12] and specifically of

---

8. See 1:10, 11; 3:15; 4:12, 28, 31; 5:11, 13; 6:18.

9. *Ptōma* is found in the NT only of a dead corpse (Matt 14:12; 24:28; Mark 6:29; 15:5; Rev 11:8, 9). However, it is used more widely for things fallen, a misfortune or calamity, injuries due to falls, fallen buildings, or a payment that falls due. See LSJ 1549.

10. LSJ 1322.

11. See Ps 18:13 [Eng. 19:12]; 21:2 [Eng. 22:1]; Job 35:15; 36:9; Wis 3:13; 10:1; Zech 9:6; Ezek 3:20; 14:11, 13; 15:8; 18:22, 24, 26; 20:27; Pss. Sol. 3:7; 13:5; 13:10; Philo, *Migr.* 170.

12. See Rom 4:25; 5:16; 11:11, 12; 2 Cor 5:19; Eph 1:7; 2:1, 5; Col 2:13.

Adam's.[13] Here then, it speaks of someone falling into sin. In context, it would especially refer to the works of the flesh listed in 5:19–21 (s.a. 5:13, 26) or submitting to the Judaizers. In terms of the latter possibility, as Paul has counseled the expulsion of people who yield to the Judaizers (4:30; 5:12), this verse may speak of the restoration of a lapsed Christian to the fellowship. Similarly, in 1 Cor 5, he urges the expulsion of the sexual sinner and others that violate the gospel through unrepentant works of the flesh (1 Cor 5:11–13, cf. 6:9–11). If this is standard practice for Paul, then this may speak of the restoration of those who have become involved without inhibition in sexual or other sins of the flesh.

The verb translated 'caught' (ESV, NIV), 'detected' (NRSV), 'discovered' (NET), 'trapped' (CEV), and 'overtaken' (RSV) is *prolambanō*. It is a compound term, blending *pro* (before) and the very common *lambanō* (seize, take, grasp). However, determining its meaning is notoriously difficult. Some lexicons assume the meaning 'caught' or 'surprised' but do not really grapple with its wide semantic range. Conversely, Liddell, Scott, and Jones rightly indicate the wide semantic range of the compound.[14]

The term is not found in the LXX. In the Pseudepigrapha, it is used for the day when the consummation *occurs* (Sib. Or. 3.569) and to *overtake* an animal while running (T. Jud. 2.5). Josephus' use is varied including[15] to anticipate and prevent,[16]

---

13. See Rom 5:15, 16, 18, 20.
14. LSJ 1488: including being used of taking money in advance or before, beginning growth earlier, to be contained in advance (passive), to take or seize beforehand, procure a vote, to take as a start, to take in preference, takeaway or take off before, assume in advance, anticipate, mental anticipation, to get a start, detect, anticipate or prejudge, precede, go before, repeat, form a preconception. G. Delling, 'προλαμβάνω,' in *TDNT* 4:14 argues that there are two main meanings: 1) Anticipate; 2) Surprise. While the former is found in the many references I discuss above, the latter meaning is not found elsewhere, and 'anticipate' is found only on occasion. Similarly, BDAG 872 limits its meaning to something with temporal priority or detect, overtake, surprise. Again, this does not cover anything like the semantic range of the term. The same problem is found in Horst Robert Balz and Gerhard Schneider, *EDNT* 3:158 where the verb is not discussed in anything like the detail I have observed.
15. As the term is slippery, a number of these are best guesses based on context.
16. See *Ant.* 2.54; 6.305; 7.276; 13.47; 18.118; *J.W.* 1.263; 3.331; 4.637; 5.479; 6.164.

to anticipate,[17] to arrive beforehand (*Ant.* 2.184), distribute (*Ant.* 5.89), receive,[18] to seize (*Ant.* 5.269; 17.233; 2.553), to be rash (*Ant.* 6.102), the origin of something (*Ant.* 15.70), to overtake (*Ant.* 16.315; *J.W.* 5.80), taste (*Ant.* 17.115), to go ahead and eat (*Ant.* 18.173), to form (*Ant.* 19.111), a military expedition (*Ag. Ap.* 1.13), and to be held (*J.W.* 1.390).

Philo uses it of grasping understanding beforehand, i.e., foreknowledge (e.g., God) (*Opif.* 16, 45), to anticipate,[19] to think previously (*Cher.* 78), to be aware beforehand (*Cher.* 118; *Agr.* 38; *Fug.* 99), to know something thoroughly (*Somn.* 1.60), to receive (*Mos.* 1.333), something expected or not (*Spec.* 1.26).

It is used twice else in the NT. Mark uses it to describe the anointing of Christ (Mark 14:8). Here, it is not completely clear what Mark has in mind as it literally reads: 'she seized before my body to anoint it for burial.' While it is common to interpret this as 'she has anointed … beforehand,' this does not capture the verb. Rather, it can speak of her actual physical act (she took my body to anoint) or she anticipated Jesus' death (she anticipated my body [broken] beforehand and anointed it for burial). In 1 Cor 11:21, Paul states of the Corinthian meals: 'for when you eat, each *takes beforehand* his own meal, and on the one hand, one is hungry, and on the other hand, one is drunk.'

This analysis shows that it is difficult to grasp Paul's intent in 6:1. We can rule out 'trapped' or 'caught' as the term is not used in this way. Similarly, 'detected' and 'discovered' seem to have no real basis. The best option would seem to be 'overtaken' (RSV), the verb used in this way (T. Jud. 2.5; Josephus, *Ant.* 16.315; *J.W.* 5.80). Otherwise, it simply means 'seized' in any transgression. If the exact nuance of the verb is unclear, the need for restoration and the concern that the restorer not to 'be tempted' enables us to at least get a good sense of Paul's intent.

So, if a member of the church is found to be engaging in sin, the spiritual should restore that person with a spirit of gentleness. 'The spiritual' here are the *pneumatikoi* (plural *pneumatikos*). Aside

---

17. See *Ant.* 15.166; *J.W.* 2.602; 4.514.
18. See *Ant.* 5.91; 18.341; *J.W.* 4.385.
19. See *Cher.* 15; *Sacr.* 18; *Somn.* 1.2; *Legat.* 208; *Prov.* 2.56.

from 1 Pet 2:5, which uses *pneumatikos* adjectivally of believers being built as a spiritual house offering spiritual sacrifices, all other uses (twenty-four times) are in Paul. It can refer to spiritual gifts (Rom 1:11; 1 Cor 12:1; 14:1).

It is used of the law which is spiritual (Rom 7:14) which is figuratively described as spiritual food and drink (1 Cor 10:3–4). It is also used for spiritual blessings or benefits in the gospel (Rom 15:27; Eph 1:3), the spiritual things sown in people through the gospel (1 Cor 9:11), spiritual songs—songs inspired by the Spirit (Eph 5:19; Col 3:16), and spiritual wisdom and understanding—wisdom granted by the Spirit (Col 1:9). Paul employs it of the spiritual resurrected body in contrast to the natural, i.e., one fully empowered by the Spirit and no longer subject to death (1 Cor 15:44, 46).

He also uses it of spiritual people, those who are imbued with the Spirit (1 Cor 2:13, 15; 3:1; 14:37). Only once does it not imply the Holy Spirit; Eph 6:12—'the *spiritual* forces of evil,' all demonic creatures. Here, as elsewhere, the masculine refers to men and women who have received the Spirit, which of course, includes all the Galatians who have saving faith (3:2, 5). So, Paul is appealing to all the Galatians, other than the sinner involved.

'Restore' is the verb *katartizō*, a verb compounding *kata*, 'according to' with *artios*, 'complete.' It can have the sense of prepare, make, create, outfit, or 'restore, mend.'[20] Here, the latter is in mind. This sense is found in wider sources, e.g., the restoration of a city after dissension (Dionysius of Halicarnassus, *Ant. rom.* 3.10.6), to restore a person from pride and fallenness (Plutarch, *Cat. Min.* 65.5), and to make peace (e.g., Herodotus, *Hist.* 5.30.1).

In the LXX, *katartizō* is used for the rebuilding of the walls of Jerusalem and the Temple and returning from Babylonian exile.[21]

---

20. BDAG 526.

21. See Ezra 4:12, 13, 16; 5:3, 9, 11; 6:14. Also to restore an inheritance (Ps 67:10 [Eng. 68:9]), restore what your right hand planted (Ps 79:16 [Eng. 80:15]); create (Exod 15:17; Ps 8:3 [Eng. 8:2]; 10:3 [Eng. 11:3]; 28:9 [Eng. 29:9]; 73:16 [Eng. 74:16], establish (Ps 16:5 [Eng. 17:5]; 17:34 [Eng. 18:33]; 88:38 [Eng. 89:37]), prepare (Ps 39:7 [Eng. 40:6]), and strengthen (Ps 67:29 [Eng. 68:28]).

Katartizō is used in the NT of the disciples mending nets (Matt 4:21; Mark 1:19) and of Christ restoring believers after suffering (1 Pet 5:10). Paul uses it in 1 Cor 1:10 of the Corinthians restored to unity of mind and in 2 Cor 13:11: 'aim for restoration.'[22]

Here, the Galatians with the Spirit are to restore a person who has been overtaken with sin. Depending on the nature of the sin, this could mean their full restoration into the community. It could also be an encouragement to the person that they are alright with God. This is a present active imperative, calling for an ongoing attitude. This is yet another direct imperative.[23]

'In a spirit of gentleness' (an attributive genitive)[24] can be the Holy Spirit, 'with the gentleness the Spirit produces' (a genitive of production). In support of this is the use of the term *prautēs* here and among the fruit of the Spirit in v. 23. Alternatively, it is 'in/with a gentle spirit,' speaking of the human spirit, the spiritual Galatians responding to the sinner with gentleness and humility. If it is the latter, in that Paul has appealed to the *pneumatikoi*, those imbued with the Spirit and draws on a fruit of the Spirit, such a response is implicitly linked to the Holy Spirit anyway. As such, the two ideas merge—led by or in step with the Spirit of gentleness (or humility), respond with the Spirit's gentleness toward the fallen sinner.

As noted concerning 5:23, the term *prautēs* can equally be translated 'humility' or 'gentleness,' humility being the underlying unction and gentleness the outworking of that inward humility. To grasp this, one might state it in this way: 'you who are spiritual restore the person with a humble and gentle spirit.'

The last clause adds a warning: 'watch out that you also are not tempted.' 'Watch out' is *skopeō*. The term speaks of looking at

---

22. Otherwise, things God has created (Matt 21:19Heb 11:3), equipped (Luke 6:40), something prepared (Rom 9:22; Heb 10:5), supply (1 Thess 3:10).

23. See further 1:8; 3:7; 4:12, 30; 5:1, 13, 15, 16; 6:2, 4, 6, 7, 11, 17.

24. Wallace, *Greek Grammar*, 86. An attributive genitive is one in which '[t]he genitive substantive specifies an attribute or innate quality of the head substantive. It is similar to a simple adjective in its semantic force, though more emphatic: it "expresses quality like an adjective indeed, but with more sharpness and distinctness."' An example would be 'body of sin' meaning a 'sinful body.' Here, 'a gentle spirit.'

something with a critical eye as does a judge (Plato, *Leg.* 11.925a; Josephus, *Ant.* 3.180), a philosopher (Plato, *Crat.* 440d; Josephus, *Ant.* 1.25; Philo, *Spec.* 3.194), and a historian (Thucydides, 1.1.3; Josephus, *Ant.* 1.108)—consider, contemplate, and investigate. It is used of avoiding danger (Aristophanes, *Thesm.* 580).[25]

In the LXX, it is used for studying ancient records (Add. Esth. E. 7) and overseeing a city's people (2 Macc 4:5). Philo uses it widely and sometimes ethically. For example, 'and let us *consider* how we might train the soul' (*Sacr.* 85). Similarly, of the body, he says, 'so then, he who is of the authority of evil, the symphony again let us *consider* in part' (*Conf.* 21) (cf. *Fug.* 25; *Somn.* 1.167). It is thus a very cognitive term, speaking of consideration, careful thought, and watching with a critical eye.

The only other NT writer to use it is Luke, who uses it ethically of Jesus stating to the crowds, 'therefore, *watch out*, lest the light which is in you is darkness' (Luke 11:33). The other five uses are in Paul. In 2 Cor 4:18, he employs it of believers contemplating what is unseen. Twice it is employed in Philippians of believers *considering* not only their own interests but the interests of others (Phil 2:4) and of the *Philippians paying careful attention* to those who live according to the pattern he has passed onto them, i.e., the Christ-pattern (2:5–8). His use in Romans 16:17 is similar to this use as he warns the Romans to '*watch out* for those who cause dissensions and offenses' in their community (Rom 16:17). Here then, while those who are spiritual are to restore the offender gently, they must also ensure that they themselves are not being tempted by sin.

Tempted is *peirazō* in wider sources means 'to make an attempt,' 'to test someone.'[26] In general terms, it has two senses: 'test' or 'tempt.' Aside from T. Sol. 15.11 and Christianized texts in the Apocalypse of Daniel (Apoc. Dan. 12.2; 13:7), *peirazō* in Jewish literature is used almost always of testing whether it is people testing God, God testing people, people testing each other, or experiencing testing.[27]

---

25. E. Fuchs, 'σκοπέω,' in *TDNT* 7:414–15.

26. H. Seesemann, 'πειράζω,' in *TDNT* 6:23.

27. God testing people (Gen 22:1; Exod 15:25; 16:4; 20:20; Deut 13:3; Judg 2:22; 3:1, 4; 2

In the NT, the term is rarely used for attempting something or self-examination, and often for testing.[28] In Matthew and Paul, *peirazō* is a descriptor of Satan— 'the tempter' (Matt 4:3; 1 Thess 3:5). The Synoptic Gospel writers and Paul each use it of Satan testing (Rev 2:10) or tempting God's people.[29] For the writer of Hebrews, Jesus was tempted fully, was without sin, and so is able to help those who are facing temptation (Heb 2:18; 4:15). Jacob also speaks of people being tempted when they yield to desire, although God is not the agent of temptation (Jas 1:13–14).

In 1 Cor 10:13, Paul speaks of God allowing temptation but also providing a path away from it. Here, it means 'tempted' warning the Galatians not to fall into sin themselves as they deal with sinners. They are to examine themselves to ensure this is not the case. This calls to mind 2 Cor 13:5: 'Test (*peirazō*) yourselves, to see whether you are in the faith. Examine yourselves.' This reminds me of Jesus' teaching concerning removing the logs from one's own eye before focusing on the speck in the eye of another (Matt 7:1–5). Paul is urging readers to remain fully humble as they deal with others caught in sin; for, but for the grace of God, we could be in the same place.

Chron 32:31; Ps 25:2 [Eng. 26:2]; Wis 3:5; 11:9; 12:26; Sir 37:27; Jdt 8:25, 26; Philo, *Leg.* 3.162; *Congr.* 163; *Somn.* 1.195). It can also have the sense of an attempt of God (Deut 4:34). *Peirazō* is also applied to wisdom testing people (Sir 4:17). It is also used of people testing God, which is very negative (Exod 17:2, 7; Num 14:22; Deut 33:8; Ps 77:41, 56 [Eng. 78:41, 56]; 94:9 [Eng. 95:9]; 105:14 [Eng. 106:14]; Wis 1:2; Jdt 8:12; Isa 7:12; Apoc. Sedr. 8.4). A test to gain God's guidance (Judg 6:39). People testing each other (1 Kings 10:1; 2 Chron 9:1; Ps 34:16 [Eng. 35:16]; Wis 2:17; Sir 13:11; Dan 1:12, 14; Philo, *Leg.* 3.167). Self-testing, a test of pleasure (Eccl 2:1), to test by wisdom (Eccl 7:24), to test death (Wis 2:24), a journey (Wis 19:5), self-examination (Sir 37:27; T. Dan 1.3), testing good and bad experiences (Sir 39:4), divine decrees to be tested (Dan 12:9), and people tested by torture (4 Macc 9:7; 15:16). None of Josephus' twenty-two uses to refer to being tempted; rather, he uses it of experience.

28. Attempt (Acts 9:26; 16:7; 24:6). Self-examination (2 Cor 13:5). Testing: of people testing Christ with questions (Matt 16:1; 19:3; 22:18, 35; Mark 8:11; 10:2; 12:15; Luke 11:16; John 8:6); Jesus testing Philip (John 6:6); people testing the Spirit (Acts 5:9); people putting God to the test (Acts 15:10; Heb 3:9), a use found in Paul (1 Cor 10:9); God testing people (Heb 11:17; Rev 3:10); and Christians testing leaders (Rev 2:2).
29. See Matt 4:1; Mark 1:13; Luke 4:2; 1 Cor 7:5; 1 Thess 3:5.

FULFILL THE LAW OF CHRIST BY BEARING EACH OTHER'S BURDENS (6:2)

Paul goes on in *Galatians 6:2*:

Bear (*bastazō*, 5:10) **one another's** (*allēlōn*,[30] 5:13) **burdens** (plural *baros*)[31] **and** (*kai*, 1:1) **in this way** (*houtōs*, 1:6) **you will fulfill**[32] (future *anaplēroō*)[33] **the law** (*nomos*, 2:16) **of Christ** (genitive *Christos*, 1:1).

As noted on 5:13, Paul delights in using 'one another' statements in his ethical teaching whether to make a positive statement (e.g., 'be slaves to one another in love,' 5:13) or negative statements as in 5:15 and 26. Here is the second of his positive 'one another' statements in Galatians. The Galatians are to 'bear one another's burdens.'

The verb is *bastazō*, used earlier in 5:10 of the Judaizer bearing the penalty for his transgression. It is used again in 6:5 of each bearing his own load, and in 6:17, of Paul bearing the marks of

---

30. Wallace, *Greek Grammar*, 351: 'The reciprocal pronoun, ἀλλήλων (*of one another*), is used to indicate an interchange between two or more groups. It is thus always *plural* and, like the reflexive pronoun, occurs only in the oblique cases. One frequently finds this pronoun in paraenetic contexts, basing the exhortation on the organic connection that believers have with the risen Christ.' (Emphasis his). Galatians 6:2 is a good example.

31. The noun βάρος (*baros*) speaks of 'weight, burden' and can mean a claim of importance (weightiness) (1 Thess 2:7) or the fullness of something, e.g., of glory (2 Cor 4:17). In its only use in Gal 6:2 it speaks of a heavy burden—'bear one another's *burden*.' Its three NT uses are all in Paul.

32. **VARIANT**: The aorist imperative *anaplērōsate* has wide support (ℵ A C Dgr K P Ψ 614 1739 syrh arm al). However, the future tense *anaplērōsete* is preferred by the UBS committee on the basis of P46 B G and the majority of other witness. Metzger, *Textual Commentary*, 531 notes that the aorist imperative likely conforms to the previous imperatives *katartizete* (6:1) and *bastazete* (6:2a). The future also fits better following *houtōs*, 'so.' This is rightly a {C} rating by Metzger, it being uncertain.

33. The verb ἀναπληρόω (*anaplēroō*) compounds *ana* (literally: 'up, up to') and *plēroō* (fill) and so speaks of something 'filled up.' All but one use is in Paul (Matt 13:14). In the one use in Galatians 6:2, it means to 'fulfil' the law of Christ, with the same meaning found in Matt 13:14 of the fulfilment of Isa 6:9–10 in Israel's rejection of Christ. Paul uses it elsewhere of someone filling a seat in church (1 Cor 14:16), someone making up financially for the absence of others (1 Cor 16:17; Phil 2:30) and filling up the measure of sins (1 Thess 2:16).

Jesus in his body (his marks of suffering on his behalf). Here, it means to carry the burdens of another.

'Load' is the noun *baros* which speaks of weight (Let. Aris. 93),[34] so figuratively, of something positive like abundance, strength (Jdt 7:4), and influence (e.g., Sir 13:2), or negatively, of a 'heavy burden,' 'oppression,' or 'sluggishness' (e.g., T. Ab. (A). 20:5), or emotional pain.[35]

In the LXX, it is used for luggage carried on a journey (Judg 18:21), while in the Testament of Abraham (B) 11.5, it is used to describe the weight of souls. Josephus and Philo use it for the weight of governing[36] and Philo of the weight of business (*Spec.* 2.102) and putting up with a virtuous person (*Prob.* 28).

In the NT, the term outside of Paul is used figuratively to describe the burden of a blisteringly hot day (Matt 20:12), the burden of the Jewish legal boundary markers on gentiles (Acts 15:28), and of the burdens that Jesus places on the readers of Revelation (Rev 2:24). Paul's other uses are of the eternal weight of glory awaiting God's faithful, which is beyond all measure in comparison to present sufferings (2 Cor 4:17). The other use is of weighty influence, which Paul did not use to make demands of the Thessalonians (1 Thess 2:7).

Here, it speaks of the burdens of suffering people carry, whether it be through their struggles with sin (6:1) or sickness. It is present imperative, amidst a cluster of imperatives and cohortative subjunctives in chapters 4 to 6 (see on 1:8). The present speaks of a habit. This appeal calls to mind the Galatians' receipt of Paul on his first visit when he was ill. Despite the great trial Paul was to them, rather than harm, repudiate, and despise him, the Galatians received him as an angel and even Christ himself (4:12–15). They were even prepared to sacrifice

---

34. S.a., Josephus, *Ant.* 3.170; 6.188 [Goliath's heavy armor]); 8.63, 244; 12.374; *J.W.* 1.507; 3.207; 4:24; *J.W.* 6.189; 7.346 (the weight of the body holding in the soul which is released at death). Also, see Philo, *Opif.* 80; *Det.* 154; *Her.* 146, 198; *Abr.* 171; *Mos.* 2.249; *Aet.* 29, 129. Philo uses it of the relative weight of one's good deeds over against the bad (*Her.* 46).

35. See LSJ 307; G. Schrenk, 'βάρος,' in *TDNT* 1:554. It is used creatively as in 2 Macc 9:10—the weight of a horrendous stench.

36. See Josephus, *Ant.* 1.461; *J.W.* 4.616; Philo, *Virt.* 70; *Legat.* 27.

their eyes for him. They heard his gospel and believed, receiving the blessing of the Spirit (3:2, 5). They bore Paul's burden, so to speak.

On the face of it, there is a contradiction between this verse and 6:5, where Paul urges them to bear their own burdens. However, in 6:5, the verb 'bear' (bastazō) is future tense speaking of the eschaton where, before God, each one will bear the burden of his/her own life. So, it is so important to test one's own work in the present as we will bear our own loads before God at the judgment (6:4). Here in 6:2, the verb is present tense. In this world of struggle and pain, each is to bear the burden of the other, helping one another through.

The final part of the verse states that 'in this way, you will fulfill the law of Christ.' 'In this way' (houtōs) refers back to the bearing of each other's burdens. 'You will fulfill' uses the verb anaplēroō, a compound verb combining ana (lit. 'up, up to') and plēroō (fill), and so, 'fill up' is its literal sense.

In wider sources, it is used among other things of filling up a void (e.g., Plato, Tim. 81b), to make up, supply (e.g., Plato, Symp. 188e), to fill up numbers in a group (e.g., Plutarch, Publ. 11), restore, to pay in full, and fulfill (see below).[37] In the NT, it is found only once outside of Paul, in Matt 13:14 where Israel's rejection of Christ fulfills Isa 6:9–10. Paul uses it of someone filling a seat of an outsider in the gathered church (1 Cor 14:16), someone making up for what cannot be supplied by absent others (1 Cor 16:17; Phil 2:30), and of the Jewish people filling up

---

37. LSJ 116. My own analysis indicates that the main use in Jewish Greek writings of anaplēroō is of the completion of a period of time (Gen 29:28; Exod 7:25; 23:26; Lev 12:6; Esth 1:5; 2:12, 15; Isa 60:20; Josephus, Ant. 8.59; Philo, Praem. 111). Other uses include to restore a wound (Gen 2:21; Philo, Leg. 2.20; 2.38 [analogy for external senses]); sins filled up (for judgment) (Gen 15:16; Philo, Her. 300 [by analogy arguments]); to finish a work (1 Kings 7:37); an overflowing river (Sir 24:26); a bird reaching full size (3 Bar. 7:3); to fill up what is lacking (T. Benj. 11.5; Philo, Spec. 1.294; Legat. 257); to enhance beauty (Let. Aris. 75); fully supply (Josephus, Ant. 5.214; 19.365); to fill a hole (Ant. 7.242), a part (Ant. 12.80), a valley (J.W. 1.145, 147; 4:13), the world (Josephus, Ant. 19.14; Philo, Somn. 1.135), or a haven (J.W. 1.412); to make up for a lack (J.W. 4.198); people selected (J.W. 5.42); to fill up a deficiency in alphabet letters (Opif. 126), the sky (Plant. 40), the mind (Mut. 168), and ill-will with joy (Ios. 206) (see also Philo, Ebr. 53).

the measure of sins (1 Thess 2:16, cf. Gen 15:16; Philo, *Her.* 300). Here, as in Matt 13:14, it means to fulfill.

'The law of Christ' is ambiguous and ironic. On the one hand, Christ is not a law and has not put in place a law in a direct sense. However, the law of Christ is written on the human heart through the Spirit. This idea, drawn from OT hope (Ezek 11:19; 36:26; Jer. 31:33), is picked up in a loose way in 2 Cor 3:3. So, Paul may have in mind the 'law' he has been referring to since 5:16, 'the law of walking by the Spirit,' 'being led by the Spirit,' 'living by the Spirit,' and 'keeping in step with the Spirit.' This is not then unlike the 'law of the Spirit of life' that has set people free from the law of sin and death (Rom 8:2). Another possibility is that Paul has in mind the sum of all laws, the 'law,' 'love your neighbor as yourself' (Gal 5:14, from Lev 19:18). Certainly, to bear one another's burdens is to act in love toward the other. Yet, equally, it is being led by the Spirit. Possibly, we should not be so fully concerned to specify what Paul precisely has in mind. He may be speaking ironically of Christ as a law, in that he is the 'consummation' of law (Rom 10:3), and as such, the only law that now exists. To bear one another's burdens is to fulfill what Jesus wants of us as his people.

DO NOT BE DECEIVED BY YOUR OWN SENSE OF IMPORTANCE (6:3)

In *Galatians 6:3*, Paul continues:

For (*gar*, 1:10) if (*ei*, 1:7) **anyone** (masculine *tis*, 1:7) **thinks** (third-person present *dokeō*,[38] 2:2) **to be** (present infinitive *eimi*, 1:7) **something** (neuter *tis*) **while being** (present participle *eimi*) **nothing** (*mēdeis*),[39] **that person deceives** (present *phrenapataō*)[40] **themselves** (*heautou*, 1:4).

---

38. This is an example of an introductory verb of perception to introduce an indirect discourse infinitive. Here, the verb is δοκεῖ (*dokei*, anyone thinks) and the infinitive εἶναι (*einai*)—'if anyone thinks to be ....' See Wallace, *Greek Grammar*, 604.

39. There are two references to the adjective μηδείς (*mēdeis*) in Galatians. In 6:3 it is neuter, 'nothing,' and in 6:17 it is masculine, 'no one.'

40. The verb φρεναπατάω (*phrenapataō*) is a hapax *legomenon*, only found in the NT in 6:3. It is also only found in Christian literature. The verb from which it is formed is

Scholars search for a connection between this verse and the previous. Aside from the *gar*, as is common in Paul's paraenetic teaching, he throws ideas together without necessarily connecting them. He does so, reinforcing a particular behavior and likely targeting something he is aware of in the community to which he writes. Hence, we do not need to find a connection between v. 2 and 3—this is an outworking of 5:26, the temptation of 6:1, or the temptation not to bear one another's burdens.[41] However, this can embrace all of these and even connect back to 5:19–21 (below). Galatians 6:2 urges that they support each other in times of trouble. Galatians 6:3 targets the problem of arrogance and false humility, a theme that continues into vv. 4–5. No doubt, there were people in the Galatians community who thought too highly of themselves. The *gar* is not causal but simply connects Paul's thoughts.

Paul uses a first-class conditional sentence (*ei* plus indicative), proposing something in the protasis for the sake of argument (see on 1:9)—'if anyone thinks to be something.' *Tis* (anyone) is nonspecific and while in the masculine, could potentially include a woman among the Galatian Christians. 'Thinks' is *dokeō*, discussed in 2:2 in a section where it is used four times of those who 'seem to be something,' '*seem* to be influential,' 'seem to be pillars.' The verb expresses subjective thought; an opinion. The second use of *tis* (neuter, so *ti*) speaks of 'something.' So, this refers to any Galatians arrogating themselves.

Hence, this targets a person with a high opinion of themselves. These people are perhaps alluded to in 5:26—people who pursue *kenodoxos*, who are proud and conceited. It also continues into the following verse, where Paul urges them to test their own

---

apataō, 'deceive, mislead' (Eph 5:6; 1 Tim 2:14; Jas 1:26). It is similar in meaning to *planaō* used in 6:7, 'do not be *deceived*.'

41. Longenecker, *Galatians*, 276 for example suggests that they should not think too highly of themselves to bear one another's burdens. Perhaps, but this potentially limits Paul's thought here. Lightfoot, *Galatians*, 216 connects this to v. 1, the sin that they may fall into being pride. Moo, *Galatians*, 379 connects this to v. 26 and the problem of *kenodoxos* (cf. Hays, 'Galatians,' 334). All of these have merit, but we should not be too specific. As I argue, the last of these has the most merit but also this connects back to the works of the flesh.

work and keep their own sense of pride personal to themselves, not before others.

'While being nothing' indicates that Paul's target is especially those who are not particularly gifted or talented but believe they are. Elsewhere, Paul urges Christians to have a realistic view of themselves. So, in Romans 12:3 he writes, 'For by the grace given to me I say to everyone among you not to think of himself more highly than he ought to think, but to think with sober judgment, each according to the measure of faith that God has assigned.' Implicit here is people knowing themselves, an important Greek maxim picked up by the Romans and many others in the world.[42] Paul goes on in Rom 12:16: 'never be wise concerning yourself.' In other words, don't be a wise guy! This recalls Prov 3:7, 'Be not wise in your own eyes; fear the Lord, and turn away from evil.' As noted, in the next verses, Paul will repudiate boasting of oneself before others.

Such a person deceives him or herself. 'Themselves' pluralizes the Greek, which is literally himself, the masculine of *heautou*. The reflexive pronoun is elsewhere used in the letter of Christ giving himself for sin (1:4) and for Paul (2:20), Peter keeping himself separate (2:12). In the next verse, it is used of testing one's own works and boasting only to oneself rather than others. There is significant teaching here on self-reflection where we put ourselves under the microscope. Elsewhere *heautou*, 'him/her/themselves' is used of the Christian life, a vital ethical term. This

---

42. The maxim originated in the Luxor Temple in Egypt. The Greek is γνῶθι σεαυτὸν (*gnōthi seauton*) and the Latin *nosce te ipsum* or *temet nosce*. The phrase was inscribed on the Temple of Apollo at Delphi (Pausanias, 10.24.1). Plato uses it extensively and is followed by a range of Greek and modern thinkers. See 'Know Thyself,' in *Wikipedia*, https://en.wikipedia.org/wiki/Know_thyself.

is so in the wider NT.[43] Paul also uses *heautou* in a range of ethical ways.[44]

43. Outside of Paul *heautou* is used in these ways: 1) Humility: Deny oneself and take up one's cross and follow Christ (Matt 16:24; Mark 8:34; Luke 9:23; 14:26–27), if not, one forfeits oneself (Luke 9:25). Humble oneself like a child (Matt 18:4), to be exalted, and vice versa (Matt 23:12; Luke 14:11; 18:14, s.a., Heb 5:4–5). Do not justify oneself before God (Luke 16:15, s.a., Luke 18:9). 2) Committed Discipleship: see above deny oneself texts; have salt in yourselves (Mark 9:50); hate one's own parents and life (Luke 14:26). 3) With Money: Provide oneself with eternal moneybags rather than storing up treasure for oneself on earth (Luke 12:21, 33) and renounce all one has (Luke 14:33), make friends for oneself with wealth (Luke 16:9). 4) Self-Deception: Do not merely hear the word and deceive oneself (Jas 1:22, 24), similarly, do not deceive yourselves saying one is sinless (1 John 1:8). 5) Holiness: Keep oneself unstained by the world (Jas 1:27). Holy women should adorn themselves with modesty (1 Pet 3:5). Keep oneself from idols (1 John 5:21). Hope in Christ and purify self as Jesus is pure (1 John 3:3). 6) Impartiality: Have no discriminations among yourselves (Jas 2:4). 7) Eternal life: Watch yourselves, so that they do not lose their reward (2 John 8). 8) Orthodoxy: Do not be as the false teachers feeding selves (Jude 12), casting foam on their own shame (Jude 13), following desires of the self (Jude 16, 18), but building up selves in the most holy faith (Jude 20), and keeping selves in the love of God (Jude 21). 9) Sin: pay attention to yourselves, that you do not fall into sin and lead others to sin (Luke 17:3). Watch yourselves that you aren't weighed down by dissipation, drunkenness (*methē*, 5:21), and the concerns of life (Luke 21:34).

44. 1) Commitment to God: Present yourselves to God as those who use their lives for righteousness' sake (Rom 6:13). Do not live to yourself but to God (Rom 14:7). People give themselves to the Lord (2 Cor 8:5). 2) Humility: Never be wise in your own selves (Rom 12:16). 'Bear with the failings of the weak, and do not please ourselves' (Rom 15:1), as 'Christ did not please himself' (Rom 15:3). Similarly, 1 Cor 10:24: 'let no one seek his own advantage, but the advantage of his neighbor.' So Stephanas and his household have devoted themselves to the service of the saints' (1 Cor 16:15). 'Let no one deceive him/herself' concerning humility (1 Cor 3:18). Avoid commending oneself but to God and others only in service (2 Cor 3:5; 4:2; 5:12; 6:4; 2 Cor 10:12, 14, 18). Consider others more significant than oneself (Phil 2:3) and be concerned for the interests of others not only one's self-interest (Phil 2:4), as did Christ who emptied himself and humbled himself (Phil 2:7–8). Timothy is a prime example, concerned not for his own interests like most, but for those of Jesus Christ (Phil 2:21–22). Work out one's own salvation, which speaks of the attitude of the Christ-hymn (Phil 2:21). Women, adorning themselves in humble clothing (1 Tim 2:9). 'Husbands love wives as they love self and as Christ loves the church (Eph 5:28, 29, 33). 3) Non-Violence: Never avenge yourselves (Rom 12:19). 4) Money and Generosity: Sharing oneself with those to whom we minister, as did Paul (1 Thess 2:8), as does a father to his children (1 Thess 2:11). Earn one's own living (2 Thess 3:12). 5) Leadership: Gain a good reputation for oneself as a Christian leader (1 Tim 3:13). Unlike the false teachers who pierce themselves through the love of money (1 Tim 6:10), store up treasure for

The verb for deceives, *phrenapataō*, is unique to Christian literature, found only in Paul in comparative literature. The associated verb *apataō* is more common and means 'deceive' and is found in Eph 5:6 (let no one deceive you with empty words), 1 Tim 2:14 (and Adam was not deceived by Satan), and Jas 1:26 (and does not bridle his tongue is deceived). Another *apataō* term, *exapataō* is also used for deception.[45] *Apatē* is utilized in Mark 4:19 of being deceived by riches. The cognate adjective *phrenapatēs* is found in Titus 1:10 of the Judaizers, who are deceivers (*phrenapatai*). Here, the problem is not satanic deception, but self-delusion. Perhaps Paul's advice to the Corinthians is sage here: 'Let no one deceive himself. If anyone among you thinks that he is wise in this age, let him become a fool that he may become wise' (1 Cor 3:18).

It is critical then that Christians spend time in prayer and in consideration of who they are in Christ. We are all God's children, and our status as such is assured. Hence, we know we are loved. We know we are wanted. We know we belong. However, we need to know our giftedness and ability to contribute as God would want. This means spending time considering who we are. We ask questions like, in my family history, what gifts and skills are seen? (We often inherit them, like the Levitical singers, where music passes across generations). What moves me? What makes me excited, angry—such things can lead us to our passions? What skills do I know I have? We can ask trusted friends to help us see what we have to offer. What vocation am I good at? What guidance in Christ have we had? As we ask these questions, we find that we do accept who we are and work out of our gifts and call. We do not fall into the trap of thinking ourselves better than we are. Nor do we consider

oneself with God (1 Tim 6:19). 6) Self-Examination: At the Lord's Supper, each should examine himself truly (1 Cor 11:28, 29, 31). Examine yourselves ... test yourselves' (2 Cor 13:5). 8) Holiness and Purity: Cleanse ourselves from every defilement of body and spirit (2 Cor 7:1). Similarly, each should control his/her own body in holiness and honor (1 Thess 4:4). Do not sow to the flesh of oneself, but the Spirit (6:8). 9) Peace: Be at peace among yourselves (1 Thess 5:13). Do not sow to the flesh of oneself, but the Spirit (6:8).

45. See Rom 7:11; 16:18; 1 Cor 3:19; 2 Cor 11:3; 2 Thess 2:3; 2 Tim 2:14.

ourselves less than what God has made us. Underlying all of this is the call to be humble Christians who are prepared to serve as slaves to one another (5:13).

Where people have an unrealistically inflated self-opinion (*kenodoxos*), this fuels the evil works of the flesh, for it is people who have a high opinion of themselves that become angry, jealous, factional, and divisive, as they consider that they should get their own way. They are so confident in their own read on things; they cannot see an alternative. They cannot let others lead because they feel they have to be involved. They resist those in leadership. They politic to get their way. They foster support. They manipulate. They want power. They believe what they are doing is justified because of their high opinion of themselves and believe that they know what God wants. They tear organizations and churches apart over time as their bitterness and divisiveness test relationships. People move on because they have had enough. The organization/church loses momentum and comes apart. One day such people look around and aside from a few people like them, there is no one left. Last one out, turn off the lights.

TEST YOUR OWN WORK AND NOT OTHERS (6:4)

In *Galatians 6:4*, Paul continues encouraging the Galatians in their work for Christ:

And (*de*, 1:15) **let each person** (*hekastos*)[46] **test** (third-person present imperative *dokimazō*)[47] **their own** (*heautou*, 1:4) **work** (*ergon*, 2:16), **and** (*kai*, 1:1) **then** (*tote*, 4:8) **to** (*eis*, 1:5) **himself** (*heautou*) **only** (*monos*, 1:23) **he has** (present *echō*, 2:4) **a boast** (*kauchēma*),[48] **and** (*kai*) **not** (*ou*, 1:1) **to** (*eis*) **another** (*heteros*, 1:6).

46. The adjective ἔκαστος (*hekastos*) means 'each, every' and is used twice in Galatians. In 6:4 and 5 it is masculine speaking of 'each person' or 'everyone' who must test his or her own work and who must carry their own load before God at the judgment.
47. The verb δοκιμάζω (*dokimazō*) means to test or prove something through testing. It is used once in Gal 6:4 in Paul's injunction to the Galatians for each person in the community to test his or her own work.
48. The noun καύχημα (*kauchēma*) means 'boast,' and is mentioned only in 6:4 in Paul's injunction that each Galatian test their own work and boast only to themselves. This speaks of pride, which is clearly an issue in the Galatian community. Boasting is a

The theme of consideration of oneself and humility rather than pride and boasting continues. *De* here is consecutive and so should be translated 'and' rather than 'but. 'Let each person test' uses the verb *dokimazō*. Each person (or everyone) is *hekastos*, which is general, inclusive of men and women. It is only used here and in the next verse indicating the generic nature of Paul's appeal—it is to everyone, to each one. *Heautou* is used twice, the reflexive pronoun indicating oneself—one's work, one's own load. It is used in the previous verse, and these two verses call for self-examination and the loneliness of standing alone before God in judgment. As noted concerning the previous verse, *heautou* is commonly used in the ethical teaching of the NT.

Dokimazō has its roots in *dokē* (watch) with *dokimos* referring to someone tested in battle, reliable, trustworthy, someone generally being tested—so someone, therefore, who is significant, recognized, esteemed, and worthy. It is used for objects, especially metals that are tested, valuable, and genuine. The verb then speaks of testing or trying something or someone, proving their worth, or accepting something as proven.[49]

In the LXX it is used of God testing people. So, David sings, 'Test (*dokimazō*) me, O Lord, and test me, purge my mind and my heart' (Ps 25:2 [Eng. 26:2], s.a. Ps 16:3 [Eng. 17:3]). Similarly, the Psalmist sings of Israel, 'For you *tested* us, O God, and purged us as refined silver' (Ps 65:10 [Eng. 65:10]). Zechariah employs the verb of God testing people in judgment (Zech 13:9, s.a. Jer 6:27; 9:7).[50] Again, in the Psalms from the glorious Ps 138 (Eng. 139): 'O Lord, you *tested* me and have known me' (Ps 138:1 [Eng. 139:1]) and '*Test* me, O God, and know my heart. Examine me and know my paths' (Ps 138:23 [139:32]). God's instruction is better than tested gold (Prov 8:10).[51] Martyrs were tested for the

particular theme of Paul, with *kauchēma* only found in his writings ten times, and once in Hebrews. The associated verb *kauchaomai* is used in 6:13–14 of the Judaizers who boast in the circumcised flesh of the Galatians, and of Paul's refusal to boast of anything except the cross of Christ.

49. See further W. Grundmann, 'δοκιμάζω,' in *TDNT* 2:256.
50. See also in Jer 11:20; 12:3; 17:10; 20:12; 3 Macc 2:6.
51. See also Prov 17:3: 'just as gold and silver are tested in a kiln, so hearts are selected before the Lord.' See also Ps 67:31 [Eng. 68:30]; 80:8 [Eng. 81:7]; Wis 3:6; Sir 2:5; 27:5;

prize of eternal life (4 Macc 17:12). In the Pseudepigrapha, the verb is regularly employed of God's testing of people and their works in the fire of final judgment.[52] Conversely, it is used for those who tested God (Ps 94:9 [Eng. 95:9], s.a. Wis 1:3).

In the non-Pauline NT, *dokimazō* is used only four times, in the sense interpret (through 'scientific' testing, observation) (Luke 12:56), trying out working animals (Luke 14:19), one's faith tested by fire (1 Pet 1:7), and of testing spirits to see if they are genuine (1 John 4:1).

Paul employs it of testing the existence of God (Rom 1:28), testing what is best before God or his will (Rom 2:18; 12:2; Eph 5:10), approving behavior (Rom 14:22), people approved for a task like the Jerusalem Collection (1 Cor 16:3; 2 Cor 8:22), for ministry (1 Thess 2:4), or for leadership (1 Tim 3:10), testing someone's love (2 Cor 8:8), to determine the best course of action (Phil 1:10), and in testing everything (1 Thess 5:21).

Similar to uses in the Pseudepigrapha, it is employed in 1 Cor 3:13 of the final judgment where, with fire, God will reveal the quality of each Christian's work for him (1 Cor 3:13). Twice to the Corinthians, as here, Paul urges self-examination. They are to examine themselves as they come together to celebrate the Eucharist, ensuring all vestiges of sinfulness and disunifying behavior are purged (1 Cor 11:28). Similarly, in 2 Cor 13:5, they are to test themselves with self-examination to ensure that they remain in the faith. Here, the tenor is similar. Rather than wait for the final judgment of their work,[53] which is coming (v. 5, cf. 1 Cor 3:13), they must test themselves and their own work now. The verb is the tenth of a sequence of imperatives running through chapters 4 to 6 (see 1:8). This speaks not only of the quality of the work but their motivations. Are they doing their

---

34:10; 34:26; 42:8; Zech 11:13. The ear tests words, and the throat tastes (tests) food (Job 34:3). A father tests a child (Wis 11:10). To investigate by testing (2 Macc 1:34; Let. Aris. 276). A person approved (2 Macc 4:3). See also T. Ash. 5.4; T. Jos. 2.6.

52. See also its use for eternal judgment, Sib. Or. 2.93; T. Ab. (A) 12.14; 13.11, 13, 14.

53. *Ergon* here is a collective singular, and so really means 'works'. See George, *Galatians*, 290.

work out of love? Are they doing their work purely to please God, or to gain the esteem of others?

Just as we need to ensure we do not have a false view of ourselves, we need to practice self-examination as part of our Christian lives. This is not to punish and judge ourselves, for we are God's children, and a prayer of contrition always reminds us that we are forgiven by God in Christ. Rather, it is to ensure that we are living faithful lives motivated only to please God and serve others in love. We then renounce all self-arrogation and the need to gain position. Earlier in Gal 1:10, Paul states that his *raison d'être* is to please God, and this is the same reason believers serve him. The Galatians who are being ripped apart by their arrogance, envy, division, dissensions, anger, and so on, have to get back to the basics and begin serving God and one another without concern for human rank, status, prestige, and honor. This is counter-cultural in a society that was all about honor and avoiding things associated with shame—such as lower status.

The second half of the verse explains the rationale behind each testing their own work. Then (*tote*) 'to himself only he has a boast.' 'Boast' is *kauchēma*, one of Paul's customary 'boasting terms.' In an honor-shame culture like the Roman world, boasting was an art form. Reputation mattered and promoting oneself was a core aspect of culture. While self-boasting was frowned upon, it was important to find ways to promote one's honor.

In Jewish culture, boasting was rejected. Paul mentions the term often, indicating that it was a real problem in his churches. Rather than any self-boasting, Paul endorses boasting in God and his Son,[54] in the glory of God (Rom 5:2), in Christ the law (which should lead to obedience to the law) (Rom 2:23), and boasting in sufferings because they produce so much good in us (Rom 5:3). He rejects humans boasting of themselves before God because of their sin,[55] gentile arrogance toward Jews (Rom 11:18), in one person over another (1 Cor 3:21), boasting of one's gifts or

---

54. See Rom 2:17; 5:11; 1 Cor 1:29, 31 [Jer 9:23–24; 1 Sam 2:10 LXX]; 2 Cor 10:16; Phil 3:3.

55. See Rom 3:27; 4:2; 1 Cor 1:29; Eph 2:9.

service before others (1 Cor 4:7) or without love (1 Cor 13:3), in sexual immorality (1 Cor 5:6), and in outward appearance (2 Cor 5:12).

At times, he speaks of boasting of his converts, the kind of beaming pride a parent has for his or her children,[56] and his converts in him (Phil 1:26). Such a boast he will have as he stands alone before God (2 Cor 1:14; Phil 2:16). He also uses boasting language ironically against those who demean him, kind of 'playing their game.' When he does, he is reluctant, describing himself as foolish in doing so and taking care to boast only of his own work and giving the ultimate glory to God.[57] The *coup de grâce* of his argument, is a catalog of suffering and weakness—badges of his service (2 Cor 11:16–12:9). He also allows pride in one's own work, not before others, but a kind of pride in the work done always glorifying God for his enabling power.[58]

In Galatians, he uses boasting language three times, all in this chapter. In 6:13, he speaks of the Judaizers' desire to have the Galatians circumcised so that they may boast in your flesh—a jibe at the circumcision of the penis while pointing to something deeper; their fallen flesh which the Judaizers are blind to. (Judaizing is to place one's trust in the flesh, cf. Phil 3:2–9). In the following verse, 6:14, Paul speaks of his determination only to boast in the cross of Christ in which he is crucified. This calls to mind other texts above which speak of God and his Son as Paul's core reason for boasting.

Here in 6:4, the Galatians are to take pride in their work and their faithfulness to God alone. This is the language of self-examination to ensure that they are faithful. Then, they can stand before God with a clear conscience and take pride in their own work. 'And not to another' translates *heteros*, with the meaning 'not to anyone else.' Like Paul who takes pride in his own work with the intent of pleasing God alone, the Galatians should do the same. Their ministry for Christ is not to please others, to

---

56. See 1 Cor 15:31; 2 Cor 7:4, 14; 8:24; 9:2, 3; 1 Thess 2:19; 2 Thess 1:4.
57. See 2 Cor 10:8, 13, 15, 16; 11:10, 12, 16–12:9.
58. See Rom 15:17; 1 Cor 9:15, 16; 2 Cor 1:12.

meet their expectations, or to gain their honor. Rather, it is to please God and to be faithful to that which one is called.

EACH WILL BEAR THEIR OWN LOAD AT THE FINAL JUDGMENT (6:5)

In *Galatians 6:5*, he gives the reason for this:

For (*gar*, 1:10) **each** (*hekastos*; 6:4) **will bear** (future *bastazō*, 5:10) **their own** (neuter *idios*, 2:2) **load** (*phortion*).[59]

The *gar* is causal, 'for, because,' with Paul giving the reason that they must test their own work. *Hekastos*, as in its only other use in Galatians in the previous verse, is inclusive—each one, men and women, Jews or Greeks, slaves or free.

'Bear' is *bastazō*, used in 5:10 of those who bear the penalty for yielding to the Judaizers or being one. In 6:17, it is used of Paul bearing in and on his body the marks of Christ. Then in v. 2, it was used of bearing one another's burdens. Here, rather than bearing one another's burdens, they are to bear their own burden. The verb in v. 2 is present, speaking of the Galatians fulfilling the call of Christ to love with humility (6:3), and giving support to one another in times of trouble, especially when facing struggles with sin (6:1). Here it is in the future tense, speaking probably of eschatological judgment where each will face God bearing the consequences for their lives. Unlike the Judaizers who will receive God's condemnation (5:10), those who live by faith will receive the wonderful reward of eternal life. This may also allude to varying degrees of reward, as is implied by 1 Cor 3:12–15, where the work (*ergon*) of each person (*hekaston*) is tested by God's judgment, with that which is consistent with the ethics, content, and praxis of the gospel, bringing reward. Others will slip through as one who has passed through a fire.

The specific term for 'burden' here is *phortion* rather than *baros*

---

59. The noun φορτίον (*phortion*) is found once in Galatians, in 6:5—'each person will bear their own burden.' The other uses are from Jesus of his burden being light (Matt 11:30), of the Jewish leaders loading people up with heavy burdens (Matt 23:4; Luke 11:46), and of a ship's cargo (Acts 27:10). This is Paul's only use.

used in v. 2, a term meaning 'weight, burden' (see on 6:2 for detail). *Phortion* is the diminutive of *phortos*,[60] meaning a ship's cargo or burden; hence, it suggests a small cargo or burden.

In wider Greek sources, it is used of things like a ship's cargo, a wagon load, freight, burden, or goods.[61] In Greek Jewish writings it is not extensively used carrying the meaning of a person being a burden to another (2 Sam 19:35; Job 7:20), the burden of sin (Ps 37:5 [Eng. 38:4], the burden of a chatterbox (Sir 21:16), a stick being a donkey's burden (Sir 30:33), burdens carried by an animal (Isa 46:1), a ship's cargo (T. Job 18:7; Josephus, *Ant.* 14.377; Philo, *Deus.* 98), goods (Josephus, *Ant.* 2.32; 2.110), or a personal sack of one's possessions (Josephus, *Ant.* 2.124, 126, 134). Matthew uses it twice and Luke once from the lips of Jesus. First, it is used of the lightness of Jesus' burden for those who in a weary state come to him (Matt 11:30). Both Luke and Matthew employ it in Jesus' rebuke of Jewish leaders who load great legal burdens on people (Matt 23:4; Luke 11:46). In Acts, Luke uses it of a ship's cargo (Acts 27:10).

There are differing interpretations of *phortion* here. Some resolve the apparent contradiction with 6:2 (bear one another's loads) noting that phortion refers to a load of everyday responsibilities while *baros* speaks of those things too hard for one person to handle.[62] However, as my discussions of the two words have shown, they are not fixed in meaning and have significant semantic overlap; hence, this is not a strong argument. Some blend the previous idea arguing that this is a general maxim with the future tense speaking of what is usually true in life for the self-sufficient person; as the NRSV puts it, 'For all must carry their own loads.'[63] Similarly, the NIV: 'for each one should carry their own load.'

60. A diminutive is a term that indicates a particularly small example of something. So, *arēn* is lamb, while *arnion* is a *little* lamb. Similarly, *pais* is a child while *paidion* is a *small* child. Hence, *phortion* connotes a small *phortos*, a *small* burden. On diminutives, see *PDSNTG* 47.

61. See further G. Fitzer, 'φορτίον,' in *TDNT* 9:86–86. It is related to the *pherō* nexus of terms (meaning 'carry, bear').

62. Dunn, *Galatians*, 322, 325.

63. Betz, *Galatians*, 303–304 argues that this was an ancient philosophical maxim related

However, as argued on 6:2 and the previous verse, the key is the shift from the present of *bastazō* in v. 2 to the future in v. 5. In the present, people are to bear one another's loads as they press on toward eternal life. In the future, on judgment day, each will stand alone having their works tested by God. Hence, in the previous verse, they should test their own work presently to ensure that they can be confident in themselves as they face God in the final judgment. So then, the tenor here is eschatological with the final judgment in mind. So, the ESV and NET translations are to be preferred: 'For each one will carry his own load' (NET); 'For each one will bear his own load' (ESV). As Moo rightly argues, 'on the day of judgment, each person will need to answer to the Lord for their conduct.'[64]

STUDENTS SHARE ALL GOOD THINGS WITH TEACHERS (6:6)

In *Galatians 6:6*, Paul gives another injunction concerning financial care of those who teach the word to them:

And (*de*, 1:15) **let the one who is taught** (present passive participle *katēcheō*)[65] **the word** (*logos*, 5:14) **share** (present active singular imperative *koinōneō*)[66] **in all** (dative neuter plural *pas*, 1:2) **good things** (dative neuter plural *agathos*)[67] **with** (*en*, 1:6) **the one who teaches** (present active participle *katēcheō*).

There are two ways of taking this verse. First, Paul could be encouraging the Galatians who are being taught the word of God to share *in* all the good things which the teacher is imparting.[68]

---

to people being self-sufficient (*autakreia*). See also Longenecker, *Galatians*, 278; Dunn, *Galatians*, 326.

64. Moo, *Galatians*, 381, s.a., Hays, '1 Corinthians,' 335.
65. The verb κατηχέω (*katēcheō*) meaning 'to teach' is found twice in Gal 6:6 of the Galatians sharing with their teacher in all good things. Paul only uses it twice else of Jews instructed from the law (Rom 2:18) and instructing others in church with things from the mind (1 Cor 14:19).
66. The one use of the verb κοινωνέω (*koinōneō*) is in 6:6 where it speaks of the Galatians sharing in good things with their teachers of the word. It is associated with *koinōnia* used of the 'right hand of *fellowship*' in 2:9.
67. The adjective ἀγαθός (*agathos*), 'good,' is used in 6:6 of 'good things' to be shared with teachers and in 6:10 of doing good to all people, especially believers. The noun *agathōsynē* is used in 5:22 of goodness as a Spirit fruit.

'All good things,' then, would be spiritual in nature—the spiritual things of the gospel. This then would be parallel to Rom 15:27 where the gentiles 'share (koinōneō) in the spiritual blessings of the Jews.' As such, this is another appeal to participate in correct teaching and not the teaching of the Judaizers.[69] The alternative, which is favored by commentators, states that the Galatians should 'share with the one teaching the word in all good things.' 'All good things' would then be material in nature. So, a parallel can be drawn from Phil 4:15: 'not one church shared with me (koinōneō) in the matter of giving and receiving, except you only.'[70] The grammar clearly favors the latter. It is the one who is taught the word who shares with the one who is teaching, rather than the converse.[71]

Connecting this to the context is challenging if we feel we need to find a connection point between the verses. Some link it to what follows in which Paul speaks of sowing. Sowing is used in 2 Cor 9:6 of material generosity toward others in need; context, the Corinthians contributing to the Jerusalem Collection. Hence, this is an example of sowing, as is 6:10, 'do good to all people, especially to those from the family of faith.'[72] Others link this back to v. 2 as an example of the Galatians bearing one another's burdens.[73] While sharing all good things with a teacher with right motives is undoubtedly an example of doing good to brothers and sowing to please the Spirit, neither of these interpretations explains why this particular verse is needed in this context. Why put it here at all? Surely, something must have caused the need for Paul to say this.

Another possibility is that this continues vv. 4–5 which emphasizes individual responsibility—self-testing, taking pride in their own work only, and final judgment. So, Moo argues:

---

68. As Moo, *Galatians*, 382 puts it. He then rejects this idea.

69. See for example, A. Oepke, *Der Brief des Paulus an die Galater*, THK (Berlin: Evangelische Verlagsanstalt, 1973), 191–93.

70. Similarly, Moo, *Galatians*, 382.

71. Dunn, *Galatians*, 327.

72. The way that contemporary English translations place this verse with what follows points to this interpretation (e.g., ESV, NET).

73. Lightfoot, *Galatians*, 217.

'This emphasis on self-reliance could, Paul realizes, easily be misinterpreted as a reason to hold back from supporting those who teach. Here, he therefore, heads off any such incorrect inference from his principle of self-examination.'[74] If we take Dunn's view of 6:5 whereby it speaks of people bearing their own material burdens being self-sufficient, this a possible interpretation. However, as Moo has argued, 6:5 is couched in the future and speaks of eschatological judgment.[75] As such, v. 5 speaks of the outcome of individual responsibility. Verse 4 speaks of self-responsibility, but there is nothing in this to lead to a person not sharing with their teacher. Hence, again we are left pondering just why this has been put here.

An alternative perspective is that aside from this being one way to bear one another's burdens and do good to all people (or live out of the fruit of the Spirit), it is not to be directly linked to the context.[76] Paul's paraenetic teaching, not everything is linked to what precedes or follows. Paul often will string together a range of commands and exhortations that can seem a little random. Take, for example, Phil 4:2–9 and 1 Thess 5:12–24. While the exhortations of Phil 4:2–20 can be connected to the problem between Euodia and Syntyche in some cases (e.g., joy, peace, anxiety), what we have is a string of Christian injunctions which speak of concerns Paul has for the Philippians based on information he has heard from emissaries, or merely so that Paul can encourage them generally—joy, gentleness, anxiety, prayer, peace, right thinking, imitation, and finances.

In 1 Thess 5:12–23, similarly, Paul gives a range of encouragements: respect and esteem those in ministry over them, be at peace, admonishment, encouragement, patience, mutual support, non-retribution, goodness, joy, prayer, gratitude, spiritual openness, prophetic awareness, testing everything, and so on. In such lists, we do not have to link

---

74. Moo, *Galatians*, 382. See also Dunn, *Galatians*, 326.
75. See the discussion above where for Moo, 6:5 speaks of eschatological judgment not self-provision in the present (an interpretation with which I agree).
76. Betz, *Galatians*, 304. See also translations which have this verse as a stand-alone paragraph (NRSV, CEV).

everything to the literary context. Rather, we can consider what might have caused Paul to put these particular injunctions in place.

Here then, it is likely because some of those among the Galatians are not providing for their teachers of the word as they should. Those with whom they are to share are those who 'teach the word,' indicating that they are authentic gospel teachers rather than Judaizers. As such, it is likely that the Judaizers are urging the Galatians to withdraw any financial support from those who are preaching a Pauline non-Judaizing gospel. Paul is then countering this, saying that they should continue to do so.

Elsewhere, although Paul himself preferred the path of self-support as a tentmaker, Paul endorses the principle that those who preach the gospel should earn their living by the gospel.[77] In fact, Paul also received support himself on occasion, especially from the Philippians (2 Cor 11:8; Phil 4:10–19). His defense of the principle that a preacher of the gospel should be supported through their ministry is particularly clear in 1 Cor 9:7–14, where he gives six arguments in support of this premise. The first three are drawn from non-religious contexts; the military and agriculture (1 Cor 9:7): a soldier serves for payment from those for whom he fights, one who plants a vineyard eats its grapes, and a shepherd who drinks from the milk of the animals. Two are drawn from the OT Scriptures and Israel's religious tradition (1 Cor 9:8–13). The first is a reference to Deut 25:4 where a working ox eats from the grain it treads (s.a. 1 Tim 5:18, below). The second refers to the priests eating from sacrificial offerings.[78] This sixth argument is from Christ who, according to

---

77. Paul's reasons for not receiving financial support are complex. They include: 1) not wishing to be a burden (2 Cor 11:9); 2) refusing patronage which required reciprocity; 3) not wishing to be identified as one who peddles the gospel for money (1 Thess 2:5); 4) as a demonstration of curtailing freedom for love (1 Cor 9); and 5) to give himself grounds for boasting before God (1 Cor 9:15–16). Paul seemed to reject accepting financial support from those to whom he initially preached but was prepared to accept support from converts when he left the context (Phil 4:10–19). He also accepts personal patronage out of love from Philemon and Phoebe (Phlm; Rom 16:1–4, s.a., Lydia, Acts 16:11).

78. See Lev 6:16, 26; 7:6; Num 5:9, 10; 18:8–20; Deut 18:1.

Paul, 'commanded that those who proclaim the gospel should get their living by the gospel' (Matt 10:10; Luke 10:4). In 1 Tim 5:18, where Deut 25:4 is again cited, Paul urges Timothy to ensure that the *presbyteroi* (elders) among them are considered worthy of double honor, especially those who labor in the word (*logos*) and in teaching (*didaskalia*). While there has been much debate over 'double honor,' the citation of Deut 25:4 alongside Matt 10:10/ Luke 10:4 suggests this speaks of material provision for these elders.[79]

Here, in Gal 6:6, Paul is reminding the Galatians that they should provide for the needs of those commissioned to teach them. They may be some from the *presbyteroi* Paul and Barnabas appointed in the Galatian churches (Acts 14:23, cf. 1 Tim 5:18). It could include others from the community with a call to teach and preach the gospel (e.g., apostles, prophets, evangelists, pastors, teachers, in Eph 4:11, s.a. 1 Cor 12:28), or they may be itinerant preachers passing through.

The specifics of the verse are worthy of comment. The verb *koinōneō* is associated with *koinōnia* used in 2:9 where Paul and Barnabas are offered the right hand of *koinōnia* (fellowship, partnership) by the Jerusalem leaders. As discussed, the *koinōn-* terms speak of partnership, including business, marriage, and other forms of personal relationship. *Koinōnia* is used in Paul of relationship with God, his Son, and Spirit,[80] symbolized by Communion (1 Cor 10:16, s.a. 1 Cor 10:18, 20),[81] and including Christ's sufferings (Phil 3:10, s.a. 2 Cor 1:7);[82] fellowship of light

---

79. See the discussion in P. H. Towner, *The Letters to Timothy and Titus*, NICNT (Grand Rapids, MI: Eerdmans, 2006), 361–64 who states '[t]he backing for the instruction that Paul gives in v. 18 suggests that at least in some cases more than respect in the form of acknowledgement—i.e., some form material compensation—might be meant' (cf. 1 Cor 9:7–14; 2 Cor 11:8–9; Gal 6:6; 1 Thess 2:7). He notes that 'double' can mean twice that given to other groups who are being supported, whether it is other non-teaching elders, deacons, or widows. Alternatively, it is figurative meaning 'more.' The details are difficult, but the overall principle is clear—they are to be financially supported.

80. See 1 Cor 1:9; 2 Cor 13:14; Phil 2:1; Rom 11:17, s.a. 1 John 1:3, 6; 2 Pet 1:4.

81. 1 Corinthians 10:18, 20 uses *koinōnos*, of a partner in idolatry and with demons (if a Christian visits a pagan temple).

82. 2 Corinthians 1:7 uses *koinōnos*, a partner in suffering. See also Rev 1:9.

and darkness, good and evil (none!) (2 Cor 6:14, s.a. 1 John 1:6), and sharing monetary resources as in the Jerusalem Collection,[83] mission partnership (Phil 1:5, 7, s.a. 2 Cor 8:23),[84] or Christian fellowship.[85]

The verb *koinōneō* (share, participate) is used outside of Paul of participating in sin (1 Tim 5:22) or wicked works (2 John 11, s.a. Rev 18:4), of Jesus participating in being flesh and blood (Heb 2:14), and of sharing in Christ's sufferings (1 Pet 4:13). Paul employs it of material generosity toward others in need (Rom 12:13), sharing in spiritual blessings (Rom 15:27), and sharing materially as the Philippians did toward Paul (Phil 4:15). He also employs the compound *synkoinōneō* (participate with, share with) of not participating in evil works (Eph 5:11), and sharing in Paul's financial struggles (Phil 4:14).

Here, it likely includes the financial edge found in a number of the references above. They are to share with their teacher their financial resources. '*All* good things' would seem to transcend the material and speak of sharing spiritually and materially with their teachers of the word. This would include fellowship itself, prayer, support (cf. 6:2), and whatever else is needed in its appropriate time. The verb is another in the string of imperatives through 4:21–6:17.[86] It is present tense speaking of an ongoing attitude of sharing.

The term used twice in this verse is not the normal Greek verb for teaching, *didaskō*; rather, Paul employs the less common *katēcheō* (from which we get the Eng. 'catechesis,' 'catechism')—first, a present passive participle; second a present active participle. The verb is late and rare, compounding *kata*

---

83. See Rom 15:26; 2 Cor 8:4; 9:13, s.a. 2 Tim 6:18 (using *koinōnikos* meaning 'giving, sharing, liberal, generous); Heb 13:16.

84. 2 Corinthians 8:23 uses *koinōnos*, partner and co-worker. Philippians 1:7 uses *synkoinōnos* of partnering with Paul in the grace of his mission (or salvation grace).

85. Acts 2:42; Gal 2:9; Phlm 6, 17, s.a. 1 John 1:7. Philemon 6 certainly includes material partnership but speaks too of the sharing of very lives. Philippians 1:5 too includes material fellowship (also Phil 4:10–19), but it is wider including engagement in mission, prayer, suffering, and unity. Philemon 17 uses *koinōnos*, partner. *Synkoinōnos* is also used of sharing in the blessings of the gospel (1 Cor 9:23, s.a., 1 Pet 5:1).

86. See 1:8, 20; 3:7; 4:12, 21, 30; 5:1, 13, 16; 6:1, 2, 4, 7, 11, 17, s.a. 5:14, 25, 26.

and *ēchos*, 'sound,' which means literally to 'sound from above.' There are two main meanings, 'to recount, to inform' or to 'teach, instruct,' as it is frequently used in Stoicism, and as it means here.[87]

Absent from the LXX, *katēcheō* is employed in other Jewish Greek sources in the sense of 'inform' (Josephus, *Life* 366; Philo, *Legat.* 198) and 'to teach,' as in the case of Jeremiah who preached and taught God's people in Babylon (4 Bar. 5:19). Luke employs the verb in the sense of 'inform' (Acts 21:21, 24) and with the meaning 'teach—so his Gospel was written to confirm the things Theophilus *had been taught* (Luke 1:4) and Apollos was instructed by Priscilla and Aquila (Acts 18:25). Paul employs it of Jews 'instructed from the law' (Rom 2:18) and his speaking in church with his mind 'in order to instruct others' (1 Cor 14:19). Here, it is employed twice of those who teach the Galatians.

The object of their teaching is the *logos*, the word, discussed more fully on 5:14 where it is used of the law being summed up in a single word (saying). Here, it is used in the more common sense of the Christian message, including the Jewish Scriptures and the subsequent teaching of Jesus particularly that of the apostles. Here it speaks not so much of the word as the gospel which brings initial conversion,[88] but as it is used more rarely of the subsequent teaching of the gospel to those who are already Christian (s.a. 1 Tim 5:17; 2 Tim 2:15; 4:2). This, of course, does not include the Judaizers, who are not to be supported, but cast out, for they violate the *logos* of God. Paul is not here subtly trying to gain their material support for himself; rather, he is speaking of those who are currently in Galatia tasked with teaching the word.

---

87. H.W. Beyer, 'κατηχέω,' in *TDNT* 3:638.
88. See e.g., 1 Cor 1:18; 2:1, 4; Eph 1:13; Col 1:5, 25; 4:3; 1 Thess 1:5–6; 2:13.

CHAPTER 31

CHAPTER THIRTY-ONE: SOW TO THE SPIRIT FOR ETERNAL LIFE (6:7–10)

We come to the final part of the body of the letter proper. Here, Paul gives a final warning, using the agricultural harvest motif. This then recalls the fruit of the Spirit, and the two sections are linked. Here he focuses on preparing to reap the fruit of the Spirit by sowing in ways that bring about the reaping of Spirit fruit. He begins with a strong warning against being deceived, for God cannot be mocked. He then gives a standard maxim that whatever one sows, one will reap, a truism for all of life that spans cultures. He will apply this to eternal fate in what follows. He returns to the flesh-Spirit antithesis used in 5:16–25. Those who sow to gratify the desires of the flesh will reap corruption; this recalls 5:19–21. Those who sow to please the Spirit will reap eternal life; this recalls 5:22–25 but adds the idea of eschatological reward. In light of this dual outcome, in vv. 9–10 he urges them not to become weary in doing good for if they do so, they will reap eternal life in due season. Hence, they must do good to all people, Christian or otherwise. Most especially, they should do good to those who are from the household of faith—the authentic Christian church.

PEOPLE REAP WHAT THEY SOW (6:7)

In *Galatians 6:7*, Paul warns the Galatians in no uncertain terms not to be deceived:

Do not be (*mē*, 1:7) **deceived** (*planaō*),[1] **God** (*Theos*, 1:1) **is not**

---

1. The verb *planaō* is used once in Galatians 6:7. It means to be led astray or deceived, so 'Do not be deceived.' It recalls 6:3 where *phrenaptaō* is used of not being self-deceived. Here, *planaō* is used of not being deceived that God will put up with their acceptance

(*ou*, 1:1) **mocked** (present passive *myktērizo*).[2] **For** (*gar*, 1:10) **whatever** (*ean*, 1:8) **a person** (*anthrōpos*, 1:1) **sows** (present subjunctive *speirō*),[3] **this** (neuter *houtos*, 2:10) **also** (*kai*, 1:1) **that person will reap** (future *therizō*).[4]

There is no connective here (asyndeton, see 2:6), Paul warning the Galatians bluntly—do not be deceived. This recalls v. 3, where, using the less common *phrenapataō*, he warns them that if anyone thinks they are something when they are not, they deceive themselves.

Here he uses a more common term *planaō*. The term means 'to lead astray' or wander in a literal sense,[5] or as here, in a figurative sense—from the right path of thinking—to deceive. In the passive as here, it means to 'be deceived, to be led astray.' The actual phrase, *mē planasthe*, is especially found in Stoic diatribes. So, Epictetus writes of those who consider him to be in suffering: 'do not deceive yourselves (*mē planasthe*), men, I am very well' (Epictetus, *Diatr.* 4.6). In the LXX, it is used widely.[6] The term

of Judaizing if indeed this is what they do (or falling into the sins of the flesh). The construct 'do not be deceived' (*mē planasthe*) is found in the warnings of 1 Cor 6:9 and 15:33.

2. The verb μυκτηρίζω (*myktērizo*) is a hapax *legomenon*, only found in 6:7. It has the sense of 'mocked, treated with contempt.' Paul then warns the Galatians, God cannot be treated contemptuously, mocked, etc. It is very rare, found only elsewhere eighteen times in the LXX and Pseudepigrapha and three times in the Apostolic Fathers.

3. The agricultural verb σπείρω (*speirō*) is used three times in Galatians metaphorically of sowing to please the Spirit or flesh and will thus reap eternal life or corruption. One reaps what one sows, a farming truism (Gal 6:7–8).

4. The agricultural verb θερίζω (*therizō*) is used four times in Gal 6:7–9 also figuratively (with *speirō* above) of reaping what one sows, whether corruption or eternal life.

5. See for example in the LXX, Gen 21:14; 37:15.

6. Examples of its used include physical wandering (e.g., Gen 21:14; Exod 14:3; Deut 22:1; Job 38:41; Sir 36:30; 51:13; Isa 35:8), misleading others physically (Deut 27:18), people deceiving others (e.g., Judg 16:10; 2 Sam 4:28; 21:9; 2 Chron 33:9) including Israel's leaders and prophets (Mic 3:5; Isa 3:12; 9:16; Ezek 13:10; 14:9), sinners leading people astray (Prov 1:10; 28:10), alcohol leading people's minds astray (1 Esdr 3:17), and of people led astray from the law (Ps 118:110, 176 [Eng. 119:110, 176]), to idolatry (Deut 4:19; 11:28; 30:17; Hos 2:14; 4:12; 8:6; Amos 2:4; Isa 44:20; Jer 23:13, 32; Ezek 44:15), or evil (Ps 57:4; 94:10 [Eng. 58:3; 95:10]). There are many uses of the term in apocryphal wisdom literature of people led astray into evil (Wis 2:21; 5:6; 11:5; 12:24; 13:6; 14:22; 15:4; 17:1; Sir 3:24; 9:7–8; 15:12; 16:23; 29:18; 31:7, 11; Tob 5:14; 10:7).

features in Jesus' parables of the stray sheep (Matt 18:12, 13, cf. 1 Pet 2:25), in Jesus' critique of the Jewish leaders as misled (Matt 22:29; Mark 12:24, 27), in Jewish critique of Jesus as a deceiver (John 7:12, s.a. 7:47), and in warnings to Christians to watch that no one leads them astray.[7]

In Hebrews, it is used literally of people wandering (Heb 11:38), hearts going astray (Heb 3:10), and Jesus as the one who deals gently with the wayward (Heb 5:2). Jacob uses it of those who wander from the truth (Jas 5:19) and utilizes this construct, 'do not be deceived' (Jas 1:16, cf. 1 John 3:7). John warns against self-deception (1 John 1:8). In Revelation, it is used frequently of the deception of Jezebel (Rev 2:20), the beast (Rev 13:14; 19:20), Babylon (Rev 18:23), and Satan the Deceiver of the nations (Rev 12:9; 20:3, 8, 10). Thrice Paul uses it for the wicked who suffer from self-deception and also deceive others (2 Tim 3:13; Tit 3:3).

Paul three times employs *mē planasthe*: 1 Cor 6:9: 'Do you not know that the unrighteous will not inherit the kingdom of God. Do not be deceived! Similarly, 1 Cor 15:33: 'Do not be deceived: "Bad company ruins good morals."' Here, Paul uses the same warning telling the Galatians not to be deceived. Just what he is focused on is made apparent in what follows. Rather than a warning against the Judaizers and their false gospel, they must not sow to please the flesh but the Spirit. To fail to do so is to mock God and to bring them into the danger of his judgment. The verb is a present passive, breaking the sequence of active imperatives from 4:21 to 6:17.[8] As with the others, it is present speaking of an ongoing attitude of sharing.

'God is not mocked' uses *myktērizō*, a *hapax legomenon* (unique in the NT) and found only in Jewish and Christian Greek literature. The term is derived from *myktēr*, 'nose,'[9] and so means to 'turn up the nose, sneer at'[10] or 'treat contemptuously.'[11] In the LXX, it is utilized of people mocking others (Prov 11:12;

7. See Matt 24:4–5, 11, 24; Mark 13:5–6; Luke 21:8, cf. 2 Pet 2:15; 1 John 2:26.
8. See 1:8, 20; 3:7; 4:12, 21, 30; 5:1, 13, 16; 6:1, 2, 4, 6, 11, 17, s.a. 5:14, 25, 26.
9. H. Preisker, 'μυκτηρίζω,' in *TDNT* 4:796.
10. LSJ 1152.
11. Preisker, 'μυκτηρίζω,' 796.

12:8) and a fool mocking a parent's instruction (Prov 15:5), their mothers (Prov 15:20), or wisdom (Prov 23:9). It is commonly used for the mockery of enemies whether it be Elijah mocking the Ba'al prophets (1 Kings 18:37), Assyria and other enemies mocking Israel,[12] Israel mocking God's prophets (2 Chron 36:16; 1 Esd 1:49; Jer 20:7) and God himself (Ezek 8:17). In Prov 1:30, it is used of people mocking God's rebuke, and in Job 22:19, their mockery of God's threatened judgment.

This is the sense here, with the Galatians being warned not to mock the threat of God's judgment by feeling that they can walk according to the flesh. There are two angles here. First, subtly this implies that they do not yield to the Judaizers and put themselves in a place of reliance on the flesh. If they yield, they are severed from Christ, fallen from grace, and will be left to sow in accordance with the flesh. This will yield destruction. Second, and more directly, they are not to claim to be in Christ and under grace but live to please the desires of the flesh outlined in 5:19–21. If they do, God and his judgment cannot be mocked. They will suffer the consequences.

The reason is then given signaled by a causal *gar*, 'because, for.' What follows is conditional; however, it is not structured as the usual conditional sentence. The combination of the neuter of the definite article *hos, ho* (the thing) plus *ean* (if) is rendered 'whatever thing,'[13] or as the context dictates, 'whatever seed.' Here, *anthrōpos* should not be translated 'man' (NIV, ESV) for it is inclusive of all humanity (nor the NET: 'for a person will reap what *he* sows'). Nor should this be turned into a second-person statement, '*you* reap what *you* sow' as in the NRSV, for this is a general truism in the third person.

The first verb is *speirō*; an agricultural verb used extensively meaning to sow seeds.[14] In the NT (fifty-two times), it features in Jesus' teaching in such places as the parable of the sower[15] and his other seed parables (Mark 4:31, 32, and parr.).[16] Jacob employs it

---

12. See 2 Kings 19:21; Ps 79:7 [Eng. 80:6]; Isa 37:22; 1 Macc 7:33.
13. See also Herm. *Mand.* 11:3: 'For, whatever is asked …'
14. BDAG 936, who notes it can also be translated scatter, disperse.
15. See, e.g., Mark 4:3, 3, 14, 15, 26, 18, 20, and parr.

once of a harvest of righteousness sown in peace (Jas 3: 18). Paul uses it of sowing spiritual seed, the gospel (1 Cor 9:11). In 1 Cor 15, it is used of the human body which, like a planted seed, dies and is raised imperishable.[17] He also employs it of God supplying seeds to a farmer (2 Cor 9:10) (see further below).

In the apodosis, the consequence is given: 'this also that person will reap.' This is the neuter of *houtos* pointing back to *ho* in the previous clause; the seed will reap a consequence. 'Reap' is *therizō*, another widely used agricultural verb speaking of reaping and harvest.[18] The term is found less often in the NT than *speirō*, twenty-one times. Jacob employs it literally of harvesters (Jas 5:4). In Revelation, it is used of judgment; God reaping the world (Rev 14:15, 16). As with *speirō*, it features in Jesus' teaching such as his encouragement toward dependence on God (Matt 6:26; Luke 12:24) and in parables like that of the Sower.[19] Paul uses it in 1 Cor 9:11 speaking of his receiving material benefit from the Corinthians after sowing spiritual seed among them (above). In 2 Cor 9:10, God will increase the Corinthian harvest of righteousness.

In 2 Cor 9:6, encouraging the Corinthians to give generously to the Jerusalem Council, as here in 6:7, Paul uses the two verbs in a truism which has similarities to Gal 6:7: 'the one who sows (*speirō*) sparingly will also reap (*therizō*) sparingly, and the one who sows (*speirō*) generously will also reap (*therizō*) generously.' Whereas here in 6:7, whatever one sows one reaps, in the Corinthians context, the amount one sows will be reaped.

Here, then, we have another maxim speaking of human activity being like the sowing of seed. This is a common idea found in differing forms in the Greco-Roman world.[20] So Plato cites Socrates as asking what an orator expects to produce when persuading people concerning behavior: 'what harvest do you

16. See also Matt 6:24; 13:3, 4, 18, 19, 20, 22, 23, 24, 27, 31, 37, 39; 25:24, 26; Luke 8:5; 12:24; 19:21, 22; John 4:36, 37.
17. See 1 Cor 15:36, 37, 42, 43, 44.
18. BDAG 453.
19. See Matt 13:3, s.a. Matt 25:24, 26; Luke 19:21, 22; John 4:36–38.
20. Longenecker, *Galatians*, 280.

suppose his oratory will reap (*therizō*) thereafter from the seed
he has sown (*speirō*)?' (*Phaedr.* 260c–d). Aristotle cites Gorgias as
saying, 'you have sown (*speirō*) these things of shame and reaped
(*therizō*) evil' (Aristotle, *Rhet.* 3c.4.5–9).[21]

In the LXX and other Jewish Greek writings, the two verbs
are used in a range of sayings that have resonances with 6:7. In
Ps 125:5 [Eng. 126:5]: 'Those sowing (*speirō*) in tears will reap
(*therizō*) in joy.' In Prov 22:8: 'The one sowing (*speirō*) wrong will
reap (*therizō*) evil.' Job writes, 'and those sowing (*speirō*) these
[wrong] things will reap (*therizō*) grief for themselves' (Job 4:8).
Similarly, in Sirach 7:3: 'Do not sow (*speirō*) in the furrows of
injustice, and you will not reap (*therizō*) them sevenfold.'[22] In T.
Levi 13:6, we read, 'and sow good things in your souls so that
you will find them in your life. For if you sow evil things, you
will reap all every tumult and tribulation.' Similarly, in 4 Ezra
4:28: 'For the evil about which you ask me has been sown, but the
harvest of it has not yet come.'

Philo loves the idea of sowing and reaping (producing) and
employs the two verbs similarly: 'the fruits of his soul which he
has sown (*speirō*) for the destruction of wisdom, though he has
not reaped (*therizō*) them' (*Deus* 166, Loeb). Similarly, in *Conf.* 21
he writes:

the mind reaps (*therizō*) what is sown (*speirō*) by its follies and
acts of cowardice and intemperance and injustice, and the
spirited part brings to the birth its fierce and raging furies and
the other evil children of its womb, and the appetite sends forth
on every side desires ever winged by childish fancy, desires
which light as chance directs on things material and immaterial
(Loeb).

Again in *Conf.* 152: 'they [Babel] dared to attack the rights of
heaven, and having sown injustice, they reaped impiety.' Finally,

---

21. Longenecker, *Galatians*, 280 also notes Demosthenes, *Cor.* 159; Cicero, *Orat.* 2.65;
Plautus, *Mer.* 71.

22. See also Hosea 10:12: to Israel writes these beautiful words of wisdom: 'Sow (*speirō*)
for yourselves for justice, gather for the fruit of life, enlighten for yourselves fruit of
knowledge, seek out the Lord until the produce of righteousness comes to us.' See also
Hag 1:6: 'you have sown (*speirō*) much and harvested little.'

in *Legat*. 293: 'Therefore they took good care not to sow (*speirō*) the seed of impiety, lest they should be compelled to reap (*therizō*) its fruits which bring utter destruction.²³ Such a maxim also has resonances with the Hindu idea of *karma*,²⁴ although without the idea of reincarnation and reward for works. Such similar ideas are unsurprising as reciprocity is self-evident across many cultures including the NT world.

Here, it covers attitude, speech, and deeds. Whatever a person does, they will reap. Similarly, Jesus said, 'with the measure you use; it will be measured to you' (Matt 7:2; Mark 4:24, s.a. Luke 6:38). This is the principle of reciprocity. In what follows, Paul will specify in more detail what he means.

SOW TO PLEASE THE SPIRIT NOT THE FLESH (6:8)

In *Galatians 6:8*, Paul begins applying the general maxim to the situation and it speaks more generally across space and time to all Christians:

For (*hoti*, 1:6), **the one sowing** (present participle *speirō*, 6:7) **to** (*eis*, 1:5) **their own** (*heautou*, 2:4) **flesh** (*sarx*, 1:16), **from** (*ek*, 1:1) **the flesh** (*sarx*) **will reap** (future *therizō*, 6:7) **destruction** (*phthora*);²⁵ **and** (*de*, 1:15) **the one sowing** (present participle *speirō*) **to** (*eis*) **the Spirit** (*pneuma*), **from** (*ek*) **the Spirit** (*pneuma*) **will reap** (future *therizō*) **life** (*zoē*)²⁶ **eternal** (*aiōnios*).²⁷

---

23. See also Philo, *Leg.* 1.80; 3.181; *Cher.* 106; *Post.* 181; *Deus* 40; *Agr.* 25; *Conf.* 196; *Fug.* 170–171 (where he takes the Jubilee of Lev 25:11 and applies it to ethics: 'That fiftieth year shall be a jubilee for you; in it you shall neither sow nor reap what grows of itself nor gather the grapes from the undressed vines'); *Mut.* 173, 269; *Somn.* 2.76; *Spec.* 1.305.
24. See Ven. Mahasi Sayadaw, 'The Theory of Karma,' http://www.buddhanet.net/e-learning/karma.htm: 'As we sow, we reap somewhere and sometime, in his life or in a future birth. What we reap today is what we have sown either in the present or in the past. The Samyutta Nikaya states: "According to the seed that's sown, So is the fruit you reap there from, Doer of good will gather good, Doer of evil, evil reaps, Down is the seed and thou shalt taste The fruit thereof."'
25. The noun φθορά (*phthora*) means 'decay,' 'corruption,' 'depravity,' and 'destruction' (BDAG 1055). It is used only in 6:8 where Paul states that the person who sows to the desires of the flesh will reap *phthora*. This speaks both of subsequent degeneration of their lives, and ultimately, eternal destruction.

The *hoti* is not so much causal as explanatory, or better, explicatory; it draws out a specific nuance of the maxim in terms of life in the flesh or Spirit. The verse is neatly balanced (antithetical parallelism) as can be seen by a transliteration:

A1 *Ho speirōn eis tēn sarpka heautou ek tēs sarkos therisei phthoran,* 'the one who sows to the flesh himself from the flesh will reap corruption'

A2 *Ho speirōn eis to pneuma ek tou pneumatos therisei zōēn aiōnion,* the one who sows to the flesh from the flesh will reap eternal life'

The only differences are due to the different articles required by the gender of the nouns, the contrasting language of flesh and Spirit, and destruction in contrast to life eternal. Paul then neatly shows how the two modes of living yield contrasting eternal outcomes.

The language calls to mind 5:16–25. The one who sows to his or her own flesh is that person who lives out of their desires and lusts. They do the works of the flesh, things like those listed in 5:19–21. They yield to their own impulses, gratifying their desires.

On the other hand, the one who sows to the Spirit speaks of those who 'walk by the Spirit,' are 'led by the Spirit,' 'live by the Spirit,' and 'keep in step with the Spirit' (5:16, 18, 25). By the Spirit's lead and empowering presence, they are to withstand the desires of the flesh that wage war against the desires of the Spirit. In the language of Romans 8, they 'walk not according to the flesh but according to the Spirit (Rom 8:4). They set their minds on the things of the Spirit, not the flesh (Rom 8:5). 'By the Spirit,' they 'put to death the deeds of the body' (Rom 8:14). As in 5:18, they are 'led by the Spirit' (Rom 8:14). The fruit of the Spirit then

---

26. The noun ζωή (*zoē*) means 'life' and is found only once in 6:8 in the construct 'life eternal,' thus speaking of the wonderful Christian gift from God of everlasting or eternal life. The associated verb *zaō*, 'live,' is used nine times in Galatians (2:14, 19–20; 3:11, 12; 5:25).

27. The adjective αἰώνιος (*aiōnios*), which literally means 'through the ages,' and so 'eternal,' is very common in biblical writings but is used only in 6:8 of 'life eternal' which will be the harvest of those who sow to please the Spirit.

is produced in their lives, such things as those listed in 5:22–23; supremely, love. They resist the impulses of their lusts. They rise above such *skybala*. When they slip and fall, they get up, dust themselves off with prayers of contrition and repentance, and they journey on following the way of the Spirit. They do not give up. Sometimes, another comes along and takes them by the hand and helps them along the way (6:1–2). Together, we walk into glory.

The two contrasting fates are found in the final phrases of the parallel statements: will reap destruction/life eternal. 'Destruction' is *phthora*. The noun is linked to is *phtheirō* used of someone who destroys God's temple being destroyed by God (1 Cor 3:17), bad company corrupting good morals (1 Cor 15:33), of deeply wronging other people (2 Cor 7:2), being corrupted from the pure worship of Christ (2 Cor 11:3) or by one's old self with its lusts (Eph 4:22), Babylon which corrupts the earth (Rev 19:2), and eternal destruction (2 Pet 2:12; Jude 10). In wider sources, *phthora* has a range of meanings including destruction as in the demolition of a building or a flood, death, shipwrecks, or financial damage. It is used in a moral sense of being led astray, ruined, to bribe, seduce, ruin, and being corrupt. In Greek philosophy, and especially Aristotle, it is an important term used dualistically of the degradation of what exists in the cosmos, of being or essentiality.[28]

We get a sense of the vividness of the term in the Greek Jewish writings where it is used of Moses who exhausts himself through work (Exod 18:18), a person in a deplorable state—the pit, destruction, death, eternal destruction (Ps 102:4 [Eng. 103:4]; Jonah 2:7), the corruption of life through idolatry (Wis 14:12, 25) or depravity (Mic 2:10), the destruction of the cosmos by God (Isa 24:3), being destroyed in a fire (Dan 3:92), a state of extreme personal distress (Dan 10:8), people and places being destroyed in war[29] or judgment (Josephus, *Ant.* 9.100; 15.301), and God destroying the flesh of the wicked (Pss. Sol. 4:6).

---

28. See for further details G. Harder, 'φθορά,' in *TDNT* 9:94.
29. See Sib. Or. 2.9; 3.336; Josephus, *Ag. Ap.* 1.9, 10; *J.W.* 2.51, 223, 447, 559; 3.528; 4.489, 551; 5.345.

Josephus uses it for the destruction of people in the flood (Josephus, *Ant.* 1.96; *Ag. Ap.* 1.130), the devastation of Dinah by rape,[30] a destructive disease sent by God,[31] and murder (Josephus, *Ag. Ap.* 2.203). Philo, in particular, employs the term often. Space precludes a full discussion; however, some of his uses include the decay of animate life (*Opif.* 58; *Post.* 164) over against the unchangeableness of God (*Leg.* 2.33), the decay of virtue (*Leg.* 1.105), death (*Leg.* 2.77; *Deus* 16), destruction caused by speech (*Cher.* 32), in vice lists of destruction (*Cher.* 92), the destruction of Egypt at the Exodus (*Sacr.* 134), rape (*Det.* 102), the consequences of ethical impurity (*Det.* 168), and the destruction of disease (*Deus* 124).

Turning to the NT, *phthora* is only employed by Peter and Paul. In 2 Pet 1:4, it speaks of the corruption of sin that riddles the world because of human lust (*epithymia*), from which believers are delivered to be participants in the divine nature. The false teachers are slaves of this corruption (2 Pet 2:19). They are like irrational animals, creatures of instinct, born to be caught and *destroyed* (2 Pet 2:12), i.e., eternal destruction.

Paul uses the term of the general degradation of the cosmos which binds the world, from which creation will be set free (1 Cor 8:21). As such, things perish with use including legal regulations (Col 2:22). In 1 Cor 15:42, it is used of the perishability of the body as it is subject to this same decay consummating in death and eternal destruction (1 Cor 15:42). So, in this state, humanity cannot enter the eternity of the kingdom, for the perishable cannot inherit the imperishable (1 Cor 15:50). *Phthora* then contrasts the present with the future.

Here *phthora* can mean the corruption that comes to a person because of their pursuit of self-gratification as they live by the flesh.[32] Such living will reap the devastation of their lives. Their identities and marriages and families will be torn apart by their sexual sin. Their wealth will be eaten away by their excessive

---

30. See Josephus, *Ant.* 1.339, s.a. *Ant.* 4.251; 5.339; 17.309; *Ag. Ap.* 2.276.
31. See *Ant.* 6.3, s.a. *Ant.* 7.324; 8.115; 10.116; 18.373; *J.W.* 6.421, 429.
32. See e.g., Lightfoot, *Galatians*, 219 who states that *phthora* 'should be taken in its primary physical sense.'

wastage on alcohol and other pleasures like gambling and entertainment. Their relationships will be torn apart by their envy, rivalry, selfish ambition, anger, and arrogance. They will plunge deeper and deeper into depravity and narcissism as they live by the desires of the flesh. They will become diseased, obese, have destroyed lungs, wrecked livers, and other consequences of an unhealthy lifestyle such as sexually transmitted diseases and cancers. The way the verse is cast means this kind of consequence is in Paul's mind, for it is 'from the flesh' that they will 'reap corruption.'

Alternatively, Paul is using *phthora* of eternal destruction. There are good reasons to consider this is the case here. First, it recalls the notion of 5:21—those who do such things will not inherit the kingdom of God. Second, it comes after 6:5, where each will bear their individual burden before God in judgment. Finally, and conclusively, it parallels 'life eternal' in the next clause—this then speaks of eternal condemnation.[33]

The third alternative, which I consider apparent, is that both dynamics are at play in the warning. If the Galatians live in accordance with the desires of the flesh, this will devastate their lives, marriages, families, and relationships. They will pay the price in this life. However, more importantly, if they go to their graves living to gratify the flesh and not by the Spirit, this will extend into an eternity of destruction. As with the warning of 5:19–21, this leaves us a little uncertain as to whether Paul means here that a seeming Christian who willingly, persistently, and unrepentantly, lives a life of the gratification of the flesh will be destroyed. Perhaps there is a point where God says, 'while you say you believe, your hideous behavior says to me that you do not. Away from me, you evildoer.' Perhaps we cannot know this answer, for if we did, we would be back in the game of measuring our good deeds against our wicked ones. This is up to God. What it does say to us is that we must persist in sowing to please the Spirit and not the flesh for the consequences of pleasing the flesh are corruption and destruction.

---

33. See e.g., Moo, *Galatians*, 38.6

In contrast to the fate of the flesh-sowers, those who live to the Spirit, i.e., live out of the unction of the Spirit toward its fruit, love, joy, peace ... etc., will reap life eternal. The term eternal is *aiōnios*, derived from *aiōn*, 'age.' While it can have the same meaning as *aiōn*, but often connotes 'eternal' in Greek writings.[34] In the LXX, it can mean ancient (for all ages past, e.g., Ps 23:7 [Eng. 24:7]).[35] It can also mean all the coming ages of human life (e.g., Gen 9:12). The sense of all the coming ages of human existence is common: an everlasting covenant (e.g., Gen 9:16; 17:13),[36] the land as an everlasting possession (Gen 17:8; Add Est C 16), God as an everlasting God (Gen 21:33),[37] commonly of a law that stands for all time (e.g., Exod 12:14; Lev 23:41; Num 19:21), an everlasting sign (Exod 31:17; Isa 55:13), everlasting disgrace (Ps 77:66 [Eng. 78:66]), and the way everlasting (Ps 138:24 [Eng. 139:24]).

In the LXX of Job 10:21, it is employed of death as the land of eternal gloom and in Jeremiah of everlasting disgrace and shame (Jer 23:40; 25:9) and sleep (Jer 28:39). Wisdom has an eternal remembrance to those who come after it (Wis 8:13) and speaks of eternal providence (Wis 17:2). In Sirach 15:6, the one who feasts with the Lord will inherit an eternal name (s.a. Isa 56:5; 1 Macc 2:51), and in Judith, eternal honor is granted from God (Jdt 13:20). In Tobit 3:6, Tobit prays, 'release me to go to the eternal home.' Redeemed Israel shall experience eternal joy (Isa 35:10; 51:11). God's salvation is eternal (Isa 45:17) as is his love (Isa 54:8; Jer 38:3), his light (Isa 60:19–20), his righteousness (Dan 9:24), and kingdom (Dan 3:100; 7:14, 27).

The notion of eternal life is rare in the LXX, with the core text being Dan 12:2: 'Many of those who sleep in the dusk shall awake, some to *everlasting life*, and some to shame and everlasting contempt' (NRSV) (s.a. 4 Macc 15:3). In 2 Macc 7:9, the hope is seen in the words of the second brother to be martyred: 'you

---

34. See H Sasse, 'αἰώνιος,' in *TDNT* 1:208.
35. See also Prov 22:28; Isa 58:12; Jer 6:16; Ezek 26:20.
36. See also Exod 31:16; Num 18:19; 25:13; 2 Sam 23:5; 1 Chron 16:17; Ps 104:10 [Eng. 105:10]; Sir 45:15; Isa 24:5; 55:3; 61:8; Jer 27:5; 39:40; Ezek 16:60; 37:26.
37. See also Job 33:12, LXX; Isa 40:28; Bar 4:8, s.a., Isa 26:4; 2 Macc 1:25; 3 Macc 6:12.

accursed wretch, you dismiss us from this present life, but the King of the universe will raise us up to an *everlasting renewal of life* because we have died for his laws' (NRSV). Conversely, the enemy of Israel will 'undergo from the divine justice eternal torment by fire' (3 Macc 9:9, NRSV).[38] Eternal life often features in the Pseudepigrapha as the reward of the righteous people and angels. Influenced by Dan 12:2, 1 En. 58:3 states: 'The righteous ones shall be in the light of the sun and the elect ones *in the light of eternal life* which has no end, and the days of the life of the holy ones cannot be numbered' (Charlesworth).[39]

The concept of eternal life is found throughout the NT and especially in the writings of John.[40] Paul employs the phrase nine times. Those who are judged by God to do good with patience, seeking glory, honor, and immortality, will receive eternal life (Rom 2:7). Because of God's grace, justification leads to eternal life through Christ (Rom 5:21). Eternal life is the end game for believers freed from sin into sanctification (Rom 6:22). Whereas the wage of sin is death, the free gift of God is eternal life (Rom 6:23). Those who believe in Christ will gain eternal life (1 Tim 1:16). Believers are to take hold of it (1 Tim 6:12). This is the Christian hope, promised before the ages (Tit 1:2), for those who have been justified by his grace (Tit 3:7). In the NT, this life begins at conversion and continues after the transformation of the believer from corruptibility to incorruptibility through death and resurrection or at the return of Christ (1 Cor 15:50–56). Eternal life is then quantitative of forever life and qualitative of the most splendid quality of life imaginable. It is an existence free from the corruption of evil in any sense of the term, whether personal or structural sin, sins of commission or omission, and

38. See also 4 Macc 10:15; 12:12; 13:15.
39. See also Odes Sol. 15:10; T. Ash. 5:2; 6:5; s.a., T. Job 4:8; T. Ab. (A) 20:15; T. Jac. 7:28; 1 En. 15:4, 6; 37:4; 40:9; 2 En. 42:2; 3 En. 18.22; Sib. Or. 1.349; 2.236; 8.255; Ques. Ezra (B) 2.
40. See Matt 19:16, 20; 25:46; Mark 10:17, 30; Luke 10:25; 18:18, 30; John 3:15, 16, 36; 4:14, 16; 4:24, 39; 6:27, 40, 47, 54, 68; 10:28; 12:25, 50; 17:2, 3; Acts 13:48; 1 John 1:2; 2:25; 3:15; 5:11, 13, 20; Jude 21. It is only absent from Hebrews and Jacob among the NT writers.

the spiritual forces of evil. It will be life without suffering, pain, enmity, and death.

The path to this life is to sow to the Spirit. In other words, it is to live the life the Spirit is urging us toward in our inner beings and through those who speak into us words infused by the Spirit's encouragement. It will be the most glorious of rewards. I am reminded of the words of Paul in Phil 1:19–26 who ponders life and death, recognizing that to die is gain but to choose life is further fruitful gospel service. Deep down, he is saying, bring it on! In the meantime, our vocation is to press on without flagging to win this prize for which we have been called heavenward. We are to pause only to help others who believe along the way as they tire and fall. Or we pause to stop and invite others to join us as we walk by the Spirit.

DO NOT TIRE OF DOING GOOD (6:9)

In *Galatians 6:9*, Paul continues drawing out what it means for them to sow to please the Spirit:

And (*de*, 1:15) **let us not** (*mē*, 1:7) **grow weary** (present passive subjunctive *enkakeō*)[41] **of doing** (present participle *poieō*, 2:10) **good** (*kalos*, 4:18), **for** (*gar*, 1:10) **in its own** (dative[42] *idios*, 2:2) **time** (dative *kairos*, 4:10), **we will reap a harvest** (first-person future plural *therizō*, 6:7) **if we do not** (*mē*) **give up** (present middle participle *eklyō*).[43]

---

41. The verb ἐγκακέω (*enkakeō*) compounds *en* (in) with the *kak-* nexus of terms which have the wider nuance of 'evil, bad.' The compound speaks of 'losing enthusiasm,' 'flagging,' and 'being discouraged,' through lack of motivation (BDAG 272). Paul uses it elsewhere on not losing heart in his ministry (2 Cor 4:1, 16), in praying for the Ephesians that they are not discouraged (Eph 3:13), and in an injunction to the Thessalonians not to grow weary in what is right (2 Thess 3:13). The one use in Galatians 6:9 is similar to the latter reference; the readers are not to lose heart or become weary of doing good.

42. This is an example of the dative of time whereby '[t]he noun in the dative indicates the *time when* the action of the main verb is accomplished. The dative routinely denotes a *point of time*, answering the question, "When?" In the eight-case system, this would be the locative of time. Though common enough, this usage is being increasingly replaced in Koine Greek with ἐν the dative.' (Wallace, *Greek Grammar*, 155).

43. The verb ἐκλύω (*eklyō*) compounds *ek* (from) and *lyō*, 'loose, untie, destroy,' and yields

This verse is linked by *de*, here used in a consecutive sense, 'and,' carrying on the thought of the previous warning to sow in accordance with the Spirit. If one does so, one will reap the harvest of eternal life. There is a neat rhythmic structure to the verse with both clauses ending with *mē* plus a compound verb beginning with epsilon (*enkakōmen, eklyomenoi*).

In the first part of the clause, Paul uses the verb *enkakeō* negated by *mē* (not), 'do not grow weary.' The verb compounds *en* (in) and *kakia*, 'evil,' 'wicked,' or 'debase.' The verb is not common, found six times in the NT, and sparingly elsewhere. It speaks of motivation for work and carries the meaning to lose enthusiasm, to flag, or to be discouraged.[44] It is found in Luke before Jesus' parable of the persistent widow: 'And he told them this parable to urge them that they should always pray and not *give up*.'

Paul uses it twice in 2 Cor 4 of his own ministry. First, in 4:1, he says, 'just as we have received mercy, having this ministry, we *do not give up*.' Similarly, in 2 Cor 4:16: 'therefore, we *do not give up*.' Three times he uses it in relation to his converts. In Eph 3:13, he prays for the Ephesians that they will not give up (Eph 3:13). Having warned the Thessalonians against idleness, he says to them using very similar language, 'but you, brothers and sisters, *do not grow weary* in doing what is right (participle *kalopoieō*).'

Here in Gal 6:9, as in 5:25, 26, and in 6:10, the verb is a hortatory subjunctive, which functions as an inclusive imperative: '*let us* not grow weary.'[45] A series of imperatives directed at the Galatians are found in 4:21–6:17. This is effectively another along with 5:14, 25, and 26.[46] As with the others, it is present speaking of an ongoing attitude of sharing.

It speaks of the Galatians not becoming weary or discouraged in doing what is right. 'What is right' uses *kalos* found in 4:18 of

---

'become weary, give out' and so 'give up' (BDAG 306). It is used by Jesus of the crowds who may become 'tired' or 'undone,' and, so need eating (Matt 15:32; Mark 8:3). Twice it is used in Heb 12 of the readers not losing heart (Heb 12:3, 5). Galatians 6:9 is Paul's only use where he urges the Galatians not to become weary of doing good so that they will reap a harvest in its time.

44. BDAG 272.
45. Wallace, *Greek Grammar*, 464.
46. See also 1:8, 20; 3:7; 4:12, 21, 30; 5:1, 13, 16; 6:1, 2, 4; 6:7, 10, 11, 17.

it being good to be zealous for a good cause. Here, it is generally speaking of doing what is right in relation to the Spirit's desires. These have been outlined in the fruit of the Spirit. Hence, it means acting in accordance with the Spirit relating to others with love, joy, peace, patience, kindness, goodness, gentleness, faithfulness, self-control, and so on. It is parallel in meaning here with the synonymous *agathos* in the next verse. Here we see again that Paul has a rich theology of works, not for salvation, but as the way in which we work out our lives as God's children.

The second half of the verse is introduced by the post-positive *gar* that here signals the grounds for doing good. The dative phrase *kairō idiō* literally states 'in its own time.' This is a good example of a dative of time that expresses a *point* in time.[47] It can be translated 'in due season' or better, 'at just the right moment.'[48] In that, theologically, God is in control of this point of time, it can be translated, 'in God's time.' However, I have chosen to retain the literal sense leaving space for interpretative ideas. This 'time' is clearly the final judgment. At this time, they will receive eternal life and reward (previous verse); they will reap what they have sown. If they have sown to the flesh and not the Spirit, they will not receive eternal life. If they have, they will.

There is a neat play on *kairos* here and in the next verse. At the right time, judgment will come, either through their death or Christ's return while they live. In the meantime, he uses *kairos* in the next verse instructing them to take every opportunity (*kairos*) to do good. If they do, their harvest is assured. The verb *therizō* is used here for the fourth time in the three verses, speaking of the final reaping of the consequences of their lives.

The final verb is the present middle participle of *eklyō*, *eklyomenoi*.[49] The verb *eklyō* compounds *ek* (from) and *lyō* (loose,

47. See Wallace, *Grammar*, 156.

48. Wallace, *Grammar*, 156 who notes this is the only example of the singular καιρῷ ἰδίῳ in the NT. The plural, however, has the same force (s.a., 1 Tim 2:6; 6:15; Titus 1:3).

49. While it can be passive, this is hardly likely here. The middle speaks of the Galatians themselves not giving up, they are the subject that '*performs or experiences the action expressed by the verb in such a way that emphasizes the subject's participation*' (Wallace, *Grammar*, 414, emphasis his).

untie, set free) and so has the sense of being loosed, set free, released.[50] Here, it is not positive but speaks of giving up doing good through losing heart (as in part one of the verse).

In the Jewish Greek sources, it has a range of meanings, including losing heart, being faint, or discouraged when facing enemies,[51] being exhausted,[52] losing heart when a loved one dies (2 Sam 4:1), or other situations of grief (T. Zeb. 2.4). Paul may have in mind something like the words of Azariah to the men of Judah and Benjamin in 2 Chron 15:7: 'and you be strong and do let your hands give up (eklyō) because these are the wages for your labor' (s.a. Neb 6:8).[53]

In the NT, the term is used by Jesus of the people in the wilderness who may 'faint' if they try to go home or to buy food (Matt 15:32; Mark 8:3). The author of Hebrews utilizes it twice, first exhorting the readers to emulate Christ and not grow weary or *lose heart* (Heb 12:3), and second, that they do not lose heart when disciplined by God (Heb 12:5). This is Paul's only use as he urges the Galatians not to become weary in their commitment to doing good. The participle is conditional and adverbial—'*if we do not lose heart*.'[54] So, if they do not lose heart or courage and continue to do so, they will reap a harvest. This harvest will

---

50. See LSJ 513. *Eklyō* is also used for unlocking something (unstringing a bow), making an end of something, and relaxing, among other meanings.
51. See Deut 20:3; Josh 18:3; 1 Sam 14:28; 2 Sam 17:2; 1 Kings 21:43 LXX; Ezra 4:4; Jdt 14:6; Jer 45:4; 1 Macc 9:8; Josephus, *Ant.* 5.134; 13.233; 17.263.
52. See 1 Sam 30:21; 2 Sam 16:2, 14; 17:29; Jer 12:5; Lam 2:19; 1 Macc 3:17; 10:82; Hist. Rech. 2:2.
53. See also other uses: to unloose a yoke or bonds from a neck or bonds (Gen 27:40; Isa 52:2; 3 Macc 6:27; Philo, *Leg.* 3.193), unloosing an arrow (Gen 49:24), release (Josh 10:6), not being weary of God's discipline (Prov 3:11), to go and provoke a friend without flagging (Prov 6:3), to be released from life (Job 19:25, LXX), the astral bodies never relaxing (Sir 43:10), hands weakened (Isa 13:7; Ezek 7:17), being weak (Isa 29:9; 46:2; Jer 30:13), weary (Isa 51:20), sound failing through weakness (Jer 4:31), faint through wounds (Lam 2:12), trees fainting (Ezek 31:15), discouraged by a vision (Dan 8:27) or a prophet (Josephus, *Ant.* 10.119), to die (4 Macc 15:24), fallen to the ground in joy (T. Job 30.1), extreme zeal released (Josephus, *Ant.* 12.231), failing eyesight (*J.W.* 1.657), to release lustful impulses (Philo, *Sacr.* 80; *Ebr.* 50), bonds of strength waned (Philo, *Sacr.* 81), weakened strength (Philo, *Sacr.* 86; *Post.* 112), the sinews of the soul unstrung (Philo, *Ios.* 61; *Decal.* 122), and to release a thought (Philo, *Flacc.* 78).
54. Wallace, *Greek Grammar*, 632.

include eternal life and God's reward (cf. 1 Cor 3:12–15) and commendation (1 Cor 4:5).

DO GOOD TO ALL PEOPLE (6:10)

Galatians 6:10 ends this section of the letter:

Therefore (*oun*, 3:5), **in light of the above** (*ara*, 2:21), **as** (*hōs*, 1:9) **we have** (*echomen*, 2:4) **opportunity** (*kairos*), **let us do**[55] (present middle subjunctive *ergazomai*)[56] **[the]**[57] **good** (neuter *agathos*, 6:6) **to** (*pros*, 1:17) **all people** (masculine plural *pas*, 1:2), **and** (*de*, 1:15) **most especially** (*malista*)[58] **to** (*pros*) **those of the household** (*oikeios*)[59] **of faith** (genitive *pistis*, 1:23).

The verse begins interestingly with the connection of two synonymous logical inferential conjunctions where one would

---

55. **VARIANT:** The verb *ergazōmetha* is widely attested. However, some witnesses read the indicative *ergazometha* (A B2 L P *al*). The indicative would follow an imperative and the hortatory subjunctive is much more likely. As Metzger, *Textual Commentary*, 530 notes, this is likely a scribal error with a scribe replacing ω with ο on the basis of pronunciation.

56. The verb ἐργάζομαι (*ergazomai*) means 'work, accomplish, carry out, do' and the latter is the meaning of the verb in 6:10—'do good.' This is the only use of *ergazomai* in Galatians. Paul elsewhere uses it another seventeen times. It is another term in Paul's works theology. Other *erg-* words used in Galatians include: *ergon*, 'works,' used eight times (works of the law, 2:16; 3:2, 5, 10; works of the flesh, 5:10; test his own work, 6:4); and *energeō*, 'be at work, work' (2:8; 3:5).

57. This is an example of the use of the article with an adjective, 'the good,' i.e., the good things. Wallace, *Greek Grammar*, 233: 'Adjectives often stand in the place of nouns, especially when the qualities of a particular group are stressed. Instances in the plural are especially frequently generic, though in both singular and plural the individualizing article occurs often enough.'

58. The adverb *malista* is the superlative of *mala*, 'very, exceedingly' (LSJ 1076), a term not found in the NT. *Malista* then means 'most of all, above all, especially, particularly, very greatly' (BDAG 613). There is one use in Galatians, in 6:10, where Paul urges the Galatians to do good to all people, and most especially those from the household of faith, i.e., the church. This would include Christians in Galatia and beyond. Paul uses it elsewhere seven times.

59. The noun οἰκεῖος (*oikeios*) is used once in Galatians. The term is related to *oik-* set of terms of which there are many (see the list of sixteen terms in O. Michel, 'οἶκος,' in *TDNT* 5.119). This term means 'persons who are related by kinship or circumstances and form a closely-knit group, *members of a household*' (BDAG 694). Galatians employs three of the *oik-* terms, the other two being *oikodomeō* ('build up what I tore down,' in 2:18) and *oikonomos* (household manager, in 4:2).

expect one: *ara oun*. *Ara* alone means 'so then, consequently, you see, as a result, so then, perhaps.'[60] *Oun*, similarly, means 'so, therefore, consequently, accordingly, so now, then.'[61] In the construct *ara oun*, *ara* expresses the logical inference and *oun* is the transition. BDAG considers this means 'so then,'[62] but the joining of the two synonyms suggests emphasis, Paul drawing their attention to this as a conclusion to what he has said in this section and perhaps the whole letter. Hence, I have translated it 'therefore, in light of the above' to try and show the force of the double conjunction, something the major English translations neglect preferring 'so then' (e.g., ESV, NRSV, NET) or 'therefore' (e.g., NIV).

'As we have opportunity,' uses the common verb *echō*, 'have, hold' (see further 2:4).[63] 'As' is *hōs*, a conjunction usually meaning 'as' (see further 1:9).[64] 'Opportunity' is *kairos*, which technically means 'time' (see further 4:10). It was used in the previous verse of the time of judgment, whenever that will be. Here, *hōs kairon* speaks of points of present time where opportunities to do good come along. Hence, it speaks of the moments of life where we find ourselves in situations where a person needs help. Biblically, one thinks of the Samaritan story where the priest and Levite have the opportunity to help the robbed and injured man by the road but do not stop. The Samaritan, on the other hand, stops to help. As the Galatians mingle in their world at work and play, they are to seize the moments gifted to them by God to do good.

'Do good' uses another *erg*– term, *ergazomai*. As noted in the translation, it is one of three *erg*-terms used in Galatians. God works in Peter and Paul's apostolic ministries (2:8), gentile converts are not required to do the 'works of the law' (2:16; 3:2, 5, 10), and they must not engage in the 'works of the flesh' (5:19). Rather, they are to repudiate such things, living by the Spirit.

60. BDAG 127.
61. BDAG 737.
62. BDAG 127.
63. See also 4:22, 27; 6:4.
64. See also 3:16; 4:12, 14; 5:14.

They are also to critically examine their own work (6:4) as they will face judgment.

The verb *ergazomai* outside of Paul in the NT is used for 'workers of lawlessness' (Matt 7:23), doing manual work (Matt 21:28, s.a. Rev 18:17) like Paul's tentmaking (Acts 18:3), working with money (Matt 25:16), work in a general sense (which must not be done on the Sabbath) (Luke 13:14), God's work through Christ (John 3:21; 5:17), Christian work, i.e., the work of God (John 6:27, 28; 9:4), working miracles (John 6:30), God doing work (Acts 13:41), and performing sin (Jas 2:9).

It is sometimes used of doing something good or beautiful. So, *ergazomai* is employed of the woman who anointed Jesus' head who 'has done a beautiful thing to me' (Matt 26:10; Mark 14:6). It is used in John of Christian work, which is to do the work of God, supremely, to believe, faith (John 6:27–29, s.a. 9:4; 2 John 8; 3 John 5). In Acts, Luke uses it of people of every nation who fear God and are 'doing righteousness' and so are acceptable to God (Acts 10:35). Similarly, the writer of Hebrews speaks of the faithful who 'worked justice' (Heb 11:33).

Paul employs the term of godly sorrow *producing* repentance (2 Cor 7:10). Otherwise, he uses it of working for wages (Rom 4:4), honest work for a living like Paul's tentmaking,[65] working in a temple (1 Cor 9:13), doing the work of God—gospel work (1 Cor 16:20), and doing works in contrast to believing (Rom 4:5). For Paul, the verb is employed of doing good (*agathon*) in Rom 2:10, something no one can do to receive eternal life. While it may be impossible to gain justification by working for this only (cf. Rom 4:5), believers are still to pursue good. So, in Romans 13:10, 'love does (*ergazomai*) no wrong to a neighbor' (Rom 13:10, s.a. Gal 5:14). Here, it is a present subjunctive which is hortatory in force (see on the previous verse). This then functions as another imperative in the sequence running from 4:21 to 6:17.[66] The present invokes a habitual attitude.

The object of the verb, as in Rom 2:10, is the adjective *agathos*,

65. See 1 Cor 4:12; 9:6; Eph 4:28; Col 3:23; 1 Thess 2:9; 4:11; 2 Thess 3:8, 10–12.
66. Cf. 5:14, s.a., 1:8, 20; 3:7; 4:12, 21, 30; 5:1, 13, 16; 6:1, 2, 4, 6, 7, 11, 17).

'good' (see on 6:6). This parallels *kalos* in the previous verse. It then means responding to opportunities to do good to all people. Good has been defined not by the Mosaic law, but by service, love, rejoicing, reconciliation, patience, kindness, goodness, humble gentleness, fidelity, and any other fruit the Spirit will produce (5:13–14, 22–24). It is not doing the works of the flesh which tear apart marriages, families, churches, and whole cities and nations (5:19–21).

It *is not* tearing one another apart like animals, living arrogantly, provocatively, and enviously (5:15, 26). It is behaving as the Galatians did when they first met the sick Paul and welcomed him as Christ himself and cared for him despite his appalling state (4:12–15). It *is* doing what the Jerusalem leaders did when they met with Paul and Barnabas, granting them the right hand of fellowship (2:1–10). It is not separating from believers on the basis of food laws but embracing one another in table fellowship—Jew with Greek, slave with free, and men with women (2:11–14; 3:28). It is restoring the transgressor humbly and gently (6:1). It is bearing one another's burdens (6:2). And, it is doing what Paul says in 1 Thess 5:15: 'See that no one repays evil with evil, but always pursue (*diōkō*) good (*agathos*) toward one another and to *all people (pantas)*.'

It must be stressed that Paul is urging them to behave this way toward all people. Hence, as they go to work each day, mingling in the Agora, the workshop, by fountains, in gymnasia, at the baths, in the schools, at the gathering of the citizens of the towns, they are to make the most of every opportunity to do good to those they encounter. This is the language of mission where God's people respond to those outside the church with goodness.

Such goodness is seen in God's healing of gentiles like the Syrian Naaman and his provision for the widow of Zarephath (Luke 4:23–27; 1 Kings 17:9; 2 Kings 5:1–14), This is how Jesus dealt with the thousands that came to him for healing and he restored them with a touch and/or word, feeding them, and sharing the message of the kingdom with them (e.g., Mark 6:30–44; 7:31–8:10; Acts 10:38). He sent his disciples into the whole world to do the same in every nation. Paul recognizes this himself, for through Abraham and his people, all the world will be blessed. This, of course, supremely happens in Christ and continues by his Spirit through his people who do good (Gal 3:8; Gen 12:1).

Jesus urged his followers to treat unbelievers with goodness, even loving their enemies and blessing those who persecute them (e.g., Matt 5:43–33; Luke 6:27–35). Paul himself said as much in Rom 12:14–18, urging the Romans to bless their enemies and live at peace with them: 'Bless those who persecute you; bless and do not curse them … Repay no one evil for evil, but give thought to do what is honorable in the sight of all. If possible, so far as it depends on you, live peaceably with all.' They are to emulate Paul, who himself emulates Christ (1 Cor 11:1), by becoming all things to all people to save some. He seeks to please everyone in everything he does, not for his own advantage, but that many may be saved (1 Cor 9:19–23; 10:33).

His prayer is that the Lord will make the Thessalonians 'increase and abound in love for one another *and for all*' (1 Thess 3:12). There is no limit on love, every gift is to be motivated by love, and love is shown to all people (1 Cor 13:1–7, 13). Everything Christians do, in any context, is to be done in love (1 Cor 16:14). We are to let our humble gentleness be known before all people (Phil 4:5). For those of us who are saved by grace through faith, God has prepared good works to do in every situation we find ourselves in (Eph 2:10). We are to exercise our gifts without favoritism,[67] for God does not show partiality (Gal 2:6; Rom 2:11).

While we live in a grossly sinful world, we do not join the world in its sin (Gal 5:19–21; Eph 4:17–5:15). Rather, we show them another way to live because God wants all people to be saved and to come to the knowledge of the truth (1 Tim 2:4).

This would potentially include the Judaizers. However, doing good to them does not include allowing them to remain engaged within Paul's churches preaching their poison. Rather, for the sake of the church, their leaven must be removed (5:7, s.a. 4:30;

---

67. See Rom 12:4–8; 1 Cor 12, 14; Eph 4:11–16.

5:13). While they will no longer engage in fellowship with them within the community, this does not mean that the Galatians believers should not reach out in grace to help them be restored (6:1). They are not to do wrong to them; rather, they are to treat them like all fallen humanity—image bearers loved by God who sent his Son to die for them.

'Especially' is *malista*, which is the superlative[68] of the adverb *mala*, 'exceedingly, very.'[69] Elsewhere, *malista* is used in Paul seven times, each time following a general statement, and drawing out a specific focal point. So, in Phil 4:22, 'all the holy people greet you, *especially* those of Caesar's household.' Again in 1 Tim 4:10, '… who (God) is the Savior of all people, *especially* of those who believe.'[70] In 1 Tim 5:17, Paul writes, 'Let the elders who rule well be considered worthy of double honor, *especially* those who labor in the word and teaching' (s.a. 2 Tim 4:13; Tit 1:10; Phlm 16). There are some resonances between 6:10 and 1 Tim 5:18: 'but if anyone does not provide for his relatives, and *especially* for members of his household (*oikeiōn*), he has denied the faith and is worse than an unbeliever.'

In such texts, as *mala* already carries a strong sense of intensification, so *malista* then, is a strong adverb. Hence, I have translated it here 'most especially …' Christians are then to do good to all people. However, most especially, they are to do so to the members of 'the household of faith.'

'Household' is *oikeios*, one of a nexus of *oik-* terms in the NT (cf. *oikodomeō*, 'build,' 2:18; *oikonomos*, 'household manager,' 4:2). *Oikeios* speaks of 'persons who are related by kinship or circumstances and form a closely-knit group, *members of a household*.'[71] It speaks in the LXX and Pseudepigrapha of members of a family, kin, and relatives.[72] The term is only found

68. A superlative concerns adjectives and adverbs and 'speaks of comparison that speaks of the highest degree. The adjective *biggest* is a superlative adjective, compared to *big* (positive) and *bigger* (comparative). Called the superlative degree.' (See *PDSNTG* 117–18). Where you have a term like *mala* which already has that sense of intensifying an idea, *malista* speaks of a very strong intensification.
69. LSJ 1076.
70. With Paul's soteriology by faith in mind, *malista* here has the sense 'only.'
71. BDAG 694.

thrice in the Paulines (see above on 1 Tim 5:8). In Eph 2:19, Paul uses it in a manner similar to this use in Galatians speaking of Jew and gentile alike as 'members of the household of God.'

Here, it is 'household of *faith* (*pistis*, see 1:23).' This is then, those who are fellow-believers, people of 'the faith' (1:23), people who do not rely on the works of the law, but who have heard the gospel with faith and who continue to walk in faith.[73] In another context, the household of faith would include all God-believers from all time, stretching back to Abel, Noah, and of course, Abraham and Sarah, who feature in this letter (esp. 3:6–14, cf. Heb 11). However, here, the focus is on those living to whom the Galatians can do good as the opportunity is given.

Critical to being Christian is that we demonstrate God's goodness by doing good to one another. The Galatians clearly are not doing so; rather, they are acting like wild animals, tearing into each other with envy, divisiveness, anger, factionalism, argument, rivalries, enmity, and arrogance (5:15, 20–21, 26). They must be restored to one another by the Spirit, living together by the fruit of the Spirit. Their *koinōnia* must be restored.

This too is missional. Mission is to be centrifugal, believers radiating out from their churches into a fallen world and shining like stars in the universe as they hold forth the word of life (Phil 2:15–16). It is also centripetal, the church, the body of Christ, the temple of the Spirit, God's very family, shining as the light to the nations. This shining is seen in our attitudes, deeds, and relationships, whereby we live out of love for one another. By such behavior, all people will know that we are Christ's disciples, as we love one another (John 13:34–35). The church is to be an attractive presence in the world, though not because of brilliant speakers, fantastic bands, awesome buildings, and packaged programs to impress the world. Though this is not all bad and

---

72. See in the LXX in Lev 18:6, 12, 13, 17; 21:2; 25:49; Num 25:5; 27:11; 1 Sam 10:14, 15, 16; Prov 17:9; Amos 6:10; Isa 3:6; 31:9; 58:7; 1 Macc 1:61; 3 Macc 6:8. In the Pseudepigrapha see 4 Ezra 7:103; T. Reu. 3:5.

73. See 2:16, 20; 3:2, 5, 22–26; 5:5, 6, 22.

has its place because we contextualize the gospel and do our very best for Jesus.

However, there is a fine line between contextualization and syncretism, where the gospel becomes merely a blend of our fallen culture and the gospel. What should really mark us is our faith, hope, and love. The way we relate to one another, sharing our lives, practicing hospitality, sharing with those in need, repudiating racism, sexism, and elitism, showing forgiveness, living humbly and gently, rejoicing in God, working through issues with grace, retaining a Christian sexual ethic with grace, showing mercy and justice, and so on, will be an attractive force to the world.

People living in the western world in the afterglow of Christendom, live in a culture that remains very salty; the gospel's influence is still strong, even if our wider society does not acknowledge this. As such, the church can seem merely like another social group as the whole culture to an extent still functions with Christian values like compassion and justice.

Yet, as our societies reject the gospel and Christendom, our cultures are changing. Corruption is on the rise. Sexual immorality is increasingly normalized. Justice is becoming compromised. Violence is permeating life in such things as terrorism and domestic violence. Racism and sexism are making a comeback. Our politics is becoming increasingly polarized and corrupted by politicians who are a million miles from the example of Christ. Yet, such things are to be expected as Christ is rejected by many—'been there, tried that!'

As this happens, the church must not sell out to such things but must press on to be even more determined to be characterized by goodness, love, purity, and more. As we model alternative communities shaped by grace and God's love and justice, we will become increasingly attractive to those seeking goodness in the world. We do not do so by compromising the gospel, but by being the gospel. May we be so! Amen!

PART VI

PART SIX: POSTSCRIPT (6:11–18)

CHAPTER THIRTY-TWO: POSTSCRIPT (6:11–18)

We come now to the conclusion of the letter to the Galatians, signaled by the absence of any connective, and Paul's personal reference to his writing. Paul's final word in the body proper was to urge them to do good to all people and, most especially other believers (6:10). Paul begins the letter-ending with a personal touch, asking them to notice the large letters with which he writes (6:11). This indicates the letter was dictated to another Christian in Antioch (unknown, see on authorship), and this functions as his signature.

He then zeros in on the central matter in the letter, circumcision. We learn more about the Judaizers. They forcibly want to circumcise them to avoid persecution, despite their not fully keeping the law. As such, it is futile to circumcise others (6:12). They want to do this so that they can boast before their persecutors (6:13). Paul repudiates such boasting, save in the cross of Jesus. By this cross, he has died to the world and the world to him (6:14). This recalls 2:19–20, where he has been crucified with Christ and now lives by his power alone. He stresses that whether one has a foreskin or not is, in reality, nothing of any consequence. What matters is a person being transformed into a new creation in God by his Spirit (6:15). For Paul, v. 16 is clearly a rule. So, for those who follow this rule, what matters is not whether someone is circumcised or not but them being a part of God's renewed creation. Paul then pronounces a blessing of peace and mercy on the Israel of God, which, I will argue is the Jewish and Gentile community of Christian saints across the whole word (6:16).

In the penultimate verse, he urges that no one continues to

cause him trouble, for he is suffering for Christ (6:17). He ends recalling 1:3 with a blessing of grace upon the Galatians and *amēn* (6:18). The passage can be divided into three: a signature (6:11), a final appeal to repudiate the Judaizers and circumcision (6:12–15), and a final blessing, appeal, and farewell (6:16–18).

SIGNATURE (6:11)

In *Galatians 6:11*, Paul begins the letter-conclusion or epistolary postscript with an appeal that they observe his personal writing:
See (second person plural aorist-imperative *eidon*, 1:19) **the large** (dative *pēlikos*)[1] **letters** (plural dative *gramma*)[2] **I write** (first person aorist *graphō*, 1:17) **to you** (plural dative *sy*, 1:3) **with [by] my own** (dative[3] *emos*, 1:13) **hand** (singular dative[3] *cheir*, 3:19).

There is no connective (asyndeton, 2:6), signaling the next section, the conclusion, or epistolary postscript. 'See' is *eidon*, used in 1:19 of Paul seeing Jacob in Jerusalem. Here, it is the second person imperative calling for them to see or observe his writing (another imperative in the letter and in the string from 4:12 through Ch. 6). 'Large' is the adjective *pēlikos*, used twice in the NT. The other use is Heb 7:4 where it refers to the greatness of Melchizedek (Abraham having tithed to him).[4] Although this is an imperative, it has a different force to the others that have been used through the paraenetic section above. It is aorist and is not behavioral, a little like 'tell me' in 4:21.

---

1. The adjective πηλίκος (*pēlikos*) means 'how large, how great.' It is used once in Paul, in Gal 6:11 of his large letters written on the Galatians' scroll. The only other NT use is in Heb 7:4 which speaks of how great Melchizedek is that Abraham tithed to him.
2. The only use of γράμμα (*gramma*), 'letter' (Eng. 'grammar') is found in Gal 6:11 of the large letters Paul writes with (cf. 2 Cor 3:7—chiseled in letters). Paul also uses it of the law, the written code (Rom 2:27, 29; 7:6; 2 Cor 3:6), and the sacred writings (2 Tim 3:15).
3. Wallace, *Greek Grammar*, 170 sees this as a dative of material; '[t]he dative substantive denotes the material that is used to accomplish the action of the verb. This use is fairly rare.' However, this could equally be one of means, as it is hard to consider a hand material.
4. It is only found three times in the LXX of how wide and long Jerusalem is (Zech 2:2) and how great a mother's suffering is as she watches her sons being tortured (4 Macc 15:22). In *Let. Aris.* 52, it is used for the largeness of an object in the Temple.

'Letters' is the plural of *gramma*, from which we get the English 'grammar' and related terms. The term has a wide range of meanings,[5] used in the NT of a financial bill (Luke 16:6, 7), what Moses wrote (John 5:47), being a person of *letters*, so learned or learning (John 7:15; Acts 26:28), a written letter (Acts 28:21), the law as a written code (Rom 2:27, 29; 7:6; 2 Cor 3:6), the sacred writings (2 Tim 3:15), and of the law being engraved in letters on stone tablets (2 Cor 3:7). Here, rather than the letter itself (large letter),[6] it simply means the large letters Paul himself has written (*graphō*, see 1:20) on the scroll of Galatians with his own (*emos*, see 2:13) hand (*cheir*, see 3:19).

The verb *graphō* is aorist, and so is an epistolary aorist, whereby the aorist is used to indicate the time of writing from the perspective of the reader after the letter is delivered and read.[7]

The reason Paul has put this here is discussed. It is generally agreed that Paul used an amanuensis or secretary for the majority of the letter. However, this verse seems to have been written by Paul.[8] There is a range of crazy ideas out there

---

5. See LSJ 358. They note that it includes what is drawn, a picture, a written character, a letter, the alphabet, to read, to articulate sound, an inscription, musical notes, a diagram, the quarters in a town, a weight, a piece of writing, papers, documents, a book, laws, rules, to have letters—learning, and so on. Such diversity is seen in the LXX where it is used for an inscription (Exod 26:39), a tattoo (Lev 19:28), a writing (1 Esd 3:13, 14), writing in general (Isa 29:11–12), a written proclamation (Esth 4:3), daily records (Esth 6:1), words (Esth 6:2), a written letter (Esth 8:5; Add Est E 17; 1 Macc 5:10), a written edict (Esther 8:10; 9:1), writings, and literature (Dan 1:4). It is also employed of place names, 'city of letters,' Keriath-sepher (Josh 15:15, 16, 49; Judg 1:11, 12), 'Spring of Letters,' En-gannim (Josh 21:29).

6. Some consider that *grammasin* here refers to the letter as a whole or his letters. However, as Longenecker, *Galatians*, 289 notes, Paul would then use *epistolē* (Rom 16:22; 1 Cor 5:9; 16:3; 2 Cor 3:1; 7:8; 10:9–11; Col 4:16; 1 Thess 5:27; 2 Thess 2:2, 15; 3:14, 17) and the term is plural.

7. Wallace, *Grammar*, 562 notes that the epistolary aorist is 'the use of the aorist indicative in the epistles in which the author self-consciously describes his letter from the time frame of the audience. The aorist indicative of πέμπω is naturally used in this sense. This category is not common, but it does have some exegetical significance.' See also 1 Cor 9:15; 2 Cor 8:17, 18, 22; 9:3, 5; Eph 6:22; Phil 2:28; Phlm 12.

8. Longenecker, *Galatians*, 289. For a fuller discussion of the role of the amanuensis see pp. lix–lxi.

concerning what it implies. One idea is that Paul had actually been crucified by being nailed through the hand.[9] This is hilarious, for if it were so, Paul would surely have listed it in his catalog of suffering in 2 Cor 11, and he is hardly likely to have been a tentmaker with crucified hands. Others have postulated Paul had some other kind of hand injury.[10] As with the previous idea, this can be ruled out instantly as he was a tentmaker who worked carefully with his hands. Another theory is that he was unskilled in writing, which again is preposterous in that he was raised in Tarsus (Acts 9:11; Gal 1:21), was a Pharisee (Phil 3:5), advanced in learning (1:14), and his letters are described as forceful (2 Cor 10:10).

The first of the two better possibilities is that this refers back to a problem with Paul's eyes (see 4:15).[11] The second possibility is that the reference to large letters speaks of their boldness and force rather than their actual size. So, Lightfoot suggests, 'The boldness of the handwriting answers to the force of the Apostle's convictions. The size of the characters will arrest the attention of his readers in spite of themselves.'[12] While we cannot be sure of the intent, I am drawn to the traditional view that this gives further indication of an eye problem. However, this does not rule out that Paul is also seeking to add emphasis to his appeal.

These next three verses bring home Paul's appeal. They make it plain what the real issue is, circumcision. They tell us something about the practice and motivations of the Judaizers—they are compelling the gentiles to be circumcised and are doing so, at least in part, to avoid persecution and to give them a reason to boast before others (either God or their persecutors). Paul repudiates their boasting, speaking of his resolve to boast only in Christ. He then states clearly what really matters; it is not whether a man is circumcised or not, but his being a new

---

9. N. Turner, *Grammatical Insights into the New Testament* (Edinburgh: T. & T. Clark, 1965), 94 based on 2:19; 6:14, 17.

10. T. Zahn, *Der Brief des Paulus an die Galater*, KNT (Leipzig: Deichert, 1905), 278.

11. Witherington, *Galatians*, 441.

12. Lightfoot, *Galatians*, 221; Longenecker, *Galatians*, 290; Dunn, *Galatians*, 335.

creation. He then blesses the Galatians and urges that no one cause him any more trouble.

THE CIRCUMCISING JUDAIZERS ARE TRYING TO AVOID PERSECUTION (6:12)

In *Galatians 6:12*, again without naming them, Paul speaks of the Judaizers:

As many as (plural *hosos*, 3:10) **want** (*thelō*, 1:7)[13] **to make a good impression** (aorist infinitive *euprosōpeō*)[14] **in** (*en*, 1:6) **the flesh** (dative sarx), **they** (plural *houtos*) **are compelling** (*anagkazō*, 2:3) **you** (plural *sy*, 1:3) **to be circumcised** (aorist passive *peritemnō*, 2:3), **only** (*monon*, 1:23) **so that** (*hina*, 1:16) **they may not** (*mē*, 1:7) **be persecuted** (present passive subjunctive *diōkō*, 1:13) **for the cross** (dative[15] *stauros*) **of Christ** (*Christos*, 1:1).

'As many as' refers indirectly to the unnamed Judaizers who are coming into the Galatian churches and forcing the Galatians to Judaize. 'Want' is *thelō*, used through Galatians, and often of what the Judaizers are wanting: 'to pervert the gospel of Christ' (1:7); 'to exclude you' (4:17); 'you to be subject to the law' (4:21); and in the next verse, 'you to be circumcised' (6:13). Otherwise, it is used of Paul's (3:2; 4:21) and the Galatians' desires, e.g., 'to be enslaved to them [*stoicheia*] again' (4:9). This is another strand of the Judaizer's desire to conform them to a 'gospel' that stands against God's will which Paul is seeking to represent (see further 1:4, 7).

---

13. The present tense verbs in this θέλουσιν and ἀναγκάζουσιν are true conative presents that refers to something in progress, being attempted. See also 5:4. See Wallace, *Greek Grammar*, 534–35.
14. The verb εὐπροσωπέω (*eyprosōpeō*) compounds *eu* (good) and *prosōpon* (face) and speaks in its only NT use in Gal 6:12 (*hapax legomenon*) of presenting a good face in the flesh, i.e., before people (with possibly a play on physical circumcision). *Prosōpon* also features in the letter of people of Judea knowing Paul in person (to the face) (1:22), God not showing favoritism (a face of a person God does not receive, 2:6), and Paul opposing Cephas to his face in Antioch (2:11).
15. The dative τῷ σταυρῷ (*tō staurō*, 'the cross') is a dative of cause (because of), '[t]he dative substantive indicates the cause or basis of the action of the verb. This usage is fairly common.' (See Wallace, *Greek Grammar*, 167). It is because of the cross of Christ that Christians are being persecuted.

Here, what they want uses a rare compound verb, *euprosōpeō*, compounding *eu* (good, well) and *prosōpon* (face), and so means 'to have a good appearance.'[16] It is extremely rare, a *hapax legomenon*. Indeed, this is its only use in comparable Jewish and Christian Greek literature. One example in wider sources is in Pausanias, who speaks of a peaceful disposition that could have stopped a war (Pausanias, *Descr.* 4.4.4). Here, it likely speaks of making a good showing,[17] impression,[18] or 'stand well'[19] before others.

'In the flesh' may have three nuances. On the one hand, it speaks of making a good showing before other people. Second, it may be a veiled reference to the circumcision of the penis which cuts the flesh and supposedly makes a good showing (at least to the Judaizers and Jews). Third, the use of flesh is ironic as flesh for Paul often speaks of human fallenness and proneness to sin. By their being circumcised, supposedly to please God and other people, Galatians are plunged into a fleshly state, in r severed from Christ (5:4). While it may have a good appearance (*euprosopeō*) in a Jewish bodily sense, and to others, it is anything but this. God, who does not receive the face (*prosōpon*) of a person (show partiality or favoritism, cf. 2:6; Rom 2:11, cf. Deut 10:17), will now see them in their fleshly state outside of God. What a horrendous irony!

In part b of the verse, these Judaizers are seeking to compel the Galatians (you) to be circumcised. The verb is *anagkazō* which is used in 2:3 of Titus not being compelled in Jerusalem to be circumcised, and in 2:14, of Peter unwittingly compelling gentiles to Judaize. Here, it is a conative present speaking of the Judaizers attempting to compel the Galatians to be circumcised.[20] As discussed in relation to 2:3, while it can have

16. E. Lohse, 'εὐπροσωπέω,' in *TDNT* 6:779.
17. BDAG 411.
18. See 'εὐπροσωπέω,' in *EDNT* 2:82.
19. See Lohse, 'εὐπροσωπέω,' 779.
20. The verb *anagkazousin* is a conative present. Wallace, *Grammar*, 534 indicates that a conative (or tendential, voluntative) present 'portrays the subject as *desiring* to do something (*voluntative*), *attempting* to do something (*conative*), or at the point of *almost doing* something (*tendential*).' It is rare. In this case, it is conative. It can be something

a softer sense, it is used to indicate some degree of force (Acts 26:11). Here, the Judaizers, unlike the Jerusalem leaders, are seeking to compel the Galatians to be circumcised. This speaks of real pressure.

If they are seeking to make a good showing toward other people by having the Judaizers circumcised, who are these people? To determine who is in view, the final clause must be examined. Here, Paul indicates that the Judaizers are motivated to avoid being persecuted (*diōkō*, see 1:13) for the cross of Christ. That is, they are avoiding persecution for believing in a crucified Messiah. Some suggest the source of this persecution is the Roman authorities (cf. Phil 1:28–29; Acts 16:16–40; 1 Thess 2:2).[21] So, the Jews want to circumcise them to bring them into the relative safety of Judaism, a *religio licita*.

However, more likely, the persecution is Jewish. The focus on the cross of Christ gets to the gist of Jewish offense at the cross, for anyone hung on a tree is accursed (see 3:13; Deut 21:23, s.a. 1 Cor 1:23). Further, in Acts 13–14, among the churches to which Paul writes this letter, although gentiles are drawn in at times, it is the Jews who initiate and sustain action against Paul and Barnabas.[22] So, more likely, the persecution is coming from the developing nationalism in Jerusalem and persecution from fellow Jews (cf. 2 Thess 2:14–16, s.a. Gal 2:12). While the Judaizers are motivated theologically, they are also seeking to soften the offense of incorporating uncircumcised gentiles into fellowship to reduce Jewish persecution.[23]

---

in progress but incomplete (a true conative) or something about to be attempted or desired (voluntative, tendential). Here, it is the latter, they are attempting to compel them.

21. B. W. Winter, *Seek the Welfare of the City: Christians as Benefactors and Citizens*, FCCGRW (Grand Rapids: Eerdmans, 1994), 137–42; J. K. Hardin, *Galatians and the Imperial Cult: A Critical Analysis of the First-Century Social Context of Paul's Letter*, WUNT 237 (Tübingen, Mohr Siebeck, 2008), 98–91.

22. See Acts 13:45, 50–51; 14:2–5, 19–20, s.a. 1 Thess 2:1–2.

23. See further Jewett, "The Agitators," 198–212.

THE LAWBREAKING JUDAIZERS WANT TO BOAST IN YOUR FLESH (6:13)

In *Galatians 6:13* Paul continues dealing with the Judaizers:

For (*gar*, 1:10) **not even** (*oude*, 1:1) **those who are circumcised** (present middle participle *peritemnō*, 2:3) **themselves** (plural *autos*, 1:1) **are keeping** (present *phylassō*)[24] **the law** (*nomos*, 2:16), **but** (*alla*, 1:1) **they want** (*thelō*, 1:7) **you** (plural *sy*, 1:3) **to be circumcised** (aorist passive infinitive *peritemnō*), **so that** (*hina*, 1:16) **they may boast** (aorist middle subjunctive third-person *kauchaomai*)[25] **in** (*en*, 1:6) **your** (*hymeteros*)[26] **flesh** (*sarx*, 1:16).

Paul now draws attention to the Judaizers' failure to uphold the law despite their being circumcised. *Gar* (for) is continuative rather than causal. The participle *peritemnomenoi* can either be present passive indicating those who 'are being circumcised' or present middle 'those who are receiving circumcision. Moo rightly recognizes that the difference is minimal.[27] While these can be those gentiles who are being circumcised by the Judaizers,[28] most likely it is the Judaizers themselves, i.e., the circumcision party.[29] At a broader level, this has in mind all who live under the law, including the Jewish people who practice circumcision as of rite.

---

24. The verb φυλάσσω (*phylassō*) has a range of meanings like 'watch, guard, protect' but its only use in Gal 6:13 means 'keep, observe, follow' the law. This the Judaizers do not do.

25. The verb καυχάομαι (*kauchaomai*) meaning 'boast,' is found twice in Gal 6:13 and 14, first of the Judaizers boasting in the flesh of the circumcised Galatians, and of Paul's refusal to boast of anything other than the cross of Christ. The noun *kauchēma* (a boast) is used in 6:4. All but two of the thirty-seven NT uses of the verb are in Paul's writings showing how important the theme is to Paul (the others being in Jacob of a lowly person boasting in being raised up [Jas 1:9] and boasting in arrogance, which is evil [Jas 4:16]).

26. The second person plural possessive pronoun ὑμέτερος (*hymeteros*) compounds the plural of *sy* (e.g., *hymas*), you with *heteros* (other) and yields 'you, your, yourself.' It is used once in Galatians 6:13. It is used eleven times in the NT and is usually possessive as here, 'your flesh.' Paul uses it five times (s.a., Rom 11:31; 1 Cor 15:31; 16:17; 2 Cor 8:8).

27. Moo, *Galatians*, 394.

28. E.g., Burton, *Galatians*, 252–53.

29. Longenecker, *Galatians*, 292; Moo, *Galatians*, 394.

They are not keeping the law. Keeping is *phylassō*, a verb used extensively across the comparative literature. It is a prison motif, speaking of guarding something, used in a range of ways in the NT.[30] At times it has the sense of keeping or observing teaching whether it is the word of God or Christ (Luke 11:28; John 12:47), the injunctions in the Jerusalem Council letter (Acts 16:4; 21:25), or instructions from Paul's letter (1 Tim 5:21). In passages like the account of the Rich Ruler, it is used of keeping or observing Israel's laws (Matt 19:20; Mark 10:20; Luke 18:21). It is used to describe Paul as he went through a Jewish ritualistic purification rite (Acts 21:24).

In Acts 7:53, Stephen accuses the Sanhedrin of receiving the law from angels, but not having kept it. In Rom 2:26, Paul employs it of those who are not circumcised by keeping the requirements of the law, something no one does perfectly. Here it is negated; these Judaizers do not keep or observe the law.

The idea of Jewish failure to keep the law is essential to Galatians. This is implied in 3:10–14 where those who rely on the works of the law for justification must do them all (Deut 27:26; Lev 18:5). Similarly, in 5:3, if anyone accepts circumcision, they are obligated to keep the whole law. As such, justification is by faith, not works of the law (2:16).

The argument of Rom 2:12–30 is that, like the gentiles, Jews too are sinners who fail to uphold the law and so justification is not through law-observance in whatever sense but through faith (esp. Rom 2:13, 17–23). Jews like gentiles are 'under sin' (Rom 3:9) and no fleshly being can be justified in the sight of God through works of the law (Rom 3:19). So, Paul's point is that these Judaizers are demanding that the Galatians be circumcised as per the law, yet they do not keep the law themselves.

---

30. *Phylassō* is used for watching over flocks (Luke 2:8), keeping someone or a place under guard (Luke 8:29; 11:21; Acts 12:4; 23:35; 28:16), being on guard of one's life (Luke 12:15; John 12:25), Jesus keeping guard over the disciples (John 17:12), Paul keeping the coats while Stephen is stoned (Acts 22:20), the Lord guarding Christians against Satan (2 Thess 3:3), keeping guard over that which has been entrusted and given (1 Tim 6:20; 2 Tim 1:12, 14), be on guard against enemies (2 Tim 4:12), God guarding Noah (2 Pet 2:5), being on guard against false teaching (2 Pet 3:17) or idols (1 John 5:21), and God guarding Christians against falling (Jude 24).

The final clause signaled by *hina* provides the purpose of the
Judaizers desiring (*thelō*) to circumcise the Galatians: 'so that they
may boast in your flesh.' Again, we have the will of the Judaizers
expressed. God's will was to send Jesus, so this is not necessary.
Paul's will is that the Galatians turn from the desires of the
Judaizers to the will of God expressed in Christ. This is the last
use of the verb in a string of references that alert us to 'the Battle
for the Wills of the Galatian Believers!' (see on 1:4, 7).

'In your flesh' here suggests their circumcised penises. Likely,
their boast is to fellow Jews who deplore the idea of
uncircumcised gentiles being incorporated into fellowship with
Jews. Earlier in 6:4, Paul uses *kauchēma* of the Galatians limiting
boasting to pride in oneself. As noted in the discussion of 6:4,
boasting was widespread in the Roman culture and Paul deals
with it through his letters, especially Romans and the Corinthian
correspondence.

As we will see in these two verses, generally speaking, Paul
repudiates all boasting other than in God, his Son, his work, and
what he has done in and through believers. This is seen in the
use of the verb used here, *kauchaomai*. Aside from Jacob, who
repudiates all boasting in arrogance as evil (Jas 4:16) other than a
lowly brother boasting in his uplifting by God (Jas 1:9), the verb
is used by Paul, thirty-five times. He employs it rhetorically in
his critique of those Jews who boast in God (Rom 2:17), the law
(Rom 2:23), and yet fail to observe the law. He also challenges
those who boast in people (1 Cor 3:21), in their gifts (1 Cor
4:7), in gifts expressed without love (1 Cor 13:3), in outward
appearance (2 Cor 5:12), and of one's works before God (Eph
2:9).

Things that are boast-worthy for a Christian include 'the hope
of the glory of God' (Rom 5:2), sufferings that produce
perseverance, character, and hope (Rom 5:3), God through Christ
(Rom 5:11; 1 Cor 1:29), in Christ,[31] other Christians to another (2
Cor 7:14; 9:2). At times he reluctantly boasts against opponents,
taking care only to speak of what he has done[32] but considering

---

31. See 1 Cor 1:31; 2 Cor 10:17, cf. Jer 9:23; 1 Sam 2:10 LXX; Phil 3:3.

himself a fool for doing so. So, he focuses on boasting in his weaknesses (2 Cor 11:30, 12:1–9).

Here, the boasting is false, the Judaizers boasting in the flesh of the circumcised Galatians. This is to be repudiated as it is unnecessary and only brings the Galatians into a position where they must uphold the whole law, something which is impossible. Boasting in the flesh is again ironical, for they are boasting in the penis when in fact, the circumcised gentile is now under the law and severed from Christ and so stands before God in a fleshly state. So, they are boasting about their lostness rather than anything gained before God. While this may make them acceptable to those Jews who are persecuting the Judaizers, it leaves the Galatians where the Judaizers are—along with all humanity in rejection of God and his Son, severed from Christ and fallen from grace (5:4). They can have no more confidence in the flesh than Paul himself could when he was the Jew par excellence (Phil 3:3–6). Rather than help, they are merely mutilating them (Phil 3:3) as they cut in on them (5:7), behaving like the Galli (5:13), leaving the Galatians in a perilous soteriological state.

BOAST ONLY IN THE CROSS BY WHICH ALL IS CRUCIFIED (6:14)

In *Galatians 6:14*, with one of the most brilliant and profound theological statements in the Scriptures, Paul shifts from the negative futile boasting of the Judaizers to boasting in what truly matters:

But (*de*, 1:15) **to me** (dative *egō*, 1:2) **may it never** (*mē*, 1:7) **be** (optative *ginomai*, 2:17) **to boast** (present middle infinitive *kauchaomai*, 6:13) **except** (*ei*, 1:7 plus *mē*) **in** (*en*, 1:6) **the cross** (*stauros*, 5:11) **of** (genitive *ho*, 1:1) **our** (genitive *egō*) **Lord** (*kyrios*, 1:3) **Jesus** (genitive *Iēsous*, 1:1) **Christ** (genitive *Christos*, 1:1), **through** (*dia*, 1:1) **whom** (genitive *hos*, 1:5) **to me** (dative *egō*) **the world** (*kosmos*, 4:3) **has been crucified** (*stauroō*, 3:1), **and I** (*kagō*, 4:12) **to the world** (dative *kosmos*).

---

32. See 2 Cor 10:8, 13, 15, 16; 11:12, 16, 18.

De is adversative here, Paul contrasting the attitude of the Judaizers with his own. Rather than boasting in the flesh of the Galatians, which is puerile, Paul responds by repudiating all boasting other than in the cross of Christ. 'May it never be' translates Paul's characteristic *mē genoito*, the negation of the optative of *ginomai*, but unusually places it mid-sentence (see further on 2:17). It is effectively a prayer that what he repudiates will never 'come to pass,' 'happen,' or 'be.' Here, what he repudiates is that he would dare to boast in anything other than Christ crucified.

The verb 'boast' is again *kauchaomai*, discussed in more detail above in relation to 6:13. While the verb *kauchasthai* here can be passive, likely it is the present middle infinitive of *kauchaomai*, with the middle adding force to Paul's personal repudiation of his own participation in such boasting.[33]

The combination of the conditional conjunction *ei* and the negative adverb *mē* (*ei mē*) is literally 'if not' and while it can mean 'but' (1:7), here as in 1:19 it yields 'except' (see further on *ei mē*, 1:7). As discussed earlier concerning 6:4 and 6:13 where boasting language is concerned, Paul repudiates all self-boasting before or over others (Rom 11:18), boasting before God for righteousness by our works (Rom 3:27; 1 Cor 1:29; Eph 2:9), boasting over our gifts as if they are self-produced (1 Cor 4:7; 13:3), in sin (1 Cor 5:6), and boasting in one person against another (1 Cor 3:21). To boast in oneself is not love (1 Cor 13:4). While at times Paul boasts reluctantly and ironically,[34] of his converts like a proud parent,[35] and his suffering,[36] and endorses taking inward pride in one's own work (6:4),[37] it is God and Christ in whom he boasts most of all.[38]

Here, it is not just Christ but his crucifixion that is the object

33. Wallace, *Grammar*, 414.
34. See 2 Cor 1:12; 2 Cor 10:8, 13–16; 11:10–12:9.
35. See 1 Cor 15:31; 2 Cor 1:14; 5:10; 7:4, 14; 2 Cor 8:24; 9:2–3; Phil 2:16; 1 Thess 2:19; 2 Thess 1:4.
36. See Rom 5:3; 2 Cor 11:11–20; 12:5, 9.
37. See also Rom 15:17; 1 Cor 9:15, 16.
38. See Rom 5:2, 11; 1 Cor 1:31; 2 Cor 10:17; Phil 1:26; 3:3.

of Paul's boasting. 'In the cross (*stauros*) of our Lord Jesus Christ' is replete with meaning (see also 5:11). Whereas the Judaizers want to circumcise the Galatians in part to avoid persecution (for themselves and/or the Galatians) (6:12), Paul boasts in the cross. Rather than seeing persecution as a problem, he sees it as identification with Christ, whereby he bears within his body the *stigmata* of Jesus (6:17). The Judaizers should not be responding this way, for being a follower of the crucified one brings suffering on his behalf, and this is basic to the call to take up one's cross and follow Jesus (Mark 8:34 and parr.). Rather than succumbing to circumcision to please the Judaizers and fit in with Judaism and avoid persecution, the Galatians are to press on persevering in their faith in a crucified Messiah who is the Savior of the world.

The cross is also mentioned in 5:11, where it is the 'offense of the cross' which is removed when someone preaches circumcision (as do the Judaizers). As discussed at some length in 5:11, crucifixion is an appalling thing to Jews and other ancients. It was repudiated as a state of accursedness (3:13; Deut 21:23), a stumbling block (5:11), shameful (Justin Martyr, *Dial.* 89:2; Heb 12:2), a miserable death (Josephus, *J.W.* 7.203), cruel and terrible (Cicero. *Verr.* 2.5.165), and more.

Yet, for Paul, it is where the glory of God is revealed. On the cross, the one who is in the form of God and equal with him in every way, who poured himself out for the world in self-emptying service and humbled himself to death for the world (Phil 2:6–11). It is where God revealed what it means to be truly human and what true divinity looks like. The cross is where Christ took the sin of fallen humanity and the pain of a busted world into himself and destroyed it in his body of death. Sinless, death could not constrain him, and he was raised by God's Spirit power and lives as the Lord Jesus Christ. Those who join him by yielding to him as cosmic Lord and savior, are swept up into him, joining all peoples of genuine faith from the past to the future. They receive from Christ his Spirit-anointing (3:2) and the status of righteous/justified (2:16), redeemed (4:5), and adopted as his children (4:5). They are incorporated into the household of faith

(6:10), the Israel of God (6:17). They are, as Paul puts it earlier, crucified with Christ and now live by faith in the Son of God and his power.

Whereas the Judaizers boast in the so-called glory of the Galatians' circumcised penises (6:13), Paul boasts in the seemingly repugnant sight of Jesus on a cross. Such a sight is appalling. His face was beaten. His naked body was covered in blood, which dripped down, staining the dusty ground beneath. His back was torn apart from a brutal flogging. His hands and feet were nailed to the timber with rusted iron. He would have pushed himself up against the nails to enable breath to flow into his straining lungs as he heaves for air. The crowds cried out in animalistic pleasure. His supporters were few and far between. The leaders of his nation mocked his so-called power. Aside from one notable exception (Mark 15:39), the Roman soldiers gambled for his clothes. Then, he breathed his last (Mark 15:37).

Whereas for the Jews and most of the world the cross is mere brutality that put an end to the messianic claims of this wannabe Messiah, for Paul, the battered and brutalized Son on the cross is glorious—the ultimate revelation of God. It is our salvation. It is our pattern for life whereby we take up a towel and cross and walk in the footsteps of the crucified Christ.

As we do, we participate in his sufferings, become like him in his death, but are at the same time empowered by resurrection power by whom we will journey onto everlasting life (Phil 3:10). Such suffering is a gift (Phil 1:29) that transforms believers to be more and more like Jesus (Rom 5:3–5). Through them, Jesus fills up suffering in his body (Col 1:24). Conversely, the circumcised penis is needless mutilation (Phil 3:2), akin to the bodily disfigurement done in the name of worship (see further 5:12). Perhaps it does help prevent persecution, but it severs us from Christ and grace (5:4). It renders the cross obsolete. And so, we may have 'gloriously' circumcised flesh, but we will go the way of all unredeemed flesh—destruction.

It is not merely the cross or the cross of Jesus; rather, Paul invokes the three-fold name of Jesus—'the cross of our Lord Jesus Christ.' Paul uses the three-fold name in key texts whether it be in his initial blessings,[39] summative declarations,[40] eschatological statements;[41] passionate appeals (Rom 15:30;1 Cor 1:10; Eph 5:10), blessings (2 Cor 1:3; Eph 1:3), prayers (Eph 1:17; 2 Thess 1:12; 2:16), thanksgivings (Col 1:3; 1 Thess 1:3), salutations (2 Thess 1:1), commands (2 Thess 3:6, 12; 1 Tim 6:3), and in farewell blessings.[42] The use of the full name adds authority, majesty, and solemnity. By making use of it here, despite Jesus dying on a cross, he remains not merely Jesus, but Israel's Messiah (Christ), and the Lord of the cosmos.

Noticeably as in another twenty-nine times in Paul,[43] it is *our* Lord Jesus Christ here—he is Lord and Christ for Paul, those with him, the Galatians, and all who name him so. While Jesus is Lord and Christ over everyone, including those who reject him who will ultimately bow to him as they face judgment (Phil 2:10–111), this is the language of inclusion and intimacy for those who *believe* he is so. That great day of bowing to God will be pure joy!

Galatians 6:14b draws out more meaning from the cross. 'Through whom' uses *dia* plus the genitive and so speaks agency, 'through, by.'[44] 'Whom' is the crucified Jesus. 'To me, the world has been crucified' uses *kosmos* (see 4:3).

Here, Paul is using *kosmos* in the sense of the peoples of the world in their fallenness and in enmity with God. This fallen world is peopled by people who in their sin are 'following the course of this world' (Eph 2:2).[45] Paul is being disciplined (1 Cor

---

39. See Rom 1:7; 1 Cor 1:3; 2 Cor 1:2; Gal 1:3; Eph 1:2; Phil 1:2; 1 Thess 1:1; 2 Thess 1:2; Phlm 3.
40. See Rom 5:11; 13:14; 15:6; 1 Cor 6:11; 8:6; 15:57; 2 Cor 8:9.
41. See 1 Cor 1:7, 8; Phil 2:11; 3:20; 1 Thess 5:9, 23; 2 Thess 2:1, 14; 1 Tim 6:14.
42. See Rom 16:20; 2 Cor 13:14; Gal 6:18; Eph 6:23–24; Phil 4:23; 1 Thess 5:28; 2 Thess 3:18; Phlm 25.
43. S.a., Rom 5:1, 11; 15:6, 30; 16:20; 1 Cor 1:2, 7, 8, 10; 15:57; 2 Cor 1:3; 8:9; Gal 6:18; Eph 1:3, 17; 5:20; 6:24; Col 1:3; 1 Thess 1:3; 5:9, 23, 28; 2 Thess 2:1, 14, 16; 2 Thess 3:6, 18; 1 Tim 6:3, 14.
44. BDAG 224.
45. On this sense of *kosmos* see also Matt 18:7; John 8:23; 12:31; 14:17, 27; 15:18–19; 17:16; Jas 1:27; 4:4; 2 Pet 1:4; 2:20; 1 John 2:15–17; 4:5; 5:4–5, 19.

11:32), so he might be set free from a world in the travail of sin along with the redeemed people of God (Rom 8:19–23).

Kosmos is also used in 4:3 of the *stoicheia* of the *world*—the elemental principles and powers of the world (cf. Col 2:8). These are those philosophical and religious ideologies and the spirits which empower them that fill the world. For the Jew, it is the Jewish religion with its enormous rituals, regulations, symbols, and interpretations of its sacred writings. For the pagan Galatians, it is their equally oppressive polytheistic and philosophical perspectives, empowered as they are by demons. Such fallen things of the world, in all their forms, are crucified to Paul. Indeed, Christ has died to the elemental powers of the world, and in Christ, so has Paul (Col 2:20).

We see Paul's outlook toward the things of the world in Philippians 3:3–11, where he speaks of his confidence in the flesh from the perspective of his Jewishness. If anyone deserves to be confident in their fleshly achievements, it is Paul. He is the quintessential Jew, an eighth-dayer where circumcision is concerned, from Israel and the esteemed tribe of Benjamin, blameless where the law is concerned, an honored Pharisee, even having persecuted the heretical Christian movement previously with a Phinehas-like zeal.

Yet for him, like Christ's determination not to exploit his absolute divinity to save a world, all such things are loss and dung (*skybala*, Phil 3:7–8). Only one thing now matters; that Christ has seized him. Now his only focus is the crucified and raised Christ—knowing him, gaining him, being found in him, believing in him for his righteousness, experiencing his power, sharing in his sufferings, and becoming like him in his death. Such a focus is it for Paul that 'to live is Christ' (Phil 1:21). Hence, the world and all its allurement are of no value, except that the world and its peoples be redeemed in Christ.

Like the man who found the pearl of great price and sold everything he had to buy it, Paul has found Jesus, or better, has been found by him. So, Paul has given up everything for him, for the world is dead to him, and he to the world in its hubris and false wisdom (cf. Matt 13:45–46). Or, like the man who found the treasure buried in the field (or better, en route to the Road to Damascus), Paul has given it all up to buy that field, and Christ is his all for all time (Matt 13:44). Even if Paul could gain the whole world, such gain is crucified to him (cf. Matt 16:26; Mark 8:36). He has chosen to hate his life in this world, and in Christ, he will keep it for eternal life (cf. John 12:25). He has been blinded and enlightened by the light of the world, and now walks in his light (cf. John 8:12). He is now determined to shine like a light in the world and inspire others to do the same (Phil 2:15). He has renounced the wisdom of this world for the wisdom of a crucified Messiah; a wisdom that shapes his whole life (1 Cor 1:20–2:12; 3:19), for this world is passing away in its present form (1 Cor 7:31). What matters for Paul are the things of the Lord and not those of the world (cf. 1 Cor 7:33–34).

This should not be misread as if Paul holds that the world has nothing good in it. He is speaking of the world in its fallen hostile-to-God sense. This world, at another level, is of supreme value. It is created by God through his Son and is being redeemed by God, again through his Son.[46] It will ultimately be liberated from its bondage to corruption (Rom 8:19–23), death defeated (1 Cor 15:26), things reconciled to God (Col 1:20) so that God is all in all (1 Cor 15:28). However, Paul is saying, the false systems of this fallen world are 'dead to me,' so to speak, and I to it.

This is profoundly challenging for us in a world that has many attractions and lures. As a lost young man in my late teens and twenties, I sought glory in sport. Deep down, it was significance I was after, honor. In a Kiwi culture at that time, achieving highly in rugby and/or cricket was the dream of many. Growing up with a dad who was a rugby and cricket man, I wanted fame through these sports. This did not satisfy my soul. Eventually, I heard God's gentle call and yielded my life to him. While many Christians glorify God in sport, one of the first things he challenged *me* to do was to give up my love of rugby and quest for honor.

After a time of wrestling with God over this, I acquiesced. He

---

46. See Rom 1:20; 8:19–23; 1 Cor 8:4–6; Eph 3:9; Col 1:15–16; 3:20; 1 Tim 4:3.

had a different plan for me, and that was to pursue him alone, learn his Word, and be one who speaks on his behalf. This still humbles me because, like Paul (1 Tim 1:13), I did not deserve this as I lived in sin. Thankfully, I gave up the sport and pursued his call. This is what it means to be a Christian. In Christ, the world is crucified to us and us to the world. Our first and only priority is Christ, his call, his direction. He could have directed me to stay in sport, as he sometimes asks of other Christians. If so, I would have done so, not for self-glory, but for him—to honor him with my effort, my character, and my determination. Further, to share him with those I played sport with, with godly attitudes, good deeds from love, and sharing Christ with wisdom and gracious conversation, seasoned with salt (Col 4:5). Christ cannot be in second place. Further, it is the crucified Christ who is our Lord. We glory in his love, humility, service, sacrifice, suffering, and death for us. We give praise every day that his bloody corpse now resurrected and scarred saves us. We seek to emulate him by seeking first him, his righteousness, and his kingdom. There is no other way to live.

WHAT MATTERS IS NOT CIRCUMCISION, BUT A NEW CREATION (6:15)

In *Galatians 6:15*, Paul sums up the meaning of the letter:

For (*gar*, 1:10) **neither**[47] (*oute*, 1:12) **circumcision** (*peritomē*, 2:7) **nor** (*oute*) **uncircumcision** (*akrobystia*, 2:7) **is** (present *eimi*, 1:7) **anything** (neuter *tis*, 1:7), **but** (*alla*, 1:1) **a new** (*kainos*)[48] **creation** (*ktisis*).[49]

---

47. **VARIANT:** Some witnesses read 'for in Christ Jesus there is neither (*en gar Christō Iēsou oute*) (see ℵ A C D F G K L P most minuscules itd, g vg syrh with * copsa, bo ethpp *al*). However, this is likely a scribal adjustment based on 5:6. The shorter and more difficult reading has good early support and is to be preferred (P46 B Ψ 33 1175 1611 1739 1908 2005 itr syrh txt, pal goth arm ethro *al*). See Metzger, *Textual Commentary*, 530) who gives it an {A} rating to excluding these words.

48. The adjective καινός (*kainos*), 'new' is used once in Gal 6:15 of a '*new* creation,' which is what matters in comparison with the state of circumcision or uncircumcision, which are of no consequence. Paul uses it seven times overall.

49. The noun κτίσις (*ktisis*), 'creation,' refers to the created order and particularly this

Gar is loosely continuative rather than causal, Paul continuing to expound on why they should repudiate circumcision. *Oute* (see 1:12) being repeated gives a 'neither … nor' construction (cf. *eite … eite*, 'either … or').

As discussed concerning 5:6, this verse has many of the same components as 1 Cor 7:19 and Gal 5:6 in that the three verses contrast circumcision and uncircumcision with new life. In 1 Cor 7:19, what matters is keeping God's commandments—not the Torah, but the law of faith and the virtues of the gospel, especially love (1 Cor 13).

In Gal 5:6, circumcision and uncircumcision produce nothing. What produces something of value is faith working itself out as love. Here, what matters is a new creation, not the state of a man's penis. We get a sense of what a new creation is for Paul; someone who lives by faith outworking as love.

Both Galatians' verses use the postpositive *gar*, merely by way of introduction. 'In Christ' is only mentioned in 5:6, but it can be assumed in 6:15. The construction 'neither circumcision … nor uncircumcision' is repeated, as is a strong contrasting conjunction *alla*, but. The verbs differ with 5:6 making the point that the state of one's foreskin *produces* nothing, whereas 6:15 avers that it *is* nothing. So then, this speaks of what is produced by a person's state with regard to circumcision, whereas 6:15 speaks of what it actually is, its ontology—it is nothing. The concluding clauses differ. In 6:16, Paul pronounces a blessing on all who follow a rule. The double use of 'neither circumcision nor uncircumcision is anything' suggests that this is the rule. Further, 'faith through love working and 'a new creation' are understandably linked. The new creation is being produced by God through the lives of believers imbued with the Spirit and overflowing with love.

Circumcision is *peritomē* and uncircumcision *akrobystia* (see on 2:7), and they here speak of the physical state of being circumcised or not—the removal of the foreskin of the penis.

world. It is used once in Galatians 6:15, a 'new creation.' Overall, Paul uses it eleven times, particularly in Romans (seven times).

Paul here states that these states are nothing ('not anything,' neuter *tis*). This comes as a little bit of a surprise in a letter where Paul has repudiated the thought that the Galatians should be circumcised by the Judaizers. If so, why write the letter at all? Yet with closer thought, Paul's thinking is coherent.

What he is saying is at an actual level, when it comes down to it, circumcision matters not. It is nothing. It is merely the removal of a small piece of skin, not unlike a haircut or cutting one's nails. It yields nothing. It brings a person no closer to God.

For the Judaizers and Jews, however, such a comment is anathema. For them, circumcision is utterly critical. A son of a faithful Jew, and for the Judaizers, a Christian, must be circumcised on the eighth day. A convert to Judaism or Judaizing Christianity must be circumcised. This is *the sign* of covenantal inclusion. Because they place so much emphasis on it and tie it to salvation and inclusion, Paul must repudiate the circumcision they advocate and demand that the new gentile Galatian converts not be circumcised. If they do, they yield not just to a small medical procedure, but they yield to circumcision as a condition of salvation and inclusion. Because of the close link of circumcision to the whole Torah, they put themselves in a place where they must do the whole law to be justified (5:3). This is implausible as it has been for Jews and all people since the law was given at Sinai. Only faith justifies and includes.

So, to concede to the Judaizers throws them into the Jewish system. This system has saved no one and never will. It is God who reaches out with grace and saves where he finds salvation faith. As such, while circumcision at one level is as meaningless as picking one's nose, to be circumcised as these Judaizers want, rips them out of Christ and grace (5:4). It severs them from dependence on Christ and being in Christ is the only way to be justified before God. So, it is not circumcision itself that is the issue, but the soteriological and ecclesiological significance they put on it that is the problem.

Understanding Paul's thought here is critical as we consider circumcision today. Although there may be such Judaizers going around the church somewhere in the world today of which I am not aware, there are no such people demanding Christians be circumcised. As such, in cultures like the Pacific Island cultures, where circumcision has become part and parcel of their lives, being circumcised is neither here nor there. It matters not. Today, other than among pious Jews who link circumcision to covenant inclusion, it really is a medical procedure that is neither here nor there. My dad was circumcised as was expected when he was a kid. I am not. It says nothing about our status before God.

What matters is spelled out in the final clause: 'but (*alla*) a new (*kainos*) creation (*ktisis*).' Whereas in 5:6 it is faith working in love, here, it is a new creation. The conjunction *alla*, as always in Galatians, introduces a strong contrast (see 1:1). New is *kainos*, one of two Greek terms for 'new,' the other being *neos*. Behm suggests *neos* in Classical Greek signifies 'what was not there before,' 'what has only just arisen or appeared.'[50] *Neos* then is what is new in time and origin, young. *Kainos*, on the other hand, tends to refer to 'what is new and distinctive' in comparison with other things.[51] It refers to something 'new in nature, different from the usual, impressive, better than the old, superior in value or attraction.'[52] As with most of these classical distinctions, by the time of the NT, such nuances are not always found. Yet, here, Behm's comment fits, Paul speaking of a new creation not as something completely new, but as the transformation of people and the cosmos.

Kainos in the NT, aside from Paul, is used of new wineskins (Matt 9:17; Mark 2:21, 22) or wine (Matt 26:29; Mark 14:25; Luke 5:38), a new garment (Luke 5:36), new teaching,[53] a new tomb (Matt 27:60; John 19:41), a new covenant (Luke 22:20; Heb 8:8, 13; 9:15), a new commandment of love,[54] a new heaven and a new earth (2 Pet 3:13; Rev 21:1), a new name (Rev 2:17; 3:12), a new Jerusalem (Rev 3:12; 21:2, 5), and a new song (Rev 5:9; 14:3).[55]

50. J. Behm, 'καινός,' in *TDNT* 3:447.
51. Behm, 'καινός,' 447.
52. Behm, 'καινός,' 447.
53. See Matt 13:52; Mark 1:27; Acts 17:19, 21.
54. See John 13:34; 1 John 2:7, 8; 2 John 5.

Paul uses *kainos* sparingly (seven times) including to describe a covenant as *new* (1 Cor 11:25; 2 Cor 3:6), a *new* person (the faithful) (Eph 2:15), and a new person (individual) (Eph 4:24). This latter use in Ephesians is another way of expressing a 'new creation.'

Outside of Paul, *ktisis* is used eleven times of creation,[56] created beings (esp. humans) (Heb 4:13), and divinely created authorities (1 Pet 2:13). Paul's use includes the creation of the world in which God can be clearly perceived (Rom 1:20); created beings who are falsely worshiped (Rom 1:25); the whole created order which is subject to futility and yearning for a freedom that will come at the realization of this age (Rom 8:19–22), from which nothing can separate a believer from God's love (Rom 8:39), over which Christ is supreme (Col 1:15), and to which Christ has been 'proclaimed' to all creation in his coming (Col 1:23).

Twice Paul speaks of a 'new creation,' the other occurrence being 2 Cor 5:17: 'therefore, if anyone is in Christ, [he/she] is a new *creation*. The old has passed away, behold, the new has come.' He also employs the verb *ktizō* to the Ephesian Christians in Eph 2:10.[57] The Ephesians are saved by grace through faith and are 'God's handiwork, created (*ktizō*) in Christ Jesus for good works which God prepared beforehand so that they might walk in them.' Similarly, in Eph 4:24, believers are to put on the new person, 'created according to God in righteousness and truthful holiness.' Ephesians 4:24 gives much detail to what Paul is speaking of in Eph 2:10—lives shaped by a godly and

---

55. The associated verb *ktizō*, 'create,' is found in Matt 19:4 (created male and female at the beginning of creation); Mark 13:19 (the beginning of the creation that God has continued to create to the present); Rev 4:11 (God created all things); and Rev 10:6 (God created heaven and what is in it). *Ktisma*, 'that which is created' is used in Jas 1:18 (created beings). *Ktizō* is also found in Rev 5:13 and 8:9 of living creatures whether in heaven or earth. *Ktistēs* is used once in 1 Pet 4:19 of God being a 'faithful creator.'

56. See Mark 10:6; 13:19; Heb 9:11; 2 Pet 3:4; Rev 3:14.

57. He also uses the verb *ktizō* of God as the creator—who alone should be worshiped (Rom 1:25), God's creation of man and woman (1 Cor 11:9), the creation of one people, Jew and gentile (Eph 2:15), the creation of all things (Eph 3:9) by Christ (Col 1:16), and food God created (1 Tim 4:3). See also *ktisma*; 'that which is created,' used in 1 Tim 4:4 of all things made by God.

christological ethic that utterly repudiates the false works of the age (Eph 4:17–6:10).

Similarly, in Col 3:10, believers are to 'take off the old self with its practices and put on the new self that is being renewed in knowledge in accordance with the image of the one who *created* it.' As with 6:15 and 2 Cor 5:17, Paul sees believers as new creations through the work of the Spirit. Their purpose is clear here, to do the works God in his providence has prepared for them, to repudiate false works of the flesh, and to live a life of ethical righteousness.

Here, as in these texts, Paul speaks of the renewal of the person who is in Christ. They are recreated by God by the power of the Spirit. First, this is a spiritual and internal renewal of the heart whereby God pours his Spirit into the person and begins the work of transformation, spiritual healing, and restoration. Sealed with the Spirit and imbued with God's love and power, they put to death the deeds of the flesh and are formed to be more and more like Christ bearing the fruit of the Spirit (5:16–26).

Second, this Spirit-work is completed at the Consummation, at which point the whole person dies and rises fully renewed and animated with nothing of sin and its consequences left. This includes full bodily renewal (esp. 1 Cor 15:35–58). The renewal of the individual believer is one central aspect of the transformation of a harvest of such people and the renewal of the world itself (Rom 8:19–23).

From the other Pauline texts discussed above, he also has in mind a transformation of attitudes, behavior, and speech. They are to renounce the works of the flesh. They are to live their lives yielded to the Spirit, shaped by his impulse, and bearing the fruit of the Spirit. They are to be the new creations God is forming them into.

Although there may be some health benefits from circumcision, there are also risks and certainly, from a theological point of view, it changes nothing. The Judaizers then should shift their focus from whether a person is circumcised or not to whether they are being formed in Christ. This calls to mind Paul's earlier motherly concern for the Galatians for whom he is again in the pains of childbirth until Christ is formed in them (4:19–20). This should be their focus.

WALK BY THE RULE OF THE GOSPEL, PEACE AND MERCY ON ALL BELIEVERS (6:16)

In *Galatians 6:16*, Paul pronounces a blessing on those who accept the 'rule' of the gospel summed up in the previous verse:

And (*kai*, 1:1) **as many as** (plural *hosos*, 3:10) **will keep in step** (future plural *stoicheō*, 5:25) **with this** (dative[58] neuter *houtos*, 2:10) **rule** (*kanōn*),[59] **peace** (*eirēnē*, 1:3) **and** (*kai*) **mercy** (*eleos*)[60] **upon** (*epi*, 3:13) **the** (accusative *ho*, 1:1) **Israel** (*Israēl*)[61] **of God** (genitive *Theos*, 1:1).

While *kai*, 'and' connects Paul's thought to the previous verse, the first part of the verse is a little unclear. He speaks of those who 'keep in step' with 'this rule.' 'Keep in step' is *stoicheō*, discussed fully on 5:25, of those who follow or keep in step with the Spirit. It is a military motif speaking of being careful to follow the rule of the Spirit and not deviate (like a soldier in rank following those ahead). Here, it is a *kanōn* that they must follow. *Kanōn* became a very important term in the later church

---

58. The dative phrase τῷ κανόνι τούτῳ (*tō kanoni toutō*, this rule) is a dative of rule whereby '[t]he dative substantive specifies the rule or code a person follows or the standard of conduct to which he or she conforms. This usage is rare.' (See Wallace, *Greek Grammar*, 157).

59. The noun κανών (*kanōn*), meaning 'rule,' 'standard,' and from which we get the English canon, is used once in Galatians 6:16. Here, it refers to the previous verse whereby Paul has stated that circumcision and uncircumcision mean nothing, but what counts is a new creation. Those who hold to this standard are blessed by Paul. Elsewhere in the NT, it is used only by Paul in 2 Cor 10 of his assignment or area of influence (2 Cor 10:13, 15, 16). The later meaning of a 'rule of faith' is not relevant to the NT uses.

60. The noun ἔλεος (*eleos*), 'mercy' is used once in Gal 6:16. Paul uses it ten times overall, always of God's mercy.

61. There is one use of the noun Ἰσραὴλ (*Israēl*) in Galatians 6:16: 'the *Israel* of God.' This is either those who are living in Christ (a renewed Israel continuous with Israel by faith before Christ), or physical Israel. Like 'all Israel will be saved' in Rom 11:26, this is fiercely debated. Paul's other uses include: 1) Physical Israel (Rom 9:6i, 27, 31; 10:19, 21; 11:2, 7, 25; 1 Cor 10:18; 2 Cor 3:7, 13; Eph 2:12; Phil 3:5); 2) Israel by faith (Rom 9:6ii); 11:26. The final category is disputed by the majority of scholars. See the commentary for further discussion.

as it grappled with true and false teaching. So, we speak of the canon of Scripture or the rule of the church—its canons.

In wider Greek use, *kanōn* is formed from the basic meaning 'a reed.' This elides into a measuring reed, rod, or staff. It is used of sticks that helped stretch the edge of a shield, the beam of a weaver, scales, architectural measures, plumb lines, lists, and tables. It was also used of a norm or the norm, as in the perfect form to be sought or an infallible criterion by which something is measured. So, in sculpture, Polycletus is regarded as the perfect human form.[62] Such norms are found in Greek music (the monochord), in writing (a canon of writers), justice (the law), and philosophy, especially for the Epicureans where logic and method were canonized. Epictetus sees the role of philosophy as finding 'the canon, the rule of the knowledge of what is true as distinct from mere appearances' (*Diatr.* 2.11).[63] He writes:

The beginning of philosophy is this: the being sensible of the disagreement of men with each other; an inquiry into the cause of this disagreement; and a disapprobation and distrust of what merely seems; a careful examination into what seems, whether it seem rightly; and the discovery of some rule (*kanōn*) which shall serve like a balance, for the determination of weights; like a square, for distinguishing straight and crooked. This is the beginning of philosophy (Epictetus, *Diatr.* 2.11.12–13). [64]

Kanōn is not used widely in Jewish Greek sources. In accordance with its etymological origin is used of a reed basket (Exod 29:32), a reed bedpost (Jdt 13:6), and a rod (Mic 7:4). It is used for creation being formed according to God's *standard* (T. Naph. 2:3). In 4 Macc 7:21, it is used in a Greek philosophical sense of the 'whole rule of philosophy,' by which one is ideally governed (s.a. Let. Aris. 2).

Josephus uses it of Josiah who lived according to the standards of David (*Ant.* 10.38). Josiah's reform was based on the

62. H. W. Beyer, 'κανών,' in *TDNT* 3:596–58.
63. Beyer, 'κανών,' 596–58.
64. Epictetus, *The Works of Epictetus: His Discourses, in Four Books, the Enchiridion, and Fragments*, ed. Thomas Wentworth Higginson (Medford, MA: Thomas Nelson and Sons, 1890), 1147. Also, see Beyer, 'κανών,' 3:598.

rediscovery of the law, and as such, it is likely that this speaks of the law as standard—a meaning he uses elsewhere (*Ag. Ap.* 2.174). Philo employs it most often among Jewish Greek writers in a diverse range of ways. In each case, it is of an external standard or rule for life or an aspect of it. These include God's sovereignty and goodness as rules for all (*Sacr.* 59), the Scriptures which contain the canons of absolute truth (*Conf.* 2), the second half of the Decalogue as rules concerning sin (*Her.* 173), teaching, nature, and practice as three rules for wisdom (*Mos.* 1.76), the law as standards for life (*Virt.* 70), God as the standard of nobility and virtue (*Virt.* 219), and 'love of God, love of virtue, love of people' as three standards for goodness (*Prob.* 83). Dominant here is the law as a *kanōn* for life.[65] The use of the term by Josephus and Philo of the law as canon may indicate that the Judaizers employed the term of the law, arguing that it is the *kanōn* of the Christian life, as it is for the Jew.

However, Paul here chooses another path. Some limit the rule to the immediately preceding clause, 'a new creation.'[66] However, as Longenecker rightly says, in context, *kanōn* is better interpreted as the whole preceding statement.[67] Yet, due to the repetition of 5:6 concerning the nothingness of circumcision and uncircumcision, the rule would most naturally refer to the statement that circumcision and uncircumcision are nothing as are its consequences (especially in light of 1 Cor 7:19 as well). Conversely, it would refer to what does matter—faith working through love and a new creation. What matters is a new creation,

---

65. Philo's other uses include the rule of truth (*Leg.* 3.233; *Det.* 125; *Ios.* 145), the musical scale (rules) (*Post.* 104), an oracle that stands as a true rule (Deut 5:31, *Gig.* 49), right standards (*Agr.* 130), standards of measurement (*Ebr.* 185), the rule of proportion (*Her.* 154, 160; *Aet.* 116), the standard of right discipline (*Fug.* 152), the rules of allegory (*Somn.* 1.73; *Spec.* 1.287), rules for civic life (*Decal.* 14), legal testimonies as rules for deciding cases (*Decal.* 140), standards of justice (*Spec.* 3.137, 164; *Aet.* 108), a correct ruler (*Post.* 28), and rules of right instruction (*Spec.* 4.115).

66. Moo, *Galatians*, 399; Bruce, *Galatians*, 273.

67. Longenecker, *Galatians*, 297. Dunn, *Galatians*, 343 suggests that this is about ethnic and ritual distinction. This limits the thought merely to horizontal cultural relations. While this is clearly part of Paul's concern, his canvass is wider.

faith, and this faith working out as love. Or what matters is yielding to the commands of God in the new covenant.

Hence, the rule or standard of the Christian life is not circumcision or Jewish legal requirements but living faith and the power of the Spirit who is forming Christ in us. This then becomes another way of saying that the Galatians are to 'walk in the Spirit,' 'be led by the Spirit,' 'live by the Spirit,' 'keep in step with the Spirit,' and 'sow to the Spirit' (5:16, 18, 25; 6:8). It is by the Spirit that they are formed into a new creation (2 Cor 5:17), and by the Spirit that they repudiate the works of the flesh, their lusts, and false desires. It is the rule of the Spirit that counts. Implicit are the nine virtues in the fruits of the Spirit as *kanōn*.

Upon those who live this way, Paul pronounces a blessing. Literally, v. 16b reads: 'peace upon them and mercy also upon the Israel of God.' The grammar of the verse is tricky. It can be read: 'peace and mercy to all who follow this rule, *even* to the Israel of God' (with the second *kai* as epexegetic).[68] Second, *kai* can be conjunctive, and the clause refers to a separate second group, 'And as for all who walk by this rule, peace and mercy be upon them, *and* upon the Israel of God' (ESV), or 'May peace come to all those who follow this standard, and mercy [*also*] to the Israel of God' (HCSB).[69]

Both renderings are grammatically plausible, and interpretation affects the greatly disputed 'Israel of God.' Is Paul here speaking in some way of Israel by descent, physical Israel? Or another Jewish group, e.g., Jewish Christians or Jewish people from all time who will be saved (epexegetic *kai*).[70] Or, is he talking about Israel as the renewed covenant people of God in Christ, the church? (conjunctive *kai*).

---

68. See Moo, *Galatians*, 400. Or, the *kai* is, as BDAG 495 puts it, explicative: 'a word or clause is connected by means of και w. another word or clause, for the purpose of explaining what goes before.'

69. Moo, *Galatians*, 400.

70. Some take this as Jewish Christians, e.g., G. Schrenk, 'Der Segenwunsch nach der Kampfepistel,' *Judaica* 6 (1950): 170–190; D. W. B. Robinson, 'Distinction Between Jewish and Gentile Believers in Galatians,' *ABR* 13 (1965): 29–48; Betz, *Galatians*, 322–33. Similarly, Bruce, *Galatians*, 274–75 suggests this is Israel destined for salvation, which is effectively the same as Betz.

It is important to begin with a discussion of the use of the term 'Israel.' The term features over 2700 times in the LXX. The first meaning is found in the origin of its name, Israel ('strive with God') given to Jacob by God as a new name. The second and dominant use of the term, overwhelmingly so, is of the people of Israel in some form or another.[71] These are the physical descendants of Israel and so Abraham, his grandfather. They have the right to belong by birth and by circumcision for a male. However, a person could be cut off for legal failure (Exod 12:15; Num 19:13; Deut 17:12). A third use of the term is of the northern tribes that split away, as opposed to Judah of the two southern tribes, including Benjamin. The fourth aspect of the names is for the land. This begins to feature more after the Conquest. So, as they entered the land, Israel, it was used of the land as a nation. So 'in Israel' is found 102 times in the ESV OT and twelve in the NRSV Apocrypha. However, in these texts it can equally mean 'in the land of Israel' or 'in/among the people of Israel.'[72] Other spatial geographical indicators showing its use of the land can be found.[73] Yet, in many of these cases, it is the land in which the people of Israel dwell. Overall, then, Israel is a people term. So, much in the same way, many confuse the idea of

---

71. An analysis of the ESV OT and NRSV Apocrypha notes that: men/sons/people/ children/of Israel is used, 710 times and twenty-seven times in the Apocrypha; Israelites thirty-eight times OT, seventeen times Apocrypha; 'tribes of Israel' forty–seven times OT, four times Apocrypha; 'God/Lord of Israel', 202 times OT, thirty times Apocrypha; 'all Israel,' 152 times, fifteen times Apocrypha; 'my people Israel,' thirty-seven times OT, once Apocrypha; 'congregation of Israel' twelve times OT, once Apocrypha; 'families of Israel,' four times OT, once in the Apocrypha; 'over Israel,' sixty–two times OT, once Apocrypha; 'O Israel,' thirty-nine times OT, eight times Apocrypha; 'offspring of Israel,' five times OT.

72. E.g., Num 18:14, 21; Josh 6:25; Judg 5:11; 6:4; 17:6; 20:6; Judg 21:25; Ruth 4:7, 14; 1 Sam 3:11; 9:9, 20; 13:13; 17:46; 26:15; 1 Kings 18:36, etc.

73. For example, 'the hill country of Israel' (s.a., Josh 11:21, cf. Josh 11:22), the valley of Israel (LXX; John 17:16), the territory of Israel (Judg 19:29; 1 Sam 11:3, 7; 2 Kings 10:32; 1 Chron 21:12), the cities of Israel (1 Sam 18:6; 1 Kings 15:20; 2 Kings 13:25), the borders of Israel (1 Sam 27:1), the waters of Israel (2 Sam 5:12), the land of Israel (2 Chron 34:7; Tob 1:4), Israel is the Lord's portion from every nation (Sir 17:17), the sanctuaries of Israel (Amos 7:9), and the border of Israel (Mal 1:5).

a church with a location or building, its dominant designation is of a people—the descendants of Israel, the grandson of Abraham.

In Pseudepigraphal use (156 times), again, we have the nuance of Israel the person, Jacob.[74] There are many references to Israel the people.[75] There are a few mentions of Israel as the northern kingdom in contrast to Judah, i.e., its people and land.[76] Israel blessed (Pss. Sol. 8:34). 'In Israel' is also found to refer to the people in the land.[77] Other references which could speak of Israel the land include 'against Israel,' i.e., the land and people (T. Iss. 5:8), the end of Israel (Liv. Proph. 15:4), throughout Israel (T. Dan 6:6, 7), upon Israel (Pss. Sol. 5:18), the synagogues of Israel (Pss. Sol. 10:7), and the land (T. Levi. 5:2; T. Jud. 25:5 S.a. Pss. Sol. 11:6, 7, 8, 9). Sometimes both are in mind with the people and land fused.[78] Josephus only uses Israel once of the people (Josephus, *Ant.* 4.180). Philo's use is more extensive but dominated by Jacob who became Israel,[79] speculation on the name 'Israel,' 'he who sees God,'[80] and especially of Israel the people.[81]

74. See T. Levi 14:2; T. Jos. 1:2; Jos. Asen. 8:10; 22:3; 25:5; 28:13.

75. E.g., Sib. Or. 1:360; 4 Ezra 5:35; T. Levi 10:2; 15:67; 17:5; 18:9; T. Jud. 21:5; T. Dan 5:4, 13; 6:4, 5; T. Naph. 7:1; T. Benj. 10:8, 10; T. Sol. 13:7; 15:14; 25:5, 6, 7; Mart. Ascen. Isa. 2:10; Jos. Asen. 23:13; Liv. Proph. 3:2, 13, 14; 4 Bar. 1:1; 6:16; 4 Bar. 9:30; Pss. Sol. 10:5, 6; 17:45; 18:1, 3). Other uses indicate a people including all of Israel (T. Reu. 6:8; T. Jos. 2:5; T. Benj. 10:11), Israel in contrast to Judah, the northern people (T. Reu. 6:11), the tribe of Israel (T. Sim. 7:2), the seed of Israel (T. Levi 4:3), the race of Israel (T. Levi 5:6, 7; T. Dan 7:13; T. Naph. 8:3; Pss. Sol 7:8), the twelve staffs of Israel (T. Naph. 5:8), the twelve tribes (T. Ab. (A) 13:6), the exile of Israel (Pss. Sol. 9:1), the Holy One of Israel, the people (T. Dan 5:13; T. Sol. 4:12), the God of Israel (T. Jos. 2:2; T. Sol. 1:13; 12:1; 13:7; 15:15; Jos. Asen. 7:5; 25:7; 4 Bar. 6:23; Pss. Sol. 4:1; 9:8; 11:1; 16:3; 18:5), the dispersion of Israel (Pss. Sol. 8:28; 9:2), the household of Israel (Pss. Sol. 9:11; 10:8; 17:42), and his servant Israel (Pss. Sol. 12:6).

76. See Mart. Ascen. Isa. 2:6, 12; 3:7, 10; Liv. Proph. 20:1.

77. See e.g., T. Reu. 1:10; T. Sim. 6:2, 5; T. Levi 6:3; 7:3; 8:16; 10:3; T. Jud. 12:8; 17:5; 22:1; 25:1; T. Zeb. 4:12; 9:5; T. Dan 1:9; T. Naph. 8:1; T. Gad 2:5; T. Jos. 18:4; Pss. Sol. 8:26.

78. Redeem Israel, people, and land (T. Levi 2:10). The salvation of Israel, similarly (T. Jud. 22:2; T. Naph. 8:2; T. Gad 8:1; T. Ash. 7:3; T. Benj. 3:8; 11:2). Peace of Israel (T. Dan 6:2). King over Israel (Pss. Sol. 17:4, 21, 42). S.a., Pss. Sol. 14:5; 17:44.

79. Jacob: *Leg.* 3.15; *Sacr.* 119; *Post.* 63; *Deus.* 121; *Ebr.* 82; *Migr.* 39; 201; *Her.* 78; *Mut.* 81, 83; *Somn.* 1.172; 2.173.

80. *Congr.* 51; *Fug.* 208; *Mut.* 81; *Somn.* 1.114, 129, 171; *Abr.* 57; *Praem.* 44; *Legat.* 4.

81. *Leg.* 2.34, 77; 3.133, 186, 212, 214; *Sac.* 118, 120, 134; *Det.* 67, 94; *Post.* 54, 89; 158; *Deus.* 144, 145; *Plant.* 59, 63; *Ebr.* 77; *Conf.* 36, 56, 72, 92, 93; *Conf.* 146, 148; *Migr.* 15,

Overwhelmingly, Israel in the OT and other Jewish Greek writings refers to a people. Only at times does it refer to the land.

In the non-Pauline NT, Israel is used of a people in most occasions whether it is God's people Israel,[82] the house of Israel,[83] the twelve tribes of Israel (Matt 19:28; 22:30; Rev 21:12), to Israel (John 1:31), a teacher of Israel (its people) (John 3:10), O Israel (Matt 12:29), his Servant Israel (Luke 1:54), the men of Israel (Acts 13:16), the God of Israel, i.e., worshiped by its people (Matt 15:31; Luke 1:68), the consolation of Israel (Luke 2:25), Israelites (Acts 2:22; 3:12; 5:35; 7:23; 21:28), elders of Israel (Acts 5:21), or repentance to Israel (Acts 5:31).

It can have a geographical sense of the land of Israel (Matt 2:20, 21), in Israel—its land and its people (Matt 8:10; 9:33; Luke 2:24; 4:25, 27; 7:9), Jesus appearing publicly in Israel (Luke 1:80), and the towns of Israel (Matt 10:23).

Some uses are ambiguous, such as King of Israel, which can mean the rule of its people and/or its land (Matt 27:42; Mark 15:32; John 1:49; 12:13). Similarly, a savior to Israel (Acts 13:23), the hope of Israel (Acts 28:20), to 'redeem Israel,' i.e., for the disciples, its land and people (Luke 24:21), or 'restore the kingdom to Israel' (Acts 2:22). The dominant use is of a people, but it is more often used of the land in the NT outside of Paul.

Like Philo, Paul never speaks of Israel as the land. Rather, he uses Israel of a people. Sometimes, this is general; *all Israelites*, the physical descendants of Abraham, Isaac, and Jacob/Isaac.[84] He is one of these people (Rom 11:1; 2 Cor 11:22; Phil 3:5). In Rom 9:6–7 we see him nuance Israel: 'For not all *those from Israel* are *Israel*, and not all are children of Abraham because they are his offspring, but "Through Isaac shall your offspring be named." The first use is in accordance with the use in Rom

---

54, 113, 125, 224; *Her.* 113, 117, 124, 279; *Cong.* 86; *Fug.* 208; *Mut.* 207; *Somn.* 1.89, 117; 2.44, 271, 280. See also the tribes of Israel (*Leg.* 2.94), the generations of Israel (*Post.* 92), the elders of Israel (*Sobr.* 19; *Migr.* 168), the house of Israel (*Somn.* 2.172), and the God of Israel (*Leg.* 3.11; *Somn.* 1.62; 2.222).

82. See Matt 2:6; 27:9; Luke 1:16; 2:32; Acts 4:10, 27; 9:15; 10:36; 13:17, 24; Rev 2:14; 7:4.

83. See Matt 10:6; 15:24; Acts 2:36; 7:42; Heb 8:8, 10.

84. See Rom 9:4, s.a. 1 Cor 10:18; 2 Cor 3:7, 13; Eph 2:12.

9:4 and other texts mentioned above. He argues that history has always shown that the children of Abraham are not all his offspring; rather, only those in the line of election through Isaac and Jacob (Rom 9:8–23). Now, the prophecies of Hos 2:23 and Isa 10:22 are being fulfilled in a remnant of Israel that is true Israel; that is, a remnant of grace and faith. Romans 4 defines this Israel, Israel of faith which is now Israel who have believed in Jesus Christ (Rom 9:30–33). This can be called 'true Israel.' So, in Rom 9:27, while there are as many Israelites as sand in the sea (Israel by descent), only a remnant will be saved, i.e., those of faith, the 'true' Israel referred to in 9:6ii.

In Rom 11:2–5, he refers again to Israel with 'true' Israel, at the time of Elijah, the 7000 who did not yield to Ba'al. This indicates that Paul thinks of Israel in two senses in the period before Christ: 1) Those who are born into Israel, Israelites by descent; 2) True Israel which is by faith. The latter includes all Jewish people who have a saving faith in Yahweh, as did Abraham. This has been argued in Gal 3:8–29. This 'Israel' includes all faithful Jews. It also includes gentiles who, like Abraham—an uncircumcised Aramaean gentile—had a faith that is credited as righteousness prior to the coming of Christ and the proclamation of the gospel.

Now that Christ has come and his gospel has been proclaimed (Rom 10:14–21), there is a remnant of Israel who is true Israel. These are Israelite believers like Paul, Peter, John, Jacob, Barnabas, the Jewish brothers and sisters with Paul in Antioch, any Jewish believers in Galatia (all mentioned in Galatians), and all other Jewish believers in all places who believe in Jesus with a saving faith.

True Israel also includes those gentiles like Titus and the gentile believers of Antioch and Galatia. Those of Israel who pursued law for righteousness did not achieve their goal, for righteousness cannot be gained by law-observance (Rom 9:31). In Rom 10:19, 21; 11:7, 11, Israel is nuanced in a third way to include not all Jews (for some have accepted Christ), but those Jews who reject Christ. In Rom 11:25, as in Rom 9:4 and 6i, they are Israelites. However, a portion of them is hardened, i.e., they reject the gospel (Rom 11:25).

In Rom 11:26, although some claim this is ethnic Israel, this is better understood as the Israel of faith referred to in 9:6ii, the true children of Abraham (cf. Gal 3; Rom 4), who include all of Israel by faith and all gentiles grafted into the Olive Tree that is Israel (Rom 11:17–24). The discussion of Paul's use of Israel makes it plain that he is speaking of Israel as a people. The question is which people of Israel is Paul referring to here? Israel by descent? Israel by faith?

In favor of Israel by descent (or another strictly Jewish group such as Jewish Christians) are these arguments.[85] First, as discussed, Paul uses *Israēl* at times for the people of Israel or those Jews who are not believers. Hence, it is certainly a reasonable interpretation.

Second, the grammar of the verse suggests Paul moves from a blessing on those who follow the rule he has outlined, which can be argued to be all genuine Christians, to another group. Which group? If the first group is the church, then this can be argued to be something different. Israel by descent or Israel who rejects Christ makes sense.

Third, the use of mercy (*eleos*) here can be argued to support this interpretation. *Eleos* speaks of 'kindness or concern expressed for someone in need, mercy, compassion, pity, clemency.'[86] *Eleos* is used in the NT of God desiring mercy toward those in need rather than sacrifice (Matt 9:13; 12:7) and mercy is one of the weightier matters of the law (Matt 23:23). Mercy toward others as a virtue is endorsed by Christ as in the Good Samaritan (Luke 10:37). Other NT writers also endorse it (Jas 2:13; 3:17). It is at times used of God's mercy toward those who fear him (Luke 1:50), toward Israel (Luke 1:54, 72, 78), toward individuals (Luke 1:58), in times of need (Heb 4:16), toward people through Christ (1 Pet 1:3; Jude 21), and as a blessing (2 John 3; Jude 2). In Paul, it used of God's action toward his elect (Rom 8:23), toward gentile believers (Rom 15:9), on all Christians (Eph 2:4; Tit 3:5), and pronounced as a blessing or in prayer

---

85. W. D. Davies, 'Paul and the People of Israel,' *NTS* 24 (1977/78): 4–39.
86. BDAG 316.

(1 Tim 1:2; 2 Tim 1:2; 2 Tim 1:16; 2 Tim 1:18). In Rom 11:28–32 Paul uses mercy of disobedient Israel:

As regards the gospel, they are enemies for your [the believing gentile Romans] sake. But as regards election, they [rejecting Israel] are beloved for the sake of their forefathers. For the gifts and the calling of God are irrevocable. For just as you [the believing gentile Romans] were at one time disobedient to God but now have received mercy because of their [rejecting Israel] disobedience, so they [rejecting Israel] too have now been disobedient in order that by the mercy shown to you [the believing gentile Romans] they [rejecting Israel] also may now receive mercy. For God has consigned all to disobedience, that he may have mercy on all.

In light of all this, it is conceivable that Paul is saying something similar here, praying for God's mercy toward disobedient Israel.

Fourth, the 'Israel of God' could have in mind the kind of thinking seen in Rom 11:29: 'For the gifts and the calling of God are irrevocable' and in other texts where Paul speaks of the privileges of Israel. So, in Rom 3:2, Israel has been entrusted with the oracles of God. In Rom 9:1–5, to them belong the adoption, the glory, the covenant, the giving of the law, the worship, the promises, the patriarchs, and Christ. They remain 'of God' even if they are rejecting him. Similarly, in Rom 11:2, God has not rejected his people—whom he foreknew. Paul here is praying that their blindness and hardness will be removed, and they will experience the mercy of God.

The alternative interpretation that Israel here is the covenant people of God by faith can also be argued and is the dominant view in biblical scholarship.[87] First, as discussed of Paul's use of

---

87. In the mid-second century Justin Martyr, *Dial.* 11 takes this view: 'If, therefore, God proclaimed a new covenant which was to be instituted, and this for a light of the nations, we see and are persuaded that men approach God, leaving their idols and other unrighteousness, through the name of Him who was crucified, Jesus Christ, and abide by their confession even unto death, and maintain piety. Moreover, by the works and by the attendant miracles, it is possible for all to understand that He is the new law, and the new covenant, and the expectation of those who out of every people wait for the good things of God. For the true spiritual Israel, and descendants of

Israēl he at times uses it of 'true Israel,' Israel by faith (Rom 9:6, 26, cf. Rom 4). Similarly, at times he speaks of the church in a parallel way. For example, Phil 3:3: 'we are the circumcision' includes all believers, Jew and Gentile, as those who are God's truly circumcised people (of the heart).

Second, as discussed, Romans 4 speaks of Abraham as the father of Jews and gentiles alike who walk in faith. Hence, Israel is redefined as all who believe in God with a saving faith before Christ toward God, and now that Christ has come and been proclaimed, toward God through Christ.

Third, the argument of Rom 9–11 heads to Rom 11 where Israel is a remnant of Jews by grace, an Olive Tree into which the gentiles are grafted, and the conclusion that all in this Olive Tree will be saved.

Fourth, the logic of Galatians leads to the conclusion that Paul has in mind all believers rather than merely Israel. So, in 3:7, those of faith are the children of Abraham. These are not those born in the physical line of Abraham, but believers, Jews or gentiles. The family of faith then includes Jews and gentiles. In this household, there is neither Jew nor Greek, slave nor free, male and female; all are one in Christ (3:28). All believers are Abraham's offspring and heirs of the promise, including the Galatians (3:29). All who believe have received the Spirit, have received adoption as God's children and heirs (4:6–7). In 4:21–31, all believers are children of the free woman Sarah—free, children of the heavenly Jerusalem, children of the Abrahamic covenant, born of the Spirit. The household of faith in 6:10 is all believers. Whether one is circumcised or not, one is a new creation, and so a part of God's people. As such, the inexorable theological logic of Galatians heads toward this being

---

Judah, Jacob, Isaac, and Abraham (who in uncircumcision was approved of and blessed by God on account of his faith, and called the father of many nations), are we who have been led to God through this crucified Christ, as shall be demonstrated while we proceed.' (ANF1, 200). See also N. A. Dahl, 'Der Name Israel: Zur Auslegung von Gal 6,16,' *Judaica* 6 (1950): 161–70; Longenecker, *Galatians*, 297–98; Martyn, *Galatians*, 1997: 574–77; Lightfoot, *Galatians*, 224–25; Hays, 'Galatians,' 345–46; Dunn, *Galatians*, 345. See for further references, Moo, *Galatians*, 401 who takes this as 'all who follow this rule' which would include gentiles and Jews.

a climactic comment redefining Israel not as the people of physical descent from Abraham and his grandson Jacob/Israel, but all peoples who have a saving faith in God.

Fifth, while mercy can fit historical Israel, as the preceding discussion of *eleos* indicates, Paul uses it of God's mercy toward gentile believers (Rom 15:9) and on all Christians (Eph 2:4; Tit 3:5). So, one can argue that Paul here asks for God's peace upon those in Galatia who read this letter and adhere to the rule stated in v. 15. Then, he pleads for mercy upon all believers in all places and times.

Finally, the genitive 'of God' in the context of Galatians is problematic for the argument that Israel here is Israel by descent in rejection of God. This speaks of ownership. Through the letter, the people of God are those of faith. Rejecting Israel is not of God; they are under the *stoicheia*, under the law, and separated from God. It seems unlikely in the flow of the letter that 'of God' would be used of rejecting Israel.

Both ideas fit, and it is difficult to argue for one over the other. On the basis of the flow of logic in Romans and Galatians, I prefer the latter argument. Both letters move through a series of arguments culminating in a climactic statement concerning Israel. In Romans, this is found in Rom 11:26: 'and so all Israel will be saved.' Here, I believe Paul means all peoples of faith in all times and places, all grafted into the one olive tree that is Israel. This includes those who believe in God before hearing the gospel of Christ. It includes all who have subsequently heard the gospel and believed in God through Christ. This people, predestined by the omniscient God, will be saved.

Similarly, in Galatians, Paul has moved through the letter arguing that there is one people of God including believing Jews and gentiles. As in the case of Rom 11:26, to argue that 6:16 is Israel by descent suddenly throws a caveat on his whole case in the two letters. Hence, I am prone to think that here Paul is speaking of God's people of faith. With that said, I hold this view of 6:16 lightly as both interpretations can work for this text.

If I am reading this correctly, the 'Israel of God' is not the 'church' per se, for it includes all of Israel *prior* to the existence

of the church, or, better, it speaks of God's people by faith from
Abel to the consummation. These people form the 'Israel of God'
for all eternity. This is not 'replacement theology' for Israel is
never replaced. Rather, it is redefined and extended. First, Paul
redefines Israel as those of faith across all time. Second, the
renewed people of God includes all who are truly Israel *prior*
to Christ's coming and the proclamation of him as Jesus Christ
Lord in any given culture. Israel has always been a people, and for
Paul, not a people of descent or of law-observance but of faith;
case in point, Abraham. No doubt he would concur with the list
of Heb 11 including those who lived prior to Abraham including
Abel, Enoch, and Noah (and others not mentioned but who also
had faith).[88] It includes gentiles like Abraham (as he was at his
call) and Rahab. Now, this people is being extended by those who
believe the gospel of Christ. It is thus an extension of Israel, not
its replacement. The emphasis is on continuity. Just as 'we are the
circumcision,' 'we are the Israel of God.' May God have mercy on
us all.

BEARING THE STIGMATA OF CHRIST (6:17)

In *Galatians 6:17*, Paul makes a personal appeal that he is no
longer troubled by the Galatians flirting with false teachers:

From now on (genitive *loipon*, 2:13), **let no one** (*mēdeis*, 6:3)
cause (first person present imperative *parechō*)[89] **trouble** (*kopos*)[90]
for me (dative *egō*, 1:2). **For** (*gar*, 1:10), **I bear** (*bastazō*, 5:10) **in**

---

88. The writer of Hebrews adds Sarah, Isaac, Jacob, Joseph, Moses, Rahab, Gideon, Barak,
Samson, Jephthah, David, Samuel, and the prophets.

89. The verb παρέχω (*parechō*) compounds *para* (beside) and *echō* (have, hold). As with
many of the *echō* compounds, it is fluid in meaning. BDAG. 776–777 notes these
meanings: 'give up,' 'offer,' 'present,' 'grant,' 'show,' 'cause,' 'make happen. In its one use
in Gal 6:17, it has the sense 'cause'—'let no one *cause* me trouble …' Paul uses it
elsewhere in Col 4:1; 1 Tim 1:4; 6:17.

90. The noun κόπος (*kopos*) is used once in Galatians 6:17. The term speaks of 'hard labor,'
'trouble,' 'difficulty,' and has the meaning 'trouble' in the verse—'let no one cause me
trouble.' Paul is challenging the Galatians to stop any rejection of him, his gospel, and
acceptance of the Judaizers. He may have the Judaizers in mind as well. Overall, Paul
uses the term eleven times.

(*en*, 1:6) **my** (genitive *egō*) **body** (dative *sōma*)[91] **the marks** (plural *stigma*)[92] **of Jesus**[93] (genitive *Iēsous*, 1:1).

There is no connective, indicating Paul is bringing the letter to an end. 'Trouble' is *kopos*, a term meaning 'work, toil, trouble.' The associated verb *kopiaō* is used in 4:11 of Paul's labor over the Galatians, his mission work among them. *Kopos* in wider Greek sources means 'beating,' 'weariness as though one had been beaten,' 'exertion,' or the 'trouble' which causes the state of feeling beaten down or wearied by things like work, extreme effort, and heat. It is applied to a soldier in battle, runners carrying messages, laborers.[94]

Such uses are found in the LXX and other Jewish Greek literature,[95] where it is used of the kinds of people Paul has in

---

91. The common term for the body, σῶμα (*sōma*), is used once in Galatians 6:17, of Paul's *body* which bears the marks of Jesus, i.e., the marks of his sufferings, his participation in the sufferings of Christ. Otherwise, it is found in Paul ninety-one times.

92. The noun στίγμα (*stigma*) (cf. English, stigma) is a hapax *legomenon*, only found in the NT in Gal 6:17 of the marks of Jesus in Paul's body. The term means 'mark, brand' and was used for slaves and tattooing (BDAG 945).

93. **VARIANT**: There is a range of alternatives to *Iēsou*, 'Jesus' (P46 A B C* 33 1070 1753) including *Christou* (P Ψ 81 255 256 442 463 1175 1319 1908 2127 copbo arm eth *al*), *kyriou Iēsou*, 'Lord Jesus' (C3 Dc K L most minuscules, followed by the Textus Receptus), *kyriou Iēsous Christou*, 'Lord Jesus Christ' (941 917 א itd al), *kyrious ēmōn Iēsou Christou*, 'our Lord Jesus Christ' (Dgr* Fgr G 104 1924 syrp goth), and *kyriou mou Iēsou Christou*, 'my Lord Jesus Christ' (Origenlat). The strong support for *Iēsou* suggests it is original and others are scribal adjustments.

94. F. Hauck, 'κοπιά ω,' in *TDNT* 3:827–88.

95. *Kopos* has a wide range including physical toil (Gen 31:42), a heavy burden of responsibility (Deut 1:12), political and/or financial oppression (Judg 10:16; Ps 54:12 [Eng. 55:11]; Hab 3:7), work (Neh 5:13, LXX; Sir 14:15; 31:28; 4 Bar. 5:6) including building idols (Sib. Or. 5:82), life's trouble in a general sense (Ps 24:18 [Eng. 25:15]; 87:16 [Eng. 88:15]; 89:10 [Eng. 90:10]; 106:12 [Eng. 107:12]; Job 5:6, 7; 11:16; Mal 2:13; 1 En. 11:1), the trouble the unrighteous experience (Ps 72:5, [Eng. 73:4, 12]; Wis 3:11), do (Mic 2:1), or cause (Sir 22:13), the struggle to understand the wicked (Ps 72:16 [Eng. 73:16]), being spoken too in weariness (Job 4:2) or speaking trouble (Zech 10:2), the labor of the righteous (Wis 10:17; Hab 1:3), the struggle to understand riddles (Sir 13:26), and Jacob's struggle with God (Hos 12:3). It is also used for Jeremiah's struggles (Jer 20:18; 51:33), trouble in war (1 Macc 10:15), food produce (1 En. 7:3), Israel's travails (4 Ezra 5:35), the labor that will produce salvation (Apoc. Sedr. 14:2), exhaustion from work or generally (T. Iss. 3:5; Josephus, *Ant.* 5.315; 7.48; 7.299; 8.244; *Life* 136), the weariness of cattle (Josephus, *Ant.* 1.336), weariness from a

mind here; people who trouble others, including, the trouble caused by wicked rulers (Ps 93:20 [Eng. 94:20] and the trouble caused by an evil person's mouth (Ps 9:28 [Eng. 10:7]; 139:10 [Eng. 140:9]).

In the NT the term is used mainly for the missional labor of Paul (including tentmaking) and others.[96] At other times, it is applied to those who cause trouble to others whether it is Judas who troubles the woman who anointed Jesus' feet (Matt 26:10; Mark 14:6) or people who bother others in the middle of the night for food (Luke 11:7), or a widow who relentlessly seeks justice from a judge (Luke 18:5).

Paul is using it in the non-missional sense here of those who are troubling him. This would, of course, include the Judaizers who are terrorizing his churches and any among the Galatians who are turning against him. Clearly, his wish is that his letter is the final word on the Judaizing problem. Soon the Jerusalem leaders would meet and deal with it, agreeing with Paul and Barnabas, and Paul would come with Silas carrying the Jerusalem Council letter to deal with the matter once and for all.

The verb is *parechō*, which compounds *para*, 'beside' and *echō*, 'to have to hold.' As with other *echō* compounds, it is fluid and widely used. The literal sense of 'bring' is found concerning bringing in financial gain or business (Acts 16:16; 19:24). It can mean to *offer* a cheek (Luke 6:29), to *grant* a favor (Luke 7:4), *become* quiet (Acts 22:2), *show* kindness (Acts 28:2), treat justly or fairly (Col 4:1), promote speculations (1 Tim 1:4), *provide* richly (1 Tim 6:17), and *show* oneself a model (Tit 2:7).

As here, it is at times paired with *kopos* on occasions such as Judas causing trouble to the woman who anointed Jesus (Matt 26:10; Mark 14:6) and in Jesus' parables of people persevering in bothering people and so being role models for prayer (Luke 11:7; 18:5). Here it is a present imperative, the final in a sequence of imperatives and hortatory subjunctives between 4:12 and this

---

journey (Josephus, *Ant.* 2.257; 3.25), an army march (Josephus, *J.W.* 5.68), or war (Josephus, *J.W.* 5.307), and the effort for virtue (Philo, *Spec.* 2.39).

96. See John 4:38; 1 Cor 3:8; 15:58; 2 Cor 6:5; 10:15; 11:23, 27; 1 Thess 1:3; 2:9; 3:5, 8; Rev 2:2; 14:13.

verse. Negated by *mē*, it yields a prohibition.[97] This then is the final appeal of the letter. It is present active and so speaks of something habitual.

As here, *parechō* is sometimes combined with *kopos*, so speaking of causing trouble, as with Judas criticizing the woman who anointed Jesus (Matt 26:10; Mark 14:6), and in Jesus' stories of people troubling others (Luke 11:7; 18:5). The imperative is present, indicating that Paul wants them to trouble him no longer.

This is followed by his reason for the desire that no one trouble him any longer. *Gar* is causal, 'for, because.' 'I bear' is *bastazō* used in 5:10 of the troublemakers bearing the penalty for their offenses, in 6:1 of bearing one another's troubles, and in 6:5 of each bearing their own load before God in judgment. Here, Paul bears the stigmata of Jesus in his body—*sōma* here is clearly referring to his physical body.

Stigmata is familiar to moderns because of the supposed phenomenon of Jesus' scars appearing on people's hands and feet.[98] Such a meaning comes later.[99]

The term comes from *stizō*, meaning to 'prick,' 'tattoo,' or 'mark' with a sharp instrument such as an engraver might use.[100] Aside from Greek Jewish writings, *stigma* is employed in a range of ways including marks on the sea (Plutarch, *Cohib. ira* 5), the writing on a message (Herodotus, *Hist.* 5.35.3) or written symbols of stone, books, or tablets (Dio Chrysostom, *Lib.* 80). It is commonly used for the markings on a skin, including animals

97. Wallace, *Greek Grammar*, 487.
98. For example, the movie *Stigmata*, Metro-Goldwyn-Mayer, 1999.
99. See Betz, 'στίγμα,' in *TDNT* 7:663 notes that Gnosticism promoted a real mark of initiation into Christianity, a hot iron on the lobe of the ear recalling baptism of fire, the branding of Roman soldiers (*signaculum saeculi*) was repudiated for Christians who bore the signum Christi from baptism. Later Christians sometimes tattooed the sign of the cross or his name on the wrist or arm, even before the sign of the cross. Some pious Christians had IHS (Jesus, Son, Savior) inscribed on the breast. The Catholic Church recognizes a number of people, including Francis of Assisi, who have supposedly borne the marks of Jesus from his crown of thorns, scourging, nail prints, or the mark of the spear in the side.
100. Betz, 'στίγμα,' 7.658.

like the griffin which has marks like that of a leopard (Pausanias, *Descr.* 8.2.7) or on a snake (Pausanias, *Descr.* 8.4.7; Hesiod, *[Scut.]* 166). It is used for marks on the skin of people including the branding irons used to mark such people as slaves (Plutarch, *Cohib. ira.* 11), the place where thieves and others are branded (Lucian, *Pisc.* 46), or brands themselves (Plutarch, *Praec. ger. rei publ.* 4). It is applied to the marks of the suffering of Hyperbolus, an Athenian politician (Plutarch, *Alc.* 13.5; *Nic.* 11.5). Appian and Plutarch use it of marks on the body such as the brand marking a slave (Appian, *Bell. civ.* 4.43; Plutarch, *Cohib. ira.* 15). Other such uses include marks from battle (Plutarch, *Herod. mal.* 42), stripes (Plutarch, *Sera* 22), sacred protective brands from the temple of Heracles (Herodotus, *Hist.* 2.113.2), tattoos (Diodorus Siculus, *Hist.* 14.30.7) including on the free woman of Thrace (Dio Chrysostom, *Orat.* 64:19), and prisoners. So, the Samians marked on the forehead with a samaena[101] and the Athenians with an owl (Plutarch, *Per.* 26.3). Xerxes marked Thebian deserters (Plutarch, *Herod. mal.* 33; Herodotus, *Hist.* 7.233.2). Lucian uses it of marks on the back and the soul (Lucian, *Cat.* 24, 28) by which one can judge another (Lucian, *Cat.* 26).

Betz adds that branded marks were also used on domestic animals and later, soldiers. This was to mark one's possessions to avoid theft. Runaway slaves were marked. A slave was even called a *stigmatias*, a 'branded one' (Xenophon, *Hell.* 5.3.24). Those who robbed temples were marked on the forehead (Plato, *Leg.* 9.854d). Caligula marked honorable citizens condemned to hard labor (Suetonius, *Caes.* 4.27.3). Such branding was used in European slavery. Such markings were universally regarded as dishonorable in the Ancient Near East.[102] Later, slaves were universally marked on the head and soldiers on the hand. Such branding was widespread in the ancient world.[103]

---

101. Plutarch explains that the *samaena* is a warship with a boar's head design at the bow and stern. The Samians were those from the island of Samos which sits off Turkey's west coast near ancient Ephesus and Patmos—where John wrote Revelation. It is a nice place to visit as I can testify.

102. Betz, 'στίγμα,' 7.658.

103. See further Betz, 'στίγμα,' 7.659.

The brand could be positive if it denoted membership of something honored, such as a particular tribe or diving being. So, Ethiopian children were marked on the knee for dedication to Apollo. One devoted to Dionysus was marked with an ivy leaf. Those devoted to Cybele were also marked, meaning perhaps some of the Galatians wore stigmata from their devotion to her. As Betz says, '[w]hen a man [person] was given the sacred mark he was dedicated to the god and became its servant, but he also came under its protection, so that he should not be molested.'[104]

In Jewish and Christian Greek sources, other than this use of Paul in the NT, it is found twice elsewhere. In the Song of Solomon 1:11, it is used of studs of silver, which will be used to adorn the body. In Pseudo-Phocylides 1:225, it is used once, of a slave branding.

Betz notes, however, that the idea of branding is attested in the OT. So, a slave can be pierced with an awl (Exod 21:6; Deut 15:16). In Isa 44:5, people of the nations will inscribe 'Yahweh's' on the hand, indicating God's ownership. God also marked Cain with a protective mark (Gen 4:15). The OT, however, generally prohibits tattoos (Lev 19:28).[105]

Here, circumcision is the stigma of Judaism; the removal of the foreskin marking the person as being 'owned' by Yahweh.[106] Hence, Paul describes circumcision as a 'seal of righteousness' (Rom 4:11).

In Revelation, the various marks referred to speak of the same kind of background. Some are marked by the Beast[107] and Babylon is marked (Rev 17:5), while others are marked by God with the seal of God (Rev 7:3; 9:4) and his name (Rev 14:1; 22:4). This is not literal but rather speaks of ownership, protection, and devotion. For Paul, the believer is sealed with the Spirit, 'marked' for eternal life (2 Cor 1:20–21; Eph 1:13–14; 4:30).

As we come to Paul's use, it speaks of the marks on his body. This does not speak of some Christian branding, but the marks

104. See further Betz, 'στίγμα,' 7.660.
105. See further Betz, 'στίγμα,' 7.660–62.
106. Betz, 'στίγμα,' 7.663.
107. See Rev 13:16, 17; 14:9, 11; 16:2; 19:20; 20:4.

inscribed on his body during his suffering.[108] These would include those things listed in 2 Cor 11 (c. AD 56), which he by this time—some eight years earlier—had experienced. Aside from his public beating and flogging in Philippi (Acts 16:22–23), most of the things listed in 2 Cor 11 had likely occurred by the time of the writing of Galatians. His list includes countless beatings often to the point of death, five times thirty-nine lashes from the Jews, three times beaten with rods (one is Philippi), once stoned (in Lystra, Acts 14:19), and three shipwrecks. He also bore the marks of his tentmaking. Such marks, unless gained on the front in war or due to religious devotion, were negative signs in the ancient world. They demonstrated that the person was a criminal of some sort, a slave, or had been defeated in conflict. In the case of Paul, they mark him as a Jesus' devotee. However, this is not branding, but the pain and scars of suffering.

For Paul, the marks of suffering on his body are the 'stigmata of Jesus.' They then speak of his service, sacrifice, and suffering for Christ. They are badges of honor. They also speak of his protection by his Lord. They stand in contrast with circumcision, which is the stigma of Israel and the Judaizers. Whereas that achieves nothing, these stigmata are signs of Paul, a new creation. The marks of suffering then are eschatological, and circumcision is no better than 'pagan branding.'[109] As with 4:8–9; 5:7, 12, Judaism-outside-of-Christ is no better than a pagan religion as it has rejected God's Son. At a deeper theological level, they indicate his participation in Christ's sufferings, his cruciform life. This is the ideal of the Christian life for Paul, not suffering for the sake of it, not a martyrdom complex, but full-on service of Christ no matter what the cost.

With such a Christ-mindset (cf. Phil 2:5), they are honorable. Stigmata was used to brand slaves; hence, they speak of his voluntary enslavement to Christ. He is branded by Christ. Similarly, such marks were used in some cultures of those who

108. Betz, 'στίγμα,' 7.663 notes older scholars who have suggested Paul had the name of Jesus tattooed on his body which misses the point. Similarly, with most scholars including Betz, see Lightfoot, *Galatians*, 225.
109. Betz, 'στίγμα,' 7.663.

served royalty, like those who served Xerxes. These stigmata of Paul indicate his service to the King of kings. Elsewhere, Paul says to honor the likes of Epaphroditus who nearly died as he delivered financial gifts from Philippi to Rome (Phil 2:29–30). Here, Paul is speaking in the same kind of way. Further, Paul states in Col 1:24 that his sufferings fill up Christ's sufferings. Hence, Paul sees Christian suffering as that of Jesus, who suffers in and with us by his Spirit. This is a glorious statement, calling us to be committed to Christ to the point of suffering for him, and in doing so, we will be marked with the honor of his stigmata.

FAREWELL (6:18)

In *Galatians 6:18*, Paul ends the letter with one of his customary final blessings for grace toward the Galatians:[110]
The grace (charis, 1:3) **of our** (plural genitive *egō*, 1:2) **Lord** (genitive *kyrios*, 1:3) **Jesus** (*Iēsous*, 1:1) **Christ** (*Christos*, 1:1) **[be] with** (*meta*, 1:18) **your** (plural genitive *sy*, 1:3) **spirit** (*pneuma* 3:2) **brothers and sisters** (vocative plural *adelphos*, 1:1), **amen** (*amēn*, 1:5).
As with 1:3, Paul prays for grace to be with the Galatians brothers and sisters. The use of the plural vocative of *adelphos*, as throughout the letter speaks of familial belonging and togetherness.[111] It reminds the Galatians that while the letter has been frank and to the point, their situation is not terminal. Paul still sees them as a family—God the Father, Jesus the Son, and Paul and all Christians, including those with him along with the Galatians, are the household of faith (6:10), the Israel of God

---

110. **VARIANT**: There is a range of alternative subscriptions: 1) *Pros Galatas*, 'to the Galatians' (א A B* C 33 466 is *pros Galatas*, 'to the Galatians;') 2) *pros Galatas egraphē*, 'I write to the Galatians' (P -φει) with some include *apo Rōmēs*, 'from Rome' (Bc K P 1908, followed by the Textus Receptus); 3) *pros Galatas eplērōthē*, 'the Galatians completed' (D); 4) *etelesthē epistolē pros Galatas*, 'the epistle to the Galatians ended' (F G); 5) *telos tēs pros Galatas. Egraphē*, 'the end of to the Galatians, I write'; 6) *egraphē apo Rōmēs hypo Paulou kai tōn adelophōn pros Galatas hoi epistolē autē*, 'I write from Rome by Paul and the brothers to the Galatians this letter' (Euthaliusmss). All are secondary.
111. See on 1:1, 2, s.a. 1:11, 19; 3:15; 4:12, 28, 31; 5:11, 13; 6:1.

(6:17). However, they must resist the Judaizers whose theological poison will see them severed from Christ and fallen from grace (5:4).

This is a prayer for them to know the fullness of his grace: to be secure in salvation, to experience his protection and providence, to know the grace of a loving Christian community, and more (see further 1:3). Recalling 5:4, where Paul warns them that to yield to circumcision as per the demands of the Judaizers is to *fall from grace*, as with the blessing of 1:3, this is a prayer that they would remain secure in grace, not compromising the gospel as per the desires of the Judaizers. They must no longer desert the God who called them by the grace of Christ through the preaching of *the* gospel (1:6). Like Paul, who was called by God's grace (1:15; 2:9), they must not render God's grace obsolete, for Christ died for them through grace (2:21).

Here, as in 1:3 and 6:14, it is the grace of our *Lord Jesus Christ*, Paul again uses the three-fold name, emphasizing Jesus' majesty and glory as Israel's Messiah and the Lord of the cosmos. Jesus and his Father is the source of all grace. This has a barb for the Judaizers who have a deficient Christology, failing to perceive that Jesus is sufficient for salvation—his grace is enough! He indeed is the conduit for God's grace, for he is the God the Son.

The particular blessing is found in three of Paul's letters, the others being Phil 4:23 and Phlm 25. In 2 Tim 4:22, there is a similar blessing, 'The Lord be with your spirit. *Grace* be with you.' While Romans ends with a long blessing, a similar blessing is found in Rom 16:20: 'the *grace* of our Lord Jesus Christ be with you,' which agrees with the final verse in the Thessalonian letters (1 Thess 5:28; 2 Thess 3:18). 1 Corinthians 16:23 includes a *grace* blessing but in a simpler form: 'the grace of the Lord Jesus be with you,' followed by a blessing of love. 2 Corinthians 13:13 includes a prayer for 'the *grace* of the Lord Jesus Christ' along with the love of God and the fellowship of the Holy Spirit. Ephesians also ends with a grace blessing for those who love Christ: '*Grace* be with all who love our Lord Jesus Christ with love incorruptible.' Colossians 4:17 and 1 Tim 6:21 include a shorter form: 'grace be with you;' and Titus, 'grace be with you all' (Tit 3:15). So, just as every letter of Paul begins with a prayer for grace, they also all include a grace blessing in the conclusions. The sandwiching of the letter with a grace blessing indicates how special grace is to Paul and how much he yearns that his converts will know it.

'With your spirit' uses *pneuma* in the singular following the plural of *sy*, 'your.' This here is not the Holy Spirit as in the other uses in Galatians (aside perhaps from 6:1 where it can be the 'spirit of gentleness').[112] Here, *pneuma* can be a collective singular, something common in Hebrew.[113] So, what is meant is 'with your spirits,' referring to the Galatians individually.[114] Alternatively, it refers to the collective spirit of the church. Either way, it speaks of the spirit as the 'God-conscious' aspect of the inner self.[115] It is that part of us with which the Spirit of God is melded. It is through the Spirit that we experience this in our spirits.

Fittingly, the final word of the letter is *amēn*, 'may it be,' used in 1:5 of Paul's short prayer that God would be glorified for all eternity. Here it consummates his prayer for Christ's grace being poured out on the Galatians. Rather than *mē genoito*, 'may it never be,' used in 2:17; 3:21; and 6:14 also cries out against any idea that Christ is a servant of sin, the law is contrary to God's promises, or that Paul would boast in anything other than the cross, *amēn* is effectively the opposite, *genoito*![116]—'may it happen, come to pass, be.' Just as Paul yearns that God is ever glorified, so he deeply desires that the Galatians know Christ's grace. This will preserve them, for God's grace is amazing and unyielding. May you know the grace of Christ as you deepen your knowledge of the Scriptures. Amen.

---

112. See 3:2, 3, 5, 14; 4:6; 5:5, 16, 17, 18, 22, 25; 6:8).
113. P. Joüon, and T. Muraoka, *A Grammar of Biblical Hebrew* (Roma: Pontificio Instituto Biblico, 2006), 466–68.
114. Similarly, Paul often uses heart as a collective singular as in Phil 1:7: 'because you have me in your *heart*,' possibly referring to the hearts of the Philippian church, Wallace, *Greek Grammar*, 196.
115. George, *Galatians*, 315.
116. See BDAG 53.

WORKS REFERENCED

Alexander, L. C. A. 'Chronology of Paul.' Pages 115–23 in *DPL*.

Arndt, William, Frederick W. Danker, and Walter Bauer. *A Greek-English Lexicon of the New Testament and Other Early Christian Literature*. Chicago: University of Chicago Press, 2000.

Arndt, William, F. Wilbur Gingrich, Frederick W. Danker, and Walter Bauer. *A Greek-English Lexicon of the New Testament and Other Early Christian Literature : A Translation and Adaption of the Fourth Revised and Augmented Edition of Walter Bauer's Griechisch-Deutsches Worterbuch Zu Den Schrift En Des Neuen Testaments Und Der Ubrigen Urchristlichen Literatur*. Chicago: University of Chicago Press, 1979.

Aune, David E. 'Religion, Greco-Roman.' Pages 917–26.

Balz, Horst Robert, and Gerhard Schneider. *Exegetical Dictionary of the New Testament*. Grand Rapids, MI.: Eerdmans, 1990–.

————. 'βασκαίνω.' Pages 208 in Volume 1 *EDNT*.

————. 'Προλαμβάνω.' Page 158 in Volume 3 *EDNT*.

————. 'συνυποκρι´νομαι.' Page 331 in Volume 1 *EDNT*.

————. 'φαρμακεία.' Page 417 in Volume 3 *EDNT*.

Barchy, S. S. 'Table Fellowship.' Pages 796–800 in *DJG*.

Barclay, John M. G. 'Jesus and Paul.' Pages 492–503 in *DPL*.

Bauer, Bruno. *Kritik der paulinischen Briefe*. Berlin: Hempel, 1852.

Baumgarten, J. 'καιρός.' Pages 232–35 in Volume 2 *EDNT*.

Baur, F. C. *Paul the Apostle of Jesus Christ, His Life and Work, His Epistles and his Doctrine*. Volume 1. Translated by E. Zeller. London: Williams and Norgate, 1876.

Betz, Otto. 'στίγμα.' Pages 657–64 in Volume 7 *TDNT*.

Behm, J. 'ἀνατίθημι (προσανατίθημι).' Pages 353–56 in Volume 1 *TDNT*.

————. 'καινός.' Pages 447–454 in Volume 3 *TDNT*.

————. 'κυρόω.' Pages 1098–1100 in Volume 3 *TDNT* 3.

————. 'ἀνόητος.' Pages 948–1022 in Volume 4 *TDNT*.

Bennett, C. E. *New Latin Grammar*. Boston; New York; Chicago, IL: Allyn and Bacon, 1908.

Betz, H. D. *Galatians: A Commentary on Paul's Letter to the Churches in Galatia*. Hermeneia. Minneapolis, MN: Fortress, 1979.

————. 'The Literary Composition and Function of Paul's Letter to the Galatians.' *NTS* 21 (1975): 353–79.

Beyer, H. W. 'κανών.' Pages 596–602 in Volume 3 *TDNT*.

————. 'κατηχέω.' Pages 638–40 in Volume 3 *TDNT*.

Blass, Friedrich, Albert Debrunner, and Robert Walter Funk. *A Greek Grammar of the New Testament and Other Early Christian Literature*. Chicago, IL: University of Chicago Press, 1961.

Bligh, J. *Galatians: A Discussion of St. Paul's Epistle*. London: St. Paul, 1969.

Bohak, G. 'Gentile Attitudes toward Jews and Judaism.' Pages 668–70 in *EDEJ*.

Bousset, Wilhelm. *Kyrios Christos: A History of the Belief in Christ from the Beginning of Christianity to Irenaeus*. Translated by J. E. Steely. Nashville: Abingdon, 1970.

Bruce, F. F. *The Acts of the Apostles: The Greek Text with Introduction and Commentary*. Grand Rapids, MI: Eerdmans, 1951.

————. *The Epistle to the Galatians: A Commentary on the Greek Text*. NIGTC. Grand Rapids, MI: Eerdmans, 1982.

Büchsel, F. 'εἰκῇ.' Pages 380–81 in Volume 2 *TDNT*.

————. 'Θυμός.' Pages 167–72 in Volume 3 *TDNT*.

Bultmann, Rudolf. 'πεισμονή.' Pages 1–11 in Volume 6 *TDNT*.

————. *Primitive Christianity in Its Contemporary Setting*. Translated by R. Fuller. London: Collins, 1960.

Burns, Joshua Ezra. "Conversion and Proselytism." Pages 484–86 in *EDEJ*.

Burton, Ernest De Witt. *A Critical and Exegetical Commentary on the Epistle to the Galatians*. ICC. New York: Charles Scribner's Sons, 1920.

Calvin, Jean. *Commentaries on the Epistles of Paul to the Galatians and Ephesians*. Edinburgh: Thomas Clark, 1854.

————. *Institutes of the Christian Religion: The Originals*. Raleigh, NC: Hayes Barton Press, 2005.

Cavallin, H. C. C. "'The Righteous Shall Live by Faith:" A Decisive Argument for the Traditional Interpretation." *ST* 32 (1978): 33–43.

Charlesworth, James H. *The Old Testament Pseudepigrapha*. Vol. 1. New York, NY; London: Yale University Press, 1983.

Ciampa, Roy E., and Brian S. Rosner. *The First Letter to the Corinthians*. PNTC. Grand Rapids, MI; Cambridge, UK: Eerdmans, 2010.

Collins, John J., and Daniel C. Harlow, eds. *The Eerdmans Dictionary of Early Judaism*. Grand Rapids, MI; Cambridge, U.K.: Eerdmans, 2010. Hansen, G. W. *Galatians*. IVPNTCS 9; Downers Grove, IL: IVP, 1994.

Dahl, N. A. 'Der Name Israel: Zur Auslegung von Gal 6, 16.' *Judaica* 6 (1950): 161–70

Davies, W. D. *Paul and Rabbinic Judaism: Some Rabbinic Elements in Paul's Theology*. London: Society for Promoting Christian Knowledge Publishing, 1955.

————. 'Paul and the People of Israel.' *NTS* 24 (1977/78): 4–39.

DeMoss, Matthew S. *Pocket Dictionary for the Study of New Testament Greek*. Downers Grove, IL: InterVarsity Press, 2001.

Delling, G. 'βασκαίνω.' Page 594–95 in Volume 1 *TDNT*.

————. 'προλαμβάνω.' Pages 14–15 in Volume 4 *TDNT*.

————. 'χρόνος.' Pages 581–93 in Volume 9 *TDNT*.

———— G. Delling, 'στοιχέω.' Pages 666–687 in Volume 7 *TDNT*.

Donfried, K. P. 'Chronology (New Testament).' Pages 1010–1022 in Volume 1 *AYBD* 1:1010–1022.

Drouhard, R. L. 'Arabia.' *LBD*.

Dunn, James D. G. *The Epistle to the Galatians*. BNTC. London: Continuum, 1993.

————. 'The New Perspective on Paul.' *BJRL* 65 (1983): 95-122.

————. 'Yet Once More— "The Works of the Law,"' *JSNT* 46 (1992): 99-107.

Easter, Matthew C. 'The *Pistis Christou* Debate: Main Arguments and Responses in Summary.' *CBR* 9.1 (2010): 33–47.

Eckman, J. P. *The Truth about Worldviews: A Biblical Understanding of Worldview Alternatives*. Wheaton, IL: Crossway Books, 2004.

Egger, J. A. 'Galatia.' *LBD*.

Epictetus, *The Works of Epictetus: His Discourses, in Four Books, the Enchiridion, and Fragments*. Edited by Thomas Wentworth Higginson. Medford, MA: Thomas Nelson and Sons, 1890.

Falk, D. K. 'Festivals and Holy Days.' Pages 636–45 in *EDEJ*.

Fee, Gordon D. *Galatians*. Pentecostal Commentary. Dorset, UK: Deo, 2007.

————. *God's Empowering Presence: The Holy Spirit in the Letters of Paul*. Peabody: Hendriksen, 1995.

Finney, David A. 'Crucifixion.' *LBD*.

Fitzer, G. 'φορτίον.' Page 84–86 in Volume 9 *TDNT*.

Fitzgerald, John T. 'Virtue/Vice Lists.' Pages 857–59 in Volume 6 *AYBD* .

Foerster, W. 'ἐχθρός.' Pages 811–15 in Volume 2 *TDNT*.

Fruchtenbaum, Arnold G. *The Messianic Jewish Epistles: Hebrews, James, First Peter, Second Peter, Jude*. 1st ed. Tustin, CA: Ariel Ministries, 2005.

Fung, Ronald Y. K. *The Epistle to the Galatians*. NICNT. Grand Rapids, MI: Eerdmans, 1988.

Fuchs, E. 'σκοπέω' Page 255 in Volume 7 *TDNT*.

Gasque, W. Ward. 'Iconium.' Pages 357–58 in Volume 3 *AYBD* .

George, Timothy. *Galatians*. NAC 30. Nashville: Broadman & Holman Publishers, 1994.

Gilbert, G. 'Jewish Attitudes Toward Gentiles.' Pages 670–73 in *EDEJ*.

Goldstein, H. 'ἀσε´λγεια.' Pages 169–70 in Volume 1 *EDNT*.

Gorman, Michael. J. *Cruciformity: Paul's Narrative Spirituality of the Cross*. Grand Rapids, MI: Eerdmans, 2001.

————. *Inhabiting the Crucified God: Kenosis, Justification, and Theosis in Paul's Narrative Soteriology*. Grand Rapids, MI: Eerdmans, 2009.

————. *Becoming the Gospel: Paul, Participation, and Mission*. Grand Rapids, MI: Eerdmans, 2015.

Giesen, H. 'ἔρις.' Pages 52–53 in Volume 2 *EDNT*.

Green, Gene L. *The Letters to the Thessalonian*. PNTC; Grand Rapids, MI; Leicester, UK: Eerdmans; Apollos, 2002.

Grundmann, W. 'δοκιμάζω.' Pages 255–60 in Volume 2 *TDNT*.

————. 'ἐγκράτεια.' Pages 339–42 in Volume 2 *TDNT*.

————. 'ἰσχύω.' Pages 397–402 in Volume 3 *TDNT*.

Guyer, M. S. 'Thessalonian.' *LBD*.

Harder, G. 'φθορά.' Pages 93–106 in Volume 9 *TDNT*.

Hardin, J. K. *Galatians and the Imperial Cult: A Critical Analysis of the First-Century Social Context of Paul's Letter*. WUNT 237. Tübingen, Mohr Siebeck, 2008.

Harrill, J. A. 'Slavery.' Pages 1124–27 in *DNTB*.

Harrington, Hannah K. 'Purity and Impurity.' Pages 1121–32 in *EDEJ*.

Hauck, Friedrich. 'κοινωνία.' Pages 789–810 in Volume 3 *TDNT*.

————. 'κοπια´ω.' Pages 827–30 in Volume 3 *TDNT*.

Hays, Richard B. 'Galatians.' Pages 181–348 in Volume XI, *The New Interpreter's Bible*. Nashville, TN: Abingdon, 2002.

————. *The Faith of Jesus Christ: An Investigation of the Narrative Substructure of Galatians 3:1–4:11*. SBLDS 56; Chico, CA: Scholars, 1983.

————.*Echoes of Scripture in the Letters of Paul*. New Haven, CT: Yale University Press, 1989.

Hendriksen, William, and Simon J. Kistemaker. *Exposition of Galatians*. Vol. 8. New Testament Commentary. Grand Rapids, MI: Baker Book House, 1953–2001.

Hengel, Martin. *Crucifixion*. Philadelphia, PA: Fortress, 1977.

Hoehner, H. W. 'Chronology.' Pages 118–22 in *DJG*.

Hong, In-Gyu. '"Being 'Under the Law' in Galatians.' *ERT* 26 (2002): 360–70.

Hooker, Morna D. "Πίστις Χριστοῦ," *NTS* 35 (1989): 321-42.

Horstmann, A. 'οἶδα.' Pages 493–94 in Volume 2 *EDNT*.

Howard, G. *Paul: Crisis in Galatia; A Study in Early Christian Theology*. SSNTM 35. Cambridge, UK: Cambridge University Press, 1979.

Hübner, H. 'χρόνος.' Pages 488–89 in Volume 3 *EDNT*.

Jewett, Robert. *A Chronology of Paul's Life*. Philadelphia, PA: Fortress Press, 1979.

————. "The Agitators and the Galatian Congregation." *NTS* 17 (1970–71): 198–212.

Johnson, Bradley T. 'Pharisees.' In *LBD*.

Joüon, P. and T. Muraoka, *A Grammar of Biblical Hebrew*. Roma: Pontificio Instituto Biblico, 2006.

Keown, Mark J. Keown, 'An Imminent Parousia and Christian Mission: Did the New Testament Writers Really Expect Jesus' Imminent Return?' pages 242–64 in *Christian Origins and the Establishment of the Early Jesus Movement*. Edited by Stanley E. Porter and Andrew W. Pitts. TENTS. ECHC 4. Leiden: Brill, 2018.

————. *Congregational Evangelism in Philippians: The Centrality of an Appeal for Gospel Proclamation to the Fabric of Philippians*. PBM. Milton Keynes: Paternoster, 2008.

————. 'Did Paul Plan to Escape from Prison? (Philippians 1:19–26),' *JSPL* 5.1 (Summer 2015): 89–108.

————. 'Porn? Ok or Not?' http://drmarkk.blogspot.co.nz/2008/05/porn-ok-or-not.html.

————. *Philippians*, EEC. Bellingham, WA: Lexham, 2017.

————. 'Preaching Christ Crucified: Cruciformity in Content and Delivery.' Pages 217–29 in *Text Messages: Preaching God's Word in a Smartphone World*. Edited by John Tucker. Eugene, Oreg.: Wipf and Stock, 2017.

Kim, S. 'Jesus, Sayings of.' Pages 474–92 in *DPL*.

Kittel, Gerhard, Geoffrey W. Bromiley, and Gerhard Friedrich, eds. *Theological Dictionary of the New Testament*. Grand Rapids, MI: Eerdmans, 1964–.

Kittel, Gerhard. 'ἀββά.' Pages 5–6 in Volume 1 *TDNT*.

————. 'δοκε´ω.' Pages 232–55 in Volume 2 *TDNT*.

Knox, J. *Chapters in the Life of Paul*. Nashville, TN: Abingdon Press, 1950.

Koehler, Ludwig, Walter Baumgartner, M. E. J. Richardson, and Johann Jakob Stamm. *The Hebrew and Aramaic Lexicon of the Old Testament*. Leiden: Brill, 1994–2000.

Kratz, R. 'ἐνιαυτός.' Pages 454–55 in Volume 1 *EDNT*.

Kroeger, Catherine C. 'Women in Greco-Roman World and Judaism.' Pages 127681 in *DNTB*.

Kuhn, H. -W. 'ἀββά.' Pages 1–2 in Volume 1 *EDNT*.

Lampe, P. 'ἵνα, hina.' Pages 188–90 in Vol 2. *EDNT* 190.

Liddell, Henry George, Robert Scott, Henry Stuart Jones, and Roderick McKenzie. *A Greek-English Lexicon*. Oxford: Clarendon Press, 1996.

Lightfoot, Joseph Barber, ed. *St. Paul's Epistle to the Galatians. A Revised Text with Introduction, Notes, and Dissertations*. 4th ed. Classic Commentaries on the Greek New Testament. London: Macmillan and Co., 1874.

Lohse, E. 'εὐπροσωπέω.' Page 768 in Volume 6 *TDNT*.

Lokkesmoe, R. 'Titus.' *LBD*.

Longenecker, Richard N. *Galatians*. WBC 41. Dallas: Word, Incorporated, 1998.

————. *Paul, Apostle of Liberty*. New York: Harper & Row, 1964.

Louw, Johannes P., and Eugene Albert Nida. *Greek-English Lexicon of the New Testament: Based on Semantic Domains*. New York: United Bible Societies, 1996. Lowery, D. D. 'Syria.' *LBD*.

Lührmann, D. *Galatians*. CCS (Minneapolis: Fortress, 1992).

Lüdemann, G. Paulus, der Heidenapostel, vol 1, Studien zur Chronologie. Göttingen: Vandenhoeck & Ruprecht, 1980.

McGuire, F. R. "Did Paul Write Galatians?" *HibJ* 66 (1967–68): 52–57.

McKnight, Scot. *Galatians*. NIVAC. Grand Rapids, MI: Zondervan, 1995.

McMillan, R. L. 'Cilicia.' In *LBD*.

Major Contributors and Editors. 'Aretas IV.' In *LBD*.

————. 'Dalmatia.' In *LBD*.

————. "Ephesians." In *LBD*.

Mare, W. H. *New Testament Background Commentary: A New Dictionary of Words, Phrases and Situations in Bible Order*. Ross-shire, UK: Mentor, 2004.

Martyn, J. L. *Galatians: A New Translation and Introduction with Commentary*. AYB 33A. New York: Doubleday, 1997.

Martyr, Justin. 'Dialogue of Justin with Trypho, a Jew.' Pages 194–270 in *The Apostolic Fathers with Justin Martyr and Irenaeus*. Edited by Alexander

Roberts, James Donaldson, and A. Cleveland Coxe. Vol. 1. The Ante-Nicene Fathers. Buffalo, NY: Christian Literature Company, 1885.

Matera, Frank J. *Galatians*. SP. Collegeville, MN: Liturgical Press, 1992.

Mattison, Mark. 'A Summary of the New Perspective on Paul. http://www.thepaulpage.com/a-summary-of-the-new-perspective-on-paul/.

Metzger, Bruce Manning, United Bible Societies. *A Textual Commentary on the Greek New Testament*. Second Edition a Companion Volume to the United Bible Societies' Greek New Testament (4th Rev. Ed.). London; New York: United Bible Societies, 1994.

Meyer, R. 'Λευ(ε)ἰτης.' Pages 239–41 in Volume 4 *TDNT*.

Michaelis, W. 'πάθημα.' Pages 930–35 in Volume 5 *TDNT*.

———. 'παρει´σακτος.' Pages 824–26 in Volume 5 *TDNT*.

Mitchell, S. 'Antioch in Pisidia.' Pages 264–65 in Volume 1 *AYBD* .

Montefiore, C. G. *Judaism and St. Paul*. London: Max Goscen, 1914.

Moo, Douglas J. *Galatians*. BECNT. Grand Rapids, MI: Baker Academic, 2013.

———. *The Epistle to the Romans*. NICNT. Grand Rapids, MI: Eerdmans, 1996.

———. *The Letter of James*. PNTC. Grand Rapids, MI; Leicester, England: Eerdmans; Apollos, 2000.

Moore, G. F. *Judaism in the First Centuries of the Christian Era: The Age of the Tannaim*. 2 vols. Cambridge, MA: Harvard University, 1927.

Morris, Leon. *Galatians: Paul's Charter of Christian Freedom*. Downers Grove, IL: InterVarsity Press, 1996.

Morrison, Michael. "Miqsat Maase Hatorah." *LBD*.

Oepke, A. *Der Brief des Paulus an die Galater*. THK. Berlin: Evangelische Verlagsanstalt, 1973.

O'Neill, J. C. The Recovery of Paul's Letter to the Galatians. London: SPCK, 1972.

Origen, 'Origen against Celsus.' Pages 395–668 in *Fathers of the Third Century: Tertullian, Part Fourth; Minucius Felix; Commodian; Origen, Parts First and Second*. Edited by Alexander Roberts, James Donaldson, and A. Cleveland Coxe. Translated by Frederick Crombie. Vol. 4 The Ante-Nicene Fathers. Buffalo, NY: Christian Literature Company, 1885.

Packer, J. I. Concise Theology: A Guide to Historic Christian Beliefs. Wheaton, IL: Tyndale House, 1993.

Patzia, Arthur G., and Anthony J. Petrotta. *Pocket Dictionary of Biblical Studies*. Downers Grove, IL: InterVarsity Press, 2002.

Pink, Arthur Walkington. *The Arthur Pink Anthology*. Bellingham, WA: Logos Bible Software, 2005.

Polhill, J. B. *Acts*. NAC 26; Nashville: Broadman & Holman Publishers, 1992.

———.*Paul and His Letters*. Nashville, TN: Broadman & Holman, 1999.

Porter, Stanley E. *Idioms of the Greek New Testament*. Sheffield: JSOT, 1999.

Porter, Stanley E., and Craig A. Evans. Dictionary of New Testament

Background: A Compendium of Contemporary Biblical Scholarship. Downers Grove, IL: InterVarsity Press, 2000.

Preisker, H. 'μυκτηρίζω.' Page 796 in Volume 4 *TDNT*.

————. 'ὀρθοποδε ω.' Page 451 in Volume 5 *TDNT*.

Ramsay, W. M. *St. Paul the Traveller and the Roman Citizen*. London: Hodder & Stoughton, 1907.

Reasoner, Mark. 'Rome and Roman Christianity.' Pages 850–55 in *DPL*.

Reed, Jeffrey T. *A Discourse Analysis of Philippians: Method and Rhetoric in the Debate over Literary Integrity*. JSNTSup Sheffield: Sheffield Academic Press, 1997.

Riesner, R. 'A Pre-Christian Jewish Mission.' Pages 211–50 in *The Mission of the Early Church to Jews and gentiles*. Edited by J. Ådna and H. Kvalbein. WUNT 127. Tübingen: Mohr Siebeck, 2000.

Rengstorf, K. H. 'ἀπόστολος.' Pages 398–447 in Volume 1 *TDNT*.

Ricks, Stephen. B. 'Abortion in Antiquity.' Pages 31–35 in Volume 1 *AYBD* 32.

Robertson, A. T. *A Grammar of the Greek New Testament in the Light of Historical Research*. Logos Bible Software, 2006.

Robinson, D. W. B. 'Distinction Between Jewish and Gentile Believers in Galatians.' *ABR* 13 (1965): 29–48.

Runge, S. E. *Discourse Grammar of the Greek New Testament: A Practical Introduction for Teaching and Exegesis*. Bellingham, WA: Lexham Press, 2010.

Rylands, L. G. *A Critical Analysis of the Four Chief Pauline Epistles*. London: Watts, 1929.

Sanday, W., and A. C. Headlam, *A Critical and Exegetical Commentary on the Epistle to the Romans*. ICC. Edinburgh: T & T. Clark, 1895.[1]

Sanders, E. P. *Paul and Palestinian Judaism: A Comparison of Patterns of Religion*. Philadelphia, PA: Fortress Press, 1977.

Sasse, H. 'αἰώνιος.' Pages 197–209 in Volume 1 *TDNT*.

Schlier, H. 'αἵρεσις.' Pages 180–85 in Volume 1 *TDNT*.

————. 'ἐκπτυ ω.' Pages 448–49 in Volume 2 *TDNT*.

Schnabel, E. J. *Early Christian Mission, Volume Two: Paul and the Early Church*. Leicester/Downers Grove, IL.: Apollos/IVP, 2004.

Schneider, G. 'παιδαγωγός.' Pages 2–3 in Volume 3 *EDNT*.

Schrenk, G. 'βάρος.' Pages 553–61 in Volume 1 *TDNT*.

————. 'Der Segenwunsch nach der Kampfepistel.' *Judaica* 6 (1950): 170–190.

Schürer, D. Emil. *Geschichte des Jüdischen Volkes im Zeitalter Jesu Christi*. Leipzig: J. C. Hinrichs'sche Buchhandlung, 1886.

Schweizer, Eduard., Peter Wülfing von Martitz, Georg Fohrer, Eduard Lohse, and Wilhelm Schneemelcher. "Υἱός, Υἱοθεσία." Pages 333–92 Volume 8 in *TDNT*.

Seesemann, H. 'πειράζω.' Pages 23–36 in Volume 6 *TDNT*.

Stählin, Gustav. 'ἀποκο πτω.' Pages 830–60 in Volume 3 *TDNT*.

Stamps, D. L. 'Children in Late Antiquity.' Pages 198–99 in *DBNT*.

Stendahl, Krister. 'The Apostle Paul and the Introspective Conscience of the West,' *HTR* 56. 3 (July 1963): 199-215.

―――. *Paul Among Jews and Gentiles.* Augsburg, AR: Fortress, 1976.

Stiles, S. J. 'Halakah.' *LBD.*

Stuart, Douglas. *Hosea–Jonah.* WBC 31; Dallas, TX: Word, 2002.

Swann, J. T. 'Levites.' *LBD.*

―――. 'Sinai.' *LBD.*

Swanson, Dennis M. 'Bibliography of Works on the New Perspective on Paul.' *TMSJ* 16/2 (Spring 2005): 317–24.

Swanson, James. *Dictionary of Biblical Languages with Semantic Domains: Hebrew. Old Testament.* Oak Harbor, WAS: Logos Research Systems, Inc., 1997.

Thielman, Frank. *From Plight to Solution: A Jewish Framework for Understanding Paul's View of the law in Galatians and Romans.* NovTSup 61. Leiden: Brill, 1989.

The Editors of Encyclopaedia Britannica. 'Anatolian Religion.' *Encyclopedia Britannica Online.* https://www.britannica.com/topic/Anatolian-religion.

The Editors of Encyclopaedia Britannica. 'Proteus.' *Encyclopedia Britannica Online.* https://www.britannica.com/topic/Proteus-Greek-mythology.

Thornhill, A. Chadwick 'Exodus.' In *LBD.*

Towner, Philip H. *The Letters to Timothy and Titus.* NICNT. Grand Rapids, MI: Eerdmans, 2006.

Tresham, A. K. 'Barnabas.' *LBD.*

Turner, D. L. *Matthew.* BECNT; Grand Rapids, MI: Baker, 2008).603–11.

Turner, N. *Grammatical Insights into the New Testament.* Edinburgh: T. & T. Clark, 1965.

Varner, William. *James.* EEC. Bellingham, WA: Lexham, 2012. von Martitz, P. W. and E. Schweizer, 'υἱοθεσία.' Pages 397–98 in Volume 8 *TDNT.*

von der Osten-Sacken, P. 'δεξιο´ς.' Pages 285–86 in Volume 1 *EDNT.*

Wallace, Daniel B. *Greek Grammar Beyond the Basics – Exegetical Syntax of the New Testament.* Grand Rapids, MI: Zondervan and Galaxie Software, 1996.

Watson, Duane F. 'Wine.' Pages 872–73 in *DJG.*

Watson, Francis. *Paul and the Hermeneutics of Faith.* CS. Edinburgh: T&T Clark, 2004.

Weber, F. *Jüdische Theologie auf Grund des Talmud und verwandter Schriften.* Leipzig: Dörffling & Franke, 1897.

―――. *System der altsynagogalen palästinischen Theologie aus Targum, Midrasch und Talmud dargestellt.* Edited by F. J. Delitzsch and G. Schnedermann. Leipzig: Dürfling & Franke, 1880.

Weima, J. A. D. 'Letters, Greco-Roman.' Pages 640–44 in *DNTB.*

Wilckens, U. 'ὑποκρίνομαι.' Pages 559–71 in Volume 8 *TDNT.*

Wilson, Todd A. *The Curse of the law and the Crisis in Galatia: Reassessing the Purpose of Galatians.* WUNT 225; Tübingen: Mohr Siebeck, 2007.

Winter, Bruce W. *Seek the Welfare of the City: Christians as Benefactors and Citizens.* FCCGRW. Grand Rapids, MI: Eerdmans, 1994.

Witherington III, Ben. *Grace in Galatia: A Commentary on St. Paul's Letter to the Galatians.* Grand Rapids, MI: Eerdmans, 1998.

―――. 'Lord.' Pages 484–92 in *DJG.*

————. *The Acts of the Apostles: A Socio-Rhetorical Commentary*. Grand Rapids, MI: Eerdmans, 1998.

Wright, N. T. '4QMMT and Paul: Justification, "Works" and Eschatology (2006).' Pages 332–35 in *Pauline Perspectives: Essays on Paul, 1978–2013*. Minneapolis, MN: Fortress Press, 2013.

————. *The Climax of the Covenant*. Minneapolis: Fortress, 1992.

————. *Paul and the Faithfulness of God*, COQG 4 (Minneapolis: Fortress Press, 2013), idem, *What Saint Paul Really Said: Was Paul of Tarsus the Real Founder of Christianity?* (Grand Rapids, MI: Eerdmans, 1997); idem, The Climax of the Covenant. Minneapolis: Fortress, 1992.

Xenophon, *Xenophon in Seven Volumes*. Translated by E. C. Marchant. Medford, MA: Harvard University Press, Cambridge, MA; William Heinemann, Ltd., London., 1923.

Zahn, T. *Der Brief des Paulus an die Galater*. KNT. Leipzig: Deichert, 1905.

See also

'Asia Minor.' http://www.sacred-texts.com/cla/orrp/orrp07.htm.

'Dies sanguinis.' *Wikipedia*. https://en.wikipedia.org/wiki/Dies_sanguinis.

'Eris (mythology).' *Wikipedia*. https://en.wikipedia.org/wiki/Eris_(mythology).

'Free City (classical antiquity).' *Wikipedia*. https://en.wikipedia.org/wiki/Free_city_(classical_antiquity).

'Galli.' *Wikipedia*. https://en.wikipedia.org/wiki/Galli.

'Greek Gods.' http://www.theoi.com/greek-mythology/greek-gods.html.

'Know Thyself.' *Wikipedia*. https://en.wikipedia.org/wiki/Know_thyself.

'List of Greek Gods and Goddesses.' http://www.gods-and-monsters.com/list-of-greek-gods-goddesses.html.

'List of Greek Mythological Figures.' *Wikipedia*. https://en.wikipedia.org/wiki/List_of_Greek_mythological_figures.

'List of Roman Deities.' *Wikipedia*. https://en.wikipedia.org/wiki/List_of_Roman_deities.

'Mutunus Tutunus.' *Wikipedia*. https://en.wikipedia.org/wiki/Mutunus_Tutunus#cite_note-1.

'Panhellenic Games.' *Wikipedia*. https://en.wikipedia.org/wiki/Panhellenic_Games.

'Priapus.' *Wikipedia*. https://en.wikipedia.org/wiki/Priapus.

'Polyaratus.' In *A Dictionary of Greek and Roman Biography and Mythology*. Edited by William Smith. http://www.perseus.tufts.edu/hopper/text?doc=Perseus%3Atext%3A1999.04.0104%3Aentry%3Dpolyaratus-bio-1

'Roman Gods List.' http://www.talesbeyondbelief.com/roman-gods/roman-gods-list.htm.

Tony Campolo>Quotes>Quotable Quote. http://www.goodreads.com/quotes/867293-i-have-three-things-i-d-like-to-say-today-first.

'Your Love O Lord,' 1999 New Spring, Vandura 2500 Songs: Crossroad Distributors Pty. Ltd.

Sayadaw, Ven. Mahasi. 'The Theory of Karma.' http://www.buddhanet.net/e-learning/karma.htm.

Stigmata. Metro-Goldwyn-Mayer. 1999.

Ingram Content Group UK Ltd.
Milton Keynes UK
UKHW022103050423
419688UK00014B/393